MORALITY, PHILOSOPHY, AND PRACTICE

HISTORICAL AND CONTEMPORARY READINGS AND STUDIES

Edited by

ABRAHAM EDEL

ELIZABETH FLOWER

FINBARR W. O'CONNOR

TEMPLE UNIVERSITY PRESS · Philadelphia

TO THE READER

Those who plan to be selective—whether by major author, by theme or problem, by school or movement, or by historical period—will find it helpful to read the chapter introductions and Chapters 5 and 7. These, taken by themselves, tell a cumulative story.

In presenting selections our object has been to maintain the integrity of the original text as far as possible. Our editorial interventions in the selections, differentiated by a larger typeface, have been primarily to summarize material that is omitted where otherwise the transitions are too abrupt. Footnotes of the selected authors are distinguished from editorial footnotes by use of letters to designate the first and numbers the second.

Temple University Press, Philadelphia 19122

First Edition
987654321
Copyright © 1989 by Random House, Inc.

LIBRARY OF CONGRESS
Library of Congress Cataloging-in-Publication Data

Morality, philosophy, and practice : historical and contemporary
 readings and studies / [compiled and edited by] Abraham Edel,
 Elizabeth Flower, Finbarr W. O'Connor.
    p. cm.
   Includes index.
   ISBN 087722-591-5
   1. Ethics   I. Edel, Abraham, 1908–   .   II. Flower, Elizabeth.
III. O'Connor, Finbarr W.
BJ1012.M63555 1988
170–dc19   88-11341
                                                    CIP

Manufactured in the United States of America

Book design by Karin Batten

ACKNOWLEDGMENTS

From *The Republic* by Plato, translated by A. D. Lindsay, 4th ed. rev. (London: J. M. Dent, 1926). Reprinted by permission of J. M. Dent.

From *Nicomachean Ethics* by Aristotle, translated by Martin Ostwald. Reprinted with permission of Macmillan Publishing Company. Copyright © 1986 by Macmillan Publishing Company. Copyright © 1962.

From *The Politics of Aristotle*, translated by Ernest Barker (1946). Reprinted by permission of Oxford University Press.

Letter to Menoeceus by Epicurus. Reprinted by permission of the publishers and the Loeb Classical Library from *Lives of Eminent Philosophers*, Vol. 2, by Diogenes Laertius, translated by R. D. Hicks, Cambridge, Mass.: Harvard University Press, 1965.

The Philosophy of Plotinus, translated by Joseph Katz, © 1950, renewed 1978. Reprinted by permission of Prentice-Hall, Inc., Englewood Cliffs, N.J.

From *Puritanism and Liberty, Being the Army Debates (1647–9) from the Clarke Manuscripts with Supplementary Documents*, ed. by A. S. P. Woodhouse (Chicago: University of Chicago Press, 1951). Reprinted by permission of University of Chicago Press and J. M. Dent.

From *Social Contract* by Jean-Jacques Rousseau, translated by G. D. H. Cole (London: J. M. Dent, 1913).

Declaration of the Rights of Woman and Citizen by Olympe de Gouges. Reprinted by permission of Schocken Books from *European Women: A Documentary History* by Eleanor S. Fiemer and John C. Font. Copyright © 1980.

The Metaphysical Principles of Virtue, translated by James Ellington, in Immanuel Kant, *Ethical Philosophy* (Cambridge and Indianapolis: Hackett Publishing Co., 1983).

Anti-Dühring by Frederick Engels (1878), translated by Emile Burns, 1939. By permission of International Publishers, New York.

From *On the Jewish Question* and *Economic and Philosophical Manuscripts of 1884* by Karl Marx from *Karl Marx, Early Writings*, translated and edited by T. B. Bottomore. Copyright © 1964. Reprinted by permission of McGraw-Hill and T. B. Bottomore.

From *The Origin of the Family, Private Property and the State* (1884) by Karl Marx (New York: International Publishers, 1942, 1972).

From *the German Ideology* by Marx and Engels (London: Lawrence & Wishart, 1965).

From *Principia Ethica* by G. E. Moore (1903). Reprinted by permission of Cambridge University Press.

From "My Early Beliefs," in *Two Memoirs* by J. M. Keynes (1949). Reprinted by permission of Augustus M. Kelley, Publishers, 300 Fairfield Rd., Fairfield, N.J. 07006

From *Language, Truth and Logic* by A. J. Ayer (London, 1936; 2nd ed. 1946). The selection is from *Language, Truth and Logic* (New York: Dover).

From "The Emotive Meaning of Ethical Terms" by Charles L. Stevenson in *Mind*, XLVI, No. 181, January 1937, pp. 16–20. Reprinted by permission of Oxford University Press.

From *Ethics* by P. H. Nowell-Smith (Penguin Books, 1954), copyright © P. H. Nowell-Smith, 1954. Reproduced by permission of Penguin Books Ltd.

Acknowledgments

From "A Plea for Excuses" by J. L. Austin in *Proceedings of the Aristotelian Society* 57 (1956–1957), pp. 1–8. © The Aristotelian Society 1956–1957. Reprinted courtesy of the Editor.

From "The Ascription of Responsibilities and Rights" by H. L. A. Hart in *Proceedings of the Aristotelian Society* 49 (1948–1949), pp. 171–175, 177–189. © The Aristotelian Society 1948–1949. Reprinted by courtesy of the Editor.

From "Approval and Disapproval" by Philippa Foot in *Law, Morality, and Society: Essays in Honour of H. L. A. Hart*, ed. by P. M. S. Hacker and J. Raz (1977). Reprinted by permission of Oxford University Press.

From "Theory of the Moral Life" by John Dewey and James H. Tufts in *Ethics*, revised edition (New York: Henry Holt and Company, 1932). Reprinted with the permission of the Center for Dewey Studies, Southern Illinois University at Carbondale.

From "Three Independent Factors in Morals" by John Dewey from *Educational Theory*, XVI, No. 3, July 1966, pp. 197–209, translated by Jo Ann Boydston. Reprinted by permission of the Board of Trustees of the University of Illinois.

From "Turning Points in Ethical Theory" and from "The Individual and the Social Order," by C. I. Lewis. Reprinted from *Collected Papers of Clarence Irving Lewis*, edited by John D. Goheen and John L. Mothershead, Jr. with the permission of the publishers, Stanford University Press, © 1970 by the Board of Trustees of the Leland Stanford Junior University.

From *Ethics*, Vol. I, pp. 218, 225–229 by Nicolai Hartmann, translated by Stanton Coit (London: George Allen & Unwin; New York: The Macmillan Company, 1932).

From "The Experience of Values" by Frithjof Bergmann in *Inquiry* 16, 3 (Autumn 1973).

From "Ethical Relativity? An Enquiry into the Psychology of Ethics," by Karl Duncker in *Mind* 48 (January 1939): 39–44. Reprinted by permission of Oxford University Press.

From *I and Thou* by Martin Buber, translated by Ronald Gregor Smith (Edinburgh: T. & T. Clark, 1937).

From *Existentialism* by Jean-Paul Sartre, translated by Bernard Frechtman (New York: Philosophical Library, 1947).

From *The Emotions: Outline of a Theory* by Jean-Paul Sartre, translated by Bernard Frechtman (New York: Philosophical Library, 1948).

From *Being and Nothingness* by Jean-Paul Sartre, translated by Hazel E. Barnes (New York: Philosophical Library, 1956).

From "Human Rights: An Appeal to Philosophers" by Felix Cohen. Originally published in the *Review of Metaphysics*, Volume 6 (1953), reprinted with permission of the publisher and of Mrs. Lucy K. Cohen.

From "Philosophy and Politics" by Ronald Dworkin in *Men of Ideas* by Bryan Magee. Copyright © 1978 by Bryan Magee. All rights reserved. Reprinted by permission of Viking Penguin Inc. and A. D. Peters & Co. Ltd.

From "Individual Rights" by Lawrence Becker from *And Justice for All*, ed. Tom Regan and Donald VanDeVeer (Totowa, N.J.: Rowman & Littlefield, 1982).

Excerpted from *In a Different Voice: Psychological Theory and Women's Development* by Carol Gilligan. Copyright © 1982 by Carol Gilligan. Excerpted by permission of Harvard University Press.

From *A Theory of Justice* by John Rawls. Excerpted by permission of the publishers from *A Theory of Justice* by John Rawls, Cambridge, Mass.: The Belknap Press of Harvard University Press, © 1971 by The President and Fellows of Harvard College and by permission of Oxford University Press.

From *Three Tests for Democracy: Personal Rights, Human Welfare, Collective Preference* by David Braybrooke. Copyright © 1983 by Random House, Inc. Reprinted by permission of the publisher.

P R E F A C E

We take the lessons of the work of moral philosophers of the past several decades to be a shift in attention from purely theoretical pursuits to concern also with the moral dimensions of institutions and practices; a new understanding of how the social, intellectual, and historical context affects the way in which problems are cast; and a new appreciation of the continuity and development of problems and proposed solutions, and so of the history of ethics. These developments, far from diminishing ethical theory or the scope of philosophical analysis, extend the arena to include how theory functions and has functioned in practice.

When the study of ethics is thus reoriented, the work of past moral philosophers is brought into fresh view. That work dealt directly with issues that arose in institutions and practices, and grappled with intellectual changes in the growth of the sciences and shifting world outlooks. Plato and Aristotle deal with the whole institutional range. Aquinas has much to say on law and authority, on money-lending and war, as well as on the reconciliation of science and religion. Hobbes throughout is facing the fundamental problem of social disorder as well as hewing out a new method for ethics in the light of the new science. Locke is concerned with property and the conditions of government while reconciling a moral outlook with a new individualism. Hume and Adam Smith deal with economic policy while establishing a moral science in a growing empiricism. In an age of revolutions that begins to think of the future and reconstruction, Bentham focuses on the critique of legislation and traditional institutions, while Kant proposes an ideal of moral development and perpetual peace. Hegel and Marx bring into view the historical matrix of human civilization. Mill deals with liberty and economic development. A fuller picture of the major figures in the history of ethics emerges when their central and more familiar works are placed side by side with their work on practical problems in the institutional areas of government, property, education, religion, social structure, and operative social ideals, as well as on ideals of personal development.

The approach through the history of ideas brings special dividends in understanding theoretical ideas. Thus utilitarianism is better understood when Bentham and Mill are separately examined, each in the context of the developing historical situation that set his problems. The important theory of rights in contemporary moral philosophy stands out in a clearer light when natural rights has been explored in its uncertain and tentative birth in the late Middle Ages, its more confident formulation in the seventeenth-century context of the Levellers and Locke, its flowering in the eighteenth-century context of Price, Burke, and Paine, and its expansion in the twentieth-century context of the United Nations Declaration and subsequent theoretical conflicts. Hobbes is more richly appreciated by placing him squarely in the center of the scientific revolution and following through the seventeenth and eighteenth centuries the reaction he provoked.

None of the moral philosophers of centuries past studied in this book saw themselves as carrying out an enterprise isolated from the broader intellectual movements of the time or from the matrix of human problems then being faced. The concern of moral theory with practical problems is as old as Plato and has been a continuing commitment of moral philosophers.

The title of this book is thus meant seriously to point to the threefold direction of our inquiry: specific moral theory, basic philosophical outlook, and human practice.

A particular delight in venturing a project that ranges widely through nooks and crannies of intellectual history is the opportunity it affords to tap the resources of congenial colleagues who cheerfully contributed their expertise. We thank, from the University of Pennsylvania, Edward Peters, Zoltan Domotor, Charles Kahn, Paul Guyer, James Ross, Martin Wolfe, and Roger Allen; from Beaver College, Anita Udell, Norman Johnston, Wayne Morra, and Steve Huber; and to Jerry Belcher for his pin-point historical leads. We are indebted to Ernan McMullin, and to Chris Macann for a translation of Nietzsche. We are grateful particularly to Jo Ann Bomze, whose eye for infelicity preserved us from many a gaffe. We have had unfailing support from the Rare Book department of the University of Pennsylvania Library, Dartmouth College Library, and Beaver College Library, where two generations of librarians, Marion Green and Maxine Bernstein, labored to find materials. Beaver College is acknowledged for providing a sabbatical leave at an opportune moment. We appreciate the helpful comments of Random House reviewers and the patience and trust of our editor, Steve Pensinger. In the final stages, Evelyn Kratrak and Fred Burns eased the labor pains of a recalcitrant manuscript with a rare sensitivity and skill. Above all, we are indebted to Jane Cullen, whose idea it all was.

Abraham Edel
Elizabeth Flower
Finbarr W. O'Connor

CONTENTS

PREFACE   v

1 **Morality and Ethics**   1

PART ONE ANCIENT AND MEDI-
EVAL WORLD   5

2 **Plato**   7

The Republic   13

3 **Aristotle**   38

The Nicomachean Ethics   42
The Politics   58

4 **Self-Mastery, Enjoyment, and the
Quest for Eternity: Philosophies in
the Graeco-Roman World**   69

HELLENISTIC PHILOSOPHICAL
SCHOOLS   70
Stoicism   73
Zeno   73
Cicero   74
De Officiis and De Legibus   74
Seneca   76
On Anger   76
Epictetus   77
The Manual   77
Discourses   78
Marcus Aurelius   79
Meditations   79

Epicureanism   81
Epicurus   81
Letter to Menoeceus   81
Lucretius   83
On the Nature of Things   83
Skepticism   86
Sextus Empiricus   86
Outlines of Pyrrhonism   86
Neoplatonism   88
Plotinus   88
Enneads   88

**GROWTH OF THE WESTERN RELI-
GIOUS ETHIC**   90
**Moral Philosophy in Biblical and Theo-
logical Writings**   91
Exodus: Decalogue   92
Job   93
Matthew: Sermon on the Mount   95
Augustine   96
Confessions and The City of God   96

5 **Themes from a Millennium**   103

6 **Intention, Law, and Will: Abelard,
Aquinas, Ockham**   110

Peter Abelard   110
Ethics or Know Thyself   111
Thomas Aquinas   116
Summa Theologica   119
William Ockham   141
Commentary on the Sentences, Seven Quodlibe-
tal Questions, and Various
Questions   144
Work of Ninety Days   152

PART TWO THE MODERN
AGE   161

**7 Stirrings of the Modern
   Age   163**

   **Religious, Social, and Scientific
      Transformations   164**
   Philosophy and Method   168

8 Thomas Hobbes   175

   Leviathan   180

**9 Cambridge Platonists, Levellers,
   and Locke   198**

   **The Cambridge Platonists: Rationalism in
      Morals   201**
   Ralph Cudworth   202
   *A Treatise Concerning Eternal and Immutable
      Morality   202*
   Henry More and Samuel Clarke   204
   An Account of Virtue   204
   *A Discourse Concerning the Unalterable Obli-
      gations of Natural Religion   205*
   An Account of Virtue   207
   Richard Cumberland   207
   A Treatise of the Laws of Nature   208
   The Levellers   209
   Putney Debates   211
   John Locke   216
   Second Treatise of Government   217

**10 English Conscience and Scottish
    Sentiment: Butler, Hume, and
    Smith   225**

   Joseph Butler   227
   Sermons   228
   David Hume   232
   *An Enquiry Concerning the Principles of
      Morals   239*
   A Treatise of Human Nature   257
   A Dialogue   258
   Political Discourses   261
   Adam Smith   264
   The Theory of Moral Sentiments   266

PART THREE THE AGE OF
REVOLUTIONS   275

**11 The Struggle Over Natural
    Rights   278**

   Jean Jacques Rousseau   279
   Social Contract   279
   Declarations   281
   Declaration of Independence   281
   *Declaration of the Rights of Man and of
      Citizens   281*
   "Othello"   282
   Essay on Negro Slavery   282
   Olympe de Gouges   283
   *Declaration of the Rights of Woman and
      Citizen   284*
   Richard Price   284
   *A Review of the Principal Questions in
      Morals   285*
   Edmund Burke   287
   *Reflections on the Revolution in
      France   289*
   Thomas Paine   292
   Rights of Man   292
   Mary Wollstonecraft   294
   *A Vindication of the Rights of
      Woman   294*
   Jeremy Bentham   296
   Anarchical Fallacies   297

12 Jeremy Bentham   298

   *An Introduction to the Principles of Morals
      and Legislation   303*
   The Rationale of Reward   316
   Deontology   317
   The Theory of Legislation   318
   Principles of International Law   321

13 Immanuel Kant   325

   *Fundamental Principles of the Metaphysic of
      Morals (Preface)   332*
   *Critique of Practical Reason
      (Conclusion)   333*

*Fundamental Principles of the Metaphysic of
  Morals* 334
Critique of Practical Reason 348
The Metaphysics of Morals 351
The Metaphysical Principles of Virtue 351
The Science of Right 358
Idea of a Universal History on a Cosmopolitical Plan 363
Perpetual Peace 365

PART FOUR THE NINETEENTH
CENTURY 367

14 G. W. F. Hegel 371

The Philosophy of History 376
The Philosophy of Right 384

15 Marxian Ethics 390

Karl Marx and Frederick Engels 390
Karl Marx 395
*A Contribution to the Critique of Political
  Economy* 395
Karl Marx and Frederick Engels 396
Manifesto of the Communist Party 396
Frederick Engels 400
Anti-Dühring 400
Karl Marx 404
On the Jewish Question 404
Karl Marx 404
*Economic and Philosophical Manuscripts of
  1844* 404
Frederick Engels 409
*The Origin of the Family, Private Property
  and the State* 409
Karl Marx and Frederick Engels 411
The German Ideology 411

16 John Stuart Mill 413

Utilitarianism 417
On Liberty 432
*Considerations on Representative
  Government* 442
Principles of Political Economy 446

**17 Darwinism and the Uses of
Evolution** 452

Charles Darwin 455
The Descent of Man 455
Herbert Spencer 460
Social Statics 460
T. H. Huxley 462
Evolution and Ethics 462
Friedrich Nietzsche 466
Beyond Good and Evil: Prelude to a Philosophy of the Future 466
Peter Kropotkin 470
Mutual Aid: A Factor of Evolution 470

**18 Ethics of Self-Realization: Green,
Bradley, Bosanquet** 474

T. H. Green 475
Prolegomena to Ethics 476
F. H. Bradley 477
Ethical Studies 477
Bernard Bosanquet 479
The Philosophical Theory of the State 480

PART FIVE THE TWENTIETH
CENTURY 485

19 The Autonomy of Ethics 490

G. E. Moore 492
Principia Ethica 492
John Maynard Keynes 501
My Early Beliefs 501

**20 Emotivism and Ordinary
Language Analysis** 504

**Logical Empiricism and the Emotive
  Theory** 505
Ordinary Language Analysis 506
A. J. Ayer 508
Language, Truth and Logic 508
Charles Leslie Stevenson 511
*The Emotive Meaning of Ethical
  Terms* 511

P. H. Nowell-Smith   515
Ethics   515
J. L. Austin   518
A Plea for Excuses   518
H. L. A. Hart   521
*The Ascription of Responsibility and
    Rights*   521
Philippa R. Foot   525
Approval and Disapproval   525

21 Pragmatism   529

Classical Pragmatists   530
John Dewey   539
Ethics, Part II: *Theory of the Moral
    Life*   539
Three Independent Factors in Morals   543
Ethics, Part II: *Theory of the Moral
    Life*   547
C. I. Lewis   549
Turning Points in Ethical Theory   549

22 Phenomenological Description and Existential Decision   555

Phenomenological Description   555
Existentialist Decision   559
Nicolai Hartmann   562
Ethics   562
Frithjof H. Bergmann   564
The Experience of Values   564
Karl Duncker   570
*Ethical Relativity? (An Enquiry into the Psy-
    chology of Ethics)*   570
Martin Buber   573
I and Thou   574

Jean-Paul Sartre   577
Existentialism   577
The Emotions: Outline of a Theory   580
Being and Nothingness   581

23 Human Rights, Justice, and Welfare   586

Human Rights   587
Justice   589
Welfare   590
*United Nations Universal Declaration of Hu-
    man Rights*   594
Felix S. Cohen   596
*Human Rights: An Appeal to
    Philosophers*   596
Ronald Dworkin   599
Philosophy and Politics   599
Lawrence C. Becker   601
Individual Rights   601
Carol Gilligan   608
In a Different Voice   608
John Rawls   609
A Theory of Justice   609
David Braybrooke   614
Three Tests for Democracy   614
Conflict or Detente   619

24 Agenda: Looking Toward the Next Century   621

Ethics and Practice   621
**Mobilizing Knowledge for
    Morality**   624

Index   632

MORALITY, PHILOSOPHY, AND PRACTICE

1

Morality and Ethics

The nature of ethics (also called ethical theory, moral theory, or moral philosophy) emerges clearly if we approach it through the way ethical reflection arises from ordinary moral perplexities and concerns in our common experience. Fortunately, none of us comes empty-handed to the study. We all bring some expertise in moral vocabulary and have definite beliefs about what is good and evil, just and unjust, moral and immoral. We think we know the virtues that make a character good and their opposing vices, and we have some ideals of a desirable community. At least we can identify shortcomings in people and community and suggest reforms. We also have some sense of moral context, setting off the moral from the nonmoral—perhaps from etiquette, taste, convention, and mere legality. We also distinguish matters of personal initiative from matters of social responsibility. This moral sensibility is acquired from parents and family, peer groups, social practices, and institutions that surround us—much as our first language is acquired.

Unavoidably, we note inconsistencies in our beliefs and conduct. Sometimes, long-held rules remain silent about new cases or are ambiguous or inadequate. Sometimes we are simply perplexed about what is right or good or obligatory; sometimes we sense a strain between what we do and what we know we ought to do, as when we pass over an ethnic joke without comment.

We also find that, unfortunately and uncomfortably, we may disagree with those closest to us—family, friends, and colleagues—on what is right, just, and fair. Are there absolute rules about promising and telling the truth, or are they dependent on the situation and consequences? For example, does an emergency justify passing off as one's own work that of another? Is it just to steal even to help others, fair not to keep a promised appointment when something very important comes up?

We may differ too about what requires individual initiative and what requires a social policy. Some people confine morality largely to

1

matters of individual decision—whether to drive after one or two drinks or to drink at all, to date someone of another religion, to live with a partner you do not intend to marry, to join a cult, to refuse to register for the draft. Others think of morality as more importantly social—taking responsibility for neighborhood poverty, for depressed classes in society, or for hunger in the world; believing it is the duty of an affluent nation to sacrifice for underdeveloped countries and to preserve resources for future generations. Among our friends, there may be agreement to consider as moral issues abortion, pornography, discrimination (racial, ethnic, and sexual), and equalizing opportunity, but disagreement about whether these are matters for individual initiative or society's responsibility.

We may indeed differ on what is properly a moral matter at all, that is, what characterizes a moral context. Some sharply separate the moral from the nonmoral. Others think that under certain conditions virtually anything can become a moral matter. For example, even etiquette can be moral when civility could forestall an open rupture in personal or diplomatic relations.

Differences are intensified in the conflicts of urban living with apparently legitimate but conflicting claims to equal opportunity. They are magnified in the encounter with other cultures. Certain cultures still allow infanticide and abandon the weak and old; others confine obligations to members of the ingroup, view women and children as property, or tolerate near serfdom. Still others regard inhospitality to the needy as morally equivalent to theft.

So durable a code as the Ten Commandments lends itself to such disagreements. Is "Thou shalt not kill" an absolute pacifist rule, or does it mean rather "Thou shalt not commit murder," which would be compatible with some justifiable killing and some just wars? Does "Honor your parents" mean care for them or obey them? If the latter, how do we resolve the conflict if a parent bids us bear

false witness on his or her behalf? Does that commandment ground a privilege not to be obliged to testify against parents, as one need not testify against a spouse? There are also puzzling omissions. Why are we told to honor our parents but they not told to take good care of their children? Why are we commanded "Thou shalt not steal" and not also "Forbear using your property in socially destructive ways"? Some rules presuppose a particular institutional context: "adultery" seems to presuppose particular patterns of marriage, and "coveting a neighbor's goods" presupposes some property system. "Bearing false witness" suggests the practices of a trial. Are the commandments unconditionally binding, or are they conditional on the promise of a reward— "that thy days may be long upon the land which the Lord, thy God, giveth thee"—or the threat of punishment—"visiting the iniquity of the fathers upon the children unto the third and fourth generations"?

Even within the same tradition, such as ours, dramatic changes have taken place in moral duties, objectives, and virtues. Thus whereas the feudal world placed great stock in loyalty and gratitude, the commercial world from the seventeenth century on gave priority to promises and contracts. The cardinal virtues that come to us from Platonic times—prudence, courage, temperance, and justice— keep uneasy company with the Calvinistic virtues of sobriety, thrift, worldly success, and property as a mark of merit. Marked shifts have taken place from the individual to the social. Thus poverty, once a matter of charity and private benevolence and philanthropy, is now generally assigned to social welfare agencies. Having fewer children, especially in desperately overpopulated countries, seems to be moving from the individual's responsibility toward an intransigent social obligation. On the other hand, sexual relations and orientation, once matters of strict social regulation, have become (at least in America) largely matters for private decision. And as the domain of private conscience about war and peace is expanded, questions of patriotism, once social, are now becoming personal.

What comes within the scope of morality has also changed over time. While the medieval world constrained price on moral grounds, laissez-faire theory beginning in the eighteenth century left it to the neutral laws of the marketplace. Recently, price regulation has once again taken on a moral complexion. Likewise, poverty, which in the colonial work ethic was regarded as a defect of character, is increasingly seen as a structural weakness of the economy that requires social provision and remedy, especially where unemployment is an unavoidable consequence of technological advance.

Now if we did not make substantive moral judgments; if we did not have moments of conscience, guilt, or remorse; if we were sure of the ingredients of a good life; if we did not prefer the quality of some kinds of associations over others, admire some characters and detest others; if we did not acknowledge some claims of others on our own conduct; if we did not resent some treatment of others as well as of ourselves, then we should have no occasion for moral concern. If we met with no differences; if customary morality, codes, and precepts led always in the same direction and adequately; if there were universal agreement as to how a life ought to be lived; if the relations were always clear between what is religious, legal, and moral; if we did not see other cultures and historical epochs living under very different moralities; if we did not acknowledge the authenticity and vitality of alternatives, we should have no need for moral reflection.

But we do. Moral theorizing begins with reflection about such concerns. We try to clarify what is at stake in these disagreements, look for grounds to validate or authorize morality, and search for fundamental notions. Sometimes we may codify and systematize precepts, rules, and laws or search for a general set of principles underlying them. Sometimes we envision ideals, even utopian views of the ideal community. In times of radical change and social distress we may examine the conflicts and seek some principles on which the situation can be reconstructed so as to do justice to various claims. In times of relative social stability we step back to examine the prevailing moral institutions and customs, the practices and the expectations generated by moral patterns, and the disparity between declared objectives and accomplishments.

Western tradition has recorded as the history of ethical theory efforts to pursue these reflections systematically and comprehensively. This is a fundamental and precious part of its heritage. There is sweep and drama in the history of such efforts, from the Socratic-Platonic search for the meaning of justice and the Aristotelian inquiry into the ingredients of the good life, through the theologically grounded systems of will and reason in Augustine and Aquinas, to the more modern secular theories, beginning with Hobbes, that develop themes of individual virtue and social good and universal moral obligation. Within this drama arise tensions and grave differences as to the nature of morality: its fundamental concepts and phenomena, controversies over how we grasp moral distinctions, what is to count as evidence, and the relation between knowing and doing. One theory may take moral law and right as fundamental (Kant); another may focus on objectives and achievements, with good as fundamental (Utilitarianism); and another may look to praise and blame, taking virtue as the central concept (Adam Smith).

Theories differ also in their view of social bonds and human nature. Theory will take a different direction depending on whether human nature is given a naturalistic psychological interpretation (Hobbes, Hume) or a biological one (Darwin), driven by fixed instincts of pleasure and pain (Bentham) or by a blind will (Nietzsche, Sartre), governed by an eminently rational will (Kant) or by reason (Aquinas). It matters too if man is thought to be essentially evil (Calvin) requiring constant restraint (Augustine) or good (Rousseau) or basically social (Aristotle) or irremediably self-interested and only reluctantly social (Hobbes); and finally, whether character is fixed or malleable.

And of course built into the theory will be some view of the world as recalcitrant or amenable to controlled change. Ancient and medieval ethics assumes that processes in the natural and in the human are to be understood by the purposes they carry out; the ethics of the seventeenth and eighteenth centuries, with the beginning of modern science, attempts to model ethics on mathematical-physical laws.

Neither ethical theory nor morality can be isolated from the social and intellectual fabric—for example, social and political changes such as the rise of nation states and the growing individualism associated with capitalism. Since the subject matter of ethics intersects with the religious, legal, and political, it is not surprising that a world that is dominantly religious formulates its ethical theory in one way, whereas one concerned with evolution constructs it in another way.

A distinctively modern issue is how ethics is related to other disciplines. In the ancient world, philosophy embraced all knowledge (in virtually every field one still receives a Ph.D., doctor of philosophy). When in modern times the sciences split from philosophy into separate guilds of specializations, their relation to ethics came into question. Inevitably, the successful deductive and experimental methods of natural science served as models for ethical inquiry. The social sciences, emerging in the eighteenth century as psychology, sociology, and economics, also significantly shaped moral theory. Psychology joined ethics to ask whether guilt, shame, remorse, and sympathy are uniquely moral emotions. Sociology joins ethics in studying morality as social control. Political science shares a concern with the forms of authority and legitimacy, as well as modes of decision and participation. History and anthropology inquire about the differences found in morality (ethical relativism) and whether there has been moral progress. And of course moral philosophy, as part of philosophy, shares problems, methods, and aspirations with logic, epistemology (theory of knowledge), and metaphysics (theory of reality).

Given the richness and complexity of the problems and materials with which ethics has worked, its history not surprisingly displays little in the way of linear direction. Its history is not readily antisepticized, as histories of science are wont to be. This is not to say that progress or maturing is indiscernible; even failed experiments contribute to the fund of learning. Ethical theories are not portraits in a gallery, relics of only antiquarian interest. Rather, they are voices in a living dialogue that clarifies options, develops alternatives, and gives clearer shape to long-held goals and ideals. The dialogue provides the vocabulary and in important measure determines the perception of present moral problems as well as the resources to meet them. The dialogue does not merely conserve, for out of it emerge innovative responses to the tax of changing situations. Out of the matrix of history an enriched view of human problems arises, a clearer understanding of fresh values: respect for all persons, aspirations to equality, human rights, universal peace, greater liberties, and participation. Each age and society contributes an overlay of different and selective readings of its own tradition. We all participate in that unfinished conversation as partners in transmuting past theory into an understanding of the present and so a shaping of the future. Ethics is not of academic interest only.

P A R T O N E

Ancient and Medieval World

Part One presents major ethical theories of ancient and medieval times. Covering about eighteen centuries, at best it can be only selective. Its major figures are Plato (Chapter 2), whose ethics, set in the first great philosophical system of Western civilization, is the first comprehensive theory that survives; Aristotle (Chapter 3), who gave technical shape to basic problems of ethics in a philosophy that challenged—and ruled—minds for centuries; and Thomas Aquinas (Chapter 6), whose synthesis of Christian and Aristotelian ideas is a monument of the Middle Ages. Chapter 4 explores the varied approaches of ancient post-Aristotelian ethics: best known are perhaps the stern Stoic ethic of self-mastery and the Epicurean ethic of quiet pleasure-seeking; it also introduces ancient skepticism and mysticism, the entry of Hebraic-Christian ideas into Western philosophy, and Augustine, a central figure of Christian ethics. Chapter 5 selects themes from the Middle Ages, while Chapter 6 presents Abelard and Ockham in addition to Aquinas.

This focus on the development of ethics in the Western world regrettably leaves unexplored other areas, particularly Islamic, Indian, and Chinese out-looks. This is not intended to convey any judgments of comparative value; it only selects paths closest to the development of the major ideas of Western moral philosophy. For the Western tradition developed the formulations, fashioned the vocabulary, and provided the intellectual tools by which people of the contemporary West grapple with their problems. The tradition is not, however, monolithic; it embraces a considerable variety of philosophical ideas, extending even to the basic conception of what ethics itself is.

Moral theory does not occur in a vacuum. It has some relevance to the kind of life led by people of the time, to their institutions, and to their problems. The development of philosophy is tied predominantly to city life and the growth of intellectual institutions. For the most part, the ancient and medieval worlds were agricultural societies with some urban life, as in Athens or Venice and, of course, the megalopolis of Rome. Most of the institutions of the period are familiar to us, although they differ from ours in many respects. For instance, the family was more often the extended family, not the nuclear one of modern times. The Greeks provided the vocabulary for political institutions—"monarchical," "aristocratic," "oligarchic," "democratic"—but early monarchy may have meant patriarchal chieftains, and the democracy of Athens was not our representative form but direct or face-to-face. In earlier periods law was tied to tradition rather than to conscious legislation; among the Romans law began to take rigorous shape, and thereafter it grew more systematically from the accumulated work of medieval courts. The existence of private property and the conflict of rich and poor continually provoked disagreements; the ancient world heard many a cry for redivision of land and abolition of debts, while the medieval world had its peasant rebellions and the mendicant friars' call for poverty as an ideal way of life. Slavery and varied forms of serfdom were not seriously questioned in these times, although it should be remembered that they involved different degrees of control from one time to another and different ideas about human beings. Women had no share in authority; for the most part society was male-dominated. Education as a formal practice was only sporadic and not for the mass. Something like the university began in the schools of Athens but became fully formed in medieval Paris and Oxford. Religion pervaded ordinary life, and in the medieval world particularly its institutions had an active, indeed sometimes a dominant, social role. Mathematics and science got started with brilliance in ancient Greece, but they were not to have firm philosophical foundations until modern times. Technology made moderate advances through individual contributions here and there, but the power of the ancient world was man power and slave power and animal power, or external water and wind power—not yet elaborately stored power.

The basic problems of survival faced by the people of this period are familiar, but their hopes for solution were more limited than ours might be. Insecurity was a constant feature of their lives; individuals and communities lived on the margin of subsistence, and the town that rose above this was likely to do so at the expense of others. The development of trade brought luxuries only to a few. War was ever present and raids by outsiders (piratical or invasion) always imminent. Rome in ancient times and feudalism in the medieval world brought some stability, but even then the dreams of what was possible were limited—they were dreams of conquest and military protection rather than of plenty and perpetual peace.

These, roughly, are the contours of life within which philosophers reflected on how life might best be led.

2

🌀

Plato
(427—347 B.C.)

Western efforts to analyze moral ideas and to construct ethical theory begin in ancient Greece. Socrates initiates the inquiry and Plato fashions the theory. The Greece of the time—the fifth and fourth centuries B.C.—had emerged from a social structure resting on extended kinship into political units, as villages grew into cities. Athens and Sparta became the two major powers. Sparta, an inland state in the southern part of Greece, became the foremost land power. Spartan society was highly regimented and largely agricultural, and depended on a large previously conquered serf (helot) population to work the land. Before the constant threat of helot revolt Spartan energies were channeled into a system of repression and control that inhibited any free cultural development. Athens became the foremost maritime power, constructing a navy to protect its trading routes. When the Persian Empire invaded Greece, the more vulnerable Athens organized the resistance and by 480 had finally defeated the invaders. For further protection Athens formed a federation of smaller cities on the Aegean Sea, which rapidly turned into

an Athenian empire. Athens became a mercantile maritime city with a sizable rural peasantry. Although slaves and foreigners had no citizen rights and women no political role, within such limitations Athens moved toward a face-to-face democracy. Lawmaking power lay with the assembly of the citizen body, and judicial power with large juries selected by lot from citizen rolls. Executive authority lay with the Council, selected by lot with rotating officers. Informal power came with leadership in the Assembly, which depended on oratory and personal influence. Pericles, during the golden age of Athens—marked by an extraordinary outpouring of cultural achievement by dramatists and sculptors, architects and city planners, poets and historians, scientists and philosophers—exercised power in just this way.

Beneath the apparent serenity of the golden age of Athenian culture, a bitter political struggle was being waged between democrats and oligarchs. As the Greek historian Thucydides makes clear, and as both Plato and Aristotle interpret the struggle, it was a conflict of the rich with the poor and it was not confined to

7

Athens but was taking place throughout the whole of the Greek world. Autocratic Sparta was a natural friend of oligarchic parties, whereas Athens sided everywhere with the democrats. The conflict led eventually to the Peloponnesian War, between Athens and Sparta, which lasted from 431 to 404 B.C., with a brief interval of peace that began in 421. We know a good deal about this war from Thucydides's history. It stands out as the conflict of two social systems with different ideals of life and character. In a funeral oration honoring the Athenian dead early in the war Pericles clarified the contrast: democratic government as against authoritarian; social, intellectual, and political freedom as against coercive discipline; rational criticism combining speech and action as against taciturnity and passivity; a rich as against an impoverished culture; though courageous in defense, a preference for peace as against a life organized for war. Sparta won the war, and only the sheer chance of conflict among the victors saved Athens from complete destruction. Sparta installed thirty oligarchs (the "thirty tyrants") to rule Athens; but they were eventually overthrown, and the restored democracy patched up a peace with Sparta.

Socrates. Socrates's life (469–399 B.C.) coincides with the age of democratic supremacy in Athens, and he lived through the Peloponnesian War. He was considered by many to be a Sophist. These Sophists were an urbane group from different parts of the Greek world who traveled among the cities earning their way by lecturing and teaching. Their success in Athens was ensured by the fact that there the ability to argue and persuade was a source of power, wealth, and success, and so those who could afford it sought out the Sophists for training in rhetoric. The techniques of argument they developed fed the growth of logic and general education. With their experience of the variety of human ways in different societies, the Sophists had a largely relativistic moral outlook. Some looked to custom, tradition, and convention as the source of human moral outlooks; others focused on the struggle for power and success.

Socrates resisted identification with the Sophists. Unlike them he refused payment, and in the Platonic dialogues he constantly criticized them. In his teaching, he said, he was simply pursuing a quest for knowledge—in matters of morality to find what was good for human beings by nature rather than by convention. Rather than lecture, he engaged in conversation, or better, *dialectic,* which begins with an idea or statement and progresses by question, answer, counterinstance, refined question, new answer, new counterinstance. He asked such questions as what is piety? What is courage, temperance, beauty, justice, friendship, love? Is virtue one or many? Is it truly knowledge? What is the good, and how do we find it? The method aims to awaken the mind. Yet some striking conclusions emerge—for example, that no one does wrong willingly: since we aim at the good, to choose the bad is a mark of ignorance; for to know what is good entails pursuing it. Virtue is, accordingly, knowledge.

These conversations are recorded in Plato's dialogues. It is not always clear to what extent they are historical. Scholars agree that the earlier dialogues are Socratic and that the later dialogues (e.g., *The Laws*) are Platonic. But in the middle ones, such as the *Republic,* we cannot always tell where Socrates ends and Plato begins.

Socrates, with his intense trust in the inquiring mind, is one of the heroes of Western thought. His inquiry, although theoretical, was also practical; for he was raising the question of how to guide our lives and how to live them. As is well known, he paid with his own life for his quest: he was tried on the charges of impiety and corrupting the youth, and was sentenced to death. Plato writes a moving account of the whole episode in three dialogues. The *Apology* is Socrates's speech defending himself at this trial. The *Crito* is his argument in jail when he refuses an opportunity to escape, on the grounds of principle—that the law should be respected even when its application is in error. The *Phaedo*, set on the last day of Socrates's life, is his conversation about immortality and ends with his drinking the hemlock. In these dialogues Socrates pictures himself as above party struggles in his quest for justice. Probably his criticism of democracy and its leaders was a factor in the hostility directed against him; he was felt to be an intellectual influence on the antidemocratic side. In any case, he was seen as stirring up criticism of traditional Athenian ways.

Plato. If his *Letters* are authentic, Plato gives an explicit account of his reaction to these events. He had hoped the thirty tyrants would reform the state, but he was disillusioned by their confiscations from and executions of opponents. When democracy was restored he was disillusioned a second time, especially by the condemnation of Socrates. What Plato wanted instead was a ruling authority that would transcend the struggle of rich and poor, of oligarchy and democracy, and act on knowledge of the public good. In brief, he wanted political and social policy to be treated as an ethical science of the good, not just as a study of the conflict of wills and desires. It was in part to promote this aim that he founded the Academy, the earliest continuing center of intellectual inquiry.

The *Republic* raises the most serious questions of the guidance and orientation of life, and explores them in depth. It is profoundly educative, irrespective of its specific answers. As might be expected, Plato's intentions here have been the subject of controversy. Some see the *Republic* as essentially a statement of general principles; others see it as a handbook for the construction of a particular type of society. It may of course be both. A practical import is indicated by its setting; for although it was probably written about 387 B.C., the events and characters mentioned suggest that it is set in the time of the temporary peace during the Peloponnesian War. This was a time when decisions about the future of Athens hung in the balance: some pressed in an imperialistic direction, while others questioned whether democracy itself was viable. The participants in the *Republic* included some well-born youths who might be expected to become leaders in Athenian politics. Glaucon and Adeimantus, who carry on most of the dialogue with Socrates, were Plato's own brothers. Thrasymachus was a hard-headed Sophist. The aged Cephalus, who represents the past and walks out when the argument gets started, was an "armaments" (spears and shields) manufacturer. His son Polemarchus, who takes up the argument for a time, was later killed by the thirty tyrants so they could confiscate his fortune. Polemarchus's brother Lysias, who is simply a bystander, subsequently became a famous orator, whose speeches survive.

While Plato wrote other dialogues that explore specific ethical issues, none is as comprehensive as the *Republic*. Nor is any other as thorough in investigating the foundations of ethical theory, especially in human nature (the psychological) and in the character of knowledge and of reality (the epistemological and the metaphysical).

Plato sees human nature as written large in the social order. Thus he looks to a theory of three social classes and the virtues that enable each class to carry out its role, to elucidate the internal structure of the individual psyche. It has three parts—reason, spirit (or mettle), and appetite. The character of his scheme is suggested by the metaphor he gives late in the book: reason is the man in us, spirit (mettle) the lion in us, and appetite the dragon in us. The dominance of one or another part determines the goals individuals have and the paths of life they pursue. The distribution of individual types and the degree to which they are virtuous determine the character of a society, that is, its constitution or way of life—aristocracy, timocracy, oligarchy, democracy, tyranny. In these terms he plots historical change among constitutions, tracing the deterioration from one to another as the dragon gains in strength. In this account Plato is offering an interpretation of the history of Greek society and its decline to his day. Table 2.1 outlines the relationship of the social classes, parts of the psyche, and varieties of goals and institutions.

Plato maintains that there are eternal Forms or Ideas which are the realities at the root of all that is, as well as the source of all genuine knowledge. He explains this from many

Classes in Society	Virtues	Human Nature (parts of the psyche)	Goals	Paths of Life	Constitutions of Society
Rulers, or top guardians; shape basic policy	Wisdom	Reason (the man in us)	The Good	Intellectual life	Aristocracy (the ideal, rule by reason)
Auxiliaries, or administrators and warriors; carry out the policies and defend society	Courage	Spirit or mettle (the lion in us)	Prestige, honor, success	Life of ambition	Timocracy (rule by the lion)
Mass of the people (farmers, producers, craftsmen)	Temperance (or self-control)	Appetite (the dragon in us)	Pleasure and bodily comforts	Pursuit of wealth (as means to pleasure)	(a) Oligarchy (b) Democracy (c) Tyranny (rule of the appetites in increasing order of lack of restraint)
	Justice, a fourth virtue, holds all classes and parts of human nature together and unifies the special virtues				

Table 2.1 Structure of the Ideal Society

different starting points. The *Phaedo* raises the question how we can judge when things are equal or unequal (for example, two sticks). Admittedly we never find two exactly equal things, hence we have never seen perfect equality. Rather we bring to our perception of things an ideal of perfect equality that we must have grasped with our intellect. Only our intellect, then, and not our senses, gives us what is really and truly equal. The same argument applies to geometrical figures—say, a triangle: the figure we draw only approximates a real triangle, which is bounded by lines that have no thickness, only length. Proofs about the properties of triangles—say, that they have an angle sum of two right angles—are carried out logically by the intellect, not by looking or by measuring with rulers and protractors. Similarly with numbers: we can break a material stick into two parts, so that a thing that was odd is now even, but we cannot break the number one into two; it remains eternally what it is and retains its oddness. Mathematics thus gives us a glimpse of entities that are eternal and unchanging. More generally: to understand what justice is as well as to understand what number is, or triangle or even chair, we have to grasp its Form. Our very knowledge of things comes through universals—as is evident in common language, which operates through words that, for the most part, indicate kinds rather than particular objects. To know the particular is to grasp the universals that make it what it is. (In modern terms, to know the particular is to know the governing laws that tell us about it. The botanist knows the tree in a way that the mere observer cannot really grasp, and the atomic physicist knows the realities of the bit of matter before him more profoundly than someone who merely stares at it.) Plato does not deny that the person who uses just his or her senses acquires beliefs and opinions about things; but belief and opinion are not knowledge. Nor is he saying that particulars do not exist but, rather, that their existence is like that of shad-

ows of a tree: they come and go, while the tree remains. Thus two orders of existence are sharply separated: on the one side is the particular, the material, the changing, found in opinion and resting on sensation; on the other side is the universal, the spiritual, the eternal, found in knowledge and resting on the intellect. Our ordinary world merely reflects eternal realities—Forms or Ideas. In sum, then, Plato provides both a theory of knowledge that makes a sharp distinction between belief and knowledge and a theory of being or what is the real that makes a correspondingly sharp distinction between appearance and reality (the Form). Our spiritual quest is to advance from shadow to substance.

The quest as Plato more fully envisages it lies in ascending a ladder of knowledge. Experience of shadows is merely the starting point; it functions to stimulate the mind and lead it on to universals (or Forms, types, or essences), whose grasp constitutes scientific knowledge of objects. The systematic development of the sciences is of the utmost importance both for its content and for its discipline. Mathematics plays a central part, for it describes things in purely intellectual terms as well as freeing the mind for purer thought. But science is not the end of the journey, for each science has basic premises that it takes for granted and that must be submitted to criticism. This criticism, much like the Socratic dialogue, is a process of *dialectic*. Out of it comes the last step, a kind of unified ultimate grasp of the reality on which the sciences converge. This is an intuitive, almost mystical, beholding of the Idea of the Good, which provides a purposive sense or meaning for all that is. All human life thus ultimately leads to the same destination, whether it is the life of action and production, the aesthetic search for beauty, or the intellectual ardor of the scientist. (This convergence is best described in Plato's *Symposium* where the search for the Good is portrayed as the essence of love.) And, of course, it is most intimately pertinent to ethics, where the attainment of the Good is the direct and explicit objective.

Plato is offering in the *Republic* nothing less than the theory of the good life, for both individuals and societies, with justice as the organizing principle. His view of ethical inquiry is broad, as is shown by the range of topics he discusses. He moves from one to the other not by order of a preassigned table of contents but under the necessities of argument as he formulates positions, proposes answers or considers alternatives, and probes underlying assumptions or suggestions. After a preliminary exploration of conventional views on the nature of justice in Book I, he raises these issues:

Book II

- The basic needs of a human community
- Individual self-sufficiency and the division of labor
- The social effects of luxury and scarcity
- War and the structure of the state
- The required character of leadership
- The education of leaders (what models are to be used for their cultural education, particularly how the gods are represented)
- The nature of the gods
- The need for strict control over the education and cultural life of the community (including literature, art, music, attitudes to health, etc.)

Book III

- The separation of the classes of society and the role of leadership

Book IV

- The central virtues of different social classes and the corresponding virtues of the individual
- The make-up of the self and the basic dynamics of life and society
- The character of justice in the individual and the society

Book V

- The institutions of the good society with respect to sex and child bearing, property, and government
- The justification of the kind of government in terms of the possession of knowledge about what is good (why philosophers should rule)

Book VI

- The nature of knowledge and its relation to belief (the nature of the real and its eternal character)

Book VII

- The search for knowledge and the contrast of the intellectual and the sensory (the myth of the cave)
- The organization of higher education for the liberation of the mind

Book VIII

- The different kinds of societies and how their basic values appear in society and in the individual
- The unavoidable degeneration from the ideal state to the chaotic society (the dynamics of historical transformations and the evaluation of aristocracy, the wealth-seeking oligarchy, and the libertarian democracy)

Book IX

- Kinds of lives and the presentation of the thoroughly unjust society and the thoroughly unjust person
- Kinds of pleasure and their evaluation

Book X

- Art and its place in society, and the need for its regulation
- The religious quest of the soul and its fate

Plato obviously finds an enormous span of disciplines necessary to working out what is justice (right and wrong, the best way of life). Beyond the purely philosophical, in modern terms his discussion ranges over topics from economics (e.g., the division of labor), political science (e.g., class structure and the justification of governmental authority), theology (e.g., the nature of the gods), sociology (e.g., the structure of institutions), psychology (e.g., the make-up of the self), anthropology (e.g., comparative values of different societies), and even psychiatry (e.g., the psychopathic personality of the tyrant). In the *Republic* are to be found a theory of social control, a medical-health model for justice, curricular proposals ranging from elementary through higher education, a philosophy of society and history, a mapping of cultural types and paths of life, a psychiatry of injustice, a psychology of pleasure, a sociology of art.

The essential power of the rulers is their ability to attain knowledge by grasping the Forms and the Form of the Good—not, like the rest of the people, acting in terms simply of belief about what appears good. This ability justifies their authority. Plato has thus launched the attempt we shall meet continually in the history of ethics: to make ethics and social policy matters of knowledge and science rather than of mere individual opinion or will.

The *Republic* [1]

In Book I Socrates's discussion with the aged Cephalus focuses first on the evils of old age and eventually on peace of mind. The value of wealth, Cephalus says, is that it helps a good man to die assured that he has done no

injustice and is "guiltless of even involuntary deceit or falsehood, and . . . quit of all our debts of sacrifice to God and of money to man." Socrates takes this to mean that justice consists in telling the truth and paying one's debts. It is soon clear that Socrates is after the principles by which life should be governed. Socrates's reply and its development raise issues of logical method as well as morality—for example, his use of counterinstances and analogies, and how he defuses the appeal to authorities (e.g., to Simonides). Socrates speaks:

[I] "What you say, Cephalus, is excellent," I said. "But as to this justice, can we quite without qualification define it as truthfulness and repayment of anything that we have received; or are these very actions sometimes just and sometimes unjust? For example, if we had been given weapons by a friend when he was of sound mind, and he went mad and reclaimed them, it would surely be universally admitted that it would not be right to give them back. Any one who did so, and who was prepared to tell the whole truth to a man in that state, would not be just." —— "You are right," he said.

"Then this is not the definition of justice—speaking the truth and restoring what we have received?"

"Yes, but it is, Socrates," broke in Polemarchus, "if we are to believe Simonides."

"Well, well," said Cephalus, "I leave the argument with you, for it is time for me to attend to the sacrifice."

"Then am I," said Polemarchus, "left to inherit your share?" —— "Certainly," he said smiling, and departed to sacrifice.

"Come, then," I said, "you who have inherited the argument, what is this saying of Simonides about justice of which you approve?" —— "That to render to every man what is owing is just," said he, "and I for one think he was right in so saying."

"Well," I said, "Simonides is one whom we cannot lightly disbelieve. He was a wise and godlike man. But as to what this saying means, you, Polemarchus, may know that; I certainly do not. For it clearly does not mean what we were just saying, repayment of what has been given to a man in pledge if the claimant is out of his senses. Yet surely

[1] The selection is from Plato, *Republic,* trans. A. D. Lindsay, 4th ed. rev. (London: J. M. Dent, 1926). The selection omits "I said" (i.e., Socrates speaking) and "he said" where the context makes clear who is talking. The bracketed numbers following passages give the pagination in Stephanus's Greek edition of Plato.

what has been given in pledge is owing, is it not?" —— "Yes."

"But we were certainly not to make repayment when the claimant is out of his senses." —— "True."

"Then Simonides apparently means something else when he says that to repay what is owing is just." —— "But assuredly he does, for he thinks that friends owe to friends to do good and no evil."

"I understand, for what is repaid is not always what is owing; when, for example, a man repays money to one who has deposited it with him, if the repayment or acceptance is harmful and the repayer and the receiver are friends. Is that what you say Simonides meant?" —— "Certainly."

"Then are we to repay to enemies whatever is owing to them?" —— "Certainly we must pay them what is owing. But I imagine that from an enemy to an enemy evil of some sort is owing, because there evil is appropriate."

"Simonides then apparently, as poets will, made a riddle on the nature of justice. For he thought, as it appears, that to pay every man what is appropriate is just; but he called that, what is owing." —— "Do you not agree?" he said.

"In heaven's name," I said, "what answer do you think he would have given us if we had asked him: 'Simonides, what that is owing and appropriate does the art called medicine render, and to whom or what?' "

"Clearly that it renders drugs and food and drink to bodies."

"And what that is owing and appropriate does the art called cookery render, and to whom or what?"

"Seasoning to dishes."

"Well, what then does the art called justice render, and to whom or what?" —— "If, Socrates, we are to be consistent, it renders benefits and injuries to friends and enemies."

"Then does he call justice doing good to friends and evil to enemies?" —— "I think so."

"But when people are ill, who, as regards health and disease, is most capable of doing good to friends and harm to enemies?" —— "A doctor."

"And when they are on a voyage, as regards the dangers of the sea?" —— "A ship captain."

"Then what about the just man? In what action and in what regard is he most capable of benefiting

his friends and harming his enemies?" —— "In wars and alliances, I imagine."

"Very good! But, my dear Polemarchus, a doctor is useless when men are not ill." —— "True."

"And a ship captain when they are not on the sea." —— "Yes."

"Then is the just man also useless when men are not at war?" —— "I cannot think so."

"Then justice is useful in peace also?" —— "It is."

"So is farming, is it not?" —— "Yes."

"In the procuring of the fruits of the earth, that is to say?" —— "Yes.". . .

"Now, then, as to justice. What need does it satisfy or what benefit procure that makes it useful in peace?" —— "It is useful in commercial dealings, Socrates."

"By commercial dealings, do you mean partnerships or something different?" —— "Yes, partnerships."

"Then in a game of draughts is the just man or the draught player a good and useful partner?" —— "The draught player."

"In bricklaying and masonry will the just man be a better and more useful partner than the builder?" —— "Certainly not."

"Then as the harp player is a better partner than the just man in playing music, in what kind of partnership will the just man be better than the harp player or the builder?" —— "In a money partnership, I imagine."

"Except, perhaps, Polemarchus, in using money, as when it comes to buying or selling a horse. Then, I imagine, the horse dealer is the better partner. Is he not?" —— "Apparently."

"And in buying or selling a ship, the shipbuilder or the captain will be the better?" —— "Probably."

"Then on which occasions of using silver and gold is the just man a more useful partner than others?" —— "In cases of depositing and keeping money safe."

"Is not that as good as saying, when there is no need to use money, but only to keep it unused?" —— "Yes."

"Then justice is useful in regard to money when money is useless?" —— "It looks like it.". . .

"Would you say the same of a shield and a harp? When they are to be kept and not used, justice is useful; but when they are to be used, the arts of fighting and of music are more useful." —— "That must be so."

"And is it not the same with everything else? When anything is to be used, justice is useless; and when it is not to be used, useful." —— "It looks like it."

"Justice, then, my friend, cannot be of any great moment if it is useful only for things that are useless. But let us consider this point. In any kind of fight, whether with fists or weapons, is not he who is cleverest in striking also cleverest in warding off blows?" —— "Certainly."

"Moreover, is not he who is clever in warding off disease also cleverest in implanting it without being found out?" —— "I think so."

"And he is an excellent guard of an army who is clever in stealing the plans of the enemy and all their dispositions?" —— "Certainly."

"Then whoever is a clever guarder of anything is also a clever thief of it?" —— "Apparently."

"Then if the just man is clever at guarding money, he is also clever at stealing it?" —— "That is certainly the drift of the argument."

"Then the just man stands revealed as a clever thief. . . . Justice, then, according to you and . . . Simonides seems to be a form of theft, for the advantage of friends and the harm of enemies. Have you not said so?" —— "Good heavens, no!" he said; "but I do not now know what I have said. Still I am of the same opinion, that justice is to help your friends and harm your enemies."

"Do you define a man's friends as those who seem to him to be trustworthy, or as those who really are whether they seem so or not, and so with his enemies?" —— "It is but natural that a man should love those whom he thinks trustworthy, and hate those whom he thinks evil."

"But do not men make mistakes in this matter so that they think many men trustworthy who are not really so, and *vice versa*?" —— "They do."

"Then to those men are not the good enemies and the bad friends?" —— "Certainly."

"But nevertheless it is just for them in those circumstances to help the evil and harm the good, is it not?" —— "Apparently."

"But are not the good just, and such as do no injustice?" —— "Yes."

"Then, according to your argument, it is just to do ill to those who do no injustice." —— "Certainly

not, Socrates. It is the argument that seems evil."

"Then is it just to harm the unjust and benefit the just?" —— "That seems a fairer conclusion than the former."

"Then, Polemarchus, for the many who have been entirely mistaken about men, it will be just to harm their friends, for some of them are evil, and to help their enemies, for some of them are good. So we shall come to a conclusion exactly contrary to what we asserted to be Simonides' meaning." —— "Yes, that is certainly the result. But let us change, for we probably did not define friend and enemy rightly."

"Where was the definition wrong, Polemarchus?" —— "In defining the friend as he who seems to be trustworthy."

"And now, what change shall we make?" —— "We shall say that he is a friend who not only is thought to be but really is trustworthy, but he who is only thought to be and is not really trustworthy is thought to be but is not really a friend. And the same change will apply to enemies."

"Then apparently according to the argument, the good man will be a friend and the bad an enemy." —— "Yes."

"Then would you have us add to our definition of justice? In other words, whereas we said previously that it was just to do good to friends and harm to enemies, shall we now further say that justice is to do good to friends when they are good, and to harm enemies when they are bad?" —— "Certainly, I think that is an excellent definition."

"Is it then," I said, "the nature of a just man to harm any human being whatever?" —— "Why, certainly. He must harm those who are wicked and enemies."

"When horses are harmed, do they become better or worse?" —— "Worse."

"Worse as horses, or worse as dogs?" —— "Worse as horses."

"And, similarly, when dogs are harmed, do they become worse as dogs and not worse as horses?" —— "Necessarily."

"Then, my good sir, shall we not say the same of men, that when harmed they become worse as men—that is, worse in human excellence?" —— "Certainly."

"But is not justice a human excellence?" —— "That, too, is indisputable."

"Then, my friend, it is also indisputable that men who are harmed become more unjust." —— "Apparently."

"Now, can musicians, by the art of music, make men unmusical?" —— "That is impossible."

"Or can horsemen by horsemanship make men worse riders?" —— "No."

"Then can just men by justice make men unjust; or, in short, can good men by virtue make men bad?" —— "No, that is impossible."

"It is not the function of heat, I imagine, to make cold, but of its opposite?" —— "Yes."

"Nor of dryness to make wet, but of its opposite?" —— "Certainly."

"Nor of the good man to do harm, but of his opposite?" —— "That is evident."

"And is not the just man good?" —— "Certainly."

"Then to harm either his friend or any man is not the function of the just man, Polemarchus, but of his opposite, the unjust?" —— "What you say seems to me indisputable, Socrates."

"Then if any man has said that it is just to restore to each man what is owing, and if that means that the just owes harm to his enemies and help to his friends, he was not a wise man, in that he said what was untrue. For we have discovered that it is never just to injure any man." —— "I agree." [331–335]

The Sophist Thrasymachus, accusing them of talking nonsense, offers a hard-boiled definition of justice in terms of the realities of practical life: Justice is simply what is in the interest of the stronger.

"Well, every government lays down laws for its own advantage—a democracy democratic, a tyranny tyrannical laws, and so on. In laying down these laws they have made it plain that what is to their advantage is just. They punish him who departs from this as a law-breaker and an unjust man. . . . In every city justice is the same. It is what is advantageous to the established government. But the established government is master, and so sound reasoning gives the conclusion that the same thing is always just—namely, what is advantageous to the stronger." [338–339]

Socrates probes the definition:

"Now tell me. Surely you regard it as just to obey the rulers. Do you not?" —— "I do."

"Then are the rulers in every city infallible, or are they liable sometimes to make mistakes?" —— "They are certainly liable to make mistakes."

"Then in their legislation will they not lay down some right and some mistaken laws?" —— "I fancy so."

"Are right laws those which are to their advantage, and mistaken laws those which are to their disadvantage?" —— "Surely."

"And their subjects must do what they order and this is justice?" —— "Yes."

"Then, according to your argument, not only is it just to do what is advantageous to the stronger, but also to do the opposite, what is not advantageous." —— "What are you saying?"

"Just what you are, I imagine. But let us look more closely. Has it not been admitted that the rulers in prescribing certain acts to the governed sometimes mistake what is best for themselves, but that at the same time it is just for the governed to do what the rulers prescribe? Has not that been admitted?" —— "I think so."

"Think also that you have admitted that it is just to do what is to the disadvantage of those who govern and are stronger. The rulers unwittingly prescribe what is to their own hurt, and you say that it is just for others to do what they have prescribed. Then, my most wise Thrasymachus, must it not necessarily follow that it is thus just to do the opposite of what you say? For obviously the weaker are commanded to do what is to the disadvantage of the stronger." —— "But, assuredly, Socrates," said Polemarchus, "that is perfectly plain." —— "No doubt," put in Cleitophon, "if you are to give witness in his favour." —— "What need is there of witness?" he said. "Thrasymachus himself acknowledges that the rulers sometimes prescribe what is to their own hurt, and that it is just for the governed to obey those commands." —— "No, Polemarchus. Thrasymachus stated that it is just to do what the rulers command." —— "Yes, and he also stated, Cleitophon, that what is to the advantage of the stronger is just, and in making these two statements he acknowledged that sometimes the stronger command the weaker over whom they rule to do what is to their disadvantage, and it follows from those admissions that what is advantageous to the stronger is no more just than what is disadvantageous." —— "But," Cleitophon said, "by what is advantageous to the stronger he meant 'what the stronger thinks is to his advantage.' And this the weaker must do, and this is his definition of justice." —— "No, that is not what he said," Polemarchus replied.

"Well, Polemarchus," I said, "it does not matter. If Thrasymachus says so now, let us take him in that sense. Tell me, Thrasymachus, was this how you wished to define justice—namely, as that which in the judgment of the stronger is advantageous to the stronger whether it be really so or not? Are we to say that this is your meaning?" —— "Most certainly not. Do you think that I call him who makes a mistake the stronger at the time of his mistake?"

"I certainly thought that that was what you meant when you admitted that the rulers are not infallible, but sometimes make mistakes." —— "Well, you are a quibbler, Socrates. When a doctor makes a mistake about his patients, do you at that moment in so far as he is mistaken call him a doctor? or do you call a man who makes a mistake in calculating an accountant at the moment of, and in respect to, his mistake? No. I fancy that is only our way of speaking. We say the doctor, or the accountant, or the writer made a mistake; but really none of these, so far as he is what we call him, ever makes a mistake. To speak precisely, since you are for being precise, every craftsman is infallible. He who makes a mistake does so where his knowledge fails him; that is, where he is no craftsman. As with craftsmen and wise men, so with a ruler; he is always infallible so long as he is a ruler, although in ordinary language we all say that the doctor made a mistake and the ruler made a mistake. Such, then, you may take it, is my answer to you now. This is the most precise form of my statement. A ruler, so far as he is a ruler, is infallible, and being infallible he prescribes what is best for himself, and this the subject must do. So that, as I said originally, to do what is advantageous to the stronger is just." [339–341]

Doubtless Socrates breathes a sigh of relief. Thrasymachus has abandoned the realistic field of the social and historical practices of real (existent) rulers and shifted to the ideal ruler, and Socrates never thereafter allows him to appeal to how actual rulers behave. He might have held his earlier ground by saying something like this: If the ruler makes a mistake, he can recover by making sure the mistaken rule is abandoned (maybe by having the courts declare it unconstitutional!). If he cannot recover, he will lose power and the new rulers will make their own rules for their own interest.

In the ensuing argument Socrates distinguishes the doctor as healer from the doctor as moneymaker (or for that matter, we may add, as medical researcher). It is not hard to pinpoint healing as the definitive function of the doctor. But underlying the controversy is the more serious question of whether justice or injustice is the more profitable for a human being. Socrates says justice, Thrasymachus injustice. Thrasymachus's ideal is the tyrant who lays down "justice" for the subjects but has the power to give full scope to his own desires, which Thrasymachus takes to be primarily acquisitive, aggressive, sexual. They both regard life as a craft, and virtue or excellence as the appropriate skill in the work of the craft; they differ only in whether justice or injustice is the requisite virtue. (The Greek word for virtue—*aretē*—is much broader than the English: literally it is the fitness or excellence for the tasks presupposed.) [2] Socrates now exploits Thrasymachus's redefinition:

"Is the doctor in the precise sense in which you have defined him a money-maker or a healer of the sick? Understand that I am asking about the real doctor." —— "A healer of the sick," he said.

"What of the ship captain? Is the genuine captain a ruler of sailors or a sailor?" —— "A ruler of sailors."

[2] The underlying assumption of both—that there is a human nature that imposes on people tasks to be accomplished and definite directions of striving—is challenged by the Skeptics (see Chapter 4) and in the twentieth century by the existentialism of Sartre (see Chapter 22).

"The fact that he sails on a ship need not, I fancy, be taken into account, nor ought we to call him a sailor; for it is not because he is on board that he is called a ship captain, but because of his skill and his authority over sailors." —— "True."

"Both for sick people and for sailors there is something which is advantageous, is there not?" —— "Certainly."

"And is it not the natural end of the art to seek after and provide this?" —— "It is."

"But is there anything advantageous to an art, except that it should be as perfect as possible?" —— "What is the meaning of your question?"

"This," I said. "If you were to ask me whether it is enough for a body to be a body, or whether it needs something more, I should reply: 'Certainly it needs something more. In fact, this is why the art of medicine has been discovered, because the body is defective and it is not enough for it to be a body; and to provide what is advantageous to it this art is established.' Do you think that such a statement would be correct?" —— "Quite correct."

"Now is medicine itself defective? In other words, does any art whatsoever need some kind of virtue or power, as eyes need sight and ears hearing, so that what is advantageous to these powers must be discovered and provided by an art which presides over the eyes and ears? Is there any such defect in art as art, so that every art needs another to discover what is advantageous to it, and that discovering art another, and so on without end? or will each art seek its own advantage? or is it unnecessary that either itself or any other art should discover what is advantageous to it and will supply its deficiency? For in truth no art is subject to any defect or mistake, and it is not the office of an art to seek the advantage of anything except its subject. So long as an art, which is strictly an art, is true to its own nature, it is correct, and is therefore without defect or blemish. Remember that we are using the words in their strict sense. Is that a true description or not?" —— "It seems true."

"Then medicine seeks what is advantageous not to medicine, but to the body." —— "Yes."

"And horsemanship what is advantageous not to horsemanship, but to horses; and no art seeks its own advantage (for it needs nothing) but the advantage of its subject." —— "So it appears."

"But, Thrasymachus, the arts govern and are masters of their subject." —— To this he agreed, though very reluctantly.

"Then no science either prescribes or seeks the advantage of the stronger, but the advantage of the weaker over which it rules?" —— This also he admitted in the end, though he tried to make a fight of it. . . .

"Then does any doctor, so far as he is a doctor, prescribe or seek the advantage of the doctor rather than of the patient? For the doctor, in the strict sense of the word, has been admitted to be the ruler of bodies, and not a money-maker. Have we not admitted that?" He agreed. . . .

"Then, Thrasymachus, no one in any kind of government will, so far as he is a ruler, prescribe or seek his own advantage but that of the subject of his craft over which he rules; all that he says and does is said and done with the subject in view, and for his advantage and good."

When we had reached this stage in the argument, and it was plain to all that the definition of justice had been turned upside down, Thrasymachus, instead of answering, said:

"Tell me, Socrates, have you a nurse?"

"Why, this!" I said. "Should you not answer rather than ask questions of that kind?" —— "Because she lets you go on snivelling, and doesn't wipe your nose when you need it, for you have not learnt from her to distinguish sheep and shepherd."

"What, in particular, makes you say that?" I said. —— "You imagine that shepherds or herdsmen look after the good of their sheep or cattle, and fatten and tend them with some other end in view than the good of their masters and themselves, and you actually think that rulers in cities, who are really rulers, do not regard their subjects just as a man his sheep, and do not night and day seek how they may profit themselves, and that only. So profoundly wise are you concerning the just and justice, and the unjust and injustice, that you are unaware that justice and the just is really the good of another, the advantage of the stronger who rules, but the self-inflicted injury of the subject who obeys; that injustice is the opposite, and rules those very simple just souls; that the governed serve the advantage of the stronger man, and by their obedience contribute to his happiness, but in no way to their own. My most simple Socrates, you must see that a just man always comes off worse than an unjust. Take, first, the case of commercial dealing, when a just and an unjust man are partners. At the dissolution of the partnership you will never find the just man with more than the unjust, but always with less. Then in politics, where there are taxes to pay, out of equal incomes the just man pays more, the unjust less. . . . Then, again, when they are in office, the just man, apart from other losses, ruins his own business by neglect, while his justice prevents him making a profit out of the public; and, in addition, he incurs the dislike of his kinsfolk and acquaintances by refusing to be unjust for their advantage. With the unjust man it is the opposite in every particular. For I am speaking, in accordance with my recent explanation, of him who is capable of aggrandisement on a large scale. . . . For if you take the most perfect injustice, you will most easily see that it makes the doer of injustice the happiest of men. . . . This is tyranny. It plunders by fraud and force alike the goods of others, sacred and holy things, private and public possessions and never pettily but always on a grand scale. Individual cases of these crimes are on detection visited with punishment and utter disgrace, and petty offenders of this sort are called temple-breakers, kidnappers, burglars, swindlers, and thieves. But those who not only despoil the citizens of their money, but capture and enslave their persons, get no such ugly names, but are called happy and blessed men, not only by their citizens, but by all who hear of their complete injustice. Men revile injustice, not because they fear to do it, but because they fear to suffer it. Therefore, Socrates, injustice, when great enough, is mightier and freer and more masterly than justice; and, as I said at the start, justice is to the advantage of the stronger, but injustice is profitable and advantageous to oneself." [341–344]

Thrasymachus attempts to leave, but the others insist on his staying, and Socrates continues:

"Thrasymachus, to look back at the argument, observe that though you began by defining the genuine doctor, you did not think the same accuracy necessary afterwards when you came to the genuine shepherd. You thought that he, so far as he is a shepherd, fattens his sheep without considering what is best for them, but with an eye to good eating, like a gourmand who is giving a banquet, or with an eye to profit, like a money-maker, not a shepherd. But surely the art of shepherding is only concerned with how it may provide what is best for that over which it presides? As for its own

interests, all that can contribute to its excellence has already been provided, so long as it is not unfaithful to its nature. This made me think that we must admit that any government, so far as it is a government, considers what is best only for that which it governs and tends, whether the government be public or private. Now, do you think that those who rule in cities, who are genuine rulers, do so willingly?" —— "No, I don't think so. I know it."

". . . Do you not notice that in the ordinary offices of state there are no voluntary rulers? They demand to be paid on the assumption that their holding office benefits not themselves, but the governed. And tell me this. Is not the test by which we always distinguish one art from another its possession of different powers? . . ." —— "Yes, that is the distinguishing test."

"And does not each of these arts give us a distinctive, not a common benefit?—medicine health, for example; navigation safety on a voyage, and so on?" —— "Certainly."

"And the art of wages gives wages, does it not? For this is its power. For you do not call medicine and navigation the same art, do you? Speaking precisely, as you suggested, if a sea captain becomes healthy because being at sea suits him, that doesn't make you call his art medicine, does it?" —— "Surely not."

"Nor do you call the art of wages medicine, I imagine, if a man gets well while earning wages?" —— "Certainly not."

"Well, would you call medicine the art of wages if a man earned wages in medical practice?" —— "No."

"Then we have agreed that the benefit of each art is confined to that art?" —— "We have."

"Then if there be any benefit which all craftsmen enjoy in common, that will clearly come from their all using as well something which is common to them all?" —— "Apparently."

"We assert, therefore, that craftsmen who earn wages derive that benefit from their use of the additional art of wages." —— He agreed reluctantly.

"Then in the case of each art this benefit, the receiving of wages, does not come from the art. If we consider carefully we shall see that health is given by the art of medicine, fees by the art of wages; a house is provided by the art of architecture, and pay by the accompanying art of wages, and so on with all the arts. Each fulfills its own function and benefits its subject. But is a craftsman benefited by his art if he does not get pay in addition?'' —— ''Apparently not.''

''Then the voluntary performance of his art does not benefit him?'' —— ''I think not.''

''Then, Thrasymachus, it is now clear that no art or government provides what is for its own benefit, but, as we said long ago, it provides and prescribes what is for the benefit of the subject, seeking the advantage of him who is weaker, not the advantage of the stronger.'' [344–346]

By comparing justice to excellence in a variety of crafts, and by pointing to the disruptive effects of injustice (even thieves must be just within the gang to be efficient), Socrates manages to silence Thrasymachus. The argument can then roll along to its climax:

''Tell me, do you think that a horse has a function?'' —— ''I do.''

''Would you define the function of a horse or of anything else as that work for which it is the indispensable or the best instrument?'' —— ''I do not understand.''

''Let me explain. Can you see with anything but your eyes?'' —— ''Of course not.''

''Or hear with anything but your ears?'' —— ''Certainly not.''

''Then could we not justly describe seeing and hearing as the functions of eyes and ears?'' —— ''Certainly.''

''Again, could not a vine shoot be cut with a carving-knife or with a chisel or with many instruments?'' —— ''Undoubtedly.''

''But with no instrument so well, I imagine, as with a pruning-knife, which is made for the purpose?'' —— ''True.''

''Then shall we not call vine dressing the function of the pruning-knife?'' —— ''We shall.''

''Now, I fancy, you will understand better what I wanted a moment ago when I asked whether the function of each thing is that for which it is the indispensable or the best instrument.'' —— ''Yes, I understand, and I agree with that definition.''

''Good. Now do you not think that everything which has a function has also a corresponding virtue? To revert to our previous instances. We say that the eyes have a function, have they not?'' —— ''They have.''

''Then have not the eyes a virtue also?'' —— ''They have.''

''Again, the ears were found to have a function, were they not?'' —— ''Yes.''

''Then have they a virtue also?'' —— ''They have.''

''Can we say the same of everything else?'' —— ''Yes.''

''Come now, could the eyes perform their proper function well if they were without their proper virtue, but had the corresponding vice instead?'' —— ''How could they? You mean probably blindness instead of sight.''

''I mean,'' I said, ''whatever their virtue be. I am not inquiring into that here. My question is whether things perform their own function well by reason of their proper virtue, badly by reason of the corresponding vice?'' —— ''It is as you say.''

''Then if ears are deprived of their proper virtue, will they not perform their proper function badly?'' —— ''Certainly.''

''Then may we make this principle of general application?'' —— ''I think so.''

''Come then, consider this point next. Has the soul a function which nothing else upon earth can perform save itself? For example, to superintend and rule and advise and so on. Is there anything except the soul to which we could assign these acts as its peculiar functions?'' —— ''Nothing.''

''Then what of life? Shall we declare it to be a function of the soul?'' —— ''Assuredly.''

''And do we say that the soul has a virtue?'' —— ''We do.''

''Then, Thrasymachus, could the soul, if deprived of its proper virtue, perform its proper functions well? Or is that impossible?'' —— ''It is impossible.''

''Of necessity an evil soul must rule and superintend badly, but a good soul will do all these things well?'' —— ''Of necessity.''

''But have we not agreed that justice is a virtue of the soul, and injustice a vice?'' —— ''We have.''

''Then the just soul and the just man will live well, but the unjust badly?'' —— ''Apparently,'' he said, ''according to your argument.'' [352–353]

In Book II Glaucon and Adeimantus, dissatisfied with the arguments presented, take over and reformulate the problem. Glaucon distinguishes kinds of goodness:

[II] ". . . Tell me now, how do you classify things we call good? Do you think that there are some which we could gladly have, not for their consequences, but because we appreciate them for their own sake; as, for example, enjoyment and those harmless pleasures which produce no further effects beyond the mere pleasurable experience?" —— "I certainly think," I said, "that there are some like that."

"Secondly, there are some which we prize both for themselves and for their consequences; as, for example, thought and sight and health. These and similar good things we appreciate for a twofold reason." —— "Yes."

"Do you recognise a third class of good things, which includes gymnastic exercises, the undergoing of medical treatment, the practice of medicine, and the other forms of money-making? These are things which we call troublesome but advantageous. We should never take them for themselves, but we accept them for the sake of the rewards and other consequences which they bring." —— "There is certainly a third class of that description. What then?"

"In which class," he said, "do you place justice?" —— "In the fairest class, I fancy," I said, "amongst those which he, who would be blessed, must love both for their own sake and for their consequences."

"That is not the opinion of most people," he said. "They place it in the troublesome class of good things, which must be pursued for the sake of the reward and the high place in public opinion which they bring, but which in themselves are irksome and to be avoided." [357–358]

Socrates is committed to the view that justice is profitable as well as inherently good. Glaucon puts the case for the opposing popular view:

"I shall proceed in this way. . . . First, I shall state what is said to be the nature and origin of justice. Then, secondly, I shall assert that all who practise it do so unwillingly, and that they do so not because justice is good, but because it is indispensable. And, thirdly, that this conduct of theirs is reasonable; for the life of the unjust man is far better than that of the just, according to their statement. . . .

". . . By nature, men say, to do injustice is good, to suffer it evil, but there is more evil in suffering injustice than there is good in inflicting it. Therefore when men act unjustly towards one another, and thus experience both the doing and the suffering, those amongst them who are unable to compass the one and escape the other, come to this opinion: that it is more profitable that they should mutually agree neither to inflict injustice nor to suffer it. Hence men began to establish laws and covenants with one another, and they called what the law prescribed lawful and just. This, then, is the origin and nature of justice. It is a mean between the best—doing injustice with impunity—and the worst—suffering injustice without possibility of requital. Thus justice, being a mean between those extremes, is looked upon with favour, not because it is good, but because the inability to inflict injustice makes it valuable. For no one who had the power to inflict injustice and was anything of a man would ever make a contract of mutual abstention from injustice with any one else. He would be mad if he did. Such, Socrates, is the nature of justice, and such is its origin, according to the popular account."

"Now, that those who practice justice do so unwillingly and from inability to inflict injustice, will be seen most clearly if we make the following supposition. Suppose we take the just and the unjust man and give each power to do whatever he will, and then follow them and see where each is led by his desires. We shall catch the just man following undisguisedly the very same road as the unjust. He would be led on by his desire to outdo his fellows: every nature naturally pursues that as good, though law compels it to turn aside and reverence equality. The impunity I refer to would be best exemplified if they could have the power possessed by the ancestor of Gyges the Lydian in the story. For they say that he was a shepherd, a servant of the reigning king of Lydia. . . . [He found a ring by which he could make himself invisible.] When he had made this discovery he at once contrived to be one of the messengers sent to the king. Arriving at the palace he seduced the queen, plotted with her against the king, killed him, and so obtained the crown.

"Now, if there were two such rings, and the just man took one and the unjust the other, no one, it is thought, would be of such adamantine nature as to abide in justice and have the strength to abstain from theft, and to keep his hands from the goods of others, when it would be in his power to steal anything he wished from the very market-place with impunity, to enter men's houses and have intercourse with whom he would, to kill or to set free whomsoever he pleased; in short, to walk among men as a god. And, in so doing, the just man would act precisely as the unjust. Both would follow the same path. This, surely, may be cited as strong evidence that no man is just willingly, but only on compulsion. Justice is not a good to the individual, for every one is unjust whenever he thinks injustice possible. Every man thinks that injustice is more profitable to the individual than justice, and thinks rightly, according to the supporters of this theory; for if any man who possessed this power we have described should yet refuse to do unjustly or to rob his fellows, all who knew of his conduct would think him the most miserable and foolish of men, but they would praise him to each other's faces, their fear of suffering injustice extorting that deceit from them. So much, then, for that. Now this question concerning the life of these two men we shall be able to decide aright only by contrasting the extremes of justice and injustice. How shall we make our contrast? In this way. Let us abstract nothing from the injustice of the unjust or from the justice of the just; each shall be perfect in his own way of life. Firstly, then, the unjust man shall be like a clever craftsman. The skilful captain or doctor can discern what is possible and what is impossible in his art. He attempts the one and leaves the other alone; and if by any chance he makes a mistake, he is able to retrieve it. Similarly the unjust man, if he is to be thoroughly unjust, shall show discernment in his unjust deeds, and shall not be found out. If he is caught, we must consider him a failure; for it is the last word in injustice to seem just without being it. To the perfectly unjust man, then, we must give perfect injustice, and abstract nothing from it. We must allow him to do the fullest injustice and be reputed truly just. If ever he makes a mistake, he must be able to retrieve it. If any of his unjust deeds are brought to light, his eloquence will be convincing in his favour. He will be able to use force where force is needed, thanks to his courage, his strength, and his resources of friends and wealth. Such is the unjust man. Beside him, in accordance with the argument, let us place our just man, a simple and noble character, one who, as Aeschylus says, desires not to seem, but to be good. The semblance, indeed, we must take from him; for if he is reputed just, he will enjoy the honours and rewards that such a reputation earns, and thus it will not be apparent, it is objected, whether he is just for justice' sake or the honours' and rewards' sake. He must be stripped of everything except justice, and made the very counterpart of the other man. He shall do no injustice, and be reputed altogether unjust, that his justice may be tested as being proof against ill-repute and its consequences, and he go on his way unchanged till death, all his life seeming unjust but being just. Thus these two will have come to the extremes of justice and of injustice, and we may judge which of them is the happier."

". . . Well, given two such characters, it is not difficult now, I fancy, to go on to discover what sort of life awaits each of them. Let me describe it. If my description is rather harsh, remember, Socrates, that those who praise injustice above justice are responsible, and not I. They will say that our just man will be scourged, racked, fettered, will have his eyes burnt out, and at last, after all manner of suffering, will be crucified, and will learn that he ought to desire not to be but to seem just. . . . [As for the unjust man] his semblance of justice brings him rule in his city. Then he may marry and give in marriage as he pleases; he may contract or enter into partnership with whom he will, and since he has no scruples against unjust dealings, he can besides make large profits. Therefore, when he enters into a contest, whether public or private, he comes out victorious and gets the better of his enemies. By so doing he becomes rich, helps his friends and harms his enemies, and on the gods he bestows sacrifices and offerings fitting and magnificent. Far better than the just man can he serve the gods or whatsoever man he please. So that even the love of the gods is more appropriately his than the just man's. Thus they say, Socrates, that at the hands of gods and men life is made richer for the unjust than for the just." [358–362]

Socrates accepts the challenge to prove that the life of justice is in itself better than that of injustice. At this point begins the constructive analysis that occupies almost the whole of the rest of the *Republic.* He shifts focus from the individual to society in order to see the operation of justice on a larger canvas. He promises to return to the individual thereafter.

The founding of the *polis* expresses the insufficiency of the individual. The material needs of food, shelter, and so forth require cooperation among people. They agree on a principle of division of labor: [3]

"[N]o two of us are by nature altogether alike. Our capacities differ. Some are fit for one work, some for another. Do you agree?" —— "I do."

"Well, then, would better work be done on the principle of one man many trades, or of one man one trade?" —— "One man one trade is better.". . .

"And so more tasks of each kind are accomplished, and the work is better and is done more easily when each man works at the one craft for which nature fits him." [370]

Soon the *polis* includes farmers, builders and other craftsmen, merchants and other shopkeepers, even sailors and importers. There is no mention of political organization. Life in this *polis* is extremely modest. Glaucon is dissatisfied with so low a level of life. Socrates observes that apparently Glaucon wants to consider not merely a city but a luxurious city and adds that perhaps there he will learn more readily what is justice and injustice.

"Then we must make our city larger. For the healthy city will not now suffice. We need one swelled in size, and full of a multitude of things which necessity would not introduce into cities. There will be all kinds of hunters and there will be the imitators; one crowd of imitators in figure and colour, and another of imitators in music; poets and their servants, rhapsodists, actors, dancers and theatrical agents; the makers of all kinds of articles,

of those used for women's adornment, for example. Then, too, we shall need more servants; or do you think we can do without footmen, wet-nurses, dry-nurses, lady's maids, barbers, and cooks and confectioners, besides? Then we shall want swineherds too; we had none in our former city—there was no need—but we shall need them along with all the others for this city. And we shall need great quantities of all kinds of cattle if people are to eat them. Shall we not?" —— "Surely."

"Then if we lead this kind of life we shall require doctors far more often than we should have in the first city?" —— "Certainly."

"Then I dare say even the land which was sufficient to support the first population will be now insufficient and too small?" —— "Yes."

"Then if we are to have enough for pasture and ploughland, we must take a slice from our neighbours' territory. And they will want to do the same to ours, if they also overpass the bounds of necessity and plunge into reckless pursuit of wealth?" —— "Yes, that must happen, Socrates."

"Then shall we go to war at that point, Glaucon, or what will happen?" —— "We shall go to war."

"And we need not say at present whether the effects of war are good or bad. Let us only notice that we have found the origin of war in those passions which are most responsible for all the evils that come upon cities and the men that dwell in them." —— "Certainly."

"Then, my friend, our city will need to be still greater, and by no small amount either, but by a whole army. It will defend all the substance and wealth we have described, and will march out and fight the invaders." —— "Why," he said, "are they not capable of doing that for themselves?"

"Certainly not," I said, "if you and the rest of us were right in the principle we agreed upon when we were shaping the city. I think we agreed, if you remember, that it was impossible for one man to work well at many crafts." —— "True."

"Well, does not the business of war seem a matter of craftsmanship?" —— "Yes, certainly."

"Then ought we to be more solicitous for the craft of shoemaking than for the craft of war?" —— "By no means."

"But did we not forbid our shoemaker to attempt to be at the same time a farmer or a weaver or house-builder? He was to be a shoemaker only, in order that our shoemaking work might be well

---

[3] This principle of division of labor differs from the modern one in that Socrates classifies people as well as jobs. For Adam Smith the principle is largely a matter of efficiency, not presuming that different people have different talents (see Chapter 10), whereas Marx takes it as a fundamental source of human alienation (see Chapter 15).

done. So with all the others: we gave each man one trade, that for which Nature had fitted him. Nothing else was to occupy his time, but he was to spend his life working at that, using all his opportunities to the best advantage and letting none go by. And is not efficiency in war more important than anything else? . . . [B]ecause the work of our guardians is the most important of all, it will demand the most exclusive attention and the greatest skill and practice." —— "I certainly think so."

"And will it not need also a nature fitted for this profession?" —— "Surely."

"Then it will be our business to do our best to select the proper persons and to determine the proper character required for the guardians of our city?" —— "Yes, we shall have to do that." [373–374]

These dramatic few pages make the transition from a stateless civil society to an organized state, on the grounds that the desire for luxury in a world of unavoidable scarcity necessitates war and calls for a ruling or guardian group to protect from enemies without and to keep order within. Socrates next turns to the selection and character of such guardians and their education. (The term "guardians" here covers both rulers and their helpers or administrators. Later, the latter are distinguished as "auxiliaries.") Education begins with the traditional gymnastics for the body and music (in the broader Greek sense, which includes literature) for the soul. Storytelling to the children comes first.

"Then do you know that the most important part of every task is the beginning of it, especially when we are dealing with anything young and tender? For then it can be most easily moulded, and whatever impression any one cares to stamp upon it sinks in." —— "Most certainly."

"Then shall we carelessly and without more ado allow our children to hear any casual stories told by any casual persons, and so to receive into their souls views of life for the most part at variance with those which we think they ought to hold when they come to man's estate?" —— "No, we shall certainly not allow that."

"Our first duty then, it seems, is to set a watch over the makers of stories, to select every beautiful story they make, and reject any that are not beautiful. Then we shall persuade nurses and mothers to tell those selected stories to the children. Thus will they shape their souls with stories far more than they can shape their bodies with their hands. But we shall have to throw away most of the stories they tell now." —— "What kind do you mean?" [337]

Stories that portray the gods as quarrelsome and deceitful should be strictly forbidden, to begin with, because they are untrue. This leads to a discussion of the nature of the gods and the criteria for censorship. The gods should be presented as good, not responsible for evil, and as unchanging in form; for being perfect, gods could not become better and would not want to become worse.

The discussion then turns to the influence of styles of music on the formation of character (the Lydian mode is regarded as soft); the development of a sense for the beautiful and appreciation for virtuous character; the avoidance of drunkenness; gymnastics, and the sort of training and diet that avoid an overathletic stupor; attitudes to medicine (no prolonged treatments). Eventually the question of who should rule is reached. The answer is the older and more experienced among those who have passed all tests and maintained the basic convictions requisite for the well-being of society. To strengthen their hand in their tasks, Socrates designs a myth, or "noble lie," for the society:

[III] " 'You in this city are all brothers,' so we shall tell our tale to them, 'but God as he was fashioning you, put gold in those of you who are capable of ruling; hence they are deserving of most reverence. He put silver in the auxiliaries, and iron and copper in the farmers and the other craftsmen. For the most part your children are of the same nature as yourselves, but because you are all akin, sometimes from gold will come a silver offspring, or from silver a gold, and so on all round. Therefore the first and weightiest command of God to the rulers is this—that more than aught else they be good guardians of and watch zealously over the offspring, seeing which of those metals is mixed in their souls; if their own offspring have an admixture of copper or iron, they must show no pity, but giving it the honour proper to its nature, set it among the artisans or the farmers; and if on the other hand in these classes children are born with an admixture of gold and silver, they shall do them honour and appoint the first to be guardians, the second to be auxiliaries. For there is an oracle that the city shall perish when it is guarded by iron or copper.' " [415]

Book IV has the major task of examining the virtues in the state, locating justice in it, and applying this analysis to the individual, with a careful demonstration that the same pattern holds. Socrates starts with the assumption that the *polis* constructed is perfect and so has all the central virtues of wisdom, courage, temperance or self-control, and justice. His strategy is to identify the elements of goodness in the state that are promoted by the first three virtues and thus isolate the remainder as the contribution of justice.

The *wisdom* of the *polis* is found in the rulers, in their knowledge of guarding (not in the special knowledge of the craftsmen or the farmers). Since the rulers are a small group, the wisdom of the city thus lies in its smallest class. The city's *courage* is in the auxiliaries, the warrior and executive class; they are imbued with the principles and attitudes conveyed by the basic education, and by their steadfastness they safeguard the mode of life. The *temperance* of the city lies in self-mastery or control of the appetites.

"[T]emperance in its action is not like courage and wisdom. The wisdom and the courage which make the city wise and courageous reside each in a particular part, but temperance is spread through the whole alike, setting in unison of the octave the weakest and the strongest and the middle class—a unison of wisdom, if you would have that; and strength, if you would have that; of numbers also, and wealth, and any other such element. So that

we may most justly say that this unanimity is temperance, the concord of the naturally worse and the naturally better as to which should rule in the city or in the individual." —— "I entirely agree with you," he said.

"Good," I answered. "Then we have descried in the city three out of the four; at least so it appears. As for the last principle which completes the virtue possessed by the city, what will it be? Obviously it will be justice." —— "Obviously.". . .

"[T]he quarry has been rolling before our feet the whole time, and we have never seen it, but have made utter fools of ourselves. Just as people sometimes go about looking for a thing which they are holding in their hands, we have been gazing somewhere miles away instead of looking at the thing before us. . . ." —— "What do you mean?"

"I mean that we seem to have been mentioning it and hearing it mentioned all this time without realizing that we were in a way describing it ourselves." —— "A long preface for one anxious to hear."

"Well, listen, and hear whether there is anything in what I say. For at the beginning when we were founding our city, the principle which we then stated should rule throughout, or at least a form of it, was, I think, justice. We stated surely, and, if you remember, have often repeated our statement, that each individual should pursue that work in this city for which his nature was naturally most fitted, each one man doing one work." —— "Yes, we did."

"But we have often said ourselves, and heard others saying, that to mind one's own business and not be meddlesome is justice." —— "Yes, we have."

"Well, then, my friend, this in some form or other is what justice seems to be, minding one's own business. . . ."

". . . Do you think it will do any notable harm to the city if a builder attempts a shoemaker's work, or a shoemaker a builder's, or if they take one another's tools or pay, or even if the same man try to do both, and there is a general interchange in such professions?" —— "No," he said.

"But I fancy when he that is by nature a craftsman or a money-maker of some kind is so elated by his wealth, or his large connections, or his bodily strength, or some such qualities, that he essays to enter the warrior class; or when one of the warriors aspires to the counseling and guardian class when he is unworthy of it, and these take one another's tools and privileges, or when the same man tries to combine all these offices, then, I fancy, you think with me that such change and meddling among those classes is death to the city?'' —— ''Most certainly.''

''Our classes are three, and meddling and interchange among them is the greatest of injuries to the city, and might justly be described as the extreme of evil-doing.'' —— ''It is exactly as you say.''

''Then will you not admit that the worst kind of evil-doing to one's own city is injustice?'' —— ''Surely.''

''This then is injustice; and conversely the opposite of this—when each class, money-makers, auxiliaries, and guardians, attends to what belongs to it, each doing its own work in the city—will be justice, and will make the city just.'' [432–434]

Socrates now moves back to the individual. He finds it plausible that the character of society comes from the character of the individuals, but he attempts a stricter psychological proof that the individual has three comparable parts. The proof rests on the phenomenon of ambivalence, a person having an inner conflict and being drawn in opposing directions. In such a case the different tendencies stem from different parts of the soul. He points to the familiar tension between a desire and the self forbidding or repressing its expression—the conflict between appetite and reason. Spirited responses, such as indignation, are distinct from both of these, as shown by cases where we are indignant against (or ashamed of) our desires even while yielding to them; and again, where we chide our own emotional responses as unreasonable. Hence there are three parts of the soul—the rational, the spirited, and the appetitive—paralleling the three classes of rulers, auxiliaries, and the mass of people. Justice then lies in the rational part, assisted by the spirited part, keeping the appetitive part in order.

''[Justice] does not concern a man's management of his own external affairs, but his internal manage-

ment of his soul, his truest self and his truest possessions. The just man does not allow the different principles within him to do other work than their own, nor the distinct classes in his soul to interfere with one another; but in the truest sense he sets his house in order, gaining the mastery over himself; and becoming on good terms with himself through discipline, he joins in harmony those different elements, like three terms in a musical scale—lowest and highest and intermediate, and any others that may lie between those—and binding together all these elements he moulds the many within him into one, temperate and harmonious. In this spirit he lives; whether he is money-making or attending to the wants of his body, whether he is engaged in politics or on business transactions of his own, throughout he considers and calls just and beautiful all conduct which pursues and helps to create this attitude of mind. The knowledge which superintends these actions is for him wisdom, while any conduct which tends to destroy this attitude is for him unjust, and the belief which inspires it ignorance.'' —— ''That is most certainly true, Socrates.''

''Good. Then if we declare that we have discovered the just man and the just city, and justice which rules in them, I fancy that we shall not be thought to be speaking altogether falsely.''. . .

''Must not [injustice] be a kind of quarrel between those three—a meddlesomeness and interference and rebellion of one part of the soul against the whole that it may gain a rule over it to which it has no right; while the whole is such by nature that that part ought to be a slave, and the other part, which is of the royal class, ought not? Such a state of affairs, I fancy, and the disturbance and confusion of these principles, we shall declare to constitute injustice and incontinence, and cowardice and ignorance, and, in a word, all wickedness?'' —— ''Yes, precisely so.''

''Then,'' I said, ''since injustice and justice are now revealed to us, is it not quite clear what it is to act unjustly and to be unjust, and what it is also to act justly?'' —— ''In what way?''

''Clearly they do not differ from healthy and diseased conditions. As those are to the body, so are acting justly and acting unjustly to the soul.'' —— ''How?''

''Surely healthy conditions produce health, and diseased conditions disease?'' —— ''Yes.''

"Well, does not just action likewise produce justice, and unjust action injustice?" —— "Necessarily."

"Now to produce health is to put the various parts of the body in their natural relations of authority or subservience to one another, while to produce disease is to disturb this natural relation." —— "Yes."

"Then to produce justice is to put the parts of the soul in their natural relations of authority or subservience, while to produce injustice is to disturb this natural relation, is it not?" —— "Surely."

"Then virtue, seemingly, will be a kind of health and beauty and good condition of the soul, vice a disease and ugliness and weakness." —— "That is true."

"Then do not fair practices conduce to the acquisition of virtue, ugly practices to the acquisition of vice?" —— "Necessarily."

"There now apparently remains for us to inquire whether it is profitable to act justly and follow fair practices and be just, and that whether the just man is recognized as such or not, or whether acting unjustly and being unjust is profitable, even if the unjust man is not punished, or reformed by correction." [443–445]

Books V–VII are a major digression. Having established the nature of justice, Socrates wants to go on next to discuss its approximations and deteriorations (Book VIII). But his hearers want him first to consider the institutions established for the life of the guardians and the auxiliaries, so he turns to the equality of men and women, family structure, property, and political structure.

[V] ". . . [I]f we find either the male or the female sex excelling the other in any art or other pursuit, then we shall say that this particular pursuit must be assigned to one and not to the other; but if we find that the difference consists simply in this, that the female conceives and the male begets, we shall not allow that that goes any way to prove that a woman differs from a man with reference to the subject of which we are speaking, and we shall still consider that our guardians and their wives ought to follow the same pursuits." —— "And quite rightly," he said. . . .

". . . [W]hen you say that one man has a natural talent for anything, and another is naturally unfitted for it, do you mean that the first learns it easily, while the second learns it with difficulty? that the first, after a little study, would find out much for himself in the subject which he has studied; but the second, in spite of much study and practice, would not even keep what he had learned? that in the one the mind would be well served by the bodily powers, in the other it would be thwarted. Are not these the only signs by which you meant to determine in any case natural talent or the want of it?" —— "No one will name any others."

"Then, do you know any human occupation in which the male sex does not in all these particulars surpass the female? Need I bore you by referring to weaving and the making of pastry and preserves, in which, indeed, the female sex is considered to excel, and where their discomfiture is most laughed at?" —— "What you say is true. Speaking generally, the one sex is easily beaten by the other all round. There are indeed many cases of women being better than men in many different employments, but, as a general rule, it is as you say."

"Then, my friend, there is no one of those pursuits by which the city is ordered which belongs to women as women, or to men as men; but natural aptitudes are equally distributed in both kinds of creatures. Women naturally participate in all occupations, and so do men; but in all women are weaker than men." —— "Certainly."

"Shall we, then, assign all occupations to men and none to women?" —— "Of course not."

"But we shall say, I fancy, that one woman is by nature fit for medicine, and another not; one musical, and another unmusical?" —— "Surely."

"And is not one woman a lover of gymnastics and of war, and another unwarlike and no lover of gymnastics?" —— "I should think so."

"And one a lover and another a hater of wisdom; one spirited, another spiritless?" —— "Yes."

"Then one woman will be capable of being a guardian and another not. For did we not select just this nature for our men guardians?" —— "We did."

"Then for the purposes of guarding the city the nature of men and women is the same, except that women are naturally weaker, men naturally stronger?" —— "Apparently."

"Then we must select women of the necessary

character to share the life of men of like character and guard the city along with them, inasmuch as they are capable and of a kindred nature?" —— "Certainly."

"Then must we not assign the same occupations to the same natures?" —— "Yes."

"So we are come round to what we said before, and allow that there is nothing unnatural in assigning music and gymnastic to the wives of the guardians [i.e., women guardians]?" —— "Most certainly."

"Then our legislation has not been an impracticable dream, seeing that we have made our law in accordance with nature? Present conditions which depart from this are evidently much more a departure from nature." [454–456]

Within the two top groups there are no private families. They constitute instead a single family. The rulers decide who is to mate with whom for procreation, apparently on eugenic grounds as determined by people's accomplishments and presumed abilities. (Deceit is used to make it seem a matter of chance or lot.) At birth, children are taken away to be raised in common, and they remain unknown to their parents. Similarly, there is among them no private property.[4]

"Then we have proved the auxiliaries' community of wives and children to be a cause of the greatest good that a city can have?" —— "Certainly we have," he said.

---

[4] Underlying both these reforms is Plato's view that private family loyalties and private property are great begetters of specialized interests. While these social transformations are revolutionary, they should not be misconstrued. Plato's communism as regards property is not Marx's: in the *Republic* the instruments of production remain in the hands of the third and largest class, which includes not just the workers but also the rich. A better comparison is to a medieval religious order, which holds land in common for its members' use and thoroughly controls their lives. If the priests were also the actual rulers and soldiers of the village, celibacy would have the same effect as Plato sought in abolishing the family, that is, it would remove all private interests. Plato might have enjoined celibacy on his rulers had he not believed that this would have meant wasting the best seed.

"Then in this we are also consistent with our former remarks. For we said, did we not, that if they were to be guardians in reality, they must not have houses or land or any other possession of their own, but must receive what they need for sustenance from the other citizens as wages for their guardianship, and lay it out in common?" —— "We were right."

"Then am I not correct in saying that these regulations, together with our former statements, will do still more to make them true guardians, and prevent the disruption of the city which would result if each man gave the name of 'mine' not to the same but to different things; if all took what they could get for themselves, and dragged it off to their different private houses; if each called a different wife and different children his own, and thus implanted in the city the individual pleasures and griefs of individuals: rather they will have one single belief concerning what is their own and be all concerned in the same purpose, and so will all be, as far as is possible, simultaneously affected by pleasure and pain?" —— "That is perfectly true."

"Further, will not lawsuits and prosecutions almost have disappeared if their own persons are their only private property and everything else is common? Will they not, therefore, be free from all those quarrels that arise among men from the possession of money, or children, or kinsmen?" —— "It is quite inevitable that they should."

"Further, no actions for forcible seizure or for assault will rightly arise among them; for we shall declare, I suppose, that it is honourable and just for equals to defend themselves against equals, so compelling them to keep themselves in condition." —— "That is right."

"Yes, and here is a further reason why this law is right. When any man is angry with another, if he may vent his anger in this way he is less likely to make a serious quarrel of it." —— "Certainly."

"Further, we shall authorise the elder to rule over and chastise all the younger." —— "Clearly."

"Also a younger man will never dare to strike or in any other way do violence to an older unless at the command of the guardians. That we may reasonably expect. And I fancy that he will not do him dishonour in any other way. For two guardians will be strong enough to prevent him—fear and shame—the shame that forbids him to lay hands on his parents, and the fear that the others will come to the rescue of the injured man, whose sons and brothers and fathers they are." —— "Yes, that will be the result."

"Then in every way our laws will make these men dwell at peace with one another?" —— "Yes, to a large extent."

"Then if they are free from dissension, there is no fear of the rest of the city quarrelling either with them or with one another?" —— "No, certainly not." [464–465]

A question now raised by the hearers—whether the ideal state is realizable—sets off what Socrates seems to regard as the most controversial issue, more controversial even than equality for women, the abolition of family and private property. For,

"Unless philosophers bear kingly rule in cities, or those who are now called kings and princes become genuine and adequate philosophers, and political power and philosophy be brought together, and unless the numerous natures who at present pursue either politics or philosophy, the one to the exclusion of the other, be forcibly debarred from this behaviour, there will be no respite from evil, my dear Glaucon, for cities, nor I fancy for humanity; nor will this constitution, which we have just described in our argument, come to that realization which is possible for it and see the light of day." [473]

Politics should be a science, not a conflict of wills and interests, and therefore, on the medical model, should be handled by "doctors." Socrates at this point brings in his heaviest philosophical armaments—epistemology and metaphysics—represented by the simile of the ship, which is intended to win a common sense assent to the authority of knowledge, and then by the famous picture of the cave.

[VI] ". . . Conceive something of this kind happening on board ship, on one ship or on several. The master is bigger and stronger than all the crew, but rather deaf and short-sighted. His seamanship is as deficient as his hearing. The sailors are quarrel-ling about the navigation. Each man thinks that he ought to navigate, though up to that time he has never studied the art, and cannot name his instructor or the time of his apprenticeship. They go further and say that navigation cannot be taught, and are ready to cut in pieces him who says that it can. They crowd round the solitary master, entreating him and offering him every inducement to entrust them with the helm. Occasionally when they fail to persuade him and others succeed, they kill those others and throw them overboard, overpower the noble master by mandragora or drink or in some other way, and bind him hand and foot. Then they rule the ship and make free with the cargo, and so drinking and feasting make just such a voyage as might be expected of men like them. Further, they compliment any one who has the skill to contrive how they may persuade or compel the master to set them over the ship, and call him a good seaman, or navigator, and a master of seamanship; any other kind of man they despise as useless. They have no notion that the true navigator must attend to the year and the seasons, to the sky and the stars and the winds, and all that concerns his craft, if he is really going to be fit to rule a ship. They do not believe that it is possible for any one to acquire by skill or practice the art of getting control of the helm, whether there is opposition or not, and at the same time to master the art of steering. If ships were managed in that way, do you not think that the true navigator would certainly be called a star gazer and a useless babbler by the crews of ships of that description?" —— "Yes, certainly," said Adeimantus.

"Now, I fancy," I said, "that if you examine the simile you will not fail to see the resemblances to cities in their attitude towards true philosophers, and you will understand what I mean." —— "Yes, certainly."

"Then propound this parable to your friend, who is astonished that philosophers are not honoured in cities, and try to persuade him that it would be much more astonishing if they were." —— "Yes, I will."

"Show him that you are right in saying that the best of the students of philosophy are useless to the world; but bid him blame for this uselessness not the good philosophers but those who do not use them. For it is not natural that the navigator should entreat the sailors to be ruled by him, or that the wise should wait at rich men's doors. The author of that sneer spoke false. The truth established by nature is that he who is ill, whether he be rich or poor, ought to wait at the doctor's door, and every man who needs to be ruled at the door of him who can rule. The ruler, if he is really good for anything, ought not to request his subjects to be ruled. But under present political conditions you will not be wrong in likening the rulers to the sailors we have just described, and those whom they call useless talkers in the air to the true navigators." [488–489]

[VII] "Then after this," I said, "liken our nature in its education and want of education to a condition which I may thus describe. Picture men in an underground cave-dwelling, with a long entrance reaching up towards the light along the whole width of the cave; in this they lie from their childhood, their legs and necks in chains, so that they stay where they are and look only in front of them, as the chain prevents them turning their heads round. Some way off, and higher up, a fire is burning behind them, and between the fire and the prisoners is a road on higher ground. Imagine a wall built along this road, like the screens which showmen have in front of the audience, over which they show the puppets." —— "I have it."

"Then picture also men carrying along this wall all kinds of articles which overtop it, statues of men and other creatures in stone and wood and other materials; naturally some of the carriers are speaking, others are silent." —— "A strange image and strange prisoners."

"They are like ourselves. For in the first place, do you think that such men would have seen anything of themselves or of each other except the shadows thrown by the fire on the wall of the cave opposite to them?" —— "How could they, if all their life they had been forced to keep their heads motionless?"

"What would they have seen of the things carried along the wall? Would it not be the same?" —— "Surely."

"Then if they were able to talk with one another, do you not think that they would suppose what they saw to be the real things?" —— "Necessarily."

"Then what if there were in their prison an echo from the opposite wall? When any one of those passing by spoke, do you imagine that they could help thinking that the voice came from the shadow passing before them?" —— "No, certainly not."

"Then most assuredly the only truth that such men would conceive would be the shadows of those manufactured articles?" —— "That is quite inevitable."

"Then consider the manner of their release from their bonds and the cure of their folly, supposing that they attained their natural destiny in some such way as this. Let us suppose one of them released, and forced suddenly to stand up and turn his head, and walk and look towards the light. Let us suppose also that all these actions gave him pain, and that he was too dazzled to see the objects whose shadows he had been watching before. What do you think he would say if he were told by some one that before he had been seeing mere foolish phantoms, while now he was nearer to being, and was turning to what in a higher degree is, and was looking more directly at it? And further, if each of the several figures passing by were pointed out to him, and he were asked to say what each was, do you not think that he would be perplexed, and would imagine that the things he had seen before were truer than those now pointed out to him?" —— "Yes, much truer."

"Then if he were forced to look at the light itself, would not his eyes ache, and would he not try to escape and turn back to things which he could look at, and think that they were really more distinct than the things shown him?" —— "Yes."

"But if some one were to drag him out up the steep and rugged ascent, and did not let go till he had been dragged up to the light of the sun, would not his forced journey be one of pain and annoyance; and when he came to the light, would not his eyes be so full of the glare that he would not be able to see a single one of the objects we now call true?" —— "Certainly, not all at once."

"Yes, I fancy that he would need time before he could see things in the world above. At first he would most easily see shadows, then the reflections in water of men and everything else, and, finally, the things themselves. After that he could look at the heavenly bodies and the sky itself by night, turning his eyes to the light of the stars and the moon more easily than to the sun or to the sun's light by day?" —— "Surely."

"Then, last of all, I fancy he would be able to look at the sun and observe its nature, not its appearances in water or on alien material, but the very sun itself in its own place?" —— "Inevitably."

"And that done, he would then come to infer

concerning it that it is the sun which produces the seasons and years, and controls everything in the sphere of the visible, and is in a manner the author of all those things which he and his fellow-prisoners used to see?'' —— ''It is clear that this will be his next conclusion.''

''Well, then, if he is reminded of his original abode and its wisdom, and those who were then his fellow-prisoners, do you not think that he will pity them and count himself happy in the change?'' —— ''Certainly.''

''Now suppose that those prisoners had among themselves a system of honours and commendations, that prizes were granted to the man who had the keenest eye for passing objects and the best memory for which usually came first, and which second, and which came together, and who could most cleverly conjecture from this what was likely to come in the future, do you think that our friend would think longingly of those prizes and envy the men whom the prisoners honour and set in authority? Would he not rather feel what Homer describes, and wish earnestly

'To live on earth a swain,
Or serve swain for hire,'

or suffer anything rather than be so the victim of seeming and live in their way?'' —— ''Yes, I certainly think that he would endure anything rather than that.''

''Then consider this point. If this man were to descend again and take his seat in his old place, would not his eyes be full of darkness because he had just come out of the sunlight?'' —— ''Most certainly.''

''And suppose that he had again to take part with the prisoners there in the old contest of distinguishing between the shadows, while his sight was confused and before his eyes had got steady (and it might take them quite a considerable time to get used to the darkness), would not men laugh at him, and say that having gone up above he had come back with his sight ruined, so that it was not worth while even to try to go up? And do you not think that they would kill him who tried to release them and bear them up, if they could lay hands on him, and slay him?'' —— ''Certainly.''

''Now this simile, my dear Glaucon, must be applied in all its parts to what we said before. . . . Whether it be actually true, God knows. But this is how it appears to me. In the world of knowledge the Form of the good is perceived last and with difficulty, but when it is seen it must be inferred that it is the cause of all that is right and beautiful in all things, producing in the visible world light and the lord of light, and being itself lord in the intelligible world and the giver of truth and reason, and this Form of the good must be seen by whosoever would act wisely in public or in private.'' —— ''I agree with you, so far as I am capable.''. . .

''Then do you think it at all surprising,'' I said, ''if one who has come from divine visions to the world of men plays a sorry part and appears very ridiculous when, with eyes still confused and before he has got properly used to the darkness that is round him, he is compelled to contend in law courts or else where concerning the shadows of the just or the images which throw those shadows, or to dispute concerning the manner in which those images are conceived by men who have never seen real justice?'' —— ''No, it is anything but surprising.'' [514–518]

''Then if these things be true, we must think thus on the subject before us—that education is not what certain of its professors declare it to be. They say, if you remember, that they put knowledge in the soul where no knowledge has been, as men putting sight into blind eyes.'' —— ''Yes, they do.''

''But our present argument shows that there resides in each man's soul this faculty and the instrument wherewith he learns, and that it is just as if the eye could not turn from darkness to light unless the whole body turned with it; so this faculty and instrument must be wheeled round together with the whole soul away from that which is becoming, until it is able to look upon and to endure being and the brighter blaze of being; and that we declare to be the good. Do we not?'' —— ''Yes.''

''Education then,'' I said, ''will be an art of doing this, an art of conversion, and will consider in what manner the soul will be turned round most easily and effectively. Its aim will not be to implant vision in the instrument of sight. It will regard it as already possessing that, but as being turned in the wrong direction, and not looking where it ought, and it will try to set this right.'' —— ''That seems probable.''

''Now most of the virtues which are commonly said to belong to the soul seem to resemble the bodily virtues. They seem to be really implanted by habit and exercise where they have not previously existed. But the virtue of wisdom evidently does in reality belong to something much more divine, which never loses its power, but which from conversion becomes useful and advantageous, or again useless and harmful." [519]

The proposed curriculum for higher education, emphasizing the development of the mind and its ascent, is heavily laden with mathematics—not to facilitate practical pursuits, but to turn the mind to purer logical thinking, appreciation of the Forms, and absorption in the eternal. The final course of study is the discipline of dialectic.

Book VIII resumes the discussion dropped at the end of Book IV—how the ideal society, if achieved, will degenerate, due to the flawed character of all existence and unavoidable human mistakes. The course of the historical descent of society (see the succession of constitutions in Table 2.1: aristocracy, timocracy, oligarchy, democracy, tyranny) is tied to how rule in the individual soul passes from reason to its lower parts. Vignettes are provided of the successive constitutions and characters, and of the match between the kind of society and the character of its members. The movement begins with the dispossession of the aristocratic rule, described in terms of the original "noble lie" with its story of the gold, silver, and iron and bronze in the different types of people.

[VIII] "When sedition had arisen, the two pairs of races began to pull different ways, the iron and bronze to money-making and possession of land and houses and gold and silver; the others, the gold and silver, since they were not in want but rich by nature, led their souls towards virtue and the old constitution. After violent conflict they came to a compromise, and distributed land and houses for private enjoyment. Those whom formerly they had protected as free men, friends and supporters, they then enslaved and treated as serfs and servants, reserving to themselves war and the duty of guarding the others." —— "I think that this is the origin of that revolution."

"Then," I asked, "will not this constitution be midway between an aristocracy and an oligarchy?" —— "Certainly."

"Such then will be the revolution. But after revolution, how will it be governed? Is it not obvious that in some respects it will imitate the earlier constitution, and in others oligarchy, inasmuch as it lies between them, and that it will also have some features of its own?" —— "Yes."

"Then in reverence towards rulers, in the abstention of its warrior element from husbandry, handicrafts, and other forms of money-making, in the establishment of common meals, and in bestowing attention on gymnastic and the exercise of war, in all these matters will it not imitate the earlier constitution?" —— "Yes."

"But will it not have many features of this kind peculiar to itself? It will distrust the wise as rulers, for its wise men will now be of mixed character, not simple and sincere as before; it will prefer spirited and more straightforward men, made more for war than for peace, will have a great admiration for military tricks and stratagems, and will always be engaging in war?" —— "Yes."

"Further, these men will be avaricious like the citizens in oligarchies, with a fierce secret passion for gold and silver. They will have storehouses and treasuries of their own where they will store their wealth in secret. They will be ringed round with dwellings, mere private nests where they may squander a lavish expenditure on their wives and whomsoever they please." —— "Very true."

"Further, they will be sparing of their money, reverencing it as men do whose money-making is in secret, but their desires will make them enjoy spending other men's money. They will pluck the fruits of pleasure in secret, running away from the law, like boys running away from their father. Compulsion and not persuasion will have controlled their education, because they have neglected the true Muse, who is accompanied by reason and philosophy, and have honoured gymnastic above music." —— "You describe a constitution compounded throughout of good and evil."

"Yes, it is a compound. But one single feature is conspicuous in it, which arises from the prevalence of the spirited element, and that is rivalry and ambition." [547–548]

"Then oligarchy, I suppose, will be the next constitution?" —— "What kind of government do you mean by oligarchy?" he asked.

"The constitution which rests on property

valuation, where the rich rule, and a poor man is debarred from office." —— "I understand."

"Then must we first declare how the change from timocracy to oligarchy comes about?" —— "Yes.". . .

"That treasure house," I said, "where each man stores his gold is the ruin of timocracy. For they begin by discovering ways of spending their money, and stretch the laws till they and their wives flout them." —— "That is probable."

"Then I fancy they watch and try to outrival one another till they make the whole population like themselves?" —— "Probably."

"From that point they make steady progress in money-making, and the more they honour money the less they honour virtue. Is there not this strife between wealth and virtue: they always incline in opposite ways in the scales of the balance?" —— "Most certainly."

"Then when in a city wealth and the wealthy are honoured, virtue and the good are slighted?" —— "Obviously."

"But men devote themselves to anything that is honoured, and neglect anything that is slighted?" —— "Yes."

"Then in process of time, from men who love victory and honour they become lovers of money-getting and of money; they give their praise and admiration to the rich man, and elect him to rule over them, but the poor man they slight?" —— "Certainly."

"Then they lay down a law which is the distinguishing feature of an oligarchic constitution. They prescribe a sum of money varying in amount as the oligarchy is more or less extreme, and proclaim all disqualified for office whose means do not amount to the prescribed sum. Either the proposal is put through by force of arms, or by threats and terrorism they manage to get an oligarchic constitution established without actual conflict. Is not that so?" —— "Yes."

"Then this is more or less the way in which it is established." [550–551]

Oligarchy becomes two cities: the city of the rich and the city of the poor, in perpetual conflict.

"Then a democracy, I fancy, comes into being when the poor have gained the day; some of the opposite party they kill, some they banish, with the rest they share citizenship and office on equal terms; and, as a general rule, office in the city is given by lot." —— "Yes, that is the establishment of democracy, whether it is effected by actual force of arms, or by the other party yielding from fear."

"Then in what fashion will they live?" I asked; "and what will be the nature of such a constitution? For, obviously, a man of similar character will turn out to be democratic." —— "Obviously."

"Then, first and foremost, they are free, the city is crammed with liberty and freedom of speech, and there is permission to do there whatever any one desires?" —— "So they say."

"Then clearly where the permissive principle rules, each man will arrange his own life to suit himself?" —— "Clearly."

"Then this constitution, I fancy, will be distinguished by the wonderful variety of men in it?" —— "Surely."

"It will turn out to be the fairest of constitutions," I said. "Like a garment of many colours of every shade and variety, this constitution will be variegated with every character, and be most fair to look upon; and possibly, just as children and women admire many-coloured things, so many people will judge this city to be fairest of all." —— "Most certainly they will."

"And it certainly is, my wonderful friend, a handy place to look for a constitution." —— "What do you mean?"

"The permissive principle allows it all kinds of constitutions, and it seems as if the man who wanted to found a city, as we have just been doing, ought to step into the democratic city and choose the style that suited him. You may go to this universal provider of constitutions, make your choice, and found your city." —— "Well, he will certainly find no lack of patterns."

"In this city there is no necessity to rule even if you are capable of ruling, or to be ruled if you don't want, or to be at war because the rest of the city is, or where the rest of the city is at peace, to observe peace if you don't wish to; if there is a law forbidding you to be a magistrate or a judge, that is no reason why you should not be both magistrate and judge if you have a mind to. Is that not a life of heavenly pleasure for the time?" —— "Perhaps," he said, "for the time."

"And is not the placid good temper of some of their condemned criminals beautiful? Under this constitution, when they have been sentenced to death or exile, they let it make no difference, but stay on and stroll about the streets; and have you never noticed how the culprit saunters round, and no one pays any attention or sees him, just as though he were a spirit from the departed?'' —— "Yes, and such a number of them too.''

"Then think of the considerateness of the city, its entire superiority to trifles, its disregard of all those things we spoke of so proudly when we were founding our city; we said that, except from altogether extraordinary natures, no one could turn out to be a good man unless his earliest years were given to noble games, and he gave himself wholly to noble pursuits. Is it not sublime how this city tramples all such things under foot, and is supremely indifferent as to what life a man has led before he enters politics? If only he assert his zeal for the multitude, it is ready to honour him.'' —— "Yes, it is perfectly splendid.''

"Then these and others of a like kind will be the marks of a democracy,'' I said. "It will be, apparently, a pleasant constitution, with no rulers and plenty of variety, distributing its peculiar kind of equality to equals and unequals impartially.'' —— "Yes, what you say is notorious.'' [557–558]

"But,'' I said, "[the democratic man] will not receive nor suffer within the ramparts the true reasoning of any one who asserts that some pleasures spring from the desires that are good and noble, but others from those that are evil, and that the former should be fostered and honoured, and the latter disciplined and enslaved. To all such remarks he shakes his head, and says that all are alike and deserving of equal honour.'' —— "Yes, that is exactly how that sort of man behaves.''

"And this is his life. Day after day he gratifies the pleasures as they come—now fluting down the primrose path of wine, now given over to teetotalism and banting; one day in hard training, the next slacking and idling, and the third playing the philosopher. Often he will take to politics, leap to his feet and do or say whatever comes into his head; or he conceives an admiration for a general, and his interests are in war; or for a man of business, and straightway that is his line. He knows no order or necessity in life; but he calls life as he conceives it pleasant and free and divinely blessed, and is ever faithful to it.'' —— "That is a perfect description of the life of a man to whom all laws are equal.'' [561]

Tyranny arises from the excess of liberty in democracy. The collapse of standards and controls opens the way to the lawless appetites (those that show themselves usually only in dreams) that take over the soul. Any means becomes acceptable. The class struggle intensifies, the rich are plundered and driven into social conspiracy, a demagogue poses as a public champion, seizes power and represses all, supported by military force. The tyrannical character is impulse-ridden, thoroughly chaotic internally, unable to have any genuine friendships with others. The tyrant becomes practically a slave of his fears and desires.

The old question of choice among the three modes of life reasserts itself: which is the happiest—the intellectual life, with its love of wisdom, the political, with its love of power, or the appetitive, with its love of bodily pleasure and the pursuit of wealth? This leads to a depth-psychological analysis of pleasure itself, in a many-pronged attempt at comparative evaluation.[5]

[IX] ". . . [W]e say that of men also there are three primary classes—the lovers of wisdom, the lovers of victory, and the lovers of gain.'' —— "Exactly so.''

"Then there are also three kinds of pleasures, one for each of the three?'' —— "Yes.''

"Now do you know,'' I said, "that if you were to ask three such men, each in turn, which of these lives is the most pleasant, each would extol his own life most highly?''. . .

"Well,'' I said, "when the discussion concerns the pleasures, and in fact the whole life, of each type of man, and the question at issue is not their relative nobility or disgracefulness, their goodness or badness, but simply and solely which is most pleasant and least painful, how can we know which of the three speaks most truly?'' —— "I can't say.''

"Well, look at the matter in this way. What is wanted for a judgment that is to turn out to be right? Are they not experience and insight and rea-

[5] A somewhat parallel discussion about the relation of quantity and quality of pleasures will be found in Mill (see Chapter 16).

son? Can you have any better test than these?''
—— ''Of course not.''

''Now, consider. There are those three men. Which of them has had most experience of all these pleasures? Do you think that the gain-lover learns the nature of truth and acquires more experience of the pleasure of knowledge than the philosopher has of the pleasure of gain?'' —— ''The cases are very different,'' he said. ''For the latter must of necessity start in childhood by testing both the other kinds; whereas there is no compulsion on the gain-lover to learn the nature of reality and taste the sweetness of this pleasure or to have any experience of it. Nay, if he had the best will in the world, he would find it no easy matter.''

''Then the philosopher far excels the gain-lover in his experience of both pleasures?'' —— ''Yes.''

''And the lover of honour also? Or has he less experience of the pleasures of honour than the other has of the pleasure derived from wisdom?'' —— ''No, honour comes to them all if they accomplish their several aims. For the rich man is honoured by many. So is the brave and the wise man. So that all have experience of the pleasure which comes from being honoured and know its nature; but it is impossible for any one but the philosopher to taste the pleasure contained in the vision of being.''

''Then so far as experience is concerned he will judge best of the three men?'' —— ''Far the best.''

''And his experience alone will involve insight?'' —— ''Certainly.''

''And, lastly, as to the necessary instrument of judgment, it is not the instrument of the gain-lover or of the honour-lover, but of the philosopher?'' —— ''What is that instrument?''

''Surely we said that judgment must be made by means of reasoning?'' —— ''Yes.''

''But reasoning is this man's special instrument?'' —— ''Surely.''

''Now, if what is being judged were best judged by means of wealth and profit, the praise and blame of the gain-lover would necessarily be the truest?'' —— ''Necessarily.''

''Or if by means of honour and victory and courage the praise of the honour- and victory-lover would be truest?'' —— ''Obviously.''

''But since they are best judged by means of experience and insight and reason——?'' —— ''It is inevitable,'' he said, ''that the praise of the philosopher and lover of reason should be truest.''

''Then of these three pleasures, will not that be the pleasantest which belongs to the part of the soul wherewith we learn, and pleasantest also the life of him amongst us in whom this part rules?'' —— ''How else? The wise man's praise is decisive, and he praises his own life.''

''What life and what pleasure does the judge declare to come second?'' —— ''Obviously the pleasure of the warrior and the honour-lover, for that is nearer him than the pleasure of the money-maker.''

''Then the gain-lover's apparently comes last?'' —— ''Of course,'' he said. [581–583]

A further argument urges the unreality of the bodily pleasures. Pleasure and pain are distinguished from a third state, one of rest or quiet. This last becomes desirable when we are in pain or under tension and so is confused with pleasure. Going from painful illness to health makes the state of health seem pleasurable, but in fact when we are in a normal condition we pay it no regard. Now the pleasures of food and sex are of such a sort: they are a cycle of repletion and depletion; their pleasure appears in coming back to normal conditions. Such intermediate pleasures as smell, which do not require a previous lack, are more real. But intellectual pleasures, in that they are genuinely cumulative and, moreover, are concerned with the eternal and not the changing, are genuinely real. Thus the mass of people are pursuing unreality. Only the wise man knows genuine pleasure. And the tyrant, driven by constant desires, is the lowest of all.[6]

Book X, returning to the nature of art, seeks

[6] This line of argument, apparently tailor-made for Plato's general scheme, has played an important part in modern psychological analyses of pleasure, though cast in other language. Thus some identify pleasure with the release from tension or the satisfaction of a need or drive. Others (e.g., Aristotle) object that this unduly concentrates on need and ignores the role of pleasure as concomitant with any successful activity. The whole argument exemplifies the way in which Plato, so early in the history of philosophy, while proceeding in the terms of his ethical argument, is constantly striking scientific pay dirt.

to justify the harsh treatment of the artist: art is a distant thirdhand copy of reality. The painter imitates or represents what he sees, which is already a copy of the true form or intellectual reality. Hence the painter deals with shadows of shadows, at third remove from the real. Similarly for poets: Homer, when he is portraying a general, is simply presenting his image of the individual who is already a secondary embodiment of true generalship. A further argument against art is that it stirs up the emotions rather than calms them. The tragedian stirs the audience, breaks down its guard and releases its emotions; as a result, the dragon among us is strengthened.[7]

At the end of Book X Socrates argues for the immortality of the soul. Religious arguments have not hitherto been utilized for his ethics; but since he feels the ethical theory is now established, "can there now be any harm in our going further and restoring to justice and the rest of virtue the rewards, in their proper number and kinds, which it renders to the soul at the hands of gods and men, both in a man's lifetime and after he is dead?" (612). What is restored is the view that the gods love the virtuous and reward them in life and beyond, in the afterlife. The soul is not merely immortal: souls also transmigrate through a succession of lives. He relates the myth of Er, who came back from an apparent death to report what happens to the dead. The climax is the choice by each soul of his or her next life.

[X] "So saying, the prophet cast the lots to all, and each man took up the lot that fell beside him, except Er. Him the prophet forbade. And as each

[7] If art had a deeper insight into truth and reality, it would be a rival of philosophy for the right to guide human life. Plato's arguments have remained a perennial challenge to subsequent aesthetic theory. Aristotle defended tragedy as providing emotional release in a way that brings deeper insight. Later Schopenhauer argued that the artist brings a deeper understanding of the real to correct the copy and makes us see what the copy represents.

took it up he knew what order in the lot he had obtained. And after this the prophet laid on the ground before them the patterns of lives, many more patterns than there were persons present. Now there were patterns of all kinds. There were lives of all living creatures, and with them all human lives. Among them were tyrannies, some lasting, others destroyed in mid course and ending in poverty and exile and beggary. There were lives of famous men also, some famed for their comeliness and beauty, or for their strength and prowess, others for their lineage and the virtues of their ancestors; similarly there were lives of unknown men; and also the lives of women. But there was no determination of soul, because of necessity the soul becomes different according as she chooses a different life. All other things were mixed with each other, and with wealth and poverty; some with disease and some with health, and there were also mean conditions of these things. And it is here, it seems, my dear Glaucon, that man's greatest danger lies; and for those reasons we must give all heed that each of us, putting aside all other learning, may search after and study this alone, if in any way he may be able to learn and discover who will give him capacity and knowledge to discern the good and evil in life, and always and everywhere to choose the better according to his ability. He will reckon up all the things we have just mentioned, taking them both together and separately, and estimate their contribution to virtue of life; and so he will know what of good or evil is worked by beauty, whether mixed with poverty or riches, and with what disposition of soul these are good and with what bad; and what of good or evil is worked by noble birth or ignoble birth, by private or public station, by strength or weakness of body, by learning or ignorance, and by all such properties as concern the soul, both natural and acquired, in their combinations with one another, so that he may be able to put these considerations together, and looking to the nature of the soul may choose the worse or the better life, calling that worse which will lead the soul into greater injustice, and that better which will lead it into greater justice. But all other considerations he will leave alone. For we have seen that this is the greatest choice both for life and beyond it. And a man when he goes to the other world must have this belief like adamant within him, in order that there also he may be unmoved by riches and evils of that sort, and may not by falling into tyranny or some such course of action, both commit himself and himself suffer in greater degree evils many and incurable, but may have knowledge to choose always the life that lies in the middle and avoid the extremes on both sides, both in this life, so far as he may, and in the life to come. For so man wins his greatest happiness." [617–619]

Those in whom the dragon is strongest grab what looks good and then despair when they see what evil their choice entails. Those of sea-soned wisdom alone make the choice that brings a peaceful and happy life. Eventually they are spared having to go the old round of succession of lives and can remain eternally with the eternal.

The *Republic* thus ends on a note that transcends this life. Subsequent thought has been left to argue whether this note is the essential point of the search for wisdom or simply the reward added as a postscript to a theory basically concerned with the organization of social life and character formation.

3

Aristotle
(384–322 B.C.)

Raphael's painting *The School of Athens* has Plato pointing upward to the heavens, while Aristotle's hand is directed toward the earth. Both sought an eternal order of things, but Plato expected it to be discovered by the intellect contemplating the Forms, whereas Aristotle wanted to find his formulae for the world by examining nature, animals, and men at work. There seems no limit to the scope of his investigations. He created the science of logic, centered on an analysis of syllogistic reasoning, which endured unchanged until the twentieth-century expansion of symbolic logic. He developed the theory of science in a solid methodological treatise. He organized and added to the biological studies of his time, paying special attention to the constitution of animal bodies, their reproduction, and the problem of the classification of species. Darwin, speaking of the biologists who influenced him, says that they were "mere schoolboys to old Aristotle." Least imaginative in his physics, even here he provided subtle analyses of space and time, infinity and continuity, and motion. The scheme of the world he constructed governed men's views up to the time of Copernicus, Galileo, and Newton. In psychology he examined the physical, physiological, and phenomenal aspects of the various modes of sense perception, and also gave an account of thinking. The *Metaphysics,* so called for having been placed after the *Physics,* is still the starting point for that controversial branch of philosophy. He surveyed and compared numerous systems of government, thus organizing political science on an empirical basis. The *Rhetoric* is a "how-to" book for statesmen and lawyers, while the *Poetics,* whose surviving part deals chiefly with tragedy, has provided aesthetic criteria for many centuries—in seventeenth-century France, for example, it was hardened into strict directions on how tragedy should be written. And there is of course the *Nicomachean Ethics,* the first systematic treatise in the field and still a living text.

Aristotle's influence has varied over the centuries. In some periods he was regarded as preeminently orthodox. For much of the medieval period he was called, simply, "the Philosopher"; to Dante, "the master of those who know." At other times he was regarded as a radical, subverting orthodox thought—as, for example, when in the thirteenth century his works were rediscovered in the West and were used by his followers to promote the claims of philosophy against theology, which led the Church to condemn his influence. After this, he came to be associated with orthodoxy and to be used dogmatically, as the major representative of traditional thought. He became the target for philosophers and scientists engaged in revolutionary thought—as his physics was attacked by Copernicus, Galileo, and Newton; his biology by Darwin; his logic by Ramus and Mill; his metaphysics and epistemology by Descartes, Bacon, Locke, and others. In the twentieth century the strong passions associated with him seem to have settled down—his thought is no longer burdened with the associations of orthodoxy and dogmatism, or with radicalism, and can again be looked at with a greater degree of neutrality; and his powerful analysis of concepts and his method of philosophizing can be regarded in its own terms.

Aristotle was born in Stagira (384 B.C.), in the northern part of Greece. At the age of seventeen he came to Plato's Academy in Athens and stayed working there for about twenty years, till about the time of Plato's death. He then left Athens and spent about a dozen years in Asia Minor, in Macedonia, and in Stagira. He returned in 335–334 and founded a school (usually called the Peripatetic school). He established a library and devoted himself to advancing science and systematizing what knowledge there was. In 323 he was charged, as Socrates had been, with corrupting the youth of Athens. He went into exile, remarking that he would not let the Athenians sin twice against philosophy. He died the following year.

By virtue of his place of birth he was never an Athenian citizen, and he remained essentially an outsider. Some of the critical points of his career were probably a consequence of his Macedonian connection. His father was physician to a king of Macedonia. A subsequent king, Philip, unified the country and gradually dominated most of the city-states of Greece. Athenian hostility to those associated with Macedonia at a time when Philip's power was most threatening to Athens may have prompted Aristotle's first departure from Athens in 348/7. During this absence Aristotle for three years tutored Philip's son, the future Alexander the Great. Philip was assassinated just as he was preparing to invade the Persian Empire, and Alexander became king. He put down a Greek rising and carried through the Persian conquest. Aristotle's return to Athens may have been made secure by the thoroughness of Alexander's repression of Greek rebellion. And Aristotle's indictment came just after Alexander's death, when Athens had immediately revolted.

As tutor to Alexander, Aristotle had the opportunity on which Plato in his own life had placed such a high value—to form the mind of a powerful future ruler. How far he succeeded is debatable. Certainly, pupil and teacher maintained friendly relations; Alexander is said to have invited Aristotle to come along on the invasion of Persia (an invitation that Aristotle refused), to have sent Aristotle specimens for biological investigation from his campaigns in far-off places, and to have ordered that all strange phenomena be reported to Aristotle. Yet on important values, they differed: whereas Aristotle looked back to the city-state (now losing its vigorous autonomy) as the ideal mode of community life, Alexander's vision was of a unified Greece and a Graeco-Persian empire.

Aristotle's ethics and political thought are set in a teleological view of the world. When examining the workings of nature as well as of humans he keeps in mind how an artist or craftsman works—from plans and designs that guide the work. The scientist's task is to discover specific designs or inherent plans in nature. A systematic scientific inquiry looks to four factors (he speaks of them as "causes" but not in our sense of the term) to explain phenomena: the *material* cause—the materials or matter involved in any thing or happening; the *formal* cause—the organization of the materials; the *efficient* cause—what stimulates or sets into motion the phenomena; and the *final* cause—the end for which a change takes place, the function for which it operates, or the culmination of a development. Aristotle brings to his ethics and politics this theory of how a scientific inquiry is to be organized: the raw materials of a morality are human capacities, both rational and appetitive—actions, passions, and feelings (the material cause); these raw materials are organized in a pattern of character and virtue (the formal cause); the older generation, by praising and blaming and by setting examples and specific standards, stimulates the development of capacities into character (the efficient cause); and the full development of human capacities is found in the life of a whole community (the final cause).

The notions of material and formal causes are relative; thus the tree is material for the lumber, and the lumber in turn is material for the house, and the house material for the city. From another point of view—regarding the process by which matter takes on a form or a thing engages in a patterned activity—matter and form may be seen as *potentiality* and *actuality*. The material is potentially what it is to become, and the form is the actuality of that becoming—as marble is potentially the statue. From this dynamic point of view, there is an inherent thrust toward realization in all that is or goes on (as if every stone longs to be a doorstep). This kind of *teleology* sees everything that is going on in terms of its end or purpose. But for Aristotle this is not a transcendent end, as Plato's Idea of the Good was the ultimate governing being of all that is. Indeed, when Aristotle applies his method to living things, his conception of the *form* is very like the modern notion of *information* that is trans-

mitted genetically through the body and guides the development of the individual to its complete or adult fulfillment along the lines laid down in the species. Nor is Aristotle's teleology a comprehensive world plan governing all detail, as in Christian theology. It is instead a species teleology—individuals develop to maturity according to the plan of the species; but external relations to other species are largely accidental, not controlled by an overall plan relating all that is going on.

The teleological note is struck in the very first sentence of the *Nicomachean Ethics*, with the assertion that all human enterprises aim at some good. This good, or these ends, are not necessarily external to the enterprise itself, as if the enterprise, or action, were without value except by virtue of the end it aims at. Aristotle sorts activities into three kinds: *theōria, praxis,* and *poiēsis*. Literally, these are contemplating, doing, and making. (The translation often given—the theoretical, the practical, and the productive—is likely to confuse a modern reader, since nothing seems more practical than manufacturing or making. But Aristotle's classification is different from the modern.) The activity of contemplation is distinguished from the other two by its object. Contemplation is directed to the eternal (or necessary), that which cannot be other than it is—God and the heavens and the fixed order of things (their essences). Science, dealing with the forms or laws of the universe, is theoretical.[1]

Both making and doing (production and practice) concern what can be otherwise, the contingent (or changing), which for Aristotle encompasses the realm of nature (including animals and humans) below the moon. These include matters we can decide about or control. Making is distinguished from doing by the fea-

[1] Puritan philosophers in the seventeenth century objected that if God created the world it could not be described as eternal, and since He did create it, what Aristotle called the theoretical was simply the human view of God's production.

ture that making concludes with a product out-side the process; the product is that for the sake of which we engage in the making, as in the crafts. By contrast, doing (*praxis*) contains its own end; it covers the activities we engage in for their own sake. Ethics and politics as inquiries are concerned with practice in this sense.[2]

Aristotle differs markedly from Plato's sharp contrast between body and soul. For Aristotle, soul (psyche) is the realization or expression of certain powers of the body. The kind of soul depends on the kind of body. He recognizes the continuities as well as the distinctions between plant, animal, and human. Mind is thus not something independent of body, but a function of thinking rooted in the complex capacities of the human being. Rationality is indeed the distinguishing human mark, but at its upper limit it involves a participation in the divine order. That order is not in opposition to the natural world but is its eternal supporting system. The Aristotelian God is impersonal, has no concern for particulars and individuals, legislates no moral code for humans, and is encountered only in pure thought.

Human nature is both rational and appetitive: it constrains what humans desire and aim at as well as the institutions that serve human needs. Aristotle does not share Plato's view of appetite as a dragon of irrational demand; appetite is rather the raw material that can be fashioned wisely in practice. Thus whereas Plato is afraid of dramatic performances because they heighten emotions and weaken rational restraints, Aristotle thinks a good tragedy rather carries through a *catharsis* or purification of the emotions by allowing

them expression; the audience leaves a tragic drama more serene and at peace, and with a deepened understanding of life's predicaments.

The final cause is not just life but the good life. Abstractly this is the life of happiness, but concretely, where people are fortunate enough to achieve it, it is a life within a community that finds fulfilment both in activities of value and in contemplation—both *praxis* and *theōria*.

The thrust of Aristotle's ethics is toward acquiring virtue, that is, developing a character that is reasonable. The formal cause is embodied in the picture he gives of the moral and intellectual virtues; the efficient cause is seen in his account of how virtue is acquired. Moral virtue lies in the grasp of the *mean* in action rather than the extreme. The doctrine of the mean is the heart of Aristotle's ethics. The idea of the mean embraces both the *just-right*, as a craftsman will cut the timber to the just-right size or a trainer assign the athlete the just-right amount of exercise, and the *balance* of opposing forces, as a statesman may find the solution to a social problem that holds opposing forces in check through compromise. The particular virtues are thus seen as cases of the mean between vices as extremes—for example, courage is a mean between cowardice and rashness, liberality between graspingness and profligacy. Practical wisdom, as distinct from the theoretical wisdom of the scientist, is the intellectual virtue that crowns the good character, for it is the ability to judge well in the discovery of the mean in facing practical problems of decision. Morality cannot be achieved by simply following rules, nor by simply intellectual learning. It requires experience and the lessons of experience. The cultivation of virtue lies in a kind of moral apprenticeship, in which the young learn to exercise judgment in the complex situations of life. Aristotle therefore assigns an important role in the process of moral maturation to men of practical wisdom, whose

---

[2] The sharpness of the practice-production distinction may reflect the aristocratic Greek attitude to manual labor as against leisure: no one who works with his hands for a living has the requisite leisure to take part in fully living the good life or to engage in politics.

praise and blame serve to shape the conceptions of the young about what is noble and praiseworthy.

The *Nicomachean Ethics* develops systematically. Book I is about the good and happiness. Book II and the first part of Book III analyze the nature of virtue. The rest of Book III through Book V treat of the particular moral virtues, ending with justice. Book VI deals with the intellectual virtues, notably practical wisdom. Book VII analyzes the character that falls short of virtue and has to handle inner conflict. Books VIII and IX deal with the varieties of interpersonal association and their values—in business, in pleasure, in common intellectual endeavor. (They are described as forms of *friendship*, which is obviously taken in a broad sense.) Book X rounds out the place of the intellectual life in human happiness and moves on to the practical life as a transition to the *Politics*.

The *Politics* is a normative continuation of the *Ethics,* employing throughout the criterion of the good life to evaluate institutions in the light of the comparative experience of different societies. In familial institutions Aristotle justifies slavery, gives women a subordinate role, and considers children largely in terms of what they are to become—their end lies in their future, not in their childhood. In economic life he favors agriculture and disparages trade; the former encourages the balanced life of human relations, whereas the latter gives undue rein to acquisitive propensities. In politics he would like aristocracy as the rule of the best; but he thinks it unrealistic in the Greek situation of his time, for there is the basic class war of the rich and the poor. The various city-states are under the oligarchic rule of the rich or the democratic rule of the poor. Both are extremes, and the solution he offers is a mean, which in this context is a balancing compromise. He works this out in some detail. The book is incomplete, breaking off in the midst of a discussion of education, in which the emphasis is on developing critical ability.

The *Nicomachean Ethics* [3]

[I, 1] Every art or applied science and every systematic investigation, and similarly every action and choice, seem to aim at some good; the good, therefore, has been well defined as that at which all things aim. But it is clear that there is a difference in the ends at which they aim: in some cases the activity is the end, in others the end is some product beyond the activity. In cases where the end lies beyond the action the product is naturally superior to the activity.

Since there are many activities, arts, and sciences, the number of ends is correspondingly large: of medicine the end is health, of shipbuilding a vessel, of strategy, victory, and of household management, wealth. In many instances several such pursuits are grouped together under a single capacity: the art of bridle-making, for example, and everything else pertaining to the equipment of a horse are grouped together under horsemanship; horsemanship in turn, along with every other military action, is grouped together under strategy; and other pursuits are grouped together under other capacities. In all these cases the ends of the master sciences are preferable to the ends of the subordinate sciences, since the latter are pursued for the sake of the former. This is true whether the ends of the actions lie in the activities themselves or, as is the case in the disciplines just mentioned, in something beyond the activities.

[2] Now, if there exists an end in the realm of action which we desire for its own sake, an end which determines all our other desires; if, in other words, we do not make all our choices for the sake of something else—for in this way the process will go on infinitely so that our desire would be futile and pointless—then obviously this end will be the good, that is, the highest good. Will not the knowledge of this good, consequently, be very important to our lives? Would it not better equip us, like archers who have a target to aim at, to hit the proper

---

[3] The selection is from Aristotle, *Nicomachean Ethics*, translated by Martin Ostwald (New York: Macmillan, 1962, 1968). The bracketed passages in the selection have been added by the translator to clarify the meaning. "Nicomachean" is generally taken to refer to Aristotle's son Nicomachus, whether by way of dedication or because he edited the work.

mark? If so, we must try to comprehend in outline at least what this good is and to which branch of knowledge or to which capacity it belongs.

This good, one should think, belongs to the most sovereign and most comprehensive master science, and politics clearly fits this description. For it determines which sciences ought to exist in states, what kind of sciences each group of citizens must learn, and what degree of proficiency each must attain. We observe further that the most honored capacities, such as strategy, household management, and oratory, are contained in politics. Since this science uses the rest of the sciences, and since, moreover, it legislates what people are to do and what they are not to do, its end seems to embrace the ends of the other sciences. Thus it follows that the end of politics is the good for man. For even if the good is the same for the individual and the state, the good of the state clearly is the greater and more perfect thing to attain and to safeguard. The attainment of the good for one man alone is, to be sure, a source of satisfaction; yet to secure it for a nation and for states is nobler and more divine. In short, these are the aims of our investigation, which is in a sense an investigation of social and political matters.

[4] [S]ince all knowledge and every choice is directed toward some good, let us discuss what is in our view the aim of politics, i.e., the highest good attainable by action. As far as its name is concerned, most people would probably agree: for both the common run of people and cultivated men call it happiness, and understand by "being happy" the same as "living well" and "doing well." But when it comes to defining what happiness is, they disagree, and the account given by the common run differs from that of the philosophers. The former say it is some clear and obvious good, such as pleasure, wealth, or honor; some say it is one thing and others another, and often the very same person identifies it with different things at different times: when he is sick he thinks it is health, and when he is poor he says it is wealth; and when people are conscious of their own ignorance, they admire those who talk above their heads in accents of greatness. Some thinkers used to believe that there exists over and above these many goods another good, good in itself and by itself, which also is the cause of good in all these things. An examination of all the different opinions would perhaps be a little

pointless, and it is sufficient to concentrate on those which are most in evidence or which seem to make some sort of sense. . . .

A student of ethics and politics must first have a proper upbringing in moral conduct.

[7] . . . Since there are evidently several ends, and since we choose some of these—e.g., wealth, flutes, and instruments generally—as a means to something else, it is obvious that not all ends are final. The highest good, on the other hand, must be something final. Thus, if there is only one final end, this will be the good we are seeking; if there are several, it will be the most final and perfect of them. We call that which is pursued as an end in itself more final than an end which is pursued for the sake of something else; and what is never chosen as a means to something else we call more final than that which is chosen both as an end in itself and as a means to something else. What is always chosen as an end in itself and never as a means to something else is called final in an unqualified sense. This description seems to apply to happiness above all else: for we always choose happiness as an end in itself and never for the sake of something else. Honor, pleasure, intelligence, and all virtue we choose partly for themselves—for we would choose each of them even if no further advantage would accrue from them—but we also choose them partly for the sake of happiness, because we assume that it is through them that we will be happy. On the other hand, no one chooses happiness for the sake of honor, pleasure, and the like, nor as a means to anything at all.

We arrive at the same conclusion if we approach the question from the standpoint of self-sufficiency. For the final and perfect good seems to be self-sufficient. However, we define something as self-sufficient not by reference to the "self" alone. We do not mean a man who lives his life in isolation, but a man who also lives with parents, children, a wife, and friends and fellow citizens generally, since man is by nature a social and political being. But some limit must be set to these relationships; for if they are extended to include ancestors, descendants, and friends of friends, they will go on to infinity. However, this point must be reserved for investigation later. For the present we define as "self-sufficient" that which taken by itself makes life something desirable and deficient in nothing. It is happiness, in our opinion, which fits this description. . . .

To call happiness the highest point is perhaps a little trite, and a clearer account of what it is, is still required. Perhaps this is best done by first ascertaining the proper function of man. For just as the goodness and performance of a flute player, a sculptor, or any kind of expert, and generally of anyone who fulfills some function or performs some action, are thought to reside in his proper function, so the goodness and performance of man would seem to reside in whatever is his proper function. Is it then possible that while a carpenter and a shoemaker have their own proper functions and spheres of action, man as man has none, but was left by nature a good-for-nothing without a function? Should we not assume that just as the eye, the hand, the foot, and in general each part of the body clearly has its own proper function, so man too has some function over and above the functions of his parts? What can this function possibly be? Simply living? He shares that even with plants, but we are now looking for something peculiar to man. Accordingly, the life of nutrition and growth must be excluded. Next in line there is a life of sense perception. But this, too, man has in common with the horse, the ox, and every animal. There remains then an active life of the rational element. The rational element has two parts: one is rational in that it obeys the rule of reason, the other in that it possesses and conceives rational rules. Since the expression "life of the rational element" also can be used in two senses, we must make it clear that we mean a life determined by the activity, as opposed to the mere possession, of the rational element. For the activity, it seems, has a greater claim to be the function of man.

The proper function of man, then, consists in an activity of the soul in conformity with a rational principle or, at least, not without it. In speaking of the proper function of a given individual we mean that it is the same in kind as the function of an individual who sets high standards for himself [spoudaios, literally "serious man"]: the proper function of a harpist, for example, is the same as the function of a harpist who has set high standards for himself. The same applies to any and every group of individuals: the full attainment of excellence must be added to the mere function. In other words, the function of the harpist is to play the harp; the function of the harpist who has high standards is to play it well. On these assumptions, if we take the proper function of man to be a certain kind of life, and if this kind of life is an activity of the soul and consists in actions performed in conjunction with the rational element, and if a man of high standards is he who performs these actions well and properly, and if a function is well performed when it is performed in accordance with the excellence appropriate to it; we reach the conclusion that the good of man is an activity of the soul in conformity with excellence or virtue, and if there are several virtues, in conformity with the best and most complete.

But we must add "in a complete life." For one swallow does not make a spring, nor does one sunny day; similarly, one day or a short time does not make a man blessed and happy. . . .

[13] Since happiness is a certain activity of the soul in conformity with perfect virtue, we must now examine what virtue or excellence is. For such an inquiry will perhaps better enable us to discover the nature of happiness. . . .

There can be no doubt that the virtue which we have to study is human virtue. For the good which we have been seeking is a human good and the happiness a human happiness. By human virtue we do not mean the excellence of the body, but that of the soul, and we define happiness as an activity of the soul. If this is true, the student of politics must obviously have some knowledge of the workings of the soul, just as the man who is to heal eyes must know something about the whole body. In fact, knowledge is all the more important for the former, inasmuch as politics is better and more valuable than medicine, and cultivated physicians devote much time and trouble to gain knowledge about the body. Thus, the student of politics must study the soul, but he must do so with his own aim in view, and only to the extent that the objects of his inquiry demand: to go into it in greater detail would perhaps be more laborious than his purposes require.

Some things that are said about the soul in our less technical discussions are adequate enough to be used here, for instance, that the soul consists of two elements, one irrational and one rational. Whether these two elements are separate, like the parts of the body or any other divisible thing, or whether they are only logically separable though in reality indivisible, as convex and concave are in the circumference of a circle, is irrelevant for our present purposes.

Of the irrational element, again, one part seems to be common to all living things and vegetative in nature: I mean that part which is responsible for nurture and growth. We must assume that some such capacity of the soul exists in everything that takes nourishment, in the embryonic stage as well as when the organism is fully developed; for this makes more sense than to assume the existence of some different capacity at the latter stage. The excellence of this part of the soul is, therefore, shown to be common to all living things and is not exclusively human. This very part and this capacity seem to be most active in sleep. For in sleep the difference between a good man and a bad is least apparent—whence the saying that for half their lives the happy are no better off than the wretched. This is just what we would expect, for sleep is an inactivity of the soul in that it ceases to do things which cause it to be called good or bad. However, to a small extent some bodily movements do penetrate to the soul in sleep, and in this sense the dreams of honest men are better than those of average people. But enough of this subject: we may pass by the nutritive part, since it has no natural share in human excellence or virtue.

In addition to this, there seems to be another integral element of the soul which, though irrational, still does partake of reason in some way. In morally strong and morally weak men we praise the reason that guides them and the rational element of the soul, because it exhorts them to follow the right path and to do what is best. Yet we see in them also another natural strain different from the rational, which fights and resists the guidance of reason. The soul behaves in precisely the same manner as do the paralyzed limbs of the body. When we intend to move the limbs to the right, they turn to the left, and similarly, the impulses of morally weak persons turn in the direction opposite to that in which reason leads them. However, while the aberration of the body is visible, that of the soul is not. But perhaps we must accept it as a fact, nevertheless, that there is something in the soul besides the rational element, which opposes and reacts against it. In what way the two are distinct need not concern us here. But, as we have

stated, it too seems to partake of reason; at any rate, in a morally strong man it accepts the leadership of reason, and is perhaps more obedient still in a self-controlled and courageous man, since in him everything is in harmony with the voice of reason.

Thus we see that the irrational element of the soul has two parts: the one is vegetative and has no share in reason at all, the other is the seat of the appetites and of desire in general and partakes of reason insofar as it complies with reason and accepts its leadership; it possesses reason in the sense that we say it is "reasonable" to accept the advice of a father and of friends, not in the sense that we have a "rational" understanding of mathematical propositions. That the irrational elements can be persuaded by the rational is shown by the fact that admonition and all manner of rebuke and exhortation are possible. If it is correct to say that the appetitive part, too, has reason, it follows that the rational element of the soul has two subdivisions: the one possesses reason in the strict sense, contained within itself, and the other possesses reason in the sense that it listens to reason as one would listen to a father.

Virtue, too, is differentiated in line with this division of the soul. We call some virtues "intellectual" and others "moral": theoretical wisdom, understanding, and practical wisdom are intellectual virtues, generosity and self-control moral virtues. In speaking of a man's character, we do not describe him as wise or understanding, but as gentle or self-controlled; but we praise the wise man, too, for his characteristic, and praiseworthy characteristics are what we call virtues.

[II, 1] Virtue, as we have seen, consists of two kinds, intellectual virtue and moral virtue. Intellectual virtue or excellence owes its origin and development chiefly to teaching, and for that reason requires experience and time. Moral virtue, on the other hand, is formed by habit, *ethos,* and its name, *ēthikē,* is therefore derived, by a slight variation, from *ethos.* This shows, too, that none of the moral virtues is implanted in us by nature, for nothing which exists by nature can be changed by habit. For example, it is impossible for a stone, which has a natural downward movement, to become habituated to moving upward, even if one should try ten thousand times to inculcate the habit by throwing it in the air; nor can fire be made to move downward, nor can the direction of any nature-given tendency be changed by habituation. Thus, the virtues are implanted in us neither by nature nor contrary to nature: we are by nature equipped with the ability to receive them, and habit brings this ability to completion and fulfillment.

Furthermore, of all the qualities with which we are endowed by nature, we are provided with the capacity first, and display the activity afterward. That this is true is shown by the senses: it is not by frequent seeing or frequent hearing that we acquired our senses, but on the contrary we first possess and then use them; we do not acquire them by use. The virtues, on the other hand, we acquire by first having put them into action, and the same is also true of the arts. For the things which we have to learn before we can do them we learn by doing: men become builders by building houses, and harpists by playing the harp. Similarly, we become just by the practice of just actions, self-controlled by exercising self-control, and courageous by performing acts of courage.

This is corroborated by what happens in states. Lawgivers make the citizens good by inculcating [good] habits in them, and this is the aim of every lawgiver; if he does not succeed in doing that, his legislation is a failure. It is in this that a good constitution differs from a bad one.

Moreover, the same causes and the same means that produce any excellence or virtue can also destroy it, and this is also true of every art. It is by playing the harp that men become both good and bad harpists, and correspondingly with builders and all other craftsmen: a man who builds well will be a good builder, one who builds badly a bad one. For if this were not so, there would be no need for an instructor, but everybody would be born as a good or a bad craftsman. The same holds true of the virtues: in our transactions with other men it is by action that some become just and others unjust, and it is by acting in the face of danger and by developing the habit of feeling fear or confidence that some become brave men and others cowards. The same applies to the appetites and feelings of anger: by reacting in one way or in another to given circumstances some people become self-controlled and gentle, and others self-indulgent and short-tempered. In a word, characteristics develop from corresponding activities. For that reason, we must see to it that our activities are of a certain kind, since any variations in them will be reflected in our characteristics. Hence it is no small matter whether one habit or another is inculcated in us from early childhood; on the contrary, it makes a considerable difference, or, rather, all the difference.

[2] The purpose of the present study is not, as it is in other inquiries, the attainment of theoretical knowledge: we are not conducting this inquiry in order to know what virtue is, but in order to become good, else there would be no advantage in studying it. For that reason, it becomes necessary to examine the problem of actions, and to ask how they are to be performed. For, as we have said, the actions determine what kind of characteristics are developed.

That we must act according to right reason is generally conceded and may be assumed as the basis of our discussion. We shall speak about it later and discuss what right reason is and examine its relation to the other virtues. But let us first agree that any discussion on matters of action cannot be more than an outline and is bound to lack precision; for as we stated at the outset, one can demand of a discussion only what the subject matter permits, and there are no fixed data in matters concerning action and questions of what is beneficial, any more than there are in matters of health. And if this is true of our general discussion, our treatment of particular problems will be even less precise, since these do not come under the head of any art which can be transmitted by precept, but the agent must consider on each different occasion what the situation demands, just as in medicine and in navigation. But although such is the kind of discussion in which we are engaged, we must do our best.

First of all, it must be observed that the nature of moral qualities is such that they are destroyed by defect and by excess. We see the same thing happen in the case of strength and of health, to illustrate, as we must, the invisible by means of visible examples: excess as well as deficiency of physical exercise destroys our strength, and similarly, too much and too little food and drink destroys our health; the proportionate amount, however, produces, increases, and preserves it. The same applies to self-control, courage, and the other virtues: the man who shuns and fears everything and never stands his ground becomes a coward, whereas a man who knows no fear at all and goes to meet every danger becomes reckless. Similarly, a man who revels in every pleasure and abstains from none becomes self-indulgent, while he who avoids every pleasure like a boor becomes what might be called insensitive. Thus we see that self-control and courage are destroyed by excess and by deficiency and are preserved by the mean. . . .

[3] An index to our characteristics is provided by the pleasure or pain which follows upon the tasks we have achieved. A man who abstains from bodily pleasures and enjoys doing so is self-controlled; if he finds abstinence troublesome, he is self-indulgent; a man who endures danger with joy, or at least without pain, is courageous; if he endures it with pain, he is a coward. For moral excellence is concerned with pleasure and pain; it is pleasure that makes us do base actions and pain that prevents us from doing noble actions. For that reason, as Plato says, men must be brought up from childhood to feel pleasure and pain at the proper things; for this is correct education.

Furthermore, since the virtues have to do with actions and emotions, and since pleasure and pain are a consequence of every emotion and of every action, it follows from this point of view, too, that virtue has to do with pleasure and pain. This is further indicated by the fact that punishment is inflicted by means of pain. For punishment is a kind of medical treatment and it is the nature of medical treatments to take effect through the introduction of the opposite of the disease. . . .

[4] However, the question may be raised what we mean by saying that men become just by performing just actions and self-controlled by practicing self-control. For if they perform just actions and exercise self-control, they are already just and self-controlled, in the same way as they are literate and musical if they write correctly and practice music.

But is this objection really valid, even as regards the arts? No, for it is possible for a man to write a piece correctly by chance or at the prompting of another: but he will be literate only if he produces a piece of writing in a literate way, and that means doing it in accordance with the skill of literary composition which he has in himself.

Moreover, the factors involved in the arts and in the virtues are not the same. In the arts, excellence lies in the result itself, so that it is sufficient if it is of a certain kind. But in the case of the virtues an act is not performed justly or with self-control if the act itself is of a certain kind, but only if in addition the agent has certain characteristics as he performs it: first of all, he must know what he is doing; secondly, he must choose to act the way he does, and he must choose it for its own sake; and in the third place, the act must spring from a firm and unchangeable character. With the exception of knowing what one is about, these considerations do not enter into the mastery of the arts; for the mastery of the virtues, however, knowledge is of little or no importance, whereas the other two conditions count not for a little but are all-decisive, since repeated acts of justice and self-control result in the possession of these virtues. In other words, acts are called just and self-controlled when they are the kind of acts which a just or self-controlled man would perform; but the just and self-controlled man is not he who performs these acts, but he who also performs them in the way just and self-controlled men do. . . .

Turning to the definition of virtue, Aristotle seeks its genus successively among emotions, capacities, and states of character or characteristics. He decides on the last.

[6] It is not sufficient, however, merely to define virtue in general terms as a characteristic: we must also specify what kind of characteristic it is. It must, then, be remarked that every virtue or excellence (1) renders good the thing itself of which it is the excellence, and (2) causes it to perform its function well. For example, the excellence of the eye makes both the eye and its function good, for good sight is due to the excellence of the eye. Likewise, the excellence of a horse makes it both good as a horse and good at running, at carrying its rider, and at facing the enemy. Now, if this is true of all things, the virtue or excellence of man, too, will be a characteristic which makes him a good man, and which causes him to perform his own function well. To some extent we have already stated how this will be true; the rest will become clear if we study what the nature of virtue is.

Of every continuous entity that is divisible into parts it is possible to take the larger, the smaller, or an equal part, and these parts may be larger, smaller, or equal either in relation to the entity itself, or in relation to us. The "equal" part is something median between excess and deficiency. By the median of an entity I understand a point equidistant from both extremes, and this point is one and the same for everybody. By the median relative to us I understand an amount neither too large nor too small, and this is neither one nor the same for everybody. To take an example: if ten is many and two is few, six is taken as the median in relation to the entity, for it exceeds and is exceeded by the same amount, and is thus the median in terms of arithmetical proportion. But the median relative to us cannot be determined in this manner: if ten pounds of food is much for a man to eat and two pounds little, it does not follow that the trainer will prescribe six pounds, for this may in turn be much or little for him to eat; it may be little for Milo and much for someone who has just begun to take up athletics. The same applies to running and wrestling. Thus we see that an expert in any field avoids excess and deficiency, but seeks the median and chooses it—not the median of the object but the median relative to us.

If this, then, is the way in which every science perfects its work, by looking to the median and by bringing its work up to that point—and this is the reason why it is usually said of a successful piece of work that it is impossible to detract from it or to add to it, the implication being that excess and deficiency destroy success while the mean safeguards it (good craftsmen, we say, look toward this standard in the performance of their work)—and if virtue, like nature, is more precise and better than any art, we must conclude that virtue aims at the median. I am referring to moral virtue: for it is moral virtue that is concerned with emotions and actions, and it is in emotions and actions that excess, deficiency, and the median are found. Thus we can experience fear, confidence, desire, anger, pity, and generally any kind of pleasure and pain either too much or too little, and in either case not properly. But to experience all this at the right time, toward the right objects, toward the right people, for the right reason, and in the right manner—that is the median and the best course, the course that is a mark of virtue.

Similarly, excess, deficiency, and the median can also be found in actions. Now virtue is concerned with emotions and actions; and in emotions and actions excess and deficiency miss the mark, whereas the median is praised and constitutes success. But both praise and success are signs of virtue or excellence. Consequently, virtue is a mean in

the sense that it aims at the median. This is corroborated by the fact that there are many ways of going wrong, but only one way which is right—for evil belongs to the indeterminate, as the Pythagoreans imagined, but good to the determinate. This, by the way, is also the reason why the one is easy and the other hard: it is easy to miss the target but hard to hit it. Here, then, is an additional proof that excess and deficiency characterize vice, while the mean characterizes virtue: for "bad men have many ways, good men but one."

We may thus conclude that virtue or excellence is a characteristic involving choice, and that it consists in observing the mean relative to us, a mean which is defined by a rational principle, such as a man of practical wisdom would use to determine it. It is the mean by reference to two vices: the one of excess and the other of deficiency. It is, moreover, a mean because some vices exceed and others fall short of what is required in emotion and in action, whereas virtue finds and chooses the median. Hence, in respect of its essence and the definition of its essential nature virtue is a mean, but in regard to goodness and excellence it is an extreme.

Not every action nor every emotion admits of a mean. There are some actions and emotions whose very names connote baseness, e.g., spite, shamelessness, envy; and among actions, adultery, theft, and murder. These and similar emotions and actions imply by their very names that they are bad; it is not their excess nor their deficiency which is called bad. It is, therefore, impossible ever to do right in performing them: to perform them is always to do wrong. In cases of this sort, let us say adultery, rightness and wrongness do not depend on committing it with the right woman at the right time and in the right manner, but the mere fact of committing such action at all is to do wrong. It would be just as absurd to suppose that there is a mean, an excess, and a deficiency in an unjust or a cowardly or a self-indulgent act. . . .

[7] However, this general statement is not enough; we must also show that it fits particular instances. For in a discussion of moral actions, although general statements have a wider range of application, statements on particular points have more truth in them: actions are concerned with particulars and our statements must harmonize with them. Let us now take particular virtues and vices. . . .

In feelings of fear and confidence courage is the mean. As for the excesses, there is no name that describes a man who exceeds in fearlessness—many virtues and vices have no name; but a man who exceeds in confidence is reckless, and a man who exceeds in fear and is deficient in confidence is cowardly.

In regard to pleasures and pains—not all of them and to a lesser degree in the case of pains—the mean is self-control and the excess self-indulgence. Men deficient in regard to pleasure are not often found, and there is therefore no name for them, but let us call them "insensitive."

In giving and taking money, the mean is generosity, the excess and deficiency are extravagance and stinginess. In these vices excess and deficiency work in opposite ways: an extravagant man exceeds in spending and is deficient in taking, while a stingy man exceeds in taking and is deficient in spending. . . .

There are also some other dispositions in regard to money: magnificence is a mean (for there is a difference between a magnificent and a generous man in that the former operates on a large scale, the latter on a small); gaudiness and vulgarity are excesses, and niggardliness a deficiency. These vices differ from the vices opposed to generosity. . . .

As regards honor and dishonor, the mean is high-mindedness, the excess is what we might call vanity, and the deficiency small-mindedness. The same relation which, as we said, exists between magnificence and generosity, the one being distinguished from the other in that it operates on a small scale, exists also between high-mindedness and another virtue: as the former deals with great, so the latter deals with small honors. For it is possible to desire honor as one should or more than one should or less than one should: a man who exceeds in his desires is called ambitious, a man who is deficient unambitious, but there is no name to describe the man in the middle. There are likewise no names for the corresponding dispositions except for the disposition of an ambitious man which is called ambition. As a result, the men who occupy the extremes lay claim to the middle position. We ourselves, in fact, sometimes call the middle person ambitious and sometimes unambitious; sometimes we praise an ambitious and at other times an unambitious man. . . .

In regard to anger also there exists an excess, a deficiency, and a mean. Although there really are no names for them, we might call the mean gentleness, since we call the man who occupies the middle position gentle. Of the extremes, let the man who exceeds be called short-tempered and his vice a short temper, and the deficient man apathetic and his vice apathy.

There are, further, three other means which have a certain similarity with one another, but differ nonetheless one from the other. They are all concerned with human relations in speech and action, but they differ in that one of them is concerned with truth in speech and action and the other two with pleasantness: (a) pleasantness in amusement and (b) pleasantness in all our daily life. We must include these, too, in our discussion, in order to see more clearly that the mean is to be praised in all things and that the extremes are neither praiseworthy nor right, but worthy of blame. Here, too, most of the virtues and vices have no name, but for the sake of clarity and easier comprehension we must try to coin names for them, as we did in earlier instances.

To come to the point; in regard to truth, let us call the man in the middle position truthful and the mean truthfulness. Pretense in the form of exaggeration is boastfulness and its possessor boastful, while pretense in the form of understatement is self-depreciation and its possessor a self-depreciator.

Concerning pleasantness in amusement, the man in the middle position is witty and his disposition wittiness; the excess is called buffoonery and its possessor a buffoon; and the deficient man a kind of boor and the corresponding characteristic boorishness.

As far as the other kind of pleasantness is concerned, pleasantness in our daily life, a man who is as pleasant as he should be is friendly and the mean is friendliness. A man who exceeds is called obsequious if he has no particular purpose in being pleasant, but if he is acting for his own material advantage, he is a flatterer. And a man who is deficient and unpleasant in every respect is a quarrelsome and grouchy kind of person.

A mean can also be found in our emotional experiences and in our emotions. Thus, while a sense of shame is not a virtue, a bashful or modest man is praised. For even in these matters we speak of one kind of person as intermediate and of another as exceeding if he is terror-stricken and abashed at everything. On the other hand, a man who is deficient in shame or has none at all is called shameless, whereas the intermediate man is bashful or modest.

Righteous indignation is the mean between envy and spite, all of these being concerned with the pain and pleasure which we feel in regard to the fortunes of our neighbors. The righteously indignant man feels pain when someone prospers undeservedly; an envious man exceeds him in that he is pained when he sees anyone prosper; and a spiteful man is so deficient in feeling pain that he even rejoices [when someone suffers undeservedly]. . . .

[III, 1] Virtue or excellence is, as we have seen, concerned with emotions and actions. When these are voluntary we receive praise and blame; when involuntary, we are pardoned and sometimes even pitied. Therefore, it is, I dare say, indispensable for a student of virtue to differentiate between voluntary and involuntary actions, and useful also for lawgivers, to help them in meting out honors and punishments.

It is of course generally recognized that actions done under constraint or due to ignorance are involuntary. An act is done under constraint when the initiative or source of motion comes from without. It is the kind of act in which the agent or the person acted upon contributes nothing. For example, a wind might carry a person somewhere [he did not want to go], or men may do so who have him in their power. But a problem arises in regard to actions that are done through fear of a greater evil or for some noble purpose, for instance, if a tyrant were to use a man's parents or children as hostages in ordering him to commit a base deed, making their survival or death depend on his compliance or refusal. Are actions of this kind voluntary or involuntary? A similar problem also arises when a cargo is jettisoned in a storm. Considering the action itself, nobody would voluntarily throw away property; but when it is a matter of saving one's own life and that of his fellow passengers, any sensible man would do so. Actions of this kind are, then, of a mixed nature, although they come closer to being voluntary than to being involuntary actions. For they are desirable at the moment of action; and the end for which an action is performed depends on the time at which it is done. Thus the terms

"voluntary" and "involuntary" are to be used with reference to the moment of action. In the cases just mentioned, the agent acts voluntarily, because the initiative in moving the parts of the body which act as instruments rests with the agent himself; and where the source of motion is within oneself, it is in one's power to act or not to act. Such actions, then, are voluntary, although in themselves they are perhaps involuntary, since nobody would choose to do any one of them for its own sake.

[That actions of this kind are considered as voluntary is also shown by the fact that] sometimes people are even praised for doing them, for example, if they endure shameful or painful treatment in return for great and noble objectives. If the opposite is the case, reproach is heaped upon them, for only a worthless man would endure utter disgrace for no good or reasonable purpose. There are some instances in which such actions elicit forgiveness rather than praise, for example, when a man acts improperly under a strain greater than human nature can bear and which no one can endure. Yet there are perhaps also acts which no man can possibly be compelled to do, but rather than do them he should accept the most terrible sufferings and death. Thus, the circumstances that compel Alcmaeon in Euripides' play to kill his own mother are patently absurd. In making a choice, it is sometimes hard to decide what advantages and disadvantages should be weighed against one another, and what losses we should endure to gain what we want; but it is even harder to abide by a decision once it is made. For as a rule, what we look forward to is painful and what we are forced to do is base. It is because of this difficulty that praise or blame depends on whether or not a man successfully resists compulsion.

What kind of actions can we say, then, are done under constraint? To state the matter without qualification, are all actions done under constraint of which the cause is external and to which the agent contributes nothing? On the other hand, actions which are in themselves involuntary, yet chosen under given circumstances in return for certain benefits and performed on the initiative of the agent— although such actions are involuntary considered in themselves, they are nonetheless voluntary under the circumstances, and because benefits are expected in return. In fact, they have a greater resemblance to voluntary actions. For actions belong among particulars, and the particular act is here performed voluntarily. But it is not easy to lay down rules how, in making a choice, two alternatives are to be balanced against one another; there are many differences in the case of particulars.

[There is a conceivable objection to this definition of "voluntary."] Suppose someone were to assert that pleasant and noble acts are performed under constraint because the pleasant and the noble are external to us and have a compelling power. But on this view, all actions would be done under constraint: for every man is motivated by what is pleasant and noble in everything he does. Furthermore, it is painful to act under constraint and involuntarily, but the performance of pleasant and noble acts brings pleasure. Finally, it is absurd to blame external circumstances rather than oneself for falling an easy prey to such attractions, and to hold oneself responsible for noble deeds, while pleasure is held responsible to one's base deeds.

It appears, thus, that an act done under constraint is one in which the initiative or source of motion comes from without, and to which the person compelled contributes nothing.

Turning now to acts due to ignorance, we may say that all of them are non-voluntary, but they are involuntary only when they bring sorrow and regret in their train: a man who has acted due to ignorance and feels no compunction whatsoever for what he has done was not a voluntary agent, since he did not know what he was doing, nor yet was he involuntary, inasmuch as he feels no sorrow. There are, therefore, two distinct types of acts due to ignorance: a man who regrets what he has done is considered an involuntary agent, and a man who does not may be called a non-voluntary agent; for as the two cases are different, it is better to give each its own name.

There also seems to be a difference between actions *due to* ignorance and acting *in* ignorance. A man's action is not considered to be due to ignorance when he is drunk or angry, but due to intoxication and anger, although he does not know what he is doing and is in fact acting in ignorance.

Now every wicked man is in a state of ignorance as to what he ought to do and what he should refrain from doing, and it is due to this kind of error that men become unjust and, in general, immoral. But an act can hardly be called involuntary if the agent is ignorant of what is beneficial. Igno-

rance in moral choice does not make an act involuntary—it makes it wicked; nor does ignorance of the universal, for that invites reproach; rather, it is ignorance of the particulars which constitute the circumstances and the issues involved in the action. It is on these that pity and pardon depend, for a person who acts in ignorance of a particular circumstance acts involuntarily.

It might, therefore, not be a bad idea to distinguish and enumerate these circumstances. They are: ignorance of (1) who the agent is, (2) what he is doing, (3) what thing or person is affected, and sometimes also (4) the means he is using, e.g., some tool, (5) the result intended by his action, e.g., saving a life, and (6) the manner in which he acts, e.g., gently or violently.

Now no one except a madman would be ignorant of all these factors, nor can he obviously be ignorant of (1) the agent; for how could a man not know his own identity? But a person might be ignorant of (2) what he is doing. For example, he might plead that something slipped out of his mouth, or that he did not know that he was divulging a secret, as Aeschylus said when he was accused of divulging the Mysteries; or again, as a man might do who discharges a catapult, he might allege that it went off accidentally while he only wanted to show it. Moreover, (3) someone might, like Merope, mistake a son for an enemy; or (4) he might mistake a pointed spear for a foil, or a heavy stone for a pumice stone. Again, (5) someone might, in trying to save a man by giving him something to drink, in fact kill him; or, (6) as in sparring, a man might intend merely to touch, and actually strike a blow.

As ignorance is possible with regard to all these factors which constitute an action, a man who acts in ignorance of any one of them is considered as acting involuntarily, especially if he is ignorant of the most important factors. The most important factors are the thing or person affected by the action and the result. An action upon this kind of ignorance is called involuntary, provided that it brings also sorrow and regret in its train.

Since an action is involuntary when it is performed under constraint or through ignorance, a voluntary action would seem to be one in which the initiative lies with the agent who knows the particular circumstances in which the action is performed.

[This implies that acts due to passion and appetite

are voluntary.] For it is perhaps wrong to call involuntary those acts which are due to passion and appetite. For on that assumption we would, in the first place, deny that animals or even children are capable of acting voluntarily. In the second place, do we perform none of the actions that are motivated by appetite and passion voluntarily? Or do we perform noble acts voluntarily and base acts involuntarily? The latter alternative is ridiculous, since the cause in both cases is one and the same. But it is no doubt also absurd to call those things which we ought to desire "involuntary." For in some cases we should be angry and there are some things for which we should have an appetite, as for example, health and learning. Moreover, we think of involuntary actions as painful, while actions that satisfy our appetite are pleasant. And finally, what difference is there, as far as involuntariness is concerned, between a wrong committed after calculation and a wrong committed in a fit of passion? Both are to be avoided; but the irrational emotions are considered no less a part of human beings than reasoning is, and hence, the actions of a man which spring from passion and appetite [are equally a part of him]. It would be absurd, then, to count them as involuntary.

The next topic is *choice*. Choice differs from appetite (which it can counter), from wish (which, unlike choice, can be for the impossible), and from opinion (which can be about the eternal, while choice is only about things within our power and realizable in action). Choice as decision calls for *deliberation*. We deliberate about what we can do about matters that involve an indeterminate element whose outcome is unpredictable. We deliberate not about ends but about the manner and means of their realization. Deliberation is like analyzing a geometrical problem: the last step in the analysis is the first in constructing the figure; so the last step in discovery is the first in the causal link we act on. The object of deliberation and that of choice are identical, the latter having been decided on the basis of deliberation. Choice may then be defined as a deliberate desire for things within our power; we arrive at a decision on the basis of deliberation, which then guides our desire.

As for *wish*, is it for what is good or what appears good? In an unqualified sense, it is for what is good (that is what the good person wishes), but for each individual it is what appears good to that person. As for responsibility, the power to act is also the power not to act; the starting point of actions is to be found within ourselves. To the objection that all seek what appears good to them, although they have no control over the appearances, Aristotle answers that if individuals are somehow responsible for their character, they are also responsible for the appearances. Of course a person might voluntarily follow a path of life until it is too late to turn back, just as one may not exercise and disobey doctor's orders until health is gone. (When you have thrown a stone, you cannot recall it.) In the end, having decided that our virtues are voluntary, Aristotle asserts the same is true for our vices.

The latter part of Book III and all of Book IV deal with particular virtues. Book V is devoted wholly to justice. In its broadest sense, justice is the whole of virtue in relation to one's fellows. (This is clearly the sense in which Plato used it.) More specifically, particular forms of justice concern distribution of goods and burdens. One type, *distributive* justice, determines the principles a just person would follow in such a distribution (ch. 3). Here Aristotle notes a social relativity: democrats want equality of free-born citizens, oligarchs apportion according to wealth or noble birth, and aristocrats (Aristotle's preference) according to excellence. Distributive justice thus lies in a "proportionate equality," not an arithmetic one. A second type is *corrective* justice, in which a just distribution that has been violated is restored in one way or another (ch. 4). A third type is *reciprocity* or fairness of exchange in economic relations (ch. 5); here he discusses the function of money as a measure in exchange. He goes on to consider political and social justice among men living under law.

One historically significant point is his attempt to distinguish what is just by nature from what is conventional. Another is his introduction of the concept of equity as providing a needed correction of the law.

[V, 7] What is just in the political sense can be subdivided into what is just by nature and what is just by convention. What is by nature just has the same force everywhere and does not depend on what we regard or do not regard as just. In what is just by convention, on the other hand, it makes originally no difference whether it is fixed one way or another, but it does make a difference once it is fixed, for example, that a prisoner's ransom shall be one mina, or that a sacrifice shall consist of a goat but not of two sheep, and all the other measures enacted for particular occasions (such as the sacrifice offered to Brasidas) and everything enacted by decree. Now, some people think that everything just exists only by convention, since whatever is by nature is unchangeable and has the same force everywhere—as, for example, fire burns both here and in Persia—whereas they see that notions of what is just change. But this is not the correct view, although it has an element of truth. Among the gods, to be sure, it is probably not true at all, but among us there are things which, though naturally just, are nevertheless changeable, as are all things human. Yet in spite of that, there are some things that are just by nature and others not by nature. It is not hard to see among the things which admit of being other than they are, which ones are by nature and which ones not by nature but by convention or agreement, although both kinds are equally subject to change. The same distinction will fit other matters as well: by nature, the right hand is the stronger, and yet it is possible for any man to become ambidextrous. What is just as determined by agreement and advantage is like measures: measures for wine and for grain are not equal everywhere; they are larger where people buy and smaller where they sell. In the same way, what is just not by nature but by human enactment is no more the same everywhere than constitutions are. Yet there is only one constitution that is by nature the best everywhere. . . .

[10] The next subject we have to discuss is equity and the equitable, and the relation of equity to justice and of the equitable to what is just. For on examination they appear to be neither absolutely identical nor generically different. Sometimes we go so far in praising a thing or a man as "equitable" that we use the word in an extended sense as a general term of praise for things in place of "good," and really mean "better" when we say "more equitable." But at other times, when we follow the logical consequences, it appears odd that the equitable should be distinct from the just and yet deserve praise. If the two terms are different, then either the just is not of great moral value, or the equitable is not just. If both are of great moral value, they are the same.

These, then, are roughly the reasons why a problem about the equitable has arisen. All our points are in a sense correct and there is no inconsistency. For the equitable is just despite the fact that it is better than the just in one sense. But it is not better than the just in the sense of being generically different from it. This means that just and equitable are in fact identical [in genus], and, although both are morally good, the equitable is the better of the two. What causes the problem is that the equitable is not just in the legal sense of "just" but as a corrective of what is legally just. The reason is that all law is universal, but there are some things about which it is not possible to speak correctly in universal terms. Now, in situations where it is necessary to speak in universal terms but impossible to do so correctly, the law takes the majority of cases, fully realizing in what respect it misses the mark. The law itself is none the less correct. For the mistake lies neither in the law nor in the lawgiver, but in the nature of the case. For such is the material of which actions are made. So in a situation in which the law speaks universally, but the case at issue happens to fall outside the universal formula, it is correct to rectify the shortcoming, in other words, the omission and mistake of the lawgiver due to the generality of his statement. Such a rectification corresponds to what the lawgiver himself would have said if he were present, and what he would have enacted if he had known [of this particular case]. That is why the equitable is both just and also better than the just in one sense. It is not better than the just in general, but better than the mistake due to the generality [of the law]. And this is the very nature of the equitable, a rectification of law where law falls short by reason of its universality.

This is also the reason why not all things are determined by law. There are some things about which it is impossible to enact a law, so that a special decree is required. For where a thing is indefinite, the rule by which it is measured is also indefinite, as is, for example, the leaden rule used in Lesbian construction work. Just as this rule is not rigid but shifts with the contour of the stone, so a decree is adapted to a given situation.

Book VI turns from the moral to the intellectual virtues. Since Aristotle's procedure is to analyze capacities by examining the objects on which they are directed, the fundamental distinction is between the rational part in us that grasps what cannot be otherwise and the one that deals with what can be otherwise. The former is theoretical (contemplative), the latter productive and practical (directed on what we may come to change or control). The major intellectual virtues of the first kind of rationality are science (aiming at the knowledge of the necessary, unchanging laws of things), intuitive intellect (furnishing first principles), and philosophic wisdom (synthesizing the two). The main virtues of the second kind are, first, art or craft or technique (exhibited in production—*poiēsis*—and aiming at a product beyond the activity itself) and, second, practical wisdom (exhibited in the decisions of action or life generally—*praxis*—where the end is contained in the action itself). Practical wisdom is thus the central intellectual virtue for ethics.

[VI, 5] We may approach the subject of practical wisdom by studying the persons to whom we attribute it. Now, the capacity of deliberating well about what is good and advantageous for oneself is regarded as typical of a man of practical wisdom— not deliberating well about what is good and advantageous in a partial sense, for example, what contributes to health or strength, but what sort of thing contributes to the good life in general. This is shown by the fact that we speak of men as having practical wisdom in a particular respect [i.e., not in an un-

qualified sense,] when they calculate well with respect to some worthwhile end, one that cannot be attained by an applied science or art. It follows that, in general, a man of practical wisdom is he who has the ability to deliberate.

Now no one deliberates about things that cannot be other than they are or about actions that he cannot possibly perform. Since, as we saw, pure science involves demonstration, while things whose starting points or first causes can be other than they are do not admit of demonstration—for such things too [and not merely their first causes] can all be other than they are—and since it is impossible to deliberate about what exists by necessity, we may conclude that practical wisdom is neither a pure science nor an art. It is not a pure science, because matters of action admit of being other than they are, and it is not an applied science or art, because action and production are generically different.

What remains, then, is that it is a truthful characteristic of acting rationally in matters good and bad for men. For production has an end other than itself, but action does not: good action is itself an end. That is why we think that Pericles and men like him have practical wisdom. They have the capacity of seeing what is good for themselves and for mankind, and these are, we believe, the qualities of men capable of managing households and states. . . .

[8] . . . While young men do indeed become good geometricians and mathematicians and attain theoretical wisdom in such matters, they apparently do not attain practical wisdom. The reason is that practical wisdom is concerned with particulars as well [as with universals], and knowledge of particulars comes from experience. But a young man has no experience, for experience is the product of a long time. In fact, one might also raise the question why it is that a boy may become a mathematician but not a philosopher or a natural scientist. The answer may be that the objects of mathematics are the result of abstraction, whereas the fundamental principles of philosophy and natural science come from experience. Young men can assert philosophical and scientific principles but can have no genuine convictions about them, whereas there is no obscurity about the essential definitions in mathematics.

Moreover, in our deliberations error is possible as regards either the universal principle or the particular fact: we may be unaware either that all heavy water is bad, or that the particular water we are faced with is heavy.

That practical wisdom is not scientific knowledge is [therefore] evident. As we stated, it is concerned with ultimate particulars, since the actions to be performed are ultimate particulars. This means that it is at the opposite pole from intelligence. For the intelligence grasps limiting terms and definitions that cannot be attained by reasoning, while practical wisdom has as its object the ultimate particular fact, of which there is perception but no scientific knowledge. This perception is not the kind with which [each of our five senses apprehends] its proper object, but the kind with which we perceive that in mathematics the triangle is the ultimate figure. For in this direction, too, we shall have to reach a stop. But this [type of mathematical cognition] is more truly perception than practical wisdom, and it is different in kind from the other [type of perception which deals with the objects proper to the various senses].

Having completed discussion of the virtues, Aristotle turns next to approximations of virtue. The virtuous person, whose knowledge is adequate and whose desires are good, is distinguished from the morally strong or self-controlled person. In the latter, knowledge of the good conflicts with evil desires, although the good prevails. The morally weak person lacks self-control: in spite of knowing the good, he yields to evil desires. (He differs from the self-indulgent or vicious man in that the latter acts on a wrong principle and follows his desires.) Socrates had previously stated the paradox that no one does evil voluntarily, since to know the good entails doing it.

[VII, 3] . . . (a) . . . "to know" has two meanings: a man is said to "know" both when he does not use the knowledge he has and when he does use it. Accordingly, when a man does wrong it will make a difference whether he is not exercising the knowledge he has [viz., that it is wrong to do what he is doing], or whether he is exercising it. In the latter case we would be baffled, but not if he acted without exercising his knowledge.

Moreover, (b) since there are two kinds of premise, [namely, universal and particular,] it may well happen that a man knows both [major and minor premise of a practical syllogism] and yet acts against his knowledge, because the [minor] premise which he uses is universal rather than particular. [In that case, he cannot apply his knowledge to his action,] for the actions to be performed are particulars. Also, there are two kinds of universal term to be distinguished: one applies to (i) the agent, and the other (ii) to the thing. For example, when a person knows that dry food is good for all men, [he may also know] (i) that he is a man, or (ii) that this kind of food is dry. But whether the particular food before him is of this kind is something of which [a morally weak man] either does not have the knowledge or does not exercise it. So we see that there will be a tremendous difference between these two ways of knowing. We do not regard it as at all strange that [a morally weak person] "knows" in the latter sense [with one term nonspecific], but it would be surprising if he "knew" in the other sense, [namely with both terms apprehended as concrete particulars].

There is (c) another way besides those we have so far described, in which it is possible for men to have knowledge. When a person has knowledge but does not use it, we see that "having" a characteristic has different meanings. There is a sense in which a person both has and does not have knowledge, for example, when he is asleep, mad, or drunk. But this is precisely the condition of people who are in the grip of the emotions. Fits of passion, sexual appetites, and some other such passions actually cause palpable changes in the body, and in some cases even produce madness. Now it is clear that we must attribute to the morally weak a condition similar to that of men who are asleep, mad, or drunk. That the words they utter spring from knowledge [as to what is good] is no evidence to the contrary. People can repeat geometrical demonstrations and verses of Empedocles even when affected by sleep, madness, and drink; and beginning students can reel off the words they have heard, but they do not yet know the subject. The subject must grow to be part of them, and that takes time. We must, therefore, assume that a man who displays moral weakness repeats the formulae [of moral knowledge] in the same way as an actor speaks his lines.

Further, (d) we may also look at the cause [of moral weakness] from the viewpoint of the science of human nature, in the following way. [In the practical syllogism,] one of the premises, the universal, is a current belief, while the other involves particular facts which fall within the domain of sense perception. When two premises are combined into one, [i.e., when the universal rule is realized in a particular case,] the soul is thereupon bound to affirm the conclusion, and if the premises involve action, the soul is bound to perform this act at once. For example, if [the premises are]: "Everything sweet ought to be tasted" and "This thing before me is sweet" ("this thing" perceived as an individual particular object), a man who is able [to taste] and is not prevented is bound to act accordingly at once.

Now, suppose that there is within us one universal opinion forbidding us to taste [things of this kind], and another [universal] opinion which tells us that everything sweet is pleasant, and also [a concrete perception], determining our activity, that the particular thing before us is sweet; and suppose further that the appetite [for pleasure] happens to be present. [The result is that] one opinion tells us to avoid that thing, while appetite, capable as it is of setting in motion each part of our body, drives us to it. [This is the case we have been looking for, the defeat of reason in moral weakness.] Thus it turns out that a morally weak man acts under the influence of some kind of reasoning and opinion, an opinion which is not intrinsically but only incidentally opposed to right reason; for it is not opinion but appetite that is opposed to right reason. And this explains why animals cannot be morally weak: they do not have conceptions of universals, but have only the power to form mental images and memory of particulars.

How is the [temporary] ignorance of a morally weak person dispelled and how does he regain his [active] knowledge [of what is good]? The explanation is the same as it is for drunkenness and sleep, and it is not peculiar to the affect of moral weakness. To get it we have to go to the students of natural science.

The final premise, consisting as it does in an opinion about an object perceived by the senses, determines our action. When in the grip of emotion, a morally weak man either does not have this premise, or he has it not in the sense of knowing it, but in the sense of uttering it as a drunken man may utter verses of Empedocles. [Because he is not in active possession of this premise,] and because

the final [concrete] term of his reasoning is not a universal and does not seem to be an object of scientific knowledge in the same way that a universal is, [for both these reasons] we seem to be led to the conclusion which Socrates sought to establish. Moral weakness does not occur in the presence of knowledge in the strict sense, and it is sensory knowledge, not science, which is dragged about by emotion. . . .

[VIII, 3] . . . [T]here are three kinds of friendship, corresponding in number to the objects worthy of affection. In each of these, the affection can be reciprocated so that the partner is aware of it, and the partners wish for each other's good in terms of the motive on which their affection is based. Now, when the motive of the affection is usefulness, the partners do not feel affection for one another *per se* but in terms of the good accruing to each from the other. The same is also true of those whose friendship is based on pleasure: we love witty people not for what they are, but for the pleasure they give us.

So we see that when the useful is the basis of affection, men love because of the good they get out of it, and when pleasure is the basis, for the pleasure they get out of it. In other words, the friend is loved not because he is a friend, but because he is useful or pleasant. Thus, these two kinds are friendship only incidentally, since the object of affection is not loved for being the kind of person he is, but for providing some good or pleasure. Consequently, such friendships are easily dissolved when the partners do not remain unchanged: the affection ceases as soon as one partner is no longer pleasant or useful to the other. Now, usefulness is not something permanent, but differs at different times. Accordingly, with the disappearance of the motive for being friends, the friendship, too, is dissolved, since the friendship owed its existence to these motives.

Friendships of this kind seem to occur most commonly among old people, because at that age men do not pursue the pleasant but the beneficial. They are also found among young men and those in their prime who are out for their own advantage. Such friends are not at all given to living in each other's company, for sometimes they do not even find each other pleasant. Therefore, they have no further need of this relationship, if they are not mutually beneficial. They find each other pleasant only to the extent that they have hopes of some good coming out of it. The traditional friendship between host and guest is also placed in this group.

Friendship of young people seems to be based on pleasure. For their lives are guided by emotion, and they pursue most intensely what they find pleasant and what the moment brings. As they advance in years, different things come to be pleasant for them. Hence they become friends quickly and just as quickly cease to be friends. For as another thing becomes pleasant, the friendship, too, changes, and the pleasure of a young man changes quickly. Also, young people are prone to fall in love, since the greater part of falling in love is a matter of emotion and based on pleasure. That is why they form a friendship and give it up again so quickly that the change often takes place within the same day. But they do wish to be together all day and to live together, because it is in this way that they get what they want out of their friendship.

The perfect form of friendship is that between good men who are alike in excellence or virtue. For these friends wish alike for one another's good because they are good men, and they are good *per se*, [that is, their goodness is something intrinsic, not incidental]. Those who wish for their friends' good for their friends' sake are friends in the truest sense, since their attitude is determined by what their friends are and not by incidental considerations. Hence their friendship lasts as long as they are good, and [that means it will last for a long time, since] goodness or virtue is a thing that lasts. In addition, each partner is both good in the unqualified sense and good for his friend. For those who are good, i.e., good without qualification, are also beneficial to one another. In the same double sense, they are also pleasant to one another: for good men are pleasant both in an unqualified sense and to one another, since each finds pleasure in his own proper actions and in actions like them, and the actions of good men are identical with or similar to one another. That such a friendship is lasting stands to reason, because in it are combined all the qualities requisite for people to be friends. . . .

Book X includes Aristotle's careful analysis of pleasure, which differs markedly from Plato's. Central to it is the distinction between an act that is complete at any moment and a movement or change that exhibits its form part by part over time. Pleasure is of the first sort, building a temple is of the second sort.

[X, 4] . . . For each sense, and similarly all thought and study, has its own pleasure and is pleasantest when it is most complete; but it is most complete when the organ is in good condition and the object the worthiest of all that fall within its range; pleasure completes the activity. Still, pleasure does not complete the activity in the same way in which the perceived object and sense perception do, when both are good, just as health and a physician are not in the same sense the cause of a man's healthy state.

That there is a pleasure for each sense is obvious, for we speak of sights and sounds as being pleasant. It is also obvious that the pleasure is greatest when the sense perception is keenest and is exercised upon the best object. As long as this is the condition of the perceived object and the perceiving subject the pleasure will last on, since there is something to act and something to be acted upon.

Pleasure completes the activity not as a characteristic completes an activity by being already inherent in it, but as a completeness that superimposes itself upon it, like the bloom of youth in those who are in their prime. So long, then, as the object of thought or of sense perception and the discriminating or studying subject are in their proper condition, there will be pleasure in the activity. For as long as that which is acted upon and that which acts remain unchanged in themselves and in their relation to one another, the same result must naturally follow.

How is it, then, that no one feels pleasure continuously? Do we get tired? [That seems to be the correct answer;] for whatever is human is incapable of continuous activity. Consequently, pleasure is not continuous, either, since it accompanies activity. And for the same reason, some things which delight us when they are new, give us less delight later on: at first our thinking is stimulated and concentrates its activity upon them. To take sight as an example, people are engrossed in what they see, but afterwards the activity is not the same but is relaxed, and as a result the pleasure loses its edge.

One is led to believe that all men have a desire for pleasure, because all strive to live. Life is an activity, and each man actively exercises his favorite faculties upon the objects he loves most. A man who is musical, for example, exercises his hearing upon tunes, an intellectual his thinking upon the subjects of his study, and so forth. But pleasure completes the activities, and consequently life, which they desire. No wonder, then, that men also aim at pleasure: each man finds that it completes his life, and his life is desirable.

We need not discuss for the present the question whether we choose life for the sake of pleasure or pleasure for the sake of life. For the two are obviously interdependent and cannot be separated: there is no pleasure without activity, and every activity is completed by pleasure.

Chapter 5 of Book X defends pleasure against criticism. Pleasure enhances worthwhile activities. When pleasure is opposed to an activity it is because the two activities are incompatible—it is not a case of pleasure versus activity. The pleasure of a good activity is a good pleasure, of a bad activity a bad pleasure. Similarly, the pleasure of a superior activity is superior to the pleasure of an inferior activity; for example, the pleasures of thought are superior to those of sense. Chapters 6–8 deal with happiness and argue that the contemplative life—the godlike activity of humans, only rarely achieved—is superior to the practical life. For the most part human well-being lies in the exercise of the virtues explored throughout the book.

The *Politics* [4]

[I, 1] Observation shows us, first, that every polis (or state) is a species of association, and, secondly, that all associations are instituted for the purpose of attaining some good—for all men do all their acts with a view to achieving something which is, in their view, a good. We may therefore hold [on

the basis of what we actually observe] that all associations aim at some good; and we may also hold that the particular association which is the most sovereign of all, and includes all the rest, will pursue this aim most, and will thus be directed to the most sovereign of all goods. This most sovereign and inclusive association is the polis, as it is called, or the political association.

The associations ruled by the statesman acting according to rule, the monarch of a kingdom, the manager of a household, and the master of slaves are different in kind, not just in numbers or power.

[2] If, accordingly, we begin at the beginning, and consider things in the process of their growth, we shall best be able, in this as in other fields, to attain scientific conclusions by the method we employ. First of all, there must necessarily be a union or pairing of those who cannot exist without one another. Male and female must unite for the reproduction of the species—not from deliberate intention, but from the natural impulse, which exists in animals generally as it also exists in plants, to leave behind them something of the same nature as themselves. Next, there must necessarily be a union of the naturally ruling element with the element which is naturally ruled, for the preservation of both. The element which is able, by virtue of its intelligence, to exercise forethought, is naturally a ruling and master element; the element which is able, by virtue of its bodily power, to do what the other element plans, is a ruled element, which is naturally in a state of slavery; and master and slave have accordingly [as they thus complete one another] a common interest. . . . The female and the slave [we may pause to note] are naturally distinguished from one another. Nature makes nothing in a spirit of stint, as smiths do when they make the Delphic knife to serve a number of purposes: she makes each separate thing for a separate end; and she does so because each instrument has the finest finish when it serves a single purpose and not a variety of purposes. . . .

The first result of these two elementary associations [of male and female, and of master and slave] is the household or family. . . . The first form of association naturally instituted for the satisfaction

---

[4] The selection is from *The Politics of Aristotle*, trans. Ernest Barker (New York: Oxford University Press, 1946). The bracketed passages in the selection are additions by the translator to elucidate the course of the argument. "Politics" should not be taken in our narrower sense. It is more like social life. *Polis* is the Greek for city, and politics is therefore the affairs of the city, or community life.

of daily recurrent needs is thus the family. . . . The next form of association—which is also the *first* to be formed from more households than one, and for the satisfaction of something more than daily recurrent needs—is the village. . . . This, it may be noted, is the reason why each Greek polis was originally ruled—as the peoples of the barbarian world still are—by kings. They were formed of persons who were already monarchically governed [i.e. they were formed from households and villages, and] households are always monarchically governed by the eldest of the kin, just as villages, when they are offshoots from the household, are similarly governed in virtue of the kinship between their members. . . . The fact that men generally were governed by kings in ancient times, and that some still continue to be governed in that way, is the reason that leads us all to assert that the gods are also governed by a king. We make the lives of the gods in the likeness of our own—as we also make their shapes. . . .

When we come to the final and perfect association, formed from a number of villages, we have already reached the polis—the association which may be said to have reached the height of full self-sufficiency; or rather [to speak more exactly] we may say that while it *grows* for the sake of mere life [and is so far, and at that stage, still short of full self-sufficiency], it *exists* [when once it is fully grown] for the sake a good life [and is therefore fully self-sufficient]. . . .

. . . [I]t is evident that the polis belongs to the class of things that exist by nature, and that man is by nature an animal intended to live in a polis. He who is without a polis, by reason of his own nature and not of some accident, is either a poor sort of being, or a being higher than man; he is like the man of whom Homer wrote in denunciation:

'Clanless and lawless and heartless is he.'

The man who is such by nature [i.e. unable to join in the society of a polis] at once plunges into a passion for war; he is in the position of a solitary advanced piece in a game of draughts.

The reason why man is a being meant for political association, in a higher degree than bees or other gregarious animals can ever associate, is evident. Nature, according to our theory, makes nothing in vain; and man alone of the animals is furnished with the faculty of language. The mere making of sounds serves to indicate pleasure and pain, and is thus a faculty that belongs to animals in general: their nature enables them to attain the point at which they have perceptions of pleasure and pain, and can signify those perceptions to one another. But language serves to declare what is advantageous and what is the reverse, and it therefore serves to declare what is just and what is unjust. It is the peculiarity of man, in comparison with the rest of the animal world, that he alone possesses a perception of good and evil, of the just and the unjust, and of other similar qualities; and it is association in [a common perception of] these things which makes a family and a polis.

[T]he polis is prior in the order of nature to the family and the individual. The reason for this is that the whole is necessarily prior [in nature] to the part. If the whole body be destroyed, there will not be a foot or a hand, except in that ambiguous sense in which one uses the same word to indicate a different thing, as when one speaks of a 'hand' made of stone; for a hand, when destroyed [by the destruction of the whole body], will be no better than a stone 'hand.' All things derive their essential character from their function and their capacity; and it follows that if they are no longer fit to discharge their function, we ought not to say that they are still the same things, but only that, by an ambiguity, they still have the same names.

We thus see that the polis exists by nature and that it is prior to the individual. [The proof of both propositions is the fact that the polis is a whole, and that individuals are simply its parts.] Not being self-sufficient when they are isolated, all individuals are so many parts all equally depending on the whole [which alone can bring about self-sufficiency]. The man who is isolated—who is unable to share in the benefits of political association, or has no need to share because he is already self-sufficient—is no part of the polis, and must therefore be either a beast or a god. . . . Man, when perfected, is the best of animals; but if he be isolated from law and justice he is the worst of all. Injustice is all the graver when it is armed injustice; and man is furnished from birth with arms [such as, for instance, language] which are intended to serve the purposes of moral prudence and virtue, but which may be used in preference for opposite ends.

That is why, if he be without virtue, he is a most unholy and savage being, and worse than all others in the indulgence of lust and gluttony. Justice [which is his salvation] belongs to the polis; for justice, which is the determination of what is just, is an ordering of the political association. . . .

[4] We may make the assumption that property is part of the household, and that the art of acquiring property is a part of household-management; and we may do so because it is impossible to live well, or indeed to live at all, unless the necessary conditions are present. We may further assume that, just as each art which has a definite sphere must necessarily be furnished with the appropriate instruments if its function is to be discharged, so the same holds good in the sphere of household management. Finally, we may also assume that instruments are partly inanimate and partly animate: the pilot, for instance, has an inanimate instrument in the rudder, and an animate instrument (for all subordinates, in every art, are of the nature of instruments) in the look-out man. On the basis of these assumptions we may conclude that each article of property is an instrument for the purpose of life; that property in general is the sum of such instruments; that the slave is an animate article of property; and that subordinates, or servants, in general may be described as instruments which are prior to other instruments [i.e. animate instruments which must first be present before other, and inanimate, instruments can be used]. There is only one condition on which we can imagine managers not needing subordinates, and masters not needing slaves. This condition would be that each [inanimate] instrument could do its own work, at the word of command or by intelligent anticipation, like the statues of Daedalus or the tripods made by Hephaestus, of which Homer relates that

> Of their own motion they entered the conclave
> of Gods on Olympus,

as if a shuttle should weave of itself, and a plectrum should do its own harp-playing. [Here, however, we must draw another distinction.] The instruments of which we have just been speaking [e.g. the shuttle] are instruments of *production;* but articles of household property [such as the slave or other chattels] are instruments of *action.* From the shuttle there issues something which is different, and exists apart, from the immediate act of its use; but from

[articles of household property, e.g.] garments or beds, there only comes the one fact of their use. We may add that, since production and action are different in kind, and both of them need their own proper instruments, those instruments must also show a corresponding difference. Life is action and not production; and therefore the slave [being an instrument for the purpose of life] is a servant in the sphere of action.

There is a further consideration [which is necessary to explain fully the nature of the slave]. An 'article of property' is a term that is used in the same sense in which the term 'part' is also used. Now a part is not only a part of something other than itself: it also belongs entirely to that other thing [and has no life or being other than that of so belonging]. It is the same with an article of property as it is with a part. Accordingly, while the master is merely the master of the slave, and does not belong to him, [having a life and being of his own beyond that of a master], the slave is not only the slave of his master; he also belongs entirely to him, [and so has no life or being other than that of so belonging].

From these considerations we can see clearly what is the nature of the slave and what is his capacity. We attain these definitions—first, that 'anybody who by his nature is not his own man, but another's, is by his nature a slave'; secondly, that 'anybody who, being a man, is an article of property, is another's man'; and thirdly, that 'an article of property is an instrument intended for the purpose of action and separable from its possessor.'

[5] . . . The soul rules the body with the sort of authority of a master: mind rules the appetite with the sort of authority of a statesman or a monarch. In this sphere [i.e. in the sphere of man's inner life] it is clearly natural and beneficial to the body that it should be ruled by the soul, and again it is natural and beneficial to the affective part of the soul that it should be ruled by the mind and the rational part; whereas the equality of the two elements, or their reverse relation, is always detrimental. What holds good in man's inner life also holds good outside it; and the same principle is true of the relation of man to animals as is true of the relation of his soul to his body. Tame animals have a better nature than wild, and it is better for all such animals that they should be ruled by man because they then get the benefit of preservation. Again,

the relation of male to female is naturally that of the superior to the inferior—of the ruling to the ruled. This general principle must similarly hold good of all human beings generally [and therefore of the relation of masters and slaves].

We may thus conclude that all men who differ from others as much as the body differs from the soul, or an animal from a man [and this is the case with all whose function is bodily service, and who produce their best when they supply such service]— all such are by nature slaves, and it is better for them, on the very same principle as in the other cases just mentioned, to be ruled by a master. A man is thus by nature a slave if he is capable of becoming (and this is the reason why he also actually becomes) the property of another, and if he participates in reason to the extent of apprehending it in another, though destitute of it himself. Herein he differs from animals, which do not apprehend reason, but simply obey their instincts. But the use which is made of the slave diverges but little from the use made of tame animals; both he and they supply their owner with bodily help in meeting his daily requirements.

[We have hitherto been speaking of mental differences.] But it is nature's intention also to erect a physical difference between the body of the freeman and that of the slave, giving the latter strength for the menial duties of life, but making the former upright in carriage and (though useless for physical labour) useful for the various purposes of civic life— a life which tends, as it develops, to be divided into military service and the occupations of peace. The contrary of nature's intention, however, often happens: there are some slaves who have the bodies of freemen—as there are others who have a freeman's soul. But if nature's intention were realized— if men differed from one another in bodily form as much as the statues of the gods [differ from the human figure]—it is obvious that we should all agree that the inferior class ought to be the slaves of the superior. And if this principle is true when the difference is one of the body, it may be affirmed with still greater justice when the difference is one of the soul; though it is not as easy to see the beauty of the soul as it is to see that of the body.

It is thus clear that, just as some are by nature free, so others are by nature slaves, and for these latter the condition of slavery is both beneficial and just.

For example, actual slaves, if prisoners of war, may not be natural slaves; in that case, slavery is conventional. (Greeks are not natural slaves.) Slavery of this sort rests on power. But in the relation of natural master and slave there is community of interest and friendship.

[9] . . . All articles of property have two possible uses. Both of these uses belong to the article as such, but they do not belong to it in the same manner, or to the same extent. The one use is proper and peculiar to the article concerned; the other is not. We may take a shoe as an example. It can be used both for wearing and for exchange. Both of these uses are uses of the shoe as such. Even the man who exchanges a shoe, in return for money or food, with a person who needs the article, is using the shoe as a shoe; but since the shoe has not been made for the purpose of being exchanged, the use which he is making of it is not its proper and peculiar use. The same is true of all other articles of property. Exchange is possible in regard to them all: it arises from the natural facts of the case, and is due to some men having more, and others less, than suffices for their needs. We can thus see that retail trade [which buys from others to sell at a profit] is not naturally a part of the art of acquisition. If that were the case, it would only be necessary to practise exchange to the extent that sufficed for the needs of both parties [and not to the extent of the making of profit by one of the parties at the expense of the other].

In the first form of association, which is the household, it is obvious that there is no purpose to be served by the art of exchange. Such a purpose only emerged when the scope of association had already been extended [until it issued in the village]. The members of the household had shared all things in common: the members of the village, separated from one another [in a number of different households], had at their disposal a number of different things, which they had to exchange with one another, as need arose, by way of barter—much as many uncivilized tribes still do to this day. On this basis things which are useful are exchanged themselves, and directly, for similar useful things, but the transaction does not go any further [that is to say, no money is involved]; wine, for instance, is given, or taken, in return for wheat, and other similar commodities are similarly bartered for one another. When used in this way, the art of exchange is not contrary to nature, nor in any way a form of the art of acquisition [in the second sense of that term defined at the beginning of this chapter]. Exchange simply served [in its first beginnings] to satisfy the natural requirements of sufficiency. None the less it was from exchange, as thus practised, that the art of acquisition [in its second sense] developed, in the sort of way we might reasonably expect. [Distant transactions were the cause.] The supply of men's needs came to depend on more foreign sources, as men began to import for themselves what they lacked, and to export what they had in superabundance; and in this way the use of a money currency was inevitably instituted. The reason for this institution of a currency was that all the naturally necessary commodities were not easily portable; and men therefore agreed, for the purpose of their exchanges, to give and receive some commodity [i.e. some form of more or less precious metal] which itself belonged to the category of useful things and possessed the advantage of being easily handled for the purpose of getting the necessities of life. Such commodities were iron, silver, and other similar metals. At first their value was simply determined by their size and weight; but finally a stamp was imposed on the metal which, serving as a definite indication of the quantity, would save men the trouble of determining the value on each occasion.

When, in this way, a currency had once been instituted, there next arose, from the necessary process of exchange [i.e. exchange between commodities, with money serving merely as a measure], the other form of the art of acquisition, which consists in retail trade [conducted for profit]. At first, we may allow, it was perhaps practised in a simple way [that is to say, money was still regarded as a measure, and not treated as a source of profit]: but in process of time, and as a result of experience, it was practised with a more studied technique, which sought to discover the sources from which, and the methods by which, the greatest profit could be made. The result has been the emergence of the view that the art of acquisition is specially concerned with currency, and that its function consists in an ability to discover the sources from which a fund of *money* can be derived. In support of this view it is urged that the art is one which produces wealth and money; indeed those who hold the view often assume that wealth is simply a fund of currency, on the ground that the art of acquisition [in the form of retail trade for profit] is concerned with currency. In opposition to this view there is another which is sometimes held. On this view currency is regarded as a sham, and entirely a convention. Naturally and inherently [the supporters of the view argue] a currency is a nonentity; for if those who use a currency give it up in favour of another, that currency is worthless, and useless for any of the necessary purposes of life. A man rich in currency [they proceed to urge] will often be at a loss to procure the necessities of subsistence; and surely it is absurd that a thing should be counted as wealth which a man may possess in abundance, and yet none the less die of starvation—like Midas in the fable, when everything set before him was turned at once into gold through the granting of his own avaricious prayer.

Basing themselves on these arguments, those who hold this latter view try to find a different conception of wealth [from that which identifies it with a fund of currency] and a different conception of the art of acquisition [from that which makes it specially concerned with currency]. They are right in making the attempt. The [natural] art of acquisition, and natural wealth, *are* different. The [natural] form of the art of acquisition is connected with the management of the household [which in turn is connected with the *general* acquisition of *all* the resources needed for its life]; but the other form is a matter only of retail trade, and it is concerned only with getting a fund of money, and that only by the method of conducting the exchange of commodities. This latter form may be held to turn on the power of currency; for currency is the starting-point, as it is also the goal, of exchange. It is a further point of difference that the wealth produced by this latter form of the art of acquisition is unlimited. [In this respect the art of acquisition, in its retail form, is analogous to other professional arts.] The art of medicine recognizes no limit in respect of the production of health, and the arts generally admit no limit in respect of the production of their ends (each seeking to produce its end to the greatest possible extent)—though medicine, and the arts generally, recognize and practise a limit to the means they use to attain their ends, since the end itself constitutes a limit. The same is true of the retail form of the art of acquisition. There is no limit to the end it seeks; and the end it seeks is wealth of the sort we have mentioned [i.e. wealth in the form of currency] and the mere acquisition of money. But the acquisition of wealth by the art of household management (as contrasted with the art of acquisition in its retail form) *has* a limit; and the object of that art is not an unlimited amount of wealth. It would thus appear, if we look at the matter in this light, that all wealth must have a limit. In actual experience, however, we see the opposite happening; and all who are engaged in acquisition increase their fund of currency without any limit or pause.

The cause of this contradiction lies in the close connexion between the two different modes of acquisition [that of the householder, and that of the retail trader]. They overlap because they are both handling the same objects and acting in the same field of acquisition; but they move along different lines—the object of the one being simply accumulation, and that of the other something quite different. This overlap of the two modes explains why some men believe that mere accumulation is the object of household management; and in the strength of that belief they stick to the idea that they must keep their wealth in currency untouched, or increase it indefinitely. But the fundamental cause of this state of mind is men's anxiety about livelihood, rather than about well-being; and since their desire for that is unlimited, their desire for the things that produce it is equally unlimited. Even those who do aim at well-being seek the means of obtaining physical enjoyments; and, as what they seek appears to depend on the activity of acquisition, they are thus led to occupy themselves wholly in the making of money. This is the real reason why the other and lower form of the art of acquisition has come into vogue. Because enjoyment depends on [the possession of] a superfluity, men address themselves to the art which produces the superfluity necessary to enjoyment; and if they cannot get what they want by the use of that art—i.e. the art of acquisition—they attempt to do so by other means, using each and every capacity in a way not consonant with its nature. The proper function of courage, for example, is not to produce money but to give confidence. The same is true of military and medical ability: neither has the function of producing money: the one has the function of producing

victory, and the other that of producing health. But those of whom we are speaking turn all such capacities into forms of the art of acquisition, as though to make money were the one aim and everything else must contribute to that aim. . . .

[13] . . . The soul has naturally two elements, a ruling and a ruled; and each has its different goodness, one belonging to the rational and ruling element, and the other to the irrational and ruled. What is true of the soul is evidently also true of the other cases [i.e. those of the household and the state]; and we may thus conclude that it is a general law that there should be naturally ruling elements and elements naturally ruled. [Just because there is a general law, operative in many spheres, there are different modes of its operation, according to the sphere in which it operates.] The rule of the freeman over the slave is one kind of rule; that of the male over the female another; that of the grown man over the child another still. It is true that all these persons [freeman and slave, male and female, the grown man and the child] possess in common the different parts of the soul; but they possess them in different ways. The slave is entirely without the faculty of deliberation; the female indeed possesses it, but in a form which remains inconclusive; and if children also possess it, it is only in an immature form. What is true [of their possessing the different parts of the soul] must similarly be held to be true of their possessing moral goodness: they must all share in it, but not in the same way—each sharing only to the extent required for the discharge of his or her function. The ruler, accordingly, must possess moral goodness in its full and perfect form [i.e. the form based on rational deliberation], because his function, regarded absolutely and in its full nature, demands a master-artificer, and reason is such a master-artificer; but all other persons need only possess moral goodness to the extent required of them [by their particular position]. It is thus clear that while moral goodness is a quality of all the persons mentioned, the fact still remains that temperance—and similarly fortitude and justice—are not, as Socrates held, the same in a woman as they are in a man. Fortitude in the one, for example, is shown in connexion with ruling; in the other, it is shown in connexion with serving; and the same is true of the other forms of goodness.

[II, 5] The next subject for consideration is

property. What is the proper system of property for citizens who are to live under an ideal constitution? Is it a system of communism, or one of private property? . . . Should use and ownership both be common? [Or should one be common and the other private?] We may note three possible alternatives. First, we may have a system under which plots of land are owned in severalty, but the crops (as actually happens among some uncivilized tribes) are brought into a common stock for the purpose of consumption. Secondly, and conversely, the land may be held in common ownership, and may also be cultivated in common, but the crops may be divided among individuals for their private use: some of the uncivilized peoples are also said to practise this second method of sharing. Thirdly, the plots and the crops [i.e. ownership and use] may both be common.

When the cultivators of the soil are a different body from the citizens who own it [as will be the case if they are serfs or slaves], the position will be different and easier to handle; but when the citizens who own the soil are also its cultivators, the problems of property will cause a good deal of trouble. If they do not share equally in work and recompense, those who do more work and get less recompense will be bound to raise complaints against those who get a large recompense and do little work. Indeed it is generally true that it is a difficult business for men to live together and to be partners in any form of human activity, but it is especially difficult to do so when property is involved. Fellow-travellers who are merely partners in a journey furnish an illustration: they generally quarrel about ordinary matters and take offence on petty occasions. So, again, the servants with whom we are most prone to take offence are those who are particularly employed in ordinary everyday services.

Difficulties such as these, and many others, are involved in a system of community of property. The present system [of private property] would be far preferable, if it were adorned by customs [in the social sphere] and by the enactment of proper laws [in the political]. It would possess the advantages of both systems, and would combine the merits of a system of community of property with those of the system of private property. [It would be the ideal]; for property *ought* to be generally and in the main private, but common in one respect [i.e. in use]. When everyone has his own separate sphere

of interest, there will not be the same ground for quarrels; and the amount of interest will increase, because each man will feel that he is applying himself to what is his own. And on such a scheme, too, moral goodness [and not, as in Plato's scheme, legal compulsion] will ensure that the property of each is made to serve the use of all, in the spirit of the proverb which says 'Friends' goods are goods in common.' Even now there are some states in which the outlines of such a scheme are so far apparent, as to suggest that it is not impossible; in well-ordered states, more particularly, there are some elements of it already existing, and others which might be added. In these states each citizen has his own property; but when it comes to the use of this property, each makes a part of it available to his friends, and each devotes still another part to the common enjoyment of all fellow-citizens. In Sparta, for example, men use one another's slaves, and one another's horses and dogs, as if they were their own; and they take provisions on a journey, if they happen to be in need, from the farms in the country-side belonging to other citizens. It is clear from what has been said that the better system is that under which property is privately owned but is put to common use; and the function proper to the legislator is to make men so disposed that they will treat property in this way.

There is a further consideration which must be taken into account. This is the consideration of pleasure. Here too [as well as in the matter of goodness] to think of a thing as your own makes an inexpressible difference. [The satisfaction of a natural feeling brings pleasure]; and it may well be that regard for oneself [and, by extension, for what is one's own] is a feeling implanted by nature, and not a mere random impulse. Self-love is rightly censured, but what is really censured is not so much love of oneself as love of oneself in excess—just as we also blame the lover of money [not so much for loving money as for loving it in excess]; the simple feeling of love for any of these things [self, or property, or money] is more or less universal. We may add that a very great pleasure is to be found in doing a kindness and giving some help to friends, or guests, or comrades; and such kindness and help become possible only when property is privately owned. But not only are these pleasures [that arising from the satisfaction of a natural feeling of self-love, and that arising from the satisfaction of our impulse to help others] impossible under a system of excessive unification of the state. The activities of two forms of goodness are also obviously destroyed. The first of these is temperance in the matter of sexual relations (it is an act of moral value to refrain from loving the wife of another in the strength of temperance): the second is liberality in the use of property. In a state which is excessively unified no man can show himself liberal, or indeed do a liberal act; for the function of liberality consists in the proper use which is made of property.

Legislation such as Plato proposes may appear to wear an attractive face and to argue benevolence. The hearer receives it gladly, thinking that everybody will feel towards everybody else some marvellous sense of fraternity—all the more as the evils now existing under ordinary forms of government (lawsuits about contracts, convictions for perjury, and obsequious flatteries of the rich) are denounced as due to the absence of a system of common property. None of these evils, however, is due to the absence of communism. They all arise from the wickedness of human nature. Indeed it is a fact of observation that those who own common property, and share in its management, are far more often at variance with one another than those who have property in severalty—though [we tend to be misled by the fact that] those who are at variance in consequence of sharing in property look to us few in number when we compare them with the mass of those who own their property privately. . . .

Questions about citizenship and the character of the state lead to a classification of constitutions. Aristotle employs two criteria. One has to do with the aims of the constitution—whether its aims are the good life for the community and its individuals or the interest of the rulers. The second criterion is the number of the rulers: one, few, or many. The combination of criteria yields six types of constitution, as shown in Table 3.1.

The constitutions in the right-hand column are perversions of those in the left-hand column. Which among the latter are desirable depends on the nature and conditions of the population and the proportion of excellence within it. Aristotle's preference is aristocracy, but he compromises on polity as a mean between the realistic contenders in his world—oligarchy and democracy.

[III, 8] . . . We have defined democracy as the sovereignty of numbers; but we can conceive a case in which the majority who hold the sovereignty in a state are the well-to-do. Similarly oligarchy is generally stated to be the sovereignty of a small number; but it might conceivably happen that the poorer classes were fewer in number than the well-to-do, and yet—in virtue of superior vigour—were the sovereign authority of the constitution. In neither case could the definition previously given of these constitutions be regarded as true. We might attempt to overcome the difficulty by combining both of the factors—wealth with paucity of numbers, and poverty with mass. On this basis oligarchy might be defined as the constitution under which the rich, being also few in number, hold the offices of the state; and similarly democracy might be defined as the constitution under which the poor, being also many in number, are in control. But this involves us in another difficulty. If our new definition is exhaustive, and there are no forms of oligarchy and democracy other than those enumerated in that definition, what names are we to give to the constitutions just suggested as conceivable—those where

	Aiming at the Good Life	Aiming at the Ruler's Interest
Rule by one	Monarchy	Tyranny
Rule by few	Aristocracy	Oligarchy
Rule by many	Polity	Democracy

Table 3.1 Types of Constitutions

the wealthy form a majority and the poor a minority, and where the wealthy majority in the one case, and the poor minority in the other, are the sovereign authority of the constitution? The course of the argument thus appears to show that the factor of number—the small number of the sovereign body in oligarchies, or the large number in democracies—is an accidental attribute, due to the simple fact that the wealthy are generally few and the poor are generally numerous. Therefore the causes originally mentioned [i.e. small and large numbers] are not in fact the real causes of the difference between oligarchies and democracies. The real ground of the difference between oligarchy and democracy is poverty and riches. It is inevitable that any constitution should be an oligarchy if the rulers under it are rulers in virtue of riches, whether they are few or many: and it is equally inevitable that a constitution under which the poor rule should be a democracy.

It happens, however, as we have just remarked, [and this is why number becomes an accidental attribute of both of these constitutions], that the rich are few and the poor are numerous. It is only a few who have riches, but all alike share in free status; and these are the real grounds on which the two parties [the oligarchical and the democratic] dispute the control of the constitution.

[IV, 11] We have now to consider what is the best constitution and the best way of life for the *majority* of states and men. In doing so we shall not employ, [for the purpose of measuring 'the best'], a standard of excellence above the reach of ordinary men, or a standard of education requiring exceptional endowments and equipment, or the standard of a constitution which attains an ideal height. We shall only be concerned with the sort of life which most men are able to share and the sort of constitution which it is possible for most states to enjoy. The 'aristocracies,' so called, of which we have just been treating, [will not serve us for this purpose: they] either lie, at one extreme, beyond the reach of most states, or they approach, at the other, so closely to the constitution called 'polity' that they need not be considered separately and must be treated as identical with it. The issues we have just raised can all be decided in the light of one body of fundamental principles. If we adopt as true the statements made in the *Ethics*—(1) that a truly happy life is a life of goodness lived in freedom from impediments, and (2) that goodness con-

sists in a mean—it follows that the best way of life [for the *majority* of men] is one which consists in a mean, and a mean of the kind attainable by every individual. Further, the same criteria which determine whether the citizen-body [i.e. all its members, considered as *individuals*] have a good or bad way of life must also apply to the constitution; for a constitution is the way of life of a citizen-body. In all states there may be distinguished three parts, or classes, of the citizen-body—the very rich; the very poor; and the middle class which forms the mean. Now it is admitted, as a general principle, that moderation and the mean are always best. We may therefore conclude that in the ownership of all gifts of fortune a middle condition will be the best. Men who are in this condition are the most ready to listen to reason. Those who belong to either extreme—the over-handsome, the over-strong, the over-noble, the over-wealthy; or at the opposite end the over-poor, the over-weak, the utterly ignoble—find it hard to follow the lead of reason. Men in the first class tend more to violence and serious crime: men in the second tend too much to roguery and petty offences; and most wrongdoing arises either from violence or roguery. It is a further merit of the middle class that its members suffer least from ambition, which both in the military and the civil sphere is dangerous to states. It must also be added that those who enjoy too many advantages—strength, wealth, connexions, and so forth—are both unwilling to obey and ignorant how to obey. This is a defect which appears in them from the first, during childhood and in home-life: nurtured in luxury, they never acquire a habit of discipline, even in the matter of lessons. But there are also defects in those who suffer from the opposite extreme of a lack of advantages: they are far too mean and poor-spirited. We have thus, on the one hand, people who are ignorant how to rule and only know how to obey, as if they were so many slaves, and, on the other hand, people who are ignorant how to obey any sort of authority and only know how to rule as if they were masters of slaves. The result is a state, not of freemen, but only of slaves and masters: a state of envy on the one side and on the other contempt. Nothing could be further removed from the spirit of friendship or the temper of a political community. Community depends on friendship; and when there is enmity instead of friendship, men will not even share the same path.

A state aims at being, as far as it can be, a society composed of equals and peers [who, as such, can be friends and associates]; and the middle class, more than any other, has this sort of composition. It follows that a state which is based on the middle class is bound to be the best constituted in respect of the elements [i.e. equals and peers] of which, on our view, a state is naturally composed. The middle classes [besides contributing, in this way, to the security of the state] enjoy a greater security themselves than any other class. They do not, like the poor, covet the goods of others; nor do others covet their possessions, as the poor covet those of the rich. Neither plotting against others, nor plotted against themselves, they live in freedom from danger; and we may well approve the prayer of Phocylides:

Many things are best for the middling:
Fain would I be of the state's middle class.

It is clear from our argument, first, that the best form of political society is one where power is vested in the middle class, and, secondly, that good government is attainable in those states where there is a large middle class—large enough, if possible, to be stronger than both of the other classes, but at any rate large enough to be stronger than either of them singly; for in that case its addition to either will suffice to turn the scale, and will prevent either of the opposing extremes from becoming dominant. It is therefore the greatest of blessings for a state that its members should possess a moderate and adequate property. Where some have great possessions, and others have nothing at all, the result is either an extreme democracy or an unmixed oligarchy; or it may even be—indirectly, and as a reaction against both of these extremes—a tyranny. Tyranny is a form of government which may grow out of the headiest type of democracy, or out of oligarchy; but it is much less likely to grow out of constitutions of the middle order, or those which approximate to them [i.e. moderate oligarchies]. . . .

[VI, 2] The underlying idea of the democratic type of constitution is liberty. (This, it is commonly said, can only be enjoyed in democracy; and this, it is also said, is the aim of every democracy.) Liberty has more than one form. One of its forms [is the political, which] consists in the interchange of ruling and being ruled. The democratic conception of justice is the enjoyment of arithmetical equality, and not the enjoyment of proportionate equality on the basis of desert. On this arithmetical conception of justice the masses must necessarily be sovereign; the will of the majority must be ultimate and must be the expression of justice. The argument is that each citizen should be on an equality with the rest; and the result which follows in democracies is that the poor—they being in a majority, and the will of the majority being sovereign—are more sovereign than the rich. Such is the first form of liberty, which all democrats agree in making the aim of their sort of constitution. The other form [is the civil, which] consists in 'living as you like.' Such a life, the democrats argue, is the function of the free man, just as the function of slaves is *not* to live as they like. This is the second aim of democracy. Its issue is, ideally, freedom from any interference of government, and, failing that, such freedom as comes from the interchange of ruling and being ruled. It contributes, in this way, to a general system of liberty based on equality.

Aristotle discusses different degrees of participation in legislative, judicial, and executive institutions.

. . . [I]f we look at the form of democracy and the sort of populace which is generally held to be specially typical, we have to connect it . . . with the conception of justice which is the recognized democratic conception—that of equality of rights for all on an arithmetical basis. Equality here *might* be taken to mean that the poorer class should exercise no greater authority than the rich, or, in other words, that sovereignty should not be exercised only by it, but equally vested in all the citizens on a numerical basis. If that were the interpretation followed, the upholders of democracy could afford to believe that equality—and liberty—was really achieved by their constitution.

[3] This raises the question, 'How is such equality actually to be secured?' Should the assessed *properties* of the citizens be divided into two equal blocks, but with one block containing 500 large and the other 1,000 small owners, and should the 1,000 and the 500 have equal voting power? Or, alternatively, should equality of this order [i.e. equality based

on property, and not on personality] be calculated on some other system—a system, for example, by which properties are divided into two equal blocks, as before, but equal numbers of representatives are then selected from the 500 owners in the one block and the 1,000 in the other, and the representatives so selected are given control of the elections [of magistrates] and the law courts? [Either system means, in effect, the basing of the constitution on property.] Now is a constitution so based the one most in accordance with justice, as justice is conceived in democracies? Or is a constitution based on numbers [i.e. on *persons*, rather than property] more truly in accordance with justice? Democrats reply by saying that justice consists in the will of a majority of persons. Oligarchs reply by saying that it consists in the will of a majority of property-owners, and that decisions should be taken on the basis of weight of property. Both of these answers involve inequality and injustice. If justice is made to consist in the will of the few [i.e. the few who own the greatest amount of property], tyranny is the logical result; for if we carry the oligarchical conception of justice to its logical consequence, a single person who owns more than all the other owners of property put together will have a just claim to be the sole ruler. If, on the other hand, justice is made to consist in the will of a majority of persons, that majority will be sure to act unjustly, as we have already noted, and to confiscate the property of the rich minority.

In this position we have to ask, in the light of the definitions of justice propounded by both sides, 'What is the sort of equality to which both sides can agree?' Both sides affirm that the will of the major part of the civic body should be sovereign. We may accept that statement; but we cannot accept it without modification. [We may modify it as follows.] There are two classes which compose the state—the wealthy class, and the poor. We may attribute sovereignty, accordingly, to the will of both these classes, or that of a majority of both. [This assumes that the wills, or the majority-wills, of the two classes are agreed.] Suppose, however, that the two classes are not agreed, and are resolved on conflicting measures. In that case we may attribute sovereignty to the will of a majority of persons *who are also the owners of a majority of property.* We may give an illustration. Suppose that there are 10 in the wealthy class, and 20 in the poor; and suppose that 6 of the 10 have arrived at a decision conflicting with that of 15 of the 20. This means that the minority of 4 in the wealthy class agrees with the majority in the poorer class, and, again, that the minority of 5 in the poorer class agrees with the majority in the wealthy class. In that case sovereignty should rest with the will of that side [be it the side of the 6 + 5, or that of the 15 + 4] whose members, on both of its elements being added together, have property in excess of that belonging to the members of the other. The result may, of course, be a deadlock, with both sides absolutely equal; but this presents no greater difficulties than those which ordinarily arise to-day when a popular assembly or a law court is equally divided. The remedy is decision by lot, or some other similar method.

To find theoretically where truth resides, in these matters of equality and justice, is a very difficult task. Difficult as it may be, it is an easier task than that of persuading men to act justly, if they have power enough to secure their own selfish interests. The weaker are always anxious for equality and justice. The strong pay no heed to either.

4

Self-Mastery, Enjoyment, and the Quest for Eternity: Philosophies in the Graeco-Roman World

The 750 years between the deaths of Alexander and Aristotle (a year apart) and the time of Augustine include the Hellenistic [1] Age in Greece and the rise and decline of Rome. Soon after Alexander's death his empire broke up into three centers: Egypt under the Ptolemies, the greater part of Asia Minor under the Seleucids, and mainland Greece itself under the Macedonian Antigonids. It was a troubled period, with numerous wars, revolts, realignments, and with little independence for the Greek cities. Rome grew to mistress of all Italy, then to conqueror of Carthage in North Africa; and by the middle of the second century B.C. it had established a protectorate over Greece and eventually became its ruler.

From now on it is a Graeco-Roman world. Rome called the political tune, but in Horace's quip, "captive Greece made her captor captive"—that is, Greek culture and Greek thought on the whole prevailed. Rome's social and cultural contributions expressed its special experience in government, especially in law; but the models for poetry and history, for tragedy and comedy, and for philosophy were Greek. The great achievements in science and technology were by Greeks: for example, Euclid's deductive systematization of geometry, Archimedes's feats of engineering and advances in physical theory, Aristarchus's suggestion of the heliocentric theory, and Eratosthenes's ingeniously simple measurement of the earth's circumference. The great library of the period was created under the Ptolemies at Alexandria in Egypt.

Also during this period Hebraic-Christian religious and ethical ideas entered the Graeco-Roman world, strengthening subversive ideas of the brotherhood of man.

This three-quarters of a millennium might be taken as a philosophical laboratory for the

---

[1] *Hellenistic* is the usual name for the period in Greece after Alexander's conquests. The earlier period (whose showpiece is fifth-century Athens) is called the *Hellenic*. It was long the fashion in Western scholarship to contrast the Hellenic and the Hellenistic as the golden age and the silver age; indeed the notion of "decadence" was sharpened on the latter. Comparative judgments of thought and art, of social values and educational importance, fell into line.

study of the relationship of varied world views
(or metaphysical outlooks) and ethical theories. The spectrum includes:

    Stoicism: a theory approximating a kind of
      pantheism, that is, a belief that divine
      spirit permeates this world rather than
      constitutes an outside governing power
    Epicureanism: a this-worldly materialism,
      seeing everything as made up of material
      atoms
    Skepticism: a theory based on sensory experi-
      ence, limiting what we can know to what
      we can experience; any attempt to assert
      an underlying reality is futile
    Neoplatonism: a school that develops Platonic
      metaphysics into a mysticism
    Hebraic-Christianity: a theism with a divine
      creator who makes the world according
      to His own plan, and gives things their
      natures and directives for their lives
    Augustinianism: a Christian theism that deli-
      neates the divine plan in detail as a histori-
      cal unfolding to a preordained culmina-
      tion

Despite their differences they share a core
of similar moral attitudes that contrasts with
the rounded community ethics of Plato and
Aristotle. We find instead an individualistic
pursuit, whether of serenity, self-control, enjoyment, or salvation. Underlying is the sense
of the brevity of life, the insecurity of the human situation, and the need for resignation
not only to the inevitable but also to the
precarious. This is readily understandable in
terms of the changes that had taken place in
Greek life. With the decline in the independence of the city-states, active participation in
city life ceased to be the moral center. Individuals were left to shift for themselves in an atmosphere of economic uncertainty, overpopulation, and class struggle. While some who clung
to the older community were led into short-
lived rebellion—ultimately to be overwhelmed
by Macedonian or Roman power—others enlisted as mercenaries in the distant wars of
the new empires. The social religions of the
old community gave way to religions in which
salvation was for the individual. While intellectuals might look to Stoicism and Epicureanism,
the masses turned to mystery religions, astro-
logical religions, Zoroastrian importations
from Persia, or variants of religions that flourished in Egypt. We do well in this period of
broad interaction throughout the whole region
to think of it as constituting the shaping of a
Mediterranean civilization rather than as a set
of separate histories. It is to this milieu that
both the Hebraic and the Christian religions
belong. Neither was isolated even in its earlier
local setting; and both had to grapple with outside influences, whether in resistance or in borrowing and self-reshaping.

This chapter falls into two parts. The first
covers the variety of schools that emerged from
the Greek philosophic experience: Stoic, Epicurean, Skeptic, Neoplatonic. The second focuses on the growth of the Western religious
ethic, from Hebraic beginnings to the full-
fledged Christian philosophy of Augustine.

HELLENISTIC PHILOSOPHICAL SCHOOLS

The Hellenistic philosophical schools are often noted for their strong practical bent. This
should not be regarded as a departure in Greek
moral philosophy. Their difference from previous theories lies less in a shift from theory to
practice than in a shift in the focus of practice.

Plato and Aristotle were oriented to practice as social policy, while the Hellenistic schools are oriented to practice as individual attitude. Still, the Hellenistic schools are by no means lacking in subtle theory.

The relation between theory and practice is complex. Just as the same behavior on the part of two persons may issue from different motives, so two ethical theories may agree in recommending the same conduct although the basis may be quite different. Thus a detached attitude to worldly goods may be recommended by one theory because it condemns worldliness, and by another because it foresees an era of scarcity ahead. Let a prospect of abundance come into view and their ethical "formulae" will yield contrasting moral judgments.

Stoicism. Stoicism was a formal philosophical school begun by Zeno (335–265 B.C.) of Citium, in Cyprus. He was shipwrecked near Athens, was impressed by the philosophical tradition there and the image of Socrates, and eventually set up his own school, which lasted for five centuries. Scholars usually divide it into three stages.

Early Stoicism, at Zeno's hands, was a revolt against the institutions and attitudes of established society. He had been influenced by the alienation of the Cynics, who, regarding all social institutions as artificial, withdrew from the social community. (The Cynic Diogenes, when Alexander introduced himself and admiringly asked whether he could do anything for him, replied, "Yes, get out of my sunlight." Alexander remarked that were he not Alexander, he would have wanted to be Diogenes.) Cleanthes (300–220 B.C.) gave Stoicism a religious or spiritual dimension. Chrysippus (280–208 B.C.) gave it a learned, systematic character. Early Stoicism, regarding each individual as a citizen of the world, was the first cosmopolitanism based on the individual rather than on world empire. On occasion, Stoic doctrine took revolutionary form. Plutarch in his *Lives*

says that the Stoic philosophy is a dangerous incentive to strong and fiery dispositions. He associates Sphaerus, one of Zeno's students, with the Spartan king Cleomenes, who tried to abolish debts and extend citizenship to slaves; and in Roman times, he associates the Stoic Blossius with the radical tribune Tiberius Gracchus, who aimed at redivision of the land.

Middle Stoicism is centered in the Roman world, with Panaetius (180–112 B.C.) and Posidonius (130–51 B.C.) as its major figures. Cicero (106–43 B.C.), though not himself a thoroughgoing Stoic, is one of our best informants on Stoicism. He reflects the Stoic turn from a Platonic-Aristotelian ethical model to a juridical model in which morality is seen as a kind of law analogous to positive law but much more fundamental—what comes down in the Western tradition as "natural law." The fact that the Roman Empire, in dealing with so many different peoples, developed the *jus gentium* (law of peoples), the law perceived as common to them all, as contrasted with the narrower law governing Roman citizens alone (*jus civile*), gave many theorists the sense that they were touching what is essential in all human beings. The Stoics played a sizable role in the theoretical development of jurisprudence. Middle Stoicism also appears to have attempted to reconcile the stern doctrine of virtue of early Stoicism with established institutions; it tried to work out the roles of different professions and human enterprises, thereby removing the revolutionary sting of early doctrine. Stoicism was concerned not only with ethics but also with logic and analyses of language, and with physics. Posidonius particularly was noted for the breadth of his learning and in this respect is sometimes compared to Aristotle.

Late Stoicism is represented by a Roman senator, a slave, and an emperor. The senator was Seneca (3 B.C.–A.D. 65). Although he had been Nero's teacher and adviser, when ordered by the emperor to commit suicide (in a note, it is said, that punned *Se neca*—Latin for "kill self"), seeing no alternative, he obeyed. The selection from Seneca, analyzing anger, shows the careful psychological inquiry of Stoic doctrine. The slave was Epictetus (A.D. 60–117): he was a freed slave and taught philosophy. Marcus Aurelius (A.D. 121–180) was one of the four emperors under whom, according to Gibbon's *History*, the empire had its most stable period. Nevertheless, in all these thinkers, the sense of insecurity is central and momentous. They focus on an individualistic inwardness; the aim of life is to maintain an inner serenity. The fact that both former slave and emperor dwell on fortitude in the face of life's vicissitudes is remarkable testimony to the need that late Stoicism was attempting to meet. It is this Stoicism that has stamped the subsequent popular meaning of the term "stoic."

Epicureanism. Epicureanism is a hedonism (from *hēdonē*, the Greek word for pleasure); it holds that the human goal and the human good is the pursuit of pleasure and the avoidance of pain. It had precursors in Aristippus and Democritus. Aristippus (fl. 395 B.C.), a disciple of Socrates, also defended a hedonism, but in his case only sensuous pleasures count. The human good is the maximizing of such pleasures; all else is valued as instrumental to this. Democritus (460–370 B.C.) held only indestructible material atoms exist, differing in size and shape and moving in space. Bodies are formed by the temporary joining of atoms. Things happen as they do because of the interaction of atoms, not because of any purposiveness in nature. Death, including that of human beings, is the separation of atoms. Pleasure and pain are gentle and rough motions of the atoms within the individual. This philosophy, the major nonteleological alternative to Plato's in the ancient world, gave a material and mechanistic interpretation of nature, offered a scientific interpretation of sensation and mind, and proposed a this-worldly ethics.

Epicurus (351–270 B.C.), starting from Democritean materialism, constructed a comprehensive philosophy spanning physics, logic, and ethics. Unfortunately most of his writings are lost. The later *Lives of the Philosophers* by Diogenes Laertius (third century A.D.) includes a life of Epicurus, as it does of Zeno, based largely on lost secondary sources. Epicurus was, however, historically fortunate in the devotion of a Roman poet, Lucretius (96–55 B.C.), whose *De Rerum Natura* (*On the Nature of Things*) militantly expounds the Epicurean system. Lucretius extols Epicurus as the man who had released mankind from the terrors of superstition—from stories of gods and punishments of the hereafter. The reasonable life is devoted to pleasant activities, as free from pain as possible, and the gentle pursuit of human aims. The selection from Lucretius shows the Epicurean conception of human powers, of the evolution of mankind as it learns from its accumulated experience, and of the best path for a peaceful life. The great Epicurean aim was *ataraxia*, tranquillity or lack of disturbance. (Ataractics is the modern medical branch that deals with tranquilizers.) "Eat, drink, and be merry today for tomorrow you die" is not Epicurean. On the contrary, the pleasures of thought and discussion are superior to those of sensation; more satisfaction can be achieved by diminishing desires than by cultivating and pursuing strong ones. "The garden of Epicurus" suggests the quiet life of the aristocrat rather than political activism; nevertheless, in its broader impact—and particularly as seen in Lucretius—Epicureanism has a strong social and equalitarian potential. Epicurus does not readily assume a predesigned system of authority; much in human life, even slavery, is a matter of accident.

Skepticism. For the formal school of Skepticism we go to Sextus Empiricus (fl. A.D. 180). He is indeed an empiricist; he is also convinced that we cannot go beyond the appearances or phenomena. Theories only speculate about alleged underlying realities. The sensible thing is to line up alternatives and to recognize that we have no decisive way of choosing between them. It is a matter of choice whether to postulate or deny a reality beyond appearances. This outlook leads to relativism: with respect to knowledge (cognitive relativism), with respect to right and wrong (moral relativism), and with respect to theories of morality (ethical relativity).

The titles of his surviving work show that Sextus grounds Skepticism comprehensively: "Against the Physicists," "Against the Logicians," "Against the Ethicists," and so on. He attacks dogmatism in all reaches of theory and provides an armory of intellectual weapons for countering it. Expressions of doubt are always in order: we can always oppose a view by saying, "On the other hand . . ." or "Why this rather than the opposite?" In ethics we can always point to the array of opposing customs, moral beliefs, and practices throughout the known world. We will be happier if we abandon the view that any one line of moral practice is "more natural" than another; such naturalness in ethics is the counterpart of the belief in a fixed reality in science.

Neoplatonism. Plotinus (A.D. 205–270) is the leading representative of this most philosophical of mysticisms. Plato had traced the ascent of the soul from sensation to pure thought and even beyond, where knowledge becomes insight into an ultimate Idea of the Good. Plotinus looks to a culminating absorption into the absolute One which draws us on. Everything stems from this ultimate One, from its *emanation* or overflowing. The obvious metaphor is the visible sun which gives off light without any apparent loss of its being. This is not a creation story in the manner of the Bible; nor is it teleological, since it lacks planning and purpose. Intelligence (universal reason, *logos*) is itself an emanation from the One. Individual souls are further emanations that crystallize into bodies. Matter has no independent being; it and the evil associated with it are as shade is to light—a privation or negation, without positive essence.

The soul or self cannot know the One because knowledge is irretrievably dualistic, dis-tinguishing between knower and known. Instead of a cognition of something beyond the self there has to be a kind of immersion and loss of self. The Neoplatonic version of how this becomes possible, through both practices and learning, is turned into a cosmic odyssey of the soul. Human life is the return journey of the soul seeking ultimate unity with the One. In this journey, beauty, knowledge, moral control, as well as varied rituals all have their place. The ultimate immersion is something that only the best of humans can achieve—and that seldom.

Stoicism

Fragments of the early Stoics state their basic view. Matter is the substance of the world; the active component in it is reason or the divine. Hence the world is alive, rational; it has soul and intelligence (Chrysippus), and the substance of God is the whole world and the heavens. To avoid necessity and still retain fate, Chrysippus distinguishes among kinds of causes: perfect and principal causes are distinct from helping and proximate ones. As pushing a cylinder, he says, does not give it its capacity for rolling, our assent is not determined by our impressions of things: assent is within our power (Cicero, *De Fato*, 41, 43). Appearances and sensations are indeed the source of truth, but thought is the source of speech and propositions. The criterion of truth is the appearance that can be established, and it comes from a real object (Diogenes Laertius).

ZENO [2]

The first impulse is that the animal look out for itself, nature from the beginning encouraging self-

---

[2] The selections are from Diogenes Laertius, *Zeno*, in *Lives of Eminent Philosophers* (DL) and from Plutarch, *De Communibus Notitiis*. The translations are by the editors of this volume.

love. . . . The first thing fitting to every animal is its own organization and its consciousness of it. . . . It rejects what is harmful and admits what is proper for it. Now some say that the first impulse in animals is toward pleasure, but the Stoics show this to be false. They say that pleasure, if it occurs, is a consequence when nature itself, having sought the things that are in harmony with its system, takes hold of them. When in animals impulse has been added, by the use of which they go toward what is proper for them, then for them what is proper according to nature is determined by what is according to impulse. But when reason has been given to rational beings in accordance with a more perfect leadership, then to live according to reason rightly becomes what is according to nature. For reason supervenes as the architect of impulse. [DL 85–86]

On account of this Zeno was the first to set as the end to live according to nature, which is to live according to virtue. For nature leads us toward this. . . . Our individual natures are part of the whole. Hence the end becomes living according to nature, which is according to our nature and according to the nature of the world, doing nothing that the common law customarily forbids, that is, the right reason that permeates everything, which is itself to be identified with Zeus. [DL 87–88]

Virtue is a harmonious disposition to be chosen on its own account, not on account of any fear or hope or something external. And happiness lies in virtue inasmuch as it directs the soul to harmony throughout life. But a rational being is perverted sometimes on account of the inducements of external affairs, sometimes on account of the pressure of associates. The starting-points that nature gives are not perverse. [DL 89]

Goods are the virtues of prudence, justice, courage, self-control, and the rest. Evils are their opposites—folly, injustice, and the rest. Things that neither benefit nor harm are neither (good nor evil): for example, life, health, pleasure, beauty, strength, wealth, good reputation, noble birth; and their opposites—death, disease, pain, ugliness, weakness, poverty, bad reputation, low birth, and the like. . . . For as the property of hot is to warm, not to cool, so it is of good to benefit, not to harm; but wealth and health benefit no more than they harm, therefore neither wealth nor health is good. [DL 102–103] [They are *indifferent*.]

There is nothing between virtue and vice. . . .

For just as a stick is either straight or twisted, so a person is either just or unjust, not more just or more unjust, and the same for the other virtues. [DL 127]

Just as a person a cubit below the surface in the sea is no less drowned than one who has sunk five hundred fathoms, so those who are near virtue are no less in vice than those who are far away. [Plutarch, *de communibus notitiis* 1063A]

Just as comedies include ridiculous remarks which in themselves are cheap but add a certain grace to the whole work, so you would find fault with evil if you took it by itself. But it is not without its purpose in the whole of things. [Chrysippus, quoted in Plutarch, *de communibus notitiis* 1065D]

Fate is defined as a causal string of things that are, or as the reason according to which the cosmos goes on. [DL 149]

CICERO

De Officiis and *De Legibus* [3]

Middle Stoicism is concerned with adjusting Stoic ideals of reason and order to existing institutions, humanizing rather than rejecting the social order. Accordingly, it appealed to the aristocratic Roman circle. A good example of the tension in this reorientation of Stoicism is given by Cicero (*De Officiis* III, 12) in the midst of a discussion of morality and expediency (*honestum*, honorable or moral; *turpe*, shameful or wrong; *utile*, useful or expedient). At a time of famine, scarcity, and high prices at Rhodes, a man brings a large cargo of grain from Alexandria. He knows other cargoes are coming and so prices will drop. He asks whether it is the appropriate thing (*officium*) for him to tell his customers or to keep quiet and get the highest price. Two Stoics debate this: Diogenes of Babylonia and his student Antipater. The latter says everything the seller knows should be told; Diogenes says that the

---

[3] The translations are by the editors of this volume.

seller should reveal only defects in the goods so far as the civil law requires—beyond that the seller may sell at the best price available, for who is wronged?

[III, 12:52] Antipater: What are you saying? You who ought to have regard for fellow-men and serve human society, and you were born under that law and have those principles of nature which you ought to obey and follow—that your welfare be the common welfare and conversely that the common welfare be your welfare—will you hide from people what benefit and plenty is at hand for them?

Diogenes will perhaps reply: It is one thing to hide; another to be silent; I do not now hide from you, if I do not tell you what is the nature of the gods or what is the highest good, which would be worth more to you than knowing the cheapness of wheat. But it is not necessary for me to tell you everything that is useful for you to hear.

Yes, it is necessary, Antipater will say, if indeed you remember that there is between men a community united by nature.

I do remember, the other says, but is that community such that a man has nothing that is his own? If that is so, nothing is ever to be sold but given away.

Cicero himself decides that full information should have been given. Likewise, it was wrong of Pompey to marry Caesar's daughter for political advancement (III, 21); and in the famous case of Fabricius, who in the war with Pyrrhus sent back a deserter who offered at a price to poison Pyrrhus—and the Roman Senate approved his decision—Cicero applauds Fabricius's firm moral response even in the light of the very highest expediency (III, 22).

The idea of a law of nature expressive of the reason that governs the world, so often invoked in the Stoic writings, is set forth most clearly in Cicero's *De Legibus*. *Lex* is used for civil law or enactment, while *ius* is what is binding, right, or just; but often there is no strict distinction. In Book I, Chapter 5, Cicero (Marcus) converses with Quintus and Atticus.

[I, 5:17] A. You do not then think that the discipline of law (*ius*) is to be drawn from the edict of the praetor, as most people now think, nor from the Twelve Tables, as people earlier thought, but from the inner profundities of philosophy?

M. Yes, for we are not considering in this discussion how to protect ourselves at law or what to answer in any specific consultation. . . . Our concern now is the cause of universal right (*ius*) and laws (*leges*), so that what we call our civil law will be confined to a small and narrow place. For the nature of right (*ius*) must be explained by us and it must be sought from the nature of man; we must consider the laws (*leges*) by which states ought to be regulated; then we have to treat of the laws (*iura*) and decrees of peoples that are prepared and written down, among them what are called the civil laws of our own people.

He quotes the definition of law from which the most learned start:

[18] . . . Law (*lex*) is the highest reason, fixed in nature, which commands what is to be done, and prohibits the opposite. That reason, when it is established and fulfilled in the mind of man, is law. Accordingly they think that law is the wisdom whose force would lie in commanding to act rightly and forbidding to do wrong. . . .

[21] M. Do you then grant us that the whole of nature is ruled by the force of the immortal gods, or by their nature, reason, power, mind, will, or any other word by which I may signify more clearly what I intend?

[23] Since nothing is better than reason, and since it is both in man and in God, the fellowship of reason is the first thing man shares with God. But those who share reason also share a common right reason. And since the latter is law, we must suppose that men are associated with the gods also in law. Furthermore, those who have a community of law (*lex*), have also a community of right (*ius*); and those who have these things in common, are to be held as of the same State. And it is much more so if in fact they obey the same authority and powers; but they do obey this heavenly order and divine mind and god of superior power; so that this whole world is to be regarded as one common State of gods and men.

SENECA

On Anger [4]

Anger is examined for its visible symptoms, its animal counterparts, and its deadly consequences among people.

[I, 1] In the other emotions there is something of the quiet and peaceful, but anger is wholly roused and consists in an assault of affliction, raging with a scarcely human greed for arms and blood and slaughter, neglecting itself as long as it can harm another, rushing upon the very spears and greedy for revenge though it drag the avenger down with it. Accordingly, some wise men have termed anger brief madness; for it is equally without self-control, unmindful of dignity, forgetful of needs, pertinacious and intent upon what it begins, shut off from reason and counsel, set into motion by trifling causes, unmanageable for discerning what is right and true, most like ruins that are smashed over what they have overwhelmed.

[5] Let us now ask whether anger is according to nature and whether it is useful and is in part to be retained. Whether it is according to nature will be clear if we look at man. What is more gentle than he is, as long as he is in a correct state of mind? What, however, is more cruel than anger? What more loving of others than man? What more dangerous than anger? Man is born for mutual aid; anger for ruin. The former wants to associate, the latter to put asunder; the one to help, the other to hurt; the one to come to the aid of even the unknown, the other to attack even the most beloved; the one is prepared to devote itself to the convenience of others, the other to descend into peril as long as it brings others down. Who therefore has greater ignorance of the nature of things than he who assigns to her best and most perfect work this wild and pernicious vice? Anger, as we said, is greedy for punishment; that a desire for it is present in the most peaceful heart of man is least in accord with his nature. For human life rests on kindness and harmony; it is bound into a compact and common assistance not by terror but by mutual love.

[7] Although anger is not natural, may it not be taken on because it has often been useful? It rouses and stimulates men's spirits and bravery accomplishes nothing great in war without it, unless the flame is kindled from it and this stimulus has agitated and sent bold men into dangers. Accordingly, some think it best to temper anger, not to eliminate it, and having curbed its overflow, to compel it into a salutary mode, and to retain as much as is needed, without which action will become sluggish and the force and vigor of spirit will be relaxed.

First, it is easier to exclude pernicious feelings than to govern them, and not to admit them than to moderate them after admission; for when they have fixed themselves in possession, they are more powerful than their governor and do not allow themselves to be cut down or diminished. Then, reason herself, to whom the reins of power have been handed, is powerful only as long as she is kept away from the perturbations; if she mixes herself with them and is polluted, she cannot restrain those whom she would have been able to drive back. For when the mind has been once unsettled and shaken, it serves that by which it is impelled. In certain matters, the beginnings are in our power, but later steps seize us by their violence and leave no retreat.

[10] Accordingly, reason will never summon to its help reckless and violent impulses, over which it will itself have no authority, and which it can never suppress unless it has opposed to them equal and similar forces, as fear against anger, anger against inertia, greed against fear. May such an evil be absent from virtue, that reason ever take refuge with the vices!

Anger is not necessary against the enemy, nor to defend one's loved ones. Its great fault is that it refuses to be ruled. Book II raises the psychological question of whether anger originates from judgment or from impulse, "that is, whether it is aroused of its own accord or whether, like many other things within us, it does not arise without our knowing it" (II, 1).

[II, 1] There is no doubt that when the appearance of injury is presented, it rouses anger; but we are asking whether the anger itself follows directly on the appearance and comes on without the mind's entering, or whether it is roused with the mind assenting. We think that it ventures nothing by itself except when the mind approves. For to accept the

[4] Translation is by the editors of this volume.

appearance of an injury received and to desire revenge for it is one thing; to add to it that the injury
ought not to have taken place and that it ought to
be avenged is another, and not an impulse of the
mind which is stirred up without our will. The former process is simple. The latter is complex and
has several parts: the mind has understood something; it is indignant, it has condemned, it is taking
vengeance: these cannot be done unless the spirit
has assented to the things by which it is moved.

[2] Why, you ask, is this question relevant? In
order that we may know what anger is. For if it is
born against our will, it will never succumb to reason.

[10] A wise man will not be angry at those who
are sinning. Why? Because he knows no one is born
wise but becomes such; he knows that very few in
every age rise to wisdom, because he holds in full
view the human condition; moreover, no sensible
person is angry at nature.

[28] Reflection on ourselves will make us more
moderate, if we take counsel with ourselves: Have
we never ourselves done something like it? Have
we never gone astray in the same way? Is it serviceable for us to condemn such things?

[29] The best remedy for anger is delay. Seek this
from anger at the outset, not that it may pardon,
but that it may judge. It has heavy first impulses;
it will cease if it waits. You will not have tried to
remove it all at once; the whole will be conquered
while it is plucked in parts.

EPICTETUS [5]

The Manual

[1] Of things that are, some are in our power,
but some are not in our power. In our power are
our understanding of things, impulse toward them,
desire, turning away, and—in a word—our own
acts. Not in our power are body, possessions, repu-
tations, offices, and—in a word—not our acts.
Again, things in our power are by nature free, un-
hindered, unimpeded; but what is not in our power
is weak, slavish, hindered, alien, or dependent on
another. Remember, therefore, that if you think
what is slavish by nature to be free and what is
alien to be your own, you will be impeded, you
will lament, you will be upset, you will blame both

gods and men; but if you think only what is yours
to be yours and what is alien to you, as indeed it
is, alien, no one will ever compel you; no one will
hinder you, you will never blame anyone, you will
accuse no one, you will do nothing against your
will, you will not have an enemy, no one will harm
you, for no harm will befall you.

[3] In the case of anything that attracts or is useful
or that you're fond of, remember to add, "What
sort of thing is it?"—from the smallest matter up.
If you are fond of a pot, say "It's a pot I am fond
of"; for when it is broken you will not be upset. If
you kiss your child or wife, say that you are kissing
a human being; for when it dies, you will not be
upset.

[5] What upsets people is not things or happenings but their opinions about them; for example,
death is nothing terrible—it would then have appeared so to Socrates, too—but this opinion about
death, that it is terrible, that's what is terrible. When
therefore we are impeded or upset or we lament,
let us never blame another, but ourselves, that is,
our opinions. It is the act of an unlearned person
to blame others where one fares badly; it's the beginning of learning to blame oneself; it's the mark
of completed learning to blame neither another nor
oneself.

[8] Seek not that what happens happens as you
wish, but wish that what happens be as it happens,
and life will flow along well.

The good things in life were just loaned to
you.

[11] Never say of anything, "I lost it," but "I returned it." Has your child died? It was returned.
Has your wife died? She was returned. "My property has been taken away." Then this too has been
returned. "But the person who took it is wicked."
Why does it concern you through whom the one
who gave it asked it back of you? While he gives
it, take care of it as another's, as travelers treat an
inn.

[16] [When you see someone weeping in sorrow,
remember that it is not the events but his reaction
to them that are responsible.] So far as words go,
do not hesitate to sympathize with him; and if it
chance that way, even to bemoan with him. But
take care not to moan within.

[17] Remember that you are an actor in a play,
the sort the playwright wants: if he wants it short,

---

[5] The translations are by the editors of this volume.

then short; if long, then long; if he wants you to act a poor man, you're to act even this cleverly; so too for a cripple, an official, a private citizen. For this is your concern, to play well the part assigned to you; to choose the part is another's role.

[26] It is possible to learn the will of nature from the things in which we do not differ from others. For example, when somebody else's slave has broken a cup, it's easy to say right off, "It's something that happens." Know then that even when your cup is broken, it is fitting that you be the same kind of person as you were when another's cup was broken. Apply this also to greater things. Another's child or wife has died. There's not one of us who would not say, "It's man's lot." But when one's own dies, immediately it's "Alas, wretched am I." But we should recall how we feel when we've heard this about others.

[28] If someone turned over your body to any chance comer, you would be outraged. But the fact that you turn over your mind to a chance comer, so that if he rail at you, it is upset and thrown into confusion—aren't you ashamed of that?

[33] Set down from now on a definite character for yourself, an image which you will preserve both when by yourself and among people. Silence for the most part, or let what is said be necessary and said in few words. But rarely, when occasion calls for speech, then speak, but not about the chance topics of conversation. . . . Let there not be much laughter, nor at many things, nor unrestrainedly.

Refuse to take an oath, if possible, altogether; if not, as far as possible.

In matters of the body, take as much as bare need requires: food, drink, clothes, house, household slaves; but cut out everything for show or luxury.

As to sex, stay pure before marriage as far as you can. If you indulge, take only what is lawful [nomimos, lawful or customary]. However, do not be disagreeable to those who indulge, or reproachful. Do not often bring up the fact that you yourself don't indulge.

If someone reports to you that a person speaks ill of you, don't defend against what was said, but answer "He didn't know the remainder of my faults, or he would not have mentioned only these."

[43] Everything has two handles, the one by which it is bearable, the other unbearable. If your brother does you an injustice, do not take it by that handle—as injustice (for taking it this way is not bearable)—but rather by the other handle: that he is your brother, that he was brought up with you, and you will be taking it by the handle by which it is bearable.

[48] The stance and character of an ordinary man is this: he never looks for benefit or harm from himself but from things outside him. The stance and character of a philosopher is this: he looks for every benefit and harm from himself. These are the marks of one who is making progress: he blames no one, he praises no one, he makes charges against no one, he says nothing about himself as being somebody or knowing something. When he is impeded or hindered, he blames himself. And if anyone praises him, he laughs in himself at the one who praises; and if anyone blames him, he offers no defense. He goes around the way sick people do, wary of disturbing any part of his constitution before it takes firm hold. He has taken away every desire from himself, and transferred aversion to only those things contrary to nature which are in our power. He deals with impulse in every context without strain. If he is thought foolish or ignorant, he does not mind. In a word, he keeps watch on himself as an enemy and lying in ambush.

Discourses

[I, 12] . . . "I want everything that seems good to me to come to pass, in whatever manner it seems good." You are mad, out of your mind. Don't you know that freedom is a noble and remarkable thing? But for me to want things as they just happen to appear good to me, this risks not only their not being noble, but being even most shameful. For how do we act in letters? Do I wish to write the name "Dion" as I want? No; but I'm taught to want it as it is proper to write it. What about music? The same. What in general, wherever there is some art or knowledge? [The same.] If it were not so, if it were fitted to the needs of each person, it would not be worth knowing anything. Is it then only in the greatest and most important matter, freedom, that it is permitted for me to want as it chances? By no means, but education lies in this: to learn to want each thing as it comes to be. And how does it come to be? As the Organizer has organized things. And he has arranged that there be summer and winter, crops and crop failure, virtue and vice, and all such opposites for the harmony of the Whole, and to each of us he gave a body and parts of the body and possessions of fellow men.

Mindful then of this order, it is proper to approach education, not in order to change the foundations (for this is not given to us, nor is it better) but in order that, things about us being disposed as they are and as they are by nature, we may ourselves keep our judgment in harmony with what comes to pass.

[II, 19] . . . Who, then, is a Stoic? As we call a statue Phidian that has been fashioned according to the art of Phidias, so show me someone fashioned according to the judgments he utters. Show me someone who is such and yet happy, who is in danger yet happy, who is dying yet happy, exiled yet happy, without reputation and yet happy. . . . Let one of you show me the spirit of a man who wants to be of one mind with God and no longer blame God or man, who wants not to fail in anything, not to fall into anything, not to be angry, not to envy, not to engage in rivalry—but why should I beat about the bush?—a man who wants to become a god instead of a man, and who in this bodily corpse is resolved upon fellowship with God.

Appollonius is quoted against those whose exercises are oriented to display:

[III, 12] . . . When you want to train for your own sake, when you are thirsty some time when it's hot, take a mouthful of cold water and spit it out—and tell no one.

[IV, 5] . . . "So-and-so reviled you." Many thanks to him for not striking. "But he also struck." Many thanks for not wounding. "But he did wound." Many thanks to him for not killing.

MARCUS AURELIUS

Meditations [6]

[II, 17] Of human life the time is a point, and the substance is in a flux, and the perception dull,

[6] The selection is from *The Thoughts of The Emperor Marcus Aurelius Antoninus*, trans. George Long, rev. ed. (London, 1873), with occasional emendations by the editors of this volume.

and the composition of the whole body subject to putrefaction, and the soul a whirl, and fortune hard to divine, and fame a thing devoid of judgment. And, to say all in a word, everything which belongs to the body is a stream, and what belongs to the soul is a dream and vapor, and life is a warfare and a stranger's sojourn, and after-fame is oblivion. What then is that which is able to conduct a man? One thing and only one—philosophy. But this consists in keeping the daemon within a man free from violence and unharmed, superior to pains and pleasures, doing nothing without a purpose, nor yet falsely and with hypocrisy, not feeling the need of another man's doing or not doing anything; and besides, accepting all that happens, and all that is allotted, as coming from thence, wherever it is, from whence he himself came; and, finally, waiting for death with a cheerful mind, as being nothing else than a dissolution of the elements of which every living being is compounded. But if there is no harm to the elements themselves in each continually changing into another, why should a man have any apprehension about the change and dissolution of all the elements? For it is according to nature, and nothing is evil which is according to nature.

[III, 4] . . . [T]he lot which is assigned to each man is carried along with him and carries him along with it. And he remembers also that every rational animal is his kinsman, and that to care for all men is according to man's nature; and a man should hold on to the opinion not of all, but of those only who confessedly live according to nature. But as to those who live not so, he always bears in mind what kind of men they are, both at home and from home, both by night and by day, and what they are, and with what men they live an impure life. Accordingly, he does not value at all the praise which comes from such men, since they are not even satisfied with themselves.

[10] [B]ear in mind that every man lives only this present time, which is an indivisible point, and that all the rest of his life is either past or it is uncertain. Short then is the time which every man lives, and small the nook of the earth where he lives; and short too the longest posthumous fame, and even this only continued by a succession of poor human beings, who will very soon die, and who know not even themselves, much less him who died long ago.

[11] To the aids which have been mentioned let this one still be added:—Make for yourself a

definition or description of the thing which is presented to you, so as to see distinctly what kind of a thing it is in its substance, in its nudity, in its complete entirety, and tell yourself its proper name, and the names of the things of which it has been compounded, and into which it will be resolved. For nothing is so productive of elevation of mind as to be able to examine methodically and truly every object which is presented to you in life, and always to look at things so as to see at the same time what kind of universe this is, and what kind of use everything performs in it, and what value everything has with reference to the whole, and what with reference to man, who is a citizen of the highest city, of which all other cities are like families; what each thing is, and of what it is composed, and how long it is the nature of this thing to endure which now makes an impression on me, and what virtue I have need of with respect to it, such as gentleness, manliness, truth, fidelity, simplicity, contentment, and the rest. Wherefore, on every occasion a man should say: this comes from god; and this is according to the apportionment and spinning of the thread of destiny, and suchlike coincidence and chance; and this is from one of the same stock, and a kinsman and partner, one who knows not however what is according to his nature. But I know; for this reason I behave toward him according to the natural law of fellowship with benevolence and justice. At the same time, however, in things indifferent I attempt to ascertain the value of each.

[IV, 3] Men seek retreats for themselves, houses in the country, seashores, and mountains; and you too are wont to desire such things very much. But this is altogether a mark of the most common sort of men, for it is in your power, whenever you choose, to retire into yourself. For nowhere either with more quiet or more freedom from trouble does a man retire than into his own soul, particularly when he has within him such thoughts that by looking into them he is immediately in perfect tranquillity; and I affirm that tranquillity is nothing else than the good ordering of the mind. Constantly then give to yourself this retreat, and renew yourself. . . .

[4] If our intellectual part is common, the reason also, in respect of which we are rational beings, is common: if this is so, common also is the reason which commands us what to do, and what not to do; if this is so, there is a common law also; if this is so, we are fellow citizens; if this is so, we are

members of some political community; if this is so, the world is in a manner a state. For of what other common political community will anyone say that the whole human race are members. And from thence, from this common political community comes also our very intellectual faculty and reasoning faculty and our capacity for law; or whence do they come? For as my earthly part is a portion given to me from certain earth, . . . so also the intellectual part comes from some source.

[7] Take away your opinion, and then there is taken away the complaint, "I have been harmed." Take away the complaint, "I have been harmed," and the harm is taken away.

[10] Consider that everything that happens, happens justly, and if you observe carefully, you will find it to be so. . . .

[V, 8] . . . [A]ccept everything which happens, even if it seem disagreeable, because it leads to this, to the health of the universe and to the prosperity and felicity of Zeus [the universe]. For he would not have brought on any man what he has brought, if it were not useful for the whole. . . .

[VI, 51] He who loves fame considers another man's activity to be his own good; and he who loves pleasure, his own sensations; but he who has understanding, considers his own acts to be his own good.

[VII, 27] Think not so much of what you have not as of what you have: but of the things which you have, select the best, and then reflect how eagerly they would have been sought, if you had them not. At the same time, however, take care that you do not, through being so pleased with them, accustom yourself to overvalue them, so as to be disturbed if ever you should not have them.

[VIII, 36] Do not disturb yourself by thinking of the whole of your life. Let not your thoughts at once embrace all the various troubles which you may expect to befall you: but on every occasion ask yourself, "What is there in this which is intolerable and past bearing?" for you will be ashamed to confess. In the next place remember that neither the future nor the past pains you, but only the present. But this is reduced to a very little, if you only circumscribe it, and chide your mind, if it is unable to hold out against even this.

[IX, 7] Wipe out imagination: check desire: extinguish appetite: keep the ruling faculty in its own power.

[X, 15] Short is the little which remains to you

of life. Live as on a mountain. For it makes no difference whether a man lives there or here, if he lives everywhere in the world as in a state. Let men see, let them know a real man who lives according to nature. If they cannot endure him, let them kill him. For that is better than to live their life.

[XII, 3] The things are three of which you are composed: a little body, a little breath (life), and intelligence. Of these the first two are yours, so far as it is your duty to take care of them; but the third alone is properly yours.

Epicureanism

EPICURUS

Letter to Menoeceus [7]

Let no one be slow to seek wisdom when he is young nor weary in the search thereof when he is grown old. For no age is too early or too late for the health of the soul. And to say that the season for studying philosophy has not yet come, or that it is past and gone, is like saying that the season for happiness is not yet or that it is now no more. Therefore, both old and young ought to seek wisdom, the former in order that, as age comes over him, he may be young in good things because of the grace of what has been, and the latter in order that, while he is young, he may at the same time be old, because he has no fear of the things which are to come. So we must exercise ourselves in the things which bring happiness, since, if that be present, we have everything, and, if that be absent, all our actions are directed toward attaining it.

Those things which without ceasing I have declared unto thee, those do, and exercise thyself therein, holding them to be the elements of right life. First believe that God is a living being immortal and blessed, according to the notion of a god indicated by the common sense of mankind; and so believing, thou shalt not affirm of him aught that is foreign to his immortality or that agrees not with

blessedness, but shalt believe about him whatever may uphold both his blessedness and his immortality. For verily there are gods, and the knowledge of them is manifest; but they are not such as the multitude believe, seeing that men do not steadfastly maintain the notions they form respecting them. Not the man who denies the gods worshipped by the multitude, but he who affirms of the gods what the multitude believes about them is truly impious. For the utterances of the multitude about the gods are not true preconceptions but false assumptions; hence it is that the greatest evils happen to the wicked and the greatest blessings happen to the good from the hand of the gods, seeing that they are always favourable to their own good qualities and take pleasure in men like unto themselves, but reject as alien whatever is not of their kind.

Accustom thyself to believe that death is nothing to us, for good and evil imply sentience, and death is the privation of all sentience; therefore a right understanding that death is nothing to us makes the mortality of life enjoyable, not by adding to life an illimitable time, but by taking away the yearning after immortality. For life has no terrors for him who has thoroughly apprehended that there are no terrors for him in ceasing to live. Foolish, therefore, is the man who says that he fears death, not because it will pain when it comes, but because it pains in the prospect. Whatsoever causes no annoyance when it is present, causes only a groundless pain in the expectation. Death, therefore, the most awful of evils, is nothing to us, seeing that, when we are, death is not come, and, when death is come, we are not. It is nothing, then, either to the living or to the dead, for with the living it is not and the dead exist no longer. But in the world, at one time men shun death as the greatest of all evils, and at another time choose it as a respite from the evils in life. The wise man does not deprecate life nor does he fear the cessation of life. The thought of life is no offence to him, nor is the cessation of life regarded as an evil. And even as men choose of food not merely and simply the larger portion, but the more pleasant, so the wise seek to enjoy the time which is most pleasant and not merely that which is longest. And he who admonishes the young to live well and the old to make a good end speaks foolishly, not merely because of the desirableness of life, but because the same exercise at once teaches to live well and to die well. Much worse is he who says that it were good not to be

[7] The selection is from Diogenes Laertius, *Lives of Eminent Philosophers*, translated by R. D. Hicks (Cambridge, Mass.: Harvard University Press, Loeb Classical Library, 1965), vol. 2, pp. 649–659.

born, but when once one is born to pass with all speed through the gates of Hades. For if he truly believes this, why does he not depart from life? It were easy for him to do so, if once he were firmly convinced. If he speaks only in mockery, his words are foolishness, for those who hear believe him not.

We must remember that the future is neither wholly ours nor wholly not ours, so that neither must we count upon it as quite certain to come nor despair of it as quite certain not to come.

We must also reflect that of desires some are natural, others are groundless; and that of the natural some are necessary as well as natural, and some natural only. And of the necessary desires some are necessary if we are to be happy, some if the body is to be rid of uneasiness, some if we are even to live. He who has a clear and certain understanding of these things will direct every preference and aversion toward securing health of body and tranquillity of mind, seeing that this is the sum and end of a blessed life. For the end of all our actions is to be free from pain and fear, and, when once we have attained all this, the tempest of the soul is laid; seeing that the living creature has no need to go in search of something that is lacking, nor to look for anything else by which the good of the soul and of the body will be fulfilled. When we are pained because of the absence of pleasure, then, and then only, do we feel the need of pleasure. Wherefore we call pleasure the alpha and omega of a blessed life. Pleasure is our first and kindred good. It is the starting-point of every choice and of every aversion, and to it we come back, inasmuch as we make feeling the rule by which to judge of every good thing. And since pleasure is our first and native good, for that reason we do not choose every pleasure whatsoever, but ofttimes pass over many pleasures when a greater annoyance ensues from them. And ofttimes we consider pains superior to pleasures when submission to the pains for a long time brings us as a consequence a greater pleasure. While therefore all pleasure because it is naturally akin to us is good, not all pleasure is choice worthy, just as all pain is an evil and yet not all pain is to be shunned. It is, however, by measuring one against another, and by looking at the conveniences and inconveniences, that all these matters must be judged. Sometimes we treat the good as an evil, and the evil, on the contrary, as a good. Again, we regard independence of outward things as a

great good, not so as in all cases to use little, but so as to be contented with little if we have not much, being honestly persuaded that they have the sweetest enjoyment of luxury who stand least in need of it, and that whatever is natural is easily procured and only the vain and worthless hard to win. Plain fare gives as much pleasure as a costly diet, when once the pain of want has been removed, while bread and water confer the highest possible pleasure when they are brought to hungry lips. To habituate one's self, therefore, to simple and inexpensive diet supplies all that is needful for health, and enables a man to meet the necessary requirements of life without shrinking, and it places us in a better condition when we approach at intervals a costly fare and renders us fearless of fortune.

When we say, then, that pleasure is the end and aim, we do not mean the pleasures of the prodigal or the pleasures of sensuality, as we are understood to do by some through ignorance, prejudice, or wilful misrepresentation. By pleasure we mean the absence of pain in the body and of trouble in the soul. It is not an unbroken succession of drinking-bouts and of revelry, not sexual love, not the enjoyment of the fish and other delicacies of a luxurious table, which produce a pleasant life; it is sober reasoning, searching out the grounds of every choice and avoidance, and banishing those beliefs through which the greatest tumults take possession of the soul. Of all this the beginning and the greatest good is prudence. Wherefore prudence is a more precious thing even than philosophy; from it spring all the other virtues, for it teaches that we cannot lead a life of pleasure which is not also a life of prudence, honour, and justice; nor lead a life of prudence, honour, and justice, which is not also a life of pleasure. For the virtues have grown into one with a pleasant life, and a pleasant life is inseparable from them.

Who, then, is superior in thy judgment to such a man? He holds a holy belief concerning the gods, and is altogether free from the fear of death. He has diligently considered the end fixed by nature, and understands how easily the limit of good things can be reached and attained, and how either the duration or the intensity of evils is but slight. Destiny, which some introduce as sovereign over all things, he laughs to scorn, affirming rather that some things happen by necessity, others by chance, others through our own agency. For he sees that necessity destroys responsibility and that chance or fortune is inconstant; whereas our own actions are free, and it is to them that praise and blame naturally attach. It were better, indeed, to accept the legends of the gods than to bow beneath that yoke of destiny which the natural philosophers have imposed. The one holds out some faint hope that we may escape if we honour the gods, while the necessity of the naturalists is deaf to all entreaties. Nor does he hold chance to be a god, as the world in general does, for in the acts of a god there is no disorder; nor to be a cause, though an uncertain one, for he believes that no good or evil is dispensed by chance to men so as to make life blessed, though it supplies the starting-point of great good and great evil. He believes that the misfortune of the wise is better than the prosperity of the fool. It is better, in short, that what is well judged in action should not owe its successful issue to the aid of chance.

Exercise thyself in these and kindred precepts day and night, both by thyself and with him who is like unto thee; then never, either in waking or in dream, wilt thou be disturbed, but wilt live as a god among men. For man loses all semblance of mortality by living in the midst of immortal blessings.

Epicurus and the Cyrenaics differ in their accounts of pleasure. The Cyrenaics limit it to a state of motion and take bodily pains to be worse than mental pains. Epicurus includes also a state of rest, and so mental as well as bodily pleasures; indeed, he regards the mental as greater than the bodily, since the mental embraces past and future as well as present.

LUCRETIUS

On the Nature of Things [8]

Books I and II expound the principles of the physical world as a set of propositions illustrated from the ordinary world. Nothing can

[8] The translation is by H. A. J. Munro, 4th ed. rev. (Cambridge, 1886), with occasional emendations by the editors of this volume.

be produced from nothing. Nature dissolves everything into its primary seeds (or, in later terms, atoms). Nothing is annihilated. In nature there are bodies and the void (empty space). Without empty space there could not be motion. Time does not exist by itself; it is an order of happenings. Bodies are either atoms or compounds of atoms; small changes of order change the resulting compound, just as shifting the letters changes a word. Existing space is unbounded; if a man got to a presumed end and hurled out a javelin, either it would keep going or else it would be stopped by matter farther out; hence, there is always something beyond. There is no design in the way things have been stationed; the order we find is the outcome of causal operation in infinite past time.

Atoms are endowed with a power of movement; they fall through the infinite void or rebound in their impact with one another. Atoms travel upward under pressure only, never on their own. The downward motion of atoms because of weight is in a straight line, but there are slight swerves at indeterminate times and places; otherwise they could never get in touch with one another, and fresh formations would be impossible. (This swerve was introduced by Epicurus.) Atoms differ in shape (and they can get hooked together), in size, and in mutual order. The number of forms is finite, but the number of atoms in any one form is infinite. Not all combinations are possible, which is why we get a definite order of species. Individual atoms do not have color; this depends on the combinations and the shapes, order, and mutual motions. Atoms are not hot or cold, nor do they have the rest of the sentient qualities. Yet, whatever has sense is composed of elements without sense.

[III, 94–97] The mind, which we often call the understanding, in which dwells the directing and governing principle of life, is no less part of the man, than hand and foot and eyes are parts of the whole living creature.

[136–146] The mind and the soul are kept together in close union and make up a single nature, but the directing principle, which we call mind and understanding, is the head, so to speak, and reigns paramount in the whole body. It has a fixed seat in the middle region of the breast: here throb fear and apprehension, about these spots dwell soothing joys; therefore here is the understanding or mind. All the rest of the soul disseminated through the whole body obeys and moves at the will and inclination of the mind. It by itself alone knows for itself, rejoices for itself, at times when the impression does not move either soul or body together with it.

But the mind when vehemently moved affects the rest of the body.

[179–188] [Mind] is extremely fine and formed of exceedingly minute bodies. . . . Nothing that is seen takes place with a velocity equal to that of the mind when it starts some suggestion and actually sets it agoing; the mind therefore is stirred with greater rapidity than any of the things whose nature stands out visible to sight. But that which is so passing nimble, must consist of seeds exceedingly round and exceedingly minute, in order to be stirred and set in motion by a small moving power.

[445–458] [T]he mind is begotten along with the body and grows up together with it and grows old along with it. For even as children go about with a tottering and weakly body, so slender sagacity of mind follows along with it; then when their life has reached the maturity of confirmed strength, the judgment too is greater and the power of mind more developed. Afterwards when the body has been shattered by the mastering might of time and the frame has drooped with its forces dulled, then the intellect halts, the tongue dotes, the mind gives way, all faculties fail and are found wanting at the same time. It naturally follows then that the whole nature of the soul is dissolved, like smoke, into the high air; since we see it is begotten along with the body and grows up along with it and . . . breaks down at the same time worn out with age.

[830–842] Death therefore to us is nothing, concerns us not a jot, since the nature of the mind is proved to be mortal. . . . [T]hus when we shall be no more, when there shall have been a separation of body and soul, out of both of which we are each formed into a single being, to us, you may be sure, who then shall be no more, nothing whatever can happen to excite sensation, not if earth shall be mingled with sea and sea with heaven.

[932–945] If the nature of things could suddenly utter a voice and in person could rally any of us in such words as these, "what has thou, O mortal, so much at heart, that thou goest to such lengths in sickly sorrows? Why bemoan and bewail death? For say thy life past and gone has been welcome to thee and thy blessings have not all, as if they were poured into a perforated vessel, run through and been lost without avail: why not then take thy departure like a guest filled with life, and with resignation, thou fool, enter upon untroubled rest? But if all that thou has enjoyed, has been squandered and lost, and life is a grievance, why seek to make any addition, to be wasted perversely in its turn and lost utterly without avail? Why not rather make an end of life and travail? For there is nothing more which I can contrive and discover for thee to give pleasure: all things are as ever the same. . . ."

[V, 195–227] [T]he nature of things has by no means been made for us by divine power: so great are the defects by which it is encumbered. . . . Of nearly two thirds [of the land] burning heat and the constant fall of frost rob mortals. What is left for tillage, even that nature by its power would overrun with thorns, unless the force of man made headway against it, accustomed for the sake of a livelihood to groan beneath the strong hoe and to cut through the earth by pressing down the plough. Unless by turning up the fruitful clods with the share and laboring the soil of the earth we stimulate things to rise, they could not spontaneously come up into the clear air; and even then sometimes when things earned with great toil now put forth their leaves over the lands and are all in blossom, either the ethereal sun burns them up with excessive heats or sudden rains and cold frosts cut them off, and the blasts of the winds waste them by a furious hurricane. . . . Why do the seasons of the year bring diseases in their train? Why stalks abroad untimely death? Then too the baby, like a sailor cast away by the cruel waves, lies naked on the ground, speechless, wanting every furtherance of life, soon as nature by the throes of birth has shed him forth from his mother's womb into the borders of light:

he fills the room with a rueful wauling [*sic*], as well he may whose destiny it is to go through in life so many ills.

This earth came into being through the encounters of conflicting material forces. Without intelligent purpose, it took form, eventually settled down, and went through transformations.

[827–836] Time changes the nature of the whole world and all things must pass on from one condition to another, and nothing continues like to itself: all things quit their bounds, all things nature changes and compels to alter. One thing crumbles away and is worn and enfeebled with age, then another comes unto honor and issues out of its state of contempt. In this way then time changes the nature of the whole world and the earth passes out of one condition into another: what once it could, it can bear no more, in order to be able to bear what before it did not bear.

Those forms of life that survived did so because of craft or courage or speed.

[1011–1027] Next after they had got themselves huts and skins and fire, and the woman united with the man passed with him into one [domicile and the duties of wedlock were] learned [by the two], and they saw an offspring born from them, then first mankind began to soften. For fire made their chilled bodies less able now to bear the frost beneath the canopy of heaven, and Venus impaired their strength, and children with their caresses soon broke down the haughty temper of parents. Then too neighbors began to join in a league of friendship mutually desiring neither to do nor to suffer harm; and asked for indulgence to children and womankind, when with cries and gestures they declared in stammering speech that meet it is for all to have mercy on the weak. And though harmony could not be established without exception, yet a very large proportion observed their agreements with good faith, or else the race of men would then have been wholly cut off, nor could breeding have continued their generations to this day.

Spoken language grew out of sounds and gestures and expression of feeling. Fire was learned from lightning striking the earth or from friction.

[1105–1160] And more and more every day men who excelled in intellect and were of vigorous understanding, would kindly show them how to exchange their former way of living for new methods. Kings began to build towns and lay out a citadel as a place of strength and of refuge for themselves, and divided cattle and lands and gave to each man in proportion to his personal beauty and strength and intellect; for beauty and vigorous strength were much esteemed. Afterwards wealth was discovered and gold found out, which soon robbed of their honors strong and beautiful alike; for men however valiant and beautiful of person generally follow in the train of the richer man. But were a man to order his life by the rules of true reason, a frugal subsistence joined to a contented mind is for him great riches; for never is there any lack of a little. But men desired to be famous and powerful, in order that their fortunes might rest on a firm foundation and they might be able by their wealth to lead a tranquil life; but in vain, since in their struggle to mount up to the highest dignities they rendered their path one full of danger; and even if they reach it, yet envy like a thunderbolt sometimes strikes and dashes men down from the highest point with ignominy into noisesome Tartarus; since the highest summits and those elevated above the level of other things are mostly blasted by envy as by a thunderbolt; so that far better it is to obey in peace and quiet than to wish to rule with power supreme and be the master of kingdoms. . . .

Kings therefore being slain, the old majesty of thrones and proud sceptres were overthrown and laid in the dust, and the glorious badge of the sovereign head bloodstained beneath the feet of the rabble mourned for its high prerogative; for that is greedily trampled on which before was too much dreaded. It would come then in the end to the lees of uttermost disorder, each man seeking for himself empire and sovereignty. Next a portion of them taught men to elect legal officers, and drew up codes, to induce men to obey the laws. For mankind, tired out with a life of brute force, lay exhausted from its feuds; and therefore the more readily it submitted of its own freewill to laws and stringent codes. For as each one moved by anger took measures to avenge himself with more severity than is now permitted by equitable laws, for this reason men grew sick of a life of brute force. Thence fear of punishment mars the prizes of life; for violence and wrong enclose all who commit them in their meshes and do mostly recoil on him from whom they began; and it is not easy for him who by his deeds transgresses the terms of the public peace to pass a tranquil and a peaceful existence. For though he eludes God and man, yet he cannot but feel a misgiving that his secret can be kept for ever. . . .

Metal was discovered, tools and arms were developed, clothing was refined, labor was divided along sex lines, plants were grafted and sown, and leisure was expanded, with newly discovered pastimes driving out the old.

[1436–1457] Those watchful guardians, sun and moon, traversing with their light all round the great revolving sphere of heaven taught men that the seasons of the year came round and that the system was carried on after a fixed plan and fixed order.

Already they would pass their life fenced about with strong towers, and the land, portioned out and marked off by boundaries, be tilled; the sea would be filled with ships scudding under sail; towns have auxiliaries and allies as stipulated by treaty, when poets began to consign the deeds of men to verse; and letters had not been invented long before. For this reason our age cannot look back to what has gone before, save where reason points out any traces.

Ships and tillage, walls, laws, arms, roads, dress, and all such like things, all the prizes, all the elegancies too of life without exception, poems, pictures, and the chiselling of fine-wrought statues, all these things practiced together with the acquired knowledge of the untiring mind taught men by slow degrees as they advanced on the way step by step. Thus time by degrees brings each several thing forth before men's eyes and reason raises it up into the borders of light; for things must be brought to light one after the other and in due order in the different

arts, until these have reached their highest point of development.

Skepticism

SEXTUS EMPIRICUS

Outlines of Pyrrhonism [9]

[I, 21–24] That we stick to appearances is clear from the things we say about the criterion of the Skeptical school. Something is called a criterion in two senses: (1) what is accepted as contributing to belief in reality and unreality (about which we shall speak in the refutation), and (2) the standard for doing, by holding to which in life we do some things and not others (which we are now discussing). We say then that the criterion of the Skeptical school is what appears, in its sense of what we call presentation. For since this lies in affection and involuntary feeling, it is not to be questioned. Therefore probably no one disputes that the underlying object is of such-and-such an appearance; the inquiry is whether it is such as it appears.

Holding then to appearances we live undogmatically with the care that is appropriate to life, since we cannot be altogether inactive. And this care appropriate to life seems to be fourfold: one consists in the guidance of nature; a second in the necessity of the passions; a third in the handing on of laws and customs; a fourth in the teaching of the arts. There is nature's guidance in that we are naturally capable of sensation and thought; necessity of the passions in that hunger leads us to food and thirst to drink; handing on of customs and laws in that we take piety pertaining to life as good and impiety as evil; teaching of the arts in that we are not inactive in the arts we practice. But we assert all this undogmatically.

[25–28] The end of the Skeptic is peace [*ataraxia*] [10] in matters of opinion and moderation of feeling in things that are unavoidable. For having embarked on philosophizing to judge beyond matters of appearance and determine which are true and which

---

[9] The translation is by the editors of this volume.
[10] *Ataraxia;* literally, lack of disturbance.

are false, so as to be at peace, he fell into contradictions of equal strength, and being unable to judge them he suspended judgment. And for him in this state of suspense, peace in matters of opinion was a consequence. For the person who believes something is fine or evil by nature is upset on every occasion: when he does not have the things that are believed to be fine, he considers that he is suffering the punishment of natural evils and pursues what he thinks to be good. And when he has acquired them he is still more upset because he is unreasonably and immoderately elated, and fearing a change he does all sorts of things in order not to lose what he judges to be good. But the person who leaves indeterminate the question of natural good or ill neither flees nor pursues vehemently; on that account he is untroubled.

[29–30] We do not consider that the Skeptic is wholly undisturbed, but we say that he is disturbed by what is unavoidable; for we grant that he is sometimes cold and thirsty and suffers in such-and-such ways. But even in these, laymen are affected by a double trouble, that is, by the feelings themselves and no less by the judgment that these circumstances are evil by nature. But the Skeptic, stripping away the additional judgment that each of these is evil by nature, escapes more moderately in these matters. That is why we say that the end of the Skeptic in dealing with beliefs is peace, but in dealing with what is unavoidable, moderate feeling.

On how to achieve the Skeptic's suspension (*epochē*):

[31–34] Speaking most generally, it is through the opposition of things. We oppose either appearances to appearances, or thoughts to thoughts, or crosswise. For example, appearances to appearances when we say, "The same tower appears round from afar, but square from nearby"; and thoughts to thoughts when to one who constructs the view that there is providence from the order of the heavens, we oppose the fact that good people often do badly while the evil do well, and infer from this that there is no providence; and thoughts to appearances, as Anaxagoras opposed to snow is white the fact that snow is frozen water and water is dark, so snow is dark. And along another line of thought we oppose sometimes present to present, as in what was said above, sometimes present to past or future;

for example, when someone proposes to us a thesis which we cannot refute, we say to him that, just as before the birth of the person who introduced the option you adopt the thesis with respect to it did not appear to be sound, though it lay hidden in nature, so it is possible that a thesis opposed to the one you are now expounding lies hidden in nature, though it does not yet appear to us; so that we ought not to agree to the thesis that now seems to be strong.

The tenth of the traditional "modes" of securing Skeptical suspension concerns ethics.

[145–150] It pertains especially to ethics, which is about ways of life and customs and laws and mythical beliefs and dogmatic opinions. Thus a way of life is a selection of a life or of some action on the part of one or many, for example, Diogenes or the Laconians. A law is a written agreement among fellow citizens, a transgressor of which is punished. A custom or usage (they do not differ) is a common tradition on some matter on the part of many people, the transgressor of which is not strictly punished; for example, there is a law that forbids adultery, but it is a custom among us not to have intercourse with a woman in public. Mythical belief is the handing on of matters that did not happen and were made up, for example among others, the stories of Cronos; for these lead many into belief. Dogmatic opinion is the handing on of something that appears to prevail through analogy or some kind of demonstration; for example, that atoms are the elements of things that are.

Now each of these we oppose sometimes to itself, sometimes to each of the others. For example, habit to habit in this way: some of the Ethiopians tattoo their offspring but we do not; and the Persians consider it fitting to wear dress that is brightly dyed and reaches down to the feet, but we think it unfitting; and the Indians have intercourse with women in public, but most other people think it to be shameful. And we oppose law to law thus: among the Romans the man who refuses his father's property does not pay his father's debts, but among the Rhodians he always pays them; and among the Tauri in Scythia there was a law that strangers be sacrificed to Artemis, but among us it is not allowed to kill a human being for a sacrifice. And we oppose way of life to way of life, when we oppose that of

Diogenes [the Cynic, who cultivated poverty] to that of Aristippus or that of the Laconians [the Spartans] to that of the Italians.

The listing of opposites continues: myth against myth, dogma against dogma (e.g., the soul is mortal against the soul is immortal); law against law (e.g., male homosexuality permissible in Persia against illegal in Rome; or adultery forbidden among us against regarded indifferently among Massegetae, marriage with sisters forbidden for us against permitted in Egypt, etc.); way of life against dogmatic opinion (e.g., athletes desiring glory and leading a strenuous life against philosophers' considering glory a base motive); myth against law (poets' telling of the gods' adulteries against man's laws forbidding it); and so on.

[III, 110–111] We have thus examined sufficiently the issue of there not being any good or evil by nature. Now let us ask whether, if these be supposed, it is possible for life to flow tranquilly and happily. Now the dogmatic philosophers say that nothing other than this is the case; on their view man is happy who hits on the good and escapes the evil; accordingly they say that practical wisdom is a kind of science of life, being capable of judging goods and evils, and productive of happiness. But the Skeptics, neither asserting nor denying anything rashly, bringing everything under critical consideration, hold that for those who accept a good and evil by nature the consequence is living unhappily, but for those who regard things as indeterminate and hold up judging, human life is easiest.

[118] Thus if one should say that nothing is by nature to be chosen or to be avoided, nor more to be avoided than chosen, each thing that happens being relative and according to differing occasions and conditions, now being set down to be chosen, now to be avoided, he will live happily and peacefully, neither being elated by the good as good, nor dejected by evil, accepting bravely what happens of necessity, and he will be freed of the turbulence that stems from the belief in which it is thought that something evil or good is present. This liberation is achieved by not judging a good or evil by nature. Therefore it is not possible to live happily if one assumes things are good or evil by nature.

Neoplatonism

PLOTINUS

Enneads [11]

[III, viii, 11] No doubt Intelligence is beautiful. It is the most beautiful of things. It is illuminated by a pure light and shines with a pure splendor; it contains the intelligible beings of which our world, in spite of its beauty, is but a shadow and an image. It lies in full resplendence because it contains nothing unintelligent or obscure or indefinite. It enjoys a blissful life. Wonder seizes him who sees it and who enters it properly and becomes one with it. Just as the view of heaven and the splendor of the stars lead one to seek and think of their author, so the contemplation of the intelligible world and the admiration it induces lead one to seek its author and to ask who has given existence to the intelligible world, where this author is, and how this author produced that world. Who is it that begot such a beautiful son as Intelligence which derives all of its fullness from its author? This supreme principle itself is neither Intelligence, nor plenitude, but is superior to them. They come after it because they need both to think and to be filled. They are close to the principle which wants nothing and does not even need to think. Nevertheless Intelligence possesses true plenitude and thought because it immediately participates in the Good. But that which is above Intelligence does not need or possess these things. Otherwise it would not be the Good.

[VI, ix, 4] [O]ur knowledge of the One comes to us neither by science nor by pure thought, as does the knowledge of other intelligible things, but by a presence which is superior to science. When the soul acquires scientific knowledge of something, she withdraws from unity and ceases being fully one; for science implies discursive reason and discursive reason implies manifoldness. She then misses the One and falls into number and multiplicity. We must therefore rise above science and never withdraw from unity. We must renounce science, the objects of science, and every other object, even

[11] The selection is from *The Philosophy of Plotinus*, translated by Joseph Katz (Englewood Cliffs, N.J.: Prentice-Hall, 1950).

beauty; for even beauty is posterior to the One and is derived from it as the daylight comes from the sun. That is why Plato says of the One that "it can neither be spoken nor written of." If we nevertheless speak of and write about it, we do so only to give direction, to stimulate towards that vision beyond discourse, as one might point out the road to somebody who desired to see some object. Instruction indeed goes as far as showing the road and guiding in the way; but to obtain the vision is the work of him who desires to obtain it.

If one does not succeed in enjoying this spectacle, if one's soul does not attain the knowledge of that life beyond, if she does not within herself feel a rapture such as that of a lover who sees the beloved object and rests within it, if, because of one's proximity to the One, one receives the true light and has one's whole soul illuminated but still in one's ascent is oppressed by a weight which hinders one's contemplation, if one does not rise in a purified state but retains within oneself something that separates one from the One, if one is not yet unified enough, if one has not yet risen so far but still is at a distance, either because of the obstacles of which we just spoke or because of the lack of such instruction as would have given one direction and confidence in the existence of things beyond, one has no one to blame but oneself and should try to become pure by detaching oneself from everything. (For the One is not absent from anything, though in another sense it is absent from all things. It is present only to those who are able to receive it and are prepared for it, so as to enter into harmony with it, to "grasp" and to "touch" it by virtue of their similarity to it, by virtue of an inner power analogous to and stemming from the One when this power is in that state in which it was when it originated from the One. Thus they will see it as far as it can become an object of contemplation.) . . .

[5] . . . There is an existence that is superior to even what is highest in the world of Being. There must indeed be an existence above Intelligence; for Intelligence does aspire to become one, but it is not one and only resembles the One. It resembles the One because it is not divided but has all its parts co-existing. On account of its proximity to the One, it did not break apart, though it dared to withdraw from it. This marvelous existence above Intelligence is the One itself which is not the same as

Being. Its unity is not the attribute of something else, as is the case with the other existences that are one. No name should really be given to it. If, however, it must be named, it may appropriately be called One, but only on the understanding that it is not a substance that possesses unity only as an attribute. Hence the One is difficult to know and is rather known by its offspring, that is, by Being. It brings Intelligence into being, and its nature is such that it is the source of the most excellent things. It is the power which begets the things while remaining within itself without undergoing any diminution. It does not pass into the things to which it gives birth because it is prior to them. We are necessarily led to call this existence the One in order to designate it to one another, to lead up with this name to an indivisible conception, and to unify our soul. But when we say that this existence is one and indivisible, it is not in the same sense that we say it of the geometrical point or the numerical unit. What is one in this latter sense is a quantitative principle which would not exist unless substance were there first and that which precedes substance and Being. It is not of this kind of unity that we must think. But we should see the analogy of things here with those beyond in regard to simplicity and the absence of manifoldness and division.

[10] . . . He who has the vision becomes, as it were, another being. He ceases to be himself, he retains nothing of himself. Absorbed in the beyond he is one with it, like a center that coincides with another center. While these two centers coincide, they are one; but they become two when they separate. It is in this sense only that we can speak of the One as something separate. Hence it is very difficult to describe this vision. For how can we represent as different from us that which did not seem, while we were contemplating it, other than ourselves but in perfect at-oneness with us?

[11] This, no doubt, is the meaning of the injunction of the mystery rites which prohibits their revelation to the uninitiated. As that which is divine is not expressible, the initiate is forbidden to talk of it to anyone who has not had the happiness of beholding it. The vision did not imply a duality, but he who saw was identical with what he saw. Hence he did not "see" it but rather was united with it. If only he could preserve the memory of what he was while thus absorbed into the One, he would, within himself, possess an image of the One. In

that state he had attained unity and contained no difference, in regard either to himself or to other beings. In his ascent there was within him no movement, no anger, desire, reason, nor thought. In sum, he was no longer himself; but swept away and filled with enthusiasm, he was tranquil, solitary, and unmoved. He did not withdraw from the One nor did he turn towards himself. He was indeed in a state of perfect stability, having, so to say, become stability itself. In this condition he busies himself no longer even with beauty. For he has risen above Beauty and has passed beyond even the choir of virtues, just as he who penetrates into the innermost sanctuary of a temple leaves behind him the statues placed in the rest of the temple. These statues are the first objects that will strike his view on his exit from the sanctuary after he has experienced the vision it offers. The intimate communion, however, is not with an image or statue (which is contemplated only when he comes out), but with that which it represents. That experience was hardly a vision, but a quite different kind of seeing, a self-transcendence, a simplification, a self-abandonment, a striving for contact, a quietude, an intentness on adaptation. This is the way one

sees in the sanctuary. Anyone who seeks to see in any other way will see nothing.

. . . When the soul descends, she will by her nature never reach complete nothingness. She will fall into evil and, in this sense, into nothingness, but not into complete nothingness. In a similar way, when the soul reverses her direction, she does not arrive at something different, but at herself. She thus is not in anything different from herself, but in herself. But as she is in herself alone and not even in the world of Being, she is in the existence beyond. We too transcend Being by virtue of the soul with which we are united. Now if one sees oneself in this state, one finds oneself an image of the One. If one rises beyond oneself, an image arising to its model, one has reached the goal of one's journey. When one falls from this vision, one will, by arousing the virtue that is within oneself, and by remembering the perfections that one possesses, regain one's lightness and through virtue rise to Intelligence, and through wisdom to the One. Such is the life of gods and of divine and blessed men, detachment from all things here below, scorn of all earthly pleasures, and flight of the alone to the alone.

GROWTH OF THE WESTERN RELIGIOUS ETHIC

As seen in the Old Testament, the Western religious ethic reaches back before classical Greek times, but some episodes have a Greek flavor—the struggle with evil (Job) and questioning whether life is worthwhile (Ecclesiastes). The New Testament falls wholly within the historical period of this chapter.

It would be overly simple to portray the growth of this religious ethic in distinct and separate stages of an initial Hebraic foundation, a Christian development, and an Islamic fringe influence, as if the Hebraic were wholly assimilated in the Christian. The Hebraic, which covers the ideas of both the Old Testament and early Christianity before the latter drew apart, goes on after the dispersion (A.D.

70), in the Talmudic writings of the rabbis. The Hellenistic period saw attempts to synthesize Hebrew religion and Platonic ideas—the most notable is that of Philo Judaeus (c. 20 B.C.–c. A.D. 40) whose philosophy is often regarded as a precursor to Neoplatonism. Beyond our present period, there is Maimonides (1135–1204), whose roots are both Aristotelian and Hebraic.

Paul shaped Christianity for a wider appeal beyond the Hebraic community and incorporated Greek influences. Hellenistic elements are evident also in the early Christian fathers—for example, Clement of Alexandria (c.150–c.213)—and Neoplatonism plays a significant part in shaping Augustine's ideas. Later the fission into Catholic and Protestant Christianity exhibits the many different philosophical strands that were to find expression in their respective theologies. Islam, since its foundation in the seventh century A.D., has been outside the Western tradition; but its influence has been strong, particularly in the theoretical interpretation of Aristotle by Moslem scholars in medieval times.

Moral Philosophy in Biblical and Theological Writings

The biblical story of Creation, of God's compact with Abraham, of the giving of the law to Moses, and so on is too well known to require recounting. The Bible, from the time of its translation and accessibility to the general European reader, has served both as a means of education and as a source of morality. It is important for ethics to recognize its many strata: biblical scholars have been able to discern different periods that correlate with the moral growth of a civilization.

The morality of the Ten Commandments embodies a distinct theoretical model, primarily a juristic or legalistic one, and in some measure a familial one. God, as Creator the Father, sets down for his people the laws as commands with sanctions. The degree of faith and trust demanded is seen in the story of Abraham, expected at God's bidding to sacrifice his son, Isaac. Medieval philosophers were quite worried by this story, since although God intervenes before Abraham obeys, in it God seemed to be violating his own commandment about killing; indeed, Abelard makes it the occasion for a judgment on God (see Chapter 6). Later the story is exploited by Kierkegaard (1813–1855) and Sartre (1905–1980): Kierkegaard to see in it the superiority of the religious over the ethical; Sartre to underscore the ultimate moral responsibility of the individual.

Abraham, says Sartre, might well decide that his God would not enjoin what the Ten Commandments forbid, and so suspect the order to be an imposture.

One issue that later divided the Hebrews concerned the stringency of the law. A second division was between those who, thinking in terms of an afterlife, pursued salvationist tendencies and those who focused on this life and godliness within it. A third was between those who emphasized God's compact with a chosen people and those who saw God's merciful concern as for all mankind (the latter increasingly the view of the later prophets). Thus in these various strands are treatments of the application of moral law, the relation of the law to the spirit as well as of body and spirit, and the extent of the moral community.

The question of what the value of life is and what one can hope from it belongs to a later stratum of the Old Testament. Ecclesiastes and Job are closer to the period of the Stoics and Epicureans, and parallel themes appear. Ecclesiastes asks whether all is in vain, whether every effort that becomes a dominant purpose in human beings is not folly, whether moderation is not the best path, for old age and death come to all of us. Job is the classic formulation in the Hebrew literature of the problem of evil—whether human sufferings are compatible with an all-powerful, all-knowing, and all-good God. At stake in such an inquiry is not theory alone but what stance ought to be taken in the presence of evil—struggle or resignation? Should one flee a plague or stay and allow God's will to prevail? And how is God's will to be identified? Is a doctor curing a patient going against God's will, or is God's will expressed through the doctor's efforts? This problem echoes throughout history, particularly at times of disaster—from plagues in ancient times to the great Lisbon earthquake of 1775 to the holocaust of World War II. Leibniz (1646–1716) made an attempt (satirized in Voltaire's *Candide*, 1759) to show that this is the best of all possible worlds, while Spinoza

(1632–1677) is driven by the problem to deny that God has any purpose for the world.

In the New Testament we find a shift from a juristic model to a model spiritual life. Two distinct features are discernible in the Sermon on the Mount. One is the overwhelming focus inward that ethically equates desires and outward behavior: to be angry is equivalent to striking, to lust is the equivalent of adultery. Such inwardness parallels the Stoic inwardness. But unlike the Stoics, the goal of the battle with oneself is not just to achieve an inner peace but to be like and at one with the divine and to achieve other-worldly salvation. The inwardness thus becomes a rejection of the worth of this world. Second, the injunction to turn the other cheek when struck releases the inherent love in the brotherhood of mankind, a love that is unqualified and not dependent on special or reciprocal treatment. This aspect of the Sermon has become in modern times the basis of pacifism, as it was developed in Tolstoy's *The Kingdom of God Is Within You*. Gandhi used it in the struggle for Indian independence; and it entered into Martin Luther King, Jr.'s, nonviolent struggle for equality of blacks in the United States.

The moral outlook of Paul, who shaped Christianity for its career in the Greek world, accents other themes. Greek philosophical elements enter, particularly Stoic. The sense of sin is stronger, as is the emphasis on the duties and the difficulty of self-control. These themes are carried over by Augustine.

Augustine (A.D. 354–430) was the most influential Christian philosophical theologian in the ancient world and remains a permanent theological-philosophical influence in the Christian tradition, Protestant as well as Catholic. He was raised in North Africa. In his youth he adopted Manicheanism, which sees the world in dualistic fashion as a struggle between spirit and an independent matter (the source of evil). Eventually converted to Christianity by his mother's influence, he served, after a time in Italy, as bishop of Hippo in North Africa.

His *Confessions* presents Augustine's inner struggles in the development of his faith. He wrote *The City of God* in response to those who blamed the Visigoths' conquest of Rome on Christianity, for having undermined the old Roman valor. In it he works out a philosophy of history to show the place of such events in a world history from the Creation to the ultimate Resurrection. Two features mark his ethical approach. First, the stress he places on the will makes a human being completely responsible, for inner feelings as well as for behavior. The selections show how far-reaching that voluntarism is. Second, his unrelenting reliance on a single criterion of human good, as a matter entirely of orientation to God, comes closest in the history of ethics to the declaration that man is not an end in himself and acquires value only insofar as he looks toward God as the sole intrinsic value. This profoundly contrasts with Kant's later declaration that every man should be treated as an end in himself.

Exodus: Decalogue [12]

[xx] 2. I *am* the Lord thy God, which have brought thee out of the land of Egypt, out of the house of bondage.

3. Thou shalt have no other gods before me.

4. Thou shalt not make unto thee any graven image, or any likeness *of anything* that *is* in heaven above, or that *is* in the earth beneath, or that *is* in the water under the earth:

5. Thou shalt not bow down thyself to them, nor serve them: for I the LORD thy God *am* a jealous God, visiting the iniquity of the fathers upon the children unto the

---

[12] The selections from the Old Testament and the New Testament are from the King James translation. Undoubtedly, there are more accurate recent translations, but the King James shaped the thought, education, literature, and language of the English-speaking world; it is still unsurpassed in its literary quality.

third and fourth *generation* of them that hate me;

6. And showing mercy unto thousands of them that love me, and keep my commandments.

7. Thou shalt not take the name of the LORD thy God in vain: for the LORD will not hold him guiltless that taketh his name in vain.

8. Remember the sabbath day, to keep it holy.

9. Six days shalt thou labour and do all thy work:

10. But the seventh day *is* the sabbath of the LORD thy God: *in it* thou shalt not do any work, thou, nor thy son, nor thy daughter, thy man-servant, nor thy maid-servant, nor thy cattle, nor the stranger that *is* within thy gates:

11. For *in* six days the LORD made heaven and earth, the sea, and all that in them *is*, and rested the seventh day: wherefore the LORD blessed the sabbath day, and hallowed it.

12. Honour thy father and thy mother: that thy days may be long upon the land which the LORD thy God giveth thee.

13. Thou shalt not kill.

14. Thou shalt not commit adultery.

15. Thou shalt not steal.

16. Thou shalt not bear false witness against thy neighbour.

17. Thou shalt not covet thy neighbour's house, thou shalt not covet thy neighbour's wife, nor his man-servant, nor his maid-servant, nor his ox, nor his ass, nor any thing that *is* thy neighbour's.

Job

The "prologue" presents Job as a model of piety. When God mentions this to Satan, the latter is skeptical, remarking that anyone would be pious when so well endowed with family and wealth. God agrees to an "experimental" test, and Satan arranges the "accidental" death of Job's children and the loss of his property. Still Job simply says, "The Lord

gave, and the Lord hath taken away; blessed be the name of the Lord" (1:21). Satan claims that it was not a satisfactory experiment, since the one crucial variable was not controlled.

[II, 4–10] Skin for skin, yea, all that a man hath will he give for his life. But put forth thine hand now, and touch his bone and his flesh, and he will curse thee to thy face. And the Lord said unto Satan, Behold, he is in thine hand; but save his life. So went Satan forth from the presence of the Lord, and smote Job with sore boils from the sole of his foot unto his crown. And he took him a potsherd to scrape himself withal; and he sat down among the ashes. Then said his wife unto him, Dost thou still retain thine integrity? curse God, and die. But he said unto her, Thou speakest as one of the foolish women speaketh. What? shall we receive good at the hand of God, and shall we not receive evil? In all this did not Job sin with his lips.

After seven days and nights of silent suffering Job finally speaks:

[III, 3–5] Let the day perish wherein I was born, and the night in which it was said, There is a man child conceived. Let that day be darkness; let not God regard it from above, neither let the light shine upon it. Let darkness and the shadow of death stain it; let a cloud dwell upon it; let the blackness of the day terrify it.

[11, 13] Why died I not from the womb? Why did I not give up the ghost when I came out of the belly? . . . For now should I have lain still and been quiet, I should have slept; then had I been at rest.

One of Job's three friends who came to comfort him with the traditional wisdom speaks:

[IV, 3–7] Behold, thou hast instructed many, and thou has strengthened the weak hands. Thy words have upholden him that was falling, and thou has strengthened the feeble knees. But now it is come upon thee, and thou faintest; it toucheth thee, and thou art troubled. Is not this thy fear, thy confidence, thy hope, and the uprightness of thy ways? Remember, I pray thee, who ever perished, being innocent? or where were the righteous cut off?

[17] Shall mortal man be more just than God? shall a man be more pure than his Maker?

[V, 17] Behold, happy is the man whom God correcteth: therefore despise not thou the chastening of the Almighty: For he maketh sore, and bindeth up: he woundeth, and his hands make whole.

Job's response stresses his desire for understanding:

[VI, 24] Teach me, and I will hold my tongue: and cause me to understand wherein I have erred.

[VII, 17–18] What is man, that thou shouldst magnify him? and that thou shouldst set thine heart upon him? And that thou shouldst visit him every morning, and try him every moment?

[21] And why dost thou not pardon my transgression, and take away mine iniquity? for now shall I sleep in the dust; and thou shalt seek me in the morning, but I shall not be.

A second friend moves the consolation a step nearer condemnation:

[VIII, 2–3] How long wilt thou speak these things? and how long shall the words of thy mouth be like a strong wind? Doth God pervert judgment? or doth the Almighty pervert justice?

[6] If thou wert pure and upright; surely now he would awake for thee, and make the habitation of thy righteousness prosperous.

[20] Behold, God will not cast away a perfect man, neither will he help the evil doers.

Job's reply appeals to the facts:

[IX, 2] I know it is so of a truth; but how should man be just with God?

[20–22] If I justify myself, mine own mouth shall condemn me: if I say, I am perfect, it shall also prove me perverse. Though I were perfect, yet would I not know my soul: I would despise my life. This is one thing, therefore I said it, He destroyeth the perfect and the wicked.

[X, 7] Thou knowest that I am not wicked; and there is none that can deliver out of thine hand.

The third friend is led into open condemnation.

[XI, 2–6] Should not the multitude of words be answered? and should a man full of talk be justified? Should thy lies make men hold their peace? and when thou mockest, shall no man make thee ashamed? For thou hast said, My doctrine is pure, and I am clean in thine eyes. But oh that God would speak, and open his lips against thee; And that he would show thee the secrets of wisdom, that they are double to that which is! Know therefore that God exacteth of thee less than thine iniquity deserveth.

Job replies.

[XII, 2–3] No doubt but ye are the people, and wisdom shall die with you. But I have understanding as well as you; I am not inferior to you: yea, who knoweth not such things as these?

[XIII, 3] Surely I would speak to the Almighty, and I desire to reason with God.

[15] Though he slay me, yet will I trust in him: but I will maintain mine own ways before him.

[23] How many are mine iniquities and sins? make me to know my transgression and my sin.

[XVI, 21] Oh that one might plead for a man with God, as a man pleadeth for his neighbour!

After another round with his friends, and a fourth man whose wrath is roused because Job justified himself rather than God (32:2), and so has added rebellion to sin (34:37), the Lord answers Job out of the whirlwind.

[XXXVIII, 2–7] Who is this that darkeneth counsel by words without knowledge? Gird up now thy loins like a man; for I will demand of thee, and answer thou me. Where wast thou when I laid the foundations of the earth? declare, if thou hast understanding. Who hath laid the measures thereof, if thou knowest? or who hath stretched the line upon it? Whereupon are the foundations thereof fastened? or who laid the corner stone thereof; when the morning stars sang together, and all the sons of God shouted for joy?

Many phenomena follow, which Job cannot even understand, much less bring into being. In the midst of this, God calls upon Job to answer.

[XL, 2–8] Shall he that contendeth with the Almighty instruct him? he that reproveth God, let him answer it. Then Job answered the Lord, and said, Behold, I am vile; what shall I answer thee? I will lay mine hand upon my mouth. Once have I spoken; but I will not answer: yea, twice; but I will proceed no further. Then answered the Lord unto Job out of the whirlwind, and said, Gird up thy loins now like a man: I will demand of thee, and declare thou unto me. Wilt thou also disannul my judgment? wilt thou condemn me, that thou mayest be righteous?

[XLII, 1–2] Then Job answered the Lord, and said, I know that thou canst do every thing, and that no thought can be withholden from thee.

[5–6] I have heard of thee by the hearing of the ear; but now mine eye seeth thee: Wherefore I abhor myself, and repent in dust and ashes.

The Lord also reprimands Job's friends for their arrogant assumption of knowledge. Job is blessed with numerous fresh children and material prosperity, and lives out a long life.

Matthew: Sermon on the Mount

[V] 3 Blessed *are* the poor in spirit: for theirs is the kingdom of heaven.

4 Blessed *are* they that mourn: for they shall be comforted.

5 Blessed *are* the meek: for they shall inherit the earth.

6 Blessed *are* they which do hunger and thirst after righteousness: for they shall be filled.

7 Blessed *are* the merciful: for they shall obtain mercy.

8 Blessed *are* the pure in heart: for they shall see God.

9 Blessed *are* the peacemakers: for they shall be called the children of God.

10 Blessed *are* they which are persecuted for righteousness' sake: for theirs is the kingdom of heaven.

11 Blessed are ye, when *men* shall revile you, and persecute *you*, and shall say all manner of evil against you falsely, for my sake.

12 Rejoice, and be exceedingly glad: for great *is* your reward in heaven: for so persecuted they the prophets which were before you.

13 Ye are the salt of the earth: but if the salt have lost his savour, wherewith shall it be salted? it is thenceforth good for nothing, but to be cast out, and to be trodden under foot of men.

16 Let your light so shine before men, that they may see your good works, and glorify your Father which is in heaven.

17 Think not that I am come to destroy the law, or the prophets: I am come not to destroy, but to fulfil.

18 For verily I say unto you, Till heaven and earth pass, one jot or one tittle shall in no wise pass from the law, till all be fulfilled.

21 Ye have heard that it was said by them of old time, Thou shalt not kill; and whosoever shall kill shall be in danger of the judgment:

22 But I say unto you, That whosoever is angry with his brother without a cause shall be in danger of the judgment: and whosoever shall say to his brother, Raca! shall be in danger of the council: but whosoever shall say, Thou fool! shall be in danger of hell fire.

27 Ye have heard that it was said by them of old time, Thou shalt not commit adultery:

28 But I say unto you, That whosoever looketh on a woman to lust after her hath committed adultery with her already in his heart.

29 And if thy right eye offend thee, pluck it out, and cast *it* from thee: for it is profitable for thee that one of thy members should perish, and not *that* thy whole body should be cast into hell.

38 Ye have heard that it hath been said, An eye for an eye, and a tooth for a tooth:

39 But I say unto you, That ye resist not evil; but whosoever shall smite thee on thy right cheek, turn to him the other also.

40 And if any man will sue thee at the law, and take away thy coat, let him have *thy* cloak also.

41 And whosoever shall compel thee to go a mile, go with him twain.

42 Give to him that asketh thee, and from him that would borrow of thee turn not thou away.

43 Ye have heard that it hath been said, Thou shalt love thy neighbour, and hate thine enemy:

44 But I say unto you, Love your enemies, bless them that curse you, do good to them that hate you, and pray for them which despitefully use you, and persecute you;

45 That ye may be the children of your Father which is in heaven: for he maketh his sun to rise

on the evil and on the good, and sendeth rain on the just and on the unjust.

46 For if ye love them which love you, what reward have ye? Do not even the publicans do the same?

[VI] 19 Lay not up for yourselves treasures upon earth, where moth and rust doth corrupt, and where thieves break through and steal:

20 But lay up for yourselves treasures in heaven, where neither moth nor rust doth corrupt, and where thieves do not break through nor steal:

24 No man can serve two masters: for either he will hate the one, and love the other: or else he will hold to the one, and despise the other. Ye cannot serve God and mammon.

[VII] 1 JUDGE not, that ye be not judged.

2 For with what judgment ye judge, ye shall be judged: and with what measure ye mete, it shall be measured to you again.

3 And why beholdest thou the mote that is in thy brother's eye, but considerest not the beam that is in thine own eye?

15 Beware of false prophets, which come to you in sheep's clothing, but inwardly they are ravening wolves.

16 Ye shall know them by their fruits. Do men gather grapes of thorns, or figs of thistles?

AUGUSTINE

Confessions [13] and The City of God [14]

[*Conf* I, 4] What art Thou then, my God? What, but the Lord God? *For who is Lord but the Lord? or who is God save our God?* Most highest, most good, most potent, most omnipotent; most merciful, yet most just; most hidden, yet most present; most beautiful, yet most strong; stable, yet incomprehensible; unchangeable, yet all-changing; never new, never old; all-renewing, and *bringing age upon the proud, and they know it not*; ever working, ever at rest; still gathering, yet nothing lacking; supporting,

[13] The translation is by E. B. Pusey (Oxford: Parker, 1840).
[14] The translation is by Marcus Dods, 1st ed. (Edinburgh: T. & T. Clark, 1871); but as noted in that edition, some of the chapters, including Chapter V, from which we quote, are translated by Rev. J. J. Smith. Texts from both works are juxtaposed by topic.

filling, and over-spreading; creating, nourishing, and maturing; seeking, yet having all things. Thou lovest, without passion; art jealous, without anxiety; repentest, yet grievest not; art angry, yet serene; changest Thy works, Thy purpose unchanged; receivest again what Thou findest; yet didst never lose; never in need, yet rejoicing in gains; never covetous, yet exacting usury. Thou receivest over and above, that Thou mayest owe; and who hath aught that is not Thine? Thou payest debts, owing nothing; remittest debts, losing nothing. And what have I now said, my God, my life, my holy joy? or what saith any man when he speaks of Thee? Yet woe to him that speaketh not, since mute are even the most eloquent.

Augustine had accepted Manichean dualism—by which matter, which exists independently, is the source of evil whereas spirit is the source of good; he later rejected it.

[*Conf* V, 20] I believed Evil also to be some such kind of substance, and to have its own foul, and hideous bulk; whether gross, which they called earth, or thin and subtile, (like the body of the air,) which they imagine to be some malignant mind, creeping through that earth. And because a piety, such as it was, constrained me to believe, that the good God never created any evil nature, I conceived two masses, contrary to one another, both unbounded, but the evil narrower, the good more expansive. And from this pestilent beginning, the other sacrilegious conceits followed on me.

[*Conf.* XII, 7] But whence had it this degree of being, but from Thee, from Whom all things are, so far forth as they are? But so much the further from Thee, as the unliker Thee; for it is not farness of place. Thou therefore, Lord . . . didst *in the Beginning*, which is of Thee, in Thy Wisdom, which was born of Thine own Substance, create something, and that out of nothing. . . . Thou wert, and nothing was there besides, out of which Thou *createst heaven and earth*; things of two sorts; one near Thee, the other near to nothing; one, to which Thou alone shouldest be superior; the other, to which nothing should be inferior.

[*CG* XI, 22] . . . We do not greatly wonder that persons, who suppose that some evil nature has been generated and propagated by a kind of opposing principle proper to it, refuse to admit that the cause of the creation was this, that the good God produced a good creation. For they believe that He was driven to this enterprise of creation by the urgent necessity of repulsing the evil that warred against Him, and that He mixed His good nature with the evil for the sake of restraining and conquering it; and that this nature of His, being thus shamefully polluted, and most cruelly oppressed and held captive, He labours to cleanse and deliver it, and with all His pains does not wholly succeed; but such part of it as could not be cleansed from that defilement is to serve as a prison and chain of the conquered and incarcerated enemy. The Manicheans would not drivel, or rather, rave in such a style as this, if they believed the nature of God to be, as it is, unchangeable and absolutely incorruptible, and subject to no injury; and if, moreover, they held in Christian sobriety, that the soul which has shown itself capable of being altered for the worse by its own will, and of being corrupted by sin, and so, of being deprived of the light of eternal truth, —that this soul, I say, is not a part of God, nor of the same nature as God, but is created by Him, and is far different from its Creator.

[23] . . . And the sinful will, though it violated the order of its own nature, did not on that account escape the laws of God, who justly orders all things for the good. For as the beauty of a picture is increased by well-arranged shadows, so, to the eye that has the skill to discern it, the universe is beautified even by sinners, though, considered by themselves, their deformity is a sad blemish.

Augustine's view of human nature and destiny focuses on an analysis of the will, its freedom and inner operations.

[*Conf.* VIII, 21] . . . The mind commands the body, and it obeys instantly; the mind commands itself, and is resisted. The mind commands the hand to be moved; and such readiness is there, that command is scarce distinct from obedience. Yet the mind is mind, the hand is body. The mind commands the mind, its own self, to will, and yet it doth not. Whence this monstrousness? and to what end? It commands itself, I say, to will, and would not command, unless it willed, and what it commands is not done. But it willeth not entirely: therefore doth it not command entirely. For so far forth it commandeth, as it willeth: and, so far forth is the thing commanded, not done, as it willeth not. For the will commandeth that there be a will; not another, but itself. But it doth not command entirely, therefore what it commandeth, is not. For were the will entire, it would not even command it to be, because it would already be. It is therefore no monstrousness partly to will, partly to nill, but a disease of the mind, that it doth not wholly rise, by truth up-borne, borne down by custom.

[*CG* XI, 9] . . . [E]vil has no positive nature; but the loss of good has received the name "evil."

[10] There is, accordingly, a good which is alone simple, and therefore alone unchangeable, and this is God. By this Good have all others been created, but not simple, and therefore not unchangeable.

[*CG* X, 24] . . . [I]t is sin which is evil, and not the substance or nature of flesh; for this, together with the human soul, could without sin be both assumed and retained, and laid down in death, and changed to something better by resurrection.

[*CG* XI, 17] . . . [D]eparture from God would be no vice, unless in a nature whose property it was to abide with God. So that even the wicked will is a strong proof of the goodness of the nature. But God, as He is the supremely good Creator of good natures, so is He of evil wills the most just Ruler; so that, while they make an ill use of good natures, He makes a good use even of evil wills.

[*CG* XIV, 7] . . . The right will is well-directed love, and the wrong will is ill-directed love. Love, then, yearning to have what is loved, is desire; and having and enjoying it, is joy; fleeing what is opposed to it, it is fear; and feeling what is opposed to it, when it has befallen it, it is sadness. Now these motions are evil if the love is evil; good if the love is good.

[*CG* V, 9] . . . What is it, then, that Cicero feared in the prescience of future things? Doubtless it was this,—that if all future things have been foreknown, they will happen in the order in which they have been foreknown; and if they come to pass in this order, there is a certain order of things foreknown by God; and if a certain order of things, then a certain order of causes, for nothing can happen which is not preceded by some efficient cause. But if there is a certain order of causes according to which everything happens which does happen, then by fate, says he, all things happen which do happen. But if this be so, then is there nothing in

our own power, and there is no such thing as freedom of will; and if we grant that, says he, then
the whole economy of human life is subverted. In
vain are laws enacted. In vain are reproaches,
praises, chidings, exhortations had recourse to; and
there is no justice whatever in the appointment of
rewards for the good, and punishments for the
wicked. And that consequences so disgraceful, and
absurd, and pernicious to humanity may not follow,
Cicero chooses to reject the foreknowledge of future
things, and shuts up the religious mind to this alternative, to make choice between two things, either
that something is in our own power, or that there
is foreknowledge,—both of which cannot be true;
but if the one is affirmed, the other is thereby denied. . . . Thus, wishing to make men free, he
makes them sacrilegious. But the religious mind
chooses both, confesses both, and maintains both
by the faith of piety. . . . It does not follow that,
though there is for God a certain order of all causes,
there must therefore be nothing depending on the
free exercise of our own wills, for our wills themselves are included in that order of causes which
is certain to God, and is embraced by His foreknowledge, for human wills are also causes of human actions; and He who foreknew all the causes
of things would certainly among those causes not
have been ignorant of our wills.

[10] . . . It is not the case, therefore, that because
God foreknew what would be in the power of our
wills, there is for that reason nothing in the power
of our wills. For He who foreknew this did not
foreknow nothing. Moreover, if He who foreknew
what would be in the power of our wills did not
foreknow nothing, but something, assuredly, even
though He did foreknow, there is something in the
power of our wills. Therefore we are by no means
compelled, either, retaining the prescience of God,
to take away the freedom of the will, or, retaining
the freedom of the will, to deny that He is prescient
of future things, which is impious. But we embrace
both. We faithfully and sincerely confess both. The
former, that we may believe well; the latter, that
we may live well. . . . For a man does not therefore
sin because God foreknew that he would sin. Nay,
it cannot be doubted but that it is the man himself
who sins when he does sin, because He, whose
foreknowledge is infallible, foreknew not that fate,
or fortune, or something else would sin, but that
the man himself would sin, who, if he wills not,

sins not. But if he shall not will to sin, even this
did God foreknow.

[CG XII, 3] . . . Things solely good, therefore,
can in some circumstances exist; things solely evil,
never; for even those natures which are vitiated
by an evil will, so far indeed as they are vitiated,
are evil, but in so far as they are natures, they are
good.

As to the fallen angels:

[6] . . . "Pride is the beginning of sin." They
were unwilling, then, to preserve their strength for
God; and as adherence to God was the condition
of their enjoying an ampler being, they diminished
it by preferring themselves to Him. This was the
first defect, and the first impoverishment, and the
first flaw in their nature, which was created, not
indeed supremely existent, but finding its blessedness in the enjoyment of the Supreme Being; whilst
by abandoning Him it should become, not indeed
no nature at all, but a nature with a less ample
existence, and therefore wretched.

If the further question be asked, What was the
efficient cause of their evil will? there is none. For
what is it which makes the will bad, when it is
the will itself which makes the action bad? And
consequently the bad will is the cause of the bad
action, but nothing is the efficient cause of the bad
will. . . . How, then, can a good thing be the efficient cause of an evil will? How, I say, can good
be the cause of evil? For when the will abandons
what is above itself, and turns to what is lower, it
becomes evil—not because that is evil to which it
turns, but because the turning itself is wicked.
Therefore it is not an inferior thing which has made
the will evil, but it is itself which has become so
by wickedly and inordinately desiring an inferior
thing. For if two men, alike in physical and moral
constitution, see the same corporeal beauty, and
one of them is excited by the sight to desire an
illicit enjoyment, while the other steadfastly maintains a modest restraint of his will, what do we
suppose brings it about, that there is an evil will
in the one and not in the other? . . . What other
account can we give of the matter than this, that
the one is willing, the other unwilling, to fall away
from chastity? And what causes this but their own
wills . . . ?

[7] Let no one, therefore, look for an efficient

cause of the evil will; for it is not efficient, but deficient, as the will itself is not an effecting of something, but a defect. For defection from that which supremely is, to that which has less of being,—this is to begin to have an evil will. Now, to seek to discover the causes of these defections,—causes, as I have said, not efficient, but deficient,—is as if someone sought to see darkness, or hear silence. . . . No other sense but the ear can perceive silence, and yet it is only perceived by not hearing. Thus, too, our mind perceives intelligible forms by understanding them; but when they are deficient, it knows them by not knowing them; for "who can understand defects?"

[8] . . . [T]he will could not become evil, were it unwilling to become so; and therefore its failings are justly punished, being not necessary, but voluntary. . . . Avarice is not a fault inherent in gold, but in the man who inordinately loves gold, to the detriment of justice, which ought to be held in incomparably higher regard than gold. . . . Pride, too, is not the fault of him who delegates power, nor of power itself, but of the soul that is inordinately enamoured of its own power, and despises the more just dominion of a higher authority.

[CG XIV, 6] The character of the human will is of moment; because, if it is wrong, these motions of the soul will be wrong, but if it is right, they will be not merely blameless, but even praiseworthy. For the will is in them all; yea, none of them is anything else than will. For what are desire and joy but a volition of consent to the things we wish? And what are fear and sadness but a volition of aversion from the things which we do not wish? But when consent takes the form of seeking to possess the things we wish, this is called desire; and when consent takes the form of enjoying the things we wish, this is called joy. In like manner, when we turn with aversion from that which we do not wish to happen, this volition is termed fear; and when we turn away from that which has happened against our will, this act of will is called sorrow. And generally in respect of all that we seek or shun, as a man's will is attracted or repelled, so it is changed and turned into these different affections. Wherefore the man who lives according to God, and not according to man, ought to be a lover of good, and therefore a hater of evil. And since no one is evil by nature, but whoever is evil is evil by vice, he who lives according to God ought to cherish

towards evil men a perfect hatred, so that he shall neither hate the man because of his vice, nor love the vice because of the man, but hate the vice and love the man.

The interpretation of emotions as acts of will, or signs of such acts, yields subtle evaluations of many situations, for example, the case of the virgins ravished by the barbarians in the sack of Rome—since it was against their will, they were faultless; any shame on their part is due to the anxiety "lest that act which could not be suffered without some sensual pleasure, should be believed to have been committed also with some assent of the will" (CG I, 16).

He does not spare himself. He tells of his prayer in early youth:

[Conf. VIII, 17] . . . "Give me chastity and continency, only not yet." For I feared lest Thou shouldest hear me soon, and soon cure me of the disease of concupiscence, which I wished to have satisfied, rather than extinguished.

An analysis of an early delinquency, when in a gang he stole pears, attempts to locate the precise point of attraction in the episode:

[Conf. II, 9] I lusted to thieve, and did it, compelled by no hunger, nor poverty, but through a cloyedness of welldoing, and a pamperedness of iniquity. . . . Nor cared I to enjoy what I stole, but joyed in the theft and sin itself.

[12] . . . Fair were those pears, but not them did my wretched soul desire; for I had store of better, and those I gathered, only that I might steal. For, when gathered, I flung them away, my only feast therein being my own sin, which I was pleased to enjoy. . . . And now, O Lord my God, I enquire what in that theft delighted me.

[14] . . . What then did I love in that theft? and wherein did I even corruptly and pervertedly imitate my Lord? Did I wish even by stealth to do contrary to Thy law, because by power I could not, so that being a prisoner, I might mimic a maimed liberty by doing with impunity things unpermitted me, a darkened likeness of Thy Omnipotency?

[16] . . . Yet alone I had not done it; such was I

then, I remember, alone I had never done it. I loved then in it also the company of the accomplices, with whom I did it? . . . But since my pleasure was not in those pears, it was in the offence itself, which the company of fellow-sinner occasioned.

[17] What then was this feeling? For of a truth it was too foul: and woe was me, who had it. But yet what was it? *Who can understand his errors?* It was the sport, which, as it were, tickled our hearts, that we beguiled, those who little thought what we were doing, and much misliked it. . . . O friendship too unfriendly! thou incomprehensible inveigler of the soul, thou greediness to do mischief out of mirth and wantonness, thou thirst of others' loss, without lust of my own gain or revenge: but when it is said, "Let's go, let's do it," we are shamed not to be shameless.

A similarly subtle inquiry into emotional effects condemns the use of music in prayer, and the distractions of vision and art, curiosity, and the desire for knowledge.

[*Conf.* X, 50] . . . Yet again, when I remember the tears I shed at the Psalmody of Thy Church, in the beginning of my recovered faith; and how at this time, I am moved, not with the singing, but with the things sung, when they are sung with a clear voice and modulation most suitable, I acknowledge the great use of this institution. Thus I fluctuate between peril of pleasure, and approved wholesomeness; inclined the rather (though not as pronouncing an irrevocable opinion) to approve of the usage of singing in the church; that so by the delight of the ears, the weaker minds may rise to the feeling of devotion. Yet when it befalls me to be more moved with the voice than the words sung, I confess to have sinned penally, and then had rather not hear music.

[53] What innumerable toys, made by divers arts and manufactures, in our apparel, shoes, utensils, and all sort of works, in pictures also and divers images, and these far exceeding all necessary and moderate use and all pious meaning, have men added to tempt their own eyes withal; outwardly following what themselves make, inwardly forsaking Him by whom themselves were made, and destroying that which themselves have been made! . . .

[54] To this is added another form of temptation more manifoldly dangerous. For besides that concupiscence of the flesh which consisteth in the delight of all senses and pleasures, wherein its slaves, who *go far from Thee,* waste and *perish,* the soul hath, through the same senses of the body, a certain vain and curious desire, veiled under the title of knowledge and learning, not of delighting in the flesh, but of making experiments through the flesh. The seat whereof being in the appetite of knowledge, and sight being the sense chiefly used for attaining knowledge, it is in Divine language called, The *lust of the eyes.*

[55] . . . From this disease of curiosity, are all those strange sights exhibited in the theatre. Hence men go on to search out the hidden powers of nature, (which is besides our end,) which to know profits not, and wherein men desire nothing but to know.

In original sin the body came to work against the spirit.

[*CG* XIII, 13] For, as soon as our first parents had transgressed the commandment, divine grace forsook them, and they were confounded at their own wickedness; and therefore they took fig-leaves (which were possibly the first that came to hand in their troubled state of mind) and covered their shame; for though their members remained the same, they had shame now where they had none before. They experienced a new motion of their flesh, which had become disobedient to them, in strict retribution of their own disobedience to God. For the soul, revelling in its own liberty, and scorning to serve God, was itself deprived of the command it had formerly maintained over the body. And because it had wilfully deserted its superior Lord, it no longer held its own inferior servant; neither could it hold the flesh subject, as it would always have been able to do had it remained itself subject to God. Then began the flesh to lust against the Spirit, in which strife we are born, deriving from the first transgression a seed of death, and bearing in our members, and in our vitiated nature, the contest or even victory of the flesh.

There is evidence of sin even in infants—graspingness, sibling hatred, and so on.

[*Conf.* I, 7] The weakness then of infant limbs, not its will, is its innocence.

The account of human history begins with the two cities:

[*CG* XIV, 1] . . . And thus it has come to pass, that though there are very many and great nations all over the earth, whose rites and customs, speech, arms, and dress, are distinguished by marked differences, yet there are no more than two kinds of human society, which we may justly call two cities, according to the language of our Scriptures. The one consists of those who wish to live after the flesh, the other of those who wish to live after the spirit.

Paul's letter to the Galatians is quoted:

[2] . . . "Now the works of the flesh are manifest, which are these: adultery, fornication, uncleanness, lasciviousness, idolatry, witchcraft, hatred, variance, emulations, wrath, strife, seditions, heresies, envyings, murders, drunkenness, revellings, and such like."

Works of the flesh are widely used to cover vices of the soul. Indeed, while the Epicureans who place men's good in bodily pleasures live for the flesh, the Stoics are no different, though they place their supreme good in the soul. In either case the source of sin is the will. The first sin is pride.

[*CG* XIV, 13] . . . And what is pride but the craving for undue exaltation? And this is undue exaltation, when the soul abandons Him to whom it ought to cleave as its end, and becomes a kind of end to itself. . . .
The devil, then, would not have ensnared man in the open and manifest sin of doing what God had forbidden, had man not already begun to live for himself. . . . By craving to be more, man becomes less; and by aspiring to be self-sufficing, he fell away from Him who truly suffices him.

From this beginning, the history of mankind is governed by predestination.

[*CG* XV, 1] . . . And these we also mystically call the two cities, or the two communities of men, of which the one is predestined to reign eternally with God, and the other to suffer eternal punishment with the devil.

Community of people is defined:

[*CG* XIX, 24] [A] people is an assemblage of reasonable beings bound together by a common agreement as to the objects of their love. . . . Yet whatever it loves, if only it is an assemblage of reasonable beings and not of beasts, and is bound together by an agreement as to the objects of love, it is reasonably called a people; and it will be a superior people in proportion as it is bound together by higher interests, inferior in proportion as it is bound together by lower.

This holds for Rome, Athens, and other places; but unless they had true religion, they could not have true justice.

[*CG* XIX, 25] For though the soul may seem to rule the body admirably, and the reason the vices, if the soul and reason do not themselves obey God, as God has commanded them to serve Him, they have no proper authority over the body and the vices. . . . The virtues which it seems to itself to possess, and by which it restrains the body and the vices that it may obtain and keep what it desires, are rather vices than virtues so long as there is no reference to God in the matter. For although some suppose that virtues which have a reference only to themselves, and are desired only on their own account, are yet true and genuine virtues, the fact is that even then they are inflated with pride, and are therefore to be reckoned vices rather than virtues.
[27] . . . [T]he peace which we enjoy in this life, whether common to all or peculiar to ourselves, is rather the solace of our misery than the positive enjoyment of felicity. Our very righteousness, too, though true in so far as it has respect to the true good, is yet in this life of such a kind that it consists rather in the remission of sins than in the perfecting of virtues. . . . But in that final peace to which all our righteousness has reference, and for the sake of which it is maintained, as our nature shall enjoy

a sound immortality and incorruption, and shall have no more vices, and as we shall experience no resistance either from ourselves or from others, it will not be necessary that reason should rule vices which no longer exist, but God shall rule the man, and the soul shall rule the body, with a sweetness and facility suitable to the felicity of a life which is done with bondage. And this condition shall there be eternal, and we shall be assured of its eternity; and thus the peace of this blessedness and the blessedness of this peace shall be the supreme good.

[28] But, on the other hand, they who do not belong to this city of God shall inherit eternal misery, which is also called the second death, because the soul shall then be separated from God its life, and therefore cannot be said to live, and the body shall be subjected to eternal pains. . . .

Augustine (CG XXI, 17) argues against those who maintain that the punishment of hell is not eternal and that (according to Origen) even the devil and his angels will ultimately be delivered from torment. He speculates (CG XXII, 29) "how the saints shall be employed when they are clothed in immortal and spiritual bodies, and when the flesh shall live no longer in a fleshly but a spiritual fashion." He confesses a lack of understanding here, but appeals to the intimation of a "peace of God which passeth all understanding" and quotes Paul: "Now we see through a glass, darkly; but then face to face." Finally, he marks out the periods of history covering the past and the future:

[CG XXII, 30] . . . The first age, as the first day, extends from Adam to the deluge; the second from the deluge to Abraham, equalling the first, not in length of time, but in the number of generations, there being ten in each. From Abraham to the advent of Christ there are, as the evangelist Matthew calculates, three periods, in each of which are fourteen generations,—one period from Abraham to David, a second from David to the captivity, a third from the captivity to the birth of Christ in the flesh. There are thus five ages in all. The sixth is now passing, and cannot be measured by any number of generations, as it has been said, "It is not for you to know the times, which the Father hath put in His own power." After this period God shall rest as on the seventh day, when He shall give us (who shall be the seventh day) rest in Himself. But there is not now space to treat of these ages; suffice it to say that the seventh shall be our Sabbath, which shall be brought to a close, not by an evening, but by the Lord's day, as an eighth and eternal day, consecrated by the resurrection of Christ, and prefiguring the eternal repose not only of the spirit, but also of the body. There we shall rest and see, see and love, love and praise. This is what shall be in the end without end. For what other end do we propose to ourselves than to attain to the kingdom of which there is no end?

5

Themes from a Millennium

The medieval world is an alien world in many ways, more remote even than that of ancient Greece. Thinkers of the period were primarily theologians and churchmen whose philosophy was in service to their theology. Where we tend to separate the moral from the religious, and moral institutions from political, economic, and legal ones, the medievals integrate them. While it is tempting to attribute this to conceptual poverty—a failure to appreciate that the political order is relevantly distinguishable from the economic—it may rather be that such distinctions were unnecessary for medieval Europeans who lived within the comprehensive institution of the universal Church. Even the theological setting of the problems might be seen as philosophical thought experiments by which the range of concepts is tested: to ask whether God can have knowledge tests the conception of knowledge; to ask whether God can command us to do evil tests whether ethics is open to appeal to authority. Our distance from the medieval can advantage us by offering a sort of prism through which to refract modern ethical ideas.

But we need some sense of the background in which the problems arise.

The millennium from the fifth century to the fifteenth saw the collapse of the Roman Empire and its revival as the Holy Roman Empire, the emergence of the Roman Church as the dominant European institution, and the rise of European nation states. The Early Middle Ages in Europe was a time of virtually unrelieved calamity. The Germanic invasions from the fourth to the sixth century destroyed the Roman Empire and with it the educational institutions on which its administration depended and which fostered philosophy. Indeed, the basic tools of the intellectual life—reading and writing—were lost to all but a few. Such intellectual life as remained was directed to preserving older achievements. Thus Isidore of Seville's (c.560–636) *Etymology*, although just a collection of authoritative sayings, was an influential source for medieval writers.

The picture is not entirely bleak. The Eastern Roman Empire, based in Byzantium, maintained Roman institutions, while across the Mediterranean, Islam was developing a highly cultivated intellectual life enriched by islands of Jewish scholarship. In Western Europe itself, the Germanic peoples contributed a tradition of law from which eventually grew common law. About 800 a brief renaissance took place when Charlemagne revived the empire, now to be called the Holy Roman Empire. Associated with Charlemagne's court were John Scotus Eriugena (810–877), the most original philosopher of the period. The empire survived Charlemagne mainly in name (attached to minor princes without imperial power), but its legislation imposing educational responsibilities on monasteries and cathedrals was responsible for the emergence of the university from cathedral schools.

Recovery began in the eleventh century when the ad hoc pattern of local agreements that characterized the previous two centuries became formalized as the feudal system. Toward the end of the century Pope Gregory VII initiated a reform of the church with the aim of diminishing secular influence in the appointment of church officials. The "investiture conflict" (1075–1122) was the first episode in a titanic and extended struggle between pope and emperor: the issue is whether secular rulers should have the right to invest bishops with the symbols of office. In the twelfth century the university appeared, either as a guild of students, as at Bologna, or as a guild of masters, as at Paris. Bologna became a center of law, both Roman law (revived by Irnerius) and canon law (founded by Gratian's *Decretum* [1140]), while Paris emphasized theology. In the thirteenth century the Church, reaching the pinnacle of its power, took on many of the characteristics of an international state. This century, too, struggled with the revolutionary impact of the recovery of Aristotle's writings.

The fourteenth century was again calamitous: serious famines early in the century, the Black Death at midcentury with an estimated death toll of one-third of the population, and the outbreak of the Hundred Years' War (1337 to 1453). Accompanying these misfortunes was a continuing decline in respect for and authority of the Church, provoked by the "Avignon papacy" (1305–1377) and then intensified by the scandal of the Schism (1378–1417), when two and sometimes three popes reigned. Calls for reform became widespread; at the beginning of the fifteenth century the "Conciliar Movement" (so called for its aim of making the pope accountable to a representative Council of Church members) succeeded in ending the Schism, but it failed to achieve the wider goals of Church reform.

A central problem for the Middle Ages was that of authority, raising itself sometimes in theological form, sometimes political, but always philosophical. In the eleventh century it was formulated as a methodological problem of theology—to what extent reason (dialectic or logic) could be used to interpret the word of God. Whether a logical critique of revelation is permissible was disputed into the twelfth century; indeed Abelard was charged with blasphemous application of reason to matters of faith. But by then the problem was becoming the competition between philosophy and theology. A crisis came with the rediscovery and translation of Aristotle's texts, for Aristotelianism was a comprehensive but naturalistic view that at significant points clashed with Christianity. The Church's repeated efforts to ban Aristotle proved futile: by the middle of the thirteenth century a vigorous school in Paris, Averroist Aristotelians, defended philosophy as the equal of theology. In this situation of institutional and faculty rivalries at the University of Paris, Thomas Aquinas undertook his monumental synthesis of Aristotle and Christian theology. A few years after Aquinas's death the Thomistic confidence in the reach of human reason was replaced by an appreciation of the limits of reason and a return to revelation.

A further problem of authority was political, namely, the conflicts of ecclesiastical and secular jurisdictions. Obedience to lawfully constituted authority had been long held a Christian obligation: "Render unto Caesar the things that are Caesar's, and unto God the things that are God's" (Matt. 22). Paul had offered a more elaborate statement of the obligation of civil obedience:

Let every soul be subject unto the higher powers. For there is no power but of God: the powers that be are ordained of God. Whosoever therefore resisteth the power, resisteth the ordinance of God; and they that resist shall receive to themselves damnation. For rulers are not a terror to good works, but to the evil. [Rom. 13:1–3]

The idea of two domains of authority, spiritual and temporal, fitted readily the Christian distinction between the flesh and the spirit. But the doctrine resulted in endless controversy as the two legal systems fought to expand their jurisdiction. In practice the domains overlapped: the pope crowned the emperor; the emperor in turn claimed the right to participate in the appointment of church officials. Issues of jurisdiction were pervasive: inside the Church, between pope, bishops, clerics, monastic orders, and laity; on the secular side, between emperor, feudal lords, and feudal vassals. Further, bishops often held secular office and owed allegiance to two different hierarchies. While in theory feudalism was pyramidal in structure, in practice the lines of allegiance overlapped in complex and ever-shifting ways.

The complex relationships characteristic of feudalism required an equally complex theory of property. We now speak of the feudal "system" and the manorial "system," but these were essentially personal and local arrangements with both economic and political dimensions. The manor was a largely self-sufficient agricultural community. Tenants owed the manorial lord crops, labor, and military support. In return, he granted tenants a plot of land, provided protection, and settled disputes. But the lord did not "own" the manor. He possessed it under the protection of a higher lord, and he was constrained by the traditional

rights of his vassals. Medievals used the term *dominium* for ownership, but it no longer could mean what it meant in Roman law—the right to use, to enjoy, and to dispose of freely, what we might call "outright ownership." In feudalism many people could have different rights to the same piece of land—one the right to live on it, another to lease, another to grow crops, another to bequeath, and so on. Each had an ownership right, but each was severely constrained by rights of the others.

The medieval treatment of property illustrates how thoroughly the moral domain pervades institutions and that a variety of sanctions are available for enforcing morality. Some practices fell within the jurisdiction of the "external forum," which included ecclesiastical and secular courts, and were enforced by legal penalties. Usury, defined by Gratian as "demanding back more than is given," was absolutely forbidden: to charge interest seemed simply exploitation of misery. Specific rules were developed to govern the marketplace. "Forestalling" (getting to the market before it was open to the public and buying before others have had the opportunity to buy) and "engrossing" (cornering the market) were condemned. The necessity of trade was acknowledged, but economic rewards should be commensurate to the labor, the risk, and the skill involved. It was considered wrong to sell an object for a higher price than one has paid to acquire it, without in any way improving it. Ecclesiastical courts were empowered to reverse a transaction where the price required by the seller was more than one and a half times the common market price.[1]

In the "internal forum"—the forum of conscience, the domain of the theologian rather than the lawyer—moral obligations were

[1] See John W. Baldwin, *The Medieval Theories of the Just Price* (Philadelphia: American Philosophical Society, 1959). This standard arose from a particular provision in Roman law, *laesio enormis*, which originally protected only an orphan selling land. Canon and Roman lawyers gradually extended it to include any buyer and any item of transaction.

enforced privately and without the public sanction of law. Here the standard of just price was what people required to maintain themselves in the necessities of their positions in life, and here also the medieval commonplace that the wealthy had obligations to the poor was enforced.

Two different Christian views of property were in contention. The moderate view was that property is natural; only its misuse is wrong. The radical view was that poverty is the ideal Christian way of life; the very possession of property is a moral evil. Monasticism represents a partial compromise: an ascetic life—of seclusion, fasting, celibacy, prayer, and nonownership—is an especially worthy choice of life, but it is not an obligation. A double code of morality thus arose, one for ordinary Christians and one, "counsels of perfection," for those who sought a more perfect life. These counsels of perfection became institutionalized as the rules of conduct for monastic orders.

The monastic life, as a natural experiment in moral living, had an enduring impact on the Christian view of morality. In the experience of the cloistered life the classification of "deadly sins" originated—pride, avarice, anger, gluttony, unchastity, envy, vainglory, gloominess, and languid indifference. Although such sins had different relevance to different categories of Christians—the lay person was to be chaste, but not necessarily celibate; the cleric and the monk were to be celibate, but the cleric need not take a vow of poverty—these categories became an established taxonomy for moral theory and, especially as formulated in penitential manuals that list sins and appropriate penances as guides in the confessional, shifted morality toward the juridical.

Running counter to this legalistic view of morality was the Judeo-Christian emphasis on inwardness. *Why* people do what they do is more important than what they do. Throughout medieval thought there is a deep-lying tension between those who emphasize love and

inward motivation, as did Augustine, and those who emphasize law and right conduct. The selection from Abelard presents arguments for the inward side—the sole basis of moral evaluation is intention. He is willing to accept as a consequence that the grounds of reward and punishment in this life are different from those of ultimate rewards and punishments. This obviously threatens the Church's claim to act as God's agent, for any slippage between the judgments it makes and God's judgment threatens to undermine its authority.

The distinctive medieval or scholastic method is early employed in Abelard's textbook, *Sic et Non* (*Yes and No*), as a pedagogical method by which conflicts of authorities are presented.[2] Thus his question 157, "That it is lawful to kill a man, and not," cites Jerome, Augustine, Isidore, and Pope Nicholas for the affirmative, and Cyprian and Augustine (again) for the negative. After Abelard the method turns into a way of reconciling authorities: it is used thus in what were to become the standard textbooks of the age, Gratian's *Decretum* in law (significantly, its full name is "The Concordance of Discordant Canons") and Peter Lombard's *Four Books of Sentences* (1150) in theology.

Medieval philosophers tended to argue from authorities; when faced with an authority they disagreed with, rather than reject it outright, they would make a distinction to preserve the wording while changing the meaning, much as a lawyer today treats an unwelcome precedent. Complexities multiplied when the disagreements among sources were great, as on the issue of natural law. In Roman law opinions on natural law included: "that which all animals have been taught by nature" (Ulpian), "what natural reason has established among all men" (Gaius), "what is common among

---

[2] We are pleased to collect together different sayings of the holy Fathers that give rise to questioning from their apparent disagreement, in order that they may provoke readers to the utmost effort in inquiring into the truth and to make them sharper from the inquiry. [Prologue]

all peoples" (Gaius), and "that which is under all circumstances fair and right" (Paulus). In canon law Gratian seemed to identify natural law and divine law.[3] But he also seemed to agree with Gaius and with Ulpian.[4] In Stoicism Cicero identified natural law with reason, while Christians readily saw in Seneca's primitive golden age, where there were no distinctions of property or status, the time before the Fall. The multiplicity of sources set the terms for medieval discussion: what is the relation of natural law to divine law, to the law of peoples, to reason, and to natural instincts?

The selection from Aquinas (Chapter 6) is a systematic account of the relationship of various kinds of law. This is not just a matter of jurisprudence but signals a fundamental philosophical-theological problem. Aquinas argues that both natural and divine law are expressions of the one basic law established by God, namely, the eternal law. Hence they had to be consistent with one another. Theologians, however, were well aware of instances in the Bible where God seemed to approve of adultery, theft, lying, and homicide. This raises questions about the nature of a law. The medievals formulated the problem as: Does law bind because of what it says or because of who imposes it? Is it right because God commands it, or does God command it because it is right?

Positions on these questions in the later Middle Ages line up as *intellectualism* or *voluntarism*. The scope of the conflict is immense. For intellectualists, God's law is the expression of God's intellect, whose object is truth. Therefore, the moral law must be rational, and the

intellect, both in God and in human beings, is superior to the will, capable of comprehending what is right and of commanding the will to seek it. The will necessarily seeks the good, and when it acts incorrectly it is because the intellect has been deceived by appearances. Since the moral law expresses the rational rather than the volitional nature of God, morality must be to some extent accessible to the human intellect.

For voluntarists, if God is not free to designate without limit anything as right or wrong, then God's omnipotence is endangered. Moral law, as it is revealed, is binding simply because it is God's will. Had God chosen otherwise, the law then revealed would bind us with equal force. Thus religion is prior to ethics. (In the example of Abraham, if God asked Abraham to sacrifice his son, then the very request makes it right.) When voluntarists discuss God's intellect and will they are also laying down a view of the relation of the human intellect to human will. Here they take the position that the will could not be free unless it were independent of the intellect: if the will must choose the good as it is presented by the intellect, then how can human beings be said to be free in their choices and hence responsible?

Metaphysically, voluntarists tend toward nominalism—the view that only individuals, not essences or general natures, exist. Where Aquinas argues that by consulting the general nature of a human being one can determine indirectly what God expects of us, for voluntarists there is no human nature as such, no shared essence. It follows that what is right for all human beings cannot be decided by consulting the characteristics of some general human nature. Epistemologically, nominalists deny the capacity of the intellect to apprehend general categories. If there is no human nature, then the concept of human nature is merely a similarity-class induced from observing individuals.

Voluntarism, then, combines a theological view of the nature of God, a theory of human

---

[3] The law of nature is that contained in the law and the Gospels, by which each is ordered to do to another what he wishes to be done to himself, and is prohibited from inflicting on another what he does not wish done to himself. [Dist I]

[4] Natural law is common to all peoples, in that it is held by the instinct of nature, not by any enactment, as for example, the union of man and woman, the generation and rearing of children, the common possession of all things and the one liberty of all men, the acquisition of those things which are taken from air and sky and sea, the restitution of an article given in trust or money loaned, and the repelling of force with force. [Dist I, canon 7]

nature, a theory of moral responsibility, and a theory of law. The last, when applied to political theory, is associated with the view that the will of the sovereign is the sole source of human law. The ultimate transformation of the medieval political order into independent sovereign states, each wielding absolute authority within its domain, can find ready justification in voluntarist political theory. Writing toward the close of the Middle Ages, William Ockham defended the voluntarist position against Aquinas on every front.

The voluntarist movement also marks the beginnings of a shift in focus from natural law to natural rights. Natural law is a system of God's universal prescriptions for mankind; from it individual rights and obligations are derived. Natural rights are primary rights with which the individual is endowed. Natural law theory tends to analyze moral questions from the point of view of duties and obligations; natural rights theories emphasize the rights of individuals.

Dating the exact moment at which the shift from natural law to natural rights occurs is a fine point of historical scholarship that is much debated.[5] Tracing the shift is made especially difficult by the fact that the shift takes place through a change in meaning in the notoriously ambiguous word *ius* (or *jus*), translatable as "law" or "right." Thus, *ius naturale* is translatable both as "natural law" and "natural right." Further, "right" itself is ambiguous. In the sense of "objective right," it connotes correctness or rightness; as "subjective right," it is a property of individuals, it is something we *have*, and it is this latter sense that is required for natural rights.

Clearly the prevailing interpretation in the thirteenth century is natural law. Aquinas, for example, discusses *ius* under his treatment of the virtue justice: " 'Right' (*ius*) or 'just' (*ius-*

tum) is a work that is matched (*adaequatum*) to another person according to some kind of equality."[6] He grants that *ius* has several meanings. Its primary meaning is "to signify the just thing itself," and then derivatively to "the art by which what is just can be known, and further to denote the place in which what is right (*ius*) is rendered . . . and further it is said that right (*ius*) is that which is rendered by one who has the office of administering justice."[7] There is here no indication that *ius* is the kind of thing that might be possessed by persons.

It is also clear that by the seventeenth century the shift has occurred and natural rights theory is well under way. Hugo Grotius (1583–1635) observes that *ius* has many meanings. In one sense it designates "that which is lawful." But the other senses include one that "concerns the person. In this sense, right [*ius*] is a moral *quality* of a person by which the person is enabled rightfully to possess something or to do something."[8] And in the same century Thomas Hobbes was to build a modern political theory on the distinction:

The names *lex* and *ius*, that is to say, law and right, are often confounded, and yet scarce are there two words of more contrary signification. For right is that liberty that law leaves us; and laws those restraints by which we agree mutually to abridge one another's liberty.[9]

Between the thirteenth century and the seventeenth many writers contributed to the shift. Francisco Suarez (1548–1617), for example, insisted on a distinction between *lex naturalis* and *ius naturale* [10] and claimed that the "true, strict

---

[5] See Richard Tuck, *Natural Rights Theories: Their Origin and Development* (New York: Cambridge University Press, 1979), and John Finnis, *Natural Law and Natural Rights* (Oxford: Clarendon Press, 1980), chapter 8.

[6] *Summa Theologica* IIaIIae, q 57, art 2 (translation by the editors of this volume).
[7] Ibid. art 1, ad 1.
[8] *De Jure Belli ac Pacis* (Paris, 1625), Bk I, ch II, 3–4 (translation by the editors of this volume.) The difficulty of translating *ius* (or *jure*) is especially acute for Grotius's title; some modern translators have rendered it as *The Law of War and Peace* and others as *The Rights of War and Peace*.
[9] *Elements of Law* II, 10. Also see *Leviathan*, ch 14.
[10] *De Legibus ac Deo Legislatore* (1612), II, ch 17.

and proper meaning" of *ius* is "a certain moral ability [*facultas*] which every man has, either over his own property or with respect to that which is due to him." [11] In analyzing *ius* as a *facultas*, Suarez was looking back at Jean Gerson (1363–1429), a follower of Ockham and a central figure in the voluntarist movement. As early as 1402 Gerson had defined *ius* as

a dispositional *facultas* or power [*potestas*], appropriate to someone and in accordance with the dictates of right reason. . . . This definition includes 'facultas or power,' since many things are in accordance with right reason which do not count as *iura* [rights] of those that have them, such as penalties for the damned or punishment for mortal sin.[12]

[11] Ibid. II, ch 2, 5 (translation by the editors of this volume).
[12] Quoted in Tuck, p. 25. It is with Gerson, Tuck believes, that the theory of natural rights fully emerges for the first time.

In regarding *ius* as a "power" Gerson, in turn, was following the lead of Ockham in *Work of Ninety Days* (see Chapter 6). Here we observe a revolutionary conceptual change taking place that required several centuries to accomplish. The terms by which the analysis of *ius* is given shifts from "the just thing itself" (Aquinas), to "power" (Ockham), then to "ability" (Gerson and Suarez), then to "quality" (Grotius), and finally, to liberty (Hobbes).

With Ockham's work in the fourteenth century we are still far from the full-bodied theory of natural rights developed by John Locke (see Chapter 9) and put to revolutionary uses in the eighteenth century (see Chapter 11), and from the dominant role rights theory achieves in the twentieth century (see Chapter 23). But in Ockham we can see the infancy of a new concept that is destined for a remarkable career.

6

Intention, Law, and Will: Abelard, Aquinas, Ockham

We present medieval ethics through the works of three figures, one from the twelfth, one from the thirteenth, and one from the fourteenth century, and each the dominating philosophical personality of his time. To the modern eye their similarities may be more salient than their differences: all three shared a Christian perspective; all three wrote as theologians as well as philosophers; and all three saw ethics as having a transcendent dimension. Yet they are very different. Abelard's brief foray into ethics takes the single task of establishing the role of intention (or consent) as the paramount ethical category. By contrast, the others treat ethics as part of a vaster philosophical project—in Aquinas's case, to establish the reach of reason, and in Ockham's case, to establish the independence of the will.

Peter Abelard
(1079–1142)

Abelard arrived in Paris just as the institution of the university was evolving from the previous cathedral schools, and he made his reputation within that university. Like a Socratic gadfly he delighted in challenging and provoking the defenders of orthodox opinion and incited many to bitter enmity, incurring along the way several condemnations for heresy. His contributions to philosophy ranged from logic and metaphysics to educational theory and ethics. Implicit in his influential *Sic et Non* was a challenge to settling arguments by credulous appeal to authorities, since he showed how authorities could be lined up on several sides of the issue. *Sic et Non* directly influenced the two most important works of the twelfth century: Gratian's *Decretum* and Peter Lombard's *Four Books of Sentences* (c.1150).

In *Ethics or Know Thyself* Abelard comes closer to an ethics of pure intention than anyone in premodern philosophy. God judges the heart, not the deed, and not just what people want to do or are inclined to do, for that comes by nature. Sin lies not in the act, nor in the injury done, but in the contempt it shows for God. Virtue cannot be external obedience to rules, it is in living for the love of God. The brief Chapter 5 asks whether it could ever be just to punish an innocent person, an issue that was to plague utilitarianism later. To Abelard the context of the issue is original sin—if, as he believes, we are not guilty of it (since we have not consented to it), is it then just that we suffer the penalty? His analysis is radical: although not guilty, we nonetheless properly suffer its penalties; the grounds for divine punishment must be distinguished from those for this-worldly punishment.

Ethics or Know Thyself [1]

[Prologue] In the study of morals we deal with the defects or qualities of mind which dispose us to bad or good actions. Defects and qualities are not only mental, but also physical. There is bodily weakness; there is also the endurance which we call strength. There is sluggishness or speed; blindness or sight. When we now speak of defects, therefore, we pre-suppose defects of the mind, so as to distinguish them from the physical ones. The defects of the mind are opposed to the qualities; injustice to justice; cowardice to constancy; intemperance to temperance.

[1] Certain defects or merits of mind have no connection with morals. They do not make human life a matter of praise or blame. Such are dull wits or quick insight; a good or a bad memory; ignorance or knowledge. Each of these features is found in good and bad alike. They have nothing to do with the system of morals, nor with making life base or honourable. To exclude these we safeguarded above the phrase 'defects of mind' by adding 'which dispose to bad actions,' that is, those defects which incline the will to what least of all either should be done or should be left undone.

[2] Defect of this mental kind is not the same thing as sin. Sin, too, is not the same as a bad action. For example, to be irascible, that is, prone or easily roused to the agitation of anger is a defect and moves the mind to unpleasantly impetuous and irrational action. This defect, however, is in the mind so that the mind is liable to wrath, even when

it is not actually roused to it. Similarly, lameness, by reason of which a man is said to be lame, is in the man himself even when he does not walk and reveal his lameness. For the defect is there though action be lacking. So, also, nature or constitution renders many liable to luxury. Yet they do not sin because they are like this, but from this very fact they have the material of a struggle whereby they may, in the virtue of temperance, triumph over themselves and win the crown. . . .

[3] Defect, then, is that whereby we are disposed to sin. We are, that is, inclined to consent to what we ought not to do, or to leave undone what we ought to do. Consent of this kind we rightly call sin. Here is the reproach of the soul meriting damnation or being declared guilty by God. What is that consent but to despise God and to violate his laws? God cannot be set at enmity by injury, but by contempt. He is the highest power, and is not diminished by any injury, but He avenges contempt of Himself. Our sin, therefore, is contempt of the Creator. To sin is to despise the Creator; that is, not to do for Him what we believe we should do for Him, or, not to renounce what we think should be renounced on His behalf. We have defined sin negatively by saying it means not doing or not renouncing what we ought to do or renounce. Clearly, then, we have shown that sin has no reality. It exists rather in *not being* than in *being*. Similarly we could define shadows by saying: The absence of light where light usually is.

Perhaps you object that sin is the desire or will to do an evil deed, and that this will or desire condemns us before God in the same way as the will to do a good deed justifies us. . . .

But diligent attention will show that we must think far otherwise of this point. We frequently err; and from no evil will at all. Indeed, the evil will itself, when restrained, though it may not be quenched, procures the palm-wreath for those who resist it. It provides, not merely the materials for combat, but also the crown of glory. It should be spoken of rather as a certain inevitable weakness than as sin. Take, for example, the case of an innocent servant whose harsh master is moved with fury against him. He pursues the servant, drawing his sword with intent to kill him. For a while the servant flies and avoids death as best he can. At last, forced all unwillingly to it, he kills his master so as not to be killed by him. Let anyone say what

---

[1] The selection is from *Abailard's Ethics*, translated by J. Ramsay McCallum (Oxford: Basil Blackwell, 1935).

sort of evil will there was in this deed. His will was only to flee from death and preserve his own life. Was this an evil will? You reply: 'I do not think this was an evil will. But the will that he had to kill the master who was pursuing him was evil.' Your answer would be admirable and acute if you could show that the servant really willed what you say that he did. But, as I insisted, he was unwillingly forced to his deed. He protracted his master's life as long as he could, knowing that danger also threatened his own life from such a crime. How, then, was a deed done voluntarily by which he incurred danger to his own life?

Your reply may be that the action was voluntary because the man's will was to escape death even though it may not have been to kill his master. This charge might easily be preferred against him. I do not rebut it. Nevertheless, as has been said, that will by which he sought to evade death, as you urge, and not to kill his master, cannot at all be condemned as bad. He did, however, fail by consenting, though driven to it through fear of death, to an unjust murder which he ought rather to have endured than committed. Of his own will, I mean, he took the sword. . . . By his rashness he risked the death and damnation of his soul. The servant's wish, then, was not to kill his master, but to avoid death. Because he *consented*, however, as he should not have done, to murder, this wrongful consent preceding the crime was sin.

Someone may interpose: 'But you cannot conclude that he wished to kill his master because, in order to escape death, he was willing to kill his master. I might say to a man; I am willing for you to have my cape so that you may give me five shillings. Or, I am glad for you to have it at this price. But I do not hand it over because I desire you to have possession of it.' No, and if a man in prison desired under duresse, to put his son there in his place that he might secure his own ransom, should we therefore admit that he wished to send his son to prison?

It was only with many a tear and groan that he consented to such a course.

The fact is that this kind of will, existing with much internal regret, is not, if I may so say, *will*, but a passive submission of mind. It is so because the man wills one thing on account of another. He puts up with *this* because he really desires *that*. A patient is said to submit to cautery or lancet that he may obtain health. . . .

Sin, therefore, is sometimes committed without an evil will. Thus sin cannot be defined as 'will.' True, you will say, when we sin under constraint, but not when we sin willingly, for instance, when we will to do something which we know ought not to be done by us. There the evil will and sin seem to be the same thing. For example, a man sees a woman; his concupiscence is aroused; his mind is enticed by fleshly lust and stirred to base desire. This wish, this lascivious longing, what else can it be, you say, than sin?

I reply: What if that wish may be bridled by the power of temperance? What if its nature is never to be entirely extinguished but to persist in struggle and not fully fail even in defeat? For where is the battle if the antagonist is away? . . . Now, for a contest, an opponent is needed who will resist, not one who simply submits. This opponent is our evil will over which we triumph when we subjugate it to the divine will. But we do not entirely destroy it. . . .

You will say, what merit have we with God in acting willingly or unwillingly? Certainly none: I reply. He weighs the intention rather than the deed in his recompense. Nor does the deed, whether it proceed from a good or an evil will, add anything to the merit, as we shall show shortly. . . .

When the Scripture says: 'Go not after your own desires' (Eccles, xviii, 30), and 'Turn from your own will' (ibid.), it instructs us not to fulfill our desires. Yet it does not say that we are to be wholly without them. It is vicious to give in to our desires; but not to have any desires at all is impossible for our weak nature.

The sin, then, consists not in desiring a woman, but in consent to the desire, and not the wish for whoredom, but the consent to the wish is damnation.

Let us see how our conclusions about sexual intemperance apply to theft. A man crosses another's garden. At the sight of the delectable fruit his desire is aroused. He does not, however, give way to desire so as to take anything by theft or rapine, although his mind was moved to strong inclination by the thought of the delight of eating. Where there is desire, there, without doubt, will exists. The man desires the eating of that fruit wherein he doubts not that there will be delight. The weakness of nature in this man is compelled to desire the fruit which, without the master's permission, he has no right to take. He conquers the desire, but does not extinguish it. Since, however, he is not enticed into consent, he does not descend to sin.

. . . It should be clear from such instances, that the wish or desire itself of doing what is not seemly is never to be called sin, but rather, as we said, the consent is sin. We consent to what is not seemly when we do not draw ourselves back from such a deed, and are prepared, should opportunity offer, to perform it completely. Whoever is discovered in this intention, though his guilt has yet to be completed in deed, is already guilty before God in so far as he strives with all his might to sin, and accomplishes within himself, as the blessed Augustine reminds us, as much as if he were actually taken in the act. . . .

Some are intensely indignant when they hear us assert that the act of sinning adds nothing to guilt or damnation before God. Their contention is that in this act of sinning a certain delight supervenes, which increases the sin, as in sexual intercourse or indulgence in food which we referred to above. Their statement is absurd unless they can prove that physical delight of this kind is itself sin, and that such pleasure cannot be taken without a sin being thereby committed. If it be as they suppose, then no one is permitted to enjoy physical pleasure. The married do not escape sin when they employ their physical privilege; nor yet the man who eats with relish his own fruits. . . .

. . . Another objection is that matrimonial intercourse and the eating of tasty food are only allowed on condition of being taken without pleasure. But, if this is so, then they are allowed to be done in a way in which they never can be done. That concession is not reasonable which concedes that a thing shall be so done as it is certain that it cannot be done. . . . Hence, I think it is plain that no natural physical delight can be set down as sin, nor can it be called guilt for men to delight in what, when it is done, must involve the feeling of delight.

For example, if anyone obliged a monk, bound in chains, to lie among women, and the monk by the softness of the couch and by contact with his fair flatterers is allured into delight, though not into consent, who shall presume to designate guilt the delight which is naturally awakened? . . .

We come, then, to this conclusion, that no one who sets out to assert that all fleshly desire is sin may say that the sin itself is increased by the doing of it. For this would mean extending the consent of the soul into the exercise of the action. In short,

one would be stained not only by consent to baseness, but also by the mire of the deed, as if what happens externally in the body could possibly soil the soul. Sin is not, therefore, increased by the doing of an action: and nothing mars the soul except what is of its own nature, namely consent. . . .

Certain acts which ought not to be done often are done, and without any sin, when, for instance, they are committed under force or ignorance. No one, I think, ignores this fact. A woman under constraint of violence, lies with another's husband. A man, taken by some trick, sleeps with one whom he supposed to be his wife, or kills a man, in the belief that he himself has the right to be both judge and executioner. Thus to desire the wife of another or actually to lie with her is not sin. But to consent to that desire or to that action is sin. . . .

Careful account will reveal that wherever actions are restricted by some precept or prohibition, these refer rather to will and consent than to the deeds themselves. Otherwise nothing relative to a person's moral merit could be included under a precept. Indeed, actions are so much the less worth prescribing as they are less in our power to do. At the same time, many things we are forbidden to do for which there exists in our will both the inclination and the consent.

The Lord God says: 'Thou shalt not kill. Thou shalt not bear false witness.' (Deut. v, 17, 20.) If we accept these cautions as being only about actions, as the words suggest, then guilt is not forbidden, but simply the activity of guilt. For we have seen that actions may be carried out without sin, as that it is not sin to kill a man or to lie with another's wife. And even the man who desires to bear false testimony, and is willing to utter it, so long as he is silent for some reason and does not speak, is innocent before the law, that is, if the prohibition in this matter be accepted literally of the action. It is not said that we should not *wish* to give false witness, or that we should not *consent* in bearing it, but simply that we should not bear false witness.

Similarly, when the law forbids us to marry or have intercourse with our sisters, if this prohibition relates to deed rather than to intention, no one can keep the commandment, for a sister, unless we recognize her, is just a woman. If a man, then, marries his sister in error, is he a transgressor for doing what the law forbade? He is not, you will reply, because, in acting ignorantly in what he did, he did not consent to a transgression. Thus a transgressor is not one who *does* what is prohibited. He is one who *consents* to what is prohibited. The prohibition is, therefore, not about action, but about consent. It is as though in saying: 'Do not do this or that' we meant: 'Do not consent to do this or that,' or 'Do not wittingly do this.'

Blessed Augustine, in his careful view of this question, reduces every sin or command to terms of charity and covetousness, and not to works. 'The law,' he says, 'inculcates nothing but charity, and forbids nothing but covetousness.' The Apostle, also, asserts: 'All the law is contained in one word: thou shalt love thy neighbour as thyself,' (Rom. xiii, 8, 10), and again, 'Love is the fulfilling of the law.' (ibid.)

Whether you actually give alms to a needy person, or charity makes you ready to give, makes no difference to the merit of the deed. The will may be there when the opportunity is not. Nor does it rest entirely with you to deal with every case of need which you encounter. Actions which are right and actions which are far from right are done by good and bad men alike. The intention alone separates the two classes of men. . . .

God considers not the action, but the spirit of the action. It is the intention, not the deed wherein the merit or praise of the doer consists. Often, indeed, the same action is done from different motives: for justice sake by one man, for an evil reason by another. Two men, for instance, hang a guilty person. The one does it out of zeal for justice; the other in resentment for an earlier enmity. The action of hanging is the same. Both men do what is good and what justice demands. Yet the diversity of their intentions causes the same deed to be done from different motives, in the one case good, in the other bad. . . .

. . . Who does not agree that sometimes what God forbids may rightly be done, while, contrarily, He may counsel certain things which of all things are least convenient? We note how He forbade certain miracles, whereby He had healed infirmities, to be made public. He set an example of humility lest any man should claim glory for the grace bestowed on him. Nevertheless, the recipients of those benefits did not cease to broadcast them, to the praise of Him who had done such things, and yet had forbidden them to be revealed. Thus we read: 'As much as He bade them not to speak, so much the more did they publish abroad, etc.' Will

you judge these men guilty of a fault who acted contrary to the command which they had received, and did so wittingly? Who can acquit them of wrongdoing, unless by finding that they did not act out of contempt for the One who commanded, but decided to do what was to His honour? How, then, did the matter stand? Did Christ command what ought not to have been commanded? Or, did the newly-healed men disobey when they should have obeyed? The command was a good thing; yet it was not good for it to be obeyed.

In the case of Abraham, also, you will accuse God for first enjoining the sacrifice of Abraham's son, and then revoking the command. Has, then, God never *wisely commanded* anything which, if *it had come about*, would not have been good? If good, you will object, why was it afterwards forbidden? But conceive that it was good for the same thing to be prescribed and also to be prohibited. God, we know, permits nothing, and does not himself consent to achieve anything apart from rational cause. Thus it is the pure intention of the command, not the execution of the action which justifies God in wisely commanding what would not in actual fact be good. God did not intend Abraham to sacrifice his son, or command this sacrifice to be put into effect. His aim was to test Abraham's obedience, constancy of faith, and love towards Him, so that these qualities should be left to us as an example. . . . There was a right intention on God's part; but it was not right for it to be put in practice. The prohibition, too, in the case of the miracles of healing was right. The object of this prohibition was not for it to be obeyed, but for an example to be given to our weak spirit in avoiding empty applause. God, in the one case enjoined an action which, if obeyed, would not have been good. In the other case, He forbade what was worth putting into fact, namely, a knowledge of Christ's miracles. The intention excuses Him in the first matter, just as the intention excuses the men who, in the second instance, were healed and did not carry out his injunction. They knew that the precept was not given to be practised, but in order that the aforenamed example of moderation in a successful miracle might be set. In keeping, then, the spirit of the command they showed, by actually disobeying no contempt for Him with whose intention they knew that they were acting.

A scrutiny of the deed rather than of the intention

will reveal, then, cases where men frequently not only wish to go against God's bidding, but carry their wish knowingly into effect, and do so without any guilt of sin. An action or a wish must not be called bad because it does not in actual fact fall in with God's command. It may well be that the doer's intention does not at all differ from the will of his divine superior. The intention exonerates Him who gave a practically unseemly command: the intention excuses the man who, out of kindness, disobeyed the command to conceal the miracle.

Briefly to summarize the above argument: Four things were postulated which must be carefully distinguished from one another.

1. Imperfection of soul, making us liable to sin.
2. Sin itself, which we decided is consent to evil or contempt of God.
3. The will or desire of evil.
4. The evil deed.

To wish is not the same thing as to fulfil a wish. Equally, to sin is not the same as to carry out a sin. In the first case, we sin by consent of the soul: the second is a matter of the external effect of an action, namely, when we fulfil in deed that whereunto we have previously consented. . . .

[5] 'The sinful action is not strictly sin; it adds nothing to the sum of sin.' Our axiom, so enunciated, falls on dissentient ears. 'Why, then,' it is asked, 'give a more severe penance for sins of commission than for guilty thoughts?' But let them reflect whether sometimes a grave penance be not imposed where no guilt called for pardon. Are there not times when we must punish those whom we know to be innocent?

A poor woman has a child at the breast. She lacks the clothing needful for herself and for the babe in the cradle. Prompted by pity, she lays the infant in her own bed so as to cherish him with her clothes. Nature, however, overcomes her, and, in sleep, she stifles the child whom she yet embraces with the greatest love. 'Have love,' says Augustine, 'and do as thou wilt.' Yet when she goes to the bishop for penance, a heavy penalty is pronounced upon her, not for the fault, but that she herself a second time, and other women, may be more careful in such a situation.

Again, a man may be accused by his enemies

before the judge, and a charge made against him whereof the judge knows that the man is innocent. His enemies, however, persist and are importunate for a hearing. On the appointed day they begin the case and adduce false witnesses to get their man convicted. By no clear reasons can the judge take exception to these witnesses; and he is compelled by law to admit them. Their proof prevails. The judge has to punish an innocent man who ought not to be punished. The accused merited no penalty; but the judge, justly in the legal aspect, had to impose one. Plainly, therefore, a man may frequently be the subject of a justifiable sentence without the anterior fault. Is it any wonder, then, if there be preceding guilt, that the subsequent act of crime should increase the penalty required by men in this life, although the guilt and not the act of crime is what begets the penalty required by God in a future life? Men judge of visible, and not of invisible fact. They do not estimate the error, so much as the effect of an action. God alone considers the spirit in which a thing is done, rather than merely what is done. He weighs accurately the guilt in our intention, and assesses our fault by a true test. . . . In punishing sin he regards not the work, but the will. We, contrarily, regard not the will, which we do not see, but the work which we do see. Frequently, therefore, by mistake, or, as we have said, under stress of law, we punish the innocent or acquit the guilty. . . .

[7] . . . We punish facts rather than faults. Injury to the soul we do not regard as so much a matter for punishment as injury to others. Our object is to avoid public mischief, rather than to correct personal mistakes. The Lord said to Peter: 'If thy brother sin against thee, correct him between thyself and him.' (Matt. xviii, 15.) 'Sin against thee.' Is the meaning here that we ought to correct and punish injuries done to us and not those done to others, as though 'against thee' meant 'not against another'? By no means. The phrase 'if he sins against thee' means that he acts publicly so as to corrupt you by his example. For if he sins against himself only, his sin, being hidden, involves in guilt merely the man himself. The sin does not, by the sinner's bad example, induce others to indiscretion. Although the evil action has no imitators, or even none who recognize it as wrong, nevertheless, in so far as it is a public act it must, in human society, be chastised more than private guilt, because it can

occasion greater mischief, and can be more destructive, by the example it sets, than the hidden failing. Everything which is likely to lead to common loss or to public harm must be punished by a greater requital. Where a sin involves more serious injury the penalty must therefore be heavier. The greater the social stumbling-block, the more stringent must be the social correction, even though the original guilt be relatively light. . . .

The punishment of public guilt is not so much a debt paid to justice as the exercise of economy. We consult the common interest, as has been said by checking social mischief. Frequently we punish minor misdeeds with major penalties. In doing so, we do not, in a spirit of pure justice ponder what guilt preceded; but, by shrewd foresight, we estimate the damage which may ensue if the deed be lightly dealt with. We reserve, therefore, sins of the soul for the divine judgment. But the effect of these sins, about which we have to determine, we follow up, by our own judgment, employing a certain economy, that is, the rule of prudence referred to above, rather than the precept of equity.

Thomas Aquinas
(1225–1274)

Aquinas was born near Naples to an illustrious family. Their ambition for him was that he should become abbot of Monte Cassino, and at the age of five he was sent to the abbey for his education. At ten he attended the University of Naples, where he became acquainted with the Dominicans, a mendicant order then considerably less prestigious than the Benedictines of Monte Cassino. Despite energetic family opposition, he joined the Dominicans and traded the high ecclesiastical office his family had envisioned for a lifelong career of teaching and writing. After study with Albert the Great (c.1200–1280), he began teaching in 1252 at the University of Paris, lecturing on philosophy and theology. He engaged in the central intellectual struggles of the day, but apart from that his life was uneventful. He died at the

age of forty-seven; in that short time he produced an astonishingly large number of major works. To this day his influence is profound, especially in scholastic philosophy where his adherents continue to identify themselves as Thomists. In the twentieth century Thomism was declared the official philosophy of the Catholic church.

Just prior to Aquinas's arrival in Paris the impact of the recovery of Aristotle's physical and metaphysical works—which had been preserved by Arab scholars—was beginning to be felt. On specific points Aristotle contradicted Christian belief. For example, he believed the world must be eternal, thereby denying the doctrine of Creation. More threatening to medieval belief than specific points of doctrinal disagreement was that Aristotelian naturalism provided a comprehensive competitor to supernatural religion. As positions were lined up when Aquinas came to Paris, the two extremes might be represented by Tertullian (c.155–c.222), who had made faith primary—"it is certain because it is impossible" [2]—while on the other side, the Arab philosopher Averroes (1126–1198) separated theology and philosophy to give the latter primacy when they were in conflict. Now in the early thirteenth century, there appeared in Paris the view that theology and philosophy provided different kinds of truth, independent of one another, reason being as authoritative as faith. Clearly it was time for a new solution to the conflict of religion and philosophy.

The motif of Aquinas's resolution of the problem, as indeed to his philosophy as a

[2] Tertullian's remark is often misunderstood (and misquoted). To those Christians who are embarrassed by the notion of God's taking on flesh he responds that God's death is no less embarrassing. "The son of God died; that is absolutely believable, because it is *ineptum* (tasteless, silly). And having been buried, he rose again; that is certain, because it is impossible (*De Carne Christi*). (See John Updike, *Roger's Version* [New York: Ballantine, 1986], p. 181.) The context suggests that Tertullian is pointing to a rule of evidence that the more unusual the phenomenon reported the more credible the testimony.

whole, is moderation, compromise, and continuity. The universe, he insisted, is intelligible and coherent, and therefore accessible to human reason. The universe disclosed by reason is the same as that grasped by revelation: theology and philosophy do not produce different *kinds* of truth; they do differ in their sources and their methods. We can infer truths about God from studying the created world, as we can also discover truth about God from revelation. Further, since revealed theology and rational theology are continuous—for revealed and reasoned truth overlap, for example, on the matter of God's existence—they *must* be consistent with each other. Where contradictions appear, the theologian-philosopher's job is to demonstrate that they are only apparent.

Aquinas refuses to opt for the primacy of either religion or philosophy. Both have their place. In his writings, particularly the *Summa Theologica*, it is far from easy to disentangle theological arguments from philosophical arguments. While he is quite clear about the distinction, he will be found defending a position equally by appeal to the authority of Scripture and of Aristotle (cited not by name but as, simply, "the Philosopher").

Similar continuities are evident in his ethics. Adopting Aristotle's teleology, he begins his ethics, as did Aristotle, with the proposition that all human beings act for an end and identifies this end as happiness. He goes beyond Aristotle to interpret the content of happiness as an intellectual vision of God, achievable in perfect form only in an afterlife. Neither intention nor kind of action is the proper object of moral judgment: an action is good, he says, only if it is good in all respects; intention is just one of four factors to be considered. He accepts from Aristotle the four virtues of prudence, justice, courage, and temperance, but adds the three theological virtues of faith, hope, and charity. His jurisprudential theory distinguishes natural law, accessible to human reason, from divine law, granted us only through revelation. Both express eternal law,

the order established by God for the universe as a whole, whether animate or inanimate, human or nonhuman. As expressions of the same law, divine law (theology) cannot conflict with natural law (philosophy).

In political theory, too, Aquinas fashions a moderate position. To many previous theologians the state is unnatural, in the sense that the necessity for common authority in secular life was the result of the fallen state of human beings; in Eden no authority was necessary. Aquinas rejects this. Human beings are naturally social and naturally subject to authority. Secular authority, even non-Christian, has a right to be obeyed (though not in matters of faith).

Excerpts cannot readily show the systematic character of Aquinas's approach to ethical questions. Figure 6.1 outlines the structure of the relevant parts of the *Summa*. In dealing with ethical issues in the two parts of Book II he always proceeds from the more to the less general. First he asks what it is that all men seek; the answer is happiness, more specifically, a vision of God. We achieve this end by actions, so he next turns to action and its sources. Actions include those proper to man (voluntary actions) and those common to man and animals (passions). Sources of action can be intrinsic or extrinsic. Intrinsic sources include powers (for example, the vegetative, the sensitive, the appetitive, the locomotive, and the intellectual) and habits. Virtues and vices are forms of habit. There are seven basic virtues: four are philosophical ("cardinal") virtues—(prudence, fortitude, wisdom, and temperance) and three theological (faith, hope, and charity). Actions have two extrinsic sources: law and grace. The continuities mentioned earlier can be seen clearly even in Aquinas's basic classification of ethical topics: to him the fact that both the theological and the philosophical virtues are habits is theoretically more significant than the fact that the one group is philosophical and the other theological. So in the treatment of virtue itself the

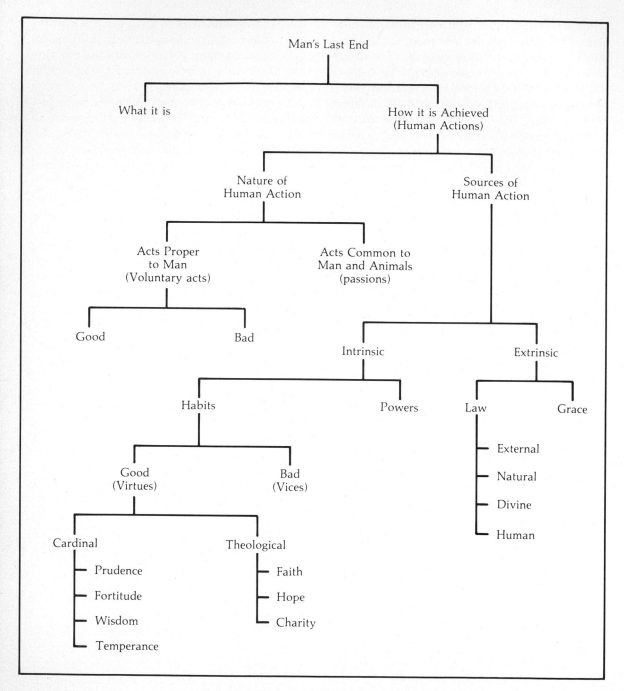

Figure 6.1 Outline of Ethics in the *Summa*

continuity of the philosophical and the theological is preserved. Similarly, although grace is wholly a theological topic, it is dealt with as an extrinsic source of human action under the same category as law, which although not entirely philosophical is largely so. All this is given in Part One of Book II of the *Summa* (cited as IaIIae). Part Two of Book II (cited as IIaIIae) applies the general theory to specific moral situations.

Summa Theologica ³

IaIIae

Questions 1–5: Treatise on the Last End. [Q1 a1] Of actions done by man those alone are properly called *human*, which are proper to man as man. Now man differs from irrational animals in this, that he is master of his actions. Wherefore those actions alone are properly called human, of which man is master. Now man is master of his actions through his reason and will; whence, too, the free-will is called the faculty and will of reason. Therefore those actions are properly called human which proceed from a deliberate will. And if any other actions befit man, they can be called actions *of a man*, but not properly *human* actions, since they are not proper to man as man.—Now it is clear that whatever actions proceed from a power, are caused by that power in accordance with the nature of its object. But the object of the will is the end and the good. Therefore all human actions must be for an end.

³ The translation is by the Fathers of the English Dominican Province (London: R. & T. Washbourne; New York: Benziger Brothers, 1911–1922). The basic unit of the *Summa* is the article, structured as follows: It begins with a question, then a series of arguments for one answer, which is almost always not Aquinas's answer, and hence this section is called the "objections." Next he gives an alternative answer, usually supporting it with a brief authoritative quotation, followed (in a section of the article called the "body") by arguments for this answer. Finally, he answers the objections. The selections, with a few exceptions, give the body of the articles. "[Q1 a1]" at the beginning of a selection means Question 1, article 1; "[a1]" at the beginning means article 1 of the question last mentioned.

Human beings are not alone in acting for an end. Irrational animals tend to an end by natural inclination. But human beings "move themselves to an end; because they have dominion over their actions, through their free will which is the *faculty of will and reason*" (a2). Although the species of an action is taken from its end, this does not exclude the possibility of alternative descriptions of the same act:

[a3] . . . [H]uman acts, whether they be considered as actions, or as passions, receive their species from the end. . . . [A]cts are called human, inasmuch as they proceed from a deliberate will. Now the object of the will is the good and the end. And hence it is clear that the principle of human acts . . . is the end. . . . And since, as Ambrose says, . . . *morality is said properly of man*, moral acts properly speaking receive their species from the end, for moral acts are the same as human acts.

Reply objection 3: One and the same act, in so far as it proceeds once from the agent, is ordained to but one proximate end, from which it has its species: but it can be ordained to several remote ends, of which one is the end of the other. It is possible, however, that an act which is one in respect of its natural species, be ordained to several ends of the will: thus this act *to kill a man*, which is but one act in respect of its natural species, can be ordained, as to an end, to the safeguarding of justice, and to the satisfying of anger: the result being that there would be several acts in different species of morality: since in one way there will be an act of virtue, in another, an act of vice. For a movement does not receive its species from that which is its terminus accidentally, but only from that which is its *per se* terminus. . . . [T]here is no reason why acts which are the same considered in their natural species, should not be diverse, considered in their moral species, and conversely.

There must be a last end:

[a4] . . . Now there is to be observed a twofold order in ends,—the order of intention, and the order of execution: and in either of these orders there must be something first. For that which is first in the order of intention, is the principle, as it were, moving the appetite; consequently, if you remove this principle, there will be nothing to move the

appetite. On the other hand, the principle in execution is that wherein operation has its beginning; and if this principle be taken away, no one will begin to work. Now the principle in the intention is the last end; while the principle in execution is the first of the things which are ordained to the end. Consequently, on neither side is it possible to go on to infinity; since if there were no last end, nothing would be desired, nor would any action have its term, nor would the intention of the agent be at rest; while if there is no first thing among those that are ordained to the end, none would begin to work at anything, and counsel would have no term, but would continue indefinitely.

Happiness is the attainment of the last end, but happiness cannot be identified with the possession of external goods, for example, wealth, honor, fame, or power:

[Q2 a4] . . . First, because, since happiness is man's supreme good, it is incompatible with any evil. Now all the foregoing can be found both in good and in evil men.—Secondly, because, since it is the nature of happiness to *satisfy of itself*, as stated in *Ethic.* i., having gained happiness, man cannot lack any needful good. But after acquiring any one of the foregoing, man may still lack many goods that are necessary to him; for instance, wisdom, bodily health, and suchlike.—Thirdly, because, since happiness is the perfect good, no evil can accrue to anyone therefrom. . . .

Is it through intellect or will that happiness is achieved?

[Q3 a4] . . . I say, then, that as to the very essence of happiness, it is impossible for it to consist in an act of the will. For . . . happiness is the attainment of the last end. But the attainment of the end does not consist in the very act of the will. For the will is directed to the end, both absent, when it desires it; and present, when it is delighted by resting therein. Now it is evident that the desire itself of the end is not the attainment of the end, but is a movement towards the end: while delight comes to the will from the end being present; and not conversely, is a thing made present, by the fact that the will delights in it. Therefore, that the end be present to him who desires it, must be due to something else than an act of the will.

This is evidently the case in regard to sensible ends. For if the acquisition of money were through an act of the will, the covetous man would have it from the very moment that he wished for it. But at that moment it is far from him; and he attains it, by grasping it in his hand, or in some like manner; and then he delights in the money got. And so it is with an intelligible end. For at first we desire to attain an intelligible end; we attain it, through its being made present to us by an act of the intellect; and then the delighted will rests in the end when attained.

So, therefore, the essence of happiness consists in an act of the intellect: but the delight that results from happiness pertains to the will. . . .

[a5] Happiness consists in an operation of the speculative rather than of the practical intellect. . . . First, because if man's happiness is an operation, it must needs be man's highest operation. Now man's highest operation is that of his highest power in respect of its highest object: and his highest power is the intellect, whose highest object is the Divine Good, which is the object, not of the practical, but of the speculative intellect. Consequently happiness consists principally in such an operation, viz., in the contemplation of Divine things. . . .

Secondly, it is evident from the fact that contemplation is sought principally for its own sake. But the act of the practical intellect is not sought for its own sake but for the sake of action: and these very actions are ordained to some end. Consequently it is evident that the last end cannot consist in the active life, which pertains to the practical intellect. . . .

Therefore the last and perfect happiness, which we await in the life to come, consists entirely in contemplation. But imperfect happiness, such as can be had here, consists first and principally in contemplation, but secondarily, in an operation of the practical intellect directing human actions and passions, as stated in *Ethic.* x.

[a8] Final and perfect happiness can consist in nothing else than the vision of the Divine Essence. . . .

Are "external goods" required for happiness?

[Q4 a7] For imperfect happiness, such as can be had in this life, external goods are necessary, not as belonging to the essence of happiness, but by serving as instruments to happiness, which consists in an operation of virtue. . . . For man needs, in this life, the necessaries of the body, both for the operation of contemplative virtue, and for the operation of active virtue, for which latter he needs also many other things by means of which to perform its operations.

On the other hand, such goods as these are nowise necessary for perfect Happiness, which consists in seeing God. . . .

Do we necessarily desire happiness?

[Q5 a8] Happiness can be considered in two ways. First according to the general notion of happiness: and thus, of necessity, every man desires happiness. For the general notion of happiness consists in the perfect good. . . . But since good is the object of the will, the perfect good of a man is that which entirely satisfies his will. Consequently to desire happiness is nothing else than to desire that one's will be satisfied. And this everyone desires. Secondly we may speak of Happiness according to its specific notion, as to that in which it consists. And thus all do not know Happiness; because they know not in what thing the general notion of happiness is found. And consequently, in this respect, not all desire it. . . .

Questions 6–48: Treatise on Human Acts.

The *Treatise on Human Acts* treats the means of achieving the final end. Actions proper to human beings are voluntary, and these are the proper subject of morality.

[Q6 a1] There must needs be something voluntary in human acts. . . . [T]he principle of some acts or movements is within the agent, or that which is moved; whereas the principle of some movements or acts is outside. For when a stone is moved upwards, the principle of this movement is outside the stone: whereas when it is moved downwards, the principle of this movement is in the stone. Now of those things that are moved by an intrinsic principle, some move themselves, some not. For since every agent or thing moved, acts or is moved for an end . . . those are perfectly moved by an intrinsic principle, whose intrinsic principle is one not only of movement but of movement for an end. Now in order for a thing to be done for an end, some knowledge of the end is necessary. Therefore, whatever so acts or is so moved by an intrinsic principle, that it has some knowledge of the end, has within itself the principle of its act, so that it not only acts, but acts for an end. . . . And consequently, since both are from an intrinsic principle, to wit, that they act and that they act for an end, the movements of such things are said to be voluntary: for the word *voluntary* implies that their movements and acts are from their own inclination. Hence it is that according to the definitions of Aristotle, Gregory of Nyssa, and Damascene, the voluntary is defined not only as having a *principle within* the agent, but also as implying *knowledge*. Therefore, since man especially knows the end of his work, and moves himself, in his acts especially is the voluntary to be found.

Although an external action commanded by the will can be the object of compulsion—your will to walk can be frustrated—the will itself properly cannot be compelled.

[a4] . . . The reason of this is that the act of the will is nothing else than an inclination proceeding from the interior principle of knowledge: just as the natural appetite is an inclination proceeding from an interior principle without knowledge. Now what is compelled or violent is from an exterior principle. Consequently it is contrary to the nature of the will's own act, that it should be subject to compulsion or violence: just as it is also contrary to the nature of a natural inclination or movement. For a stone may have an upward movement from violence, but that this violent movement be from its natural inclination is impossible. In like manner a man may be dragged by force: but it is contrary to the very notion of violence, that he be thus dragged of his own will.

An action compelled by force is involuntary. An action done from fear is essentially voluntary. Concupiscence does not excuse (a7), but the effect of ignorance is more complex:

[a8] If ignorance cause involuntariness, it is in so far as it deprives one of knowledge, which is a necessary condition of voluntariness, as was declared above (A.1). But it is not every ignorance

that deprives one of this knowledge. Accordingly, we must take note that ignorance has a threefold relationship to the act of the will: in one way, *concomitantly*; in another, *consequently*; in a third way, *antecedently*.—*Concomitantly*, when there is ignorance of what is done; but, so that even if it were known, it would be done. For then, ignorance does not induce one to wish this to be done, but it just happens that a thing is at the same time done and not known. . . . [Consider the case of a man who kills an enemy whom he wishes to kill, but at the time he thinks he is killing a stag.] [I]gnorance of this kind . . . does not cause involuntariness, since it is not the cause of anything that is repugnant to the will; but it causes *non-voluntariness,* since that which is unknown cannot be actually willed. Ignorance is *consequent* to the act of the will, in so far as ignorance itself is voluntary: and this happens in two ways. . . . First, [when] the act of the will is brought to bear on the ignorance: as when a man wishes not to know, that he may have an excuse for sin, or that he may not be withheld from sin. . . . [T]his is called *affected ignorance.*—Secondly, ignorance is said to be voluntary, when it regards that which one can and ought to know: for in this sense *not to act* and *not to will* are said to be voluntary. . . . And ignorance of this kind happens, either when one does not actually consider what one can and ought to consider;—this is called *ignorance of evil choice*, and arises from some passion or habit: or when one does not take the trouble to acquire the knowledge which one ought to have; in which sense, ignorance of the general principles of law, which one ought to know, is voluntary, as being due to negligence.—Accordingly if, in either of these ways, ignorance is voluntary, it cannot cause involuntariness simply. Nevertheless, it causes involuntariness in a certain respect, inasmuch as it precedes the movement of the will towards the act, which movement would not be, if there were knowledge. Ignorance is *antecedent* to the act of the will, when it is not voluntary, and yet is the cause of man's willing what he would not will otherwise. Thus a man may be ignorant of some circumstance of his act, which he was not bound to know, the result being that he does that which he would not do, if he knew of that circumstance; for instance, a man, after taking proper precaution, may not know that someone is coming along the road, so that he shoots an arrow and slays a passer-by. Such ignorance causes involuntariness simply.

An action's *circumstances*—"*who* did it? *What* was done? *Where* was it done? By what *means*? *Why*? *How*? *When*?"—are morally relevant (a2), but not of equal importance (a4):

[Q7 a2] Circumstances come under the consideration of the theologian. . . . First, because the theologian considers human acts, inasmuch as man is thereby directed to Happiness. Now, everything that is directed to an end should be proportionate to that end. But acts are made proportionate to an end by means of a certain commensurateness, which results from the due circumstances. Hence, the theologian has to consider the circumstances.— Secondly, because the theologian considers human acts according as they are found to be good or evil, better or worse: and this diversity depends on circumstances, as we shall see further on (Q18, AA10, 11). . . .

[a4] . . . Now, the motive and object of the will is the end. Therefore that circumstance is the most important of all which touches the act on the part of the end, viz., the circumstance *why*: and the second in importance, is that which touches the very substance of the act, viz., the circumstance *what he did*. As to the other circumstances, they are more or less important, according as they more or less approach to these.

On the will (Q8) and its relation to the intellect (Q9):

[Q8 a1] The will is a rational appetite. Now every appetite is only of something good. The reason of this is that the appetite is nothing else than an inclination of a person desirous of a thing towards that thing. Now every inclination is to something like and suitable to the thing inclined. Since, therefore, everything, inasmuch as it is being and substance, is a good, it must needs be that every inclination is to something good. And hence it is that the Philosopher says (*Ethic* i.) that *the good is that which all desire.*

But it must be noted that, since every inclination results from a form, the natural appetite results from a form existing in the nature of things: while the sensitive appetite, as also the intellective or rational appetite, which we call the will, follows from an apprehended form. Therefore, just as the natural appetite tends to good existing in a thing; so the animal or voluntary appetite tends to a good which is apprehended. Consequently, in order that the will tend to anything, it is requisite, not that this be good in very truth, but that it be apprehended as good. Wherefore the Philosopher says (*Phys.* ii.) that *the end is a good, or an apparent good.*

[Q9 a1] A thing requires to be moved by something in so far as it is in potentiality to several things; for that which is in potentiality needs to be reduced to act by something actual; and to do this is to move. Now a power of the soul is seen to be in potentiality to different things in two ways: first, with regard to acting and not acting; secondly, with regard to this or that action. Thus the sight sometimes sees actually, and sometimes sees not: and sometimes it sees white, and sometimes black. It needs therefore a mover in two respects: viz., as to the exercise or use of the act, and as to the determination of the act. . . .

The motion of the subject itself is due to some agent. And since every agent acts for an end . . . the principle of this motion lies in the end. And hence it is that the art which is concerned with the end, by its command moves the art which is concerned with the means: just as the *art of sailing commands the art of shipbuilding* (*Phys.* ii.). Now good in general, which has the nature of an end, is the object of the will. Consequently, in this respect, the will moves the other powers of the soul to their acts: for we make use of the other powers when we will. . . .

On the other hand, the object moves, by determining the act, after the manner of a formal principle, whereby in natural things actions are specified, as heating by heat. Now the first formal principle is universal *being* and *truth*, which is the object of the intellect. And therefore by this kind of motion the intellect moves the will, as presenting its object to it.

Questions 18–21 contain the core of Aquinas's ethics. The introduction gives the plan of attack.

[Q18] We must now consider the good and evil of human acts. First, how a human act is good or evil; secondly, what results from the good or evil of a human act, as merit or demerit, sin and guilt.

Under the first head there will be a threefold consideration: the first will be of the good and evil of human acts, in general; the second, of the good

and evil of internal acts; the third, of the good and evil of external acts.

Actions can have four kinds of goodness: from its fullness of being (a1), from its object (a2), its circumstances (a3), and its end (a4).

[a1] . . . [E]very action has goodness, in so far as it has being: whereas it is lacking in goodness, in so far as it is lacking in something that is due to its fulness of being; and thus it is said to be evil: for instance if it lacks the quantity determined by reason, or its due place, or something of the kind.

[a2] . . . Now the first thing that belongs to the fulness of being seems to be that which gives a thing its species. And just as a natural thing has its species from its form, so an action has its species from its object, as movement from its term. And therefore, just as the primary goodness of a natural thing is derived from its form, which gives it its species, so the primary goodness of a moral action is derived from its suitable object: hence some call such an action *good in its genus*; for instance, *to make use of what is one's own.* And just as, in natural things, the primary evil is when a generated thing does not realize its specific form (for instance, if instead of a man, something else be generated); so the primary evil in moral actions is that which is from the object, for instance, *to take what belongs to another.* And this action is said to be *evil in its genus*, genus here standing for species, just as we apply the term *mankind* to the whole human species.

[a3] In natural things, it is to be noted that the whole fulness of perfection due to a thing, is not from the mere substantial form, that gives it its species; since a thing derives much from supervening accidents, as man does from shape, colour, and the like; and if any one of these accidents be out of due proportion, evil is the result. So is it with action. For the plenitude of its goodness does not consist wholly in its species, but also in certain additions which accrue to it by reason of certain accidents: and such are its due circumstances. Wherefore if something be wanting that is requisite as a due circumstance the action will be evil.

[a4] The disposition of things as to goodness is the same as their disposition as to being. Now in some things the being does not depend on another, and in these it suffices to consider their being absolutely. But these are things the being of which depends on something else, and hence in their regard

we must consider their being in its relation to the cause on which it depends. Now just as the being of a thing depends on the agent and the form, so the goodness of a thing depends on its end. . . . [H]uman actions . . . have a measure of goodness from the end on which they depend, besides that goodness which is in them absolutely.

Accordingly a fourfold goodness may be considered in a human action. First, that which, as an action, it derives from its genus; because as much as it has of action and being so much has it of goodness. . . . Secondly, it has goodness according to its species; which is derived from its suitable object. Thirdly, it has goodness from its circumstances, in respect, as it were, of its accidents. Fourthly, it has goodness from its end, to which it is compared as to the cause of its goodness.

Reply objection 3: Nothing hinders an action that is good in one of the ways mentioned above, from lacking goodness in another way. And thus it may happen that an action which is good in its species or in its circumstances, is ordained to an evil end, or vice versa. However, an action is not good simply, unless it is good in all those ways: since *evil results from any single defect, but good from the complete cause*, as Dionysius says. . . .

Does the end of an action determine its species as good or evil?

[a6] . . . [I]n a voluntary action, there is a twofold action, viz., the interior act of the will, and the external action: and each of these actions has its object. The end is properly the object of the interior act of the will: while the object of the external action, is that on which the action is brought to bear. Therefore, just as the external action takes its species from the object on which it bears: so the interior act of the will takes its species from the end, as from its own proper object.

Now that which is on the part of the will is formal in regard to that which is on the part of the external action: because the will uses the limbs to act as instruments; nor have external actions any measure of morality, save in so far as they are voluntary. Consequently the species of a human act is considered formally with regard to the end, but materially with regard to the object of the external action. Hence the Philosopher says (*Ethic.* v.) that *he who steals that he may commit adultery, is, strictly speaking, more adulterer than thief.*

Can actions be morally indifferent?

[a9] It sometimes happens that an action is indifferent in its species; but considered in the individual it is good or evil. . . . [A] moral action . . . derives its goodness not only from its object, whence it takes its species; but also from the circumstances, which are its accidents, as it were. . . . And every individual action must needs have some circumstance that makes it good or bad, at least in respect of the intention of the end. For since it belongs to the reason to direct; if an action that proceeds from deliberate reason be not directed to the due end, it is, by that fact alone, repugnant to reason, and is specifically evil. But if it be directed to a due end it is in accord with reason; wherefore it is specifically good. . . . Consequently every human action that proceeds from deliberate reason, if it be considered in the individual, must be good or bad.

If, however, it does not proceed from deliberate reason, but from some act of the imagination, as when a man strokes his beard, or moves his hand or foot; such an action, properly speaking, is not moral or human; since this depends on the reason. Hence it will be indifferent, as standing apart from the genus of moral actions.

What would normally be counted as circumstances can change the species of an action (a10), but not all circumstances have this effect (a11):

[a10] . . . [T]hat which, in one action, is taken as a circumstance added to the object that specifies the action, can again be taken by the directing reason, as the principal condition of the object that determines the action's species. Thus to appropriate another's property is specified by reason of the property being *another's*, and in this respect it is placed in the species of theft; and if we consider that action also in its bearing on place or time, then this will be an additional circumstance. But since the reason can direct as to place, time, and the like, it may happen that the condition as to place, in relation to the object, is considered as being in disaccord with reason: for instance, reason forbids damage to be done to a holy place. Consequently to steal from a holy place has an additional repugnance to the order of reason. And thus place, which was first of all considered as a circumstance, is

considered here as the principal condition of the object, and as itself repugnant to reason. And in this way, whenever a circumstance has a special relation to reason, either for or against, it must needs specify the moral action whether good or bad.

[a11] . . . [I]t happens sometimes that a circumstance does not regard a special order of reason in respect of good or evil, except on the supposition of another previous circumstance, from which the moral action takes its species of good or evil. Thus to take something in a large or small quantity, does not regard the order of reason in respect of good or evil, except a certain other condition be presupposed, from which the action takes its malice or goodness; for instance, if what is taken belongs to another, which makes the action to be discordant with reason. Wherefore to take what belongs to another in a large or small quantity, does not change the species of the sin. Nevertheless it can aggravate or diminish the sin. . . .

Question 19, on "internal acts" (acts of the will), inquires whether an erring conscience [4] obliges (a5) or excuses (a6).

[Q19 a5] . . . [S]ome distinguished three kinds of actions: for some are good generically; some are

---

[4] Earlier conscience had been defined as an act rather than a power:

[Ia Q79 a13] . . . This is evident both from the very name and from those things which in the common way of speaking are attributed to conscience. For conscience, according to the very nature of the word, implies the relation of knowledge to something: for conscience may be resolved into *cum alio scientia, i.e.,* knowledge applied to an individual case. But the application of knowledge to something is done by some act. . . .

But sometimes by conscience is meant something else— *synderesis:*

[Q79 a12] *Synderesis* is not a power but a habit. . . . Now it is agreed that, as the speculative reason argues about speculative things, so the practical reason argues about practical things. Therefore we must have, bestowed on us by nature, not only speculative principles, but also practical principles. Now the first speculative principles bestowed on us by nature do not belong to a special power, but to a special habit, which is called the *understanding of principles,* as the Philosopher explains (*Ethic.* vi.). Wherefore the first practical principles, bestowed on us by nature, do not belong to a special power, but to a special natural habit, which we call *synderesis.* Whence *synderesis* is said to incite to good, and to murmur at evil, inasmuch as through first principles we proceed to discover, and judge of what we have discovered. . . .

indifferent; some are evil generically. And they say that if reason or conscience tell us to do something which is good generically, there is no error: and in like manner if it tell us not to do something which is evil generically. . . . On the other hand if a man's reason or conscience tell him that he is bound by precept to do what is evil in itself; or that what is good in itself, is forbidden, then his reason or conscience errs. In like manner if a man's reason or conscience tell him, that what is indifferent in itself, for instance to raise a straw from the ground, is forbidden or commanded, his reason or conscience errs. They say, therefore, that reason or conscience, when erring in matters of indifference, either by commanding or by forbidding them, binds. . . . But they say that when reason or conscience errs in commanding what is evil in itself, or in forbidding what is good in itself and necessary for salvation, it does not bind; wherefore in such cases the will which is at variance with erring reason or conscience is not evil.

But this is unreasonable. For in matters of indifference, the will that is at variance with erring reason or conscience, is evil in some way on account of the object, on which the goodness or malice of the will depends; not indeed on account of the object according as it is in its own nature; but according as it is accidentally apprehended by reason as something evil to do or to avoid. . . . [F]rom the very fact that a thing is proposed by the reason as being evil, the will by tending thereto becomes evil. And this is the case not only in indifferent matters, but also in those that are good or evil in themselves. For not only indifferent matters can receive the character of goodness or malice accidentally; but also that which is good, can receive the character of evil, or that which is evil, can receive the character of goodness, on account of the reason apprehending it as such. For instance, to refrain from fornication is good: yet the will does not tend to this good except in so far as it is proposed by the reason. If, therefore, the erring reason propose it as an evil, the will tends to it as to something evil. Consequently the will is evil, because it wills evil, not indeed that which is evil in itself, but that which is evil accidentally, through being apprehended as such by the reason. . . . We must therefore conclude that, absolutely speaking, every will at variance with reason, whether right or erring, is always evil.

[a6] [The question, "whether an erring conscience

excuses,"] depends on what has been said above about ignorance. For it was said (Q6 A8) that ignorance sometimes causes an act to be involuntary, and sometimes not. . . . [W]hen ignorance causes an act to be involuntary, it takes away the character of moral good and evil; but not, when it does not cause the act to be involuntary. . . . [W]hen ignorance is in any way willed, either directly or indirectly, it does not cause the act to be involuntary. And I call that ignorance *directly* voluntary, to which the act of the will tends: and that, *indirectly* voluntary, which is due to negligence, by reason of a man not wishing to know what he ought to know. . . .

If then reason or conscience err with an error that is voluntary . . . then such an error of reason or conscience does not excuse the will, that abides by that erring reason or conscience, from being evil. But if the error arise from ignorance of some circumstance, and without any negligence, so that it cause the act to be involuntary, then that error of reason or conscience excuses the will, that abides by that erring reason, from being evil. For instance, if erring reason tell a man that he should go to another man's wife, the will that abides by that erring reason is evil; since this error arises from ignorance of the Divine Law, which he is bound to know. But if a man's reason errs in mistaking another for his wife, and if he wish to give her her right when she asks for it, his will is excused from being evil: because this error arises from ignorance of a circumstance, which ignorance excuses, and causes the act to be involuntary.

Question 20, on external actions, inquires whether their goodness depends wholly on the will (a2), and whether consequences are relevant (a5).

[Q20 a1] External actions may be said to be good or bad in two ways. First, in regard to their genus, and the circumstances connected with them: thus the giving of alms, if the required conditions be observed, is said to be good. Secondly, a thing is said to be good or evil, from its relation to the end: thus the giving of alms for vainglory is said to be evil. Now, since the end is the will's proper object, it is evident that this aspect of good or evil, which the external action derives from its relation to the end, is to be found first of all in the act of the will,

whence it passes to the external action. On the other hand, the goodness or malice which the external action has of itself, on account of its being about due matter and its being attended by due circumstances, is not derived from the will, but rather from the reason. . . .

[a2] . . . [F]or a thing to be evil, one single defect suffices, whereas, for it to be good simply, it is not enough for it to be good in one point only, it must be good in every respect. If therefore the will be good, both from its proper object and from its end, it follows that the external action is good. But if the will be good from its intention of the end, this is not enough to make the external action good: and if the will be evil either by reason of its intention of the end, or by reason of the act willed, it follows that the external action is evil.

[a5] The consequences of an action are either foreseen or not. If they are foreseen, it is evident that they increase the goodness or malice. . . .

But if the consequences are not foreseen, we must make a distinction. Because if they follow from the nature of the action, and in the majority of cases, in this respect, the consequences increase the goodness or malice of that action: for it is evident that an action is specifically better, if better results can follow from it; and specifically worse, if it is of a nature to produce worse results.—On the other hand, if the consequences follow by accident and seldom, then they do not increase the goodness or malice of the action: because we do not judge of a thing according to that which belongs to it by accident. . . .

On the relation of the right and the good:

[Q21 a1] Evil is more comprehensive than sin, as also is good than right. For every privation of good, in whatever subject, is an evil: whereas sin consists properly in an action done for a certain end, and lacking due order to that end. Now the due order to an end is measured by some rule. In things that act according to nature, this rule is the natural force that inclines them to that end. When therefore an action proceeds from a natural force, in accord with the natural inclination to an end, then the action is said to be right. . . .

Now in those things that are done by the will, the proximate rule is the human reason, while the supreme rule is the Eternal Law. When, therefore, a human action tends to the end, according to the order of reason and of the Eternal Law, then that action is right: but when it turns aside from that rectitude, then it is said to be a sin. . . . Hence it follows that a human action is right or sinful by reason of its being good or evil.

[a2] Just as evil is more comprehensive than sin, so is sin more comprehensive than blame. For an action is said to deserve praise or blame, from its being imputed to the agent. . . . Now an action is imputed to an agent, when it is in his power, so that he has dominion over it: and this is the case in all voluntary acts. . . . Hence it follows that good or evil, in voluntary actions alone, renders them worthy of praise or blame: and in suchlike actions, evil, sin and guilt are one and the same thing.

[a3] We speak of merit and demerit, in relation to retribution, rendered according to justice. Now, retribution according to justice is rendered to a man, by reason of his having done something to another's advantage or hurt. . . .

It is therefore evident that a good or evil action deserves praise or blame, in so far as it is in the power of the will: that it is right or sinful, according as it is ordained to the end; and that its merit or demerit depend on the retribution of justice to another.

The rest of the *Treatise on Human Acts* (Questions 22–48) deals with the passions, "acts common to man and other animals," for example, love, hatred, concupiscence, pleasure, pain, sorrow, fear, and anger. Human beings act both from voluntary choice and from passion, so ethics must account for both.

Questions 49–89: Treatise on Habit.

The springs or sources of human action include the internal (habits) and the external (law and grace). Virtues and vices are habits.

[Q49 a4] [H]abit implies a disposition in relation to a thing's nature, and to its operation or end, by reason of which disposition a thing is well or ill disposed thereto. Now for a thing to need to be disposed to something else, three conditions are necessary. . . . [First] that which is disposed should be distinct from that to which it is disposed; and

so, it should be related to it as potentiality is to act. . . . [Second] that which is in a state of potentiality in regard to something else, be capable of determination in several ways and to various things. Whence if something be in a state of potentiality in regard to something else, but in regard to that only, there we find no room for disposition and habit. . . . [Third] in disposing the subject to one of those things to which it is in potentiality, several things should concur, capable of being adjusted in various ways: so as to dispose the subject well or ill to its form or to its operation. Wherefore the simple qualities of the elements which suit the natures of the elements in one single fixed way, are not called dispositions or habits, but *simple qualities:* but we call dispositions or habits, such things as health, beauty, and so forth, which imply the adjustment of several things which may vary in their relative adjustability. . . .

[Q54 a3] . . . [A] good habit is one which disposes to an act suitable to the agent's nature, while an evil habit is one which disposes to an act unsuitable to nature. Thus, acts of virtue are suitable to human nature, since they are according to reason, whereas acts of vice are discordant from human nature, since they are against reason. . . .

[Q55, a1] Virtue denotes a certain perfection of a power. Now a thing's perfection is considered chiefly in regard to its end. But the end of power is act. Wherefore power is said to be perfect, according as it is determinate to its act.

Now there are some powers which of themselves are determinate to their acts; for instance, the active natural powers. And therefore these natural powers are in themselves called virtues. But the rational powers, which are proper to man, are not determinate to one particular action, but are inclined indifferently to many: and they are determinate to acts by means of habits, as is clear from what we have said above (Q49 A4). Therefore human virtues are habits.

Augustine's definition of virtue is acceptable—"a good quality of the mind, by which we live righteously, of which no one can make bad use, which God forms in us, without us"—provided it is emended by substituting "habit" for "quality" (Q55 a4). Virtues are either intellectual or moral.

[Q58 a3] Human virtue is a habit perfecting man in view of his doing good deeds. Now, in man there are but two principles of human actions, viz., the intellect or reason and the appetite. . . . Consequently every human virtue must needs be a perfection of one of these principles. Accordingly if it perfects man's speculative or practical intellect in order that his deed may be good, it will be an intellectual virtue: whereas if it perfects his appetite, it will be a moral virtue. . . .

[Q57 a1] . . . [A] habit . . . may be called a virtue for two reasons: first, because it confers aptness in doing good; secondly, because besides aptness, it confers the right use of it. [It is only in the first sense that intellectual virtues are virtues.] For it does not follow that, if a man possess a habit of speculative science, he is inclined to make use of it, but he is made able to consider the truth in those matters of which he has scientific knowledge:—that he make use of the knowledge which he has, is due to the motion of his will. . . .

Intellectual virtues include wisdom, science, art, understanding, and especially prudence:

[a5] Prudence is a virtue most necessary for human life. For a good life consists in good deeds. Now in order to do good deeds, it matters not only what a man does, but also how he does it; to wit, that he do it from right choice and not merely from impulse or passion. And, since choice is about things in reference to the end, rectitude of choice requires two things; namely, the due end, and something suitably ordained to that due end. Now man is suitably directed to his due end by a virtue which perfects the soul in the appetitive part, the object of which is the good and the end. And to that which is suitably ordained to the due end man needs to be rightly disposed by a habit in his reason, because counsel and choice, which are about things ordained to the end, are acts of the reason. Consequently an intellectual virtue is needed in the reason, to perfect the reason, and make it suitably affected towards things ordained to the end; and this virtue is prudence. Consequently prudence is a virtue necessary to lead a good life.

[Q58 a4] Moral virtue can be without some of the intellectual virtues, viz., wisdom, science, and art; but not without understanding and prudence. Moral virtue cannot be without prudence, because it is a habit of choosing, i.e., making us choose well. Now in order that a choice be good, two things are required. First, that the intention be directed to a due end; and this is done by moral virtue, which inclines the appetitive faculty to good according to reason, which is a due end. Secondly, that man take rightly those things which have reference to the end: and this he cannot do unless his reason counsel, judge and command aright, which is the function of prudence. . . . Wherefore there can be no moral virtue without prudence: and consequently neither can there be without understanding. For it is by virtue of understanding that we know self-evident principles both in speculative and in practical matters. Consequently just as right reason in speculative matters, in so far as it proceeds from naturally known principles, presupposes the understanding of those principles, so also does prudence, which is the right reason about things to be done.

[a5] Other intellectual virtues can, but prudence cannot, be without moral virtue. The reason for this is that prudence is the right reason about things to be done (and this, not merely in general, but also in particular). . . . Now right reason demands principles from which reason proceeds to argue. And when reason argues about particular cases, it needs not only universal but also particular principles. As to universal principles of action, man is rightly disposed by the natural understanding of principles, whereby he understands that he should do no evil; or again by some practical science. But this is not enough in order that man may reason aright about particular cases. For it happens sometimes that the aforesaid universal principle, known by means of understanding or science, is destroyed in a particular case by reason of a passion: thus to one who is swayed by concupiscence, when he is overcome thereby, the object of his desire seems good, although it is opposed to the universal judgment of his reason. Consequently, as by the habit of natural understanding or of science, man is made to be rightly disposed in regard to the universal principles of action; so, in order that he be rightly disposed with regard to the particular principles of action, viz., the ends, he needs to be perfected by certain habits, whereby it becomes connatural, as it were, to man to judge aright of the end. This is done by moral virtue: for the virtuous man judges aright of the end of virtue. . . . Consequently the

right reason about things to be done, viz., prudence, requires man to have moral virtue.

The four moral ("cardinal") virtues can be described in two ways.

[Q61 a3] [First] any virtue that causes good in reason's act of consideration, may be called prudence; every virtue that causes the good of right and due in operations, be called justice; every virtue that curbs and represses the passions, be called temperance; and every virtue that strengthens the mind against any passions whatever, be called fortitude. . . . [In the second way of speaking] prudence is the virtue which commands; justice, the virtue which is about due actions between equals; temperance, the virtue which suppresses desires for the pleasures of touch; and fortitude, the virtue which strengthens against dangers of death. . . .

Questions 90–108: Treatise on Law.

Law, an extrinsic source of action, is defined (Q90) and then classified in four kinds.

[Q90 a1] Law is a rule and measure of acts, whereby man is induced to act or is restrained from acting: for *lex* (law) is derived from *ligare* (to bind), because it binds one to act. Now the rule and measure of human acts is the reason, which is the first principle of human acts . . . ; since it belongs to the reason to direct to the end, which is the first principle in all matters of action, according to the Philosopher (*Phys.* ii). Now that which is the principle in any genus, is the rule and measure of that genus: for instance, unity in the genus of numbers, and the first movement in the genus of movements. Consequently it follows that law is something pertaining to reason.

Reply Objection 1: Since law is a kind of rule and measure, it may be in something in two ways. First, as in that which measures and rules: and since this is proper to reason, it follows that, in this way, law is in the reason alone.—Secondly, as in that which is measured and ruled. In this way, law is in all those things that are inclined to something by reason of some law: so that any inclination arising from a law, may be called a law, not essentially, but by participation as it were. . . .

[a2] . . . Now as reason is a principle of human acts, so in reason itself there is something which is the principle in respect of all the rest: wherefore to this principle chiefly and mainly law must needs be referred.—Now the first principle in practical matters, which are the object of the practical reason, is the last end: and the last end of human life is bliss or happiness. . . . Consequently the law must needs regard principally the relationship to happiness. Moreover, since every part is ordained to the whole, as imperfect to perfect; and since one man is a part of the perfect community, the law must needs regard properly the relationship to universal happiness. Wherefore the Philosopher . . . mentions both happiness and the body politic: for he says (*Ethic.* v.) that we call those legal matters *just, which are adapted to produce and preserve happiness and its parts for the body politic*: since the state is a perfect community, as he says in *Polit.* i.

Now in every genus, that which belongs to it chiefly is the principle of the others, and the others belong to that genus in subordination to that thing: thus fire, which is chief among hot things, is the cause of heat in mixed bodies, and these are said to be hot in so far as they have a share of fire. Consequently, since the law is chiefly ordained to the common good, any other precept in regard to some individual work, must needs be devoid of the nature of a law, save in so far as it regards the common good. Therefore every law is ordained to the common good.

[a3] . . . Now to order anything to the common good, belongs either to the whole people, or to someone who is the viceregent of the whole people. And therefore the making of a law belongs either to the whole people or to a public personage who has care of the whole people: since in all other matters the directing of anything to the end concerns him to whom the end belongs.

[a4] [A] law is imposed on others by way of a rule and measure. Now a rule or measure is imposed by being applied to those who are to be ruled and measured by it. Wherefore, in order that a law obtain the binding force which is proper to a law, it must needs be applied to the men who have to be ruled by it. Such application is made by its being notified to them by promulgation. Wherefore promulgation is necessary for the law to obtain its force.

Thus from the four preceding articles, the definition of law may be gathered; and it is nothing else than an ordinance of reason for the common good, made by him who has care of the community, and promulgated.

On eternal law:

[Q91 a1] [A] law is nothing else but a dictate of practical reason emanating from the ruler who governs a perfect community. Now it is evident, granted that the world is ruled by Divine Providence . . . that the whole community of the universe is governed by Divine Reason. Wherefore the very Idea of the government of things in God the Ruler of the universe, has the nature of a law. And since the Divine Reason's conception of things is not subject to time but is eternal, . . . therefore it is that this kind of law must be called eternal.

[Q93 a1] Just as in every artificer there pre-exists a type of the things that are made by his art, so too in every governor there must pre-exist the type of the order of those things that are to be done by those who are subject to his government. . . . Now God, by His wisdom, is the Creator of all things, in relation to which He stands as the artificer to the products of his art. . . . Moreover He governs all the acts and movements that are to be found in each single creature. . . . Wherefore as the type of the Divine Wisdom, inasmuch as by It all things are created, has the character of art, exemplar or idea; so the type of Divine Wisdom, as moving all things to their due end, bears the character of law. Accordingly the eternal law is nothing else than the type of Divine Wisdom, as directing all actions and movements.

[a3] [L]aw denotes a kind of plan directing acts towards an end. Now wherever there are movers ordained to one another, the power of the second mover must needs be derived from the power of the first mover; since the second mover does not move except in so far as it is moved by the first. Wherefore we observe the same in all those who govern, so that the plan of government is derived by secondary governors from the governor in chief: thus the plan of what is to be done in a state flows from the king's command to his inferior administrators. . . . Since then the eternal law is the plan of government in the Chief Governor, all the plans of government in the inferior governors must be derived from the eternal law. But these plans of inferior governors are all other laws besides the eter-

nal law. Therefore all laws, in so far as they partake of right reason, are derived from the eternal law. . . .

[a5] . . . Now just as man . . . impresses a kind of inward principle of action on the man that is subject to him, so God imprints on the whole of nature the principles of its proper actions. . . . Consequently irrational creatures are subject to the eternal law, through being moved by Divine providence; but not, as rational creatures are, through understanding the Divine commandment.

On natural law: its definition (Q91 a2, Q94 a1), self-evidence (Q94 a2), universality (a4), and changeability (a5), and its relation to the "Old Law" (Old Testament) (Q100 a1) and to the Ten Commandments (a3):

[Q91 a2] . . . [I]t is evident that all things partake somewhat of the eternal law, in so far as, namely, from its being imprinted on them, they derive their respective inclinations to their proper acts and ends. Now among all others, the rational creature is subject to Divine providence in the most excellent way, in so far as it partakes of a share of providence, by being provident both for itself and for others. Wherefore it has a share of the Eternal Reason, whereby it has a natural inclination to its proper act and end: and this participation of the eternal law in the rational creature is called the natural law. . . . [T]he light of natural reason, whereby we discern what is good and what is evil, which is the function of the natural law, is nothing else than an imprint on us of the Divine light. It is therefore evident that the natural law is nothing else than the rational creature's participation of the eternal law.

Strictly natural law is not a habit, but in a sense it is:

[Q94 a1] . . . [T]he term habit may be applied to that which we hold by a habit: thus faith may mean that which we hold by faith. And accordingly, since the precepts of the natural law are sometimes considered by reason actually, while sometimes they are in the reason only habitually, in this way the natural law may be called a habit. . . .

[a2] [T]he precepts of the natural law are to the

practical reason, what the first principles of demonstrations are to the speculative reason; because both are self-evident principles. Now a thing is said to be self-evident in two ways: first, in itself; secondly, in relation to us. Any proposition is said to be self-evident in itself, if its predicate is contained in the notion of the subject: although, to one who knows not the definition of the subject, it happens that such a proposition is not self-evident. For instance, this proposition, *Man is a rational being*, is, in its very nature, self-evident, since who says *man*, says a *rational being*: and yet to one who knows not what a man is, this proposition is not self-evident. Hence . . . certain axioms or propositions are universally self-evident to all; and such are those propositions whose terms are known to all, as, *Every whole is greater than its part*, and *Things equal to one and the same are equal to one another*. But some propositions are self-evident only to the wise, who understand the meaning of the terms of such propositions: thus to one who understands that an angel is not a body, it is self-evident that an angel is not circumscriptively in a place: but this is not evident to the unlearned, for they cannot grasp it.

Now a certain order is to be found in those things that are apprehended universally. For that which, before aught else, falls under apprehension, is *being*, the notion of which is included in all things whatsoever a man apprehends. Wherefore the first indemonstrable principle is that *the same thing cannot be affirmed and denied at the same time*, which is based on the notion of *being* and *not-being:* and on this principle all others are based. . . . Now as *being* is the first thing that falls under the apprehension simply, so *good* is the first thing that falls under the apprehension of the practical reason, which is directed to action: since every agent acts for an end under the aspect of good. Consequently the first principle in the practical reason is one founded on the notion of good, viz., that *good is that which all things seek after*. Hence this is the first precept of law, that *good is to be done and ensued, and evil is to be avoided*. All other precepts of the natural law are based upon this: so that whatever the practical reason naturally apprehends as man's good (or evil) belongs to the precepts of the natural law as something to be done or avoided.

Since, however, good has the nature of an end, and evil, the nature of a contrary, hence it is that all those things to which man has a natural inclination, are naturally apprehended by reason as being good, and consequently as objects of pursuit, and their contraries as evil, and objects of avoidance. Wherefore according to the order of natural inclinations, is the order of the precepts of the natural law. Because in man there is first of all an inclination to good in accordance with the nature which he has in common with all substances: inasmuch as every substance seeks the preservation of its own being, according to its nature: and by reason of this inclination, whatever is a means of preserving human life, and of warding off its obstacles, belongs to the natural law. Secondly, there is in man an inclination to things that pertain to him more specially, according to that nature which he has in common with other animals: and in virtue of this inclination, those things are said to belong to the natural law, *which nature has taught to all animals*, such as sexual intercourse, education of offspring, and so forth. Thirdly, there is in man an inclination to good, according to the nature of his reason, which nature is proper to him: thus man has a natural inclination to know the truth about God, and to live in society: and in this respect, whatever pertains to this inclination belongs to the natural law; for instance, to shun ignorance, to avoid offending those among whom one has to live, and other such things regarding the above inclination.

[a4] [T]o the natural law belong those things to which a man is inclined naturally: and among these it is proper to man to be inclined to act according to reason. Now the process of reason is from the common to the proper. The speculative reason, however, is differently situated in this matter, from the practical reason. For, since the speculative reason is busied chiefly with necessary things, which cannot be otherwise than they are, its proper conclusions, like the universal principles, contain the truth without fail. The practical reason, on the other hand, is busied with contingent matters, about which human actions are concerned: and consequently, although there is necessity in the general principles, the more we descend to matters of detail, the more frequently we encounter defects. Accordingly then in speculative matters truth is the same in all men, both as to principles and as to conclusions: although the truth is not known to all as regards the conclusions, but only as regards the principles which are called common notions. But in matters of action, truth or practical rectitude is

not the same for all, as to matters of detail, but only as to the general principles: and where there is the same rectitude in matters of detail, it is not equally known to all.

It is therefore evident that, as regards the general principles whether of speculative or of practical reason, truth or rectitude is the same for all, and is equally known by all. As to the proper conclusions of the speculative reason, the truth is the same for all, but is not equally known to all: thus it is true for all that the three angles of a triangle are together equal to two right angles, although it is not known to all. But as to the proper conclusions of the practical reason, neither is the truth or rectitude the same for all, nor, where it is the same, is it equally known by all. Thus it is right and true for all to act according to reason: and from this principle it follows as a proper conclusion, that goods entrusted to another should be restored to their owner. Now this is true for the majority of cases: but it may happen in a particular case that it would be injurious, and therefore unreasonable, to restore goods held in trust; for instance if they are claimed for the purpose of fighting against one's country. And this principle will be found to fail the more, according as we descend further into detail, *e.g.*, if one were to say that goods held in trust should be restored with such and such a guarantee, or in such and such a way; because the greater the number of conditions added, the greater the number of ways in which the principle may fail, so that it be not right to restore or not to restore.

Consequently we must say that the natural law, as to general principles, is the same for all, both as to rectitude and as to knowledge. But as to certain matters of detail, which are conclusions, as it were, of those general principles, it is the same for all in the majority of cases, both as to rectitude and as to knowledge; and yet in some few cases it may fail, both as to rectitude, by reason of certain obstacles (just as natures subject to generation and corruption fail in some few cases on account of some obstacle), and as to knowledge, since in some the reason is perverted by passion, or evil habit, or an evil disposition of nature: thus formerly, theft, although it is expressly contrary to the natural law, was not considered wrong among the Germans, as Julius Caesar relates (*De Bello Gall.* vi.)

[a5] A change in the natural law may be understood in two ways. First, by way of addition. In this sense nothing hinders the natural law from being changed: since many things for the benefit of human life have been added over and above the natural law, both by the Divine law and by human laws.

Secondly, a change in the natural law may be understood by way of subtraction, so that what previously was according to the natural law, ceases to be so. In this sense, the natural law is altogether unchangeable in its first principles: but in its secondary principles, which . . . are certain detailed proximate conclusions drawn from the first principles, the natural law is not changed so that what it prescribes be not right in most cases. But it may be changed in some particular cases of rare occurrence, through some special causes hindering the observance of such precepts. . . .

[Q100 a1] . . . [S]ince the moral precepts are about matters which concern good morals; and since good morals are those which are in accord with reason; and since also every judgment of human reason must needs be derived in some way from natural reason; it follows, of necessity, that all the moral precepts belong to the law of nature; but not all in the same way. For there are certain things which the natural reason of every man, of its own accord and at once, judges to be done or not to be done: *e.g.*, *Honour thy father and thy mother*, and *Thou shalt not kill, Thou shalt not steal*: and these belong to the law of nature absolutely.—And there are certain things which, after a more careful consideration, wise men deem obligatory. Such belong to the law of nature, yet so that they need to be inculcated, the wiser teaching the less wise: *e.g.*, *Rise up before the hoary head, and honour the person of the aged man*, and the like.—And there are some things, to judge of which, human reason needs Divine instruction, whereby we are taught about the things of God: *e.g.*, *Thou shalt not make to thyself a graven thing, nor the likeness of anything; Thou shalt not take the name of the Lord thy God in vain*.

[a3] . . . [T]wo kinds of precepts are not reckoned among the precepts of the decalogue: viz., first general principles, for they need no further promulgation after being once imprinted on the natural reason to which they are self-evident; as, for instance, that one should do evil to no man, and other similar principles:—and again those which the careful reflection of wise men shows to be in accord with reason: since the people receive these principles

from God, through being taught by wise men. Nevertheless both kinds of precepts are contained in the precepts of the decalogue; yet in different ways. For the first general principles are contained in them, as principles in their proximate conclusions; while those which are known through wise men are contained, conversely, as conclusions in their principles.

On human law:

[Q91 a3] . . . [J]ust as, in the speculative reason, from naturally known indemonstrable principles, we draw the conclusions of the various sciences, the knowledge of which is not imparted to us by nature, but acquired by the efforts of reason, so too it is from the precepts of the natural law, as from general and indemonstrable principles, that the human reason needs to proceed to the more particular determination of certain matters. These particular determinations, devised by human reason, are called human laws, provided the other essential conditions of law be observed, as stated above (Q 90, AA 2, 3, 4). . . .

[Q95 a1] [M]an has a natural aptitude for virtue; but the perfection of virtue must be acquired by man by means of some kind of training. . . . [A] man needs to receive this training from another, whereby to arrive at the perfection of virtue. And as to those young people who are inclined to acts of virtue, by their good natural disposition, or by custom, or rather by the gift of God, paternal training suffices, which is by admonitions. But since some are found to be depraved, and prone to vice, and not easily amenable to words, it was necessary for such to be restrained from evil by force and fear, in order that, at least, they might desist from evil-doing, and leave others in peace, and that they themselves, by being habituated in this way, might be brought to do willingly what hitherto they did from fear, and thus become virtuous. Now this kind of training, which compels through fear of punishment, is the discipline of laws. Therefore, in order that man might have peace and virtue, it was necessary for laws to be framed. . . .

[a2] As Augustine says (*De Lib. Arb.* i.), *that which is not just seems to be no law at all*: wherefore the force of a law depends on the extent of its justice. Now in human affairs a thing is said to be just, from being right, according to the rule of reason.

But the first rule of reason is the law of nature. . . . Consequently every human law has just so much of the nature of law, as it is derived from the law of nature. But if in any point it deflects from the law of nature, it is no longer a law but a perversion of law.

But it must be noted that something may be derived from the natural law in two ways: first, as a conclusion from premises, secondly, by way of determination of certain generalities. The first way is like to that by which, in sciences, demonstrated conclusions are drawn from the principles: while the second mode is likened to that whereby, in the arts, general forms are particularized as to details: thus the craftsman needs to determine the general form of a house to some particular shape. Some things are therefore derived from the general principles of the natural law, by way of conclusions; *e.g.*, that *one must not kill* may be derived as a conclusion from the principle that *one should do harm to no man*: while some are derived therefrom by way of determination; *e.g.*, the law of nature has it that the evildoer should be punished; but that he be punished in this or that way, is a determination of the law of nature.

Accordingly both modes of derivation are found in the human law. But those things which are derived in the first way, are contained in human law not as emanating therefrom exclusively, but have some force from the natural law also. But those things which are derived in the second way, have no other force than that of human law.

[a4] . . . [P]ositive law is divided into the *law of nations* and *civil law*, according to the two ways in which something may be derived from the law of nature. [T]o the law of nations belong those things which are derived from the law of nature, as conclusions from premises, *e.g.*, just buyings and sellings, and the like, without which men cannot live together, which is a point of the law of nature, since man is by nature a social animal, as is proved in *Polit.* i. But those things which are derived from the law of nature by way of particular determination, belong to the civil law, according as each state decides on what is best for itself. . . .

Reply Objection 1: The law of nations is indeed, in some way, natural to man, in so far as he is a reasonable being, because it is derived from the natural law by way of a conclusion that is not very remote from its premisses. Wherefore men easily agreed thereto. Nevertheless it is distinct from natural law, especially from that natural law which is common to all animals.

[Q96 a1] Whatever is for an end should be proportionate to that end. Now the end of law is the common good. . . . Hence human laws should be proportionate to the common good. . . .

[a2] . . . [A] measure should be homogeneous with that which it measures. . . . Wherefore laws imposed on men should also be in keeping with their condition, for, as Isidore says (*Etym.* ii.), law should be *possible both according to nature, and according to the customs of the country.* . . .

Now human law is framed for a number of human beings, the majority of whom are not perfect in virtue. Wherefore human laws do not forbid all vices, from which the virtuous abstain, but only the more grievous vices, from which it is possible for the majority to abstain; and chiefly those that are to the hurt of others, without the prohibition of which human society could not be maintained: thus human law prohibits murder, theft, and suchlike.

[a3] . . . [T]here is no virtue whose acts cannot be prescribed by the law. Nevertheless human law does not prescribe concerning all the acts of every virtue: but only in regard to those that are ordainable to the common good. . . .

Does human law bind in conscience?

[a4] Laws framed by man are either just or unjust. If they be just, they have the power of binding in conscience, from the eternal law whence they are derived. . . . Now laws are said to be just, both from the end, when, to wit, they are ordained to the common good,—and from their author, that is to say, when the law that is made does not exceed the power of the lawgiver,—and from their form, when, to wit, burdens are laid on the subjects, according to an equality of proportion and with a view to the common good. For, since one man is a part of the community, each man, in all that he is and has, belongs to the community; just as a part, in all that it is, belongs to the whole; wherefore nature inflicts a loss on the part, in order to save the whole: so that on this account, such laws as these, which impose proportionate burdens, are just and binding in conscience, and are legal laws.

On the other hand, laws may be unjust in two ways: first, by being contrary to human good, through being opposed to the things mentioned above:—either in respect of the end, as when an authority imposes on his subjects burdensome laws, conducive, not to the common good, but rather to his own cupidity or vainglory;—or in respect of the author, as when a man makes a law that goes beyond the power committed to him;—or in respect of the form, as when burdens are imposed unequally on the community, although with a view to the common good. The like are rather acts of violence than laws. . . . Wherefore such laws do not bind in conscience, except perhaps in order to avoid scandal or disturbance, for which cause a man should even yield his right. . . .

Secondly, laws may be unjust through being opposed to the Divine good: such are the laws of tyrants inducing to idolatry, or to anything else contrary to the Divine law: and laws of this kind must nowise be observed, because, as stated in Acts v. 29, *we ought to obey God rather than men.*

The scope and limits of subjects' obligation to obey rulers is further discussed elsewhere in IIaIIae: in Question 104 ("Of Obedience") and Question 42 ("Of Sedition")

[IIaIIae Q104 a5] . . . [A] subject is not bound to obey his superior, if the latter command him to do something wherein he is not subject to him. For Seneca says (*De Beneficiis* iii.): *It is wrong to suppose that slavery falls upon the whole man: for the better part of him is excepted. His body is subjected and assigned to his master, but his soul is his own.* Consequently in matters touching the internal movement of the will man is not bound to obey his fellow-man, but God alone.

Nevertheless man is bound to obey his fellow-man in things that have to be done externally by means of the body: and yet, since by nature all men are equal, he is not bound to obey another man in matters touching the nature of the body, for instance in those relating to the support of his body or the begetting of his children. Wherefore servants are not bound to obey their masters, nor children their parents, in the question of contracting marriage or of remaining in the state of virginity or the like. But in matters concerning the disposal of actions and human affairs, a subject is bound to obey his superior within the sphere of his authority; for instance, a soldier must obey his general in matters relating to war, a servant his master in matters touching the execution of the duties of his service, a son his father in matters relating to the conduct of his life and the care of the household; and so forth.

[IIaIIae Q42 a2] *Reply Objection 3:* A tyrannical government is not just, because it is directed, not to the common good, but to the private good of the ruler. . . . Consequently there is no sedition in disturbing a government of this kind, unless indeed the tyrant's rule be disturbed so inordinately, that his subjects suffer greater harm from the consequent disturbance than from the tyrant's government. Indeed it is the tyrant rather that is guilty of sedition, since he encourages discord and sedition among his subjects, that he may lord over them more securely; for this is tyranny, being conducive to the private good of the ruler, and to the injury of the multitude.

On divine law:

[Q91 a4] Besides the natural and the human law it was necessary for the directing of human conduct to have a Divine law. And this for four reasons. First, . . . since man is ordained to an end of eternal happiness which is inproportionate to man's natural faculty, . . . it was necessary that . . . man should be directed to his end by a law given by God.

Secondly, because, on account of the uncertainty of human judgment, especially on contingent and particular matters, different people form different judgments on human acts; whence also different and contrary laws result. In order, therefore, that man may know without any doubt what he ought to do and what he ought to avoid, it was necessary for man to be directed in his proper acts by a law given by God, for it is certain that such a law cannot err.

Thirdly, . . . man is not competent to judge of interior movements, that are hidden, but only of exterior acts which appear: and yet for the perfection of virtue it is necessary for man to conduct himself aright in both kinds of acts. Consequently human law could not sufficiently curb and direct interior acts; and it was necessary for this purpose that a Divine law should supervene.

Fourthly, because . . . human law cannot punish or forbid all evil deeds: since while aiming at doing away with all evils, it would do away with many good things, and would hinder the advance of the common good, which is necessary for human intercourse. In order, therefore, that no evil might remain unforbidden and unpunished, it was necessary for the Divine law to supervene, whereby all sins are forbidden.

IIaIIae

In IIaIIae Aquinas analyzes in detail the seven virtues and their opposing vices. The treatment ranges from the quite theoretical (e.g., Q47 a2 asks if prudence is a virtue of the theoretical or practical reason—his answer: practical reason) to the mundane (e.g., Q68 a2 asks whether justice requires accusations to be in writing—he answers yes). The selection and framing of the topics is revealing for the practical problems of the age. Thus under the topic of faith, Q10 a1 inquires whether unbelief is a sin (answer: no, if it is only a matter of ignorance; yes, if it involves obduracy and opposition); and Q11 a3 asks whether heretics should be tolerated (answer: "they deserve not only to be separated from the Church by excommunication, but also to be severed from the world by death," although the church should also be merciful).

Question 31, treating beneficence as a case of charity, shows Aquinas's insistence on the relevance of circumstances.

[Q31 a2] . . . [S]ince the love of charity extends to all, beneficence also should extend to all, but according as time and place require: because all acts of virtue must be modified with a view to their due circumstances.

[a3] . . . Now one man's connexion with another may be measured in reference to the various matters in which men are engaged together; (thus the intercourse of kinsmen is in natural matters, that of fellow-citizens is in civic matters, that of the faithful is in spiritual matters, and so forth): and various benefits should be conferred in various ways according to these various connexions, because we ought in preference to bestow on each one such benefits

as pertain to the matter in which, speaking simply, he is most closely connected with us. And yet this may vary according to the various requirements of time, place, or matter in hand: because in certain cases one ought, for instance, to succour a stranger, in extreme necessity, rather than one's own father, if he is not in such urgent need.

On war: Can war, a vice opposed to charity, be just?

[Q40 a1] In order for a war to be just, three things are necessary. First, the authority of the sovereign by whose command the war is to be waged. For it is not the business of a private individual to declare war. . . . And as the care of the common weal is committed to those who are in authority, it is their business to watch over the common weal of the city, kingdom or province subject to them. And just as it is lawful for them to have recourse to the sword in defending that common weal against internal disturbances, when they punish evil-doers, . . . so too, it is their business to have recourse to the sword of war in defending the common weal against external enemies. . . .

Secondly, a just cause is required, namely that those who are attacked, should be attacked because they deserve it on account of some fault. . . .

Thirdly, it is necessary that the belligerents should have a rightful intention, so that they intend the advancement of good, or the avoidance of evil. Hence Augustine says (*De Verb. Dom.*): *True religion looks upon as peaceful those wars that are waged not for motives of aggrandisement, or cruelty, but with the object of securing peace, of punishing evil-doers, and of uplifting the good.* For it may happen that the war is declared by the legitimate authority, and for a just cause, and yet be rendered unlawful through a wicked intention. Hence Augustine says (*Contra Faust.* xxii.): *The passion for inflicting harm, the cruel thirst for vengeance, an unpacific and relentless spirit, the fever of revolt, the lust of power, and suchlike things, all these are rightly condemned in war.*

On justice: Justice is the social virtue connected with equality:

[Q57 a1] It is proper to justice . . . to direct man in his relations with others: because it denotes a kind of equality, as its very name implies; indeed we are wont to say that things are adjusted when they are made equal. . . . On the other hand the other virtues perfect man in those matters only which befit him in relation to himself. . . .

In one sense, justice is natural; in another conventional:

[a2] [T]he *right* or the *just* is a work that is adjusted to another person according to some kind of equality. Now a thing can be adjusted to a man in two ways: first by its very nature, as when a man gives so much that he may receive equal value in return, and this is called *natural right*. In another way a thing is adjusted or commensurated to another person, by agreement, or by common consent, when, to wit, a man deems himself satisfied, if he receives so much. This can be done in two ways: first by private agreement, as that which is confirmed by an agreement between private individuals; secondly, by public agreement, as when the whole community agrees that something should be deemed as though it were adjusted and commensurated to another person, or when this is decreed by the prince who is placed over the people, and acts in its stead, and this is called *positive right*.

Justice constrains the judgments we make of one another. It is unjust to judge another on the basis of suspicion alone (Q60 a3); indeed, justice requires us to give people the benefit of the doubt (a4).

[Q61 a1] [P]articular justice is directed to the private individual, who is compared to the community as a part to the whole. Now a twofold order may be considered in relation to a part. In the first place there is the order of one part to another, to which corresponds the order of one private individual to another. This order is directed by commutative justice, which is concerned about the mutual dealings between two persons. In the second place there is the order of the whole towards the parts, to which corresponds the order of that which belongs to the community in relation to each single person. This order is directed by distributive justice, which distributes common goods proportionately. Hence there are two species of justice, distributive and commutative.

"Respect of persons" violates distributive justice.

[Q63 a1] . . . For the equality of distributive justice consists in allotting various things to various persons in proportion to their personal dignity. Accordingly, if one considers that personal property by reason of which the thing allotted to a particular person is due to him, this is respect not of the person but of the cause. . . . For instance if you promote a man to a professorship on account of his having sufficient knowledge, you consider the due cause, not the person; but if, in conferring something on someone, you consider in him not the fact that what you give him is proportionate or due to him, but the fact that he is this particular man (e.g. Peter or Martin), then there is respect of the person, since you give him something not for some cause that renders him worthy of it, but simply because he is this person. And any circumstance that does not amount to a reason why this man be worthy of this gift, is to be referred to his person: for instance if a man promote someone to a prelacy or a professorship, because he is rich or because he is a relation of his, it is respect of persons. It may happen, however, that a circumstance of person makes a man worthy as regards one thing, but not as regards another: thus consanguinity makes a man worthy to be appointed heir to an estate, but not to be chosen for a position of ecclesiastical authority: wherefore consideration of the same circumstance of person will amount to respect of persons in one matter and not in another. It follows, accordingly, that respect of persons is opposed to distributive justice in that it fails to observe due proportion. Now nothing but sin is opposed to virtue: and therefore respect of persons is a sin.

Commutative justice requires that one not be injured by one's neighbor or state. Murder, therefore, is an injustice. But what about other takings of life—of animals for food (Q64 a1), capital punishment (a2), suicide (a5), in self-defense (a7—notable for its statement of the doctrine of double effect)?

[Q64 a1] There is no sin in using a thing for the purpose for which it is. Now the order of things is such that the imperfect are for the perfect, even as in the process of generation nature proceeds from imperfection to perfection. Hence it is that just as in the generation of a man there is first a living thing, then an animal, and lastly a man, so too things, like the plants, which merely have life, are all alike for animals, and all animals are for man. Wherefore it is not unlawful if man use plants for the good of animals, and animals for the good of man. . . .

Now the most necessary use would seem to consist in the fact that animals use plants, and men use animals, for food, and this cannot be done unless these be deprived of life: wherefore it is lawful both to take life from plants for the use of animals, and from animals for the use of men. . . .

[a2] . . . Now every part is directed to the whole, as imperfect to perfect, wherefore every part is naturally for the sake of the whole. For this reason we observe that if the health of the whole body demands the excision of a member, through its being decayed or infectious to the other members, it will be both praiseworthy and advantageous to have it cut away. Now every individual person is compared to the whole community, as part to whole. Therefore if a man be dangerous and infectious to the community, on account of some sin, it is praiseworthy and advantageous that he be killed in order to safeguard the common good. . . .

[a5] It is altogether unlawful to kill oneself, for three reasons. First, because everything naturally loves itself, the result being that everything naturally keeps itself in *being*, and resists corruption so far as it can. Wherefore suicide is contrary to the inclination of nature, and to charity whereby every man should love himself. Hence suicide is always a mortal sin, as being contrary to the natural law and to charity.

Secondly, because every part, as such, belongs to the whole. Now every man is part of the community, and so, as such, he belongs to the community. Hence by killing himself he injures the community. . . .

Thirdly, because life is God's gift to man, and is subject to His power, Who kills and makes to live. Hence whoever takes his own life, sins against God, even as he who kills another's slave, sins against that slave's master, and as he who usurps to himself judgment of a matter not entrusted to him. For it belongs to God alone to pronounce sentence of death and life. . . .

[a7] Nothing hinders one act from having two effects, only one of which is intended, while the other is beside the intention. Now moral acts take their species according to what is intended. . . . Accordingly the act of self-defence may have two effects, one is the saving of one's life, the other is the slaying of the aggressor. Therefore this act, since one's intention is to save one's own life, is not unlawful, seeing that it is natural to everything to keep itself in *being*, as far as possible. And yet, though proceeding from a good intention, an act may be rendered unlawful, if it be out of proportion to the end. Wherefore if a man, in self-defence, uses more than necessary violence, it will be unlawful: whereas if he repel force with moderation his defence will be lawful. . . . Nor is it necessary for salvation that a man omit the act of moderate self-defence in order to avoid killing the other man, since one is bound to take more care of one's own life than of another's. But . . . it is not lawful for a man to intend killing a man in self-defence, except for such as have public authority, who while intending to kill a man in self-defence, refer this to the public good, as in the case of a soldier fighting against the foe, and in the minister of the judge struggling with robbers, although even these sin if they be moved by private animosity.

On property: The possession of private property is just (Q66 a1, a2), but it can be taken justly in case of need (a7).

[Q66 a1] External things can be considered in two ways. First, as regards their nature, and this is not subject to the power of man, but only to the power of God Whose mere will all things obey. Secondly, as regards their use, and in this way, man has a natural dominion over external things, because, by his reason and will, he is able to use them for his own profit, as they were made on his account: for the imperfect is always for the sake of the perfect. . . .

[a2] Two things are competent to man in respect of exterior things. One is the power to procure and dispense them, and in this regard it is lawful for man to possess property. Moreover this is necessary to human life for three reasons. First because every man is more careful to procure what is for himself

alone than that which is common to many or to all: since each one would shirk the labour and leave to another that which concerns the community. . . . Secondly, because human affairs are conducted in more orderly fashion if each man is charged with taking care of some particular thing himself, whereas there would be confusion if everyone had to look after any one thing indeterminately. Thirdly, because a more peaceful state is ensured to man if each one is contented with his own. Hence it is to be observed that quarrels arise more frequently where there is no division of the things possessed.

The second thing that is competent to man with regard to external things is their use. In this respect man ought to possess external things, not as his own, but as common, so that, to wit, he is ready to communicate them to others in their need. . . .

Reply objection 1: Community of goods is ascribed to the natural law, not that the natural law dictates that all things should be possessed in common, and that nothing should be possessed as one's own: but because the division of possessions is not according to the natural law, but rather arose from human agreement which belongs to positive law. . . . Hence the ownership of possessions is not contrary to the natural law, but an addition thereto devised by human reason.

[a7] Things which are of human right cannot derogate from natural right or Divine right. Now according to the natural order established by Divine providence, inferior things are ordained for the purpose of succouring man's needs by their means. Wherefore the division and appropriation of things which are based on human law, do not preclude the fact that man's needs have to be remedied by means of these very things. Hence whatever certain people have in superabundance is due, by natural law, to the purpose of succouring the poor. . . .

Since, however, there are many who are in need, while it is impossible for all to be succoured by means of the same thing, each one is entrusted with the stewardship of his own things, so that out of them he may come to the aid of those who are in need. Nevertheless, if the need be so manifest and urgent, that it is evident that the present need must be remedied by whatever means be at hand (for instance when a person is in some imminent danger, and there is no other possible remedy), then it is lawful for a man to succour his own need by means of another's property, by taking it either openly or secretly: nor is this properly speaking theft or robbery.

The justice of judicial proceedings is a matter of commutative justice (Q 67). Punishments issuing from secular courts (Q68 a1) "are sought, not for their own sake, because this is not the final time of retribution, but in their character of medicine, conducing either to the amendment of the sinner, or to the good of the commonwealth whose calm is ensured by the punishment of evil-doers." The accuser who fails to prove the case risks punishment himself, since "the equality of justice requires that a man should himself suffer whatever harm he has intended to be inflicted on another" (a4).

Under no circumstances is a defendant permitted to lie, even when the truth risks his condemnation (Q69 a1) (no Fifth Amendment right).

Question 71 considers the role of lawyers: are they obliged to represent the poor? (The answer applies also to physicians.)

[Q71 a1] Since defence of the poor man's suit belongs to the works of mercy . . . no man is sufficient to bestow a work of mercy on all those who need it. Wherefore, as Augustine says (*De Doct. Christ.* i.), *since one cannot do good to all, we ought to consider those chiefly who by reason of place, time, or any other circumstance, by a kind of chance are more closely united to us.* He says *by reason of place*, because one is not bound to search throughout the world for the needy that one may succour them; and it suffices to do works of mercy to those one meets with. . . . He says also *by reason of time*, because one is not bound to provide for the future needs of others, and it suffices to succour present needs. . . . Lastly he says, *or any other circumstance*, because one ought to show kindness to those especially who are by any tie whatever united to us. . . .

It may happen however that these circumstances concur, and then we have to consider whether this particular man stands in such a need that it is not easy to see how he can be succoured otherwise,

and then one is bound to bestow the work of mercy on him. If, however, it is easy to see how he can be otherwise succoured, either by himself, or by some other person still more closely united to him, or in a better position to help him, one is not bound so strictly to help the one in need that it would be a sin not to do so: although it would be praiseworthy to do so where one is not bound to. Therefore an advocate is not always bound to defend the suits of the poor, but only when the aforesaid circumstances concur, else he would have to put aside all other business, and occupy himself entirely in defending the suits of poor people. The same applies to a physician with regard to attendance on the sick.

Question 77 deals with economic transactions: is it unjust to sell something for more than its worth (a1), to sell a defective product (a2), not to disclose defects (a3), or to profit from trade (a4)? Usury is condemned (Q78 a1), though only on the part of the lender, not of the borrower (a4).

(Q77 a1) It is altogether sinful to have recourse to deceit in order to sell a thing for more than its just price, because this is to deceive one's neighbour so as to injure him. . . . But, apart from fraud, we may speak of buying and selling in two ways. First, as considered in themselves, and from this point of view, buying and selling seem to be established for the common advantage of both parties. . . . Now whatever is established for the common advantage, should not be more of a burden to one party than to another, and consequently all contracts between them should observe equality of thing and thing. Again, the quality of a thing that comes into human use is measured by the price given for it, for which purpose money was invented. Therefore if either the price exceed the quantity of the thing's worth, or, conversely, the thing exceed the price, there is no longer the equality of justice: and consequently, to sell a thing for more than its worth, or to buy it for less than its worth, is in itself unjust and unlawful.

Secondly we may speak of buying and selling, considered as accidentally tending to the advantage of one party, and to the disadvantage of the other:

for instance, when a man has great need of a certain thing, while another man will suffer if he be without it. In such a case the just price will depend not only on the thing sold, but on the loss which the sale brings on the seller. And thus it will be lawful to sell a thing for more than it is worth in itself, though the price paid be not more than it is worth to the owner. Yet if the one man derive a great advantage by becoming possessed of the other man's property, and the seller be not at a loss through being without that thing, the latter ought not to raise the price, because the advantage accruing to the buyer, is not due to the seller, but to a circumstance affecting the buyer. Now no man should sell what is not his, though he may charge for the loss he suffers.

On the other hand if a man find that he derives great advantage from something he has bought, he may, of his own accord, pay the seller something over and above: and this pertains to his honesty.

Reply objection 1: [H]uman law is given to the people among whom there are many lacking virtue, and it is not given to the virtuous alone. Hence human law was unable to forbid all that is contrary to virtue; and it suffices for it to prohibit whatever is destructive of human intercourse, while it treats other matters as though they were lawful, not by approving of them, but by not punishing them. Accordingly, if without employing deceit the seller disposes of his goods for more than their worth, or the buyer obtains them for less than their worth, the law looks upon this as licit, and provides no punishment for so doing, unless the excess be too great, because then even human law demands restitution to be made, for instance if a man be deceived in regard to more than half the amount of the just price of a thing.

[a3] It is always unlawful to give anyone an occasion of danger or loss, although a man need not always give another the help or counsel which would be for his advantage in any way; but only in certain fixed cases, for instance when someone is subject to him, or when he is the only one who can assist him. Now the seller who offers goods for sale, gives the buyer an occasion of loss or danger, by the very fact that he offers him defective goods, if such defect may occasion loss or danger to the buyer:—loss, if, by reason of this defect, the goods are of less value, and he takes nothing off the price on that account:—danger, if this defect

either hinder the use of the goods or render it hurtful, for instance, if a man sells a lame for a fleet horse, a tottering house for a safe one, rotten or poisonous food for wholesome. Wherefore if suchlike defects be hidden, and the seller does not make them known, the sale will be illicit and fraudulent, and the seller will be bound to compensation for the loss incurred.

On the other hand, if the defect be manifest, for instance if a horse have but one eye, or if the goods though useless to the buyer, be useful to someone else, provided the seller take as much as he ought from the price, he is not bound to state the defect of the goods, since perhaps, on account of that defect the buyer might want him to allow a greater rebate than he need. Wherefore the seller may look to his own indemnity, by withholding the defect of the goods.

[a4] A tradesman is one whose business consists in the exchange of things. [E]xchange of things is twofold: one, natural as it were, and necessary, whereby one commodity is exchanged for another, or money taken in exchange for a commodity, in order to satisfy the needs of life. Suchlike trading, properly speaking, does not belong to tradesmen, but rather to housekeepers or civil servants who have to provide the household or the state with the necessaries of life. The other kind of exchange is either that of money for money, or of any commodity for money, not on account of the necessities of life, but for profit, and this kind of exchange, properly speaking, regards tradesmen according to the Philosopher (*Polit.* i.). The former kind of exchange is commendable because it supplies a natural need: but the latter is justly deserving of blame, because, considered in itself, it satisfies the greed for gain, which knows no limit and tends to infinity. Hence trading, considered in itself, has a certain debasement attaching thereto, in so far as, by its very nature, it does not imply a virtuous or necessary end. Nevertheless gain which is the end of trading, though not implying, by its nature, anything virtuous or necessary, does not, in itself, connote anything sinful or contrary to virtue: wherefore nothing prevents gain from being directed to some necessary or even virtuous end, and thus trading becomes lawful. Thus, for instance, a man may intend the moderate gain which he seeks to acquire by trading for the upkeep of his household, or for the assistance of the needy: or again, a man may

take to trade for some public advantage, for instance, lest his country lack the necessaries of life, and seek gain, not as an end, but as payment for his labour.

[Q78 a1] To take usury for money lent is unjust in itself, because this is to sell what does not exist, and this evidently leads to inequality which is contrary to justice.

In order to make this evident, we must observe that there are certain things the use of which consists in their consumption: thus we consume wine when we use it for drink, and we consume wheat when we use it for food. Wherefore in suchlike things the use of the thing must not be reckoned apart from the thing itself, and whoever is granted the use of the thing, is granted the thing itself; and for this reason, to lend things of this kind is to transfer the ownership. Accordingly if a man wanted to sell wine separately from the use of the wine, he would be selling the same thing twice, or he would be selling what does not exist, wherefore he would evidently commit a sin of injustice. In like manner he commits a sin of injustice who lends wine or wheat, and asks for double payment, viz., one, the return of the thing in equal measure, the other, the price of the use, which is called usury.

On the other hand there are things the use of which does not consist in their consumption: thus to use a house is to dwell in it, not to destroy it. Wherefore in such things, both may be granted: for instance, one man may hand over to another the ownership of his house while reserving to himself the use of it for a time, or vice versa, he may grant the use of the house, while retaining the ownership. For this reason a man may lawfully make a charge for the use of his house, and, besides this, revendicate the house from the person to whom he has granted its use, as happens in renting and letting a house.

Now money . . . was invented chiefly for the purpose of exchange: and consequently the proper and principal use of money is its consumption or alienation whereby it is sunk in exchange. Hence it is by its very nature unlawful to take payment for the use of money lent, which payment is known as usury: and just as a man is bound to restore other ill-gotten goods, so is he bound to restore the money which he has taken in usury.

[a4] It is by no means lawful to induce a man to sin, yet it is lawful to make use of another's sin

for a good end, since even God uses all sin for some good. . . .

Accordingly, . . . it is by no means lawful to induce a man to lend under a condition of usury: yet it is lawful to borrow for usury from a man who is ready to do so and is a usurer by profession; provided the borrower have a good end in view, such as the relief of his own or another's need. Thus too it is lawful for a man who has fallen among thieves to point out his property to them (which they sin in taking) in order to save his life. . . .

William Ockham
(c.1285–1347)

Ockham was born in Surrey, England. As a young man he joined the Franciscan order, and studied theology at Oxford. He never became Master of Theology because John Lutterell, chancellor of Oxford, opposed his ideas. Denounced by Lutterell as a heretic, Ockham was summoned to Avignon to answer the charges. The Franciscan minister general, Michael Cesena, was then at Avignon disputing with Pope John XXII, about the nature of Franciscan poverty. Ockham studied the matter at Michael's request and concluded that the pope was heretical. In 1328 they both fled from Avignon to seek refuge at Pisa with Emperor Louis of Bavaria. Subsequently Ockham accompanied Louis to Munich; here he issued tracts taking the emperor's side against the pope. He died at Munich, probably a victim of the plague.

Ockham's writings fall into two distinct periods. His philosophical and theological works, completed by 1328, include *Commentary on the Sentences*, *Seven Quodlibetal Questions*, *Various Questions*, and (perhaps his masterpiece) *Sum of Logic*. The political and polemical works, written after his flight from Avignon, include *Work of Ninety Days* and *Dialogue*.

The tone of fourteenth-century thought differs markedly from that of the thirteenth.

Thirteenth-century scholastics are predominantly realist: the objects of knowledge are common natures in individuals; the intellect is competent to abstract these natures, which reflect divine ideas archetypal in creation and underlie the order of the universe. Fourteenth-century thinkers reject this realism both on theological grounds—for the attribution of ideas to God is contrary to God's unity, freedom, and power—and on philosophical grounds. For Ockham, the general and abstract concepts we use do not describe something general or abstract outside the mind but are merely the product of the mind's capacity to signify collections of individuals; in this sense he is a nominalist. He deploys his famous "razor"—"plurality is to be affirmed only where necessary" —to cut out what he regards as pseudoexplanatory entities, and devotes a good deal of his logic to showing how statements apparently about these entities—relations, universals, time, place—can be reduced to statements about individuals, for example, statements about "humanity" can be reduced to statements about individual human beings. (Other assumed entities fare less well: for example, the notion of final causes in the natural world—as in Aquinas's eternal law—is dismissed as pure metaphor.)

In the absence of common natures there are no physical or metaphysical necessities. The range of the possible is what is possible to God, and this is anything that is not a logical contradiction. Within the limits of the logically possible, our universe is radically contingent, for God could have created others (and in Ockham's view, may have). It follows that causal relations cannot be necessary. In our experience smoke always follows fire, and so we say fire causes smoke; but God can present us with the experience of fire without smoke, since they are separable (or "absolute") events. Hence there is no necessary connection between fire and smoke; to say fire causes smoke is only to generalize actual sequences we observe.

This is not to say that Ockham is a skeptic. There is order, but we discover it by experience, not just by reason. In this regard Ockham employs a critical distinction he takes from Duns Scotus: between God's absolute and ordained power. God's absolute power is unlimited; but as a matter of fact God has created an ordered universe and chooses to act by the laws already laid down (the ordination). We may therefore rely on the laws (that is, regular sequences) we do discover. Ockham operates at two different levels, sharply distinguishing the theological and philosophical. God's omnipotence is an article of faith, not philosophically demonstrable (as indeed, the existence of God as unique first cause is indemonstrable). As a theologian he reminds the philosopher that what appear to be necessary relations are merely sequences; as a philosopher he insists that these sequences are nevertheless genuine.

The same two levels appear in Ockham's ethical voluntarism, and the same radical contingency. Since God does not create in virtue of any archetypal idea of human nature, the moral laws ordained could have been otherwise. If God commanded truth telling, it is not because lying is necessarily wrong; it is simply God's choice so to command. God can even command that He be hated. Ockham defines good and evil in terms of the obligatory,[5] and the obligatory in terms of commands and imperatives,[6] and thus is clearly aligned with those who take the right rather than the good as primary. But—and here we move to the other level—since God has ordained, there *is* a moral order. There are actions that are intrinsically virtuous, "while stands the divine command" (a phrase he constantly invokes). Here

[5] "Evil is nothing other than to do something to whose opposite someone is obliged to do. Which obligation does not apply to God, for he is obliged to the doing of nothing" [*Sent* II, q 4].
[6] Even suggesting, in the fifth degree of virtue, a conception of the categorical imperative.

Ockham speaks of "right reason": "Every right will is in conformity with right reason." [7] Here also Ockham's empiricism plays a role, for he identifies "right reason" as prudence, whose principles, he insists, can be learned only in experience.

Counterpart to his theological voluntarism is a psychological voluntarism in the emphasis on freedom as the distinctive feature of human beings and an emphasis on will rather than intellect. Whereas the intellect, once it grasps the truth, must assent, the will is a free power. [8] This cannot be proven by reason, but it is a matter of experience that "however much reason may dictate something, still the will can will it or not will it or reject it" [9] If the will were incapable of rejecting natural inclinations or the intellect, human beings would be capable only of errors of judgment, not of sin. The will can refuse even happiness. Ockham, therefore, rejects Aquinas's argument that the will necessarily chooses the good. In this sense the will is free and primary.

Ockham's political writings are polemics in the struggle between emperor and pope. From this struggle emerged ideas of representation and constitutionalism initially directed to church governance but later extended to the secular domain. Joining Ockham on the anti-papal side was Marsilius of Padua (1275/1280–1342), for whom the church is the "whole body of the faithful" within which all are equal. Privileges and exemptions enjoyed by the clergy are matters entirely within the jurisdiction of secular powers. Equality extends even to questions of scriptural interpretation: the authority is held by the whole church; but since it is

practically impossible to consult the whole body, Marsilius called for the establishment of a general council with a membership (both clergy and laity) elected on a basis of proportional representation and offered one of the first clear statements of popular sovereignty:

The legislator . . . is the people or the whole body of citizens, or the weightier part thereof, through its election or will expressed by words in the general assembly of the citizens, commanding or determining that something be done or omitted with regard to human civil acts, under a temporal pain or punishment. [10]

Ockham takes a similar view of the church and the right of representation, but he is not interested in substituting the emperor for the pope. Both have a limited power. He advocates what seems to be a right of due process even against the emperor:

He also has dominion over things of others to the extent that for cause and for the common utility of the people and on account of a crime of the possessor he can take them away from the possessors and appropriate them for himself or give them to others. Yet he cannot do this arbitrarily at will, but [only] on account of guilt of the possessors, or for cause or for the common utility. [11]

Work of Ninety Days was written (in ninety days) as a response to the pope on the issue of clerical poverty. The followers of Saint Francis ("Friars Minor") understood their vow of poverty to go beyond the earlier monastic renunciation of private property to the renunciation of even community property. But as the Franciscan order expanded, it inevitably accumulated property—to the dismay of some of

---

[7] He immediately reminds us that the ultimate basis remains the divine will: "But by the very fact that the divine will wills this, right reason dictates that it is to be willed" [*Sent* I, dist 41, q 1].

[8] "I call liberty a power by which I am able indifferently and contingently to do diverse things, such that I can cause or not cause the very same effect while apart from this power nothing else is different" [*Quod* I, q 16].

[9] *Quod* I, q 16.

[10] *Defensor Pacis*, trans. Alan Gewirth (Toronto: University of Toronto Press, 1980), Discourse I, ch XII, 3.

[11] *Dialogue*, Part III, tr 2, bk 2, ch 23. (Translated by the editors of this volume from Guillelmus De Occam, *Opera Plurima*, facsimile of Lyons, 1495 edition [Gregg Press, 1962], vol. I.)

its members. In 1279 an agreement had been made with Pope Nicholas III whereby he would hold the *dominium* (ownership) of the goods used by Franciscans; since they would own nothing, he would give them permission to use what they needed. Disputes continued in the order over whether mere nonownership constituted poverty as a way of life. Pope John XXII's decretal *Ad conditorem canonem* (1322) withdrew this agreement and invited them to resume ownership. Considering this as undermining everything that made it distinctive, the order appealed, but to no avail. John's final rejection of the Franciscan case, *Quia vir reprobus* (1329), asserted that property is of divine origin. It is this that *Work of Ninety Days* seeks to refute. This debate is significant in that it marks a transition from natural law to natural rights.

Ockham clearly uses *ius* in the sense of subjective right: he speaks of *ius utendi*, which is the right to use something, and of *ius agendi*, the right to take legal action. These are not natural rights. *Ius naturale*, on the other hand, which normally would be translated as "natural law," he seems to understand as a natural right (the right to use the property of other people when necessary to keep ourselves alive). It shares at least two characteristics of the later more fully developed conception of natural rights: we cannot renounce it and it is independent of any legal arrangement (not established by human agreements and not enforceable in law). Ironically, Ockham seems to have no intention of arguing for such a right; it is simply assumed in his argument that the Friars' just use of property does not require that they have a legal right.

Ockham never wrote a systematic treatise on ethics as such. His views on voluntarism, prudence and right reason, moral virtues, and ethical theory are presented here in selections from *Commentary on the Sentences* (*Sent*), *Seven Quodlibetal Questions* (*Quod*), and *Various Questions* (*VQ*); his views on property and rights, in selections from *Work of Ninety Days*.

Commentary on the Sentences, Seven Quodlibetal Questions, and Various Questions [12]

Voluntarism

[*Sent* II, q 20] The powers of the soul . . . namely, intellect and will, . . . are the same really, both among themselves and in relation to the essence of the soul. . . . The intellect is no more distinguished from the will than God is from God, or Socrates from Socrates; for [the intellect] is distinguished from the will neither in reality nor by reason. But in this way the one substance of the soul can have distinct acts in respect to which it can have different denominations: for as it performs or can perform an act of understanding, it is called intellect; as an act of willing, the will. [*OT* V, 435: 5–8; 436:6–12]

Taking will for that which is designated by the word or concept, that is, as a principle performing the act of will (and similarly for the intellect), in this sense the will is not nobler than the intellect, any more than the will is nobler than the will, for they are altogether the same. But taking both in terms of the total signification of their names, it can be admitted that the will is nobler than the intellect, because the act of loving, which is connoted by the will, is nobler than the act of understanding, which is connoted by the intellect. Also [in another sense] it can be admitted that the intellect is prior to the will, because the act of understanding, which is connoted by the intellect, is prior to the act of willing, which is connoted by the will; for the act of understanding is a partial efficient cause in relation to the act of willing, and can exist naturally without the act of willing, but not conversely. But that priority does not confer perfection on that which is first, nor imperfection on that which is later. [441:6–442:3]

[*Sent* I, dist 1, q 6] The will contingently and freely . . . enjoys the final end shown in general, because it can love happiness and not love it, and it can

[12] Translated by the editors of this volume from the Latin text of the critical edition, Guillelmi De Ockham, *Opera Philosophica et Theologica* (St. Bonaventure, N.Y.: The Franciscan Institute, 1967–1983). All the selections come from *Opera Theologica* (*OT*). The numbers in brackets give the volume number, pagination, and line numbers of this edition.

desire happiness for itself and not desire it. A persuasive argument is this: that can be rejected by the will which the intellect can dictate be rejected; but the intellect can believe no happiness is possible, for it can believe only in a state that in fact appears to us possible, and therefore it can reject all that which appears to us incompatible with that state; and consequently, it can reject happiness. The major is manifest, because although . . . the will does not conform necessarily to the judgment of reason, it can conform with the judgment of reason—whether correct or erroneous. [*OT* I, 503:7–19]

Furthermore, whoever can effectually will the antecedent can will what is known or thought to be the consequent. But someone can effectually will not to exist, and can know evidently that not to be blessed is a consequence of not existing; therefore, he can will not to be blessed, and consequently reject happiness. The assumption is clear because many using reason—both the faithful who believe in a future life as well as infidels with no belief in a future life—have killed themselves and exposed themselves to death; therefore, they willed not to exist. [504:1–9]

Acts are good or evil by their relation to commands and obligation.

[*Sent* I, dist 47, q 1] The same act [can be] both good and bad: as for instance the same act is just when it is done justly by one person and unjust when done unjustly by another. Hence, if the same [act] is commanded by a superior to one subordinate and prohibited to another, and both of them do it, the same act will be just when done by the one in obedience to the command of his superior and unjust when done by the other transgressing the command of the superior. . . .

And just as [an act] totally the same can be done by one justly and by another unjustly, so an act totally the same can be done badly by a man and justly and well by God. . . . Because, for an act to be bad is nothing but that it is done badly by someone, and for an act to be good is nothing but that it is done well by someone. And so should the same act be done badly by a man and well by God, the same act will be good and bad. Nor does this seem any more contradictory than saying the same man is a father and a son, similar and dissimi-

lar in relation to different things. [*OT* IV, 683:10–684:5]

[*Quod* III, q 15] Difformity is not the lack of justice nor of due rectitude in an act, but the lack of due rectitude in the will, which is to say nothing but that the will is obliged to perform some act according to the divine command and does not. And therefore rightness of an act is nothing else than the act itself, which ought to be performed according to right reason. [*OT* IX, 261:89–94]

God's freedom extends even to commanding evil.

[*Sent* II, q 15] And that God could cause in a created will an act of hating God . . . is proved: for God can cause anything absolute [independently existing] without anything else which is not the same as that absolute. But the act of hating God in so far as any absolute in it is concerned, is not the same as difformity and evil in the act; therefore God can cause whatever is absolute in the act of hating or rejecting God, without causing some difformity or evil in the act; therefore, etc. [*OT* V, 342:8–15]

If you say that then God sins and is evil, for he does not will to concur with a good act, I answer: a man never sins unless he is bound to do what he does not do, or because he does what he ought not to. By that reason a person becomes indebted. But God is not bound to anything, nor obligated as if indebted, and therefore he cannot do what he ought not, nor not do what he ought. [343:16–22]

Although perhaps hatred, stealing, adultery, and the like, have evil circumstances connected with them, according to the common law, inasmuch as they are done by someone who by divine command is obliged to the contrary, nevertheless as far as anything absolute in those acts is concerned, they can be performed by God without any evil circumstance attached. And indeed, they can be performed meritoriously by a man here on earth if they fall under a command of God, just as now in fact the opposites fall under a command. But while stands the divine command to their opposite, someone cannot perform such acts meritoriously or well, for they cannot be performed meritoriously unless they fall under a divine command. But opposites cannot simultaneously fall under a divine command. If thus they were performed meritoriously by a man here on earth, then they would not be said to be nor named theft, adultery, hatred, etc., for these names signify such acts, not absolutely, but by connotation or by letting it be understood that he who does such acts is obliged to the opposite by divine command. And therefore, in regard to the total significa-tion of their names, they signify evil circumstances. [352:3–19]

An act can be done well, when caused by one [person], while if done by another can only be evil. The total reason is that one cause is obliged to the opposite act, and the other is not. . . . The created will is obliged by command of God to love God, and therefore while that command stands, it cannot act well by hating God or by causing an act of ha-tred. . . . And this is so because it is obliged by command of God to the opposite act. Nor, while the first command stands, can God command him-self to the opposite. But God is obligated to cause no act, therefore, he can cause any absolute act whatsoever, and its opposite, without any evil of guilt. And therefore, just as he can totally cause an act of loving without goodness or moral evil—for moral goodness or evil connotes that the agent is obliged to that act or its opposite—so for the same reason he can totally cause an act of hating God without any moral evil, because God is obligated to the causing of no act. [353:2–18]

[*Quod* III, q 14] If you should say that God can command that for a time he not be loved, because he can command that the intellect be so intent on study (and similarly the will) that for this time it can think not at all of God: I accept that the will then is performing an act of loving God; and then either the act is virtuous—which cannot be said, since it is performed contrary to the command of God—or else it is not virtuous, in which case . . . the act of loving God above all is not virtuous.

I respond: if God can command this, as it seems he can do without contradiction, then I say that the will cannot for that time perform such an act; because from the very fact that it performs such an act, the will loves God above all and conse-quently fulfills the divine command; because this is what it is to love God above all—to love whatever God wishes to be loved, and by the fact that thus it loves, it would not fulfill the divine command in the case, and consequently, in so loving, loves God and does not love God, and fulfills and does

not fulfill the divine command. [*OT* IX, 256:74–257:91]

Even so, there must be intrinsically good acts and intrinsically evil acts, and these must be acts of the will.

[*VQ* q 7, art 1] Some acts are necessarily and in-trinsically virtuous. Proof: it is impossible that some contingently virtuous act—namely, one that indif-ferently can be called virtuous or vicious—should be determinately virtuous on account of the new addition of some act not necessarily virtuous, for by no contingently virtuous act . . . does another act become determinately virtuous or is so denomi-nated. If it did, that second act, which is contin-gently virtuous, will be determinately virtuous ei-ther through some other act that is necessarily virtuous or through an act contingently virtuous. If the former, then by the same reasoning it must stop at the second [act], and then the proposition—that some act in humans is necessarily virtuous—is established. If the second, there will be an infinite regress, or else it will stop at some necessarily virtu-ous act, and thus the proposition is established.

But acts of a man—both external and internal (for instance, to understand and to will)—the willing of which is an indifferent act, are contingently virtu-ous. Example: to go to church on account of an obligatory end is first a virtuous act, and given the same act, to go on account of an evil end is vicious; consequently, it is contingently virtuous. It is the same for understanding and speculating: to under-stand on account of an obligatory end will be virtu-ous; afterward, given the same act in the intellect but the intention changed, namely that such an act is continued on account of an undue end, the specu-lation will be vicious, and consequently that specu-lation is contingently virtuous.

I say therefore that we must grant that there is some act from the first necessarily virtuous, which is an act from the first praiseworthy and perfectly circumstanced, and is so virtuous that it cannot be-come vicious; just as to will to do something because it is a divine command is so virtuous that it cannot become vicious, while the divine command stands. And from such an act is generated virtue. [*OT* VIII, 327:99–328:129]

Other than an act of the will no act is intrinsically

virtuous or vicious: first, because any other act, while remaining the same, can be indifferently praiseworthy and blameworthy—praiseworthy first when it conforms to a right volition, and blameworthy afterward when it conforms to a vicious volition. Second, because no act is vicious unless it be voluntary and in the power of the will, for sin is truly voluntary, etc; but an external act can first be in the power of the will, for instance that someone can let go at the precipice, and afterward while descending can reject that act simply meritoriously for the sake of God. [329:145–330:155]

An intrinsically good act conforms to right reason and is performed for the sake of right reason. Hence, only habits of the will (not acts or bodily habits) are virtues.

[*Sent* III, q 11] A habit is called virtuous only by some extrinsic denomination, namely, insofar as it inclines to a virtuous act that is properly virtuous. But no act whatever is properly and intrinsically virtue. Proof: if it were, it would be so only on account of conformity with right reason. But this is not valid. First, because then an act of any organ you like would be properly virtuous, because it can be performed in conformity with right reason; and consequently moral virtues would be placed subjectively in the hand of a scribe and in the mouth of a singer, because from such acts frequently performed a habit can be generated; and yet no one places virtues in such organs. Second, because an animal can be directed in his actions by someone having right reason as appetite, and yet no one posits virtue in an animal. . . . Third, when something receives opposite denominations, while remaining wholly unchanged, neither denomination is intrinsic to it, but extrinsic; but an act of the sensitive part is of such a kind; therefore, etc. The assumption is clear: because someone can go to church to celebrate mass or pray, on account of the glory and praise of God. This act of walking is said then to be virtuous. He can continue the very same act of walking wholly unchanged, and change only the act of will and intend an evil end, for instance, to will for vainglory to walk to church to celebrate mass and pray. Then this act—numerically the same and not different in itself from that which before was said to be virtuous—is said to be vicious;

thus it is capable of having opposite denominations, but not intrinsically, it is plain; therefore extrinsically. Therefore no act nor habit of a sensitive part is said to be virtuous or vicious unless by some extrinsic denomination. [*OT* VI, 359:10–361:1]

Only an act of the will is praiseworthy or blameworthy; therefore only it is virtuous. Therefore only a habit generated from such an act is virtuous. This is confirmed by the Philosopher, *Ethics* III, where he says that no act is blameworthy unless it is in our power. For instance, no one blames a man born blind because he is blind. But if he is blind by a sin of his own, then he is culpable. [366:2–9]

Against the objection that moral virtue is primarily in right reason (not the will):

If God were to perform in my will an act in conformity with right reason, while my will does nothing, the act would not be meritorious or virtuous. And therefore for an act to be good it is required that it be in the power of the will of him whose act it is. Similarly, an act is virtuous no more on account of right reason than because of the end or other circumstance, because just as right reason is partial object of a virtuous or vicious act, so sometimes is the end and time. And yet no one asserts that the primary goodness of an act is from its end or from time. Only an act of will is primarily imputable as primarily morally good or evil. And afterwards, the will is denominated good or bad by the mediation of an act, and sometimes the act is also denominated by an extrinsic denomination. [389:19–390:6]

Prudence and Right Reason

The identification of right reason with prudence raises the question of how prudence is related to practical knowledge and to ethics.

[*Sent* III, q 12] If you ask whether any practical knowledge whatever can be called prudence, I answer no—because practical knowledge, especially scientific, concerns universal and necessary things. Prudence, however, concerns rather particular things we can do. Hence, the difference between them is of the kind [that differentiates] experience and art, because art is about universals and experience about particulars. Hence all prudence is practical, but not the converse. [*OT* VI, 419:15–420:2]

[*VQ*, q 6, art 10] Ethics is taken in two senses: First, for all scientific knowledge which is possible to have evidently through teaching (*doctrina*). And this proceeds from self-evident principles, such as, "every benefactor is to be benefited, but anyone who frees someone from death is a benefactor, therefore all such is to be benefited." In the other sense, ethics is evident scientific knowledge, which is held by, and only by, experience, and in no way evidently through teaching. For example, "any person irascible on such an occasion is to be soothed and mollified by pretty words," cannot be known evidently except through experience, namely, the evident knowledge that man has by experience of many singular propositions, for instance, that this person is to be soothed, and that person, and so on for individuals.

Similarly, prudence has two senses: properly it means evident knowledge of some singular proposition that is held solely by experience. For example, the evident knowledge: "this person is to be soothed by pretty words," which is evident by virtue of the contingent [proposition]: "he is soothed in such and such a way," and this is known through experience. In another sense [prudence] is taken commonly for the evident knowledge of some universal practical [proposition] which is known solely through experience, as that every irascible person is to be mollified thus.

Taking ethics in the first sense—for evident scientific knowledge which can be acquired evidently through teaching—it is distinguished from prudence in both its senses. For whichever prudence means, it can be acquired only through experience. Taking ethics in the second sense, ethics and prudence are commonly said to be the same. . . . Even so, it is to be distinguished from prudence properly speaking, because prudence (in this sense) is about singulars whereas the other is about universals. . . .

From this it is clear that John [Duns Scotus] does not do well to assign the difference between ethics and prudence primarily to this: that ethics is of universals and directs only remotely and mediately, while prudence is of particulars and directs immediately and from nearby. First, he supposes that ethics directs only by the mediation of prudence, which is false. For someone can have evident knowledge

of some universal proposition through teaching, such as: "every benefactor is to be benefited," and evident knowledge of some contingent proposition subsumed under the universal proposition, and this by experience—for instance, that this is the benefactor because I saw him do it—which knowledge is not prudence since it is not directive. From this it follows evidently that he is to be benefited. And the knowledge of this particular proposition directs immediately the practice following, internal and external. And nevertheless knowledge of this conclusion is not prudence because it is acquired through teaching and not by experience. Second, [Scotus] supposes that since it is of universals, ethics does not direct immediately, and that prudence, since it is of particulars, directs immediately, meaning by this that in regard to practice every particular directs more immediately than the universal, which is false. For to direct in practice is nothing other than to cause practice. Now knowledge of a universal proposition can immediately cause practice, just as does knowledge of a particular proposition. For instance, it is clear that the knowledge of the major universal and of the minor particular equally direct the following practice, because both are partial causes in relation to knowledge of the particular conclusion that directs immediately or causes the practice. So that neither knowledge causes before the other, but both equally cause immediately that knowledge which immediately directs in practice, so that they are the cause of the cause. [*OT* VIII, 281:220–284:280]

Moral Virtues

How virtues are connected to prudence, and among themselves:

[*Sent* III, q 12] In regard to the connection of virtues, I say one thing when speaking of habits in the sensitive part, and another of those in the rational part. Speaking of the former habits, I say they are not connected. . . . The reason is that habits are generated from acts. Now, however, someone can have an act generative of one habit and frequently perform it, although he does not have an act generative of another. Thus someone can have an act of temperance, although not of fortitude. [*OT* VI, 420:11–421:2]

Of habits in the rational part, there is first the

difficulty of the connection of prudence with the moral virtues. And concerning this I say that it is not contradictory that prudence exist without the moral virtues. Proof: any act whatever is compatible with an act opposite in virtue and can generate a habit without virtue. But an act of prudence is of such a kind. Proof: the will can will the opposite of that which is dictated by reason. Hence if the intellect dictates that all that is sweet is to be tasted, the will can disagree with reason and will the opposite. It can indeed interrupt any action. But the act by which the will chooses the opposite of that dictated by reason is contrary to the judgment of reason, and consequently it is a vicious action. Therefore, prudence can stand without an act of that virtue. And as it is argued thus in regard to one virtue, so it is to be argued in regard to any at all.

The second difficulty concerns the connection of moral virtues to prudence. About this I say that perfect moral virtue cannot exist without prudence, and consequently there is necessarily a connection between moral virtues and prudence. Proof: it is the nature of perfect virtue and its act that it be performed in conformity with right reason (as defined by the Philosopher [*Ethics* II]): right reason, however, is prudence in an act or in habit. [420:9–422:7]

The third difficulty concerns the connection of virtues among themselves. About this I say that . . . virtues are connected. But their connection can be understood in two ways: in one way, they are connected among themselves formally, so that when one virtue is present, according to imperfect or perfect degree, by that fact another is to be posited, according to imperfect or perfect degree; in another way, the connection can be understood as dispositive, or inclinative, or principative.

In the first way of speaking, they are not connected, either in imperfect or perfect degree. The reason is . . . that virtue is generated from determinate acts. Now, however, it is possible for someone to perform an act of one virtue while thinking nothing at all of another virtue. Therefore, it is possible that one be generated without the other, and it can be increased to the maximum without acquiring the other virtue.

In the second way of speaking, I say that they are connected in two ways: in one way, as regards the general practical principles of all virtue, partial premises implying practical conclusions by whose possession acts of virtue can (and without them cannot) be performed in the will. Example: this is one such principle: "Everything dictated by right reason for the right end, and so on for other circumstances, is to be done." Another: "Every good dictated by right reason is to be loved." These and many others are common principles of all virtue; without them a virtuous act cannot be performed. And just as these principles are common, the habits of these principles (called [habits] of prudence) are common, so that the knowledge of that common principle is the immediate partial cause of knowledge of the particular conclusion. And I speak of actual knowledge on both sides. If it is argued, "everything dictated by right reason is to be loved; but right reason dictates that father and mother and God are to be loved; therefore, father is to be loved," the actual knowledge of the principle, namely, the major, is a partial efficient cause in relation to actual knowledge of the conclusion, "father is to be loved," inasmuch as it is dictated by right reason. And thus it is a partial cause of knowledge of one practical conclusion in particular. Thus in respect to anything whatever afterwards, the actual knowledge of this conclusion in particular is partial efficient cause of the virtuous willing, so that this knowledge, along with the will, are sufficient efficient causes in respect to that virtuous practice.

In the other way of speaking they are connected by inclination and disposition; thus, he who possesses one virtue perfectly has an inclination and partially efficient principle in respect to all virtues. Example: if someone has virginal chastity perfectly—but not fortitude, for he has never performed an act of fortitude—and is threatened with death or wounds or flogging unless he fornicate, then if he elects to undergo whipping, wounds, and all torments before he will fornicate, that choice or election is the first act of fortitude. And in respect to that act the act of virginal chastity or the habit is the immediate partial efficient cause. And I believe further that the act of chastity is the cause of the other act immediately and the habit mediately. From that first act of choosing torments over loss of chastity, fortitude is generated. In this way one act of the will can be the efficient cause in respect to another. And as it is concerning fortitude, so it is concerning every moral virtue.

From this it is clear that no moral virtue contradicts another. In fact, each is a principle of and a partial efficient cause of the other. The reason is that every perfect moral virtue is in conformity with right reason; otherwise it would not be virtue. Now, contraries and formal contradictories are never in conformity with right reason. Therefore those virtues are not contradictory. And therefore the chastity of the virgin and the chastity of the married person are not contradictory, but one inclines to the other as a partial principle, so that the act of one inclines to the act of the other, and this I say speaking of internal acts which are virtuous properly and intrinsically. [424:6–427:8]

Right reason is required for actual and perfect virtue. And therefore a madman and a drunk and children, who do not have the use of reason, do not sin before God, because no one sins ignorantly according to Augustine. Hence the drunk, not having the use of reason, if he commits adultery does not sin, for, although he has the will and the intention in relation to such an act, yet he does not have the right rule of reason, and therefore does not sin. [428:13–18]

How moral virtues are generated:

[VQ, q 7, art 2, dist 2] Certain moral habits are generated from acts formally imperative of execution. Certain [others] are generated from acts relating to the same objects, but which are only equivalently, not formally, imperative of execution, for such a habit does not incline to these acts when there is an impediment to its execution. When all impediments are removed, then the habit inclines of necessity to such acts.

Example of the first: someone wills patiently to undergo death in defense of the faith, and upon being threatened with death commands the faculties to undergo such pain without rebellion. This command is nothing but to will actually without contradiction to undergo death when death is presented. Another example is: someone with many riches actually wills to give them to the poor for the love of God and, the impediment having been removed, actually commands the executive faculties to carry it out. That command is not other than so to will actually to give, all impediments having been removed; no doubt if there is an impediment, then he could not reasonably will to give absolutely but only conditionally, namely, if such an impediment were absent.

Example of the second: someone wills to undergo death in defense of the faith if he is threatened with death and there is no impediment. Similarly, as regards the other example, someone wills freely to give riches for the love of God, if he has them and there is no other impediment; but because he does not have [riches], he cannot reasonably actually absolutely give them because of the impediment. This willing is an imperative act, not formally but only equivalently.

From these acts are generated habits of distinct species; first, because of the distinction of the specific objects, for one act has an impediment for its object which the other—that which is formally imperative—does not have; second, because however greatly the habit generated from equivalently imperative acts is intensified, [even] to infinity, it never inclines to a formally imperative act. The distinction is clear from the separability of acts, for someone can do an equivalently imperative act, even if he never does a formally imperative act. [OT VIII, 333:76–334:109]

There are five degrees of virtue:

[dist 3] Justice, and every single virtue, . . . has five degrees, not of the same species, but of different species.

The first degree is when someone wishes to do a just deed in conformity with right reason directing such deeds to be done according to the due circumstances respecting precisely that deed, on account of the honorableness of the deed itself as an end. For instance, the intellect says that such a just deed is to be done in such a place and such a time for the sake of the honor of the deed itself or for the sake of peace or some other such, and the will performs the act of willing such deeds in conformity with the dictate of the intellect.

The second degree is when the will wishes to do just deeds according to the aforementioned right rule, and further with the intention of in no way forsaking it for anything whatever that is contrary to right reason, not even for death, if right reason dictates that such a deed is not to be forsaken for death. For example, a man wills so to honor his father according to the aforementioned right rule in regard to time and place, etc., with the intention and the will not to forsake this honor for death, if it threaten.

The third degree is when someone wills to do such a deed according to the aforementioned right reason with the aforementioned intention, and further wills to do such a deed according to the aforementioned circumstances precisely and only because such is the rule of right reason.

The fourth degree is when [someone] wills to do such a deed according to all the conditions and circumstances aforementioned, and further, precisely for the sake of the love of God; for example, because thus it is dictated by the intellect, that such deeds be done precisely for the sake of the love of God. And this degree alone is the perfect and true moral virtue of which the Saints speak.

That this is properly moral virtue is clear. First, since it is generated from moral acts and inclines to similar acts and directs to acts in respect to the same objects, it properly pertains to moral virtue. Second, because a change of end does not change virtue insofar as morality and nonmorality is concerned, because in respect to different ends there can be diverse moral virtues, and here only the end is changed from the aforementioned degrees. Third, because the opposite vice is properly moral vice.

The fifth degree is when someone elects to do such a deed according to the aforementioned conditions, except for the end—when indifferently it can be done for the sake of God as the end, and for the sake of honor or peace or some other such— and further he elects to do such a deed as an act formally, not just equivalently, commanded. If then he elects by an act formally commanded to do or to suffer something which by its own nature exceeds the common state of humans and is contrary to natural inclination, or where such a deed neither exceeds the common state of man nor is contrary to the natural inclination in so far as the nature of the act is concerned, but is contrary to natural inclination by some circumstances, then such a formally commanded act, I say, is generative of heroic virtue or is done from heroic virtue. . . .

Example of the first: someone threatened by death or burning for the defense of the faith actually wills by a formally commanded act to undergo death or burning. Example of the second: someone so habituated to justice that for nothing contrary to right reason will he choose to desert justice and do injustice, chooses fire or perpetual imprisonment rather than do injustice. Here to reject injustice does not exceed the common state of mankind, but to reject

it thus, as regards this circumstance which is universal right reason, exceeds the common state of humankind. If then he wills by an act formally commanding the performance of an external act to enter the fire rather than desert justice, he uses heroic virtue perfectly, both in the first case and the second. [334:111–337:180]

[dist 6] Some acts are good or bad generically, some circumstantially, and some by a meritorious principle. Example of an act good generically: to pray, to give alms, or to will such absolutely without any circumstance, good or bad. Example of a [generically] bad act: to will to steal, to will to fornicate, absolutely without any circumstance, good or bad. . . . Example of [a circumstantially good act]: to will to abstain according to circumstances dictated by right reason for the sake of honor as end or for the conservation of nature or some other end meant by the pagan philosopher. Example of [a circumstantially bad act]: to will to fornicate against right reason, in an undue place, etc., and for the sake of lust as end. Example of [an act good by meritorious principle]: to will to control [oneself] according to right reason and other circumstances, and for the sake of the honor of God because such an act is accepted by God. [338:212–339:229]

Ethical Theory

Can there be a demonstrative science of morals?

[*Quod* II, q 14] Moral doctrine has many parts, of which one is positive and the other is nonpositive. Positive moral science is that which contains laws, human and divine, which obligate to the pursuit or the avoidance of those things which are neither good nor bad unless they be prohibited or commanded by a superior to whom it belongs to establish laws.

Nonpositive moral science is that which, without any command of a superior, directs human acts; just as principles known through themselves or by experience direct, as for instance, that anything honorable should be done and anything dishonorable should be avoided, and principles of that kind of which Aristotle spoke in moral philosophy.

Positive moral science, of which jurisprudence is an example, is not a demonstrative science, . . . for the arguments of jurisprudence are founded on positive human laws, which are not accepted as propositions known evidently.

But nonpositive moral discipline is a demonstrative science. Proof: knowledge [that proceeds by] deducing conclusions syllogistically from principles known through themselves or by experience is demonstrative, knowledge and the discipline of morals is of such a kind; therefore, etc. The major is manifest. The minor is proved: there are many principles known through themselves in moral philosophy, for instance, that the will ought to conform itself to right reason, that all blameworthy evil is to be avoided, and such like. Similarly, many principles are known through experience, as is clear to any one who follows experience.

And in addition I say that this science is more certain than many others, in that any one can have more experience from his own actions than from others'. From which it is clear that this science is very refined, useful, and evident. [OT IX, 177:18–178:47]

Work of Ninety Days [13]

In this work Ockham aims to refute, point by point, the arguments of Pope John XXII in *Quia vir reprobus*. Each chapter begins with a section of the pope's document, which Ockham then proceeds to analyze. Ockham purports to be merely reporting the position of Michael Cesena and the other dissident Franciscans and so speaks in the third person ("they say," "the combatants respond"). The argument involves intricate legal meanings of words like "use," "factual use," "right of use," "dominion," "right," "just," "mine," and so forth. In Chapter 2 Ockham establishes definitions of terms used throughout the argument.

Of *factual use* they say that it is the act of using some external thing, like to inhabit, to eat, to drink, to ride, to wear clothing, and such like. [99–100]

[13] Translated by the editors of this volume from the Latin text in Guillelmi De Ockham, *Opera Politica* (Manchester: Manchester University Press); vol. I, ed. H. S. Offler (1974), vol II. ed. R. F. Bennett and H. S. Offler (1963). The numbers in brackets give line numbers of this edition.

Rightful use is a positive and determinate right established by human arrangement by which one has the lawful power and authority to use the things of another, keeping safe their substance. Whence and thus it is defined in law: *Use is the right of using things of another, keeping safe their substance.* But use so called can be divided into bare use and usufruct. (a) *Bare use* is when one has the right of using something of another's, keeping safe its substance, but this is not the right to sell to another, lease it, nor give it away for nothing; thus when one leases a house, one has the right to inhabit it with one's family, but one cannot sell nor give it away or lease it to another. . . . (b) *Usufruct* is a fuller right to the things belonging to another, keeping safe their substance; because he who has the usufruct can not merely use the thing itself, but has a whole right of his own to sell to, give away or lease to another. . . . However rightful use is understood, it is always a certain right and not the act of using. Whence he who leases a house to inhabit it, has the rightful use of the house, although he may be outside the house and he may not be inhabiting it actually. [127–152]

Right of use (*ius utendi*) is the lawful power of using an external thing of which one ought not to be deprived unwillingly without fault of one's own or without reasonable cause, and if one is deprived, one can meet the depriver in court. "Lawful power" is included to distinguish it from unlawful power, by which a thief often uses the things of another. . . . "Without fault etc." is included to distinguish it from a favor (*gratia*), by which often the lawful power of using something is granted to someone, and by which, nevertheless, at the pleasure of the giver and without any fault of one's own or reason, one can be licitly deprived solely because he who granted the power revokes it. Thus poor people invited by a rich man can lawfully use the food and drink placed before them; still, the inviter can at his own pleasure remove them, and if he does, the invited cannot on that account meet the inviter in court, nor do they have any action against him. [155–167]

[On *simple users*]: the word "user" is made from the word "use" and therefore, just as the word "use" has two meanings—namely, rightful use and factual use (and indeed it may have other senses)—so the word "user" can also be taken in two ways. In one sense—to correspond with the word "use" in its meaning of rightful use—a person is called a "user" who has the rightful use, just as that person is called "proprietor" who has the proprietorship of a thing. And then he who has bare use is called a "simple user," or who at least has no right beyond rightful use; and in that sense . . . the Friars Minor are not simple users because they are not users in that sense, since they do not have rightful use, of which there is discussion in jurisprudence, but never in theology. In another sense, it is possible to take this word "user" in a sense to correspond with the word "use" as it is taken for "factual use"; and in this sense he is said to be a "user" who has factual use of a thing; but a person is said to be a simple user if he has or can have factual use of a thing through the absence of all right on the basis of which one is enabled to litigate in court either for the thing or for the factual use of the thing, either in his own name or in the name of his own association. And in that sense . . . the Friars Minor are simple users. [217–235]

[On *dominion*]: words of this sort—"dominion," "master," "lord," "dominate"—are taken ambiguously for various powers, and in various senses. They have one sense for instance in moral philosophy, another in natural philosophy, another whenever spoken of popularly, and another in jurisprudence. . . .

In moral philosophy the word "dominion" often means the power by which one can freely perform contrary acts; and thus they say that man is a master and has dominion over his own actions; but brutes do not have dominion over their own acts. . . . In another sense such words are taken for the habit of virtue, by which one rules one's own passions according to right reason. . . . In another sense, such words are taken for forcible and acquired rule over some people who cannot nor dare not resist such rule. . . . So also whenever it is said popularly that a woman dominates her man, and a servant his master, and a companion his companion. In another sense, words like these are taken for the power of ruling some thing in an appropriate way, and thus sometimes it is said that a boy lords it over the horse of his master. [262–288]

In jurisprudence such words are taken in another sense, namely, for some special power of claiming some temporal thing and of defending and keeping and of disposing it; "some special power" because it may be that any power of claiming a temporal

thing etc. is called dominion in law, yet not every such power of claiming etc. is called dominion. For instance, he who has rented a house has in some way the power to claim the house, if he is expelled unlawfully, and also of defending it, if someone will have tried to rob him in it; he has also the power of inhabiting the house, and otherwise of disposing of the house, not however on account of the fact that he is distinguished to have dominion. Therefore, not every power of claiming a temporal thing etc. is called dominion. And yet it is plain that dominion is the power of claiming a temporal thing, etc. It is necessary therefore to seek a proper definition or description of dominion, of which mention is frequently made in jurisprudence.

. . . They make a distinction in regard to dominion as it is taken in jurisprudence: One [form of] dominion of temporal things is divine, which at present they do not mean; the other is human dominion, and that is twofold: one is that which belonged to human beings in the state of innocence from natural or divine law; of which it is said of the first parents in Genesis I: "Rule over the fish of the sea and the fowls of the air and all living animals that move upon the earth." The other belongs to human beings from positive law or from human arrangement; and of that dominion mention is frequently made in civil and canon law. And dominion so taken can be understood in two senses, namely either generally or liberally and particularly or strictly.

[They] define or describe dominion taken generally or liberally in this way: "Dominion is the principal human power of claiming some temporal thing and of defending it in a human court." "Human power" separates this dominion from divine dominion. "Principal" separates dominion from bare use and usufruct and from every other right which anyone has from the principal lord, and even from the power of the agent, who has the power to claim a thing in the name of another. It may be that he who has bare use and usufruct has the power to claim the thing and even to defend it, but he has the power from another, who relinquished his own use or usufruct, and kept the first right to himself without acquiring a new right. . . . "In a human court" separates this dominion from the dominion that belongs to humans by natural right (*iure naturale*) or by preeminent divine law; it also separates this dominion from every favor and license to use some thing, though indeed, taking the words strictly, favors and licenses are excluded by "of claiming."

Thus in this general meaning of dominion, prelates and churchmen have dominion over ecclesiastical things. . . . Indeed in the decretal *Exiit qui seminat* of Nicholas III it is held expressly that everything that the Friars Minor use he received into the dominion and propriety of the Roman church. [293–367]

In another sense dominion is taken more strictly . . . : *Dominion is the principal human power of claiming a temporal thing in court and of dealing with it in every way that is not prohibited by natural law.* And by the last part is excluded the right to temporal things that clerics are acknowledged to have; because although they may have the principal power of claiming etc. they cannot nevertheless dispose of ecclesiastical property at their own pleasure, and the laity can dispose of their temporal property in many ways from which clerics are thoroughly forbidden.

This therefore is the strictest definition of dominion . . . and by however much some right to temporal things recedes from that definition, by that much it recedes from the fullness of dominion. Hence, however much someone is more or less limited to certain ways of disposing and of dealing with his own property, it is plain that by that amount more or less he has dominion in those things. [389–402]

But churchmen do not have this kind of dominion in whatever temporal things are offered to God by the faithful. Because all clerics are restricted so to certain ways of disposing of ecclesiastical property that if they dispose and deal with that property otherwise, they sin mortally, unless perhaps through ignorance or some other way they can be excused; besides, if they should otherwise hand over the property of the church, bequeath it or part with it in some way other than that which is allowed to them, the property can be revoked by a judge. [423–429]

[On *proprietorship*]: In jurisprudence, that is to say in civil law and in canon law, proprietorship is taken more often for dominion of a thing, so that dominion and proprietorship are the same. [436–438]

Such words as "mine," "yours," "his/hers," "to have," and words similar in meaning, are taken in many places ambiguously. Sometimes they mean dominion and proprietorship. . . . Sometimes such words mean the lawful power of using some thing or the use of a thing, or the delegation of some thing for the use of someone. Thus it is said popularly that the person invited to the inn "has" the inn, and often he says, "This is my inn," of which, nevertheless, he has neither dominion nor proprietorship. And of this latter sense of such words, since it is employed of the dominion and reign of Christ, many examples are admitted. Therefore, for the present I pass it over. [442–452]

Chapter 61 challenges John XXII's argument that to use something implies the right to use it, even in the case of a license or permission: if you are permitted to use the property of another by permission, that gives you a *right of use* in it. In response, Ockham makes two distinctions ("right of use" can be a natural right or a positive right; a license can be revocable or irrevocable), offers four arguments against the view that the possession of permission implies a right of use, and finally argues that the possession of a right of use does not imply a legal right.

First they say that right of use has two senses: one is the natural right of use; the other is the positive right of use. The natural right of use is common to all human beings, because it is held from nature, not by some later constitution. Nevertheless, although every human being may have this right of use all the time, he does not have this right of use in things at every time. That is to say, those who have no property, whether private or in common, although they may have the right of use in property of others, they have this right only during the time of extreme necessity, when, by virtue of a natural right, they can lawfully use every thing present at hand without which it is not possible to save their lives. But at another time they cannot use the property of others by the authority of that right. The other [right of use] is the positive right of use, which is held by virtue of some constitution or human agreement. (This right of use was discussed above in the second chapter.) Hence, this right of use is nothing but a certain lawful power to take some action in relation to an external temporal thing, of which one cannot be deprived unwillingly, without fault and reasonable cause, and such that if one is deprived, one can meet the unjust depriver in a court. That indeed the positive right of use is such a lawful power is clear: because nothing unlawful ought to be reckoned a right of any sort, as Isidore says in the first distinction: "But right (*ius*) is so called because it is just." Also, that no one should be deprived unwillingly of such a right of use without fault and without a reasonable cause is clear: for every right of use is a right. But no one ought to be deprived of a right of one's own without fault and without a reasonable cause. . . . That the unwillingly deprived can meet the unjust depriver in court is also clear from this: that anyone can pursue his own positive right in court, nor does he who pursues his own right do an injustice to another person. He, therefore, who is deprived unjustly of such a right of use can meet the depriver in court. Again, he to whom an injustice is done can meet the injurer in the presence of a judge, especially if he has not renounced such an action; but the person who is deprived of such a right of use without fault and reasonable cause is done an injustice; therefore, he can meet the injurer in court, if he has not renounced such an action. And thus he who has such a right of use can meet the unjust depriver in court. [34–67]

Second, they make a distinction in regard to license (*licentia*). Because there is a certain license which cannot be revoked by the granter—as when a religious prelate gives someone under his authority license to enter another order, which he cannot revoke later. And by such a license, a certain right is acquired. The other is the license which can be revoked at the pleasure of the person giving it; and by that license no right seems to be acquired.

Third, these combatants attack the assertion of [John XXII] when he suggests that someone can have a right of use, that is a license to use, without the right to take legal action. They show, first, that not every license to use is the right of use; and, second, that he who has the right of use in some determinate thing has the right to take legal action.

They show the first primarily thus: According to Nicholas III in the decretal *Exiit*, the Friars Minor in using things given to them by the faithful have in these things no right of use for that time, and yet, they do have license to use those same things for that time. Therefore, license to use is not the

right of use. The antecedent is clear from the aforementioned Nicholas who says: "Nor by this, that they renounced the proprietorship of use and the dominion of anything whatever, is it demonstrated that the simple use of every thing is renounced. . . . The moderate use . . . of things necessary both to the sustenance of life and to the carrying out of the offices of their station (excepting that which is added about money below) is granted to the Friars. These things the Friars are lawfully able to use for the duration of the license granted." From these words one may infer evidently that in granting the Friars the license to use things he bestowed nothing of right to them, and consequently, license to use is not the right of use and the grant of the former does not necessarily bestow the latter.

But perhaps someone will say that the above . . . scarcely contains the truth. . . . For the Friars do have the right of use in the things that they use; because they cannot renounce the natural right of use, since [Nicholas] says "it is not at all precluded to the Friars that at the moment of extreme necessity life should be provided with the sustenance of nature by the right of heaven (*ius poli*)." It appears false, therefore, that the Friars have nothing as a matter of right in such things.

To this they say that, although the Friars Minor do not have a certain positive right to the things they use, they do have a certain right to them, namely natural right, although not always for that time when they use them. And therefore, Nicholas does not say that the Friars have nothing [as a matter] of right in such things; but he says that the use, which the Friars do have in things, gives them nothing of right. . . . From the fact that the Friars use things in the way of common property, nothing of right is attributed to them; with that, however, it is plain that they have some right from elsewhere—namely, natural right; but they have that right only for the time of extreme necessity. And from this it is clear that a license to use is not a right of use. Because the Friars have license to use things for a time other than the time of extreme necessity; but they do not have any right whatever to use except for the time of extreme necessity; therefore, license to use is not the right of use. . . . Nicholas III says the Friars Minor renounce proprietorship and dominion of anything; but he never says that they renounce all right to anything. Because it is permitted to renounce proprietorship and the power to appropriate; but no one is permitted to renounce the natural right of use, because anyone has the right of use at any time from natural right, but not everyone has that right for every time, but only for the time of extreme necessity.

Second: If the license to use is the right of use, then whoever has a special license to use has a special right of use. But every religious has a special license to use many things, which license every other person is without. Therefore, every religious has a special right. But a special right, which belongs to one person alone, is a private property right; therefore, every religious has a right to private property, and thus every religious is to be regarded as a proprietor.

Third: A slave has the license to use the property of his master; and yet he does not have the right of use in those same things; therefore, not every license to use is the right of use.

Fourth: No one is to be deprived of his right without cause and without fault. But often a person can be deprived of a license to use without fault and without cause; therefore, not every license to use is a right of use.

[Against the claim that right of use implies a legal right]: He who has a positive right of use in a determinate thing has the right to take legal action. . . . He who can sue for the recovery of his own property has the right to take legal action, because a judicial suit for recovery cannot exist without the right to take legal action. But he who has the right of use in something can sue to recover it if it is taken away. Every person is permitted to sue for the recovery of his property, at least in connection with standing debts, hence clerics and monks also can sue for the recovery of community property, at least with the license of their superiors. And just as they can sue for their own common property, so also can they sue for their rights. Therefore, whoever has the right of use in a determinate thing, at any rate a positive right, has the right to take legal action. [89–173]

Chapter 65 begins with a summary of the argument to be challenged:

[John XXII] sets out to prove according to reason that he who has permission to use some thing has the right of use in it. . . . The argument is like this: He who uses something by a license from another, not by right, uses it either justly or unjustly, or neither justly nor unjustly. If unjustly, this agrees with the constitution *Ad conditorem;* if justly, then it is by right; . . . if it is neither just nor unjust, this cannot be said; because every human act is just or unjust.

. . . In order to refute this argument they first make a distinction in regard to right; . . . third, they show how in different senses different people are said to possess temporal things; fourth, they review briefly a certain distinction regarding "just" and "justice" and "justly"; fifth, they respond to the form of the aforementioned argument.

Concerning the first they say that this word "right" (*ius*) is taken sometimes for legal right (*ius fori*) and sometimes for right of heaven (*ius poli*).[14] . . . As evidence of this distinction, legal right is called "just," which is explicitly constituted by agreement or ordinance, whether human or divine; hence it will be possible to call legal right a right of custom, in a broad sense of "custom." And of this right the Decretals say (di. vi.): "In truth, customary right arose after natural law, by which humans coming together as one began to act in the same way," from which it is to be understood that this law (*ius*) is constituted through a human agreement or ordinance: after which agreement or ordinance, whether by custom or statute, it ought not to be violated at the pleasure of anyone whatever. . . . [14–48]

The right of heaven (*ius poli*), however, is called natural equity. Apart from any human, and indeed of pure positive divine, arrangement, right of heaven is in harmony with right reason, whether purely natural right reason or right reason taken from those things that are divinely revealed to us. On account of this, this right is sometimes called natural right (*ius naturale*), because every natural right pertains to right of heaven. Sometimes it is called divine right, for many things that are not in agreement with pure natural right reason are in agreement with right reason taken from what is

---

[14] The terms *ius fori* and *ius poli* were often used in the Middle Ages to mark the distinction of jurisdiction between the external forum (*ius fori*)—i.e., the domain of courts, civil and ecclesiastical—and the internal forum (*ius poli*)—i.e., the domain of conscience and confessional.

divinely revealed to us. Thus the following is in agreement with right reason taken from the beliefs proclaimed by the Gospel—those persons who do not have whence they may be sustained otherwise are to be sustained from the goods of those to whom [the Gospel] preaches. This, however, cannot be proven by purely natural reason, just as reason is not sufficient to prove that these beliefs preached are true, useful, and necessary to those to whom they preach. [76–89]

Third, they show in how many ways temporal things are said to belong to different people: [first], temporal things are said to be some people's by virtue of merit; and in this way everything belongs to the just, that is, the worthy just possess everything; and in that sense no temporal thing belongs to an impious person, because he is not worthy even of the bread which he eats. And therefore, because God made everything for the just, it is said that in another sense that everything belongs to the just by divine right. . . . that is, the just alone are worthy of all terrestrial things. In a second sense, temporal things are said to belong to some people by the obligation of necessity or honesty, because evidently from right reason they are owed them. And in that sense superfluous things of rich people belong to the poor and indigent, because evidently the rich are bound to be endowed with things superfluous to them. . . . And thus the goods of the church are said to belong to the poor. And those things that are said to belong to some people can be said to be theirs by divine right; because by divine right the possessors of them are bound to give them up to such indigents. In a third sense, temporal things are said to belong to some people by right of heaven, and sometimes at the same time by legal right and by good conscience. Thus those things which someone uses in a time of extreme necessity are his, whether they are his by legal right or not. In a fourth sense, things are said to belong by the sincerity of conscience. And thus temporal things are said to be theirs who are moved not by avarice or bad intentions but by reason; in this sense, however, things do not belong to those who keep them from avarice or bad intentions. . . . In a fifth sense, some temporal things are said to belong to some people by legal right alone. And this sense includes many others: because things belong by legal right either as propriety and dominion or as bare use or as usufruct, and

perhaps in other ways. And in this sense things can belong, even though they do not belong in any of the four aforementioned ways; accordingly, the avaricious hold many things, of which they are unworthy, by legal right. . . .

From this it is clear that different people are known to possess temporal things in different senses. Certain people possess temporal things by legal right: as for example those who possess temporal things by human or divine positive laws. Certain people possess temporal things by right of heaven: as for example, those who possess and use temporal things in a time of extreme necessity. Some possess by a good conscience. Some, however, possess temporal things by no right and not by a good conscience, as for example, tyrants, usurers and others who possess temporal things unjustly.

Fourth, [there are various senses of] "justice," "just," and "justly." For one is particular justice distinct from other virtues; one is legal justice; the other is justice whose performance conforms to right reason. And thus an act is said to be just or unjust in three senses, and in three senses it is said that something is done justly or unjustly.

Fifth, [in regard to John XXII's premise,] "He to whom is granted a license (which is not a right) to use some thing, uses it justly, or unjustly, or neither justly nor unjustly," they say that if "justly" is taken in the first sense, according to which something is said to be done justly because it is from particular justice, which is a virtue distinct from other virtues—in this sense, he uses neither justly nor unjustly; for in this sense of "justice" and "just" many acts are both meritorious and demeritorious that are neither just nor unjust, although they are good or evil, and praiseworthy or blameworthy; for an act of chastity is in this sense neither just nor unjust. If however "justly" is taken in the third sense, they say that he who has the license to use does use the thing justly, for he uses it in conformity with right reason. And therefore they concede that he uses it as a matter of right, not however by legal right, but by right of heaven; for everything that happens rightly but without a legal right is by right of heaven. Whence to act by right is nothing but to act morally well, and to use by right is to use morally well, just as to possess by right is to possess morally well.

Perhaps someone may say that such a person [a licensee] does not use the thing granted him by right of heaven, just as for instance he does not possess by right of heaven; for no one uses a thing by right of heaven except one who uses such a thing in a time of extreme necessity. . . . To this they say that, although . . . it is lawful by right of heaven for anyone in a time of extreme necessity to use what is necessary to natural sustenance, [this is not to deny] that some in other situations can use things by right of heaven.

As the evidence of this they say that to use temporal things pertains to the right of nature (*ius naturae*), which no one can lawfully renounce; however it does not pertain to natural right (*ius naturale*) in such a way that he cannot in many cases be limited and in some manner confined, and that he is not free from being hindered. Just as according to Isidore (di. 1, c. *Ius naturale*): "The common possession of everything and one liberty of all" pertains to natural law, and yet that law is limited in some way, for temporal things are appropriated and many [persons] are subjected to slavery; still that natural right cannot be totally voided, for temporal things can never be appropriated except that they ought to be common in time of need. Thus the power to use temporal things can be limited in some way by human law and the private will of a free man, and sometimes it is not free from hindrance in the act of using—thus someone can vow to abstain from things of the flesh; so also men are prohibited from using the property of others. However, the power to use temporal things cannot be totally eradicated. And therefore by right of heaven anyone can use any temporal thing whose use is prohibited neither by the right of nature nor by human law nor by divine law nor by private deed. And therefore in a time of extreme necessity anyone can by right of heaven use any temporal thing, without which he cannot conserve his own life; for he is not obliged not to use a temporal thing in this case, neither by any law whatever nor by any private deed.

Where, on the other hand, in using some temporal determinate thing someone is hindered only by the fact that it belongs to another (because no one ought to use another's property, to which he has no right beyond natural right, that is, beyond the case of extreme necessity when he is due the use, against the owner's will), the owner's permission alone, expressed through a license, suffices for the use of the thing by right of heaven. But the permission, and consequently the license, only removes the impediment prohibiting its use to him who has the natural right to use, and no new right is conferred on him. Therefore, in this way, the permitted, or the licensed, can use another's property by right of heaven. That indeed by such licensing no new right is conferred is proved by an argument like this: every right is either divine or human; and if human, is either natural and of heaven, or a positive and legal right. But it is clear that by such permission or license a divine right is not conferred, nor a right of heaven or natural right; therefore, if some right is conferred on the recipient of the license, such a right belongs to legal right; therefore, such a person uses a thing by legal right—which is clearly false. Because by every legal right one is enabled to litigate in court; but such a person [a licensee] has no right by which he is empowered to litigate in court; therefore, he does not use the thing by a legal right. Hence he uses solely by right of heaven. It is when he is licensed or permitted that it is first lawful for him to use such a thing by right of heaven, and not before; for in that way is removed the natural right prohibiting him from using, and before it, it was not at all removed. From this it is clear that the Friars Minor, if they do not have a positive right to things common to them and to all other believers, use whatever they use lawfully by right of heaven and not by legal right, to the extent that they are outside the time of extreme necessity. For they cannot renounce using the right of heaven to use. They can, however, vow that they wish to have nothing of their own or a private right in temporal things, and therefore they can use nothing by legal right. If they must use the property of another, it is necessary to remove the prohibition, which is removed by the permission of license of him to whom it belongs to give permission or a license; the prohibition being removed, they can act by right of heaven. If however they use something that has been given up by the occupant or held for the destitute, they use by right of heaven itself. For in respect to such a thing, there is no natural right prohibition against using. [115–251]

[John XXII speaks] disjunctively or equivalently of right of heaven and legal right. Right of heaven, however, is nothing but a power in conformity with right reason in the absence of an agreement; legal right is a power from agreement, sometimes conforming to right reason and sometimes not. But no one possesses a thing well, unless he possess it according to right reason. And thus he who possesses well possesses either by right of heaven or by legal right; and he who possesses by right of heaven possesses well; but not everyone, who possesses by legal right possesses well. From which it follows that the aforementioned words about legal right to this extent cannot be understood; because many things are possessed by legal right that are not possessed well, and many things are possessed well that are not possessed by legal right. That indeed many things are possessed by legal right that are not possessed well is clear from [the case of] avaricious people, who possess many things by legal right that they do not possess well, and of many things, that they possess by right, that nevertheless they use badly, and consequently do not possess

well. . . . . Some people possess their private property badly; and consequently they possess many things by legal right that yet are possessed badly. It is clear that indeed many things are possessed well that are possessed not at all by legal right. For he who is declared an heir, possesses well the things of another before the inheritance is completed, and yet before the completed inheritance possesses nothing by legal right; therefore, many things are possessed well that nevertheless are possessed by no legal right. Therefore, the above chapters speak not only of legal right but also of right of heaven; and thus from those it is not possible to conclude that he who uses another's property by license from the other uses by legal right, but it is sufficient for his using by right of heaven. [272–298]

P A R T   T W O

The Modern Age

The passage from medieval to modern times exhibits a dramatic shift in the way that ethical problems are understood. By David Hume's death in 1776, the medieval spirit has quite vanished. The geography of the world is known. The Renaissance and the Reformation are past. The scientific revolution has taken place, and science is already established as an institution of immense prestige and influence. In the continuing conflicts of science and religion, science will not again be threatened in its very existence. The industrial revolution is in the offing and laissez faire is emerging. Chapter 7 describes the historical background for the change from medievalism to the modern era: the Reformation, the scientific revolution, and the major philosophical models of rationalism and empiricism.

Thomas Hobbes (Chapter 8) is the first serious proponent of modern ethical theory. All the themes of the modern era are found in his work: his ethics and political theory are secular, his psychology is naturalistic, his effort to found a science of natural justice reflects the geometrical and empirical methods of the new physical sciences, and the grudging democracy of his political thought comes to grips with modern problems of power and the emerging claims of popular sovereignty.

Hobbes set the agenda for the ethical theories of the next two centuries. His views of morality as conventional—merely the product of agreements— and of human nature as egoistic became the subject of bitter and continued controversy. Criticisms of Hobbes came in two waves. The first (Chapter 9) opposed his contractualism. The Cambridge Platonists appealed to self-evident principles of morality as the axioms of a geometrical treatment of ethics, in which moral obligations would be derived deductively from necessary and fundamental truths. The Levellers advanced the modern tradition of natural rights as prior to any agreements, while John Locke assumed there existed a natural morality prior to the social contract and found a place for both basic rights and agreements.

A second response to Hobbes challenged his view of human nature (Chapter 10). Bishop Butler argued that benevolence and conscience are as deeply rooted in human nature as self-love. Following Butler, and attempting to ground their analyses in a scientific conception of human nature, the moral sense theorists, represented here by David Hume and Adam Smith, criticized Hobbes for too intellectualist a psychology. Against his egoism they claimed that human nature is governed as much by feelings and emotions as by reason; by sympathy and a natural concern for other people as by calculation.

7

❧

Stirrings of the Modern Age

This chapter gives the historical setting of modern ethical theory—its problems and its interplay with the new intellectual tools being forged in political theory, economics, religion, law, mathematics, and physical science. Vast institutional changes—cultural as well as social—mark the transition from medieval to modern. The Reformation illustrates how new ideas in religion interact with practical considerations in the economic, political, and cultural spheres. How ethics is related to science and comes to grips with the new scientific methods becomes a critical issue, and for this we need to consider what these centuries took science to be. The proper use of method is debated in science, in philosophy, and in legal theory.

The compass, the printing press, and gunpowder—the three inventions that, as Francis Bacon remarked, changed the world—appeared in Europe in the fifteenth century; to Bacon's list we may add the telescope. Gunpowder doomed the medieval way of warfare

and its underlying feudal relationships. The compass made possible the great ocean voyages of the late fifteenth and early sixteenth centuries, resulting in a flow of new wealth into Europe that led to the development of a money economy and a new powerful urban trading class. The printing press, in making popular access to the Bible possible, provided a ready audience for the spread of ideas of Protestant Reform. And, of course, the telescope was the instrument through which the new science was forged.

The Renaissance reacted against medieval religiosity, gloominess, and bookishness. It began in fourteenth-century Italy and touched other countries at different times. Renaissance writers celebrated human achievements, especially the humanism of classical Greece—the view that the human being and things human are intrinsically valuable, for their own sake and not merely as they reflect God. (The phrase "dignity of the human person" originated in this period.) Renaissance culture celebrated energy, joy, buoyancy, individual-ism, this-worldliness, naturalism.[1]

Religious, Social, and Scientific Transformations

Protestant Reformation. On October 31, 1517, Martin Luther (1483–1546) set in motion a movement that would fractionate Christen-dom. Luther's immediate protest was against the selling of indulgences; but the deeper re-volt fed from frustrations within the church, caused by the failure of successive reform movements, and allied itself with a dissenting strain in Christianity running from Augustine to Abelard to Ockham. Luther's protest echoes Abelard's inwardness; as Luther put it, "bap-tism, Gospel, and faith, these alone make spiritual and Christian people." The early Protestants saw themselves largely not as revo-lutionaries challenging authority as such, but as true believers challenging a corrupted au-thority and calling for a return to a simpler and purer Christianity.

Within a generation Protestant churches, or "denominations," proliferated: Lutheran, An-glican, Calvinist, Anabaptist, and many oth-ers. Basic was the right of the individual to decide what God demands of him. To be sure, the early Protestants scarcely carried this through in practice. Luther translated the Bible so that the peasants could read it for them-selves; but when, in the German Peasant Re-bellion, they couched their demands ("Twelve Articles")—the right of each parish to choose its own priest, reduction of tithes paid to clergy, and the right of peasants to take game and wood from forests—in biblical language, Luther was horrified and took the side of the German princes against them. Jean Calvin (1509–1564), led a theocracy in Geneva, where the political, economic, and intellectual life was dominated by a church. Geneva was as intoler-ant of dissent as the medieval church. Still, in affirming the right of individual conscience to decide, the Reformation contributed to and benefited from Renaissance individualism. The developing theme of nationalism was further reinforced by the growth of national (Protes-tant) churches, with princes often claiming the right to decide the religion of their people.

Of direct significance to the history of morals was the shift in the patterns of virtue that developed in some forms of Calvinism, par-ticularly among Puritans. The other-worldly emphasis of medieval morality condemned working for material success because it dis-tracted from the life of the spirit. Much as Cal-vinist theology held salvation to be a free gift of divine grace, not an earned reward, para-doxically it emphasized industry, thrift, disci-pline, hard work, and postponement of con-sumption, and came to see material success as a sign of salvation. By encouraging the accu-mulation of capital and the growth of the com-mercial and industrial middle class, Puritanism played a large part in the development of capitalism.[2]

---

[1] Petrarch's "Ascent of Mont Ventoux" records his awe at the majesty of the scene from its summit. Then, opening a copy of Augustine's *Confessions*, he reads, "And men go to admire the high mountains, the vast floods of the sea, the huge streams of the rivers, the circumference of the ocean, and the revolutions of the stars—and desert themselves."

Petrarch is overcome by guilt: "I was stunned, I confess. I bade my brother, who wanted to hear more, not to molest me, and closed the book, angry with myself that I still admired earthly things." His initial enjoyment of nature is pure Renaissance; his guilt is medieval. (Trans. Hans Nachod, in E. Cassirer et. al., *The Renaissance Philosophy of Man* [Chicago: Chicago University Press, 1948], p. 41.)

[2] This controversial thesis was propounded by Max Weber, *The Protestant Ethic and the Spirit of Capitalism* (1904–1905). See also R. H. Tawney, *Religion and the Rise of Capitalism* (1926). Critics point to other significant factors—for exam-ple, a population decrease in the fifteenth century and increase in the sixteenth, and the exclusion of Puritans from politics and the professions, which forced them into commerce. Weber's point was that before Calvinism the established religious order was hostile to commerce and profit making.

The New Economics. Medieval economic theory, which assumed an agricultural and non-commercial economy, gave way to a new theory, "mercantilism." It was early formulated by Thomas Mun (1571–1641), and its practice is exemplified best by the policies of Jean-Baptiste Colbert (1619–1683), minister of finance to King Louis XIV. The central thesis of mercantilism is that national wealth and power reside in the possession of gold and silver. Balance of trade, then, becomes a critical matter of state policy. Exports, which bring in gold and silver, should be encouraged and imports discouraged. Mercantilists advocate heavy protective tariffs, which require central regulation of national trade. Now monarchs, themselves struggling to consolidate power, were perfectly placed to provide such regulation, and so in them the new economic theory found appreciative allies. Mercantilism was attractive also to the commercial classes, for central national regulation of trade was likely to diminish the power of the landed nobility. Hence, though for different reasons, national rulers and the commercial classes were allied against the remnants of feudalism.

Mercantilist theory lasted well into the eighteenth century. By then the commercial classes had come to believe that central state economic regulation was inimical to their interests. On theoretical grounds it was challenged by the "physiocrats"—French philosopher-economists—who emphasized freedom of trade, *laissez faire*,[3] and it was eventually overthrown by Scottish economists led by Hume and Smith. Whereas mercantilists, like the medievals, took economic life to be subject to human control, eighteenth-century economists began to think of economic phenomena as operating under natural laws (no more alterable than laws of physics). The job of economic theory is to describe these laws; restrictive economic regulation that seeks to abrogate them is unwarranted.

The New Politics. Even before the Reformation, Machiavelli (1469–1527) sounded a new note in political thought based neither on natural law nor on the Scriptures, but on a descriptive account of how human beings behave, especially as revealed in history. The role of political analysis is to describe the means by which rulers secure stability. Ethical and religious considerations are secondary: although it is desirable that the ruler be perceived as a good person, if circumstances require cruelty, violence, or dishonesty (and in Machiavelli's opinion, they often do), then moral scruples should not stand in the way. What matters is that the actions and policies of the ruler be effective.

Machiavelli's lead in divorcing politics from morals and religion was not taken up immediately. The sixteenth and seventeenth centuries continued to be dominated by a priori methods and appeals to natural law. Even so, the trend was toward secularizing natural law and interpreting it as the rational rules implicit in social interactions.

The pivotal political concepts of the period were *sovereignty* and *contract*. The development of independent nation states required a concept by which national associations could be distinguished from other kinds: sovereignty, for which Jean Bodin's (1530–1596) definition—"supreme power over citizens and subjects, unrestrained by the laws"—served the purpose and became the standard text. Debates over sovereignty revolved around two issues: its location and its limits. On location, three positions were held. For monarchists, kings only were sovereign. Others favored popular sovereignty, but some attributed it to institutions, such as parliament or estates, while others located it in individual citizens with the right of consent. On limits, some held that by its nature sovereignty is unlimited, for the lawgiver must be above the law (Hobbes).

---

[3] The label comes from a Physiocrat maxim: *Laisser faire, laisser passer, le monde va de lui-même*—"Let people produce, let them move about; the world goes on of itself."

Others limited sovereignty by higher laws (e.g., Bodin has the sovereign bound by natural law, divine law, and the law of nations) or by individuals' natural rights (Locke). For Spinoza (1632–1677) the sovereign's only right is to do what will increase individual freedom.

The notion of an original contract in a state of nature served different functions. On one side it grounded doctrines of popular sovereignty, helped define limits of government, and justified resistance to tyrannical rule. On the other side it was employed by monarchists; for example, Richard Hooker (1553–1600) defended Tudor monarchy on the ground that once the people have consented to surrender sovereignty they must obey.

The character of the state of nature was disputed: for Hobbes it is a nonmoral state of peril and insecurity; for Locke it is a moral condition requiring organization; Rousseau (1712–1778) pictures natural man as strictly nonmoral but endowed with feelings of compassion until perverted by society. Some interpreted it as presocial, others as merely prepolitical. Its theoretical status was also controverted; but whether a historical event or a theoretical construct, it represented a search for forces hidden in human nature generating an invariant order behind the appearances, much as physicists sought universal forces for physical nature generally.

The Scientific Revolution. The Renaissance and the Reformation, still in many respects medieval, looked to books for authority—classical Greek authors in one case, the Bible in the other. The more decisive break came in science, especially celestial and terrestrial mechanics. The new science thoroughly secularized human knowledge—human reason is competent to forge the fundamental laws of the universe—and this program eventually is carried through to political science, law, psychology, economics, and ethics. The scientific revolution was clearly on its way in the fifteenth century with a climax in Newton's

work which secured the authority of science in the intellectual world.

Nicolaus Copernicus (1473–1543) led the way by challenging the reigning geocentric (Ptolemaic) astronomy, which held that the earth is an unmoving center around which planets revolve. The ancients had asked: if the earth moves, why is it that objects dropped on earth fall vertically? And why is it that objects on the surface of the earth do not fly off into space? [4] But the geocentric hypothesis also faced difficulties, particularly the phenomenon of retrogression—occasionally planets seem to move backward in relation to the background of fixed stars. To account for this, astronomers hypothesized that planets moved in epicycles [5] —an increasingly cumbersome theory as new celestial observations required epicycles on epicycles. Fifteenth-century Arab and Spanish observation tables complicated the Ptolemaic theory even more. Convinced that the laws of the universe must be simple and harmonious, Copernicus calculated what the observations would be if the earth and planets moved around the sun; the resulting account fit the data and was simpler. Copernicus's posthumous *On Revolutions* (1543) included a preface by a friend suggesting that Copernicus was offering merely a computing device by which planetary positions could be calculated, and not a true description. The text was sufficiently ambiguous that the church did not react immediately. But it was aware of the danger: the central importance of human beings in the universe seemed at stake; for if God created the universe for man, surely He would have placed man at its center?

The church did react when Giordano Bruno (1543–1600) espoused heliocentrism and attacked the traditional picture, which Copernicus had retained, of fixed stars embedded in

[4] The alternative view, heliocentrism, had its ancient defenders, for example, Aristarchus.
[5] An epicycle is a circle around a circle; for example, if a dog runs around a man who is walking in a circle, the dog's motion is epicyclic.

an enormous crystalline sphere. Bruno believed stars are independent suns, each with its own solar system, scattered through infinite space, and that our earth is not the only locus of the drama of salvation. For his views Bruno was burned at the stake, and the Church officially condemned the "Copernican hypothesis."

Like Copernicus, Johann Kepler (1571–1630) possessed an almost mystical conviction that laws governing planetary motion must be simple: nothing less would do justice to God's creation. Kepler was fortunate in having access to even more accurate observations made by Tycho Brahe (1546–1601), and for years he searched for mathematical patterns in the data. Initially he was led astray by the assumption that the planets must have circular orbits (since circles are perfect figures). After many failures, he tried noncircular orbits and saw the pattern, formulated in three famous laws. The third law—the square of the time it takes a planet to orbit the sun (its year), divided by the cube of the planet's average distance from the sun, equals 1—was a spectacular and utterly unexpected insight. But the first law—planets move in elliptical orbits, with the sun at one focus—was revolutionary: it broke with the circular pattern that had gone unchallenged since the Greeks.

Galileo Galilei (1564–1642) used a telescope to challenge the Aristotelian view that there is a fundamental distinction between heavenly and earthly bodies, that they are composed of different stuff and subject to different laws. He could *see* that Jupiter had four satellites, just as the earth has a moon, and that the moon had mountains; he concluded that all these were of a uniform stuff. Galileo invited his colleagues to see for themselves, but they refused to look, or, if they looked, to believe, attributing the observations to distortions by a deceptive instrument.

Galileo's work in dynamics, the science of moving bodies, is as important as his contributions to astronomy. On the Aristotelian view,

as popularly understood, the velocity of falling bodies is a function of their weight: the heavier a body is, the faster it falls. By experiments Galileo ascertained the actual acceleration of particular falling bodies. For example, he rolled a ball down an inclined plane; varying the inclination of the board and measuring times and distances, he found that the distance traveled by the ball was always proportional to the square of the time. He invented a geometric method of representation of motion that enabled him to derive several laws, the most important of which is the law of falling bodies. Here the fundamental note of the new science had been sounded: geometry wedded to experiment.

Philosophy is written in this grand book, the universe, which stands continually open to our gaze. But the book cannot be understood unless one first learns to comprehend the language and read the letters in which it is composed. It is written in the language of mathematics, and its characters are triangles, circles, and other geometrical figures without which it is humanly impossible to understand a single word of it; without these, one wanders about in a dark labyrinth.[6]

Galileo's *Dialogue on the Two Chief World-Systems* (1632), treating the Copernican model as a physical theory, brought him to the attention of the Inquisition. He was summoned to Rome, forced to recant, and lived out his life under house arrest. It remained for René Descartes (1596–1650) to generalize Galileo's theory and methods. Descartes's invention of analytical geometry brought together two hitherto independent domains, algebra and geometry, thus enabling the power of algebraic calculations to be applied to problems of space.[7]

About a century and a half after Coperni-

---

[6] *The Assayer*, from *Discoveries and Opinions of Galileo*, ed. and trans. Stillman Drake (Garden City, N.Y.: Doubleday Anchor, 1957), pp. 237–238.
[7] His countryman Pierre Fermat (1601–1665) at least shares credit for the discovery.

cus's death, developments in astronomy and physics culminated in the most celebrated book of the age, *Mathematical Principles of Natural Philosophy* (1687), by its most celebrated scientist, Isaac Newton (1642–1727). Previously the connection between Kepler's third law and Galileo's laws of motion had not been apparent. The *Principles*, modeled roughly on Euclid's *Elements*, with an initial set of definitions (mass, momentum, force) and three "axioms" or laws of motion, demonstrated the connection. Newton generalized Galileo's laws of motion, including a more precise formulation of the principle of inertia (Newton's first law), and was able to show that were planetary bodies to obey the laws of motion, they would describe exactly the elliptical orbits Kepler had discovered. The *Principles* also formulated the law of universal gravitation, according to which every particle of matter in the universe attracts every other with a force proportional to the product of their masses and inversely proportional to the square of the distance between them. Newton assumed that all bodies, down to their smallest parts, are extended, hard, impenetrable, mobile, and inert. All bodies gravitate toward one another—this, he said, is a matter of experiment and astronomical observation—but since gravity diminishes with the square of the distance, gravity is not essential to a body in the way in which its inertia is. Inertia and universal gravitation together are sufficient to explain curved motion, both on earth (as Galileo had shown) and in planetary orbits (as Kepler had calculated).

The *Principles* gathered together in one system the achievements of Copernicus, Galileo, and Descartes. It established once and for all the utility of mathematics in the service of discovering truth about the physical universe. It established that the laws governing the solar system were the same as those governing bodies on earth. It demonstrated the power of mechanical, nonteleological explanation by offering a coherent account of bodies in terms of mass particles. It announced the discovery of a new powerful mathematical tool—the calculus. All nature suddenly seemed accessible to the human mind. In Pope's famous line, "God said, 'Let Newton be,' and all was light."

The picture one is left with, after Newton, has been called the "billiard ball universe." The physical universe is characterized entirely by time, space, material points, and forces. It consists of small, solid particles, inert but always in motion, bound together by gravitational forces and the laws of motion, and elastically rebounding from one another as they collide. A physical event is to be analyzed as motion of these particles. The system is utterly deterministic: given the position, velocity, and mass of all the particles in any closed system, the future configurations of the system can be calculated. Although Newton had established this model only for physical motion, his demonstration was so powerful that afterwards the search was on for similar explanations in all areas—from studies of electromagnetism, gases, and light, to psychology and economics. Making a subject matter "scientific" came to mean finding the "atoms" of it and quantifying the operating forces and the laws of their operation. Not until Darwin will another model of comparable influence make an appearance.

Philosophy and Method

Thus the years from Copernicus to Newton consolidated new ways to discover truth about the world. Their successes were undeniable. Galileo had wedded mathematics (Euclidean geometry) to observation and experiment. In Galileo's case, the mathematics was Euclidean geometry; Descartes added analytical geometry, and Newton (and Leibniz) contributed the calculus. Philosophy debated whether mathematics or experience was to be generalized as a model for all knowledge. The debate eventually hardened into two competing interpretations: rationalism and empiricism.

Rationalism. Rationalism, appreciating the clarity and certainty that mathematics (especially Euclidean geometry) provides, generalized it as a method for securing all knowledge. Starting from axioms guaranteed true by reason, the rest of knowledge can then be deduced as theorems. The classic defense of rationalism is still that of Descartes. It is less his substantial contributions to mathematics that give him his eminent place in modern thought than his expansion of the mathematical method, as a model for all knowledge, for its clarity, certainty, rigor, and the power of the deductive relationships between the axioms and the theorems. His vision was of a new science constructed entirely from mathematical principles, combining the best of the mathematical sciences, algebra and geometry.

[A]s I considered the matter carefully it gradually came to light that all those matters only were referred to Mathematics in which order and measurement are investigated, and that it makes no difference whether it be in numbers, figures, stars, sounds or any other object that the question of measurement arises. I saw consequently that there must be some general science to explain that element as a whole which gives rise to problems about order and measurement, restricted as these are to no special subject matter. This, I perceived, was called 'Universal Mathematics.' . . .[8]

This aim of a universal science built on mathematical principles rested on a view of geometry different from that held today: then geometry was understood as a kind of physics that provides a true description of the world. Its axioms state properties of the physical world, are self-evident and necessarily true.

For the Cartesian project the critical point is its beginning: how to guarantee the truth of the initial axioms? Descartes's answer was to test axiom candidates by the "method of doubt." Any belief about which he could conceivably be mistaken was to be set aside; thus, set aside were all beliefs based on sense perception (any one of which could be an hallucination) and even arithmetical statements (since they could be produced in us by the actions of an evil and all-powerful genius). One belief alone survived: the famous *cogito, ergo sum*— "I think, therefore I am." This is an indubitable truth, and what makes it so is only its clarity and distinctness.

I term that clear which is present and apparent to an attentive mind, in the same way as we assert that we see objects clearly when, being present to the regarding eye, they operate upon it with sufficient strength. But the distinct is that which is so precise and different from all other objects that it contains within itself nothing but what is clear.[9]

Accordingly, he formulates the general rule that what is apprehended clearly and distinctly is known to be true with certainty and hence can serve as an axiom for the universal science. It is grasped immediately, or intuited, as a

conception which an unclouded and attentive mind gives us so readily and distinctly that we are wholly freed from doubt about that which we understand.[10]

The requirement that these conceptions be distinct means that they must be the simplest of ideas. With these simple ideas as base, complex ideas, or theorems, are derived by deduction. Deduction is not essentially different from intuition, since it consists of step-by-step intuitions. Thus knowledge, whether simple or derivative, is intuitive.

Simple ideas must be innate. A famous passage of the *Meditations* illustrates from our knowledge of a piece of wax. We may think of the wax as having a particular taste, color,

[8] *Rules for the Direction of the Mind*, in *The Philosophical Works of Descartes*, ed. and trans. Elizabeth S. Haldane and G. R. T. Ross (Cambridge: University Press, 1972), vol 1, p. 13.

[9] *The Principles of Philosophy*, in *The Philosophical Works of Descartes*, vol I, p. 237.
[10] *Rules for the Direction of the Mind*, p. 7.

odor, size, and shape; yet placing the wax near fire quickly changes these properties, and we still know it as wax. How, then, do we know the wax, if it does not need *this* shape, *this* color, *this* odor?

Let us attentively consider this, and, abstracting from all that does not belong to the wax, let us see what remains. Certainly nothing remains excepting a certain extended thing which is flexible and movable. But what is the meaning of flexible and movable? Is it not that I imagine that this piece of wax being round is capable of becoming square and of passing from a square to a triangular figure? No, certainly it is not that, since I imagine it admits of an infinitude of similar changes, and I nevertheless do not know how to compass the infinitude by my imagination, and consequently this conception which I have of the wax is not brought about by the faculty of imagination. . . . We must then grant that I could not even understand through the imagination what this piece of wax is, and that it is my mind alone which perceives it.[11]

The concept of wax, with an infinite variety of possible sizes and shapes, cannot be wholly experiential. It depends on the prior understanding of extension, flexibility, and movability, wholly intellectual concepts.

Clarity and distinctness also determine real properties of the world. Only quantitative properties (e.g., extension, movability), those capable of mathematical description, pass this test. Color, smell, and taste are not distinctly conceived and are therefore phenomenal properties.[12] Matter is extension (three-dimensional) and motion is the source of all change in matter. Therefore, mathematical physics is the fundamental science, and mathematics the key to nature. Over the next two centuries physics developed along the lines laid down by Descartes. Qualitative change is explained

by showing how it emerges from more fundamental quantitative changes in the underlying material reality—the primary qualities of fundamental particles of matter. The universe is a machine, subject to mechanical laws.

There is an exception (apart from God) to this mechanical picture—the human mind. Since mind is separately conceivable clearly and distinctly, it is not material. The indubitable truth that survives the methodic doubt, my own existence, is the existence of a mind, not of a body: knowledge of the body could be hallucinatory. Mind and body differ in intrinsic properties, since the self is inherently active whereas matter is inherently inert. This dualism has the difficulty of explaining how such distinct realities could interact. (Descartes has mind and body interact in the pineal gland.) His formulation of the problem was to have long-lasting ramifications, particularly for moral theorists trying to deal with human behavior on scientific grounds; for if science applies only to material bodies, then immaterial mind lies beyond its methods and explanations.

Of the three classic rationalists of the seventeenth century, Descartes, Spinoza, and Leibniz (1646–1716), Spinoza alone extended the deductive model to moral theory. Although generally a Continental view, still rationalism had an impact in England, even on Hobbes. Lord Herbert of Cherbury (1583–1648), a friend of Hobbes, sought the foundation of ethics in "Common Notions" that "must be deemed not so much the outcome of experience as principles without which we should have no experience at all."[13] They are "inscribed" in us by nature, although they can be more or less common:

Those principles are in the highest degree common, which are common to all men and are common even beyond our species; such as the law of self-preserva-

---

[11] *Meditations on First Philosophy*, in *The Philosophical Works of Descartes*, vol I, pp. 154–155.
[12] This distinction was later named by John Locke the distinction of *primary* and *secondary* qualities and became a familiar position in modern science and philosophy.

[13] *De Veritate* (1624), trans. Meyrick H. Carre (Bristol: J. W. Arrowsmith, 1937), p. 132.

tion and the desire for happiness. Those are less common, the objects of which are uncertain or obscure. And those principles are least common which are hindered by prejudice or which possess objects that are seldom brought into conformity, so that they cannot be termed Common because the conditions required for the conformation of our truths are absent. I do not call these notions common because they are revealed in every man, whether he will or no; they are termed common because they would be so but for the fact that we ourselves prevent them entering our minds.[14]

But the clearest attempt to derive moral principles from a self-evident foundation is found in the Cambridge Platonists (see Chapter 9).

Empiricism. Where rationalism sought certainty by deduction from innate ideas or self-evident principles, empiricism employs inductive inference from observation and experiment based on sensible experience to secure knowledge as at best probable.

The classic formulation of philosophical empiricism is found in the three British philosophers John Locke (1632–1704) (Chapter 9), George Berkeley (1685–1753), and David Hume (1711–1776) (Chapter 10). The empiricist tradition is strong in British thought, reaching back to Roger Bacon in the thirteenth century. But among Descartes's contemporaries, Francis Bacon (1561–1626) was the strongest advocate.

Bacon lived in the England of Elizabeth I and Shakespeare. Man of letters, judge, scholar, government official, and scientist, under the stimulus of the cultural freedom of Elizabethan England, he set out to expand the intellectual world. Central is his view of knowledge as utilitarian, for by it man's wretched state can be improved: "I am labouring to lay the foundation, not of any sect or doctrine, but of human utility and power." [15] He criticizes current reduction of ways of knowing

to the syllogism; we should confront nature directly. Of course, experience can be biased by a host of misinterpretations and prejudices ("idols"), such as the tendency to adopt beliefs according to our desires, to attribute intention to natural phenomena, to suffer from illusion, and to mistake metaphors for literal descriptions. To learn from experience, we must purge ourselves of such prejudices, including socially biased observations and stereotyping.

Bacon offers an early analysis of induction: "that form of demonstration which upholds the sense, and closes with nature." [16] It cannot be the simple collecting of instances; simple enumeration is a "puerile thing." A proper method should establish "a true and lawful marriage between the empirical and the rational faculty." [17] The proper relation of reason and experience is shown in the famous analogy:

Those who have handled sciences have been either men of experiment or men of dogmas. The men of experiment are like the ant; they only collect and use; the reasoners resemble spiders, who make cobwebs out of their own substance. But the bee takes a middle course; it gathers its materials from the flowers of the garden and of the field, but transforms and digests it by a power of its own.[18]

Bacon is frequently charged with oversimplifying induction. While he does seem to underestimate mathematics, he clearly anticipates the experimental method, insisting that induction proceed from systematic observation and experiment to truths of limited generality, and from these to more general truths, and so on, and he proposes rules ("tables") by which observations can be transformed into scientific truths.

Bacon's contemporaries included many who were successfully using such methods. Wil-

---

[14] Ibid., pp. 126–127.
[15] *The Great Instauration,* in *The Philosophical Works of Francis Bacon,* ed. John M. Robertson (London: George Routledge, 1905), p. 247.

[16] Ibid., p. 249.
[17] Ibid., p. 246.
[18] *Novum Organum,* in *The Philosophical Works of Francis Bacon,* aphorism xcv, p. 288.

liam Gilbert's *De Magnete* (1600) reports seventeen years' research on magnetism, including an ingenious experiment to prove that the earth is a great magnet, implying that it is a natural object not excluded by its size from the physical laws governing the behavior of bodies on its surface. Gilbert stresses the navigational utility of knowledge of magnetism—for example, for improving the compass and determining latitude. Certainly the Baconian spirit rings clear in William Harvey's (1578–1657) preface to *On the Motion of the Heart and the Blood in Animals* (1628): "I profess both to learn and to teach anatomy, not from books but from dissections; not from the positions of philosophers but from the fabric of nature." Observation establishes the uniform flow of blood; experiments with ligatures establish that blood in the arteries always flows away from, and that in the veins toward, the heart. Further experiment shows that the heart propels in half an hour an amount greater than the quantity of blood in the whole body. Harvey concludes that blood must circulate from the heart to the arteries to the veins and back to the heart. The explanation is thoroughly mechanical: the heart is a muscle that expels when it contracts and receives when it expands—no appeal whatsoever to the "spirits" postulated by ancient anatomical theory.

Observational and experimental science grew apace in the seventeenth century. New instruments became available—microscope, telescope, thermometer, barometer, air pump, pendulum clock (just consider that Galileo had to conduct his experiments without an accurate clock). Scientific societies were established to provide for exchange of ideas among the larger numbers of people involved. In 1657 two disciples of Galileo, Viviani and Torricelli, established the Accademia del Cimento in Florence to carry out experiments. In England, the Royal Society, originating as informal gatherings of adherents of Francis Bacon's experimental philosophy, was formalized under royal charter in 1662. Its members included William Petty (1623–1687), who investigated the statistics of population and mortality rates; Robert Boyle (1627–1691), whose law states the relation between volume and pressure of a gas held at constant temperature, and Robert Hooke (1635–1703), who discovered the law of elasticity.

The French Academie des Sciences grew from informal meetings held in the monastic cell of Father Mersenne (1588–1648). Mersenne served virtually as a clearing house for new ideas, husbanding and publicizing much of the innovative effort of such young scientists as Descartes, Galileo, Hobbes, Fermat, Grotius, Pascal, and Gassendi (who represented Democritean and Epicurean materialism as an alternative to Descartes's physics). Mersenne passed on information, encouraged publication, and in various ways facilitated communication. He translated Galileo's *Mechanics* and Herbert of Cherbury's *De Veritate*, and arranged the publication of Hobbes's *De Cive*. The scientific tradition of quick publication, open inquiry, and submission to criticism by peers owes much to Mersenne's activities at this pivotal point in the history of science, when science was becoming institutionalized.

When toward the close of the century Newton's work appeared, Newton did not speak in one voice and so did little to settle the philosophical battle between empiricists and rationalists. He sets out the theory in a geometrical way, states the laws of motion as differential equations, and deduces consequences from his general laws. Where Kepler had induced the elliptical shape of the planetary orbits from observation, Newton deduces the shape from equations. On the other side, he also employs observation—his predictions are observational. He makes no appeal to innate ideas as such and disclaims "hypotheses," for

whatever is not deduced from the phenomena is to be called an hypothesis; and hypotheses, whether metaphysical or physical, whether of occult qualities or mechanical, have no place in experimental philosophy. In this philosophy particular propositions are inferred from the phenomena, and afterwards rendered general by induction.[19]

Thus Newtonianism was sufficiently rich that arguments from it could be extracted for both sides.

Newton's influence was felt everywhere in the eighteenth century. To be Newtonian was to be certified for entry into respectable discourse. His model was exploited everywhere— for example, by Locke in psychology to analyze perception and knowledge; by Berkeley for a social physics, and by Hume and Smith, among others, in ethics and economics (the moral sciences).

Legal Theory. Legal theory illustrates the conflict of method: for Grotius, geometry is the model; for Coke, although legal interpretation requires methods unique to the law, it is broadly inductive as reflecting accumulating experience.

In law, there are two strikingly different traditions. In Roman law, the law is laid down in a code—for example, the Justinian Code— so that the job of the jurist or lawyer is to determine the proper fit of a case to an already existing law. Here legal reasoning is deductive: starting from the law and a premise describing the case, the object is to deduce a conclusion from these premises. By contrast, in the British common law tradition law is made cumulatively—each decision adds to the body of authority determining future cases. Legal reasoning is inductive: the jurist argues from precedent, to exhibit a rule relevant to the present case by way of similarities and analogies with past cases.

The rationalist-deductive tradition is illustrated in Hugo Grotius (1583–1645), a Dutch jurist and statesman. Appalled by the violence of his time, particularly by the Thirty Years' War, and by the claims made for the absolute sovereignty of the state—memories were still fresh of Machiavelli's appeal to "reasons of state" to justify acts of state interest—Grotius argued that the domain of natural law applies not just to individuals but to states, and to relations between states, even in time of war.

Law is either natural or volitional. The natural law is grounded in the fact that human beings are naturally social, naturally impelled to seek society, and rational:

The law of nature is a dictate of right reason, which points out that an act, according as it is or is not in conformity with rational nature, has in it a quality of moral baseness or moral necessity; and that, in consequence, such an act is either forbidden or enjoined by the author of nature, God.[20]

This law of nature is self-evident, necessary, and unchangeable, even in the sense, he says, that it cannot be changed by God.[21] Natural law can be applied only by strict deduction from first principles with the rigor of mathematics:

I have made it my concern to refer the proofs of things touching the law of nature to certain fundamental conceptions which are beyond question, so that no one can deny them without doing violence to himself.[22]

Volitional law—which includes *ius gentium*, interpreted by Grotius as international law, or the legal relations *between* nations—is not strictly deducible from first principles. It is changeable, and based primarily on agreements.

---

[19] *Mathematical Principles of Natural Philosophy*, trans. Andrew Motte and revised by Florian Cajori (Berkeley: University of California Press, 1934), Book III, General Scholium.

[20] *De Jure Belli ac Pacis* (The Law of War and Peace) (1625), trans. Francis W. Kelsey (Indianapolis: Bobbs-Merrill, 1925), bk I, ch. 1, sec. x, 1.
[21] A remark in ibid., *Prolegomena*, sec. 11, that the law of nature would remain valid even if God did not exist—a thought "which cannot be conceded without the utmost wickedness"—led later writers to see in Grotius the first step to a modern secularized version of natural law.
[22] Ibid., *Prolegomena*, sec. 39.

By contrast, Sir Edward Coke (1552–1634), a chief justice of the King's Bench, moves in an empirical direction. His standing in legal history rests on a relentless campaign he waged in favor of common law as the fundamental law of England, securing the ancient rights of "Englishmen." He revered the common law as "the perfection of reason." As interpreters of this common law, judges and lawyers become final arbiters of right, against the king and even Parliament.

[I]n many cases the common law will control acts of parliament, and sometimes adjudge them to be utterly void; for when an act of parliament is against common right and reason, or repugnant, or impossible to be performed, the common law will control it and adjudge such act to be void.[23]

In this appeal to a fundamental law Coke resembles Grotius; both speak of it as the law of reason. But Grotius looks to human nature for the law of nature; Coke looks instead to the authority of precedents: "Let us now peruse our ancient authors, for out of the old fields must come the new corn." [24] To appro-

priate the past, Coke immersed himself in medieval precedents to produce his famous *Reports* as an authoritative record. Only lawyers are competent to interpret and apply these precedents, to determine from a collection of cases what the common underlying principle is. The content of the common law is thus elusive, at least to the nonlawyer.[25] But it is quite clear that the interpretative method is not deductive, building on principles evident to all rational beings.

[23] Bonham's Case (1610), in Roscoe Pound and Theodore F. T. Plucknett (eds.), *Readings on the History and System of the Common Law*, 3rd ed. (Rochester N.Y.: The Lawyers Co-operative Publishing Company, 1927), p. 33.

[24] Quoted in Theodore F. T. Plucknett, *A Concise History of the Common Law* (Rochester N.Y.: The Lawyers Co-operative Publishing Company, 1929), p. 51.

[25] Coke's *Reports* includes this account of a famous confrontation he had with King James, which turned on the claims Coke made for the need for lawyers to interpret the common law:

Then the King said that he thought the law was founded upon reason, and that he and others had reason as well as the judges: to which it was answered by me [Coke], that true it was, that God had endowed his Majesty with excellent science, and great endowment of nature; but his Majesty was not learned in the laws of his realm of England, and causes which concern the life, or inheritance, or goods or fortunes of his subjects, are not to be decided by natural reason, but by the artificial reason and judgment of law, which law is an art which requires long study and experience, before that a man can attain to the cognizance of it; and that the law was the golden met wand and measure to try the causes of the subjects and which protected his Majesty in safety and peace; with which the King was greatly offended and said that then he should be under the law, which was treason to affirm, as he said: to which I said that Bracton saith, *quod Rex non debet esse sub homine, sed sub Deo et lege* [the king ought not to be under man, but under God and the law].

(Quoted in Pound and Plucknett, *Readings on the History and System of the Common Law*, p. 187.)

8

Thomas Hobbes
(1588—1679)

Hobbes's work falls clearly on this side of the watershed just sketched—the great historical changes in living, in economic and social organization, that in tandem with the scientific and technological advances ushered in the distinctively modern. He is looking to a society that reflects a competitive individualism with its base in a growing market economy; and his writings do much to entrench and justify it. Above all, his moral theory, expressed maturely in *Leviathan*, breaks radically with the medieval outlook. Morality has been thoroughly secularized, and moral law is assimilated to physical law. Gone is virtually all reference to a transcendent or immanent purpose that provides standards or goals for human conduct or to a justice that is independent of human enactment. Hobbes resolutely limits himself to causes that belong to this world and to explanations that are plausibly experiential. Abandoned even is the appeal to the divine origin of moral and civil authority, the divine right of kings; it is replaced by secular needs and forces. His is already a functional view of institutions, including the national state and

an acknowledged plurality of religions. Good is no longer an intrinsic source of attraction; rather we label as good whatever we are attracted to. Even when Hobbes couches moral ideas in a traditional vocabulary, they are given a fresh twist: for example, *jus naturale* has the cash value of biological survival. And the virtues are no longer the feudal ones of gratitude and contentment with one's status; these give way to promise keeping and contract performance.

The very impudence of his comprehensive "grand plan" comes with a modern stamp. Human unaided reason is competent to penetrate the structure of nature and frame its workings in general laws that allow prediction and hence possible control. Starting with the principle that all that is, is matter, and all that happens, motion, Hobbes attempts to account for human behavior, society, speech, perception and action, knowledge, and even philosophy. He projects nothing less than the extension of the mathematical-empirical methods that had proved so successful in celestial and terrestrial mechanics to explain all phenomena. The grand plan contains three parts: of body, of man, and of civil society. Physics studies the consequences of the qualities (properties) of bodies in motion. A related mechanistic (physiological) psychology studies man as a particular kind of natural body with distinctive motions—desires and passions—and endowed with special properties—foresight and the ability to guide action in the light of such foresight. Ethics is a kind of physics of human attempts to satisfy desires—a sort of social physics that brings man and society under the same principles of motion as were applicable to bodies in general—while political or civil philosophy, the natural science of justice, studies such individuals in association as they generate (cause) the artificial body politic, that is, the Commonwealth or Leviathan.

To emphasize Hobbes's modernity does not mean, of course, that his theories were without anticipation, nor that they did not take shape in interplay with his contemporaries, but rather that he dealt with so much that is of present interest. The materialism that he (with Gassendi) was refurbishing was as old as Democritus and Epicurus (see Chapter 4). Like Machiavelli he sought to justify absolute sovereign power, and like Bodin he searched for natural laws that determine social behavior. He was concerned with method, especially the algebraicizing of geometry by Fermat and Descartes that gave such general power to the deductive method (although he rejected absolutely, on materialistic grounds, the Cartesian dualism of mind and matter). He followed Grotius's effort to combine deductive and inductive method for understanding mores and the law (although he rejected Grotius's view that man is social by nature). Above all he was indebted to Galileo, for method, for discoveries about motion, and for ideas about sensation; indeed Hobbes rather thought of himself as generalizing Galileo's mechanics.

Hobbes speaks across the centuries with wit and irony. It is easy to imagine him reading *Scientific American*—approving models of artificial intelligence or the mechanics of brain physiology in perception and emotion—or writing to the *Sunday Times* correcting misinterpretations of his own still debated themes. He would debate conscientious objection and civil disobedience, governmental responsibility toward the poor, crime in the streets, and the omnipresent threats of taxation and war, cold and hot. He sees no remedy for conflict between nations in the absence of power to enforce peace and agreements; and in the case of civil war he seeks arrangements for amnesty that would not leave the country deprived of its exiled talent.

Hobbes was singularly advantaged by his setting for the role he was to play. Born into Elizabeth's England while it was under threat from the Spanish Armada, he was educated at Oxford as the Tudors gave way to the Stuart James I. Oxford at the time was dominated by scholastic logic, Aristotelian physics, and medieval biology. Even then the university atmosphere was one of tension—between competing religious allegiances, and between Commons and Crown. On graduation he became a tutor (in effect, a companion) to the young William Cavendish, later earl of Devonshire. This gave him access to the seat of power, intellectual as well as political. He served briefly as Lord Bacon's secretary. He later insisted, perhaps too strenuously, that his philosophy owed Bacon little. Perhaps it did not directly, but they shared a functional view of knowledge that begins with sensation and remains true to experience. They both agreed, too, on the practical aims of philosophy; but while Bacon's assertion that knowledge is power reflected a belief in the ready advance in knowledge, for Hobbes knowledge issued from fear and anxiety about the future. (For Bacon the value of the science of navigation was doubtless the riches of a new world; for Hobbes, that it helps avoid calamities.) Through the Cavendishes Hobbes was in touch with the literary circle that included Ben Jonson and with scientific circles, especially

Herbert of Cherbury, William Petty, and William Harvey. (Indeed, Hobbes seems to have taken the clue for his mechanistic and ideomotor account of sensation and action from Harvey's discovery of the circulation of the blood.)

Connections with the Cavendish family also provided Hobbes the opportunity for his first visit to the Continent, accompanying William on the grand tour. This visit (1610–1612) awakened him to the vitality of Continental thought, largely unnoticed at Oxford. Once returned to England, he translated Thucydides's *History of the Peloponnesian War*, from which he took the lesson of the disasters of civil strife.

Two further trips (1629–1631 and 1634–1637) marked a decisive turn in Hobbes's interest and his recognition as a philosopher. In Paris he was received cordially by Father Mersenne. It is probable that in Mersenne's circle Hobbes first learned of Grotius's *De Jure Belli ac Pacis*, and it is certain that there he came to appreciate Euclid and the importance of geometry as providing a general method for reasoning. Geometry at that time was allied to motion and mechanics, that is to say, was interpreted as dealing with the dynamic generation of figures. Hobbes also then worked on problems of motion in optics and physiology. For example, he speculated that without movement of the eyes the image would disappear; and he wondered whether sensation generally might not be explained causally by motion transmitted from external objects along the nerves (strings). With such ideas in mind, he sought out Galileo in Florence, at that time under house detention by the Inquisition, and visited him almost daily for several months. In the end Hobbes's interest in sensation and perception went beyond Galileo's. For Hobbes the motion involved in sensation, meeting a brain already in motion, gives rise to images (phantasms), and then an equal and opposite motion outward along the nerves accounts both for the belief in external objects and for action. The external stimulus also affects the *vital mo-*

tions, such as the activity of the heart: when the stimulus is helpful (increases vitality), there is a motion or endeavor (an *appetite* or a *desire*) toward what causes it; when the stimulus hinders vital motion, there arises a motion away or *aversion*. Appetites and aversions are objective designations of what is experienced on the subjective side as pleasure and pain. We call good what satisfies, and hence what is good is relative to the individual. When modified by those distinctive capacities—of reasoning in regulated sequence, of foreseeing, of learning by experience—desires and appetites can be postponed or altered for long-term satisfaction.

By the time Hobbes returned to England in 1637 he had the full outline of his "grand plan" well in hand, but he was deflected from its orderly realization by the imminence of civil strife. Accordingly, moved by the immediate importance of the ethical and political part, he turned to it first, providing just enough of the psychology to support it. In the spring of 1640 he circulated a manuscript, a "Little Treatise," arguing that many of the powers then in contention between Charles I and Parliament, including the vital one of taxation and the controversial one of a uniform prayer book, were indissolubly annexed to the sovereign. Parliament was seriously irked, and not without some reason Hobbes felt himself in danger. So a fourth time he left England, not to return for eleven years.

Mersenne welcomed him back into the old circle, and once again Hobbes became deeply involved in philosophic debate. Mersenne arranged the publication of *De Cive* (1642) which amplified the "Little Treatise." Other works of his were published in Europe. They all bear virtually the same message as *Leviathan*, which was composed during his last years in exile.

Leviathan is best known for how it shaped the theory of the social contract. In a state of nature every man has an unlimited right to everything (effectively no secure right to anything). There is neither justice nor injustice, and self-preservation is the only rule. In such a state of anarchy, there is no culture, commerce, civilization, law, no mine and thine (i.e., no property); in the famous phrase, life would be "solitary, poor, nasty, brutish, and short." But men are led by reason and by passion—the fear of death and injury, the desire and hope for a long and pleasant life—to lift themselves out of this state of insecurity. They do this by relinquishing a part of their unlimited rights on the condition that others do so as well, that is, by promising or contracting mutually. This contract enstates political society and morality. Reason advises obedience to certain laws of nature, among which are to seek peace, to keep contracts or promises, and to be content with as much liberty for oneself as is allowed to others. Since self-interest may on occasion dictate the breaking of the covenant, a coercive political power is needed as a guardian of the covenant and the surrendered rights. In effect, each man surrenders the exclusive rights of self-government to an authority or sovereign. The wills of all are thus united in a single will, which establishes the Commonwealth; but once established, the authority of the sovereign (who is not party to the contract) is all-encompassing and it determines the means of peace, censorship, the interpretation of law and property, the established religion, and what is just and what is right. Reserved to the individual is only the right of self-defense and the right not to incriminate oneself, since self-preservation was the ground for the original contract. Strictly speaking, sovereignty and authority may be vested in an assembly of men, but Hobbes's clear preference is for a monarchy, in the instance, the Stuarts.

Leviathan has four parts. The accounts of method and human nature form *Of Man* (Part I); that of ethics and politics, *Of Commonwealth* (Part II). The remainder, more than half of the book—*Of a Christian Commonwealth* and *Of the Kingdom of Darkness* (Parts III and IV)—deals with the relation between religion, church, the Scriptures, and civil authority. Hobbes was facing a situation in which civil strife—at least in its more overt form—revolved around the political claims of Puritan, Presbyterian, Anglican, and Catholic; it was crossed by the issue of private conscience versus civil law. He shows by ingenious and pyrotechnic analysis of the Scriptures how all that he has offered about seeking peace, undivided sovereignty, and the supremacy of the civil authority is supported by the Bible. Hence the state religion must be determined by the sovereign, and even the correct interpretation of the Bible. Anarchy threatens if such questions are left to private conscience or particular sects inflamed by the passions of religious conviction and self-righteousness. The need to preserve the social order takes precedence over the pretensions of any clergy. The individual's salvation is not menaced, since the onus then rests with the king, and sovereignty is itself required by the Bible. Nor is the requirement for the individual onerous: outward conformity in speech and act (prayer and rituals) is all that is demanded; belief or thought cannot be coerced. Hobbes's account of institutional religion is not delicately etched.

Traditional religions and theology have exploited the fears and anxieties of imaginary things, unlike earthquakes and fire, to gain power and authority. They introduced demons, ghosts, fairies, and incorporeal spirits, and mixed with the Scriptures diverse relics of religion and much of the vain and erroneous philosophy of the Greeks, especially Aristotle. Thus they made it appear that the Kingdom of God is of this world and sanctions a religious power as distinct from the civil state. Gods that are products of fear must be distinguished from the one God that is a postulate of science, the efficient cause of all things. But much can be done scientifically before appealing to God. Indeed God's attributes are not matters to be proven, not matters of truth at all, but attributes that express our intention to reverence and honor Him. In sum, for the individual's salvation, the two virtues are obedience to laws and faith in Christ. The former takes care of and relieves him of responsibility for the present; the latter secures a remission of sins for the past.

Leviathan was published in London in 1651, when Cromwell was in power. The years of Hobbes's exile had seen momentous changes in English political life. By 1644 the fortunes of the Civil War had clearly turned against Charles I, and by 1649 he had been beheaded. Charles's son, later to be Charles II, had fled to Paris, where a growing number of royalists gathered around him. Hobbes moved in this circle, even tutoring the prince in mathematics. Hobbes was already suspect for his views, especially with the French Catholics and the exiled Anglicans. Even so, he thought to present a copy of *Leviathan* to the prince and was apparently amazed that his friends discouraged this because, among other, things it included the conditions under which and at

what point of time it is that a subject becomes obliged to the conqueror . . . if a man, when his country is conquered, be out of it, he is not conquered, nor subject: but if at his return he submit to the government, he is bound to obey it. [*Leviathan*, "A Review and Conclusion"]

By mid-century Hobbes was restive, perhaps thinking about returning home. With Mersenne's death in 1648 his group had lost its focus, and the Cavendish family had returned to England on the promise of abstaining from politics. Feeling harassed now in Paris, Hobbes left secretly for London in the winter of 1651 and made his submission to the Cromwellians. With the Restoration in 1660 he might have faced a fresh problem, but Charles II, recognizing his old tutor in the street, welcomed him to court but prohibited him from publishing "tendentious books" in England (the works continued to appear abroad).

Hobbes died after nineteen more years of enjoyable wrangling on matters mathematical, literary, and legal, and themes of liberty and necessity. The voluminous *Dialogue between a Philosopher and a Student of the Common Laws of England*, mainly applying the theory of the *Leviathan* to the specific case of the law, challenged Coke's claims that the law is the common law, that reason is the life of the law, and that only lawyers by their specialized study are in a position to grasp it. On the contrary, says Hobbes, custom is not necessarily rational, nor precedent necessarily binding. It is the sovereign's recognition of what law intends that makes it the law; the interpretation that he commands is positive law.

Hobbes's work was enormously influential. Even in his own day Europe recognized it as a powerful, if dangerous, force. His theories were controversial in Dutch political circles. He influenced Continental rationalists: Spinoza profoundly in his account of emotions, and Leibniz especially in his theory of method. Pufendorf owes him much. In the next century the French read him, and Diderot included a laudatory account of Hobbes in the *Encyclopédie*.

In his own country in his own time he was equally famous, or infamous. The popular mind laid the London fire and plague at the door of his atheistic philosophy; he narrowly missed a parliamentary charge of heresy. Among the intellectuals, some misunderstood or willfully misinterpreted him, turning attacks on him to their own advantage. But others in that century and the next recognized the serious issues he had raised, especially the arbitrary and conventional character of morality, its enstatement by the contract, and the character of popular consent (see Chapter 9). The eighteenth century was particularly concerned with amplifying or correcting his view of human nature—often supplementing his egoism with the recognition of more benign sentiments, such as sympathy, benevolence, and humanity (see Chapter 10). In the nineteenth century, the utilitarians began to rehabilitate his reputation. They shared his hedonism but sought to mute the egoism (see Chapters 12 and 16). And they appreciated his view of law as command and his effort to make a science of legislation and morals. It was a utilitarian, Molesworth, who issued the collected works of Hobbes.

In the twentieth century, at least in the popular mind, Hobbes's reputation has taken on a destiny of its own as stereotyping a gross self-interested hedonism. But to the more serious-minded he presents problems of interpretation; for example, is his an ethical hedonism, a psychological hedonism, or indeed no hedonism at all?

Leviathan [1]

Part I: Of Man

VI. Of the Interior Beginnings of Voluntary Motions; Commonly Called the Passions; and the Speeches by Which They Are Expressed

There be in animals, two sorts of *motions* peculiar to them: one called *vital;* begun in generation, and continued without interruption through their whole life; such as are the *course* of the *blood,* the *pulse,* the *breathing,* the *concoction, nutrition, excretion,* etc., to which motions there needs no help of imagination: the other is *animal motion,* otherwise called *voluntary motion;* as to *go,* to *speak,* to *move* any of our limbs, in such manner as is first fancied in our minds. That sense is motion in the organs and interior parts of man's body, caused by the action of the things we see, hear, etc.; and that fancy is but the relics of the same motion, remaining after sense, has been already said in the first and second chapters. And because *going, speaking,* and the like voluntary motions, depend always upon a precedent thought of *whither, which way,* and *what;* it is evident, that the imagination is the first internal beginning of all voluntary motion. . . . These small beginnings of motion, within the body of man, before

they appear in walking, speaking, striking, and other visible actions, are commonly called ENDEAVOR.

This endeavor, when it is toward something which causes it, is called APPETITE, or DESIRE; the latter, being the general name; and the other oftentimes restrained to signify the desire of food, namely *hunger* and *thirst.* And when the endeavor is fromward something, it is generally called AVERSION. These words, *appetite* and *aversion,* we have from the Latins; and they both of them signify the motions, one of approaching, the other of retiring. . . .

That which men desire, they are also said to LOVE: and to HATE those things for which they have aversion. So that desire and love are the same thing; save that by desire, we always signify the absence of the object; by love, most commonly the presence of the same. So also by aversion, we signify the absence; and by hate, the presence of the object.

Of appetites and aversions, some are born with men; as appetite of food, appetite of excretion, and exoneration, which may also and more properly be called aversions, from somewhat they feel in their bodies; and some other appetites, not many. The rest, which are appetites of particular things, proceed from experience, and trial of their effects upon themselves or other men. For of things we know not at all, or believe not to be, we can have no further desire, than to taste and try. But aversion we have for things, not only which we know have hurt us, but also that we do not know whether they will hurt us, or not. . . .

And because the constitution of a man's body is in continual mutation, it is impossible that all the same things should always cause in him the same appetites, and aversions: much less can all men consent, in the desire of almost any one and the same object.

But whatsoever is the object of any man's appetite or desire, that is it which he for his part calls *good:* and the object of his hate and aversion, *evil;* and of his contempt, *vile* and *inconsiderable.* For these words of good, evil, and contemptible, are ever used with relation to the person that uses them: there being nothing simply and absolutely so; nor any common rule of good and evil, to be taken from the nature of the objects themselves; but from the person of the man, where there is no commonwealth; or, in a commonwealth, from the person

[1] London, 1651. The selection is based on Sir William Molesworth's edition of the *Complete Works* (1839–1845), with some emendation and modernization by the editors of this volume.

that represents it; or from an arbitrator or judge, whom men disagreeing shall by consent set up, and make his sentence the rule thereof.

. . . [O]f good there be three kinds; good in the promise, that is *pulchrum;* good in effect, as the end desired, which is called *jucundum, delightful;* and good as the means, which is called *utile, profitable;* and as many of evil: for *evil* in promise, is that they call *turpe;* evil in effect, and end, is *molestum, unpleasant, troublesome;* and evil in the means, *inutile, unprofitable, hurtful.*

As, in sense, that which is really within us, is, as I have said before, only motion, caused by the action of external objects, but in appearance; to the sight, light and color; to the ear, sound; to the nostril, odor, etc.: so, when the action of the same object is continued from the eyes, ears, and other organs to the heart, the real effect there is nothing but motion, or endeavor; which consists in appetite, or aversion, to or from the object moving. But the appearance, or sense of that motion, is that we either call *delight,* or *trouble of mind.*

This motion, which is called appetite, and for the appearance of it *delight,* and *pleasure,* seems to be a corroboration of vital motion, and a help thereunto; and therefore such things as caused delight, were not improperly called *jucunda,* . . . from helping or fortifying; and the contrary, *molesta, offensive,* from hindering, and troubling the motion vital.

Pleasure therefore, or *delight,* is the appearance, or sense of good; and *molestation,* or *displeasure,* the appearance, or sense of evil. And consequently all appetite, desire, and love, is accompanied with some delight more or less; and all hatred and aversion, with more or less displeasure and offense.

Of pleasures or delights, some arise from the sense of an object present; and those may be called *pleasure of sense.* . . . Others arise from the expectation, that proceeds from foresight of the end, or consequence of things; whether those things in the sense please or displease. And these are *pleasures of the mind* of him that draws those consequences, and are generally called JOY. In the like manner, displeasures are some in the sense, and called PAIN; others in the expectation of consequences, and are called GRIEF.

These simple passions called *appetite, desire, love, aversion, hate, joy* and *grief,* have their names for divers considerations diversified. As first, when they one succeed another, they are diversely called from the opinion men have of the likelihood of attaining what they desire. Secondly, from the object loved or hated. Thirdly, from the consideration of many of them together. Fourthly, from the alteration or succession itself.

For example: *Hope* is appetite when the opinion of attaining is present, *despair,* when it is absent. *Fear* is aversion with the opinion of hurt, *courage,* the same with the hope of avoiding that hurt by resistance. *Anger* is sudden courage. Anger for a hurt done to another is *indignation.* Grief, for the discovery of some defect of ability, is *shame* (which discovers itself in blushing). Grief for the calamity of another, is *pity;* and when it arises from the imagination that a like calamity may befall himself, is *compassion.*

Grief, for the success of a competitor in wealth, honor, or other good, if it be joined with endeavor to enforce our own abilities to equal or exceed him, is called EMULATION: but joined with endeavor to supplant, or hinder a competitor, ENVY.

When in the mind of man, appetites, and aversions, hopes, and fears, concerning one and the same thing, arise alternately; and divers good and evil consequences of the doing, or omitting the thing propounded, come successively into our thoughts; so that sometimes we have an appetite to it; sometimes an aversion from it; sometimes hope to be able to do it; sometimes despair, or fear to attempt it; the whole sum of desires, aversions, hopes and fears continued till the thing be either done, or thought impossible, is that we call DELIBERATION.

Therefore of things past, there is no *deliberation;* because manifestly impossible to be changed: nor of things known to be impossible, or thought so; because men know, or think such deliberation vain. But of things impossible, which we think possible, we may deliberate; not knowing it is in vain. And it is called *deliberation;* because it is a putting an end to the *liberty* we had of doing, or omitting, according to our own appetite, or aversion.

This alternate succession of appetites, aversions, hopes and fears, is no less in other living creatures than in man: and therefore beasts also deliberate.

Every *deliberation* is then said to *end,* when that whereof they deliberate, is either done, or thought impossible; because till then we retain the liberty of doing, or omitting; according to our appetite, or aversion.

In *deliberation*, the last appetite, or aversion, immediately adhering to the action, or to the omission thereof, is that we call the WILL; the act, not the faculty, of *willing*. And beasts that have *deliberation*, must necessarily also have *will*. The definition of the *will*, given commonly by the Schools, that it is a *rational appetite*, is not good. For if it were, then could there be no voluntary act against reason. For a *voluntary act* is that, which proceeds from the *will*, and no other. But if instead of a rational appetite, we shall say an appetite resulting from a precedent deliberation, then the definition is the same that I have given here. *Will*, therefore, *is the last appetite in deliberating*. And though we say in common discourse, a man had a will once to do a thing, that nevertheless he forebore to do; yet that is properly but an inclination, which makes no action voluntary; because the action depends not of it, but of the last inclination, or appetite. For if the intervenient appetites, make any action voluntary; then by the same reason all intervenient aversions, should make the same action involuntary; and so one and the same action, should be both voluntary and involuntary.

By this it is manifest, that not only actions that have their beginning from covetousness, ambition, lust, or other appetites to the thing propounded; but also those that have their beginning from aversion, or fear of those consequences that follow the omission, are *voluntary actions*.

The forms of speech by which the passions are expressed, are partly the same, and partly different from those, by which we express our thoughts. And first, generally all passions may be expressed *indicatively*; as *I love, I fear, I joy, I deliberate, I will, I command*: but some of them have particular expressions by themselves, which nevertheless are not affirmations, unless it be when they serve to make other inferences, besides that of the passion they proceed from. Deliberation is expressed *subjunctively*; which is a speech proper to signify suppositions, with their consequences: as, *if this be done, then this will follow*: and differs not from the language of reasoning, save that reasoning is in general words; but deliberation for the most part is of particulars. The language of desire, and aversion, is *imperative*; as *do this, forbear that*; which when the party is obliged to do, or forbear, is *command*; otherwise *prayer*; or else *counsel*.

The language of vain-glory, of indignation, pity and revengefulness, *optative*: but of the desire to know, there is a peculiar expression called *interrogative*; as, *what is it, when shall it, how is it done*, and *why so*? other language of the passions I find none: for cursing, swearing, reviling, and the like, do not signify as speech; but as the actions of a tongue accustomed.

These forms of speech, I say, are expressions, or voluntary significations of our passions: but certain signs they be not; because they may be used arbitrarily, whether they that use them, have such passions or not. The best signs of passions present, are either in the countenance, motions of the body, actions, and ends, or aims, which we otherwise know the man to have.

And because in deliberation, the appetites, and aversions, are raised by foresight of the good and evil consequences, and sequels of the action whereof we deliberate; the good or evil effect thereof depends on the foresight of a long chain of consequences, of which very seldom any man is able to see the end. But for so far as a man sees, if the good in those consequences be greater than the evil, the whole chain is that which writers call *apparent*, or *seeming good*. And contrarily, when the evil exceeds the good, the whole is *apparent*, or *seeming evil*: so that he who has by experience, or reason, the greatest and surest prospect of consequences, deliberates best himself; and is able when he will, to give the best counsel unto others.

Continual success in obtaining those things which a man from time to time desires, that is to say, continual prospering, is that men call FELICITY; I mean the felicity of this life. For there is no such thing as perpetual tranquillity of mind, while we live here; because life itself is but motion, and can never be without desire, nor without fear, no more than without sense. . . .

The form of speech whereby men signify their opinion of the goodness of anything, is PRAISE. That whereby they signify the power and greatness of anything, is MAGNIFYING. . . .

VIII. Of the Virtues Commonly Called Intellectual; and Their Contrary Defects

VIRTUE generally, in all sorts of subjects, is somewhat that is valued for eminence; and consists in comparison. For if all things were equal in all men, nothing would be prized. And by *virtues intellectual*, are always understood such abilities of the mind, as men praise, value, and desire should be in themselves; and go commonly under the name of a *good wit*; though the same word *wit*, be used also, to distinguish one certain ability from the rest.

These *virtues* are of two sorts; *natural*, and *acquired*. By natural, I mean not, that which a man has from his birth: for that is nothing else but sense; wherein men differ so little one from another, and from brute beasts, as it is not to be reckoned amongst virtues. But I mean, that *wit*, which is gotten by use only, and experience; without method, culture, or instruction. This NATURAL WIT, consists principally in two things; *celerity of imagining*, that is, swift succession of one thought to another; and *steady direction* to some approved end. On the contrary a slow imagination, makes that defect, or fault of the mind, which is commonly called DULLNESS, *stupidity*. . . .

And this difference of quickness, is caused by the difference of men's passions; that love and dislike, some one thing, some another: and therefore some men's thoughts run one way, some another; and are held to, and observe differently the things that pass through their imagination. And whereas in this succession of men's thoughts, there is nothing to observe in the things they think on, but either in what they be *like one another*, or in what they be *unlike*, or *what they serve for*, or *how they serve to such a purpose*; those that observe their similitudes, in case they be such as are but rarely observed by others, are said to have a *good wit*; by which, in this occasion is meant, a *good fancy*. But they that observe their differences, and dissimilitudes; which is called *distinguishing*, and *discerning*, and *judging* between thing and thing; in case such discerning be not easy, are said to have a *good judgment*; and particularly in matter of conversation and business, wherein, times, places, and persons are to be discerned, this virtue is called DISCRETION. . . .

The secret thoughts of a man run over all things, holy, profane, clean, obscene, grave, and light, without shame, or blame; which verbal discourse cannot do, farther than the judgment shall approve of the time, place, and persons. An anatomist, or a physician may speak, or write his judgment of unclean things: because it is not to please, but profit: but for another man to write his extravagant, and pleasant fancies of the same, is as if a man, from being tumbled into the dirt, should come and present himself before good company. And it is the want of discretion that makes the difference. . . .

When the thoughts of a man, that has a design in hand, running over a multitude of things, observes how they conduce to that design; or what design they may conduce unto; if his observations be such as are not easy, or usual, this wit of his is called PRUDENCE; and depends on much experience, and memory of the like things, and their consequences heretofore. In which there is not so much difference of men; as there is in their fancies and judgment; because the experience of men equal in age, is not much unequal, as to the quantity; but lies in different occasions; every one having his private designs. To govern well a family, and a kingdom, are not different degrees of prudence; but different sorts of business. . . . A plain husbandman is more prudent in affairs of his own house, than a privy-councilor in the affairs of another man. . . .

As for *acquired wit*, I mean acquired by method and instruction, there is none but reason; which is grounded on the right use of speech, and produces the sciences. . . .

The causes of this difference of wits are in the passions . . . which are different, not only from the difference of men's complexions; but also from their difference of customs, and education.

The passions that most of all cause the difference of wit, are principally, the more or less desire of power, of riches, of knowledge, and of honor. All which may be reduced to the first, that is, desire of power. For riches, knowledge, and honor, are but several sorts of power.

And therefore, a man who has no great passion for any of these things; but is, as men term it, indifferent; though he may be so far a good man, as to be free from giving offense; yet he cannot possibly have either a great fancy, or much judgment. For the thoughts are to the desires, as scouts, and spies, to range abroad, and find the way to the things desired: all steadiness of the mind's motion, and all quickness of the same, proceeding from thence: for as to have no desire, is to be dead: so to have weak passions, is dullness; and to have passions indifferently for everything, GIDDINESS, and *distraction*; and to have stronger and more vehement passions for anything, than is ordinarily seen in others, is that which men call MADNESS. . . .

X. Of Power, Worth, Dignity, Honor, and Worthiness

The power *of a man*, to take it universally, is his present means; to obtain some future apparent good; and is either *original* or *instrumental*.

Natural power, is the eminence of the faculties of body, or mind: as extraordinary strength, form, prudence, arts, eloquence, liberality, nobility. *Instrumental* are those powers, which acquired by these, or by fortune, are means and instruments to acquire more; as riches, reputation, friends, and the secret working of God, which men call good luck. For the nature of power, is in this point, like to fame, increasing as it proceeds; or like the motion of heavy bodies, which the further they go, make still the more haste.

The greatest of human powers, is that which is compounded of the powers of most men, united by consent, in one person, natural, or civil, that has the use of all their powers depending on his will; such as is the power of a commonwealth: or depending on the wills of each particular; such as is the power of a faction or of divers factions leagued. Therefore to have servants, is power; to have friends, is power: for they are strengths united.

Other sources of power include riches, reputation of power, popularity, affability (since it gains love), science, and arts of public use (technology).

The *value* or WORTH of a man is, as of all other things, his price; that is to say, so much as would be given for the use of his power: and therefore is not absolute; but a thing dependent on the need and judgment of another. An able conductor of soldiers, is of great price in time of war present, or imminent; but in peace not so. A learned and uncorrupt judge, is much worth in time of peace; but not so much in war. And as in other things, so in men, not the seller, but the buyer determines the price. For let a man, as most men do, rate themselves at the highest value they can; yet their true value is no more than it is esteemed by others.

The manifestation of the value we set on one another, is that which is commonly called honoring and dishonoring. To value a man at a high rate, is to *honor* him; at a low rate, is to *dishonor* him. But high, and low, in this case, is to be understood by comparison to the rate that each man sets on himself.

The public worth of a man, which is the value set on him by the commonwealth, is that which men commonly call *dignity*.

WORTHINESS is a thing different from the worth, or value of a man; and also from his merit, or desert, and consists in a particular power, or ability for that, whereof he is said to be worthy; which particular ability, is usually named FITNESS, or *aptitude*.

For he is worthiest to be a commander, to be a judge, or to have any other charge, that is best fitted, with the qualities required to the well discharging of it; and worthiest of riches, that has the qualities most requisite for the well using of them: any of which qualities being absent, one may nevertheless be a worthy man, and valuable for something else. Again, a man may be worthy of riches, office, and employment, that nevertheless, can plead no right to have it before another; and therefore cannot be said to merit or deserve it. For merit presupposes a right, and that the thing deserved is due by promise: of which I shall say more hereafter, when I shall speak of contracts.

XIII. Of the Natural Condition of Mankind as Concerning Their Felicity, and Misery

Nature has made men so equal, in the faculties of the body, and mind; as that though there be found one man sometimes manifestly stronger in body, or of quicker mind than another; yet when all is reckoned together, the difference between man, and man, is not so considerable, as that one man can thereupon claim to himself any benefit, to which another may not pretend, as well as he. For as to the strength of body, the weakest has strength enough to kill the strongest, either by secret machination, or by confederacy with others, that are in the same danger with himself.

And as to the faculties of the mind, setting aside the arts grounded upon words, and especially that skill of proceeding upon general, and infallible rules, called science; which very few have, and but in few things; as being not a native faculty, born with us; nor attained, as prudence, while we look after somewhat else, I find yet a greater equality amongst men, than that of strength. For prudence, is but experience; which equal time, equally bestows on all men, in those things they equally apply themselves unto. That which may perhaps make such equality incredible, is but a vain conceit of one's own wisdom, which almost all men think they have in a greater degree, than the vulgar; that is, than all men but themselves, and a few others, whom by fame, or for concurring with themselves, they approve. For such is the nature of men, that howsoever they may acknowledge many others to be more witty, or more eloquent, or more learned; yet they will hardly believe there be many so wise as themselves; for they see their own wit at hand, and other men's at a distance. But this proves rather that men are in that point equal, than unequal. For there is not ordinarily a greater sign of the equal distribution of any thing, than that every man is contented with his share.

From this equality of ability, arises equality of hope in the attaining of our ends. And therefore if any two men desire the same thing, which nevertheless they cannot both enjoy, they become enemies; and in the way to their end, which is principally their own conservation, and sometimes their delectation only, endeavor to destroy, or subdue one another. And from hence it comes to pass, that where an invader has no more to fear, than another man's single power; if one plant, sow, build, or possess a convenient seat, others may probably be expected to come prepared with forces united, to dispossess, and deprive him, not only of the fruit of his labor, but also of his life, or liberty. And the invader again is in the like danger of another.

And from this diffidence of one another, there is no way for any man to secure himself, so reasonable, as anticipation; that is, by force, or wiles, to master the persons of all men he can, so long, till he see no other power great enough to endanger him: and this is no more than his own conservation requires, and is generally allowed. Also because there be some, that taking pleasure in contemplating their own power in the acts of conquest, which they pursue farther than their security requires; if others, that otherwise would be glad to be at ease within modest bounds, should not by invasion increase their power, they would not be able, long time, by standing only on their defense, to subsist. And by consequence, such augmentation of dominion over men being necessary to a man's conservation, it ought to be allowed him.

Again, men have no pleasure, but on the contrary a great deal of grief, in keeping company, where there is no power able to over-awe them all. For every man looks that his companion should value him, at the same rate he sets upon himself: and upon all signs of contempt, or undervaluing, naturally endeavors, as far as he dares, (which amongst them that have no common power to keep them in quiet, is far enough to make them destroy each other), to extort a greater value from his contemners, by damage; and from others, by the example.

So that in the nature of man, we find three principal causes of quarrel. First, competition; secondly, diffidence; thirdly, glory.

The first, makes men invade for gain; the second, for safety; and the third, for reputation. The first use violence, to make themselves masters of other men's persons, wives, children, and cattle; the second, to defend them; the third, for trifles, as a word, a smile, a different opinion, and any other sign of undervalue, either direct in their persons, or by reflection in their kindred, their friends, their nation, their profession, or their name.

Hereby it is manifest, that during the time men live without a common power to keep them all in awe, they are in that condition which is called war; and such a war, as is of every man, against every man. For WAR, consists not in battle only, or the act of fighting; but in a tract of time, wherein the will to contend by battle is sufficiently known: and therefore the notion of *time*, is to be considered in the nature of war; as it is in the nature of weather. For as the nature of foul weather, lies not in a shower or two of rain; but in an inclination thereto of many days together: so the nature of war, consists not in actual fighting; but in the known disposition thereto, during all the time there is no assurance to the contrary. All other time is PEACE.

Whatsoever therefore is consequent to a time of war, where every man is enemy to every man; the same is consequent to the time, wherein men live without other security, than what their own strength, and their own invention shall furnish them withal. In such condition, there is no place for industry; because the fruit thereof is uncertain: and consequently no culture of the earth; no navigation, nor use of the commodities that may be imported by sea; no commodious building; no instruments of moving, and removing, such things as require much force; no knowledge of the face of the earth; no account of time; no arts; no letters; no society; and which is worst of all, continual fear, and danger of violent death; and the life of man, solitary, poor, nasty, brutish, and short.

It may seem strange to some man, that has not well weighed these things; that nature should thus dissociate, and render men apt to invade, and destroy one another: and he may therefore, not trusting to this inference, made from the passions, desire perhaps to have the same confirmed by experience. Let him therefore consider with himself, when taking a journey, he arms himself, and seeks to go well accompanied; when going to sleep, he locks his doors; when even in his house he locks his chests; and this when he knows there be laws, and public officers, armed, to revenge all injuries shall be done him; what opinion he has of his fellow-subjects, when he rides armed; of his fellow citizens, when he locks his doors; and of his children, and servants, when he locks his chests. Does he not there as much accuse mankind by his actions, as I do by my words? But neither of us accuse man's nature in it. The desires, and other passions of man, are in themselves no sin. No more are the actions, that proceed from those passions, till they know a law that forbids them: which till laws be made they cannot know: nor can any law be made, till they have agreed upon the person that shall make it.

It may peradventure be thought, there was never such a time, nor condition of war as this; and I believe it was never generally so, over all the world: but there are many places, where they live so now. For the savage people in many places of America, except the government of small families, the concord whereof depends on natural lust, have no government at all; and live at this day in that brutish manner, as I said before. Howsoever, it may be perceived what manner of life there would be, where there were no common power to fear, by the manner of life, which men that have formerly lived under a peaceful government, use to degenerate into, in a civil war.

But though there had never been any time, wherein particular men were in a condition of war one against another; yet in all times, kings, and persons of sovereign authority, because of their independency, are in continual jealousies, and in the state and posture of gladiators; having their weapons pointing, and their eyes fixed on one another; that is, their forts, garrisons, and guns upon the frontiers of their kingdoms; and continual spies upon their neighbors; which is a posture of war. But because they uphold thereby, the industry of their subjects; there does not follow from it, that misery, which accompanies the liberty of particular men.

To this war of every man, against every man, this also is consequent; that nothing can be unjust. The notions of right and wrong, justice and injustice have there no place. Where there is no common power, there is no law: where no law, no injustice. Force, and fraud, are in war the two cardinal virtues. Justice, and injustice are none of the faculties neither of the body, nor mind. If they were, they might be in a man that were alone in the world, as well as his senses, and passions. They are qualities, that relate to men in society, not in solitude. It is consequent also to the same condition, that there be no propriety, no dominion, no *mine* and *thine* distinct; but only that to be every man's, that he can get; and for so long, as he can keep it. And thus much for the ill condition, which man by mere nature is actually placed in; though with a possibility to come out of it, consisting partly in the passions, partly in his reason.

The passions that incline men to peace, are fear of death; desire of such things as are necessary to commodious living; and a hope by their industry to obtain them. And reason suggests convenient articles of peace, upon which men may be drawn to agreement. These articles, are they, which otherwise are called the Laws of Nature: whereof I shall speak more particularly, in the two following chapters.

XIV. Of the First and Second Natural Laws, and of Contracts

The RIGHT OF NATURE, which writers commonly call *jus naturale*, is the liberty each man has, to use his own power, as he will himself, for the preservation of his own nature; that is to say, of his own life; and consequently, of doing anything, which in his own judgment, and reason, he shall conceive to be the aptest means thereunto.

By LIBERTY, is understood, according to the proper signification of the word, the absence of external impediments: which impediments, may oft take away part of a man's power to do what he would; but cannot hinder him from using the power left him, according as his judgment, and reason shall dictate to him.

A LAW OF NATURE, *lex naturalis*, is a precept or general rule, found out by reason, by which a man is forbidden to do that, which is destructive of his life, or takes away the means of preserving the same; and to omit that, by which he thinks it may be best preserved. For though they that speak of this subject, use to confound *jus*, and *lex*, right and *law*: yet they ought to be distinguished; because RIGHT, consists in liberty to do, or to forbear; whereas LAW, determines, and binds to one of them: so that law, and right, differ as much, as obligation, and liberty; which in one and the same matter are inconsistent.

And because the condition of man, as has been declared in the precedent chapter, is a condition of war of every one against every one; in which case every one is governed by his own reason; and there is nothing he can make use of, that may not be a help unto him, in preserving his life against his enemies; it follows, that in such a condition, every man has a right to every thing; even to one another's body. And therefore, as long as this natural right of every man to every thing endures, there can be no security to any man, how strong or wise soever he be, of living out the time, which nature ordinarily allows men to live. And consequently it is a precept, or general rule of reason, *that every man, ought to endeavor peace, as far as he has hope of obtaining it; and when he cannot obtain it, that he may seek, and use, all helps, and advantages of war.* The first branch of which rule, contains the first, and fundamental law of nature; which is, *to seek peace, and follow it.* The second, the sum of the right of nature; which is, *by all means we can, to defend ourselves.*

From this fundamental law of nature, by which men are commanded to endeavor peace, is derived this second law; *that a man be willing, when others are so too, as far forth, as for peace, and defense of himself he shall think it necessary, to lay down this right to all things; and be contented with so much liberty against other men, as he would allow other men against himself.* For as long as every man holds this right, of doing any thing he likes; so long are all men in the condition of war. But if other men will not lay down their right, as well as he; then there is no reason for anyone, to divest himself of his: for that were to expose himself to prey, which no man is bound to, rather than to dispose himself to peace. This is that law of the Gospel; *whatsoever you require that others should do to you, that do ye to them.* And that law of all men, *quod tibi fieri non vis, alteri ne feceris* ["that which you wish not to be done to you, do not to another"].

To *lay down* a man's *right* to any thing, is to *divest* himself of the *liberty,* of hindering another of the benefit of his own right to the same. For he that renounces, or passes away his right, gives not to any other man a right which he had not before; because there is nothing to which every man had not right by nature: but only stands out of his way, that he may enjoy his own original right, without hindrance from him; not without hindrance from another. So that the effect which redounds to one man, by another man's defect of right, is but so much diminution of impediments to the use of his own right original.

Right is laid aside, either by simply renouncing it; or by transferring it to another. By *simply* RENOUNCING; when he cares not to whom the benefit thereof redounds. By TRANSFERRING; when he intends the benefit thereof to some certain person, or persons. And when a man has in either manner abandoned, or granted away his right; then he is said to be OBLIGED, or BOUND, not to hinder those, to whom such right is granted, or abandoned, from the benefit of it: and that he *ought,* and it is his DUTY, not to make void that voluntary act of his own: and that such hindrance is INJUSTICE, and INJURY, as being *sine jure;* the right being before renounced, or transferred. So that *injury,* or *injustice,* in the controversies of the world, is somewhat like to that, which in the disputations of scholars is called *absurdity.* For as it is there called an absurdity, to contradict what one maintained in the beginning; so in the world, it is called injustice, and injury, voluntarily to undo that, which from the beginning he had voluntarily done. The way by which a man either simply renounces, or transfers his right, is a declaration, or signification, by some voluntary and sufficient sign, or signs, that he does so renounce, or transfer; or has so renounced, or transferred the same, to him that accepts it. And these signs are either words only, or actions only; or, as it happens most often, both words, and actions. And the same are the BONDS, by which men are bound, and obliged: bonds, that have their strength, not from their own nature, for nothing is more easily broken than a man's word, but from fear of some evil consequence upon the rupture.

Whensoever a man transfers his right, or renounces it; it is either in consideration of some right reciprocally transferred to himself; or for some other good he hopes for thereby. For it is a voluntary act: and of the voluntary acts of every man, the object is some *good to himself*. And therefore there be some rights, which no man can be understood by any words, or other signs, to have abandoned, or transferred. As first a man cannot lay down the right of resisting them, that assault him by force, to take away his life; because he cannot be understood to aim thereby, at any good to himself. The same may be said of wounds, and chains, and imprisonment; both because there is no benefit consequent to such patience; as there is to the patience of suffering another to be wounded, or imprisoned: as also because a man cannot tell, when he sees men proceed against him by violence, whether they intend his death or not. And lastly the motive, and end for which this renouncing, and transferring of right is introduced, is nothing else but the security of a man's person, in his life, and in the means of so preserving life, as not to be weary of it. And therefore if a man by words, or other signs, seem to despoil himself of the end, for which those signs were intended; he is not to be understood as if he meant it, or that it was his will; but that he was ignorant of how such words and actions were to be interpreted.

The mutual transferring of right, is that which men call CONTRACT.

There is difference between transferring of right to the thing; and transferring, or tradition, that is delivery of the thing itself. For the thing may be delivered together with the translation of the right; as in buying and selling with ready-money; or exchange of goods, or lands: and it may be delivered some time after.

Again, one of the contractors, may deliver the thing contracted for on his part, and leave the other to perform his part at some determinate time after, and in the mean time be trusted; and then the contract on his part, is called PACT, or COVENANT: or both parts may contract now, to perform hereafter: in which cases, he that is to perform in time to come, being trusted, his performance is called *keeping of promise*, or faith; and the failing of performance, if it be voluntary, *violation of faith*.

When the transferring of right, is not mutual: but one of the parties transfers, in hope to gain thereby friendship, or service from another, or from his friends; or in hope to gain the reputation of charity, or magnanimity; or to deliver his mind from the pain of compassion; or in hope of reward in heaven; this is not contract, but GIFT, FREE-GIFT, GRACE: which words signify one and the same thing.

Signs of contract are either *express*, or *by inference*. Express, are words spoken with understanding of what they signify: and such words are either of the time *present*, or *past*; as, *I give, I grant, I have given, I have granted, I will that this be yours*: or of the future; as, *I will give, I will grant*: which words of the future are called PROMISE. . . .

In contracts, the right passes, not only where the words are of time present, or past, but also where they are of the future: because all contract is mutual translation, or change of right; and therefore he that promises only, because he has already received the benefit for which he promises, is to be understood as if he intended the right should pass: for unless he had been content to have his words so understood, the other would not have performed his part first. And for that cause, in buying, and selling, and other acts of contract, a promise is equivalent to a covenant; and therefore obligatory.

He that performs first in the case of a contract, is said to MERIT that which he is to receive by the performance of the other; and he has it as *due*. Also when a prize is propounded to many, which is to be given to him only that wins; or money is thrown amongst many, to be enjoyed by them that catch it; though this be a free gift; yet so to win, or so to catch, is to *merit*, and to have it as DUE. . . .

If a covenant be made, wherein neither of the parties perform presently, but trust one another; in the condition of mere nature, which is a condition of war of every man against every man, upon any reasonable suspicion, it is void: but if there be a common power set over them both, with right and force sufficient to compel performance, it is not void. For he that performs first, has no assurance the other will perform after; because the bonds of words are too weak to bridle men's ambition, avarice, anger, and other passions, without the fear of some coercive power; which in the condition of mere nature, where all men are equal, and judges of the justness of their own fears, cannot possibly be supposed. And therefore he which performs first, does but betray himself to his enemy; contrary to the right, he can never abandon, of defending his life, and means of living.

But in a civil estate, where there is a power set up to constrain those that would otherwise violate their faith, that fear is no more reasonable; and for that cause, he which by the covenant is to perform first, is obliged so to do.

The cause of fear, which makes such a covenant invalid, must be always something arising after the covenant made; as some new fact, or other sign of the will not to perform: else it cannot make the covenant void. For that which could not hinder a man from promising, ought not to be admitted as a hindrance of performing.

He that transfers any right, transfers the means of enjoying it, as far as lies in his power. As he that sells land, is understood to transfer the herbage, and whatsoever grows upon it; nor can he that sells a mill turn away the stream that drives it. And they that give to a man the right of government in sovereignty, are understood to give him the right of levying money to maintain soldiers; and of appointing magistrates for the administration of justice.

To make covenants with brute beasts, is impossible; because not understanding our speech, they understand not, nor accept of any translation of right; nor can translate any right to another: and without mutual acceptation, there is no covenant.

To make covenant with God, is impossible, but by mediation of such as God speaks to, either by revelation supernatural, or by his lieutenants that govern under him, and in his name: for otherwise we know not whether our covenants be accepted, or not. And therefore they that vow anything contrary to any law of nature, vow in vain; as being a thing unjust to pay such vow. And if it be a thing commanded by the law of nature, it is not the vow, but the law that binds them.

The matter, or subject of a covenant, is always something that falls under deliberation; for to covenant, is an act of the will; that is to say, an act, and the last act of deliberation; and is therefore always understood to be something to come; and which is judged possible for him that covenants, to perform.

And therefore, to promise that which is known to be impossible, is no covenant. But if that prove impossible afterwards, which before was thought possible, the covenant is valid, and binds, though not to the thing itself, yet to the value; or, if that also be impossible, to the unfeigned endeavor of performing as much as is possible: for to more no man can be obliged.

Men are freed of their covenants two ways; by performing; or by being forgiven. For performance, is the natural end of obligation; and forgiveness, the restitution of liberty; as being a retransferring of that right, in which the obligation consisted.

Covenants entered into by fear, in the condition of mere nature, are obligatory. For example, if I covenant to pay a ransom, or service for my life, to an enemy; I am bound by it: for it is a contract, wherein one receives the benefit of life; the other is to receive money, or service for it; and consequently, where no other law, as in the condition of mere nature, forbids the performance, the covenant is valid. Therefore prisoners of war, if trusted with the payment of their ransom, are obliged to pay it: and if a weaker prince, make a disadvantageous peace with a stronger, for fear; he is bound to keep it; unless, as has been said before, there arises some new, and just cause of fear, to renew the war. And even in commonwealths, if I be forced to redeem myself from a thief by promising him money, I am bound to pay it, till the civil law discharge me. For whatsoever I may lawfully do without obligation, the same I may lawfully covenant to do through fear; and what I lawfully covenant, I cannot lawfully break.

A former covenant makes void a later. . . .

A covenant not to defend myself from force, by force, is always void. For, as I have showed before, no man can transfer, or lay down his right to save himself from death, wounds, and imprisonment, the avoiding whereof is the only end of laying down any right; and therefore the promise of not resisting force, in no covenant transfers any right; nor is obliging. For though a man may covenant thus, *unless I do so, or so, kill me;* he cannot covenant thus, *unless I do so, or so, I will not resist you, when you come to kill me.* For man by nature chooses the lesser evil, which is danger of death in resisting; rather than the greater, which is certain and present death in not resisting. And this is granted to be true by all men, in that they lead criminals to execution, and prison, with armed men, notwithstanding that such criminals have consented to the law, by which they are condemned.

A covenant to accuse oneself, without assurance of pardon, is likewise invalid. For in the condition of nature, where every man is judge, there is no place for accusation: and in the civil state, the accusation is followed with punishment; which being force, a man is not obliged not to resist. The same is also true, of the accusation of those, by whose condemnation a man falls into misery; as of a father, wife, or benefactor. For the testimony of such an accuser, if it be not willingly given, is presumed to be corrupted by nature; and therefore not to be received: and where a man's testimony is not to be credited, he is not bound to give it. Also accusations upon torture, are not to be reputed as testimonies. For torture is to be used but as means of conjecture, and light, in the further examination, and search of truth: and what is in that case confessed, tends to the ease of him that is tortured; not to the informing of the torturers: and therefore ought not to have the credit of a sufficient testimony: for whether he deliver himself by true, or false accusation, he does it by the right of preserving his own life.

The force of words, being, as I have formerly noted, too weak to hold men to the performance of their covenants; there are in man's nature, but two imaginable helps to strengthen it. And those are either a fear of the consequence of breaking their word; or a glory, or pride in appearing not to need to break it. This latter is a generosity too rarely found to be presumed on, especially in the pursuers of wealth, command, or sensual pleasure; which are the greatest part of mankind. The passion to be reckoned upon, is fear; whereof there be two very general objects: one, the power of spirits invisible; the other, the power of those men they shall therein offend. Of these two, though the former be the greater power, yet the fear of the latter is commonly the greater fear. The fear of the former is in every man, his own religion: which has place in the nature of man before civil society. The latter has not so; at least not place enough, to keep men to their promises; because in the condition of mere nature, the inequality of power is not discerned, but by the event of battle. So that before the time of civil society, or in the interruption thereof by war, there is nothing can strengthen a covenant of peace agreed on, against the temptations of avarice, ambition, lust, or other strong desire, but the fear of that invisible power, which they every one worship as God; and fear as a revenger of their perfidy. All therefore that can be done between two men not subject to civil power, is to put one another to swear by the God he fears: which *swearing*, or OATH, is a *form of speech, added to a promise; by which he that promises, signifies, that unless he perform, he renounces the mercy of his God, or calls to him for vengeance on himself.* . . .

It appears also, that the oath adds nothing to the obligation. For a covenant, if lawful, binds in the sight of God, without the oath, as much as with it: if unlawful, binds not at all; though it be confirmed with an oath.

XV. Of Other Laws of Nature

From that law of nature, by which we are obliged to transfer to another, such rights, as being retained, hinder the peace of mankind, there follows a third; which is this, *that men perform their covenants made*: without which, covenants are in vain, and but empty words; and the right of all men to all things remaining, we are still in the condition of war.

And in this law of nature, consists the fountain and original of JUSTICE. For where no covenant has preceded, there has no right been transferred, and every man has right to every thing; and consequently, no action can be unjust. But when a covenant is made, then to break it is *unjust*: and the definition of INJUSTICE, is no other than *the not performance of covenant*. And whatsoever is not unjust, is *just*.

But because covenants of mutual trust, where there is a fear of not performance on either part, as has been said in the former chapter, are invalid; though the original of justice be the making of covenants; yet injustice actually there can be none, till the cause of such fear be taken away; which while men are in the natural condition of war, cannot be done. Therefore before the names of just, and unjust can have place, there must be some coercive power, to compel men equally to the performance of their covenants, by the terror of some punishment, greater than the benefit they expect by the breach of their covenant; and to make good that propriety, which by mutual contract men acquire, in recompense of the universal right they abandon: and such power there is none before the erection of a commonwealth. And this is also to be gathered out of the ordinary definition of justice in the Schools: for they say, that *justice is the constant will of giving to every man his own*. And therefore where there is no *own*, that is no propriety, there is no injustice; and where there is no coercive power erected, that is, where there is no commonwealth, there is no propriety; all men having right to all things: therefore where there is no commonwealth, there nothing is unjust. So that the nature of justice, consists in keeping of valid covenants: but the validity of covenants begins not but with the constitution of a civil power, sufficient to compel men to keep them: and then it is also that propriety begins.

Various arguments are directed against the view that justice—the keeping of covenants—is contrary to reason. It cannot be reasonable to keep or break covenants according to whether it is beneficial or not; this would subvert the principles on which any society is founded, and must end by depriving the individual of any of its benefits. Even in war one needs to keep faith with one's confederates in defense, since it is a condition for keeping allies together. And where rebellion (a breach of covenant) is taken as a means, it gives example to others to gain sovereignty in the same way; hence rebellion is against self-preservation. Faith must be kept even with heretics. Justice is the surest way of preserving our lives and therefore is a rule of reason and a law of nature.

Justice as applied to acts is somewhat different from that applied to men and manners. A single act does not destroy a man's character as just or unjust, whence the notion of justice as a virtue.

Justice of actions, is by writers divided into *commutative* and *distributive:* and the former they say consists in proportion arithmetical; the latter in proportion geometrical. Commutative therefore, they place in the equality of value of the things contracted for; and distributive, in the distribution of equal benefit, to men of equal merit. As if it were injustice to sell dearer than we buy; or to give more to a man than he merits. The value of all things contracted for, is measured by the appetite of the contractors: and therefore the just value, is that which they be contented to give. And merit, besides that which is by covenant, where the performance on one part, merits the performance of the other part, and falls under justice commutative, not distributive, is not due by justice; but is rewarded of grace only. And therefore this distinction, in the sense wherein it used to be expounded, is not right. To speak properly, commutative justice, is the justice, of a contractor; that is, a performance of covenant, in buying, and selling; hiring, and letting to hire; lending, and borrowing; exchanging, bartering, and other acts of contract.

And distributive justice, the justice of an arbitrator; that is to say, the act of defining what is just. Wherein, being trusted by them that make him arbitrator, if he perform his trust, he is said to distribute to every man his own: and this is indeed just distribution, and may be called, though improperly, distributive justice; but more properly equity; which also is a law of nature, as shall be shown in due place.

Other laws follow quickly: (4) *Gratitude: "that a man which receives benefit from another of mere grace, endeavor that he which gives it, have no reasonable cause to repent him of his goodwill";* (5) *Complaisance: "that every man strive to accommodate himself to the rest";* (6) *Pardon: "that upon caution of the future time, a man ought to pardon the offenses past of them that repenting, desire it."*

A seventh is, *that in revenges,* that is, retribution of evil for evil, *men look not at the greatness of the evil past, but the greatness of the good to follow.* Whereby we are forbidden to inflict punishment with any other design, than for correction of the offender, or direction of others. For this law is consequent to the next before it, that commands pardon, upon security of the future time. Besides, revenge without respect to the example, and profit to come, is a triumph, or glorying in the hurt of another, tending to no end; for the end is always somewhat to come; and glorying to no end, is vain-glory, and contrary to reason, and to hurt without reason, tends to the introduction of war; which is against the law of nature; and is commonly styled by the name of *cruelty.*

And because all signs of hatred, or contempt, provoke to fight; insomuch as most men choose rather to hazard their life, than not to be revenged; we may in the eighth place, for a law of nature, set down this precept, *that no man by deed, word, countenance, or gesture, declare hatred, or contempt of another.* The breach of which law, is commonly called *contumely.*

The question who is the better man, has no place in the condition of mere nature; where, as has been shown before, all men are equal. The inequality that now is, has been introduced by the laws civil. . . . For there are very few so foolish, that had not rather govern themselves, than be governed by others: nor when the wise in their own conceit, contend by force, with them who distrust their own wisdom, do they always, or often, or almost at any time, get the victory. If nature therefore have made men equal, that equality is to be acknowledged: or if nature have made men unequal; yet because men that think themselves equal, will not enter into conditions of peace, but upon equal terms, such equality must be admitted. And therefore for the ninth law of nature, I put this, *that every man acknowledge another for his equal by nature.* The breach of this precept is *pride.*

On this law, depends another, *that at the entrance into conditions of peace, no man require to reserve to himself any right, which he is not content should be reserved to every one of the rest.* As it is necessary for all men that seek peace, to lay down certain rights of nature; that is to say, not to have liberty to do all they list: so it is necessary for man's life, to retain some; as right to govern their own bodies; enjoy air, water, motion, ways to go from place to place; and all things else, without which a man cannot live, or not live well. If in this case, at the making of peace, men require for themselves, that which they would not have to be granted to others, they do contrary to the precedent law, that commands the acknowledgment of natural equality, and therefore also against the law of nature. The observers of this law, are those we call *modest,* and the breakers *arrogant.* . . .

Also if *a man be trusted to judge between man and man,* it is a precept of the law of nature, *that he deal equally between them.* For without that, the controversies of men cannot be determined but by war. He therefore that is partial in judgment, does what in him lies, to deter men from the use of judges, and arbitrators; and consequently, against the fundamental law of nature, is the cause of war.

The observance of this law, from the equal distribution to each man, of that which in reason belongs to him, is called EQUITY, and, as I have said before, distributive justice: the violation, *acception of persons.*

And from this follows another law, *that such things as cannot be divided, be enjoyed in common, if it can be; and if the quantity of the thing permit, without stint; otherwise proportionably to the number of them that have*

right. For otherwise the distribution is unequal, and contrary to equity.

But some things there be, that can neither be divided, nor enjoyed in common. Then, the law of nature, which prescribes equity, requires, *that the entire right; or else, making the use alternate, the first possession, be determined by lot.* For equal distribution, is of the law of nature; and other means of equal distribution cannot be imagined. . . .

It is also a law of nature, *that all men that mediate peace, be allowed safe conduct.* For the law that commands peace, as the *end,* commands intercession, as the *means;* and to intercession the means is safe conduct.

And because, though men be never so willing to observe these laws, there may nevertheless arise questions concerning a man's action; first, whether it were done, or not done; secondly, if done, whether against the law, or not against the law; the former whereof, is called a question *of fact;* the latter a question *of right,* therefore unless the parties to the question, covenant mutually to stand to the sentence of another, they are as far from peace as ever. This other to whose sentence they submit is called an ARBITRATOR. And therefore it is of the law of nature, *that they that are at controversy, submit their right to the judgment of an arbitrator.*

And seeing every man is presumed to do all things in order to his own benefit, no man is a fit arbitrator in his own cause: and if he were never so fit; yet equity allowing to each party equal benefit, if one be admitted to be judge, the other is to be admitted also; and so the controversy, that is, the cause of war, remains, against the law of nature.

For the same reason no man in any cause ought to be received for arbitrator, to whom greater profit, or honor, or pleasure apparently arises out of the victory of one party, than of the other: for he has taken, though an unavoidable bribe, yet a bribe; and no man can be obliged to trust him. And thus also the controversy, and the condition of war remains, contrary to the law of nature. . . .

These are the laws of nature, dictating peace, for a means of the conservation of men in multitudes; and which only concern the doctrine of civil society. There be other things tending to the destruction of particular men; as drunkenness, and all other parts of intemperance; which may therefore also be reckoned amongst those things which the law of nature has forbidden; but are not necessary to be mentioned, nor are pertinent enough to this place.

And though this may seem too subtle a deduction of the laws of nature, to be taken notice of by all men; whereof the most part are too busy in getting food, and the rest too negligent to understand; yet to leave all men inexcusable, they have been contracted into one easy sum, intelligible even to the meanest capacity; and that is, *Do not that to another, which thou wouldst not have done to thyself;* which shows him, that he has no more to do in learning the laws of nature, but, when weighing the actions of other men with his own, they seem too heavy, to put them into the other part of the balance, and his own into their place, that his own passions, and self-love, may add nothing to the weight; and then there is none of these laws of nature that will not appear unto him very reasonable.

The laws of nature oblige *in foro interno;* that is to say, they bind to a desire they should take place: but *in foro externo;* that is, to the putting them in act, not always. For he that should be modest, and tractable, and perform all he promises, in such time, and place, where no man else should do so, should but make himself a prey to others, and procure his own certain ruin, contrary to the ground of all laws of nature, which tend to nature's preservation. And again, he that having sufficient security, that others shall observe the same laws towards him, observes them not himself, seeks not peace, but war; and consequently the destruction of his nature by violence.

And whatsoever laws bind *in foro interno*, may be broken, not only by a fact contrary to the law, but also by a fact according to it, in case a man think it contrary. For though his action in this case, be according to the law; yet his purpose was against the law; which, where the obligation is *in foro interno*, is a breach.

The laws of nature are immutable and eternal; for injustice, ingratitude, arrogance, pride, iniquity, acception of persons, and the rest, can never be made lawful. For it can never be that war shall preserve life, and peace destroy it.

The same laws, because they oblige only to a desire, and endeavor, I mean an unfeigned and constant endeavor, are easy to be observed. For in that they require nothing but endeavor, he that endeavors their performance, fulfills them; and he that fulfills the law, is just.

And the science of them, is the true and only moral philosophy. For moral philosophy is nothing else but the science of what is *good,* and *evil,* in the conversation, and society of mankind. *Good,* and *evil,* are names that signify our appetites, and aversions; which in different tempers, customs, and doctrines of men, are different: and divers men, differ not only in their judgment, on the senses of what is pleasant, and unpleasant to the taste, smell, hearing, touch, and sight; but also of what is conformable, or disagreeable to reason, in the actions of common life. Nay, the same man, in divers times, differs from himself; and one time praises, that is, calls good, what another time he dispraises, and calls evil: from whence arise disputes, controversies, and at last war. And therefore so long as a man is in the condition of mere nature, which is a condition of war, as private appetite is the measure of good, and evil: and consequently all men agree on this, that peace is good, and therefore also the way, or means of peace, which, as I have showed before, are *justice, gratitude, modesty, equity, mercy,* and the rest of the laws of nature, are good; that is to say; *moral virtues;* and their contrary *vices,* evil. Now the science of virtue and vice, is moral philosophy; and therefore the true doctrine of the laws of nature, is the true moral philosophy. But the writers of moral philosophy, though they acknowledge the same virtues and vices; yet not seeing wherein consisted their goodness; nor that they come to be praised, as the means of peaceable, sociable, and comfortable living, place them in a mediocrity of passions: as if not the cause, but the degree of daring, made fortitude; or not the cause, but the quantity of a gift, made liberality.

These dictates of reason, men used to call by the name of laws, but improperly: for they are but conclusions, or theorems concerning what conduces to the conservation and defense of themselves; whereas law, properly, is the word of him, that by right has command over others. But yet if we consider the same theorems, as delivered in the word of God, that by right commands all things; then are they properly called laws.

Part II: Of Commonwealth
XVII. Of the Causes, Generation, and Definition of a Commonwealth

The final cause, end, or design of men, who naturally love liberty, and dominion over others, in the introduction of that restraint upon themselves, in which we see them live in commonwealths, is the foresight of their own preservation, and of a more contented life thereby; that is to say, of getting themselves out from that miserable condition of war, which is necessarily consequent, as has been shown in chapter xiii, to the natural passions of men, when there is no visible power to keep them in awe, and tie them by fear of punishment to the performance of their covenants, and observation of those laws of nature set down in the fourteenth and fifteenth chapters.

For the laws of nature, as *justice, equity, modesty, mercy,* and, in sum, *doing to others, as we would be done to,* of themselves, without the terror of some power, to cause them to be observed, are contrary to our natural passions, that carry us to partiality, pride, revenge, and the like. And covenants, without the sword, are but words, and of no strength to secure a man at all. Therefore notwithstanding the laws of nature, which every one has then kept, when he has the will to keep them, when he can do it safely, if there be no power erected, or not great enough for our security; every man will, and may lawfully rely on his own strength and art, for caution against all other men. And in all places, where men have lived by small families, to rob and spoil one another, has been a trade, and so far from being reputed against the law of nature, that the greater spoils they gained, the greater was their honor; and men observed no other laws therein, but the laws of honor; that is, to abstain from cruelty, leaving to men their lives, and instruments of husbandry. And as small families did then; so now do cities and kingdoms which are but greater families, for their own security, enlarge their dominions, upon all pretenses of danger, and fear of invasion, or assistance that may be given to invaders, and endeavor as much as they can, to subdue, or weaken their neighbors, by open force, and secret arts, for want of other caution, justly; and are remembered for it in after ages with honor.

Bees and ants live sociably with one another; yet they have no need of centralized power. Why cannot man do the same? Bees do not compete for honor, and thus envy, hatred and war do not arise among them. Lacking reason, they do not criticize the administration of their common business or strive to reform it this way or that, and thereby bring it to distraction and civil war. Moreover,

the agreement of these creatures is natural; that of men, is by covenant only, which is artificial: and therefore it is no wonder if there be somewhat else required, besides covenant, to make their agreement constant and lasting; which is a common power, to keep them in awe, and to direct their actions to the common benefit.

The only way to erect such a common power, as may be able to defend them from the invasion of foreigners, and the injuries of one another, and thereby to secure them in such sort, as that by their own industry, and by the fruits of the earth, they may nourish themselves and live contentedly; is, to confer all their power and strength upon one man, or upon one assembly of men, that may reduce all their wills, by plurality of voices, unto one will: which is as much as to say, to appoint one man, or assembly of men, to bear their person; and every one to own, and acknowledge himself to be author of whatsoever he that so bears their person, shall act, or cause to be acted, in those things which concern the common peace and safety; and therein to submit their wills, every one to his will, and their judgments, to his judgment. This is more than consent, or concord; it is a real unity of them all, in one and the same person, made by covenant of every man with every man, in such manner, as if every man should say to every man, *I authorize and give up my right of governing myself, to this man, or to this assembly of men, on this condition, that thou give up thy right to him, and authorize all his actions in like manner.* This done, the multitude so united in one person, is called a COMMONWEALTH, in Latin CIVITAS. This is the generation of that great LEVIATHAN, or rather, to speak more reverently, of that *mortal god,* to which we owe under the *immortal God,* our peace and defense. For by this authority, given him by every particular man in the commonwealth, he has the use of so much power and strength conferred on him, that by terror thereof, he is enabled to perform the wills of them all, to peace at home, and mutual aid against their enemies abroad. And in him consists the essence of the commonwealth; which, to define it, is *one person, of whose acts a great multitude, by mutual covenants one with another, have made themselves every one the author, to the end he may use the strength and means of them all, as he shall think expedient, for their peace and common defense.*

And he that carries this person, is called SOVEREIGN, and said to have *sovereign power;* and every one besides, his SUBJECT.

The attaining to this sovereign power, is by two ways. One, by natural force. . . . The other, is when men agree amongst themselves, to submit to some man, or assembly of men, voluntarily, on confidence to be protected by him against all others. This latter, may be called a political commonwealth, or commonwealth by *institution;* and the former, a commonwealth by *acquisition.* . . .

XXI. Of the Liberty of Subjects

LIBERTY, OR FREEDOM, signifies, properly, the absence of opposition; by opposition, I mean external impediments of motion; and may be applied no less to irrational, and inanimate creatures, than to rational. For whatsoever is so tied, or environed, as it cannot move but within a certain space, which space is determined by the opposition of some external body, we say it has not liberty to go further. And so of all living creatures, whilst they are imprisoned, or restrained, with walls, or chains; and of the water whilst it is kept in by banks, or vessels, that otherwise would spread itself into a larger space, we use to say, they are not at liberty, to move in such manner, as without those external impediments they would. But when the impediment of motion, is in the constitution of the thing itself, we use not to say; it wants the liberty; but the power to move; as when a stone lies still, or a man is fastened to his bed by sickness.

And according to this proper, and generally received meaning of the word, a FREEMAN, *is he, that in those things, which by his strength and wit he is able to do, is not hindered to do what he has a will to.* . . . [F]rom the use of the word *free-will,* no liberty can be inferred of the will, desire, or inclination, but the liberty of the man; which consists in this, that he finds no stop, in doing what he has the will, desire, or inclination to do.

Fear and liberty are consistent; as when a man throws his goods into the sea for *fear* the ship should sink, he does it nevertheless very willingly, and may refuse to do it if he will; it is therefore the action of one that was *free:* so a man sometimes pays his debt, only for *fear* of imprisonment, which because nobody hindered him from detaining, was the action of a man at *liberty.* And generally all actions which men do in commonwealths, for *fear* of the law, are actions, which the doers had *liberty* to omit.

Liberty, and *necessity* are consistent: as in the water, that has not only *liberty,* but a *necessity* of descending by the channel; so likewise in the actions which men voluntarily do: which, because they proceed from their will, proceed from *liberty;* and yet, because every act of man's will, and every desire, and inclination proceeds from some cause, and that from another cause, in a continual chain, whose first link is in the hand of God the first of all causes, proceed from *necessity.* So that to him that could see the connection of those causes, the *necessity* of all men's voluntary actions, would appear manifest. And therefore God, that sees, and disposes all things, sees also that the *liberty* of man in doing what he will, is accompanied with the *necessity* of doing that which God will, and no more, nor less. For though men may do many things, which God does not command, nor is therefore author of them; yet they can have no passion, nor appetite to anything, of which appetite God's will is not the cause. And did not his will assure the *necessity* of man's will, and consequently of all that on man's will depends, the *liberty* of men would be a contradiction, and impediment to the omnipotence and *liberty* of God. And this shall suffice, as to the matter in hand, of that natural *liberty,* which only is properly called *liberty.*

But as men, for the attaining of peace, and conservation of themselves thereby, have made an artificial man, which we call a commonwealth; so also have they made artificial chains, called *civil laws,* which they themselves, by mutual covenants, have fastened at one end, to the lips of that man, or assembly, to whom they have given the sovereign power; and at the other end to their own ears. These bonds, in their own nature but weak, may nevertheless be made to hold, by the danger, though not by the difficulty of breaking them.

In relation to these bonds only it is, that I am to speak now, of the *liberty* of *subjects.* For seeing there is no commonwealth in the world, wherein there be rules enough set down, for the regulating of all the actions, and words of men; as being a thing impossible: it follows necessarily, that in all kinds of actions by the laws praetermitted, men have the liberty, of doing what their own reasons shall suggest, for the most profitable to themselves. . . . The liberty of a subject, lies therefore only in those things, which in regulating their actions, the sovereign has praetermitted: such as is the liberty to buy, and sell, and otherwise contract with one another; to choose their own abode, their own diet, their own trade of life, and institute their children as they themselves think fit; and the like.

Nevertheless we are not to understand, that by such liberty, the sovereign power of life and death, is either abolished, or limited. For it has been already shown, that nothing the sovereign representative can do to a subject, on what pretense soever, can properly be called injustice, or injury; because every subject is author of every act the sovereign does; so that he never wants right to anything, otherwise, than as he himself is the subject of God, and bound thereby to observe the laws of nature. And therefore it may, and does often happen in commonwealths, that a subject may be put to death, by the command of the sovereign power; and yet neither do the other wrong. . . .

The liberty, whereof there is so frequent and honorable mention, in the histories, and philosophy of the ancient Greeks, and Romans, and in the writings, and discourse of those that from them have received all their learning in the politics, is not the liberty of particular men; but the liberty of the commonwealth. . . .

But it is an easy thing, for men to be deceived, by the specious name of liberty; and for want of judgment to distinguish, mistake that for their private inheritance, and birth-right, which is the right of the public only. And when the same error is confirmed by the authority of men in reputation for their writings on this subject, it is no wonder if it produce sedition, and change of government. In these western parts of the world, we are made to receive our opinions concerning the institution, and rights of commonwealths, from Aristotle, Cicero, and other men, Greeks and Romans, that living under popular states, derived those rights, not from the principles of nature, but transcribed them into their books, out of the practice of their own commonwealths, which were popular; as the grammarians describe the rules of language, out of the practice of the time; or the rules of poetry, out of the poems of Homer and Virgil. . . .

To come now to the particulars of the true liberty of a subject; that is to say, what are the things, which though commanded by the sovereign, he may nevertheless, without injustice, refuse to do; we are to consider, what rights we pass away, when we make a commonwealth. . . .

If the sovereign command a man, though justly condemned, to kill, wound, or maim himself; or not to resist those that assault him; or to abstain from the use of food, air, medicine, or any other thing, without which he cannot live; yet has that man the liberty to disobey.

If a man be interrogated by the sovereign, or his authority, concerning a crime done by himself, he is not bound, without assurance of pardon, to confess it; because no man, as I have shown in [Chapter XIV], can be obliged by covenant to accuse himself.

Again, the consent of a subject to sovereign power, is contained in these words, *I authorize, or take upon me, all his actions;* in which there is no restriction at all, of his own former natural liberty: for by allowing him to *kill me,* I am not bound to kill myself when he commands me. It is one thing to say, *kill me, or my fellow, if you please;* another thing to say, *I will kill myself, or my fellow.* It follows therefore, that

No man is bound by the words themselves, either to kill himself, or any other man; and consequently, that the obligation a man may sometimes have, upon the command of the sovereign to execute any dangerous, or dishonorable office, depends not on the words of our submission; but on the intention, which is to be understood by the end thereof. When therefore our refusal to obey, frustrates the end for which the sovereignty was ordained; then there is no liberty to refuse: otherwise there is.

Upon this ground, a man that is commanded as a soldier to fight against the enemy, though his sovereign have right enough to punish his refusal with death, may nevertheless in many cases refuse, without injustice; as when he substitutes a sufficient soldier in his place: for in this case he deserts not the service of the commonwealth. And there is allowance to be made for natural timorousness; not only to women, of whom no such dangerous duty is expected, but also to men of feminine courage. When armies fight, there is on one side, or both, a running away; yet when they do it not out of treachery, but fear, they are not esteemed to do it unjustly, but dishonorably. For the same reason, to avoid battle, is not injustice, but cowardice. But he that enrolls himself a soldier, or takes imprest money, takes away the excuse of a timorous nature; and is obliged, not only to go to the battle, but also not to run from it, without his captain's leave. And when the defense of the commonwealth, requires at once the help of all that are able to bear arms, every one is obliged; because otherwise the institution of the commonwealth, which they have not the purpose, or courage to preserve, was in vain.

To resist the sword of the commonwealth, in defense of another man, guilty, or innocent, no man has liberty; because such liberty, takes away from the sovereign, the means of protecting us; and is therefore destructive of the very essence of government. But in case a great many men together, have already resisted the sovereign power unjustly, or committed some capital crime, for which every one of them expects death, whether have they not the liberty then to join together, and assist, and defend one another? Certainly they have: for they but defend their lives, which the guilty man may as well do, as the innocent. There was indeed injustice in the first breach of their duty; their bearing of arms subsequent to it, though it be to maintain what they have done, is no new unjust act. And if it be only to defend their persons, it is not unjust at all. But the offer of pardon takes from them, to whom it is offered, the plea of self-defense, and makes their perseverance in assisting, or defending the rest, unlawful.

As for other liberties, they depend on the silence of the law. In cases where the sovereign has prescribed no rule, there the subject has the liberty to do, or forbear, according to his own discretion. And therefore such liberty is in some places more, and in some less; and in some times more, in other times less, according as they that have the sovereignty shall think most convenient. As for example, there was a time, when in England a man might enter into his own land, and dispossess such as wrongfully possessed it, by force. But in aftertimes, that liberty of forcible entry, was taken away by a statute made, by the king, in parliament. And in some places of the world, men have the liberty of many wives: in other places, such liberty is not allowed.

If a subject have a controversy with his sovereign, of debt, or of right of possession of lands or goods, or concerning any service required at his hands,

or concerning any penalty, corporal, or pecuniary, grounded on a precedent law; he has the same liberty to sue for his right, as if it were against a subject; and before such judges, as are appointed by the sovereign. For seeing the sovereign demands by force of a former law, and not by virtue of his power; he declares thereby, that he requires no more, than shall appear to be due by that law. The suit therefore is not contrary to the will of the sovereign; and consequently the subject has the liberty to demand the hearing of his cause; and sentence, according to that law. But if he demand, or take anything by pretense of his power; there lies, in that case, no action of law; for all that is done by him in virtue of his power, is done by the authority of every subject, and consequently he that brings an action against the sovereign, brings it against himself. . . .

The obligation of subjects to the sovereign, is understood to last as long, and no longer, than the power lasts, by which he is able to protect them. For the right men have by nature to protect themselves, when none else can protect them, can by no covenant be relinquished. The sovereignty is the soul of the commonwealth; which once departed from the body, the members do no more receive their motion from it. The end of obedience is protection; which, wheresoever a man sees it, either in his own, or in another's sword, nature applies his obedience to it, and his endeavor to maintain it. And though sovereignty, in the intention of them that make it, be immortal; yet is it in its own nature, not only subject to violent death, by foreign war; but also through the ignorance, and passions of men, it has in it, from the very institution, many seeds of a natural mortality, by intestine discord. . . .

If a monarch subdued by war, render himself subject to the victor; his subjects are delivered from their former obligation, and become obliged to the victor. But if he be held prisoner, or have not the liberty of his own body; he is not understood to have given away the right of sovereignty; and therefore his subjects are obliged to yield obedience to the magistrates formerly placed, governing not in their own name, but in his. For, his right remaining, the question is only of the administration; that is to say, of the magistrates and officers; which, if he have not means to name, he is supposed to approve those, which he himself had formerly appointed.

9

Cambridge Platonists, Levellers, and Locke

In ethics, as in politics, seventeenth-century thinkers in England experimented with theories and systems, almost as if to test how far they could go to break with the past. The counters of theory were old: nature, reason, equality, the divine, even contract, and so on. But their interpretations poured new wine—at times intoxicating revolutionary wine—into old conceptual bottles. Hobbes employed all these ideas in a novel way, yet not without restraint. Nature was raw and without morality, yet natural laws could guide among its necessities. Reason reckoned scientifically with experience, advising men on what to fear and what to expect. The divine was pushed into the background and put at the service of civil authority. Contract became the great carrier of individualism, the magical category that transmuted nature into morality and made possible the individual's ordered pursuit of his desires; but the contract put the individual under almost but not quite limitless authority.

The response to Hobbes was immediate and violent. He was attacked from every side—from pulpit, Parliament, and pub. Natural disasters were laid at his door as God's retribution for his atheistic immorality. Beyond the calumnies and refutations there were serious replies; and with only the mildest distortion the next two centuries can be understood as reacting to Hobbes's bold theories. The seventeenth century responded mainly to his view of morality as contractual—to the overtones of arbitrariness and conventionalism in its standards of right and wrong. It was left to the empiricism of the next century to answer Hobbes's view of human nature with a more sophisticated analysis of complex affections and a greater appreciation of moral, social, and aesthetic sensibilities.

Of course many among the Calvinist sects of Hobbes's time, including the Puritans and Presbyterians in Cromwell's camp, could well acquiesce in his view of human nature—often outdoing him in describing man's depravity and vileness after the Fall. But where Hobbes lifts man out of this corrupt state by human contracts, they see man rescued only by the voluntary covenant or contract that God offered the regenerate. Without grace no conduct could be moral; no works could be morally good unless the doer were a Christian of a particular sect.

Neither Hobbes nor those consulted in the present chapter were playing conceptual chess. At issue in England were survival, emergence of a new order, rebellion, civil war. If they believed themselves to be stating eternal truths of morality, the question of the period was where these truths would lead. Hobbes was attacked from opposite sides: from the old order for basing authority on a precarious empirical ground, instead of the divine right of kings, and from the other side for conceding too much to rulers. Each of the three views that follow selects among the conceptual counters, reinterprets its chosen ideas, and leads to startlingly different views of morality.

As the multiple sects vied in dogmatic intolerance, it seemed to some that the moral life and questions of moral conduct had been completely lost in the internecine disputes. A group of men, most educated as Puritans but many of whom became Anglican clergy centered primarily at Cambridge, took up arms against both Hobbes and the narrow Puritans. Called "latitudinarians" for their tolerance, they were reacting as much against the view that a man need be a Christian to be moral as they were against Hobbes's conventionalism. They brought Plato to bear against the dogmatisms of the sectarian consciences as well as against Hobbes's egoism. Their Platonism, it should be added, was deeply modified by Neoplatonism and the Christian interpretations of Plato, as well as by Renaissance humanism.

The Cambridge Platonists oppose Hobbes with moral truths of reason, in the mathematical spirit of an enlarged Cartesian rationalism. Deeply religious, they emphasize divine reason, not the divine will of an Ockham or, for that matter, of Descartes. Human reason can

grasp and state these truths. They demote, however, rather than reinterpret contract: it cannot enstate morality because it presupposes the moral integrity of keeping promises.

The moral and political philosophies of this age in Britain played a part in the great constitutional crisis from which the parliamentary system was forged and power wrested from the monarchy; the issues at stake and two of the more detailed episodes are worth looking at for how they are intertwined with the ideas of the Levellers and of Locke.

Throughout the Stuart monarchy—James I, who succeeded Elizabeth in 1603; Charles I, who was beheaded in the Civil War (1649); Charles II, who ascended the throne in the Restoration of 1660 after Cromwell's death; and James II, whose brief reign ended in the revolution of 1688—the political, religious, and economic spheres of the nation were permeated with conflict. The political struggle focused on whether the king could rule alone as against rule by the Commons. The claim for personal rule took shape in the theory of the divine right of kings, advanced by James I himself in *The True Law of Free Monarchy* (1598). Increasingly the Commons became a cohesive force, using its acknowledged sole power of voting taxes to consolidate and expand its rights. The first two Stuarts tried to rule without it, by irregular levies, but the attempt only spurred resistance. Bacon supported the monarchy whereas Coke (in his later career) looked to the common law as an authoritative system binding even the king. In the competition of religious faiths, Catholicism had been driven from official recognition as England established its national Anglican church. Although any movement toward Catholicism occasioned parliamentary and popular resistance, it had underground strength and provided the strongest support for personal royal rule. Like Anglicans, Presbyterians wanted a national church, but one organized around presbyters (not bishops) and synods, and so opposed personal rule. They were strong in Scotland and from the 1640s constituted a majority in Parliament. The double outlook of Presbyterianism makes understandable its wavering role in the Civil War; when the king appeared likely to grant concessions to parliamentary rule, it shifted to the royal side. An overlapping classification distinguishes Puritans and Independents, the former wishing to purify Anglicanism while the Independents ("Congregationalists" in the succeeding century) opposed a national church and wanted independent churches governed by private groups of devotees, thus inclining toward religious liberty. Independents had strength in the parliamentary army of the Civil War and carried the war to its conclusion. This was also the period when the Quakers came on the religious scene, and on the radical wing were a variety of other sects, comparable to the Anabaptists on the Continent, among whom ideas of individual freedom and social radicalism are to be found.

Historians have looked for specific socioeconomic groupings to identify with the diversity of religious and philosophical outlooks. Broadly speaking, the social changes met commercial needs—the growth of trade and finance, increasing use of land for commercial production, removal of older and arbitrary restraints and exactions. Each specific change as it takes place, however, is carried through by a coalition of interests and outlooks, and often within any single outlook there is a division on the direction of practical policy.

The Levellers came front stage in 1647–1649, in the latter part of the Civil War. Cromwell's victories over the party of Charles I in the Civil War had shaken the nation and awakened demands for some share in governance. Agitation was alive in London and in the army. Parliament was negotiating with the defeated king, but the army—led by Cromwell, who hoped the monarchy could be preserved but with Parliament sovereign—was in control. Early in 1647 the rank and file—fearing the

terms of a settlement—elected delegates (called "agitators," in the sense of representatives or agents) to speak for them. In June the army seized the king and in August occupied London. The Leveller movement, with considerable strength in London and in the army, issued a manifesto, "Agreement of the People," an important early model of a written constitution. The manifesto was debated at meetings of the General Council of the Army at Putney in October and November. The record of the meeting shows clearly the opposing positions among the advocates of parliamentary sovereignty. Here we have a struggle over the direction of policy by those holding the power and, though conscious of the variety of forces around them, fully aware that power can be put at the immediate service of the policy they decide—if they can prevail in the army, which, as we shall see, the Levellers were unable to do.

The Levellers' moral ideas emerge in this immediately practical situation. The overthrow of the old order, it is said, has brought men back to the natural order: people have God-given natural rights, including the right of free Englishmen to elect representatives to a sovereign Parliament. They appeal to the light of reason, assume equality, and reject contracts or customs that violate natural rights. This formulation is new, militant, and to many in that day, subversive.

The historical context of Locke's political philosophy is far different. Cromwell's constitutional experiments with a commonwealth ended with the Restoration of Charles II. His first Parliament, the "Cavalier Parliament," systematically set to repeal the laws of the Commonwealth. Yet Charles pursued a cautious policy and could not wholly restore the old order. The Test Act (1673) excluded both Catholics and Puritans (thereafter called "dissenters") from public office and eventually from the professions. Still, his reign was alive with suspicions of a revival of Catholicism and the undermining of parliamentary sovereignty. Hereditary succession pointed to James, duke of York, an acknowledged Catholic, as Charles's heir. The leader of the opposition to York was Locke's patron, Lord Ashley, later earl of Shaftesbury, an advocate of parliamentary rule. Shaftesbury's career fluctuated from high office (lord chancellor in 1672, president of the Privy Council in 1679) to a year in the Tower of London in between, and later trial, acquittal, and flight to Holland (1682), where he died a year later. In 1685 James succeeded Charles, after a rebellion in favor of the duke of Monmouth (a Protestant and natural son of Charles) had been crushed. When James had a son, which promised another Catholic king for Protestant England, Parliament invited William of Orange to take the throne, which he did in a bloodless revolution thereafter known as the Glorious Revolution of 1688. The Succession Act finally resolved the succession question—in the future it was to be by parliamentary consent, not hereditary succession alone. Rights of free speech and frequent meetings of Parliament were established. In short, after a century of struggle and revolt, the Whig program was to be the constitutional structure of England.

Locke's role on the parliamentary side was sufficiently prominent that he felt it prudent to flee to Holland and live there for five years under an assumed name. He returned to England in 1689, where his *Two Treatises* was published (although dated 1690). It was once generally accepted that the *Second Treatise* was written in 1689, after the revolution. It is now thought that he wrote it in 1679–1681, during the height of the succession crisis, making it a revolutionary document from a man out of power and not an after-the-fact justification of the victorious party. The points in Locke's doctrine that had the most practical implications for his historical situation are the emphasis on consent and contract, the defense of property rights, and the justification of revolution.

Locke is the great orchestrator of the moral categories of his age. In contrast to Hobbes,

divine purposes are manifest in an already moral state of nature. The contract is trimmed down to deal only with those natural rights that individuals cannot enforce alone. Reason sounds sometimes like that of the Cambridge Platonists, but more often it is fully experiential. Consent, like the "engagements" urged by Cromwell's side against the Levellers, legitimizes the accumulation of property beyond immediate consumption. The divine stands ready to justify rebellion when extreme tyranny leaves no choice.

The Cambridge Platonists: Rationalism in Morals

Although scarcely household names today, in their own time the Cambridge Platonists were academics of substance and influence, especially as teachers of those who founded Harvard. Some were more theologian than philosopher, for example Benjamin Whichcote (1609–1683), who was the initiator; but among the more philosophic were Ralph Cudworth (1617–1688) and Henry More (1614–1689). Richard Cumberland (1631–1718) and Samuel Clarke (1675–1729) were on the fringe and not always reckoned in the group. The philosophers often made contributions to science and were elected to the Royal Society.

While not averse to revelation, they held that the essence of religion was a morality based on natural law that was knowable by methods not significantly different from those of the sciences, especially mathematics. This opened for them the resources of the new philosophy, particularly the rationalism that appealed to the geometric or the deductive model. They all agreed on a kind of Platonic notion that there exists a moral order as a part of the structure of the world.

The exact nature and description of that moral order, however, as well as the way it was known, are matters on which they differed.

We shall not follow here their somewhat ponderous accounts cast in the prolix style of the century. Brief selections can convey points that significantly influenced moral philosophy. Their effort to frame morals on a deductive pattern that begins with self-evident and self-certifying truths stands out as a prototype of rationalism in ethics.[1] Together with Locke they provided the texts for the colleges of colonial America and the vocabulary that justified the American Revolution.

Insofar as the Cambridge Platonists insisted that moral principles have the same universality and reality as mathematical principles, they were not so much exploiting an analogy as presenting a view of the world order that included both the objects of ethics and the objects of mathematics. Of course, there could be no conflict between ethics and science, since both deal with the objective world order created by God.

There is, however, a disability (shared by classical rationalism) that was soon to be felt. There is no provision for adjudicating disagreement where conflicting truths are offered as intuitive. For example, between Locke's "life, liberty, and property" and Jefferson's "life, liberty, and the pursuit of happiness" an unresolvable debate could arise. In the long run the viability of comparing moral axioms to mathematical axioms depends on what the nature of mathematics is taken to be (see Kant, Chapter 13, and the positivists, Chapter 20).

RALPH CUDWORTH

A Treatise Concerning Eternal and Immutable Morality [2]

A Treatise Concerning Eternal and Immutable Morality was published long after Cudworth's

death, but his ideas were well known through his teaching and prior works. Indeed his stature was such that at Cromwell's invitation he preached a sermon before Parliament pleading for religious toleration.

Cudworth presents the major arguments of the school. Democritean materialism, Epicurean hedonism, and Protagorean relativism are simply wrong; when joined in Hobbes's philosophy they are disastrously wrong. Like Plato, he disparages the sensible: it is unable to give more than fancies and mere appearances. Intellection or knowledge of a different sort is required to penetrate to the immutable essence and the nature of things and their unchangeable relations to one another—moral as well as mathematical. "Everything is what it is and not another thing."

[Bk I, ch 2, sec 1] [M]oral good and evil, just and unjust, honest and dishonest . . . cannot possibly be arbitrary things, made by will without nature; because it is universally true, that things are what they are, not by will but by nature. As for example, things are white by whiteness, and black by blackness, triangular by triangularity . . . like by likeness, and equal by equality, that is, by such certain natures of their own. Neither can Omnipotence itself (to speak with reverence) by mere will make a thing white or black without whiteness or blackness . . . or things like or equal to one another without the natures of likeness and equality. The reason whereof is plain, because all these things imply a manifest contradiction; that things should be what they are not. . . .

[sec 2] And since a thing cannot be made any thing by mere will without a being or nature, every thing must be necessarily and immutably determined by its own nature. . . . For though the will and power of God have an absolute, infinite and unlimited command upon the existences of all created things to make them to be, or not to be at pleasure; yet when things exist, they are what they are, this or that, absolutely or relatively, not by will or arbitrary command, but by the necessity of their own nature. . . . Wherefore the natures of justice and injustice cannot be arbitrarious things, that may be applicable by will indifferently to any actions or dispositions whatsoever.

---

[1] To see rationalism in ethics developed in a fully systematic way, we have to go to the Continent, especially to Spinoza's *Ethica in Ordine Geometrico Demonstrata* (1677).
[2] London, 1731. The selection is from *A Treatise Concerning Eternal and Immutable Morality* (Andover, N.Y.: Gould & Newman, 1838), pp. 13–18.

Cudworth, like Descartes, is proceeding deductively, but where Descartes started from the *Cogito* and the perfection of God, Cudworth maintains that there could be no reasoning without recognizing that there are immutable principles by which reasoning itself is carried on, nor any judgment of perfection without criteria. The eternal truths that Cudworth takes to be self-evident supply such principles and the standard of comparison upon which particular judgments are made.

The strategy employed against arbitrary will is also directed against Hobbes's theory of the contract. If morality were enstated by the contract, then whence comes the morality that makes obligatory the original contractual promise?

[sec 3] [I]f we well consider it, we shall find that even in positive commands themselves, mere will doth not make the thing commanded just or debitum, obligatory, or beget and create any obligation to obedience; but that it is natural justice or equity, which gives to one the right or authority of commanding, and begets in another duty and obligation to obedience. . . . For it was never heard of, that any one founded all his authority of commanding others, and others' obligation or duty to obey his commands, in a law of his own making, that men should be bound or obliged to obey him. Wherefore since the thing willed in all laws is not that men should be required, obliged, or bound to obey; this thing cannot be the product of the mere will of the commander, but it must proceed from something else; namely, the right or authority of the commander, which is founded in natural justice and equity, and an antecedent obligation to obedience in the subjects; which things are not made by laws, but pre-supposed before all laws to make them valid: And if it should be imagined, that any one should make a positive law to require that others should be obliged, or bound to obey him, every one would think such a law ridiculous and absurd; for if they were obliged before, then this law would be in vain, and to no purpose; and if they were not before obliged, then they could not be obliged by any positive law, because they were not previously bound to obey such a person's commands:

so that obligation to obey all positive laws is older than all laws, and previous or antecedent to them. . . . And if this were not morally good and just in its own nature before any positive command of God, that God should be obeyed by his creatures, the bare will of God himself could not beget an obligation upon any to do what he willed and commanded.

In extending the argument to God's will here Cudworth is touching the quick of voluntarism (see Ockham, Chapter 6): If God's command, too, presupposes the prior obligation to obey it, then morality cannot be wholly founded on God's will.

The moral distinctions of good and evil, just and unjust, right and wrong are anticipations of morality, springing not from certain rules or propositions arbitrarily printed on the soul as on a book, but from some more inward and vital principle in intellectual beings, whereby these have within themselves a natural determination to do some things and avoid others.

[sec 4] Wherefore that common distinction betwixt . . . things that are therefore commanded because they are good and just, and things that are therefore good and just, because they are commanded, stands in need of a right explication. . . . [In the case of the latter], it is not the mere will and pleasure of him that commandeth, that obligeth to do positive things commanded, but the intellectual nature of him that is commanded. Wherefore the difference of these things lies wholly in this, that there are some things which the intellectual nature obligeth to per se, of itself, and directly, absolutely and perpetually, and these things are called naturally good and evil; other things there are which the same intellectual nature obligeth to by accident only, and hypothetically, upon condition of some voluntary action either of our own or some other persons, by means whereof those things which were in their own nature indifferent, falling under something that is absolutely good or evil, and thereby acquiring a new relation to the intellectual Nature, do for the time become debita or illicita. . . . As for example, to keep faith and perform covenants, is that which natural justice obligeth to

absolutely; therefore ex hypothesi, upon the supposition, that any one maketh a promise, which is a voluntary act of his own, to do something which he not before obliged to by natural justice, upon the intervention of this voluntary act of his own, that indifferent thing promised falling now under something absolutely good, and becoming the matter of promise and covenant, standeth for the present in a new relation to the rational nature of the promiser, and becometh for the time a thing which ought to be done by him, or which he is obliged to do. . . .

[sec 5] . . . [W]hen a man covenanteth or promiseth to do an indifferent thing which by natural justice he was not bound to do, the virtue of doing it consisteth not in the materiality of the action promised, but in the formality of keeping faith and performing covenants. Wherefore in positive commands, the will of the commander doth not create any new moral entity, but only diversely modifies and determines that general duty or obligation of natural justice to obey lawful authority and keep oaths and covenants. . . .

HENRY MORE AND SAMUEL CLARKE

Henry More, in *An Account of Virtue*, and Samuel Clarke, in *A Discourse Concerning the Unalterable Obligations of Natural Religion*, exploit the parallels between mathematics and moral knowledge more robustly than Cudworth. Their standing in the scientific community gave special prominence to their views. More was a fellow of the Royal Society and he confronted not only Hobbes's materialism but also Cartesian mechanism and the sharp separation of spirit from matter, on the ground that such separation could not adequately account for the interpenetration of mind and matter exhibited in purposive or thought-guided activity. He holds a more unified view of the world; extension is a common property of both matter and spirit, while the essence of spirit is self-activity. He appeals to mystical sources for these ideas, but he also appeals to scientific sources in his studies of magnetism and "electrics."

Clarke, a younger colleague of Newton, introduced Newtonian physics and mathematics as part of the regular curriculum at Cambridge. He defended Newton in a controversy with Leibniz over space and time, and over the threat Newton's theories posed for religion. Boyle and the Newtonians generally maintained that the scientific advances and Newtonian theory enhanced rather than derogated religious belief. Natural theology, science, and morals all exhibit the rational, and therefore the divine, structure of the world.

In their use of the mathematical parallel, More and Clarke differ from one another and also from Cudworth. More appeals to fairly specific principles (*Noemata*) on the analogy of arithmetic, while Clarke looks rather to relations and proportions.

An Account of Virtue [3]

[Bk I, ch IV, sec 2] From this magazine therefore let us draw forth a flock of such Principles, as being immediately and irresistibly true, need no proof; such, I mean, as all Moral Reason may in a sort have reference unto; even as all Mathematical Demonstrations are found in some *first undeniable Axioms*. And because these Principles arise out of that Faculty, which the Greeks call *Nous,* that signifies the Mind or Intellect; and that the Words *Noema* and *Noemata* derive therefrom, and properly signify Rules intellectual: we do not therefore improperly style the Rules that hereafter follow, *Moral Noema's*. But, lest any should fancy them to be morose and impracticable, I must here affirm, they propose nothing for good, which at the same time is not grateful also, and attended with delight.

Noema I. Good is that which is grateful, and congruous and well-suited to any Being, which hath life

---

[3] Originally published as *Enchiridion Ethicum* ("Handbook of Ethics"), London, 1667. The selection is from *An Account of Virtue, or Dr. Henry More's Abridgment of Morals*, trans. Edward Southwell, 2d ed. (London: Benjamin Tooke, 1701), pp. 20–27.

and Perception, or that contributes in any degree to the preservation of it.

Noema IV. One Good may excel another in Quality, or Duration, or in both.

This is self-evident: yet it may be illustrated from this absurdity, that otherwise one Life would not be better, nor one sort of Happiness greater than another: so as Gods, Angels, Men, Horses, and the vilest Worm, would be happy alike: which none but a mad man can fancy. And as to duration, there is no scruple therefore.

Noema XVII. 'Tis good for a man to have where-withal to live well and happily.

Noema XVIII. If it be good for one man to have wherewithal to be happy; evidently, 'tis twice as good for two men to be happy, thrice for three, a thousand times for a thousand; and so of the rest.

Noema XIX. 'Tis better that one man be disabled from living voluptuously, than that another should live in want and calamity.

Noema XX. 'Tis good to obey the Magistrate in things indifferent, even where there is no penalty to disobey.

[sec 4] These and such like *sayings* may justly be called *Moral Axioms* or Noema's: for they are so clear and evident of themselves that, if men consider impartially they need no manner of Deduction or Argument, but they are agreed to as soon as heard. And thus we are prepared, as with so many Touchstones, to let the inquisitive know what *Right Reason* is. For in short, *it is that which by certain and necessary Consequences, is at length resolved into some intellectual Principle that is immediately true.* [pp. 20–27]

A Discourse Concerning the Unalterable Obligations of Natural Religion [4]

[I, sec 1] That there are differences of things; and different relations, respects or proportions, of some

[4] Samuel Clarke, *A Discourse Concerning the Unalterable Obligations of Natural Religion and the Truth and Certainty of the Christian Revelation* (London, 1706). The selection is from the 4th ed. corrected (London, 1716).

things towards others; is as evident and undeniable, as that one magnitude or number, is greater, equal to, or smaller than another. That from these different relations of different things, there necessarily arises an agreement or disagreement of some things with others, or a fitness or unfitness of the application of different things or different relations one to another; is likewise as plain, as that there is any such thing as proportion or disproportion in geometry and arithmetic, or uniformity or difformity in comparing together the respective figures of bodies. Further, that there is a fitness or suitableness of certain circumstances to certain persons, and an unsuitableness of others; founded in the nature of things and the qualifications of persons, antecedent to all positive appointment whatsoever; Also, that from the different relations of different persons one to another, there necessarily arises a fitness or unfitness of certain manners of behaviour of some persons towards others: is as manifest, as that the properties which flow from the essences of different mathematical figures, have different congruities or incongruities between themselves; or that, in mechanicks, certain weights or powers have very different forces, and different effects one upon another, according to their different distances, or different positions and situations in respect of each other. . . . [I]n men's dealing and conversing one with another, it is undeniably more fit, absolutely and in the nature of the thing itself, that all men should endeavour to promote the universal good and welfare of all; than that all men should be continually contriving the ruin and destruction of all. 'Tis evidently more fit, even before all positive bargains and compacts, that men should deal one with another according to the known rules of justice and equity; than that every man for his own present advantage, should without scruple disappoint the most reasonable and equitable expectations of his neighbours, and cheat and defraud, or spoil by violence, all others without restraint. Lastly, it is without dispute more fit and reasonable in itself, that I should preserve the life of an innocent man that happens at any time to be in my power; or deliver him from any imminent danger, tho' I have never made any promise so to do; than that I should suffer him to perish, or take away his life, without any reason or provocation at all.

These things are so notoriously plain and self-evident, that nothing but the extremest stupidity of mind, corruption of manners, or perverseness of spirit can possibly make any man entertain the least doubt concerning them. For a man endued with reason, to deny the truth of these things; is the very same thing, as if a man that has the use of his sight, should at the same time that he beholds the sun, deny that there is any such thing as light in the world; or as if a man that understands geometry or arithmetic, should deny the most obvious and known proportions of lines or numbers, and perversely contend that the whole is not equal to all its parts, or that a square is not double to a triangle of equal base and height. Any man of ordinary capacity, and unbiased judgment, plainness and simplicity; who had never read, and had never been told, that there were men and philosophers, who had in earnest asserted and attempted to prove, that there is no natural and unalterable difference between good and evil; would at the first hearing be as hardly persuaded to believe, that it could ever really enter into the heart of any intelligent man, to deny all natural difference between right and wrong; as he would be to believe, that ever there could be any geometer who would seriously and in good earnest lay it down as a first principle, that a crooked line is as straight as a right one. . . . [pp. 36–40]

There remains the problem of a possible gap between perceiving the good and acting in conformity to the perception. In Hobbes, motivation issued from self-interest; Clarke and More take a different approach from Hobbes and from one another. Clarke assumes that the will is oriented to the perception, unless there is ignorance. Savages may go astray; they act according to their perceptions, but their perceptions are as faulty as their ignorance of mathematics. Education and maturity are of course required. We may assume that God's will corresponds directly to his reason; in the case of man it may be different, and this is where punishment becomes relevant.

[sec 3] . . . For originally and in reality, it is as natural and (morally speaking) necessary, that the will should be determined in every action by the reason of the thing, and the right of the case; as it is natural and (absolutely speaking) necessary, that the understanding should submit to a demonstrated truth. And it is as absurd and blame-worthy, to mistake negligently plain right and wrong, that is, to understand the proportions of things in morality to be what they are not; or wilfully to act contrary to known justice and equity, that is, to will things to be what they are not and cannot be; as it would be absurd and ridiculous for a man in arithmetical matters, ignorantly to believe that *twice two is not equal to four*; or wilfully and obstinately to contend, against his own clear knowledge, that *the whole is not equal to all its parts*. The only difference is, that assent to a plain speculative truth, is not in a man's power to with-hold; but to act according to the plain right and reason of things, this he may, by the natural liberty of his will, forbear. But the one he ought to do; and it is as much his plain and indispensable duty; as the other he cannot but do, and 'tis the necessity of his nature to do it. . . . [p. 50]

. . . [B]y the reason of his mind, he cannot but be compelled to own and acknowledge, that there is really such an obligation indispensably incumbent upon him; even at the same time that in the actions of his life he is endeavouring to throw it off and despise it. For the judgment and conscience of a man's own mind, concerning the reasonableness and fitness of the thing, that his actions should be conformed to such and such a rule or law; is the truest and formallest obligation; even more properly and strictly so, than any opinion whatsoever of the authority of the giver of a law, or any regard he may have to its sanction by rewards and punishments. For whoever acts contrary to this sense and conscience of his own mind, is necessarily self-condemned; and the greatest and strongest of all obligations is that, which a man cannot break through without condemning himself. . . . So far therefore as men are conscious of what is right and wrong, so far they are under an obligation to act accordingly; and consequently that eternal rule of right, which I have been hitherto describing, 'tis evident ought as indispensably to govern men's actions, as cannot but necessarily determine their assent. [pp. 53–54]

[sec 7] . . . [I]t does not at all follow, either that a good man ought to have no respect to rewards and punishments, or that rewards and punishments are not absolutely necessary to maintain the practice of virtue and righteousness in this present world.

. . . [T]he practice of vice, is accompanied with great temptations and allurements of pleasure and profit; and the practice of virtue is often threatened with great calamities, losses, and sometimes even with death itself. And this alters the question, and destroys the practice of that which appears so reasonable in the whole speculation, and introduces a necessity of rewards and punishments. For though virtue is unquestionably worthy to be chosen for its own sake, even without any expectation of reward; yet it does not follow that it is therefore entirely self-sufficient, and able to support a man under all kinds of sufferings, and even death itself, for its sake; without any prospect of future recompence. [pp. 92–93]

More's account of motivation appeals to the *boniform faculty* which integrates the intellectual with the voluntary.

An Account of Virtue

[Bk I, ch 2, sec 5] . . . The desires of the soul fly not to their object, as it is intelligible, but as it is good or congruous, or grateful, or at least tending to these ends; and so filling the mind with all the joys and pleasure it can comprehend. Hence it is plain, that supreme happiness is not barely to be placed in the intellect; but her proper seat must be called the *Boniform Faculty of the Soul:* namely, a faculty of that divine composition and supernatural texture, as enables us to distinguish not only what is simply and absolutely the best, but to relish it and to have pleasure in that alone. Which faculty much resembles that part of the will which moves towards that which we judge to be absolutely the best, when, as it were with an unquenchable thirst and affection it is hurried on towards so pleasing an object; and being in possession of it, is swallowed up in satisfaction that cannot be expressed.

[6] He therefore who acts according to this faculty, conforms to *the best and divinest thing that is in us.* And this, as Aristotle notes, is necessary unto happiness: . . . "such inward working and conformity to virtue's law, is that which denominates true happiness." . . .

[7] Wherefore, we think, happiness should be seated rather in that *boniform faculty* we spoke of;

since it is the most elevated and most divine faculty of the soul. . . .

[8] We do therefore mention in our definition of happiness, *the pleasure which the mind enjoys from a sense of virtue.* . . . [pp. 6–8]

[Bk II, ch 9, sec 16] Therefore, I say, this most simple divine sense and feeling in the *boniform faculty of the soul,* is that rule or boundary whereby reason is examined and approves herself. For if she [reason] offers or affirms anything that is contrary to the sense and feeling 'tis spurious and dishonest; if congruous to it, 'tis orthodox, fit and just. So that we need not invent any other *external* Idea of Good. . . . [p. 157]

RICHARD CUMBERLAND

Although associated with the Platonists at Cambridge and like them counted among the "latitude men," Cumberland stands apart. He sympathized with their search for universal natural laws of morality known by reason independently of revealed religion, with their coupling moral and mathematical laws, and with their earnest efforts to refute Hobbes. He was wary, however, of their tilt toward innateness, since he saw this as a very weak base from which to confront Hobbes.

His *De Legibus Naturae* (1672) was the earliest serious examination of Hobbes's thought, but he is here considered last, because his alternative avenue to the fundamental laws or propositions as well as his view of universal happiness as the standard of morality allies him rather with the next century's utilitarianism. His appeals to physiology and biology (sophisticated for the day), including the continuities of human with higher animals, anticipate the evolutionary theorists of the nineteenth century.

Cumberland is self-consciously extending Grotius's view of natural law, but he shifts the method. Instead of looking for the universal and immutable moral principles as they are exhibited in the consensus of customs, laws, and institutions of civilized society, or of deducing them from the social nature of man, he takes our knowledge of these laws to be derived from experience—generalizing from particular observations to more general principles and finally to the fundamental propositions or axioms. Thus we may all know that a man may be killed by the lack of food or by the excessive loss of blood; we may note the long dependence of the young of higher animals, and the longer dependence of children; we may observe the likely consequences of actions and their effects upon others; and we come to the knowledge of even mathematics and the nature of God by way of reasoning grounded in experience.

A Treatise of the Laws of Nature [5]

Human benevolence has natural roots:

[Ch 2, sec 20] Animals are incited to endeavour the propagation of their own species, by the force of the same causes which preserve the life of every individual, so that these two are connected by a tie evidently natural. Hence it is that animals of the same species but different sexes are united by a strong friendship, whence they perform to one another many mutual good offices, and that offspring is propagated which they love and cherish as their own blood. . . . The connexion is very close between the propagation of the species and that natural affection which excites to an endeavour of nourishing the young when brought forth. . . . Their offspring cannot be preserved except animals of the same species mutually cultivate peace or benevolence. They naturally desire that this benevolence may be as long continuance, as they wish to their offspring: in such benevolence, which is extensive and durable, consists the pursuit of the common good of the whole species. [p. 128]

In effect, the nature of things and the structure of the world impresses on us its organization, uniformities, and relations. We know the operations of reason itself from an examination of, or reflection on, these operations; and so we come to understand too the place of rational agents, their capacities, and their appropriate relations. We can see the natural impulse of affection in sexual love and between parent and child; the latter, when matured, habitual and reasoned about, is expressed as compassion and a natural concern for the felicity of others and for the common good.

Thus all we see in nature, from the mechanism of propagation to interpersonal dependencies, suggests that people are created to cooperate. The large size of the human brain shows that we are able both to subordinate passions to reason and to direct voluntary action by foreseen long-range consequences. The ease with which we communicate our affections and feelings is suggested by the expressiveness of our countenance (speech aside) and by the pleasure and the heightening of our physiological systems as we observe the enjoyments of others and enjoy the sympathy others show us. The human species would be an anomaly if conservation in its best estate were not its end. Hobbes's initial thesis about the right of everyone to everything is thus unnecessary:

[Ch 2, sec 17] It is evident from the inward frame of animals that it is necessary to their preservation that they take to themselves only a few things to satisfy their hunger and thirst, and to repel the inclemency of the weather, and leave the rest of fruitful Mother Earth's abundant productions to those to whom they may be useful. Thus the quantity of the bodies of animals, which is naturally limited, limits their appetites, to seek only a few things necessary for themselves, leaving the rest to the use of others; whence *naturally* arises some kind of division of things, among several animals, in which is laid the foundation of that concord and mutual benevolence which we are inquiring after. For on this account, that self-love, which is natural to animals, is limited and satisfied in the manner I have now shewn, there is no inducement to their opposing

[5] Richard Cumberland, *De Legibus Naturae* (London, 1672). The selection is from Richard Cumberland, *A Treatise of the Laws of Nature*, trans. John Maxwell (London, 1727).

the preservation of others, either by debarring them from a free use of what is not necessary to themselves, or even by refusing to lend them their labour, when it is of no further use to themselves. But they are rather, on the contrary, thence disposed to *assist* others, whether from the *pleasure*, though it were not supposed very great, which they receive from the society of others, or from the *hope* of their afterwards rewarding them with a like assistance. *Animals* (I believe) are sensible, I am sure men cannot be ignorant, that when once they have provided themselves with necessaries, there remains nothing that can be of greater advantage to them, than *tranquillity* and the *society* of animals of their own kind, which can be procured or preserved, only by benevolence towards them. [p. 124]

Accordingly the fundamental principle, the fountain of all natural laws—an axiom that is, like those of mathematics, certain, immutable, eternal—is:

[Ch 1, sec 4] *The greatest benevolence of every rational agent towards all, forms the happiest state of each and all, as far as it is in their power; and is necessarily requisite in the happiest state they can attain; and therefore the common good is the supreme law.*

The reader is to observe that I nowhere understand by the name of *benevolence* that languid and lifeless volition of theirs which effects nothing of what they are said to desire, but that only, by force whereof we execute as speedily and thoroughly as we are able what we heartily desire. We may likewise also comprehend in this word that affection by which we desire things grateful to our superiors, which is particularly distinguished by the name of *piety*, towards God, our country, and our parents. [pp. 41–42]

Among "all rational beings" Cumberland means to include God as well as man. He suggests that "benevolence is both the intrinsic cause of present, and the efficient cause of future happiness, and is a necessary requisite for both." We cannot control all external factors involved in achieving happiness, and people have different abilities for promoting the public good, but the law of nature is suffi-

ciently observed if each person does what he is able.

Cumberland is here dealing with a new idea. His benevolence is not Christian charity, not even the commandment to love thy neighbor. Nor again is he resurrecting the Greek notion of the social virtues of friendship or liberality. He is introducing the public good in a novel way. And this good has priority over right— right deeds and right rules are those that conduce to the public good. Even civil laws are valid simply because they are effective as means of securing the common happiness. The general law of nature suggests a natural law of universal justice, mandating and preserving a division of rights, especially the rights of men to have those advantages continued to them whereby they may perfect themselves and be useful to others. A division of obligations is also required. The particular rights and obligations reflect the good will, love of peace, and toleration respected by all the Cambridge men.

A stumbling block for later utilitarianism is why the good of others should have a claim on our own actions, especially if we ask nothing of them. Underlying Cumberland's view is the optimistic assumption that individual interest and the social good are identical, after an analogy to organisms in which the health of the whole depends on the cooperative functioning of all the parts. On the other hand, natural laws (and it does not matter whether they are stated as commands, laws, or what is to be done) issue from God and are supported by rewards and punishments that are also built into the structure of the world. Yet universal justice and benevolence are obligatory not because God commands them; He commands them because they are just and good.

The Levellers

The period 1647–1649 was marked by extraordinary political and religious agitation as people sensed a decisive turning point for the English constitution was at hand. This is also the time when the Levellers burst onto the stage to play a brief and incandescent part in history. The royalist forces had been defeated, but promonarchical feelings were still influential, and many, including Cromwell, were seeking a compromise between king and Parliament. The Levellers had their opportunity to turn the revolution decisively at debates of the General Council of the Army at Putney, where they presented the manifesto, "Agreement of the People."

The position of the Levellers, seen in their literature and in the agitation of such leaders as John Lilburne and Richard Overton, was basically a democratic one. Lilburne declared:

[A]ll and every particular and individual man and woman . . . are, and were, by nature all equal and alike in power, dignity, authority, and majesty, none of them having by nature any authority, dominion, or magisterial power one over or above another; neither have they, nor can they exercise any, but merely by institution or donation, that is to say, by mutual agreement or consent. . . .[6]

The "native rights" they proclaimed included civil liberties—free speech, equal treatment of all persons, the right not to incriminate oneself in criminal cases. They wanted the right of free Englishmen to elect representatives to Parliament. This demand, which had been only haltingly indicated in the "Agreement of the People," came immediately to the fore in the Putney debates. Arguing for the Levellers are Colonel Thomas Rainborough and Agitator Edward Sexby from the army, and Maximilian Petty and John Wildman, civilians from London. Representing the army command are Oliver Cromwell and his son-in-law Henry Ireton.

The latter argue against extending the vote to people who do not have a stake in the kingdom; the vote belongs properly only to landholders and holders of trading rights, who have a permanent interest, not to the propertyless. To give everyone the vote is to destroy property and to upset existing social institutions—to break the historical contracts ("engagements") people have made.

The Leveller political demand, while radical for the time, was in fact much more limited than it sounds to modern ears. The concept of free Englishmen, or Englishmen "who have not lost their birthright" (as Petty put it in the debate) did not cover persons who took alms or servants, who were regarded as having surrendered their power of decision to their masters. What is more, the concept of servant then embraced all those who worked for others for pay, as contrasted with independent artisans and workers.[7] The question of votes for women was not 'raised. The focal extension of the franchise would be to free workmen. The Levellers appear to assume that free labor is a natural property right comparable to land. But the argument goes beyond matters of the franchise; it raises forcibly the injustice of political and social privileges for wealth. Ireton argues that only men who have a paramount

[6] *The Free-Man's Freedom Vindicated* (1646), from *Puritanism and Liberty, Being the Army Debates (1647–49) from the Clarke Manuscripts with Supplementary Documents*, ed. A. S. P. Woodhouse (Chicago: University of Chicago Press, 1951), p. 317.

[7] For a careful study of the concrete meaning of the Leveller demands and the different interpretations of modern scholars about the movement, see C. B. McPherson, *The Political Theory of Possessive Individualism: Hobbes to Locke* (Oxford: Clarendon Press, 1962), Chapter 3. See also his appendix on the distribution and voting rights of social classes at the time of the debates. One reviewer, Peter Laslett, objected that "servant" meant more narrowly a person who lived in his master's house and so would not apply to a wage earner heading his own household (*Historical Journal*, 7, no. 1). Still, in the second *Agreement of the People* (December 10, 1648), the Levellers distinguish servants from wage earners, asking that the vote be extended to "natives or denizens of England, such as have subscribed to this Agreement, not persons receiving alms, but such as are assessed ordinarily towards the relief of the poor; not servants to, nor receiving wages from, any particular person" (Woodhouse, *Puritanism and Liberty*, p. 357).

interest in the kingdom—landholders, holders of trading rights, but not the propertyless—should elect representatives. Otherwise the propertyless, being most numerous, will be in a position to dominate the propertied.[8] The Levellers deny that they are against property; it is not their aim, as their opponents charge, to "level" property. But the fact that they are known to history by the label placed on them by their opposition makes them an early victim of what we would now call propaganda.

Shortly after the debates the General Council of the Army was suppressed. In the next year the Civil War flared again as the king got fresh assistance from the Scots. Cromwell defeated the Scottish army, then purged Parliament of those inclined to the king. In 1649 Charles I was tried and executed, and a republic was proclaimed. In that year, too, the Levellers revolted and the movement was finally crushed. Rainborough had been assassinated the previous year by royalists.

Putney Debates [9]

The debate opened on October 28, 1647. The aim of the Levellers and Agitators was to impeach Cromwell and his allies among the generals for having reneged on previous agreements ("engagements"). The debate immediately takes on a curiously ironic twist, for Ireton turns on them the argument that their more fundamental aim of constitutional reform on the basis of natural right more generally

threatens engagements (that is, the rights to property based upon contracts). Ireton insists that his position, not theirs, pays due regard to engagements and established agreements as the foundation of social order. The Levellers, he charges, propose to upset engagements by dogmatic principles of justice.

Ireton: . . . There is no other foundation of right I know, of right to [any] one thing from another man, no foundation of that [particular] justice or that [particular] righteousness, but this general justice, and this general ground of righteousness, that we should keep covenant one with another. Covenants freely made, freely entered into, must be kept one with another. Take away that, I do not know what ground there is of anything you can call any man's right. I would very fain know what you gentlemen, or any other, do account the right you have to anything in England—anything of estate, land or goods, that you have, what ground, what right you have to it. What right hath any man to anything if you lay not [down] that principle, that we are to keep covenant? If you will resort only to the Law of Nature, by the Law of Nature you have no more right to this land, or anything else, than I have. I have as much right to take hold of anything that is for my sustenance, [to] take hold of anything that I have a desire to for my satisfaction, as you. But here comes the foundation of all right that I understand to be betwixt men, as to the enjoying of one thing or not enjoying of it: we are under a contract, we are under an agreement, and that agreement is what a man has for matter of land that he hath received by a traduction from his ancestors, which according to the law does fall upon him to be his right. That [agreement is] that he shall enjoy, he shall have the property of, the use of, the disposing of [the land], with submission to that general authority which is agreed upon amongst us for the preserving of peace, and for the supporting of this law. This I take to be [the foundation of all right] for matter of land. For matter of goods, that which does fence me from that [right] which another man may claim by the Law of Nature, of taking my goods, that which makes it mine really and civilly, is the law. That which makes it unlawful originally and radically is only this: because that

---

[8] This fear pervades later historical struggles for extension of the franchise and lies behind the unwillingness to surrender property qualifications for voting. Compare the discussion by Hamilton, Jay, and Madison in *The Federalist* (1787–1788), particularly Essay 10, dealing with the danger of a propertyless faction becoming a majority.

[9] The selection is from Woodhouse, *Puritanism and Liberty*, pp. 26–27, 52–56, 62–63, 69. (The Clarke Manuscripts is a record taken in shorthand by someone, presumed to be William Clarke, present at the debate.) The First "Agreement of the People," read at the debates, is derived from pp. 443–445.

man is in covenant with me to live together in peace one with another, and not to meddle with that which another is possessed of, but that each of us should enjoy, and make use of, and dispose of, that which by the course of law is in his possession, and [another] shall not by violence take it away from him. This is the foundation of all the right any man has to anything but to his own person. This is the general thing: that we must keep covenant one with another when we have contracted one with another. And if any difference arise among us, it shall be thus and thus: that I shall not go with violence to prejudice another, but with submission to this way. And therefore when I hear men speak of laying aside all engagements to [consider only] that wild or vast notion of what in every man's conception is just or unjust, I am afraid and do tremble at the boundless and endless consequences of it. What [are the principles] you apply to this paper? You say, 'If these things in this paper, in this engagement, be just, then'—say you—'never talk of any [prior] engagement, for if anything in that engagement be against this, your engagement was unlawful; consider singly this paper, whether it be just.' In what sense do you think this is just? There is a great deal of equivocation [as to] what is just and unjust.

Wildman: [Y]ou take away the substance of the question. Our [sense] was, that an unjust engagement is rather to be broken than kept. . . . I make a question whether any engagement can be [binding] to an unjust thing. [If] a man may promise to do that which is never so much unjust, a man may promise to break all engagements and duties. But [I say] this: we must lay aside the consideration of engagements, so as not to take in that as one ground of what is just or unjust amongst men in this case. . . .

After further and inconclusive discussion, a committee is established to look into the proposal brought by the Levellers and the meeting adjourns. The meeting reconvenes the next day, and after some introductory debate the Leveller document, "Agreement of the People," is read to the gathering.

(First) "Agreement of the People"
We declare:

I. That the people of England, being at this day very unequally distributed by counties, cities, and boroughs, for the election of their deputies in Parliament, ought to be more indifferently proportioned, according to the number of the inhabitants; the circumstances whereof, for number, place, and manner, are to be set down before the end of this present Parliament.

II and III ask for biennial Parliaments.

IV. That the power of this, and all future Representatives of this nation is inferior only to theirs who choose them, and doth extend, without the consent or concurrence of any other person or persons, to the enacting, altering, and repealing of laws; to the erecting and abolishing of offices and courts; to the appointing, removing, and calling to account magistrates and officers of all degrees; to the making war and peace; to the treating with foreign states; and generally to whatsoever is not expressly or impliedly reserved by the represented to themselves.

Which are as followeth:
1. That matters of religion, and the ways of God's worship, are not at all entrusted by us to any human power, because therein we cannot remit or exceed a tittle of what our consciences dictate to be the mind of God, without wilful sin; nevertheless the public way of instructing the nation (so it be not compulsive) is referred to their discretion.

2. That the matter of impressing and constraining any of us to serve in the wars is against our freedom, and therefore we do not allow it in our representatives. . . .

3. That after the dissolution of this present Parliament, no person be at any time questioned for anything said or done in reference to the late public differences, otherwise than in execution of the judgments of the present representatives, or House of Commons.

4. That in all laws made, or to be made, every person may be bound alike, and that no tenure, estate, charter, degree, birth, or place, do confer any exemption from the ordinary course of legal proceedings, whereunto others are subjected.

5. That as the laws ought to be equal, so they must be good, and not evidently destructive to the safety and well-being of the people.

These things we declare to be our native rights. . . .

On request, the first article is read again. It becomes the focus of the rest of the debate. Ireton wonders what representation of "the people of England . . . according to the number of inhabitants" means. If it means equality of the vote, he is against it.

Ireton: . . . 'The people of England,' &c. And this doth make me think that the meaning is, that every man that is an inhabitant is to be equally considered, and to have an equal voice in the election of those representers . . . and if that be the meaning, then I have something to say against it. . . .

The Levellers respond:

Petty: We judge that all inhabitants that have not lost their birthright should have an equal voice in elections.

Rainborough: . . . For really I think that the poorest he that is in England hath a life to live, as the greatest he; and therefore, truly, sir, I think it's clear, that every man that is to live under a government ought first by his own consent to put himself under that government; and I do think that the poorest man in England is not at all bound in a strict sense to that government that he hath not had a voice to put himself under. . . . I should doubt whether he was an Englishman or no, that should doubt of these things.

Ireton: . . . [I]f you make this the rule I think you must fly for refuge to an absolute natural right, and you must deny all civil right. . . . I think that no person hath a right to an interest or share in the disposing of the affairs of the kingdom, and in determining or choosing those that shall determine what laws we shall be ruled by here—no person hath a right to this, that hath not a permanent fixed interest in this kingdom, and those persons together are properly the represented of this kingdom, and consequently are [also] to make up the representers of this kingdom, who taken together do comprehend whatsoever is of real or permanent interest in the kingdom. And I am sure otherwise I cannot tell what any man can say why a foreigner coming in amongst us—or as many as will coming in amongst us, or by force or otherwise settling themselves here, or at least by our permission having a being here—why they should not as well lay claim to it as any other. We talk of birthright. Truly [by] birthright there is thus much claim. Men may justly have by birthright, by their very being born in England, that we should not seclude them out of England, that we should not refuse to give them air and place and ground, and the freedom of the highways and other things, to live amongst us—not any man that is born here, though by his birth there come nothing at all (that is part of the permanent interest of this kingdom) to him. That I think is due to a man by birth. But that by a man's being born here he shall have a share in that power that shall dispose of the lands here, and of all things here, I do not think it a sufficient ground. I am sure if we look upon that which is the utmost (within [any] man's view) of what was originally the constitution of this kingdom, upon that which is most radical and fundamental, and which if you take away, there is no man hath any land, any goods, [or] any civil interest, that is this: that those that choose the representers for the making of laws by which this state and kingdom are to be governed, are the persons who, taken together, do comprehend the local interest of this kingdom; that is, the persons in whom all land lies, and those in corporations in whom all trading lies. This is the most fundamental constitution of this kingdom and [that] which if you do not allow, you allow none at all. This constitution hath limited and determined it that only those shall have voices in elections. It is true, as was said by a gentleman near me, the meanest man in England ought to have [a voice in the election of the government he lives under—but only if he has some local interest.] I say this: that those that have the meanest local interest—that man that hath but forty shillings a year, he *hath* as great voice in the election of a knight for the shire as he that hath ten thousand a year, or more if he had never so much; and therefore there is that regard had to it. But this [local interest], still the constitution of this government hath had an eye to (and what other government hath not an eye to this?) It doth not relate to the interest of the kingdom if it do not lay the foundation of the power that's given to the representers, in those who have a permanent and a local interest in the kingdom, and who taken all together do comprehend the whole [interest of the kingdom]. There is all the reason and justice that can be, [in this]: if I will come to live in a kingdom, being a foreigner to it, or live in a kingdom, having no permanent interest in it, [and] if I will desire as a stranger, or claim as one freeborn here, the air, the free passage of highways, the protection of laws, and all such things—if I will either desire them or claim them, [then] I (if I have no permanent interest in that kingdom) must submit to those laws and those rules [which they shall choose], who, taken together, do comprehend the whole interest of the kingdom. And if we shall go to take away this, we shall plainly go to take away all property and interest that any man hath either in land by inheritance, or in estate by possession, or anything else—[I say], if you take away this fundamental part of the civil constitution.

Rainborough: . . . I do hear nothing at all that can convince me, why any man that is born in England ought not to have his voice in election of burgesses. It is said that if a man have not a permanent interest, he can have no claim; and [that] we must be no freer than the laws will let us be, and that there is no [law in any] chronicle will let us be freer than that we [now] enjoy. Something was said to this yesterday. I do think that the main cause why Almighty God gave men reason, it was that they should make use of that reason, and that they should improve it for that end and purpose that God gave it them. And truly, I think that half a loaf is better than none if a man be anhungry: [this gift of reason without other property may seem a small thing], yet I think there is nothing that God hath given a man that any [one] else can take from him. And therefore I say, that either it must be the Law of God or the law of man that must prohibit the meanest man in the kingdom to have this benefit as well as the greatest. I do not find anything in the Law of God, that a lord shall choose twenty burgesses, and a gentleman but two, or a poor man may choose none: I find no such thing in the Law of Nature, nor in the Law of Nations. But I do find that all Englishmen must be subject to English laws, and I do verily believe that there is no man but will say that the foundation of all law lies in the people, and if [it lie] in the people, I am to seek for this exemption.

Rainborough denies that equality of representation implies a danger to property: after all, God said, "Thou shalt not steal," and this implies property. The Levellers are for the vote, not for anarchy. Cromwell, seeking to placate him, points out that anarchy may not be intended, but the consequences of the new rule might tend that way.

Petty: . . . I would fain know, if we were to begin a government, [whether you would say], 'You have not forty shillings a year, therefore you shall not have a voice.' Whereas before there was a government every man had such a voice, and afterwards, and for this very cause, they did choose representatives, and put themselves into forms of government that they may preserve property, and therefore it is not to destroy it, [to give every man a voice].

Ireton: . . . To that which this gentleman spake last. The main thing that he seemed to answer was this: that he would make it appear that the going about to establish this government, [or] such a government, is not a destruction of property, nor does not tend to the destruction of property, because the people's falling into a government is for the preservation of property. What weight there [is in it] lies in this: since there is a falling into a government, and government is to preserve property, therefore this cannot be against property.

Ireton's objection is not to *some* extension of equality, but to

the introducing of men into an equality of interest in this government, who have no property in this kingdom, or who have no local permanent interest in it. For if I had said that I would not wish at all that we should have any enlargement of the bounds of those that are to be the electors, then you might have excepted against it. But [what I said was] that I would not go to enlarge it beyond all bounds, so that upon the same ground you may admit of so many men from foreign states as would outvote you. The objection lies still in this. I do not mean that I would have it restrained to that proportion [that now obtains], but to restrain it still to men who have a local, a permanent interest in the kingdom, who have such an interest that they may live upon it as freeman, and who have such an interest as is fixed upon a place, and is not the same equally everywhere. If a man be an inhabitant upon a rack rent for a year, for two years, or twenty years, you cannot think that man hath any fixed or permanent interest. That man, if he pay the rent that his land is worth, and hath no advantage but what he hath by his land, is as good a man, may have as much interest in another kingdom as here. . . . But if you go beyond this law, if you admit any man that hath a breath and being, I did show you how this will destroy property. It may come to destroy property thus. You may have such men chosen, or at least the major part of them, [as have no local and permanent interest]. Why may not those men vote against all property? [Again] you may admit strangers by this rule, if you admit them once to inhabit, and those that have interest in the land may be voted out of their land. It may destroy property that way. But here is the rule that you go by. You infer this to be the right of the people, of every inhabitant, because man hath such a right in nature, though it be not of necessity for the preserving of his being: [and] therefore you are to overthrow the most fundamental constitution for this. By the same rule, show me why you will not, by the same right of nature, make use of anything that any man hath, [though it be not] for the necessary sustenance of men. Show me what you will stop at; wherein you will fence any man in a property by this rule.

Rainborough: I desire to know how this comes to be a property in some men, and not in others.

Colonel [Nathaniel] Rich: I confess [there is weight] in [Ireton's objection]; for you have five to one in this kingdom that have no permanent interest. Some men [have] ten, some twenty servants, some more, some less. If the master and servant shall be equal electors, then clearly those that have no interest in the kingdom will make it their interest to choose those that have no interest. It may happen, that the majority may by law, not in a confusion, destroy property; there may be a law enacted, that there shall be an equality of goods and estate.

He suggests a compromise: some, but not equal, representation for the poor.

Ireton: If the principle upon which you move this alteration . . . do destroy all kind of property or whatsoever a man hath by human constitution, [I cannot consent to it]. The Law of God doth not give me property, nor the Law of Nature, but property is of human constitution. I have a property and this I shall enjoy. Constitution founds property. If either the thing itself that you press or the consequence [of] that you press [do destroy property], though I shall acquiesce in having no property, yet I cannot give my heart or hand to it; because it is a thing evil in itself and scandalous to the world, and I desire this Army may be free from both.

Sexby: I see that though liberty were our end, there is a degeneration from it. We have engaged in this kingdom and ventured our lives, and it was all for this: to recover our birthrights and privileges as Englishmen; and by the arguments urged there is none. There are many thousands of us soldiers that have ventured our lives; we have had little propriety in the kingdom as to our estates, yet we have had a birthright. But it seems now, except a man hath a fixed estate in this kingdom, he hath no right in this kingdom. I wonder we were so much deceived. If we had not a right to the kingdom, we were mere mercenary soldiers.

Ireton replies that what they fought against was a one-man tyranny; some men even without representation fought to have the benefits that Parliament brought: an ordered law and the opportunity to rise and to acquire estates.

During these years of the Civil War, there were others to the left of the Levellers in the interpretation of natural law and the rights of Englishmen. The *Diggers* were a sect who held that from the time of the Norman conquest the current institutions—private property, law, the priesthood—had exploited free Englishmen. The old order now being overthrown, they could go back to communal property, to which they had a natural right under the natural law. Pacific in their methods, they tried to plant in the unused land but were dispersed by violence.

After the Restoration the more radical movements receded. The central issue debated was the establishment and preservation of parliamentary sovereignty as against the revived argument for the divine right of kings. The revolution of 1688 adopted a theory closer to Ireton than to the Levellers, though it had a complex appeal to nature as well as consent. The central philosophical figure here, John Locke, took property qualification for granted. The question continued to be argued well into the nineteenth century.

John Locke
(1632–1704)

Locke is a recognized parent of modern epistemology and psychology. Aspiring in his major work, *An Essay Concerning Human Understanding* (1690), to extend Newtonian principles to the mind, he was influential in France, Scotland, Ireland, and America, as well as in his native England. The magnificent ambiguity of his work made it possible for different philosophical schools to claim him. The French Enlightenment concentrated on how he related sensation to physiology, and so found in his work a philosophical materialism; Berkeley and Hume turned the same sensationalism into a phenomenalist idealism and skepticism, and the Scottish school (Reid) traced from it a common sense realism.

The *Essay* touches on ethics at but a few points: the denial that there are innate or inborn moral principles; the channeling of our understanding of the good to the psychology of pleasure and pain; the classification of moral law as divine (sanctioned by God), political, and social (sanctioned by opinion and reputation, praise and blame); finally, the suggestion that morality could be organized as a deductive system:

I doubt not but from self-evident propositions, by necessary consequences, as incontestible as those in mathematics, the measures of right and wrong might be made out, to anyone that will apply himself with the same indifferency and attention to the one as he does to the other of these sciences.[10]

The clearest expression of his moral theory is in the *Two Treatises of Government*, his other important (though less voluminous) work, which provides the framework and assumptions for his theory of fundamental rights. In the United States it provided an apt ethicopolitical background for the Declaration of Independence and for the fresh organization of government. It remains a foundational document for contractarian ethics.

Commentators have often noted a possible conflict between the empiricism of the *Essay* and the seeming rationalism of the *Second Treatise*, with its theory of ultimate (axiomatic) rights. Some subtle reconciliation may be possible by taking the notions of liberty and property as part of the definition of being a person or individual; in that case, morality might be regarded as derivable from the nature of man. That such a deductive system was not always felt to be incompatible with learning through experience is clear at least in the case of Hobbes.

In setting forth the theory of the social contract the *Second Treatise* expresses an individualist view of liberties and natural rights. Locke's presentation of the contract is fighting an intellectual battle on two fronts. One is against the divine right of kings, as conceived in Sir Robert Filmer's *Patriarcha*, which denies any contractual basis for government. At the outset, Locke says that Filmer's view amounts to this: "That all government is absolute monarchy; and the ground he builds on is this: That no man is born free," that man is born to slavery and is incapable of more than that. On the other side, Locke's theory takes issue with Hobbes: the state of nature is already moral and is not to be "confounded" with the state of war. (Locke apparently took seriously Cudworth's criticism that the social contract

[10] *An Essay Concerning Human Understanding*, Bk IV, ch 1, sec 18.

assumes a prior morality.) Moreover, the contract is a limited one between people and sovereign; natural rights (life, liberty, and markedly property) are not given up, only the right to judge and punish infractions. Unlike Hobbes, Locke grants the possibility of trespass by the executive (or monarch), so that individuals may rightfully as a last resort appeal to God and take up arms against tyranny.

Second Treatise of Government [11]

Chapter 1 begins with a summary of what has been established in the *First Treatise.*

Ch I: The Introduction

[Sec 1] It having been shown in the foregoing discourse,

(1) That Adam had not, either by natural right of fatherhood, or by positive donation from God, any such authority over his children or dominion over the world as is pretended.

(2) That if he had, his heirs yet had no right to it.

(3) That if his heirs had, there being no law of nature nor positive law of God that determines which is the right heir in all cases that may arise, the right of succession, and consequently of bearing rule, could not have been certainly determined.

(4) That if even that had been determined, yet the knowledge of which is the eldest line of Adam's posterity, being so long since utterly lost, that in the races of mankind and families of the world there remains not to one above another the least pretence to be the eldest house, and to have the right of inheritance.

All these premises having, as I think, been clearly made out, it is impossible that the rulers now on earth should make any benefit, or derive any the least shadow of authority from that which is held to be the fountain of all power. . . .

Ch II: Of the State of Nature

[4] To understand political power right, and derive it from its original, we must consider what state

all men are naturally in, and that is, a *state of perfect freedom* to order their actions, and dispose of their possessions and persons as they think fit, within the bounds of the law of nature, without asking leave, or depending upon the will of any other man.

A *state* also of *equality,* wherein all the power and jurisdiction is reciprocal, no one having more than another; there being nothing more evident than that creatures of the same species and rank, promiscuously born to all the same advantages of nature, and the use of the same faculties, should also be equal one amongst another, without subordination or subjection; unless the Lord and Master of them all should, by any manifest declaration of His Will, set one above another, and confer on him, by an evident and clear appointment, an undoubted right to dominion and sovereignty.

[5] This *equality* of men by nature, the judicious Hooker looks upon as so evident in itself, and beyond all question, that he makes it the foundation of that obligation to mutual love amongst men on which he builds the duties they owe one another, and from whence he derives the great maxims of *justice* and *charity.* . . .

[6] But though this be a *state of liberty,* yet it is *not a state of licence;* though man in that state have an uncontrollable liberty to dispose of his person or possessions, yet he has not liberty to destroy himself, or so much as any creature in his possession, but where some nobler use than its bare preservation calls for it. The *state of nature* has a law of nature to govern it, which obliges every one: and reason, which is that law, teaches all mankind, who will but consult it, that being all *equal and independent,* no one ought to harm another in his life, health, liberty, or possessions: for men being all the workmanship of one omnipotent and infinitely wise Maker—all the servants of one sovereign Master, sent into the world by His order, and about His business—they are His property, whose workmanship they are, made to last during His, not one another's pleasure. And being furnished with like faculties, sharing all in one community of nature, there cannot be supposed any such *subordination* among us, that may authorize us to destroy one another, as if we were made for one another's uses, as the inferior ranks of creatures are for ours. Every one, as he is *bound to preserve himself,* and not to quit his station wilfully, so by the like reason, when his own preservation comes not in competition,

---

[11] London, 1690. The selection is from the sixth edition, 1764, with some modernization of spelling and punctuation by the editors of this volume.

ought he, as much as he can, to *preserve the rest of mankind*, and may not, unless it be to do justice on an offender, take away, or impair the life, or what tends to the preservation of the life, the liberty, health, limb, or goods of another.

[7] And that all men may be restrained from invading others' rights, and from doing hurt to one another, and the law of nature be observed, which willeth the peace and *preservation of all mankind*, the *execution* of the law of nature is, in that state, put into every man's hands, whereby every one has a right to punish the transgressors of that law to such a degree as may hinder its violation. For the *law of nature* would, as all other laws that concern men in this world, be in vain, if there were no body that in the state of nature had a *power to execute* that law, and thereby preserve the innocent and restrain offenders. And if any one in the state of nature may punish another for any evil he has done, every one may do so. For in that *state of perfect equality*, where naturally there is no superiority or jurisdiction of one over another, what any may do in prosecution of that law, every one must needs have a right to do.

[8] And thus, in the state of nature, *one man comes by a power over another*; but yet no absolute or arbitrary power to use a criminal when he has got him in his hands, according to the passionate heats, or boundless extravagancy of his own will; but only to retribute to him so far as calm reason and conscience dictate, what is proportionate to his transgression, which is so much as may serve for *reparation* and *restraint*. For these two are the only reasons why one man may lawfully do harm to another, which is that we call *punishment*. In transgressing the law of nature, the offender declares himself to live by another rule than that of reason and common equity, which is that measure God has set to the actions of men, for their mutual security; and so he becomes dangerous to mankind; the tie which is to secure them from injury and violence, being slighted and broken by him. Which being a trespass against the whole species, and the peace and safety of it, provided for by the law of nature, every man upon this score, by the right he hath to preserve mankind in general, may restrain, or where it is necessary, destroy things noxious to them, and so may bring such evil on any one who hath transgressed that law, as may make him repent the doing of it, and thereby deter him, and by his example others, from doing the like mischief. And in this

case, and upon this ground, *every man hath a right to punish the offender, and be executioner of the law of nature.*

[9] I doubt not but this will seem a very strange doctrine to some men: but before they condemn it, I desire them to resolve me, by what right any prince or state can put to death or *punish an alien* for any crime he commits in their country. It is certain their laws, by virtue of any sanction they receive from the promulgated will of the legislative, reach not a stranger. They speak not to him, nor, if they did, is he bound to hearken to them. The legislative authority, by which they are in force over the subjects of that commonwealth, hath no power over him. Those who have the supreme power of making laws in England, France or Holland are, to an Indian, but like the rest of the world—men without authority. And therefore, if by the law of nature every man hath not a power to punish offences against it, as he soberly judges the case to require, I see not how the magistrates of any community can *punish an alien* of another country; since, in reference to him, they can have no more power than what every man naturally may have over another.

[10] Besides the crime which consists in violating the law, and varying from the right rule of reason, whereby a man so far becomes degenerate, and declares himself to quit the principles of human nature, and to be a noxious creature, there is commonly *injury* done to some person or other, and some other man receives damage by his transgression: in which case he who hath received any damage has—besides the right of punishment common to him with other men—a particular right to seek *reparation* from him that has done it. And any other person who finds it just may also join with him that is injured, and assist him in recovering from the offender so much as may make satisfaction for the harm he has suffered.

[11] From these *two distinct rights*—the one of *punishing* the crime *for restraint* and preventing the like offence, which right of punishing is in every body; the other of taking *reparation*, which belongs only to the injured party—comes it to pass that the magistrate, who by being magistrate hath the common right of punishing put into his hands, can often, where the public good demands not the execution of the law, *remit* the punishment of criminal offences by his own authority, but yet cannot *remit* the satisfaction due to any private man for the damage he has received. That, he who has suffered the damage

has a right to demand in his own name, and he alone can remit: the damnified person has this power of appropriating to himself the goods or service of the offender, *by right of self-preservation*, as every man has a power to punish the crime, to prevent its being committed again, *by the right he has of preserving all mankind*, and doing all reasonable things he can in order to that end. And thus it is, that every man in the state of nature has a power to kill a murderer, both *to deter* others from doing the like injury (which no reparation can compensate) by the example of the punishment that attends it from every body, and also to secure men from the attempts of a criminal who, having renounced reason—the common rule and measure God hath given to mankind—hath, by the unjust violence and slaughter he hath committed upon one, declared war against all mankind, and therefore may be destroyed as a lion or a tiger, one of those wild savage beasts with whom men can have no society nor security. And upon this is grounded that great law of nature, "Whoso sheddeth man's blood, by man shall his blood be shed." And Cain was so fully convinced that every one had a right to destroy such a criminal, that, after the murder of his brother, he cries out, "Every one that findeth me shall slay me"; so plain was it writ in the hearts of all mankind.

[14] It is often asked as a mighty objection, *where are*, or ever were there any *men in such a state of nature*? To which it may suffice as an answer at present, that since all princes and rulers of *independent* governments all through the world are in a state of nature, it is plain the world never was, nor ever will be, without numbers of men in that state. I have named all governors of *independent communities*, whether they are, or are not, in league with others: for it is not every compact that puts an end to the state of nature between men, but only this one of agreeing together mutually to enter into one community, and make one body politic; other promises, and compacts, men may make one with another, and yet still be in the state of nature. The promises and bargains for truck, etc., between the two men in the desert island (mentioned by Garcilasso de la Vega, in his history of Peru), or between a Swiss and an Indian in the woods of America, are binding to them, though they are perfectly in a state of nature, in reference to one another: for truth and keeping of faith belongs to men as men, and not as members of society.

Ch III: Of the State of War

[16] The *state* of *war* is a state of *enmity* and *destruction*: and therefore declaring by word or action, not a passionate and hasty, but a sedate settled design upon another man's life, *puts him in a state of war* with him against whom he has declared such an intention, and so has exposed his life to the other's power to be taken away by him, or any one that joins with him in his defence, and espouses his quarrel; it being reasonable and just I should have a right to destroy that which threatens me with destruction; for *by the fundamental law of nature, man being to be preserved* as much as possible, when all cannot be preserved, the safety of the innocent is to be preferred: and one may destroy a man who makes war upon him, or has discovered an enmity to his being, for the same reason that he may kill a wolf or a lion; because such men are not under the ties of the common law of reason, have no other rule but that of force and violence, and so may be treated as beasts of prey, those dangerous and noxious creatures that will be sure to destroy him whenever he falls into their power.

[17] . . . He that, in the state of nature *would take away the freedom* that belongs to any one in that state, must necessarily be supposed to have a design to take away everything else, that *freedom* being the foundation of all the rest; as he that in the state of society would take away the *freedom* belonging to those of that society or commonwealth must be supposed to design to take away from them everything else, and so be looked on as *in a state of war*.

[19] And here we have the plain *difference between the state of nature and the state of war*, which however some men have confounded, are as far distant, as a state of peace, good will, mutual assistance, and preservation, and a state of enmity, malice, violence, and mutual destruction, are one from another. Men living together according to reason, without a common superior on earth, with authority to judge between them, is *properly the state of nature*. But force, or a declared design of force, upon the person of another, where there is no common superior on earth to appeal to for relief, *is the state of war*: and it is the want of such an appeal gives a man the right of war even against an *aggressor*, though he be in society and a fellow subject. Thus, a *thief* whom I cannot harm, but by appeal to the law, for having stolen all that I am worth, I may kill, when he sets on me to rob me but of my horse

or coat; because the law, which was made for my preservation, where it cannot interpose to secure my life from present force, which, if lost, is capable of no reparation, permits me my own defence, and the right of war, a liberty to kill the aggressor, because the aggressor allows not time to appeal to our common judge, nor the decision of the law, for remedy in a case where the mischief may be irreparable. Want of a common judge with authority, puts all men in a state of nature: force without right upon a man's person makes a state of war, both where there is, and is not, a common judge.

[20] But when the actual force is over, the *state of war ceases* between those that are in society, and are equally on both sides subjected to the fair determination of the law; because then there lies open the remedy of appeal for the past injury, and to prevent future harm: but where no such appeal is, as in the state of nature, for want of positive laws, and judges with authority to appeal to, the state of war once begun, continues, with a right to the innocent party to destroy the other whenever he can, until the aggressor offers peace, and desires reconciliation on such terms as may repair any wrongs he has already done, and secure the innocent for the future; nay, where an appeal to the law, and constituted judges, lies open, but the remedy is denied by a manifest perverting of justice, and a barefaced wresting of the laws to protect or indemnify the violence or injuries of some men, or party of men, *there* it is hard to imagine anything but a *state of war*: for wherever violence is used, and injury done, though by hands appointed to administer justice, it is still violence and injury, however coloured with the name, pretences, or forms of law, the end whereof being to protect and redress the innocent, by an unbiassed application of it, to all who are under it; wherever that is not *bona fide* done, *war is made* upon the sufferers, who having no appeal on earth to right them, they are left to the only remedy in such cases—an appeal to heaven.

[21] To avoid this *state of war* (wherein there is no appeal but to heaven, and wherein every the least difference is apt to end, where there is no authority to decide between the contenders) is one great reason of men's putting themselves into society, and quitting the state of nature: for where there is an authority, a power on earth, from which relief can be had by *appeal*, there the continuance of the *state of war* is excluded, and the controversy is de-

cided by that power. Had there been any such court, any superior jurisdiction on earth, to determine the right between Jephtha and the Ammonites, they had never come to a *state of war*: but we see he was forced to appeal to heaven. "The Lord the Judge," says he, "be judge this day between the children of Israel and the children of Ammon" (Judg. xi. 27); and then prosecuting, and relying on his *appeal*, he leads out his army to battle. And, therefore, in such controversies, where the question is put, "Who shall be judge?" it cannot be meant, who shall decide the controversy; every one knows what Jephtha here tells us, that "the Lord the Judge" shall judge. Where there is no judge on earth, the appeal lies to God in Heaven. That question then cannot mean, who shall judge, whether another hath put himself in a *state of war* with me, and whether I may, as Jephtha did, *appeal to Heaven* in it? Of that I myself can only be judge in my own conscience, as I will answer it, at the great day, to the Supreme Judge of all men.

The transition from natural law to natural rights is rapid. Locke began with natural law and its obligations or duties not to harm others in specific respects, and added the ability of reason to discern the right rule. Section 7 already speaks of "invading others' rights." There is also the derivation of the individual's right in the state of nature to execute the natural law, that is, to punish an aggressor. The individual is of course essential to the idea of consent; both are central in the social contract.

Ch IV: Of Slavery

[22] The *natural liberty* of man is to be free from any superior power on earth, and not to be under the will or legislative authority of man, but to have only the law of nature for his rule. The *liberty of man*, in society, is to be under no other legislative power but that established by consent in the commonwealth; nor under the dominion of any will, or restraint of any law, but what that legislative shall enact, according to the trust put in it.

When Locke moves on to discuss property (Chapter V) he is already concentrating on it as a right and how it is begotten through other rights.

Ch V: Of Property

[25] Whether we consider natural *reason*, which tells us that men, being once born, have a right to their preservation, and consequently to meat and drink and such other things as nature affords for their subsistence: or *revelation*, which gives us an account of those grants God made of the world to Adam, and to Noah and his sons; it is very clear that God, as King David says (Psal. cxv. 16) "has given the earth to the children of men," given it to mankind in common. But this being supposed, it seems to some a very great difficulty, how any one should ever come to have a *property* in anything. . . . I shall endeavour to show, how men might come to have a *property* in several parts of that which God gave to mankind in common, and that without any express compact of all the commoners.

[27] Though the earth, and all inferior creatures, be common to all men, yet every man has a *property* in his own *person*: this nobody has any right to but himself. The *labour* of his body, and the *work* of his hands, we may say, are properly his. Whatsoever then he removes out of the state that nature hath provided and left it in, he hath mixed his *labour* with, and joined to it something that is his own, and thereby makes it his *property*. It being by him removed from the common state nature hath placed it in, it hath by this *labour* something annexed to it, that excludes the common right of other men: for this *labour* being the unquestionable property of the labourer, no man but he can have a right to what that is once joined to, at least where there is enough, and as good, left in common for others.

Locke pinpoints the precise moment at which something becomes property: as soon as we pick up acorns under an oak or gather apples from a tree they become ours, with the first labor of appropriation, not when you later boil or eat them. The law of nature sets limits to appropriation: We are given property to *enjoy*; hence, "As much as any one can make use of to any advantage of life before it spoils, so much he may by his labour fix a property in: whatever is beyond this, is more than his share, and belongs to others. Nothing was made by God for man to spoil or destroy" (31). Our rights of appropriation are also limited to what we can use. These need not be signifi-

cant limitations, "since there is land enough in the world to suffice double the inhabitants." Further, "the invention of money and the tacit agreement of men to put a value on it intro-duced—by consent—larger possessions and a right to them" (36).

[50] But since gold and silver, being little useful to the life of man in proportion to food, raiment, and carriage, has its *value* only from the consent of men, whereof *labour* yet makes, in great part, *the measure*, it is plain that men have agreed to a disproportionate and unequal *possession of the earth*, they having, by a tacit and voluntary consent found out a way how a man may fairly possess more land than he himself can use the product of, by receiving in exchange for the overplus gold and silver which may be hoarded up without injury to anyone; these metals not spoiling or decaying in the hands of the possessor. This partage of things in an inequality of private possessions, men have made practicable out of the bounds of society, and without compact, only by putting a value on gold and silver, and tacitly agreeing in the use of money: for in govern-ments, the laws regulate the right of property, and the possession of land is determined by positive constitutions.

Throughout the rest of the work important rights are generated. This involves explaining what the natural equality of men entails as well as what happens when a political society is formed by contract.

Ch VI: Of Paternal Power

[54] Though I have said above (Chap. II) *That all men by nature are equal*, I cannot be supposed to understand all sorts of *equality: age* or *virtue* may give men a just precedency: *excellency of parts* and *merit* may place others above the common level: *birth* may subject some, and *alliance* or *benefits* oth-ers, to pay an observance to those to whom nature, gratitude, or other respects, may have made it due: and yet all this consists with the *equality*, which all men are in, in respect of jurisdiction or dominion one over another, which was the *equality* I there spoke of, as proper to the business in hand, being that *equal right*, that every man hath, *to his natural*

freedom, without being subjected to the will or authority of any other man.

Ch VIII: Of the Beginning of Political Societies

[99] Whosoever therefore out of a state of nature unite into a *community*, must be understood to give up all the power necessary to the ends for which they unite into society to the *majority* of the community, unless they expressly agreed in any number greater than the majority. And this is done by barely agreeing to *unite into one political society*, which is *all the compact* that is, or needs be, between the individuals that enter into or make up a *commonwealth*. And thus that, which begins and actually *constitutes a political society*, is nothing but the consent of any number of freemen capable of a majority to unite and incorporate into such a society. And this is that, and that only, which did, or could give beginning to any *lawful government* in the world.

The "ends of political society and government" (Chapter IX), are "the mutual *preservation* of . . . lives, liberties and estates, which I call by the general name, *property*" (123). This sets limits on what government may do. If it trespasses too far, the question of "the dissolution of government" (Chapter XIX) and revolution arises: the key point is who is to judge, for example, between king and legislative body. "To this I reply, *The people shall be judge;* for who shall be judge whether his trustee or deputy acts well, and according to the trust reposed in him, but he who deputes him, and must, by having deputed him, have still a power to discard him, when he fails in his trust?" (240). Ultimately God, to whom each side may appeal, is judge: "He alone, it is true, is Judge of the right. But *every man* is *judge* for himself, as in all other cases, so in this, whether another hath put himself into a state of war with him, and whether he should appeal to the Supreme Judge" (241).

The dissolution of a government involves not the dissolution of society but either the construction of government in a new form or simply a change of governors.

*   *   *

Taken as a whole, the *Second Treatise* marks a shift of emphasis from natural law—as it was found in the Stoics, in Aquinas, or in Hooker's (1553–1600) *Laws of Ecclesiastical Polity* (published 1594–1662)—to natural rights, considered as an individual endowment, a kind of initial moral capital for the enterprise of life. After Locke, the grounding of rights in the natural law began to give way to a pluralism of rights inherent in the individual, derived generally from self-preservation or well-being and increasingly asserted independently on grounds of rational self-evidency.

Doubtless the shift (perhaps not altogether accomplished by Locke, although often credited to him by his successors) was in line with philosophic methods that need to start from self-evident principles. But it was certainly abetted by the demands of the developing individualism that argued for the rights of conscience (Locke himself wrote on behalf of religious toleration), freedom of speech and expression (advocated by Milton's *Areopagitica* [1644], at least for intellectuals), some extension of civil rights, including representation (though Locke clearly asked for less than the Levellers), and the increasingly successful efforts of the commercial world to reduce restraints on individual trade. We shall meet natural rights again both in the eighteenth century, in the moral justification of the American and French revolutions, and in the twentieth century, in the form of human rights.

Locke's *Treatise* and his *Essay* were both published in the last decade of the seventeenth century; but the *Treatise* closes the century that is ending, while the *Essay* opens the door to the century about to begin. What changes is the arena in which philosophy is spelled out. Seventeenth-century moral philosophy focuses on what it takes to be the realities of the world, whether physical movement, divine law, or Platonic universals. The arena of the eighteenth century is the mental world, and its counters are the psychological operations of the mind. Even a conception as common as reason takes on different form. For seventeenth-century philosophers reason is for the most part a light shining on the real, whether it lights up ethical axioms, natural law, or natural rights. Reason in the eighteenth century becomes reflection, an operation of the mind, putting in order its ideas and abstracting from them. And where reason is demoted, its place is taken by other elements, chiefly feelings and sentiments.

In this shift from the metaphysical to the epistemological, the path lies through Locke's psychological explorations in his immensely influential *Essay Concerning Human Understanding* (1690). In true Newtonian spirit Locke sets out to catalogue the elements of his subject matter, "to examine our own abilities, and see what objects our understandings were, or were not, fitted to deal with." [12] There is no evidence for innate ideas. In a famous metaphor he states the fundamental principle of empiricism:

Let us then suppose the mind to be, as we say, white paper, void of all characters, without any ideas; how comes it to be furnished? Whence comes it by that vast store, which the busy and boundless fancy of man has painted on it with an almost endless variety? Whence has it all the materials of reason and knowledge? To this I answer, in one word, from experience. In that all our knowledge is founded, and from that it ultimately derives itself. Our observation, employed either about external sensible objects, or about the internal operations of our minds, perceived and reflected on by ourselves, is that which supplies our understandings with all the materials of thinking. These two are the fountains of knowledge, from whence all the ideas we have, or can naturally have, do spring. [13]

If knowledge of the external world is experiential, then it must come from simple ideas of sensation. The objects of these ideas are qualities perceived through the five senses, that is, color, solidity, odor, taste, and so on.

The external physical universe is really composed of particles, mass-points. The qualities these particles have, independent of the human observer—"primary qualities," those that Newton found capable of mathematical treatment—are solidity, extension, figure, motion or rest, and number. Ideas produced by action of the primary qualities are "resemblances of them, and their patterns do really exist in the bodies themselves." [14] Not all ideas are of this sort. Many—heat, color, taste, for example—are "secondary qualities," effects produced in us by the powers things have by virtue of their primary qualities (as a rapid motion of particles gives the idea of heat, while slow motion produces the idea of cold). The relation of a secondary quality and the object is not a matter of resemblance, but causal only.

Simple ideas of reflection, for example, thinking and willing, are what appear in the mind as it reflects on its own operations. Simple ideas can be combined, compared, and abstracted to make up complex ideas. The mind is capable also of contemplating (holding an idea before it for some time), remembering, and naming. Moral ideas, such as gratitude, obligation, hypocrisy, a lie, are "mixed modes," complex ideas that combine simple ideas of different kinds and involve a reference to good and evil, that is, to pleasure and pain.

Locke's distinction between primary and secondary qualities quickly came under attack. George Berkeley (1685–1753) accused Locke in effect of a failure of nerve for not carrying through his own empiricist program; for the distinction between primary and secondary qualities is itself not an object of experience; and further, the causal relation and resemblance between ideas and objects outside of us cannot be established by experience. If the distinction between primary and secondary qualities is dropped, then all our ideas (experiences) are in the same boat, the question of correspondence disappears, and there is no

---

[12] *Essay*, "The Epistle to the Reader."
[13] Ibid., Bk II, ch 1, sec 2.

[14] Ibid., Bk I, ch 8, sec 15.

reason to invoke the notion of matter as a strange metaphysical support for primary qualities, nor to look to any outside causal support for ideas. Hume (See Chapter 10) directed against mind the same fire that Berkeley had against matter, leaving as the major philosophical task the analysis of impressions (experiences) and ideas. Other philosophers devoted their efforts rather to extended reaches of experience, adding to the perceptual the experience of interpersonal relations, morality, and aesthetic qualities. They faced these as encountered realities, not as interior effects of some hidden causes. Much of the moral philosophy of the eighteenth century conveys this sense of the exploration of experience. Whatever direction eighteenth-century moral philosophy was to take, the basis would lie in an analysis of human nature as psychological foundation.

Eighteenth-century sentiment philosophers, although they accepted the basic thrust of Locke's empiricism, felt that his view of experience was overintellectualized and discounted the richness of emotional life—the affections, passions, and sentiments, including interpersonal ones; further, they contended that Locke's concept of experience failed to make clear the status of moral and aesthetic experience and properties.

10

English Conscience and Scottish Sentiment: Butler, Hume, and Smith

Philosophers in the seventeenth century turned from attacking Hobbes's contractualism to criticizing his egoism. Putting aside the will of God as the foundation of morality, they accepted Hobbes's lead in grounding morality in human nature itself. Even Joseph Butler, clearly committed to a religious ethics, argues from within the constraints of human nature. Egoism had been elegantly restated by Bernard Mandeville (1670–1733). His provoking *The Fable of the Bee, or Private Vices, Public Benefits* (1714) "demonstrated" that selfish desires—for gourmet foods, for luxuries, for the envy of others—feed the dynamics of the economy and of social progress. Thus Mandeville's cynical paradox: life would become marginal and pitiful without a basis of such private vices. If such accounts were to be corrected, a whole science of human nature had to be fashioned afresh.

The model of investigation was of course Newtonian, as developed by Locke but going into the richer human capabilities that he had neglected or insufficiently explored. The spirit of this expanded Newtonianism is intimated in a popular essay by Bishop Berkeley, "The Bond of Society," which uses the Newtonian notion of attraction to explain social relationships:

From the contemplation of the order, motion, and cohesion of natural bodies, philosophers are now agreed that there is a mutual attraction between the most distant parts at least of this solar system. All those bodies that revolve round the sun are drawn towards each other and towards the sun, by some secret, uniform and never-ceasing principle. Hence it is that the earth (as well as the other planets) without flying off in a tangent line, constantly rouls about the sun, and the moon about the earth, without deserting her companion in so many thousand years. And as the larger systems of the universe are held together by this cause, so likewise the particular globes derive their cohesion and consistence from it. Now, if we carry our thoughts from the corporeal to the moral world, we may observe in the Spirits or Minds of men a like principle of attraction, whereby they are drawn together in communities, clubs, families, friendships, and all the various species of society. As in bodies, where the quantity is the same, the attraction is strongest between those which are placed nearest to each other, so is it likewise in the minds of men, *ceteris paribus*, between those which are most nearly related. Bodies that are placed at the distance of many millions of miles may nevertheless attract and constantly operate on each other, although this action do not shew itself by an union or approach of those distant bodies, so long as they are withheld by the contrary forces of other bodies, which, at the same time, attract them different ways, but would, on the supposed removal of all other bodies, mutually approach and unite with each other. The like holds with regard to the human soul, whose affection towards the individuals of the same species who are distantly related to it, is rendered inconspicuous by its more powerful attraction towards those who have a nearer relation to it. But as those are removed the tendency which before lay concealed doth gradually disclose itself.

A man who has no family is more strongly attracted towards his friends and neighbours; and, if absent from these, he naturally falls into an acquaintance with those of his own city or country who chance to be in the same place. Two Englishmen meeting at Rome or Constantinople soon run into a familiarity. And in China or Japan Europeans would think their being so a good reason for their uniting in particular converse. Further, in case we suppose ourselves translated into Jupiter or Saturn, and there to meet a Chinese or other most distant native of our own planet, we should look on him as a near relation, and readily commence a friendship with him. These are natural reflections, and such as may convince us that we are linked by an imperceptible chain to every individual of the human race.

The several great bodies which compose the solar system are kept from joining together at the common center of gravity by the rectilinear motions the Author of nature hath impressed on each of them, which concurring with the attractive principle, form their respective orbits round the sun: upon the ceasing of which motions, the general law of gravitation that is now thwarted would shew itself by drawing them all into one mass. After the same manner in the parallel case of society, private passions and motions of the soul do often obstruct the operation of that benevolent uniting instinct implanted in human nature, which, notwithstanding, doth still exert, and will not fail to shew itself when those obstructions are taken away.

The mutual gravitation of bodies cannot be ex-

plained any other way than by resolving it into the immediate operation of God, who never ceases to dispose and actuate his creatures in a manner suitable to their respective beings. So neither can that reciprocal attraction in the minds of men be accounted for by any other cause. It is not the result of education, law, or fashion; but is a principle originally engrafted in the very first formation of the soul by the Author of our nature.

And as the attractive power in bodies is the most universal principle which produceth innumerable effects, and is a key to explain the various phenomena of nature; so the corresponding social appetite in human souls is the great spring and source of moral actions. This it is that inclines each individual to an intercourse with his species, and models every one to that behaviour which best suits with the common well-being. Hence that sympathy in our nature whereby we feel the pains and joys of our fellow-creatures. Hence that prevalent love in parents towards their children, which is neither founded on the merit of the object, nor yet on self-interest. It is this that makes us inquisitive concerning the affairs of distant nations which can have no influence on our own. It is this that extends our care to future generations, and excites us to acts of beneficence towards those who are not yet in being, and consequently from whom we can expect no recompence. In a word, hence arises that diffusive sense of humanity so unaccountable to the selfish man who is untouched with it, and is, indeed, a sort of monster or anomalous production.[1]

The initial thesis of the expanded "moral sciences" was that egoistic psychology is an oversimplification of human nature. Even the egoistic, they argued, had been misanalyzed. What Lord Shaftesbury (1671–1713) and Francis Hutcheson (1694–1747) early in the century appreciated was the variety and complexity of human response, especially to beauty, nature, and others. They turned attention to aesthetics, noting, for example, the richness of the notions of the sublime and even the ugly. They also found aesthetic qualities in interpersonal responses (in sympathy and in benevolence). There were doubtless reactive aspects to their expanded view. In the background as they

[1] *The Guardian,* August 5, 1713.

wrote was the ugly side to the social changes then being experienced in Britain: cities in disorder upsetting the natural environment, the breakdown of established methods for dealing with the unemployed and those in want; greed and the promise of gain seeming to emerge as the closest human bond.

This was also a period of growing wealth and rapid expansion of the arts as well as the sciences—the age of Richardson and Fielding, who shaped the novel and who explored in it the subtlety of human social behavior. Style became a focus of morals and manners as well as of literature, a spirit that became a feature even of philosophical writing.

The philosophers who carried out this sensitive exploration of human nature have been inappropriately grouped together as "moral sense intuitionists." They do not all talk of the direct or intuitive grasp of moral truths. Indeed, their unity is more in their confrontation with Hobbes than in substance: human tendencies toward virtuous and benevolent actions are as natural and as solid as those directed to advancing self-interest. They agree in allowing human beings scope for nonselfish motivation, but they differ in where they locate this capacity. Some, such as Shaftesbury (who did speak of the "moral sense"), are impressed by the feelings we have for beauty generally and for beauty in the moral. Others, such as Butler, attend to the cognitive aspects of the moral judgment, sketching the multiple ways we perceive and respond to the multiple features of the world. Others again, like Hutcheson, turn their analysis more directly to the affections themselves, making morality more a matter of affective responses than of rational apprehension. In still others, such as Hume and Smith, the Newtonian model emerges in full strength: they are scientists of the human response, searching for the laws underlying its action and reaction.

For the most part, the lead in these moral sciences had passed to Scotland—in law, medicine, economics, science, and philosophy: not just Hutcheson, Hume, and Smith, but others such as Henry Home (Lord Kames), Thomas Reid, Adam Ferguson, and Dugald Stewart. These, along with the French of the *Encyclopédie*, advanced Locke's agenda into fresh fields.

There is an interesting progression in the three philosophies examined in this chapter, if we attend to the relations of self-interest and the other-regarding attitude that appears sometimes as benevolence and sometimes as utilitarian furthering of the common interest. Butler disinfects self-interest by setting it off from the passions and making self-love a reasonable reckoning of the individual's overall well-being; he can then claim that the verdicts of conscience (embodying the general well-being) tend to coincide with those of self-interest. Hume allows the utilitarian aspect to spread over the whole field of justice; it is a purely instrumental virtue. Even more, utility explains why appreciations take the form they do, although utility does not enter into the feelings themselves. Smith, too, lets utilitarian considerations have their place in the underlying, "gravitational," principles of human response; but more than Hume, he insists on the aesthetic rather than the utilitarian character of the responses. More important, Smith's partition of the self-interested and the aesthetic yields two different sciences—the science of political economy and the science of morals.

If a label were needed, "sentiment theorists" might do. They did investigate the sentiments and the affective aspects of human experience, as contrasted with the prior emphasis on the cognitive and the rational. Whether the sentiments were seen as the affective aspects of reason or as affection vying with reason seems to depend largely on the kind of psychology to which they adhered.

Joseph Butler
(1692–1752)

Butler moved from Presbyterianism to Anglicanism, eventually becoming bishop of Durham. The first of his two major works, *Fifteen*

Sermons Preached at the Rolls Chapel (1726), analyzed human nature; the second, *Analogy of Religion* (1736), attempted a reconciliation of deism (though he attacks it) with revelation. Other more popular sermons show his attitude toward social problems: he recognized the changes in economic life but disparaged the pursuit of wealth insofar as it expresses pecuniary greed. On the whole he inclined to accept status based on birth but insisted on its responsibilities:

How unhappy a choice then do those rich men make, who sacrifice all these high prerogatives of their state, to the wretched purposes of dissoluteness and vanity, or to the sordid itch of heaping up, to no purpose at all; whilst in the mean time they stand charged with the important trust, in which they are thus unfaithful, and of which a strict account remains to be given![2]

Calling for charity ("not mere good humor, but kind inclinations with judgment considering the proper means") for distressed seamen and "poor manufacturers" ("all who are employed in any labour whatever belonging to trade and commerce"), he wants them treated as if they had been household servants:

If any of your domestic servants were disabled by sickness, there is none of you but would think himself bound to do somewhat for their relief. Now these seamen and manufacturers are employed in your immediate business. They are servants of merchants, and other principal traders; as much your servants as if they lived under your roof: though by their not doing so, the relation is less in sight.[3]

While Butler's moral philosophy undoubtedly is religious, the *Sermons* approach it psychologically. The strategy is to establish an authoritative order, without invoking external divine authority and indeed before raising the question of the supreme authority of con-

science. He distinguishes four elements—passions, self-love, benevolence, and conscience—and argues that there is no principled or general opposition between them. Hobbes mistakenly confused self-love, which is a long-range principle, with the passions. Self-love has authority over the passions, indeed, but some passions (e.g., a desire for revenge) may work contrary to self-love, while others may assist self-love. He need only go on in the same way to further elements that have even higher authority: compassion, as authentic a passion as any appetite concerned with private goods; benevolence, which is directed to public goods and has a status similar to that of self-love; and conscience, which involves reason and is the most authoritative element in human nature. For the most part the dictates of cool self-love coincide with those of conscience. We often assume the pursuit of our own interests must be opposed to that of others' interest. This is due to our mistaken habit of thinking in terms of property (Sermon XI).

The criticisms of Hobbes's analysis of human nature are best seen in Sermon I (particularly in its long footnotes) and Sermon II.

Sermons [4]

Sermon I

From this review and comparison of the nature of man as respecting self, and as respecting society, it will plainly appear, that *there are as real and the same kind of indications in human nature, that we were made for society and to do good to our fellow-creatures; as that we were intended to take care of our own life and health and private good: and that the same objections lie against one of these assertions, as against the other.* For,

First, There is a natural principle of *benevolence* [b]

---

[2] Sermon VI (March 31, 1748), in *The Works of Joseph Butler*, ed. the Right Honorable W. E. Gladstone (Oxford: Clarendon Press; New York: Macmillan & Co., 1896), vol. II, p. 396.
[3] Ibid., p. 392.

[4] The selection is from *Works*, vol. II. Butler's first footnote to Sermon I, footnote *a*, is omitted.
[b] Suppose a man of learning to be writing a grave book upon *human nature*, and to show in several parts of it that he had an insight into the subject he was considering; amongst other things, the following one would require to be accounted for; the appearance of benevolence or good-will in men towards each other in the instances of natural relation, and in others [Hobbes, *On Human Nature*, ix, 7]. Cautious of being deceived with outward show,

in man; which is in some degree to *society*, what *self-love* is to the *individual*. And if there be in mankind any disposition to friendship; if there be any such thing as compassion, for compassion is momentary love; if there be any such thing as the paternal or filial affections; if there be any affection in human nature, the object and end of which is the good of another; this is itself benevolence, or the love of another. Be it ever so short, be it in ever so low a degree, or ever so unhappily confined; it proves the assertion, and points out what we were designed for, as really as though it were in a higher degree and more extensive.

I must however remind you that though benevo-

lence and self-love are different; though the former tends most directly to public good, and the latter to private: yet they are so perfectly coincident, that the greatest satisfactions to ourselves depend upon our having benevolence in a due degree; and that self-love is one chief security of our right behaviour towards society. It may be added, that their mutual coinciding, so that we can scarce promote one without the other, is equally a proof that we were made for both.

Secondly, This will further appear, from observing that the *several passions* and *affections*, which are distinct [c] both from benevolence and self-love, do

---

he retires within himself to see exactly, what that is in the mind of man from whence this appearance proceeds; and, upon deep reflection, asserts the principle in the mind to be only the love of power, and delight in the exercise of it. Would not every body think here was a mistake of one word for another? that the philosopher was contemplating and accounting for some other *human actions*, some other behaviour of man to man? And could any one be thoroughly satisfied, that what is commonly called benevolence or good-will was really the affection meant, but only by being made to understand that this learned person had a general hypothesis, to which the appearance of good-will could no otherwise be reconciled?

That what has this appearance is often nothing but ambition; that delight in superiority often (suppose always) mixes itself with benevolence, only makes it more specious to call it ambition than hunger, of the two: but in reality that passion does no more account for the whole appearances of good-will, than this appetite does. Is there not often the appearance of one man's wishing that good to another, which he knows himself unable to procure him; and rejoicing in it, though bestowed by a third person? And can love of power any way possibly come in to account for this desire or delight? Is there not often the appearance of men's distinguishing between two or more persons, preferring one before another, to do good to, in cases where love of power cannot in the least account for the distinction and preference? For this principle can no otherwise distinguish between objects, than as it is a greater instance and exertion of power to do good to one rather than to another.

Again, suppose good-will in the mind of man to be nothing but delight in the exercise of power: men might indeed be restrained by distant and accidental considerations; but these restraints being removed, they would have a disposition to, and delight in mischief as an exercise and proof of power: and this disposition and delight would arise from, or be the same principle in the mind, as a disposition to, and delight in charity. Thus cruelty, as distinct from envy and resentment, would be exactly the same in the mind of man as good-will: that one tends to the happiness, the other to the misery of our fellow-creatures, is, it seems, merely an accidental circumstance, which the mind has not the least regard to. These are

the absurdities which even men of capacity run into, when they have occasion to belie their nature, and will perversely disclaim that image of God which was originally stamped upon it, the traces of which, however faint, are plainly discernible upon the mind of man.

If any person can in earnest doubt, whether there be such a thing as good-will in one man towards another; (for the question is not concerning either the degree or extensiveness of it, but concerning the affection itself:) let it be observed, that *whether man be thus, or otherwise constituted, what is the inward frame in this particular*, is a mere question of fact or natural history, not provable immediately by reason. It is therefore to be judged of and determined in the same way other facts or matters of natural history are: by appealing to the external senses, or inward perceptions, respectively, as the matter under consideration is cognizable by one or the other: by arguing from acknowledged facts and actions; for a great number of actions in the same kind, in different circumstances, and respecting different objects, will prove, to a certainty, what principles they do not, and, to the greatest probability, what principles they do proceed from: and lastly, by the testimony of mankind. Now that there is some degree of benevolence amongst men, may be as strongly and plainly proved in all these ways, as it could possibly be proved, supposing there was this affection in our nature. And should any one think fit to assert, that resentment in the mind of man was absolutely nothing but reasonable concern for our own safety, the falsity of this, and what is the real nature of that passion, could be shewn in no other ways than those in which it may be shown, that there is such a thing in *some degree* as *real* good-will in man towards man. It is sufficient that the seeds of it be implanted in our nature by God.

There is, it is owned, much left for us to do upon our own heart and temper; to cultivate, to improve, to call it forth, to exercise it in a steady, uniform manner. This is our work: this is virtue and religion.

[c] Every body makes a distinction between self-love, and the several particular passions, appetites, and affections; and yet they are often confounded again. That they are totally different, will be seen by any one who will distinguish between the passions and appetites *themselves*, and *endeavouring* after the means of their gratification. Consider the appetite of hunger, and the desire of esteem: these

in general contribute and lead us to *public* good as really as to *private*. It might be thought too minute and particular, and would carry us too great a length, to distinguish between and compare together the several passions or appetites distinct from benevolence, whose primary use and intention is the security and good of society; and the passions distinct from self-love, whose primary intention and design is the security and good of the individual.[d] It is enough to the present argument, that desire of esteem from others, contempt and esteem of

being the occasion both of pleasure and pain, the coolest *self-love*, as well as the appetites and passions themselves, may put us upon making use of the *proper methods of obtaining* that pleasure, and avoiding that pain; but the *feelings themselves*, the pain of hunger and shame, and the delight from esteem, are no more self-love than they are any thing in the world. Though a man hated himself, he would as much feel the pain of hunger as he would that of the gout: and it is plainly supposable there may be creatures with self-love in them to the highest degree, who may be quite insensible and indifferent (as men in some cases are) to the contempt and esteem of those, upon whom their happiness does not in some further respects depend. And as self-love and the several particular passions and appetites are in themselves totally different; so, that some actions proceed from one, and some from the other, will be manifest to any who will observe the two following very supposable cases. One man rushes upon certain ruin for the gratification of a present desire: nobody will call the principle of this action self-love. Suppose another man to go through some laborious work upon promise of a great reward, without any distinct knowledge what the reward will be: this course of action cannot be ascribed to any particular passion.

The former of these actions is plainly to be imputed to some particular passion or affection, the latter as plainly to the general affection or principle of self-love. That there are some particular pursuits or actions concerning which we cannot determine how far they are owing to one, and how far to the other, proceeds from this, that the two principles are frequently mixed together, and run up into each other.

[d] If any desire to see this distinction and comparison made in a particular instance, the appetite and passion now mentioned may serve for one. Hunger is to be considered as a private appetite; because the end for which it was given us is the preservation of the individual. Desire of esteem is a public passion; because the end for which it was given us is to regulate our behaviour towards society. The respect which this has to private good is as remote as the respect that has to public good: and the appetite is no more self-love, than the passion is benevolence. The object and end of the former is merely food; the object and end of the latter is merely esteem: but the latter can no more be gratified, without contributing to the good of society; than the former can be gratified, without contributing to the preservation of the individual.

them, love of society as distinct from affection to the good of it, indignation against successful vice, that these are public affections or passions; have an immediate respect to others, naturally lead us to regulate our behaviour in such a manner as will be of service to our fellow-creatures. If any or all of these may be considered likewise as private affections, as tending to private good; this does not hinder them from being public affections too, or destroy the good influence of them upon society, and their tendency to public good. It may be added, that as persons without any conviction from reason of the desireableness of life, would yet of course preserve it merely from the appetite of hunger; so by acting merely from regard (suppose) to reputation, without any consideration of the good of others, men often contribute to public good. In both these instances they are plainly instruments in the hands of another, in the hands of Providence, to carry on ends, the preservation of the individual and good of society, which they themselves have not in their view or intention. The sum is, men have various appetites, passions, and particular affections, quite distinct both from self-love and from benevolence: all of these have a tendency to promote both public and private good, and may be considered as respecting others and ourselves equally and in common: but some of them seem most immediately to respect others, or tend to public good; others of them most immediately to respect self, or tend to private good: as the former are not benevolence, so the latter are not self-love: neither sort are instances of our love either to ourselves or others; but only instances of our Maker's care and love both of the individual and the species, and proofs that he intended we should be instruments of good to each other, as well as that we should be so to ourselves.

Thirdly, There is a principle of reflection in men, by which they distinguish between, approve and disapprove their own actions. We are plainly constituted such sort of creatures as to reflect upon our own nature. The mind can take a view of what passes within itself, its propensions, aversions, passions, affections, as respecting such objects, and in such degrees; and of the several actions consequent thereupon. In this survey it approves of one, disapproves of another, and towards a third is affected in neither of these ways, but is quite indifferent.

This principle in man, by which he approves or disapproves his heart, temper, and actions, is conscience; for this is the strict sense of the word, though sometimes it is used so as to take in more. And that this faculty tends to restrain men from doing mischief to each other, and leads them to do good, is too manifest to need being insisted upon. Thus a parent has the affection of love to his children: this leads him to take care of, to educate, to make due provision for them; the natural affection leads to this: but the reflection that it is his proper business, what belongs to him, that it is right and commendable so to do; this added to the affection becomes a much more settled principle, and carries him on through more labour and difficulties for the sake of his children, than he would undergo from that affection alone, if he thought it, and the course of action it led to, either indifferent or criminal. This indeed is impossible, to do that which is good, and not to approve of it; for which reason they are frequently not considered as distinct, though they really are: for men often approve of the actions of others, which they will not imitate, and likewise do that which they approve not. It cannot possibly be denied, that there is this principle of reflection or conscience in human nature. Suppose a man to relieve an innocent person in great distress; suppose the same man afterwards, in the fury of anger, to do the greatest mischief to a person who had given no just cause of offence; to aggravate the injury, add the circumstances of former friendship, and obligation from the injured person; let the man who is supposed to have done these two different actions, coolly reflect upon them afterwards, without regard to their consequences to himself: to assert that any common man would be affected in the same way towards these different actions, that he would make no distinction between them, but approve or disapprove them equally, is too glaring a falsity to need being confuted. There is therefore this principle of reflection or conscience in mankind.

It is needless to compare the respect it has to private good, with the respect it has to public; since it plainly tends as much to the latter as to the former, and is commonly thought to tend chiefly to the latter. This faculty is now mentioned merely as another part in the inward frame of man, pointing out to us in some degree what we are intended for, and as what will naturally and of course have some

influence. The particular place assigned to it by nature, what authority it has, and how great influence it ought to have, shall be hereafter considered. [pp. 35–43]

But allowing all this, it may be asked, "Has not man dispositions and principles within, which lead him to do evil to others, as well as to do good? Whence come the many miseries else, which men are the authors and instruments of to each other?" These questions, so far as they relate to the foregoing discourse, may be answered by asking, Has not man also dispositions and principles within, which lead him to do evil to himself, as well as good? Whence come the many miseries else, sickness, pain, and death, which men are the instruments and authors of to themselves?

It may be thought more easy to answer one of these questions than the other, but the answer to both is really the same; that mankind have ungoverned passions which they will gratify at any rate, as well to the injury of others, as in contradiction to known private interest: but that as there is no such thing as self-hatred, so neither is there any such thing as ill-will in one man towards another, emulation and resentment being away; whereas there is plainly benevolence or good-will: there is no such thing as love of injustice, oppression, treachery, ingratitude; but only eager desires after such and such external goods; which, according to a very ancient observation, the most abandoned would choose to obtain by innocent means, if they were as easy, and as effectual to their end: that even emulation and resentment, by any one who will consider what these passions really are in nature, will be found nothing to the purpose of this objection.

And that the principles and passions in the mind of man, which are distinct both from self-love and benevolence, primarily and most directly lead to right behaviour with regard to others as well as himself, and only secondarily and accidentally to what is evil. Thus, though men, to avoid the shame of one villainy, are sometimes guilty of a greater, yet it is easy to see, that the original tendency of shame is to prevent the doing of shameful actions; and its leading men to conceal such actions when done, is only in consequence of their being done; i.e. of the passion's not having answered its first end.

If it be said, that there are persons in the world,

who are in great measure without the natural affections towards their fellow-creatures: there are likewise instances of persons without the common natural affections to themselves: but the nature of man is not to be judged of by either of these, but by what appears in the common world, in the bulk of mankind. [pp. 45–48]

Sermon II

Now what is it which renders such a rash action [following an appetite, though foreseeing that ruin will follow] unnatural? Is it that he went against the principle of reasonable and cool self-love, considered *merely* as a part of his nature? No: for if he had acted the contrary way, he would equally have gone against a principle, or part of his nature, namely, passion or appetite. But to deny a present appetite, from foresight that the gratification of it would end in immediate ruin or extreme misery, is by no means an unnatural action: whereas to contradict or go against cool self-love for the sake of such gratification, is so in the instance before us. Such an action then being unnatural; and its being so not arising from a man's going against a principle or desire barely, nor in going against that principle or desire which happens for the present to be strongest; it necessarily follows that there must be some other difference or distinction to be made between these two principles, passion and cool self-love, than what I have yet taken notice of.

And this difference, not being a difference in strength or degree, I call a difference in *nature* and in *kind*. And since, in the instance still before us, if passion prevails over self-love, the consequent action is unnatural; but if self-love prevails over passion, the action is natural: it is manifest that self-love is in human nature a superior principle to passion. This may be contradicted without violating that nature; but the former cannot. So that, if we will act conformably to the economy of man's nature, reasonable self-love must govern. Thus, without particular consideration of conscience, we may have a clear conception of the *superior nature* of one inward principle to another; and see that there really is this natural superiority, quite distinct from degrees of strength and prevalency. . . .

All this is no more than the distinction, which every body is acquainted with, between *mere power* and *authority*: only instead of being intended to ex-

press the difference between what is possible, and what is lawful in civil government; here it has been shown applicable to the several principles in the mind of man. Thus that principle, by which we survey, and either approve or disapprove our own heart, temper, and actions, is not only to be considered as what is in its turn to have some influence; which may be said of every passion, of the lowest appetites: but likewise as being superior; as from its very nature manifestly claiming superiority over all others: insomuch that you cannot form a notion of this faculty, conscience, without taking in judgment, direction, superintendency. This is a constituent part of the idea, that is, of the faculty itself: and, to preside and govern, from the very economy and constitution of man, belongs to it. Had it strength, as it has right; had it power, as it has manifest authority; it would absolutely govern the world. [pp. 61–64]

David Hume
(1711–1776)

In the eighteenth-century controversy between reason and the proponents of sentiment, if Butler's allegiance was to the former, Hume's was to the latter. Hume's debt in several major respects is to Francis Hutcheson (1694–1747), who was mentor to a whole generation of Scottish philosophers. Hutcheson pursued further the avenue opened up by Locke's account of reflection as a human power and of ideas of reflection as indicative of our abilities to analyze our own operations. Locke had too quickly closed this line of inquiry by referring a rich variety of materials to pleasures and pains and self-interest. Hutcheson's *Inquiry into the Original of Our Ideas of Beauty and Virtue* (1725) argues that as we have a visual capacity by which we are naturally capable of seeing color so we have an aesthetic sense, an "internal sense," by which we naturally delight in order and harmony. Analogously, there is a "moral sense," which is gratified and pleased by the sight of benevolence and virtue and displeased by the sight of vice. Our judgment of virtue reflects the distinctive feeling of moral pleasure we experience upon observing a virtuous act. Since we may appreciate an act contrary to self-interest, the feeling is dispassionate and disinterested.

This moral sense is self-referring, but not self-interested, and so helps explain how human beings can be moved to act for pleasure without being selfish. Seeing one person being kind to another, you are pleased. You respond by reenacting the pleasure, by being benevolent to another person; your act in turn pleases some other who responds by being benevolent, and so on. In this way benevolence sympathetically spreads through social groups. Hutcheson was much concerned about the relation of virtue to happiness and attempted to quantify it, giving one of the first statements of the principle of utility:

In comparing the moral qualities of actions, in order to regulate our election among various actions proposed, or to find which of them has the greatest moral excellency, we are led by our moral sense of virtue to judge thus: that in equal degrees of happiness, expected to proceed from the action, the virtue is in proportion to the number of persons to whom the happiness shall extend (and here the dignity, or moral importance of persons may compensate numbers); and in equal numbers, the virtue is as the quantity of the happiness, or natural good; or that the virtue is in a compound ratio of the quantity of good, and number of enjoyers. And in the same manner, the moral evil, or vice, is as the degree of misery and number of sufferers; so that that action is best, which procures the greatest happiness for the greatest numbers.[5]

Hume attended Edinburgh University, leaving it at age fourteen or fifteen, which was not uncommon for the time. By 1739, he had published his philosophical masterpiece, *A Treatise of Human Nature*. Its reception, falling "dead born from the press," deeply disappointed him. In 1741–1742 he tried again, with *Essays, Moral and Political*, and was encouraged

by its modest success. Convinced that the failure of the *Treatise* was due to its style, he recast its epistemological sections as *An Enquiry Concerning Human Understanding* (1748), and (with serious revisions) its sections on moral philosophy as *An Enquiry Concerning the Principles of Morals* (1751). *Political Discourses* (1752) and *History of England* (Vol I, 1754) gained him the literary reputation he sought. In 1757 came *Four Dissertations*, and, posthumously, *Dialogues Concerning Natural Religion* (1779).

While his main interests lay in philosophy, science, politics, economics, and literature, he served also as librarian at the Faculty of Advocates in Edinburgh, as secretary to the British ambassador to Paris (where he seems to have been a social lion), and as undersecretary of state for Scotland. In his short autobiography, *My Own Life* (1776), he described himself as

a man of mild dispositions, of command of temper, of an open, social, and cheerful humour, capable of attachment, but little susceptible of enmity, and of great moderation in all my passions. Even my love of literary fame, my ruling passion, never soured my temper, notwithstanding my frequent disappointments.[6]

Hume's philosophy little reflects his personal amiability: his work is a profound critique that devastated the landscape of eighteenth-century thought. As Newton observed the motions of physical bodies in order to detect the general principles that would explain apparently unrelated events, so Hume aspired to observe human behavior and to divine the principles that would explain it: Why do human beings reason as they do? Why do they feel as they do? How are they motivated and why? Writing from inside the tradition of British empiricism, but taking it well beyond any of his predecessors, he relied on two critical tools: experience and the association of ideas.

[5] *Inquiry*, Treatise II, Concerning Good and Evil, sec 3, 8.

[6] *My Own Life*, reprinted in David Hume, *Essays: Moral, Political, and Literary*, ed. T. H. Green and T. H. Grose (London: Longmans, Green, 1875), pp. 7–8.

In *An Abstract of a Treatise of Human Nature* (1740), writing in the third person, he catalogues the elements, defines empiricism and notes its consequences:

Our author [Hume] begins with some definitions. He calls a *perception* whatever can be present to the mind, whether we employ our senses, or are actuated with passion, or exercise our thought and reflection. He divides our perceptions into two kinds, viz. *impressions* and *ideas*. When we feel a passion or emotion of any kind, or have the images of external objects conveyed by our senses; the perception of the mind is what he calls an *impression*, which is a word that he employs in a new sense. When we reflect on a passion or an object which is not present, this perception is an *idea*. *Impressions*, therefore, are our lively and strong perceptions; *ideas* are the fainter and weaker. . . .

[A]ll our ideas, or weak perceptions, are derived from our impressions, or strong perceptions, and . . . we can never think of any thing which we have not seen without us, or felt in our own minds.

. . . Accordingly, whenever any idea is ambiguous, [Hume] has always recourse to the impression, which must render it clear and precise. And when he suspects that any philosophical term has no idea annexed to it (as is too common) he always asks *from what impression that idea is derived?* And if no impression can be produced, he concludes that the term is altogether insignificant.[7]

If a complex idea is not reducible to simple ideas, and if those simple ideas are not derived in turn from specific impressions, then the complex idea is meaningless.

For the second critical tool, he observes that perceptions in the mind do not succeed one another randomly:

[I]f anything can entitle the author to so glorious a name as that of an *inventor*, it is the use he makes

of the principle of the association of ideas. . . . [T]here is a secret tie or union among particular ideas, which causes the mind to conjoin them more frequently together, and makes the one, upon its appearance, introduce the other. [The principles of association] are the only links that bind the parts of the universe together, or connect us with any person or object exterior to ourselves.[8]

Ideas are associated if they have one of three relations—resemblance, contiguity, or cause and effect:

A picture naturally leads our thoughts to the original [resemblance]: The mention of one apartment in a building naturally introduces an enquiry or discourse concerning the others [contiguity]: and if we think of a wound, we can scarcely forbear reflecting on the pain which follows it [cause and effect].[9]

Through these associations alone is knowledge constructed.

With these two instruments—the rooting of ideas in impressions and the association of ideas as an explanatory principle—Hume launched a far-reaching critique of the foundations of knowledge. Rationalism bears the brunt of the attack, in particular its reliance on *absolutes*, *necessary* connections, *indubitable* principles, *self-evident* truths. But the empirical base from which the attack was launched also suffers from the fallout. Hume's discussion of science and causality undermines the confidence with which we rely on past experience to address the future (induction). While rationalism and empiricism had been battling for the hearts and minds of philosophers, Hume takes on both parties and undercuts their foundations. It is no wonder that he left his contemporaries frustrated and even angry, suspecting a genial atheism and an immoral skepticism, yet admiring of his analytic skills.

Still, the subtitle of his *Treatise*, "Being an

[7] *An Abstract of A Treatise of Human Nature*, ed. J. M. Keynes and P. Sraffa (Cambridge: Cambridge University Press, 1938), pp. 8–11. This was an anonymous review of Book I of the *Treatise*. Not until the twentieth century was it established conclusively that Hume himself had been its author.

[8] Ibid., pp. 31–32.
[9] *An Enquiry Concerning Human Understanding*, ed. L. A. Selby-Bigge (Oxford: Clarendon Press, 1894), sec III, p. 24.

Attempt to Introduce the Method of Experimental Reasoning into Moral Subjects," might have reassured them that he had also constructive aims. Through the principle of association of ideas he is prepared to offer guiding principles of human and social life—habit and custom—which in the end emerge as a traditionalism.

Rationalists attribute too great a scope to human reason, especially when, in metaphysics, they assert the reality of selves and substances. "The only method of freeing learning, at once, from . . . abstruse [metaphysical] questions, is to enquire seriously into the nature of human understanding, and show, from an exact analysis of its powers and capacity, that it is by no means fitted for such remote and abstruse subjects." [10] Thus, the concepts of self and substance are subjected to the test, "from what impression is the idea derived?" To those, like Descartes, who had held that the mind or the self is given directly in experience, Hume responds:

For my part, when I enter most intimately into what I call *myself*, I always stumble on some particular perception or other, of heat or cold, light or shade, love or hatred, pain or pleasure. I never can catch *myself* at any time without a perception, and never can observe any thing but the perception. . . . I may venture to affirm of the rest of mankind, that they are nothing but a bundle or collection of different perceptions, which succeed each other with an inconceivable rapidity, and are in perpetual flux and movement. . . . The mind is a kind of theatre, where several perceptions successively make their appearance; pass, re-pass, glide away, and mingle in an infinite variety of postures and situations.[11]

Berkeley, who had argued that we cannot know what the world is really like because we are limited to experience, still appealed to mind. Hume turns the same argument against Berkeley, for experience does not extend to minds, or to God.

Recognizing that mathematics had been the great stronghold of rationalism's defense of necessary truth, he concedes to it necessary truth, but the necessity lies only between our ideas, not between events or objects in the world. Necessary truth about the world, traditionally the search of metaphysicians, is entirely inaccessible to human reason. Truths about the world are "matters of fact," which are merely probable.

All the objects of human reason or enquiry may naturally be divided into two kinds, to wit, *Relations of Ideas,* and *Matters of Fact.* Of the first kind are the sciences of Geometry, Algebra, and Arithmetic; and in short, every affirmation which is either intuitively or demonstratively certain. . . . Propositions of this kind are discoverable by the mere operation of thought, without dependence on what is anywhere existent in the universe. . . . Matters of fact . . . are not ascertained in the same manner; nor is our evidence of their truth, however great, of a like nature with the foregoing. The contrary of every matter of fact is still possible; because it can never imply a contradiction. . . . *That the sun will not rise tomorrow* is no less intelligible a proposition, and implies no more contradiction than the affirmation, *that it will rise.* We should in vain, therefore, attempt to demonstrate its falsehood. . . . It may, therefore, be a subject worthy of curiosity, to enquire what is the nature of that evidence which assures us of any real existence and matter of fact, beyond the present testimony of our senses, or the records of our memories. . . . All reasonings concerning matters of fact seem to be founded on the relation of *Cause and Effect.*[12]

Hume's attack on necessary relations may have been welcomed by empiricists, traditionally hostile to metaphysics and encouraging to science. To Hume, however, necessary

---

[10] Ibid., sec I, p. 12.
[11] *A Treatise of Human Nature,* ed. L. A. Selby-Bigge (Oxford: Clarendon Press, 1896), Bk I, Part IV, sec 6, pp. 252–253.

[12] *Enquiry Concerning Human Understanding,* sec IV, part 1, pp. 25–26.

relations are also implicit in science, with its talk of laws and of causality. Indeed, our knowledge of matters of fact is pervaded by causality. Hume invites us to consider the apparently simple inference we make that a friend is in Paris from the fact that we receive a letter from him postmarked Paris: it involves a sequence of causal judgments—that he wrote the letter, that he mailed it, that it was transported, and so on. Causality is also invoked by laws of nature such as those of physics, and they establish our confidence in the order and stability of the physical universe. If necessary relations cannot be established, then causal judgments, which seem to depend on them, also become questionable, for to say A causes B is to say that the occurrence of A *necessitates* the occurrence of B, and on what impression can this necessary connection between cause and effect be based? The impact of one billiard ball on another is paradigmatic:

Here is a billiard-ball lying on the table, and another ball moving towards it with rapidity. They strike; and the ball, which was formerly at rest, now acquires a motion. This is as perfect an instance of the relation of cause and effect as any which we know, either by sensation or by reflection. Let us therefore examine it. 'Tis evident, that the two balls touched one another before the motion was communicated, and that there was no interval betwixt the shock and the motion. *Contiguity* in time and place is therefore a requisite circumstance to the operation of all causes. 'Tis evident likewise, that the motion, which was the cause, is prior to the motion, which was the effect. *Priority* in time, is therefore another requisite circumstance in every cause. But this is not all. Let us try any other balls of the same kind in a like situation, and we shall always find, that the impulse of the one produces motion in the other. Here therefore is a *third* circumstance, *viz.* that of a *constant conjunction* betwixt the cause and effect. Every object like the cause, produces always some object like the effect. Beyond these three circumstances of contiguity, priority, and constant conjunction, I can discover nothing in this cause.[13]

Thus if by causality we mean a necessary connection between the two events, we have no experiential support for claiming to know that one causes the other. Yet we are entitled to claim A caused B if we remember that the only evidence we can have are the three conditions of contiguity, priority, and constant conjunction.

The relation of causality to induction raises another problem: can we know that the conjunction of A and B in the past, upon which we rely for a causal connection, will continue? The problem of making causal judgments is generalized to a problem for all reasoning from experience: "in all reasonings from experience, there is a step taken by the mind which is not supported by any argument or process of the understanding." [14] Reasoning from experience assumes the future will be like the past, that is, that nature exhibits uniformities. That assumption is not justifiable by reason, for to deny it is not contradictory; neither is it justifiable by experience:

To say it is experimental, is begging the question. For all inferences from experience suppose, as their foundation, that the future will resemble the past. . . . If there be any suspicion that the course of nature may change, and that the past may be no rule for the future, all experience becomes useless, and can give rise to no inference or conclusion.[15]

Hume is not satisfied just to show that causal necessities are indemonstrable, nor with showing that the uniformity of nature is unjustifiable. It is a fact that people do attribute necessity to the causal relation. Why do we find it so natural to say the second billiard ball *must* move? The association of ideas provides an explanation: I associate the idea of the motion of the first ball with the idea of the motion of the second if I see one following the other, and if I experience the occurrence of the two motions in that order a sufficient number of times, I begin to *expect* the effect upon my

[13] *Abstract*, pp. 11–12.

[14] *Enquiry Concerning Human Understanding*, sec V, part 1, p. 41.
[15] Ibid., sec IV, part 2, pp. 37–38.

experiencing the cause. The necessity I attribute to the relationship among the events is in fact a psychological connection between my ideas of the events.

Similarly, in the case of induction, why do we persist in reasoning from experience? Again, he appeals to association of ideas: It is because of

Custom or *Habit*. For wherever the repetition of any particular act or operation produces a propensity to renew the same act or operation, without being impelled by any reasoning or process of the understanding, we always say, that this propensity is the effect of *Custom*.[16]

Uniformity of nature is unprovable, but we can explain why we are impelled to believe it. Hume does not inquire why custom has this effect, any more than Newton felt compelled to inquire why gravity has the effect it does. It is sufficient to understand how it works. However, Hume does ask what the nature of the *belief* is that results from the operation of custom. What distinguishes the mere possession of an idea from a belief? Only a feeling:

Whenever any object is presented to the memory or senses, it immediately, by the force of custom, carries the imagination to conceive that object, which is usually conjoined to it; and this conception is attended with a feeling or sentiment, different from the loose reveries of the fancy. In this consists the whole nature of belief.[17]

Belief is thus not a matter of choice.

Sentiment in morals parallels the role of custom in induction. Reason cannot stir us to action; only feelings and passions can do this. Yet the function of moral judgments is to influence and direct conduct. "Reason is, and ought only to be the slave of the passions, and can never pretend to any other office than to serve and obey them." [18] Still, reason is not without

a role—both scientific and critical—in matters of morality. Reason can determine that social utility is the ground on which we approve and disapprove, praise and blame. Reason can also correct our moral judgments in the light of discovered utilities. (In the case of benevolence, each instance can be shown to be useful and approved; while in the case of justice, it is the overall system of stable rules that is useful and approved.)

Why do we approve of utility? For this Hume looks to sentiment, but between the *Treatise* and the *Enquiry* there is a shift in his views. In the *Treatise* the sentiment is sympathy:

No quality of human nature is more remarkable, both in itself and in its consequences, than that propensity we have to sympathize with others, and to receive by communication their inclinations and sentiments, however different from, or even contrary to our own. . . . To this principle we ought to ascribe the great uniformity we may observe in the humours and turn of thinking of those of the same nation. . . . A cheerful countenance infuses a sensible complacency and serenity into my mind; as an angry or sorrowful one throws a sudden damp upon me. . . .

When any affection is infused by sympathy, it is at first known only by its effects, and by those external signs in the countenance and conversation, which convey an idea of it. This idea is presently converted into an impression, and acquires such a degree of force and vivacity, as to become the very passion itself, and produce an equal emotion, as any original affection. . . .

'Tis evident that the idea, or rather impression of ourselves is always intimately present with us, and that our consciousness gives us so lively a conception of our own person, that 'tis not possible to imagine, that any thing can in this particular go beyond it. Whatever object, therefore, is related to ourselves must be conceived with a like vivacity of conception, according to the foregoing principles.[19]

It is evident that people are affected by others' happiness and pain. To sympathize with

[16] Ibid., sec V, part 1, p. 43.
[17] Ibid., sec V, part 2, p. 48.
[18] *Treatise*, Bk II, part III, sec 3, p. 415.
[19] Ibid., Bk II, part I, sec 11, pp. 316–317.

another's pain is to feel pain yourself. The *Treatise* attempts to explain the psychological mechanism by which people are affected by others' happiness and pain, without having recourse to a special faculty or a moral sense (as Hutcheson did). In the *Enquiry* the emphasis shifts away from sympathy toward benevolence, "a feeling for the happiness of mankind and a resentment of their misery," which he accepts without attempting to explain its psychological construction.[20]

Another problem, which in modern philosophy has come to be called the "is-ought" problem, is raised in the *Treatise* in a brief paragraph (see p. 257 below). Hume complains that too many writers move from factual statements to normative statements without attending explicitly to the nature of the move. The interpretation of the "is-ought" paragraph is controversial. Did he intend to deny that there was any evidential relation by which we can infer or deduce what we ought to do from the facts of the situation? Was he merely reiterating the point that since reason alone cannot move us, a sentiment is required; or that the inference is possible only if a special sophisticated form

of argument is used; or that the inference is possible if a special meaning is assigned to "ought"? The issue, and Hume's stand on it, remain a matter of present interest and controversy.

Hume has little respect for natural law or natural rights in versions that make them dependent on self-evidence or on unobservable properties. Similarly, his attitude to the social contract—a "philosophical fiction"[21]—is that there is no evidence it ever took place; in any case there is no need to appeal to an original contract in order to justify obedience to the state: there may be societies founded on a contract or on consent, but obedience stems primarily from habit and custom.

> Man, born in a family, is compelled to maintain society, from necessity, from natural inclination, and from habit. . . . Habit soon consolidates what other principles of human nature had imperfectly founded; and men, once accustomed to obedience, never think of departing from that path in which they and their ancestors have constantly trod, and to which they are confined by so many urgent and visible motives.[22]

And if persons now consent to the sovereign,

> [T]hey imagine not that their consent gives their prince a title: But they willingly consent, because they think that, from long possession, he has acquired a title, independently of their choice or inclination.[23]

Undue emphasis on contract and consent jeopardizes the habit of obedience. Only extraordinary circumstances justify disobedience to established government: ordinarily resistance means civil war, which is worse than tyranny. So, although disobedience is theoretically conceivable, he will "always incline to their side who draw the bond of allegiance

---

[20] In the *Treatise* he had denied such a feeling: "[T]here is no such passion in human minds as the love of mankind merely as such, independent of personal qualities, of services, or of relation to ourself" (Bk III, part II, sec 1, p. 481). His explanation of sympathy in the *Treatise* faces a profound epistemological difficulty: you learn of the other person's pain by having an idea of it, and he had earlier distinguished ideas from impressions by the quality of force and vivacity they have. Emotions are impressions, so the idea of pain differs from pain in vivacity. How, then, does the idea of pain become transformed into the emotion pain? His answer is by its association with our *impression* of the self. But his analysis of the self denies there is such an impression. The "enlivening" needed to change the idea into the impression of pain cannot be delivered through the mere idea of the self. So his account of self and his account of sympathy are in serious conflict. In an appendix later added to the *Treatise* he laments: "[U]pon a more strict review of the section concerning *personal identity*, I find myself involv'd in such a labyrinth, that, I must confess, I neither know how to correct my former opinions, nor how to render them consistent" (p. 633).

[21] *An Enquiry Concerning the Principles of Morals*, ed. L. A. Selby-Bigge (Oxford: Clarendon Press, 1894), sec III, part I, p. 189.
[22] "Of the Origin of Government," in *Essays*, pp. 113, 115.
[23] "Of the Original Contract," in *Essays*, p. 451.

very close." [24] Legitimacy of government itself does not rest on one single basis—although consent is relevant, so is succession, and possession. If government is doing its job reasonably well, it is legitimate.

An Enquiry Concerning the Principles of Morals sets the problem as the disagreements between those theories that look to reason alone to adjudicate moral judgments, and those that look to feelings or sentiment. Hume insists on a role for feelings of approval and disapproval, but he also rejects a specifically moral sense and argues for utility as the underlying principle for virtues. The central virtues are benevolence and justice. In the eighteenth century benevolence became the counter to self-love; benevolence, no less than self-love, is rooted in human nature. Hume's method of "experimentally" observing the pattern and language of actual moral approvals and analyzing them for underlying principles results in a deep appreciation of the social dimension of moral judgments and, particularly, of justice. His analysis of justice—as a purely instrumental virtue justified by its social consequences—gives him a major role in the debate that includes Bentham in the late eighteenth century, Mill in the nineteenth century, and Rawls in the twentieth century. The problem of accounting for justice on the grounds of utility continues to vex moral philosophy.

An Enquiry Concerning the Principles of Morals [25]

I: Of the General Principles of Morals

. . . There has been a controversy started of late . . . concerning the general foundation of Morals; whether they be derived from Reason, or from Sentiment; whether we attain the knowledge of them by a chain of argument and induction, or by an immediate feeling and finer internal sense; whether, like all sound judgement of truth and falsehood, they should be the same to every rational intelligent being; or whether, like the perception of beauty and deformity, they be founded entirely on the particular fabric and constitution of the human species. [p. 170]

It must be acknowledged, that both sides of the question are susceptible of specious arguments. Moral distinctions, it may be said, are discernible by pure *reason*: else, whence the many disputes that reign in common life, as well as in philosophy, with regard to this subject: the long chain of proofs often produced on both sides; the examples cited, the authorities appealed to, the analogies employed, the fallacies detected, the inferences drawn, and the several conclusions adjusted to their proper principles. Truth is disputable; not taste: what exists in the nature of things is the standard of our judgement; what each man feels within himself is the standard of sentiment. Propositions in geometry may be proved, systems in physics may be controverted; but the harmony of verse, the tenderness of passion, the brilliancy of wit, must give immediate pleasure. No man reasons concerning another's beauty; but frequently concerning the justice or injustice of his actions. In every criminal trial the first object of the prisoner is to disprove the facts alleged, and deny the actions imputed to him: the second to prove, that, even if these actions were real, they might be justified, as innocent and lawful. It is confessedly by deductions of the understanding, that the first point is ascertained: how can we suppose that a different faculty of the mind is employed in fixing the other?

On the other hand, those who would resolve all moral determinations into *sentiment*, may endeavour to show, that it is impossible for reason ever to draw conclusions of this nature. To virtue, say they, it belongs to be *amiable*, and vice *odious*. This forms their very nature or essence. But can reason or argumentation distribute these different epithets to any subjects, and pronounce beforehand, that this must produce love, and that hatred? Or what other reason can we ever assign for these affections, but the original fabric and formation of the human mind, which is naturally adapted to receive them?

[24] "Of Passive Obedience," in *Essays*, p. 461.
[25] First printed 1751. The selection is from the posthumous edition of 1777, reprinted in *Hume's Enquiries*, ed. L. A. Selby-Bigge (Oxford: Clarendon Press, 1894).

The end of all moral speculations is to teach us our duty; and, by proper representations of the deformity of vice and beauty of virtue, beget correspondent habits, and engage us to avoid the one, and embrace the other. But is this ever to be expected from inferences and conclusions of the understanding, which of themselves have no hold of the affections or set in motion the active powers of men? They discover truths: but where the truths which they discover are indifferent, and beget no desire or aversion, they can have no influence on conduct and behaviour. What is honourable, what is fair, what is becoming, what is noble, what is generous, takes possession of the heart, and animates us to embrace and maintain it. What is intelligible, what is evident, what is probable, what is true, procures only the cool assent of the understanding; and gratifying a speculative curiosity, puts an end to our researches.

Extinguish all the warm feelings and prepossessions in favour of virtue, and all disgust or aversion to vice: render men totally indifferent towards these distinctions; and morality is no longer a practical study, nor has any tendency to regulate our lives and actions.

These arguments on each side (and many more might be produced) are so plausible, that I am apt to suspect, they may, the one as well as the other, be solid and satisfactory, and that *reason* and *sentiment* concur in almost all moral determinations and conclusions. The final sentence, it is probable, which pronounces characters and actions amiable or odious, praise-worthy or blameable; that which stamps on them the mark of honour or infamy, approbation or censure; that which renders morality an active principle and constitutes virtue our happiness, and vice our misery: it is probable, I say, that this final sentence depends on some internal sense or feeling, which nature has made universal in the whole species. For what else can have an influence of this nature? But in order to pave the way for such a sentiment, and give a proper discernment of its object, it is often necessary, we find, that much reasoning should precede, that nice distinctions be made, just conclusions drawn, distant comparisons formed, complicated relations examined, and general facts fixed and ascertained. Some species of beauty, especially the natural kinds, on their first appearance, command our affection and approbation; and where they fail of this effect, it is impossible for any reasoning to redress their influence, or

adapt them better to our taste and sentiment. But in many orders of beauty, particularly those of the finer arts, it is requisite to employ much reasoning, in order to feel the proper sentiment; and a false relish may frequently be corrected by argument and reflection. There are just grounds to conclude, that moral beauty partakes much of this latter species, and demands the assistance of our intellectual faculties, in order to give it a suitable influence on the human mind.

But though this question, concerning the general principles of morals, be curious and important, it is needless for us, at present, to employ farther care in our researches concerning it. For if we can be so happy, in the course of this enquiry, as to discover the true origin of morals, it will then easily appear how far either sentiment or reason enters into all determinations of this nature.[a] In order to attain this purpose, we shall endeavour to follow a very simple method: we shall analyse that complication of mental qualities, which form what, in common life, we call Personal Merit: we shall consider every attribute of the mind, which renders a man an object either of esteem and affection, or of hatred and contempt; every habit or sentiment or faculty, which, if ascribed to any person, implies either praise or blame, and may enter into any panegyric or satire of his character and manners. The quick sensibility, which, on this head, is so universal among mankind, gives a philosopher sufficient assurance, that he can never be considerably mistaken in framing the catalogue, or incur any danger of misplacing the objects of his contemplation: he needs only enter into his own breast for a moment, and consider whether or not he should desire to have this or that quality ascribed to him, and whether such or such an imputation would proceed from a friend or an enemy. The very nature of language guides us almost infallibly in forming a judgement of this nature; and as every tongue possesses one set of words which are taken in a good sense, and another in the opposite, the least acquaintance with the idiom suffices, without any reasoning, to direct us in collecting and arranging the estimable or blameable qualities of men. The only object of reasoning is to discover the circumstances on both sides, which are common to these qualities; to observe that particular in which the estimable qualities agree on the one hand, and the blameable on the

---

[a] See Appendix I.

other; and thence to reach the foundation of ethics, and find those universal principles, from which all censure or approbation is ultimately derived. As this is a question of fact, not of abstract science, we can only expect success, by following the experimental method, and deducing general maxims from a comparison of particular instances. The other scientific method, where a general abstract principle is first established, and is afterwards branched out into a variety of inferences and conclusions, may be more perfect in itself, but suits less the imperfection of human nature, and is a common source of illusion and mistake in this as well as in other subjects. Men are not cured of their passion for hypotheses and systems in natural philosophy, and will hearken to no arguments but those which are derived from experience. It is full time they should attempt a like reformation in all moral disquisitions; and reject every system of ethics, however subtle or ingenious, which is not founded on fact and observation.

We shall begin our enquiry on this head by the consideration of the social virtues, Benevolence and Justice. The explication of them will probably give us an opening by which the others may be accounted for. [pp. 171–175]

II: Of Benevolence

. . . [N]o qualities are more intitled to the general good-will and approbation of mankind than beneficence and humanity, friendship and gratitude, natural affection and public spirit, or whatever proceeds from a tender sympathy with others, and a generous concern for our kind and species. These wherever they appear, seem to transfuse themselves, in a manner, into each beholder, and to call forth, in their own behalf, the same favourable and affectionate sentiments, which they exert on all around.

We may observe that, in displaying the praises of any humane, beneficent man, there is one circumstance which never fails to be amply insisted on, namely, the happiness and satisfaction, derived to society from his intercourse and good offices. To his parents, we are apt to say, he endears himself by his pious attachment and duteous care still more than by the connexions of nature. His children never feel his authority, but when employed for their advantage. With him, the ties of love are consolidated by beneficence and friendship. The ties

of friendship approach, in a fond observance of each obliging office, to those of love and inclination. His domestics and dependants have in him a sure resource; and no longer dread the power of fortune, but so far as she exercises it over him. From him the hungry receive food, the naked clothing, the ignorant and slothful skill and industry. Like the sun, an inferior minister of providence he cheers, invigorates, and sustains the surrounding world. [p. 178]

As these topics of praise never fail to be employed, and with success, where we would inspire esteem for any one; may it not thence be concluded, that the utility, resulting from the social virtues, forms, at least, a *part* of their merit, and is one source of that approbation and regard so universally paid to them? [p. 176]

In all determinations of morality, this circumstance of public utility is ever principally in view; and wherever disputes arise, either in philosophy or common life, concerning the bounds of duty, the question cannot, by any means, be decided with greater certainty, than by ascertaining, on any side, the true interests of mankind. If any false opinion, embraced from appearances, has been found to prevail; as soon as farther experience and sounder reasoning have given us juster notions of human affairs, we retract our first sentiment, and adjust anew the boundaries of moral good and evil.

Giving alms to common beggars is naturally praised; because it seems to carry relief to the distressed and indigent: but when we observe the encouragement thence arising to idleness and debauchery, we regard that species of charity rather as a weakness than a virtue. [p. 180]

Upon the whole, then, it seems undeniable, *that* nothing can bestow more merit on any human creature than the sentiment of benevolence in an eminent degree; and *that a part*, at least, of its merit arises from its tendency to promote the interests of our species, and bestow happiness on human society. . . .

How considerable a *part* of their merit we ought to ascribe to their utility, will better appear from future disquisitions;[b] as well as the reason, why this circumstance has such a command over our esteem and approbation.[c] [pp. 181–182]

---

[b] Sections III and IV.
[c] Section V.

III: Of Justice

That Justice is useful to society, and consequently that *part* of its merit, at least, must arise from that consideration, it would be a superfluous undertaking to prove. That public utility is the *sole* origin of justice, and that reflections on the beneficial consequences of this virtue are the *sole* foundation of its merit; this proposition, being more curious and important, will better deserve our examination and enquiry.

Let us suppose that nature has bestowed on the human race such profuse *abundance* of all *external* conveniencies, that, without any uncertainty in the event, without any care or industry on our part, every individual finds himself fully provided with whatever his most voracious appetites can want, or luxurious imagination wish or desire. His natural beauty, we shall suppose, surpasses all acquired ornaments: the perpetual clemency of the seasons renders useless all clothes or covering: the raw herbage affords him the most delicious fare; the clear fountain, the richest beverage. No laborious occupation required: no tillage: no navigation. Music, poetry, and contemplation form his sole business: conversation, mirth, and friendship his sole amusement.

It seems evident that, in such a happy state, every other social virtue would flourish, and receive tenfold increase; but the cautious, jealous virtue of justice would never once have been dreamed of. For what purpose make a partition of goods, where every one has already more than enough? Why give rise to property, where there cannot possibly be any injury? Why call this object *mine*, when upon the seizing of it by another, I need but stretch out my hand to possess myself to what is equally valuable? Justice, in that case, being totally useless, would be an idle ceremonial, and could never possibly have place in the catalogue of virtues.

We see, even in the present necessitous condition of mankind, that, wherever any benefit is bestowed by nature in an unlimited abundance, we leave it always in common among the whole human race, and make no subdivisions of right and property. Water and air, though the most necessary of all objects, are not challenged as the property of individuals; nor can any man commit injustice by the most lavish use and enjoyment of these blessings. In fertile extensive countries, with few inhabitants, land is regarded on the same footing. . . . [pp. 183–184]

Again; suppose, that, though the necessities of human race continue the same as at present, yet the mind is so enlarged, and so replete with friendship and generosity, that every man has the utmost tenderness for every man, and feels no more concern for his own interest than for that of his fellows; it seems evident, that the use of justice would, in this case, be suspended by such an extensive benevolence, nor would the divisions and barriers of property and obligation have ever been thought of. Why should I bind another, by a deed or promise, to do me any good office, when I know that he is already prompted, by the strongest inclination, to seek my happiness, and would, of himself, perform the desired service; except the hurt, he thereby receives, be greater than the benefit accruing to me? in which case, he knows, that, from my innate humanity and friendship, I should be the first to oppose myself to his imprudent generosity. [pp. 184–185]

Relationships among family members approximate such "enlarged affections."

[L]et us reverse the foregoing suppositions; and carrying everything to the opposite extreme, consider what would be the effect of these new situations. Suppose a society to fall into such want of all common necessaries, that the utmost frugality and industry cannot preserve the greater number from perishing, and the whole from extreme misery; it will readily, I believe, be admitted, that the strict laws of justice are suspended, in such a pressing emergence, and give place to the stronger motives of necessity and self-preservation. Is it any crime, after a shipwreck, to seize whatever means or instrument of safety one can lay hold of, without regard to former limitations of property? Or if a city besieged were perishing with hunger; can we imagine, that men will see any means of preservation before them, and lose their lives, from a scrupulous regard to what, in other situations, would be the rules of equity and justice? The use and tendency of that virtue is to procure happiness and security, by preserving order in society: but where the society is ready to perish from extreme necessity, no greater evil can be dreaded from violence and injustice; and every man may now provide for himself by all the means which prudence can dictate, or humanity permit. The public, even in less urgent necessities, opens granaries, without the consent of proprietors; as justly supposing, that the authority of magistracy may, consistent with equity, extend so far: but were any number of men to assemble, without the tie of laws or civil jurisdiction; would an equal partition of bread in a famine, though effected by power and even violence, be regarded as criminal or injurious? [pp. 186–187]

The rage and violence of public war; what is it but a suspension of justice among the warring parties, who perceive, that this virtue is now no longer of any *use* or advantage to them? The laws of war, which then succeed to those of equity and justice, are rules calculated for the *advantage* and *utility* of that particular state, in which men are now placed. And were a civilized nation engaged with barbarians, who observed no rules even of war, the former must also suspend their observance of them, where they no longer serve to any purpose; and must render every action or rencounter as bloody and pernicious as possible to the first aggressors.

Thus, the rules of equity or justice depend entirely on the particular state and condition in which men are placed, and owe their origin and existence to that utility, which results to the public from their strict and regular observance. Reverse, in any considerable circumstance, the condition of men: Produce extreme abundance or extreme necessity: Implant in the human breast perfect moderation and humanity, or perfect rapaciousness and malice: By rendering justice totally *useless*, you thereby totally destroy its essence, and suspend its obligation upon mankind.

The common situation of society is a medium amidst all these extremes. We are naturally partial to ourselves, and to our friends; but are capable of learning the advantage resulting from a more equitable conduct. Few enjoyments are given us from the open and liberal hand of nature; but by art, labour, and industry, we can extract them in great abundance. Hence the ideas of property become necessary in all civil society: Hence justice derives its usefulness to the public: And hence alone arises its merit and moral obligation. [pp. 187–188]

[T]he *philosophical* fiction of the *state of nature* . . . is painted out as a state of mutual war and violence, attended with the most extreme necessity. On the first origin of mankind, we are told, their ignorance and savage nature were so prevalent, that they could give no mutual trust, but must each depend upon himself and his own force or cunning for protection and security. No law was heard of: No rule of justice known: No distinction of property regarded: Power was the only measure of right; and a perpetual war of all against all was the result of men's untamed selfishness and barbarity.

Whether such a condition of human nature could ever exist, or if it did, could continue so long as to merit the appellation of a *state*, may justly be doubted. Men are necessarily born in a family-society, at least; and are trained up by their parents to some rule of conduct and behaviour. But this must be admitted, that, if such a state of mutual war and violence was ever real, the suspension of all laws of justice, from their absolute inutility, is a necessary and infallible consequence. [pp. 189–190]

If we examine the *particular* laws, by which justice is directed, and property determined; we shall still be presented with the same conclusion. The good of mankind is the only object of all these laws and regulations. Not only it is requisite, for the peace and interest of society, that men's possessions should be separated; but the rules, which we follow, in making the separation, are such as can best be contrived to serve farther the interests of society.

We shall suppose that a creature, possessed of reason, but unacquainted with human nature, deliberates with himself what rules of justice or property would best promote public interest, and establish peace and security among mankind: His most obvious thought would be, to assign the largest possessions to the most extensive virtue, and give every one the power of doing good, proportioned to his inclination. In a perfect theocracy, where a being, infinitely intelligent, governs by particular volitions, this rule would certainly have place, and might serve to the wisest purposes: But were mankind to execute such a law; so great is the uncertainty of merit, both from its natural obscurity, and from the self-conceit of each individual, that no determinate rule of conduct would ever result from it; and the total dissolution of society must be the immediate consequence. . . . [pp. 192–193]

It must, indeed, be confessed, that nature is so liberal to mankind, that, were all her presents equally divided among the species, and improved by art and industry, every individual would enjoy all the necessaries, and even most of the comforts of life; nor would ever be liable to any ills, but such as might accidentally arise from the sickly frame and constitution of his body. It must also be confessed, that, wherever we depart from this equality, we rob the poor of more satisfaction than we add to the rich, and that the slight gratification of a frivolous vanity, in one individual, frequently costs more than bread to many families, and even provinces. . . .

But historians, and even common sense, may inform us, that, however specious these ideas of *perfect* equality may seem, they are really, at bottom, *impracticable;* and were they not so, would be extremely *pernicious* to human society. Render possessions ever so equal, men's different degrees of art, care, and industry will immediately break that equality. Or if you check these virtues, you reduce society to the most extreme indigence; and instead of preventing want and beggary in a few, render it unavoidable to the whole community. The most rigorous inquisition too is requisite to watch every inequality on its first appearance; and the most severe jurisdiction, to punish and redress it. But besides, that so much authority must soon degenerate into tyranny, and be exerted with great partialities; who can possibly be possessed of it, in such a situation as is here supposed? Perfect equality of possessions, destroying all subordination, weakens extremely the authority of magistracy, and must reduce all power nearly to a level, as well as property.

We may conclude, therefore, that, in order to establish laws for the regulation of property, we must be acquainted with the nature and situation of man; must reject appearances, which may be false, though specious; and must search for those rules, which are, on the whole, most *useful* and *beneficial.* . . .

Who sees not, for instance, that whatever is produced or improved by a man's art or industry ought, for ever, to be secured to him, in order to give encouragement to such *useful* habits and accomplishments? That the property ought also to descend to children and relations, for the same *useful* purpose? . . .

Examine the writers on the laws of nature; and you will always find, that, whatever principles they set out with, they are sure to terminate here at last, and to assign, as the ultimate reason for every rule

which they establish, the convenience and necessities of mankind. . . .

What other reason, indeed, could writers ever give, why this must be *mine* and that *yours;* since uninstructed nature surely never made any such distinction? The objects which receive those appellations are, of themselves, foreign to us; they are totally disjoined and separated from us; and nothing but the general interests of society can form the connexion.

Sometimes the interests of society may require a rule of justice in a particular case; but may not determine any particular rule, among several, which are all equally beneficial. In that case, the slightest *analogies* are laid hold of, in order to prevent that indifference and ambiguity, which would be the source of perpetual dissension. Thus possession alone, and first possession, is supposed to convey property, where no body else has any preceding claim and pretension. Many of the reasonings of lawyers are of this analogical nature, and depend on very slight connexions of the imagination.

Does any one scruple, in extraordinary cases, to violate all regard to the private property of individuals, and sacrifice to public interest a distinction, which had been established for the sake of that interest? The safety of the people is the supreme law: All other particular laws are subordinate to it, and dependent on it: And if, in the *common* course of things, they be followed and regarded; it is only because the public safety and interest *commonly* demand so equal and impartial an administration. [pp. 193–196]

In general we may observe that all questions of property are subordinate to the authority of civil laws, which extend, restrain, modify, and alter the rules of natural justice, according to the particular *convenience* of each community. The laws have, or ought to have, a constant reference to the constitution of government, the manners, the climate, the religion, the commerce, the situation of each society. . . .

What is a man's property? Anything which it is lawful for him, and for him alone, to use. *But what rule have we, by which we can distinguish these objects?* Here we must have recourse to statutes, customs, precedents, analogies, and a hundred other circumstances; some of which are constant and inflexible, some variable and arbitrary. But the ultimate point, in which they all professedly terminate, is the interest and happiness of human society. Where this enters not into consideration, nothing can appear more whimsical, unnatural, and even superstitious, than all or most of the laws of justice and of property. [pp. 196–198]

These reflections are far from weakening the obligations of justice, or diminishing anything from the most sacred attention to property. On the contrary, such sentiments must acquire new force from the present reasoning. For what stronger foundation can be desired or conceived for any duty, than to observe, that human society, or even human nature, could not subsist without the establishment of it; and will still arrive at greater degrees of happiness and perfection, the more inviolable the regard is, which is paid to that duty?

The dilemma seems obvious: As justice evidently tends to promote public utility and to support civil society, the sentiment of justice is either derived from our reflecting on that tendency, or like hunger, thirst, and other appetites, resentment, love of life, attachment to offspring, and other passions, arises from a simple original instinct in the human breast, which nature has implanted for like salutary purposes. If the latter be the case, it follows, that property, which is the object of justice, is also distinguished by a simple original instinct, and is not ascertained by any argument or reflection. But who is there that ever heard of such an instinct? Or is this a subject in which new discoveries can be made? We may as well expect to discover, in the body, new senses, which had before escaped the observation of all mankind. [pp. 200–201]

What alone will beget a doubt concerning the theory, on which I insist, is the influence of education and acquired habits, by which we are so accustomed to blame injustice, that we are not, in every instance, conscious of any immediate reflection on the pernicious consequences of it. The views the most familiar to us are apt, for that very reason, to escape us; and what we have very frequently performed from certain motives, we are apt likewise to continue mechanically, without recalling, on every occasion, the reflections, which first determined us. The convenience, or rather necessity, which leads to justice is so universal, and everywhere points so much to the same rules, that the habit takes place in all societies; and it is not without some scrutiny, that we are able to ascertain its true origin. . . .

Thus we seem, upon the whole, to have attained a knowledge of the force of that principle here insisted on, and can determine what degree of esteem or moral approbation may result from reflections on public interest and utility. The necessity of justice to the support of society is the sole foundation of that virtue; and since no moral excellence is more highly esteemed, we may conclude that this circumstance of usefulness has, in general, the strongest energy, and most entire command over our sentiments. It must, therefore, be the source of a considerable part of the merit ascribed to humanity, benevolence, friendship, public spirit, and other social virtues of that stamp; as it is the sole source of the moral approbation paid to fidelity, justice, veracity, integrity, and those other estimable and useful qualities and principles. It is entirely agreeable to the rules of philosophy, and even of common reason; where any principle has been found to have a great force and energy in one instance, to ascribe to it a like energy in all similar instances. This indeed is Newton's chief rule of philosophizing. [pp. 203–204]

Appendix III, "Some Farther Considerations with Regard to Justice," contrasts benevolence and justice, and attacks those who see the foundation of justice as convention.

The social virtues of humanity and benevolence exert their influence immediately by a direct tendency or instinct, which chiefly keeps in view the simple object, moving the affections, and comprehends not any scheme or system, nor the consequences resulting from the concurrence, imitation, or example of others. A parent flies to the relief of his child; transported by that natural sympathy which actuates him, and which affords no leisure to reflect on the sentiments or conduct of the rest of mankind in like circumstances. A generous man cheerfully embraces an opportunity of serving his friend. . . . In all these cases the social passions have in view a single individual object, and pursue the safety or happiness alone of the person loved and esteemed. With this they are satisfied: in this they acquiesce. And as the good, resulting from their benign influence, is in itself complete and entire, it also excites the moral sentiment of approbation, without any reflection on farther consequences, and without any more enlarged views of the concurrence or imitation of the other members of society. . . .

The case is not the same with the social virtues of justice and fidelity. They are highly useful, or indeed absolutely necessary to the well-being of mankind: but the benefit resulting from them is not the consequence of every individual single act; but arises from the whole scheme or system concurred in by the whole, or the greater part of the society. General peace and order are the attendants of justice or a general abstinence from the possessions of others; but a particular regard to the particular right of one individual citizen may frequently, considered in itself, be productive of pernicious consequences. The result of the individual acts is here, in many instances, directly opposite to that of the whole system of actions; and the former may be extremely hurtful, while the latter is, to the highest degree, advantageous. Riches, inherited from a parent, are, in a bad man's hand, the instrument of mischief. The right of succession may, in one instance, be hurtful. Its benefit arises only from the observance of the general rule; and it is sufficient, if compensation be thereby made for all the ills and inconveniences which flow from particular characters and situations. [pp. 303–304]

The happiness and prosperity of mankind, arising from the social virtue of benevolence and its subdivisions, may be compared to a wall, built by many hands, which still rises by each stone that is heaped upon it, and receives increase proportional to the diligence and care of each workman. The same happiness, raised by the social virtue of justice and its subdivisions, may be compared to the building of a vault, where each individual stone would, of itself, fall to the ground; nor is the whole fabric supported but by the mutual assistance and combination of its corresponding parts.

All the laws of nature, which regulate property, as well as all civil laws, are general, and regard alone some essential circumstances of the case, without taking into consideration the characters, situations, and connexions of the person concerned, or any particular consequences which may result from the determination of these laws in any particular case which offers. They deprive, without scruple, a beneficent man of all his possessions, if acquired by mistake, without a good title; in order to bestow them on a selfish miser, who has already heaped up immense stores of superfluous riches. Public utility requires that property should be regulated by general inflexible rules; and though such rules are adopted as best serve the same end of public utility, it is impossible for them to prevent all particular hardships, or make beneficial consequences result from every individual case. It is sufficient, if the whole plan or scheme be necessary to the support of civil society, and if the balance of good, in the main, do thereby preponderate much above that of evil. Even the general laws of the universe, though planned by infinite wisdom, cannot exclude all evil or inconvenience in every particular operation.

It has been asserted by some, that justice arises from Human Conventions, and proceeds from the voluntary choice, consent, or combination of mankind. If by *convention* be here meant a *promise* (which is the most usual sense of the word) nothing can be more absurd than this position. The observance of promises is itself one of the most considerable parts of justice, and we are not surely bound to keep our word because we have given our word to keep it. But if by convention be meant a sense of common interest; which sense each man feels in his own breast, which he remarks in his fellows, and which carries him, in concurrence with others, into a general plan or system of actions, which tends to public utility; it must be owned, that, in this sense, justice arises from human conventions. For if it be allowed (what is, indeed, evident) that the particular consequences of a particular act of justice may be hurtful to the public as well as to individuals; it follows that every man, in embracing that virtue, must have an eye to the whole plan or system, and must expect the concurrence of his fellows in the same conduct and behaviour. Did all his views terminate in the consequences of each act of his own, his benevolence and humanity, as well as his self-love, might often prescribe to him measures of conduct very different from those which are agreeable to the strict rules of right and justice.

Thus, two men pull the oars of a boat by common convention for common interest, without any promise or contract: thus gold and silver are made the measures of exchange; thus speech and words and language are fixed by human convention and agreement. Whatever is advantageous to two or more persons, if all perform their part; but what loses all advantage if only one perform, can arise from no other principle. There would otherwise be no motive for any one of them to enter into that scheme of conduct. [pp. 305–307]

IV: Of Political Society

Utility is also the basis of political society: "the sole foundation of the duty of allegiance is the *advantage,* which it procures to society, by preserving peace and order among mankind" (p. 205). Similarly, utility explains the rule of the Laws of Nations that ambassadors be protected, and the rules of chastity: "The long and helpless infancy of man requires the combination of parents for the subsistence of their young; and that combination requires the virtue of chastity or fidelity to the marriage bed. Without such a *utility,* it will readily be owned, that such a virtue would never have been thought of" (pp. 206–207). Why, then, do the rules of chastity apply also to persons beyond the age of childbearing? *"General rules are often extended beyond the principle whence they first arise; and this in all matters of taste and sentiment. . . . The imagination is influenced by associations of ideas; which, though they arise at first from the judgement, are not easily altered by every particular exception that occurs to us"* (p. 207). Even robbers and pirates have rules among themselves, because of utility, which is "the foundation of most of the laws of good manners; a kind of lesser morality, calculated for the ease of company and conversation" (p. 209).

V: Why Utility Pleases

Given the pervasive appeal to utility in common life, one might expect to find it everywhere in moral philosophy.

But perhaps the difficulty of accounting for these effects of usefulness, or its contrary, has kept philosophers from admitting them into their systems of ethics, and has induced them rather to employ any other principle, in explaining the origin of moral good and evil. But it is no just reason for rejecting any principle, confirmed by experience, that we cannot give a satisfactory account of its origin, nor are able to resolve it into other more general principles. And if we would employ a little thought on the present subject, we need be at no loss to account for the influence of utility, and to deduce it from principles, the most known and avowed in human nature.

From the apparent usefulness of the social virtues, it has readily been inferred by sceptics, both ancient and modern, that all moral distinctions arise from education, and were, at first, invented, and afterwards encouraged, by the art of politicians, in order to render men tractable, and subdue their natural ferocity and selfishness, which incapacitated them for society. This principle, indeed, of precept and education, must so far be owned to have a powerful influence, that it may frequently increase or diminish, beyond their natural standard, the sentiments of approbation or dislike; and may even, in particular instances, create, without any natural principle, a new sentiment of this kind; as is evident in all superstitious practices and observances: But that *all* moral affection or dislike arises from this origin, will never surely be allowed by any judicious enquirer. Had nature made no such distinction, founded on the original constitution of the mind, the words, *honourable* and *shameful, lovely* and *odious, noble* and *despicable,* had never had place in any language; nor could politicians, had they invented these terms, ever have been able to render them intelligible, or make them convey any idea to the audience. . . .

The social virtues must, therefore, be allowed to have a natural beauty and amiableness, which, at first, antecedent to all precept or education, recommends them to the esteem of uninstructed mankind, and engages their affections. And as the public utility of these virtues is the chief circumstance, whence they derive their merit, it follows, that the end, which they have a tendency to promote, must be some way agreeable to us, and take hold of some natural affection. It must please, either from considerations of self-interest, or from more generous motives and regards.

It has often been asserted, that, as every man has a strong connexion with society, and perceives the impossibility of his solitary subsistence, he becomes, on that account, favourable to all those habits or principles, which promote order in society, and insure to him the quiet possession of so inestimable a blessing. . . .

This deduction of morals from self-love, or a regard to private interest, is an obvious thought. . . .

[Y]et is not this an affair to be decided by authority, and the voice of nature and experience seems plainly to oppose the selfish theory.

We frequently bestow praise on virtuous actions, performed in very distant ages and remote countries; where the utmost subtilty of imagination would not discover any appearance of self-interest, or find any connexion of our present happiness and security with events so widely separated from us.

A generous, a brave, a noble deed, performed by an adversary, commands our approbation; while in its consequences it may be acknowledged prejudicial to our particular interest.

Where private advantage concurs with general affection for virtue, we readily perceive and avow the mixture of these distinct sentiments, which have a very different feeling and influence on the mind. We praise, perhaps, with more alacrity, where the generous humane action contributes to our particular interest: But the topics of praise, which we insist on, are very wide of this circumstance. And we may attempt to bring over others to our sentiments, without endeavouring to convince them, that they reap any advantage from the actions which we recommend to their approbation and applause. [pp. 213–216]

It is but a weak subterfuge, when pressed by these facts and arguments, to say, that we transport ourselves, by the force of imagination, into distant ages and countries, and consider the advantage, which we should have reaped from these characters, had we been contemporaries, and had any commerce with the persons. It is not conceivable, how a *real* sentiment or passion can ever arise from a known *imaginary* interest; especially when our *real* interest is still kept in view, and is often acknowledged to be entirely distinct from the imaginary, and even sometimes opposite to it.

A man, brought to the brink of a precipice, cannot look down without trembling; and the sentiment of *imaginary* danger actuates him, in opposition to the opinion and belief of *real* safety. But the imagination is here assisted by the presence of a striking object; and yet prevails not, except it be also aided by novelty, and the unusual appearance of the object. Custom soon reconciles us to heights and precipices, and wears off these false and delusive terrors. The reverse is observable in the estimates which we form of characters and manners; and the more we habituate ourselves to an accurate scrutiny of morals, the more delicate feeling do we acquire of the most minute distinctions between vice and virtue. Such frequent occasion, indeed, have we, in common life, to pronounce all kinds of moral determinations, that no object of this kind can be new or unusual to us; nor could any *false* views or prepossessions maintain their ground against an experience, so common and familiar. Experience being chiefly what forms the associations of ideas, it is impossible that any association could establish and support itself, in direct opposition to that principle.

Usefulness is agreeable, and engages our approbation. This is a matter of fact, confirmed by daily observation. But, *useful?* For what? For somebody's interest, surely. Whose interest then? Not our own only: For our approbation frequently extends farther. It must, therefore, be the interest of those, who are served by the character or action approved of; and these we may conclude, however remote, are not totally indifferent to us. By opening up this principle, we shall discover one great source of moral distinctions. [pp. 217–218]

Self-love is a principle in human nature of such extensive energy, and the interest of each individual is, in general, so closely connected with that of the community, that those philosophers were excusable, who fancied that all our concern for the public might be resolved into a concern for our own happiness and preservation. They saw every moment, instances of approbation or blame, satisfaction or displeasure towards characters and actions; they denominated the objects of these sentiments, *virtues*, or *vices*; they observed, that the former had a tendency to increase the happiness, and the latter the misery of mankind; they asked, whether it were possible that we could have any general concern for society, or any disinterested resentment of the welfare or injury of others; they found it simpler to consider all these sentiments as modifications of self-love; and they discovered a pretence, at least, for this unity of principle, in that close union of interest, which is so observable between the public and each individual.

But notwithstanding this frequent confusion of interests, it is easy to attain what natural philosophers, after Lord Bacon, have affected to call the *experimentum crucis*, or that experiment which points out the right way in any doubt or ambiguity. We have found instances, in which private interest was separate from public; in which it was even contrary: And yet we observed the moral sentiment to continue, notwithstanding this disjunction of interests.

And wherever these distinct interests sensibly concurred, we always found a sensible increase of the sentiment, and a more warm affection to virtue, and detestation of vice, or what we properly call, *gratitude* and *revenge*. Compelled by these instances, we must renounce the theory, which accounts for every moral sentiment by the principle of self-love. We must adopt a more public affection, and allow, that the interests of society are not, even on their own account, entirely indifferent to us. Usefulness is only a tendency to a certain end; and it is a contradiction in terms, that anything pleases as means to an end, where the end itself no wise affects us. If usefulness, therefore, be a source of moral sentiment, and if this usefulness be not always considered with a reference to self; it follows, that, everything, which contributes to the happiness of society, recommends itself directly to our approbation and good-will. Here is a principle, which accounts, in great part, for the origin of morality: And what need we seek for abstruse and remote systems, when there occurs one so obvious and natural? [d]

[d] It is needless to push our researches so far as to ask, why we have humanity or a fellow-feeling with others. It is sufficient, that this is experienced to be a principle in human nature. We must stop somewhere in our examination of causes; and there are, in every science, some general principles, beyond which we cannot hope to find any principle more general. No man is absolutely indifferent to the happiness and misery of others. The first has a natural tendency to give pleasure; the second, pain. This every one may find in himself. It is not probable, that these principles can be resolved into principles more simple and universal, whatever attempts may have been made to that purpose. But if it were possible, it belongs not to the present subject; and we may here safely consider these principles as original: happy, if we can render all the consequences sufficiently plain and perspicuous!
[In a footnote in Appendix II ("Of Self-Love") Hume elaborates a further distinction regarding benevolence.] Benevolence naturally divides into two kinds, the *general* and the *particular*. The first is, where we have no friendship or connexion or esteem for the person, but feel only a general sympathy with him or a compassion for his pains, and a congratulation with his pleasures. The other species of benevolence is founded on an opinion of virtue, on services done us, or on some particular connexions. Both these sentiments must be allowed real in human nature: but whether they will resolve into some nice considerations of self-love, is a question more curious than important. The former sentiment, to wit, that of general benevolence, or humanity, or sympathy, we shall have occasion frequently to treat of in the course of this enquiry; and I assume it as real, from general experience, without any other proof. [p. 298]

Have we any difficulty to comprehend the force of humanity and benevolence? Or to conceive, that the very aspect of happiness, joy, prosperity, gives pleasure; that of pain, suffering, sorrow, communicates uneasiness? The human countenance, says Horace, borrows smiles or tears from the human countenance. Reduce a person to solitude, and he loses all enjoyment, except either of the sensual or speculative kind; and that because the movements of his heart are not forwarded by correspondent movements in his fellow-creatures. The signs of sorrow and mourning, though arbitrary, affect us with melancholy; but the natural symptoms, tears and cries and groans, never fail to infuse compassion and uneasiness. And if the effects of misery touch us in so lively a manner; can we be supposed altogether insensible or indifferent towards its causes; when a malicious or treacherous character and behaviour are presented to us?

We enter, I shall suppose, into a convenient, warm, well-contrived apartment: We necessarily receive a pleasure from its very survey; because it presents us with the pleasing ideas of ease, satisfaction, and enjoyment. The hospitable, good-humoured, humane landlord appears. This circumstance surely must embellish the whole; nor can we easily forbear reflecting, with pleasure, on the satisfaction which results to every one from his intercourse and good-offices.

His whole family, by the freedom, ease, confidence, and calm enjoyment, diffused over their countenances, sufficiently express their happiness. I have a pleasing sympathy in the prospect of so much joy, and can never consider the source of it, without the most agreeable emotions.

He tells me, that an oppressive and powerful neighbour had attempted to dispossess him of his inheritance, and had long disturbed all his innocent and social pleasures. I feel an immediate indignation arise in me against such violence and injury.

But it is no wonder, he adds, that a private wrong should proceed from a man, who had enslaved provinces, depopulated cities, and made the field and scaffold stream with human blood. I am struck with horror at the prospect of so much misery, and am actuated by the strongest antipathy against its author.

In general, it is certain, that, wherever we go, whatever we reflect on or converse about, everything still presents us with the view of human happiness or misery, and excites in our breast a sympathetic movement of pleasure or uneasiness. In our serious occupations, in our careless amusements, this principle still exerts its active energy. [pp. 218–221]

If any man from a cold insensibility, or narrow selfishness of temper, is unaffected with the images of human happiness or misery, he must be equally indifferent to the images of vice and virtue: As, on the other hand, it is always found, that a warm concern for the interests of our species is attended with a delicate feeling of all moral distinctions; a strong resentment of injury done to men; a lively approbation of their welfare. In this particular, though great superiority is observable of one man above another; yet none are so entirely indifferent to the interest of their fellow-creatures, as to perceive no distinctions of moral good and evil in consequence of the different tendencies of actions and principles. How, indeed, can we suppose it possible in any one, who wears a human heart, that if there be subjected to his censure, one character or system of conduct, which is beneficial, and another which is pernicious to his species or community, he will not so much as give a cool preference to the former, or ascribe to it the smallest merit or regard? Let us suppose such a person ever so selfish; let private interest have ingrossed ever so much his attention; yet in instances, where that is not concerned, he must unavoidably feel *some* propensity to the good of mankind, and make it an object of choice, if everything else be equal. Would any man, who is walking along, tread as willingly on another's gouty toes, whom he has no quarrel with, as on the hard flint and pavement? There is here surely a difference in the case. We surely take into consideration the happiness and misery of others, in weighing the several motives of action, and incline to the former, where no private regards draw us to seek our own promotion or advantage by the injury of our fellow-creatures. And if the principles of humanity are capable, in many instances, of influencing our actions, they must, at all times, have *some* authority over our sentiments, and give us a general approbation of what is useful to society, and blame of what is dangerous or pernicious. The degrees of these sentiments may be the subject of controversy; but the reality of their existence, one should think, must be admitted in every theory or system. [pp. 225–226]

A statesman or patriot, who serves our own country in our own time, has always a more passionate regard paid to him, than one whose beneficial influence operated on distant ages or remote nations; where the good, resulting from his generous humanity, being less connected with us, seems more obscure, and affects us with a less lively sympathy. We may own the merit to be equally great, though our sentiments are not raised to an equal height, in both cases. The judgement here corrects the inequalities of our internal emotions and perceptions; in like manner, as it preserves us from error, in the several variations of images, presented to our external senses. The same object, at a double distance, really throws on the eye a picture of but half the bulk; yet we imagine that it appears of the same size in both situations; because we know that on our approach to it, its image would expand on the eye, and that the difference consists not in the object itself, but in our position with regard to it. And, indeed, without such a correction of appearances, both in internal and external sentiment, men could never think or talk steadily on any subject; while their fluctuating situations produce a continual variation on objects, and throw them into such different and contrary lights and positions.

The more we converse with mankind, and the greater social intercourse we maintain, the more shall we be familiarized to these general preferences and distinctions, without which our conversation and discourse could scarcely be rendered intelligible to each other. Every man's interest is peculiar to himself, and the aversions and desires, which result from it, cannot be supposed to affect others in a like degree. General language, therefore, being formed for general use, must be moulded on some more general views, and must affix the epithets of praise or blame, in conformity to sentiments, which arise from the general interests of the community. And if these sentiments, in most men, be not so strong as those, which have a reference to private good; yet still they must make some distinction, even in persons the most depraved and selfish; and must attach the notion of good to a beneficent conduct, and of evil to the contrary. Sympathy, we shall allow, is much fainter than our concern for ourselves, and sympathy with persons remote from us much fainter than that with persons near and contiguous; but for this very reason it is necessary for us, in our calm judgements and discourse concerning the characters of men, to neglect all these differences, and render our sentiments more public and social. Besides, that we ourselves often change our situation in this particular, we every day meet with persons who are in a situation different from us, and who could never converse with us were we to remain constantly in that position and point of view, which is peculiar to ourselves. The intercourse of sentiments, therefore, in society and conversation, makes us form some general unalterable standard, by which we may approve or disapprove of characters and manners. And though the heart takes not part entirely with those general notions, nor regulates all its love and hatred by the universal abstract differences of vice and virtue, without regard to self, or the persons with whom we are more intimately connected; yet have these moral differences a considerable influence, and being sufficient, at least for discourse, serve all our purposes in company, in the pulpit, on the theatre, and in the schools.

Thus, in whatever light we take this subject, the merit, ascribed to the social virtues, appears still uniform, and arises chiefly from that regard, which the natural sentiment of benevolence engages us to pay to the interests of mankind and society. . . . [pp. 227–230]

Social utility does not account for all the virtues we approve. There are three other categories of approval: qualities approved of because they benefit the possessor (section VI)—for example, discretion, industry, frugality, temperance, sobriety, constancy, perseverance, forethought, considerateness, secrecy, order, presence of mind, quickness of expression, facility of expression; qualities immediately agreeable to the possessor (section VII)—for example, cheerfulness, greatness of mind, courage, tranquillity, delicacy of taste, and benevolence; and qualities immediately agreeable to others (section VIII)—for example, ingenuity, modesty, cleanliness, and the rules of good manners or politeness. The conclusion (section IX) gives an example with all four grounds of approval.

VI: Qualities Useful to Ourselves

Now as these advantages are enjoyed by the person possessed of the character, it can never be *self-love* which renders the prospect of them agreeable to us, the spectators, and prompts our esteem and approbation. No force of imagination can convert us into another person, and make us fancy, that we, being that person, reap benefit from those valuable qualities, which belong to him. Or if it did, no celerity of imagination could immediately transport us back, into ourselves, and make us love and esteem the person, as different from us. Views and sentiments, so opposite to known truth and to each other, could never have place, at the same time, in the same person. All suspicion, therefore, of selfish regards, is here totally excluded. It is a quite different principle, which actuates our bosom, and interests us in the felicity of the person whom we contemplate. Where his natural talents and acquired abilities give us the prospect of elevation, advancement, a figure in life, prosperous success, a steady command over fortune, and the execution of great or advantageous undertakings; we are struck with such agreeable images, and feel a complacency and regard immediately arise towards him. The ideas of happiness, joy, triumph, prosperity, are connected with every circumstance of his character, and diffuse over our minds a pleasing sentiment of sympathy and humanity. [p. 234]

VII: Of Qualities Immediately Agreeable to Ourselves

[These are] mental qualities, which, without any utility or any tendency to farther good, either of the community or of the possessor, diffuse a satisfaction on the beholders, and procure friendship and regard. Their immediate sensation, to the person possessed of them, is agreeable. Others enter into the same humour, and catch the sentiment, by a contagion or natural sympathy; and as we cannot forbear loving whatever pleases, a kindly emotion arises towards the person who communicates so much satisfaction. . . . [pp. 250–251]

The merit of benevolence, arising from its utility, and its tendency to promote the good of mankind, has been already explained, and is, no doubt, the source of a *considerable* part of that esteem, which is so universally paid to it. But it will also be allowed, that the very softness and tenderness of the sentiment, its engaging endearments, its fond expressions, its delicate attentions, and all that flow of mutual confidence and regard, which enters into a warm attachment of love and friendship: it will be allowed, I say, that these feelings, being delightful in themselves, are necessarily communicated to the spectators, and melt them into the same fondness and delicacy. The tear naturally starts in our eye on the apprehension of a warm sentiment of this nature: our breast heaves, our heart is agitated, and every humane tender principle of our frame is set in motion, and gives us the purest and most satisfactory enjoyment. [p. 257]

As a certain proof that the whole merit of benevolence is not derived from its usefulness, we may observe, that in a kind way of blame, we say, a person is *too good;* when he exceeds his part in society, and carries his attention for others beyond the proper bounds. In like manner, we say a man is *too high-spirited, too intrepid, too indifferent about fortune:* reproaches, which really, at bottom, imply more esteem than many panegyrics. Being accustomed to rate the merit and demerit of characters chiefly by their useful or pernicious tendencies, we cannot forbear applying the epithet of blame, when we discover a sentiment, which rises to a degree, that is hurtful; but it may happen, at the same time, that its noble elevation, or its engaging tenderness so seizes the heart, as rather to increase our friendship and concern for the person. [p. 258]

IX: Conclusion

. . . What [is] so natural . . . as the following dialogue? You are very happy, we shall suppose one to say, addressing himself to another, that you have given your daughter to Cleanthes. He is a man of honour and humanity. Every one, who has any intercourse with him, is sure of *fair* and *kind* treatment.[e] I congratulate you too, says another, on the promising expectations of this son-in-law; whose assiduous application to the study of the laws, whose quick penetration and early knowledge both of men and business, prognosticate the greatest honours and advancement.[f] You surprise me, replies a third, when you talk of Cleanthes as a man of business and application. I met him lately in a circle of the gayest company, and he was the very life and soul of our conversation: so much wit with good manners; so much gallantry without af-

fectation; so much ingenious knowledge so genteelly delivered, I have never before observed in any one.[g] You would admire him still more, says a fourth, if you knew him more familiarly. That cheerfulness, which you might remark in him, is not a sudden flash struck out by company: it runs through the whole tenor of his life, and preserves a perpetual serenity on his countenance, and tranquillity in his soul. He has met with severe trials, misfortunes as well as dangers; and by his greatness of mind, was still superior to all of them.[h] The image, gentlemen, which you have here delineated of Cleanthes, cried I, is that of accomplished merit. Each of you has given a stroke of the pencil to his figure; and you have unawares exceeded all the pictures drawn by Gratian or Castiglione. A philosopher might select this character as a model of perfect virtue. [pp. 269–270]

It seems a happiness in the present theory, that it enters not into that vulgar dispute concerning the *degrees* of benevolence or self-love, which prevail in human nature; a dispute which is never likely to have any issue, both because men, who have taken part, are not easily convinced, and because the phenomena, which can be produced on either side, are so dispersed, so uncertain, and subject to so many interpretations, that it is scarcely possible accurately to compare them, or draw from them any determinate inference or conclusion. It is sufficient for our present purpose, if it be allowed, what surely, without the greatest absurdity cannot be disputed, that there is some benevolence, however small, infused into our bosom; some spark of friendship for human kind; some particle of the dove kneaded into our frame, along with the elements of the wolf and serpent. Let these generous sentiments be supposed ever so weak; let them be insufficient to move even a hand or finger of our body, they must still direct the determinations of our mind, and where everything else is equal, produce a cool preference of what is useful and serviceable to mankind, above what is pernicious and dangerous. A *moral distinction,* therefore, immediately arises; a general sentiment of blame and approbation; a tendency, however faint, to the objects of

---

[e] Qualities useful to others.
[f] Qualities useful to the person himself.

[g] Qualities immediately agreeable to others.
[h] Qualities immediately agreeable to the person himself.

the one, and a proportionable aversion to those of the other. . . . [pp. 270–271]

If moral approvals are based on feelings, when are they feelings of *moral* approval?

. . . The notion of morals implies some sentiment common to all mankind, which recommends the same object to general approbation, and makes every man, or most men, agree in the same opinion or decision concerning it. It also implies some sentiment, so universal and comprehensive as to extend to all mankind, and render the actions and conduct, even of the persons the most remote, an object of applause or censure, according as they agree or disagree with that rule of right which is established. These two requisite circumstances belong alone to the sentiment of humanity here insisted on. The other passions produce in every breast, many strong sentiments of desire and aversion, affection and hatred; but these neither are felt so much in common, nor are so comprehensive, as to be the foundation of any general system and established theory of blame or approbation.

When a man denominates another his *enemy*, his *rival*, his *antagonist*, his *adversary*, he is understood to speak the language of self-love, and to express sentiments, peculiar to himself, and arising from his particular circumstances and situation. But when he bestows on any man the epithets of *vicious* or *odious* or *depraved*, he then speaks another language, and expresses sentiments, in which he expects all his audience are to concur with him. He must here, therefore, depart from his private and particular situation, and must choose a point of view, common to him with others; he must move some universal principle of the human frame, and touch a string to which all mankind have an accord and symphony. If he mean, therefore, to express that this man possesses qualities, whose tendency is pernicious to society, he has chosen this common point of view, and has touched the principle of humanity, in which every man, in some degree, concurs. While the human heart is compounded of the same elements as at present, it will never be wholly indifferent to public good, nor entirely unaffected with the tendency of characters and manners. And though this affection of humanity may not generally be es-

teemed so strong as vanity or ambition, yet, being common to all men, it can alone be the foundation of morals, or of any general system of blame or praise. One man's ambition is not another's ambition, nor will the same event or object satisfy both; but the humanity of one man is the humanity of every one, and the same object touches this passion in all human creatures.

But the sentiments, which arise from humanity, are not only the same in all human creatures, and produce the same approbation or censure; but they also comprehend all human creatures; nor is there any one whose conduct or character is not, by their means, an object to every one of censure or approbation. . . . [pp. 272–273]

Another spring of our constitution, that brings a great addition of force to moral sentiment, is the love of fame; which rules, with such uncontrolled authority, in all generous minds, and is often the grand object of all their designs and undertakings. By our continual and earnest pursuit of a character, a name, a reputation in the world, we bring our own deportment and conduct frequently in review, and consider how they appear in the eyes of those who approach and regard us. This constant habit of surveying ourselves, as it were, in reflection, keeps alive all the sentiments of right and wrong, and begets, in noble natures, a certain reverence for themselves as well as others, which is the surest guardian of every virtue. . . . [p. 276]

Having explained the moral *approbation* attending merit or virtue, there remains nothing but briefly to consider our interested *obligation* to it, and to inquire whether every man, who has any regard to his own happiness and welfare, will not best find his account in the practice of every moral duty. If this can be clearly ascertained from the foregoing theory, we shall have the satisfaction to reflect, that we have advanced principles, which not only, it is hoped, will stand the test of reasoning and inquiry, but may contribute to the amendment of men's lives, and their improvement in morality and social virtue. . . . [pp. 278–279]

. . . [W]hat theory of morals can ever serve any useful purpose, unless it can show, by a particular detail, that all the duties which it recommends, are also the true interest of each individual? The peculiar advantage of the foregoing system seems to be, that it furnishes proper mediums for that purpose.

That the virtues which are immediately *useful* or *agreeable* to the person possessed of them, are desirable in a view to self-interest, it would surely be superfluous to prove. . . . [p. 280]

Whatever contradiction may vulgarly be supposed between the *selfish* and *social* sentiments or dispositions, they are really no more opposite than selfish and ambitious, selfish and revengeful, selfish and vain. It is requisite that there be an original propensity of some kind, in order to be a basis to self-love, by giving a relish to the objects of its pursuit; and none more fit for this purpose than benevolence or humanity. . . . [p. 281]

Treating vice with the greatest candour, and making it all possible concessions, we must acknowledge that there is not, in any instance, the smallest pretext for giving it the preference above virtue, with a view of self-interest; except, perhaps, in the case of justice, where a man, taking things in a certain light, may often seem to be a loser by his integrity. And though it is allowed that, without a regard to property, no society could subsist; yet according to the imperfect way in which human affairs are conducted, a sensible knave, in particular incidents, may think that an act of iniquity or infidelity will make a considerable addition to his fortune, without causing any considerable breach in the social union and confederacy. That *honesty is the best policy,* may be a good general rule, but is liable to many exceptions; and he, it may perhaps be thought, conducts himself with most wisdom, who observes the general rule, and takes advantage of all the exceptions.

I must confess that, if a man think that this reasoning much requires an answer, it would be a little difficult to find any which will to him appear satisfactory and convincing. If his heart rebel not against such pernicious maxims, if he feel no reluctance to the thoughts of villainy or baseness, he has indeed lost a considerable motive to virtue; and we may expect that this practice will be answerable to his speculation. But in all ingenuous natures, the antipathy to treachery and roguery is too strong to be counterbalanced by any views of profit or pecuniary advantage. Inward peace of mind, consciousness of integrity, a satisfactory review of our own conduct; these are circumstances, very requisite to happiness, and will be cherished and cultivated by every honest man, who feels the importance of them. [pp. 282–283]

Hume postponed to Appendix I the more technical treatment of the question with which the *Enquiry* began:

Appendix I: Concerning Moral Sentiment

[We may resume the question first started, and] examine how far either *reason* or *sentiment* enters into all decisions of praise or censure.

One principal foundation of moral praise being supposed to lie in the usefulness of any quality or action, it is evident that *reason* must enter for a considerable share in all decisions of this kind; since nothing but that faculty can instruct us in the tendency of qualities and actions, and point out their beneficial consequences to society and to their possessor. . . .

But though reason, when fully assisted and improved, be sufficient to instruct us in the pernicious or useful tendency of qualities and actions; it is not alone sufficient to produce any moral blame or approbation. Utility is only a tendency to a certain end; and were the end totally indifferent to us, we should feel the same indifference towards the means. It is requisite a *sentiment* should here display itself, in order to give a preference to the useful above the pernicious tendencies. This sentiment can be no other than a feeling for the happiness of mankind, and a resentment of their misery; since these are the different ends which virtue and vice have a tendency to promote. Here therefore *reason* instructs us in the several tendencies of actions, and *humanity* makes a distinction in favour of those which are useful and beneficial.

This partition between the faculties of understanding and sentiment, in all moral decisions, seems clear from the preceding hypothesis. But I shall suppose that hypothesis false: it will then be requisite to look out for some other theory that may be satisfactory; and I dare venture to affirm that none such will ever be found, so long as we suppose reason to be the sole source of morals. To prove this, it will be proper to weigh the five following considerations.

I. . . . Examine the crime of *ingratitude*, for instance; which has place, wherever we observe goodwill, expressed and known, together with good-offices performed, on the one side, and a return of ill-will or indifference, with ill-offices or neglect on the other: anatomize all these circumstances, and examine, by your reason alone, in what consists the demerit or blame. You will never come to any issue or conclusion.

Reason judges either of *matter of fact* or of *relations*. Enquire then, *first*, where is that matter of fact which we here call *crime*; point it out; determine the time of its existence; describe its essence or nature; explain the sense or faculty to which it discovers itself. It resides in the mind of the person who is ungrateful. He must, therefore, feel it, and be conscious of it. But nothing is there, except the passion of ill-will or absolute indifference. You cannot say that these, of themselves, always, and in all circumstances, are crimes. No, they are only crimes when directed towards persons who have before expressed and displayed good-will towards us. Consequently, we may infer, that the crime of ingratitude is not any particular individual *fact*; but arises from a complication of circumstances, which, being presented to the spectator, excites the *sentiment* of blame, by the particular structure and fabric of his mind.

This representation, you say, is false. Crime, indeed, consists not in a particular *fact*, of whose reality we are assured by *reason*; but it consists in certain *moral relations*, discovered by reason, in the same manner as we discover by reason the truths of geometry or algebra. But what are the relations, I ask, of which you here talk? In the case stated above, I see first good-will and good-offices in one person; then ill-will and ill-offices in the other. Between these, there is a relation of *contrariety*. Does the crime consist in that relation? But suppose a person bore me ill-will or did me ill-offices; and I, in return, were indifferent towards him, or did him good-offices. Here is the same relation of *contrariety*; and yet my conduct is often highly laudable. Twist and turn this matter as much as you will, you can never rest the morality on relation; but must have recourse to the decisions of sentiment. [pp. 285–288]

. . . The hypothesis which we embrace is plain. It maintains that morality is determined by sentiment. It defines virtue to be *whatever mental action or quality gives to a spectator the pleasing sentiment of approbation*; and vice the contrary. We then proceed to examine a plain matter of fact, to wit, what actions have this influence. We consider all the circumstances in which these actions agree, and thence endeavour to extract some general observations with regard to these sentiments. If you call this metaphysics, and find anything abstruse here, you need only conclude that your turn of mind is not suited to the moral sciences.

II. When a man, at any time, deliberates concerning his own conduct (as, whether he had better, in a particular emergence, assist a brother or a benefactor), he must consider these separate relations, with all the circumstances and situations of the persons, in order to determine the superior duty and obligation; and in order to determine the proportion of lines in any triangle, it is necessary to examine the nature of that figure, and the relation which its several parts bear to each other. But notwithstanding this appearing similarity in the two cases, there is, at bottom, an extreme difference between them. A speculative reasoner concerning triangles or circles considers the several known and given relations of the parts of these figures; and thence infers some unknown relation, which is dependent on the former. But in moral deliberations we must be acquainted beforehand with all the objects, and all their relations to each other; and from a comparison of the whole, fix our choice or approbation. No new fact to be ascertained; no new relation to be discovered. All the circumstances of the case are supposed to be laid before us, ere we can fix any sentence of blame or approbation. If any material circumstance be yet unknown or doubtful, we must first employ our inquiry or intellectual faculties to assure us of it; and must suspend for a time all moral decision or sentiment. While we are ignorant whether a man were aggressor or not, how can we determine whether the person who killed him be criminal or innocent? But after every circumstance, every relation is known, the understanding has no further room to operate, nor any object on which it could employ itself. The approbation or blame which then ensues, cannot be the work of the judgement, but of the heart; and is not a speculative proposition or affirmation, but an active feeling or sentiment. . . .

Hence the great difference between a mistake of *fact* and one of *right*; and hence the reason why the one is commonly criminal and not the other. When Oedipus killed Laius, he was ignorant of the relation, and from circumstances, innocent and involuntary, formed erroneous opinions concerning the action which he committed. But when Nero killed Agrippina, all the relations between himself and the person, and all the circumstances of the fact, were previously known to him; but the motive of revenge, or fear, or interest, prevailed in his savage heart over the sentiments of duty and humanity. And when we express that detestation against him to which he himself, in a little time, became insensible, it is not that we see any relations, of which he was ignorant; but that, for the rectitude of our disposition, we feel sentiments against which he was hardened from flattery and a long perseverance in the most enormous crimes. In these sentiments then, not in a discovery of relations of any kind, do all moral determinations consist. Before we can pretend to form any decision of this kind, everything must be known and ascertained on the side of the object or action. Nothing remains but to feel, on our part, some sentiment of blame or approbation; whence we pronounce the action criminal or virtuous.

III. This doctrine will become still more evident, if we compare moral beauty with natural, to which in many particulars it bears so near a resemblance. It is on the proportion, relation, and position of parts, that all natural beauty depends; but it would be absurd thence to infer, that the perception of beauty, like that of truth in geometrical problems, consists wholly in the perception of relations, and was performed entirely by the understanding or intellectual faculties. In all the sciences, our mind from the known relations investigates the unknown. But in all decisions of taste or external beauty, all the relations are beforehand obvious to the eye; and we thence proceed to feel a sentiment of complacency or disgust, according to the nature of the object, and disposition of our organs.

Euclid has fully explained all the qualities of the circle; but has not in any proposition said a word of its beauty. The reason is evident. The beauty is not a quality of the circle. It lies not in any part of the line, whose parts are equally distant from a common centre. It is only the effect which that figure produces upon the mind, whose peculiar fabric of structure renders it susceptible of such sentiments. In vain would you look for it in the circle, or seek it, either by your senses or by mathematical reasoning, in all the properties of that figure. [pp. 289–292]

IV. Inanimate objects may bear to each other all the same relations which we observe in moral agents; though the former can never be the object of love or hatred, nor are consequently susceptible of merit or iniquity. A young tree, which over-tops and destroys its parent, stands in all the same relations with Nero, when he murdered Agrippina; and if morality consisted merely in relations, would no doubt be equally criminal.

V. It appears evident that the ultimate ends of human actions can never, in any case, be accounted for by *reason*, but recommend themselves entirely to the sentiments and affections of mankind, without any dependence on the intellectual faculties. Ask a man *why he uses exercise;* he will answer, *because he desires to keep his health*. If you then enquire, *why he desires health*, he will readily reply, *because sickness is painful*. If you push your enquiries farther, and desire a reason *why he hates pain*, it is impossible he can ever give any. This is an ultimate end, and is never referred to any other object.

. . . It is impossible there can be a progress *in infinitum*; and that one thing can always be a reason why another is desired. Something must be desirable on its own account, and because of its immediate accord or agreement with human sentiment and affection.

Now as virtue is an end, and is desirable on its own account, without fee and reward, merely for the immediate satisfaction which it conveys; it is requisite that there should be some sentiment which it touches, some internal taste or feeling, or whatever you may please to call it, which distinguishes moral good and evil, and which embraces the one and rejects the other.

Thus the distinct boundaries and offices of *reason* and of *taste* are easily ascertained. The former conveys the knowledge of truth and falsehood: the latter gives the sentiment of beauty and deformity, vice and virtue. The one discovers objects as they really stand in nature, without addition or diminution: the other has a productive faculty, and gilding or staining all natural objects with the colours, borrowed from internal sentiment, raises in a manner a new creation. Reason being cool and disengaged, is no motive to action, and directs only the impulse received from appetite or inclination, by showing us the means of attaining happiness or avoiding misery: Taste, as it gives pleasure or pain, and thereby constitutes happiness or misery, becomes a motive to action, and is the first spring or impulse to desire and volition. . . . [pp. 293–294]

A Treatise of Human Nature [26]

The foregoing appendix corresponds to the section in the *Treatise* called "Moral Distinctions Not Derived from Reason," which concludes with a famous passage, the *locus classicus* for the "is-ought" problem: May descriptions ever, logically, yield prescriptions? May one derive norms from facts? If a valid argument has an "ought" statement in its conclusion, must it also have an "ought" statement among its premises?

The simplest reading of the passage, perhaps, is that it denies that facts can be relevant to obligations. But it is not a simple matter. Hume himself is not loath to draw policy conclusions about money and government in his economic and political writings, and supports them by generalizations of psychology about the effect of habit on individuals' behavior and of custom on social behavior. He appreciates the complexity of facts. Further, there is the question of what "ought" means to him: an ethics that locates the springs of virtuous action in pleasurable feelings of approval is likely to be hard put to find a place for a strong sense of obligation, such as doing what is right because it is right. And if the treatment of induction is analogous, his point might be that the connection between "is" and "ought" is possible, but only with the assistance of a mediating sentiment, not on the basis of reason alone.

. . . But can there be any difficulty in proving, that vice and virtue are not matters of fact, whose existence we can infer by reason? Take any action allowed to be vicious: Wilful murder, for instance. Examine it in all lights, and see if you can find that matter of fact, or real existence, which you call *vice*. In whichever way you take it, you find only certain passions, motives, volitions and thoughts.

[26] First printed 1739–1740. The selection is from *A Treatise of Human Nature*, ed. L. A. Selby-Bigge (Oxford: Clarendon Press, 1896), Bk III, Part I, sec I, pp. 468–470.

There is no other matter of fact in the case. The vice entirely escapes you, as long as you consider the object. You never can find it, till you turn your reflexion into your own breast, and find a sentiment of disapprobation, which arises in you towards this action. Here is a matter of fact; but 'tis the object of feeling, not of reason. It lies in yourself, not in the object. So that when you pronounce any action or character to be vicious, you mean nothing, but that from the constitution of your nature you have a feeling or sentiment of blame from the contemplation of it. Vice and virtue, therefore, may be compared to sounds, colours, heat and cold, which, according to modern philosophy, are not qualities in objects, but perceptions in the mind: And this discovery in morals, like that other in physics, is to be regarded as a considerable advancement of the speculative sciences; though, like that too, it has little or no influence on practice. Nothing can be more real, or concern us more, than our own sentiments of pleasure and uneasiness; and if these be favourable to virtue, and unfavourable to vice, no more can be requisite to the regulation of our conduct and behaviour.

I cannot forbear adding to these reasonings an observation, which may, perhaps, be found of some importance. In every system of morality, which I have hitherto met with, I have always remarked, that the author proceeds for some time in the ordinary way of reasoning, and establishes the being of a God, or makes observations concerning human affairs; when of a sudden I am surprized to find, that instead of the usual copulations of propositions, *is*, and *is not*, I meet with no proposition that is not connected with an *ought*, or an *ought not*. This change is imperceptible; but is, however, of the last consequence. For as this *ought*, or *ought not*, expresses some new relation or affirmation, 'tis necessary that it should be observed and explained; and at the same time that a reason should be given, for what seems altogether inconceivable, how this new relation can be a deduction from others, which are entirely different from it. But as authors do not commonly use this precaution, I shall presume to recommend it to the readers; and am persuaded, that this small attention would subvert all the vulgar systems of morality, and let us see, that the distinction of vice and virtue is not founded merely on the relations of objects, nor is perceived by reason.

A Dialogue [27]

A Dialogue, the whimsical exchange between Palamedes and the narrator, was a contribution to the emerging social sciences in its appreciation of the particular social settings of virtues. It argues that although societies may differ in what they count as a social virtue, social utility is a uniform principle underlying the differences.

It opens with Palamedes describing a country, Fourli, he has visited,

whose inhabitants have ways of thinking, in many things, particularly in morals, diametrically opposite to ours. When I came among them, I found that I must submit to double pains; first to learn the meaning of the terms in their language, and then to know the import of those terms, and the praise or blame attached to them. After a word had been explained to me, and the character, which it expressed, had been described, I concluded, that such an epithet must necessarily be the greatest reproach in the world; and was extremely surprised to find one in a public company, apply it to a person, with whom he lived in the strictest intimacy and friendship. *You fancy*, said I, one day, to an acquaintance, *that* Changuis *is your mortal enemy: I love to extinguish quarrels; and I must, therefore, tell you, that I heard him talk of you in the most obliging manner.* But to my great astonishment, when I repeated Changuis's words, though I had both remembered and understood them perfectly, I found, that they were taken for the most mortal affront, and that I had very innocently rendered the breach between these persons altogether irreparable. [p. 289]

Palamedes also met Alcheic, a person universally admired in Fourli.

One evening he invited me, as an amusement, to bear him company in a serenade, which he in-

tended to give to Gulki, which whom, he told me, he was extremely enamoured; and I soon found that his taste was not singular: For we met many of his rivals, who had come on the same errand. I very naturally concluded, that this mistress of his must be one of the finest women in town; and I already felt a secret inclination to see her, and be acquainted with her. [Gulki turned out to be a young man, but Alcheic's relationship with him was approved of by all the good company in town, and even] Alcheic's wife (who by-the-by happened also to be his sister) was no wise scandalized by this species of infidelity.

Much about the same time I discovered (for it was not attempted to be kept a secret from me or any body) that Alcheic was a murderer and a parricide, and had put to death an innocent person, the most nearly connected with him, and whom he was bound to protect and defend by all the ties of nature and humanity. When I asked, with all the caution and deference imaginable, what was his motive for this action; he replied coolly, that he was not then so much at ease in his circumstances as he is at present, and that he had acted, in that particular, by the advice of all his friends.

Having heard Alcheic's virtue so extremely celebrated, I pretended to join him in the general voice of acclamation, and only asked, by way of curiosity, as a stranger, which of all his noble actions was most highly applauded; and I soon found, that all sentiments were united in giving the preference to the assassination of Usbek. This Usbek had been to the last moment Alcheic's intimate friend, had laid many high obligations upon him, had even saved his life on a certain occasion, and had, by his will, which was found after the murder, made him heir to a considerable part of his fortune. Alcheic, it seems, conspired with about twenty or thirty more, most of them also Usbek's friends; and falling all together on that unhappy man, when he was not aware, they had torne him with a hundred wounds; and given him that reward for all his past favours and obligations. Usbek, said the general voice of the people, had many great and good qualities: His very vices were shining, magnificent, and generous: But this action of Alcheic's sets him far above Usbek in the eyes of all judges of merit; and is one of the noblest that ever perhaps the sun shone upon. . . . [pp. 290–291]

I have lately received a letter from a correspon-

[27] First printed in the first edition of the *Enquiry Concerning the Principles of Morals* (1751). The selection is from David Hume, *Essays: Moral, Political, and Literary*, ed. T. H. Green and T. H. Grose (London: Longmans, Green, 1875), vol II.

dent in Fourli, by which I learn, that, since my departure, Alcheic, falling into a bad state of health, has fairly hanged himself; and has died universally regretted and applauded in that country. So virtuous and noble a life, says each Fourlian, could not be better crowned than by so noble an end. . . . [p. 291]

[The narrator is shocked]: such barbarous and savage manners are not only incompatible with a civilized, intelligent people, . . . but are scarcely compatible with human nature. . . .

Have a care, cried he, have a care! You are not aware that you are speaking blasphemy, and are abusing your favourites, the Greeks, especially the Athenians, whom I have couched, all along, under these bizarre names I employed. If you consider aright, there is not one stroke of the foregoing character, which might not be found in the man of highest merit at Athens, without diminishing in the least from the brightness of his character. The amours of the Greeks, their marriages, and the exposing of their children cannot but strike you immediately. The death of Usbek is an exact counter-part to that of Caesar. [p. 292]

Similarly, by our morality, Brutus and Cassius should be considered traitors and assassins, although "they are, perhaps, the highest characters of all antiquity."

. . . And I think I have fairly made it appear, that an Athenian man of merit might be such a one as with us would pass for incestuous, a parricide, an assassin, an ungrateful, perjured traitor, and something else too abominable to be named; not to mention his rusticity and ill-manners. And having lived in this manner, his death might be entirely suitable: He might conclude the scene by a desperate act of self-murder, and die with the most absurd blasphemies in his mouth. And notwithstanding all this, he shall have statues, if not altars, erected to his memory. . . .

I might have been aware, replied I, of your artifice. You seem to take pleasure in this topic: and are indeed the only man I ever knew, who was well acquainted with the ancients and did not extremely admire them. But instead of attacking their philosophy . . . you now seem to impeach their morals, and accuse them of ignorance in a science, which is the only one, in my opinion, in which

they are not surpassed by the moderns. . . . Your representation of things is fallacious. You have no indulgence for the manners and customs of different ages. Would you try a Greek or Roman by the common law of England? Hear him defend himself by his own maxims; and then pronounce.

There are no manners so innocent or reasonable, but may be rendered odious or ridiculous, if measured by a standard unknown to the persons; especially, if you employ a little art or eloquence, in aggravating some circumstances, and extenuating others, as best suits the purpose of your discourse. All these artifices may easily be retorted on you. Could I inform the Athenians, for instance, that there was a nation, in which adultery, both active and passive, so to speak, was in the highest vogue and esteem: In which every man of education chose for his mistress a married woman, the wife, perhaps, of his friend and companion; and valued himself upon these infamous conquests, . . . In which every man also took a pride in his tameness and facility with regard to his own wife, and was glad to make friends or gain interest by allowing her to prostitute her charms; and even, without any such motive, gave her full liberty and indulgence: I ask, what sentiments the Athenians would entertain of such a people; they who never mentioned the crime of adultery but in conjunction with robbery and poisoning? Which would they admire most, the villainy or the meanness of such a conduct? [pp. 293–294]

Palamedes recognizes this nation as the French.

. . . But I give you thanks for helping me out with my argument. I had no intention of exalting the moderns at the expence of the ancients. I only meant to represent the uncertainty of all these judgements concerning characters; and to convince you, that fashion, vogue, custom, and law, were the chief foundation of all moral determinations. The Athenians surely, were a civilized, intelligent people, if ever there were one; and yet their man of merit might, in this age, be held in horror and execration. The French are also, without doubt, a very civilized, intelligent people; and yet their man of merit might, with the Athenians, be an object of the highest contempt and ridicule, and even hatred. And what renders the matter more extraordinary: These two people are supposed to be the most similar in their national character of any in ancient and modern times; and while the English flatter themselves that they resemble the Romans, their neighbours on the continent draw the parallel between themselves and those polite Greeks. What wide difference, therefore, in the sentiments of morals, must be found between civilized nations and Barbarians, or between nations whose characters have little in common? How shall we pretend to fix a standard for judgments of this nature?

By tracing matters, replied I, a little higher, and examining the first principles, which each nation establishes, of blame or censure. The Rhine flows north, the Rhone south; yet both spring from the *same* mountain, and are also actuated, in their opposite directions, by the *same* principle of gravity. The different inclinations of the ground, on which they run, cause all the difference of their courses.

In how many circumstances would an Athenian and a French man of merit certainly resemble each other? Good sense, knowledge, wit, eloquence, humanity, fidelity, truth, justice, courage, temperance, constancy, dignity of mind: These you have all omitted; in order to insist only on the points, in which they may, by accident, differ. Very well: I am willing to comply with you; and shall endeavour to account for these differences from the most universal, established principles of morals.

The Greek loves, I care not to examine more particularly. I shall only observe, that, however blameable, they arose from a very innocent cause, the frequency of the gymnastic exercises among that people; and were recommended, though absurdly, as the source of friendship, sympathy, mutual attachment, and fidelity; qualities esteemed in all nations and all ages.

The marriage of half-brothers and sisters seems no great difficulty. Love between the nearer relations is contrary to reason and public utility; but the precise point, where we are to stop, can scarcely be determined by natural reason; and is therefore a very proper subject for municipal law or custom. . . .

Had you asked a parent at Athens, why he bereaved his child of that life, which he had so lately given it. It is because I love it, he would reply; and regard the poverty which it must inherit from me, as a greater evil than death, which it is not capable of dreading, feeling, or resenting.

How is public liberty, the most valuable of all blessings, to be recovered from the hands of an usurper or tyrant, if his power shields him from public rebellion, and our scruples from private vengeance? That his crime is capital by law, you acknowledge: And must the highest aggravation of his crime, the putting of himself above law, form his full security? You can reply nothing, but by showing the great inconveniences of assassination; which could any one have proved clearly to the ancients, he had reformed their sentiments in this particular.

[As for French gallantry: they] have resolved to sacrifice some of the domestic to the sociable pleasures; and to prefer ease, freedom, and an open commerce, to a strict fidelity and constancy. These ends are both good, and are somewhat difficult to reconcile; nor need we be surprised, if the customs of nations incline too much, sometimes to the one side, sometimes to the other. . . . [pp. 296–298]

You see then, continued I, that the principles upon which men reason in morals are always the same; though the conclusions which they draw are often very different. That they all reason aright with regard to this subject, more than with regard to any other, it is not incumbent on any moralist to show. It is sufficient, that the original principles of censure or blame are uniform, and that erroneous conclusions can be corrected by sounder reasoning and larger experience. Though many ages have elapsed since the fall of Greece and Rome; though many changes have arrived in religion, language, laws, and customs; none of these revolutions has ever produced any considerable innovation in the primary sentiments of morals, more than in those of external beauty. Some minute differences, perhaps, may be observed in both. Horace celebrates a low forehead, and Anacreon joined eye-brows: But the Apollo and the Venus of antiquity are still our models for male and female beauty; in like manner as the character of Scipio continues our standard for the glory of heroes, and that of Cornelia for the honour of matrons.

It appears, that there never was any quality recommended by any one, as a virtue or moral excellence, but on account of its being *useful*, or *agreeable* to a man *himself*, or to *others*. For what other reason can ever be assigned for praise or approbation? Or where would be the sense of extolling a *good* character or action, which, at the same time, is allowed to be *good for nothing*? All the differences, therefore, in morals, may be reduced to this one general foundation, and may be accounted for by the different views, which people take of these circumstances. [p. 299]

Political Discourses [28]

Hume achieved literary fame not for his philosophical works but for essays in a lighter vein, on criticism, economics, politics. *Political Discourses* was such a book of essays, "the only work of mine that was successful on the first publication." [29]

The practical import of his political ideas can be seen in "Idea of a Perfect Commonwealth," influential for the writing of the United States Constitution. In contrast to Hobbes and Locke, Hume does not begin in a presocietal state but thrusts us instead into the middle of an ongoing government, directing his remarks at the inadequacies of the British parliamentary system. He justifies his ideal commonwealth not by showing that it remedies injustices among men in the state of nature, but (paralleling his treatment of justice and benevolence) by showing its utility in representing the will and interest of its citizens. He proposes—intending it as reform, not revolutionary—a complex three-tiered structure with offices and functions spelled out.

Idea of a Perfect Commonwealth

. . . An established government has an infinite advantage, by that very circumstance of its being established; the bulk of mankind being governed by authority, not reason, and never attributing authority to anything that has not the recommendation of antiquity. To tamper, therefore, in this affair, or try experiments merely upon the credit of supposed argument and philosophy, can never be the

part of a wise magistrate, who will bear a reverence to what carries the marks of age; and though he may attempt some improvements for the public good, yet will he adjust his innovations, as much as possible, to the ancient fabric, and preserve entire the chief pillars and supports of the constitution. [p. 480]

The proposal is this: Let the territory be divided into 100 counties of 100 parishes. In each parish let the freeholders of 20 pounds a year and householders worth 500 pounds meet annually to elect the county representative. Let each 100 county representatives elect 10 county magistrates and 1 senator. Let the 100 senators be "endowed with the whole executive power of the commonwealth; the power of peace and war, of giving order to generals, admirals, and ambassadors, and, in short, all the prerogatives of a British King, except his negative" (pp. 482–483). Let the senators elect from among themselves a protector, "who represents the dignity of the commonwealth and presides in the senate," six commissioners and members of six councils, and appoint ambassadors and judicial officials. Let the county representatives "possess the whole legislative power of the commonwealth; the greater number of counties deciding the question; and where these are equal, let the senate have the casting vote" (p. 483). No elected official is to be salaried.

The following political aphorisms may explain the reason of these orders.

The lower sort of people and small proprietors are good judges enough of one not very distant from them in rank or habitation; and therefore, in their parochial meetings, will probably choose the best, or nearly the best representative: But they are wholly unfit for county-meetings, and for electing into the higher offices of the republic. Their ignorance gives the grandees an opportunity of deceiving them. . . .

All free governments must consist of two councils, a lesser and greater; or, in other words, of a senate and people. The people . . . would want

---

[28] Edinburgh, 1752. The selections are from David Hume, *Essays: Moral, Political, and Literary*, ed. T. H. Green and T. H. Grose (London: Longmans, Green, 1875), vol I, Part II. The term "political" should not be taken in our narrower sense. The essays deal as much with economics as with politics.

[29] "My Own Life," *Essays*, p. 4.

wisdom, without the senate: the senate, without the people, would want honesty. . . .

. . . [A]ll numerous assemblies, however composed, are mere mob, and swayed in their debates by the least motive. This we find confirmed by daily experience. When an absurdity strikes a member, he conveys it to his neighbour, and so on, till the whole be infected. Separate this great body; and though every member be only of middling sense, it is not probable, that any thing but reason can prevail over the whole. Influence and example being removed, good sense will always get the better of bad among a number of people. [pp. 487–488]

In economics Hume argues that mercantilism is inherently self-defeating. Wealth involves the nation as a whole, and should include the standard of living of laborers and level of industrial activity. The economic system is intimately woven in the sociopolitical fabric, and it is justified by how it improves men's lives, not by its improvement of the balance of trade. The next two selections exhibit Hume's technical criticism of mercantilism. A third shows how he weaves his moral views into an analysis of what might appear to be a strict economic issue, namely, whether "vicious luxury" is economically beneficial to a nation. In effect he offers a moral justification for commercial and industrial society on the grounds that economic growth contributes to the happiness of individuals and makes society more humane.

Of Commerce

The same method of reasoning will let us see the advantage of *foreign* commerce, in augmenting the power of the state, as well as the riches and happiness of the subject. It encreases the stock of labour in the nation; and the sovereign may convert what share of it he finds necessary to the service of the public. Foreign trade, by its imports, furnishes materials for new manufactures; and by its exports, it produces labour in particular commodities, which could not be consumed at home. In short, a kingdom, that has a large import and export, must abound more with industry, and that

employed upon delicacies and luxuries, than a kingdom which rests contented with its native commodities. It is, therefore, more powerful, as well as richer and happier. The individuals reap the benefit of these commodities, so far as they gratify the senses and appetites. And the public is also a gainer, while a greater stock of labour is, by this means, stored up against any public exigency; that is, a greater number of laborious men are maintained, who may be diverted to the public service, without robbing any one of the necessaries, or even the chief conveniences of life. [p. 295]

Of the Balance of Trade

It is very usual, in nations ignorant of the nature of commerce, to prohibit the exportation of commodities, and to preserve among themselves whatever they think valuable and useful. They do not consider, that, in this prohibition, they act directly contrary to their intention; and that the more is exported of any commodity, the more will be raised at home, of which they themselves will always have the first offer. [pp. 330–331]

The same jealous fear, with regard to money, has also prevailed among several nations; and it required both reason and experience to convince any people, that these prohibitions serve to no other purpose than to raise the exchange against them, and produce a still greater exportation.

These errors, one may say, are gross and palpable: But there still prevails, even in nations well acquainted with commerce, a strong jealousy with regard to the balance of trade, and a fear, that all their gold and silver may be leaving them. This seems to me, almost in every case, a groundless apprehension; and I should as soon dread, that all our springs and rivers should be exhausted, as that money should abandon a kingdom where there are people and industry. Let us carefully preserve these latter advantages; and we need never be apprehensive of losing the former. [p. 331]

Suppose four-fifths of all the money in Great Britain to be annihilated in one night, . . . what would be the consequence? Must not the price of all labour and commodities sink in proportion, and everything be sold as cheap as they were in [past] ages? What nation could then dispute with us in any foreign market, or pretend to navigate or to sell manufactures at the same price, which to us would afford sufficient profit? In how little time, therefore, must this bring back the money which we had lost, and raise us to the level of all the neighbouring nations? Where, after we have arrived, we immediately lose the advantage of the cheapness of labour and commodities; and the farther flowing in of money is stopped by our fulness and repletion.

Again, suppose, that all the money of Great Britain were multiplied fivefold in a night, must not the contrary effect follow? Must not all labour and commodities rise to such an exorbitant height, that no neighbouring nations could afford to buy from us; while their commodities, on the other hand, became comparatively so cheap, that, in spite of all the laws which could be formed, they would be run in upon us, and our money flow out; till we fall to a level with foreigners, and lose that great superiority of riches, which had laid us under such disadvantages?

Now, it is evident, that the same causes, which would correct these exorbitant inequalities, were they to happen miraculously, must prevent their happening in the common course of nature, and must for ever, in all neighbouring nations, preserve money nearly proportionable to the art and industry of each nation. All water, wherever it communicates, remains always at a level. Ask naturalists the reason; they tell you, that, were it to be raised in any one place, the superior gravity of that part not being balanced, must depress it, till it meet a counterpoise; and that the same cause, which redresses the inequality when it happens, must for ever prevent it, without some violent external operation. [p. 333]

In short, a government has great reason to preserve with care its people and its manufactures. Its money, it may safely trust to the course of human affairs, without fear or jealousy. Or if it ever give attention to this latter circumstance, it ought only to be so far as it affects the former. [p. 345]

Of Refinement in the Arts

[An] advantage of industry and of refinements in the mechanical arts, is, that they commonly produce some refinements in the liberal [arts]; nor can one be carried to perfection without being accompanied, in some degree, with the other. The same age, which produces great philosophers and politicians, renowned generals and poets, usually abounds with skilful weavers, and ship-carpenters. We cannot reasonably expect, that a piece of woollen cloth will be brought to perfection in a nation, which is ignorant of astronomy, or where ethics are neglected. The spirit of the age affects all the arts; and the minds of men, being once roused from their lethargy, and put into a fermentation, turn themselves on all sides, and carry improvements into every art and science. Profound ignorance is totally banished, and men enjoy the privilege of rational creatures, to think as well as to act, to cultivate the pleasures of the mind as well as those of the body.

The more these refined arts advance, the more sociable men become: nor is it possible, that, when enriched with science, and possessed of a fund of conversation, they should be contented to remain in solitude, or live with their fellow-citizens in that distant manner, which is peculiar to ignorant and barbarous nations. They flock into cities; love to receive and communicate knowledge; to show their wit or their breeding; their taste in conversation or living, in clothes or furniture. Curiosity allures the wise; vanity the foolish; and pleasure both. . . . So that, beside the improvements which they receive from knowledge and the liberal arts, it is impossible but they must feel an encrease of humanity, from the very habit of conversing together, and contribute to each other's pleasure and entertainment. Thus *industry, knowledge,* and *humanity,* are linked together by an indissoluble chain, and are found, from experience as well as reason, to be peculiar to the more polished, and, what are commonly denominated, the more luxurious ages. [pp. 301–302]

Let us consider what we call vicious luxury. No gratification, however sensual, can of itself be esteemed vicious. A gratification is only vicious, when it engrosses all a man's expence, and leaves no ability for such acts of duty and generosity as are required by his situation and fortune. Suppose, that he correct the vice, and employ part of his expence in the education of his children, in the support of his friends, and in relieving the poor: would any prejudice result to society? On the contrary, the same consumption would arise; and that labour, which, at present, is employed only in producing a slender gratification to one man, would relieve the necessitous, and bestow satisfaction on hundreds. The same care and toil that raise a dish of peas at Christmas, would give bread to a whole family during six months. To say, that, without a vicious luxury, the labour would not have been employed at all, is only to say, that there is some other defect in human nature, such as indolence, selfishness, inattention to others, for which luxury, in some measure, provides a remedy; as one poison may be an antidote to another. But virtue, like wholesome food, is better than poisons, however corrected.

Suppose the same number of men, that are present in Great Britain, with the same soil and climate; I ask, is it not possible for them to be happier, by the most perfect way of life that can be imagined, and by the greatest reformation that Omnipotence itself could work in their temper and disposition? To assert, that they cannot, appears evidently ridiculous. As the land is able to maintain more than all its present inhabitants, they could never, in such a Utopian state, feel any other ills than those which arise from bodily sickness; and these are not the half of human miseries. All other ills spring from some vice, either in ourselves or others; and even many of our diseases proceed from the same origin. Remove the vices, and the ills follow. You must only take care to remove all the vices. If you remove part, you may render the matter worse. By banishing *vicious* luxury, without curing sloth and an indifference to others, you only diminish industry in the state, and add nothing to men's charity or their generosity. Let us, therefore, rest contented with asserting, that two opposite vices in a state may be more advantageous than either of them alone; but let us never pronounce vice in itself advantageous. . . .

I thought this reasoning necessary, in order to give some light to a philosophical question, which has been much disputed in England. I call it a *philosophical* question, not a *political* one. For whatever may be the consequence of such a miraculous transformation of mankind, as would endow them with every species of virtue, and free them from every species of vice; this concerns not the magistrate, who aims only at possibilities. He cannot cure every vice by substituting a virtue in its place. Very often he can only cure one vice by another; and in that case, he ought to prefer what is least pernicious to society. Luxury, when excessive, is the source of many ills; but is in general preferable to sloth and idleness, which would commonly succeed in its place, and are more hurtful both to private persons

and to the public. When sloth reigns, a mean uncultivated way of life prevails amongst individuals, without society, without enjoyment. And if the sovereign, in such a situation, demands the service of his subjects, the labour of the state suffices only to furnish the necessaries of life to the labourers, and can afford nothing to those who are employed in the public service. [pp. 307–309]

Adam Smith
(1723–1790)

Adam Smith is best known for *The Wealth of Nations* (1776) and thus as the father of classical economics. This has overshadowed *The Theory of Moral Sentiments* (1759), a highly systematic exploration of sympathy, the situations in which it is exercised, and the way in which the moral concepts are grounded in complex combinations of sympathetic reactions. The contrast between economic motives and moral sympathy has led some scholars to speak of "the Adam Smith problem," namely, how to reconcile these two pictures of man. But human beings are certainly sufficiently complex to have many sentiments that jostle one another. Further, a person may engage at different times in different enterprises, in each of which different propensities dominate. There scarcely seems a problem here if rational economic man and moral man are isolated in order to study separately the consequences from each—much as a physicist may separate for study the laws of motion and the laws of friction but still reckons with both when describing the motion of a particular object in a particular medium. If there is a conflict, it is social: with growing commercialism, interpersonal relations were increasingly assigned to two distinct provinces—business relationships carried on for profit and ordinary human relationships involving care and concern. The task of reconciliation, for Smith, thus becomes the task of showing that egoism and altruism tend to the same overall result.

Here the utilitarian element begins to play a role. *The Wealth of Nations* gives men a new picture of their world, showing how the work they do fits into the social fabric; how the market keeps society together; how the dynamics of interacting self-interest and competition (guided by the providential "invisible hand") provide for society and its well-being through the increased productivity that ensues. *The Theory of Moral Sentiments* underscores this lesson:

For what purpose is all the toil and bustle of this world? what end of avarice, ambition, of the pursuit of wealth, of power, and preeminence? It has its ultimate justification in the welfare of the common man.

The book's larger theme is that the built-in connections of moral sentiments and feelings tie the common man to his fellows.

Sympathy is the basic moral phenomenon. It is not just an introspected feeling, but a cognitive sympathy that includes causes, situations, and behaviors. It is an independent phenomenon, reducible neither to other sentiments nor to calculations of expediency. *Moral Sentiments* exhibits the variety of moral distinctions or concepts as complex interrelated sympathetic reactions of different sorts: from propriety (or fitness) to merit and demerit, duty, and finally virtue. The book concludes with a review of the different systems of moral philosophy, classified in the light of his own theory.

Smith's debt to his friend Hume is considerable. Just as *The Wealth of Nations* develops leads provided by Hume's essay "Of the Balance of Trade," so *Moral Sentiments* follows Hume on the centrality of sympathy. There are, however, critical differences in the moral theory. Where Hume's notion of sympathy is individualistic, Smith's develops the interpersonal and communicative mutuality; and where Hume stresses the emotive in the notion, Smith's appeal to an ideal spectator allows him to introduce a cognitive and genuinely judgmental aspect to our approvals of the conduct and character of others, and ultimately of ourselves. They share a similar general model of inquiry, stemming from the general impact of Newton on the Scottish Enlightenment, and a broad conception of the scope of moral philosophy.

Smith's life was placid and uneventful, apparently without crises. Born in the fishing and mining village of Kircaldy, north of Edinburgh, he was educated at Glasgow and then Oxford. Scottish universities were then among the most intellectually vigorous centers in Europe; Oxford was in decline, with wretched professorial standards leaving the students to seek intellectual stimulus for themselves. In Glasgow he had ample opportunity to observe the advance of a prosperous industrialism, active in the Atlantic trade, shipbuilding, and the iron and engineering industries, as well as in the distillation of spirits, and with a virtual monopoly of the sale of raw and refined sugar. Thus, in contrast to the physiocrats, he saw that manufacturing, not just agriculture, is a source of wealth. He returned to Glasgow as professor of logic, and later of moral philosophy, which then embraced not only ethics and jurisprudence but also natural theology and political economy.

Smith resigned his professorship in 1763 to serve—on an extended visit to Europe, especially France—as tutor to the young duke of Buccleuch. In France he came to know the physiocrats, especially Quesney, and the circle of the Encyclopedists—Turgot, d'Alembert, Helvetius, and others. He returned to Edinburgh, where he spent his time in study and writing. On visits to London he was welcomed into the circles of Samuel Johnson, Franklin, Burke, and Gibbon. And of course his association with Hume was continual. Though criticized for this friendship, Smith showed himself loyal, humane, and principled. He died a year after the outbreak of the French Revolution.

The Theory of Moral Sentiments [30]

Sympathy, the building-block of Smith's theory, is defined as our fellow feeling with any passion in another when in imagination we place ourselves in the other's situation. We can see, for example, that the other person is grieving, but our sympathy is imperfect until we know the causes. We are always pleased when others share our passions, whether the passion be agreeable or disagreeable. On the whole, though, we are more concerned that people share our dislikes than that they share our likes.

Part I deals with *propriety* of actions:

[Pt I, sec I, ch 3] When the original passions of the person principally concerned are in perfect concord with the sympathetic emotions of the spectator, they necessarily appear to this last just and proper, and suitable to their objects; and, on the contrary, when, upon bringing the case home to himself, he finds that they do not coincide with what he feels, they necessarily appear to him unjust and improper, and unsuitable to the causes which excite them. To approve of the passions of another, therefore, as suitable to their objects, is the same thing as to observe that we entirely sympathize with them; and not to approve of them as such, is the same thing as to observe that we do not entirely sympathize with them. The man who resents the injuries that have been done to me, and observes that I resent them precisely as he does, necessarily approves of my resentment. The man whose sympathy keeps time to my grief, cannot but admit the reasonableness of my sorrow. He who admires the same poem or the same picture, and admires them exactly as I do, must surely allow the justness of my admiration. He who laughs at the same joke, and laughs along with me, cannot well deny the propriety of my laughter. On the contrary, the person who, upon these different occasions, either feels no such emotion as that which I feel, or feels none that bears any proportion to mine, cannot avoid disapproving my sentiments on account of their dis-

sonance with his own. If my animosity goes beyond what the indignation of my friend can correspond to; if my grief exceeds what his most tender compassion can go along with; if my admiration is either too high or too low to tally with his own; if I laugh loud and heartily when he only smiles, or, on the contrary, only smile when he laughs loud and heartily; in all these cases, as soon as he comes from considering the object, to observe how I am affected by it, according as there is more or less disproportion between his sentiments and mine, I must incur a greater or less degree of his disapprobation: and upon all occasions his own sentiments are the standards and measures by which he judges of mine.

To approve of another man's opinions is to adopt those opinions, and to adopt them is to approve of them. If the same arguments which convince you, convince me likewise, I necessarily approve of your conviction; and if they do not, I necessarily disapprove of it: neither can I possibly conceive that I should do the one without the other. To approve or disapprove, therefore, of the opinions of others is acknowledged, by every body, to mean no more than to observe their agreement or disagreement with our own. But this is equally the case with regard to our approbation or disapprobation of the sentiments or passions of others. [pp. 39–41]

In the suitableness or unsuitableness, in the proportion or disproportion which the affection seems to bear to the cause or object which excites it, consists the propriety or impropriety, the decency or ungracefulness of the consequent action.

In the beneficial or hurtful nature of the effects which the affection aims at, or tends to produce, consists the merit or demerit of the action, the qualities by which it is entitled to reward, or is deserving of punishment.

Philosophers have, of late years, considered chiefly the tendency of affections, and have given little attention to the relation which they stand in to the cause which excites them. In common life, however, when we judge of any person's conduct, and of the sentiments which directed it, we constantly consider them under both these aspects. When we blame in another man the excesses of love, of grief, of resentment, we not only consider the ruinous effects which they tend to produce, but the little occasion which was given for them. The merit of his favourite, we say, is not so great, his misfortune is not so dreadful, his provocation is

[30] First published 1759. The selection is from Adam Smith, *The Theory of Moral Sentiments*, 12th ed. (Glasgow: R. Chapman, 1809).

not so extraordinary as to justify so violent a passion. We should have indulged, we say, perhaps, have approved of the violence of his emotion, had the cause been in any respect proportioned to it.

When we judge in this manner of any affection as proportioned or disproportioned to the cause which excites it, it is scarce possible that we should make use of any other rule or canon, but the correspondent affection in ourselves. If upon bringing the case home to our own breast, we find that the sentiments which it gives occasion to, coincide and tally with our own, we necessarily approve of them, as proportioned and suitable to their objects; if otherwise, we necessarily disapprove of them, as extravagant and out of proportion.

Every faculty in one man is the measure by which he judges of the like faculty in another. I judge of your sight by my sight, of your ear by my ear, of your reason by my reason, of your resentment by my resentment, of your love by my love. I neither have, nor can have, any other way of judging about them. [pp. 42–43]

Many passions are explored for their propriety: bodily passions, passions that are derived from special habits of the imagination (e.g., patterns of love), unsocial passions (including our reactions to villains and heroes in dramas), social passions, selfish passions, and so on. Our moral sentiments are often distorted by the disposition to admire the rich and to despise or neglect the poor. A note clarifies the notion of sympathy:

[Sec III, ch 1] It has been objected to me, that as I found the sentiment of approbation, which is always agreeable, upon sympathy, it is inconsistent with my system to admit any disagreeable sympathy. I answer, that in the sentiment of approbation there are two things to be taken notice of; first, the sympathetic passion of the spectator; and, secondly, the emotion which arises from his observing the perfect coincidence between this sympathetic passion in himself, and the original passion in the person principally concerned. This last emotion, in which the sentiment of approbation properly consists, is always agreeable and delightful. The other may either be agreeable or disagreeable, according to the nature of the original passion, whose features it must always, in some measure retain. [p. 80]

In his survey of systems of moral philosophy (Part VII) Smith adds important insights into the nature of "sympathy." Those systems that deduce the principle of approbation from self-love neglect the independence and nonreducibility of sympathy: "Though sympathy is very properly said to arise from an imaginary change of situations with the person principally concerned, yet this imaginary change is not supposed to happen to me in my own person and character, but in that of the person with whom I sympathize" (sec III, ch 1, pp. 427–428). To condole with your loss of a son, then, is not to imagine what I should suffer in such an eventuality, but what I should suffer if I were you. "My grief, therefore, is entirely upon your account, and not in the least upon my own. It is not, therefore, in the least selfish." Thus a man may sympathize with a woman in childbed, though it is impossible that he should conceive himself as suffering her pains in his own person. "That whole account of human nature, however, which deduces all sentiments and affections from self-love, which has made so much noise in the world, but which, so far as I know, has never yet been fully and distinctly explained, seems to me to have arisen from some confused misapprehension of the system of sympathy." (p. 428)

Part II turns to *merit* and *demerit*: Whereas propriety dealt with the affection in relation to its cause or object, merit and demerit—"the qualities of deserving reward, and of deserving punishment"—deal with "the beneficial" (merit) "or hurtful" (demerit) "effects which the affection proposes or tends to produce."

[Pt II, sec I, ch 1] . . . The sentiment which most immediately and directly prompts us to reward, is gratitude; that which most immediately and directly prompts us to punish, is resentment.

To us, therefore, that action must appear to deserve reward, which appears to be the proper and approved object of gratitude; as, on the other hand, that action must appear to deserve punishment, which appears to be the proper and approved object of resentment.

To reward is to recompence, to remunerate, to return good for good received. To punish, too, is to recompence, to remunerate, though in a different manner; it is to return evil for evil that has been done.

There are some other passions, besides gratitude and resentment, which interest us in the happiness or misery of others; but there are none which so directly excite us to be the instruments of either. The love and esteem which grow upon acquaintance and habitual approbation, necessarily lead us to be pleased with the good fortune of the man who is the object of such agreeable emotions, and consequently, to be willing to lend a hand to promote it. Our love, however, is fully satisfied, though his good fortune should be brought about without our assistance. All that this passion desires is to see him happy, without regarding who was the author of his prosperity. But gratitude is not to be satisfied in this manner. If the person to whom we own many obligations is made happy without our assistance, though it pleases our love, it does not content our gratitude. Till we have recompensed him, till we ourselves have been instrumental in promoting his happiness, we feel ourselves still loaded with that debt which his past services have laid upon us.

The hatred and dislike, in the same manner, which grow upon habitual disapprobation, would often lead us to take a malicious pleasure in the misfortune of the man whose conduct and character excite so painful a passion. But though dislike and hatred harden us against all sympathy, and sometimes dispose us even to rejoice at the distress of another, yet if there is no resentment in the case, if neither we nor our friends have received any great personal provocation, these passions would not naturally lead us to wish to be instrumental in bringing it about. Though we could fear no punishment in consequence of our having had some hand in it, we would rather that it should happen by other means. To one under the dominion of violent hatred, it would be agreeable perhaps to hear, that the person whom he abhorred and detested was killed by some accident. But if he had the least spark of justice, which, though this passion is not very favourable to virtue, he might still have, it would hurt him excessively to have been himself, even

without design, the occasion of this misfortune. Much more would the very thought of voluntarily contributing to it, shock him beyond all measure. He would reject with horror even the imagination of so execrable a design; and if he could imagine himself capable of such an enormity, he would begin to regard himself in the same odious light in which he had considered the person who was the object of his dislike. But it is quite otherwise with resentment: if the person who had done us some great injury, who had murdered our father or our brother, for example, should soon afterwards die of a fever, or even be brought to the scaffold upon account of some other crime, though it might sooth our hatred, it would not fully gratify our resentment. Resentment would prompt us to desire, not only that he should be punished, but that he should be punished by our means, and upon account of that particular injury which he had done to us. Resentment cannot be fully gratified unless the offender is not only made to grieve in his turn, but to grieve for that particular wrong which we have suffered from him. He must be made to repent and be sorry for this very action, that others, through fear of the like punishment, may be terrified from being guilty of the like offence. The natural gratification of this passion tends, of its own accord, to produce all the political ends of punishment; the correction of the criminal, and the example to the public. [pp. 105–107]

[Ch 2] To be the proper and approved object either of gratitude or resentment, can mean nothing but to be the object of that gratitude, and of that resentment, which naturally seems proper, and is approved of.

But these, as well as all the other passions of human nature, seem proper, and are approved of, when the heart of every impartial spectator entirely sympathizes with them, when every indifferent bystander entirely enters into, and goes along with them.

He, therefore, appears to deserve reward, who, to some person or persons, is the natural object of a gratitude which every human heart is disposed to beat time to, and thereby applaud: and he, on the other hand, appears to deserve punishment, who in the same manner is to some person or persons the natural object of a resentment which the breast of every reasonable man is ready to adopt and sympathize with. To us, surely, that action must appear to deserve reward, which every body who knows of it would wish to reward, and therefore delights to see rewarded: and that action must as surely appear to deserve punishment, which every body who hears of it is angry with, and upon that account rejoices to see punished. [p. 108]

The sense of merit arises from an indirect sympathy with the gratitude of the person acted upon (Chapter 5). We have, of course, first to approve the motives of the benefactor. The sense of merit, then, involves two distinct emotions: "a direct sympathy with the sentiments of the agent, and an indirect sympathy with the gratitude of those who receive the benefit of his actions" (p. 115). Comparably, in the case of demerit, there is a want of sympathy or an antipathy to the affections and motives of the agent and an indirect sympathy with the resentment of the sufferer.

[Sec II, "Of Justice and Beneficence," ch 1] Actions of a beneficent tendency, which proceed from proper motives, seem alone to require a reward; because such alone are the approved object of gratitude, or excite the sympathetic gratitude of the spectator.

Actions of a hurtful tendency, which proceed from improper motives, seem alone to deserve punishment; because such alone are the approved objects of resentment, or excite the sympathetic resentment of the spectator. [p. 120]

He who does not recompense his benefactor is disapproved of by every impartial spectator; there is no fellow feeling with the selfishness of his motives. But he does no positive hurt. Resentment, on the other hand, seems to have been given to us by nature for defense against injury. It prompts us to beat off the mischief and to retaliate, to make the offender repent and to deter him thereafter. It must be reserved for such purposes, and the spectator would not go along with it for any other purpose.

Justice is distinct from all the other social virtues. Injustice does positive hurt to particular persons from motives we naturally disap-

prove of and is therefore the proper object of resentment. Accordingly we feel that force may with propriety be employed to secure the rules of justice. In the case of violations of beneficence, we feel that blame, not force, may be employed.

Feelings also shift with the impact of accidental factors (as it shifts from the victim to the perpetrator who is about to be punished). Consequences do play a serious part, but what matters is not their goodness or badness, but the reactions of our feelings to those affected.

Part III turns to the way our sentiments are reflected upon ourselves and how the sense of duty emerges. There is no break in continuity:

[Ch 1] [W]e either approve or disapprove of our own conduct, according as we feel that, when we place ourselves in the situation of another man, and view it, as it were, with his eyes, and from his station, we either can or cannot entirely enter into, and sympathize with the sentiments and motives which influenced it. [p. 160]

The love of praise is distinguished from that of praiseworthiness: we feel mortified when we are praised without deserving it. Different classes of men react differently to praise and blame. For example, mathematicians are indifferent to the reception of their work by the public. An elaborate and striking example shows that the authority of conscience is not in fact governed by actual pains we feel.

[Ch 3] . . . [T]o the selfish and original passions of human nature, the loss or gain of a very small interest of our own, appears to be of vastly more importance, excites a much more passionate joy or sorrow, a much more ardent desire or aversion, than the greatest concern of another with whom we have no particular connexion. His interests, as long as they are surveyed from his station, can never be put into the balance with our own, can never restrain us from doing whatever may tend to promote our own, how ruinous soever to him. Before we can make any proper comparison of those opposite interests, we must change our position. We must view them, neither from our own place nor yet from his, neither with our own eyes nor yet with his, but from the place and with the eyes of a third person, who has no particular connexion with either, and who judges with impartiality between us. Here, too, habit and experience have taught us to do this so easily and so readily, that we are scarce sensible that we do it; and it requires, in this case too, some degree of reflection, and even of philosophy, to convince us, how little interest we should take in the greatest concerns of our neighbour, how little we should be affected by whatever relates to him, if the sense of propriety and justice did not correct the otherwise natural inequality of our sentiments.

Let us suppose that the great empire of China, with all its myriads of inhabitants, was suddenly swallowed up by an earthquake, and let us consider how a man of humanity in Europe, who had no sort of connexion with that part of the world, would be affected upon receiving intelligence of this dreadful calamity. He would, I imagine, first of all, express very strongly his sorrow for the misfortune of that unhappy people, he would make many melancholy reflections upon the precariousness of human life, and the vanity of all the labours of man, which could thus be annihilated in a moment. He would too, perhaps, if he was a man of speculation, enter into many reasonings concerning the effects which this disaster might produce upon the commerce of Europe, and the trade and business of the world in general. And when all this fine philosophy was over, when all these humane sentiments had been once fairly expressed, he would pursue his business or his pleasure, take his repose or his diversion, with the same ease and tranquillity as if no such accident had happened. The most frivolous disaster which could befal himself would occasion a more real disturbance. If he was to lose his little finger to-morrow, he would not sleep to-night; but, provided he never saw them, he will snore with the most profound security over the ruin of a hundred millions of his brethren, and the destruction of that immense multitude seems plainly an object less interesting to him, than this paltry misfortune of his own. To prevent, therefore, this paltry misfortune to himself, would a man of humanity be willing to sacrifice the lives of a hundred million, of his brethren, provided he had never seen them? Hu-

man nature startles with horror at the thought, and the world, in its greatest depravity and corruption, never produced such a villain as could be capable of entertaining it. But what makes this difference? when our passive feelings are almost always so sordid and so selfish, how comes it that our active principles should often be so generous and so noble? When we are always so much more deeply affected by whatever concerns ourselves, than by whatever concerns other men; what is it which prompts the generous, upon all occasions, and the mean upon many, to sacrifice their own interest to the greater interests of others? It is not the soft power of humanity, it is not that feeble spark of benevolence which Nature has lighted up in the human heart, that is thus capable of counteracting the strongest impulses of self-love. It is a stronger power, a more forcible motive, which exerts itself upon such occasions. It is reason, principle, conscience, the inhabitant of the breast, the man within, the great judge and arbiter of our conduct. It is he who, whenever we are about to act so as to affect the happiness of others, calls to us, with a voice capable of astonishing the most presumptuous of our passions, that we are but one of the multitude, in no respect better than any other in it; and that when we prefer ourselves so shamefully and so blindly to others, we become the proper objects of resentment, abhorrence, and execration. It is from him only that we learn the real littleness of ourselves, and of whatever relates to ourselves, and the natural misrepresentations of self-love can be corrected only by the eye of this impartial spectator. It is he who shows us the propriety of generosity and the deformity of injustice; the propriety of resigning the greatest interests of our own, for the yet greater interests of others; and the deformity of doing the smallest injury to one another, in order to obtain the greatest benefit to ourselves. It is not the love of our neighbour, it is not the love of mankind, which upon many occasions prompts us to the practice of those divine virtues. It is a stronger love, a more powerful affection, which generally takes place upon such occasions; the love of what is honourable and noble, of the grandeur, and dignity, and superiority of our own characters.

When the happiness or misery of others depends in any respect upon our conduct, we dare not, as self-love might suggest to us, prefer the interest of one to that of many. The man within immediately calls to us, that we value ourselves too much and other people too little, and that, by doing so, we render ourselves the proper object of the contempt and indignation of our brethren. Neither is this sentiment confined to men of extraordinary magnanimity and virtue. It is deeply impressed upon every tolerably good soldier, who feels that he would become the scorn of his companions, if he could be supposed capable of shrinking from danger, or of hesitating, either to expose or to throw away his life, when the good of the service required it.

One individual must never prefer himself so much even to any other individual, as to hurt or injure that other, in order to benefit himself, though the benefit to the one should be much greater than the hurt or injury to the other. The poor man must neither defraud nor steal from the rich, though the acquisition might be much more beneficial to the one than the loss could be hurtful to the other. The man within immediately calls to him, in this case too, that he is no better than his neighbour, and that by his unjust preference he renders himself the proper object of the contempt and indignation of mankind: as well as of the punishment which that contempt and indignation must naturally dispose them to inflict, for having thus violated one of those sacred rules, upon the tolerable observation of which depend the whole security and peace of human society. There is no commonly honest man who does not more dread the inward disgrace of such an action, the indelible stain which it would for ever stamp upon his own mind, than the greatest external calamity which, without any fault of his own, could possibly befal him; and who does not inwardly feel the truth of that great stoical maxim, that for one man to deprive another unjustly of any thing, or unjustly to promote his own advantage by the loss or disadvantage of another, is more contrary to nature, than death, than poverty, than pain, than all the misfortunes which can affect him, either in his body, or in his external circumstances. [pp. 187–190]

[Ch 4] . . . Our continual observations upon the conduct of others, insensibly lead us to form to ourselves certain general rules, concerning what is fit and proper either to be done or to be avoided. Some of their actions shock all our natural sentiments. We hear every body about us express the like detestation against them. This still further confirms, and even exasperates our natural sense of their defor-

mity. It satisfies us that we view them in the proper light, when we see other people view them in the same light. We resolve never to be guilty of the like, nor ever, upon any account, to render ourselves in this manner the objects of universal disapprobation. We thus naturally lay down to ourselves a general rule, that all such actions are to be avoided, as tending to render us odious, contemptible, or punishable, the objects of all those sentiments for which we have the greatest dread and aversion. Other actions, on the contrary, call forth our approbation, and we hear every body around us express the same favourable opinion concerning them. Every body is eager to honour and reward them. They excite all those sentiments for which we have by nature the strongest desire; the love, the gratitude, the admiration of mankind. We become ambitious of performing the like; and thus naturally lay down to ourselves a rule of another kind, that every opportunity of acting in this manner is carefully to be sought after.

It is thus that the general rules of morality are formed. They are ultimately founded upon experience of what, in particular instances, our moral faculties, our natural sense of merit and propriety, approve, or disapprove of. We do not originally approve or condemn particular actions; because, upon examination, they appear to be agreeable or inconsistent with a certain general rule. The general rule, on the contrary, is formed, by finding from experience, that all actions of a certain kind, or circumstanced in a certain manner, are approved or disapproved of. To the man who first saw an inhuman murder committed from avarice, envy, or unjust resentment, and upon one too that loved and trusted the murderer, who beheld the last agonies of the dying person, who heard him, with his expiring breath, complain more of the perfidy and ingratitude of his false friend, than of the violence which had been done to him, there could be no occasion, in order to conceive how horrible such an action was, that he should reflect, that one of the most sacred rules of conduct was what prohibited the taking away the life of an innocent person, that this was a plain violation of that rule, and consequently a very blameable action. His detestation of this crime, it is evident, would arise instantaneously and antecedent to his having formed to himself any such general rule. The general rule, on the contrary, which he might afterwards form, would be founded upon the detestation which he felt necessarily arise in his own breast, at the thought of this, and every other particular action of the same kind. [pp. 216–217]

The sense of duty—the regard to the general rules of conduct that provides for the bulk of mankind the only principle by which to direct their actions—helps us resist temptation and makes us men of honor (Chapter 5). Since the moral sentiments were plainly intended to be the governing principles of human nature, the rules they prescribe are to be regarded as the commands and laws of the deity. The original purpose of the deity appears to have been the happiness of mankind, and obedience to the rules bring it about. Yet there is no exact coincidence between what nature yields and what men's sentiments would favor. Justice has its familiar special position:

[Ch 6] . . . The rules of justice may be compared to the rules of grammar; the rules of the other virtues, to the rules which critics lay down for the attainment of what is sublime and elegant in composition. The one, are precise, accurate, and indispensable. The other, are loose, vague, and indeterminate, and present us rather with a general idea of the perfection we ought to aim at, than afford us any certain and infallible directions for acquiring it. [pp. 239–240]

Part IV, "The Effect of Utility upon the Sentiment of Approbation," shows how utilitarianism fails. Nature is moderately well adjusted so that our sentiments do point to the good. They do not calculate the good, but rather fix on the beauty which such a picture of nature presents; it is more like the beauty of a machine or a well-ordered system. Smith differs from Hume,

the same ingenious and agreeable author who first explained why utility pleases. . . . But I still affirm, that it is not the view of this utility or hurtfulness which is either the first or principal source of our approbation and disapprobation. These sentiments are no doubt enhanced and enlivened by the per-

ception of the beauty or deformity which results from this utility or hurtfulness. But still, I say, they are originally and essentially different from this perception. [Ch 2, pp. 256–257]

Part VI discusses *virtue*, considering a person's character, first, as it affects his own happiness (prudence, health, security, fortune, reputation, sincerity, capacity for friendship, politeness, industry and frugality, and so on), and second, as it affects the happiness of others. Crucial to affecting the happiness of others is a disposition to help and not to hurt. The exercise of beneficence moves through circles that start with family and goes on to wider kinship, friends, and beyond. Under love of country, reverence for the constitution is distinguished from the desire to render one's fellow citizens happy. Foreign war and civil strife occasion public spirit, but in the latter case the admiration of one faction is countered by the hatred of the other. "The glory which is acquired by foreign war is, upon this account, almost always more pure and more splendid than that which can be acquired in civil faction" (Sec II, ch 2, p. 316). It is difficult to exhibit a universal benevolence; it cannot bring happiness to a person unless he is convinced of a divine providence directed at all times to the greatest quantity of happiness.

[Ch 3] The administration of the great system of the universe, however, the care of the universal happiness of all rational and sensible beings, is the business of God and not of man. To man is allotted a much humbler department, but one much more suitable to the weakness of his powers, and to the narrowness of his comprehension; the care of his own happiness, of that of his family, his friends, his country: that he is occupied in contemplating the more sublime, can never be an excuse for his neglecting the more humble department; and he must not expose himself to the charge which Avidius Cassius is said to have brought, perhaps unjustly, against Marcus Antoninus; that while he employed himself in philosophical speculations, and contemplated the prosperity of the universe, he neglected that of the Roman empire. The most sublime speculation of the contemplative philosopher can scarce compensate the neglect of the smallest active duty. [pp. 322–323]

The outcome foreshadows *The Wealth of Nations*, in which the pursuit of self-interest in a world of unrestrained international commerce is counted on to produce the same effects as would universal benevolence. Where people are free to pursue private gain without state regulation, the "invisible hand" will establish an equilibrium of natural liberty where people will produce what others want and cheaper production is encouraged for the economic advantage it bestows on the producer.

All systems either of preference or of restraint, therefore, being thus completely taken away, the obvious and simple system of natural liberty establishes itself of its own accord. Every man, as long as he does not violate the laws of justice, is left perfectly free to pursue his own interest his own way, and to bring both his industry and capital into competition with those of any other man, or order of men. The sovereign is completely discharged from a duty, in the attempting to perform which he must always be exposed to innumerable delusions, and for the proper performance of which no human wisdom or knowledge could ever be sufficient; the duty of superintending the industry of private people, and of directing it towards the employments most suitable to the interest of the society. According to the system of natural liberty, the sovereign has only three duties to attend to; three duties of great importance, indeed, but plain and intelligible to common understandings: first, the duty of protecting the society from the violence and invasion of other independent societies; secondly, the duty of protecting, as far as possible, every member of the society from the injustice or oppression of every other member of it, or the duty of establishing an exact administration of justice; and, thirdly, the duty of erecting and maintaining certain public works and certain public institutions, which it can never be for the interest of any individual, or small number of individuals, to erect and maintain; because the profit could never repay the expence to any individual or small number of individuals, though it may frequently do much more than repay it to a great society.[31]

In the language of *Moral Sentiments*, for a government to intervene further is to trespass on the business of God.

[31] Adam Smith, *An Inquiry into the Nature and Causes of The Wealth of Nations* (1776; New York: Random House, Modern Library, 1937), p. 651.

PART THREE

The Age of Revolutions

The congruence of political, industrial, technological, social, and intellectual transformations within a relatively limited time is striking enough to constitute an age of revolutions. If the American was rather more political, and the British industrial and technological, there was no mistaking the French as a social revolution. And as for the intellectual transformations, they went on everywhere, although at different paces.

In France, the conflict of social ideas was sharp. The old order, still strongly feudal, remained in power during the greater part of the eighteenth century. Critiques and trenchant visions of new ways of life—both often under censorship—were more extreme, although often disguised. The traditional acceptance of suffering as the due of man born in original sin was met with philosophies of reason and progress that would wipe the slate clean and fashion man afresh. The wit of a Voltaire (1694–1778) is biting, the primitivism of a Rousseau is sentimental, the materialism of a Holbach (1723–1789) or a Diderot (1713–1784) is outspoken and deterministic. The intellectual revolution of the French Enlightenment was thus mature by the time the political revolution broke out.

When the Revolution erupted in 1789 the pace of the collapse of the old order profoundly shocked Europe: the Bastille was stormed in July, the Declaration of the Rights of Man and of Citizens was proclaimed in August, and by October Louis XVI had been imprisoned. Even so, the Revolution initially followed a moderate course of liberal political and economic reform; it was extreme only in contrast to the order of privilege it was replacing. In this phase it inspired ideals of liberty, equality, and fraternity beyond the borders of France, and set forth the rights of man. By 1792 a second phase had begun as the French, beset by threats of invasion on behalf of the monarchy, declared a republic and entered a war that was to last twenty-three years; in the following year they executed Louis. Under the press of demands by the people of Paris to defend and deepen the Revolution, the government between 1792 and 1794 organized a citizen army, repelled invasion, and

moved outward to spread the Revolution. In the process it resorted to the
Terror, for which it is more remembered than for its broader democratic
program. It lost liberal sympathies abroad; even a figure as radical as Thomas
Paine came to be seen as conservative by contrast. The overthrow of Robespierre and the Jacobin leadership in 1794 led to a Directory dependent on
the army, and eventually to the rise of Napoleon as first consul (1799) and
as emperor (1804). The consolidation of the bourgeois revolution and the
provision of its legal, economic, and social institutions was the work of the
Napoleonic period. The energy unleashed by the Revolution and the sweep
of its reforms—from the Republic's abolition of feudalism and its declaration
that slaves of French colonies were to be citizens of France, to Napoleon's
abolition of the Holy Roman Empire and his institution of an entirely new
legal system modeled on the Roman—threatened the social order continent-
wide. Not until 1815 and Waterloo did other nations feel safe again; but
the ideas unleashed in 1789 were not to be contained.

England had had its political revolutions in the seventeenth century and
appeared more stable in the eighteenth. Its new order, although now only
a century old, was already being transmuted into almost immemorial tradition. In the last quarter of the century the industrial revolution intensified;
the effects of urbanization and of the doubling of population, and all the
disruptions of industrialism, were beginning to be felt at the same time as
its promises. The intellectual revolution, spreading from the Scottish Enlightenment and stimulated by the French, had already prepared the blueprints
of change by the time the critical fourth quarter of the century arrived. Soon
there was added a full-blown utilitarianism in Jeremy Bentham's demands
for criticism of all human institutions. On the surface the English way of
life—as dissected in Jane Austen's (1775–1817) novels—was peaceful and
comfortable. Beneath, however, a serious social crisis simmered: the Luddite
uprisings took place in 1811 and again in 1826. The government, abetted
by the war hysteria of the Napoleonic threat, undertook a repression extraordinary in English history: the suspension of habeas corpus in 1794, the ban-
ning of trade unions in 1799, the Peterloo Massacre in 1819. At first the
French Revolution met sympathy in England, particularly among the Whig-
gish reformers—proud of their own tradition of liberty and inclined to contrast
it favorably with French autocracy. As events in France became more bloody,
however, sympathies changed and demands for reform were dampened, to
take voice again when the war ended. The industrial-utilitarian interests
prospered and moved into political power with the legislative reforms of
1832.

The most systematic European philosophy of the age is that of Immanuel
Kant, whose major works are of the 1780s and 1790s. He is an Enlightenment
figure, but with a difference: he is already witnessing the culminating revolution—elsewhere. Although reflecting all the themes and aspirations of the
Enlightenment, the work of this spectator from a remote city in a not yet
unified Germany rocked all foundations. His influence was immediate and
profound.

The three philosophies to be considered in this part were catalysts of change. Vigorous doctrines of natural rights spearheaded the American and French revolutions (Chapter 11). The utilitarianism of Jeremy Bentham aspired to develop criteria for the wholesale critique of the institutions of the past and for the reconstruction of the institutions of the future (Chapter 12). Kant, in his own quiet way, revolutionized all branches of thought (Chapter 13).

In view of the usual tendency to pit Bentham against Kant, it is instructive to look for similarities between them. When theories as different as natural rights, utilitarianism, and Kantianism converge on a fundamental moral egalitarianism it is likely that we are dealing with an element in morality whose historical time is coming—even if at a snail's pace.

Such intellectual changes of revolutionary proportions do not stop with the passing of the age of revolutions. From the point of view of moral philosophy, the questions raised thereafter and the types of avenues explored have a markedly fresh tone even when they deal with old themes.

11

❧

The Struggle Over Natural Rights

In the seventeenth century natural rights, growing out of an individualism associated with the social contract, recast the traditional idea of natural law. By the last quarter of the eighteenth century, the appeal to natural rights had become the moral voice of the American and French revolutions. Although divinity is still in the background, the epistemological status of natural rights comes to the fore as the emphasis falls on their intuitive grasp. Thus in the American Declaration of Independence the rights are self-evident and unalienable; in the French Declaration of the Rights of Man and of Citizens they are natural, imprescriptible, and unalienable (and sacred).

Rousseau is the clearest bridge to the oncoming age of revolutions. Notorious in his time— a universal stimulus and a universal irritant— he was extraordinarily influential in literature, education, ethics, and politics. He countered an Age of Reason with a romantic primacy of emotions and a thesis of natural man corrupted by the growth of civilization, yet with a conviction that proper education from childhood (for girls as well as boys—but not the same) could meliorate the corruption. He has some claim to be the first forthright democratic theorist in that he propounded the sovereignty of the people on the basis of complete equality and considered the conditions under which it might find genuine expression. His concept of "the general will"—sharply distinguished from "the will of all," that is, the sum of particular interests—became a counter of political struggle in large countries, although his models were ancient Greece and Rome as well as his own Swiss cantons. Thus at the opening of an age of revolution kindled on declarations of the individual's natural rights, Rousseau sowed within that individualism the seeds of a social outlook. His theory of general will might point to a public well-being that reconciles individual and community and that might save democracy from particular and factional interests; on the other hand, it might yield a "tyranny of the majority" or (in twentieth-century terms) an "authoritarian" ideology.

In an atmosphere charged by the American and French declarations, demands for the abolition of slavery intensified. The selection from

"Othello" thus argues that slavery is inconsistent with the principles of American independence. Similarly, the declarations inspired hopes for women's equality—as is illustrated in the selection from Olympe de Gouges.

Among the philosophically inclined, the notion of natural rights met an uneasy reception, but the play of argument and counterargument in the eighteenth century develops broader options than those of the previous century (as presented by the Levellers and Locke). Richard Price, who regards moral principles of right as open to a direct rational insight (much as the Cambridge Platonists had done), preached a sermon commemorating the English Revolution of 1688 and interpreting the fundamental rights of Englishmen. It is memorable in part for stirring Edmund Burke to write *Reflections on the Revolution in France* (1790) in opposition to natural rights, especially as the grounds for revolution. In turn, Burke's *Reflections* roused Thomas Paine to answer with *Rights of Man* (1791). Mary Wollstonecraft, also a friend of Price, had earlier responded to Burke in *A Vindication of the Rights of Men* (1790), but her more notable *A Vindication of the Rights of Woman* (1792) called for an extension of rights to women. This work fully accepts Locke's association of rights and rationality, but in exploring the condition of women it shows a rare appreciation of the subtle working of social institutions and their consequences. Meanwhile, commenting on the French Declaration, Bentham calls natural rights nonsense and restricts the idea of rights to the legal context and to moral rules established on a utilitarian basis.

Jean Jacques Rousseau
(1712–1778)

Social Contract (1762) [1]

[Bk I, ch 1] Man is born free; and everywhere he is in chains. One thinks himself the master of

[1] Translated by G. D. H. Cole (London: J. M. Dent, 1913).

others, and still remains a greater slave than they. How did this change come about? I do not know. What can make it legitimate? That question I think I can answer.

[Ch 6] "The problem is to find a form of association which will defend and protect with the whole common force the person and goods of each associate, and in which each, while uniting himself with all, may still obey himself alone, and remain as free as before." This is the fundamental problem of which the *Social Contract* provides the solution.

The clauses of this contract . . . may be reduced to one—the total alienation of each associate, together with all his rights, to the whole community; for, in the first place, as each gives himself, absolutely, the conditions are the same for all; and, this being so, no one has any interest in making them burdensome to others.

Moreover, the alienation being without reserve, the union is as perfect as it can be. . . .

[E]ach man, in giving himself to all, gives himself to nobody; and as there is no associate over which he does not acquire the same right as he yields others over himself, he gains an equivalent for everything he loses, and an increase of force for the preservation of what he has.

[The social contract essentially] reduces itself to the following terms:

> Each of us puts his person and all his power in common under the supreme direction of the general will, and, in our corporate capacity, we receive each member as an indivisible part of the whole.

At once, in place of the individual personality of each contracting party, this act of association creates a moral and collective body, composed of as many members as the assembly contains voters, and receiving from this act its unity, its common identity, its life, and its will. . . .

[Ch 7] This formula shows us that the act of association comprises a mutual undertaking between the public and the individuals, and that each individual, in making a contract, as we may say, with himself, is bound in a double capacity; as a member of the Sovereign he is bound to the individuals, and as a member of the State to the Sovereign. . . .

In order then that the social compact may not be an empty formula, it tacitly includes the undertaking, which alone can give force to the rest, that whoever refuses to obey the general will shall be compelled to do so by the whole body. This means nothing less than that he will be forced to be free; for this is the condition which, by giving each citizen to his country, secures him against all personal dependence. . . .

[Ch 8] The passage from the state of nature to the civil state produces a very remarkable change in man, by substituting justice for instinct in his conduct, and giving his actions the morality they had formerly lacked. Then only, when the voice of duty takes the place of physical impulses and right of appetite, does man, who so far had considered only himself, find that he is forced to act on different principles, and to consult his reason before listening to his inclinations. Although, in this state, he deprives himself of some advantages which he got from nature, he gains in return others so great, his faculties are so stimulated and developed, his ideas so extended, his feelings so ennobled, and his whole soul so uplifted, that, did not the abuses of this new condition often degrade him below that which he left, he would be bound to bless continually the happy moment which took him from it for ever, and, instead of a stupid and unimaginative animal, made him an intelligent being and a man.

[Above all, he gains] moral liberty, which alone makes him truly master of himself; for the mere impulse of appetite is slavery, while obedience to a law which we prescribe to ourselves is liberty.

In Book II, Rousseau declares that sovereignty is inalienable and indivisible. As general will, it is infallible, but

[Bk II, ch 3] it does not follow that the deliberations of the people are always equally correct. Our will is always for our own good, but we do not always see what that is; the people is never corrupted, but it is often deceived, and on such occasions only does it seem to will what is bad.

There is often a great deal of difference between the will of all and the general will; the latter considers only the common interest, while the former takes private interest into account, and is no more than a sum of particular wills: but take away from these same wills the pluses and minuses that cancel one another, and the general will remains as the sum of the differences.

If, when the people, being furnished with adequate information, held its deliberations, the citizens had no communication one with another, the grand total of the small differences would always give the general will, and the decision would always be good. But when factions arise, and partial associations are formed at the expense of the great association, the will of each of these associations becomes general in relation to its members, while it remains particular in relation to the State: it may then be said that there are no longer as many votes as there are men, but only as many as there are associations. The differences become less numerous and give a less general result. Lastly, when one of these associations is so great as to prevail over all the rest, the result is no longer a sum of small differences, but a single difference; in this case there is no longer a general will, and the opinion which prevails is purely particular.

It is therefore essential, if the general will is to be able to express itself, that there should be no partial society within the State, and that each citizen should think only his own thoughts. . . . But if there are partial societies, it is best to have as many as possible and to prevent them from being unequal. . . . These precautions are the only ones that can guarantee that the general will shall be always enlightened, and that the people shall in no way deceive itself.

The state has absolute power over its members; they should immediately render any service it demands. But the state cannot impose fetters that are useless to the community.

[Ch 4] The undertakings which bind us to the social body are obligatory only because they are mutual; and their nature is such that in fulfilling them we cannot work for others without working for ourselves. Why is it that the general will is always in the right, and that all continually will the happiness of each one, unless it is because there is not a man who does not think of "each" as meaning him, and consider himself in voting for all? This proves that equality of rights and the idea of justice which such equality creates originate in the preference each man gives to himself, and accordingly in the very nature of man. It proves that the general will, to be really such, must be general in its object as well as its essence; that it must both come from all and apply to all; and that it loses its natural rectitude when it is directed to some particular and determinate object. . . .

. . . So long as the subjects have to submit only to conventions of this sort, they obey no one but their own will; and to ask how far the respective rights of the Sovereign and the citizens extend, is to ask up to what point the latter can enter into undertakings with themselves, each with all, and all with each.

[Ch 11] [The ends of legislation are liberty and equality]: liberty, because all particular dependence means so much force taken from the body of the State, and equality, because liberty cannot exist without it.

The social contract requires unanimity; subsequently majority votes bind.

[Bk IV, ch 2] . . . But it is asked how a man can be both free and forced to conform to wills that are not his own. How are the opponents at once free and subject to laws they have not agreed to?

I retort that the question is wrongly put. The citizen gives his consent to all the laws, including those which are passed in spite of his opposition, and even those which punish him when he dares to break any of them. The constant will of all the members of the State is the general will; by virtue of it they are citizens and free. When in the popular assembly a law is proposed, what the people is asked is not exactly whether it approves or rejects the proposal, but whether it is in conformity with the general will, which is their will. Each man, in giving his vote, states his opinion on that point; and the general will is found by counting votes. When therefore the opinion that is contrary to my own prevails, this proves neither more nor less than that I was mistaken, and that what I thought to be the general will was not so. If my particular opinion had carried the day I should have achieved the opposite of what was my will; and it is in that case that I should not have been free.

Declarations

Declaration of Independence (1776)

Preamble

. . . We hold these truths to be self-evident, that all men are created equal, that they are endowed by their Creator with certain unalienable Rights, that among these are Life, Liberty, and the pursuit of Happiness. That to secure these rights, Governments are instituted among Men, deriving their just powers from the consent of the governed, That whenever any Form of Government becomes destructive of these ends, it is the Right of the People to alter or to abolish it, and to institute a new Government, laying its foundations on such principles and organizing its powers in such form, as to them shall seem most likely to effect their Safety and Happiness.

Declaration of the Rights of Man and of Citizens (1789) [2]

The Representatives of the people of FRANCE, formed into a National Assembly, considering that ignorance, neglect, or contempt of human rights, are the sole causes of public misfortunes and corruptions of government, have resolved to set forth, in a solemn declaration, these natural, imprescriptible, and unalienable rights: that this declaration, being constantly present to the minds of the members of the body social, they may be ever kept attentive to their rights and their duties: that the acts of the legislative and executive powers of government, being capable of being every moment compared with the end of political institutions, may be more respected: and also, that the future claims of the citizens, being directed by simple and incontestible principles, may always tend to the maintenance of the constitution, and the general happiness.

For these reasons, the NATIONAL ASSEMBLY doth recognize and declare, in the presence of the Supreme Being, and with the hope of His blessing

[2] The translation is that given by Thomas Paine in *Rights of Man* (London: J. S. Jordan, 1791), pp. 110–113.

and favor, the following *sacred* rights of men and of citizens:

I. *Men are born, and always continue free, and equal in respect of their rights. Civil distinctions, therefore, can be founded only on public utility.*

II. *The end of all political associations is the preservation of the natural and imprescriptible rights of man; and these rights are liberty, property, security, and resistance of oppression.*

III. *The nation is essentially the source of all sovereignty; nor can any INDIVIDUAL, or ANY BODY OF MEN, be entitled to any authority which is not expressly derived from it.*

IV. Political Liberty consists in the power of doing whatever does not injure another. The exercise of the natural rights of every man, has no other limits than those which are necessary to secure to every *other* man the free exercise of the same rights; and these limits are determinable only by the law.

V. The law ought to prohibit only actions hurtful to society. What is not prohibited by the law, should not be hindered; nor should anyone be compelled to that which the law does not require.

VI. The law is an expression of the will of the community. All citizens have a right to concur, either personally, or by their representatives, in its formation. It should be the same to all, whether it protects or punishes; and *all being equal in its sight, are equally eligible to all honours, places, and employments, according to their different abilities, without any other distinction than that created by their virtues and talents.*

VII. No man should be accused, arrested, or held in confinement, except in cases determined by the law, and according to the forms which it has prescribed. All who promote, solicit, execute, or cause to be executed, arbitrary orders, ought to be punished; and every citizen called upon or apprehended by virtue of the law, ought immediately to obey, and renders himself culpable by resistance.

VIII. The law ought to impose no other penalties but such as are absolutely and evidently necessary: and no one ought to be punished, but in virtue of a law promulgated before the offence, and legally applied.

IX. Every man being presumed innocent till he has been convicted, whenever his detention becomes indispensable, all rigour to him, more than is necessary to secure his person, ought to be provided against by the law.

X. No man ought to be molested on account of his opinions, not even on account of his *religious* opinions, provided his avowal of them does not disturb the public order established by the law.

XI. The unrestrained communication of thoughts and opinions being one of the most precious rights of man, every citizen may speak, write, and publish freely, provided he is responsible for the abuse of this liberty in cases determined by the law.

XII. A public force being necessary to give security to the rights of men and of citizens, that force is instituted for the benefit of the community, and not for the particular benefit of the persons with whom it is entrusted.

XIII. A common contribution being necessary for the support of the public force, and for defraying the other expences of government, it ought to be divided equally among the members of the community, according to their abilities.

XIV. Every citizen has a right, either by himself or his representative, to a free voice in determining the necessity of public contributions, the appropriation of them, and their amount, mode of assessment, and duration.

XV. Every community has the right to demand of all its agents, an account of their conduct.

XVI. Every community in which a separation of powers and a security of rights is not provided for, wants a constitution.

XVII. The right to property being inviolable and sacred, no one ought to be deprived of it, except in cases of evident public necessity legally ascertained, and on condition of a previous just indemnity.

"Othello"

Essay on Negro Slavery (1788) [3]

When the united colonies revolted from Great Britain, they did it upon this principle, "that all men are by nature and of right ought to be free."—

---

[3] *American Museum.* Reprinted from *Great Documents in Black American History,* ed. George Ducas (New York: Praeger, 1970). The anonymous author was a free black from Maryland, sometimes thought to be Benjamin Banneker.

After a long, successful, and glorious struggle for liberty, during which they manifested the firmest attachment to the rights of mankind, can they so soon forget the principles that then governed their determinations? Can Americans, after the noble contempt they expressed for tyrants, meanly descend to take up the scourge? Blush, ye revolted colonies, for having apostasized from your own principles.

Slavery, in whatever point of light it is considered, is repugnant to the feelings of nature, and inconsistent with the original rights of man. It ought, therefore, to be stigmatized for being unnatural; and detested for being unjust. 'Tis an outrage to providence and an affront offered to divine Majesty, who has given to man his own peculiar image.—That the Americans, after considering the subject in this light—after making the most manly of all possible exertions in defense of liberty—after publishing to the world the principle upon which they contended, viz., "that all men are by nature and of right ought to be free," should still retain in subjection a numerous tribe of the human race merely for their own private use and emolument, is, of all things, the strongest inconsistency, the deepest reflection on our conduct, and the most abandoned apostasy that ever took place since the Almighty fiat spoke into existence this habitable world. So flagitious a violation can never escape the notice of a just Creator, whose vengeance may be now on the wing, to disseminate and hurl the arrows of destruction. . . .

The practice of stealing or bartering for human flesh is pregnant with the most glaring turpitude, and the blackest barbarity of disposition.—For can any one say that this is doing as he would be done by? Will such a practice stand the scrutiny of this great rule of moral government? Who can, without the complicated emotions of anger and impatience, suppose himself in the predicament of a slave? . . . .

Slavery unquestionably should be abolished, particularly in this country; because it is inconsistent with the declared principles of the American Revolution. The sooner, therefore, we set about it the better. . . .

Beyond rights and justice, appeal is also made to consequences:

It would not be difficult to show, were it necessary, that America would soon become a richer and more happy country provided this step was adopted. That corrosive anguish of persevering in anything improper, which now embitters the enjoyments of life, would vanish as the mist of a foggy morn doth before the rising sun. . . .

Upon no better principle do we plunder the coasts of Africa and bring away its wretched inhabitants as slaves than that by which the greater fish swallows up the lesser. . . .

In 1829, when hopes that the Declaration would lead to the abolition of slavery had been frustrated, David Walker addressed his famous *Appeal* to fellow blacks bitterly condemning the "moderate" proposals to return blacks—both free and slave—to Africa. The *Appeal* ends with a point-by-point commentary on the Preamble to the Declaration of Independence, asking, "See your declaration, Americans! Do you understand your own language?" The American Revolution had been provoked by "a long train of abuses," but "Now, Americans! I ask you candidly, was your sufferings under Great Britain one hundredth part as cruel and tyrannical as you have rendered ours under you?" [4]

Olympe de Gouges
(1748–1793)

Olympe de Gouges (Marie Gouze) was an early supporter of the French Revolution, but soon came to feel that its Declaration excluded women—although during the revolutionary period women did gain important legal reforms. She published her own declaration, modeled on the 1789 Declaration. For her opposition to the Jacobins she was guillotined.

[4] *Great Documents in Black American History,* p. 103.

Declaration of the Rights of Woman and Citizen (1790) [5]

The mothers, daughters, sisters, representatives of the nation, ask to constitute a National Assembly. Considering that ignorance, forgetfulness or contempt of the rights of women are the sole causes of public miseries, and of corruption of governments, they have resolved to set forth in a solemn declaration, the natural, unalterable and sacred rights of woman, so that this declaration, being ever present to all members of the social body, may unceasingly remind them of their rights and their duties; in order that the acts of women's power, as well as those of men, may be judged constantly against the aim of all political institutions, and thereby be more respected for it, in order that the complaints of women citizens, based henceforth on simple and indisputable principles, may always take the direction of maintaining the Constitution, good morals and the welfare of all.

In consequence, the sex superior in beauty and in courage in maternal suffering recognizes and declares, in the presence of and under the auspices of the Supreme Being, the following rights of woman and of the woman citizen:

I. Woman is born free and remains equal to man in rights. Social distinctions can be based only on common utility.

II. The aim of every political association is the preservation of the natural and imprescriptible rights of man and woman. These rights are liberty, prosperity, security and above all, resistance to oppression.

III. The source of all sovereignty resides essentially in the Nation, which is nothing but the joining together of Man and Woman; no body, no individual, can exercise authority that does not emanate expressly from it.

IV. Liberty and justice consist in giving back to others all that belongs to them; thus the only limits on the exercise of woman's natural rights are the perpetual tyranny by which man opposes her; these limits must be reformed by the laws of nature and of reason.

VI. Law must be the expression of the general will: all citizens, men and women alike, must personally or through their representatives concur in its formation; it must be the same for all; all citizens, men and women alike, being equal before it, must be equally eligible for all high offices, positions and public employments, according to their abilities, and without distinctions other than their virtues and talents.

VII. No woman can be an exception: she will be accused, apprehended and detained in cases determined by law; women, like men, will obey this rigorous rule.

X. No one ought to be disturbed for one's opinions, however fundamental they are; since a woman has the right to mount the scaffold, she must also have the right to address the House, provided her interventions do not disturb the public order as it has been established by law.

Afterword

Woman, wake up! The alarm bell of reason is making itself heard throughout the universe; recognize your rights. The powerful empire of nature is no longer beset by prejudices, fanaticism, superstition and lies. The torch of truth has dispelled all clouds of stupidity and usurpation. The enslaved man multiplied his forces but has had to resort to yours to break his chains. Once free he became unjust to his female companion. O women! women, when will you stop being blind? What advantages have you received from the Revolution? . . .

Richard Price
(1723–1791)

Richard Price was a minister, known for his mathematical studies of population and financial statistics as well as for his philosophical writing. A friend of many of the leaders of the American Revolution, he actively supported their cause. *A Review of the Principal Questions in Morals* defends moral intuition: ideas of *right* and *wrong* are simple and directly grasped, and principles of right and wrong are similarly immediate and even self-evident.

[5] Reprinted from *European Women: A Documentary History 1789–1945*, ed. Eleanor S. Riemer and John C. Font (New York: Schocken Books, 1980), pp. 63–66.

Such an approach furnishes a hospitable environment for natural rights. The defense of a natural rights theory against utilitarian attack developed its own standard move, stated clearly in the selection, of pointing to the absurdity of denying natural rights on utilitarian grounds.

A Review of the Principal Questions in Morals (1787) [6]

[Ch. VII] . . . Taking possession of an object, and disposing of it as I please, abstracted from all particular circumstances attending such conduct, is innocent; but suppose the object was before possessed by another, the fruit of whose labour it was, and who consents not to be deprived of it, and then this conduct becomes wrong; not merely upon the account of its consequences, but *immediately* wrong.—Taking to ourselves any of the means of enjoyment, when quite loose from our fellow-creatures, or not related to them in any of the ways which determine property, cannot be the same with doing this, when the contrary is true; nor is it possible to frame the same moral judgment concerning an action in these different circumstances.—That *first possession, prescription, donation, succession*, &c. should be circumstances which alter the *nature of a case*, determine right and wrong, and induce obligation, where otherwise we should have been free, is not less conceivable than that benefits received, private or publick interest, the will of certain beings, or any of the other considerations before insisted on, should have this effect. There is no other account to be given of this, than that "such is truth, such the nature of things." And this account, wherever it distinctly appears, is ultimate and satisfactory, and leaves nothing further for the mind to desire.

The limbs, the faculties, and lives of persons are *theirs*, or to be reckoned amongst their *properties*, in much the same sense and upon the same grounds with their external goods and acquisitions. The former differ from the latter, no more than the latter differ among themselves. The right to them is obtained in different ways, but is equally real and cer-

[6] First published 1758. The selection is from 3rd ed. rev. (London, 1787), pp. 264–271.

tain. And if, antecedently to society and conventions entered into for common convenience, there is no property of the latter kind, and it is naturally indifferent in what manner what we take and detain is related to another; it will be hard to shew that the same is not true of the other kind of property, or that in reality there can be any right to any thing.

Were nothing meant, when we speak of the *rights* of beings, but that it is for the general utility, that they should have the exclusive enjoyment of such and such things; then, where this is not concerned, a man has no more right to his liberty or his life, than to objects the most foreign to him; and having no property, can be no object of injurious or unjust treatment. Supposing two men to live together, without being at all connected with or known to the rest of the world; one of them could possess nothing that did not in reason lie quite open to the seizure of the other, nothing that was *his*, or that he could properly *give* away: There would be nothing wrong in the most wanton and unprovoked invasion or destruction of the enjoyments of the one by the other, supposing this in the other's power, and that in any circumstances he knew he should gain as much by it as the other would lose. What little reason then have we, upon these principles, for rejecting the opinion that a state of nature is a state of war?

These observations may be more clearly applied to independent societies of men, who are to be looked upon as in a state of nature with respect to one another, and amongst whom it is very strange (as whatever one of them can take from the other may be equally useful to both) that the notions of *property* and *injustice* should prevail almost as much as amongst private persons, if these notions are not natural, or if derived wholly from the consideration of publick good. But besides, if publick good be the sole measure and foundation of *property* and of the *rights* of beings, it would be absurd to say *innocent* beings have a right to exemption from misery, or that they may not be made in any degree miserable, if but the smallest degree of *prepollent* good can arise from it. Nay, any number of innocent beings might be placed in a state of absolute and eternal misery, provided amends is made for their misery by producing at the same time a greater number of beings in a greater degree happy. For wherein would this be worse than producing a less rather than a greater degree of good, or than producing the excess only of the happiness above the misery, without any degree of the latter? What makes the difference between communicating happiness to a *single being* in such a manner, as that it shall be only the excess of his enjoyments above his sufferings; and communicating happiness to a *system of beings* in such a manner that a *great* number of them shall be totally miserable, but a *greater* number happy? Would there be nothing in such a procedure that was not right and just; especially could we conceive the sufferings of the unhappy part to be, in any way, the occasion or means of greater happiness to the rest? Is a man, be his relations or kindnesses to another what they will, capable of receiving no injury from him by any actions not detrimental to the publick? Might a man innocently ruin any number of his fellow-creatures, provided he causes in a greater degree the good of others? Such consequences are plainly shocking to our natural sentiments; but I know not how to avoid them on the principles I am examining.—It is indeed far from easy to determine what degree of superior good would compensate the irreparable and undeserved ruin of *one* person; or what overbalance of happiness would be great enough to justify the absolute misery of one innocent being.[a] Be these things however as they will; there is at least enough in the considerations now proposed to shew that publick happiness cannot be the sole standard and measure of justice and injustice. But without having recourse to them, the decision of this question might perhaps be rested entirely on the determination any impartial person shall find himself obliged to give in the following case.—Imagine any object which cannot be divided or enjoyed in common by two persons, and which also would be of equal advantage to both: Is it not fit, setting aside all distant consequences, that the *first possessor*, or he whose skill and labour had procured it, should have the use and enjoyment of it rather than the other? The affirmative in this case is very obvious; and he who admits it, cannot think that there is no such origin of property as I have assigned.

Price's sermon "A Discourse on the Love of Our Country," delivered on November 4, 1789, to the Society for Commemorating the [1688] Revolution in Great Britain, declares the principles of the 1688 revolution as: "First; the right to liberty of conscience in religious matters. Secondly; the right to resist power when abused, And Thirdly; the right to chuse our own governors; to cashier them for misconduct; and to frame a government for ourselves." [7] He calls for a love of country that would not be as hitherto a love of domination. Offensive wars are always unlawful. The doctrines of passive obedience, nonresistance, and the divine right of kings are all equally odious. He concluded, "I have lived to see the rights of man better understood than ever; and nations panting for liberty, which seemed to have lost the idea of it." [8] The appendix to the publication of this sermon includes "The Declaration of Rights, which has been agreed to by the National Assembly of France, and sanctioned by the King, and which forms the Basis of the new Constitution of France contains such an authority for some of the sentiments in the foregoing Discourse, and holds out to the world an instruction on the subject of Civil Government of such consequence, that I cannot help inserting here the following Translation of it." [9] Price objects to the proviso in clauses X and XI that the avowal of religious beliefs and the publication of ideas should be freely permitted provided they do not provoke public disorder, for that proviso could be used by the established power against any criticism of its doctrines. He suggests an alternative formulation:

That every man has a right to profess and practise, without molestation or the loss of any civil privilege, that mode of religious faith and worship which he thinks most acceptable to his Maker; and also to

---

[a] There are some actions, says *Cicero*, so foul, that a good man would not do them to save his country. *De Officiis*, Lib. I, Chap. XLV.—He praises *Fabius*, the Roman general, for sending back to *Pyrrhus* a deserter, who had offered privately to poison him for a proper reward from the *Romans*.

[7] *A Miscellany of Tracts and Pamphlets*, ed. A. C. Ward (London: Oxford University Press, 1927), p. 466.
[8] Ibid., p. 476.
[9] Ibid., p. 480.

discuss freely by speaking, writing, and publishing all speculative points, provided he does not by any *overt* act or *direct* invasion of the rights of others, break the peace, or attempt to injure any one in his person, property, or good name.[10]

Edmund Burke
(1729–1797)

Although now remembered above all as a champion of political conservativism, Burke saw himself, and was seen by contemporaries, as a reformer. In his lengthy career as member of Parliament (1765–1794) Burke spoke on the side of reform across the full spectrum of issues then vexing Parliament.[11]

For two decades he led efforts to reform British policy in India, as carried on by the East India Company, which had become, "a state in the guise of a merchant," culminating in the (unsuccessful) impeachment for corruption of Warren Hastings, Governor General of Bengal and India. To defend Hastings's conduct, Burke argued, was to claim that "actions in Asia do not bear the same moral qualities which the same actions would bear in Europe." [12] This Burke saw as a form of "geographical morality," according to which,

the duties of men, in public and in private situations, are not to be governed by their relation to the great Governor of the Universe, or by their relation to mankind, but by climates, degrees of longitude, parallels, not of life, but of latitudes: as if, when you have crossed the equinoctial, all the virtues die, as they say some insects die when they cross the line. . . .

This geographical morality we do protest against.

. . . [We] declare that the laws of morality are the same everywhere, and that there is no action which would pass for an act of extortion, of peculation, of bribery, and of oppression in England, that is not an act of extortion, of peculation, of bribery, and oppression in Europe, Asia, Africa, and all the world over.[13]

In the continuing debates on Catholic emancipation, Burke unwaveringly spoke for extending the electoral franchise to them and for relieving them of the burdens of the penal laws. No society of genuine liberty would "doom any part of the people to a permanent slavery."

. . . It is but too true, that the love, and even the very idea, of genuine liberty is extremely rare. It is but too true that there are many whose whole scheme of freedom is made up of pride, perverseness, and insolence. They feel themselves in a state of thraldom, they imagine that their souls are cooped and cabined in, unless they have some man or some body of men dependent on their mercy. This desire of having some one below them descends to those who are the very lowest of all; and a Protestant cobbler, debased by his poverty, but exalted by his share of the ruling church, feels a pride in knowing it is by his generosity alone that the peer whose footman's instep he measures is able to keep his chaplain from a jail. This disposition is the true source of the passion which many men in very humble life have taken to the American war. *Our* subjects in America; *our* colonies; *our* dependants.[14]

Laws "proscribing the citizens by denominations and general descriptions" are fundamentally unjust:

Crimes are the acts of individuals, and not of denominations: and therefore arbitrarily to class men under general descriptions, in order to proscribe and punish them in the lump for a presumed delinquency, of which perhaps but a part, perhaps none

---

[10] Ibid., p. 484.

[11] An exception was his opposition to extending the franchise, a favorite cause of reformers. Burke argued that representation should not be numerical, but "virtual," that is, representation by interest.

[12] *Speech in Opening the Impeachment of Warren Hastings, Second Day* (February 16, 1788), *The Works of the Right Honorable Edmund Burke*, rev. ed. (Boston: Little, Brown, 1865–1866), vol. IX, p. 447.

[13] Ibid., pp. 447–448.

[14] *Speech at Bristol Previous to the Election* (September 6, 1780), *Works*, vol. II, pp. 416–417.

at all, are guilty, is indeed a compendious method, and saves a world of trouble about proof; but such a method, instead of being law, is an act of unnatural rebellion against the legal dominion of reason and justice.[15]

In economics, he took a laissez-faire (in contemporary terms, the liberal) view. Writing from retirement to Prime Minister William Pitt, he opposed proposals for government intervention to control wages and prices in order to protect laborers. Such intervention would be an attempt to overrule "the laws of commerce, which are the laws of Nature, and consequently the laws of God."[16] Wages should be left to the marketplace. "Labor is a commodity like every other, and rises or falls according to the demand,"[17] and is governed by a version of the invisible hand:

[I]n the case of the farmer and the laborer, their interests are always the same, and it is absolutely impossible that their free contracts can be onerous to either party. . . .
    It is therefore the first and fundamental interest of the laborer, that the farmer should have a full incoming profit on the product of his labor. The proposition is self-evident; and nothing but the malignity, perverseness, and ill-governed passions of mankind, and particularly the envy they bear to each other's prosperity, could prevent their seeing and acknowledging it, with thankfulness to the benign and wise Disposer of all things, who obliges men, whether they will or not, in pursuing their own selfish interests, to connect the general good with their own individual success.[18]

On relations with America, he spoke for conciliation ("prudent management") and against the use of force, "a feeble instrument, for preserving a people so numerous, so active, so growing, so spirited as this, in a profitable and

subordinate connection with us."[19] Americans, as "descendants of Englishmen," are "not only devoted to liberty, but to liberty according to English ideas and on English principles,"[20] and hence ought to be admitted "into an interest in the Constitution."[21]

In view of all this, contemporaries were surprised by Burke's passionate onslaught on the French revolutionaries in *Reflections*. Burke believed it is fundamentally mistaken to see an analogy between the natural rights claimed by the French Revolution and those upon which the British Constitution was founded (as Price had argued in his sermon). Burke had always distinguished reform, of which he approved, from revolution. A free society, he thought, is composed of fragile institutions resting on custom and tradition. Change is inevitable, but its prudent management is a delicate task. Indeed, the "one eminent criterion which above all the rest distinguishes a wise government from an administration weak and improvident" is "well to know the best time and manner of yielding what it is impossible to keep."[22]

Early reformations are amicable arrangements with a friend in power; late reformations are terms imposed upon a conquered enemy: early reformations are made in cool blood; late reformations are made under a state of inflammation. In that state of things the people behold in government nothing that is respectable. They see the abuse, and they will see nothing else. They fall into the temper of a furious populace provoked at the disorder of a house of ill-fame; they never attempt to correct or regulate; they go to work by the shortest way: they abate the nuisance, they pull down the house.[23]

---

[15] Ibid., p. 418.
[16] *Thoughts and Details on Scarcity* (1795), *Works*, vol. V, p. 157.
[17] Ibid., p. 136.
[18] Ibid., pp. 139–141.

[19] *Speech on Moving His Resolutions for Conciliation with the Colonies* (March 22, 1775), *Works*, vol. II, p. 118.
[20] Ibid., p. 120.
[21] Ibid., p. 141.
[22] *Speech on A Plan for Economical Reform* (February 11, 1780), *Works*, vol. II, pp. 278–279.
[23] Ibid., p. 280.

Revolutions, once restraints are removed, release destructive passions and end in tyranny.
This, Burke thought, is what is in prospect
for the French Revolution.

Although set in the context of current
events, Burke's *Reflections* offers a philosophy
of social process as well as a critique of the
doctrine of natural rights.

Reflections on the Revolution in France (1790) [24]

. . . Circumstances (which with some gentlemen
pass for nothing) give in reality to every political
principle its distinguishing color and discriminating
effect. The circumstances are what render every civil
and political scheme beneficial or noxious to mankind. Abstractedly speaking, government, as well
as liberty, is good. . . .

When I see the spirit of liberty in action, I see a
strong principle at work; and this, for a while, is
all I can possibly know of it. The wild gas, the fixed
air, is plainly broke loose: but we ought to suspend
our judgment until the first effervescence is a little
subsided. . . . The effect of liberty to individuals
is, that they may do what they please: we ought
to see what it will please them to do, before we
risk congratulations, which may be soon turned into
complaints. . . . [pp. 240–242]

Burke differs with Price on the interpretation
of the 1688 revolution. It aimed to restore older
laws and liberties that were being violated, not
to fabricate new forms.

The very idea of the fabrication of a new government is enough to fill us with disgust and horror.
We wished at the period of the Revolution, and
do now wish, to derive all we possess as *an inheritance from our forefathers*. . . . All the reformations
we have hitherto made have proceeded upon the
principle of reference to antiquity; and I hope, nay,
I am persuaded, that all those which possibly may
be made hereafter will be carefully formed upon
analogical precedent, authority, and example. [p.
272]

24 The selection is from *Works*, vol. III (1866).

. . . Believe me, Sir, those who attempt to level,
never equalize. In all societies consisting of various
descriptions of citizens, some description must be
uppermost. The levellers, therefore, only change
and pervert the natural order of things. . . . [p.
295]

Nothing is a due and adequate representation of
a state, that does not represent its ability, as well
as its property. But as ability is a vigorous and active
principle, and as property is sluggish, inert, and
timid, it never can be safe from the invasions of
ability, unless it be, out of all proportion, predominant in the representation. It must be represented,
too, in great masses of accumulation, or it is not
rightly protected. The characteristic essence of property, formed out of the combined principles of its
acquisition and conservation, is to be *unequal*. The
great masses, therefore, which excite envy, and
tempt rapacity, must be put out of the possibility
of danger. Then they form a natural rampart about
the lesser properties in all their gradations. . . .
[pp. 297–298]

Revolutionaries, dissatisfied with the present system of representation, are bent on destruction.

Something they must destroy, or they seem to
themselves to exist for no purpose. One set is for
destroying the civil power through the ecclesiastical;
another for demolishing the ecclesiastic through the
civil. They are aware that the worst consequences
might happen to the public in accomplishing this
double ruin of Church and State; but they are so
heated with their theories, that they give more than
hints that this ruin, with all the mischiefs that must
lead to it and attend it, and which to themselves
appear quite certain, would not be unacceptable to
them, or very remote from their wishes. . . .

It is no wonder, therefore, that, with these ideas
of everything in their Constitution and government
at home, either in Church or State, as illegitimate
and usurped, or at best as a vain mockery, they
look abroad with an eager and passionate enthusiasm. Whilst they are possessed by these notions,
it is vain to talk to them of the practice of their
ancestors, the fundamental laws of their country, the fixed form of a Constitution whose merits
are confirmed by the solid test of long experience
and an increasing public strength and national

prosperity. They despise experience as the wisdom of unlettered men; and as for the rest, they have wrought under ground a mine that will blow up, at one grand explosion, all examples of antiquity, all precedents, charters, and acts of Parliament. They have "the rights of men." Against these there can be no prescription; against these no argument [25] is binding: these admit no temperament and no compromise: anything withheld from their full demand is so much of fraud and injustice. Against these their rights of men let no government look for security in the length of its continuance, or in the justice and lenity of its administration. The objections of these speculatists, if its forms do not quadrate with their theories, are as valid against such an old and beneficent government as against the most violent tyranny or the greenest usurpation. They are always at issue with governments, not on a question of abuse, but a question of competency and a question of title. I have nothing to say to the clumsy subtilty of their political metaphysics. Let them be their amusement in the schools. . . .

Far am I from denying in theory, full as far is my heart from withholding in practice, (if I were of power to give or to withhold,) the *real* rights of men. In denying their false claims of right, I do not mean to injure those which are real, and are such as their pretended rights would totally destroy. If civil society be made for the advantage of man, all the advantages for which it is made become his right. It is an institution of beneficence; and law itself is only beneficence acting by a rule. Men have a right to live by that rule; they have a right to justice, as between their fellows, whether their fellows are in politic function or in ordinary occupation. They have a right to the fruits of their industry, and to the means of making their industry fruitful. They have a right to the acquisitions of their parents, to the nourishment and improvement of their offspring, to instruction in life and to consolation in death. Whatever each man can separately do, without trespassing upon others, he has a right to do for himself; and he has a right to a fair portion of all which society, with all its combinations of skill and force, can do in his favor. In this partnership all men have equal rights; but not to equal things. He that has but five shillings in the partnership has as good a right to it as he that has five hundred

pounds has to his larger proportion; but he has not a right to an equal dividend in the product of the joint stock. And as to the share of power, authority, and direction which each individual ought to have in the management of the state, that I must deny to be amongst the direct original rights of man in civil society; for I have in my contemplation the civil social man, and no other. It is a thing to be settled by convention.

If civil society be the offspring of convention, that convention must be its law. That convention must limit and modify all the descriptions of constitution which are formed under it. Every sort of legislative, judicial, or executory power are its creatures. They can have no being in any other state of things; and how can any man claim, under the conventions of civil society, rights which do not so much as suppose its existence,—rights which are absolutely repugnant to it? One of the first motives to civil society, and which becomes one of its fundamental rules, is, *that no man should be judge in his own cause.* By this each person has at once divested himself of the first fundamental right of uncovenanted man, that is, to judge for himself, and to assert his own cause. He abdicates all right to be his own governor. He inclusively, in a great measure, abandons the right of self-defence, the first law of Nature. Men cannot enjoy the rights of an uncivil and of a civil state together. That he may obtain justice, he gives up his right of determining what it is in points the most essential to him. That he may secure some liberty, he makes a surrender in trust of the whole of it.

Government is not made in virtue of natural rights, which may and do exist in total independence of it,—and exist in much greater clearness, and in a much greater degree of abstract perfection; but their abstract perfection is their practical defect. By having a right to everything they want everything. Government is a contrivance of human wisdom to provide for human *wants*. Men have a right that these wants should be provided for by this wisdom. Among these wants is to be reckoned the want, out of civil society, of a sufficient restraint upon their passions. Society requires not only that the passions of individuals should be subjected, but that even in the mass and body, as well as in the individuals, the inclinations of men should frequently be thwarted, their will controlled, and their passions brought into subjection. This can only be

---

[25] Some editions have "agreement."

done *by a power out of themselves*, and not, in the exercise of its function, subject to that will and to those passions which it is its office to bridle and subdue. In this sense the restraints on men, as well as their liberties, are to be reckoned among their rights. But as the liberties and the restrictions vary with times and circumstances, and admit of infinite modifications, they cannot be settled upon any abstract rule; and nothing is so foolish as to discuss them upon that principle.

The moment you abate anything from the full rights of men each to govern himself, and suffer any artificial, positive limitation upon those rights, from that moment the whole organization of government becomes a consideration of convenience. This it is which makes the constitution of a state, and the due distribution of its powers, a matter of the most delicate and complicated skill. It requires a deep knowledge of human nature and human necessities, and of the things which facilitate or obstruct the various ends which are to be pursued by the mechanism of civil institutions. The state is to have recruits to its strength and remedies to its distempers. What is the use of discussing a man's abstract right to food or medicine? The question is upon the method of procuring and administering them. In that deliberation I shall always advise to call in the aid of the farmer and the physician, rather than the professor of metaphysics.

The science of constructing a commonwealth, or renovating it, or reforming it, is, like every other experimental science, not to be taught *a priori*. Nor is it a short experience that can instruct us in that practical science; because the real effects of moral causes are not always immediate, but that which in the first instance is prejudicial may be excellent in its remoter operation, and its excellence may arise even from the ill effects it produces in the beginning. The reverse also happens; and very plausible schemes, with very pleasing commencements, have often shameful and lamentable conclusions. . . . [I]t is with infinite caution that any man ought to venture upon pulling down an edifice which has answered in any tolerable degree for ages the common purposes of society. . . . [pp. 306–312]

The pretended rights of these theorists are all extremes; and in proportion as they are metaphysically true, they are morally and politically false. The rights of men are in a sort of *middle*, incapable of definition, but not impossible to be discerned.

The rights of men in governments are their advantages; and these are often in balances between differences of good,—in compromises sometimes between good and evil, and sometimes between evil and evil. . . . [p. 313]

Burke's historical and traditional approach emphasizes compromise and experience, with a repeatedly provoking eloquence. For example, he is thankful for the "cold sluggishness of our national character" (p. 344), which keeps Englishmen in the old ways; they are not converts of Rousseau, Voltaire, or Helvetius.

. . . We know that *we* have made no discoveries, and we think that no discoveries are to be made, in morality,—nor many in the great principles of government, nor in the ideas of liberty, which were understood long before we were born. [p. 345]

You see, Sir, that in this enlightened age I am bold enough to confess that we are generally men of untaught feelings: that, instead of casting away all our old prejudices, we cherish them to a very considerable degree; and, to take more shame to ourselves, we cherish them because they are prejudices; and the longer they have lasted, and the more generally they have prevailed, the more we cherish them. We are afraid to put men to live and trade each on his own private stock of reason; because we suspect that the stock in each man is small, and that the individuals would do better to avail themselves of the general bank and capital of nations and of ages. . . . [p. 346]

An "established church, an established monarchy, an established aristocracy, and an established democracy, each in the degree it exists, and in no greater" (p. 352) are the best ways to keep appetites and passions from erupting. Existent privileges, whatever they are, are thus an asset.

Society is, indeed, a contract. Subordinate contracts for objects of mere occasional interest may be dissolved at pleasure; but the state ought not to be considered as nothing better than a partnership agreement in a trade of pepper and coffee, calico or tobacco, or some other such low concern, to be taken up for a little temporary interest, and to be dissolved by the fancy of the parties. It is to be looked on with other reverence; because it is not a partnership in things subservient only to the gross animal existence of a temporary and perishable nature. It is a partnership in all science, a partnership in all art, a partnership in every virtue and in all perfection. As the ends of such a partnership cannot be obtained in many generations, it becomes a partnership not only between those who are living, but between those who are living, those who are dead, and those who are to be born. Each contract of each particular state is but a clause in the great primeval contract of eternal society, linking the lower with the higher natures, connecting the visible and invisible world, according to a fixed compact sanctioned by the inviolable oath which holds all physical and all moral natures each in their appointed place. . . . [p. 359]

Thomas Paine
(1737–1809)

Paine came to America with letters of introduction from Franklin, whom he had met in London. He never forgot the wretchedness and evils of poverty among the working classes that he had witnessed in England. Almost a year after his arrival, he wrote *Common Sense,* the first public cry for independence; it stirred Americans toward the Declaration. His further writing was important during the war in rallying support when the war situation was desperate. After the Revolution, he returned to Europe where he wrote *Rights of Man,* to answer Burke's *Reflections.* Charged with sedition in England, he escaped to France. During the Terror there he was arrested, to be freed and honored once again after the fall of Robespierre. Unable to live under Napoleon, he returned to America where he died in obscurity.

Paine epitomized the Age of Reason and its faith that reason could remedy evils and ensure progress. He was especially concerned to protect minorities and proposed institutions such as public education, unemployment in-

surance, poor relief, and old age pensions. In advancing these he carried out hard-headed analyses of populations, conditions, and taxation. *Rights of Man* defends natural rights, as distinct from advantageous rights. It is a theory of the limits of government.

Rights of Man (1791) [26]

Hitherto we have spoken only (and that but in part) of the natural rights of man. We have now to consider the civil rights of man, and to shew how the one originates from the other. Man did not enter into society to become *worse* than he was before, nor to have fewer rights than he had before, but to have those rights better secured. His natural rights are the foundation of all his civil rights. . . .

. . . Natural rights are those which appertain to man in right of his existence. Of this kind are all the intellectual rights, or rights of the mind, and also all those rights of acting as an individual for his own comfort and happiness, which are not injurious to the natural rights of others.—Civil rights are those which appertain to man in right of his being a member of society. Every civil right has for its foundation some natural right pre-existing in the individual, but to the enjoyment of which his individual power is not, in all cases, sufficiently competent. Of this kind are all those which relate to security and protection.

From this short review, it will be easy to distinguish between that class of natural rights which man retains after entering into society, and those which he throws into the common stock as a member of society.

The natural rights which he retains, are all those in which the *power* to execute is as perfect in the individual as the right itself. Among this class, as is before mentioned, are all the intellectual rights, or rights of the mind: consequently, religion is one of those rights. The natural rights which are not retained, are all those in which, though the right is perfect in the individual, the power to execute them is defective. They answer not his purpose.

[26] *Rights of Man* was published in two parts, Part One in 1791 and Part Two in 1792. The selection is from Thomas Paine, *Rights of Man* (London: J. S. Jordan, 1971).

A man, by natural right, has a right to judge in his own cause; and so far as the right of the mind is concerned, he never surrenders it: But what availeth it him to judge, if he has not power to redress? He therefore deposits this right in the common stock of society, and takes the arm of society, of which he is a part, in preference and in addition to his own. Society *grants* him nothing. Every man is a proprietor in society, and draws on the capital as a matter of right.

From those premises, two or three certain conclusions will follow.

First, That every civil right grows out of a natural right; or, in other words, is a natural right exchanged.

Secondly, That civil power, properly considered as such, is made up of the aggregate of that class of the natural rights of man, which becomes defective in the individual in point of power, and answers not his purpose; but when collected to a focus, becomes competent to the purpose of every one.

Thirdly, That the power produced from the aggregate of natural rights, imperfect in power in the individual, cannot be applied to invade the natural rights which are retained in the individual, and in which the power to execute is as perfect as the right itself.

We have now, in a few words, traced man from a natural individual to a member of society, and shewn, or endeavored to shew, the quality of the natural rights retained, and of those which are exchanged for civil rights. Let us now apply those principles to governments.

In casting our eyes over the world, it is extremely easy to distinguish the governments which have arisen out of society, or out of the social compact, from those which have not: but to place this in a clearer light than what a single glance may afford, it will be proper to take a review of the several sources from which governments have arisen, and on which they have been founded.

They may be all comprehended under three heads.

First, Superstition.

Secondly, Power.

Thirdly, the common interests of society, and the common rights of man.

The first was a government of priestcraft, the second of conquerors, and the third of reason. [pp. 48–51]

Paine takes issue with Burke's elitism:

When I contemplate the natural dignity of man; when I feel (for Nature has not been kind enough to me to blunt my feelings) for the honour and happiness of its character, I become irritated at the attempt to govern mankind by force and fraud, as if they were all knaves and fools. . . . [pp. 51–52]

The universal right of conscience is distinguished from governmental toleration of religious beliefs. To grant freedom is presumptuous where freedom inherently belongs.

The French Constitution hath abolished or renounced *Toleration,* and *Intolerance* also, and hath established UNIVERSAL RIGHT OF CONSCIENCE.

Toleration is not the *opposite* of Intoleration, but is the *counterfeit* of it. Both are despotisms. The one assumes to itself the right of with-holding Liberty of Conscience, and the other of granting it. The one is the pope, armed with fire and faggot, and the other is the pope selling or granting indulgences. The former is church and state, and the latter is church and traffic.

But Toleration may be viewed in a much stronger light. Man worships not himself, but his Maker; and the liberty of conscience which he claims, is not for the service of himself, but of his God. In this case, therefore, we must necessarily have the associated idea of two beings; the *mortal* who renders the worship, and the IMMORTAL BEING who is worshipped. Toleration therefore, places itself not between man and man, nor between church and church, nor between one denomination of religion and another, but between God and man; between the being who worships, and the being who is worshipped; and by the same act of assumed authority by which it tolerates man to pay his worship, it presumptuously and blasphemously sets up itself to tolerate the Almighty to receive it.

Were a bill brought into any Parliament, entitled, "An ACT to tolerate or grant liberty to the Almighty to receive the worship of a Jew or a Turk," or "to prohibit the Almighty from receiving it," all men would startle, and call it blasphemy. There would be an uproar. The presumption of toleration in religious matters would then present itself unmasked: but the presumption is not the less because the name of "Man" only appears to those laws, for the associated idea of the *worshipper* and the *worshipped* cannot be separated.—Who, then, art thou, vain dust and ashes! by whatever name thou art called, whether a King, a Bishop, a Church, or a State, a Parliament, or any thing else, that obtrudest thine insignificance between the soul of man and its Maker? Mind thine own concerns. If he believes not as thou believest, it is a proof that thou believest not as he believeth, and there is no earthly power can determine between you. [pp. 74–75]

Mary Wollstonecraft
(1759–1797)

Wollstonecraft overcame poverty and prejudice to achieve fame as an author. *Thoughts on the Education of Daughters* (1786) gained her entry to a radical circle that included her publisher, Joseph Johnston, as well as Price, Paine, Joseph Priestley, William Blake, William Wordsworth, and William Godwin. After writing *A Vindication of the Rights of Woman* she emigrated to France, where she expected to live in equality and freedom. When the promise of the Revolution turned sour, she returned to England in 1795, where she married Godwin. She died of complications attendant upon the birth of a daughter, Mary, who became Shelley's wife.

Rights of Woman argues that since women are rational beings human rights extend to them too. The work is notable for an appreciation of how socialization works to make women dependent and turns them to emotion ("sensibility") rather than to reason.

A Vindication of the Rights of Woman (1792) [27]

[Ch I, The Rights and Involved Duties of Mankind Considered] In the present state of society it appears necessary to go back to first principles in search of the most simple truths, and to dispute with some prevailing prejudice every inch of ground. To clear my way, I must be allowed to ask some plain questions, and the answers will probably appear as unequivocal as the axioms on which reasoning is built; though, when entangled with various motives of action, they are formally contradicted, either by the words or conduct of men.

In what does man's pre-eminence over the brute creation consist? The answer is as clear as that a half is less than the whole; in Reason.

What acquirement exalts one being above another? Virtue; we spontaneously reply.

For what purpose were the passions implanted? That man by struggling with them might attain a degree of knowledge denied to the brutes; whispers Experience.

Consequently the perfection of our nature and capability of happiness, must be estimated by the degree of reason, virtue, and knowledge, that distinguish the individual, and direct the laws which bind society: and that from the exercise of reason, knowledge and virtue naturally flow, is equally undeniable, if mankind be viewed collectively.

The rights and duties of man thus simplified, it seems almost impertinent to attempt to illustrate truths that appear so incontrovertible. . . . [pp. 15–16]

[Ch III] . . . It is time to effect a revolution in female manners—time to restore to them their lost dignity—and make them, as a part of the human species, labour by reforming themselves to reform the world. It is time to separate unchangeable morals from local manners. . . . [pp. 92–93]

[Ch IV, Observations on the State of Degradation to Which Woman is Reduced by Various Causes] . . . The stamina [28] of immortality, if I may be allowed the phrase, is the perfectibility of human reason. . . . Reason is, consequentially, the simple power of improvement; or, more properly speaking, of discerning truth. Every individual is in this respect a world in itself. More or less may be conspicuous in one being than another; but the nature of reason must be the same in all, if it be an emanation of divinity, the tie that connects the creature with the Creator; for, can that soul be stamped with the heavenly image, that is not perfected by the exercise

[27] The selection is from Mary Wollstonecraft, *A Vindication of the Rights of Woman, with Strictures on Political and Moral Subjects* (London: J. Johnson, 1792).

[28] Other editions give "stamen."

of its own reason? Yet outwardly ornamented with elaborate care, and so adorned to delight man, . . . the soul of woman is not allowed to have this distinction, and man, ever placed between her and reason, she is always represented as only created to see through a gross medium, and to take things on trust. But dismissing these fanciful theories, and considering woman as a whole, let it be what it will, instead of a part of man, the inquiry is whether she has reason or not. If she has, which, for a moment, I will take for granted, she was not created merely to be the solace of man, and the sexual should not destroy the human character. . . . [pp. 110–112]

The power of generalizing ideas, of drawing comprehensive conclusions from individual observations, is the only acquirement, for an immortal being, that really deserves the name of knowledge. . . .

This power has not only been denied to women; but writers have insisted that it is inconsistent, with a few exceptions, with their sexual character. Let men prove this, and I shall grant that woman only exists for man. I must, however, previously remark, that the power of generalizing ideas, to any great extent, is not very common amongst men or women. But this exercise is the true cultivation of the understanding; and every thing conspires to render the cultivation of the understanding more difficult in the female than the male world. [p. 114]

The present social order systematically degrades woman under the guise of respecting her.

Pleasure is the business of woman's life, according to the present modification of society, and while it continues to be so, little can be expected from such weak beings. Inheriting, in a lineal descent from the first fair defect in nature, the sovereignty of beauty, they have, to maintain their power, resigned the natural rights, which the exercise of reason might have procured them, and chosen rather to be short-lived queens than labour to obtain the sober pleasures that arise from equality. Exalted by their inferiority (this sounds like a contradiction), they constantly demand homage as women, though experience should teach them that the men who pride themselves upon paying this arbitrary insolent respect to the sex, with the most scrupulous exact-

ness, are most inclined to tyrannize over, and despise, the very weakness they cherish. . . . [pp. 116–117]

In short, women, in general, as well as the rich of both sexes, have acquired all the follies and vices of civilization, and missed the useful fruit. It is not necessary for me always to premise, that I speak of the condition of the whole sex, leaving exceptions out of the question. Their senses are inflamed, and their understandings neglected, consequently they become the prey of their senses, delicately termed sensibility. . . . [p. 129]

And will moralists pretend to assert, that this is the condition in which one half of the human race should be encouraged to remain with listless inactivity and stupid acquiescence? . . . [p. 131]

Property distinctions damage social relations between men and women and parents and children.

[Ch IX, Of the Pernicious Effects Which Arise from the Unnatural Distinctions Established in Society] From the respect paid to property flow, as from a poisoned fountain, most of the evils and vices which render this world such a dreary scene to the contemplative mind. . . .

One class presses on another; for all are aiming to procure respect on account of their property: and property, once gained, will procure the respect due only to talents and virtue. . . .

. . . There must be more equality established in society, or morality will never gain ground, and this virtuous equality will not rest firmly even when founded on a rock, if one half of mankind be chained to its bottom by fate, for they will be continually undermining it through ignorance or pride. . . . [pp. 320–321]

[T]he most respectable women are the most oppressed. . . . How many women thus waste life away the prey of discontent, who might have practised as physicians, regulated a farm, managed a shop, and stood erect, supported by their own industry, instead of hanging their heads surcharged with the dew of sensibility that consumes the beauty to which at first it gave lustre. . . . [p. 340]

[Ch. XI, Duty to Parents] [R]espect for parents, is, generally speaking, . . . only a selfish respect for property. The father who is blindly obeyed, is obeyed from sheer weakness, or from motives that degrade the human character.

A great proportion of the misery that wanders, in hideous forms around the world, is allowed to rise from the negligence of parents; and still these are the people who are most tenacious of what they term a natural right, though it be subversive of the birth-right of man, the right of acting according to the direction of his own reason. [p. 352]

Summarizing the argument:

[Ch XIII, sec VI] Moralists have unanimously agreed, that unless virtue be nursed by liberty, it will never attain due strength—and what they say of man I extend to mankind, insisting that in all cases morals must be fixed on immutable principles; and, that the being cannot be termed rational or virtuous who obeys any authority, but that of reason.

To render women truly useful members of society, I argue that they should be led, by having their understandings cultivated on a large scale, to acquire a rational affection for their country, founded on knowledge, because it is obvious that we are little interested about what we do not understand. And to render this general knowledge of due importance, I have endeavoured to show that private duties are never properly fulfilled unless the understanding enlarges the heart; and that public virtue is only an aggregate of private. . . . [p. 445]

That women at present are by ignorance rendered foolish or vicious, is, I think, not to be disputed; and, that the most salutary effects tending to improve mankind might be expected from a REVOLUTION in female manners, appears, at least with a face of probability, to rise out of the observation. For as marriage has been termed the parent of those endearing charities which draw man from the brutal herd, the corrupting intercourse that wealth, idleness, and folly, produce between the sexes, is more universally injurious to morality than all the other vices of mankind collectively considered. . . . [p. 447]

Asserting the rights which women in common with men ought to contend for, I have not attempted to extenuate their faults; but to prove them to be the natural consequence of their education and station in society. If so, it is reasonable to suppose that they will change their character, and correct their vices and follies, when they are allowed to be free in a physical, moral, and civil sense.[a]

Let woman share the rights and she will emulate the virtues of man; for she must grow more perfect when emancipated, or justify the authority that chains such a weak being to her duty.—If the latter, it will be expedient to open a fresh trade with Russia for whips: a present which a father should always make to his son-in-law on his wedding day, that a husband may keep his whole family in order by the same means; and without any violation of justice reign, wielding this sceptre, sole master of his house, because he is the only being in it who has reason:—the divine, indefeasible earthly sovereignty breathed into man by the Master of the universe. Allowing this position, women have not any inherent rights to claim, and by the same rule, their duties vanish, for rights and duties are inseparable.

Jeremy Bentham
(1748–1832)

Although wholly supportive of the aims of the American and French revolutionaries, Bentham was provoked by the reasons they gave—the appeal to natural rights. On the American declarations of rights he wrote:

Who can help lamenting, that so rational a cause should be rested upon reasons, so much fitter to beget objections, than to remove them?

But with men who are unanimous and hearty about *measures*, nothing so weak but may pass in the character of a *reason*: nor is this the first instance in the world, where the conclusion has supported the premises, instead of the premises the conclusion.[29]

[a] I had further enlarged on the advantages which might reasonably be expected to result from an improvement in female manners, towards the general reformation of society; but it appeared to me that such reflections would more properly close the last volume. [Unfortunately that volume never appeared.]

[29] *An Introduction to the Principles of Morals and Legislation* (1789; 2nd rev. ed. London, 1823; Oxford: Clarendon Press, 1876), Chapter XVII, note 27, p. 336.

The very notion of such rights lies entirely out of his system (see Chapter 12), ruled out by the basic utilitarian thesis that the greatest happiness of the greatest number is the standard for right and good. Hence the civil, political, and legal rights that a society establishes are to be justified by an empirical appeal to consequences under the conditions of time and place, not by the clarion call of natural inherence. While he regards natural rights as nonsense, he advocates many of the freedoms they secure. His positive notion of rights is that they are *conclusions* drawn in the light of utilitarian investigation about what kinds of claims should be supported by government; they are not self-evident first premises from which moral deductions can be made. His essay "Anarchical Fallacies" responds to the French Declaration of Rights of 1789.

Anarchical Fallacies [30]

. . . In proportion to the want of happiness resulting from the want of rights, a reason exists for wishing that there were such things as rights. But reasons for wishing there were such things as rights, are not rights;—a reason for wishing that a

[30] The essay was named and published in French by Etienne Dumont as part of *Tactique des Assemblees legislative* (1816). It was first published in English in *The Works of Jeremy Bentham*, ed. John Bowring (London, 1843), vol. II. The selection is from the latter edition, p. 501.

certain right were established, is not that right—want is not supply—hunger is not bread.

That which has no existence cannot be destroyed—that which cannot be destroyed cannot require anything to preserve it from destruction. *Natural rights* is simple nonsense: natural and imprescriptible rights, rhetorical nonsense,—nonsense upon stilts. But this rhetorical nonsense ends in the old strain of mischievous nonsense: for immediately a list of these pretended natural rights is given, and those are so expressed as to present to view legal rights. And of these rights, whatever they are, there is not, it seems, any one of which any government *can*, upon any occasion whatever, abrogate the smallest particle.

So much for terrorist language. What is the language of reason and plain sense upon this same subject? That in proportion as it is *right* or *proper*, *i.e.* advantageous to the society in question, that this or that right—a right to this or that effect—should be established and maintained, in that same proportion it is *wrong* that it should be abrogated: but that as there is no *right*, which ought not be maintained so long as it is upon the whole advantageous to the society that it should be maintained, so there is no right which, when the abolition of it is advantageous to society, should not be abolished. To know whether it would be more for the advantage of society that this or that right should be maintained or abolished, the time at which the question about maintaining or abolishing is proposed, must be given, and the circumstances under which it is proposed to maintain or abolish it; the right itself must be specifically described, not jumbled with an undistinguishable heap of others, under any such vague general terms as property, liberty, and the like.

12

Jeremy Bentham

(1748–1832)

Pleasure has had a venerable career in ethics, sometimes offered as an explanatory account of how people act (psychological hedonism), and sometimes as a moral theory of how they ought to act (ethical hedonism). For the Cyrenaics and Epicureans pleasure was the goal of life, and so the good. Seneca saw it as a mark of successful desire, Augustine as a mark of consent to an occurring action. Eighteenth-century hedonism was given added vigor by material advances that offered people more pleasure in greater security. As the idea of pleasure became assimilated to that of happiness, its ethical use was explored in a number of different directions. Universal hedonism (the general happiness) was sanctioned theologically, as in the work of Richard Cumberland and William Paley (1743–1805), and given a more secular version as the objective of government in Thomas Jefferson and his associates. Some, such as Hume, discovered social utility at the basis of customary morality and justice. Bentham weaves universal hedonism and utility together and fleshes them out in a thoroughly naturalistic way. Starting with an all-encompassing egoistic hedonism—nature has placed man under two sovereign masters, pleasure and pain, that determine both what he does and what he ought to do—Bentham constructs a theory of general happiness or welfare. He distinguishes utility as a property of things and (what he is proposing) utility as the consequences for happiness of those concerned; the latter he advances as a test for moral action and a practicable standard for social policy, especially legislation. When the parties concerned are the general public, the standard becomes the general happiness or the greatest happiness of the greatest number. The term "utilitarianism" applies to this complex ethical theory that Bentham fashioned.

Utilitarianism is not utopian, nor is it to be brought about by natural laws operating through custom or an "unseen hand," but by reform based on a firm knowledge of human motivation and the operations (both actual and nominal) of institutions. Hence there is the need, which Bentham addressed, for some objective way, ideally quantitative, of calculating the pleasure-pain consequences of action.

Bentham's life spanned enormous changes: the American Revolution and the French, with its far more radical impact—in a single day it banished serfdom. Britain, a century before, had had its civil war, and was now facing an industrial revolution, marked with unrest and dislocation, and above all the advancing economic power of a middling class and their still unfulfilled press for political power. Bentham and the group that gathered around him provided the intellectual leadership for the parliamentary reforms that extended the franchise. He died just as the success of the Reform Bill of 1832 was ensured.

Bentham was educated at Westminster and Oxford, from which he graduated at the age of sixteen. From a family of attorneys and early destined for the law, he was associated with the legal profession throughout his life, although he did not practice. His early study of British law—which he regarded as brutal and inefficient, arbitrary and biased, charged with obscure language and subterfuge, and so costly that only one in ten could expect remedy—caused him to recoil from the then entrenched view of William Blackstone (1723–1780), who revered British institutions as the very embodiment of reason. Bentham's first work, *A Fragment on Government* (1776), was an attack on Blackstone's view. Rejecting appeals to mere tradition, and all "arbitrary principles," such as natural rights (see Chapter 11), he found in the "principle of utility"—that the end of legislation was the greatest happiness of people—a sounder basis for law and morality. It is somewhat uncertain where he picked up the phrase—it was in the air and had been used by Francis Hutcheson, Cesare Beccaria (1738–1794), Joseph Priestley (1733–1804), and Claude Adrien Helvetius (1715–1771). What Bentham added was "the discovery" that while this principle does not describe what people and Parliament do, it is the premise underlying all debate and justification of policy.

He set to work on a "constitutional code"

that proposed a structure for legal institutions, from constitutional law through penal and civil law, with detailed prescriptions for administration of all the departments of government down to the times for court sittings, the appropriate furniture and equipment for a courtroom, and judicial robes. It was a plan for the new order. All his works were related to this—as part of the vast project, as theoretical bases for it, as strategies for realizing it, or as critiques of opposing programs and proposals.

Radical (but not violent) thought was increasing everywhere: slavery was under attack, under the leadership of William Wilberforce (1759–1833); John Howard (1726–1790) had exposed the conditions of prisons and poorhouses. The new economics challenged traditional restraints on the marketplace, and democratic political reforms were being urged. Bentham took part in many such movements. He accepted the new economics; indeed his *Defence of Usury* (1787) went beyond Smith to apply *laissez faire* to money and to urge removal of all limits on interest.[1] He welcomed the growth of technology, trusting the future to take care of its results. An inventor, like his brother Samuel, he was impatient with bureaucratic vested interests that hindered new technologies—work that could more easily be done with a new mechanical device was a social waste. His fertile mind knew no boundaries—from chemical experiments in a homemade laboratory (to the loud dismay of his neighbors) to proposals for canals in Panama and Suez. He planned a model prison—a circular building so devised as to have light and air everywhere, and called the *panopticon* because the guards at the center could have a view of all the cells without being themselves seen—together with a detailed scheme of

---

[1] *Truth versus Ashhurst* (1823) condemns what he regarded as irrational constraints on the freedom to work and trade (reprinted in *The Works of Jeremy Bentham*, ed. John Bowring [Edinburgh: Tait, 1838–1843], Vol. V, pp. 231–237).

management.[2] Its acceptance in England was frustrated, but it influenced Holland, Cuba, Mexico, and the United States. He had hoped that reforms could be left to segments of the ruling class, such as Lord Shelburne's circle in England or, abroad, to enlightened monarchs like Catherine of Russia. But disappointed, he turned to democratic political action. He favored the French revolutionaries, who made him a French citizen in 1792; but he soured on the revolution with the Terror. In 1808 he linked his work with that of James Mill. Around them gathered a group called "philosophical radicals" for their advocacy of wholesale utilitarian reform. The *Westminster Review* was founded as its organ. The group played the role of intellectual spearhead for social reform, including more frequent elections, the elimination of "rotten boroughs," a secret ballot, and extension of the suffrage. (Bentham virtually alone supported suffrage for women.)

To provide an objective way for evaluating laws and institutions as well as personal morality, Bentham works out a calculus of happiness—the so-called *felicific calculus*. Its intent is simple: we all make choices judging the comparative value of alternatives. To make our comparisons more precise requires examining not only the dimensions in terms of which we measure a lot (or consignment) of pleasure or pain, but such conditions for application as specific and variable circumstances, intentions, likely consequences, and variable tastes or inclinations. In some respects, the twentieth century is in a better position to appreciate Bentham's efforts. For, where measurement used to be thought of as belonging exclusively to the physical sciences, modern social science has familiarized us with mathematical techniques of grading, ordering, and measuring

features of human interaction. Again, the development of utility theory has shown not only the importance of ordering values and mapping the probabilities of alternative scenarios but also the need to combine the two measures in one. And recently, the use of computers has familiarized us with the need for analytical precision in programming the variety of factors that play a part in decision making. We do not go far astray if we think of Bentham's direction as preparing moral decisions or ethical evaluations for computer programming. Indeed his correlation of increased happiness with increased wealth (within certain limits) parallels the usual political assumption that the happiness of the community is raised if income, and so the standard of living, is higher. He sometimes sees wrong action as essentially a mistake in moral arithmetic. This is not as bizarre for legislation and institution building as it may seem for individual decision making.

Serious reform requires an understanding of the uses and abuses of language. He criticizes its emotionally charged character; for example, the same motive may be described as "avarice," "frugality," "covetousness," and "industry." A neutral formulation is "pecuniary interest"; but even this, as with any noun-substantive, is an abstraction or "fiction." Bentham sometimes writes as if he opposes all fictions, vehemently condemning the fictions lawyers use to mask their procedures. But abstractions can be innocuous, and in any case, abstraction is indispensable for communication. He proposes a method of "paraphrasis," by which sentences using fictional terms are analyzed into sentences referring to particular real entities, situations, and happenings in the natural world—for example, "pecuniary interest" is paraphrased by referring to particular pleasures or desires for wealth. When Bentham speaks of "disposition" as "a kind of fictitious entity," he does not mean it is imaginary but what we might call a "construct," as when we speak of the average

[2] *Works*, vol. XI, pp. 99–100. The plan is of course wholly paternalistic, insofar as a prison system controls the whole life; but it is concerned for the physical and general well-being of the prisoners.

consumer or the gross national product. But some fictions are "fabulous," when they have no paraphrase in particular real things: "these phantastic denominations are a sort of paper currency: if we know how at any time to change them and get sterling in their room, it is well: if not we are deceived, and . . . we possess nothing but nonsense." [3]

In law particularly, fictions, when not transparent, can be malicious subterfuges. So too in ethics. Terms such as "obligation," "right," "sovereign," "community," "the social contract," and "natural law" must be paraphrased to see what they mean or whether there is a meaning at all. Thus "rights" can be paraphrased in terms of specific laws or commands, and these in turn paraphrased in terms of pain (the sanctions entailed in violation of the law). Hence legal rights are blameless falsehoods, capable of analysis, with a termination in real things. They are a sort of paper currency, acceptable if we know how to change them. No such reduction is possible for "natural rights," whose violation outside the legal context carries no consequences; they are therefore fabulous fictions. The "general welfare" also ought not to be reified; it means merely the interests of the people involved, not something in addition. Even so grand an ethical concept as "justice" is "nothing more than an imaginary instrument" to forward certain purposes of benevolence. So too, the social contract is a fiction, not a historical fact. It has its uses and abuses: it is easier to publicize breaches of contract than breaches of the greatest happiness principle; but it yields indifferently grounds justifying obedience to the sovereign and the right of revolution.

Bentham faces two difficult problems: the meaning of happiness and the transition from an egoistic to a universal hedonism. By happi-

ness Bentham means, simply, pleasure and the absence of pain, directly experienced by the individual. He was led to this largely by David Hartley's (1705–1757) psychology in which the existence and intensity of pleasures were correlated with the strength of physiological vibrations. Pleasure and pain are thus objective states, in principle capable of cardinal measurement by an impartial investigator in units (later called "utils") that allow interpersonal comparison. (Thus the 10 utils gained by one person can be compared with the 5 utils gained by another: the first is advantaged twice as much as the second.) A later economist, F. Y. Edgeworth, building on Bentham's idea, speculated in 1881 about a "hedonimeter" as a kind of political thermometer that could take readings directly.

Yet whenever Bentham approaches the question of deciding what is a person's pleasure, he insists that each individual knows his own pleasures and pains best and that no one else can decide them. In practice, then, the measurement of happiness becomes a matter of votes and individual preferences. This way of viewing it reinforces a basic individualism, in the sense that no knowledge about human beings can override an individual's preferences. This aspect of Bentham's interpretation is seen in the later development of marginalist economics in the last half of the nineteenth century. Faced with the principle of decreasing marginal utility—each additional unit of a commodity increases its utility to the individual by a decreasing amount—economists came to argue that ordinal measures of an individual's preferences are adequate for economic analysis. From actual choices consumers make between alternative commodities, Vilfredo Pareto in 1896–1897 constructed "indifference curves" that map the consumer's preferences. These ordinal measures still make interpersonal comparison difficult and leave as a central task of modern economics the derivation of a "social welfare function" by which optimal

---

[3] *The Limits of Jurisprudence Defined*, ed. Charles Warren Everett (New York: Columbia University Press, 1945), p. 57.

social choices can be derived from individual preferences.[4]

The second problem is justifying a social ethics on individualist foundations. This is a major difficulty for any social system that is to make its allocations on the basis of some function of individual satisfactions and interests. Bentham insists that the foundation must be laid in individual psychology, in the study of motives. These motives derive from the "sovereign masters," pleasure and pain, but acquire a rich social overlay woven by our associations and expectations. These reckon not only with the interests of the living but also with the consequences for future generations as well as with the reputation of the dead and even the interests of animals. Natural and social forces help the transition from individual to social happiness: a certain *fusion of human interests*, through sympathy; a *natural identity of interest* by which each person pursuing his own interest in the long run advances the common interest; and an *artificial identification of interests*, achieved by legislative sanctions.

The domain of law differs from that of private morality (or "private deontology") in that the legislator has the power to compel by punishment while the deontologist can only persuade.[5] Punishment must be immediately forthcoming, must fit the crime, and must look to the class of action (e.g., petty theft, forgery,

corruption of public office). Actions objectionable solely on the ground of taste ought not to be matters of political control. Whereas the art of legislation creates a coincidence of private interest and public good, the deontologist indicates the course of individual action most likely to lead to private happiness when such a coincidence obtains. Bentham criticizes past moralists for glorifying sacrifice; it is an impractical effort. Much more needs to be done to educate people on what leads to their own happiness:

Men must be persuaded, enlightened, taught little by little, to distinguish the different degrees of utility, and to proportion their benevolence to the extent of its object. The best model is traced by Fenelon in that sentence which paints his heart: "I prefer my family to myself, my country to my family, mankind to my country."[6]

Bentham's writings were influential in France, Spain, Russia, and the Americas. In England intellectual recognition and practical impact, though slower, reached well through the nineteenth century. To use the idea of well-being or happiness as the aim of social policy may be commonplace today, but it was revolutionary in Bentham's time. The tradition had been privilege, the privileges of the established (in England the landed) class, and this is precisely what was being challenged in the appeal to general welfare. Of course a utilitarian might defend a system of privileged inequality, as indeed the theologian William Paley did. Paley maintained, as the revolution in France was stimulating unrest in England, that it was best for all when the lord had his extensive domain, for to protect this was also to protect the peasant in his hovel. Any attack on privilege would upset all security, and all would lose. Since God wanted the happiness of his people, to know God's will required figuring out what would produce the greatest happiness.

---

[4] In the twentieth century the notion of a cardinal measure of utility was revived by a philosopher, Frank Ramsey (*The Foundations of Mathematics and Other Essays*, 1931), and by John von Neumann and Oskar Morgenstern (*Theory of Games and Economic Behavior*, 1944). They proposed a technique whereby an individual's utilities can be inferred by observing what gambles the person is willing to take. The problem of measuring utilities has ramifications beyond economics and has spread to statistical decision theory, game theory, social psychology, and political science, as well as moral philosophy.

[5] Bentham's views in Chapter XVII of *Principles* might be compared to Kant's distinction of virtue and right and to Mill's attempt to distinguish a domain of permissible public regulation from one of inviolable private decision (see Chapters 13 and 16).

[6] *The Theory of Legislation*, trans. Richard Hildreth, ed. C. K. Ogden (London: Kegan Paul, Trench, Trubner, 1931), p. 431.

Since the nineteenth century was to make a sharp contrast between liberty and equality, and the twentieth (in its argument over the welfare state) to pit liberty against security, it is illuminating to see Bentham's treatment of these tangled concepts. Security is, of course, a prime concern. Our social living runs on the reliability of expectations, on the predictability of associations built on habit and custom, on contracts, promises, and property. Even language cannot be used capriciously, but needs to have the kind of stability, of generated expectation, that provides security to communication. Bentham regards liberty as a branch of security: personal liberty as security against certain injuries that affect the person, and political liberty as security against injustice from ministers of government. Every law, by invoking penalties, cuts down on liberty, and this has to be evaluated on utilitarian grounds.

Equality is basic to Bentham's calculus of happiness. Every person is to be counted as one and no more than one. Nobody can demand more because of a greater capacity for pleasure or sensitivity to pain; there are no special privileges or benefits outside the results of the reckoning. Among the ends of civil law, however, equality is secondary to security, since attempts to equalize property upset expectations and diminish productivity. Nevertheless, the achievement of greater equality in distribution does provide greater general happiness.

Bentham's social philosophy thus has a double potential. On the one hand, he makes room for positive action by the state to advance social welfare: inheritance taxation to achieve greater equality in distribution, provision for education, care of the poor, and the reduction of privilege and its egregious polarization of wealth and poverty. On the other hand, he recognizes that there is a cost to all governmental action in the limitation of liberty, and he accepts the economic liberalism as worked out by Hume and Adam Smith. Excepting where gross disutility exists, he is committed to the view that the best way to secure general happiness is through minimal governmental intrusion. The combination of both potentials provided a basis for the liberal movements of the nineteenth century.

An Introduction to the Principles of Morals and Legislation [7]

Ch I: Of the Principle of Utility

i. Nature has placed mankind under the governance of two sovereign masters, *pain* and *pleasure*. It is for them alone to point out what we ought to do, as well as to determine what we shall do. On the one hand the standard of right and wrong, on the other the chain of causes and effects, are fastened to their throne. They govern us in all we do, in all we say, in all we think: every effort we can make to throw off our subjection, will serve but to demonstrate and confirm it. In words a man may pretend to abjure their empire: but in reality he will remain subject to it all the while. The *principle of utility* [a] recognises this subjection, and assumes it for the foundation of that system, the object of which is to rear the fabric of felicity by the hands of reason and of law. Systems which attempt to question it, deal in sounds instead of sense, in caprice instead of reason, in darkness instead of light.

But enough of metaphor and declamation: it is not by such means that moral science is to be improved.

ii. The principle of utility is the foundation of the present work: it will be proper therefore at the outset to give an explicit and determinate account

---

[7] Printed in 1780, first published London, 1789; 2nd rev. ed., London, 1823. The selection is from Jeremy Bentham, *An Introduction to the Principles of Morals and Legislation* (Oxford: Clarendon Press, 1876).

[a] To this denomination has of late been added, or substituted, the *greatest happiness* or *greatest felicity* principle: this for shortness, instead of saying at length *that principle* which states the greatest happiness of all those whose interest is in question, as being the right and proper, and only right and proper and universally desirable, end of human action: of human action in every situation, and in particular in that of a functionary or set of functionaries exercising the powers of Government. . . .

of what is meant by it. By the principle [b] of utility
is meant that principle which approves or disapproves of every action whatsoever, according to the
tendency which it appears to have to augment or
diminish the happiness of the party whose interest
is in question: or, what is the same thing in other
words, to promote or to oppose that happiness. I
say of every action whatsoever; and therefore not
only of every action of a private individual, but of
every measure of government.

iii. By utility is meant that property in any object,
whereby it tends to produce benefit, advantage,
pleasure, good, or happiness, (all this in the present
case comes to the same thing) or (what comes again
to the same thing) to prevent the happening of mischief, pain, evil, or unhappiness to the party whose
interest is considered: if that party be the community in general, then the happiness of the community: if a particular individual, then the happiness
of that individual.

iv. The interest of the community is one of the
most general expressions that can occur in the
phraseology of morals: no wonder that the meaning
of it is often lost. When it has a meaning, it is this.
The community is a fictitious *body,* composed of
the individual persons who are considered as constituting as it were its *members.* The interest of the
community then is, what?—the sum of the interests
of the several members who compose it.

v. It is in vain to talk of the interest of the community, without understanding what is the interest
of the individual.[c] A thing is said to promote the
interest, or to be *for* the interest, of an individual,
when it tends to add to the sum total of his pleasures: or, what comes to the same thing, to diminish
the sum total of his pains.

vi. An action then may be said to be conformable
to the principle of utility, or, for shortness sake,

to utility, (meaning with respect to the community
at large) when the tendency it has to augment the
happiness of the community is greater than any it
has to diminish it.

vii. A measure of government (which is but a
particular kind of action, performed by a particular
person or persons) may be said to be conformable
to or dictated by the principle of utility, when in
like manner the tendency which it has to augment
the happiness of the community is greater than any
which it has to diminish it.

viii. When an action, or in particular a measure
of government, is supposed by a man to be conformable to the principle of utility, it may be convenient, for the purposes of discourse, to imagine a
kind of law or dictate, called a law or dictate of
utility: and to speak of the action in question, as
being conformable to such law or dictate.

x. Of an action that is conformable to the principle of utility, one may always say either that it is
one that ought to be done, or at least that it is not
one that ought not to be done. One may say also,
that it is right it should be done; at least that it is
not wrong it should be done: that it is a right action;
at least that it is not a wrong action. When thus
interpreted, the words *ought,* and *right* and *wrong,*
and others of that stamp, have a meaning: when
otherwise, they have none.

xi. Has the rectitude of this principle been ever
formally contested? It should seem that it had, by
those who have not known what they have been
meaning. Is it susceptible of any direct proof? it
should seem not: for that which is used to prove
every thing else, cannot itself be proved: a chain
of proofs must have their commencement somewhere. To give such proof is as impossible as it is
needless.

xii. Not that there is or ever has been that human
creature breathing, however stupid or perverse,
who has not on many, perhaps on most occasions
of his life, deferred to it. By the natural constitution
of the human frame, on most occasions of their
lives men in general embrace this principle, without
thinking of it: if not for the ordering of their own
actions, yet for the trying of their own actions, as
well as of those of other men. There have been, at
the same time, not many, perhaps, even of the most
intelligent, who have been disposed to embrace
it purely and without reserve. There are even
few who have not taken some occasion or other to

[b] The word principle is . . . a term of very vague and
very extensive signification: it is applied to any thing
which is conceived to serve as a foundation or beginning
to any series of operations: in some cases, of physical
operations; but of mental operations in the present case.

The principle here in question may be taken for an act
of the mind; a sentiment; a sentiment of approbation; a
sentiment which, when applied to an action, approves
of its utility, as that quality of it by which the measure
of approbation or disapprobation bestowed upon it ought
to be governed.

[c] Interest is one of those words, which not having any
superior *genus,* cannot in the ordinary way be defined.

quarrel with it, either on account of their not understanding always how to apply it, or on account of some prejudice or other which they were afraid to examine into, or could not bear to part with. For such is the stuff that man is made of: in principle and in practice, in a right track and in a wrong one, the rarest of all human qualities is consistency.

xiii. When a man attempts to combat the principle of utility, it is with reasons drawn, without his being aware of it, from that very principle itself.[d] His arguments, if they prove any thing, prove not that the principle is *wrong*, but that, according to the applications he supposes to be made of it, it is *misapplied*. Is it possible for a man to move the earth? Yes; but he must first find out another earth to stand upon.

xiv. To disprove the propriety of it by arguments is impossible; but, from the causes that have been mentioned, or from some confused or partial view

[d] 'The principle of utility, (I have heard it said) is a dangerous principle: it is dangerous on certain occasions to consult it.' This is as much as to say, what? that it is not consonant to utility, to consult utility: in short, that it is *not* consulting it, to consult it.

Addition by the Author, July 1822.

Not long after the publication of the Fragment on Government, anno 1776, in which, in the character of an all-comprehensive and all-commanding principle, the principle of *utility* was brought to view, one person by whom observation to the above effect was made was *Alexander Wedderburn*, at that time Attorney or Solicitor General. . . . 'This principle (said Wedderburn) is a dangerous one.' Saying so, he said that which, to a certain extent, is strictly true: a principle, which lays down, as the only *right* and justifiable end of Government, the greatest happiness of the greatest number—how can it be denied to be a dangerous one? dangerous it unquestionably is, to every government which has for its *actual* end or object, the greatest happiness of a certain *one,* with or without the addition of some comparatively small number of others, whom it is matter of pleasure or accommodation to him to admit, each of them, to a share in the concern, on the footing of so many junior partners. *Dangerous* it therefore really was, to the interest—the sinister interest—of all those functionaries, himself included, whose interest it was, to maximize delay, vexation, and expense, in judicial and other modes of procedure, for the sake of the profit, extractible out of the expense. In a Government which had for its end in view the greatest happiness of the greatest number, Alexander Wedderburn might have been Attorney General and then Chancellor: but he would not have been Attorney General with £15,000 a year, nor Chancellor, with a peerage with a veto upon all justice, with £25,000 a year, and with 500 sinecures at his disposal, under the name of Ecclesiastical Benefices, besides *et caeteras.*

of it, a man may happen to be disposed not to relish it. Where this is the case, if he thinks the settling of his opinions on such a subject worth the trouble, let him take the following steps, and at length, perhaps, he may come to reconcile himself to it.

1. Let him settle with himself, whether he would wish to discard this principle altogether; if so, let him consider what it is that all his reasonings (in matters of politics especially) can amount to?

2. If he would, let him settle with himself, whether he would judge and act without any principle, or whether there is any other he would judge and act by?

3. If there be, let him examine and satisfy himself whether the principle he thinks he has found is really any separate intelligible principle; or whether it be not a mere principle in words, a kind of phrase, which at bottom expresses neither more nor less than the mere averment of his own unfounded sentiments; that is, what in another person he might be apt to call caprice?

4. If he is inclined to think that his own approbation or disapprobation, annexed to the idea of an act, without any regard to its consequences, is a sufficient foundation for him to judge and act upon, let him ask himself whether his sentiment is to be a standard of right and wrong, with respect to every other man, or whether every man's sentiment has the same privilege of being a standard to itself?

5. In the first case, let him ask himself whether his principle is not despotical, and hostile to all the rest of human race?

6. In the second case, whether it is not anarchial, and whether at this rate there are not as many different standards of right and wrong as there are men? and whether even to the same man, the same thing, which is right to-day, may not (without the least change in its nature) be wrong to-morrow? and whether the same thing is not right and wrong in the same place at the same time? and in either case, whether all argument is not at an end? and whether, when two men have said, 'I like this,' and 'I don't like it,' they can (upon such a principle) have any thing more to say?

7. If he should have said to himself, No: for that the sentiment which he proposes as a standard must be grounded on reflection, let him say on what particulars the reflection is to turn? if on particulars having relation to the utility of the act, then let him say whether this is not deserting his own

principle, and borrowing assistance from that very one in opposition to which he sets it up: or if not on those particulars, on what other particulars?

8. If he should be for compounding the matter, and adopting his own principle in part, and the principle of utility in part, let him say how far he will adopt it?

9. When he has settled with himself where he will stop, then let him ask himself how he justifies to himself the adopting it so far? and why he will not adopt it any farther?

10. Admitting any other principle than the principle of utility to be a right principle, a principle that is right for a man to pursue; admitting (what is not true) that the word *right* can have a meaning without reference to utility, let him say whether there is any such thing as a *motive* that a man can have to pursue the dictates of it: if there is, let him say what that motive is, and how it is to be distinguished from those which enforce the dictates of utility: if not, then lastly let him say what it is this other principle can be good for?

Ch II: Of Principles Adverse to That of Utility

Chapter II elaborates the challenges from the ascetic and the anarchic principles. Asceticism, which disparages pleasure, appears an indirect route for its very pursuit. Its advocates usually look to the pleasure of being honored for despising pleasure. Religious asceticism, fearing God's punishment for pursuing pleasure, is trying to avoid pain. In any case, to enhance pain can scarcely serve as a principle of government!

The despotic or anarchic path, the principle of *sympathy* and *antipathy*, makes arbitrary feelings the basis of judgment. This arbitrariness is at the bottom of most ethical theories that rely on intuition, conscience, common sense, alleged right reason, moral truth, and so on. Utility, on the contrary, by opening moral judgments to empirical investigation, furnishes a scientific approach.

Ch III: Of the Four Sanctions or Sources of Pain and Pleasure

Chapter III examines pleasure and pain as efficient causes or means (not as final causes or ends), that is, as sanctions attached to conduct. Sanctions take four forms: physical (pleasure-pain consequences of actions according to natural processes); political (such consequences at the hand of the law); moral (in this context defined as stemming from popular opinions or reactions to what one does); and religious (from presumed response of deity in this or afterlife).

Ch IV: Value of a Lot of Pleasure or Pain, How to Be Measured

i. Pleasures then, and the avoidance of pains, are the *ends* which the legislator has in view: it behoves him therefore to understand their *value*. Pleasures and pains are the *instruments* he has to work with: it behoves him therefore to understand their force, which is again, in other words, their value.

ii. To a person considered *by himself*, the value of a pleasure or pain considered *by itself*, will be greater or less, according to the four following circumstances.

1. Its *intensity*.
2. Its *duration*.
3. Its *certainty* or *uncertainty*.
4. Its *propinquity* or *remoteness*.

iii. These are the circumstances which are to be considered in estimating a pleasure or a pain considered each of them by itself. But when the value of any pleasure or pain is considered for the purpose of estimating the tendency of any *act* by which it is produced, there are two other circumstances to be taken into account; these are,

5. Its *fecundity*, or the chance it has of being followed by sensations of the *same* kind: that is, pleasures, if it be a pleasure: pains, if it be a pain.

6. Its *purity*, or the chance it has of *not* being followed by sensations of the *opposite* kind: that is, pains, if it be a pleasure: pleasures, if it be a pain.

These two last, however, are in strictness scarcely to be deemed properties of the pleasure or the pain itself; they are not, therefore, in strictness to be taken into the account of the value of that pleasure or that pain. They are in strictness to be deemed properties only of the act, or other event, by which such pleasure or pain has been produced; and accordingly are only to be taken into the account of the tendency of such act or such event.

iv. To a *number* of persons, with reference to each

of whom the value of a pleasure or a pain is considered, it will be greater or less, according to seven circumstances: to wit, the six preceding ones. . . .

And one other; to wit:

7. Its *extent;* that is, the number of persons to whom it *extends;* or (in other words) who are affected by it.

v. To take an exact account then of the general tendency of any act, by which the interests of a community are affected, proceed as follows. Begin with any one person of those whose interests seem most immediately to be affected by it: and take an account,

1. Of the value of each distinguishable *pleasure* which appears to be produced by it in the *first* instance.

2. Of the value of each *pain* which appears to be produced by it in the *first* instance.

3. Of the value of each pleasure which appears to be produced by it *after* the first. This constitutes the *fecundity* of the first *pleasure* and the *impurity* of the first *pain.*

4. Of the value of each *pain* which appears to be produced by it after the first. This constitutes the *fecundity* of the first *pain* and the *impurity* of the first pleasure.

5. Sum up all the values of all the *pleasures* on the one side, and those of all the pains on the other. The balance, if it be on the side of pleasure, will give the *good* tendency of the act upon the whole, with respect to the interests of that *individual* person; if on the side of pain, the *bad* tendency of it upon the whole.

6. Take an account of the *number* of persons whose interests appear to be concerned; and repeat the above process with respect to each. *Sum up* the numbers expressive of the degrees of *good* tendency, which the act has, with respect to each individual, in regard to whom the tendency of it is *good* upon the whole: do this again with respect to each individual, in regard to whom the tendency of it is *bad* upon the whole. Take the *balance;* which, if on the side of *pleasure*, will give the general *good tendency* of the act, with respect to the total number or community of individuals concerned; if on the side of pain, the general *evil tendency*, with respect to the same community.

vi. It is not to be expected that this process should be strictly pursued previously to every moral judgment, or to every legislative or judicial operation. It may, however, be always kept in view: and as

near as the process actually pursued on these occasions approaches to it, so near will such process approach to the character of an exact one.

vii. The same process is alike applicable to pleasure and pain, in whatever shape they appear: and by whatever denomination they are distinguished: to pleasure, whether it be called *good* (which is properly the cause or instrument of pleasure) or *profit* (which is distant pleasure, or the cause or instrument of distant pleasure,) or *convenience,* or *advantage, benefit, emolument, happiness,* and so forth: to pain, whether it be called *evil,* (which corresponds to *good*) or *mischief,* or *inconvenience,* or *disadvantage,* or *loss,* or *unhappiness,* and so forth.

viii. Nor is this a novel and unwarranted, any more than it is a useless theory. In all this there is nothing but what the practice of mankind, wheresoever they have a clear view of their own interest, is perfectly conformable to. An article of property, an estate in land, for instance, is valuable, on what account? On account of the pleasures of all kinds which it enables a man to produce, and what comes to the same thing the pains of all kinds which it enables him to avert. But the value of such an article of property is universally understood to rise or fall according to the length or shortness of the time which a man has in it: the certainty or uncertainty of its coming into possession: and the nearness or remoteness of the time at which, if at all, it is to come into possession. As to the *intensity* of the pleasures which a man may derive from it, this is never thought of, because it depends upon the use which each particular person may come to make of it; which cannot be estimated till the particular pleasures he may come to derive from it, or the particular pains he may come to exclude by means of it, are brought to view. For the same reason, neither does he think of the *fecundity* or *purity* of those pleasures.

Thus much for pleasure and pain, happiness and unhappiness, in *general.* We come now to consider the several particular kinds of pain and pleasure.

Ch V: Pleasures and Pains, Their Kinds

i. . . . . Pains and pleasures may be called by one general word, interesting perceptions. Interesting perceptions are either simple or complex. The simple ones are those which cannot any one of them be resolved into more: complex are those which are resolvable into divers simple ones. A complex interesting perception may accordingly be composed either, 1. Of pleasures alone: 2. Of pains alone: or, 3. Of a pleasure or pleasures, and a pain or pains together. What determines a lot of pleasure, for example, to be regarded as one complex pleasure, rather than as divers simple ones, is the nature of the exciting cause. Whatever pleasures are excited all at once by the action of the same cause, are apt to be looked upon as constituting all together but one pleasure.

The simple pleasures (ii) are the pleasures of sense, wealth, skill, amity, a good name, power, piety, benevolence, malevolence, memory, imagination, expectation, the pleasures dependent on association, and those of relief. The simple pains (iii) are the pains of privation, of the senses, of awkwardness, enmity, an ill name, of piety, benevolence, malevolence, of memory, imagination, expectation, and those dependent on association. A detailed examination of each of these concludes:

xxxii. Of the above list there are certain pleasures and pains which suppose the existence of some pleasure or pain of some other person, to which the pleasure or pain of the person in question has regard: such pleasures and pains may be termed *extra-regarding*. Others do not suppose any such thing: these may be termed *self-regarding*. The only pleasures and pains of the extra-regarding class are those of benevolence and those of malevolence: all the rest are self-regarding.

xxxiii. Of all these several sorts of pleasures and pains, there is scarce any one which is not liable, on more accounts than one, to come under the consideration of the law. Is an offence committed? it is the tendency which it has to destroy, in such or such persons, some of these pleasures, or to produce some of these pains, that constitutes the mischief of it, and the ground for punishing it. It is the prospect of some of these pleasures, or of security from some of these pains, that constitutes the motive or temptation, it is the attainment of them that constitutes the profit of the offence. Is the offender to be punished? It can be only by the production of one or more of these pains, that the punishment can be inflicted.

Ch VI: Of Circumstances Influencing Sensibility

Individuals differ greatly in their pleasure-pain reactions, and in how circumstances influence their sensibilities. These circumstances are:

vi. . . . 1. Health. 2. Strength. 3. Hardiness. 4. Bodily imperfection. 5. Quantity and quality of knowledge. 6. Strength of intellectual powers. 7. Firmness of mind. 8. Steadiness of mind. 9. Bent of inclination. 10. Moral sensibility. 11. Moral biases. 12. Religious sensibility. 13. Religious biases. 14. Sympathetic sensibility. 15. Sympathetic biases. 16. Antipathetic sensibility. 17. Antipathetic biases. 18. Insanity. 19. Habitual occupations. 20. Pecuniary circumstances. 21. Connexions in the way of sympathy. 22. Connexions in the way of antipathy. 23. Radical frame of body. 24. Radical frame of mind. 25. Sex. 26. Age. 27. Rank. 28. Education. 29. Climate. 30. Lineage. 31. Government. 32. Religious profession.

Each is considered in great detail, concluding, as usual, with a consideration of how the analysis might be used.

xliii. These circumstances, all or many of them, will need to be attended to as often as upon any occasion any account is taken of any quantity of pain or pleasure, as resulting from any cause. Has any person sustained an injury? they will need to be considered in estimating the mischief of the offence. Is satisfaction to be made to him? they will need to be attended to in adjusting the *quantum* of that satisfaction. Is the injurer to be punished? they will need to be attended to in estimating the force of the impression that will be made on him by any given punishment.

Chapters VII–XI deal with action and its circumstances (VII), intention (VIII), consciousness (IX), motive (X), and disposition (XI).

Ch VII: Of Human Actions in General

i. The business of government is to promote the happiness of the society, by punishing and rewarding. That part of its business which consists in punishing, is more particularly the subject of penal law. In proportion as an act tends to disturb that happiness, in proportion as the tendency of it is pernicious, will be the demand it creates for punishment. What happiness consists of we have already seen: enjoyment of pleasures, security from pains.

ii. The general tendency of an act is more or less pernicious, according to the sum total of its consequences: that is, according to the difference between the sum of such as are good, and the sum of such as are evil.

iii. It is to be observed, that here, as well as henceforward, wherever consequences are spoken of, such only are meant as are *material*. Of the consequences of any act, the multitude and variety must needs be infinite: but such of them only as are material are worth regarding. Now among the consequences of an act, be they what they may, such only, by one who views them in the capacity of a legislator, can be said to be material,[e] as either consist of pain or pleasure, or have an influence in the production of pain or pleasure.

Material circumstances are partly dependent on the intention.

vi. In every transaction, therefore, which is examined with a view to punishment, there are four articles to be considered: 1. The *act* itself, which is done. 2. The *circumstances* in which it is done. 3. The *intentionality* that may have accompanied it. 4. The *consciousness*, unconsciousness, or false consciousness, that may have accompanied it.

Also to be considered is the motive that gives birth to the act and the disposition it indicates.

In general, actions are of many kinds: positive and negative, external and internal, transitive (having effects beyond the agent) and intransitive, and others. A continued act is not the same as a repetition of acts (of which a habit or practice is a special case). Hence no universal answer can be given to when one act has ended and another begun: "A man is wounded in two fingers at one stroke—Is it

one wound or several? A man is beaten at 12 o'clock, and again at 8 minutes after 12—Is it one beating or several? You beat one man, and instantly in the same breath you beat another—Is this one beating or several? In any of these cases it may be *one*, perhaps, as to some purposes, and *several* as to others" (xx).

Ch VIII: Of Intentionality

xiii. It is frequent to hear men speak of a good intention, of a bad intention. . . . Strictly speaking, nothing can be said to be good or bad, but either in itself; which is the case only with pain or pleasure: or on account of its effects; which is the case only with things that are the causes or preventives of pain and pleasure. But in a figurative and less proper way of speech, a thing may also be styled good or bad, in consideration of its cause. Now the effects of an intention to do such or such an act, are the same objects which we have been speaking of under the appellation of its *consequences*: and the causes of intention are called *motives*. A man's intention then on any occasion may be styled good or bad, with reference either to the consequences of the act, or with reference to his motives. . . . But the goodness or badness of the consequences depend upon the circumstances. Now the circumstances are no objects of the intention. A man intends the act: and by his intention produces the act: but as to the circumstances, he does not intend *them*: he does not, inasmuch as they are circumstances of it, produce them. If by accident there be a few which he has been instrumental in producing, it has been by former intentions, directed to former acts, productive of those circumstances as the consequences: at the time in question he takes them as he finds them. Acts, with their consequences, are objects of the will as well as of the understanding: circumstances, as such, are objects of the understanding only. All he can do with these, as such, is to know or not to know them: in other words, to be conscious of them, or not conscious. . . .

Ch IX: Of Consciousness

xiii. In ordinary discourse, when a man does an act of which the consequences prove mischievous, it is a common thing to speak of him as having

[e] Or *of importance*.

acted with a good intention or with a bad intention.
. . . The act, though eventually it prove mischievous, is said to be done with a good intention, when it is supposed to issue from a motive which is looked upon as a good motive . . . But the nature of the consequences intended, and the nature of the motive which gave birth to the intention, are objects which, though intimately connected, are perfectly distinguishable. The intention might therefore with perfect propriety be styled a good one, whatever were the motive. It might be styled a good one, when not only the consequences of the act *prove* mischievous, but the motive which gave birth to it *was* what is called a bad one. To warrant the speaking of the intention as being a good one, it is sufficient if the consequences of the act, had they proved what to the agent they seemed likely to be, *would* have been of a beneficial nature. . . .

Ch X: Of Motives

i. [*Motives* are important because it is] an acknowledged truth that every kind of act . . . is apt to assume a different character, and be attended with different effects, according to the nature of the *motive* which gives birth to it.

iii. [A motive is] any thing whatsoever, which, by influencing the will of a sensitive being, is supposed to serve as a means of determining him to act, or voluntarily to forbear to act, upon any occasion.

"Motive" is ambiguous. Literally it refers to "any of those really existing incidents from whence the act in question is supposed to take its rise" (iv). Figuratively it refers to "a certain fictitious entity, a passion, an affection of the mind, an ideal being which upon the happening of any such incident is considered as operating upon the mind, and prompting it to take that course, towards which it is impelled by the influence of such incident" (e.g., avarice, indolence, benevolence). Literal motives may be *interior*—"the *internal* perception of any individual lot of pleasure or pain, the expectation of which is looked upon as calculated to determine you to act in such or such a manner"— or *exterior*—an external event, "the happening whereof is regarded as having a tendency to

bring about the perception of such pleasure or such pain" (v). Motives can also be either *in esse* or *in prospect*: For example, a fire breaks out in a neighbor's house; apprehensive of its reaching your house, you run from it.

vi. . . . The event of the fire's breaking out in your neighbour's house is an external motive, and that in *esse*: the idea or belief of the probability of the fire extending to your own house, that of your being burnt if you continue, and the pain you feel at the thought of such a catastrophe, are all so many internal events, but still in *esse*: the event of the fire's actually extending to your own house, and that of your being actually burnt by it, external motives in prospect: the pain you would feel at seeing your house a burning, and the pain you would feel while you yourself were burning, internal motives in prospect. . . .

ix. . . . A motive is substantially nothing more than pleasure or pain, operating in a certain manner.

x. Now, pleasure is in *itself* a good: nay, even setting aside immunity from pain, the only good: pain is in itself an evil; and, indeed, without exception, the only evil; or else the words good and evil have no meaning. And this is alike true of every sort of pain, and of every sort of pleasure. It follows, therefore, immediately and incontestibly, that *there is no such thing as any sort of motive that is in itself a bad one.*

It is common, though inaccurate, to speak of good and bad motives. If a motive is good, it is so on account of its tendency to produce pleasure or avert pain, and every motive may give birth to both pleasure and pain. Verbal difficulties arise for any analysis of motive, for the name of a motive calls forth other associations, conveying the idea of approbation or disapprobation.

xiii. . . . Now there are certain motives which, unless in a few particular cases, have scarcely any other name to be expressed by but such a word as is used only in a good sense. This is the case, for example, with the motives of piety and honour. The consequence of this is, that if, in speaking of such a motive, a man should have occasion to apply the epithet bad to any actions which he mentions as apt to result from it, he must appear to be guilty of a contradiction in terms. . . .

Similarly, *lust* and *avarice* are used only in a bad sense. *Sexual desire, curiosity, compassion,* and *piety* could in some instances be labeled *lust, prying, weakness,* and *intolerance,* although in other instances they are clearly virtuous. Names of motives can be classified into good, bad, and neutral uses, corresponding to the different kinds of pleasures and pains. For example:

xxii. To the pleasures of the moral sanction, or, as they may otherwise be called, the pleasures of a good name, corresponds a motive which, in a neutral sense, has scarcely yet obtained any adequate appellative. It may be styled, the love of reputation. It is . . . neither more nor less than the desire of ingratiating one's self with, or, as in this case we should rather say, of recommending one's self to, the world at large. In a good sense, it is termed honour, or the sense of honour. . . . In particular cases, it is styled the love of glory. In a bad sense, it is styled, in some cases, false honour; in others, pride; in others, vanity. In a sense not decidedly bad, but rather bad than otherwise, ambition. In an indifferent sense, in some cases, the love of fame: in others, the sense of shame. And, as the pleasures belonging to the moral sanction run undistinguishably into the pains derived from the same source, it may also be styled, in some cases, the fear of dishonour, the fear of disgrace, the fear of infamy, the fear of ignominy, or the fear of shame.

xxv. To the pleasures of sympathy corresponds the motive which, in a neutral sense, is termed good-will. The word sympathy may also be used on this occasion: though the sense of it seems to be rather more extensive. In a good sense, it is styled benevolence: and in certain cases, philanthropy; and, in a figurative way, brotherly love; in others, humanity; in others, charity; in others, pity and compassion; in others, mercy; in others, gratitude; in others, tenderness; in others, patriotism; in others, public spirit. Love is also employed in this as in so many other senses. In a bad sense, it has no

name applicable to it in all cases: in particular cases it is styled partiality. . . .

1. A man who has set a town on fire is apprehended and committed: out of regard or compassion for him, you help him to break prison. In this case the generality of people will probably scarcely know whether to condemn your motive or to applaud it: those who condemn your conduct, will be disposed rather to impute it to some other motive: if they style it benevolence or compassion, they will be for prefixing an epithet, and calling it false benevolence or false compassion. 2. The man is taken again, and is put upon his trial: to save him you swear falsely in his favour. People, who would not call your motive a bad one before, will perhaps call it so now. . . . 5. You find a man on the point of starving: you relieve him; and save his life. In this case your motive will by every body be accounted laudable, and it will be termed compassion, pity, charity, benevolence. Yet in all these cases the motive is the same: it is neither more nor less than the motive of good-will.

xxxiii. The only way, it should seem, in which a motive can with safety and propriety be styled good or bad, is with reference to its effects in each individual instance; and principally from the intention it gives birth to. . . .

Ch XI: Of Human Dispositions in General

Unlike motives, dispositions can be characterized as good or bad. A disposition is

i. a kind of fictitious entity, feigned for the convenience of discourse, in order to express what there is supposed to be *permanent* in a man's frame of mind, where, on such or such an occasion, he has been influenced by such or such a motive, to engage in an act, which, as it appeared to him, was of such or such a tendency.

ii. It is with disposition as with every thing else: it will be good or bad according to its effects: according to the effects it has in augmenting or diminishing the happiness of the community. . . .

iii. [Dispositions can be meritorious or mischievous, the latter when a man] is *presumed* to be more apt to engage, or form intentions of engaging, in acts which are *apparently* of a pernicious tendency, than in such as are apparently of a beneficial tendency.

iv. I say presumed: for, by the supposition, all that appears is one single action, attended with one single train of circumstances: but from that degree of consistency and uniformity which experience has shown to be observable in the different actions of the same person, the probable existence (past or future) of a number of acts of a similar nature, is naturally and justly inferred from the observation of one single one. . . .

vi. [These inferences depend on two further facts], both of them sufficiently verified by experience: The one is, that in the ordinary course of things the consequences of actions commonly turn out conformable to intentions. A man who sets up a butcher's shop, and deals in beef, when he intends to knock down an ox, commonly does knock down an ox; though by some unlucky accident he may chance to miss his blow and knock down a man. . . .

vii. The other is, that a man who entertains intentions of doing mischief at one time is apt to entertain the like intentions at another.

The disposition is inferred from the combination of the apparent tendency of the action and its motive, but an inference is not always possible. From the combination tendency good and motive self-regarding (e.g., a baker sells bread to a hungry man who pays for it), no inference is possible. From tendency bad and motive self-regarding (e.g., a man steals bread from the bakery), a mischievous disposition can be inferred. From tendency good and motive good will (e.g., a baker gives a poor man bread as a gift), a beneficent disposition may be inferred. In the fourth case, tendency bad and motive good will, the inference depends on how apparent the tendency is: (Bentham's view of the case may be compared with Kant's—see Chapter 13).

xiii. It may be thought, that a case of this sort cannot exist; and that to suppose it, is a contradiction in terms. For the act is one, which, by the supposition, the agent knows to be a mischievous one. How then can it be, that good-will, that is, the desire of doing good, could have been the motive that led him into it? To reconcile this, we must advert to the distinction between enlarged benevolence and confined. The motive that led him into it, was that of confined benevolence. Had he followed the dictates of enlarged benevolence, he would not have done what he did. Now, although he followed the dictates of that branch of benevolence, which in any single instance of its exertion is mischievous, when opposed to the other, yet, as the cases which call for the exertion of the former are, beyond comparison, more numerous than those which call for the exertion of the latter, the disposition indicated by him, in following the impulse of the former, will often be such as in a man, of the common run of men, may be allowed to be a good one upon the whole.

xiv. *Example I.* A man with a numerous family of children, on the point of starving, goes into a baker's shop, steals a loaf, divides it all among the children, reserving none of it for himself. It will be hard to infer that that man's disposition is a mischievous one upon the whole. Alter the case, give him but one child, and that hungry perhaps, but in no imminent danger of starving: and now let the man set fire to a house full of people, for the sake of stealing money out of it to buy the bread with. The disposition here indicated will hardly be looked upon as a good one.

Chapter XII directs the inquiry to mischievous acts. (This doubtless reflects Bentham's concern with punishment, which—rather than reward, although he recognizes its appropriateness—is central in the criminal law. More and more the rest of the work deals with offenses and punishment.)

Ch XII: Of the Consequences of a Mischievous Act

ii. The tendency of an act is mischievous when the consequences of it are mischievous; that is to say, either the certain consequences or the probable. The consequences, how many and whatsoever they may be, of an act, of which the tendency is mischievous, may, such of them as are mischievous, be conceived to constitute one aggregate body, which may be termed the mischief of the act.

iii. This mischief may frequently be distinguished, as it were, into two shares or parcels: the one containing what may be called the primary mischief; the other, what may be called the secondary. That share may be termed the *primary*, which is sustained by an assignable individual, or a multitude of assignable individuals. That share may be termed the *secondary*, which, taking its origin from the former, extends itself either over the whole community, or over some other multitude of unassignable individuals.

v. [Secondary mischief consists of pain or danger.] The pain which it produces is a pain of apprehension: a pain grounded on the apprehension of suffering such mischiefs or inconveniences, whatever they may be, as it is the nature of the primary mischief to produce. It may be styled, in one word, the *alarm*. The danger is the *chance*, whatever it may be, which the multitude it concerns may in consequence of the primary mischief stand exposed to, of suffering such mischiefs or inconveniencies. For danger is nothing but the chance of pain, or, what comes to the same thing, of loss of pleasure.

The remaining chapters apply the analytic apparatus of the ethical theory to the moral and legal aspects of punishment. The very idea of offense is construed in a utilitarian way: no intrinsic feature of an act makes it an offense. Offenses are made by the community in the light of the kind of conduct that is detrimental to it (XVI, ii). That there should be recognized offenses in a community is itself a judgment of moral and legal policy; that particular acts should be deemed offenses is a more specific similar judgment. Chapter XVII addresses the relationship of law to morality, their domains and their limits.

Ch XVII: Of the Limits of the Penal Branch of Jurisprudence

ii. Ethics at large may be defined, the art of directing men's actions to the production of the greatest possible quantity of happiness, on the part of those whose interest is in view.

iii. . . . Ethics, in as far as it is the art of directing a man's own actions, may be styled the *art of self-government*, or *private ethics*.

iv.   What other agents then are there, which, at the same time that they are under the influence of

man's direction, are susceptible of happiness? They are of two sorts: 1. Other human beings who are styled persons. 2. Other animals, which, on account of their interests having been neglected by the insensibility of the ancient jurists, stand degraded into the class of *things*.[f] . . .

vi. As to ethics in general, a man's happiness will depend, in the first place, upon such parts of his behaviour as none but himself are interested in; in the next place, upon such parts of it as may affect the happiness of those about him. In as far as his happiness depends upon the first-mentioned part of his behaviour, it is said to depend upon his *duty to himself*. Ethics then, in as far as it is the art of directing a man's actions in this respect, may be termed the art of discharging one's duty to one's self: and the quality which a man manifests by the discharge of this branch of duty (if duty it is to be called) is that of *prudence*. In as far as his happiness, and that of any other person or persons whose interests are considered, depends upon such parts of his behaviour as may affect the interests of those about him, it may be said to depend upon his *duty to others*; or, to use a phrase now somewhat anti-

[f] Under the Gentoo and Mahometan religions, the interests of the rest of the animal creation seem to have met with some attention. Why have they not, universally, with as much as those of human creatures, allowance made for the difference in point of sensibility? Because the laws that are have been the work of mutual fear; a sentiment which the less rational animals have not had the same means as man has of turning to account. Why *ought* they not? No reason can be given. . . . The day has been, I grieve to say in many places it is not yet past, in which the greater part of the species, under the denomination of slaves, have been treated by the law exactly upon the same footing as, in England for example, the inferior races of animals are still. The day *may* come, when the rest of the animal creation may acquire those rights which never could have been withholden from them but by the hand of tyranny. The French have already discovered that the blackness of the skin is no reason why a human being should be abandoned without redress to the caprice of a tormentor. It may come one day to be recognised, that the number of the legs, the villosity of the skin, or the termination of the *os sacrum*, are reasons equally insufficient for abandoning a sensitive being to the same fate. What else is it that should trace the insuperable line? Is it the faculty of reason, or, perhaps, the faculty of discourse? But a full-grown horse or dog is beyond comparison a more rational, as well as a more conversable animal, than an infant of a day, or a week, or even a month, old. But suppose the case were otherwise, what would it avail? the question is not, Can they *reason*? nor, Can they *talk*? but, Can they *suffer*?

quated, his *duty to his neighbour*. Ethics then, in as far as it is the art of directing a man's actions in this respect, may be termed the art of discharging one's duty to one's neighbour. Now the happiness of one's neighbour may be consulted in two ways: 1. In a negative way, by forbearing to diminish it. 2. In a positive way, by studying to increase it. A man's duty to his neighbour is accordingly partly negative and partly positive: to discharge the negative branch of it, is *probity:* to discharge the positive branch, *beneficence.*

vii. It may here be asked, How it is that upon the principle of private ethics, legislation and religion out of the question, a man's happiness depends upon such parts of his conduct as affect, immediately at least, the happiness of no one but himself: this is as much as to ask, What motives (independent of such as legislation and religion may chance to furnish) can one man have to consult the happiness of another? by what motives, or, which comes to the same thing, by what obligations, can he be bound to obey the dictates of *probity* and *beneficence*? In answer to this, it cannot but be admitted, that the only interests which a man at all times and upon all occasions is sure to find *adequate* motives for consulting, are his own. Notwithstanding this, there are no occasions in which a man has not some motives for consulting the happiness of other men. In the first place, he has, on all occasions, the purely social motive of sympathy or benevolence: in the next place, he has, on most occasions, the semi-social motives of love of amity and love of reputation. The motive of sympathy will act upon him with more or less effect, according to the *bias* of his sensibility: the two other motives, according to a variety of circumstances, principally according to the strength of his intellectual powers, the firmness and steadiness of his mind, the quantum of his moral sensibility, and the characters of the people he has to deal with.

viii. Now private ethics has happiness for its end: and legislation can have no other. . . . Thus far, then, private ethics and the art of legislation go hand in hand. The end they have, or ought to have, in view, is of the same nature. . . . Where then lies the difference? In that the acts which they ought to be conversant about, though in a great measure, are not *perfectly and throughout* the same. There is no case in which a private man ought not to direct his own conduct to the production of his own happi-

ness, and of that of his fellow-creatures: but there are cases in which the legislator ought not (in a direct way at least, and by means of punishment applied immediately to particular *individual* acts) to attempt to direct the conduct of the several other members of the community. Every act which promises to be beneficial upon the whole to the community (himself included) each individual ought to perform of himself: but it is not every such act that the legislator ought to compel him to perform. Every act which promises to be pernicious upon the whole to the community (himself included) each individual ought to abstain from of himself: but it is not every such act that the legislator ought to compel him to abstain from.

ix. Where then is the line to be drawn?—We shall not have far to seek for it. The business is to give an idea of the cases in which ethics ought, and in which legislation ought not (in a direct manner at least) to interfere. If legislation interferes in a direct manner, it must be by punishment. Now the cases in which punishment . . . ought not to be inflicted . . . are of four sorts: 1. Where punishment would be groundless. 2. Where it would be inefficacious. 3. Where it would be unprofitable. 4. Where it would be needless. Let us look over all these cases, and see whether in any of them there is room for the interference of private ethics, at the same time that there is none for the direct interference of legislation.

Neither ethics nor law applies where punishment is *groundless,* where there is no evil in the act. Punishment is *inefficacious* where there is a defect of timing (e.g., ex post facto laws) and

xi. . . . where the will could not be deterred from any act, even by the extraordinary force of artificial punishment: as in the cases of extreme infancy, insanity, and perfect intoxication: of course, therefore, it could not by such slender and precarious force as could be applied by private ethics. . . . It is evident, that in these cases, if the thunders of the law prove impotent, the whispers of simple morality can have but little influence.

Cases where punishment is *unprofitable,* when the evil of the punishment exceeds that of the offense,

xii. . . . are the cases which constitute the great field for the exclusive interference of private ethics. . . .

xiii. Punishment . . . may be unprofitable in both or either of two ways: 1. By the expense it would amount to, even supposing the application of it to be confined altogether to delinquency: 2. By the danger there may be of its involving the innocent in the fate designed only for the guilty. . . .

When the likelihood of detection is small, it must be balanced by increasing the magnitude of punishment; but the exact balance is mere guesswork. And where the "seducing motive" is strong, exemplary punishment, however harsh, is unprofitable.

It seems to be partly owing to some such considerations, that fornication, for example, or the illicit commerce between the sexes, has commonly either gone altogether unpunished, or been punished in a degree inferior to that in which, on other accounts, legislators might have been disposed to punish it.[8]

Punishment is unprofitable also when it endangers the innocent, a danger arising primarily from the difficulty of defining clearly the nature of the act to be punished. Thus legislators are reluctant to control by law such actions as rudeness, treachery, or ingratitude.

xv. For the sake of obtaining the clearer idea of the limits between the art of legislation and private ethics, it may now be time to call to mind the distinctions above established with regard to ethics in general. The degree in which private ethics stands in need of the assistance of legislation, is different in the three branches of duty above distinguished. Of the rules of moral duty, those which seem to stand least in need of the assistance of legislation are the rules of *prudence*. It can only be through some defect on the part of the understanding, if a man be ever deficient in point of duty to himself. . . . It is a standing topic of complaint, that a man knows too little of himself. Be it so: but is it so certain that the legislator must know more? . . . All he can hope to do, is to increase the efficacy of private ethics, by giving strength and direction to the influence of the moral sanction. With what chance of success, for example, would a legislator go about

---

[8] It was otherwise with homosexuality, an "offence against taste." Bentham was appalled by the severity with which convicted homosexuals were treated. It is now known that he devoted many manuscript pages to this topic, none of which he dared publish, and some of which have become available just in the twentieth century. (See Jeremy Bentham, "Offences Against Taste," in *The Theory of Legislation*, ed. C. K. Ogden, pp. 476–497, and Louis Crompton, *Byron and Greek Love* [Berkeley: University of California Press, 1985], pp. 12–62, 251–283.)

As seen in these manuscript notes, his treatment of the topic is a case study in his method. Initially his attention is drawn to the topic by the fact that since, from a utilitarian viewpoint, there is little harm to the practice, he regards its legal proscription as fundamentally arbitrary. "To destroy a man there should certainly be some better reason than mere dislike to his Taste" (Quoted in Crompton, p. 27). From 1774 to 1825 he returns repeatedly to the topic, growing more radical in his conclusions as he brings to bear his growing interest in language and the social psychology of prejudice.

In manuscripts dated 1814–1816 he attempts to explain why the topic arouses such violent emotions. In part it is a matter of language: "It is by the power of names—of signs originally arbitrary and insignificant—that imagination has in good measure been guided" (Ogden, p. 482). From words such as *unnatural* and *impure* "has flowed a mass of misery altogether beyond the reach of calculation" (Ogden, p. 482).

The truth is that by the epithet *unnatural*, when applied to any human act or thought, the only matter of which it affords any indication that can be depended upon is the existence of a sentiment of disapprobation, accompanied with passion in the breast of the person by whom it is employed. [Ogden, p. 479]

As a remedy he seeks a more neutral, scientific vocabulary, distinguishing types of sexual intercourse as *regular* and *irregular*, rather than *natural* and *unnatural*, and suggests we speak of *improlific* appetite instead of *unnatural* appetite.

But it goes beyond language. Why is it, he asks, that in England, where it is simply unthinkable that any significant minority of the population would approve of executing heretics, executing homosexuals is "considered as a public good, every idea of mercy a public injury" (Ogden, p. 492)? Englishmen abhor the Spanish *auto de fe*, where heretics are burned alive.

Yet in a subject of infinitely less importance, for a difference not in opinon, but merely in taste . . . will the same man with indefensible satisfaction behold the same punishment inflicted on a fellow-countryman in every other respect void of offense. For heresy in religion, no; but for heresy in taste, what can be more reasonable? [Ogden, p. 492]

For an explanation he turns to social psychology. In asceticism two motives combine to produce intolerance: a love

to extirpate drunkenness and fornication by dint of legal punishment? Not all the tortures which ingenuity could invent would compass it: and, before he had made any progress worth regarding, such a mass of evil would be produced by the punishment, as would exceed, a thousand-fold, the utmost possible mischief of the offence. . . . All that he can do then, against offences of this nature, with any prospect of advantage, in the way of direct legislation, is to subject them, in cases of notoriety, to a slight censure, so as thereby to cover them with a slight shade of artificial disrepute.

xviii. The rules of *probity* are those, which in point of expediency stand most in need of assistance on the part of the legislator, and in which, in point of fact, his interference has been most extensive. There are few cases in which it *would* be expedient to punish a man for hurting *himself*: but there are few cases, if any, in which it would *not* be expedient to punish a man for injuring his neighbour. With regard to that branch of probity which is opposed to offences against property, private ethics depends in a manner for its very existence upon legislation. Legislation must first determine what things are to be regarded as each man's property, before the general

rules of ethics, on this head, can have any particular application. The case is the same with regard to offences against the state. . . .

xix. As to the rules of beneficence, these, as far as concerns matters of detail, must necessarily be abandoned in great measure to the jurisdiction of private ethics. . . . The limits of the law on this head seem, however, to be capable of being extended a good deal farther than they seem ever to have been extended hitherto. In particular, in cases where the person is in danger, why should it not be made the duty of every man to save another from mischief, when it can be done without prejudicing himself, as well as to abstain from bringing it on him. . . .[8]

The *fusion of human interests*, the first mode of reconciling the utility principle with the initial psychological hedonism, is illustrated in the preceding selection by the role assigned to the social motive of sympathy. The *artificial identification of interests* is illustrated below from *Rationale of Reward*, and the *natural identity of interests* in morality is illustrated from the *Deontology*.

The Rationale of Reward [9]

Bk I, Ch IV: Of the Union of Interest with Duty, and of Self-Executing Laws

. . . .

The legislator should, say they, endeavour to unite interest with duty: this accomplished, they consider perfection as attained. But how is this union to be brought about?—what constitutes it? To create a duty and affix a punishment to the violation of it, is to unite a man's interest with his duty,

---

of reputation (for "maintaining a line of conduct such as men in general do not maintain") and a love of amity (the desire to ingratiate oneself with the Almighty). The first alone produces in the ascetic only "the determination to abstain for his own part from all such inexcusable gratifications: after producing antipathy towards the obnoxious act, there it should stop and should not proceed so far onwards as to attach upon the agent." But the love of amity requires that one recommend oneself to the Almighty,

and for recommending oneself to any person's favour no method more effectual can be found than to take and treat as his enemies all that person's enemies. When the person whose enemies are to be dealt with as our own is no more than a human being, charity may interpose and apply a bridle; but when that person is the Almighty himself, no such bridle is necessary or so much as proper and admissible. He being infinite, such ought to be our love, such consequently our hatred for his enemies, such consequently the determination by which that hatred is manifested, gratified, demonstrated.

Thus, then, we have an antipathy—an antipathy towards the person—naturally produced and wound up to the highest pitch. [Ogden, p. 481]

This is a remarkable passage for an era when the standard analysis of homosexuality was satisfied to dismiss it as unnatural. For Bentham, what needs explanation is not why people have "improlific" appetites, but a social phenomenon—labeled homophobia in the twentieth century.

[8] A woman's head-dress catches fire: water is at hand: a man, instead of assisting to quench the fire, looks on, and laughs at it. A drunken man, falling with his face downwards into a puddle, is in danger of suffocation: lifting his head a little on one side would save him: another man sees this and lets him lie. A quantity of gunpowder lies scattered about a room: a man is going into it with a lighted candle: another, knowing this, lets him go in without warning. Who is there that in any of these cases would think punishment misapplied?

[9] First printed London, 1825. The selection is from *Works*, Vol. II, p. 199.

and even to unite it more strongly than by any prospect of reward. . . .

. . . [T]he idea designed to be expressed is, the existence of such a provision in the law, as that conformity to it shall be productive of certain benefits which will cease of themselves so soon as the law ceases to be observed. . . .

This connexion between duty and interest is to a high degree attained in the case of pensions and places held during pleasure. Let us suppose, for example, that the continuance of the pension is made to depend upon the holder's paying at all times absolute obedience to the will of his superior. The pensioner ceases to give satisfaction; the pension ceases. There are none of the embarrassments and uncertainties attendant on ordinary procedure; there are no complaints of disobedience made against persons thus circumstanced. It is against the extreme efficacy of this plan, rather than against its weakness, that complaints are heard.

In some countries, by the revenue laws, and particularly in the case of the customhouse duties, it is not uncommon to allow the officers, as a reward, a portion of the goods seized by them in the act of being smuggled. This is the only mode that has appeared effectually to combat the temptations to which they are perpetually exposed. The price which it would be worth while for individuals to offer to the officers for connivance, can scarcely equal, upon an average, the advantage they derive from the performance of their duty. So far from there being any apprehension of their being remiss in its discharge, when every instance of neglect is followed by immediate punishment, the danger is, lest they should be led to exceed their duty, and the innocent should be exposed to suspicion and vexation.

The legislator should enact *laws which will execute themselves*. What is to be understood by this? Speaking with precision, no law can execute itself. In a state of insulation, a law is inoperative: to produce its desired effects, it must be supported and enforced by some other law, which, in its turn, requires for its support the assistance of other laws. It is thus that a body of laws forms a group, or rather a circle, in which each is reciprocally supported and supports. When it is said, therefore, that the law executes itself, it is not meant that it can subsist without the assistance of other laws, but that its provisions are so arranged that punishment immediately follows its violation, unaided by

any form of procedure; that to one offence, another more easily susceptible of proof, or more severely punished, is substituted.

Mr. Burke's law [10] . . . is justly entitled to be ranked under this head. The clause which forbids the ministers and treasurers to pay themselves till all other persons have been paid, possesses in effect the properties of a punishment annexed to any retardation of payments—a punishment which commences with the offence, which lasts as long as the offence, which is inflicted without need of procedure; in a word, a punishment, the imposition of which does not require the intervention of any third person.

Deontology [11]

The business of the Deontologist is to bring forth, from the obscurity in which they have been buried,

---

[10] The reference is to an idea proposed by Edmund Burke in 1780 as part of a larger program of economic reform. Responding to complaints that the government was slow in paying its employees and when funds were insufficient, preference was given to friends of the powerful, Burke moved a bill to establish "an invariable order in all payments, which will prevent partiality, which will give preference to services, not according to the importunity of the demandant, but the rank and order of their utility or their justice" ("Speech on Economical Reform" [February 11, 1780], in *The Works of the Right Honorable Edmund Burke*, rev. ed. [Boston: Little, Brown, 1865], vol II, p. 287).

Bentham commends the ingenuity of the scheme:

How would an ordinary legislator have acted? He would have enacted that every one should be paid in proportion to the receipts; and that his regulations might not be wanting in form, he would have added a direct punishment for its breach, without inquiring if it were easy to be eluded or not. Mr. Burke acted differently: he arranged the different officers in classes; he prepared a table of preference, in which the order is the inverse of the credit which they might be supposed to possess. The noble lords, with the prime minister at their head, bring up the rear, and are prohibited from touching a single shilling of their pay, till the lowest scullion has received every penny of his. [p. 198]

[11] *Deontology* was issued by John Bowring (London, 1834) and described as from the manuscripts of Jeremy Bentham. Bowring's edition took liberties, particularly with the wording. Of the four passages here, the first and fourth appear in substantially similar form in the new critical edition, ed. Amnon Goldworth (Oxford: Clarendon Press, 1983, pp. 193, 278). The other two do not appear at all.

those points of duty, in which, by the hands of nature, a man's interests have been associated with his enjoyments,—in which his own well-being has been connected, combined, and identified, with the well-being of others; to give, in a word, to the social, all the influence of the self-regarding motive. [I, p. 23]

Aristocratic moral judgments tend to the arbitrary principle, democratic to the utility principle:

. . . In misdeeds affecting *persons*, for example, the democratic sanction tolerates boxing, the trying to hurt; not duelling, trying to kill: while the aristocratic tolerates and rewards trying to kill. Of misdeeds affecting *property*, the democratic sanction gives preference to the debts due to a tradesman over those due to a gamester; the aristocratic sanction decides directly the reverse: the democratic sanction punishes swindling in all its shapes; the aristocratic rewards it in the case and situation of a man of landed and entailed estate. In the democratic scale of reprobation, the mischievous stands above the ridiculous; in the aristocratic, the ridiculous above the mischievous. The democratic refers, or is at least constantly tending, more and more, to refer every thing to the standard of utility, to the greatest-happiness principle; the aristocratical, as much, as far, and as long as possible, to the standard of taste,—constituting itself the arbiter of taste. [I, p. 91]
. . . Vice may be defined to be a miscalculation of chances: a mistake in estimating the value of pleasures and pains. It is false moral arithmetic; and there is the consolation of knowing that, by the application of a right standard, there are few moral questions which may not be resolved, with an accuracy and a certainty not far removed from mathematical demonstration. [I, p. 131]

The reconciliation of the self-regarding and the extra-regarding, and the grounding of benevolence involve a variety of processes and natural sanctions: the desire for approbation which becomes indissolubly linked with our physical wants and can hardly be detached from the idea of a personal pleasure (II, p. 37), the apprehension of resentment on the part of others, the possibility of unexpected return through appreciation of our acts, the actual pleasure of doing good to others which is strengthened by habit, the recognition of mutual dependence, and so on. The argument is even allowed to assume an acquisitive cast:

By every act of virtuous beneficence which a man exercises, he contributes to a sort of fund, a savings-bank, a depository of general good-will, out of which services of all sorts may be looked for, as about to flow from other hands into his; if not positive services, at any rate negative services; services consisting in the forbearance to vex him by annoyances with which he might otherwise have been vexed. [II, p. 260]

Growing wisdom in morality is expected to exhibit the truth that mutual doing of good expresses a natural identity of interest for human beings.

The Theory of Legislation [12]

In *Principles of the Civil Code*, Part I, utilitarian doctrine is applied to fundamental institutions and basic policies underlying practice. The four subordinate ends for civil law are subsistence, abundance, equality, and security. The last is the preeminent end, inherently forward-looking. Liberty in its various forms is a branch of security—for example, personal liberty as security against certain kinds of injury affecting the person. In case of conflict of ends, security should prevail. Men's needs are sufficiently powerful to motivate efforts for subsistence without the law; and "abundance is formed little by little by the continued opera-

---

[12] Assembled from Bentham's manuscripts by Etienne Dumont, translated into French and published as *Traites de Legislation civile et penale* (Paris, 1802). Dumont's French version was subsequently translated back into English as *The Theory of Legislation* by Richard Hildreth (London, 1840). The selection is from the 1864 edition, pp. 99, 103–104, 110–113, 132–133.

tion of the same causes which produce subsistence." (There is no point in calling abundance luxury.)

"Equality ought not to be favoured except in the cases in which it does not interfere with security; in which it does not thwart the expectations which the law itself has produced, in which it does not derange the order already established." Underlying is the view that security leads to productivity, whereas equality upsets it: equality brought about by changing an existent inequality will not last and the fear of further enforced redistribution will inhibit production. In general, a perfect equality of rights would upset all legislation, as the laws are constantly establishing inequalities—giving rights to one person imposes obligations on others. Inequality is implied in subordination, for example, of son to father. A general slogan of equality stirs the multitude.

In calculating the effect of wealth upon happiness, it matters whether the wealth has always been in the hands of the holder, is leaving his hands, or is coming into them. Several theses are set down (Chapter VI) in the calculation of happiness, the third interpretable as a statement of the diminishing marginal utility of money:

Each portion of wealth has a corresponding portion of happiness.
Of two individuals with unequal fortunes, he who has the most wealth has the most happiness.
The excess in happiness of the richer will not be so great as the excess of his wealth.
The nearer the actual proportion approaches to equality, the greater will be the total mass of happiness.

Equality is desirable where it does not interfere with security. Insurance is a movement toward equalization of losses; the state's indemnifying victims of public calamities or war is justified, indeed, indemnification of victims reduces the effect of offenses against property.

Security and property are accomplishments of law.

Ch VII: Of Security

. . . Law alone has done that which all the natural sentiments united have not the power to do. Law alone is able to create a fixed and durable possession which merits the name of property. Law alone can accustom men to bow their heads under the yoke of foresight, hard at first to bear, but afterwards light and agreeable. Nothing but law can encourage men to labours superfluous for the present, and which can be enjoyed only in the future. Economy has as many enemies as there are dissipators—men who wish to enjoy without giving themselves the trouble of producing. Labour is too painful for idleness; it is too slow for impatience. Fraud and injustice secretly conspire to appropriate its fruits. Insolence and audacity think to ravish them by open force. Thus security is assailed on every side—ever threatened, never tranquil, it exists in the midst of alarms. The legislator needs a vigilance always sustained, a power always in action, to defend it against this crowd of indefatigable enemies.

Law does not say to man, *Labour, and I will reward you;* but it says: *Labour, and I will assure to you the enjoyment of the fruits of your labour—that natural and sufficient recompense which without me you cannot preserve; I will insure it by arresting the hand which may seek to ravish it from you.* If industry creates, it is law which preserves; if at the first moment we owe all to labour, at the second moment, and at every other, we are indebted for everything to law.

To form a precise idea of the extent which ought to be given to the principle of security, we must consider that man is not like the animals, limited to the present, whether as respects suffering or enjoyment; but that he is susceptible of pains and pleasures by anticipation; and that it is not enough to secure him from actual loss, but it is necessary also to guarantee him, as far as possible, against future loss. It is necessary to prolong the idea of his security through all the perspective which his imagination is capable of measuring.

This presentiment, which has so marked an influence upon the fate of man, is called *expectation.* It is hence that we have the power of forming a general plan of conduct; it is hence that the successive instants which compose the duration of life are not like isolated and independent points, but become continuous parts of a whole. *Expectation* is a chain which unites our present existence to our future existence, and which passes beyond us to the generation which is to follow. The sensibility of man extends through all the links of this chain.

The principle of security extends to the maintenance of all these expectations; it requires that events, so far as they depend upon laws, should conform to the expectations which law itself has created.

Every attack upon this sentiment produces a distinct and special evil, which may be called a *pain of disappointment*.

It is a proof of great confusion in the ideas of lawyers, that they have never given any particular attention to a sentiment which exercises so powerful an influence upon human life. The word *expectation* is scarcely found in their vocabulary. Scarce a single argument founded upon that principle appears in their writings. They have followed it, without doubt, in many respects; but they have followed it by instinct rather than by reason. If they had known its extreme importance they would not have failed to *name* it and to mark it, instead of leaving it unnoticed in the crowd.

Ch VIII: Of Property

The better to understand the advantages of law, let us endeavour to form a clear idea of *property*. We shall see that there is no such thing as natural property, and that it is entirely the work of law.

Property is nothing but a basis of expectation; the expectation of deriving certain advantages from a thing which we are said to possess, in consequence of the relation in which we stand towards it.

There is no image, no painting, no visible trait, which can express the relation that constitutes property. It is not material, it is metaphysical; it is a mere conception of the mind.

To have a thing in our hands, to keep it, to make it, to sell it, to work it up into something else; to use it—none of these physical circumstances, nor all united, convey the idea of property. A piece of stuff which is actually in the Indies may belong to me, while the dress I wear may not. The aliment which is incorporated into my very body may belong to another, to whom I am bound to account for it.

The idea of property consists in an established expectation; in the persuasion of being able to draw such or such an advantage from the thing possessed, according to the nature of the case. Now

this expectation, this persuasion, can only be the work of law. I cannot count upon the enjoyment of that which I regard as mine, except through the promise of the law which guarantees it to me. It is law alone which permits me to forget my natural weakness. It is only through the protection of law that I am able to inclose a field, and to give myself up to its cultivation with the sure though distant hope of harvest.

But it may be asked, What is it that serves as a basis to law, upon which to begin operations, when it adopts objects which, under the name of property, it promises to protect? Have not men, in the primitive state, a *natural* expectation of enjoying certain things,—an expectation drawn from sources anterior to law?

Yes. There have been from the beginning, and there always will be, circumstances in which a man may secure himself, by his own means, in the enjoyment of certain things. But the catalogue of these cases is very limited. The savage who has killed a deer may hope to keep it for himself, so long as his cave is undiscovered; so long as he watches to defend it, and is stronger than his rivals; but that is all. How miserable and precarious is such a possession! If we suppose the least agreement among savages to respect the acquisitions of each other, we see the introduction of a principle to which no name can be given but that of law. A feeble and momentary expectation may result from time to time from circumstances purely physical; but a strong and permanent expectation can result only from law. That which, in the natural state, was an almost invisible thread, in the social state becomes a cable.

Property and law are born together, and die together. Before laws were made there was no property; take away laws, and property ceases.

As regards property, security consists in receiving no check, no shock, no derangement to the expectation founded on the laws, of enjoying such and such a portion of good. The legislator owes the greatest respect to this expectation which he has himself produced. When he does not contradict it, he does what is essential to the happiness of society; when he disturbs it, he always produces a proportionate sum of evil.

Ch IX: Answer to an Objection

But perhaps the laws of property are good for those who have property, and oppressive to those who have none. The poor man, perhaps, is more miserable than he would be without laws.

The laws, in creating property, have created riches only in relation to poverty. Poverty is not the work of the laws; it is the primitive condition of the human race. The man who subsists only from day to day is precisely the man of nature—the savage. The poor man, in civilized society, obtains nothing, I admit, except by painful labour; but, in the natural state, can he obtain anything except by the sweat of his brow? . . .

Where security and equality are opposed, the former should prevail. Yet means should be found to reconcile them; for example, the law can intervene though regulating testamentary power—presumably through death duties—to prevent excessive individual accumulation of wealth. Similarly, slavery can be slowly disposed of.[13] On the other hand, some forms of security have to be sacrificed for other forms of security—e.g., taxation for defense (Chapters X–XIII). Chapter XIV deals with providing for the indigent.

Ch XIV: Of Some Cases Liable to Be Contested

[W]e may lay it down as a general principle that the legislator ought to establish a regular contribution for the wants of indigence, it being understood that those only are to be regarded as indigent who are in want of what is absolutely necessary. From this definition of the indigent, it follows that their title as indigent is stronger than the title of the proprietor of superfluities as proprietor. For the pain of death, which would presently fall upon the starving poor, would be always a more serious evil than the pain of disappointment which falls upon the rich when a portion of his superfluity is taken from him.[a]

In the amount of the legal contribution we ought not to go beyond what is simply necessary. To go beyond that would be taxing industry for the support of idleness. Those establishments which fur-

nish more than is absolutely necessary are not good, except so far as they are supported at the expense of individuals, for individuals can make a discrimination in the distribution of these aids, and apply them to specific classes.

Public support for the arts and sciences is permissible: the sums involved are relatively small, and the addition to general levies sufficiently imperceptible to avoid alarm.

In one field after another traditional rules are examined in terms of their consequences for happiness, for example, incest rules: some of them serve useful purposes in preserving intrafamilial harmony and in protecting females from the stronger males (Part II, Chapter V). There are good reasons to allow divorce and to adjust the law to avoid possible consequent evils.

Principles of International Law [14]

The first essay presents a general perspective on how to reconcile national and international interests. The fourth offers a plan for universal and perpetual peace. Addressed in large part to England and France, as leading powers, it seeks to prove that they will gain by free trade, freeing their colonies, and limiting their armed forces. It proposes a common judicial court and a Congress of nations. Compliance is to be achieved primarily through publicity (just as publicity in national politics diminishes the influence of "sinister interests" and "inspection" encourages good behavior on the part of prisoners in the panopticon).

Essay I: Objects of International Law

If a citizen of the world had to prepare an universal international code, what would he propose to himself as his object? It would be the common and equal utility of all nations: this would be his inclination and his duty. Would or would not the duty

---

[13] Slave ownership was abolished in the British Empire in 1834, gradually, and with compensation to the owners.
[a] When this tax is put upon a regular footing, and each proprietor knows beforehand what he must contribute, the pain of disappointment vanishes, and gives place to another, different in its nature, and less in degree.

[14] From *Works*, Vol. II, pp. 537–538 (Essay I) and 546–547, 552, 554–555 (Essay IV).

of a particular legislator, acting for one particular nation, be the same with that of the citizen of the world? That moderation, which would be a virtue in an individual acting for his own interests, would it become a vice, or treason, in a public man commissioned by a whole nation? Would it be sufficient for him to pursue in a strict or generous manner their interests as he would pursue his own?—or would it be proper, that he should pursue their interests as he would pursue his own, or ought he so to regulate his course in this respect as they would regulate theirs, were it possible for them to act with a full knowledge of all circumstances? And in this latter case, would the course he would pursue be unjust or equitable? What ought to be required of him in this respect?

Whatever he may think upon these questions—how small soever may be the regard which it may be wished that he should have for the common utility, it will not be the less necessary for him to understand it. This will be necessary for him on two accounts: In the first place, that he may follow this object in so far as his particular object is comprised in it;—secondly, that he may frame according to it, the expectations that he ought to entertain, the demands he ought to make upon other nations. For, in conclusion, the line of common utility once drawn, this would be the direction towards which the conduct of all nations would tend—in which their common efforts would find least resistance—in which they would operate with the greatest force—and in which the equilibrium once established, would be maintained with the least difficulty. . . .

But ought the sovereign of a state to sacrifice the interests of his subjects for the advantage of foreigners? Why not?—provided it be in a case, if there be such an one, in which it would have been praiseworthy in his subjects to make the sacrifice themselves.

Probity itself, so praiseworthy in an individual, why should it not be so in a whole nation? Praiseworthy in each one, how can it be otherwise in all? . . .

The end of the conduct which a sovereign ought to observe relative to his own subjects—the end of the internal laws of a society—ought to be the greatest happiness of the society concerned. This is the end which individuals will unite in approving, if they approve of any. It is the straight line—the shortest line—the most natural of all those by which it is possible for a sovereign to direct his course. . . .

The same holds for any end that nations will unite in approving.

Hence in order to regulate his proceedings with regard to other nations, a given sovereign has no other means more adapted to attain his own particular end, than the setting before his eyes the general end—the most extended welfare of all the nations on the earth. . . .

For greater simplicity, let us therefore substitute everywhere this object to the other:—and though unhappily there has not yet been any body of law which regulates the conduct of a given nation, in respect to all other nations on every occasion, as if this had been, or say rather, as if this ought to be, the rule,—yet let *us* do as much as is possible to establish one.

1. The first object of international law for a given nation:—Utility general, in so far as it consists in doing no injury to the other nations respectively, saving the regard which is proper to its own well-being.

2. Second object:—Utility general, in so far as it consists in doing the greatest good possible to other nations, saving the regard which is proper to its own well-being.

3. Third object:—Utility general, in so far as it consists in the given nation not receiving any injury from other nations respectively, saving the regard due to the well-being of these same nations.

4. Fourth object:—Utility general, in so far as it consists in such state receiving the greatest possible benefit from all other nations, saving the regard due to the well-being of these nations.

It is to the two former objects that the duties which the given nation ought to recognise may be referred. It is to the two latter that the rights which it ought to claim may be referred. But if these same rights shall in its opinion be violated, in what manner, by what means shall it apply, or seek for satisfaction? There is no other mode but that of war. But war is an evil—it is even the complication of all other evils.

5. Fifth object:—In case of war, make such arrangements, that the least possible evil may be

produced, consistent with the acquisition of the good which is sought for.

Expressed in the most general manner, the end that a disinterested legislator upon international law would propose to himself, would therefore be the greatest happiness of all nations taken together.

Essay IV: A Plan for an Universal and Perpetual Peace

The purpose is to recommend "three grand objects,—simplicity of government, national frugality, and peace." Fourteen propositions are laid down, among them:

I. That it is not the interest of Great Britain to have any foreign dependencies whatsoever.

II. That it is not the interest of Great Britain to have any treaty of alliance, offensive or defensive, with any other power whatever.

IV. That it is not the interest of Great Britain to keep up any naval force beyond what may be sufficient to defend its commerce against pirates. [p. 546]

All of these also apply to France.

XI. That supposing Great Britain and France thoroughly agreed, the principal difficulties would be removed to the establishment of a plan of general and permanent pacification for all Europe.

XII. That for the maintenance of such a pacification, general and perpetual treaties might be formed, limiting the number of troops to be maintained. [p. 547]

The moral feelings of men in matters of national morality are still so far short of perfection, that in the scale of estimation, justice has not yet gained the ascendancy over force. Yet this prejudice may, in a certain point of view, by accident, be rather favourable to this proposal than otherwise. Truth, and the object of this essay, bid me to say to my countrymen, it is for you to begin the reformation—it is you that have been the greatest sinners. But the same considerations also lead me to say to them, you are the strongest among nations: though justice be not on your side, force is; and it is your force that has been the main cause of your injustice. If the measure of moral approbation had been brought to perfection, such positions would have been far

from popular, prudence would have dictated the keeping them out of sight, and the softening them down as much as possible.

Humiliation would have been the effect produced by them on those to whom they appeared true—indignation on those to whom they appeared false. But, as I have observed, men have not yet learned to tune their feelings in unison with the voice of morality in these points. They feel more pride in being accounted strong, than resentment at being called unjust: or rather, the imputation of injustice appears flattering rather than otherwise, when coupled with the consideration of its cause. I feel it in my own experience; but if *I*, listed as I am as the professed and hitherto the only advocate in my own country in the cause of justice, set a less value on justice than is its due, what can I expect from the general run of men?

Proposition XIII.—That the maintenance of such a pacification might be considerably facilitated, by the establishment of a common court of judicature, for the decision of differences between the several nations, although such court were not to be armed with any coercive powers.

It is an observation of somebody's, that no nation ought to yield any evident point of justice to another. This must mean, evident in the eyes of the nation that is to judge,—evident in the eyes of the nation called upon to yield. What does this amount to? That no nation is to give up anything of what it looks upon as its rights—no nation is to make any concessions. Wherever there is any difference of opinion between the negociators of two nations, war is to be the consequence.

While there is no common tribunal, something might be said for this. Concession to notorious injustice invites fresh injustice.

Establish a common tribunal, the necessity for war no longer follows from difference of opinion. Just or unjust, the decision of the arbiters will save the credit, the honour of the contending party.

Can the arrangement proposed be justly styled visionary, when it has been proved of it—that

1. It is the interest of the parties concerned.

2. They are already sensible of that interest.

3. The situation it would place them in is no new one, nor any other than the original situation they set out from. [p. 552]

The proceedings of [the Tribunal] should all be public.

Its power would consist,—1. In reporting its opinion; 2. In causing that opinion to be circulated in the dominions of each state; . . . 3. After a certain time, in putting the refractory state under the ban of Europe. [p. 554]

Events in a war between Sweden and Russia are cited as evidence of the power of publicity: manifestoes circulated by Russia caused the Swedish army to turn against the war and the king of Sweden was forced to concede. This occurred despite the manifestoes being the enemy's, and therefore less authoritative than they would be if produced by a Congress of nations.

There might, perhaps, be no harm in regulating, as a last resource, the contingent to be furnished by the several states for enforcing the decrees of the court. But the necessity for the employment of this resource would, in all human probability, be superseded for ever by having recourse to the much more simple and less burthensome expedient, of introducing into the instrument by which such court was instituted, a clause guaranteeing the liberty of the press in each state, in such sort, that the diet might find no obstacle to its giving, in every state, to its decrees, and to every paper whatever which it might think proper to sanction with its signature, the most extensive and unlimited circulation.

Proposition XIV.—That secresy in the operations of the foreign department in England ought not to be endured, being altogether useless, and equally repugnant to the interests of liberty and peace. [p. 554]

I take at once the boldest and the broadest ground—I lay down two propositions:—

1. That in no negociation, and at no period of any negociation, ought the negociations of the cabinet in this country to be kept secret from the public at large; much less from parliament and after inquiry made in parliament.

2. That whatever may be the case with preliminary negociations, such secresy ought never to be maintained with regard to treaties actually concluded.

In both cases, to a country like this, such secresy is equally mischievous and unnecessary.

It is mischievous. Over measures of which you have no knowledge, you can apply no controul. Measures carried on without your knowledge you cannot stop,—how ruinous soever to you, and how strongly soever you would disapprove of them if you knew them. Of negociations with foreign powers carried on in time of peace, the principal terminations are treaties of alliance, offensive or defensive, or treaties of commerce. But by one accident or another, everything may lead to war.

That in new treaties of commerce as such, there can be no cause for secresy, is a proposition that will hardly be disputed. Only such negociations, like all others, may eventually lead to war, and everything connected with war, it will be said, may come to require secresy.

But rules which admit of a minister's plunging the nation into a war against its will, are essentially mischievous and unconstitutional.

It is admitted that ministers ought not to have it in their power to impose taxes on the nation against its will. It is admitted that they ought not to have it in their power to maintain troops against its will. But by plunging it into war without its knowledge they do both.

Parliament may refuse to carry on a war after it is begun:—Parliament may remove and punish the minister who has brought the nation into a war.

Sorry remedies these; add them both together, their efficacy is not worth a straw. Arrestment of the evil, and punishment of the authors, are sad consolations for the mischief of a war, and of no value as remedies in comparison with prevention. [pp. 554–555]

13

❧

Immanuel Kant

(1724—1804)

Kant was born and lived his entire life in Koenigsberg, Prussia. He was brought up in a strict Lutheran pietism and studied and taught at the university. Though far from the rapidly modernizing areas of an industrializing England and a France in social transition, he was intellectually a citizen of the world, abreast of the most advanced science and of the political and historical transformations. He inherited the riches of eighteenth-century Enlightenment: its view of an orderly Newtonian world with universal laws, its cosmopolitan individualism, its sense of progress, and its confidence in reason. He consolidated its achievements and profoundly reshaped modern philosophy.

Kant's early work was in natural philosophy as physicists were beginning to give a historical turn to Newtonian science by applying it to questions of development and change. In 1754 Kant attempted to estimate how much the earth's axial rotation had been slowed by the friction of tides. His *Universal Natural History*

and Theory of the Heavens (1755) showed that Newtonian laws could explain how the present constitution of the universe developed from the simplest state of the material world. Kant was thus the originator of what is now called the "Kant-Laplace nebular hypothesis," according to which the solar system evolved from a rotating mass of incandescent gas; he went further to try to explain the development of that mass itself.

He came late in life to formulate the "critical philosophy"—so called for the three major *Critiques*—of *Pure Reason* (1781), *of Practical Reason* (1788), *of Judgment* (1790)—in which he forged an intellectual revolution. He appreciated that both rationalism and empiricism express part of the truth; the problem was to reconcile their strengths, to weave the lessons of each into a whole cloth. What he succeeded in doing was to make an entirely new fabric that changed the face of philosophy. The Critical Philosophy is neither wholly rationalist nor wholly empiricist, but it finds an essential place both for the universal and the necessary and for experience.[1] What he achieved he regarded as a Copernican revolution,[2] except that where Copernicus had displaced man from his central position in the universe, Kant returns him, if not to his former glory, at least to a constructive and legislative role in his knowledge.

He asks, as regards science and morals, what the preconditions are that make these possible: what allows us to interrogate nature, to find it intelligible and lawlike, and what is required for morality to be possible? He answers that the order we find in nature we find because we have first put it there ourselves; it is not the order of a world independent of our knowing but the order making of our minds that we explore: "The order and uniformity in the phenomena we call Nature, we ourselves bring into them and never had we found them there had we not first put them there."[3] He is not arguing that sensible experience is unnecessary but that it is our understanding which ensures that the phenomena will be law-abiding. Similarly, in the domain of morals, he accepts from the beginning that we are subject to and can be motivated by duty, and asks what is required for this to be the case. He

answers that only those who are capable of legislating for themselves are capable of moral obligation. We find a moral order because we ourselves construct it, under universal and objective constraints that apply to any rational being.

Kant's approach gives ethics a momentous turn. Unlike ancient philosophies that focus on the whole good life, his juridical view of morality as laws or rules narrows it to questions of right and obligation. Nature, as the Newtonians had shown, is governed by universal laws. Reason applied to experience can discover these laws and predict what will be. Experience can test these predictions. Moral laws, however, tell us not what is or will be but what *ought* to be; hence they are not tested by what we do or what happens. Criteria for moral laws can be secured only by a refined analysis of our moral consciousness. Kant argues that what is right or wrong in a particular choice can be determined by eliciting the maxim or proposed principle of an action and asking whether it can be consistently willed in universal legislation. That involves regarding every person as an end, not as a means only, and mankind as a community of ends.

This analysis may not sound new. It echoes the Stoics on law and Augustine on will, and doubtless others. But it is thoroughly distinctive and thoroughly revolutionary: to understand how, we need to see his moral theory set in the context of his philosophy as a whole.

Critique of Pure Reason focuses on the analysis of knowledge itself and man's active role in its construction. What is needed is "a critical inquiry into the faculty of reason, with reference to the cognitions to which it strives to attain *without the aid of experience*."[4] He explores forms of intuition and categories and schemas that organize experience, for exam-

---

[1] That all our knowledge begins with experience there can be no doubt. . . . But, though all our knowledge begins with experience, it by no means follows, that all arises out of experience. [*Critique of Pure Reason*, 2d ed. (1787), trans. J. M. D. Meiklejohn (London: G. Bell, 1924), p. 1.]

[2] We here propose to do just what Copernicus did in attempting to explain the celestial movements. When he found that he could make no progress by assuming that all the heavenly bodies revolved round the spectator, he reversed the process, and tried the experiment of assuming that the spectator revolved, while the stars remained at rest. We may make the same experiment with regard to the intuition of objects. If the intuition must conform to the nature of the objects, I do not see how we can know anything of them *a priori*. If, on the other hand, the object conforms to the nature of our faculty of intuition, I can then easily conceive the possibility of such an *a priori* knowledge. [Ibid., "Preface to the Second Edition," p. xxix.]

[3] *Critique of Pure Reason*, 1st ed. (1781), 124 (translation by the editors of this volume).

[4] *Critique of Pure Reason*, 2d ed. (1787), trans. Meiklejohn, "Preface to the Second Edition," p. xix.

ple, space and time—by which we locate events and objects—and principles such as causality, that govern our search for order in time. Such principles are not established by experience; it can scarcely prove, for example, that every event necessarily and universally has a cause. And yet such an assumption is essential to science.[5] Kant's view is that such principles are fixed forms provided by reason itself, indeed, the indispensable basis of the possibility of any experience. The sensory material, of course, comes to us from without, but it is blind until structured by the forms; similarly, mere forms are empty until provided with sensory material.

Accordingly we are constrained within the realm of experience. The world of which we are conscious, whose framework is constituted by the categories of reason and whose material is provided by the senses, is the *phenomenal* world. Science is to have a free hand to explore this world of phenomena, as well as the different faculties or powers exercised in its construction. But we must resist the temptation to claim knowledge of a world of reality (a *noumenal* world) underlying and independent of this knowledge of phenomena. The temptation is strong. We think we know mind (because we are fixed in our categories) and matter (because sensory experience is coerced). And because we have such a rich panoply of ideas for experience, we conjure realities out of them. We are, says Kant in a striking metaphor, like the doves, feeling the air's resistance as they fly, imagining how much more rapidly they could fly if there were no air.

Old-style metaphysics, creating entities in a domain beyond experience from categories intended to organize experience, leads only to transcendental illusions. Kant constructs opposing arguments from traditional metaphysical claims, such as that the world had to have a beginning and that it could not have had a beginning. Proofs of the existence of God, the freedom of the will, and the immortality of the soul lie beyond our competence.

The critical method by thus securing science and banishing metaphysics displaces God and freedom as objects of possible knowledge and so threatens morality and religion. Yet if there is one conviction that pervades Kant's writings it is that freedom is an indispensable basis for morality. Free will is implicit in the moral judgment that a person *could have acted otherwise*, without which we could not blame him. If his action is simply a causal resultant, as science treats every phenomenon, then moral judgment is irrelevant. Kant here offers another turn, arguing that it is sufficient to show that freedom is a requirement of practical reason and that it is possible; then we can be justified in accepting it, even if it is, strictly,

---

[5] Some of Kant's technical terminology should be noted, because it enters at a few points in his ethical writings as well. A statement is *analytic* if its predicate is already contained in its subject—e.g., "every effect has a cause," in which "effect" already means something caused. A statement is *synthetic* if the predicate is not contained in the subject—e.g., "every event has a cause," where the idea of an event as a happening in time does not contain the idea of being caused. A statement is *a priori* if either we know it prior to experience or experience is not required to validate it—e.g., "7 plus 5 equals 12" (we do not count objects to establish this). A statement is *a posteriori* if validation requires experience—e.g., "grass is green in summer." Now of the four possible combinations of these two distinctions, there is no difficulty with (1) *analytic a priori* statements—indeed all analytic statements are *a priori*. Nor is there any difficulty with (2) *synthetic a posteriori* statements—all *a posteriori* statements are synthetic in that they tell us something new about their subjects. Hence, (3) *analytic a posteriori* statements are not possible and can be eliminated. But what about (4) *synthetic a priori* statements? They are mysterious in that we learn something definite not contained in the subject and yet not given by experience. They include such important propositions as "every event has a cause" (and for Kant, "7 plus 5 equals 12"). Accordingly, Kant's technical formulation of the basic question of the *Critique of Pure Reason* is "How are *synthetic a priori* propositions possible?" He believes his fundamental assertion in ethics—that a good will governs itself by universal laws—is *synthetic a priori*.

unprovable.[6] Similarly, we may in scientific investigation use an unprovable principle regulatively. For example, although we cannot prove that nature is simple or that it is infinitely complex, the latter fruitfully regulates our inquiries, for it leads us to dig deeper, whereas the former tends to make us content with the discovery of simple elements. Kant pursues something of the same essential strategy, though infinitely more complex an argument, to legitimate concepts of purpose and design, plan and function, and to secure for ethics the metaphysical trio of freedom of the will, God, and immortality [7]—although none of these can be said properly to be established as knowledge.

Kant's systematic treatment of morality is found in two further works at either end of *Practical Reason: Grundlegung zur Metaphysik der Sitten* (*Fundamental Principles of the Metaphysic of Morals*—hereafter *Fundamental Principles*) [8] (1785) and *Metaphysik der Sitten* (*The Metaphysics of Morals*) (1797), for which *Fundamental Principles* had been intended as an introduction. The former investigates and establishes the supreme principle underlying morality presupposed in common judgments; the latter applies the principle to law (justice) and virtue.

Where Bentham takes practical reason as the intelligent computation of consequences—thus building morality around notions of good and experience—and understands by "good will" benevolence and generosity of spirit, Kant's understanding of reason, indeed his whole project, is different from that of any who preceded him. While acknowledging that men are naturally drawn to pleasure and happiness, he argues that it is irrelevant to the determination of what is right or obligatory and works with a vastly different notion of good will.

Fundamental Principles begins with the difficult claim that there is nothing unqualifiedly good save a good will, that is, when the motive is directed not toward the satisfaction of needs or interests, objectives or purposes, and the intention or maxim is to do what is obligated by morality. At stake is the motive, the ground of decision, and not the consequences. The decision of the virtuous or good will derives from nothing less than sheer respect for the law itself, because it is acknowledged as absolutely and universally binding. If the good will took its goodness from something outside itself—from something empirical—then it would lose its necessary and universal character. If we were wholly rational—unmoved by inclination and desire—the moral law would be like a law of nature; but since we are human too, it is felt as command or imperative. Moral precepts—unlike those of skill or prudence, which are contingent on particular ends or objectives—are *categorical*.

Kant provides various (in his view, equivalent) formulations of the categorical imperative. The initial statement focuses on reason as legislative: "Act only on that maxim whereby thou canst at the same time will that it should become a universal law." It provides a test for the maxim or principle of action that a person proposes in a given case. If the maxim passes the test—if it can be consistently willed as a universal law—then it becomes an objective moral law. Other formulae stress different

---

[6] This is "the enigma of the critical philosophy, viz. how we *deny* objective *reality* to the supersensible use of the *categories* in speculation, and yet *admit* this *reality* with respect to the objects of pure practical reason" [*Critique of Practical Reason* (1788), trans. Thomas Kingsmill Abbott (London: Longmans, Green, 1879), Preface, p. 108.].

[7] The argument for God is roughly this: we find ourselves under an obligation to match happiness with duty, for the *summum bonum*, or highest good, is a morally good life properly rewarded. Thus we say that a villain ought not to be happy nor a good man miserable. We ought then to work for such a result. But if we ought to, then—since *ought* implies *can*—we postulate in our moral judgment that the *summum bonum* is achievable, at least in principle. But nature and the empirical world do not guarantee this. Hence we must assume, as a postulate, not as knowledge, that a judging God exists. A comparable argument is offered for postulating immortality.

[8] Also translated as *Groundwork* and *Grounding*.

aspects of the moral situation. One, often called the "human imperative," is cast in terms of the end of action: that every person be treated as an end, as intrinsically valuable, and not only as a means. While the initial formula exhibits the universality and equality inherent in the moral, this exhibits the dignity and worth of humanity. Another version centers on the autonomy of the person in a community of moral persons; it sees moral action as issuing from the autonomous legislation of the agent for a kingdom of ends (persons). The major bent of Kant's formulations, especially the last, can be interpreted as the condition for a moral community, generating those practices and institutions that are indispensable for autonomy.

Kant's conception of freedom as autonomy falls into neither of the two traditionally opposing views of causality and indeterminism; it is rather a kind of self-determination in which will as practical reason both legislates the moral law and executes decision out of a rational respect for the moral law.

The possibility of freedom suggests two perspectives on human beings: we are both phenomenal and noumenal, and the notion of reason pertains to both. On the one hand, we live in a natural, nonmoral world—a phenomenal world amenable to scientific laws and description. Like most philosophers, Kant takes reason itself as a universal capacity of man; but for him reason is a law giver, in the sense that sensible experience must conform to the forms or categories provided by the understanding. Here reason functions speculatively and theoretically. Scientific laws are causal and descriptive and include those of psychology and anthropology (such generalizations as Bentham and others offered). On the other hand, we also live in an intelligible moral world. Even the common man shares a sense of obligation that is not motivated by pleasure or inclinations and that indeed often runs counter to self-interest or even sympathy and benevolence—witness the prevalence of the

Golden Rule. Reason here is functioning not constitutively but in its practical capacity, as decision making or willing what is to be done.

All this departs from the tradition in ethics that takes *good* as the basic concept.

This is the proper place to explain the paradox of method in a critique of Practical Reason, namely, *that the concept of good and evil must not be determined before the moral law (of which it seems as if it must be the foundation), but only after it and by means of it.*[9]

To start with good and evil leaves no way to distinguish the good from the pleasant, nor good and evil from "weal" and "woe," in short, questions of goodness from questions of welfare. On the other hand, to start with duty or obligation focuses the moral good on the character of the will exhibited in action, a narrower and rational conception of good and evil appropriate to morals. Hence it is not the concept of good that determines the moral law, but the moral law that first determines the concept of good and makes possible the equation of the absolute good with a good will.

To read Kant exclusively from the *Critiques* and *Fundamental Principles* is to find an austere portrayal of duty virtually unrelieved by reference to consequences and practice or to happiness (the search for which, if not strictly moral, is at least humanly justifiable) or to sentiments such as sympathy and benevolence, or to social institutions in their historical development. Other works—among them *The Metaphysics of Morals*—may not obliterate the austerity but at least mute it. Kant writes passable poetry, encourages cheerfulness in educating children, and is concerned with the care of animals and the environment, with the moral objectives of government and legislation, and with international responsibilities for peace and progress. And in all the works on morality, we should not overlook the reverence with which he

---

[9] *Critique of Practical Reason*, trans. Abbott, 183.

writes about our capacity for disinterested self-government free from coercion and even from causal laws and about rational humanity:

But man as a person, i.e., as the subject of a morally-practical reason, is exalted above all price. For as such a one (*homo noumenon*) he is not to be valued merely as a means to the ends of other people, or even to his own ends, but is to be prized as an end in himself. This is to say, he possesses a dignity (an absolute inner worth) whereby he exacts the respect of all other rational beings in the world, can measure himself against each member of his species, and can esteem himself on a footing of equality with them.[10]

The Metaphysics of Morals serves as a bridge between the formal critical philosophy and practice.[11] Part One, *Right,* considers law or justice, and is limited to those obligations to others where performance is owed and where nonperformance is a wrong. Part Two, *Virtue,* concerns ends such as self-perfection and happiness in their relation to character. *Right* is about what can be sanctioned by external means (for the law attempts only to alter conduct, not change the will) and *Virtue* is about what is internally sanctioned by a sense of duty. Neither part appeals to "anthropology"—to actual legal systems, to existing political authority, to customary moralities—for the problem, even in these works, continues to be not the examination of existing norms but what ought to be.

Virtue is closer to the moral theory already laid down, but the perspective is considerably softened. Duties of virtue permit a latitude to the moral agent. Only the "fantastically virtuous person" carries morality into all domains of life. Although we have a duty to the happiness of other people, it must be on their terms and on their judgment of what makes them happy, not ours; and we are not obligated to self-sacrifice. Above all, *Virtue* makes clear that the application of the categorical imperative is not direct. The complexity of practice lies beyond the reach of systematic ethics and calls for training in judgment ("casuistics") and experience.

Right considers the conditions under which the voluntary acts of any one person may be harmonized, by external sanctions, with the will of every other person under the general law of freedom. There is only the one right, even in a stateless or nonjuridical society, namely, to be free from the constraining will of another, compatible of course with a like freedom for others. This autonomy entails the right to live in peace, freedom of speech, and protection of property.

Kant's view of property—as a distinction between *mine* and *thine*—is broad and complex. Ownership is not an observable relation between a person and, for example, an object, but a social relation whereby one is empowered to exclude others from the use or enjoyment of an object. This implies an obligation on others to respect what is rightfully mine, so that anyone who uses it without my consent does me an injury. Property broadly covers promise and contract, for I may be said to own the free will of another with respect to the performance of a specific act. It also covers certain status relationships, as when a man speaks of *his* family, which entails certain rights and obligations.

These various rights are not enacted by a civil society, but they can be guaranteed only in a civil or political state; and insofar as effective freedom is possible only in this way, it is a moral duty to join in and help fashion a

---

[10] *The Metaphysical Principles of Virtue,* trans. James Ellington, in Immanuel Kant, *Ethical Philosophy* (Indianapolis/Cambridge: Hackett, 1983), p. 97.

[11] It originally (1797) appeared in two parts, which were put together in the second edition. The regrettable absence of a uniform English translation makes it difficult to preserve the parallelism of the German titles: *Metaphysische Anfangsgründe der Rechtslehre* (translated variously as *Metaphysical Rudiments of Jurisprudence, The Metaphysical Elements of Justice,* or *The Science of Right*—hereafter *Right*) and *Metaphysische Anfangsgründe der Tugendlehre* (*The Metaphysical Principles of Virtue, Metaphysical Rudiments of Morality,* or *Doctrine of Virtue*—hereafter *Virtue*).

juridical state. The social contract is not a historical event; but it can serve to express the assumed consent essential to the rightness of a constitution (the moral relations that weave the members into a community) and to guide legislators in constructing laws that could have sprung from the united will of a people.

The most developed form of a state is a constitutional republic with divided powers—legislative, executive, and judicial. The legislative is crucial, and from the one intrinsic right of freedom there follows the right to participate in legislation, to obey only those laws to which one has consented—in effect, to be a citizen. The republican form shows the social underpinnings of the categorical imperative—not merely that I can will my maxim to become a universal law, but that the binding force derives from a community where everyone legislates for all. The injunction to treat everyone as an end and not solely as a means militates against paternalism and explains why criminal justice is not deterrent.

There are tensions in Kant's social theory. The freedom or autonomy at the base of law has two faces: individualistic self-reliance with independence from the compulsion of others and a communal obligation to others that approximates Rousseau's general will. Similarly, authoritarian and conservative strains fit uneasily with the democratic and liberal: on the one hand, he excludes from full citizenship women, servants, hired workmen, and all who may be regarded as dependent; insists on retributive justice (*jus talionis*, an eye for an eye) in all criminal cases; and denies the right of revolution. On the other hand, he is the spokesman for equality, for the right of everyone to live in peace, a sympathizer with the American and French revolutions, and an outspoken defender of the assorted liberties others claimed as natural. Above all, there is a faith, with reservations to be sure, in the perfectability of human beings and their institutions.

Kant's writings on history and politics carry the early developmental interest into human affairs. He tries to relate regulative principles from morality, such as the ideal of moral progress of the human race, to the operation of causes in the phenomenal world—the material interests and passions operating on the social scene. It is almost as if he were scanning the way in which a Kantian morality might unfold from the operations of a Hobbesian world. In the process of presenting the vista of a universal history and the possibility of a world federation bringing perpetual peace he launches ideas that came to greater fruition in Hegel and then in Marx. His practical judgments on current affairs are consistently appreciative of the American and French revolutions for the opportunities they opened up, and of science for making possible greater well-being and liberty. Although condemning the extremes of the Terror, he did not allow these to reverse his judgment that the revolution had marked fundamental advances. And for all his stress on legality as a moral attitude, he did not fail to recognize that progress was sometimes the consequence of illegal action.

Clearly the use of regulative principles in history and politics has a teleological dimension. Underlying it is the tension between the mechanical order of the physical world and the order of freedom and ideal purpose found in organic nature and in works of art. Relations between parts of an organism or a symphony are comprehensible only in terms of a purposive framework—of means or conditions for the existence of the whole—as if they had been produced under the guidance of an end. Similarly, historical understanding must accommodate itself both to a microscopic causality and a macroscopic teleology. Kant is not describing particular events of history, which are random and without pattern; he is rather searching for a clue that there is a direction in history measured by increase in freedom. There are two assumptions: that nature does nothing in vain and works economically, and that the talents and capacities of human beings are not vested in a single person or in a single generation. We must then look for nature's carrying out of their realization not in one period or in one finite group but in the whole of the world and the whole of posterity.

Kant's view of religion reverses the accepted relation of religion to ethics. To base morality on the will of God is to make it as *heteronomous* (having an outside basis) as basing it on science. Instead of morality resting on religion, religion rests on morality. Morality tells us what religious views have to be to make morality tenable. Indeed, our ideas of God and divine properties are presuppositions of moral consciousness. This thesis was historical dynamite that had immediate influence: Protestantism welcoming it for its emphasis on faith, Catholicism condemning it and placing Kant on the Index of forbidden books. In humanistic movements it encouraged a sympathetic interpretation of religion as a symbolic expression of human needs. In Kant's home territory, his *Radical Evil in Human Nature* (1792) led the king of Prussia to demand that he write no more on religious matters. (After the king's death Kant considered himself no longer bound by his promise and continued the work in *Religion Within the Limits of Reason Alone* [1793].) It may seem strange that Kant expresses no regret for a human situation in which a *knowledge* of God's existence and properties is inaccessible, but he actually thinks it is better so. A remarkable passage in *Practical Reason* holds that if we had such knowledge, then "*God* and *eternity* with their *awful majesty* would stand unceasingly *before our eyes*"; [12] our natural inclinations being what they are, we would act from fear or hope, not from duty.

Difficult as Kant's writings are, they were immediately hailed as momentous and inspired important intellectual movements. In general, one may say that he left everything different from what it had been. It was a new

world, with new beginnings. But it could not long rest where he had left it.

Fundamental Principles of the Metaphysic of Morals [13]

Preface

The metaphysics of morals presents a pure moral philosophy cleared of the empirical psychological and anthropological elements:

Every one must admit that if a law is to have moral force, *i.e.*, to be the basis of an obligation, it must carry with it absolute necessity; that, for example, the precept, 'Thou shalt not lie,' is not valid for men alone, as if other rational beings had no need to observe it; and so with all the other moral laws properly so called; that, therefore, the basis of obligation must not be sought in the nature of man, or in the circumstances in the world in which he is placed, but *a priori* simply in the conceptions of pure reason; and although any other precept which is founded on principles of mere experience may be in certain respects universal, yet in as far as it rests even in the least degree on an empirical basis, perhaps only as to a motive, such a precept, while it may be a practical rule, can never be called a moral law.

Thus not only are moral laws with their principles essentially distinguished from every other kind of practical knowledge in which there is anything empirical, but all moral philosophy rests wholly on its pure part. When applied to man, it does not borrow the least thing from the knowledge of man himself (anthropology), but gives laws *a priori* to him as a rational being. No doubt these laws require a judgment sharpened by experience, in order on the one hand to distinguish in what cases they are applicable, and on the other to procure for them access to the will of the man, and effectual influence on conduct; since man is acted on by so many incli-

---

[12] *Critique of Practical Reason*, trans. Abbott, 294.

[13] The selection is from *Kant's Critique of Practical Reason and Other Works on the Theory of Ethics*, trans. Thomas Kingsmill Abbott, 2d ed. (London: Longmans, Green, 1879). Abbott used the Rosenkranz and Schubert edition of Kant; the bracketed numbers following passages in the selection refer to the pagination of that edition.

nations that, though capable of the idea of a practical pure reason, he is not so easily able to make it effective *in concreto* in his life. [5–6]

The analysis starts with the common idea of duty and moral law. The aim is to proceed in a way parallel to Newton's analysis of motion, as explained in the "Conclusion" of *Critique of Practical Reason*.

Critique of Practical Reason [14]

Conclusion

Two things fill the mind with ever new and increasing admiration and awe, the oftener and the more steadily we reflect on them: *the starry heavens above and the moral law within.* I have not to search for them and conjecture them as though they were veiled in darkness or were in the transcendent region beyond my horizon; I see them before me and connect them directly with the consciousness of my existence. The former begins from the place I occupy in the external world of sense, and enlarges my connexion therein to an unbounded extent with worlds upon worlds and systems of systems, and moreover into limitless times of their periodic motion, its beginning and continuance. The second begins from my invisible self, my personality, and exhibits me in a world which has true infinity, but which is traceable only by the understanding, and with which I discern that I am not in a merely contingent but in a universal and necessary connexion, as I am also thereby with all those visible worlds. The former view of a countless multitude of worlds annihilates as it were my importance as an *animal creature*, which after it has been for a short time provided with vital power, one knows not how, must again give back the matter of which it was formed to the planet it inhabits (a mere speck in the universe). The second on the contrary infinitely elevates my worth as an *intelligence* by my personality, in which the moral law reveals to me a life

independent on animality and even on the whole sensible world, at least so far as may be inferred from the destination assigned to my existence by this law, a destination not restricted to conditions and limits of this life, but reaching into the infinite.

But though admiration and respect may excite to inquiry, they cannot supply the want of it. What then is to be done in order to enter on this in a useful manner and one adapted to the loftiness of the subject? Examples may serve in this as a warning, and also for imitation. The contemplation of the world began from the noblest spectacle that the human senses present to us, and that our understanding can bear to follow in their vast reach; and it ended—in astrology. Morality began with the noblest attribute of human nature, the development and cultivation of which give a prospect of infinite utility; and ended—in fanaticism or superstition. So it is with all crude attempts where the principal part of the business depends on the use of reason, a use which does not come of itself, like the use of the feet, by frequent exercise, especially when attributes are in question which cannot be directly exhibited in common experience. But after the maxim had come into vogue, though late, to examine carefully beforehand all the steps that reason purposes to take, and not to let it proceed otherwise than in the track of a previously well considered method, then the study of the structure of the universe took quite a different direction, and thereby attained an incomparably happier result. The fall of a stone, the motion of a sling, resolved into their elements and the forces that are manifested in them, and treated mathematically, produced at last that clear and henceforward unchangeable insight into the system of the world, which as observation is continued may hope always to extend itself, but need never fear to be compelled to retreat.

This example may suggest to us to enter on the same path in treating of the moral capacities of our nature, and may give us hope of a like good result. We have at hand the instances of the moral judgment of reason. By analysing these into their elementary conceptions, and in default of *mathematics* adopting a process similar to that of *chemistry*, the *separation* of the empirical from the rational elements that may be found in them, by repeated experiments on common sense, we may exhibit both *pure*, and learn with certainty what each part can accomplish of itself, so as to prevent on the one hand the errors

---

[14] The selection is from *Kant's Critique of Practical Reason and Other Works on the Theory of Ethics*, trans. Thomas Kingsmill Abbott, 2d ed. (London: Longmans, Green, 1879).

of a still *crude* untrained judgment, and on the other hand (what is far more necessary) the *extravagances of genius,* by which, as by the adepts of the philosopher's stone, without any methodical study or knowledge of nature, visionary treasures are promised and the true are thrown away. In one word, science (critically undertaken and methodically directed) is the narrow gate that leads to the true *doctrine of practical wisdom,* if we understand by this not merely what one ought to *do,* but what ought to serve *teachers* as a guide to construct well and clearly the road to wisdom which every one should travel, and to secure others from going astray. Philosophy must always continue to be the guardian of this science, and although the public does not take any interest in its subtle investigations, it must in the resulting *doctrines,* which such an examination first puts in a clear light. [312–315]

Fundamental Principles of the Metaphysic of Morals [15]

First Section: Transition from the Common Rational Knowledge of Morality to the Philosophical

Nothing can possibly be conceived in the world, or even out of it, which can be called good without qualification, except a Good Will. Intelligence, wit, judgment, and the other *talents* of the mind, however they may be named, or courage, resolution, perseverance, as qualities of temperament, are undoubtedly good and desirable in many respects; but these gifts of nature may also become extremely bad and mischievous if the will which is to make use of them, and which, therefore, constitutes what is called *character,* is not good. It is the same with the *gifts of fortune.* Power, riches, honour, even health, and the general well-being and contentment with one's condition which is called *happiness,* inspire pride, and often presumption, if there is not a good will to correct the influence of these on the mind, and with this also to rectify the whole principle of acting and adapt it to its end. The sight of a being who is not adorned with a single feature of a pure and good will, enjoying unbroken prosper-

ity, can never give pleasure to an impartial rational spectator. Thus a good will appears to constitute the indispensable condition even of being worthy of happiness.

There are even some qualities which are of service to this good will itself, and may facilitate its action, yet which have no intrinsic unconditional value, but always presuppose a good will, and this qualifies the esteem that we justly have for them, and does not permit us to regard them as absolutely good. Moderation in the affections and passions, self-control and calm deliberation are not only good in many respects, but even seem to constitute part of the intrinsic worth of the person; but they are far from deserving to be called good without qualification, although they have been so unconditionally praised by the ancients. For without the principles of a good will, they may become extremely bad, and the coolness of a villain not only makes him far more dangerous, but also immediately makes him more abominable in our eyes than he would have been without it.

A good will is good not because of what it performs or effects, not by its aptness for the attainment of some proposed end, but simply by virtue of the volition, that is, it is good in itself, and considered by itself is to be esteemed much higher than all that can be brought about by it in favour of any inclination, nay even of the sum total of all inclinations. Even if it should happen that, owing to special disfavour of fortune, or the niggardly provision of a step-motherly nature, this will should wholly lack power to accomplish its purpose, if with its greatest efforts it should yet achieve nothing, and there should remain only the good will (not, to be sure, a mere wish, but the summoning of all means in our power), then, like a jewel, it would still shine by its own light, as a thing which has its whole value in itself. Its usefulness or fruitlessness can neither add nor take away anything from this value. It would be, as it were, only the setting to enable us to handle it the more conveniently in common commerce, or to attract to it the attention of those who are not yet connoisseurs, but not to recommend it to true connoisseurs, or to determine its value.

There is, however, something so strange in this idea of the absolute value of the mere will [that] we will examine this idea from this point of view.

In the physical constitution of an organized being,

[15] Abbott translation (1879).

we assume it as a fundamental principle that no organ for any purpose will be found in it but what is also the fittest and best adapted for that purpose. Now in a being which has reason and a will, if the proper object of nature were its *conservation*, its *welfare*, in a word, its *happiness*, then nature would have hit upon a very bad arrangement in selecting the reason of the creature to carry out this purpose. For all the actions which the creature has to perform with a view to this purpose, and the whole rule of its conduct, would be far more surely prescribed to it by instinct, and that end would have been attained thereby much more certainly than it ever can be by reason. . . .

. . . [O]ur existence has a different and far nobler end, for which, and not for happiness, reason is properly intended, and which must, therefore, be regarded as the supreme condition to which the private ends of man must, for the most part, be postponed.

For as reason is not competent to guide the will with certainty in regard to its objects and the satisfaction of all our wants (which it to some extent even multiplies), this being an end to which an implanted instinct would have led with much greater certainty; and since, nevertheless, reason is imparted to us as a practical faculty, *i.e.*, as one which is to have influence on the *will*, therefore, admitting that nature generally in the distribution of her capacities has adapted the means to the end, its true destination must be to produce a *will*, not merely good as a *means* to something else, but *good in itself*, for which reason was absolutely necessary. This will then, though not indeed the sole and complete good, must be the supreme good and the condition of every other, even of the desire of happiness. . . .

We have then to develop the notion of a will which deserves to be highly esteemed for itself, and is good without a view to anything further, a notion which exists already in the sound natural understanding, requiring rather to be cleared up than to be taught, and which in estimating the value of our actions always takes the first place, and constitutes the condition of all the rest. In order to do this we will take the notion of duty, which includes that of a good will, although implying certain subjective restrictions and hindrances. These, however, far from concealing it, or rendering it unrecognisable, rather bring it out by contrast, and make it shine forth so much the brighter.

I omit here all actions which are already recognised as inconsistent with duty, although they may be useful for this or that purpose, for with these the question whether they are done *from duty* cannot arise at all, since they even conflict with it. I also set aside those actions which really conform to duty, but to which men have *no* direct *inclination*, performing them because they are impelled thereto by some other inclination. For in this case we can readily distinguish whether the action which agrees with duty is done *from duty*, or from a selfish view. It is much harder to make this distinction when the action accords with duty, and the subject has besides a *direct* inclination to it. For example, it is always a matter of duty that a dealer should not overcharge an inexperienced purchaser, and wherever there is much commerce the prudent tradesman does not overcharge, but keeps a fixed price for every one, so that a child buys of him as well as any other. Men are thus *honestly* served; but this is not enough to make us believe that the tradesman has so acted from duty and from principles of honesty: his own advantage required it; it is out of the question in this case to suppose that he might besides have a direct inclination in favour of the buyers, so that, as it were, from love he should give no advantage to one over another. Accordingly the action was done neither from duty nor from direct inclination, but merely with a selfish view.

On the other hand, it is a duty to maintain one's life; and, in addition, every one has also a direct inclination to do so. But on this account the often anxious care which most men take for it has no intrinsic worth, and their maxim has no moral import. They preserve their life *as duty requires*, no doubt, but not *because duty requires*. On the other hand, if adversity and hopeless sorrow have completely taken away the relish for life; if the unfortunate one, strong in mind, indignant at his fate rather than desponding or dejected, wishes for death, and yet preserves his life without loving it—not from inclination or fear, but from duty—then his maxim has a moral worth.

To be beneficent when we can is a duty; and besides this, there are many minds so sympathetically constituted that without any other motive of vanity or self-interest, they find a pleasure in spreading joy around them, and can take delight in the satisfaction of others so far as it is their own work. But I maintain that in such a case an action of this kind, however proper, however amiable it may be, has nevertheless no true moral worth, but is on a level with other inclinations, *e.g.*, the inclination to honour, which, if it is happily directed to that which is in fact of public utility and accordant with duty, and consequently honourable, deserves praise and encouragement, but not esteem. For the maxim wants the moral import, namely, that such actions be done *from duty*, not from inclination. Put the case that the mind of that philanthropist were clouded by sorrow of his own, extinguishing all sympathy with the lot of others, and that while he still has the power to benefit others in distress he is not touched by their trouble because he is absorbed with his own; and now suppose that he tears himself out of this dead insensibility, and performs the action without any inclination to it, but simply from duty, then first has his action its genuine moral worth. Further still; if nature has put little sympathy in the heart of this or that man; if he, supposed to be an upright man, is by temperament cold and indifferent to the sufferings of others, perhaps because in respect of his own he is provided with the special gift of patience and fortitude, and supposes, or even requires, that others should have the same—and such a man would certainly not be the meanest product of nature—but if nature had not specially framed him for a philanthropist, would he not still find in himself a source from whence to give himself a far higher worth than that of a good-natured temperament could be? Unquestionably. It is just in this that the moral worth of the character is brought out which is incomparably the highest of all, namely, that he is beneficent, not from inclination, but from duty.

To secure one's own happiness is a duty, at least indirectly; for discontent with one's condition under a pressure of many anxieties and amidst unsatisfied wants might easily become a great *temptation to transgression of duty*. . . .

It is in this manner, undoubtedly, that we are to understand those passages of Scripture also in which we are commanded to love our neighbour, even our enemy. For love, as an affection, cannot be commanded, but beneficence for duty's sake; even though we are not impelled to it by any inclination, nay, are even repelled by a natural and unconquerable aversion. This is *practical* love, and not *pathological*, a love which is seated in the will, and not in the propensions of sense, in principles of action and not of tender sympathy; and it is this love alone which can be commanded.

The second proposition [a] is: That an action done from duty derives its moral worth, *not from the purpose* which is to be attained by it, but from the maxim by which it is determined, and therefore does not depend on the realization of the object of the action, but merely on the *principle of volition* by which the action has taken place, without regard to any object of desire. It is clear from what precedes that the purposes which we may have in view in our actions, or their effects regarded as ends and springs of the will, cannot give to actions any unconditional or moral worth. In what then can their worth lie, if it is not to consist in the will and in reference to its expected effect? It cannot lie anywhere but in the *principle of the will* without regard to the ends which can be attained by the action. For the will stands between its *a priori* principle which is formal, and its *a posteriori* spring which is material, as between two roads, and as it must be determined by something, it follows that it must be determined by the formal principle of volition when an action is done from duty, in which case every material principle has been withdrawn from it.

The third proposition, which is a consequence of the two preceding, I would express thus: *Duty is the necessity of acting from respect for the law.* I may have *inclination* for an object as the effect of my proposed action, but I cannot have *respect* for it, just for this reason, that it is an effect and not an energy of will. Similarly, I cannot have respect for inclination, whether my own or another's; I can at most if my own, approve it; if another's, sometimes even love it; *i.e.*, look on it as favourable to my own interest. It is only what is connected with my will as a principle, by no means as an effect—what does not subserve my inclination, but overpowers it, or at least in case of choice excludes it from its calculation—in other words, simply the law of itself, which can be an object of respect, and hence a command. Now an action done from duty must wholly exclude the influence of inclination, and with it every object of the will, so that nothing remains which can determine the will except objectively the

[a] [The first proposition was that to have moral worth an action must be done from duty.]

law, and subjectively *pure respect* for this practical law, and consequently the maxim [b] to follow this law even to the thwarting of all my inclinations.

Thus the moral worth of an action does not lie in the effect expected from it, nor in any principle of action which requires to borrow its motive from this expected effect. For all these effects—agreeableness of one's condition, and even the promotion of the happiness of others—could have been also brought about by other causes, so that for this there would have been no need of the will of a rational being; it is in this, however, alone that the supreme and unconditional good can be found. The preeminent good which we call moral can therefore consist in nothing else than *the conception of law* in itself, *which certainly is only possible in a rational being*, in so far as this conception, and not the expected effect, determines the will. This is a good which is already present in the person who acts accordingly, and we have not to wait for it to appear first in the result. [c]

But what sort of law can that be, the conception of which must determine the will, even without paying any regard to the effect expected from it, in order that this will may be called good absolutely and without qualification? As I have deprived the will of every impulse which could arise to it from obedience to any law, there remains nothing but the universal conformity of its actions to law in general, which alone is to serve the will as a principle, *i.e.*, I am never to act otherwise than so *that I could also will that my maxim should become a universal law.* Here now, it is the simple conformity to law in general, without assuming any particular law applicable to certain actions, that serves the will as its principle, and must so serve it, if duty is not to be a vain delusion and a chimerical notion. The common reason of men in its practical judgments perfectly coincides with this, and always has in view the principle here suggested. Let the question be, for example: May I when in distress make a promise with the intention not to keep it? I readily distinguish here between the two significations which the question may have: Whether it is prudent, or whether it is right, to make a false promise. The former may undoubtedly often be the case. I see clearly indeed that it is not enough to extricate myself from a present difficulty by means of this subterfuge, but it must be well considered whether there may not hereafter spring from this lie much greater inconvenience than that from which I now free myself, and as, with all my supposed *cunning*, the consequences cannot be so easily foreseen but that credit once lost may be much more injurious to me than any mischief which I seek to avoid at present, it should be considered whether it would not be more *prudent* to act herein according to a universal maxim, and to make it a habit to promise nothing except with the intention of keeping it. But it is soon clear to me that such a maxim will still only be based on the fear of consequences. Now it is a wholly different thing to be truthful from duty, and to be so from apprehension of injurious consequences. In the first case, the very notion of the action already implies a law for me; in the second case, I must first look about elsewhere to see what results may be combined with it which would affect myself. For to deviate from the principle of duty is beyond all doubt wicked; but to be unfaithful to my maxim of prudence may often be very advantageous to me, although to abide by it is certainly

---

[b] A *maxim* is the subjective principle of volition. The objective principle (*i.e.*, that which would also serve subjectively as a practical principle to all rational beings if reason had full power over the faculty of desire) is the practical *law*.
[c] It might here be objected to me that I take refuge behind the word *respect* in an obscure feeling instead of giving a distinct solution of the question by a concept of the reason. But although respect is a feeling, it is not a feeling *received* through influence, but is *self-wrought* by a rational concept, and, therefore, is specifically distinct from all feelings of the former kind, which may be referred either to inclination or fear. What I recognise immediately as a law for me, I recognise with respect. This merely signifies the consciousness that my will is *subordinate* to a law, without the intervention of other influences on my sense. The immediate determination of the will by the law, and the consciousness of this is called *respect*, so that this is regarded as an *effect* of the law on the subject, and not as the *cause* of it. Respect is properly the conception of a work which thwarts my self-love. Accordingly it is something which is considered neither as an object of inclination nor of fear, although it has something analogous to both. The *object* of respect is the *law* only, and that, the law which we impose on *ourselves*, and yet recognise as necessary in itself. As a law, we are subjected to it without consulting self-love; as imposed by us on ourselves, it is a result of our will. In the former aspect it has an analogy to fear, in the latter to inclination. Respect for a person is properly only respect for the law (of honesty, &c.,) of which he gives us an example. . . .

safer. The shortest way, however, and an unerring one, to discover the answer to this question whether a lying promise is consistent with duty, is to ask myself, Should I be content that my maxim (to extricate myself from difficulty by a false promise) should hold good as a universal law, for myself as well as for others? and should I be able to say to myself, 'Every one may make a deceitful promise when he finds himself in a difficulty from which he cannot otherwise extricate himself'? Then I presently become aware that while I can will the lie, I can by no means will that lying should be a universal law. For with such a law there would be no promises at all, since it would be in vain to allege my intention in regard to my future actions to those who would not believe this allegation, or if they over hastily did so would pay me back in my own coin. Hence my maxim, as soon as it should be made a universal law, would necessarily destroy itself.

I do not therefore need any far-reaching penetration to discern what I have to do in order that my will may be morally good. Inexperienced in the course of the world, incapable of being prepared for all its contingencies, I only ask myself: Canst thou also will that thy maxim should be a universal law? If not, then it must be rejected, and that not because of a disadvantage accruing from it to myself or even to others, but because it cannot enter as a principle into a possible universal legislation, and reason extorts from me immediate respect for such legislation. I do not indeed as yet *discern* on what this respect is based (this the philosopher may inquire), but at least I understand this, that it is an estimation of the worth which far outweighs all worth of what is recommended by inclination, and that the necessity of acting from *pure* respect for the practical law is what constitutes duty, to which every other motive must give place, because it is the condition of a will being good *in itself,* and the worth of such a will is above everything.

Thus then, without quitting the moral knowledge of common human reason, we have arrived at its principle. And although no doubt common men do not conceive it in such an abstract and universal form, yet they always have it really before their eyes, and use it as the standard of their decision. . . . [W]e do not need science and philosophy to know what we should do to be honest and good, yea even wise and virtuous. . . .

Still there is need for a defense of common moral knowledge:

Innocence is indeed a glorious thing, only, on the other hand, it is very sad that it cannot well maintain itself, and is easily seduced. On this account even wisdom—which otherwise consists more in conduct than in knowledge—yet has need of science, not in order to learn from it, but to secure for its precepts admission and permanence. . . .

Thus is the *common reason of man* compelled to go out of its sphere, and to take a step into the field of a *practical philosophy.* . . . [11–26]

Second Section: Transition from Popular Moral Philosophy to the Metaphysic of Morals

We can never be sure that the maxim of a right action rests on moral grounds: it is always possible that a secret impulse of self-love is the actual determining cause of the will. Still, we can be sure that "reason of itself, independent on all experience, ordains what ought to take place" (30). Its law is valid "not merely for man, but for all *rational creatures generally,* not merely under certain contingent conditions or with exceptions, but *with absolute necessity*" (30). Such absolute and necessary law cannot be inferred from experience. Moralists go astray who attempt to construct morality (as a kind of moral cocktail) out of "at one time the special destination of human nature (including, however, the idea of a rational nature generally,) at one time perfection, at another happiness, here moral sense, there fear of God, a little of this, and a little of that, in marvellous mixture" (33). Morality needs psychology and anthropology for its application, but not for its determination.

Everything in nature works according to laws. Rational beings alone have the faculty of acting according *to the conception* of laws, that is according to principles, *i.e.,* have a *will.* Since the deduction of actions from principles requires *reason,* the will is nothing but practical reason. If reason infallibly determines the will, then the actions of such a being which are recognised as objectively necessary are subjectively necessary also; *i.e.*, the will is a faculty to choose *that only* which reason independent on inclination recognises as practically necessary, *i.e.*, as good. But if reason of itself does not sufficiently determine the will, if the latter is subject also to subjective conditions (particular impulses) which do not always coincide with the objective conditions; in a word, if the will does not *in itself* completely accord with reason (which is actually the case with men), then the actions which objectively are recognised as necessary are subjectively contingent, and the determination of such a will according to objective laws is *obligation*, that is to say, the relation of the objective laws to a will that is not thoroughly good, is conceived as the determination of the will of a rational being by principles of reason, but which the will from its nature does not of necessity follow.

The conception of an objective principle, in so far as it is obligatory for a will, is called a command (of reason), and the formula of the command is called an Imperative.

All imperatives are expressed by the word *ought* [or *shall*], and thereby indicate the relation of an objective law of reason to a will, which from its subjective constitution is not necessarily determined by it (an obligation). They say that something would be good to do or to forbear, but they say it to a will which does not always do a thing because it is conceived to be good to do it. That is practically *good*, however, which determines the will by means of the conceptions of reason, and consequently not from subjective causes, but objectively, that is, on principles which are valid for every rational being as such. It is distinguished from the *pleasant*, as that which influences the will only by means of sensation from merely subjective causes, valid only for the sense of this or that one, and not as a principle of reason, which holds for every one.

A perfectly good will would therefore be equally subject to objective laws (viz., of good), but could not be conceived as *obliged* thereby to act lawfully, because of itself from its subjective constitution it can only be determined by the conception of good. Therefore no imperatives hold for the Divine will, or in general for a *holy* will; *ought* is here out of place, because the volition is already of itself necessarily in unison with the law. Therefore imperatives are only formulae to express the relation of objective laws of all volition to the subjective imperfection

of the will of this or that rational being, *e.g.*, the human will.

Now all *imperatives* command either *hypothetically* or *categorically*. The former represent the practical necessity of a possible action as means to something else that is willed (or at least which one might possibly will). The categorical imperative would be that which represented an action as necessary of itself without reference to another end, *i.e.*, as objectively necessary. [36–38]

General principles are either of *skill* (concerning an end regardless of whether it is rational or good), of *prudence* (concerning happiness), or of morality (the categorical imperative) which concerns "not the matter of the action, or its intended result, but its form and the principle of which it is itself a result; and what is essentially good in it consists in the mental disposition, let the consequence be what it may" (40–41). Imperatives may also be classified as technical, pragmatic, and moral.

Now arises the question, how are all these imperatives possible? This question does not seek to know how the accomplishment of the action ordained by the imperative can be conceived, but merely how the obligation of the will which the imperative expresses, can be thought. No special explanation is needed to show how an imperative of skill is possible. Whoever wills the end, wills also (so far as reason decides his conduct) the means in his power which are indispensably necessary thereto. This proposition is, as regards the volition, analytical; for, in willing an object as my effect, there is already thought the causality of myself as an acting cause, that is to say, the use of the means. . . .

If it were only equally easy to give a definite conception of happiness, the imperatives of prudence would correspond exactly with those of skill, and would likewise be analytical. For in this case as in that, it could be said, whoever wills the end, wills also (according to the dictate of reason necessarily) the indispensable means thereto which are in his power. But, unfortunately, the notion of happiness is so indefinite that although every man wishes to attain it, yet he never can say definitely and consistently what it is that he really wishes and wills. The reason of this is that all the elements which belong to the notion of happiness are altogether empirical, *i.e.*, they must be borrowed from experience, and nevertheless the idea of happiness requires an absolute whole, a maximum of welfare in my present and all future circumstances. Now it is impossible that the most clear-sighted, and at the same time most powerful being (supposed finite) should frame to itself a definite conception of what he really wills in this. Does he will riches, how much anxiety, envy, and snares might he not thereby draw upon his shoulders? Does he will knowledge and discernment, perhaps it might prove to be only an eye so much the sharper to show him so much the more fearfully the evils that are now concealed from him, and that cannot be avoided, or to impose more wants on his desires which already give him concern enough. Would he have long life, who guarantees to him that it would not be a long misery? Would he at least have health; how often has uneasiness of the body restrained from excesses into which perfect health would have allowed one to fall? and so on. In short he is unable, on any principle, to determine with certainty what would make him truly happy; because to do so he would have need to be omniscient. We cannot therefore act on any definite principles to secure happiness, but only on empirical counsels, *ex. gr.*, of regimen, frugality, courtesy, reserve, &c., which experience teaches do, on the average, most promote well-being. Hence it follows that the imperatives of prudence do not strictly speaking command at all, that is, they cannot present actions objectively as practically *necessary*; that they are rather to be regarded as counsels (*consilia*) than precepts (*praecepta*) of reason, that the problem to determine certainly and universally what action would promote the happiness of a rational being is completely insoluble, and consequently no imperative respecting it is possible which should, in the strict sense, command to do what makes happy; because happiness is not an ideal of reason but of imagination, resting solely on empirical grounds, and it is vain to expect that these should define an action by which one could attain the totality of a series of consequences which is really endless. This imperative of prudence would however be an analytical proposition if we assume that the means to happiness could be certainly assigned; for it is distin-

guished from the imperative of skill only by this, that in the latter the end is merely possible, in the former it is given; as however both only ordain the means to that which we suppose to be willed as an end, it follows that the imperative which ordains the willing of the means to him who wills the end is in both cases analytical. Thus there is no difficulty in regard to the possibility of an imperative of this kind either.

On the other hand the question, how the imperative of *morality* is possible, is undoubtedly one, the only one, demanding a solution, as this is not at all hypothetical, and the objective necessity which it presents cannot rest on any hypothesis, as is the case with the hypothetical imperatives. Only here we must never leave out of consideration that we *cannot* make out *by any example*, in other words empirically, whether there is such an imperative at all, but it is rather to be feared that all those which seem to be categorical may yet be at bottom hypothetical. For instance, when the precept is: Thou shalt not promise deceitfully; and it is assumed that the necessity of this is not a mere counsel to avoid some other evil, so that it should mean: thou shalt not make a lying promise, lest if it become known thou shouldst destroy thy credit; but that an action of this kind must be regarded as evil in itself, so that the imperative of the prohibition is categorical; then we cannot show with certainty in any example that the will was determined merely by the law, without any other spring of action, although it may appear to be so. For it is always possible that fear of disgrace, perhaps also obscure dread of other dangers, may have a secret influence on the will. Who can prove by experience the non-existence of a cause when all that experience tells us is that we do not perceive it? But in such a case the so-called moral imperative, which as such appears to be categorical and unconditional, would in reality be only a pragmatic precept; drawing our attention to our own interests, and merely teaching us to take these into consideration.

We shall therefore have to investigate *a priori* the possibility of a categorical imperative, as we have not in this case the advantage of its reality being given in experience, so that [the elucidation of] its possibility should be requisite only for its explanation, not for its establishment. In the meantime it may be discerned beforehand that the categorical imperative alone has the import of a practical Law;

all the rest may indeed be called *principles* of the will but not laws, since whatever is only necessary for the attainment of some arbitrary purpose may be considered as in itself contingent, and we can at any time be free from the precept if we give up the purpose; on the contrary the unconditional command leaves the will no liberty to choose the opposite, consequently it alone carries with it that necessity which we require in a law.

Secondly, in the case of this categorical imperative or law of morality, the difficulty (of discerning its possibility) is a very profound one. It is an *a priori* synthetical practical proposition, and as there is so much difficulty in discerning the possibility of speculative propositions of this kind, it may readily be supposed that the difficulty will be no less with the practical.

In this problem we will first inquire whether the mere conception of a categorical imperative may not perhaps supply us also with the formula of it, containing the proposition which alone can be a categorical imperative; for even if we know the tenor of such an absolute command, yet how it is possible will require further special and laborious study; which we postpone to the last section.

When I conceive a hypothetical imperative in general, I do not know beforehand what it will contain, until I am given the condition. But when I conceive a categorical imperative I know at once what it contains. For as the imperative contains, besides the law, only the necessity of the maxim [d] conforming to this law, while the law contains no condition restricting it, there remains nothing but the general statement that the maxim of the action should conform to a universal law, and it is this conformity alone that the imperative properly represents as necessary.

There is therefore but one categorical imperative, namely this: *Act only on that maxim whereby thou canst at the same time will that it should become a universal law.*

Now if all imperatives of duty can be deduced from this one imperative as from their principle, then although it should remain undecided whether what is called duty is not merely a vain notion,

yet at least we shall be able to show what we understand by it and what this notion means.

Since the universality of the law according to which effects are produced constitutes what is properly called *nature* in the most general sense (as to form), that is the existence of things so far as it is determined by general laws, the imperative of duty may be expressed thus: *Act as if the maxim of thy action were to become by thy will a Universal Law of Nature.*

We will now enumerate a few duties, adopting the usual division of them into duties to ourselves and to others, and into perfect and imperfect duties.[e]

1. A man reduced to despair by a series of misfortunes feels wearied of life, but is still so far in possession of his reason that he can ask himself whether it would not be contrary to his duty to himself to take his own life. Now he inquires whether the maxim of his action could become a universal law of nature. His maxim is: From self-love I adopt it as a principle to shorten my life when its longer duration is likely to bring more evil than satisfaction. It is asked then simply whether this principle of self-love can become a universal law of nature? Now we see at once that a system of nature of which it should be a law to destroy life by the very feeling which is designed to impel to the maintenance of life would contradict itself, and therefore could not exist as a system of nature; hence that maxim cannot possibly exist as a universal law of nature and consequently would be wholly inconsistent with the supreme principle of all duty.

2. Another finds himself forced by necessity to borrow money. He knows that he will not be able to repay it, but sees also that nothing will be lent to him, unless he promises stoutly to repay it in a definite time. He desires to make this promise, but he has still so much conscience as to ask himself: Is it not unlawful and inconsistent with duty to get out of a difficulty in this way? Suppose however that he resolves to do so: then the maxim of his action would be expressed thus: When I think my-

---

[d] A MAXIM is a subjective principle of action . . . the principle on which the subject *acts;* but the law is the objective principle valid for every rational being, and is the principle on which it *ought to act* that is an imperative.

[e] It must be noted here that I reserve the division of duties for a future *metaphysic of morals;* so that I give it here only as an arbitrary one (in order to arrange my examples). For the rest, I understand by a perfect duty, one that admits no exception in favour of inclination, and then I have not merely external but also internal perfect duties. . . .

self in want of money, I will borrow money and promise to repay it, although I know that I never can do so. Now this principle of self-love or of one's own advantage may perhaps be consistent with my whole future welfare; but the question now is, Is it right? I change then the suggestion of self-love into a universal law, and state the question thus: How would it be if my maxim were a universal law? Then I see at once that it could never hold as a universal law of nature, but would necessarily contradict itself. For supposing it to be a universal law that every one when he thinks himself in a difficulty should be able to promise whatever he pleases, with the purpose of not keeping his promise, the promise itself would become impossible, as well as the end that one might have in view in it, since no one would consider that anything was promised to him, but would ridicule all such statements as vain pretences.

3. A third finds in himself a talent which with the help of some culture might make him a useful man in many respects. But he finds himself in comfortable circumstances, and prefers to indulge in pleasure rather than to take pains in enlarging and improving his happy natural capacities. He asks, however, whether his maxim of neglect of his natural gifts, besides agreeing with his inclination to indulgence, agrees also with what is called duty? He sees then that a system of nature could indeed subsist with such a universal law, though men (like the South Sea islanders) should let their talents rust, and resolve to devote their lives merely to idleness, amusement, and propagation of their species, in a word to enjoyment; but he cannot possibly *will* that this should be a universal law of nature, or be implanted in us as such by a natural instinct. For, as a rational being, he necessarily wills that his faculties be developed, since they serve him for all sorts of possible purposes, and have been given him for this.

4. A fourth, who is in prosperity, while he sees that others have to contend with great wretchedness and that he could help them, thinks: What concern is it of mine? Let every one be as happy as heaven pleases or as he can make himself; I will take nothing from him nor even envy him, only I do not wish to contribute anything either to his welfare or to his assistance in distress! Now no doubt if such a mode of thinking were a universal law, the human race might very well subsist, and doubtless

even better than in a state in which every one talks of sympathy and good will, or even takes care occasionally to put it into practice, but on the other side, also cheats when he can, betrays the rights of men or otherwise violates them. But although it is possible that a universal law of nature might exist in accordance with that maxim, it is impossible to *will* that such a principle should have the universal validity of a law of nature. For a will which resolved this would contradict itself, inasmuch as many cases might occur in which one would have need of the love and sympathy of others, and in which by such a law of nature, sprung from his own will, he would deprive himself of all hope of the aid he desires.

These are a few of the many actual duties, or at least what we regard as such, which obviously fall into two classes on the one principle that we have laid down. We must be *able to will* that a maxim of our action should be a universal law. This is the canon of the moral appreciation of the action generally. Some actions are of such a character, that their maxim cannot without contradiction be even *conceived* as a universal law of nature, far from it being possible that we should *will* that it *should* be so. In others this intrinsic impossibility is not found, but still it is impossible to *will* that their maxim should be raised to the universality of a law of nature, since such a will would contradict itself. It is easily seen that the former violate strict or rigorous (inflexible) duty; the latter only laxer (meritorious) duty. Thus it has been completely shown how all duties depend as regards the nature of the obligation (not the object of the action) on the same principle.

If now we attend to ourselves on occasion of any transgression of duty, we shall find that we in fact do not will that our maxim should be a universal law, for that is impossible for us; on the contrary we will that the opposite should remain a universal law, only we assume the liberty of making an *exception* in our own favour or (just for this time only) in favour of our inclination. [41–51]

That there is such an imperative has not yet been proven a priori. And it cannot be done empirically.

The will is conceived as a faculty of determining oneself to action *in accordance with the conception of certain laws*. And such a faculty can be found only in rational beings. Now that which serves the will as the objective ground of its self-determination is the *end*, and if this is assigned by reason alone, it must hold for all rational beings. On the other hand, that which merely contains the ground of possibility of the action of which the effect is the end, this is called the *means*. The subjective ground of the desire is the *spring*, the objective ground of the volition is the *motive*; hence the distinction between subjective ends which rest on springs, and objective ends which depend on motives that hold for every rational being. Practical principles are *formal* when they abstract from all subjective ends, they are *material* when they assume these, and therefore particular springs of action. The ends which a rational being proposes to himself at pleasure as *effects* of his actions (material ends) are all only relative, for it is only their relation to the particular desires of the subject that gives them their worth, which therefore cannot furnish principles universal and necessary for all rational beings and for every volition, that is to say practical laws. Hence all these relative ends can give rise only to hypothetical imperatives.

Supposing, however, that there were something *whose existence* has *in itself* an absolute worth, something which being *an end in itself*, could be a source of definite laws, then in this and this alone would lie the source of a possible categorical imperative, *i.e.*, a practical law. Now I say: man and generally any rational being *exists* as an end in himself, *not merely as a means* to be arbitrarily used by this or that will, but in all his actions, whether they concern himself or other rational beings, must always be regarded at the same time as an end. All objects of the inclinations have only a conditional worth, for if the inclinations and the wants founded on them did not exist, then their object would be without value. But the inclinations themselves being sources of want, are so far from having an absolute worth for which they should be desired, that on the contrary it must be the universal wish of every rational being to be wholly free from them. Thus the worth of any object which is *to be acquired* by our action is always conditional. Beings whose existence depends not on our will but on nature's, have nevertheless, if they are irrational beings, only a relative value as means, and are therefore called *things*; rational beings on the contrary, are called *persons*, because their very nature points them out as ends in themselves, that is as something which must not be used merely as means, and so far there-

fore restricts freedom of action (and is an object of respect). These, therefore, are not merely subjective ends whose existence has a worth *for us* as an effect of our action, but *objective ends*, that is things whose existence is an end in itself; an end moreover for which no other can be substituted, which they should subserve *merely* as means, for otherwise nothing whatever would possess *absolute worth*; but if all worth were conditioned and therefore contingent, then there would be no supreme practical principle of reason whatever.

If then there is a supreme practical principle or, in respect of the human will, a categorical imperative, it must be one which, drawn from the conception of that which is necessarily an end for every one because it is *an end in itself*, constitutes an *objective* principle of will, and can therefore serve as a universal practical law. The foundation of this principle is: *rational nature exists as an end in itself*. Man necessarily conceives his own existence as being so; so far then, this is a *subjective* principle of human actions. But every other rational being regards its existence similarly, just on the same rational principle that holds for me: [f] so that it is at the same time an objective principle, from which as a supreme practical law all laws of the will must be capable of being deduced. Accordingly the practical imperative will be as follows: *So act as to treat humanity, whether in thine own person or in that of any other, in every case as an end withal, never as a means only.* [55–57]

This formulation of the imperative yields the same results as the previous formulation for the four examples: suicide treats oneself as a means to escape painful circumstances; a false promise uses another merely as means; the neglect of our capacities may be consistent with maintaining humanity as an end in itself, but not with advancing that end; lack of concern for others harmonizes only negatively, not positively and fully, with humanity as an end in itself.

This principle, that humanity and generally every rational nature is *an end in itself*, (which is the su-

[f] This proposition is here stated as a postulate. The grounds of it will be found in the concluding section.

preme limiting condition of every man's freedom of action), is not borrowed from experience, *firstly*, because it is universal, applying as it does to all rational beings whatever, and experience is not capable of determining anything about them; *secondly*, because it does not present humanity as an end to men (subjectively) that is as an object which men do of themselves actually adopt as an end; but as an objective end, which must as a law constitute the supreme limiting condition of all our subjective ends, let them be what we will; it must therefore spring from pure reason. In fact the objective principle of all practical legislation lies (according to the first principle) in *the rule* and its form of universality which makes it capable of being a law (say, *e.g.,* a law of nature); but the *subjective* principle is in the *end*; now by the second principle the subject of all ends is each rational being, inasmuch as it is an end in itself. Hence follows the third practical principle of the will, which is the ultimate condition of its harmony with universal practical reason, viz: the idea of *the will of every rational being as a universally legislative will.*

On this principle all maxims are rejected which are inconsistent with the will being itself universal legislator. Thus the will is not subject simply to the law, but so subject that it must be regarded *as itself giving the law,* and on this ground only, subject to the law (of which it can regard itself as the author).

In the previous imperatives, namely, that based on the conception of the conformity of actions to general laws, as in a *physical system of nature,* and that based on the universal *prerogative* of rational beings as *ends* in themselves—these imperatives just because they were conceived as categorical, excluded from any share in their authority all admixture of any interest as a spring of action; they were however only *assumed* to be categorical, because such an assumption was necessary to explain the conception of duty. But we could not prove independently that there are practical propositions which command categorically, nor can it be proved in this section; one thing however could be done, namely to indicate in the imperative itself by some determinate expression, that in the case of volition from duty all interest is renounced, which is the specific criterion of categorical as distinguished from hypothetical imperatives. This is done in the present (third) formula of the principle, namely in the idea of the will of every rational being as a *universally legislating will.*

For although a will *which is subject to laws* may be attached to this law by means of an interest, yet a will which is itself a supreme lawgiver cannot possibly depend on any interest, since a will so dependent would itself still need another law restricting the interest of its self-love by the condition that it should be valid as universal law. [59–61]

The conception of the will of every rational being as one which must consider itself as giving in all the maxims of its will universal laws, so as to judge itself and its actions from this point of view—this conception leads to another which depends on it and is very fruitful, namely that of *a kingdom of ends.*

By a *kingdom* I understand the union of different rational beings in a system by common laws. Now since it is by laws that ends are determined as regards their universal validity, hence, if we abstract from the personal differences of rational beings and likewise from all the content of their private ends, we shall be able to conceive all ends combined in a systematic whole (including both rational beings as ends in themselves, and also the special ends which each may propose to himself), that is to say, we can conceive a kingdom of ends, which on the preceding principles is possible.

For all rational beings come under the *law* that each of them must treat itself and all others *never merely as means,* but in every case *at the same time as ends in themselves.* Hence results a systematic union of rational beings by common objective laws, *i.e.,* a kingdom which may be called a kingdom of ends, since what these laws have in view is just the relation of these beings to one another as ends and means. It is certainly only an ideal.

A rational being belongs as a *member* to the kingdom of ends when although giving universal laws in it he is also himself subject to these laws. He belongs to it *as sovereign,* when while giving laws he is not subject to the will of any other.

A rational being must always regard himself as giving laws in a kingdom of ends which freedom of the will makes possible, whether it be as member or as sovereign. He cannot, however, maintain the latter position merely by the maxims of his will, but only in case he is a completely independent being without wants and with unrestricted power adequate to his will.

Morality consists then in the reference of all action

to the legislation which alone can render a kingdom of ends possible. This legislation must be capable of existing in every rational being, and of emanating from his will, so that the principle of this will, is never to act on any maxim which could not without contradiction be also a universal law, and accordingly always so to act *that the will could at the same time regard itself as giving in its maxims universal laws.* If now the maxims of rational beings are not by their own nature coincident with this objective principle, then the necessity of acting on it is called practical obligation, *i.e., duty.* Duty does not apply to the sovereign in the kingdom of ends, but it does to every member of it and to all in the same degree.

The practical necessity of acting on this principle, *i.e.,* duty does not rest at all on feelings, impulses or inclinations, but solely on the relation of rational beings to one another, a relation in which the will of a rational being must always be regarded as *legislative* since otherwise it could not be conceived as *an end in itself.* Reason then refers every maxim of the will, regarding it as legislating universally, to every other will and also to every action towards oneself; and this not on account of any other practical motive or any future advantage, but from the idea of the *dignity* of a rational being, obeying no law but that which he himself also gives.

In the kingdom of ends everything has either Value or Dignity. Whatever has a value can be replaced by something else which is *equivalent;* whatever on the other hand is above all value, and therefore admits of no equivalent, has a dignity.

Whatever has reference to the general inclinations and wants of mankind has a *market value;* whatever without presupposing a want, corresponds to a certain taste, that is to a satisfaction in the mere purposeless play of our faculties, has a *fancy value;* but that which constitutes the condition under which alone anything can be an end in itself, this has not merely a relative worth, *i.e.,* value, but an intrinsic worth, that is, *dignity.*

Now morality is the condition under which alone a rational being can be an end in himself, since by this alone is it possible that he should be a legislating member in the kingdom of ends. Thus morality, and humanity as capable of it, is that which alone has dignity. Skill and diligence in labour have a market value; wit, lively imagination, and humour have a fancy value; on the other hand, fidelity to promises, benevolence from principle (not from in-

stinct) have an intrinsic worth. Neither nature nor art contains anything which in default of these it could put in their place, for their worth consists not in the effects which spring from them, not in the use and advantage which they secure, but in the disposition of mind, that is the maxims of the will which are ready to manifest themselves in such actions, even though they should not have the desired effect. These actions also need no recommendation from any subjective taste or sentiment, that they may be looked on with immediate favour and satisfaction: they need no immediate propension or feeling for them; they exhibit the will that performs them as an object of an immediate respect, and nothing but reason is required to *impose* them on the will; not to *flatter* it into them, which in the case of duties would be a contradiction. This estimation therefore shows that the worth of such a disposition is dignity, and places it infinitely above all value, with which it cannot for a moment be brought into comparison or competition without as it were violating its sanctity.

What then is it which justifies virtue or the morally good disposition, in making such lofty claims? It is nothing less than the privilege it secures to the rational being of participating in the giving of universal laws, by which it qualifies him to be a member of a possible kingdom of ends, a privilege to which he was already destined by his own nature as being an end in himself, and on that account legislating in the kingdom of ends; free as regards all laws of physical nature, and obeying those only which he himself gives, and by which his maxims can belong to a system of universal law, to which at the same time he submits himself. For nothing has any worth except what the law assigns it. Now the legislation itself which assigns the worth of everything, must for that very reason possess dignity, that is an unconditional incomparable worth, and the word *respect* alone supplies a becoming expression for the esteem which a rational being must have for it. *Autonomy* then is the basis of the dignity of human and of every rational nature. [62–66]

The autonomy of the will is the supreme principle of morality.

Autonomy of the will is that property of it by which it is a law to itself (independently on any property of the objects of volition). The principle of autonomy then is: Always so to choose that the same volition shall comprehend the maxims of our choice as a universal law. [71]

Heteronomy of the will is the source of all spurious principles of morality:

The will in that case does not give itself the law, but it is given by the object through its relation to the will. This relation whether it rests on inclination or on conceptions of reason only admits of hypothetical imperatives: I ought to do something *because I wish for something else.* [72]

Theories based on happiness or perfection or even divine will are examples.

The principle of *private happiness,* however, is the most objectionable, not merely because it is false, and experience contradicts the supposition that prosperity is always proportioned to good conduct, nor yet merely because it contributes nothing to the establishment of morality—since it is quite a different thing to make a prosperous man and a good man, or to make one prudent and sharp-sighted for his own interests, and to make him virtuous—but because the springs it provides for morality are such as rather undermine it and destroy its sublimity, since they put the motives to virtue and to vice in the same class, and only teach us to make a better calculation, the specific difference between virtue and vice being entirely extinguished. [74]

The appeal to a divine will is circular:

[W]e have no intuition of the divine perfection, and can only deduce it from our own conceptions, the most important of which is that of morality, and our explanation would thus be involved in a gross circle; and, in the next place, if we avoid this, the only notion of the Divine will remaining to us is a conception made up of the attributes of desire of glory and dominion, combined with the awful conceptions of might and vengeance, and any system of morals erected on this foundation would be directly opposed to morality. [75]

Section II, like Section I, has been merely analytical: showing that the autonomy of the will is the foundation of the ordinarily received notion of morality. The possibility of that foundation, and its necessity, is a matter whose

proof lies beyond the metaphysic of morals and requires a critical examination of practical reason.

In the concluding section we shall give the principal outlines of this critique as far as is sufficient for our purpose. [77]

Third Section: Transition from the Metaphysic of Morals to the Critique of Pure Practical Reason

The Concept of Freedom is the Key That Explains the Autonomy of the Will. The will is a kind of causality belonging to living beings in so far as they are rational, and *freedom* would be this property of such causality that it can be efficient, independently on foreign causes *determining* it; just as *physical necessity* is the property that the causality of all irrational beings has of being determined to activity by the influence of foreign causes.

The preceding definition of freedom is *negative,* and therefore unfruitful for the discovery of its essence; but it leads to a *positive* conception which is so much the more full and fruitful. Since the conception of causality involves that of laws, according to which, by something that we call cause, something else, namely the effect, must be produced [laid down]; hence, although freedom is not a property of the will depending on physical laws, yet it is not for that reason lawless; on the contrary it must be a causality acting according to immutable laws, but of a peculiar kind; otherwise a free will would be an absurdity. Physical necessity is a heteronomy of the efficient causes, for every effect is possible only according to this law, that something else determines the efficient cause to exert its causality. What else then can freedom of the will be but autonomy, that is the property of the will to be a law to itself? But the proposition: The will is in every action a law to itself, only expresses the principle, to act on no other maxim than that which can also have as an object itself as a universal law. Now this is precisely the formula of the categorical imperative and is the principle of morality, so that a free will and a will subject to moral laws are one and the same.

On the hypothesis then of freedom of the will, morality together with its principle follows from it by mere analysis of the conception. However the latter is still a synthetic proposition; viz., an absolutely good will is that whose maxim can always include itself regarded as a universal law; for this property of its maxim can never be discovered by analysing the conception of an absolutely good will. Now such synthetic propositions are only possible in this way; that the two cognitions are connected together by their union with a third in which they are both to be found. The *positive* concept of freedom furnishes this third cognition, which cannot, as with physical causes, be the nature of the sensible world (in the concept of which we find conjoined the concept of something in relation as cause to *something else* as effect). We cannot now at once show what this third is to which freedom points us, and of which we have an idea *a priori*, nor can we make intelligible how the concept of freedom is shown to be legitimate from principles of pure practical reason, and with it the possibility of a categorical imperative; but some further preparation is required.

Freedom. Must Be Presupposed as a Property of the Will of All Rational Beings. It is not enough to predicate freedom of our own will, from whatever reason, if we have not sufficient grounds for predicating the same of all rational beings. For as morality serves as a law for us only because we are *rational beings*, it must also hold for all rational beings, and as it must be deduced simply from the property of freedom, it must be shown that freedom also is a property of all rational beings. It is not enough then to prove it from certain supposed experiences of human nature (which indeed is quite impossible, and it can only be shown *a priori*), but we must show that it belongs to the activity of all rational beings endowed with a will. Now I say every being that cannot act except *under the idea of freedom* is just for that reason in a practical point of view really free, that is to say all laws which are inseparably connected with freedom have the same force for him as if his will had been shown to be free in itself by a proof theoretically conclusive.[8] Now I affirm that we must attribute to every rational being

which has a will that it has also the idea of freedom and acts entirely under this idea. For in such a being we conceive a reason that is practical, that is has causality in reference to its objects. Now we cannot possibly conceive a reason consciously receiving a bias from any other quarter with respect to its judgments, for then the subject would ascribe the determination of its judgment not to its own reason, but to an impulse. It must regard itself as the author of its principles independent on foreign influences. Consequently as practical reason or as the will of a rational being it must regard itself as free, that is to say, the will of such a being cannot be a will of its own except under the idea of freedom. This idea must therefore in a practical point of view be ascribed to every rational being. [78–81]

Why should I subject myself and other rational beings—that is, those who have sensibility and whose springs may counter the rational—to this principle? The moral law is presupposed in the idea of freedom, and we can have an interest in being worthy of happiness. But whence does the moral law derive its obligation? We have here a sort of circle: we assume freedom to conceive ourselves as subject to moral laws, and we afterwards consider ourselves subject to these laws because we have attributed freedom to ourselves. The solution is that we look at ourselves in two different ways—when we think of ourselves as free and when we think of our actions as effects. (This is the fundamental move Kant establishes in the *Critique of Pure Reason*.) To view our actions as effects is to view them as *phenomena;* to postulate freedom is to reach to *noumena* or things in themselves. But since we cannot *know* noumena, we can only *postulate* or demand freedom, for without it morality makes no sense.

Therefore freedom is only an Idea [ideal conception] of Reason, and its objective reality in itself is doubtful, while nature is a *concept* of the *understanding* which proves, and must necessarily prove its reality in examples of experience.

There arises from this a dialectic of Reason, since the freedom attributed to the will appears to

---

[8] I adopt this method of assuming freedom merely *as an idea* which rational beings suppose in their actions, in order to avoid the necessity of proving it in its theoretical aspect also. The former is sufficient for my purpose; for even though the speculative proof should not be made out, yet a being that cannot act except with the idea of freedom is bound by the same laws that would oblige a being who was actually free. Thus we can escape here from the onus which presses on the theory.

contradict the necessity of nature, and placed between these two ways Reason for *speculative purposes* finds the road of physical necessity much more beaten and more appropriate than that of freedom, yet for *practical purposes* the foot-path of freedom is the only one on which it is possible to make use of reason in our conduct; hence it is just as impossible for the subtlest philosophy as for the commonest reason of men to argue away freedom. Philosophy must then assume that no real contradiction will be found between freedom and physical necessity of the same human actions, for it cannot give up the conception of nature any more than that of freedom. [90]

Critique of Practical Reason [16]

The problem just considered cannot be avoided by treating freedom as a psychological property.

[T]here are still many who think that they can explain this freedom on empirical principles, like any other physical faculty, and treat it as a *psychological* property, the explanation of which only requires a more exact study of the *nature of the soul* and of the motives of the will, and not as a *transcendental* predicate of the causality of a being that belongs to the world of sense (which is really the point). They thus deprive us of the grand revelation which we obtain through practical reason by means of the moral law, the revelation, namely, of a supersensible world by the realization of the otherwise transcendent concept of freedom, and by this deprive us also of the moral law itself, which admits no empirical principle of determination. [224]

Misunderstandings of freedom are explored.

When I say of a man who commits a theft that by the physical law of causality this deed is a necessary result of the determining causes in preceding time, then it was impossible that it could not have happened; how then can the judgment, according to the moral law, make any change, and suppose that it could have been omitted, because the law

says that it ought to have been omitted; that is, how can a man be called quite free at the same moment, and with respect to the same action in which he is subject to an inevitable physical necessity? . . . In fact, in the question about the freedom which must be the foundation of all moral laws and the consequent responsibility, it does not matter whether the principles which necessarily determine causality by a physical law reside *within* the subject or *without* him, or in the former case whether these principles are instinctive or are conceived by reason, if, as is admitted by these men themselves, these determining ideas have the ground of their existence in time and in the *antecedent state*, and this again in an antecedent, etc. Then it matters not that these are internal; it matters not that they have a psychological and not a mechanical causality, that is, produce actions by means of ideas, and not by bodily movements; they are still *determining principles* of the causality of a being whose existence is determinable in time, and therefore under the necessitation of conditions of past time, which therefore when the subject has to act, are *no longer in his power*. This may imply psychological freedom (if we choose to apply this term to a merely internal chain of ideas in the mind), but it involves physical necessity, and therefore leaves no room for *transcendental freedom*, which must be conceived as independence on everything empirical, and, consequently, on nature generally, whether it is an object of the internal sense considered in time only, or of the external in time and space. Without this freedom (in the latter and true sense), which alone is practical *a priori*, no moral law and no moral imputation are possible. [226–227]

In this view now the rational being can justly say of every unlawful action that he performs, that he could very well have left it undone; although as appearance it is sufficiently determined in the past, and in this respect is absolutely necessary; for it, with all the past which determines it, belongs to the one single phenomenon of his character which he makes for himself, in consequence of which he imputes the causality of those appearances to himself as a cause independent on sensibility. [228–229]

A striking example shows that the moral law and practical reason force upon us the idea of freedom:

---

[16] Abbott translation (1879).

Suppose some one asserts of his lustful appetite that when the desired object and the opportunity are present it is quite irresistible. [Ask him]:—if a gallows were erected before the house where he finds this opportunity, in order that he should be hanged thereon immediately after the gratification of his lust, whether he could not then control his passion; we need not be long in doubt what he would reply. Ask him however:—if his sovereign ordered him on pain of the same immediate execution to bear false witness against an honourable man, whom the prince might wish to destroy under a plausible pretext, would he consider it possible in that case to overcome his love of life, however great it may be. He would perhaps not venture to affirm whether he would do so or not, but he must unhesitatingly admit that it is possible to do so. He judges, therefore, that he can do a certain thing because he is conscious that he ought, and he recognizes that he is free, a fact which but for the moral law he would never have known. [141]

Respect for the moral law should not be interpreted as a feeling or sentiment comparable to sympathy or love.

Since then for the purpose of giving the moral law influence over the will, we must not seek for any other motives that might enable us to dispense with the motive of the law itself, because that would produce mere hypocrisy, without consistency; and it is even *dangerous* to allow other motives, (for instance, that of interest) even to co-operate *along with* the moral law; hence nothing is left us but to determine carefully in what way the moral law becomes a motive, and what effect this has upon the faculty of desire. For as to the question how a law can be directly and of itself a determining principle of the will (which is the essence of morality) this is, for human reason, an insoluble problem and identical with the question: how a free will is possible. Therefore what we have to show *a priori* is, not why the moral law in itself supplies a motive, but what effect it, as such, produces (or, more correctly speaking, must produce) on the mind.

The essential point in every determination of the will by the moral law is that being a free will it is determined simply by the moral law, not only without the co-operation of sensible impulses, but even

to the rejection of all such, and to the checking of all inclinations so far as they might be opposed to that law. So far, then, the effect of the moral law as a motive is only negative, and this motive can be known *a priori* to be such. For all inclination and every sensible impulse is founded on feeling, and the negative effect produced on feeling (by the check on the inclinations) is itself feeling; consequently, we can see *a priori* that the moral law, as a determining principle of the will, must by thwarting all our inclinations produce a feeling which may be called pain; and in this we have the first, perhaps the only instance, in which we are able from *a priori* considerations to determine the relation of a cognition (in this case of pure practical reason) to the feeling of pleasure or displeasure. [196–197]

[O]ur nature as sensible beings is such that the matter of desire (objects of inclination, whether of hope or fear) first presents itself to us; and our pathologically affected self, although it is in its maxims quite unfit for universal legislation, yet, just as if it constituted our entire self, strives to put its pretensions forward first and to have them acknowledged as the first and original. This propensity to make ourselves in the subjective determining principles of our choice serve as the objective determining principle of the will generally, may be called *self-love*, and if this pretends to be legislative as an unconditional practical principle it may be called *self-conceit*. Now the moral law, which alone is truly objective (namely, in every respect), entirely excludes the influence of self-love on the supreme practical principle, and indefinitely checks the self-conceit that prescribes the subjective conditions of the former as laws. Now whatever checks our self-conceit in our own judgment, humiliates; therefore the moral law inevitably humbles every man when he compares with it the physical propensities of his nature. That, the idea of which as a *determining principle of our will* humbles us in our self-consciousness, awakes *respect* for itself, so far as it is itself positive, and a determining principle. Therefore the moral law is even subjectively a cause of respect. [198–199]

While the moral law, therefore, is a formal determining principle of action by practical pure reason . . . it is also a subjective determining principle, that is, a motive to this action, inasmuch as it has influence on the morality of the subject, and produces a feeling conducive to the influence of the law on the will. There is here in the subject no *antecedent* feeling tending to morality. For this is impossible, since every feeling is sensible, and the motive of moral intention must be free from all sensible conditions. On the contrary, while the sensible feeling which is at the bottom of all our inclinations is the condition of that impression which we call respect, the cause that determines it lies in the pure practical reason. . . . For by the fact that the conception of the moral law deprives self-love of its influence and self-conceit of its illusion, it lessens the obstacle to pure practical reason, and produces the conception of the superiority of its objective law to the impulses of the sensibility; and thus, by removing the counterpoise, it gives relatively greater weight to the law in the judgment of reason. . . . Thus the respect for the law is not a motive to morality, but is morality itself subjectively considered as a motive, inasmuch as pure practical reason, by rejecting all the rival pretensions of self-love, gives authority to the law which now alone has influence. [200–201]

Respect applies always to persons only—not to things. The latter may arouse inclination, and if they are animals (*e.g.,* horses, dogs, etc.) even *love* or *fear*, like the sea, a volcano, a beast of prey; but never *respect.* Something that comes nearer to this feeling is *admiration*, and this as an affection, astonishment, can apply to things also, *ex. gr.*, lofty mountains, the magnitude, number, and distance of the heavenly bodies, the strength and swiftness of many animals, etc. But all this is not respect. A man also may be an object to me of love, fear, or admiration, even to astonishment, and yet not be an object of respect. His jocose humour, his courage and strength, his power from the rank he has amongst others, may inspire me with sentiments of this kind, but still inner respect for him is wanting. *Fontenelle* says, "I bow before a great man, but my mind does not bow." I would add, before an humble, plain man in whom I perceive uprightness of character in a higher degree than I am conscious of in myself, *my mind bows* whether I choose it or not, and though I bear my head never so high that he may not forget my superior rank. Why is this? Because his example exhibits to me a law that humbles my self-conceit when I compare it with my conduct; a law, the *practicability* of obedience to which I see proved by fact before my eyes. Now I may even be conscious of a like degree of upright-

ness, and yet the respect remains. For since in man all good is defective, the law made visible by an example still humbles my pride, my standard being furnished by a man whose imperfections, whatever they may be, are not known to me as my own are, and who therefore appears to me in a more favourable light. *Respect* is a *tribute* which we cannot refuse to merit, whether we will or not; we may indeed outwardly withhold it, but we cannot help feeling it inwardly. [201–202]

The consciousness of a *free* submission of the will to the law, yet combined with an inevitable constraint put upon all inclinations, though only by our own reason, is respect for the law. The law that demands this respect and inspires it is clearly no other than the moral (for no other precludes all inclinations from exercising any direct influence on the will). An action which is objectively practical according to this law, to the exclusion of every determining principle of inclination, is *duty*, and this by reason of that exclusion includes in its concept practical *obligation*, that is, a determination to actions, however *reluctantly* they may be done. [206] [17]

---

[17] Kant's interpretation of respect became the starting point for different sociopsychological investigations of the nature of morality, as is shown in the following passage from Jean Piaget's *The Moral Judgment of the Child*, trans. Marjorie Gabain (New York: The Free Press, 1965), pp. 374–375:

The conception which M. Bovet has formed of respect is equally removed from that urged by Kant and that expounded by Durkheim. In Kant's view respect is not an ordinary feeling arising like any other under the influence of a person or thing. Its appearance is occasioned by the moral law in a manner which is inexplicable, and if we feel respect for certain individuals, we do so, in so far as they incarnate, as it were, this very law. According to M. Bovet, on the contrary, the law is not the source of respect. It is respect for persons which causes the commands coming from these persons to acquire the force of law in the spirit that feels respect. Thus respect is the source of law. In Durkheim's view as in Kant's there is no respect for individuals; it is in so far as the individual obeys the rule that he is respected. But this rule, far from emanating from reason, results as does respect itself, from the authority of the group. In a sense, then, law is the daughter of respect, but of the respect of the individual for the group. To this M. Bovet answers that if in adult society respect for the man and respect for the rule are in fact indissoluble, in the child the former can be seen to precede the latter.

The Metaphysics of Morals [18]

The metaphysics of morals, which works out duties that embody the categorical imperative, is divided into the doctrine of virtue and the doctrine of right (law). A common "Introduction" makes clear that although both doctrines involve empirical assumptions, they still provide *a priori* principles. Experience shows that men have ends (happiness, perfection) and that they require society; but the principles of virtue show which ends are duties, and the principles of right show how the freedom of the will of each can coexist with that of others. The principles in one area are particularized in specific virtues, while those of the other are particularized in fields of obligation (property, contract, etc.). Beyond all this lies moral anthropology. It contains only "the subjective conditions in human nature hindering as well as favoring the performance of the laws of the metaphysics of morals" (217). It treats of the strengthening and propagation of morality, for example in education.

[A]ll duties, simply because they are duties, belong to ethics. But their legislation is not therefore always contained in ethics. . . . Ethics teaches only that if the incentive which juridical legislation connects with that duty, namely, external constraint, were absent, the idea of duty alone would still be sufficient as an incentive. For if this were not so, and if the legislation itself were not juridical and the duty arising from it thus not properly a juridical duty [*Rechtspflicht*] (in contradistinction to a duty of virtue [*Tugendpflicht*]), then keeping faith (in accordance with one's promise in a contract) would be put in the same class with actions of benevolence and the obligation to them, and this certainly must not happen. It is not a duty of virtue to keep one's promise, but a juridical duty, one which we can

be compelled to perform. Nevertheless, it is a virtuous action (proof of virtue) to do so where no constraint is to be feared. The doctrine of right and the doctrine of virtue [*Rechtslehre und Tugendlehre*] are distinguished, therefore, not so much by their different duties as by the difference in the legislation which connects the one or the other incentive with the law. [219–220]

The Metaphysical Principles of Virtue [19]

Introduction

The doctrine of right had to do merely with the formal condition of external freedom. . . . Ethics, on the other hand, supplies in addition a matter (an object of free choice), namely, an *end* of pure reason which is at the same time represented as an objectively necessary end, i.e., as a duty for man. . . .

An end is an object of choice (of a rational being); by means of the representation of such an end, choice is determined to an action to produce the object. Now, I can indeed be forced by others to actions which are directed as means to an end, but I can never be forced by others to have an end; I alone can make something an end for myself. If, however, I am also obligated to make something which lies in the concepts of practical reason an end for myself, and if, therefore, besides the formal determining ground of choice (such as right contains) I am obligated to have in addition a material determining ground, i.e., an end that can be opposed to the end derived from sensible impulses, then this would be the concept of an end which is in itself a duty. . . .

For this reason ethics can also be defined as the system of the ends of pure practical reason. End and duty distinguish the two parts of the general doctrine of morals. That ethics contains duties which one cannot be (physically) forced by others

---

[18] The selection for the General Introduction to *The Metaphysics of Morals* is from *The Metaphysical Principles of Virtue*, trans. James Ellington, in Immanuel Kant, *Ethical Philosophy* (Indianapolis/Cambridge: Hackett, 1983). The bracketed numbers following the selection give the pagination of the Prussian Academy of Berlin edition of Kant.

[19] The selection is from *The Metaphysical Principles of Virtue*, trans. James Ellington, in Immanuel Kant, *Ethical Philosophy* (Indianapolis/Cambridge: Hackett, 1983). The bracketed numbers following passages in the selection give the pagination of the Prussian Academy of Berlin edition of Kant.

to observe is merely the consequence of the fact that ethics is a doctrine of ends, for being forced to have ends or to determine them contradicts itself. [380–381]

How is it possible that an end is also a duty?

One can think of the relation of an end to a duty in two ways: either starting from the end to find the maxim of the actions which are in accordance with duty; or, conversely, commencing with the maxim to find the end which is at the same time a duty. The doctrine of right proceeds in the first way. What end a person proposes for his action is left up to his free choice. But the maxim of his action is determined a priori, namely, so that the freedom of the agent can be consistent with the freedom of every other person according to a universal law.

Ethics, however, takes the opposite way. It cannot start from the ends which a man may propose to himself . . . for that would be to take empirical grounds for his maxims, and such grounds furnish no concept of duty, inasmuch as this concept (the categorical "ought") has its root in pure reason alone. If one's maxims were to be adopted according to such ends (which are all selfish), then one could not properly speak of the concept of duty at all. Thus in ethics the concept of duty will lead to ends, and the maxims regarding the ends which we ought to set before ourselves must be founded on moral principles. [382]

A duty of this kind is a "duty of virtue." The ends that are also duties are "one's own perfection and the happiness of others." These cannot be reversed:

For one's own happiness is an end which, to be sure, all men do have (by virtue of the impulse of their nature), but this end can never without contradiction be regarded as a duty. What everyone of himself already inevitably wants does not belong under the concept of duty, because a duty is a constraint to an end that is not gladly adopted. It is, therefore, a contradiction to say that one is obligated to promote his own happiness with all his powers. [386]

The laws that ethics gives govern not actions but their maxims. It follows that ethical duties

are of broad obligation, whereas those of right are of strict obligation.

For if the law can command only the maxim of actions and not the actions themselves, then this is a sign that the law leaves in its obedience (observance) a latitude for free choice, i.e., it cannot definitely assign in what way and to what extent something should be brought about by an action directed to an end which is at the same time a duty. But by a broad duty is not understood a permission to make exceptions to the maxim of the actions, but only the permission to limit one maxim of duty by another (e.g., the general love of one's neighbor by the love of one's parents); and this in fact broadens the field for the practice of virtue. [390]

The duty to cultivate morality within ourselves might appear to be a strict duty, but even here only the maxim is commanded.

For it is not possible for man to look so far into the depths of his own heart as ever to be entirely certain, even in one single action, of the purity of his moral purpose and the sincerity of his mental disposition, although he has no doubt at all about its legality. [392]

Similarly for beneficence:

That beneficence is a duty results from the fact that since our self-love cannot be separated from our need to be loved by others (to obtain help from them in case of need), we therefore make ourselves an end for others; and this maxim can never be obligatory except by qualifying as a universal law and, consequently, through a will to make others our ends. Hence the happiness of others is an end which is at the same time a duty.

But while I should sacrifice a part of my welfare to others without any hope of recompense because it is my duty, yet it is impossible to set definite limits on how far this is to go. Much depends upon what the true need of each one would be according to his own feelings, and it must be left to each one to determine this need for himself. For to sacrifice one's own happiness, one's true needs, in order to promote the happiness of others would be a self-contradictory maxim if made a universal law.

Therefore, this duty is only a broad one; it has a latitude within which we may do more or less without being able to assign definite limits to it. The law holds only for maxims, not for definite actions. [393]

Conflict of duties is not possible.

[A] duty can have only a single ground of obligation. And if two or more proofs of the ground are adduced, then this is a sure sign that either no valid proof at all has yet been given or that there are several distinct duties which have been regarded as one.

For all moral proofs can as philosophical ones only be adduced by means of rational knowledge from concepts and not, as in mathematics, through the construction of concepts. Mathematics allows a plurality of proofs for one and the same proposition, because in a priori intuition there can be several determinations of the nature of an object all of which lead back to the very same ground. If one proof of the duty of veracity, for instance, were first drawn from the harm that a lie causes other men, and then another from the worthlessness of a liar and the violation of his self-respect, what would be proved in the first argument is a duty of benevolence and not a duty of veracity, that is to say, not the duty for which a proof was required, but another duty. But if in giving a plurality of proofs for one and the same proposition one consoles himself with the thought that the plurality of reasons will make up for the lack of weight in each taken separately, then this is a very unphilosophical expedient, which betrays artifice and dishonesty; for various insufficient reasons placed beside one another do not produce certainty, or even probability. [403]

On virtue:

Virtue is the strength of man's maxim in obeying his duty. All strength is known only by the obstacles it can overcome; and in the case of virtue the obstacles are the natural inclinations, which can come into conflict with moral purpose. And since it is man himself who puts these obstacles in the way of his maxims, virtue is not merely self-constraint (for that might be an effort of one inclination to constrain another), but is, moreover, a constraint according to a principle of internal freedom and,

consequently, by the mere representation of his duty according to its formal law. [394]

The true strength of virtue is the mind at rest, with a deliberate and firm resolution to bring its law into practice. . . . That man who will admit nothing to be morally indifferent and strews his steps with duties, as with traps, and will not allow it to be a matter of indifference whether one eats meat or fish, drinks beer or wine, when both agree with him—a micrology which, if adopted into the doctrine of virtue, would make its dominion a tyranny—that man can be called fantastically virtuous.

Remark. Virtue is always in progress and yet always begins at the beginning. The first follows from the fact that, objectively considered, virtue is an ideal and unattainable; but yet constantly to approximate it is nevertheless a duty. The second is founded subjectively upon the nature of man, which is affected by inclinations. Under the influence of these inclinations virtue, with its maxims adopted once for all, can never settle into a state of rest and inactivity; if it is not rising, it inevitably declines. This is so because moral maxims, unlike technical ones, cannot be based on habit (for basing a maxim on habit belongs to the physical nature of the determination of the will). But even if the *exercise* of moral maxims were to become a habit, the subject would thereby lose the freedom of adopting his maxims; this freedom, however, is the character of an action done from duty. [409]

The doctrine of virtue is not sufficient for application to particular cases. Unlike law, ethics requires judgment, and for this *casuistics* is required.

Ethics . . . because of the latitude which it allows for its imperfect duties, inevitably leads to questions which call upon the faculty of judgment to decide how a maxim is to be applied in particular cases, and in such a way that this faculty suggests in turn a (subordinate) maxim (concerning which one may again ask for a principle for applying this maxim to cases at hand). And so ethics gets into a casuistics, of which the doctrine of right knows nothing.

Casuistics is neither a science nor a part thereof; if it were, it would be a dogmatics. It is not so much a doctrine as to how something is to be found, as an exercise in how the truth is to be sought.

Accordingly, it is interwoven fragmentarily and not systematically with ethics, i.e., it is added to the system like scholia. [411]

(Subsequently Kant adds "casuistical questions" to his discussion of particular duties to illustrate the type of issue to be dealt with when applying the maxims.)

Duties of virtue are classified as "duties to oneself" and "duties to others." Duties to oneself can be perfect or imperfect. It is an imperfect duty to ourselves that we cultivate our natural and moral perfection. Suicide, self-abuse, immoderate use of food and drink, lying, avarice, and servility violate perfect duties to oneself. The argument on suicide illustrates the basic strategy: it is not an appeal to the effect of a suicide on other people.

Man cannot deprive himself of his personality so long as one speaks of duties, thus so long as he lives. That man ought to have the authorization to withdraw himself from all obligation, i.e., to be free to act as if no authorization at all were required for this withdrawal, involves a contradiction. To destroy the subject of morality in his own person is tantamount to obliterating from the world, as far as he can, the very existence of morality itself; but morality is, nevertheless, an end in itself. Accordingly, to dispose of oneself as a mere means to some end of one's own liking is to degrade the humanity in one's person (*homo noumenon*), which, after all, was entrusted to man (*homo phaenomenon*) to preserve. [422–423]

Suicide is never permissible when one considers only human nature as such, in abstraction from particular circumstances and motivations, but the casuistical questions suggest a variety of considerations relevant to application:

Is committing suicide permitted in anticipation of an unjust death sentence from one's superior? Even if the sovereign permitted such a suicide (as Nero permitted of Seneca)? . . .

Bitten by a mad dog, a man already felt hydrophobia coming upon him. He declared that since he

had never known anybody cured of it, he would destroy himself in order that, as he said in his testament, he might not in his madness (which he already felt gripping him) bring misfortune to other men too. The question is whether or not he did wrong.

Whoever decides to let himself to be inoculated against smallpox risks his life on an uncertainty, although he does it to preserve his life. Accordingly, he is in a much more doubtful position with regard to the law of duty than is the mariner, who does not in the least create the storm to which he entrusts himself. Rather, the former invites an illness which puts him in the danger of death. Consequently, is smallpox inoculation allowed? [423–424]

Self-abuse and immoderate use of food and drink are degrading to the human personality and interfere with our capacity to pursue our own ends. But Kant's most vehement eloquence is directed against lying:

Concerning Lying. The greatest violation of man's duty to himself considered only as a moral being (the humanity in his person) is the opposite of veracity: lying (*aliud lingua promptum, aliud pectore inclusum genere*).[a] That no intentional untruth in the expression of one's thoughts can avoid this harsh name in ethics, which derives no authorization from harmlessness, is clear of itself (although in the doctrine of right it bore the name only when it violated another's right). For dishonor (to be an object of moral contempt), which goes with lying, accompanies also the liar, like his shadow. Lying can be either external or internal. By the former, man makes himself an object of contempt in the eyes of others; but by the latter, which is still worse, he makes himself contemptible in his own eyes and violates the dignity of humanity in his own person. The injury to other people which can arise from lying has nothing to do with this vice (for that would be merely a violation of one's duty to others) and so does not come into consideration here, nor does even the injury one brings upon himself; for then lying, insofar as it is merely a fault of prudence, would be contrary to the pragmatic maxim but not to the moral maxim, and so could not be regarded

[a] ["When what the tongue utters is different from what is in the heart." Sallust, *The War with Cataline* 10.5.]

as a violation of duty at all. Lying is the throwing away and, as it were, the obliteration of one's dignity as a human being. A man who does not himself believe what he says to another (even if it be only a person existing in idea) has even less worth than if he were a mere thing; for because of the thing's property of being useful, the other person can make some use of it, since it is a thing real and given. But to communicate one's thoughts to someone by words which (intentionally) contain the opposite of what one thinks is an end directly contrary to the natural purposiveness of his capacity to communicate his thoughts. In so doing, he renounces his personality and, as a liar, manifests himself as a mere deceptive appearance of a man, not as a true man. Veracity in one's statements is called honesty, and when these statements are at the same time promises, sincerity. But veracity in general is called uprightness. [429]

Internal lying, that is, self-deception, is also contemptible.

Man insofar as he is a moral being (*homo noumenon*) cannot use himself insofar as he is a physical being (*homo phaenomenon*) as a mere means (as a talking machine) not bound to an internal purpose (the communication of thought); but he is bound to the condition of being in accord with the declaration of the moral being, and is obligated to himself to be truthful. One lies when, for instance, he professes a belief in a future World Judge though he can really find no such belief within himself, but rather by so acknowledging in thought such a Searcher of Hearts, convinces himself that it can do no harm and may even be useful, in order at all events to insinuate himself into such a one's favor. Or if he is not in doubt about this, yet he may flatter himself for having inner reverence for His law, even though he feels no other incentive than fear of punishment.

Insincerity is simply want of conscientiousness, i.e., want of candor in confessing before one's internal judge, who is thought of as another person. For instance, strictly considered, insincerity is already involved when, out of self-love, a wish is taken as a deed because the wish has an essentially good end in view; and the internal lie, although it is contrary to man's duty to himself, receives here the name of a weakness, even as the wish of a

lover to find nothing but good qualities in his beloved makes him oblivious to her obvious faults. However, this insincerity in one's declarations, practiced against oneself, deserves the strongest censure; for once the highest principle of veracity has been violated, from such a rotten spot (the falsity which seems to be rooted in human nature) the evil of untruthfulness spreads itself also into one's relationships with other men. [430–431]

Casuistical Questions. Can an untruth from mere politeness (e.g., "your most obedient servant" at the end of a letter) be taken as lying? Nobody is deceived by it. An author asks one of his readers, "How do you like my work?" To be sure, the answer might be given in an illusory way inasmuch as one might jest concerning the captiousness of such a question. But who always has his wits about him? The slightest hesitation with the answer is already a mortification for the author. May one flatter him, then? [431] [20]

The duty not to lie applies particularly with respect to ourselves. We are all innate judges of ourselves:

Every man has a conscience and finds himself observed by an internal judge, who threatens him and keeps him in awe (respect combined with fear). This authority watching over the laws within him is not something which he himself (arbitrarily) creates, but is incorporated in his being. If he tries to run away, his conscience follows him like his shadow. . . .

This original intellectual and (as a representation of duty) moral predisposition called conscience has the peculiarity that though this whole matter is an

---

[20] Kant's "A Supposed Right to Tell Lies from Benevolent Motives" is an extreme case of rule-absolutism with respect to truth telling; it argues that you should tell the truth to (or refuse to answer) a would-be murderer asking whether his intended victim is in your house. As usual in Kant's thought, there are depths below depths. His argument suggests that he is most concerned with the insecurity and uncertainty of things: a lie might accidentally contribute to the murder (if the intended victim is running away and the lie leads the murderer to the escape path) and be a source of guilt. But if truth telling yields evil consequences, they are accidental.

affair of man with himself, man sees himself, nevertheless, compelled to conduct this affair as though at the bidding of another person. For the business here is the conduct of a lawsuit (*causa*) before a tribunal. But if the man accused by his conscience is represented as one and the same with the judge, then such a mode of representation is absurd in a court of justice; for in that event, the accuser would certainly lose every time. Therefore, as far as all man's duties are concerned, his conscience will have to suppose someone other than himself to be the judge of his actions, if his conscience is not to contradict itself. This other may be a real person or merely an ideal one which reason creates for itself.

Such an ideal person (the authorized judge of conscience) must be a searcher of hearts, for the court of justice is set up in our inmost selves. At the same time he must be all-obligating: he must be, or be conceived as, a person in relation to whom all duties are to be regarded as commands by him, because conscience is the internal judge of all free actions. Now, since such a moral being must at the same time possess all authority (over heaven and earth), for otherwise he could not give proper effect to his laws (something which the office of judge necessarily requires), and since such a moral being possessing power over all is called *God*, so conscience must be conceived as the subjective principle of being accountable to God for one's deeds. [438–439]

Our treatment of animals involves our duty to ourselves:

Even more intimately opposed to man's duty to himself is a savage and at the same time cruel treatment of that part of creation which is living, though lacking reason (animals). For thus is compassion for their suffering dulled in man, and thereby a natural predisposition very serviceable to morality in one's relations with other men is weakened and gradually obliterated. However, man is authorized to put animals to adroit and painless slaughter or to make them do hard work, as long as it is not beyond their strength (work such as men themselves often have to put up with). On the other hand, physical experiments involving excruciating pain for animals and conducted merely for the sake of speculative inquiry (when the end might also be achieved without such experiments) are to be abhorred. Even gratitude for the long-performed service of an old horse or dog (just as if they were members of the household) belongs indirectly to a man's duty, namely, his duty *regarding* these animals; but directly considered, such a duty is always only his duty *to* himself. [443]

Duties to other people are divided into duties to others "considered simply as men" and duties taking into account their circumstances. The basic duties to other people are those of love and those of respect. Although both are required for human association, they work in different directions.

When the laws of duty (not laws of nature) concerning the external relationships of men to one another are under consideration, we regard ourselves as being in a moral (intelligible) world in which, by analogy with the physical world, the association of rational beings (on earth) is effected through attraction and repulsion. According to the principle of *mutual love* they are directed constantly to approach one another; by the principle of *respect* which they owe one another they are directed to keep themselves at a distance. Should one of these great moral forces sink, "so then would nothingness (immorality) with gaping throat drink up the whole realm of (moral) beings like a drop of water." [449]

By love and respect is not intended a feeling. Love is "the maxim of benevolence; and this maxim results in beneficence" (449). Respect is "the maxim that limits our self-esteem by the dignity of humanity in another person; hence it is understood in the practical sense" (449). The duty to love others is "the duty to make the ends of others (as long as they are not immoral) my own" (450). The duty to respect others is "contained in the maxim, degrade no other man merely as a means to personal ends (do not require another person to throw himself away in order to pander to one's own ends)" (450).

Duties of love are beneficence ("the maxim to make the happiness of others an end for oneself" [452]), gratitude, and sympathy.

For a rich man (abundantly provided with the means for promoting the happiness of others, i.e., provided with means above and beyond his own needs), beneficence is hardly even to be held as his meritorious duty, though he does obligate the one he benefits. The satisfaction with which he thus provides himself, and which costs him no sacrifice, is a kind of reveling in moral feelings. Furthermore, he must carefully avoid any appearance of intending to obligate the other person, lest he not render a true benefit, inasmuch as by his act he expresses that he wants to lay an obligation upon the receiver (which always humbles the one obligated in his own eyes.) Rather, the benefactor must express himself as being obligated or honored by the other's acceptance, treating the duty merely as a debt he owes, if he cannot (though it is better when he can) carry out his beneficence completely in secret. This virtue is greater when the means for beneficence are limited, and when the benefactor is strong enough to silently assume the burden which he spares the other; he then can truly be regarded as morally rich. [453]

[To *feel* pity or compassion is not directly a duty, but] active sympathizing with their lot is a duty. To this end it accordingly is an indirect duty to cultivate our natural (sensitive) feelings for others, and to make use of them as so many means for sympathy based on moral principles and the feeling appropriate to them. Thus it is a duty not to avoid places where the poor, who lack the most necessary things, are to be found; instead, it is a duty to seek them out. It is a duty not to shun sickrooms or prisons and so on in order to avoid the pain of compassion, which one may not be able to resist. For this feeling, though painful, nevertheless is one of the impulses placed in us by nature for effecting what the representation of duty might not accomplish by itself.

Casuistical Questions. Would it not be better for the world's welfare if all morality in human beings were restricted exclusively to juridical duties (but done with the greatest conscientiousness), and if benevolence were counted among things morally indifferent? It is not too easy to see what consequence such a thing might have for the happiness of human beings. But in such a case the world would, at all events, lack a great moral ornament, namely, the love of mankind. To represent the world as a beautiful moral whole in its complete perfection, this love of mankind is required for its own sake, without any advantages (of happiness) being counted upon. [457–458]

Each duty of love has a corresponding vice: envy (corresponding to beneficence), ingratitude (gratitude), and malice (sympathy). To omit a duty of love is simply to lack virtue; to omit a duty of respect is vicious and does injury to another. The duties of respect, therefore, are negative: they are divided into the duty to avoid pride, calumny, and mockery. Above all, respect avoids contempt for other people.

Thus far the discussion has taken into account only human nature in the abstract. Something more is required to apply the principles:

In a system of pure ethics, these duties of virtue can indeed give no occasion for a separate chapter, for they do not contain principles obligating men to one another and thus cannot properly yield a part of *The Metaphysical Principles of Virtue.* They are only rules qualified according to the differences in the subjects to which the principle of virtue (which is formal) may be applied in cases issuing from experience (the material); and therefore they admit of no assuredly complete classification, as do no empirical divisions. Nevertheless, just as a "Transition from the Metaphysics of Nature to Physics," [b] having its own special rules, is required, so something similar is rightfully required of *The Metaphysics of Morals,* namely, applying pure principles of duty to cases of experience so as to schematize them, as it were, and to set them forth ready for morally-practical use. What conduct is proper toward men according to the moral purity or depravity of their conditions? What is proper in crude or refined circumstances? What to the unlearned or to the learned? And if to the latter, then what is appropriate to them in the use of their knowledge as educated (polished) members of society or as specialists in their own fields (professional intellectuals)? And for the latter, again, what is fitting for those whose knowledge proceeds from technique

[b] [An unfinished work by Kant, part of the *Opus Postumum.*]

or more from the spirit [*Geist*] and from taste? What conduct is suitable according to distinctions of status, age, sex, state of health, affluence or poverty, and so on? These considerations do not provide so many kinds of ethical obligation (for there is only one kind, namely, that of virtue in general), but only kinds of application (corollaries). They cannot, then, be set up as sections of ethics and as members of its systematic division (which must follow a priori from a concept of reason), but can only be appended to it. But even these applications belong to a complete presentation of the system. [468–469]

The Science of Right [21]

Introduction: General Definitions and Divisions

1. The conception of RIGHT,—as referring to a corresponding obligation which is the moral aspect of it, in the *first* place, has regard only to the external and practical relation of one person to another, in so far as they can have influence upon each other, immediately or mediately, by their *actions* as facts. 2. [T]he conception of right does not indicate the relation of the action of an individual to the *wish* or the mere desire of another, as in acts of benevolence or of unkindness, but only the relation of his free action to the freedom of *action* of the other. 3. [I]n this reciprocal relation of voluntary actions, the conception of right does not take into consideration the *matter* of the act of will in so far as the end which any one may have in view in willing it, is concerned. In other words, it is not asked in a question of right whether any one on buying goods for his own business realizes a profit by the transaction or not; but only the *form* of the transaction is taken into account, in considering the relation of the mutual acts of will. Acts of will or voluntary choice are thus regarded only in so far as they are *free*, and as to whether the action of one can harmonize with the freedom of another, according to a universal law.

Right, therefore, comprehends the whole of the conditions under which the voluntary actions of any one person can be harmonized in reality with the voluntary actions of every other person, according to a universal law of freedom.

[The] *Universal Principle of Right* [is] "Every action is *right* which in itself, or in the maxim on which it proceeds, is such that it can co-exist along with the freedom of the will of each and all in action, according to a universal law." [pp. 44–45]

To have a right implies the title to compel violators.

It is clear that the assertion of such a right is not to be understood objectively as being in accordance with what a law would prescribe, but merely subjectively, as proceeding on the assumption of how a sentence would be pronounced by a court in the case. There can, in fact, be no *criminal law* assigning the penalty of death to a man who, when shipwrecked and struggling in extreme danger for his life, and in order to save it, may thrust another from a plank on which he had saved himself. For the punishment threatened by the law could not possibly have greater power than the fear of the loss of life in the case in question. Such a penal law would thus fail altogether to exercise its intended effect; for the threat of an evil which is still *uncertain*—such as death by a judicial sentence—could not overcome the fear of an evil which is *certain*, as drowning is in such circumstances. An act of violent self-preservation, then, ought not to be considered as altogether beyond condemnation; it is only to be adjudged as exempt from punishment. [pp. 52–53]

Rights can be classified as natural or positive, innate or acquired (there is just one innate right: "an innate EQUALITY belonging to every man which consists in his right to be independent of being bound by others to anything more than that to which he may also reciprocally bind them [p. 56])," and public or private. The last is the more fundamental classification.

For it is not the "*social* state" but the "*civil* state" that is opposed to the "state of nature"; for in the "state of nature" there may well be society of some

---

[21] The selection is from *The Philosophy of Law: an Exposition of the Fundamental Principles of Jurisprudence as the Science of Right*, trans. W. W. Hastie (Edinburgh: T. & T. Clark, 1887), with some modernization by the editors of this volume.

kind, but there is no "civil" society, as an institution securing the mine and thine by public laws. It is thus that right, viewed under reference to the state of nature, is specially called private right. [p. 58]

Part First: Private Right

[The juridical postulate of practical reason is:] It is possible to have any external object of my will as mine. In other words, a maxim to this effect— were it to become law—that any object on which the will can be exerted must remain objectively in itself *without an owner*, as "res nullius," is contrary to the principle of right.

. . . It is therefore an assumption *a priori* of the practical reason to regard and treat every object within the range of my free exercise of will as objectively a possible mine or thine.

This postulate may be called "a permissive law" of the practical reason, as giving us a special title which we could not evolve out of the mere conceptions of right generally. And this title constitutes the right to impose upon all others an obligation, not otherwise laid upon them, to abstain from the use of certain objects of our free choice, because we have already taken them into our possession. [pp. 62–63]

6. Deduction of the conception of a purely juridical Possession of an External Object. The question, "How is an *external mine and thine* possible?" resolves itself into this other question: "How is a *merely juridical* or *rational* possession possible?" And this second question resolves itself again into a third: "How is a *synthetic* proposition in right possible *a priori?*"

All propositions of right—as juridical propositions—are propositions *a priori*, for they are practical laws of reason. But the juridical proposition *a priori* respecting *empirical possession* is *analytical*; for it says nothing more than what follows by the principle of contradiction, from the conception of such possession; namely, that if I am the holder of a thing in the way of being physically connected with it, any one interfering with it without my consent— as, for instance, in wrenching an apple out of my hand—affects and detracts from my freedom as that which is internally mine; and consequently the maxim of his action is in direct contradiction to the axiom of right. . . .

On the other hand, the proposition expressing the possibility of the possession of a thing external to me, after abstraction of all the conditions of empirical possession in space and time—consequently . . . goes beyond these limiting conditions; and because this proposition asserts a possession even without physical holding, as necessary to the conception of the external mine and thine, it is *synthetical*. . . .

In this manner, for instance, the act of taking possession of a particular portion of the soil, is a mode exercising the private free-will without being an act of *usurpation*. The possessor founds upon the innate right of *common possession* of the surface of the earth, and upon the universal will corresponding *a priori* to it, which allows a *private possession* of the soil; because what are mere things would be otherwise made in themselves and by a law into unappropriable objects. Thus a first appropriator acquires originally by primary possession a particular portion of the ground; and by right (*jure*) he resists every other person who would hinder him in the private use of it, although while the "state of nature" continues, this cannot be done by juridical means (*de jure*), because a public law does not yet exist.

And although a piece of ground should be regarded as free, or declared to be such, so as to be for the public use of all without distinction, yet it cannot be said that it is thus free by nature and *originally* so, prior to any juridical act. For there would be a real relation already incorporated in such a piece of ground by the very fact that the possession of it was denied to any particular individual; and as this public freedom of the ground would be a prohibition of it to every particular individual, this presupposes a common possession of it which cannot take effect without a contract. . . .

This *original* community of the soil and of the things upon it, is an idea which has objective and practical juridical reality and is entirely different from the idea of a *primitive* community of things, which is a fiction. For the latter would have had to be *founded* as a form of society, and must have taken its rise from a contract by which all renounced the right of private possession, so that by uniting the property owned by each into a whole, it was thus transformed into a common possession. But had such an event taken place, history must have presented some evidence of it. To regard such a procedure as the original mode of taking possession, and to hold that the particular possessions of every individual may and ought to be grounded upon it, is evidently a contradiction. . . .

Simple physical possession, or holding of the soil, involves already certain relations of right to the thing, although it is certainly not sufficient to enable me to regard it as mine. Relative to others, so far as they know, it appears as a first possession in harmony with the law of external freedom; and, at the same time, it is embraced in the universal original possession which contains *a priori* the fundamental principle of the possibility of a private possession. Hence to disturb the first occupier or holder of a portion of the soil in his use of it, is a lesion or wrong done to him. The first taking of possession has therefore a title of right (*titulus possessionis*) in its favour, which is simply the principle of the original common possession; and the saying that "It is well for those who are in possession," when one is not bound to authenticate his possession, is a principle of natural right that establishes the juridical act of taking possession, as a ground of acquisition upon which every first possessor may found. [pp. 67–71]

8. *To have anything External as one's own is only possible in a Juridical or Civil state of Society under the regulation of a public legislative Power.* If, by word or deed, I declare my will that some external thing shall be mine, I make a declaration that every other person is obliged to abstain from the use of this object of my exercise of will; and this imposes an obligation which no one would be under, without such a juridical act on my part. But the assumption of this act, at the same time involves the admission that I am obliged reciprocally to observe a similar abstention towards every other in respect of what is externally theirs; for the obligation in question arises from a universal rule regulating the external juridical relations. Hence I am not obliged to let alone what another person declares to be externally his, unless every other person likewise secures me by a guarantee that he will act in relation to what is mine, upon the same principle. This guarantee of reciprocal and mutual abstention from what belongs to others, does not require a special juridical act for its establishment, but is already involved in the conception of an external obligation of right, on account of the universality and consequently the reciprocity of the obligatoriness arising from a universal rule.—Now,

a single will, in relation to an external and consequently contingent possession, cannot serve as a compulsory law for all, because that would be to do violence to the freedom which is in accordance with universal laws. Therefore it is only a will that binds every one, and as such a common, collective, and authoritative will, that can furnish a guarantee of security to all. But the state of men under a universal, external, and public legislation, conjoined with authority and power, is called the civil state. There can therefore be an external mine and thine only in the civil state of society. [pp. 76–77]

41. *Public Justice as related to the Natural and the Civil state.* The juridical state is that relation of men to one another which contains the conditions, under which it is alone possible for every one to obtain the right that is his due. The formal principle of the possibility of actually *participating* in such right, viewed in accordance with the idea of a universally legislative will, is PUBLIC JUSTICE. Public justice may be considered in relation either to the possibility, or actuality, or necessity of the possession of objects—regarded as the matter of the activity of the will—according to laws. It may thus be divided into *protective justice, commutative justice,* and *distributive justice.* In the *first* mode of justice, the law declares merely what relation is internally *right* in respect of form; in the *second,* it declares what is likewise externally in accord with a law in respect of the object, and what possession is rightful; and in the *third,* it declares what is right, and what is *just,* and to what extent, by the judgment of a court in any particular case coming under the given law. [p. 155]

Part Second: Public Right

46. *The Legislative Power and the Members of the State.* The legislative power, viewed in its rational principle, can only belong to the united will of the people. For, as all right ought to proceed from this power, it is necessary that its laws should be unable to do wrong to any one whatever. Now, if any *one* individual determines anything in the state in contradistinction to *another,* it is always possible that he may perpetrate a wrong on that other; but this is never possible when *all* determine and decree what is to be Law to themselves. "*Volenti non fit*

injuria.'' Hence it is only the united and consenting will of all the people—in so far as each of them determines the same thing about all, and all determine the same thing about each—that ought to have the power of enacting law in the state.

Citizenship carries three attributes:

1. Constitutional FREEDOM, as the right of every citizen to have to obey no other law than that to which he has given his consent or approval; 2. Civil EQUALITY, as the right of the citizen to recognize no one as a superior among the people in relation to himself, except in so far as such a one is as subject to *his* moral power to impose obligations, as that other has power to impose obligations upon him; and 3. Political INDEPENDENCE, as the right to owe his existence and continuance in society not to the arbitrary will of another, but to his own rights and powers as a member of the commonwealth, and, consequently, the possession of a civil personality, which cannot be represented by any other than himself.

. . . The last of the three qualities involved, necessarily constitutes the distinction between *active* and *passive* citizenship; although the latter conception appears to stand in contradiction to the definition of a citizen as such. The following examples may serve to remove this difficulty. The apprentice of a merchant or tradesman, a servant who is not in the employ of the state, a minor, all women, and, generally, every one who is compelled to maintain himself not according to his own industry, but as it is arranged by others (the state excepted), are without civil personality, and their existence is only, as it were, incidentally included in the state. The woodcutter whom I employ on my estate; the smith in India who carries his hammer, anvil, and bellows into the houses where he is engaged to work in iron, as distinguished from the European carpenter or smith, who can offer the independent products of his labour as wares for public sale; the resident tutor as distinguished from the schoolmaster; the ploughman as distinguished from the farmer and such like, illustrate the distinction in question. In all these cases, the former members of the contrast are distinguished from the latter by being mere subsidiaries of the commonwealth and not active members of it, because they are of necessity commanded and protected by others, and consequently possess

no political self-sufficiency in themselves. Such dependence on the will of others and the consequent inequality are, however, not inconsistent with the freedom and equality of the individuals *as men* helping to constitute the people. Much rather is it the case that it is only under such conditions, that a people can become a state and enter into a civil constitution. But all are not equally qualified to exercise the right of the suffrage under the constitution, and to be full citizens of the state, and not mere passive subjects under its protection. For, although they are entitled to demand to be treated by all the other citizens according to laws of natural freedom and equality, as *passive* parts of the state, it does not follow that they ought themselves to have the right to deal with the state as active members of it, to reorganize it, or to take action by way of introducing certain laws. All they have a right in their circumstances to claim, may be no more than that whatever be the mode in which the positive laws are enacted, these laws must not be contrary to the natural laws that demand the freedom of all the people and the equality that is conformable thereto; and it must therefore be made possible for them to raise themselves from this passive condition in the state to the condition of active citizenship. [pp. 166–169]

49. Distinct Functions of the Three Powers. Autonomy of the State
A. Right of the Supreme Power. Treason; Dethronement; Revolution; Reform. [T]he supreme power in the state has only rights, and no (compulsory) duties towards the subject.—Further, if the ruler or regent, as the organ of the supreme power, proceeds in violation of the laws, as in imposing taxes, recruiting soldiers, and so on, contrary to the law of equality in the distribution of the political burdens, the subject may oppose *complaints* and *objections* to this injustice, but not active resistance. . . .

Resistance on the part of the people to the supreme legislative power of the state, is in no case legitimate; for it is only by submission to the universal legislative will, that a condition of law and order is possible. Hence there is no right of sedition, and still less of rebellion, belonging to the people. And least of all, when the supreme power is embodied in an individual monarch, is there any justification, under the pretext of his abuse of power, for seizing his person or taking away his life. . . . The slightest attempt of this kind is *high treason;* and a traitor of this sort who aims at the *overthrow* of his country may be punished, as a political parricide, even with death. It is the duty of the people to bear any abuse of the supreme power, even then though it should be considered to be unbearable. And the reason is, that any resistance of the highest legislative authority can never but be contrary to the law, and must even be regarded as tending to destroy the whole legal constitution. In order to be entitled to offer such resistance, a public law would be required to permit it. But the supreme legislation would by such a law cease to be supreme, and the people as subjects would be made sovereign over that to which they are subject; which is a contradiction. [pp. 175–177]

C. *Relief of the Poor. Foundling Hospitals. The Church.* [The state is permitted to exact taxes for the welfare of the poor.] The people have in fact united themselves by their common will into a society, which has to be perpetually maintained; and for this purpose they have subjected themselves to the internal power of the state, in order to preserve the members of this society even when they are not able to support themselves. By the fundamental principle of the state, the government is justified and entitled to compel those who are able, to furnish the means necessary to preserve those who are not themselves capable of providing for the most necessary wants of nature. For the existence of persons with property in the state, implies their submission under it for protection and the provision by the state of what is necessary for their existence; and accordingly the state founds a right upon an obligation on their part to contribute of their means for the preservation of their fellow-citizens. This may be carried out by taxing the property or the commercial industry of the citizens, or by establishing funds and drawing interest from them, not for the wants of the state as such, which is rich, but for those of the people. And this is not to be done merely by *voluntary* contributions, but by *compulsory* exactions as state-burdens, for we are here considering only the *right* of the state in relation to the people. [pp. 186–187]

E. *The Right of Punishing and of Pardoning.* . . . Juridical punishment can never be administered merely as a means for promoting another good either with regard to the criminal himself or to civil society, but must in all cases be imposed only because the individual on whom it is inflicted *has committed a crime.* For one man ought never to be dealt with merely as a means subservient to the purpose of another. . . . Against such treatment his inborn personality has a right to protect him, even although he may be condemned to lose his civil personality. He must first be found guilty and *punishable,* before there can be any thought of drawing from his punishment any benefit for himself or his fellow-citizens. The penal law is a categorical imperative; and woe to him who creeps through the serpent-windings of utilitarianism to discover some advantage that may discharge him from the justice of punishment, or even from the due measure of it, according to the Pharisaic maxim: "It is better that *one* man should die than that the whole people should perish." For if justice and righteousness perish, human life would no longer have any value in the world.—What, then, is to be said of such a proposal as to keep a criminal alive who has been condemned to death, on his being given to understand that if he agreed to certain dangerous experiments being performed upon him, he would be allowed to survive if he came happily through them? It is argued that physicians might thus obtain new information that would be of value to the commonweal. But a court of justice would repudiate with scorn any proposal of this kind if made to it by the medical faculty; for justice would cease to be justice, if it were bartered away for any consideration whatever.

But what is the mode and measure of punishment by which public justice takes as its principle and standard? It is just the principle of equality, by which the pointer of the scale of justice is made to incline no more to the one side than the other. It may be rendered by saying that the undeserved evil which any one commits on another is to be regarded as perpetrated on himself. Hence it may be said: "If you slander another, you slander yourself; if you steal from another, you steal from yourself; if you strike another, you strike yourself; if you kill another, you kill yourself." This is the right of retaliation (*jus talionis*); and properly understood, it is the only principle which in regulating a public court, as distinguished from mere private judgement, can definitely assign both the quality and the quantity of a just penalty. All other standards are wavering and uncertain. . . . But whoever has committed murder must *die*. There is, in this case, no judicial substitute or surrogate, that can be given or taken for the satisfaction of justice. There is no *likeness* or proportion between life, however painful, and death; and therefore there is no equality between the crime of murder and the retaliation of it but what is judicially accomplished by the execution of the criminal. His death, however, must be kept free from all maltreatment that would make the humanity suffering in his person loathsome or abominable. Even if a civil society resolved to dissolve itself with the consent of all its members . . . the last murderer lying in prison ought to be executed before the resolution was carried out. This ought to be done in order that every one may realize the desert of his deeds, and that bloodguiltiness may not remain upon the people; for otherwise they might all be regarded as participators in the murder as a public violation of justice. [pp. 195–198]

As to the objection of Beccaria who, moved by sentimentality, argues against capital punishment on the ground that it could not be part of the original civil contract, for no one would consent to die:

All this is mere sophistry and perversion of right. No one undergoes punishment because he has willed to be punished, but because he has willed *a punishable action;* for it is in fact no punishment when any one experiences what he wills, and it is impossible for any one to *will* to be punished. To say, "I will to be punished, if I murder any one," can mean nothing more than, "I submit myself along with all the other citizens to the laws;" and if there are any criminals among the people, these laws will include penal laws. [p. 201]

The book ends with a plea for perpetual peace.

If one cannot prove that a thing *is,* he may try to prove that it is *not*. And if he succeeds in doing neither (as often occurs), he may still ask whether it is in his *interest* to *accept* one or other of the alternatives hypothetically, from the theoretical or the practical point of view. In other words, a hypothesis may be accepted either in order to explain a certain phenomenon (as in astronomy to account for the retrogression and stationariness of the planets), or in order to attain a certain end, which again may be either *pragmatic* as belonging merely to the sphere of art, or *moral* as involving a purpose which it is a duty to adopt as a maxim of action. Now it is evident that the assumption of the practicability of such an end, though presented merely as a theoretical and problematical judgment, may be regarded as constituting a duty; and hence it is so regarded in this case. For although there may be no positive obligation to believe in such an end, yet even if there were not the least theoretical probability of action being carried out in accordance with it, so long as its impossibility cannot be demonstrated, there still remains a duty incumbent upon us with regard to it.

Now, as a matter of fact, the morally practical reason utters within us its irrevocable *veto*: *"There shall be no war."* So there ought to be no war, neither between me and you in the condition of nature, nor between us as members of states which, although internally in a condition of law, are still externally in their relation to each other in a condition of lawlessness; for this is not the way by which any one should prosecute his right. Hence the question no longer is as to whether perpetual peace is a real thing or not a real thing, or as to whether we may not be deceiving ourselves when we adopt the former alternative, but we must *act* on the supposition of its being real. [pp. 229–230]

Idea of a Universal History on a Cosmopolitical Plan [22]

The evolutionary outlook of Kant's earliest work in physics resurfaces in late works on human history and the prospect of progress. *Universal History*, not intended to predict the course of world development, expounds a regulative idea that shows both the direction in which it is our duty to strive and the grounds for reasonable hope.

[22] Originally published 1784. Translated by Thomas De Quincey, *London Magazine*, October 1824. The selection is from *The Collected Writings of Thomas De Quincey*, ed. David Masson (Edinburgh: Adam and Charles Black, 1890), vol. IX, pp. 428–444.

Whatsoever difference there may be in our no-tions of the *freedom of the will* metaphysically consid-ered, it is evident that the manifestations of this will, viz. human actions, are as much under the control of universal laws of nature as any other physical phenomena. It is the province of History to narrate these manifestations; and, let their causes be ever so secret, we know that History, simply by taking its station at a distance and contemplating the agency of the human will upon a large scale, aims at unfolding to our view a regular stream of tendency in the great succession of events,—so that the very same course of incidents which, taken sep-arately and individually, would have seemed per-plexed, incoherent, and lawless, yet viewed in their connexion and as the actions of the human *species* and not of independent beings, never fail to dis-cover a steady and continuous, though slow, de-velopment of certain great predispositions in our nature. Thus, for instance, deaths, births, and marriages, considering how much they are sepa-rately dependent on the freedom of the human will, should seem to be subject to no law according to which any calculation could be made beforehand of their amount: and yet the yearly registers of these events in great countries prove that they go on with as much conformity to the laws of nature as the oscillations of the weather. These, again, are events which in detail are so far irregular that we cannot predict them individually; and yet, taken as a whole series, we find that they never fail to support the growth of plants, the currents of rivers, and other arrangements of nature in a uniform and uninter-rupted course. Individual men, and even nations, are little aware that, whilst they are severally pursu-ing their own peculiar and often contradictory pur-poses, they are unconsciously following the guid-ance of a great natural purpose which is wholly unnoticed by themselves, and are thus promoting and making efforts for a great process which, even if they perceived it, they would little regard.

Considering that men, taken collectively as a body, do not proceed, like brute animals, under the law of an instinct, nor yet again, like rational cosmopolites, under the law of a preconcerted plan, one might imagine that no systematic history of their actions (such, for instance, as the history of bees or beavers) could be possible. At the sight of the actions of man displayed on the great stage of the world, it is impossible to escape a certain degree of disgust: with all the occasional indications

of wisdom scattered here and there, we cannot but perceive the whole sum of these actions to be a web of folly, childish vanity, and often even of the idlest wickedness and spirit of destruction. Hence, at last, one is puzzled to know what judgment to form of our species, so conceited of its high advan-tages. In such a perplexity there is no resource for the philosopher but this,—that, finding it impossi-ble to presume in the human race any *rational* pur-pose of its own, he must endeavour to detect some *natural* purpose in such a senseless current of hu-man actions; by means of which a history of crea-tures that pursue no plan of their own may yet admit a systematic form as the history of creatures that are blindly pursuing a plan of nature. Let us now see whether we can succeed in finding out a clue to such a history, leaving it to nature to produce a man capable of executing it,—just as she produced a Kepler who unexpectedly brought the eccentric courses of the planets under determinate laws, and afterwards a Newton who explained these laws out of a universal ground in Nature:—

Proposition the First

All tendencies of any creature to which it is predisposed by Nature, are destined in the end to develop themselves perfectly and agreeably to their final purpose.

External as well as internal (or anatomical) exami-nation confirms this remark in all animals. An organ which is not to be used, a natural arrangement that misses its purpose, would be a contradiction in physics. Once departing from this fundamental proposition, we have a Nature no longer tied to laws, but objectless and working at random; and a cheerless reign of Chance steps into the place of Reason.

Proposition the Second

In Man, as the sole rational creature upon earth, those tendencies which have the use of his reason for their object are destined to obtain their perfect development in the species only, and not in the individual. [Reason needs trials and practices and accumulation of knowledge, far beyond one person's lifetime.]

Proposition the Third

It is the will of Nature that Man should owe to himself alone everything which transcends the mere mechanic con-stitution of his animal existence, and that he should be susceptible of no other happiness or perfection than what he has created for himself, instinct apart, through his own reason. [Nature's purpose was not that man might live in pleasure, but that he might make himself worthy of living in pleasure by wrestling with difficulties. We must assume a race of rational animals destined to a perfect development of their tendencies, immortal as a species.]

Proposition the Fourth

The means which Nature employs to bring about the development of all the tendencies she has laid in Man is the antagonism of these tendencies in the social state— no farther, however, than to that point at which this antagonism becomes the cause of social arrangements founded in law. [This "unsocial sociality" is the conflict of gregarious and antigregarious inclinations. Competition among men awakens their powers.]

. . . In this way arise the first steps from the savage state to the state of culture, which consists peculiarly in the social worth of Man. Talents of every kind are now unfolded, taste formed, and by gradual increase of light a preparation is made for such a mode of thinking as is capable of converting the rude natural tendency to moral distinctions into determinate practical principles, and finally of exalting a social concert that had been *pathologically* extorted from the mere necessities of situation into a *moral* union founded on the reasonable choice. [But for such antisocial propensities man would have remained on a low level, like sheep.] Thanks, therefore, to Nature for the enmity, for the jealous spirit of envious competition, for the insatiable thirst after wealth and power! . . .

Proposition the Fifth

The highest problem for the Human Species, to the solution of which it is irresistibly urged by natural impulses, is the establishment of a universal Civil Society founded on the empire of political justice.

Proposition the Sixth

This problem is at the same time the most difficult of all, and the one which is latest solved by man. [Because of our inclinations, we need a master, not another person, who also needs a master; it requires notions of a just constitution, great experience, and above all a will favorably disposed to the adoption of such a constitution. Many fruitless trials may be expected.]

Proposition the Seventh

The problem of the establishment of a perfect Constitution of Society depends upon the problem of a system of International Relations adjusted to law, and apart from this latter problem cannot be solved. [The same lawless strife once existent among individuals recurs among states, in their external relations. We are advanced in culture as to arts and sciences; we are civilized, but not sufficiently moralized.]

Proposition the Eighth

The History of the Human Species as a whole may be regarded as the unravelling of a hidden Plan of Nature for accomplishing a perfect State of Civil Constitution for society in its internal relations (and, as the condition of that, by the last proposition, in its external relations also) as the sole state of society in which the tendencies of human nature can be all and fully developed. [There are some traces of this unraveling. States are now so interconnected that none can become culturally stationary without declining in power and influence compared with the rest. Civil liberty cannot be arrested without affecting trade. This liberty gradually is extended, personal restriction diminished, and religious liberty established. Enlightenment is advanced. War itself becomes too expensive. There is a stirring toward the formation of a great primary state-body.]

Proposition the Ninth

A philosophical attempt to compose a Universal History, in the sense of a Cosmopolitical History, upon a plan tending to unfold the purpose of Nature in a perfect Civil Union of the Human Species (instead of the present imperfect union), is to be regarded as possible, and as capable even of helping forward this very purpose of Nature.

Perpetual Peace [23]

When Kant published *Perpetual Peace* (1795) the United States had a federal constitution and the French Revolution was a half-dozen years in process. A listing of the main points of the plan suggests its direction.

[23] Translated by M. Campbell Smith (London: Allen & Unwin, 1903).

First Section: Containing the Preliminary Articles of Perpetual Peace Between States

1. No treaty of peace shall be regarded as valid, if made with the secret reservation of material for a future war.
2. No state having an independent existence—whether it be great or small—shall be acquired by another through inheritance, exchange, purchase or donation.
3. Standing armies shall be abolished in course of time.
4. No national debts shall be contracted in connection with the external affairs of the state [as against loans for internal economic development].
5. No state shall violently interfere with the constitution and administration of another. [In the anarchy of civil war, however, interference is permitted.]
6. No state at war with another shall countenance such modes of hostility as would make mutual confidence impossible in a subsequent state of peace: such are the employment of assassins or of poisoners, breaches of capitulation, the instigating and making use of treachery in the hostile state. [This rules out wars of total extermination, and the use of spies, for it would carry over into peace.]

Second Section: Containing the Definitive Articles of a Perpetual Peace Between States

I.   The civil constitution of each state shall be republican. ["Republican" is opposed to "despotic." Democracy is always despotic; a republican form of administration requires a representative system. Maintaining peace requires basic participation in the law by the citizens, who if they thought about war would realize that they were bringing down its miseries and costs on themselves.]

II. The law of nations shall be founded on a federation of free states. [The proposal is a federation, not a superstate; it will make a covenant of peace guaranteeing peace to the states.]

III. The rights of men, as citizens of the world, shall be limited to the conditions of universal hospitality. [This establishes the minimal right not to be treated as an enemy, although not necessarily as a guest either. This is directed against the plundering of strangers by pirates and the abusive treatment of colonizing countries.]

The supplements and appendixes look for supporting evidence of possible development in the manifest purposes of nature and the convergence of trends, ask for a quiet place for philosophers in giving advice to statesmen, and deal again with the problem of theory and practice in the form of alleged disagreement between morals and politics. Kant unmasks political tricks and arguments, and as a climax proposes a transcendental formula of public right:

All actions relating to the rights of other men are wrong, if the maxims from which they follow are inconsistent with publicity. [p. 185]

The Nineteenth Century

The major ethical theories of the nineteenth century are characterized by the growing roles they assign to change and the problems it raises. Kant, in the previous period, had dealt with change in the generation of the heavens and, of course, in his outline of universal history. But this barely suggests what the nineteenth century did with development and evolution. For Hegel, early in the century, every phase of life and culture is seen in its patterned movement and is understood as part of an inexorable world process, but this movement is appreciated only retrospectively. By mid-century Marx turns to the future, seeking control of human destiny through a knowledge of the direction of development. Even revised utilitarianism in Mill adds some historical orientation to its Benthamite origins.

It is the Darwinian theory of evolution, however, that most significantly revises ways of regarding human life. It plays the liberating role in biology that Newtonian physics had played in the seventeenth century, generating new models for thought and opening a new path for naturalizing morality. The conception of change is quite different from the eighteenth-century idea of progress, which for the most part was linear, was directed to a finite end, and presupposed fixed species. Darwinian evolution is open, and even though it is lawlike, there is no predicting how species change. Its vision of an open world in time rocked traditional ideas of stable foundations as strongly as Giordano Bruno's spectacle of infinite worlds had shaken the outlook of an earlier age. Not surprisingly, many moral philosophers seize upon evolution and give it a special turn—whether the Social Darwinism inaugurated by Spencer, the mutual aid of the anarchists, or the Nietzschean will to power. Even a philosophical idealism that set out to block the naturalizing of man and to confront the intensified individualism of the century had to make fresh philosophical and ethical moves.

Part Four focuses on the distinctively new in moral philosophy of the nineteenth century. But not to be overlooked are the continuing older moral philosophies and their responses to the new. Stable religious moralities of the Western world flourished. Roused by the theory of evolution and its apparent challenge to biblical authority, for the most part they fought bitter battles against it. There were also religious thinkers who were receptive to any scientific advance as an advance in understanding God's plan. And throughout the century novel directions in the relation of religion and ethics were offered, as in Kierkegaard's individualistic emphasis on the particular and the inner as against Hegelian "system"; or Feuerbach's humanistic rein-terpretation of religion in terms of human needs; or Comte's positivism, which he took to be the last stage in a historical development from animism and theology through a metaphysical stage to a scientific outlook.

There is a complex interaction between moral thinking and the historical events of the century. Social movements called for the analysis of socioethical ideals. The dynamic factor is a growing industrial capitalism associated with a liberal individualistic philosophy. It confronts the old order of the landed class; but it also begins to be faced by demands of the working class for some share in the new material and social gains. These confrontations vary markedly in different countries; they take different shape in Continental West-ern Europe (particularly Germany, Austria, and Italy), in France, and in Britain.

In Western Europe, with the defeat of Napoleon, the old order was re-stored. The liberal aspirations of the middle class had been kindled by Napo-leon's conquests, but the revolutionary wave of 1848 failed either to liberalize politics or to unseat the landed power. Particularly in Germany and in Italy, nationalistic aims and ideals crossed these struggles. In Germany it was not liberalism but Prussian autocratic power that unified the nation by 1870. In general, throughout Western Europe, capitalism with its philosophy of liberalism was still the revolutionary idea, and liberalism was regarded as the enemy wherever the landed class was dominant. Papal encyclicals show this attitude clearly: the faithful are warned against liberalism—for its secular tendencies, its individualism, its subversion of order and authority, its selfish aggressiveness and worldliness.

In France, the intensity of the Revolution and the sharpness of the social change led to a polarization of thought throughout the nineteenth century and into the twentieth. But however strong the intellectual battles, the social issue had been settled by the Revolution. It was too late for a restoration of the old order, and after the defeat of Napoleon the restoration lasted for only a brief period. From 1830 on, bourgeois power is secure and is main-tained whether under republican or imperial politics. Indeed a major confron-tation now is with the left. At the time of the *Communist Manifesto* in 1848, Marx and Engels were already anticipating the collapse of capitalism. But the civil strife of 1848 in France ended in the empire of Napoleon III. Engels subsequently admitted that if he and Marx had had the later statistical tools, they would have been less confident about the collapse of capitalism. Never-theless, 1848 had brought forward some novel elements of social experimenta-tion. The next revolution in France, the Paris Commune of 1870–1871, was greeted by Marx as the first really independent revolution of the working class, no longer in alliance with the middle class. He accordingly hastened to examine what new institutions of communal organization the Parisians had created before they were crushed with the support of the Prussian victors of the Franco-Prussian War. Thereafter, the socioethical ideals struggling in France were particularly clear: a religious traditionalism on the right, an individualistic liberalism in the center, and a materialist socialism on the left.

In Britain, where *laissez faire* had become established early and the industrial segment of capitalism had come to power in the expansion of the vote in 1832, the confrontation with the left is less overt. The effort to expand social welfare takes place largely within the framework of liberalism itself. The struggle of the broader mass of the people for emancipation and participation is nevertheless continuous—from the Chartist demands for votes for working-men in the 1840s through the growth of unionism and the foundation of a labor party with a program of social equality and economic welfare. John Stuart Mill, whose refined utilitarianism is the central liberal philosophy of the century, thought that capitalism had not yet had a chance to show what it could accomplish; it was still too laden with older traditional ideas. Mill was especially attracted by its individualism. Later in the century a more social form of liberalism challenged the intense individualism that impeded state welfare action. At the same time different stages in the development of capitalism itself posed different analytic problems for moral philosophy: for example, whereas *laissez faire* called for analyses of liberty and free trade and the limits of state action, the empire building and intensified nationalism of the end of the century called for an ethics of loyalty, of identification with the state, and even of state power.

If there is a single ethical idea that dominates the new moral philosophies it is *freedom*. Each assigns it a central place, reinterpreting it to fit its preferred pattern or discovering some fresh aspect of its complexities. For Hegel, freedom characterizes not so much individual action as whole social formations; it develops in history driven by the contradictions of each successive period. For Marx, freedom is the striving of mankind to make a fit home in the natural world, to give concreteness to human values by a growing social control. To Mill freedom is a characteristic of the individual fashioning a plan of life; it is spontaneity and inventiveness overcoming the sloth of tradition and habit. In the diverse ethical systems that took up the evolutionary idea, freedom is Spencer's aggressive competitiveness, or Nietzsche's equally assertive will to power, or the radical individualism of anarchist theory in the spontaneous mutual effort to overcome the oppression of power. At the end of the century, the neo-Hegelians struggle with the difficulties of egoistic freedom and the needs of social organization to elicit a wholesome freedom, seeking, as it were, the higher synthesis of the movements of the century.

It is philosophically important, therefore, to be sensitive to how changing responses give a different quality to the same ethical concept; no socioethical concept, such as freedom and liberty, or equality, or democracy, can be given a finished abstract analysis that will continue to fit a changing social scene. Take, for example, the complex associated with the spread of the democratic idea—the dynamic phenomenon of mass pressure toward greater participation and a share in political power, education, and the gains of industry. At the time of Mill's *On Liberty* antidemocratic thinkers are still attacking the concept of liberty as a whole, even in its rudimentary form of untrammeled freedom of thought and expression. Thus James Fitzjames Stephen's *Liberty, Equality, Fraternity* (1873) objects to the idea of liberty, for it assumes a stance of neutrality: no serious ideational question allows such a stance. With some virulence he gives a religious example:

I cannot understand how a man who is not a Roman Catholic can regard a real Roman Catholic with absolute neutrality. A man who really thinks that a wafer is God Almighty; and who really believes that rational men owe any sort of allegiance to any kind of priest, is either right—in which case the man who differs from him ought to repent in sackcloth and ashes—or else he is wrong, in which case he is the partizan of a monstrous imposture.[1]

Not surprisingly, he condemns the whole idea of democracy as an expression of resentment by the poor.

On the other hand, as democracy gains social strength, liberty assumes a different cast: it is now contrasted with equality, and the defense of liberty becomes the defense of society and the rule of the fit against "leveling." The concept requires a historical date, with contextual reference, to be understood. Yet the correlation of social context and ethical ideas is by no means simple. If a relation is sought—and some relation is recognized in the usual formulation that ethics is a practical discipline—it is often necessary to trace the variety of relations in historical detail.

---

[1] James Fitzjames Stephen, *Liberty, Equality, Fraternity*, 2d ed., London, 1874; reprinted, ed. R. J. White (Cambridge: Cambridge University Press, 1967), p. 105.

14

G. W. F. Hegel

(1770–1831)

Hegel was born in a Germany that was still a patchwork of principalities, but when the Enlightenment and ideas of freedom were spreading in Europe. He was expected to study for the Lutheran ministry, but instead he turned to an academic career in philosophy. He had a passion for Greek culture, from tragedy to philosophy, admired the Greek *polis* as a balanced communal life, and saw Sophocles's *Antigone* as the essence of freedom—conflict, fate, and the acceptance of inexorable necessity. After he had spent several years as a private tutor in Switzerland and then in Frankfurt, his writing won him a place as *privatdozent* at the University of Jena. Here he witnessed Napoleon's entry into the city, which he, with other intellectuals, felt as a vital move in world history and which he hoped would bring liberalization, constitutional government, and free inquiry. The turbulent events closed the university. Hegel worked as an editor and then as principal of a high school in Nuremberg, during which time he published *The Science of Logic* (1812–1816). His *Phenomenology of Spirit* had already appeared in 1807. In 1816 he became a professor at Heidelberg, and two years later he succeeded Fichte at the University of Berlin. There he wrote many of his major works (including *The Philosophy of Right,* 1821) and inspired a large group of disciples, but he died in the cholera epidemic of 1831. He was regarded as having synthesized and redirected the history of philosophy and, after a temporary eclipse, his philosophy has remained a recognized turning point. Moreover, the scope and breadth of his learning—he dealt with philosophy, art, mathematics, economics, and jurisprudence—inspired attempts to apply his philosophy in many disciplines; in his tradition, culture becomes as much a subject for philosophical treatment as knowledge or reality.

Hegel's outlook on practical life emphasized community as the fully developed form of human living; individual feelings, intentions, and ideals are merely subjectivity; objectivity comes with their finding a place in human social life. He was thus wary of the individualism that shut people out of communal participation or that dissolved communal ties; hence he criticized the British poor laws as inadequate and misguided. He was also suspicious of the movement toward electoral reform, so dear to the hearts of the utilitarians, as likely to intensify private interests at the cost of the sacrifice of a unified society.

At this time the German-speaking area was fragmented, with Prussia beginning to challenge the leadership of Austria. There had already been considerable experience of the halting character of liberalization—freedom for the serfs but little improvement in the lot of the peasantry, promises of a constitution but hopes thwarted by devious performance, forward-looking monarchs but with reactionary successors. The French occupation, at first greeted as a harbinger of modernization and liberalization, soon became felt as an outside imposition, stirring counterfeelings of national identity. This was accentuated by Prussia's growing drive to unify the German-speaking communities outside Austria. And much of this occurred after the Congress of Vienna, which deliberately sought to turn back the clock on the equalitarian democratic movement that the French Revolution had inspired in Europe.

Hegel wove together the threads of political unity and national aspiration, of liberal participation and general education. He supported Prussian leadership in a unified Germany and advocated a constitutional monarchy as the appropriate form of a developed state. When he speaks of the state, however, he has in mind not just a political organization but the nation as a people sharing culture, language, literature, historical tradition, and art. He and Kant thus faced in different directions: Kant toward the growing unity of mankind, Hegel toward what was to become the rampant nationalism of the nineteenth and twentieth centuries.

The difficulty of Hegel's work is legendary. If in Goethe and Kant the classic struggles with the romantic, in Hegel romanticism prevails. Hegel's vision is that of a dynamic social process at work in the world. Largely unconscious pressures shape social institutions, government, moralities, and religions, in organic connection. The influence of Hegel was wide and varied. It was to give Continental social sciences a very different impetus than that found in the mainly empirical trends of British and American social thought. Marx thought he had only to put Hegel right side up to yield a materialistic, rather than idealistic, view. There was also a substantial neo-Hegelian movement in ethics and social philosophy in Britain—particularly in the works of F. H. Bradley (1846–1924) and Bernard Bosanquet (1848–1923). It was a dramatic and comprehensive, indeed heroic, view of the world that held in its spell for a time at the turn of the century even such analytic philosophers as Bertrand Russell (1872–1970) and G. E. Moore (1873–1958). And in America, the St. Louis Hegelians gave a very middle-class interpretation of Hegel's moral theory.

Since Hegel is admittedly so difficult, the first thing is to get some hold on his thinking in terms of the philosophical tradition. This can be done in various ways. One is to move from the familiar to the unfamiliar by comparing Hegel to a philosopher with whom he had serious intellectual connections. Suppose we try this and ask not how he makes certain moves out of Kant but what moves we would have to make out of Aristotle to approach Hegel.

Aristotle's world view is teleological—looking to ends or purposes for explanation—but it is a species teleology: individuals in their development toward maturity embody the plan found in their species; from seed to adult each is governed by the species groundplan. External relations among individuals to other species and the rest of nature are largely accidental; there is no overall plan to relate all that is going on in the world. To move toward Hegel, expand the teleology to the whole of the world. Include not only individual careers but careers of whole peoples and their relations to other nations; in short, include the history of both nature and man in a total world plan.

Aristotle's is an eternal scheme: the world has always existed, structured as it is. Holding it together is a divine self-consciousness in which God thinks himself and so has before him the essence of the world. For Hegel, see this as a process spread over time: history is the development of self-consciousness. Reason (Idea, Spirit) is in the continuing process of actualizing itself. The human philosophic mind seeks to grasp the plan from the course of historical events. Nature itself falls within the historical plan. Matter, so often opposed to Spirit, shares in the plan in its blind way; it is itself simply the extreme alienation of Spirit, a phase in which Spirit is most other than its essential self. Hegel sometimes seems out of step with the traditional supernaturalistic religion. He occasionally sees religion as one phase of the development of self-consciousness. And by embracing everything within a single process, his view skirts pantheism—that is, identifying God and nature, as Spinoza's had done.

In Aristotle, actuality (or reality) is found in the fulfilling of potentialities by the individuals acting or developing according to their plans or essences. Actuality therefore is not equivalent to just existing or happening, for this may be a matter of accident. In Hegel, reality is identified with the working out of the world plan; the unfolding of this Reason marks the essential. Actuality or reality does not then consist in mere happenings but in happenings that are (so to speak) actions that contribute to the plot of the drama. Thus for Hegel aims or principles or ideals held by people are mere potentiality until they enter into existence as governing the course of events. An ideal that is by-passed by events has no reality, it is merely subjective, and it was merely potential. Mere existence is not enough if it plays no part in what is coming into being.

For Aristotle, individuals are social animals—they act *in* communities. For Hegel, the actors *are* the communities or nations. (His strong sense of the cultural and the social in the make-up of the individual has been a permanent influence in the development of the social sciences.) He thus by-passes the intense individualism that preassigns a character to the individual as such, that endows him with antecedent rights and the ability to bargain and contract, and that seeks explanations of events in terms of the mutual interaction of individuals. F. H. Bradley puts it bluntly when he asserts that both the individual and the society, taken by themselves, are vicious abstractions.

Communities can be described as having two different kinds of unity: first, a contemporaneous or synchronic pattern, what we currently refer to as the cultural pattern; second, the temporal or diachronic pattern, exhibited in the succession of societies over historical time. For Hegel, the diachronic pattern is basic, since the cultural pattern is determined by the particular stage of the historical pattern that is due at that particular point. For example, if the historical development calls for the growth of individualism in all its institutions and ideals, an anthropologist simply describing the pattern at that period will find it an individualistic culture. *The Philosophy of History* works out the dialectic of the diachronic pattern. It focuses on the growth of the idea of freedom which is the essence of Spirit as the growth of self-consciousness. It goes from the ancient Eastern societies, in which only the ruler is free, to the modern Germanic world, in which men are free in their integration within the state.

The conception of *dialectic* that governs Hegel's method and the organization of his presentation is many sided. It is already familiar in a Socratic dialogue as a form of argument, and in Plato as a method of pushing further back in examining the basic assumptions of a science (see Chapter 2). There dialectic was a method of thinking, of reason at work. In the growth of philosophical idealism, however, reason becomes transformed from method to metaphysics, from simply the way people think to the structure of reality—reason, so to speak, becomes Reason (cf. Plotinus, Chapter 4). Correspondingly, when Hegel thinks of dialectic, it is not just the order of our thinking but the order of historical unfolding, since history is itself a rational process. Hence in Hegel, in the analysis of the synchronic structure and in that of the diachronic, whether the concern is with phases or with successive stages, the dialectic is shown in the order of analysis—first the *thesis,* then its opposite, *antithesis,* then the *synthesis;* for example, first the external law, then the inner conscience, and then the unified social self.

There is no mystery about such historical transformations as took place for *dialectic.* Similar transformations are going on today. For example, the simple idea of *dialogue,* which means just a conversation in which each person pays some attention to what the other is saying and directs his remarks as an answer, has begun to be used as a psychological process of interpersonal relations going far beyond mere communication. It blossoms into a whole attitude toward others, the heart and soul of human awareness (cf. Buber, Chapter 22). The general idea of dialectic fits readily the order in which our ideas grow and are presented. If we try to give a history of any field—say, music—we often follow the account of one type with that of opposing tendencies and look for the influence of both within some subsequent style. Indeed, the interplay of rationalism and empiricism in the history of the growth of science was presented this way here (see Chapter 7) as a matter of course. Philosophical disputes about the nature of dialectic have been common after Hegel; but they usually concern more detailed doctrines of method and principles by which the character of reality is to be determined. That such notions can be taken to hold not only for the way people think in expanding their ideas but for describing actual processes can be seen from contemporary ways of dealing with interaction—for example, with feedback systems, where one

part of the process is described in terms of what it does to the other parts and what happens to those other parts determines what changes take place in the original parts. The whole idea of systems analysis may perhaps be seen as a refinement of traditional ideas of dialectic.

Hegel was concerned with both the temporal-historical aspects and the systematic-interrelational aspects of the dialectical method. On the whole his most successful and insightful analyses were of the latter sort, particularly in dealing with the interplay of ideas and qualities of feeling in individual consciousness (as in his *Phenomenology*) and in his study of the interactive character of institutional forms (as in his *Philosophy of Right*). Later Hegelians (Chapter 18) moved away from the temporal and stressed rather the unified systematic character of the totality, the whole of reality; for example, they saw the whole of reality as a system of truth, and since full reality and full truth lie only in the whole, all beliefs are partly true and partly false and are to be assessed by the degree of truth they contain. Whatever the epistemological merit of this view, Hegelianism brought a distinctive approach to the history of philosophy as itself a development—with the consequence that different philosophical outlooks are to be searched for the partial truths they contain and how they contribute to a growing consciousness—and it prompted a philosophical generosity toward the diversity of systems. On the other hand, the Marxian use of the idea of dialectic (Chapter 15) never loses sight of the particular temporal-historical context in order to interpret what is going on.

In metaphysics, Hegel works out the idealistic option from Kant. Fichte had started along this path. For Kant, our idea of reality (*noumena, things in themselves,* the *transcendental subject* pointed to in the sense of "I think," *Reason* both theoretical and practical) stemmed ultimately from either the fact of sense as given from outside or the activity of the mind in construction and organization of experience in theory and practice. Fichte boldly unified all sources. As the distinction between the phenomenal and the real itself wore thin or was broken down, philosophy was again faced with the question of characterizing the Reality now so familiarly embraced. For some, including Hegel, Reality was modeled on the nature of thought, as Reason or Spirit being realized in nature and history. Others—Schopenhauer (1788–1860) and Nietzsche (1844–1900)—focused on the active world of practice: reason is secondary, manipulated by the Will, and so Reality is characterized ultimately as Will.

Hegel's ethical theory is most fully presented in his *Philosophy of Right* (sometimes translated as *The Philosophy of Law*). Its concern is less a dialectic of history than a dialectic of concepts as they unfold in experience. The first stage (*Moment*) is Abstract Right, dealing with law and rights of individuals and the obligations they are subject to independently of motivation; the second, Morality (*Moralität*), deals with the inward aspects of obligations; and the third, Ethical Life (*Sittlichkeit*), synthesizes the best of the other two.

Abstract Right has the barest of content. Freedom (free will) is expressed by the self entering into the world of natural objects: it claims *property*, the products of one's labor (including broadly also talents and so aesthetic production, hence everything that can be called "mine"). This outward shape given by the claim of ownership is a symbolic act; it involves recognition by others as well as by myself; and of course it also makes my extended self vulnerable to forces of nature and others' claims at the same time as it makes the object a means or vehicle for me. Moreover, what is mine involves my right to relinquish or alienate my property in exchange, and admits *contract*. Thus a further step has been taken in the meaning of wills, in constituting a common will.

Conflicts in the use of property among extended selves give rise to contradictions: not only unintended *wrongs* (done without malice) but intentional fraud and deceit and breaking of contracts. Wrong, though negating right, is parasitic upon it, for where there is no right, there is no wrong. Punishment then is not an evil per se, but an undoing, a wrong redressed. It is the negation of a negation. A criminal does not wish to be punished, but he is a responsible citizen within a system that he uses, and so has quite literally the right to be punished; insofar as he is moral, he will approve such punishment.

Abstract Right provides the necessary but not the sufficient conditions for organized rational life. As a mere bearer of rights one lives under the external conditions of needs and laws. There is also an inward side to this self as it develops; for as persons we are active, self-determining in willing private ends and purposes. This is the stage of Morality. At the outset an agent may regard himself responsible only for what he imputes to himself as his *own* (proprietory) act, for specific acts he has designed and whose consequences he foresees. But such self-limitation will not do, for consequences do not stop where our finite foresight does. We live in an objective world; just as the criminal benefits when his act has fewer evil consequences, so the good man must also suffer when his purposes have few good results. Thus we must look beyond the narrow confines of purposes taken narrowly to the pattern or character behind isolated acts, that is, we must look beyond our purposes to our intentions—purposes made comprehensive by such a pattern. Our intentions are given shape and meaning by our permanent dispositions; their satisfaction can be regarded as well-being or happiness.

At this point comes the recognition that such objectives are not local; a worth has to be found in the ends moral beings recommend to themselves. At this level we may first take a stand on duty for duty's sake, but this is an empty abstraction; concrete objects are always in view and motives always mixed. No act is done purely out of duty. Even appeal to the larger notion of self-legislation or universal moral law, as in Kant, remains abstract and insufficient; it sets the autonomy of the individual against objective considerations, as well as against the social and truly Ethical world. Sincerity and self-legislation are not enough. Our ideals may be repudiated by nature; we have to find our ideals latent in the world and responsive to the deeper conditions on which morality itself depends. Rights and duties, even conscience, are not the private possessions of individuals.

The final stage, or synthesis, is Social Philosophy. It attempts to reconcile the antagonism, as well as the constructive features, of Abstract Right—providing only the external conditions for organized society—and Morality—which develops the inward acquiescence to obligation, but remains individualistic and formal. Only as this dichotomy of the individual/social is overcome will there be a truly ethical world. This means the recognition not so much that the individual is social, but that the social is *in* the individual. The individual here finds his satisfaction of purposes and intentions in the institutions that frame a common life; and his freedom is realized by accepting the ends of the rational community as his own.

From this point on Hegel moves into the social world of institutions and organizations. The three major institutions are the family, the associations of civil society, and the state. In the *family* the interests of members are organically related and are reinforced by loyalty. But the individual may develop interests that are different and possibly in conflict with family interests. Then he will join or form *associations*—business, sport, fraternal, etc. Again, such associations are bound only by external ties; they are not held together by sentiment and readily dissolve when the objectives are no longer shared. It is the *state* alone that can provide the structure and the opportunity for freedom needed for the full development of the person. All this is integral to ethics, not an application of a prior completed ethics.

The selections begin with *The Philosophy of History*, to give the overall view, and then turn to *The Philosophy of Right* (1821) as an account from which we can get a clear view of Hegel's moral theory. The former was left incomplete, because of Hegel's death. The version given here was constructed by his son, partly from Hegel's manuscript materials and partly from notes taken by others of Hegel's lectures. Nevertheless, it can be taken as a fair indication of his theoretical aspirations.

The Philosophy of History [1]

Introduction

The only Thought which Philosophy brings with it to the contemplation of History, is the simple conception of *Reason*; that Reason is the Sovereign of the World; that the history of the world, therefore, presents us with a rational process. This conviction and intuition is a hypothesis in the domain of history as such. In that of Philosophy it is no hypothesis. It is there proved by speculative cognition, that Reason—and this term may here suffice us, without investigating the relation sustained by the Universe to the Divine Being—is *Substance*, as well as *Infinite Power*; its own *Infinite Material* underlying all the natural and spiritual life which it originates, as also the *Infinite Form*—that which sets this Material in motion. On the one hand, Reason is the *substance* of the Universe; viz., that by which and in which all reality has its being and subsistence. On the other hand, it is the *Infinite Energy* of the Universe; since Reason is not so powerless as to be incapable of producing anything but a mere ideal, a mere intention—having its place outside reality, nobody knows where; something separate and abstract, in the heads of certain human beings. It is *the infinite complex of things*, their entire Essence and Truth. It is its own material which it commits to its own Active Energy to work up; not needing, as finite action does, the conditions of an external material of given means from which it may obtain its support, and the objects of its activity. It supplies

[1] The translation is by J. Sibree, from the second edition of 1840, ed. Dr. C. Hegel (New York: P. F. Collier and Son, 1900).

its own nourishment, and is the object of its own operations. While it is exclusively its own basis of existence, and absolute final aim, it is also the energizing power realizing this aim; developing it not only in the phenomena of the Natural, but also of the Spiritual Universe—the History of the World. That this "Idea" or "Reason" is the *True*, the *Eternal*, the absolutely *powerful* essence; that it reveals itself in the World, and that in that World nothing else is revealed but this and its honor and glory—is the thesis which, as we have said, has been proved in Philosophy, and is here regarded as demonstrated. [pp. 52–53]

Pious persons are encouraged to recognize, in particular circumstances, something more than mere chance; to acknowledge the guiding hand of God: *e.g.* when help has unexpectedly come to an individual in great perplexity and need. But these instances of providential design are of a limited kind, and concern the accomplishment of nothing more than the desires of the individual in question. But in the history of the World, the *Individuals* we have to do with are *Peoples*; Totalities that are States. We cannot, therefore, be satisfied with what we may call this "peddling" view of Providence, to which the belief alluded to limits itself. Equally unsatisfactory is the merely abstract, undefined belief in a Providence, when that belief is not brought to bear upon the details of the process which it conducts. On the contrary, our earnest endeavor must be directed to the recognition of the ways of Providence, the means it uses, and the historical phenomena in which it manifests itself; and we must show their connection with the general principle above mentioned. . . . The time must eventually come for understanding that rich product of active Reason, which the History of the World offers to us. It was for a while the fashion to profess admiration for the wisdom of God, as displayed in animals, plants, and isolated occurrences. But, if it be allowed that Providence manifests itself in such objects and forms of existence, why not also in Universal History. This is deemed too great a matter to be thus regarded. But Divine Wisdom, *i.e.* Reason, is one and the same in the great as in the little. [pp. 58–59]

Three topics are to be examined: the abstract characteristics of Spirit, the means that Spirit uses to realize its Idea, and the shape that the perfect embodiment of Spirit assumes, that is, the State. Spirit is the opposite of Matter. The essence of Matter is gravity; that of Spirit is Freedom.

It is a result of speculative Philosophy, that Freedom is the sole truth of Spirit. Matter possesses gravity in virtue of its tendency toward a central point. It is essentially composite; consisting of parts that *exclude* each other. It seeks its Unity; and therefore exhibits itself as self-destructive, as verging toward its opposite [an indivisible point]. If it could attain this, it would be Matter no longer, it would have perished. It strives after the realization of its Idea; for in Unity it exists *ideally*. Spirit, on the contrary, may be defined as that which has its centre in itself. It has not a unity outside itself, but has already found it; it exists *in* and *with* itself. Matter has its essence out of itself; Spirit is *self-contained existence* (Bei-sich-selbst-seyn). Now this is Freedom, exactly. For if I am dependent, my being is referred to something else which I am not; I cannot exist independently of something external. I am free, on the contrary, when my existence depends upon myself. This self-contained existence of Spirit is none other than self-consciousness—consciousness of one's own being. Two things must be distinguished in consciousness; first, the fact *that I know*; secondly, *what I know*. In *self* consciousness these are merged in one; for Spirit *knows itself*. It involves an appreciation of its own nature, as also an energy enabling it to realize itself; to make itself *actually* that which it is *potentially*. According to this abstract definition it may be said of Universal History, that it is the exhibition of Spirit in the process of working out the knowledge of that which it is potentially. And as the germ bears in itself the whole nature of the tree, and the taste and form of its fruits, so do the first traces of Spirit virtually contain the whole of that History. The Orientals have not attained the knowledge that Spirit—Man *as such*—is free; and because they do not know this, they are not free. They only know that *one is free*. But on this very account, the freedom of that one is only caprice; ferocity—brutal recklessness of passion, or a mildness and tameness of the desires, which is itself only an accident of Nature—mere caprice like the former.—That *one* is therefore only a Despot; not a *free man*. The consciousness of Freedom first arose among the Greeks, and therefore they were free; but they, and the Romans likewise, knew only that *some* are free—not man as such. Even Plato

and Aristotle did not know this. The Greeks, therefore, had slaves; and their whole life and the maintenance of their splendid liberty, was implicated with
the institution of slavery: a fact, moreover, which
made that liberty on the one hand only an accidental, transient and limited growth; on the other hand,
constituted it a rigorous thraldom of our common
nature—of the Human. The German nations, under
the influence of Christianity, were the first to attain
the consciousness, that man, as man, is free: that
it is the *freedom* of Spirit which constitutes its essence. This consciousness arose first in religion, the
inmost region of Spirit; but to introduce the principle into the various relations of the actual world,
involves a more extensive problem than its simple
implantation; a problem whose solution and application require a severe and lengthened process of
culture. In proof of this, we may note that slavery
did not cease immediately on the reception of Christianity. Still less did liberty predominate in States;
or Governments and Constitutions adopt a rational
organization, or recognize freedom as their basis.
That application of the principle to political relations; the thorough molding and interpenetration
of the constitution of society by it, is a process identical with history itself. I have already directed attention to the distinction here involved, between a
principle as such, and its *application; i.e.* its introduction and carrying out in the actual phenomena of
Spirit and Life. This is a point of fundamental importance in our science, and one which must be
constantly respected as essential. And in the same
way as this distinction has attracted attention in
view of the *Christian* principle of self-consciousness—Freedom; it also shows itself as an essential
one, in view of the principle of Freedom *generally*.
The History of the world is none other than the
progress of the consciousness of Freedom; a progress whose development according to the necessity
of its nature, it is our business to investigate. [pp.
62–64]

As to the means Spirit uses to carry out its
Idea: the actions of men proceed from their
needs, passions, character, and talents—or noble patriotism—but this is a small part (p. 65).
Our subjective designs are only a potentiality.
"That some conception of mine should be developed into act and existence, is my earnest

desire: I wish to assert my personality in connection with it: I wish to be satisfied by its
execution" (pp. 67–68). It must in some way
be *my* object; I must find *my* satisfaction. Indeed nothing is accomplished without interest
on the part of the actors: "We may affirm absolutely that *nothing great in the World* has been
accomplished without *passion*" (p. 69). Human
action thus motivated furnishes the instrumen-
talities of the Idea. The Idea and the complex
of human passions are the warp and woof of
universal history.

The building of a house is, in the first instance,
a subjective aim and design. On the other hand
we have, as means, the several substances required
for the work—Iron, Wood, Stones. The elements
are made use of in working up this material: fire
to melt the iron, wind to blow the fire, water to
set wheels in motion, in order to cut the wood,
etc. The result is, that the wind, which has helped
to build the house, is shut out by the house; so
also are the violence of rains and floods, and the
destructive powers of fire, so far as the house is
made fireproof. The stones and beams obey the law
of gravity—press downward—and so high walls are
carried up. Thus the elements are made use of in
accordance with their nature, and yet to co-operate
for a product, by which their operation is limited.
Thus the passions of men are gratified; they develop
themselves and their aims in accordance with their
natural tendencies, and build up the edifice of human society; thus fortifying a position for Right and
Order *against themselves*. [p. 73]

Caesar . . . belongs essentially to this category
[world-historical individuals]. Caesar was contending for the maintenance of his position, honor, and
safety; and, since the power of his opponents included the sovereignty over the provinces of the
Roman Empire, his victory secured for him the conquest of that entire Empire; and he thus became
(though leaving the form of the constitution) the
Autocrat of the State. That which secured for him
the execution of a design, which in the first instance
was of negative import—the Autocracy of Rome—
was, however, at the same time an independently
necessary feature in the history of Rome and of
the world. It was not then his private gain merely,
but an unconscious impulse that occasioned the

accomplishment of that for which the time was ripe. Such are all great historical men—whose own particular aims involve those large issues which are the will of the World-Spirit. They may be called Heroes, inasmuch as they have derived their purposes and their vocation, not from the calm, regular course of things, sanctioned by the existing order; but from a concealed fount—one which has not attained to phenomenal, present existence—from that inner Spirit, still hidden beneath the surface, which, impinging on the outer world as on a shell, bursts it in pieces, because it is another kernel than that which belonged to the shell in question. They are men, therefore, who appear to draw the impulse of their life from themselves; and whose deeds have produced a condition of things and a complex of historical relations which appear to be only *their* interest, and *their* work.

Such individuals had no consciousness of the general Idea they were unfolding, while prosecuting those aims of theirs; on the contrary, they were practical, political men. But at the same time they were thinking men, who had an insight into the requirements of the time—*what was ripe for development*. This was the very Truth for their age, for their world; the species next in order, so to speak, and which was already formed in the womb of time. It was theirs to know this nascent principle; the necessary, directly sequent step in progress, which their world was to take; to make this their aim, and to expend their energy in promoting it. World-historical men—the Heroes of an epoch—must, therefore, be recognized as its clear-sighted ones; *their* deeds, *their* words are the best of that time. Great men have formed purposes to satisfy themselves, not others. Whatever prudent designs and counsels they might have learned from others, would be the more limited and inconsistent features in their career; for it was they who best understood affairs; from whom *others* learned, and approved, or at least acquiesced in—their policy. For that Spirit which had taken this fresh step in history is the inmost soul of all individuals; but in a state of unconsciousness which the great men in question aroused. Their fellows, therefore, follow these soul-leaders; for they feel the irresistible power of their own inner Spirit thus embodied. If we go on to cast a look at the fate of these World-Historical persons, whose vocation it was to be the agents of the World-Spirit—we shall find it to have been no happy one. They attained no calm enjoyment; their whole life was labor and trouble; their whole nature was naught else but their master-passion. When their object is attained they fall off like empty hulls from the kernel. They die early, like Alexander; they are murdered, like Caesar; transported to St. Helena, like Napoleon. This fearful consolation—that historical men have not enjoyed what is called happiness, and of which only private life (and this may be passed under very various external circumstances) is capable—this consolation those may draw from history, who stand in need of it; and it is craved by Envy—vexed at what is great and transcendent—striving, therefore, to depreciate it, and to find some flaw in it. Thus in modern times it has been demonstrated *ad nauseam* that princes are generally unhappy on their thrones; in consideration of which the possession of a throne is tolerated, and men acquiesce in the fact that not themselves but the personages in question are its occupants. The Free Man, we may observe, is not envious, but gladly recognizes what is great and exalted, and rejoices that it exists.

. . . [T]hese historical men . . . are *great* men, because they willed and accomplished something great; not a mere fancy, a mere intention, but that which met the case and fell in with the needs of the age. This mode of considering them also excludes the so-called "psychological" view, which—serving the purpose of envy most effectually—contrives so to refer all actions to the heart—to bring them under such a subjective aspect—as that their authors appear to have done everything under the impulse of some passion, mean or grand—some *morbid craving*—and on account of these passions and cravings to have been not moral men. Alexander of Macedon partly subdued Greece, and then Asia; therefore he was possessed by a *morbid craving* for conquest. . . . What pedagogue has not demonstrated of Alexander the Great—of Julius Caesar—that they were instigated by such passions, and were consequently immoral men?—whence the conclusion immediately follows that he, the pedagogue, is a better man than they, because he has not such passions. . . . These psychologists are particularly fond of contemplating those peculiarities of great historical figures which appertain to them as private persons. . . . "No man is a hero to his valet-de-chambre," is a well-known proverb; I have added—and Goethe repeated it ten years later—

"but not because the former is no hero, but because the latter is a valet." He takes off the hero's boots, assists him to bed, knows that he prefers champagne, etc. Historical personages waited upon in historical literature by such psychological valets, come poorly off; they are brought down by these their attendants to a level with—or rather a few degrees below the level of—the morality of such exquisite discerners of spirits. . . .

A World-historical individual is not so unwise as to indulge a variety of wishes to divide his regards. He is devoted to the One Aim, regardless of all else. It is even possible that such men may treat other great, even sacred interests, inconsiderately; conduct which is indeed obnoxious to moral reprehension. But so mighty a form must trample down many an innocent flower—crush to pieces many an object in its path.

The special interest of passion is thus inseparable from the active development of a general principle: for it is from the special and determinate and from its negation that the Universal results. Particularity contends with its like, and some loss is involved in the issue. *It* is not the general idea that is implicated in opposition and combat, and that is exposed to danger. It remains in the background, untouched and uninjured. This may be called the *cunning of reason*—that it sets the passions to work for itself, while that which develops its existence through such impulsion pays the penalty, and suffers loss. For it is *phenomenal* being that is so treated, and of this, part is of no value, part is positive and real. The particular is for the most part of too trifling value as compared with the general: individuals are sacrificed and abandoned. The Idea pays the penalty of determinate existence and of corruptibility, not from itself, but from the passions of individuals.

But though we might tolerate the idea that individuals, their desires and the gratification of them, are thus sacrificed, and their happiness given up to the empire of chance, to which it belongs; and that, as a general rule, individuals come under the category of means to an ulterior end—there is one aspect of human individuality which we should hesitate to regard in that subordinate light, even in relation to the highest; since it is absolutely no subordinate element, but exists in those individuals as inherently eternal and divine. I mean *morality, ethics, religion*. Even when speaking of the realization of the great ideal aim by means of individuals, the *subjective* element in them—their interest and that of their cravings and impulses, their views and judgments, though exhibited as the merely formal side of their existence—was spoken of as having an infinite right to be consulted. The first idea that presents itself in speaking of *means* is that of something external to the object, and having no share in the object itself. But merely natural things—even the commonest lifeless objects—used as means, must be of such a kind as adapts them to their purpose; they must possess something in common with it. Human beings least of all sustain the bare external relation of mere means to the great ideal aim. Not only do they, in the very act of realizing it, make it the occasion of satisfying personal desires, whose purport is diverse from that aim—but they share in that ideal aim itself; and are for that very reason objects of their own existence; not *formally* merely as the world of living beings generally is—whose individual life is essentially subordinate to that of man, and is properly used *up* as an instrument. Men, on the contrary, are objects of existence to themselves, as regards the intrinsic import of the aim in question. To this order belongs that in them which we would exclude from the category of mere means—Morality, Ethics, Religion. That is to say, man is an object of existence in himself only in virtue of the Divine, that is in him—that which was designated at the outset as *Reason;* which, in view of its activity and power of self-determination, was called *Freedom*. And we affirm—without entering at present on the proof of the assertion—that Religion, Morality, etc., have their foundation and source in that principle, and so are essentially elevated above all alien necessity and chance. And here we must remark that individuals, to the extent of their freedom, are responsible for the depravation and enfeeblement of morals and religion. This is the seal of the absolute and sublime destiny of man—that he knows what is good and what is evil; that his Destiny *is* his very ability to will either good or evil—in one word, that he is the subject of moral imputation, imputation not only of evil, but of good; and not only concerning this or that particular matter, and all that happens *ab extra*, but *also* the good and evil attaching to his individual freedom. The brute alone is simply innocent. . . .

. . . Nothing, as before remarked, is now more common than the complaint that the *ideals* which imagination sets up are not realized—that these glorious dreams are destroyed by cold actuality. These Ideals—which in the voyage of life founder on the rocks of hard reality—may be in the first instance only subjective, and belong to the idiosyncrasy of the individual, imagining himself the highest and wisest. Such do not properly belong to this category. For the fancies which the individual in his isolation indulges, cannot be the model for universal reality; just as *universal* law is not designed for the units of the mass. These as such may, in fact, find their interests decidedly thrust into the background. But by the term "Ideal," we also understand the ideal of Reason, of the Good, of the True. Poets, as *e.g.* Schiller, have painted such ideals touchingly and with strong emotion, and with the deeply melancholy conviction that they could not be realized. In affirming, on the contrary, that the Universal Reason *does* realize itself, we have indeed nothing to do with the individual empirically regarded. That admits of degrees of better and worse, since here chance and speciality have received authority from the Idea to exercise their monstrous power. Much, therefore, in particular aspects of the grand phenomenon might be found fault with. This subjective fault-finding—which, however, only keeps in view the individual and its deficiency, without taking notice of Reason pervading the whole—is easy; and inasmuch as it asserts an excellent intention with regard to the good of the whole, and seems to result from a kindly heart, it feels authorized to give itself airs and assume great consequence. It is easier to discover a deficiency in individuals, in states, and in Providence, than to see their real import and value. [pp. 76–83]

The argument concludes:

The insight then to which—in contradistinction from those ideals—philosophy is to lead us, is, that the real world is as it ought to be—that the truly good—the universal divine reason—is not a mere abstraction, but a vital principle capable of realizing itself. This *Good*, this *Reason*, in its most concrete form, is God. God governs the world; the actual working of his government—the carrying out of his plan—is the History of the World. This plan philosophy strives to comprehend. [p. 84]

This can be reconciled with ordinary views.

The religion, the morality of a limited sphere of life—that of a shepherd or a peasant, *e.g.*—in its intensive concentration and limitation to a few perfectly simple relations of life—has infinite worth; the same worth as the religion and morality of extensive knowledge, and of an existence rich in the compass of its relations and actions. This inner focus—this simple region of the claims of subjective freedom—the home of volition, resolution, and action—the abstract sphere of conscience—that which comprises the responsibility and moral value of the individual, remains untouched; and is quite shut out from the noisy din of the World's History. [But] whatever in the world possesses claims as noble and glorious, has nevertheless a higher existence above it. The claim of the World-Spirit rises above all special claims. [p. 85]

The form that Spirit assumes in reality is seen in the development of the State—the third of the three topics previously announced.

What is the material in which the Ideal of Reason is wrought out? The primary answer would be—Personality itself—human desires—Subjectivity generally. In human knowledge and volition, as its material element, Reason attains positive existence. We have considered subjective volition where it has an object which is the truth and essence of a reality; viz. where it constitutes a great world-historical passion. As a subjective will, occupied with limited passions, it is dependent, and can gratify its desires only within the limits of this dependence. But the subjective will has also a substantial life—a reality—in which it moves in the region of *essential* being, and has the essential itself as the object of its existence. This essential being is the union of the *subjective* with the *rational* Will: it is the moral Whole, the *State*, which is that form of reality in which the individual has and enjoys his freedom; but on the condition of his recognizing, believing in and willing that which is common to the Whole. And this must not be understood as if the subjective will of the social unit attained its gratification and enjoyment through that common Will; as if this were a means provided for its benefit; as if the individual, in his relations to other individuals, thus limited his freedom, in order that this universal limitation—the mutual constraint of all—might secure a small space of liberty for each. Rather, we affirm, are Law, Morality, Government, and they alone, the positive reality and completion of Freedom. Freedom of a low and limited order is mere caprice, which finds its exercise in the sphere of particular and limited desires.

Subjective volition—Passion—is that which sets men in activity, that which effects "practical" realization. The Idea is the inner spring of action; the State is the actually existing, realized moral life. For it is the Unity of the universal, essential Will, with that of the individual; and this is "Morality." The Individual living in this unity has a moral life; possesses a value that consists in this substantiality alone. Sophocles in his Antigone, says, "The divine commands are not of yesterday, nor of to-day; no, they have an infinite existence, and no one could say whence they came." The laws of morality are not accidental, but are the essentially Rational. It is the very object of the State that what is essential in the practical activity of men, and in their dispositions, should be duly recognized; that it should have a manifest existence, and maintain its position. It is the absolute interest of Reason that this moral Whole should exist; and herein lies the justification and merit of heroes who have founded states—however rude these may have been. In the history of the World, only those peoples can come under our notice which form a state. For it must be understood that this latter is the realization of Freedom, *i.e.* of the absolute final aim, and that it exists for its own sake. It must further be understood that all the worth which the human being possesses—all spiritual reality, he possesses only through the State. For his spiritual reality consists in this, that his own essence—Reason—is objectively present to him, that it possesses objective immediate existence for him. Thus only is he fully conscious; thus only is he a partaker of morality—of a just and moral social and political life. For Truth is the Unity of the universal and subjective Will; and the Universal is to be found in the State, in its laws, its universal and rational arrangements. The State is the Divine Idea as it exists on Earth. We have in it, therefore, the object of History in a more definite shape than before; that in which Freedom obtains objectivity, and lives in the enjoyment of this objectivity. For Law is the objectivity of Spirit; volition in its true form. Only that will which obeys law, is free; for it obeys itself—it is independent and so free. When the State or our country constitutes a community of existence; when the subjective will of man submits to laws—the contradiction between Liberty and Necessity vanishes. [pp. 86–87]

The development of the idea of the State belongs to jurisprudence. One erroneous view is that man is free by nature but is limited by society. The state of nature is merely one of natural conditions and untamed impulses. The family, as one substantial being, provides a feeling of unity. Also erroneous is the conception that the people alone have reason and insight, and know what justice is. Each popular faction may represent itself as the people, but what constitutes the State is a matter of science, not popular decision (p. 92). The State should not be considered simply abstractly. Generically it exists in its citizenry; specifically it is embodied in individual will and activity. It should be seen as a whole, not one-sidedly, as for example when it is regarded merely as a constitution.

There are three stages of freedom in the consciousness of people:

Among the forms of this conscious union *Religion* occupies the highest position. In it, Spirit—rising above the limitations of temporal and secular existence—becomes conscious of the Absolute Spirit, and in this consciousness of the self-existent Being, renounces its individual interest. . . . The religious concentration of the soul appears in the form of feeling; it nevertheless passes also into reflection; a form of worship (*cultus*) is a result of reflection. [p. 99]

A second form of the union of subjective and objective in the human spirit is art. "This advances farther into the realm of the actual and sensuous than Religion." Its noblest work is representing the form of God, and secondarily that which is divine and spiritual generally. But the true is the object not only of conception and feeling, as in religion, nor of intuition as in art, but of the thinking faculty in philosophy. "This is consequently the highest, freest, and wisest phase" (p. 99).

Summing up what has been said of the State, we find that we have been led to call its vital principle, as actuating the individuals who compose it—Morality. The State, its laws, its arrangements, constitute the rights of its members; its natural features, its mountains, air, and waters, are *their* country, their fatherland, their outward material property; the history of this State, *their* deeds; what their ancestors have produced belongs to them and lives in their memory. All is their possession, just as they are possessed by it; for it constitutes their existence, their being.

Their imagination is occupied with the ideas thus presented, while the adoption of these laws, and of a fatherland so conditioned is the expression of their will. It is this matured totality which thus constitutes *one* Being, the spirit of *one* People. To it the individual members belong; each unit is the Son of his Nation, and at the same time—in as far as the State to which he belongs is undergoing development—the Son of his Age. None remains behind it, still less advances beyond it. This spiritual Being (the Spirit of his Time) is his; he is a representative of it; it is that in which he originated, and in which he lives. Among the Athenians the word Athens had a double import; suggesting primarily, a complex of political institutions, but no less, in the second place, that Goddess who represented the Spirit of the People and its unity.

This Spirit of a People is a *determinate* and particular Spirit, and is, as just stated, further modified by the degree of its historical development. This Spirit, then, constitutes the basis and substance of those other forms of a nation's consciousness which have been noticed. For Spirit in its self-consciousness must become an object of contemplation to itself, and objectivity involves, in the first instance, the rise of differences which make up a total of distinct spheres of objective spirit; in the same way as the Soul exists only as the complex of its faculties, which in their form of concentration in a simple unity produce that Soul. It is thus *One Individuality* which, presented in its essence as God, is honored and enjoyed in *Religion;* which is exhib-

ited as an object of sensuous contemplation in *Art;* and is apprehended as an intellectual conception, in *Philosophy*. In virtue of the original identity of their essence, purport, and object, these various forms are inseparably united with the Spirit of the State. Only in connection with this particular religion, can this particular political constitution exist; just as in such or such a State, such or such a Philosophy or order of Art. [pp. 102–103]

A philosophical history starts where rationality begins to manifest itself in the world's affairs (p. 110). (The earlier periods present no subjective history, no annals [p. 113].) Every step in the process has its determinate peculiar principle. This is the idiosyncrasy of Spirit, that each period shows a peculiar national genius: "Its religion, its polity, its ethics, its legislation, and even its science, art, and mechanical skill, all bear its stamp" (p. 116). We should not hold against great men "the Litany of private virtues—modesty, humility, philanthropy and forbearance" (p. 120). The temporal development of Spirit is summed up: "The principles of the successive phases of Spirit that animate the Nations in a necessitated gradation, are themselves only steps in the development of the one universal Spirit, which through them elevates and completes itself to a self-comprehending *totality*" (p. 133).

The plan of development is carried into a historical sketch of the ancient Orient, the story of Greece and Rome, and the Germanic world. It is the story of freedom, from one to many, to all in the state. America does not have a real State, "for a real State and a real Government arise only after a distinction of classes has arisen, when wealth and poverty become extreme, and when such a condition of things presents itself that a large portion of the people can no longer satisfy its necessities in the way in which it has been accustomed so to do" (p. 141). America still has the outlet of colonization. "What *has* taken place in the New World up to the present time is only an echo of the Old World—the expression of a foreign Life; and as a Land of the Future, it has no interest for us here" (p. 143). The historian's concern is with what has been or what is, while the philosopher's is with eternal existence or Reason.

The future is apparently, then, not in Hegel's province. The essentially retrospective attitude is clearly expressed in the concluding words of the whole book—that the History of the World as the realization of Spirit is the true Theodicaea, the justification of God in History. "What has happened, and is happening every day, is not only not 'without God,' but is essentially His Work" (p. 569). It is this retrospective, rather than activist, attitude that Marx had in mind when he remarked: "The philosophers have only *interpreted* the world, in various ways; the point, however, is to *change* it."[2]

The Philosophy of Right [3]

The Philosophy of Right traces the dialectic of personhood from the legal or abstract sense of person through the inward aspect of private conscience to the concrete life of man in society, in which his nature is fully realized.

At the bare minimum, the individual, set off from things, has the formal power of entering relations with them. This makes him in the legal sense a person. He gets a purchase in the real world by projecting his will on things in ownership.

44. A person has the right to direct his will upon any object, as his real and positive end. The object thus becomes his. As it has no end in itself, it re-

ceives its meaning and soul from his will. Mankind has the absolute right to appropriate all that is a thing. . . .

A man may own anything, because he is a free will, and is therefore self-contained and self-dependent. But the mere object is of an opposite nature. Every man has the right to turn his will upon a thing or make the thing an object of his will, that is to say, to set aside the mere thing and recreate it as his own. As the thing is in its nature external, it has no purpose of its own and contains no infinite reference to itself; it is external to itself. . . . Only the will is the unlimited and absolute, while all other things in contrast with the will are merely relative. . . .

49. In my relation to external things, the rational element is that it is I who own property. But the particular element on the other hand is concerned with ends, wants, caprices, talents, external circumstances, etc. Upon them, it is true, mere abstract possession depends, but they in this sphere of abstract personality are not yet identical with freedom. Hence what and how much I possess is from the standpoint of right a matter of indifference.

If we can speak of several persons, when as yet no distinction has been drawn between one person and another, we may say that in personality all persons are equal. But this is an empty tautological proposition, since a person abstractedly considered is not as yet separate from others, and has no distinguishing attribute. . . . This equality would be only the equality of abstract persons as such, and would exclude all reference to possession, which is the basis of inequality. Sometimes the demand is made for equality in the division of the soil of the earth, and even of other kinds of wealth. Such a claim is superficial, because differences of wealth are due not only to the accidents of external nature but also to the infinite variety and difference of mind and character. . . . We cannot say that nature is unjust in distributing wealth and property unequally, because nature is not free and, therefore, neither just nor unjust. It is in part a moral desire that all men should have sufficient income for their wants, and when the wish is left in this indefinite form it is well-meant, although it, like everything merely well-meant, has no counterpart in reality. . . .

. . . Here the assertion that the property of every man ought in justice to be equal to that of every other is false, since justice demands merely that

[2] Karl Marx, *Theses on Feuerbach*, XI, in *Marx and Engels: Basic Writings on Politics and Philosophy*, ed. Lewis S. Feuer (Garden City, New York: Doubleday, Anchor, 1959), p. 245.
[3] The selection is from *Hegel's Philosophy of Right*, trans. S. W. Dyde (London: George Bell and Sons, 1896).

every one should have property. Indeed, amongst persons variously endowed inequality must occur, and equality would be wrong. . . .

50. It is a self-evident and, indeed, almost superfluous remark that an object belongs to him who is accidentally first in possession of it. . . .

. . . He is rightful owner, not because he is first, but because he is a free will. . . .

51. In order to fix property as the outward symbol of my personality, it is not enough that I represent it as mine and internally will it to be mine; I must also take it over into my possession. The embodiment of my will can then be recognized by others as mine. . . .

There are various ways in which I can signify my ownership—by first possession, by use or consumption, by mixing my labor with it, and finally by relinquishing property. The property relation is not really firm until recognized by others, that is, it involves the consenting will of others. Thus the relation between things becomes a relation between wills.

The objectification of the common will forms the basis of contract. Hegel here parts company with social contract theories, since contracts underlie only our relations with respect to particular external things, namely those things which are not intrinsically connected with the will. Thus marriage is wrongly described as a contract (Hegel considers Kant's view here scandalous); and similarly for family and state. Contract, however, has still to do with legal rather than moral rights; secret intentions and moral dispositions of the parties are not relevant. Individuals can, however, have conflicting legal grounds for claiming the same things.

86. . . . The first form of wrong [the unintentional] negates only the particular will; but pays respect to the general right; it is thus the slightest of all forms of wrong. When I say that a rose is not red, I still admit that the object has colour. I thus do not deny the species, colour, but only the particular colour, red. It is the same here with right. Everybody wills the right, and for him the right only shall take place; his wrong consists in his holding that what he wills is right.

Fraud and crime are more serious intentional wrongs that violate contract and property. They are wrong in so far as they annul or cancel a willing.

92. Since it is only in so far as the will has visible existence that it is the idea and so really free . . . force or violence destroys itself forthwith in its very conception. It is a manifestation of will which cancels or supersedes a manifestation or visible expression of will. Force or violence, therefore, is, according to this abstract treatment of it, devoid of right.

93. Since it in its very conception destroys itself, its principle is that it must be cancelled by violence. Hence it is not only right but necessary that a second exercise of force should annul and supersede the first.

94. Abstract right is a right to use force. A wrong done to this right is a force exercised against my liberty realized in an external thing. . . .

100. The injury which the criminal experiences is inherently just because it expresses his own inherent will, is a visible proof of his freedom and is his right. But more than that, the injury is a right of the criminal himself, and is implied in his realized will or act. In his act, the act of a rational being, is involved a universal element, which by the act is set up as a law. . . .

The injury done the criminal is the completion of his own deed, and is called for by justice to the criminal himself. Yet only insofar as the criminal is morally aware can he accept his punishment. Such awareness constitutes the move from the legal to the moral, from external compulsion to inward verdict. This internal judgment, going beyond self-interest, ushers in a new dimension, in contrast to abstract right. In this new dimension the agent first regards himself as responsible merely for his immediate objective, that is, the consequences purposed.

118. An act, when it has become an external reality, and is connected with a varied outer necessity, has manifold consequences. These consequences, being the visible shape, whose soul is the end of action, belong to the act. But at the same time the

inner act, when realized as an end in the external world, is handed over to external forces, which attach to it something quite different from what it is in itself, and thus carry it away into strange and distant consequences. It is the right of the will to adopt only the first consequences, since they alone lie in the purpose.

The division of consequences into necessary and accidental is not accurate, because the inner necessity, involved in the finite, is realized as a necessity which is external, a necessity, that is to say, implying a relation of separate things, which are independent, indifferent to one another, and only externally connected. The principle "In acting neglect the consequences," and the principle "Judge an act by its consequences, and make them the standard of what is right and good," belong both alike to the abstract understanding. The consequences are the native form of the act, simply manifest its nature, and are nothing but the act itself. The act cannot scorn and disown them. Yet amongst the consequences is included that which is only externally attached to them and has no fellowship with the act itself.

A subsequent section, "The Good and Conscience," criticizes Kant for having limited himself to the subjective dimension of merely universalized intention. Kant's theory of duty is an empty formalism. Particular duties can be determined only by importing something further into the empty formal principle. Virtually any immoral act can be justified on Kant's formulation; it is only insofar as property and life are to be respected on other grounds that theft and murder are self-contradictory.

134. Since an act requires its own special content and definite end, and duty in the abstract contains no such end, there arises the question, What is duty? No answer is at once forthcoming, except "To do right, and to consider one's own well-being, and the general well-being, the well-being of others."

. . . The universal good cannot, if abstractly taken, be realized. If it is to be realized, it must be given a particular content.

135. . . . In so far as duty is the universal or essence of the moral consciousness, and merely refers itself to itself within itself, it is only an abstract universality, and has for its characteristic an identity without content, an abstract positive, an absence of definite character.

It is important to be clear that the pure unconditioned self-direction of the will is the root of duty. This doctrine of volition attained to a firm basis and starting-point first of all in the Kantian philosophy through the thought of the infinite autonomy of the will. Yet if this merely moral standpoint does not pass into the conception of the ethical system, this philosophical acquisition is reduced to empty formalism, and moral science is converted into mere rhetoric about duty for duty's sake. From such a position can be derived no inherent doctrine of duties. Materials, it is true, may be introduced from without, and in this way specific duties may be secured; but from duty, whose characteristic is an absence of contradiction or formal concord with itself, a characteristic which is no more than the establishment of abstract indefiniteness, no specific duties can be deduced. Nor, further, if any specific content of action comes up for consideration, is there in this principle any way of judging whether it is a duty or not. On the contrary, all manner of wrong and immoral acts may be by such a method justified.

The more detailed Kantian statement, the suitability of an act to be presented as a universal rule, implies indeed the more concrete notion of a condition, but really contains no other principle than absence of contradiction, or formal identity. The rule that there should be no private property contains of itself no contradiction, nor does the proposition that this or that particular nation or family should not exist, or that no one should live at all. Only if it is really fixed and assumed that private property and human life should exist and be respected, is it a contradiction to commit theft or murder. There can be no contradiction except of something that exists or of a content, which is assumed to be a fixed principle. Only such a content can an act agree with or contradict. But duty which must be willed only as such, and not for the sake of a content, is a formal identity excluding all content and specific character. . . .

Although we exalted the standpoint of the Kantian philosophy, in so far as it nobly insists that duty should accord with reason, yet its weakness is that it lacks all organic filling. The proposition,

"Consider if thy maxim can be set up as a universal rule" would be all right, if we already had definite rules concerning what should be done. A principle that is suitable for universal legislation already presupposes a content. . . .

Neither of the opposing attitudes to the developing scope of responsibility—intention or consequence—is sufficient. The individual's conscious reckoning of purpose may grow into a fuller conception of his good, but even this will not do unless he moves beyond his individual self. The individual does not abandon his good and his freedom but concretizes it in the social context by identifying with a social group. In this way alone does a man become genuinely a person.

The account moves from family to civic community to the state. The family is unified by affection and love; the interests of its members are subordinated to the ongoing familial interests. With maturity the young gain loyalties that are directed outward into business associations, unions, religious organizations, and other corporations. But such loyalties are ephemeral and external. They may come into conflict with one another and with the family loyalty. The state builds on the kind of affection and feeling that cements the family and also on the shared objectives which hold together other associations. The state, the greatest of social achievements, is the source of all morality, not by returning individuals the greatest dividends, nor by guaranteeing individual liberties, but by giving expression to their common life.

The selections have purchased perhaps too ready intelligibility at a considerable cost to the sweep of Hegel's view of freedom. His account also addresses practical questions—for example, slavery, the social character of needs, poverty, and work.

57. . . . We may set aside the justification of slavery based upon the argument that it originates in superior physical force, the taking of prisoners

in war, the saving and preserving of life, upbringing, education, or bestowal of kindnesses. These reasons all rest ultimately on the ground that man is to be taken as a merely natural being, living, or, it may even be, choosing a life which is not adequate to his conception. Upon the same footing stands the attempted justification of ownership as merely the status of masters, as also all views of the right to slaves founded on history. The assertion of the absolute injustice of slavery on the contrary, clinging to the conception that man, as spiritual, is free of himself, is also a one-sided idea, since it supposes man to be free by nature. In other words, it takes as the truth the conception in its direct and unreflective form rather than the idea. This antinomy, like all others, rests upon the external thinking, which keeps separate and independent each of two aspects of a single complete idea. In point of fact, neither aspect, if separated from the other, is able to measure the idea, and present it in its truth. It is the mark of the free spirit that it does not exist merely as conception or naturally, but that it supersedes its own formalism, transcending thereby its naked natural existence, and gives to itself an existence, which, being its own, is free.

Hence the side of the antinomy, which maintains the conception of freedom, is to be preferred, since it contains at least the necessary point of departure for the truth. The other side . . . has in it nothing reasonable or right at all. The standpoint of the free will, with which right and the science of right begin, is already beyond the wrong view that man is simply a natural being, who, as he cannot exist for himself, is fit only to be enslaved. This untrue phenomenon had its origin in the circumstance that the spirit had at that time just attained the level of consciousness. . . .

If we hold fast to the side that man is absolutely free, we condemn slavery. Still it depends on the person's own will, whether he shall be a slave or not, just as it depends upon the will of a people whether or not it is to be in subjection. Hence slavery is a wrong not simply on the part of those who enslave or subjugate, but of the slaves and subjects themselves. Slavery occurs in the passage from the natural condition of man to his true moral and social condition. It is found in a world where a wrong is still a right. Under such a circumstance the wrong has its value and finds a necessary place.

66. Some goods, or rather substantive phases of

life are inalienable, and the right to them does not perish through lapse of time. These comprise my inner personality and the universal essence of my consciousness of myself, and are personality in general, freedom of will in the broadest sense, social life and religion.

What the spirit is in conception, or implicitly, it should also be in actuality; it should be a person, that is to say, be able to possess property, have sociality and religion. This idea is itself the conception of spirit. . . . In this very conception . . . lies the possibility of opposition between what it is only implicitly, and what it is only explicitly. In the will this opposition is the possibility of evil, but in general it is the possibility of the alienation of personality and substantive being; and this alienation may occur either unconsciously or intentionally.—Examples of the disposal of personality are slavery, vassalage, inability to own property or lack of complete control over it. Relinquishment of reason, sociality, morality or religion occurs in superstition; it occurs also if I delegate to others the authority to prescribe for me what kind of acts I shall commit, as when one sells himself for robbery, murder, or the possibility of any other crime; it occurs when I permit others to determine what for me shall be duty or religious truth.

194. . . . It has been held that man as to want is free in a so-called state of nature, in which he has only the so-called simple wants of nature, requiring for their satisfaction merely the means furnished directly and at random by nature. In this view no account is taken of the freedom which lies in work, of which more hereafter. Such a view is not true, because in natural want and its direct satisfaction the spiritual is submerged by mere nature. Hence, a state of nature is a state of savagery and slavery. Freedom is nowhere to be found except in the return of spirit and thought to itself, a process by which it distinguishes itself from the natural and turns back upon it.

195. This liberation is formal, since the particular side of the end remains the fundamental content. The tendency of the social condition indefinitely to increase and specialize wants, means, and enjoyments, and to distinguish natural from unrefined wants, has no limits. Hence arises luxury, in which the augmentation of dependence and distress is in its nature infinite. It operates upon an infinitely unyielding material, namely, an external means, which

has the special quality of being the possession of the free will. Hence it meets with the most obdurate resistance.

Diogenes in his completely cynical character is properly only a product of Athenian social life. That which gave birth to him was the public opinion, against which his behaviour was directed. His way of life was therefore not independent, but occasioned by his social surroundings. It was itself an ungainly product of luxury. Wherever luxury is extreme, there also prevail distress and depravity, and cynicism is produced in opposition to over-refinement.

242. The subjective element of poverty, or generally the distress, to which the individual is by nature exposed, requires subjective assistance, both in view of the special circumstances, and out of sympathy and love. Here, amidst all general arrangements, morality finds ample room to work. But since the assistance is in its own nature and in its effects casual, the effort of society shall be to discover a general remedy for penury and to do without random help.

Haphazard almsgiving and such foundations as the burning of lamps beside holy images, etc., are replaced by public poor-houses, hospitals, street lighting, etc. To charity enough still remains. It is a false view for charity to restrict its help to private methods and casual sentiment and knowledge, and to feel itself injured and weakened by regulations binding upon the whole community. On the contrary, the public system is to be regarded as all the more complete, the less remains to be done by special effort.

244. When a large number of people sink below the standard of living regarded as essential for the members of society, and lose that sense of right, rectitude, and honour which is derived from self-support, a pauper class arises, and wealth accumulates disproportionately in the hands of a few.

Hegel goes on to examine alternative economic policies, reverting occasionally to moral aspects; for example:

253. . . . In the corporation the assistance received by poverty loses its lawless character, and the humiliation wrongly associated with it. The opulent, by performing their duty to their associates, lose their pride, and cease to stir up envy in others.

Integrity receives its due honour and recognition.

196. The instrument for preparing and acquiring specialized means adequate to specialized wants is labour. By labour the material, directly handed over by nature for these numerous ends, is specialized in a variety of ways. This fashioning of the material gives to the means value and purpose, so that in consumption it is chiefly human products and human effort that are used up.

198. The universal and objective in work is to be found in the abstraction which, giving rise to the specialization of means and wants, causes the specialization also of production. This is the division of labour. By it the labour of the individual becomes more simple, his skill in his abstract work greater, and the amount he produces larger. The result of the abstraction of skill and means is that men's interdependence or mutual relation is completed. It becomes a thorough necessity. Moreover, the abstraction of production causes work to be continually more mechanical, until it is at last possible for man to step out and let the machine take his place.

15

Marxian Ethics

Karl Marx
(1818–1883)

Frederick Engels
(1820–1895)

The close association of Marx, son of a law-yer, and Engels, son of a cotton manufacturer, had momentous social consequences. As a university student Marx gravitated toward a group of left-wing Hegelians who, with many other intellectuals, were restive under the authoritarianism of the Prussian government—its failure to grant the long-promised constitution, its constraints on freedom of the press, and above all its interference in university teaching. Marx abandoned the study of law for philosophy; he wrote a thesis on the materialism of Democritus and Epicurus. He went beyond the radicalism of the Hegelians who, though not averse to direct political action, were more concerned with liberating people from religious dogma, in their view an obstacle to human progress. Marx focused on economic

ills. His radical activities ending any hope of an academic career, he became an editor of a journal in the Rhineland. Soon driven out by government pressure he moved to Paris, where his writings and activities in socialist circles eventually led to his expulsion at the initiative of the Prussian government. After a time in Belgium he moved to London, where he spent the rest of his life, living with his wife and children generally in poverty and substantially supported by Engels.

Frederick (Friedrich) Engels's radicalism stemmed from an early sympathy with the impoverished condition of workers. His contact with his father's business in his native town in Germany and later in Manchester, where his father's business carried him, led him to immerse himself in economics and to become active in the socialist movement. He had done a lot of writing by the time he met Marx, whose work he had admired. They found that they shared the same analysis of Hegelianism, the same criticisms of the Hegelians, and the same view that economic conditions are primary. They both took from Hegel the idea of a logical development in history, and they replaced the romantic dialectic of Spirit with a dialectic of material conditions (this reversal is what Marx meant when he said that Hegel needed only to be turned upside down). From these agreements stemmed their lifelong collaboration.

They early collaborated on a series of critiques, largely of the younger Hegelians, fragments of which were published eventually as *The German Ideology*. Published in entirety only in the twentieth century, it provides striking models of the social critique of intellectual production. At the instance of the Communist League they helped establish, they wrote the *Manifesto of the Communist Party* just in time for the revolutions that swept Europe beginning in 1848. They took an active part in this revolutionary movement in southern Germany. When the revolution failed, they turned to building up a European-wide socialist movement, often underground. There were many conflicts over doctrinal approach, particularly with anarchism; earlier Marx had written a critique of Pierre Joseph Proudhon and later he clashed with Michael Bakunin for leadership of the international movement.

Marx spent a good part of his time in the British Museum, absorbing the mass of economic materials that entered into his major writings—*A Contribution to the Critique of Political Economy* (1859) and the first volume of *Capital* (1867). (After Marx's death the later volumes of *Capital* were put together by Engels from accumulated manuscripts.) A large part of his writings analyzed current happenings and conditions, for example, the Paris Commune in 1871, the growing tensions between the industrial North and the slave-holding agrarian South in America, and conditions in Ireland and India. Marx (and often Engels) wrote articles for the *New-York Tribune* from 1851 to 1862. There is also a mass of correspondence between Marx and Engels and between them and others. All of this constitutes a vast body of materials that since then has often been mined for the relation of theory and prac-

tice. For example, Marx's *Economic and Philosophical Manuscripts of 1844*, resurrected in the twentieth century, shows the humanistic roots of Marxian theory. It helped to shake the stereotypes of Marxism that then prevailed and entered into the mid-twentieth century breakup of a monolithic Marxism, for example, in the development of Marxian humanism in Yugoslavia.[1]

Engels also wrote influential works of a more systematic character. His *Anti-Dühring* (1878), in attacking the comprehensive philosophy of Eugen Dühring, was compelled to match its scope—from metaphysics and epistemology to ethics and social theory. His *Origin of the Family, Private Property and the State* (1884) shows how the evaluation of institutions and attitudes is dealt with from a Marxian standpoint. Such writings of Engels address directly many of the traditional problems of ethical theory.

Marxian ethics is a highly distinctive theory. Most ethical theories hope to state general moral principles or ends as the inner citadel of the theory and then to deal with practical affairs as applications of the principles. Marxian theory holds that no general ends or principles can really be understood apart from the complex sociohistorical context in which they function: the modes of production and distribution, the material changes taking place in technology, the drift of social institutions and their stresses, and the alignment of classes and the specific grounds of their battles. These do not merely provide a scene of application for eternal or perennial principles; they give ethical ideas their meaning.

In Marxian theory moralities and ethical

---

[1] Yugoslavian philosophers employed the central Marxian concept of *praxis* (free self-conscious practical activity, embodying social ends and goods as well as responsibilities) in an effort to democratize political action and to give workers a direct hand in the control of industry. See Mihailo Marković, *From Affluence to Praxis: Philosophy and Social Criticism* (Ann Arbor: University of Michigan Press, 1974) and Gajo Petrovic, *Marx in the Mid-Twentieth Century* (Garden City, N.Y.: Doubleday Anchor Books, 1967).

ideas are part of a *superstructure* that is both institutional and ideational, resting on a basic material or economic structure. These notions are part of its general philosophy of history and social science, which, to oversimplify, works as follows. If we wish to describe a society, the life of a definite people, the Marxian says that we should begin by mapping the way the people manages to survive—how it provides its food, shelter, and clothing; how it manages communication, reproduces itself, and so forth. This gives the material basis of the society. It is called the *economic base* and refers not to money but to the concrete activities of production, exchange, and the like. The theory then divides the base into the *forces of production* (the technology, skills, and organization by which things needed are actually produced) and the *relations of production* (the way in which production is controlled and distribution determined, how exchange takes place, whether and in what way production is planned, etc.). The former yields the classification of societies and periods that historians refer to as the Stone Age, the Bronze Age, the farming society, the industrial society, and so on. The latter yields the historical mapping of societies as landed (e.g., feudal) or capitalist or socialist. It may be objected that starting this way makes strong assumptions about human life. Why not start with, say, God's purposes (as Augustine did) or human psychology (as Bentham did) or the autonomy of moral law (as Kant did)? Marxian theory is frank about such assumptions: the human being is material, of the same matter as physics studies, though more complex and developed; humans evolve (in the familiar Darwinian conception); thinking is an interaction of an expanded human brain and nervous system with features of the environment; and intellectual production, in spite of its intrinsic joys, always has practical import. There is thus no room in Marxian theory for a God or for abstract ideals as forces in human life. Institutions have been strengthened and developed by beliefs in God and ideals, but beliefs and ideals, particularly their specific shapes at specific times, are what is to be explained.

Part of this metaphysical background is the view that change is a permanent feature of existence. This is true not merely for the physical background of life but for institutions, ideas, qualities of life and feeling—in short, everything. Even the categories by which societies are described change meaning as the forms they refer to undergo change. Capitalism in its early days was small business, individually owned, in transition from the crafts to manufacturing; capitalism today is large-scale, corporate, verging into high technology, with giant financial organization that reaches into controlling interests. The meaning of capitalism at a given time is determined by its sociohistorical relations. The same holds for democracy, family, rural community, law, and any concept dealing with types of social organization or social philosophy, as for example, conservatism or liberalism.

The superstructure also contains two sorts of content: institutions and intellectual productions. The roster of institutions includes social organizations (family and kinship systems, village or urban community), political and legal forms, religion, education, and so on. These also continually undergo change, as new institutions and practices emerge and transform the interrelationships among them. Intellectual products include art, science, literature, philosophy, theology, morality, myths, and symbols—in effect, how we see our world. While these are not always sharply divided from the institutions—for example, religious doctrines are part of religious institutions, and legal theories shade into legal institutions and practices—still, intellectual production has its own career.

The four-tier division—forces of production, relations of production, institutions, and consciousness—is used to understand and explain social phenomena, particularly social change and its dynamics. Marx analyzed in great detail the shift from feudalism to capitalism. The dynamics are provided by the contradiction that emerges between the forces of production and the relations of production, and the resulting conflict of classes. The contradiction arises when the forces of production change without a corresponding change in the relations of production, so that the latter hinders the operation of the former. Thus Marx sees production in nineteenth-century capitalism becoming increasingly organized and large-scale, in fact internally socialized by high division of labor and machinery, while the relations of production remain individualized, socially planless, generating confusion and recurrent depressions. Relations of production cannot be changed easily, for the classes in power will not readily give up a control that profits them, however harmful it is to society at large. Historically, classes appear when labor becomes efficient enough and human knowledge great enough to yield a surplus. Those who own and control the means of production (land, factories, etc.) appropriate the surplus as profit while those who have nothing to offer but their labor (peasants, factory-workers, etc.) are exploited through their necessities. Under capitalism the antagonism of classes is unavoidable because profit comes ultimately from appropriation of the fruits of labor. (The attempt to demonstrate this is the crucial theme of Marx's *Capital*.)

When a class comes to power, because it is able to do more for human progress than its predecessor, it is revolutionary and changes the relations, institutions, and forms of thought of the old order to fit its economic base. How the *bourgeoisie* (Marx's term for the commercial and industrial class) overcame the old feudal order is vividly summarized in the *Manifesto*. The contributions of such a class to progress, however, involve changes in the productive base of the society—witness the technological and organizational development of the economic world under capitalism—and in due course again the need to change the relations of production arises. But this the class in power will not allow, for its domination is tied to the now older ways. Moreover, another class, the *proletariat*, is forming as the bearer of the new and emerging ways. Just as the bourgeoisie confronted the older feudal landed class, so the proletariat struggles with the bourgeoisie. In the *Critique of Political Economy* Marx describes the intensity and scope of the class struggle: it is carried out not only in the economic sphere but in all institutions and modes of thought. The eventual outcome is either the victory of the new or else a common ruin, which Marxians generally expect to avoid. The new class consolidates gradually; the basic antagonism of interests ensures the growth of consciousness and organization and increasingly active struggle. In this revolutionary period the transformation usually becomes violent because the old class is unwilling to give way. A class in decline has nothing to offer but obstruction to human progress.

Morality—the conception of a good life, obligations and responsibilities, and ideals—is part of the superstructure. Different moralities in a given society reflect different classes, expressing their needs and interests. The dominant morality of a society is the morality of the dominant class. Thus feudal morality stressed loyalty, gratitude, and contentment with one's allotted place, acceptance of suffering, and resignation. Bourgeois morality promulgated, in religious or in outright secular form, the virtues of individual success, cleanliness, justice, keeping contracts, initiative, prudence, and thrift (which becomes hoarding when the economic need is for spending); it championed an open world with eventual opportunity for everyone. The fullest exploration of a morality would therefore distinguish those parts that rest on the character of productive processes (e.g., punctuality and precision as

virtues in a machine age), the relations of production (e.g., individualistic-aggressive success morality in the capitalist world, though
corporate capitalism may tinker with ideas of
loyalty), the particular stage of the class conflict
(for example, when conflict is so intense that
it is likely to tear society apart, ideals of social
harmony may be tailored to reconcile classes),
and the parts that express the self-conscious
emerging class (as ideals of cooperation and
solidarity in the proletariat).

In spite of its sociology of ethics, Marxian
theory does not finally come to rest in a moral
relativism. It finds an all-human morality in
the direction and growth of human striving.
In the early *Economic and Philosophical Manuscripts of 1844* Marx seemed to talk of intrinsically human forms of expression that different
class interests had distorted and that could be
freed only in a classless society. In the later
theory the all-human morality is seen instead
in the growth of the idea of freedom as the
continuous struggle to broaden the scope of
knowledge and control in the pursuit of human values. (In the selection from Engels this
is tied to the Hegelian rather than to the older
metaphysical conception of freedom.)

While the growth of such freedom has
emerged as a product of class struggle, its full
development can come only with the classless
society. Indeed this signals the entry of mankind from prehistory to genuine history, when
humans can plan their destiny. The significance of the proletariat lies in its being the
last of the classes. Just as the bourgeoisie in
their ideals of liberty, equality, and fraternity
spoke in the name of all humankind because
they were fighting against the restrictive controls of the feudal world, so the proletariat will
give content to all-human ideals, not because
it is less concerned with its own interests but
because the socialization of production which
is in its interest will release production for all.
Hence its interests coincide, and its success
will coincide, with those of humankind.

The moral vantage point for normative judgment is thus seen as the interest of the class
that contains the most progressive elements
for humankind. Particular moral judgments
may become exceedingly complex. Take, for
example, Marx's retrospective analysis of the
morality of slavery. It is easy to judge that
slavery is wrong because of what it does to
human beings, yet the emergence of slavery
as an institution can be seen to mark a step
forward relative to the period. In ancient times
the introduction of slavery had the result that
conquered enemies were kept alive, which had
become feasible because by then the slave's
labor could produce an excess beyond his own
survival needs. (Marx seems to assume that
no real alternative—say, a program of human
cooperation—might have worked at that
point.) With the advance of techniques of production, slavery quickly became retrograde
(despite the length of time needed to abolish
it). Similarly for exploitation, "wage slavery":
it is progressive when it gives employment to
uprooted peasants, retrograde when it works
to prevent a full use of human resources for
the general interest. In the *Manifesto* Marx admires the accomplishments of capitalism even
while portraying its excessive human costs; but
he urges its abolition once he finds that socialism could better provide for well-being. Finally, once the vista of a classless society comes
into view, it becomes possible to speculate on
changes in institutional forms and the shape
of ideals. Engels on the future of love, in *The
Origin of the Family, Private Property and the
State,* is a good example.

Marxian theory applies historical materialism to the development of ethics itself. Marx
thought that his whole theory could have been
proposed only in the nineteenth century,
when production was sufficiently advanced to
find such theoretical expression. So too, theories of morality reflect the stage of general development and the diversity of interests. He
analyzes various ethical theories in such terms.

His estimate of Bentham is here offered in illustration.

KARL MARX

A Contribution to the Critique of Political Economy [2]

Preface

. . . I was led by my studies to the conclusion that legal relations as well as forms of state could neither be understood by themselves, nor explained by the so-called general progress of the human mind, but that they are rooted in the material conditions of life, which are summed up by Hegel after the fashion of the English and French of the eighteenth century under the name "civic society;" the anatomy of that civic society is to be sought in political economy. The study of the latter which I had taken up in Paris, I continued at Brussels whither I emigrated on account of an order of expulsion issued by Mr. Guizot. The general conclusion at which I arrived and which, once reached, continued to serve as the leading thread in my studies, may be briefly summed up as follows: In the social production which men carry on they enter into definite relations that are indispensable and independent of their will; these relations of production correspond to a definite stage of development of their material powers of production. The sum total of these relations of production constitutes the economic structure of society—the real foundation, on which rise legal and political superstructures and to which correspond definite forms of social consciousness. The mode of production in material life determines the general character of the social, political and spiritual processes of life. It is not the consciousness of men that determines their existence, but, on the contrary, their social existence determines their consciousness. At a certain stage of their development, the material forces of production in society come in conflict with the existing relations of production, or—what is but a legal expression for the same thing—with the property relations within which they had been at work before. From forms of development of the forces of production these relations turn into their fetters. Then comes the period of social revolution. With the change of the economic foundation the entire immense superstructure is more or less rapidly transformed. In considering such transformations the distinction should always be made between the material transformation of the economic conditions of production which can be determined with the precision of natural science, and the legal, political, religious, aesthetic or philosophic—in short ideological forms in which men become conscious of this conflict and fight it out. Just as our opinion of an individual is not based on what he thinks of himself, so can we not judge of such a period of transformation by its own consciousness; on the contrary, this consciousness must rather be explained from the contradictions of material life, from the existing conflict between the social forces of production and the relations of production. No social order ever disappears before all the productive forces, for which there is room in it, have been developed; and new higher relations of production never appear before the material conditions of their existence have matured in the womb of the old society. Therefore, mankind always takes up only such problems as it can solve; since, looking at the matter more closely, we will always find that the problem itself arises only when the material conditions necessary for its solution already exist or are at least in the process of formation. In broad outlines we can designate the Asiatic, the ancient, the feudal, and the modern bourgeois methods of production as so many epochs in the progress of the economic formation of society. The bourgeois relations of production are the last antagonistic form of the social process of production—antagonistic not in the sense of individual antagonism, but of one arising from conditions surrounding the life of individuals in society; at the same time the productive forces developing in the womb of bourgeois society create the material conditions for the solution of that antagonism. This social formation constitutes, therefore, the closing chapter of the prehistoric stage of human society. [pp. 11–13]

---

[2] The selection is from the second German edition, trans. N. I. Stone (Chicago: Charles H. Kerr, 1904); originally published 1859.

KARL MARX AND FREDERICK ENGELS

Manifesto of the Communist Party [3]

I: Bourgeois and Proletarians

The history of all hitherto existing society is the history of class struggles.

Freeman and slave, patrician and plebeian, lord and serf, guild-master and journeyman, in a word, oppressor and oppressed, stood in constant opposition to one another, carried on an uninterrupted, now hidden, now open fight, a fight that each time ended, either in a revolutionary re-constitution of society at large, or in the common ruin of the contending classes.

In the earlier epochs of history, we find almost everywhere a complicated arrangement of society into various orders, a manifold gradation of social rank. In ancient Rome we have patricians, knights, plebeians, slaves; in the middle ages, feudal lords, vassals, guild-masters, journeymen, apprentices, serfs; in almost all of these classes, again, subordinate gradations.

The modern bourgeois society that has sprouted from the ruins of feudal society, has not done away with class antagonisms. It has but established new classes, new conditions of oppression, new forms of struggle in place of the old ones.

Our epoch, the epoch of the bourgeoisie, possesses, however, this distinctive feature; it has simplified the class antagonisms. Society as a whole is more and more splitting up into two great hostile camps, into two great classes directly facing each other: Bourgeoisie and Proletariat.

From the serfs of the middle ages sprang the chartered burghers of the earliest towns. From these burgesses the first elements of the bourgeoisie were developed.

The discovery of America, the rounding of the Cape, opened up fresh ground for the rising bourgeoisie. The East-Indian and Chinese markets, the colonization of America, trade with the colonies, the increase in the means of exchange and in commodities generally, gave to commerce, to navigation, to industry, an impulse never before known, and thereby, to the revolutionary element in the tottering feudal society, a rapid development.

The feudal system of industry, under which industrial production was monopolized by closed guilds, now no longer sufficed for the growing wants of the new markets. The manufacturing system took its place. The guild-masters were pushed on one side by the manufacturing middle-class; division of labor between the different corporate guilds vanished in the face of division of labor in each single workshop.

Meantime the markets kept ever growing, the demand, ever rising. Even manufacture no longer sufficed. Thereupon, steam and machinery revolutionized industrial production. The place of manufacture was taken by the giant, Modern Industry, the place of the industrial middle-class, by industrial millionaires, the leaders of whole industrial armies, the modern bourgeois.

Modern industry has established the world-market, for which the discovery of America paved the way. This market has given an immense development to commerce, to navigation, to communication by land. This development has, in its turn, reacted on the extension of industry; and in proportion as industry, commerce, navigation, railways extended, in the same proportion the bourgeoisie developed, increased its capital, and pushed into the background every class handed down from the Middle Ages.

We see, therefore, how the modern bourgeoisie is itself the product of a long course of development, of a series of revolutions in the modes of production and of exchange.

Each step in the development of the bourgeoisie was accompanied by a corresponding political advance of that class. [pp. 12–14]

The bourgeoisie, historically, has played a most revolutionary part.

The bourgeoisie, wherever it has got the upper hand, has put an end to all feudal, patriarchal, idyllic relations. It has pitilessly torn asunder the motley feudal ties that bound man to his "natural superiors," and has left remaining no other nexus between man and man than naked self-interest, than callous "cash payment." It has drowned the most heavenly ecstasies of religious fervor, of chivalrous enthusiasm, of philistine sentimentalism, in the icy water of egotistical calculation. It has resolved personal

[3] The translation is by Samuel Moore (London: 1888), revised by Moore with Engels; originally published London, 1848. The selection is from *The Communist Manifesto* (Chicago: Charles H. Kerr, 1912).

worth into exchange value, and in place of the numberless indefeasible chartered freedoms, has set up that single, unconscionable freedom—Free Trade. In one word, for exploitation, veiled by religious and political illusions, it has substituted naked, shameless, direct, brutal exploitation.

The bourgeoisie has stripped of its halo every occupation hitherto honored and looked up to with reverent awe. It has converted the physician, the lawyer, the priest, the poet, the man of science, into its paid wage-laborers.

The bourgeoisie has torn away from the family its sentimental veil, and has reduced the family relation to a mere money relation. . . .

The bourgeoisie cannot exist without constantly revolutionizing the instruments of production, and thereby the relations of production, and with them the whole relations of society. [pp. 15–16]

The bourgeoisie has subjected the country to the rule of the towns. It has created enormous cities, has greatly increased the urban population as compared with the rural, and has thus rescued a considerable part of the population from the idiocy of rural life. . . .

The bourgeoisie, during its rule of scarce one hundred years, has created more massive and more colossal productive forces than have all preceding generations together. . . .

We see then: the means of production and of exchange on whose foundation the bourgeoisie built itself up, were generated in feudal society. At a certain stage in the development of these means of production and of exchange, the conditions under which feudal society produced and exchanged, the feudal organization of agriculture and manufacturing industry, in one word, the feudal relations of property became no longer compatible with the already developed productive forces; they became so many fetters. They had to burst asunder; they were burst asunder.

Into their places stepped free competition, accompanied by a social and political constitution adapted to it, and by the economical and political sway of the bourgeois class.

A similar movement is going on before our own eyes. Modern bourgeois society with its relations of production, of exchange and of property, a society that has conjured up such gigantic means of production and of exchange, is like the sorcerer, who is no longer able to control the powers of the nether world whom he has called up by his spells. For many a decade past the history of industry and commerce is but the history of the revolt of modern productive forces against modern conditions of production, against the property relations that are the conditions for the existence of the bourgeoisie and of its rule. It is enough to mention the commercial crises that by their periodical return put on its trial, each time more threateningly, the existence of the entire bourgeois society. In these crises a great part not only of the existing products, but also of the previously created productive forces, are periodically destroyed. In these crises there breaks out an epidemic that, in all earlier epochs, would have seemed an absurdity—the epidemic of over-production. Society suddenly finds itself put back into a state of momentary barbarism; it appears as if a famine, a universal war of devastation had cut off the supply of every means of subsistence; industry and commerce seem to be destroyed; and why? Because there is too much civilization, too much means of subsistence, too much industry, too much commerce. The productive forces at the disposal of society no longer tend to further the development of the conditions of bourgeois property; on the contrary, they have become too powerful for these conditions, by which they are fettered, and so soon as they overcome these fetters, they bring disorder into the whole of bourgeois society, endanger the existence of bourgeois property. The conditions of bourgeois society are too narrow to comprise the wealth created by them. And how does the bourgeoisie get over these crises? On the one hand by enforced destruction of a mass of productive forces; on the other, by the conquest of new markets, and by the more thorough exploitation of the old ones. That is to say, by paving the way for more extensive and more destructive crises, and by diminishing the means whereby crises are prevented.

The weapons with which the bourgeoisie felled feudalism to the ground are now turned against the bourgeoisie itself.

But not only has the bourgeoisie forged the weapons that bring death to itself; it has also called into existence the men who are to wield those weapons—the modern working-class—the proletarians.

In proportion as the bourgeoisie, i.e., capital, is developed, in the same proportion is the proletariat, the modern working-class, developed, a class of laborers, who live only so long as they find work, and who find work only so long as their labor increases capital. These laborers, who must sell themselves piecemeal, are a commodity, like every other article of commerce, and are consequently exposed to all the vicissitudes of competition, to all the fluctuations of the market. [pp. 18–21]

The plight of the workers under capitalism is described and the stages of the development of the proletariat from individual revolt against the machine, through growing labor organization, to political consciousness. The ruling class begins to dissolve, a portion of it (especially of bourgeois ideologists) going over to the proletariat.

Of all the classes that stand face to face with the bourgeoisie today, the proletariat alone is a really revolutionary class. The other classes decay and finally disappear in the face of modern industry; the proletariat is its special and essential product. [Eventually], society can no longer live under this bourgeoisie, in other words, its existence is no longer compatible with society. [pp. 26–29]

Communists are the most advanced section of the working class parties.

II. Proletarians and Communists

The theoretical conclusions of the Communists are in no way based on ideas or principles that have been invented, or discovered, by this or that would-be universal reformer.

They merely express, in general terms, actual relations springing from an existing class struggle, from a historical movement going on under our very eyes. The abolition of existing property relations is not at all a distinctive feature of Communism.

All property relations in the past have continually been subject to historical change consequent upon the change in historical conditions.

The French Revolution, for example, abolished feudal property in favor of bourgeois property.

The distinguishing feature of Communism is not the abolition of property generally, but the abolition of bourgeois property. But modern bourgeois private property is the final and most complete expression of the system of producing and appropriating products, that is based on class antagonism, on the exploitation of the many by the few.

In this sense, the theory of the Communists may be summed up in the single sentence: Abolition of private property.

We Communists have been reproached with the desire of abolishing the right of personally acquiring property as the fruit of a man's own labor, which property is alleged to be the ground work of all personal freedom, activity and independence.

Hard-won, self-acquired, self-earned property! Do you mean the property of the petty artisan and of the small peasant, a form of property that preceded the bourgeois form? There is no need to abolish that; the development of industry has to a great extent already destroyed it, and is still destroying it daily.

Or do you mean modern bourgeois private property?

But does wage-labor create any property for the laborer? Not a bit. It creates capital, i.e., that kind of property which exploits wage-labor, and which cannot increase except upon condition of getting a new supply of wage-labor for fresh exploitation. Property, in its present form, is based on the antagonism of capital and wage-labor. Let us examine both sides of this antagonism.

To be a capitalist, is to have not only a purely personal, but a social status in production. Capital is a collective product, and only by the united action of many members, nay, in the last resort, only by the united action of all members of society, can it be set in motion.

Capital is therefore not a personal, it is a social power.

When, therefore, capital is converted into common property, into the property of all members of society, personal property is not thereby transformed into social property. It is only the social character of the property that is changed. It loses its class-character.

Let us now take wage-labor.

The average price of wage-labor is the minimum wage, i.e., that quantum of the means of subsistence, which is absolutely requisite to keep the laborer in bare existence as a laborer. What, therefore, the wage-laborer appropriates by means of his labor, merely suffices to prolong and reproduce a bare existence. We by no means intend to abolish this personal appropriation of the products of labor, an appropriation that is made for the maintenance and reproduction of human life, and that leaves no surplus wherewith to command the labor of others. All that we want to do away with is the miserable character of this appropriation, under which the laborer lives merely to increase capital, and is allowed to live only insofar as the interest of the ruling class requires it.

In bourgeois society, living labor is but a means to increase accumulated labor. In Communist society, accumulated labor is but a means to widen, to enrich, to promote the existence of the laborer.

In bourgeois society, therefore, the past dominates the present; in Communist society, the present dominates the past. In bourgeois society capital is independent and has individuality, while the living person is dependent and has no individuality.

And the abolition of this state of things is called by the bourgeois, abolition of individuality and freedom! And rightly so. The abolition of bourgeois individuality, bourgeois independence, and bourgeois freedom is undoubtedly aimed at.

By freedom is meant, under the present bourgeois conditions of production, free trade, free selling and buying.

But if selling and buying disappears, free selling and buying disappears also. This talk about free selling and buying, and all the other "brave words" of our bourgeoisie about freedom in general, have a meaning, if any, only in contrast with restricted selling and buying, with the fettered traders of the Middle Ages, but have no meaning when opposed to the Communistic abolition of buying and selling, of the bourgeois conditions of production, and of the bourgeoisie itself.

You are horrified at our intending to do away with private property. But in your existing society, private property is already done away with for nine-tenths of the population; its existence for the few is solely due to its non-existence in the hands of those nine-tenths. You reproach us, therefore, with intending to do away with a form of property, the necessary condition for whose existence is, the non-existence of any property for the immense majority of society.

In one word, you reproach us with intending to do away with your property. Precisely so; that is just what we intend.

From the moment when labor can no longer be converted into capital, money, or rent, into a social power capable of being monopolized, i.e., from the moment when individual property can no longer be transformed into bourgeois property, into capital, from that moment, you say, individuality vanishes.

You must, therefore, confess that by "individual" you mean no other person than the bourgeois, than the middle-class owner of property. This person must, indeed, be swept out of the way, and made impossible.

Communism deprives no man of the power to appropriate the products of society: all that it does is to deprive him of the power to subjugate the labor of others by means of such appropriation.

It has been objected, that upon the abolition of private property all work will cease, and universal laziness will overtake us.

According to this, bourgeois society ought long ago to have gone to the dogs through sheer idleness; for those of its members who work, acquire nothing, and those who acquire anything, do not work. The whole of this objection is but another expression of the tautology: that there can no longer be any wage-labor when there is no longer any capital.

All objections urged against the Communistic mode of producing and appropriating material products, have, in the same way, been urged against the Communistic modes of producing and appropriating intellectual products. Just as, to the bourgeois, the disappearance of class property is the disappearance of production itself, so the disappearance of class culture is to him identical with the disappearance of all culture.

That culture, the loss of which he laments, is, for the enormous majority, a mere training to act as a machine.

But don't wrangle with us so long as you apply, to our intended abolition of bourgeois property, the standard of your bourgeois notions of freedom, culture, law, etc. Your very ideas are but the outgrowth of the conditions of your bourgeois production and bourgeois property, just as your jurisprudence is but the will of your class made into a law for all, a will, whose essential character and direction are determined by the economic conditions of existence of your class.

The selfish misconception that induces you to transform into eternal laws of nature and of reason, the social forms springing from your present mode of production and form of property—historical relations that rise and disappear in the progress of production—this misconception you share with every ruling class that has preceded you. What you see clearly in the case of ancient property, what you admit in the case of feudal property, you are of course forbidden to admit in the case of your own bourgeois form of property.

Abolition of the family! Even the most radical flare up at this infamous proposal of the Communists.

On what foundation is the present family, the bourgeois family, based? On capital, on private gain. In its completely developed form this family exists only among the bourgeoisie. But this state of things finds its complement in the practical absence of the family among the proletarians, and in public prostitution.

The bourgeois family will vanish as a matter of course when its complement vanishes, and both will vanish with the vanishing of capital.

Do you charge us with wanting to stop the exploitation of children by their parents? To this crime we plead guilty.

But, you will say, we destroy the most hallowed of relations, when we replace home education by social.

And your education! Is not that also social, and determined by the social conditions under which you educate, by the intervention, direct or indirect, of society by means of schools, etc.? The Communists have not invented the intervention of society in education; they do but seek to alter the character of that intervention, and to rescue education from the influence of the ruling class.

The bourgeois clap-trap about the family and education, about the hallowed co-relation of parent and child, becomes all the more disgusting, the more, by the action of Modern Industry, all family ties among the proletarians are torn asunder, and their children transformed into simple articles of commerce and instruments of labor.

But you Communists would introduce community of women, screams the whole bourgeoisie in chorus.

The bourgeois sees in his wife a mere instrument of production. He hears that the instruments of production are to be exploited in common, and, naturally, can come to no other conclusion, than that the lot of being common to all will likewise fall to the women.

He has not even a suspicion that the real point aimed at is to do away with the status of women as mere instruments of production. [pp. 31–37]

FREDERICK ENGELS

Anti-Dühring [4]

The selections deal with the class character of morality, the analysis of equality as an ethical concept, and the nature of freedom.

Ch IX: Morality and Law. Eternal Truths

If we have not made much progress with truth and error, we can make even less with good and bad. This antithesis belongs exclusively to the domain of morals, that is, a domain belonging to the history of mankind, and it is precisely in this field that final and ultimate truths are most sparsely sown. The conceptions of good and bad have varied so much from nation to nation and from age to age that they have often been in direct contradiction to each other. But all the same, someone may object, good is not bad and bad is not good; if good is confused with bad there is an end to all morality, and everyone can do and leave undone whatever he cares. . . . But the matter cannot be so simply disposed of. If it was such an easy business there would certainly be no dispute at all over good and bad; everyone would know what was good and what was bad. But how do things stand today? What morality is preached to us today? There is first Christian-feudal morality, inherited from past periods of faith; and this again has two main subdivisions, Catholic and Protestant moralities, each of which in turn has no lack of further subdivisions from the Jesuit-Catholic and Orthodox-Protestant to loose "advanced" moralities. Alongside of these we find the modern bourgeois morality and with it too the proletarian morality of the future, so that in the most advanced European countries alone the past, present and future provide three great groups of moral theories which are in force simultaneously and alongside of one another. Which is then the true one? Not one of them, in the sense of having

[4] The selection is from Frederick Engels, *Herr Eugen Dühring's Revolution in Science* (*Anti-Dühring*), trans. Emile Burns (New York: International Publishers, 1939); originally published 1878.

absolute validity; but certainly that morality which contains the maximum of durable elements is the one which, in the present, represents the overthrow of the present, represents the future: that is, the proletarian.

But when we see that the three classes of modern society, the feudal aristocracy, the bourgeoisie and the proletariat, each have their special morality, we can only draw the conclusion, that men, consciously or unconsciously, derive their moral ideas in the last resort from the practical relations on which their class position is based—from the economic relations in which they carry on production and exchange.

But nevertheless there is much that is common to the three moral theories mentioned above—is this not at least a portion of a morality which is externally fixed? These moral theories represent three different stages of the same historical development, and have therefore a common historical background, and for that reason alone they necessarily have much in common. Even more. In similar or approximately similar stages of economic development moral theories must of necessity be more or less in agreement. From the moment when private property in movable objects developed, in all societies in which this private property existed there must be this moral law in common: Thou shalt not steal. Does this law thereby become an eternal moral law? By no means. In a society in which the motive for stealing has been done away with, in which therefore at the very most only lunatics would ever steal, how the teacher of morals would be laughed at who tried solemnly to proclaim the eternal truth: Thou shalt not steal!

We therefore reject every attempt to impose on us any moral dogma whatsoever as an eternal, ultimate and forever immutable moral law on the pretext that the moral world too has its permanent principles which transcend history and the differences between nations. We maintain on the contrary that all former moral theories are the product, in the last analysis, of the economic stage which society had reached at that particular epoch. And as society has hitherto moved in class antagonisms, morality was always a class morality; it has either justified the domination and the interests of the ruling class, or, as soon as the oppressed class has become powerful enough, it has represented the revolt against this domination and the future interests of the oppressed. That in this process there

has on the whole been progress in morality, as in all other branches of human knowledge, cannot be doubted. But we have not yet passed beyond class morality. A really human morality which transcends class antagonisms and their legacies in thought becomes possible only at a stage of society which has not only overcome class contradictions but has even forgotten them in practical life. [pp. 103–105]

Ch X: Morality and Law. Equality

The idea that all men, as men, have something in common, and that they are therefore equal so far as these common characteristics go, is of course primeval. But the modern demand for equality is something entirely different from that; this consists rather in deducing from those common characteristics of humanity, from that equality of men as men, a claim to equal political or social status for all human beings, or at least for all citizens of a state or all members of a society. Before the original conception of relative equality could lead to the conclusion that men should have equal rights in the state and in society, before this conclusion could appear to be something even natural and self-evident, however, thousands of years had to pass and did pass. In the oldest primitive communities equality of rights existed at most for members of the community; women, slaves and strangers were excluded from this equality as a matter of course. Among the Greeks and Romans the inequalities of men were of greater importance than any form of equality. It would necessarily have seemed idiotic to the ancients that Greeks and barbarians, freemen and slaves, citizens and dependents, Roman citizens and Roman subjects (to use a comprehensive term) should have a claim to equal political status. Under the Roman Empire all these distinctions gradually disappeared, except the distinction between freemen and slaves, and in this way there arose, for the freemen at least, that equality as between private individuals on the basis of which Roman law developed—the completest elaboration of law based on private property which we know. But so long as the distinction between freemen and slaves existed, there could be no talk of drawing legal conclusions from the fact of general equality *as men*; and we saw this again quite recently, in the slave-owning states of the North American Union.

Christianity knew only *one* point in which all men were equal: that all were equally born in original sin—which corresponded perfectly with its character as the religion of the slaves and the oppressed. Apart from this is recognised, at most, the equality of the elect, which however was only stressed at the very beginning. The traces of common ownership which are also found in the early stages of the new religion can be ascribed to the solidarity of a proscribed sect rather than to real equalitarian ideas. Within a very short time the establishment of the distinction between priests and laymen put an end even to this tendency to Christian equality. The overrunning of Western Europe by the Germans abolished for centuries all ideas of equality, through the gradual building up of a complicated social and political hierarchy such as had never before existed. But at the same time the invasion drew Western and Central Europe into the course of historical development, created for the first time a compact cultural area, and within this area also for the first time a system of predominantly national states exerting mutual influence on each other and mutually holding each other in check. Thereby it prepared the ground on which alone the question of the equal status of men, of the rights of man, could at a later period be raised.

The feudal middle ages also developed in its womb the class which was destined in the future course of its evolution to be the standard-bearer of the modern demand for equality: the bourgeoisie. Itself in its origin one of the "estates" of the feudal order, the bourgeoisie developed the predominantly handicraft industry and the exchange of products within feudal society to a relatively high level, when at the end of the fifteenth century the great maritime discoveries opened to it a new and more comprehensive career. Trade beyond the confines of Europe, which had previously been carried on only between Italy and the Levant, was now extended to America and India, and soon surpassed in importance both the mutual exchange between the various European countries and the internal trade within each separate country. American gold and silver flooded Europe and forced its way like a disintegrating element into every fissure, hole and pore of feudal society. Handicraft industry could no longer satisfy the rising demand; in the leading industries of the most advanced countries it was replaced by manufacture.

But this mighty revolution in the economic conditions of life in society was not followed immediately by any corresponding change in its political structure. The state order remained feudal, while society became more and more bourgeois. Trade on a large scale, that is to say, international and, even more, world trade, requires free owners of commodities who are unrestricted in their movements and have equal rights as traders to exchange their commodities on the basis of laws that are equal for them all, at least in each separate place. The transition from handicraft to manufacture presupposes the existence of a number of free workers—free on the one hand from the fetters of the guild and on the other from the means whereby they could themselves utilise their labour power: workers who can contract with their employers for the hire of their labour power, and as parties to the contract have rights equal with his. And finally the equality and equal status of all human labour, because and in so far as it is *human* labour, found its unconscious but clearest expression in the law of value of modern bourgeois economics, according to which the value of a commodity is measured by the socially necessary labour embodied in it.[a] But where economic relations required freedom and equality of rights, the political system opposed them at every step with guild restrictions and special privileges. Local privileges, differential duties, exceptional laws of all kinds affected in trading not only foreigners or people living in the colonies, but often enough also whole categories of the nationals of each country; the privileges of the guilds everywhere and ever anew formed barriers to the path of development of manufacture. Nowhere was the path open and the chances equal for the bourgeois competitors—and yet this was the first and ever more pressing need.

The demand for liberation from feudal fetters and the establishment of equality of rights by the abolition of feudal inequalities was bound soon to assume wider dimensions from the moment when the economic advance of society first placed it on the order of the day. If it was raised in the interests of industry and trade, it was also necessary to demand the same equality of rights for the great mass of the peasantry who, in every degree of bondage from total serfdom upwards, were compelled to give

[a] This tracing of the origin of the modern ideas of equality to the economic conditions of bourgeois society was first developed by Marx in *Capital*. [*Note by F. Engels.*]

the greater part of their labour time to their feudal lord without payment and in addition to render innumerable other dues to him and to the state. On the other hand, it was impossible to avoid the demand for the abolition also of feudal privileges, the freedom from taxation of the nobility, the political privileges of the various feudal estates. And as people were no longer living in a world empire such as the Roman Empire had been, but in a system of independent states dealing with each other on an equal footing and at approximately the same degree of bourgeois development, it was a matter of course that the demand for equality should assume a general character reaching out beyond the individual state, that freedom and equality should be proclaimed as *human rights*. And it is significant of the specifically bourgeois character of these human rights that the American Constitution, the first to recognize the rights of man, in the same breath confirmed the slavery of the coloured races in America: class privileges were proscribed, race privileges sanctified.

As is well known, however, from the moment when, like a butterfly from the chrysalis, the bourgeoisie arose out of the burghers of the feudal period, when this "estate" of the Middle Ages developed into a class of modern society, it was always and inevitably accompanied by its shadow, the proletariat. And in the same way the bourgeois demand for equality was accompanied by the proletarian demand for equality. From the moment when the bourgeois demand for the abolition of class *privileges* was put forward, alongside of it appeared the proletarian demand for the abolition of the *classes themselves*—at first in religious form, basing itself on primitive Christianity, and later drawing support from the bourgeois equalitarian theories themselves. The proletarians took the bourgeoisie at their word: equality must not be merely apparent, must not apply merely to the sphere of the state, but must also be real, must be extended to the social and economic sphere. And especially since the time when the French bourgeoisie, from the Great Revolution on, brought bourgeois equality to the forefront, the French proletariat has answered it blow for blow with the demand for social and economic equality, and equality has become the battle-cry particularly of the French proletariat.

The demand for equality in the mouth of the proletariat has therefore a double meaning. It is either—

as was especially the case at the very start, for example in the peasants' war—the spontaneous reaction against the crying social inequalities, against the contrast of rich and poor, the feudal lords and their serfs, surfeit and starvation; as such it is the simple expression of the revolutionary instinct, and finds its justification in that, and indeed only in that. Or, on the other hand, the proletarian demand for equality has arisen as the reaction against the bourgeois demand for equality, drawing more or less correct and more far-reaching demands from this bourgeois demand, and serving as an agitational means in order to rouse the workers against the capitalists on the basis of the capitalists' own assertions; and in this case it stands and falls with bourgeois equality itself. In both cases the real content of the proletarian demand for equality is the demand for the *abolition of classes*. Any demand for equality which goes beyond that, of necessity passes into absurdity. . . .

The idea of equality, therefore, both in its bourgeois and in its proletarian form, is itself a historical product, the creation of which required definite historical conditions which in turn themselves presuppose a long previous historical development. It is therefore anything but an eternal truth. [pp. 113–118]

Ch XI: Morality and Law. Freedom and Necessity

Hegel was the first to state correctly the relation between freedom and necessity. To him, freedom is the appreciation of necessity. "Necessity is *blind only in so far as it is not understood.*" Freedom does not consist in the dream of independence of natural laws, but in the knowledge of these laws, and in the possibility this gives of systematically making them work towards definite ends. This holds good in relation both to the laws of external nature and to those which govern the bodily and mental existence of men themselves—two classes of laws which we can separate from each other at most only in thought but not in reality. Freedom of the will therefore means nothing but the capacity to make decisions with real knowledge of the subject. Therefore the *freer* a man's judgment is in relation to a definite question, with so much the greater *necessity* is the content of this judgment determined; while the uncertainty, founded on ignorance, which seems to make an arbitrary choice among many different and conflicting possible decisions, shows by this precisely that it is not free, that it is controlled by the very object it should itself control. Freedom therefore consists in the control over ourselves and over external nature which is founded on knowledge of natural necessity; it is therefore necessarily a product of historical development. [p. 125]

KARL MARX

On the Jewish Question [5]

This essay (1843) is noteworthy for the account of human rights as an expression of only political emancipation, not of the more developed human emancipation, a distinction that anticipates the fuller treatment in the *Economic and Philosophical Manuscripts* of the following year. The content of the rights of a citizen (political rights) is "*participation* in the *community* life, in the *political* life of the community, the life of the state" (p. 23). The rights of man, which include equality, liberty, security, and property, are simply the rights of egoistic man, "of man separated from other men and from the community" (p. 24). For example:

Liberty is . . . the right to do everything which does not harm others. The limits within which each individual can act without harming others are determined by law, just as the boundary between two fields is marked by a stake. It is a question of the liberty of man regarded as an isolated monad, withdrawn into himself. . . . [L]iberty as a right of man is not founded upon the relations between man and man, but rather upon the separation of man from man. It is the right of such separation. The right of the *circumscribed* individual, withdrawn into himself. [pp. 24–25]

The right of property is . . . the right to enjoy one's fortune and to dispose of it as one will; without regard for other men and independently of society. It is the right of self-interest. This individual liberty, and its application, form the basis of civil society. It leads every man to see in other men, not the *realization*, but rather the *limitation* of his own liberty. It declares above all the right "to enjoy and to dispose of *as one will*, one's goods and revenues, the fruits of one's work and industry." [p. 25]

None of the supposed rights of man, therefore, go beyond the egoistic man, man as he is, as a member of civil society; that is, an individual separated from the community, withdrawn into himself, wholly preoccupied with his private interest and acting in accordance with his private caprice. Man is far from being considered, in the rights of man, as a species-being; on the contrary, species-life itself—society—appears as a system which is external to the individual and as a limitation of his original independence. The only bond between men is natural necessity, need and private interest, the preservation of their property and their egoistic persons. [p. 26]

Political emancipation is a reduction of man, on the one hand to a member of civil society, an *independent* and *egoistic* individual, and on the other hand, to a *citizen*, to a moral person.

Human emancipation will only be complete when the real, individual man has absorbed into himself the abstract citizen; when as an individual man, in his everyday life, in his work, and in his relationships, he has become a *species-being;* and when he has recognized and organized his own powers (*forces propres*) as *social* powers so that he no longer separates this social power from himself as *political* power. [p. 31]

KARL MARX

Economic and Philosophical Manuscripts of 1844 [6]

Manuscript I

Alienated Labour

Private property is a result of a fundamental *alienation*, of which there are four kinds: First, workers are alienated from the *product* of their work:

---

[5] The selection is from *Karl Marx, Early Writings,* trans. and ed. T. B. Bottomore (New York: McGraw-Hill, 1964).

[6] The selection is from *Karl Marx, Early Writings,* trans. and ed. T. B. Bottomore (New York: McGraw-Hill, 1964).

[T]he worker is related to the *product of his labour* as to an *alien* object. For it is clear on this presupposition that the more the worker expends himself in work the more powerful becomes the world of objects which he creates in face of himself, the poorer he becomes in his inner life, and the less he belongs to himself. It is just the same as in religion. The more of himself man attributes to God the less he has left in himself. The worker puts his life into the object, and his life then belongs no longer to himself but to the object. The greater his activity, therefore, the less he possesses. What is embodied in the product of his labour is no longer his own. The greater this product is, therefore, the more he is diminished. The *alienation* of the worker in his product means not only that his labour becomes an object, assumes an *external* existence, but that it exists independently, *outside* himself, and alien to him, and that it stands opposed to him as an autonomous power. The life which he has given to the object sets itself against him as an alien and hostile force. [pp. 122–123]

(The alienation of the worker in his object is expressed as follows in the laws of political economy: the more the worker produces the less he has to consume; the more value he creates the more worthless he becomes; the more refined his product the more crude and misshapen the worker; the more civilized the product the more barbarous the worker; the more powerful the work the more feeble the worker; the more the work manifests intelligence the more the worker declines in intelligence and becomes a slave of nature.) [pp. 123–124]

Second, the worker is alienated from the process, from productive activity.

What constitutes the alienation of labour? First, that the work is *external* to the worker, that it is not part of his nature; and that, consequently, he does not fulfil himself in his work but denies himself, has a feeling of misery rather than well-being, does not develop freely his mental and physical energies but is physically exhausted and mentally debased. The worker, therefore, feels himself at home only during his leisure time, whereas at work he feels homeless. His work is not voluntary but imposed, *forced labour*. It is not the satisfaction of a need, but only a *means* for satisfying other needs. Its alien character is clearly shown by the fact that

as soon as there is no physical or other compulsion it is avoided like the plague. . . . Finally, the external character of work for the worker is shown by the fact that it is not his own work but work for someone else, that in work he does not belong to himself but to another person. [pp. 124–125]

[Third], Man is a species-being [a] not only in the sense that he makes the community (his own as well as those of other things) his object both practically and theoretically, but also (and this is simply another expression for the same thing) in the sense that he treats himself as the present, living species, as a *universal* and consequently free being. [p. 126]

Since alienated labour: (1) alienates nature from man; and (2) alienates man from himself, from his own active function, his life activity; so it alienates him from the species. It makes *species-life* into a means of individual life. In the first place it alienates species-life and individual life, and secondly, it turns the latter, as an abstraction, into the purpose of the former, also in its abstract and alienated form.

For labour, *life activity*, *productive life*, now appear to man only as *means* for the satisfaction of a need, the need to maintain his physical existence. Productive life is, however, species-life. It is life creating life. In the type of life activity resides the whole character of a species, its species-character; and free, conscious activity is the species-character of human beings. Life itself appears only as a *means of life*. [p. 127]

The practical construction of an *objective world*, the *manipulation* of inorganic nature, is the confirmation of man as a conscious species-being, i.e. a being who treats the species as his own being or himself as a species-being. Of course, animals also produce. They construct nests, dwellings, as in the case of bees, beavers, ants, etc. But they only produce what is strictly necessary for themselves or their young.

---

[a] The terms "species-life" and "species-being" are derived from Feuerbach. In the first chapter of *The Essence of Christianity* (1841) Feuerbach discusses the nature of man, and argues that man is to be distinguished from animals not by "consciousness" as such, but by a particular kind of consciousness. Man is not only conscious of himself as an individual; he is also conscious of himself as a member of the human species, and so he apprehends a "human essence" which is the same in himself and in other men. According to Feuerbach this ability to conceive of "species" is the fundamental element in the human power of reasoning: "Science is the consciousness of species." . . . [*Bottomore's note*] [p. 13]

They produce only in a single direction, while man produces universally. They produce only under the compulsion of direct physical needs, while man produces when he is free from physical need and only truly produces in freedom from such need. . . .

It is just in his work upon the objective world that man really proves himself as a *species-being*. This production is his active species-life. By means of it nature appears as *his* work and his reality. The object of labour is, therefore, the *objectification of man's species-life*; for he no longer reproduces himself merely intellectually, as in consciousness, but actively and in a real sense, and he sees his own reflection in a world which he has constructed. While, therefore, alienated labour takes away the object of production from man, it also takes away his *species-life*, his real objectivity as a species-being, and changes his advantage over animals into a disadvantage in so far as his inorganic body, nature, is taken from him. [pp. 127–128]

[Fourth], *man* is *alienated* from other *men*. When man confronts himself he also confronts *other* men. . . .

In general, the statement that man is alienated from his species-life means that each man is alienated from others, and that each of the others is likewise alienated from human life.

Human alienation, and above all the relation of man to himself, is first realized and expressed in the relationship between each man and other men. Thus in the relationship of alienated labour every man regards other men according to the standards and relationships in which he finds himself placed as a worker.

We began with an economic fact, the alienation of the worker and his production. We have expressed this fact in conceptual terms as *alienated labour*, and in analysing the concept we have merely analysed an economic fact. [p. 129]

[T]hrough alienated labour the worker creates the relation of another man, who does not work and is outside the work process, to this labour. The relation of the worker to work also produces the relation of the capitalist (or whatever one likes to call the lord of labour) to work. *Private property* is, therefore, the product, the necessary result, of *alienated labour*, of the external relation of the worker to nature and to himself.

Private property is thus derived from the analysis of the concept of *alienated labour*; that is, alienated man, alienated labour, alienated life, and estranged man.

[A]lthough private property appears to be the basis and cause of alienated labour, it is rather a consequence of the latter, just as the gods are *fundamentally* not the cause but the product of confusions of human reason. At a later stage, however, there is a reciprocal influence. [p. 131]

[It follows that it is a mistake simply to seek an increase in wages; that would be] nothing more than a *better remuneration of slaves.*

[I]t also follows that the emancipation of society from private property, from servitude, takes the political form of the *emancipation of the workers*; not in the sense that only the latter's emancipation is involved, but because this emancipation includes the emancipation of humanity as a whole. For all human servitude is involved in the relation of the worker to production, and all the types of servitude are only modifications or consequences of this relation. [pp. 132–133]

Manuscript III

Private Property and Communism

Communism is the "positive expression of the abolition of private property" (p. 152). Mere abolition ("crude communism") is not enough.

[In "crude communism"] the domination of material property looms so large that it aims to destroy everything which is incapable of being possessed by everyone as private property. It wishes to eliminate talent, etc. by *force*. Immediate physical possession seems to it the unique goal of life and existence. The role of *worker* is not abolished, but is extended to all men. The relation of private property remains the relation of the community to the world of things. Finally, this tendency to oppose general private property to private property is expressed in an animal form; *marriage* (which is incontestably a form of *exclusive private property*) is contrasted with the community of women, in which women become communal and common property. One may say that this idea of the *community of women* is the *open secret* of this entirely crude and unreflective communism. Just as women are to pass from marriage to universal prostitution, so the whole world of wealth (i.e.

the objective being of man) is to pass from the relation of exclusive marriage with the private owner to the relation of universal prostitution with the community. This communism, which negates the *personality* of man in every sphere, is only the logical expression of private property, which is this negation. [p. 153]

True communism develops the social nature of human beings:

It is, therefore, the return of man himself as a *social*, i.e. really human, being, a complete and conscious return which assimilates all the wealth of previous development. Communism as a fully developed naturalism is humanism and as a fully developed humanism is naturalism. It is the *definitive* resolution of the antagonism between man and nature, and between man and man. It is the true solution of the conflict between existence and essence, between objectification and self-affirmation, between freedom and necessity, between individual and species. It is the solution of the riddle of history and knows itself to be this solution. [p. 155]

It is above all necessary to avoid postulating "society" once again as an abstraction confronting the individual. The individual *is* the *social being*. The manifestation of his life—even when it does not appear directly in the form of a communal manifestation, accomplished in association with other men—is, therefore, a manifestation and affirmation of *social life*. Individual human life and species-life are not different things, even though the mode of existence of individual life is necessarily either a more *specific* or a more *general* mode of species-life, or that of species-life a [more] *specific* or more *general* mode of individual life. [p. 158]

[T]he positive supersession of private property, i.e. the *sensuous* appropriation of the human essence and of human life, of objective man and of human *creations*, by and for man, should not be taken only in the sense of *immediate*, exclusive *enjoyment*, or only in the sense of *possession* or *having*. Man appropriates his manifold being in an all-inclusive way, and thus as a whole man. All his *human* relations to the world—seeing, hearing, smelling, tasting, touching, thinking, observing, feeling, desiring, acting, loving—in short, all the organs of his individuality, like the organs which are directly communal in form, are in their objective action (their *action in*

relation to the object) the appropriation of this object, the appropriation of human reality. The way in which they react to the object is the confirmation of *human reality*. It is human effectiveness and human *suffering*, for suffering humanly considered is an enjoyment of the self for man. [p. 159]

The supersession of private property is, therefore, the complete *emancipation* of all the human qualities and senses. It is such an emancipation because these qualities and senses have become *human*, from the subjective as well as the objective point of view. The eye has become a *human* eye when its *object* has become a *human*, social object, created by man and destined for him. The senses have, therefore, become directly theoreticians in practice. They relate themselves to the thing for the sake of the thing, but the thing itself is an *objective human* relation to itself and to man, and vice versa. Need and enjoyment have thus lost their *egoistic* character and nature has lost its mere *utility* by the fact that its utilization has become *human* utilization. [p. 160]

Let us next consider the subjective aspect. Man's musical sense is only awakened by music. The most beautiful music has no meaning for the non-musical ear, is not an object for it, because my object can only be the confirmation of one of my own faculties. It can only be so for me in so far as my faculty exists for itself as a subjective capacity, because the meaning of an object for me extends only as far as the sense extends (only makes sense for an appropriate sense). For this reason, the *senses* of social man are *different* from those of non-social man. . . . The cultivation of the five senses is the work of all previous history. [p. 161]

Needs, Production, and Division of Labour

Under capitalism human needs are perverted.

We have seen the importance which must be attributed, in a socialist perspective, to the *wealth* of human needs. . . . Within the system of private property it has the opposite meaning. Every man speculates upon creating a *new* need in another in order to force him to a new sacrifice, to place him in a new dependence, and to entice him into a new kind of pleasure and thereby into economic ruin. Everyone tries to establish over others an alien power in order to find there the satisfaction of his own egoistic need. With the increasing mass of objects, therefore, the realm of alien entities to which man is subjected also increases. Every new product is a new *potentiality* of mutual deceit and robbery. Man becomes increasingly poor as a man; he has increasing need of *money* in order to take possession of the hostile being. The power of his *money* diminishes directly with the growth of the quantity of production, i.e. his need increases with the increasing *power* of money. The need for money is, therefore, the real need created by the modern economic system, and the only need which it creates. The *quantity* of money becomes increasingly its only important quality. Just as it reduces every entity to an abstraction, so it reduces itself in its own development to a *quantitative* entity. Excess and immoderation become its true standard. This is shown subjectively, partly in the fact that the expansion of production and of needs becomes an *ingenious* and always *calculating* subservience to inhuman, depraved, unnatural and *imaginary* appetites. Private property does not know how to change crude need into *human* need; its *idealism* is *fantasy, caprice* and *fancy*. No eunuch flatters his tyrant more shamefully or seeks by more infamous means to stimulate his jaded appetite, in order to gain some favour, than does the eunuch of industry, the entrepreneur, in order to acquire a few silver coins or to charm the gold from the purse of his dearly beloved neighbour. (Every product is a bait by means of which the individual tries to entice the essence of the other person, his money. Every real or potential need is a weakness which will draw the bird into the lime. Universal exploitation of human communal life. . . .) The entrepreneur accedes to the most depraved fancies of his neighbour, plays the role of pander between him and his needs, awakens unhealthy appetites in him, and watches for every weakness so that later on he may claim the remuneration for this labour of love. [pp. 168–169]

. . . [B]y reckoning as the general standard of life (general because it is applicable to the mass of men) the *most impoverished* life conceivable, [the political economist] turns the worker into a being who has neither senses nor needs, just as he turns his activity into a pure abstraction from all activity. Thus all working-class *luxury* seems to him blameworthy, and everything which goes beyond the most abstract need (whether it be a passive enjoyment or a manifestation of personal activity) is re-

garded as a *luxury*. Political economy, the science of *wealth*, is, therefore, at the same time, the science of renunciation, of privation and of saving, which actually succeeds in depriving man of fresh *air* and of physical *activity*. This science of a marvellous industry is at the same time the science of *asceticism*. Its true ideal is the *ascetic* but *usurious* miser and the *ascetic* but *productive* slave. Its moral ideal is the *worker* who takes a part of his wages to the savings bank. It has even found a servile art to embody this favourite idea, which has been produced in a sentimental manner on the stage. Thus, despite its worldly and pleasure-seeking appearance, it is a truly moral science, and the most moral of all sciences. Its principal thesis is the renunciation of life and of human needs. The less you eat, drink, buy books, go to the theatre or to balls, or to the public house, and the less you think, love, theorize, sing, paint, fence, etc. the more you will be able to save and the *greater* will become your treasure which neither moth nor dust will corrupt—your *capital*. The less you *are*, the less you express your life, the more you *have*, the greater is your *alienated* life and the greater is the saving of your alienated being. Everything which the economist takes from you in the way of life and humanity, he restores to you in the form of *money* and *wealth*. [pp. 170–171]

Everything which you own must be made *venal*, i.e. useful. Suppose I ask the economist: am I acting in accordance with economic laws if I earn money by the sale of my body, by prostituting it to another person's lust . . . or if I sell my friends to the Moroccans (and the direct sale of men occurs in all civilized countries in the form of the trade in conscripts)? He will reply: you are not acting contrary to my laws, but you must take into account what Cousin Morality and Cousin Religion have to say. My *economic* morality and religion have no objection to make, but . . . But then whom should we believe, the economist or the moralist? The morality of political economy is *gain*, work, thrift and sobriety—yet political economy promises to satisfy my needs. The political economy of morality is the riches of a good conscience, of virtue, etc., but how can I be virtuous if I am not alive and how can I have a good conscience if I am not aware of anything? The nature of alienation implies that each sphere applies a different and contradictory norm, that morality does not apply the same norm as political economy, etc., because each of them is a particular alienation of man; each is concentrated upon a specific area of alienated activity and is itself alienated from the other. [p. 173]

Money

Money undermines all human relations:

Money, since it has the *property* of purchasing everything, of appropriating objects to itself, is, therefore, the *object par excellence*. . . . [It] is the *pander* between need and object, between human life and the means of subsistence. But *that which* mediates *my* life mediates also the existence of other men for me. It is for me the *other* person. [pp. 189–190]

That which exists for me through the medium of *money*, that which I can pay for (i.e. which money can buy), that *I am*, the possessor of the money. My own power is as great as the power of money. The properties of money are my own (the possessor's) properties and faculties. What I *am* and *can do* is, therefore, not at all determined by my individuality. I *am* ugly, but I can buy the most beautiful woman for myself. Consequently, I am not *ugly*, for the effect of ugliness, its power to repel, is annulled by money. As an individual I am *lame*, but money provides me with twenty-four legs. Therefore, I am not lame. I am a detestable, dishonourable, unscrupulous and stupid man, but money is honoured and so also is its possessor. Money is the highest good, and so its possessor is good. Besides, money saves me the trouble of being dishonest; therefore, I am presumed honest. I am *stupid*, but since money is *the real mind* of all things, how should its possessor be stupid? Moreover, he can buy talented people for himself, and is not he who has power over the talented more talented than they? I who can have, through the power of money, *everything* for which the human heart longs, do I not possess all human abilities? Does not my money, therefore, transform all my incapacities into their opposites?

If *money* is the bond which binds me to *human* life, and society to me, and which links me with nature and man, is it not the bond of all *bonds*? Is it not, therefore, also the universal agent of separation? It is the real means of both *separation* and *union*, the galvano-*chemical* power of society. [pp. 191–192]

Money, then, appears as a *disruptive* power for the individual and for the social bonds, which claim

to be self-subsistent *entities*. It changes fidelity into infidelity, love into hate, hate into love, virtue into vice, vice into virtue, servant into master, stupidity into intelligence and intelligence into stupidity.

Since money, as the existing and active concept of value, confounds and exchanges everything, it is the universal *confusion and transposition* of all things, the inverted world, the confusion and transposition of all natural and human qualities. [p. 193]

Let us assume *man* to be *man*, and his relation to the world to be a human one. Then love can only be exchanged for love, trust for trust, etc. If you wish to enjoy art you must be an artistically cultivated person; if you wish to influence other people you must be a person who really has a stimulating and encouraging effect upon others. Every one of your relations to man and to nature must be a *specific expression*, corresponding to the object of your will, of your *real individual* life. If you love without evoking love in return, i.e. if you are not able, by the *manifestation* of yourself as a loving person, to make yourself a *beloved person*, then your love is impotent and a misfortune. [pp. 193–194]

FREDERICK ENGELS

The Origin of the Family, Private Property and the State [7]

In the vast majority of cases, therefore, marriage remained up to the close of the middle ages what it had been from the start—a matter which was not decided by the partners. . . . That the mutual affection of the people concerned should be the one paramount reason for marriage, outweighing everything else, was and always had been absolutely unheard of in the practice of the ruling classes; that sort of thing only happened in romance—or among the oppressed classes, who did not count.

Such was the state of things encountered by capitalist production when it began to prepare itself, after the epoch of geographical discoveries, to win world power by world trade and manufacture. One would suppose that this manner of marriage exactly

[7] Originally published 1884; 4th ed., 1891. The selection is from Frederick Engels, *The Origin of the Family, Private Property and the State* (New York: International Publishers, 1942; 1972), pp. 141–145.

suited it, and so it did. And yet—there are no limits to the irony of history—capitalist production itself was to make the decisive breach in it. By changing all things into commodities, it dissolved all inherited and traditional relationships, and in place of time-honored custom and historic right, it set up purchase and sale, "free" contract. . . .

But a contract requires people who can dispose freely of their persons, actions, and possessions, and meet each other on the footing of equal rights. To create these "free" and "equal" people was one of the main tasks of capitalist production. Even though at the start it was carried out only half-consciously, and under a religious disguise at that, from the time of the Lutheran and Calvinist Reformation the principle was established that man is only fully responsible for his actions when he acts with complete freedom of will, and that it is a moral duty to resist all coercion to an immoral act. But how did this fit in with the hitherto existing practice in the arrangement of marriages? Marriage according to the bourgeois conception was a contract, a legal transaction, and the most important one of all because it disposed of two human beings, body and mind, for life. Formally, it is true, the contract at that time was entered into voluntarily; without the assent of the persons concerned, nothing could be done. But everyone knew only too well how this assent was obtained and who were the real contracting parties in the marriage. But if real freedom of decision was required for all other contracts, then why not for this? Had not the two young people to be coupled also the right to dispose freely of themselves, of their bodies and organs? Had not chivalry brought sex love into fashion, and was not its proper bourgeois form, in contrast to chivalry's adulterous love, the love of husband and wife? And if it was the duty of married people to love each other, was it not equally the duty of lovers to marry each other and nobody else? Did not this right of the lovers stand higher than the right of parents, relations, and other traditional marriage brokers and matchmakers? If the right of free, personal discrimination broke boldly into the Church and religion, how should it halt before the intolerable claim of the older generation to dispose of the body, soul, property, happiness, and unhappiness of the younger generation? . . .

So it came about that the rising bourgeoisie, especially in Protestant countries where existing conditions had been most severely shaken, increasingly

recognized freedom of contract also in marriage, and carried it into effect in the manner described. Marriage remained class marriage, but within the class the partners were conceded a certain degree of freedom of choice. And on paper, in ethical theory and in poetic description, nothing was more immutably established than that every marriage is immoral which does not rest on mutual sexual love and really free agreement of husband and wife. In short, the love marriage was proclaimed as a human right, and indeed not only as a *droit de l'homme*, one of the rights of man, but also, for once in a way, as *droit de la femme*, one of the rights of woman.

This human right, however, differed in one respect from all other so-called human rights. While the latter in practice remain restricted to the ruling class (the bourgeoisie) and are directly or indirectly curtailed for the oppressed class (the proletariat), in the case of the former the irony of history plays another of its tricks. The ruling class remains dominated by the familiar economic influences and therefore only in exceptional cases does it provide instances of really freely contracted marriages, while among the oppressed class, as we have seen, these marriages are the rule.

Full freedom of marriage can therefore only be generally established when the abolition of capitalist production and of the property relations created by it has removed all the accompanying economic considerations which still exert such a powerful influence on the choice of a marriage partner. For then there is no other motive left except mutual inclination.

And as sexual love is by its nature exclusive—although at present this exclusiveness is fully realized only in the woman—the marriage based on sexual love is by its nature individual marriage. . . . If now the economic considerations also disappear which made women put up with the habitual infidelity of their husbands—concern for their own means of existence and still more for their children's future—then, according to all previous experience, the equality of woman thereby achieved will tend infinitely more to make men really monogamous than to make women polyandrous.

But what will quite certainly disappear from monogamy are all the features stamped upon it through its origin in property relations; these are, in the first place, supremacy of the man and secondly, the indissolubility of marriage. The supremacy of the man in marriage is the simple consequence of his economic supremacy, and with the abolition of the latter will disappear of itself. The indissolubility of marriage is partly a consequence of the economic situation in which monogamy arose, partly tradition from the period when the connection between this economic situation and monogamy was not yet fully understood and was carried to extremes under a religious form. Today it is already broken through at a thousand points. If only the marriage based on love is moral, then also only the marriage is moral in which love continues. But the intense emotion of individual sex love varies very much in duration from one individual to another, especially among men, and if affection definitely comes to an end or is supplanted by a new passionate love, separation is a benefit for both partners as well as for society—only people will then be spared having to wade through the useless mire of a divorce case.

What we can now conjecture about the way in which sexual relations will be ordered after the impending overthrow of capitalist production is mainly of a negative character, limited for the most part to what will disappear. But what will there be new? That will be answered when a new generation has grown up: a generation of men who never in their lives have known what it is to buy a woman's surrender with money or any other social instrument of power; a generation of women who have never known what it is to give themselves to a man from any other considerations than real love or to refuse to give themselves to their lover from fear of the economic consequences. When these people are in the world, they will care precious little what anybody today thinks they ought to do; they will make their own practice and their corresponding public opinion about the practice of each individual—and that will be the end of it.

KARL MARX AND FREDERICK ENGELS

The German Ideology [8]

The selection on the idea of utility, and particularly Bentham's idea, illustrates how Marx and Engels apply their theory not simply to morality but to ethics. They are not alone in

[8] From *The German Ideology* (London: Lawrence & Wishart, 1965). It was written in 1845–1846.

thinking ethics cannot be evaluated solely in intellectual terms. Nietzsche, for example, expected a theory to reveal the psychological-moral make-up of the moral philosopher. Marx and Engels examine the social and historical bases and development of even the most abstract categories or central ideas.

The apparent stupidity of merging all the manifold relationships of people in the *one* relation of usefulness, this apparently metaphysical abstraction arises from the fact that, in modern bourgeois society, all relations are subordinated in practice to the one abstract monetary-commercial relation. This theory came to the fore with Hobbes and Locke at the same time as the first and second English revolutions, those first battles by which the bourgeoisie won political power. It is to be found even earlier, of course, among writers on political economy, as a tacit premise. . . . In Holbach, all the activity of individuals in their mutual intercourse, e.g., speech, love, etc., is depicted as a relation of utility and utilisation. Hence the actual relations that are presupposed here are speech, love, the definite manifestations of definite qualities of individuals. Now these relations are supposed not to have the meaning *peculiar* to them but to be the expression and manifestation of some third relation introduced in their place, the *relation of utility or utilisation*. This *paraphrasing* ceases to be meaningless and arbitrary only when these relations have validity for the individual not on their own account, not as self-activity, but rather as disguises, though by no means disguises of the category of utilisation, but of an actual third aim and relation which is called the relation of utility.

The verbal masquerade only has meaning when it is the unconscious or deliberate expression of an actual masquerade. In this case, the utility relation has a quite definite meaning, namely, that I derive benefit for myself by doing harm to someone else; further, in this case the use that I derive from some relation is in general alien to this relation, just as we saw above in connection with ability that from each ability a product alien to it was demanded, a relation determined by social relations—and this is precisely the relation of utility. All this is actually the case with the bourgeois. For him only *one* relation is valid on its own account—the relation of exploitation; all other relations have validity for him only insofar as he can include them under this one relation, and even where he encounters relations which cannot be directly subordinated to the relation of exploitation, he does at least subordinate them to it in his imagination. [pp. 448–450]

The theory which for the English still was simply the registration of a fact becomes for the French a philosophical system. This generality devoid of positive content, such as we find it in Helvétius and Holbach, is essentially different from the substantial comprehensive view which is first found in Bentham and Mill. The former corresponds to the struggling, still undeveloped bourgeoisie, the latter to the ruling, developed bourgeoisie.

The content of the theory of exploitation that was neglected by Helvétius and Holbach was developed and systematised by the Physiocrats—who worked at the same time as Holbach; but as they took as their basis the undeveloped economic relations of France where feudalism, under which landownership plays the chief role, was still not broken, they remained in thrall to the feudal outlook insofar as they declared landownership and land cultivation to be that [productive force] which determines the whole structure of society.

The theory of exploitation owes its further development in England to Godwin, and especially to Bentham, who gradually re-incorporated the economic content which the French had neglected, in proportion as the bourgeoisie succeeded in asserting itself both in England and in France. Godwin's *Political Justice* was written during the terror, and Bentham's chief works during and after the French Revolution and the development of large-scale industry in England. The complete union of the theory of utility with political economy is to be found, finally, in Mill.

At an earlier period political economy had been the subject of inquiry either by financiers, bankers and merchants, i.e., in general by persons directly concerned with economic relations, or by persons with an all-round education like Hobbes, Locke and Hume, for whom it was of importance as a branch of encyclopaedic knowledge. Thanks to the Physio-crats, political economy for the first time was raised to the rank of a special science and has been treated as such ever since. As a special branch of science it absorbed the other relations—political, juridical, etc.—to such an extent that it reduced them to economic relations. But it considered this subordination of all relations to itself only one aspect of these relations, and thereby allowed them for the rest an independent significance also outside political economy. The complete subordination of all existing relations to the relation of utility, and its unconditional elevation to be the sole content of all other relations, we find for the first time in Bentham, where, after the French Revolution and the development of large-scale industry, the bourgeoisie no longer appears as a special class, but as the class whose conditions of existence are those of the whole society.

When the sentimental and moral paraphrases, which for the French were the entire content of the utility theory, had been exhausted, all that remained for its further development was the question how individuals and relations were to be used, to be exploited. Meanwhile the reply to this question had already been given in political economy; the only possible step forward was by inclusion of the economic content. Bentham achieved this advance. But the idea had already been stated in political economy that the chief relations of exploitation are determined by production by and large, independently of the will of individuals who find them already in existence. Hence, no other field of speculative thought remained for the utility theory than the attitude of individuals to these important relations, the private exploitation of an already existing world by individuals. On this subject Bentham and his school indulged in lengthy moral reflections. Thereby the whole criticism of the existing world provided by the utility theory also moved within a narrow compass. Prejudiced in favour of the conditions of the bourgeoisie, it could criticise only those relations which had been handed down from a past epoch and were an obstacle to the development of the bourgeoisie. [pp. 452–453]

16

❧

John Stuart Mill

(1806–1873)

John Stuart Mill was the son of the incomparably versatile James Mill (1773–1836), whose fame was established by the groundbreaking *History of India* (1817), groundbreaking in that instead of the usual mostly political history it gave a full account of the social milieu—customs, religions, and patterns of belief. James Mill's educational theory shared the same broad outlook: education requires an understanding of the whole man, physical resources, and impact of the environment as well as institutional patterns; the job of the educator is socially critical. His *Analysis of the Phenomena of the Human Mind* (1829) extended the association of ideas to include sentiments and pointed to an experimental dimension for psychology. Articles he wrote for the Supplement to the *Encyclopaedia Britannica* (1816–1823)—applying utilitarian principles to topics such as prison reform, government, jurisprudence, the press, and education—influenced public debates in the 1820s and prepared the way for the reforms of the 1830s. Until replaced by his son's work, his *Elements of Political Economy* (1821) represented for the pub-

lic the best statement of utilitarian economics.

The "philosophical radicals"—orthodox Benthamites and a larger group of writers and members of Parliament interested in social and political reform, including the economist David Ricardo (1772–1823) and the jurist John Austin (1790–1859)—were brought together largely due to his organizational efforts.

James Mill became equally famous for organizing his son's education, which was carried forward across the same table at which James wrote the *History*. The education included Greek by age three, Latin by age eight, and soon—as John Stuart became a frequent visitor to the Bentham household—the whole range of social and legal thought. In 1823 John Stuart began his thirty-two-year service in the East India Company, which during the latter part of his employment involved making British government policy for the whole of India. Only indefatigable work habits (doubtless established by his education) made possible the prodigious amount of writing he did at the same time, spanning ethics and politics, logic, epistemology, and economics. *A System of Logic*

(1843) gained him the reputation of the leading logician of his age; *Principles of Political Economy* (1848) became for several generations the standard textbook of classical economics. After his retirement from the East India Company he served one term in Parliament (he refused to campaign, relenting to deliver one speech on the condition that he also make a speech to a group of working-class people, who did not have the vote). His political life was marked particularly for his activity in favor of extending the franchise and suffrage for women.

His theoretical and practical activity made him the outstanding spokesman for Utilitarianism in the nineteenth century and, retrospectively, the central figure in classical liberalism. He did not adopt Benthamism wholesale: he reframed the theory to remedy its shortcomings; he modified it in the light of developing knowledge of history, the nature of experience, society, and methodology; and he refashioned it to face the newer social problems that became manifest after the reforms of 1832.

His major essay on Bentham couples appreciation and critique. Bentham is

the great *subversive*, or, in the language of Continental philosophers, the great *critical* thinker of his age and country. [Bentham] has swept away the accumulated cobwebs of centuries; he has untied knots which the efforts of the ablest thinkers, age after age, had only drawn tighter; and it is no exaggeration to say of him, that, over a great part of the field, he was the first to shed the light of reason.[1]

Still, Bentham's very limited experience had led him to portray human life and character in the crudest terms: in his "Table of the Springs of Action" words such as "conscience," "principle," "moral duty," are synonyms for "love of reputation." There is no real grasp of the inner life.

Mill recognizes that Bentham's concern was

[1] "Bentham," *London and Westminster Review*, August 1838. Reprinted in John Stuart Mill, *Dissertations and Discussions: Political, Philosophical, and Historical* (Boston: William V. Spencer, 1865), vol. I, pp. 359, 392.

with legislation and institutional reconstruction rather than with the finer texture of character formation and the structure of individual morality. Mill himself has the task, therefore, of showing the subtler shades of feeling, of toning down Bentham's stark idea of community as only a collection of individuals. He does this in part in an informal way in *Utilitarianism* (first printed as separate essays in *Frazer's Magazine*), defending utilitarian theory against various objections; since he has a wider intellectual audience in mind, it is scarcely likely that he intended the kind of minute technical and methodological scrutiny that generations of philosophers were to give these essays.

Some of the emendations and amplifications of utilitarianism that Mill introduces have subsequent importance. In place of the list of sanctions that Bentham offered, classified by their sources (physical, governmental, religious, and public opinion), Mill distinguishes the external from the internal sanctions. The latter is the inner feeling of obligation, which can come from many sources. And basic among them is the social feeling, the desire to be in unity with our fellow creatures, which involves a concern with their well-being. Mill also reconsiders the notion of happiness, adding qualitative distinctions of pleasures to the quantitative explored by Bentham. To orthodox Benthamites this undermined Bentham's program of objective policy decision and introduced subjective arbitrariness.

In attempting to offer proofs of utilitarianism Mill goes beyond Bentham, who had been content to argue that a utilitarian standard underlies all other theories as well as people's practical evaluations. In *Utilitarianism* (Chapter 4) Mill offers as proof what some later philosophers (Bradley and Moore, for example) attacked as logical fallacies: first, that we can argue from what is desired to what is desirable, and second, that we can argue from everyone pursuing his own happiness to all pursuing the general happiness. The first he rests on an analogy between such manifest predicates (those occasioned in an actual experiencing) as *is seen* and *is desired* and such dispositional predicates as *is visible* and *is desirable*. The critics pointed to the disanalogy: "desirable" means *worthy of* desire, whereas "visible" means *capable of* being seen. And in the second case, the shift from the distributive pursuit of happiness to the collective seems an obvious example of the fallacy of composition.

On the other hand, Mill has here not been without his supporters, who say that he wrought better than he thought. Very sophisticated problems are involved in the relation of dispositionals, induction, and learning by experience in matters of conduct as well as of science. In Mill's own *Logic* the relation of the descriptive to the normative is carefully expounded. Book VI, dealing with the moral sciences, distinguishes Art and Science. Laws of Science are cast in indicatives, whereas precepts or rules of Art are in imperatives. Art proposes some end to be achieved as desirable: thus, in medicine, health is presupposed; in architecture, shelter, beauty, and comfort; and in ethics, the pursuit of happiness in human living. Whereas while Science informs Art of the means required to achieve its end, it is for Art to decide whether action on that end is then desirable. In general, while Science pursues the various effects of one cause, Art has to trace the effect it is interested in to diversified causes and conditions. In this, Art, after it has learned from its corresponding Science how to achieve its end, has to take account of its resources for performance. Art has, in short, to appeal to the sciences to justify its precepts or imperatives. The relations of arts and sciences therefore prove to be highly complex. Mill's analysis may even suggest that there is a continual interrelation between art and science, between theory and practice, rather than just a coordination in which art, having scientific advice, makes an isolated decision.

Ethics or morality is the art corresponding to the sciences of human nature and society;

hence the method of ethics is simply that of art or practice in general. How Mill himself practices what he preaches here can be seen directly in his ethical and social writings. Whether dealing with justice, liberty, forms of government, or types of economy, he is intent on formulating the dominant ends involved, the best of inductive knowledge that may throw light on their achievement, the resources of human nature or society that can be invoked to achieve those ends according to our best knowledge, and finally the decision as to which principles or rules are best under the given conditions. A great deal of his work is directed toward establishing secondary principles for utilitarianism. Later moral philosophers have labeled this "rule utilitarianism," as contrasted with "act utilitarianism"—the latter thinking of utilitarian reckoning as ideally directed afresh to each particular case, while the former is concerned primarily with rules or practices.

The discussion of justice in Chapter 5 of *Utilitarianism* shows his method at work. In various fields of life that invoke the idea of justice, secondary principles can be understood better and reconstructed better if we see them not as entrenched and absolute principles but as empirical efforts, making use of the resources of human feeling, to attain the general well-being. Similarly, basic individual freedom in thought and action is defended in *On Liberty* on the grounds of the importance for general well-being of an almost absolute adherence to a principle of liberty. The principle is not justified as a natural or God-given or intuitively inalienable right. Again, in *Considerations on Representative Government*, the normative ground of selecting among political forms— how far in experience they can be shown to produce an educated populace—is explicit and pervasive; indeed, in effect it defines the enterprise of constitution making. And in *The Subjection of Women* (1869) he has the even more uphill struggle to work out principles that will bring equality to women, more uphill because he regards all the existing discriminations as wrong and constituting one of the chief hindrances to human improvement.

Mill is consistent in his reliance on the lessons of experience, whether they come from all our individual lives and deal with our feelings and tendencies, or from the macroscopic experience of groups and peoples in the long run. At the same time this commits him to altering principles or their applications insofar as their shape rested in part on what was previously taken to be relevant knowledge. For example, in his *Autobiography* he says that he started out as a firm believer in private property and democracy, but he and Harriet Taylor (who became his wife)

were now much less democrats than I had been, because so long as education continues to be so wretchedly imperfect, we dreaded the ignorance and especially the selfishness and brutality of the mass; but our ideal of ultimate improvement went far beyond Democracy, and would class us decidedly under the general designation of Socialists.[2]

Ultimately, as the selections from *Representative Government* (1861) and *Principles of Political Economy* (1848) make clear, the description of these changes is very much exaggerated; his views developed slowly as particular doctrines were refined or proved outworn by experience. His initial laissez faire rested on the idea that production and distribution and exchange were all subject to natural law, so that they could not be altered. Thus, for example, if the so-called Iron Law of Wages held and there was a fixed distribution between capital and labor, then there was little point in organizing for higher wages, since prices would go up and depress them again to their natural level. Only after the seventh edition of his *Political Economy* did he decide that the Iron Law was less than iron. He wrote in a review:

There is no law of nature making it inherently impossible for wages to rise to the point of absorbing

not only the funds which he [the capitalist] had intended to devote to carrying on his business, but the whole of what he allows for his private expenses, beyond the necessaries of life. The real limit to the rise is the practical consideration, how much would ruin him or drive him to abandon the business: not the inexorable limits of the wages-fund.[3]

In fact Mill had earlier reached the conclusion that forms of distribution and exchange were cultural and so alterable. Contemporary with Mill were many experiments in communal and utopian living; there were also notable theorists who advocated various ways of reorganizing society. The lines between the various forms of communism and socialism were not drawn as they are today. When Mill discusses them, he does not appear to have in mind Marx or Engels. He is thinking especially of Robert Owen, the successful capitalist who had shown it was possible to improve the conditions of workmen and still make a profit, and who experimented with small-scale communes, rejecting capitalism as the embodiment of greed. Or else Mill is thinking of Charles Fourier, who devised socialist communities and had considerable influence in French radical groups. In general, Mill thought that while socialism and communism were high ideals, free capitalism had not been given a sufficient trial because there were too many holdovers from older ways. What appealed to him about capitalism was its individualism, and he accepted the necessity for competition.

Individualism is the recurrent motif. Whereas it had meant freeing every individual by extending his liberties—economic, civil, political, personal—Mill now began to fear the onrush of equalitarianism as likely to bring conformism. Evident in his works is an ambivalence between his hopes for democracy and his fears of what it might become under current conditions. In his long review (1840)

[2] *Autobiography* (London, 1873; Indianapolis: Bobbs-Merrill, 1957), p. 148.

[3] "Thornton on Labour and Its Claims," *Fortnightly Review*, May 1869. Reprinted in John Stuart Mill, *Essays on Economics and Society*, ed. J. M. Robson (Toronto: University of Toronto Press, 1967), p. 645.

of Alexis de Tocqueville's *Democracy in America* (1835–1840) he agrees that there is a growing conformism in America, but he finds it also growing in Britain and attributes it not to political form but to the impact of bourgeois economic life. All in all, Mill represents a remarkable illustration in practice of the relation of beliefs about society and its processes to ethical formations and social policies. The study of his ethics in depth has remained a natural introduction to the real complexities of the field.

Representative Government and his several writings culminating in *The Subjection of Women* were, in their historical context, part of the campaign for further extension of voting rights and citizen rights. But more fundamentally, the themes that underlie his writings reflect how the historical situation had altered since utilitarianism was being consolidated by Bentham and James Mill. The working class had emerged as an independent force bidding for admission to political and social processes—first in Chartism in the 1840s, then in socialist and communist movements. The changed atmosphere can be seen if we look back at James Mill's attitude to the relation of the middle class and the working class. In the *Encyclopaedia Britannica* article, "Government," he considers the objection "that the people are not capable of acting agreeably to their interest." The aristocracy are no more capable, he says; but the people at least would be guided by the "advice and example" of the "middle rank of society," and he concludes:

It is altogether futile with regard to the foundation of good government to say that this or the other portion of the people, may at this or the other time, depart from the wisdom of the middle rank. It is enough that the great majority of the people never cease to be guided by that rank; and we may, with some confidence, challenge the adversaries of the people to produce a single instance to the contrary in the history of the world.[4]

[4] James Mill, *Essays on Government, Jurisprudence, Liberty of the Press, and Law of Nations*, ed. Philip Wheelwright (Garden City, N.Y.: Doubleday, Doren, 1935), p. 210.

Mid-nineteenth century history rapidly rendered such confidence obsolete. The Benthamite victories of the 1830s were followed by the riots and revolutions of the 1840s, so the luxury of his father's supreme confidence was no longer open to John Stuart Mill. His thought had to grapple with the whole array of new issues—with an estimation of the consequences of altered economic and social systems, with the likely career of the working class and the possibilities of education, with the conflict and balance of capital and labor, with the dangers of conformity and the maintenance of initiative and excellence, with the need for pivotal secondary principles within a utilitarian framework, with the role and limitations of state action in social institutions as well as economic ones. And it is something of a paradox that the same criticism he offered against Bentham—an insufficient concern with character and selfhood—came in turn to be offered against his utilitarianism by the Idealist philosophers, who, whether in the social liberalism of T. H. Green (1836–1882) or the conservatism of F. H. Bradley (1846–1924) and B. Bosanquet (1848–1923), were prepared to give the state a greater share in providing conditions for the moral cultivation of the individual (see Chapter 18).

Utilitarianism [5]

Chapter I: General Remarks

There are few circumstances among those which make up the present condition of human knowledge, more unlike what might have been expected, or more significant of the backward state in which speculation on the most important subjects still lingers, than the little progress which has been made in the decision of the controversy respecting the criterion of right and wrong. From the dawn of phi-

[5] *Utilitarianism* first appeared as essays in three issues of *Frazer's Magazine* (October–December, 1861) and was then reprinted as a separate volume in 1863. The selection is from 5th ed. (London: Longmans, Green, Reader, and Dyer, 1874).

losophy, the question concerning the *summum bonum,* or, what is the same thing, concerning the foundation of morality, has been accounted the main problem in speculative thought, has occupied the most gifted intellects, and divided them into sects and schools, carrying on a vigorous warfare against one another. And after more than two thousand years the same discussions continue, philosophers are still ranged under the same contending banners, and neither thinkers nor mankind at large seem nearer to being unanimous on the subject, than when the youth Socrates listened to the old Protagoras, and asserted (if Plato's dialogue be grounded on a real conversation) the theory of utilitarianism against the popular morality of the so-called sophist.

It is true that similar confusion and uncertainty, and in some cases similar discordance, exist respecting the first principles of all the sciences, not excepting that which is deemed the most certain of them, mathematics; without much impairing, generally indeed without impairing at all, the trustworthiness of the conclusions of those sciences. An apparent anomaly, the explanation of which is, that the detailed doctrines of a science are not usually deduced from, nor depend for their evidence upon, what are called its first principles. Were it not so, there would be no science more precarious, or whose conclusions were more insufficiently made out, than algebra; which derives none of its certainty from what are commonly taught to learners as its elements, since these, as laid down by some of its most eminent teachers, are as full of fictions as English law, and of mysteries as theology. The truths which are ultimately accepted as the first principles of a science, are really the last results of metaphysical analysis, practised on the elementary notions with which the science is conversant; and their relation to the science is not that of foundations to an edifice, but of roots to a tree, which may perform their office equally well though they be never dug down to and exposed to light. But though in science the particular truths precede the general theory, the contrary might be expected to be the case with a practical art, such as morals or legislation. All action is for the sake of some end, and rules of action, it seems natural to suppose, must take their whole character and colour from the end to which they are subservient. When we engage in a pursuit, a clear and precise conception of what we are pursu-

ing would seem to be the first thing we need, instead of the last we are to look forward to. A test of right and wrong must be the means, one would think, of ascertaining what is right or wrong, and not a consequence of having already ascertained it.

The difficulty is not avoided by having recourse to the popular theory of a natural faculty, a sense or instinct, informing us of right and wrong. For—besides that the existence of such a moral instinct is itself one of the matters in dispute—those believers in it who have any pretensions to philosophy, have been obliged to abandon the idea that it discerns what is right or wrong in the particular case in hand, as our other senses discern the sight or sound actually present. [pp. 1–3]

To inquire how far the bad effects of this deficiency have been mitigated in practice, or to what extent the moral beliefs of mankind have been vitiated or made uncertain by the absence of any distinct recognition of an ultimate standard, would imply a complete survey and criticism of past and present ethical doctrine. It would, however, be easy to show that whatever steadiness or consistency these moral beliefs have attained, has been mainly due to the tacit influence of a standard not recognised. Although the non-existence of an acknowledged first principle has made ethics not so much a guide as a consecration of men's actual sentiments, still, as men's sentiments, both of favour and of aversion, are greatly influenced by what they suppose to be the effects of things upon their happiness, the principle of utility, or as Bentham latterly called it, the greatest happiness principle, has had a large share in forming the moral doctrines even of those who most scornfully reject its authority. Nor is there any school of thought which refuses to admit that the influence of actions on happiness is a most material and even predominant consideration in many of the details of morals, however unwilling to acknowledge it as the fundamental principle of morality, and the source of moral obligation. I might go much further, and say that to all those *a priori* moralists who deem it necessary to argue at all, utilitarian arguments are indispensable. It is not my present purpose to criticize these thinkers; but I cannot help referring, for illustration, to a systematic treatise by one of the most illustrious of them, the *Metaphysics of Ethics,* by Kant. This remarkable man, whose system of thought will long remain one of the landmarks in the history of philosophical speculation, does, in the treatise in question, lay down an universal first principle as the origin and ground of moral obligation; it is this:— 'So act, that the rule on which thou actest would admit of being adopted as a law by all rational beings.' But when he begins to deduce from this precept any of the actual duties of morality, he fails, almost grotesquely, to show that there would be any contradiction, any logical (not to say physical) impossibility, in the adoption by all rational beings of the most outrageously immoral rules of conduct. All he shows is that the *consequences* of their universal adoption would be such as no one would choose to incur.

On the present occasion, I shall, without further discussion of the other theories, attempt to contribute something towards the understanding and appreciation of the Utilitarian or Happiness theory, and towards such proof as it is susceptible of. It is evident that this cannot be proof in the ordinary and popular meaning of the term. Questions of ultimate ends are not amenable to direct proof. Whatever can be proved to be good, must be so by being shown to be a means to something admitted to be good without proof. The medical art is proved to be good, by its conducing to health; but how is it possible to prove that health is good? The art of music is good, for the reason, among others, that it produces pleasure; but what proof is it possible to give that pleasure is good? If, then, it is asserted that there is a comprehensive formula, including all things which are in themselves good, and that whatever else is good, is not so as an end, but as a mean, the formula may be accepted or rejected, but is not a subject of what is commonly understood by proof. We are not, however, to infer that its acceptance or rejection must depend on blind impulse, or arbitrary choice. There is a larger meaning of the word proof, in which this question is as amenable to it as any other of the disputed questions of philosophy. The subject is within the cognizance of the rational faculty; and neither does that faculty deal with it solely in the way of intuition. Considerations may be presented capable of determining the intellect either to give or withhold its assent to the doctrine; and this is equivalent to proof.

. . . [I]t is a preliminary condition of rational acceptance or rejection, that the formula should be correctly understood. I believe that the very imperfect notion ordinarily formed of its meaning, is the chief obstacle which impedes its reception; and that could it be cleared, even from only the grosser misconceptions, the question would be greatly simplified, and a large proportion of its difficulties removed. [pp. 4–7]

Chapter II: What Utilitarianism Is

The creed which accepts as the foundation of morals, Utility, or the Greatest Happiness Principle, holds that actions are right in proportion as they tend to promote happiness, wrong as they tend to produce the reverse of happiness. By happiness is intended pleasure, and the absence of pain; by unhappiness, pain, and the privation of pleasure. To give a clear view of the moral standard set up by the theory, much more requires to be said; in particular, what things it includes in the ideas of pain and pleasure; and to what extent this is left an open question. But these supplementary explanations do not affect the theory of life on which this theory of morality is grounded—namely, that pleasure, and freedom from pain, are the only things desirable as ends; and that all desirable things (which are as numerous in the utilitarian as in any other scheme) are desirable either for the pleasure inherent in themselves, or as means to the promotion of pleasure and the prevention of pain. [pp. 9–10]

. . . It must be admitted, however, that utilitarian writers in general have placed the superiority of mental over bodily pleasures chiefly in the greater permanency, safety, uncostliness, &c., of the former—that is, in their circumstantial advantages rather than in their intrinsic nature. And on all these points utilitarians have fully proved their case; but they might have taken the other, and, as it may be called, higher ground, with entire consistency. It is quite compatible with the principle of utility to recognise the fact, that some *kinds* of pleasure are more desirable and more valuable than others. It would be absurd that while, in estimating all other things, quality is considered as well as quantity, the estimation of pleasures should be supposed to depend on quantity alone.

If I am asked, what I mean by difference of quality in pleasures, or what makes one pleasure more valuable than another, merely as a pleasure, except its being greater in amount, there is but one possible answer. Of two pleasures, if there be one to which all or almost all who have experience of both give a decided preference, irrespective of any feeling of moral obligation to prefer it, that is the more desirable pleasure. If one of the two is, by those who are competently acquainted with both, placed so far above the other that they prefer it, even though knowing it to be attended with a greater amount of discontent, and would not resign it for any quantity of the other pleasure which their nature is capable of, we are justified in ascribing to the preferred enjoyment a superiority in quality, so far outweighing quantity as to render it, in comparison, of small account.

Now it is an unquestionable fact that those who are equally acquainted with, and equally capable of appreciating and enjoying, both, do give a most marked preference to the manner of existence which employs their higher faculties. Few human creatures would consent to be changed into any of the lower animals, for a promise of the fullest allowance of a beast's pleasures; no intelligent human being would consent to be a fool, no instructed person would be an ignoramus, no person of feeling and conscience would be selfish and base, even though they should be persuaded that the fool, the dunce, or the rascal is better satisfied with his lot than they are with theirs. They would not resign what they possess more than he, for the most complete satisfaction of all the desires which they have in common with him. If they ever fancy they would, it is only in cases of unhappiness so extreme, that to escape from it they would exchange their lot for almost any other, however undesirable in their own eyes. A being of higher faculties requires more to make him happy, is capable probably of more acute suffering, and is certainly accessible to it at more points, than one of an inferior type; but in spite of these liabilities, he can never really wish to sink into what he feels to be a lower grade of existence. We may give what explanation we please of this unwillingness; we may attribute it to pride . . . ; we may refer it to the love of liberty and personal independence, an appeal to which was with the Stoics one of the most effective means for the inculcation of it; to the love of power, or to the love of excitement, both of which do really enter into and contribute to it: but its most appropriate appellation is a sense of dignity, which all human beings possess in one form or other, and in some, though by no means in exact, proportion to their higher faculties, and which is so essential a part of the happiness of those

in whom it is strong, that nothing which conflicts with it could be, otherwise than momentarily, an object of desire to them. Whoever supposes that this preference takes place at a sacrifice of happiness—that the superior being, in anything like equal circumstances, is not happier than the inferior—confounds the two very different ideas, of happiness, and content. It is indisputable that the being whose capacities of enjoyment are low, has the greatest chance of having them fully satisfied; and a highly-endowed being will always feel that any happiness which he can look for, as the world is constituted, is imperfect. But he can learn to bear its imperfections, if they are at all bearable; and they will not make him envy the being who is indeed unconscious of the imperfections, but only because he feels not at all the good which those imperfections qualify. It is better to be a human being dissatisfied than a pig satisfied; better to be Socrates dissatisfied than a fool satisfied. And if the fool, or the pig, is of a different opinion, it is because they only know their own side of the question. The other party to the comparison knows both sides. [pp. 11–14]

. . . On a question which is the best worth having of two pleasures, or which of two modes of existence is the most grateful to the feelings, apart from its moral attributes and from its consequences, the judgment of those who are qualified by knowledge of both, or, if they differ, that of the majority among them, must be admitted as final. And there needs be the less hesitation to accept this judgment respecting the quality of pleasures, since there is no other tribunal to be referred to even on the question of quantity. What means are there of determining which is the acutest of two pains, or the intensest of two pleasurable sensations, except the general suffrage of those who are familiar with both? Neither pains nor pleasures are homogeneous, and pain is always heterogeneous with pleasure. What is there to decide whether a particular pleasure is worth purchasing at the cost of a particular pain, except the feelings and judgment of the experienced? When, therefore, those feelings and judgment declare the pleasures derived from the higher faculties to be preferable *in kind*, apart from the question of intensity, to those of which the animal nature, disjoined from the higher faculties, is susceptible, they are entitled on this subject to the same regard. [pp. 15–16]

The remainder of the chapter explains what utilitarianism is by meeting major criticisms and by commenting on its fundamental notions. The first objection is that happiness cannot be the rational purpose of human life and action because, first, "it is unattainable," and second, "men can do *without* happiness" (p. 17).

. . . If by happiness be meant a continuity of highly pleasurable excitement, it is evident enough that this is impossible. A state of exalted pleasure lasts only moments, or in some cases, and with some intermissions, hours or days, and is the occasional brilliant flash of enjoyment, not its permanent and steady flame. Of this the philosophers who have taught that happiness is the end of life were as fully aware as those who taunt them. The happiness which they meant was not a life of rapture; but moments of such, in an existence made up of few and transitory pains, many and various pleasures, with a decided predominance of the active over the passive, and having as the foundation of the whole, not to expect more from life than it is capable of bestowing. A life thus composed, to those who have been fortunate enough to obtain it, has always appeared worthy of the name of happiness. And such an existence is even now the lot of many, during some considerable portion of their lives. The present wretched education, and wretched social arrangements, are the only real hindrance to its being attainable by almost all.

. . . Next to selfishness, the principal cause which makes life unsatisfactory, is want of mental cultivation. A cultivated mind—I do not mean that of a philosopher, but any mind to which the fountains of knowledge have been opened, and which has been taught, in any tolerable degree, to exercise its faculties—finds sources of inexhaustible interest in all that surrounds it; in the objects of nature, the achievements of art, the imaginations of poetry, the incidents of history, the ways of mankind past and present, and their prospects in the future. It is possible, indeed, to become indifferent to all this, and that too without having exhausted a thousandth part of it; but only when one has had from the beginning no moral or human interest in these things, and has sought in them only the gratification of curiosity.

Now there is absolutely no reason in the nature of things why an amount of mental culture sufficient to give an intelligent interest in these objects of contemplation, should not be the inheritance of every one born in a civilized country. As little is there an inherent necessity that any human being should be a selfish egotist, devoid of every feeling or care but those which centre in his own miserable individuality. Something far superior to this is sufficiently common even now, to give ample earnest of what the human species may be made. Genuine private affections, and a sincere interest in the public good, are possible, though in unequal degrees, to every rightly brought up human being. In a world in which there is so much to interest, so much to enjoy, and so much also to correct and improve, every one who has this moderate amount of moral and intellectual requisites is capable of an existence which may be called enviable; . . . Yet no one whose opinion deserves a moment's consideration can doubt that most of the great positive evils of the world are in themselves removable, and will, if human affairs continue to improve, be in the end reduced within narrow limits. Poverty, in any sense implying suffering, may be completely extinguished by the wisdom of society, combined with the good sense and providence of individuals. Even that most intractable of enemies, disease, may be indefinitely reduced in dimensions by good physical and moral education, and proper control of noxious influences; while the progress of science holds out a promise for the future of still more direct conquests over this detestable foe. And every advance in that direction relieves us from some, not only of the chances which cut short our own lives, but, what concerns us still more, which deprives us of those in whom our happiness is wrapt up. As for vicissitudes of fortune, and other disappointments connected with worldly circumstances, these are principally the effect either of gross imprudence, of ill-regulated desires, or of bad or imperfect social institutions. All the grand sources, in short, of human suffering are in a great degree, many of them almost entirely, conquerable by human care and effort. . . . [pp. 18–22]

To the objection that utilitarianism is a selfish doctrine:

. . . The utilitarian morality does recognise in human beings the power of sacrificing their own greatest good for the good of others. It only refuses to admit that the sacrifice is itself a good. A sacrifice which does not increase, or tend to increase, the sum total of happiness, it considers as wasted. The only self-renunciation which it applauds, is devotion to the happiness, or to some of the means of happiness, of others; either of mankind collectively, or of individuals within the limits imposed by the collective interests of mankind.

[T]he happiness which forms the utilitarian standard of what is right in conduct, is not the agent's own happiness, but that of all concerned. As between his own happiness and that of others, utilitarianism requires him to be as strictly impartial as a disinterested and benevolent spectator. In the golden rule of Jesus of Nazareth, we read the complete spirit of the ethics of utility. To do as one would be done by, and to love one's neighbour as oneself, constitute the ideal perfection of utilitarian morality. As the means of making the nearest approach to this ideal, utility would enjoin, first, that laws and social arrangements should place the happiness, or (as speaking practically it may be called) the interest, of every individual, as nearly as possible in harmony with the interest of the whole; and secondly, that education and opinion, which have so vast a power over human character, should so use that power as to establish in the mind of every individual an indissoluble association between his own happiness and the good of the whole; especially between his own happiness and the practice of such modes of conduct, negative and positive, as regard for the universal happiness prescribes: so that not only he may be unable to conceive the possibility of happiness to himself, consistently with conduct opposed to the general good, but also that a direct impulse to promote the general good may be in every individual one of the habitual motives of action, and the sentiments connected therewith may fill a large and prominent place in every human being's sentient existence. . . . [pp. 24–25]

Some objectors say that the standard of utility is too high.

They say it is exacting too much to require that people shall always act from the inducement of promoting the general interests of society. But this is to mistake the very meaning of a standard of morals, and to confound the rule of action with the motive of it. It is the business of ethics to tell us what are our duties, or by what test we may know them; but no system of ethics requires that the sole motive of all we do shall be a feeling of duty; on the contrary, ninety-nine hundredths of all our actions are done from other motives, and rightly so done, if the rule of duty does not condemn them. It is the more unjust to utilitarianism that this particular misapprehension should be made a ground of objection to it, inasmuch as utilitarian moralists have gone beyond almost all others in affirming that the motive has nothing to do with the morality of the action, though much with the worth of the agent. He who saves a fellow creature from drowning does what is morally right, whether his motive be duty, or the hope of being paid for his trouble: he who betrays the friend that trusts him is guilty of a crime, even if his object be to serve another friend to whom he is under greater obligations. . . . [p. 26]

Again, defenders of utility often find themselves called upon to reply to such objections as this—that there is not time, previous to action, for calculating and weighing the effects of any line of conduct on the general happiness. This is exactly as if any one were to say that it is impossible to guide our conduct by Christianity, because there is not time, on every occasion on which anything has to be done, to read through the Old and New Testaments. The answer to the objection is, that there has been ample time, namely, the whole past duration of the human species. During all that time mankind have been learning by experience the tendencies of actions; on which experience all the prudence, as well as all the morality of life, is dependent. People talk as if the commencement of this course of experience had hitherto been put off, and as if, at the moment when some man feels tempted to meddle with the property or life of another, he had to begin considering for the first time whether murder and theft are injurious to human happiness. . . . There is no difficulty in proving any ethical standard whatever to work ill, if we suppose universal idiocy to be conjoined with it, but on any hypothesis short of that, mankind must by this time have acquired positive beliefs as to the effects of some actions on their happiness; and the beliefs which have thus come down are the rules of morality for the multitude, and for the philosopher until he has succeeded in finding better. . . . The corollaries from the principle of utility, like the precepts of every practical art, admit of indefinite improvement, and, in a progressive state of the human mind, their improvement is perpetually going on. But to consider the rules of morality as improvable, is one thing; to pass over the intermediate generalizations entirely, and endeavour to test each individual action directly by the first principle, is another. It is a strange notion that the acknowledgment of a first principle is inconsistent with the admission of secondary ones. To inform a traveller respecting the place of his ultimate destination, is not to forbid the use of landmarks and direction-posts on the way. . . . Nobody argues that the art of navigation is not founded on astronomy, because sailors cannot wait to calculate the Nautical Almanack. Being rational creatures, they go to sea with it ready calculated; and all rational creatures go out upon the sea of life with their minds made up on the common questions of right and wrong, as well on many of the far more difficult questions of wise and foolish. . . . Whatever we adopt as the fundamental principle of morality, we require subordinate principles to apply it by: the impossibility of doing without them, being common to all systems, can afford no argument against any one in particular. . . .

The remainder of the stock arguments against utilitarianism mostly consist in laying to its charge the common infirmities of human nature, and the general difficulties which embarrass conscientious persons in shaping their course through life. We are told that an utilitarian will be apt to make his own particular case an exception to moral rules, and, when under temptation, will see an utility in the breach of a rule, greater than he will see in its observance. But is utility the only creed which is able to furnish us with excuses for evil doing, and means of cheating our own conscience? . . . It is not the fault of any creed, but of the complicated nature of human affairs, that rules of conduct cannot be so framed as to require no exceptions, and that hardly any kind of action can safely be laid down as either always obligatory or always condemnable. There is no ethical creed which does not temper the rigidity of its laws, by giving a certain latitude, under the moral responsibility of the agent, for accommodation to peculiarities of circumstances; and under every creed, at the opening thus made, self-deception and dishonest casuistry get in. There exists no moral system under which there do not arise unequivocal cases of conflicting obligation. These are the real difficulties, the knotty points both in the theory of ethics, and in the conscientious guidance of personal conduct. . . . [I]t can hardly be pretended that any one will be the less qualified for dealing with them, from possessing an ultimate standard to which conflicting rights and duties can be referred. If utility is the ultimate source of moral obligations, utility may be invoked to decide between them when their demands are incompatible. Though the application of the standard may be difficult, it is better than none at all: while in other systems, the moral laws all claiming independent authority, there is no common umpire entitled to interfere between them; their claims to precedence one over another rest on little better than sophistry, and unless determined, as they generally are, by the unacknowledged influence of considerations of utility, afford a free scope for the action of personal desires and partialities. We must remember that only in these cases of conflict between secondary principles is it requisite that first principles should be appealed to. There is no case of moral obligation in which some secondary principle is not involved; and if only one, there can seldom be any real doubt which one it is, in the mind of any person by whom the principle itself is recognised. [pp. 34–38]

Chapter III: Of the Ultimate Sanction of the Principle of Utility

The question is often asked, and properly so, in regard to any supposed moral standard—What is its sanction? what are the motives to obey it? or more specifically, what is the source of its obligation? whence does it derive its binding force? It is a necessary part of moral philosophy to provide the answer to this question; which, though frequently assuming the shape of an objection to the utilitarian morality, as if it had some special applicability to that above others, really arises in regard to all standards. It arises, in fact, whenever a person is called on to *adopt* a standard or refer morality to any basis on which he has not been accustomed to rest it. For the customary morality, that which education and opinion have consecrated, is the only one which presents itself to the mind with the feeling of being *in itself* obligatory; and when a person is asked to believe that this morality *derives* its obligation from some general principle round which custom has not thrown the same halo, the assertion is to him a paradox; the supposed corollaries seem to have a more binding force than the original theorem; the superstructure seems to stand better without, than with, what is represented as its foundation. He says to himself, I feel that I am bound not to rob or murder, betray or deceive; but why am I bound to promote the general happiness? If my own happiness lies in something else, why may I not give that the preference? [pp. 39–40]

The principle of utility either has, or there is no reason why it might not have, all the sanctions which belong to any other system of morals. Those sanctions are either external or internal. Of the external sanctions it is not necessary to speak at any length. They are, the hope of favour and the fear of displeasure from our fellow creatures or from the Ruler of the Universe, along with whatever we may have of sympathy or affection for them or of love and awe of Him, inclining us to do his will independently of selfish consequences. There is evidently no reason why all these motives for observance should not attach themselves to the utilitarian morality, as completely and as powerfully as to any other. . . .

So far as to external sanctions. The internal sanction of duty, whatever our standard of duty may be, is one and the same—a feeling in our own mind; a pain, more or less intense, attendant on violation of duty, which in properly-cultivated moral natures rises, in the more serious cases, into shrinking from it as an impossibility. This feeling, when disinterested, and connecting itself with the pure idea of duty, and not with some particular form of it, or with any of the merely accessory circumstances, is the essence of Conscience; though in that complex phenomenon as it actually exists, the simple fact is in general all encrusted over with collateral associations, derived from sympathy, from love, and still more from fear; from all the forms of religious feeling; from the recollections of childhood and of all our past life; from self-esteem, desire of the esteem of others, and occasionally even self-abasement. This extreme complication is, I apprehend, the origin of the sort of mystical character which, by a tendency of the human mind of which there are many other examples, is apt to be attributed to the idea of moral obligation, and which leads people to believe that the idea cannot possibly attach itself to any other objects than those which, by a supposed mysterious law, are found in our present ex-

perience to excite it. Its binding force, however, consists in the existence of a mass of feeling which must be broken through in order to do what violates our standard of right, and which, if we do nevertheless violate that standard, will probably have to be encountered afterwards in the form of remorse. Whatever theory we have of the nature or origin of conscience, this is what essentially constitutes it.

. . . Undoubtedly this sanction has no binding efficacy on those who do not possess the feelings it appeals to; but neither will these persons be more obedient to any other moral principle than to the utilitarian one. On them morality of any kind has no hold but through the external sanctions. Meanwhile the feelings exist, a fact in human nature, the reality of which, and the great power with which they are capable of acting on those in whom they have been duly cultivated, are proved by experience. No reason has ever been shown why they may not be cultivated to as great intensity in connexion with the utilitarian as with any other rule of morals. [pp. 40–43]

It is not necessary, for the present purpose, to decide whether the feeling of duty is innate or implanted. . . . If there be anything innate in the matter, I see no reason why the feeling which is innate should not be that of regard to the pleasures and pains of others. . . . If so, the intuitive ethics would coincide with the utilitarian, and there would be no further quarrel between them. . . .

On the other hand, if, as is my own belief, the moral feelings are not innate, but acquired, they are not for that reason the less natural. It is natural to man to speak, to reason, to build cities, to cultivate the ground, though these are acquired faculties. The moral feelings are not indeed a part of our nature, in the sense of being in any perceptible degree present in all of us; but this, unhappily, is a fact admitted by those who believe the most strenuously in their transcendental origin. Like the other acquired capacities above referred to, the moral faculty, if not a part of our nature, is a natural outgrowth from it; capable, like them, in a certain small degree, of springing up spontaneously; and susceptible of being brought by cultivation to a high degree of development. . . . [pp. 44–45]

But there *is* this basis of powerful natural sentiment; and this it is which, when once the general happiness is recognised as the ethical standard, will constitute the strength of the utilitarian morality. This firm foundation is that of the social feelings of mankind; the desire to be in unity with our fellow creatures, which is already a powerful principle in human nature, and happily one of those which tend to become stronger, even without express inculcation, from the influences of advancing civilization. The social state is at once so natural, so necessary, and so habitual to man, that, except in some unusual circumstances or by an effort of voluntary abstraction, he never conceives himself otherwise than as a member of a body; and this association is riveted more and more, as mankind are further removed from the state of savage independence. Any condition, therefore, which is essential to a state of society, becomes more and more an inseparable part of every person's conception of the state of things which he is born into, and which is the destiny of a human being. Now, society between human beings, except in the relation of master and slave, is manifestly impossible on any other footing than that the interests of all are to be consulted. Society between equals can only exist on the understanding that the interests of all are to be regarded equally. And since in all states of civilization, every person, except an absolute monarch, has equals, every one is obliged to live on these terms with somebody; and in every age some advance is made towards a state in which it will be impossible to live permanently on other terms with anybody. In this way people grow up unable to conceive as possible to them a state of total disregard of other people's interests. They are under a necessity of conceiving themselves as at least abstaining from all the grosser injuries, and (if only for their own protection) living in a state of constant protest against them. They are also familiar with the fact of co-operating with others, and proposing to themselves a collective, not an individual, interest, as the aim (at least for the time being) of their actions. So long as they are co-operating, their ends are identified with those of others; there is at least a temporary feeling that the interests of others are their own interests. Not only does all strengthening of social ties, and all healthy growth of society, give to each individual a stronger personal interest in practically consulting the welfare of others; it also leads him to identify his *feelings* more and more with their good, or at least with an ever greater degree of practical consideration for it. He comes, as though

instinctively, to be conscious of himself as a being who *of course* pays regard to others. The good of others becomes to him a thing naturally and necessarily to be attended to, like any of the physical conditions of our existence. Now, whatever amount of this feeling a person has, he is urged by the strongest motives both of interest and of sympathy to demonstrate it, and to the utmost of his power encourage it in others; and even if he has none of it himself, he is as greatly interested as any one else that others should have it. Consequently, the smallest germs of the feeling are laid hold of and nourished by the contagion of sympathy and the influences of education; and a complete web of corroborative association is woven round it, by the powerful agency of the external sanctions. . . .

. . . This feeling in most individuals is much inferior in strength to their selfish feelings, and is often wanting altogether. But to those who have it, it possesses all the characters of a natural feeling. It does not present itself to their minds as a superstition of education, or a law despotically imposed by the power of society, but as an attribute which it would not be well for them to be without. This conviction is the ultimate sanction of the greatest-happiness morality. This it is which makes any mind, of well-developed feelings, work with, and not against, the outward motives to care for others, afforded by what I have called the external sanctions; and when those sanctions are wanting, or act in an opposite direction, constitutes in itself a powerful internal binding force, in proportion to the sensitiveness and thoughtfulness of the character; since few but those whose mind is a moral blank, could bear to lay out their course of life on the plan of paying no regard to others except so far as their own private interest compels. [pp. 46–51]

Chapter IV: Of What Sort of Proof the Principle of Utility is Susceptible

It has already been remarked, that questions of ultimate ends do not admit of proof, in the ordinary acceptation of the term. To be incapable of proof by reasoning is common to all first principles; to the first premises of our knowledge, as well as to those of our conduct. But the former, being matters of fact, may be the subject of a direct appeal to the faculties which judge of fact—namely, our senses, and our internal consciousness. Can an appeal be made to the same faculties on questions of practical ends? Or by what other faculty is cognizance taken of them?

Questions about ends are, in other words, questions what things are desirable. The utilitarian doctrine is, that happiness is desirable, and the only thing desirable, as an end; all other things being only desirable as means to that end. What ought to be required of this doctrine—what conditions is it requisite that the doctrine should fulfil—to make good its claim to be believed?

The only proof capable of being given that an object is visible, is that people actually see it. The only proof that a sound is audible, is that people hear it: and so of the other sources of our experience. In like manner, I apprehend, the sole evidence it is possible to produce that anything is desirable, is that people do actually desire it. If the end which the utilitarian doctrine proposes to itself were not, in theory and in practice, acknowledged to be an end, nothing could ever convince any person that it was so. No reason can be given why the general happiness is desirable, except that each person, so far as he believes it to be attainable, desires his own happiness. This, however, being a fact, we have not only all the proof which the case admits of, but all which it is possible to require, that happiness is a good: that each person's happiness is a good to that person, and the general happiness, therefore, a good to the aggregate of all persons. Happiness has made out its title as *one* of the ends of conduct, and consequently one of the criteria of morality.

But it has not, by this alone, proved itself to be the sole criterion. To do that, it would seem, by the same rule, necessary to show, not only that people desire happiness, but that they never desire anything else. Now it is palpable that they do desire things which, in common language, are decidedly distinguished from happiness. They desire, for example, virtue, and the absence of vice, no less really than pleasure and the absence of pain. The desire of virtue is not as universal, but it is as authentic a fact, as the desire of happiness. And hence the opponents of the utilitarian standard deem that they have a right to infer that there are other ends of human action besides happiness, and that happiness is not the standard of approbation and disapprobation.

But does the utilitarian doctrine deny that people desire virtue, or maintain that virtue is not a thing to be desired? The very reverse. It maintains not only that virtue is to be desired, but that it is to be desired disinterestedly, for itself. . . . The ingredients of happiness are very various, and each of them is desirable in itself, and not merely when considered as swelling an aggregate. The principle of utility does not mean that any given pleasure, as music, for instance, or any given exemption from pain, as for example health, are to be looked upon as means to a collective something termed happiness, and to be desired on that account. They are desired and desirable in and for themselves; besides being means, they are a part of the end. Virtue, according to the utilitarian doctrine, is not naturally and originally part of the end, but it is capable of becoming so; and in those who love it disinterestedly it has become so, and is desired and cherished, not as a means to happiness, but as a part of their happiness. [pp. 52–55]

It results from the preceding considerations, that there is in reality nothing desired except happiness. Whatever is desired otherwise than as a means to some end beyond itself, and ultimately to happiness, is desired as itself a part of happiness, and is not desired for itself until it has become so. Those who desire virtue for its own sake, desire it either because the consciousness of it is a pleasure, or because the consciousness of being without it is a pain, or for both reasons united. . . .

We have now, then, an answer to the question, of what sort of proof the principle of utility is susceptible. If the opinion which I have now stated is psychologically true—if human nature is so constituted as to desire nothing which is not either a part of happiness or a means of happiness, we can have no other proof, and we require no other, that these are the only things desirable. If so, happiness is the sole end of human action, and the promotion of it the test by which to judge of all human conduct; from whence it necessarily follows that it must be the criterion of morality, since a part is included in the whole.

And now to decide whether this is really so; whether mankind do desire nothing for itself but that which is a pleasure to them, or of which the absence is a pain; we have evidently arrived at a question of fact and experience, dependent, like all similar questions, upon evidence. It can only be determined by practised self-consciousness and self-observation, assisted by observation of others. I believe that these sources of evidence, impartially consulted, will declare that desiring a thing and finding it pleasant, aversion to it and thinking of it as painful, are phenomena entirely inseparable, or rather two parts of the same phenomenon; in strictness of language, two different modes of naming the same psychological fact: that to think of an object as desirable (unless for the sake of its consequences), and to think of it as pleasant, are one and the same thing; and that to desire anything, except in proportion as the idea of it is pleasant, is a physical and metaphysical impossibility. [pp. 57–58]

Chapter V: On the Connexion Between Justice and Utility

In all ages of speculation, one of the strongest obstacles to the reception of the doctrine that Utility or Happiness is the criterion of right and wrong, has been drawn from the idea of Justice. The powerful sentiment, and apparently clear perception, which that word recalls with a rapidity and certainty resembling an instinct, have seemed to the majority of thinkers to point to an inherent quality in things; to show that the Just must have an existence in Nature as something absolute—generically distinct from every variety of the Expedient, and, in idea, opposed to it, though (as is commonly acknowledged) never, in the long run, disjoined from it in fact.

In the case of this, as of our other moral sentiments, there is no necessary connexion between the question of its origin, and that of its binding force. That a feeling is bestowed on us by Nature, does not necessarily legitimate all its promptings. The feeling of justice might be a peculiar instinct, and might yet require, like our other instincts, to be controlled and enlightened by a higher reason. If we have intellectual instincts, leading us to judge in a particular way, as well as animal instincts that prompt us to act in a particular way, there is no necessity that the former should be more infallible in their sphere than the latter in theirs: it may as well happen that wrong judgments are occasionally suggested by those, as wrong actions by these. But though it is one thing to believe that we have natural feelings of justice, and another to acknowledge them as an ultimate criterion of conduct, these two

opinions are very closely connected in point of fact. Mankind are always predisposed to believe that any subjective feeling, not otherwise accounted for, is a revelation of some objective reality. Our present object is to determine whether the reality, to which the feeling of justice corresponds, is one which needs any such special revelation; whether the justice or injustice of an action is a thing intrinsically peculiar, and distinct from all its other qualities, or only a combination of certain of those qualities, presented under a peculiar aspect. For the purpose of this inquiry, it is practically important to consider whether the feeling itself, of justice and injustice, is *sui generis* like our sensations of colour and taste, or a derivative feeling, formed by a combination of others. . . .

To throw light upon this question, it is necessary to attempt to ascertain what is the distinguishing character of justice, or of injustice: what is the quality, or whether there is any quality, attributed in common to all modes of conduct designated as unjust (for justice, like many other moral attributes, is best defined by its opposite), and distinguishing them from such modes of conduct as are disapproved, but without having that particular epithet of disapprobation applied to them. . . .

To find the common attributes of a variety of objects, it is necessary to begin by surveying the objects themselves in the concrete. Let us therefore advert successively to the various modes of action, and arrangements of human affairs, which are classed, by universal or widely spread opinion, as Just or as Unjust. . . .

In the first place, it is mostly considered unjust to deprive any one of his personal liberty, his property, or any other thing which belongs to him by law. . . . [I]t is just to respect, unjust to violate, the *legal rights* of any one. . . .

Secondly; the legal rights of which he is deprived, may be rights which *ought* not to have belonged to him; in other words, the law which confers on him these rights, may be a bad law. . . . We may say, therefore, that a second case of injustice consists in taking or withholding from any person that to which he has a *moral right*.

Thirdly, it is universally considered just that each person should obtain that (whether good or evil) which he *deserves;* and unjust that he should obtain a good, or be made to undergo an evil, which he does not deserve. . . .

Fourthly, it is confessedly unjust to *break faith* with any one: to violate an engagement, either express or implied, or disappoint expectations raised by our own conduct, at least if we have raised those expectations knowingly and voluntarily. . . .

Fifthly, it is, by universal admission, inconsistent with justice to be *partial;* to show favour or preference to one person over another, in matters to which favour or preference do not properly apply. Impartiality, however, does not seem to be regarded as a duty in itself, but rather as instrumental to some other duty; for it is admitted that favour and preference are not always censurable, and indeed the cases in which they are condemned are rather the exception than the rule. A person would be more likely to be blamed than applauded for giving his family or friends no superiority in good offices over strangers, when he could do so without violating any other duty; and no one thinks it unjust to seek one person in preference to another as a friend, connexion, or companion. Impartiality where rights are concerned is of course obligatory, but this is involved in the more general obligation of giving to every one his right. A tribunal, for example, must be impartial, because it is bound to award, without regard to any other consideration, a disputed object to the one of two parties who has the right to it. There are other cases in which impartiality means, being solely influenced by desert; as with those who, in the capacity of judges, preceptors, or parents, administer reward and punishment as such. There are cases, again, in which it means, being solely influenced by consideration for the public interest; as in making a selection among candidates for a government employment. Impartiality, in short, as an obligation of justice, may be said to mean, being exclusively influenced by the considerations which it is supposed ought to influence the particular case in hand; and resisting the solicitation of any motives which prompt to conduct different from what those considerations would dictate.

Nearly allied to the idea of impartiality, is that of *equality;* which often enters as a component part both into the conception of justice and into the practice of it, and, in the eyes of many persons, constitutes its essence. But in this, still more than in any other case, the notion of justice varies in different persons, and always conforms in its variations to their notion of utility. Each person maintains that equality is the dictate of justice, except where he

thinks that expediency requires inequality. The justice of giving equal protection to the rights of all, is maintained by those who support the most outrageous inequality in the rights themselves. Even in slave countries it is theoretically admitted that the rights of the slave, such as they are, ought to be as sacred as those of the master; and that a tribunal which fails to enforce them with equal strictness is wanting in justice; while, at the same time, institutions which leave to the slave scarcely any rights to enforce, are not deemed unjust, because they are not deemed inexpedient. Those who think that utility requires distinctions of rank, do not consider it unjust that riches and social privileges should be unequally dispensed; but those who think this inequality inexpedient, think it unjust also. Whoever thinks that government is necessary, sees no injustice in as much inequality as is constituted by giving to the magistrate powers not granted to other people. Even among those who hold levelling doctrines, there are as many questions of justice as there are differences of opinion about expediency. Some Communists consider it unjust that the produce of the labour of the community should be shared on any other principle than that of exact equality; others think it just that those should receive most whose needs are greatest; while others hold that those who work harder, or who produce more, or whose services are more valuable to the community, may justly claim a larger quota in the division of the produce. And the sense of natural justice may be plausibly appealed to in behalf of every one of these opinions.

Among so many diverse applications of the term Justice, which yet is not regarded as ambiguous, it is a matter of some difficulty to seize the mental link which holds them together, and on which the moral sentiment adhering to the term essentially depends. . . .

. . . There can, I think, be no doubt that the *idée mère*, the primitive element, in the formation of the notion of justice, was conformity to law. . . .

. . . [T]he idea of legal constraint is still the generating idea of the notion of justice, though undergoing several transformations before that notion, as it exists in an advanced state of society, becomes complete.

The above is, I think, a true account, as far as it goes, of the origin and progressive growth of the idea of justice. But we must observe, that it contains, as yet, nothing to distinguish that obligation from moral obligation in general. For the truth is, that the idea of penal sanction, which is the essence of law, enters not only into the conception of injustice, but into that of any kind of wrong. We do not call anything wrong, unless we mean to imply that a person ought to be punished in some way or other for doing it; if not by law, by the opinion of his fellow creatures; if not by opinion, by the reproaches of his own conscience. This seems the real turning point of the distinction between morality and simple expediency. It is a part of the notion of Duty in every one of its forms, that a person may rightfully be compelled to fulfil it. Duty is a thing which may be *exacted* from a person, as one exacts a debt. Unless we think that it might be exacted from him, we do not call it his duty. Reasons of prudence, or the interest of other people, may militate against actually exacting it; but the person himself, it is clearly understood, would not be entitled to complain. There are other things, on the contrary, which we wish that people should do, which we like or admire them for doing, perhaps dislike or despise them for not doing, but yet admit that they are not bound to do; it is not a case of moral obligation; we do not blame them, that is, we do not think that they are proper objects of punishment. How we come by these ideas of deserving and not deserving punishment, will appear, perhaps, in the sequel; but I think there is no doubt that this distinction lies at the bottom of the notions of right and wrong; that we call any conduct wrong, or employ instead, some other term of dislike or disparagement, according as we think that the person ought, or ought not, to be punished for it; and we say that it would be right to do so and so, or merely that it would be desirable or laudable, according as we would wish to see the person whom it concerns, compelled or only persuaded and exhorted, to act in that manner.

This, therefore, being the characteristic difference which marks off, not justice, but morality in general, from the remaining provinces of Expediency and Worthiness; the character is still to be sought which distinguishes justice from other branches of morality. Now it is known that ethical writers divide moral duties into two classes, denoted by the ill-chosen expressions, duties of perfect and of imperfect obligation; the latter being those in which, though the act is obligatory, the particular occasions of performing it are left to our choice; as in the case of charity or beneficence, which we are indeed bound to practise, but not towards any definite person, nor at any prescribed time. In the more precise language of philosophic jurists, duties of perfect obligation are those duties in virtue of which a correlative *right* resides in some person or persons; duties of imperfect obligation are those moral obligations which do not give birth to any right. I think it will be found that this distinction exactly coincides with that which exists between justice and the other obligations of morality. . . . It seems to me that this feature in the case—a right in some person, correlative to the moral obligation—constitutes the specific difference between justice, and generosity or beneficence. Justice implies something which it is not only right to do, and wrong not to do, but which some individual person can claim from us as his moral right. No one has a moral right to our generosity or beneficence, because we are not morally bound to practise those virtues towards any given individual. . . . Wherever there is a right, the case is one of justice, and not of the virtue of beneficence: and whoever does not place the distinction between justice and morality in general where we have now placed it, will be found to make no distinction between them at all, but to merge all morality in justice.

[W]e are ready to enter on the inquiry, whether the feeling, which accompanies the idea, is attached to it by a special dispensation of nature, or whether it could have grown up, by any known laws, out of the idea itself; and in particular, whether it can have originated in considerations of general expediency.

I conceive that the sentiment itself does not arise from anything which would commonly, or correctly, be termed an idea of expediency; but that though, the sentiment does not, whatever is moral in it does.

We have seen that the two essential ingredients in the sentiment of justice are, the desire to punish a person who has done harm, and the knowledge or belief that there is some definite individual or individuals to whom harm has been done.

Now it appears to me, that the desire to punish a person who has done harm to some individual, is a spontaneous outgrowth from two sentiments, both in the highest degree natural, and which either are or resemble instincts; the impulse of self-defence, and the feeling of sympathy. [pp. 62–76]

The sentiment of justice, in that one of its elements which consists of the desire to punish, is thus, I conceive, the natural feeling of retaliation or vengeance, rendered by intellect and sympathy applicable to those injuries, that is, to those hurts, which wound us through, or in common with, society at large. This sentiment, in itself, has nothing moral in it; what is moral is, the exclusive subordination of it to the social sympathies, so as to wait on and obey their call. For the natural feeling tends to make us resent indiscriminately whatever any one does that is disagreeable to us; but when moralized by the social feeling, it only acts in the directions conformable to the general good: just persons resenting a hurt to society, though not otherwise a hurt to themselves, and not resenting a hurt to themselves, however painful, unless it be of the kind which society has a common interest with them in the repression of. [pp. 77–78]

To recapitulate: the idea of justice supposes two things; a rule of conduct, and a sentiment which sanctions the rule. The first must be supposed common to all mankind, and intended for their good. The other (the sentiment) is a desire that punishment may be suffered by those who infringe the rule. There is involved, in addition, the conception of some definite person who suffers by the infringement; whose rights (to use the expression appropriated to the case) are violated by it. And the sentiment of justice appears to me to be, the animal desire to repel or retaliate a hurt or damage to oneself, or to those with whom one sympathizes, widened so as to include all persons, by the human capacity of enlarged sympathy, and the human conception of intelligent self-interest. From the latter elements, the feeling derives its morality; from the former, its peculiar impressiveness, and energy of self-assertion.

. . . When we call anything a person's right, we mean that he has a valid claim on society to protect him in the possession of it, either by the force of law, or by that of education and opinion. . . .

To have a right, then, is, I conceive, to have something which society ought to defend me in the possession of. If the objector goes on to ask why it ought, I can give him no other reason than general utility. If that expression does not seem to convey a sufficient feeling of the strength of the obligation, nor to account for the peculiar energy of the feeling,

it is because there goes to the composition of the sentiment, not a rational only but also an animal element, the thirst for retaliation; and this thirst derives its intensity, as well as its moral justification, from the extraordinarily important and impressive kind of utility which is concerned. The interest involved is that of security, to every one's feelings the most vital of all interests. Nearly all other earthly benefits are needed by one person, not needed by another; and many of them can, if necessary, be cheerfully foregone, or replaced by something else; but security no human being can possibly do without; on it we depend for all our immunity from evil, and for the whole value of all and every good, beyond the passing moment; since nothing but the gratification of the instant could be of any worth to us, if we could be deprived of everything the next instant by whoever was momentarily stronger than ourselves. Now this most indispensable of all necessaries, after physical nutriment, cannot be had, unless the machinery for providing it is kept unintermittedly in active play. Our notion, therefore, of the claim we have on our fellow-creatures to join in making safe for us the very groundwork of our existence, gathers feelings round it so much more intense than those concerned in any of the more common cases of utility, that the difference in degree (as is often the case in psychology) becomes a real difference in kind. The claim assumes that character of absoluteness, that apparent infinity, and incommensurability with all other considerations, which constitute the distinction between the feeling of right and wrong and that of ordinary expediency and inexpediency. The feelings concerned are so powerful, and we count so positively on finding a responsive feeling in others (all being alike interested), that *ought* and *should* grow into *must*, and recognised indispensability becomes a moral necessity, analogous to physical, and often not inferior to it in binding force. [pp. 79–81]

If a utilitarian account of justice is not correct, one would expect to find clear principles, like mathematical truths. In fact different notions of justice contend with one another in field after field: in criminal law: should punishment be retributive or deterrent? and how should punishment be made proportionate to the offense? in wages: should remuneration be according to effort or abilities or work done? in taxation: should tax be proportionate to means, should it be graduated, or should equal contributions be exacted from all? "From these confusions there is no other mode of extrication than the utilitarian" (p. 88).

. . . Justice is a name for certain classes of moral rules, which concern the essentials of human well-being more nearly, and are therefore of more absolute obligation, than any other rules for the guidance of life; and the notion which we have found to be of the essence of the idea of justice, that of a right residing in an individual, implies and testifies to this more binding obligation.

The moral rules which forbid mankind to hurt one another (in which we must never forget to include wrongful interference with each other's freedom) are more vital to human well-being than any maxims, however important, which only point out the best mode of managing some department of human affairs. They have also the peculiarity, that they are the main element in determining the whole of the social feelings of mankind. It is their observance which alone preserves peace among human beings: if obedience to them were not the rule, and disobedience the exception, every one would see in every one else a probable enemy, against whom he must be perpetually guarding himself. . . . Thus the moralities which protect every individual from being harmed by others, either directly or by being hindered in his freedom of pursuing his own good, are at once those which he himself has most at heart, and those which he has the strongest interest in publishing and enforcing by word and deed. . . .

The same powerful motives which command the observance of these primary moralities, enjoin the punishment of those who violate them; and as the impulses of self-defence, of defence of others, and of vengeance, are all called forth against such persons, retribution, or evil for evil, becomes closely connected with the sentiment of justice, and is universally included in the idea. Good for good is also one of the dictates of justice; and this, though its social utility is evident, and though it carries with it a natural human feeling, has not at first sight that obvious connexion with hurt or injury, which, existing in the most elementary cases of just and unjust, is the source of the characteristic intensity of the sentiment. But the connexion, though less obvious, is not less real. He who accepts benefits, and denies a return of them when needed, inflicts a real hurt, by disappointing one of the most natural and reasonable of expectations, and one which he must at least tacitly have encouraged, otherwise the benefits would seldom have been conferred. The important rank, among human evils and wrongs, of the disappointment of expectation, is shown in the fact that it constitutes the principal criminality of two such highly immoral acts as a breach of friendship and a breach of promise. Few hurts which human beings can sustain are greater, and none wound more, than when that on which they habitually and with full assurance relied, fails them in the hour of need; and few wrongs are greater than this mere withholding of good; none excite more resentment, either in the person suffering, or in a sympathizing spectator. The principle, therefore, of giving to each what they deserve, that is, good for good as well as evil for evil, is not only included within the idea of Justice as we have defined it, but is a proper object of that intensity of sentiment, which places the Just, in human estimation, above the simply Expedient. [pp. 88–91]

The thesis that social utility determines principles of justice is applied to other current maxims of justice. The ideal of judicial impartiality is connected with the notion of equality, and even with Bentham's dictum, "everybody to count for one, nobody for more than one."

. . . The equal claim of everybody to happiness in the estimation of the moralist and the legislator, involves an equal claim to all the means of happiness, except in so far as the inevitable conditions of human life, and the general interest, in which that of every individual is included, set limits to the maxim; and those limits ought to be strictly construed. . . . All persons are deemed to have a *right* to equality of treatment, except when some recognised social expediency requires the reverse. And hence all social inequalities which have ceased to be considered expedient, assume the character not of simple inexpediency, but of injustice, and appear so tyrannical, that people are apt to wonder how they ever could have been tolerated; forgetful that they themselves perhaps tolerate other inequalities under an equally mistaken notion of expediency, the correction of which would make that which they approve seem quite as monstrous as what they have at last learnt to condemn. . . .

It appears from what has been said, that justice is a name for certain moral requirements, which, regarded collectively, stand higher in the scale of social utility, and are therefore of more paramount obligation, than any others; though particular cases may occur in which some other social duty is so important, as to overrule any one of the general maxims of justice. Thus, to save a life, it may not only be allowable, but a duty, to steal, or take by force, the necessary food or medicine, or to kidnap, and compel to officiate, the only qualified medical practitioner. In such cases, as we do not call anything justice which is not a virtue, we usually say, not that justice must give way to some other moral principle, but that what is just in ordinary cases is, by reason of that other principle, not just in the particular case. By this useful accommodation of language, the character of indefeasibility attributed to justice is kept up, and we are saved from the necessity of maintaining that there can be laudable injustice.

The considerations which have now been adduced resolve, I conceive, the only real difficulty in the utilitarian theory of morals. It has always been evident that all cases of justice are also cases of expediency: the difference is in the peculiar sentiment which attaches to the former, as contradistinguished from the latter. If this characteristic sentiment has been sufficiently accounted for; if there is no necessity to assume for it any peculiarity of origin; if it is simply the natural feeling of resentment, moralized by being made coextensive with the demands of social good; and if this feeling not only does but ought to exist in all the classes of cases to which the idea of justice corresponds; that idea no longer presents itself as a stumbling-block to the utilitarian ethics. Justice remains the appropriate name for certain social utilities which are vastly more important, and therefore more absolute and imperative, than any others are as a class (though not more so than others may be in particular cases); and which, therefore, ought to be, as well as naturally are, guarded by a sentiment not only different in degree, but also in kind; distinguished from the milder feeling which attaches to the mere idea of promoting human pleasure or convenience, at once by the more definite nature of its commands, and by the sterner character of its sanctions. [pp. 93–96]

On Liberty [6]

The thesis is given in the epitaph at the head of the essay, from Wilhelm von Humboldt's *Sphere and Duties of Government*:

The grand, leading principle, towards which every argument unfolded in these pages directly converges, is the absolute and essential importance of human development in its richest diversity.

To expand happiness requires material and cultural progress; to achieve these requires inventiveness; inventiveness comes only with a characteristic individualism that allows of rich diversity and is unconstrained; such diversity is achievable only with liberty. Hence a principle of liberty is the pivotal point in an ethic that aims at expanded happiness for mankind.

Chapter I: Introductory

Originally, the struggle was between Liberty and Authority. In societies where rulers and ruled were distinct, liberty meant limiting the power of the rulers, first by the device of acknowledged political rights (with rebellion as the sanction) and later by the instrument of constitutional checks. Eventually people turned against the whole idea of being ruled and developed the conception of self-rule by revocable or elected governments. This changed the focus of Liberty, since a nation need not be protected against its own will. Experience showed, however, that even in self-government those who exercise power are not always those over whom it is exercised. Self-government is not "the government of each by himself, but of each by all the rest.

[6] London, 1859. The selection is from John Stuart Mill, *On Liberty* (Boston: Ticknor and Fields, 1863).

The will of the people, moreover, practically means the will of the most numerous or the most active *part* of the people; the majority, or those who succeed in making themselves accepted as the majority" (pp. 12–13). It is therefore legitimate to take precautions against the tyranny of the majority by finding "a limit to the legitimate interference of collective opinion with individual independence" (p. 14). Restraints on the actions of other people, by law or opinion, are of course required, and the rules for these are variable and become customary. Standards for these, even when worked out by philosophers, are still matters of opinion, sometimes of prejudice. "Wherever there is an ascendant class, a large portion of the morality of the country emanates from its class interests, and its feelings of class superiority. The morality between Spartans and Helots, between planters and negroes, between princes and subjects, . . . between men and women, has been for the most part the creation of these class interests and feelings" (p. 17).

The likings and dislikings of society, or of some powerful portion of it, are thus the main thing which has practically determined the rules laid down for general observance, under the penalties of law or opinion. And in general, those who have been in advance of society in thought and feeling, have left this condition of things unassailed in principle, however they may have come into conflict with it in some of its details. They have occupied themselves rather in inquiring what things society ought to like or dislike, than in questioning whether its likings or dislikings should be a law to individuals. [pp. 18–19]

The general issue has been addressed only in matters of religious liberty. The problem should be addressed on a higher ground.

The object of this Essay is to assert one very simple principle, as entitled to govern absolutely the dealings of society with the individual in the way of compulsion and control, whether the means used be physical force in the form of legal penalties, or the moral coercion of public opinion. That principle is, that the sole end for which mankind are warranted, individually or collectively, in interfering with the liberty of action of any of their number, is self-protection. That the only purpose for which power can be rightfully exercised over any member of a civilized community, against his will, is to prevent harm to others. His own good, either physical or moral, is not a sufficient warrant. He cannot rightfully be compelled to do or forbear because it will be better for him to do so, because it will make him happier, because, in the opinions of others, to do so would be wise, or even right. These are good reasons for remonstrating with him, or reasoning with him, or persuading him, or entreating him, but not for compelling him, or visiting him with any evil, in case he do otherwise. To justify that, the conduct from which it is desired to deter him must be calculated to produce evil to some one else. The only part of the conduct of any one, for which he is amenable to society, is that which concerns others. In the part which merely concerns himself, his independence is, of right, absolute. Over himself, over his own body and mind, the individual is sovereign.

It is, perhaps, hardly necessary to say that this doctrine is meant to apply only to human beings in the maturity of their faculties. We are not speaking of children, or of young persons below the age which the law may fix as that of manhood or womanhood. Those who are still in a state to require being taken care of by others, must be protected against their own actions as well as against external injury. For the same reason, we may leave out of consideration those backward states of society in which the race itself may be considered as in its nonage. The early difficulties in the way of spontaneous progress are so great, that there is seldom any choice of means for overcoming them; and a ruler full of the spirit of improvement is warranted in the use of any expedients that will attain an end, perhaps otherwise unattainable. Despotism is a legitimate mode of government in dealing with barbarians, provided the end be their improvement, and the means justified by actually effecting that end. Liberty, as a principle, has no application to any state of things anterior to the time when mankind have become capable of being improved by free and equal discussion. Until then, there is nothing for them but implicit obedience to an Akbar or a Charlemagne, if they are so fortunate as to find one. But as soon as mankind have attained the capacity of being guided to their own improvement by conviction or persuasion (a period long since reached in all nations with whom we need here concern ourselves), compulsion, either in the direct form or in that of pains and penalties for noncompliance, is no longer admissible as a means to their own good, and justifiable only for the security of others.

It is proper to state that I forego any advantage which could be derived to my argument from the idea of abstract right, as a thing independent of utility. I regard utility as the ultimate appeal on all ethical questions; but it must be utility in the largest sense, grounded on the permanent interests of man as a progressive being. Those interests, I contend, authorize the subjection of individual spontaneity to external control, only in respect to those actions of each, which concern the interest of other people. If any one does an act hurtful to others, there is a *prima facie* case for punishing him, by law, or, where legal penalties are not safely applicable, by general disapprobation. There are also many positive acts for the benefit of others, which he may rightfully be compelled to perform; such as, to give evidence in a court of justice; to bear his fair share in the common defence, or in any other joint work necessary to the interest of the society of which he enjoys the protection; and to perform certain acts of individual beneficence, such as saving a fellow creature's life, or interposing to protect the defenceless against ill-usage, things which whenever it is obviously a man's duty to do, he may rightfully be made responsible to society for not doing. A person may cause evil to others not only by his actions but by his inaction, and in either case he is justly accountable to them for the injury. The latter case, it is true, requires a much more cautious exercise of compulsion than the former. To make any one answerable for doing evil to others, is the rule; to make him answerable for not preventing evil, is, comparatively speaking, the exception. Yet there are many cases clear enough and grave enough to justify that exception. In all things which regard the external relations of the individual, he is *de jure* amenable to those whose interests are concerned, and if need be, to society as their protector. There are often

good reasons for not holding him to the responsibility; but these reasons must arise from the special expediencies of the case: either because it is a kind of case in which he is on the whole likely to act better, when left to his own discretion, than when controlled in any way in which society have it in their power to control him; or because the attempt to exercise control would produce other evils, greater than those which it would prevent. When such reasons as these preclude the enforcement of responsibility, the conscience of the agent himself should step into the vacant judgment-seat, and protect those interests of others which have no external protection; judging himself all the more rigidly, because the case does not admit of his being made accountable to the judgment of his fellow-creatures.

But there is a sphere of action in which society, as distinguished from the individual, has, if any, only an indirect interest; comprehending all that portion of a person's life and conduct which affects only himself, or, if it also affects others, only with their free, voluntary, and undeceived consent and participation. When I say only himself, I mean directly, and in the first instance; for whatever affects himself, may affect others *through* himself; and the objection which may be grounded on this contingency, will receive consideration in the sequel. This, then, is the appropriate region of human liberty. It comprises, first, the inward domain of consciousness; demanding liberty of conscience, in the most comprehensive sense; liberty of thought and feeling; absolute freedom of opinion and sentiment on all subjects, practical or speculative, scientific, moral, or theological. The liberty of expressing and publishing opinions may seem to fall under a different principle, since it belongs to that part of the conduct of an individual which concerns other people; but, being almost of as much importance as the liberty of thought itself, and resting in great part on the same reasons, is practically inseparable from it. Secondly, the principle requires liberty of tastes and pursuits; of framing the plan of our life to suit our own character; of doing as we like, subject to such consequences as may follow; without impediment from our fellow-creatures, so long as what we do does not harm them, even though they should think our conduct foolish, perverse, or wrong. Thirdly, from this liberty of each individual, follows the liberty, within the same limits, of combination among individuals; freedom to unite, for any purpose not involving harm to others: the persons combining being supposed to be of full age, and not forced or deceived.

No society in which these liberties are not, on the whole, respected, is free, whatever may be its form of government; and none is completely free in which they do not exist absolute and unqualified. The only freedom which deserves the name, is that of pursuing our own good in our own way, so long as we do not attempt to deprive others of theirs, or impede their efforts to obtain it. Each is the proper guardian of his own health, whether bodily, or mental and spiritual. Mankind are greater gainers by suffering each other to live as seems good to themselves, than by compelling each to live as seems good to the rest. [pp. 22–29]

Chapter II: Of the Liberty of Thought and Discussion

Toward the end of the chapter the argument is summarized:

First, if any opinion is compelled to silence, that opinion may, for aught we can certainly know, be true. To deny this is to assume our own infallibility.

Secondly, though the silenced opinion be an error, it may, and very commonly does, contain a portion of truth; and since the general or prevailing opinion on any subject is rarely or never the whole truth, it is only by the collision of adverse opinions that the remainder of the truth has any chance of being supplied.

Thirdly, even if the received opinion be not only true, but the whole truth; unless it is suffered to be, and actually is, vigorously and earnestly contested, it will, by most of those who receive it, be held in the manner of a prejudice, with little comprehension or feeling of its rational grounds. And not only this, but, fourthly, the meaning of the doctrine itself will be in danger of being lost, or enfeebled, and deprived of its vital effect on the character and conduct: the dogma becoming a mere formal profession, inefficacious for good, but cumbering the ground, and preventing the growth of any real and heartfelt conviction, from reason or personal experience. [pp. 101–102]

Among the objections dealt with in the course of the argument are these:

. . . Judgment is given to men that they may use it. Because it may be used erroneously, are men to be told that they ought not to use it at all? . . . We may, and must, assume our opinion to be true for the guidance of our own conduct: and it is assuming no more when we forbid bad men to pervert society by the propagation of opinions which we regard as false and pernicious.

I answer, that it is assuming very much more. There is the greatest difference between presuming an opinion to be true, because, with every opportunity for contesting it, it has not been refuted, and assuming its truth for the purpose of not permitting its refutation. Complete liberty of contradicting and disproving our opinion, is the very condition which justifies us in assuming its truth for purposes of action. [pp. 39–40]

[It is also objected that there are] certain beliefs, so useful, not to say indispensable to well-being, that it is as much the duty of governments to uphold those beliefs, as to protect any other of the interests of society. . . . This mode of thinking makes the justification of restraints on discussion not a question of the truth of doctrines, but of their usefulness; and flatters itself by that means to escape the responsibility of claiming to be an infallible judge of opinions. But those who thus satisfy themselves, do not perceive that the assumption of infallibility is merely shifted from one point to another. The usefulness of an opinion is itself matter of opinion: as disputable, as open to discussion, and requiring discussion as much, as the opinion itself. . . . [Indeed], the truth of an opinion is part of its utility. [pp. 45–46]

Some people are reconciled to persecution by their belief in the dictum that truth always triumphs over persecution. This is nothing but idle sentimentality. "History teems with instances of truth put down by persecution" (p. 56).

. . . [I]t is not the minds of heretics that are deteriorated most, by the ban placed on all inquiry which does not end in the orthodox conclusions. The greatest harm done is to those who are not heretics, and whose whole mental development is cramped, and their reason cowed, by the fear of heresy. Who can compute what the world loses in the multitude of promising intellects combined with timid characters, who dare not follow out any bold, vigorous, independent train of thought, lest it should land them in something which would admit of being considered irreligious or immoral? [pp. 65–66]

Finally, there are those who would permit freedom of expression but only on condition that "the manner be temperate, and do not pass the bounds of fair discussion." It is impossible to decide where these bounds are. But a more fundamental objection is that

the principal offences of the kind are such as it is mostly impossible, unless by accidental self-betrayal, to bring home to conviction. The gravest of them is, to argue sophistically, to suppress facts or arguments, to misstate the elements of the case, or misrepresent the opposite opinion. But all this, even to the most aggravated degree, is so continually done in perfect good faith, by persons who are not considered, and in many other respects may not deserve to be considered, ignorant or incompetent, that it is rarely possible on adequate grounds conscientiously to stamp the misrepresentation as morally culpable; and still less could law presume to interfere with this kind of controversial misconduct. With regard to what is commonly meant by intemperate discussion, namely, invective, sarcasm, personality, and the like, the denunciation of these weapons would deserve more sympathy if it were ever proposed to interdict them equally to both sides; but it is only desired to restrain the employment of them against the prevailing opinion: against the unprevailing they may not only be used without general disapproval, but will be likely to obtain for him who uses them the praise of honest zeal and righteous indignation. Yet whatever mischief arises from their use, is greatest when they are employed against the comparatively defenceless; and whatever unfair advantage can be derived by any opinion from this mode of asserting it, accrues almost exclusively to received opinions. The worst offence of this kind which can be committed by a polemic, is to stigmatize those who hold the contrary opinion as bad and immoral men. To calumny of this sort, those who hold any unpopular opinion are pecu-

liarly exposed, because they are in general few and uninfluential, and nobody but themselves feels much interest in seeing justice done them; but this weapon is, from the nature of the case, denied to those who attack a prevailing opinion: they can neither use it with safety to themselves, nor, if they could, would it do anything but recoil on their own cause. In general, opinions contrary to those commonly received can only obtain a hearing by studied moderation of language, and the most cautious avoidance of unnecessary offence, from which they hardly ever deviate even in a slight degree without losing ground: while unmeasured vituperation employed on the side of the prevailing opinion, really does deter people from professing contrary opinions, and from listening to those who profess them. For the interest, therefore, of truth and justice, it is far more important to restrain this employment of vituperative language than the other; and, for example, if it were necessary to choose, there would be much more need to discourage offensive attacks on infidelity, than on religion. It is, however, obvious that law and authority have no business with restraining either, while opinion ought, in every instance, to determine its verdict by the circumstances of the individual case; condemning every one, on whichever side of the argument he places himself, in whose mode of advocacy either want of candor, or malignity, bigotry, or intolerance of feeling manifest themselves; but not inferring these vices from the side which a person takes, though it be the contrary side of the question to our own: and giving merited honor to every one, whatever opinion he may hold, who has calmness to see and honesty to state what his opponents and their opinions really are, exaggerating nothing to their discredit, keeping nothing back which tells, or can be supposed to tell, in their favor. This is the real morality of public discussion. [pp. 102–106]

Chapter III: Of Individuality, as One of the Elements of Well-being

Does freedom of thought and discussion carry over into complete freedom of action?

. . . No one pretends that actions should be as free as opinions. On the contrary, even opinions lose their immunity, when the circumstances in which they are expressed are such as to constitute their expression a positive instigation to some mischievous act. An opinion that corn-dealers are starvers of the poor, or that private property is robbery, ought to be unmolested when simply circulated through the press, but may justly incur punishment when delivered orally to an excited mob assembled before the house of a corn-dealer, or when handed about among the same mob in the form of a placard. Acts, of whatever kind, which, without justifiable cause, do harm to others, may be, and in the more important cases absolutely require to be, controlled by the unfavorable sentiments, and, when needful, by the active interference of mankind. The liberty of the individual must be thus far limited; he must not make himself a nuisance to other people. But if he refrains from molesting others in what concerns them, and merely acts according to his own inclination and judgment in things which concern himself, the same reasons which show that opinion should be free, prove also that he should be allowed, without molestation, to carry his opinions into practice at his own cost. . . . As it is useful that while mankind are imperfect there should be different opinions, so is it that there should be different experiments of living; that free scope should be given to varieties of character, short of injury to others; and that the worth of different modes of life should be proved practically, when any one thinks fit to try them. It is desirable, in short, that in things which do not primarily concern others, individuality should assert itself. [pp. 107–109]

. . . No one's idea of excellence in conduct is that people should do absolutely nothing but copy one another. . . . On the other hand, it would be absurd to pretend that people ought to live as if nothing whatever had been known in the world before they came into it; as if experience had as yet done nothing towards showing that one mode of existence, or of conduct, is preferable to another. Nobody denies that people should be so taught and trained in youth, as to know and benefit by the ascertained results of human experience. But it is the privilege and proper condition of a human being, arrived at the maturity of his faculties, to use and interpret experience in his own way. . . . The traditions and customs of other people are, to a certain extent, evidence of what their experience has taught *them;* presumptive evidence, and as

such, have a claim to his deference: but, in the first place, their experience may be too narrow; or they may not have interpreted it rightly. Secondly, their interpretation of experience may be correct, but unsuitable to him. . . . Thirdly, . . . to conform to custom, merely *as* custom, does not educate or develop in him any of the qualities which are the distinctive endowment of a human being. The human faculties of perception, judgment, discriminative feeling, mental activity, and even moral preference, are exercised only in making a choice. He who does anything because it is the custom, makes no choice. He gains no practice either in discerning or in desiring what is best. The mental and moral, like the muscular powers, are improved only by being used. . . .

He who lets the world, or his own portion of it, choose his plan of life for him, has no need of any other faculty than the ape-like one of imitation. He who chooses his plan for himself, employs all his faculties. He must use observation to see, reasoning and judgment to foresee, activity to gather materials for decision, discrimination to decide, and when he has decided, firmness and self-control to hold to his deliberate decision. And these qualities he requires and exercises exactly in proportion as the part of his conduct which he determines according to his own judgment and feelings is a large one. It is possible that he might be guided in some good path, and kept out of harm's way, without any of these things. But what will be his comparative worth as a human being? It really is of importance, not only what men do, but also what manner of man they are that do it. Among the works of man, which human life is rightly employed in perfecting and beautifying, the first in importance surely is man himself. Supposing it were possible to get houses built, corn grown, battles fought, causes tried, and even churches erected and prayers said, by machinery—by automatons in human form—it would be a considerable loss to exchange for these automatons even the men and women who at present inhabit the more civilized parts of the world, and who assuredly are but starved specimens of what nature can and will produce. Human nature is not a machine to be built after a model, and set to do exactly the work prescribed for it, but a tree, which requires to grow and develop itself on all sides, according to the tendency of the inward forces which make it a living thing.

. . . To a certain extent it is admitted, that our understanding should be our own: but there is not the same willingness to admit that our desires and impulses should be our own likewise; or that to possess impulses of our own, and of any strength, is anything but a peril and a snare. Yet desires and impulses are as much a part of a perfect human being, as beliefs and restraints: and strong impulses are only perilous when not properly balanced; when one set of aims and inclinations is developed into strength, while others, which ought to coexist with them, remain weak and inactive. It is not because men's desires are strong that they act ill; it is because their consciences are weak. There is no natural connection between strong impulses and a weak conscience. The natural connection is the other way. To say that one person's desires and feelings are stronger and more various than those of another, is merely to say that he has more of the raw material of human nature, and is therefore capable, perhaps of more evil, but certainly of more good. Strong impulses are but another name for energy. Energy may be turned to bad uses; but more good may always be made of an energetic nature, than of an indolent and impassive one. Those who have most natural feeling are always those whose cultivated feelings may be made the strongest. The same strong susceptibilities which make the personal impulses vivid and powerful, are also the source from whence are generated the most passionate love of virtue, and the sternest self-control. It is through the cultivation of these, that society both does its duty and protects its interests: not by rejecting the stuff of which heroes are made, because it knows not how to make them. A person whose desires and impulses are his own—are the expression of his own nature, as it has been developed and modified by his own culture—is said to have a character. One whose desires and impulses are not his own, has no character, no more than a steam-engine has a character. If, in addition to being his own, his impulses are strong, and are under the government of a strong will, he has an energetic character. Whoever thinks that individuality of desires and impulses should not be encouraged to unfold itself, must maintain that society has no need of strong natures—is not the better for containing many persons who have much character—and that a high general average of energy is not desirable.

In some early states of society, these forces might be, and were, too much ahead of the power which society then possessed of disciplining and controlling them. There has been a time when the element of spontaneity and individuality was in excess, and the social principle had a hard struggle with it. The difficulty then was, to induce men of strong bodies or minds to pay obedience to any rules which required them to control their impulses. To overcome this difficulty, law and discipline, like the Popes struggling against the Emperors, asserted a power over the whole man, claiming to control all his life in order to control his character—which society had not found any other sufficient means of binding. But society has now fairly got the better of individuality; and the danger which threatens human nature is not the excess, but the deficiency, of personal impulses and preferences. Things are vastly changed, since the passions of those who were strong by station or by personal endowment were in a state of habitual rebellion against laws and ordinances, and required to be rigorously chained up to enable the persons within their reach to enjoy any particle of security. In our times, from the highest class of society down to the lowest, every one lives as under the eye of a hostile and dreaded censorship. Not only in what concerns others, but in what concerns only themselves, the individual, or the family, do not ask themselves—what do I prefer? or, what would suit my character and disposition? or, what would allow the best and highest in me to have fair play, and enable it to grow and thrive? They ask themselves, what is suitable to my position? what is usually done by persons of my station and pecuniary circumstances? or (worse still) what is usually done by persons of a station and circumstances superior to mine? I do not mean that they choose what is customary, in preference to what suits their own inclination. It does not occur to them to have any inclination, except for what is customary. Thus the mind itself is bowed to the yoke: even in what people do for pleasure, conformity is the first thing thought of; they like in crowds; they exercise choice only among things commonly done: peculiarity of taste, eccentricity of conduct, are shunned equally with crimes: until by dint of not following their own nature, they have no nature to follow: their human capacities are withered and starved: they become incapable of any strong wishes or native pleasures, and are generally without either opinions or feelings of home growth, or properly their own. Now is this, or is it not, the desirable condition of human nature? [pp. 111–119]

An atmosphere of freedom is important for the cultivation of genius, whose worth to mankind is obvious.

. . . At present individuals are lost in the crowd. In politics it is almost a triviality to say that public opinion now rules the world. The only power deserving the name is that of masses, and of governments while they make themselves the organ of the tendencies and instincts of masses. This is as true in the moral and social relations of private life as in public transactions. Those whose opinions go by the name of public opinion, are not always the same sort of public: in America, they are the whole white population; in England, chiefly the middle class. But they are always a mass, that is to say, collective mediocrity. And what is a still greater novelty, the mass do not now take their opinions from dignitaries in Church or State, from ostensible leaders, or from books. Their thinking is done for them by men much like themselves, addressing them or speaking in their name, on the spur of the moment, through the newspapers. I am not complaining of all this. I do not assert that anything better is compatible, as a general rule, with the present low state of the human mind. But that does not hinder the government of mediocrity from being mediocre government. No government by a democracy or a numerous aristocracy . . . ever did or could rise above mediocrity, except in so far as the sovereign Many have let themselves be guided . . . by the counsels and influence of a more highly gifted and instructed One or Few. The initiation of all wise or noble things, comes and must come from individuals; generally at first from some one individual. The honor and glory of the average man is that he is capable of following that initiative; that he can respond internally to wise and noble things, and be led to them with his eyes open. I am not countenancing the sort of "hero-worship" which applauds the strong man of genius for forcibly seizing on the government of the world and making it do his bidding in spite of itself. . . . It does seem, however, that when the opinions of masses of merely average men are everywhere become or becoming the dominant power, the counterpoise and corrective to that tendency would be, the more and more pronounced individuality of those who stand on the higher eminences of thought. It is in these circumstances most especially, that exceptional individuals, instead of being deterred, should be encouraged in acting differently from the mass. In other times there was no advantage in their doing so, unless they acted not only differently, but better. In this age the mere example of non-conformity, the mere refusal to bend the knee to custom, is itself a service. Precisely because the tyranny of opinion is such as to make eccentricity a reproach, it is desirable, in order to break through that tyranny, that people should be eccentric. Eccentricity has always abounded when and where strength of character has abounded; and the amount of eccentricity in a society has generally been proportional to the amount of genius, mental vigor, and moral courage which it contained. That so few now dare to be eccentric, marks the chief danger of the time.

I have said that it is important to give the freest scope possible to uncustomary things, in order that it may in time appear which of these are fit to be converted into customs. But independence of action, and disregard of custom are not solely deserving of encouragement for the chance they afford that better modes of action, and customs more worthy of general adoption, may be struck out; nor is it only persons of decided mental superiority who have a just claim to carry on their lives in their own way. There is no reason that all human existences should be constructed on some one, or some small number of patterns. If a person possesses any tolerable amount of common sense and experience, his own mode of laying out his existence is the best, not because it is the best in itself, but because it is his own mode. Human beings are not like sheep; and even sheep are not undistinguishably alike. A man cannot get a coat or a pair of boots to fit him, unless they are either made to his measure, or he has a whole warehouseful to choose from: and is it easier to fit him with a life than with a coat, or are human beings more like one another in their whole physical and spiritual conformation than in the shape of their feet? If it were only that people have diversities of taste, that is reason enough for not attempting to shape them all after one model. But different persons also require different conditions for their spiritual development; and can no more exist healthily in the same moral, than all the variety of plants can in the same physical, atmosphere and climate. The same things which are helps to one person towards the cultivation of his higher nature, are hindrances to another. The same mode of life is a healthy excitement to one, keeping all his faculties of action and enjoyment in their best order, while to another it is a distracting burden, which suspends or crushes all internal life. Such are the differences among human beings in their sources of pleasure, their susceptibilities of pain, and the operation on them of different physical and moral agencies, that unless there is a corresponding diversity in their modes of life, they neither obtain their fair share of happiness, nor grow up to the mental, moral, and aesthetic stature of which their nature is capable. [pp. 127–131]

Chapter IV: Of the Limits to the Authority of Society over the Individual

What, then, is the rightful limit to the sovereignty of the individual over himself? Where does the authority of society begin? [p. 144]

Though society is not founded on a contract, and though no good purpose is answered by inventing a contract in order to deduce social obligations from it, every one who receives the protection of society owes a return for the benefit, and the fact of living in society renders it indispensable that each should be bound to observe a certain line of conduct towards the rest. This conduct consists, first, in not injuring the interests of one another; or rather certain interests, which, either by express legal provision or by tacit understanding, ought to be considered as rights; and secondly, in each person's bearing his share (to be fixed on some equitable principle) of the labors and sacrifices incurred for defending the society or its members from injury and molestation. . . . Nor is this all that society may do. The acts of an individual may be hurtful to others, or wanting in due consideration for their welfare, without going the length of violating any of their constituted rights. The offender may then be justly punished by opinion, though not by law. . . . [W]hen a person's conduct affects the interests of no persons besides himself, or needs not affect them unless they like . . . there should be perfect freedom, legal and social, to do the action and stand the consequences. [pp. 144–146]

The thesis is not one of selfish indifference to others. "But disinterested benevolence can find other instruments to persuade people to their good, than whips and scourges, either of the literal or the metaphorical sort" (p. 146). Nevertheless, individuals do know best about themselves.

. . . We have a right . . . to act upon our unfavorable opinion of any one, not to the oppression of his individuality, but in the exercise of ours. We are not bound, for example, to seek his society; we have a right to avoid it (though not to parade the avoidance), for we have a right to choose the society most acceptable to us. We have a right, and it may be our duty, to caution others against him, if we think his example or conversation likely to have a pernicious effect on those with whom he associates. . . . In these various modes a person may suffer very severe penalties at the hands of others, for faults which directly concern only himself; but he suffers these penalties only in so far as they are the natural, and, as it were, the spontaneous consequences of the faults themselves, not because they are purposely inflicted on him for the sake of punishment. [pp. 149–150]

This is far different from the way we deal with acts injurious to others; here not only the acts but the dispositions leading to them are properly immoral, and subject to reprobation, "but they are only a subject of moral reprobation when they involve a breach of duty to others. . . . What are called duties to ourselves are not socially obligatory" (p. 152).

The distinction here pointed out between the part of a person's life which concerns only himself, and that which concerns others, many persons will refuse to admit. How (it may be asked) can any part of the conduct of a member of society be a matter of indifference to the other members? No person is an entirely isolated being; it is impossible for a person to do anything seriously or permanently hurtful to himself, without mischief reaching at least to his near connections, and often far beyond them. If he injures his property, he does harm to those who directly or indirectly derived support from it, and usually diminishes, by a greater or less amount, the general resources of the community. If he deteriorates his bodily or mental faculties, he not only brings evil upon all who depended on him for any portion of their happiness, but disqualifies himself for rendering the services which he owes to his fellow-creatures generally. [p. 154]

I fully admit that the mischief which a person does to himself, may seriously affect, both through their sympathies and their interests, those nearly connected with him, and in a minor degree, society at large. When, by conduct of this sort, a person is led to violate a distinct and assignable obligation to any other person or persons, the case is taken out of the self-regarding class, and becomes amenable to moral disapprobation in the proper sense of the term. If, for example, a man, through intemperance or extravagance, becomes unable to pay his debts, or, having undertaken the moral responsibility of a family, becomes from the same cause incapable of supporting or educating them, he is deservedly reprobated, and might be justly punished; but it is for the breach of duty to his family or creditors, not for the extravagance. . . . No person ought to be punished simply for being drunk; but a soldier or a policeman should be punished for being drunk on duty. Whenever, in short, there is a definite damage, or a definite risk of damage, either to an individual or to the public, the case is taken out of the province of liberty, and placed in that of morality or law.

But with regard to the merely contingent, or, as it may be called, constructive injury which a person causes to society, . . . the inconvenience is one which society can afford to bear, for the sake of the greater good of human freedom. [It is not as if] society had no means of bringing its weaker members up to its ordinary standard of rational conduct, except waiting till they do something irrational, and then punishing them, legally or morally, for it. Society has had absolute power over them during all the early portion of their existence: it has had the whole period of childhood and nonage in which to try whether it could make them capable of rational conduct in life. . . . If society lets any considerable number of its members grow up mere children, incapable of being acted on by rational consideration of distant motives, society has itself to blame for the consequences. [pp. 156–159]

What the powers of education, the ascendancy of authority, and natural penalties did not accomplish, is not improved by enforcing obedience in the personal concerns of individuals.

But the strongest of all the arguments against the interference of the public with purely personal conduct, is that when it does interfere, the odds are that it interferes wrongly, and in the wrong place.

Society is likely to be right on conduct affecting others but not necessarily on the self-regarding conduct of majorities.

There are many who consider as an injury to themselves any conduct which they have a distaste for, and resent it as an outrage to their feelings; as a religious bigot, when charged with disregarding the religious feelings of others, has been known to retort that they disregard his feelings, by persisting in their abominable worship or creed. But there is no parity between the feeling of a person for his own opinion, and the feeling of another who is offended at his holding it; no more than between the desire of a thief to take a purse, and the desire of the right owner to keep it.

. . . [T]o extend the bounds of what may be called moral police, until it encroaches on the most unquestionably legitimate liberty of the individual, is one of the most universal of all human propensities. [pp. 161–164]

Thus, experiments to prohibit alcohol in some of the American states are objectionable, as are attempts to suppress Mormon institutions such as polygamy.

. . . So long as the sufferers by the bad law do not invoke assistance from other communities, I cannot admit that persons entirely unconnected with them ought to step in and require that a condition of things with which all who are directly interested appear to be satisfied, should be put an end to because it is a scandal to persons some thousands of miles distant, who have no part of concern in it. [p. 179]

Chapter V: Applications

Here numerous institutional problems are examined. For example, individual losses are not to be counted as interfering with liberty when they occur in competitive institutions:

. . . In many cases, an individual, in pursuing a legitimate object, necessarily and therefore legitimately causes pain or loss to others, or intercepts a good which they had a reasonable hope of obtaining. Such oppositions of interest between individuals often arise from bad social institutions, but are unavoidable while those institutions last; and some would be unavoidable under any institutions. [p. 182]

Trade is a social act and therefore does not come under the protection of the liberty principle: "This is the so-called doctrine of Free Trade, which rests on grounds different from, though equally solid with, the principle of individual liberty asserted in this Essay" (p. 183). Economics settles empirically such questions as whether there should be fixed prices. Individuals are free to regulate themselves, but within limits—a person should not be allowed to sell himself into slavery. "The principle of freedom cannot require that he should be free not to be free" (p. 199).

It is not contrary to liberty to require parents to see that their children are educated. Perhaps an examination should be given to children and the father fined if the child is not up to standard, with the fine used for further education. But education concentrated in the hands of the state is inimical to the desired diversity of character. Neither is it contrary to liberty (although it may be inadvisable) to forbid marriage where the means of supporting a family are lacking.

I have reserved for the last place a large class of questions respecting the limits of government interference [where] the reasons against interference do not turn upon the principle of liberty: the question is not about restraining the actions of individuals, but about helping them: it is asked whether the government should do, or cause to be done, something for their benefit, instead of leaving it to be done by themselves, individually, or in voluntary combination. [pp. 210–211]

Government interference is objectionable in three cases: First, where individuals can do the thing better by themselves (these include industrial and commercial enterprises); second, where it would be educational for individuals to do it, even if government officials might do it better, for example, service on juries and participation in local and municipal elections.

The third and most cogent reason for restricting the interference of government, is the great evil of adding unnecessarily to its power. Every function superadded to those already exercised by the government, causes its influence over hopes and fears to be more widely diffused, and converts, more and more, the active and ambitious part of the public into hangers-on of the government. . . . If the roads, the railways, the banks, the insurance offices, the great joint-stock companies, the universities, and the public charities, were all of them branches of the government; if, in addition, the municipal corporations and local boards, with all that now devolves on them, became departments of the central administration; if the employees of all these different enterprises were appointed and paid by the government, and looked to the government for every rise in life; not all the freedom of the press and popular constitution of the legislature would make this or any other country free otherwise than in name. And the evil would be greater, the more efficiently and scientifically the administrative machinery was constructed—the more skilful the arrangements for obtaining the best qualified hands and heads with which to work it. [pp. 213–214]

. . . [T]he practical principle in which safety resides, the ideal to be kept in view, the standard by which to test all arrangements [is] the greatest dissemination of power consistent with efficiency; but the greatest possible centralization of information, and diffusion of it from the centre. [p. 220]

If the state devotes everything to perfecting its machinery, it will lose the vital power of its people.

Considerations on Representative Government [7]

Mill's concern with the vital power of the people continues to be central. In a sober re-

[7] London, 1861. The selection is from 2d ed. (London: Parker, 1861).

view of political institutions—as neither a machine to be given ends nor an organism that as it grows cannot be tampered with—he focuses on the conditions that are requisite to their operation, constantly contrasting the essential active participation of people with their passive acquiescence. "The people for whom the form of government is intended must be willing to accept it; or at least not so unwilling, as to oppose an insurmountable obstacle to its establishment. They must be willing and able to do what is necessary to keep it standing. And they must be willing and able to do what it requires of them to enable it to fulfil its purposes" (p. 5). The "criterion of a good form of government" (Chapter II) is an educational one: "the degree in which it tends to increase the sum of good qualities in the governed, collectively and individually; since, besides that their well-being is the sole object of government, their good qualities supply the moving force which works the machinery" (p. 30). These embrace general mental and moral development directed to public affairs.

Chapter III: That the Ideally Best Form of Government is Representative Government

It has long (perhaps throughout the entire duration of British freedom) been a common form of speech, that if a good despot could be ensured, despotic monarchy would be the best form of government. I look upon this as a radical and most pernicious misconception of what good government is; which, until it can be got rid of, will fatally vitiate all our speculations on government.

The supposition is, that absolute power, in the hands of an eminent individual, would ensure a virtuous and intelligent performance of all the duties of government. Good laws would be established and enforced, bad laws would be reformed; the best men would be placed in all situations of trust; justice would be as well administered, the public burthens would be as light and as judiciously imposed, every branch of administration would be as purely and as intelligently conducted, as the circumstances of the country and its degree of intellectual and moral cultivation would admit. I am willing, for the sake of the argument, to concede all this; but I must

point out how great the concession is; how much more is needed to produce even an approximation to these results, than is conveyed in the simple expression, a good despot. Their realization would in fact imply, not merely a good monarch, but an all-seeing one. . . . But the argument can do without even this immense item in the account. Suppose the difficulty vanquished. What should we then have? One man of superhuman mental activity managing the entire affairs of a mentally passive people. Their passivity is implied in the very idea of absolute power. The nation as a whole, and every individual composing it, are without any potential voice in their own destiny. They exercise no will in respect to their collective interests. All is decided for them by a will not their own, which it is legally a crime for them to disobey. What sort of human beings can be formed under such a regimen? What development can either their thinking or their active faculties attain under it? On matters of pure theory they might perhaps be allowed to speculate, so long as their speculations either did not approach politics, or had not the remotest connexion with its practice. On practical affairs they could at most be only suffered to suggest; and even under the most moderate of despots, none but persons of already admitted or reputed superiority could hope that their suggestions would be known to, much less regarded by, those who had the management of affairs. [pp. 45–47]

Leaving things to the Government, like leaving them to Providence, is synonymous with caring nothing about them, and accepting their results, when disagreeable, as visitations of Nature. [p. 49]

[T]he ideally best form of government is that in which the sovereignty, or supreme controlling power in the last resort, is vested in the entire aggregate of the community; every citizen not only having a voice in the exercise of that ultimate sovereignty, but being, at least occasionally, called on to take an actual part in the government, by the personal discharge of some public function, local or general. [p. 53]

In popular government the rights and interests of an individual are safeguarded by his being able to stand up for them. General prosperity is promoted by the amount and variety of personal energies. If an exclusive class has power, there is the danger of its overlooking the interests of the ruled, even if not deliberately, and of seeing them differently than they do themselves. This is illustrated in the persistent attempts to keep workers' wages low by law.

. . . If we now pass to the influence of the form of government upon character, we shall find the superiority of popular government over every other to be, if possible, still more decided and indisputable.

This question really depends upon a still more fundamental one—viz., which of two common types of character, for the general good of humanity, it is most desirable should predominate—the active, or the passive type; that which struggles against evils, or that which endures them; that which bends to circumstances, or that which endeavours to bend circumstances to itself.

The commonplaces of moralists, and the general sympathies of mankind, are in favour of the passive type. Energetic characters may be admired, but the acquiescent and submissive are those which most men personally prefer. The passiveness of our neighbours increases our own sense of security, and plays into the hands of our wilfulness. Passive characters, if we do not happen to need their activity, seem an obstruction the less in our own path. A contented character is not a dangerous rival. Yet nothing is more certain, than that improvement in human affairs is wholly the work of the uncontented characters; and, moreover, that it is much easier for an active mind to acquire the virtues of patience than for a passive one to assume those of energy. [pp. 58–59]

The striving, go-ahead character of England and the United States is only a fit subject of disapproving criticism, on account of the very secondary objects on which it commonly expends its strength. In itself it is the foundation of the best hopes for the general improvement of mankind. [pp. 63–64]

Government by one or a few favors a passive type of character; government by the many favors the active self-helping type.

From these accumulated considerations it is evident, that the only government which can fully satisfy all the exigencies of the social state, is one in which the whole people participate; that any participation, even in the smallest public function, is useful; that the participation should everywhere be as great as the general degree of improvement of the community will allow; and that nothing less can be ultimately desirable, than the admission of all to a share in the sovereign power of the state. But since all cannot, in a community exceeding a single small town, participate personally in any but some very minor portions of the public business, it follows that the ideal type of a perfect government must be representative. [p. 69]

Chapter VI: Of the Infirmities and Dangers to which Representative Government is Liable

All government is subject to two positive evils:

. . . first, general ignorance and incapacity, or, to speak more moderately, insufficient mental qualifications, in the controlling body; secondly, the danger of its being under the influence of interests not identical with the general welfare of the community. [p. 110]

[Concerning the second]: One of the greatest dangers, therefore, of democracy, as of all other forms of government, lies in the sinister interest of the holders of power: it is the danger of class legislation; of government intended for (whether really effecting it or not) the immediate benefit of the dominant class, to the lasting detriment of the whole. . . .

If we consider as a class, politically speaking, any number of persons who have the same sinister interest,—that is, whose direct and apparent interest points towards the same description of bad measures; the desirable object would be that no class, and no combination of classes likely to combine, should be able to exercise a preponderant influence in the government. A modern community, not divided within itself by strong antipathies of race, language, or nationality, may be considered as in the main divisible into two sections, which, in spite of partial variations, correspond on the whole with two divergent directions of apparent interest. Let us call them (in brief general terms) labourers on the one hand, employers of labour on the other: including however along with employers of labour, not only retired capitalists, and the possessors of inherited wealth, but all that highly paid description of labourers (such as the professions) whose education and way of life assimilate them with the rich, and whose prospect and ambition it is to raise themselves into that class. With the labourers, on the other hand, may be ranked those smaller employers of labour, who by interests, habits, and educational impressions, are assimilated in wishes, tastes, and objects to the labouring classes; comprehending a large proportion of petty tradesmen. In a state of society thus composed, if the representative system could be made ideally perfect, and if it were possible to maintain it in that state, its organization must be such, that these two classes, manual labourers and their affinities on one side, employers of labour and their affinities on the other, should be, in the arrangement of the representative system, equally balanced, each influencing about an equal number of votes in Parliament: since, assuming that the majority of each class, in any difference between them, would be mainly governed by their class interests, there would be a minority of each in whom that consideration would be subordinate to reason, justice, and the good of the whole; and this minority of either, joining with the whole of the other, would turn the scale against any demands of their own majority which were not such as ought to prevail. The reason why, in any tolerably constituted society, justice and the general interest mostly in the end carry their point, is that the separate and selfish interests of mankind are almost always divided; some are interested in what is wrong, but some, also, have their private interest on the side of what is right: and those who are governed by higher considerations, though too few and weak to prevail against the whole of the others, usually after sufficient discussion and agitation become strong enough to turn the balance in favour of the body of private interests which is on the same side with them. The representative system ought to be so constituted as to maintain this state of things. [pp. 127–129]

Chapter VII, "Of True and False Democracy; Representation of All, and Representation of the Majority Only," argues that the minority should have some representation and considers favorably newly suggested schemes of proportional representation. The argument in Chapter VIII, on the then current agitation in England for further extension of the franchise, shows the double pull of, on the one hand, the aim of extending and intensifying democracy, and on the other, the fear of the results (if not accompanied by popular education) and the quality of participation.

Chapter VIII: Of the Extension of the Suffrage

. . . [I]t is a personal injustice to withhold from any one, unless for the prevention of greater evils, the ordinary privilege of having his voice reckoned in the disposal of affairs in which he has the same interest as other people. If he is compelled to pay, if he may be compelled to fight, if he is required implicitly to obey, he should be legally entitled to be told what for; to have his consent asked, and his opinion counted at its worth, though not at more than its worth. There ought to be no pariahs in a full-grown and civilized nation; no persons disqualified, except through their own default. Every one is degraded, whether aware of it or not, when other people, without consulting him, take upon themselves unlimited power to regulate his destiny. And even in a much more improved state than the human mind has ever yet reached, it is not in nature that they who are thus disposed of should meet with as fair play as those who have a voice. [p. 166]

The ability to read, write, and perform the common operations of arithmetic is of great importance. Greater knowledge, though desirable, in the current state of educational opportunity cannot be insisted upon. "The attempt, at present, would lead to partiality, chicanery, and every kind of fraud" (p. 168). Mill also offers the principle that "the assembly which votes the taxes, either general or local, should be elected exclusively by those who pay something towards the taxes imposed" (p. 169). Those who contribute nothing to the taxes may too freely dispose of what would be gotten from other people. Thus, "the receipt of parish relief should be a peremptory disqualification for the franchise" (p. 170). Similarly for an "uncertified bankrupt" and the like. He hopes such groups will diminish in the long run, so that suffrage will become practically universal.

Mill does not make a strict rule of one man one vote. In principle, he would allow greater mental quality, greater education, higher professional ability—but not greater property—to bring greater weight in voting.[8] Any such plural vote should "be open to the poorest individual in the community to claim its privileges, if he can prove that, in spite of all difficulties and obstacles, he is, in point of intelligence, entitled to them" (p. 177). (He suggests a voluntary examination.)

[Differences of sex are] as entirely irrelevant to political rights, as difference in height, or in the colour of the hair. All human beings have the same interest in good government; the welfare of all is alike affected by it, and they have equal need of a voice in it to secure their share of its benefits. [p. 182]

Principles of Political Economy [9]

Books I deals with production. This domain is governed by laws of economics, unalterable by human will. But—"and this is perhaps the biggest *but* in economics" [10] —the domain of distribution is quite different.

Book II, Distribution

Chapter 1, Of Property

. . . The laws and conditions of the Production of Wealth, partake of the character of physical truths. There is nothing optional, or arbitrary in them. Whatever mankind produce, must be produced in the modes, and under the conditions, im-

posed by the constitution of external things, and by the inherent properties of their own bodily and mental structure. Whether they like it or not, their productions will be limited by the amount of their previous accumulation, and, that being given, it will be proportional to their energy, their skill, the perfection of their machinery, and their judicious use of the advantages of combined labor. Whether they like it or not, a double quantity of labor will not raise, on the same land, a double quantity of food, unless some improvement takes place in the processes of cultivation. . . .

It is not so with the Distribution of Wealth. That is a matter of human institution solely. The things once there, mankind, individually or collectively, can do with them as they like. They can place them at the disposal of whomsoever they please, and on whatever terms. Further, in the social state, in every state except total solitude, any disposal whatever of them can only take place by the consent of society, or rather of those who dispose of its active force. Even what a person has produced by his individual toil, unaided by any one, he cannot keep, unless by the permission of society. Not only can society take it from him, but individuals could and would take it from him, if society only remained passive; if it did not either interfere *en masse*, or employ and pay people for the purpose of preventing him from being disturbed in the possession. The distribution of wealth, therefore, depends on the laws and customs of society. The rules by which it is determined, are what the opinions and feelings of the ruling portion of the community make them, and are very different in different ages and countries; and might be still more different, if mankind so chose.

The opinions and feelings of mankind, doubtless, are not a matter of chance. They are consequences of the fundamental laws of human nature, combined with the existing state of knowledge and experience, and the existing condition of social institutions and intellectual and moral culture. But the laws of the generation of human opinions are not within our present subject. They are part of the general theory of human progress, a far larger and more difficult subject of inquiry than political economy. We have here to consider, not the causes, but the consequences of the rules according to which wealth may be distributed. Those, at least, are as little arbitrary, and have as much the character

---

[8] England did indeed have plural voting into the mid-twentieth century in the form of university seats for Parliament, so that graduates would have a double vote—for the university seat and for their locality of residence.

[9] London, 1848. The selection is from John Stuart Mill, *Principles of Political Economy*, rev. ed. (New York: The Colonial Press, 1899), 2 vols.

[10] Robert L. Heilbroner, *The Worldly Philosophers*, rev. ed. (New York: Simon and Schuster, 1961), p. 108.

of physical laws, as the laws of production. Human beings can control their own acts, but not the consequences of their acts either to themselves or to others. Society can subject the distribution of wealth to whatever rules it thinks best; but what practical results will flow from the operation of those rules, must be discovered, like any other physical or mental truths, by observation and reasoning. [Vol. I, pp. 196–197]

On private property and socialism:

[2] If private property were adopted, we must presume that it would be accompanied by none of the initial inequalities and injustices which obstruct the beneficial operation of the principle in old societies. Every full-grown man or woman, we must suppose, would be secured in the unfettered use and disposal of his or her bodily and mental faculties; and the instruments of production, the land and tools, would be divided fairly among them, so that all might start, in respect to outward appliances, on equal terms. It is possible also to conceive that in this original apportionment, compensation might be made for the injuries of nature, and the balance redressed by assigning to the less robust members of the community advantages in the distribution, sufficient to put them on a par with the rest. But the division, once made, would not again be interfered with; individuals would be left to their own exertions and to the ordinary chances, for making an advantageous use of what was assigned to them. If individual property, on the contrary, were excluded, the plan which must be adopted would be to hold the land and all instruments of production as the joint property of the community, and to carry on the operations of industry on the common account. The direction of the labor of the community would devolve upon a magistrate or magistrates, whom we may suppose elected by the suffrages of the community, and whom we must assume to be voluntarily obeyed by them. The division of the produce would in like manner be a public act. The principle might either be that of complete equality, or of apportionment to the necessities or deserts of individuals, in whatever manner might be conformable to the ideas of justice or policy prevailing in the community. . . .

The assailants of the principle of individual property may be divided into two classes: those whose

scheme implies absolute equality in the distribution of the physical means of life and enjoyment, and those who admit inequality, but grounded on some principle, or supposed principle, of justice or general expediency, and not, like so many of the existing social inequalities, dependent on accident alone. [pp. 198–200]

Mill regards both as "communism" in a highly general sense. The first class is illustrated by Robert Owen, and the second by the formula that all should work according to their capacity and receive according to their wants. Socialism generally is characterized as including the social ownership of land and the means of production.

[3] Whatever may be the merits or defects of these various schemes, they cannot be truly said to be impracticable. No reasonable person can doubt that a village community, composed of a few thousand inhabitants cultivating in joint ownership the same extent of land which at present feeds that number of people, and producing by combined labor and the most improved processes the manufactured articles which they required, could raise an amount of productions sufficient to maintain them in comfort; and would find the means of obtaining, and if need be, exacting, the quantity of labor necessary for this purpose, from every member of the association who was capable of work.

The objection ordinarily made to a system of community of property and equal distribution of the produce, that each person would be incessantly occupied in evading his fair share of the work, points, undoubtedly, to a real difficulty. But those who urge this objection, forget to how great an extent the same difficulty exists under the system on which nine-tenths of the business of society is now conducted. The objection supposes, that honest and efficient labor is only to be had from those who are themselves individually to reap the benefit of their own exertions. But how small a part of all the labor performed in England, from the lowest paid to the highest, is done by persons working for their own benefit. From the Irish reaper or hodman to the chief justice or the minister of state, nearly all the work of society is remunerated by day wages or fixed salaries. A factory operative has less personal interest in his work than a member of a Communist association, since he is not, like him, working for a partnership of which he is himself a member. It will no doubt be said, that though the laborers themselves have not, in most cases, a personal interest in their work, they are watched and superintended, and their labor directed, and the mental part of the labor performed, by persons who have. Even this, however, is far from being universally the fact. In all public, and many of the largest and most successful private undertakings, not only the labors of detail, but the control and superintendence are intrusted to salaried officers. And though the "master's eye," when the master is vigilant and intelligent, is of proverbial value, it must be remembered that in a Socialist farm or manufactory, each laborer would be under the eye not of one master, but of the whole community. . . . I am not undervaluing the strength of the incitement given to labor when the whole or a large share of the benefit of extra exertion belongs to the laborer. But under the present system of industry this incitement, in the great majority of cases, does not exist. If Communistic labor might be less vigorous than that of a peasant proprietor, or a workman laboring on his own account, it would probably be more energetic than that of a laborer for hire, who has no personal interest in the matter at all. The neglect by the uneducated classes of laborers for hire, of the duties which they engage to perform, is in the present state of society most flagrant. Now it is an admitted condition of the Communist scheme that all shall be educated: and this being supposed, the duties of the members of the association would doubtless be as diligently performed as those of the generality of salaried officers in the middle or higher classes. [pp. 200–202]

A communist association would direct ambition and activity toward the general benefit rather than toward self-regarding interests.

. . . The same cause, so often assigned in explanation of the devotion of the Catholic priest or monk to the interest of his order—that he has no interest apart from it—would, under Communism, attach the citizen to the community. And independently of the public motive, every member of the association would be amenable to the most universal, and one of the strongest of personal motives, that of public opinion. . . . A contest, who can do most for the common good, is not the kind of competition which Socialists repudiate. [pp. 202–203]

Were subsistence to be guaranteed, overpopulation might be a danger; but it would be more directly felt and more directly faced in a socialist society. The difficulty of apportioning the labor among people is a difficulty common to many systems, not just the socialist.

. . . We must remember too that Communism, as a system of society, exists only in idea; that its difficulties, at present, are much better understood than its resources; and that the intellect of mankind is only beginning to contrive the means of organizing it in detail, so as to overcome the one and derive the greatest advantage from the other.

If, therefore, the choice were to be made between Communism with all its chances, and the present state of society with all its sufferings and injustices; if the institution of private property necessarily carried with it as a consequence, that the produce of labor should be apportioned as we now see it, almost in an inverse ratio to the labor—the largest portions to those who have never worked at all, the next largest to those whose work is almost nominal, and so in a descending scale, the remuneration dwindling as the work grows harder and more disagreeable, until the most fatiguing and exhausting bodily labor cannot count with certainty on being able to earn even the necessaries of life; if this, or Communism, were the alternative, all the difficulties, great or small, of Communism would be as dust in the balance. But to make the comparison applicable, we must compare Communism at its best, with the *régime* of individual property, not as it is, but as it might be made. The principle of private property has never yet had a fair trial in any country; and less so, perhaps, in this country than in some others. The social arrangements of modern Europe commenced from a distribution of property which was the result, not of just partition, or acquisition by industry, but of conquest and violence: and notwithstanding what industry has been doing for many centuries to modify the work of force, the system still retains many and large traces of its origin. The laws of property have never yet conformed to the principles on which the justification of private property rests. They have made property of things which never ought to be property, and absolute property where only a qualified property ought to exist. They have not held the balance fairly between human beings, but have heaped impediments upon some, to give advantage to others; they have purposely fostered inequalities, and prevented all from starting fair in the race. That all should indeed start on perfectly equal terms, is inconsistent with any law of private property: but if as much pains as has been taken to aggravate the inequality of chances arising from the natural working of the principle, had been taken to temper that inequality by every means not subversive of the principle itself; if the tendency of legislation had been to favor the diffusion, instead of the concentration of wealth— to encourage the subdivision of the large masses, instead of striving to keep them together; the principle of individual property would have been found to have no necessary connection with the physical and social evils which almost all Socialist writers assume to be inseparable from it.

Private property, in every defence made of it, is supposed to mean, the guarantee to individuals, of the fruits of their own labor and abstinence. The guarantee to them of the fruits of the labor and abstinence of others, transmitted to them without any merit or exertion of their own, is not of the essence of the institution, but a mere incidental consequence, which when it reaches a certain height, does not promote, but conflicts with the ends which render private property legitimate. To judge of the final destination of the institution of property, we must suppose everything rectified, which causes the institution to work in a manner opposed to that equitable principle, of proportion between remuneration and exertion, on which in every vindication of it that will bear the light, it is assumed to be grounded. We must also suppose two conditions realized, without which neither Communism nor any other laws or institutions could make the condition of the mass of mankind other than degraded and miserable. One of these conditions is, universal education; the other, a due limitation of the numbers of the community. With these, there could be no poverty, even under the present social institutions: and these being supposed, the question of Socialism is not, as generally stated by Socialists, a question of flying to the sole refuge against the evils which now bear down humanity; but a mere question of comparative advantages, which futurity must determine. We are too ignorant either of what individual agency in its best form, or Socialism in its best form, can accomplish, to be qualified to decide which of the two will be the ultimate form of human society. [pp. 204–206]

[4] . . . It is for experience to determine how far or how soon any one or more of the possible systems of community of property will be fitted to substitute itself for the "organization of industry" based on private ownership of land and capital. In the meantime we may, without attempting to limit the ultimate capabilities of human nature, affirm, that the political economist, for a considerable time to come, will be chiefly concerned with the conditions of existence and progress belonging to a society founded on private property and individual competition; and that the object to be principally aimed at in the present stage of human improvement, is not the subversion of the system of individual property, but the improvement of it, and the full participation of every member of the community in its benefits. [pp. 212–213]

Book IV, Influence of the Progress of Society on Production and Distribution

Chapter VII, On the Probable Futurity of the Laboring Classes

[1] . . . When I speak, either in this place or elsewhere, of "the laboring classes," or of laborers as a "class," I use those phrases in compliance with custom, and as descriptive of an existing, but by no means a necessary or permanent state of social relations. I do not recognize as either just or salutary, a state of society in which there is any "class" which is not laboring; any human beings, exempt from bearing their share of the necessary labors of human life, except those unable to labor, or who have fairly earned rest by previous toil. So long, however, as the great social evil exists of a non-laboring class, laborers also constitute a class, and may be spoken of, though only provisionally, in that character. [Vol. II, p. 265]

Two views are held of the laboring class: dependence and protection, and self-dependence. On the first, the higher class does the thinking; the relation is "affectionate tutelage on the one side, respectful and grateful deference on the other" (p. 266). This is a backward-looking ideal that has never been realized. Further, "What is there in the present state of society to make it natural that human beings, of ordinary strength and courage, should glow with the warmest gratitude and devotion in return for protection?" (p. 268). The beginnings of reading and education for labor, together with the modern system of production, make only self-dependence feasible.

[7] I agree, then, with the Socialist writers in their conception of the form which industrial operations tend to assume in the advance of improvement; . . . [But] I utterly dissent from the most conspicuous and vehement part of their teaching, their declamations against competition. [p. 297]

Even so, Mill limits the scope of competition in two ways. First, he resists taking competition as the sole explanatory factor of economic behavior: there is also the principle of "custom or usage." There are cases where competition is in no way hindered by monopolies or by governmental interference, but where "prices . . . are much higher in some places than in others not far distant, without its being possible to assign any other cause than that it has always been so: the customers are used to it, and acquiesce in it" (Bk II, Ch IV, 3; vol I, p. 240). Second, he proposes a criterion by which departures from laissez faire would be justified:

Book V: On the Influence of Government

Chapter XI, Of the Grounds and Limits of the Laisser-faire or Non-intervention Principle

[7] . . . Letting alone . . . should be the general practice: every departure from it, unless required by some great good, is a certain evil. . . . [p. 451]
. . . But we must now . . . direct our attention to cases, in which [the general objections to government intervention] are altogether absent, while those which can never be got rid of entirely, are overruled by counter-considerations of still greater importance.

We have observed that, as a general rule, the business of life is better performed when those who have an immediate interest in it are left to take their own course, uncontrolled either by the mandate of the law or by the meddling of any public functionary. The persons, or some of the persons, who do the work, are likely to be better judges than the government, of the means of attaining the particular end at which they aim. Were we to suppose, what is not very probable, that the government has possessed itself of the best knowledge which had been acquired up to a given time by the persons most skilled in the occupation; even then, the individual agents have so much stronger and more direct an interest in the result, that the means are far more likely to be improved and perfected if left to their uncontrolled choice. But if the workman is generally the best selector of means, can it be affirmed with the same universality, that the consumer, or person served, is the most competent judge of the end? Is the buyer always qualified to judge of the commodity? If not, the presumption in favor of the competition of the market does not apply to the case; and if the commodity be one, in the quality of which society has much at stake, the balance of advantages may be in favor of some mode and degree of intervention, by the authorized representatives of the collective interest of the state.

[8] Now, the proposition that the consumer is a competent judge of the commodity, can be admitted only with numerous abatements and exceptions. He is generally the best judge (though even this is not true universally) of the material objects produced for his use. These are destined to supply some physical want, or gratify some taste or inclination, respecting which wants or inclinations there is no appeal from the person who feels them; or they are the means and appliances of some occupation, for the use of the persons engaged in it, who may be presumed to be judges of the things required in their own habitual employment. But there are other things of the worth of which the demand of the market is by no means a test; things of which the utility does not consist in ministering to inclinations, nor in serving the daily uses of life, and the want of which is least felt where the need is greatest. This is peculiarly true of those things which are

chiefly useful as tending to raise the character of human beings. The uncultivated cannot be competent judges of cultivation. Those who most need to be made wiser and better, usually desire it least, and if they desired it, would be incapable of finding the way to it by their own lights. It will continually happen, on the voluntary system, that, the end not being desired, the means will not be provided at all, or that, the persons requiring improvement having an imperfect or altogether erroneous conception of what they want, the supply called forth by the demand of the market will be anything but what is really required. Now any well-intentioned and tolerably civilized government may think without presumption that it does or ought to possess a degree of cultivation above the average of the community which it rules, and that it should therefore be capable of offering better education and better instruction to the people, than the greater number of them would spontaneously demand. Education,

therefore, is one of those things which it is admissible in principle that a government should provide for the people. The case is one to which the reasons of the non-interference principle do not necessarily or universally extend. [pp. 453–455]

[15] It may be said generally, that anything which it is desirable should be done for the general interests of mankind or of future generations, or for the present interests of those members of the community who require external aid, but which is not of a nature to remunerate individuals or associations for undertaking it, is in itself a suitable thing to be undertaken by government: though, before making the work their own, governments ought always to consider if there be any rational probability of its being done on what is called the voluntary principle, and if so, whether it is likely to be done in a better or more effectual manner by government agency, than by the zeal and liberality of individuals. [p. 478]

17

🌿

Darwinism and the Uses of Evolution

Charles Darwin's (1809–1882) theory of biological evolution stimulated a reassessment that was as revolutionary as the work of Newton. In Newton's mechanical model of the physical universe, the mind could still be seen in Cartesian fashion as standing outside it, with a destiny of its own. Darwinian evolution put human beings solidly within the evolutionary process. To many, shaken by the change, it seemed that Darwinism had moved humans from "a little below the angels to a little above the apes." It had profound effects on religious and ethical theory.

The basic possibilities the theory opened up went far beyond what Darwin himself envisaged. His was a limited aim: to discover the process by which species changed and fresh species emerged. His theory involved the convergence of a number of factors: unceasing reduplication of individuals, minute variations from parental stock (*natural variation*), limited nourishment, leading inevitably to a *struggle for existence*. This Darwin regarded as the doctrine of Malthus applied to the whole realm of animal and vegetable. The problem, as he saw it, was to account for the direction in which forms developed. For this he looked to *natural selection* as the primary mechanism: in the competition for existence those variations that confer an advantage make more likely survival of the individuals possessing them and of their progeny. New species thus appear by chance adaptation, and they survive or not as their variations are favorable or not.

The challenge to orthodox thinking was felt immediately. Initially evolution was a thesis about the development of biological forms, about how earlier and later stages were related, and proposing a principle by which the later came out of the earlier. Whether life itself could be explained in comparable ways as developing from inorganic matter was a separate further question. Still, in coming into conflict with the literal biblical story of the creation of the separate species in their modern form, Darwinism presented a challenge to supernatural authority. In the second place, deism had pushed back the role of the divine in the world (from retail to wholesale business, in William James's quip), perhaps as a response to the impressive Newtonian accomplishments. Deists held that God had created the world, furnished its laws, and allowed it to operate without intervention (with perhaps occasional corrections). After Darwin, there may still be an order, but if the order reflects the orderer (as in the design argument for God), then God seems the manager of a slaughterhouse. Against the deist picture of perfectly harmonious nature, economical and benevolent, the Darwinian picture is of a nature bungling, uneconomical, red in tooth and claw.

Most critical for ethics, however, Darwinism jeopardized the distinctive nature of human beings. If what separates us from the animal world—reason, conscience, consciousness, and consciousness of self—can be accounted for naturalistically, then we seem to have lost our centrality. Darwin was not alone here. Other scientific advances concerning the relation of life and inorganic matter—for example, Wöhler's synthesis of urea (1828) and subsequent studies of the carbon molecule and the relation of carbon compounds and proteins— combined with the theory of biological evolution to point toward a broader naturalism. Hitherto in ethics, while some looked to human nature as a source of evil and many more saw human nature as the source of sympathy and mutuality, they had agreed that it was fixed. Now for Darwin human instincts are simply response structures that have become stabilized in the past development of the species insofar as they contributed to survival; under changed conditions they may be harmful. In human nature there are different layers and different tendencies, and we cannot assume that they are all harmoniously related. In any case they have no special moral status.

Darwin recognizes the novelty of his approach to the moral sense. In *The Descent of Man* (1871) he says that no one else has approached it exclusively from the side of natural history. Previous moral philosophers may have looked with awe at the moral consciousness (as Kant did); or taken for granted the sympathetic feelings as the base of morals (as Hume and Smith did); or shifted the base to the work of reason or our cognitive equipment, taking it for granted (as Mill did) that the flexible nature of our sentiments can be counted on to provide stronger feelings for the more serious obligations.

After Darwin the scene changes. The concept of the good loses its direct attachment to that of human nature. To some degree it shifts to an attachment to the idea of the human situation, which in evolutionary terms makes the struggle for survival a primary criterion. Darwin himself simply offers a minimal biological interpretation of the general good—reproductive continuation, with healthy offspring possessing perfect faculties. In the early twentieth century (see Chapter 21) some philosophers attempt to let the good go on its own, just as Kant had sought autonomy for duty; others seek to relate it to the growth of knowledge in a continued effort to read an ethical scenario out of the biological story.

Thus Herbert Spencer (1820–1903) defended a laissez faire capitalism in terms of the *survival of the fittest* (a phrase he coined). Sickly as a child, he was educated at home, and, often left to his own inclinations, he studied mechanics, politics, religion, and (selectively) philosophy. He became a schoolmaster, then chief engineer for the London and Birmingham railroad, where he was intrigued by the fossils turned up in railroad beds. Finally he found his niche in writing, first as editor of the prestigious *Economist* where he came to know the intellectual leaders of the day—including George Eliot, Thomas Carlyle, and T. H. Huxley. From then he devoted himself to writing and produced an enormous corpus. Even before Darwin's *Origin of Species*, Spencer had published *Social Statics* (1851), with strong evolutionary themes. He welcomed Darwin's *Origin*, but he saw evolution as a cosmic process and tried to track the shape it took in all areas— metaphysics, biology, psychology, sociology, and ethics.

Spencer's ethical theory provides an evolutionary base for utilitarianism. Where Bentham treats the pursuit of pleasure and the avoidance of pain as ultimate facts, Spencer looks to evolutionary function and asks us to speculate on what evolution would have been like if what was harmful to survival had been pleasant and conduct helpful to survival painful. Humans would not have survived without pain as a warning signal. Evolution works so that

there will eventually be achieved the greatest individuation along with the greatest mutual dependence—an equilibrium of such kind that each, in fulfilling the wants of his own life, will spontaneously aid in fulfilling the wants of all other lives.[1]

The issue of egoism versus altruism will thereby be overcome. Evolution itself, however, goes on in the *struggle for existence* and the *survival of the fittest*. The extreme individualism from which Spencer derived the individual's rights, especially property rights, limited the state to little more than a policeman's function. Laissez faire capitalism is most in line with evolutionary processes that allow the "fittest" to come to the top; nothing can be done through organized social welfare without ruining the fundamentals of society. His antistatism led him in the latter part of the century to oppose also the imperialistic wars for colonies.

Under the label "Social Darwinism," Spencer's evolutionary philosophy had considerable vogue in America as a justification of economic individualism and business supremacy. Its influence reached even the Supreme Court: witness Justice Holmes's acid rebuke to the majority in *Lochner* (1904): "The Fourteenth Amendment does not enact Mr. Herbert Spencer's *Social Statics*."

T. H. Huxley (1825–1895), a staunch evolutionist, delivered a famous Romanes Lecture,

"Evolution and Ethics" (1893), which broke with Darwin on the relation of ethics to evolution. Where Darwin regards the moral sentiments as of great value to human survival and considers specifically how they manage intermittently to prevail over immediate and pressing appetites, Huxley severs ethics from evolution. Old ingrained responses coming down from the violent struggle for existence are far from an asset to an ethical management of life in a civilized world. The lecture contrasts the carefully tended garden and the jungle—the one is ethics, the other nature, and nature makes constant inroads on ethics.

Whether Friedrich Nietzsche (1844–1900) is to be counted as making use of Darwinian evolutionary theory is a fine point of historical scholarship. Certainly he can be enrolled among those for whom the idea of a changing human world with a biological explanatory base underlies philosophical thought. Most of his remarks on Darwin, however, challenge the view that the struggle for existence (i.e., for life and survival) is fundamental. Instead, the biological struggle is an expression of the psychical will to power. The will to procreate is not a will to life but a will to power. Similarly, the will to pursue an end and for that matter the drive to knowledge are expressions of a drive to dominate. Humans are divided into the few strong and the many weak. Both have the will to power, but in the latter it is frustrated and turned into submissive obedience. The weak make submission a virtue, both to exalt themselves and to tame the strong. The Hebraic-Christian religious tradition expresses this weakness of the masses. To the biblical warning "unless ye become as little children, ye shall not enter the kingdom of heaven," he replies, "But we have no wish whatever to enter the kingdom of heaven: we have become men—so we want the earth." The weakness of the masses is perpetuated by modern democratic and socialist movements. As against these, he looks for the evolutionary emergence of the superman.

Nietzsche's aphoristic style sometimes ob-

[1] *Principles of Ethics*, (New York: D. Appleton, 1896), vol I, p. vii.

scures the fact that he has a well-developed view of how to approach ethics. That view is markedly phenomenological: it looks for the different qualities of feeling and different shades in consciousness. He sets theoretical problems in the context of the historical struggle that he takes to be fundamental. He sees in other theories psychological symptoms of the place the author takes in the historical struggle between the strong and the weak, thus offering a psychological dimension to ethical theory rivaling Marx's sociohistorical analysis.

Prince Peter Kropotkin (1842–1921), a leading philosophical anarchist, is critical of the Darwinian emphasis on struggle among the species as overlooking the cooperativeness that runs through evolution. Building on Darwin's view of sociality, he offers as the guiding thread a principle of solidarity that is stronger than mere love or sympathy. *Mutual Aid* traces this principle in animal life and human history, and how it survives the distortions of power inherent in the growth of the state.

Proposals about which unavoidable path of human development is morally necessary are legion. As scientific advances amplify Darwinian evolutionary theory into the underlying genetic mechanisms, new genetically oriented bases for understanding morality are proposed. A twentieth-century example is sociobiology, which takes almost literally Samuel Butler's remark that a chicken is an egg's way of making an egg.[2] As one researcher put it, the genes do not care whether they take the shape of a giraffe or an assistant professor— they are simply going about their own expansive business. As part of that business, the sociobiologist dreams of understanding morals in human life, especially altruism, in terms of animal and insect life. Whether this is a new illumination or simply a more sophisticated dress for old arguments is the subject of contemporary debate. The problem is fast moving

beyond general sociobiological argument for, with the growing scope of genetic engineering, an alterable human nature comes into view. Rather than large-scale explanatory projections, an exact estimation of the particular impact of culture and the particular action of genetic equipment becomes essential.

One thing in any case is clear: after Darwin the problems of moral philosophy are different. Evolution and the interpretation of evolution become a constituent part of any serious ethical theory.

Charles Darwin
(1809–1882)

The Descent of Man [3]

Ch IV. Comparison of the Mental Powers of Man and the Lower Animals—continued

I fully subscribe to the judgment of those writers who maintain that of all the differences between man and the lower animals, the moral sense or conscience is by far the most important. This sense, as Mackintosh remarks, "has a rightful supremacy over every other principle of human action;" it is summed up in that short but imperious word *ought*, so full of high significance. It is the most noble of all the attributes of man, leading him without a moment's hesitation to risk his life for that of a fellow-creature; or after due deliberation, impelled simply by the deep feeling of right or duty, to sacrifice it in some great cause. Immanuel Kant exclaims, "Duty! Wondrous thought, that workest neither by fond insinuation, flattery, nor by any threat, but merely by holding up thy naked law in the soul, and so extorting for thyself always reverence, if not always obedience; before whom all appetites are dumb, however secretly they rebel; whence thy original?"

This great question has been discussed by many

[2] See E. O. Wilson, *Sociobiology: The New Synthesis* (Cambridge, Mass.: Belknap Press, 1975).

[3] Published 1871; 2d ed. 1874. The selection is from Charles Darwin, *The Descent of Man and Selection in Relation to Sex* (London: John Murray, 1898), vol. I. The footnotes are here selected and edited.

writers of consummate ability; and my sole excuse for touching on it is the impossibility of here passing it over; and because, as far as I know, no one has approached it exclusively from the side of natural history. The investigation possesses, also, some independent interest, as an attempt to see how far the study of the lower animals throws light on one of the highest psychical faculties of man.

The following proposition seems to me in a high degree probable—namely, that any animal whatever, endowed with well-marked social instincts,[a] the parental and filial affections being here included, would inevitably acquire a moral sense or conscience, as soon as its intellectual powers had become as well, or nearly as well, developed as in man. For, *firstly*, the social instincts lead an animal to take pleasure in the society of its fellows, to feel a certain amount of sympathy with them, and to perform various services for them. The services may be of a definite and evidently instinctive nature, or there may be only a wish and readiness, as with most of the higher social animals, to aid their fellows in certain general ways. But these feelings and services are by no means extended to all the individuals of the same species, only to those of the same association. *Secondly*, as soon as the mental faculties had become highly developed, images of all past actions and motives would be incessantly passing through the brain of each individual; and that feeling of dissatisfaction, or even misery, which invariably re-

sults, as we shall hereafter see, from any unsatisfied instinct, would arise, as often as it was perceived that the enduring and always present social instinct had yielded to some other instinct, at the time stronger, but neither enduring in its nature nor leaving behind it a very vivid impression. It is clear that many instinctive desires, such as that of hunger, are in their nature of short duration; and after being satisfied, are not readily or vividly recalled. *Thirdly*, after the power of language had been acquired, and the wishes of the community could be expressed, the common opinion how each member ought to act for the public good would naturally become in a paramount degree the guide to action. But it should be borne in mind that, however great weight we may attribute to public opinion, our regard for the approbation and disapprobation of our fellows depends on sympathy, which, as we shall see, forms an essential part of the social instinct, and is indeed its foundation-stone. *Lastly*, habit in the individual would ultimately play a very important part in guiding the conduct of each member; for the social instinct, together with sympathy, is, like any other instinct, greatly strengthened by habit, and so consequently would be obedience to the wishes and judgment of the community. These several subordinate propositions must now be discussed, and some of them at considerable length.

It may be well first to premise that I do not wish to maintain that any strictly social animal, if its intellectual faculties were to become as active and as highly developed as in man, would acquire exactly the same moral sense as ours. In the same manner as various animals have some sense of beauty, though they admire widely different objects, so they might have a sense of right and wrong, though led by it to follow widely different lines of conduct. If, for instance, to take an extreme case, men were reared under precisely the same conditions as hive-bees, there can hardly be a doubt that our unmarried females would, like the worker-bees, think it a sacred duty to kill their brothers, and mothers would strive to kill their fertile daughters; and no one would think of interfering.[b] Nevertheless, the bee,

---

[a] Sir B. Brodie, after observing that man is a social animal, asks the pregnant question, "Ought not this to settle the disputed question as to the existence of a moral sense?" . . . Mr. J. S. Mill speaks, in his celebrated work, "Utilitarianism," of the social feelings as a "powerful natural sentiment," and as "the natural basis of sentiment for utilitarian morality." Again he says, "Like the other acquired capacities above referred to, the moral faculty, if not a part of our nature, is a natural outgrowth from it; capable, like them, in a certain small degree, of springing up spontaneously." But in opposition to all this, he also remarks, "if, as is my own belief, the moral feelings are not innate, but acquired, they are not for that reason less natural." It is with hesitation that I venture to differ at all from so profound a thinker, but it can hardly be disputed that the social feelings are instinctive or innate in the lower animals; and why should they not be so in man? Mr. Bain and others believe that the moral sense is acquired by each individual during his lifetime. On the general theory of evolution this is at least extremely improbable. The ignoring of all transmitted mental qualities will, as it seems to me, be hereafter judged as a most serious blemish in the works of Mr. Mill.

[b] Mr. H. Sidgwick remarks, "a superior bee, we may feel sure, would aspire to a milder solution of the population question." Judging, however, from the habits of many or most savages, man solves the problem by female infanticide, polyandry, and promiscuous intercourse; therefore it may well be doubted whether it would be by a milder

or any other social animal, would gain in our supposed case, as it appears to me, some feeling of right or wrong, or a conscience. For each individual would have an inward sense of possessing certain stronger or more enduring instincts, and others less strong or enduring; so that there would often be a struggle as to which impulse should be followed; and satisfaction, dissatisfaction, or even misery would be felt, as past impressions were compared during their incessant passage through the mind. In this case an inward monitor would tell the animal that it would have been better to have followed the one impulse rather than the other. The one course ought to have been followed, and the other ought not; the one would have been right, and the other wrong; but to these terms I shall recur.

Sociability.—Animals of many kinds are social; we find even distinct species living together; for example, some American monkeys; and united flocks of rooks, jackdaws, and starlings. Man shows the same feeling in his strong love for the dog, which the dog returns with interest. Everyone must have noticed how miserable horses, dogs, sheep, etc., are when separated from their companions, and what strong mutual affection the two former kinds, at least, show on their reunion. It is curious to speculate on the feelings of a dog, who will rest peacefully for hours in a room with his master or any of the family, without the least notice being taken of him; but if left for a short time by himself, barks or howls dismally. We will confine our attention to the higher social animals; and pass over insects, although some of these are social, and aid one another in many important ways. The most common mutual service in the higher animals is to warn one another of danger by means of the united senses of all. Every sportsman knows, as Dr. Jaeger re-

marks, how difficult it is to approach animals in a herd or troop. Wild horses and cattle do not, I believe, make any danger-signal; but the attitude of any one of them who first discovers an enemy warns the others. Rabbits stamp loudly on the ground with their hind feet as a signal; sheep and chamois do the same with their forefeet, uttering likewise a whistle. . . . [pp. 148–153]

The all-important emotion of sympathy is distinguished from that of love. Adam Smith was mistaken when he attributed the basis of sympathy to our "strong retentiveness of former states of pain or pleasures" (p. 162) so that our suffering raised by seeing someone else's suffering impels us to relieve them. Sympathy is greater with a beloved person.

The explanation may lie in the fact that, with all animals, sympathy is directed solely towards the members of the same community, and therefore towards known, and more or less beloved members, but not to all the individuals of the same species. [Whatever the origin of this complex feeling] it will have been increased through natural selection; for those communities which included the greatest number of the most sympathetic members, would flourish best, and rear the greatest number of offspring.

It is, however, impossible to decide in many cases whether certain social instincts have been acquired through natural selection, or are the indirect result of other instincts and faculties, such as sympathy, reason, experience, and a tendency to imitation; or again, whether they are simply the result of long-continued habit. [p. 163]

The crucial question is:

Why should a man feel that he ought to obey one instinctive desire rather than another? Why is he bitterly regretful, if he has yielded to a strong sense of self-preservation, and has not risked his life to save that of a fellow-creature? or why does he regret having stolen food from hunger? [p. 168]

Perhaps self-sacrificing actions are spontaneous and result from the greater strength of the social or maternal instincts. Where they do not prevail it is clear that they have not

---

method. Miss Cobbe, in commenting on the same illustration, says, the *principles* of social duty would be thus reversed; and by this, I presume, she means that the fulfilment of a social duty would tend to the injury of individuals; but she overlooks the fact, which she would doubtless admit, that the instincts of the bee have been acquired for the good of the community. She goes so far as to say that if the theory of ethics advocated in this chapter were ever generally accepted, "I cannot but believe that in the hour of their triumph would be sounded the knell of the virtue of mankind!" It is to be hoped that the belief in the permanence of virtue on this earth is not held by many persons on so weak a tenure.

acquired greater strength than instincts of self-preservation, hunger, lust, and the like. But they are persistent, and continue to be felt after the action is over.

The instinct of self-preservation is not felt except in the presence of danger; and many a coward has thought himself brave until he has met his enemy face to face. The wish for another man's property is perhaps as persistent a desire as any that can be named; but even in this case the satisfaction of actual possession is generally a weaker feeling than the desire: many a thief, if not an habitual one, after success has wondered why he stole some article.[c]

A man cannot prevent past impressions often repassing through his mind; he will thus be driven to make a comparison between the impressions of past hunger, vengeance satisfied, or danger shunned at other men's cost, with the almost ever-present instinct of sympathy, and with his early knowledge of what others consider as praiseworthy or blamable. This knowledge cannot be banished from his mind, and from instinctive sympathy is esteemed of great moment. He will then feel as if he had been balked in following a present instinct or habit, and this with all animals causes dissatisfaction, or even misery.

[c] Enmity or hatred seems also to be a highly persistent feeling, perhaps more so than any other that can be named. Envy is defined as hatred of another for some excellence or success; and Bacon insists (Essay ix.), "Of all other affections envy is the most importune and continual." Dogs are very apt to hate both strange men and strange dogs, especially if they live near at hand, but do not belong to the same family, tribe, or clan; this feeling would thus seem to be innate, and is certainly a most persistent one. It seems to be the complement and converse of the true social instinct. From what we hear of savages, it would appear that something of the same kind holds good with them. If this be so, it would be a small step in any one to transfer such feelings to any member of the same tribe if he had done him an injury and had become his enemy. Nor is it probable that the primitive conscience would reproach a man for injuring his enemy: rather it would reproach him if he had not revenged himself. To do good in return for evil, to love your enemy, is a height of morality to which it may be doubted whether the social instincts would, by themselves, have ever led us. It is necessary that these instincts, together with sympathy, should have been highly cultivated and extended by the aid of reason, instruction, and the love or fear of God, before any such golden rule would ever be thought of and obeyed.

[T]he swallow affords an illustration, though of a reversed nature, of a temporary, though for the time strongly persistent, instinct conquering another instinct which is usually dominant over all others. At the proper season these birds seem all day long to be impressed with the desire to migrate; their habits change; they become restless, are noisy, and congregate in flocks. While the mother-bird is feeding, or brooding over her nestlings, the maternal instinct is probably stronger than the migratory; but the instinct which is the more persistent gains the victory, and at last, at a moment when her young ones are not in sight, she takes flight and deserts them. When arrived at the end of her long journey, and the migratory instinct has ceased to act, what an agony of remorse the bird would feel, if, from being endowed with great mental activity, she could not prevent the image constantly passing through her mind, of her young ones perishing in the bleak north from cold and hunger.

At the moment of action man will no doubt be apt to follow the stronger impulse; and though this may occasionally prompt him to the noblest deeds, it will more commonly lead him to gratify his own desires at the expense of other men. But after their gratification, when past and weaker impressions are judged by the ever-enduring social instinct, and by his deep regard for the good opinion of his fellows, retribution will surely come. He will then feel remorse, repentance, regret, or shame; this latter feeling, however, relates almost exclusively to the judgment of others. He will consequently resolve more or less firmly to act differently for the future; and this is conscience; for conscience looks backward, and serves as a guide for the future.

The nature and strength of the feelings which we call regret, shame, repentance, or remorse, depend apparently not only on the strength of the violated instinct, but partly on the strength of the temptation, and often still more on the judgment of our fellows. How far each man values the appreciation of others, depends on the strength of his innate or acquired feeling of sympathy, and on his own capacity for reasoning out the remote consequences of his acts. Another element is most important, although not necessary—the reverence or fear of the Gods or Spirits believed in by each man; and this applies especially in cases of remorse. Several critics have objected that, though some slight regret or repentance may be explained by the view advocated in this chapter, it is impossible thus to account for the soul-shaking feeling of remorse. But I can see little force in this objection. My critics do not define what they mean by remorse, and I can find no definition implying more than an overwhelming sense of repentance. Remorse seems to bear the same relation to repentance as rage does to anger, or agony to pain. It is far from strange that an instinct so strong and so generally admired as maternal love should, if disobeyed, lead to the deepest misery, as soon as the impression of the past cause of disobedience is weakened. Even when an action is opposed to no special instinct, merely to know that our friends and equals despise us for it is enough to cause great misery. Who can doubt that the refusal to fight a duel through fear has caused many men an agony of shame? Many a Hindoo, it is said, has been stirred to the bottom of his soul by having partaken of unclean food. [pp. 172–175]

The habit of self-command may be inherited.

Thus at last man comes to feel, through acquired and perhaps inherited habit, that it is best for him to obey his more persistent impulses. The imperious word *ought* seems merely to imply the consciousness of the existence of a rule of conduct, however it may have originated. [p. 177]

On virtue and good:

The virtues which must be practised, at least generally, by rude men, so that they may associate in a body, are those which are still recognised as the most important. [pp. 178–179]

The term, general good, may be defined as the rearing of the greatest number of individuals in full vigour and health, with all their faculties perfect, under the conditions to which they are subjected. [The greatest happiness principle can serve as a secondary guide.] Thus the reproach is removed of laying the foundation of the noblest part of our nature in the base principle of selfishness. [pp. 185–186]

Ch V. On the Development of the Intellectual and Moral Faculties During Primeval and Civilised Times

But another and much more powerful stimulus to the development of the social virtues is afforded by the praise and the blame of our fellow-men. To the instinct of sympathy, as we have already seen, it is primarily due that we habitually bestow both praise and blame on others, while we love the former and dread the latter when applied to ourselves; and this instinct no doubt was originally acquired, like all the other social instincts, through natural selection. At how early a period the progenitors of man, in the course of their development, became capable of feeling and being impelled by the praise or blame of their fellow-creatures, we cannot, of course, say. But it appears that even dogs appreciate encouragement, praise, and blame. The rudest savages feel the sentiment of glory, as they clearly show by preserving the trophies of their prowess, by their habit of excessive boasting, and even by the extreme care which they take of their personal appearance and decorations; for unless they regarded the opinion of their comrades, such habits would be senseless.

They certainly feel shame at the breach of some of their lesser rules, and apparently remorse, as shown by the case of the Australian who grew thin and could not rest from having delayed to murder some other woman, so as to propitiate his dead wife's spirit. Though I have not met with any other recorded case, it is scarcely credible that a savage who will sacrifice his life rather than betray his tribe, or one who will deliver himself up as a prisoner rather than break his parole, would not feel remorse in his inmost soul if he had failed in a duty which he held sacred.

We may therefore conclude that primeval man, at a very remote period, was influenced by the praise and blame of his fellows. It is obvious that the members of the same tribe would approve of conduct which appeared to them to be for the general good, and would reprobate that which appeared evil. To do good unto others—to do unto others as ye would they should do unto you—is the foundation-stone of morality. It is, therefore, hardly possible to exaggerate the importance, during rude times, of the love of praise and the dread of blame. A man who was not impelled by any deep, instinctive feeling to sacrifice his life for the good of others, yet was roused to such actions by a sense of glory, would by his example excite the same wish for glory in other men, and would strengthen by exercise the noble feeling of admiration. He might thus do far more good to his tribe than by begetting offspring with a tendency to inherit his own high character.

With increased experience and reason, man perceives the more remote consequences of his actions, and the self-regarding virtues, such as temperance, chastity, etc., which during early times are, as we have before seen, utterly disregarded, come to be highly esteemed or even held sacred. I need not, however, repeat what I have said on this head in the fourth chapter. Ultimately our moral sense or conscience becomes a highly complex sentiment—originating in the social instincts, largely guided by the approbation of our fellow-men, ruled by reason, self-interest, and in later times by deep religious feelings, and confirmed by instruction and habit. [pp. 201–203]

Herbert Spencer
(1820–1903)

Social Statics [4]

Ch XXV: Poor Laws

[6] Pervading all nature we may see at work a stern discipline, which is a little cruel that it may be very kind. That state of universal warfare maintained throughout the lower creation, to the great perplexity of many worthy people, is at bottom the most merciful provision which the circumstances admit of. It is much better that the ruminant animal, when deprived by age of the vigour which made its existence a pleasure, should be killed by some beast of prey, than that it should linger out a life made painful by infirmities, and eventually die of starvation. By the destruction of all such, not only is existence ended before it becomes burdensome, but room is made for a younger generation capable of the fullest enjoyment; and, moreover, out of the very act of substitution happiness is derived for a tribe of predatory creatures. Note further, that their carnivorous enemies not only remove from herbivorous herds individuals past their prime, but also weed out the sickly, the malformed, and the least

fleet or powerful. By the aid of which purifying process, as well as by the fighting, so universal in the pairing season, all vitiation of the race through the multiplication of its inferior samples is prevented; and the maintenance of a constitution completely adapted to surrounding conditions, and therefore most productive of happiness, is ensured.

The development of the higher creation is a progress toward a form of being capable of a happiness undiminished by these drawbacks. It is in the human race that the consummation is to be accomplished. Civilization is the last stage of its accomplishment. And the ideal man is the man in whom all the conditions of that accomplishment are fulfilled. Meanwhile the well-being of existing humanity, and the unfolding of it into this ultimate perfection, are both secured by that same beneficent, though severe discipline, to which the animate creation at large is subject: a discipline which is pitiless in the working out of good: a felicity-pursuing law which never swerves for the avoidance of partial and temporary suffering. The poverty of the incapable, the distresses that come upon the imprudent, the starvation of the idle, and those shoulderings aside of the weak by the strong, which leave so many "in shallows and in miseries" are the decrees of a large, far-seeing benevolence. It seems hard that an unskilfulness which with all his efforts he cannot overcome, should entail hunger upon the artisan. It seems hard that a labourer incapacitated by sickness from competing with his stronger fellows, should have to bear the resulting privations. It seems hard that widows and orphans should be left to struggle for life or death. Nevertheless, when regarded not separately, but in connection with the interests of universal humanity, these harsh fatalities are seen to be full of the highest beneficence—the same beneficence which brings to early graves the children of diseased parents, and singles out the low-spirited, the intemperate, and the debilitated as the victims of an epidemic.

There are many very amiable people—people over whom in so far as their feelings are concerned we may fitly rejoice—who have not the nerve to look this matter fairly in the face. Disabled as they are by their sympathies with present suffering, from duly regarding ultimate consequences, they pursue a course which is very injudicious, and in the end even cruel. We do not consider it true kindness in a mother to gratify her child with sweetmeats that

---

[4] London, 1851. The selection is from Herbert Spencer, *Social Statics* (New York: D. Appleton, 1886).

are certain to make it ill. We should think it a very foolish sort of benevolence which led a surgeon to let his patient's disease progress to a fatal issue, rather than inflict pain by an operation. Similarly, we must call those spurious philanthropists, who, to prevent present misery, would entail greater misery upon future generations. All defenders of a poor-law must, however, be classed amongst such. That rigorous necessity which, when allowed to act on them, becomes so sharp a spur to the lazy, and so strong a bridle to the random, these paupers' friends would repeal, because of the wailings it here and there produces. Blind to the fact, that under the natural order of things society is constantly excreting its unhealthy, imbecile, slow, vacillating, faithless members, these unthinking, though well-meaning, men advocate an interference which not only stops the purifying process, but even increases the vitiation—absolutely encourages the multiplication of the reckless and incompetent by offering them an unfailing provision, and *dis*courages the multiplication of the competent and provident by heightening the prospective difficulty of maintaining a family. And thus, in their eagerness to prevent the really salutary sufferings that surround us, these sigh-wise and groan-foolish people bequeath to posterity a continually increasing curse.

Returning again to the highest point of view, we find that there is a second and still more injurious mode in which law-enforced charity checks the process of adaptation. To become fit for the social state, man has not only to lose his savageness, but he has to acquire the capacities needful for civilized life. Power of application must be developed; such modification of the intellect as shall qualify it for its new tasks must take place; and, above all, there must be gained the ability to sacrifice a small immediate gratification for a future great one. The state of transition will of course be an unhappy state. Misery inevitably results from incongruity between constitution and conditions. All these evils, which afflict us, and seem to the uninitiated the obvious consequences of this or that removable cause, are unavoidable attendants on the adaptation now in progress. Humanity is being pressed against the inexorable necessities of its new position—is being moulded into harmony with them, and has to bear the resulting unhappiness as best it can. The process *must* be undergone, and the sufferings *must* be endured. [pp. 352–355]

[8] We find, then, that the verdict given by the law of state-duty against a public provision for the indigent is enforced by sundry independent considerations. A critical analysis of the alleged rights, for upholding which a poor-law is defended, shows them to be fictitious. Nor does the plea that a poor-law is a means of distributing compensation for wrongs done to the disinherited people turn out to be valid. The assumption that only by law-administered relief can physical destitution be met, proves to be quite analogous to the assumption that spiritual destitution necessitates a law-administered religion; and consistency requires those who assert the sufficiency of voluntary effort in the one case to assert it in the other also. The substitution of a mechanical charity for charity prompted by the heart is manifestly unfavourable to the growth of men's sympathies, and therefore adverse to the process of adaptation. Legal bounty further retards adaptation by interposing between the people and the conditions to which they must become adapted, so as partially to suspend those conditions. And, to crown all, we find, not only that a poor-law must necessarily fail to diminish popular suffering, but that it must inevitably increase that suffering, both directly by checking the production of commodities, and indirectly by causing a retrogression of character, which painful discipline must at some future day make good. [p. 360]

Ch XXVI: National Education

[1] In the same way that our definition of state-duty forbids the state to administer religion or charity, so likewise does it forbid the state to administer education. Inasmuch as the taking away, by government, of more of a man's property than is needful for maintaining his rights, is an infringement of his rights, and therefore a reversal of the government's function toward him; and inasmuch as the taking away of his property to educate his own or other people's children is not needful for the maintaining of his rights; the taking away of his property for such a purpose is wrong.

Should it be said that the rights of the children are involved, and that state-interposition is required to maintain these, the reply is that no cause for such interposition can be shown until the children's rights have been violated, and that their rights are not violated by a neglect of their education. For, as repeatedly explained, what we call rights are merely arbitrary subdivisions of the general liberty to exercise the faculties; and that only can be called an infringement of rights which actually diminishes this liberty—cuts off a previously existing power to pursue the objects of desire. Now the parent who is careless of a child's education does not do this. The liberty to exercise the faculties is left intact. Omitting instruction in no way takes from a child's freedom to do whatsoever it wills in the best way it can; and this freedom is all that equity demands. Every aggression, be it remembered—every infraction of rights, is necessarily *active*; whilst every neglect, carelessness, omission, is as necessarily *passive*. Consequently, however wrong the nonperformance of a parental duty may be—however much it is condemned by that secondary morality— the morality of beneficence—it does not amount to a breach of the law of equal freedom, and cannot therefore be taken cognizance of by the state. [pp. 360–361]

T. H. Huxley
(1825–1895)

Evolution and Ethics [5]

Prolegomena

[III] . . . No doubt . . . man, physical, intellectual, and moral, is as much a part of nature, as purely a product of the cosmic process, as the humblest weed.

But if, following up this admission, it is urged that, such being the case, the cosmic process cannot be in antagonism with that horticultural process which is part of itself—I can only reply, that if the conclusion that the two are antagonistic is logically absurd, I am sorry for logic, because, as we have seen, the fact is so. The garden is in the same position as every work of man's art; it is a result of the cosmic process working through and by human

energy and intelligence; and, as is the case with every other artificial thing set up in the state of nature, the influences of the latter are constantly tending to break it down and destroy it. [pp. 11–12]

[IV] Not only is the state of nature hostile to the state of art of the garden; but the principle of the horticultural process, by which the latter is created and maintained, is antithetic to that of the cosmic process. The characteristic feature of the latter is the intense and unceasing competition of the struggle for existence. The characteristic of the former is the elimination of that struggle, by the removal of the conditions which give rise to it. The tendency of the cosmic process is to bring about the adjustment of the forms of plant life to the current conditions; the tendency of the horticultural process is the adjustment of the conditions to the needs of the forms of plant life which the gardener desires to raise.

The cosmic process uses unrestricted multiplication as the means whereby hundreds compete for the place and nourishment adequate for one; it employs frost and drought to cut off the weak and unfortunate; to survive, there is need not only of strength, but of flexibility and of good fortune.

The gardener, on the other hand, restricts multiplication; provides that each plant shall have sufficient space and nourishment; protects from frost and drought; and, in every other way attempts to modify the conditions, in such a manner as to bring about the survival of those forms which most nearly approach the standard of the useful, or the beautiful, which he has in his mind.

If the fruits and the tubers, the foliage and the flowers thus obtained, reach, or sufficiently approach, that ideal, there is no reason why the *status quo* attained should not be indefinitely prolonged. So long as the state of nature remains approximately the same, so long will the energy and intelligence which created the garden suffice to maintain it. However, the limits within which this mastery of man over nature can be maintained are narrow. If the conditions of the cretaceous epoch returned, I fear the most skilful of gardeners would have to give up the cultivation of apples and gooseberries; while, if those of the glacial period once again obtained, open asparagus beds would be superfluous, and the training of fruit trees against the most favourable of south walls, a waste of time and trouble.

[5] Thomas H. Huxley, *Evolution and Ethics and Other Essays* (New York: D. Appleton, 1897). "Prolegomena" was added for the publication of the lecture (1894).

But it is extremely important to note that, the state of nature remaining the same, if the produce does not satisfy the gardener, it may be made to approach his ideal more closely. Although the struggle for existence may be at end, the possibility of progress remains. In discussions on these topics, it is often strangely forgotten that the essential conditions of the modification, or evolution, of living things are variation and hereditary transmission. [pp. 13–15]

[X] I see no reason to doubt that, at its origin, human society was as much a product of organic necessity as that of the bees. The human family, to begin with, rested upon exactly the same conditions as those which gave rise to similar associations among animals lower in the scale. Further, it is easy to see that every increase in the duration of the family ties, with the resulting co-operation of a larger and larger number of descendants for protection and defence, would give the families in which such modification took place a distinct advantage over the others. And, as in the hive, the progressive limitation of the struggle for existence between the members of the family would involve increasing efficiency as regards outside competition.

But there is this vast and fundamental difference between bee society and human society. In the former, the members of the society are each organically predestined to the performance of one particular class of functions only. . . .

Among mankind, on the contrary, there is no such predestination to a sharply defined place in the social organism. However much men may differ in the quality of their intellects, the intensity of their passions, and the delicacy of their sensations, it cannot be said that one is fitted by his organization to be an agricultural labourer and nothing else, and another to be a landowner and nothing else. Moreover, with all their enormous differences in natural endowment, men agree in one thing, and that is their innate desire to enjoy the pleasures and to escape the pains of life; and, in short, to do nothing but that which it pleases them to do, without the least reference to the welfare of the society into which they are born. That is their inheritance (the reality at the bottom of the doctrine of original sin) from the long series of ancestors, human and semi-human and brutal, in whom the strength of this innate tendency to self-assertion was the condition of victory in the struggle for existence. That is the

reason of the *aviditas vitae*—the insatiable hunger for enjoyment—of all mankind, which is one of the essential conditions of success in the war with the state of nature outside; and yet the sure agent of the destruction of society if allowed free play within.

The check upon this free play of self-assertion, or natural liberty, which is the necessary condition for the origin of human society, is the product of organic necessities of a different kind from those upon which the constitution of the hive depends. One of these is the mutual affection of parent and offspring, intensified by the long infancy of the human species. [pp. 26–28]

Conscience, the man within, "is the watchman of society, charged to restrain the antisocial tendencies of the natural man within the limits required by social welfare (p. 30)." Law and morals thus restrain the struggle for existence between men in society, but the sympathy inherent in the Golden Rule cannot be carried to an extreme: "What would become of the garden if the gardener treated all the weeds and slugs and birds and trespassers as he would like to be treated, if he were in their place?" (pp. 32–33). The ethical process has advanced far in man, and the progressive modification of civilization is a different process from the competitive struggle in evolution of the species. But no matter how far it goes it cannot root out the inherent equipment that each man brings with him, which reflects the struggle with nature. It is a constant struggle against the state of nature to advance the state of art of an organized polity.

Evolution and Ethics

. . . Where the cosmopoietic energy works through sentient beings, there arises, among its other manifestations, that which we call pain or suffering. This baleful product of evolution increases in quantity and in intensity, with advancing grades of animal organization, until it attains its highest level in man. Further, the consummation is not reached in man, the mere animal; nor in man, the whole or half savage; but only in man, the member of an organized polity. And it is a necessary consequence of his attempt to live in this way; that is, under those conditions which are essential to the full development of his noblest powers.

Man, the animal, in fact, has worked his way to the headship of the sentient world, and has become the superb animal which he is, in virtue of his success in the struggle for existence. The conditions having been of a certain order, man's organization has adjusted itself to them better than that of his competitors in the cosmic strife. In the case of mankind, the self-assertion, the unscrupulous seizing upon all that can be grasped, the tenacious holding of all that can be kept, which constitute the essence of the struggle for existence, have answered. For his successful progress, throughout the savage state, man has been largely indebted to those qualities which he shares with the ape and the tiger; his exceptional physical organization; his cunning, his sociability, his curiosity, and his imitativeness; his ruthless and ferocious destructiveness when his anger is roused by opposition.

But, in proportion as men have passed from anarchy to social organization, and in proportion as civilization has grown in worth, these deeply ingrained serviceable qualities have become defects. After the manner of successful persons, civilized man would gladly kick down the ladder by which he has climbed. He would be only too pleased to see 'the ape and tiger die.' But they decline to suit his convenience; and the unwelcome intrusion of these boon companions of his hot youth into the ranged existence of civil life adds pains and griefs, innumerable and immeasurably great, to those which the cosmic process necessarily brings on the mere animal. In fact, civilized man brands all these ape and tiger promptings with the name of sins; he punishes many of the acts which flow from them as crimes; and, in extreme cases, he does his best to put an end to the survival of the fittest of former days by axe and rope.

I have said that civilized man has reached this point; the assertion is perhaps too broad and general; I had better put it that ethical man has attained thereto. The science of ethics professes to furnish us with a reasoned rule of life; to tell us what is right action and why it is so. Whatever differences of opinion may exist among experts, there is a general consensus that the ape and tiger methods of the struggle for existence are not reconcilable with sound ethical principles.

The hero of our story descended the bean-stalk, and came back to the common world, where fare and work were alike hard; where ugly competitors were much commoner than beautiful princesses; and where the everlasting battle with self was much less sure to be crowned with victory than a turn-to with a giant. We have done the like. Thousands upon thousands of our fellows, thousands of years ago, have preceded us in finding themselves face to face with the same dread problem of evil. They also have seen that the cosmic process is evolution; that it is full of wonder, full of beauty, and, at the same time, full of pain. They have sought to discover the bearing of these great facts on ethics; to find out whether there is, or is not, a sanction for morality in the ways of the cosmos. [pp. 50–53]

. . . The thief and the murderer follow nature just as much as the philanthropist. Cosmic evolution may teach us how the good and the evil tendencies of man may have come about; but, in itself, it is incompetent to furnish any better reason why what we call good is preferable to what we call evil than we had before. Some day, I doubt not, we shall arrive at an understanding of the evolution of the aesthetic faculty; but all the understanding in the world will neither increase nor diminish the force of the intuition that this is beautiful and that is ugly.

There is another fallacy which appears to me to pervade the so-called "ethics of evolution." It is the notion that because, on the whole, animals and plants have advanced in perfection of organization by means of the struggle for existence and the consequent 'survival of the fittest'; therefore men in society, men as ethical beings, must look to the same process to help them towards perfection. I suspect that this fallacy has arisen out of the unfortunate ambiguity of the phrase 'survival of the fittest.' 'Fittest' has a connotation of 'best'; and about 'best' there hangs a moral flavour. In cosmic nature, however, what is 'fittest' depends upon the conditions. Long since, I ventured to point out that if our hemisphere were to cool again, the survival of the fittest might bring about, in the vegetable kingdom, a population of more and more stunted and humbler and humbler organisms, until the 'fittest' that survived might be nothing else but lichens, diatoms, and such microscopic organisms as those which give red snow its colour; while, if it became hotter, the pleasant valleys of the Thames and Isis might be uninhabitable by any animated beings save those that flourish in a tropical jungle. They, as the fittest, the best adapted to the changed conditions, would survive.

Men in society are undoubtedly subject to the cosmic process. As among other animals, multiplication goes on without cessation, and involves severe competition for the means of support. The struggle for existence tends to eliminate those less fitted to adapt themselves to the circumstances of their existence. The strongest, the most self-assertive, tend to tread down the weaker. But the influence of the cosmic process on the evolution of society is the greater the more rudimentary its civilization. Social progress means a checking of the cosmic process at every step and the substitution for it of another, which may be called the ethical process; the end of which is not the survival of those who may happen to be the fittest, in respect of the whole of the conditions which obtain, but of those who are ethically the best.

As I have already urged, the practice of that which is ethically best—what we call goodness or virtue—involves a course of conduct which, in all respects, is opposed to that which leads to success in the cosmic struggle for existence. In place of ruthless self-assertion it demands self-restraint; in place of thrusting aside, or treading down, all competitors, it requires that the individual shall not merely respect, but shall help his fellows; its influence is directed, not so much to the survival of the fittest, as to the fitting of as many as possible to survive. It repudiates the gladiatorial theory of existence. It demands that each man who enters into the enjoyment of the advantages of a polity shall be mindful of his debt to those who have laboriously constructed it; and shall take heed that no act of his weakens the fabric in which he has been permitted to live. Laws and moral precepts are directed to the end of curbing the cosmic process and reminding the individual of his duty to the community, to the protection and influence of which he owes, if not existence itself, at least the life of something better than a brutal savage.

It is from neglect of these plain considerations that the fanatical individualism of our time attempts to apply the analogy of cosmic nature to society. Once more we have a misapplication of the stoical injunction to follow nature; the duties of the individual to the state are forgotten, and his tendencies to self-assertion are dignified by the name of rights.

It is seriously debated whether the members of a community are justified in using their combined strength to constrain one of their number to contribute his share to the maintenance of it; or even to prevent him from doing his best to destroy it. The struggle for existence, which has done such admirable work in cosmic nature, must, it appears, be equally beneficent in the ethical sphere. Yet if that which I have insisted upon is true; if the cosmic process has no sort of relation to moral ends; if the imitation of it by man is inconsistent with the first principles of ethics; what becomes of this surprising theory?

Let us understand, once for all, that the ethical progress of society depends, not on imitating the cosmic process, still less in running away from it, but in combating it. It may seem an audacious proposal thus to pit the microcosm against the macrocosm and to set man to subdue nature to his higher ends; but I venture to think that the great intellectual difference between the ancient times with which we have been occupied and our day, lies in the solid foundation we have acquired for the hope that such an enterprise may meet with a certain measure of success. [pp. 80–83]

The civilizing process has been successful, particularly its role in the growth of knowledge over the preceding two centuries. But

the theory of evolution encourages no millennial anticipations. If, for millions of years, our globe has taken the upward road, yet, some time, the summit will be reached and the downward route will be commenced. . .

Moreover, the cosmic nature born with us and, to a large extent, necessary for our maintenance, is the outcome of millions of years of severe training, and it would be folly to imagine that a few centuries will suffice to subdue its masterfulness to purely ethical ends. Ethical nature may count upon having to reckon with a tenacious and powerful enemy as long as the world lasts. [p. 85]

Still, intelligence and will, guided by knowledge, may do much, and much may be done to change the nature of man himself.

Fifty years after this lecture, Julian Huxley gave another Romanes Lecture, "Evolutionary Ethics," examining the consequences of his grandfather's admission that the gardener himself is part of the evolutionary process. As suggested by the title, the theme is no longer the relation of two external processes—evolution and ethics—but the study of ethics itself as part of the process, employing biology and all the social sciences. As the notochord is succeeded by the skeleton, conscience, with its peremptory guilt feeling, is a rudimentary development in the child to be succeeded by reason, which makes finer discriminations; in its yes-no sharpness conscience is like the biological processes that can be only wholly on or off. Julian carries his evolutionary view beyond the content of morality into ethical theory itself, suggesting that ethics has had different historical aims—first it expressed the human need for solidarity, as a way of survival; then, with group survival gaining in strength, it turned to securing class domination; and now it has the task of fashioning the human attitudes and institutions required by a planetary community.

Friedrich Nietzsche
(1844–1900)

Beyond Good and Evil: Prelude to a Philosophy of the Future [6]

Sections 257–260 offer a more or less systematic account of master and slave moralities. Section 228 criticizes British ethical theory.

[257] Every heightening of the type "Man" has hitherto been the work of an aristocratic society—and it will be so again and again—a society which believes in a long ladder of rank ordering and difference in value between Man and Man and which requires slavery in some sense or other. Without

[6] Translated by Christopher E. Macann for this volume.

that *pathos of distance* which grows out of the ingrained distinction of status, out of the continual outlook and condescension of the ruling caste with regard to subordinates and instruments and out of their equally constant practice of obeying and commanding, of keeping down and keeping at a distance, that other more mysterious pathos could not have arisen either, that longing for an ever new widening of distances within the soul itself, the formation of ever higher, rarer, more remote, more extended, more comprehensive states, in short, precisely that heightening of the type "Man," the continued "self-overcoming of Man," to take up a moral formula in a supra moral sense. To be sure, one should not give in to humanitarian illusions about the historical origins of an aristocratic society (and therefore of the presuppositions of that heightening of the type "Man"): The truth is hard. Let us state unsparingly how hitherto every higher culture on earth has begun. Men who still possess a natural nature, barbarians in that frightful understanding of the word, men of prey, still in possession of unbroken strength of will and lust for power, threw themselves upon weaker, more civilized, more peaceful races, merchants perhaps, or cattle breeders, or upon old mellow cultures in whom precisely the conclusive life force was fizzling out in a brilliant fireworks of culture and corruption. In the beginning the noble caste was always the barbarian caste; their superiority did not consist primarily in physical strength but in strength of soul. They were the more complete human beings (which also means, at every level, the "more complete beasts").

[258] Corruption, as the expression of the fact that anarchy threatens within the instincts and that the foundation of the affects, namely "life," has been shattered. Corruption is something completely different, depending upon the life form in which it manifests itself. When, for example, an aristocracy, like that of France at the beginning of the revolution, throws away its privileges with sublime contempt and sacrifices itself to an excess of moral feeling, that is corruption—it was really only the final act of that centuries-old corruption by virtue of which it had given up its lordly prerogatives step by step and had lowered itself to a mere function of the monarchy (in the end, even to a mere decoration and show-piece). What is essential to a good and healthy aristocracy, however, is that it should not feel itself to be a *function*, whether of the mon-

archy or of the commonwealth, but to be the highest meaning and justification thereof,—that therefore it accepts with a good conscience the sacrifice of innumerable individuals who, for its sake, must be suppressed and reduced down to incomplete beings, to slaves, to instruments. Its fundamental belief must precisely be that society is not supposed to exist for the sake of society, but only as the foundation and scaffolding upon which a select kind of being can be elevated to its higher task and, in general, to a higher *existence*: on an analogy with those sun-seeking vines of Java—they are called Sipo Matador—which encircle an oak with their arms so long and so often that, in the end, high above it but supported by it, they can unfold their crowns in the open light and display their happiness.

[259] To refrain from injury, from violence and exploitation, and put one's will on a par with that of the Other; in a certain rough sense this may result in good conduct among individuals when the relevant conditions are given (namely, in so far as they are actually similar in strength and standards of value and belong together within one body). As soon, however, as one tries to extend this principle, where possible to the point of being the *fundamental principle of society*, it would immediately prove to be what it is, namely, a will to the denial of life, a principle of dissolution and disintegration. Here one has to think one's way right to the very heart of the matter and resist all sentimental weakness. Life itself is *essentially* appropriation, injury, overpowering of the alien and the weak, suppression, hardness, imposition of one's own ways, incorporation and, at least, putting it mildly, exploitation,—but why should one always use precisely those words which, from ages past, have been stamped with a slanderous intent? Even that body within which, as was previously supposed, the individuals treat each other as equals—and this takes place in every healthy aristocracy—must itself, if it is to be a living and not a dying body, do all that towards other bodies which the individuals within it refrain from doing to each other. It will have to be the incarnation of the will to power, it will strive to grow, reach out around itself, draw to itself and gain predominance—not out of any morality or immorality but because it lives and because life is precisely will to power. On no point, however, is the common consciousness of Europeans more resistant to instruction than on this; people now rave everywhere, and

even in the guise of science, about the coming condition of society in which the "exploitive element" will disappear—which sounds to me as if they promised to invent a way of life which would dispense with all organic functions. The "exploitation" does not belong to a corrupt or imperfect and primitive society, but inheres in the essence of the living, as a basic organic function. It is a consequence of the genuine will to power which is precisely the will to life.—Granted that this may be an innovation, *qua* theory,—as a reality, it is the *fundamental fact* of all history. Let us be honest with ourselves, at least to this extent!

[260] In the course of a tour through the many finer and coarser moralities which have hitherto held sway on earth or which still hold sway, I have found that certain traits recurred regularly together and were connected with one another:—until I finally hit upon two basic types and one basic distinction. There is *master morality* and *slave morality*;—I should add at once that in all higher and more mixed cultures one also finds attempts at a mediation of both moralities; and, even more frequently, the interpenetration and mutual misunderstanding of them, indeed sometimes their close juxtaposition—even in the same human being, within one soul. The discrimination of moral values has either originated in a ruling class which delighted in its distinction from the ruled—or among the ruled, slaves and dependents of every kind.

In the first instance, when it is the rulers who determine the concept "good," it is the exalted, proud states of mind which are experienced as conferring distinction and determining the rank order. The eminent human being separates himself from those beings in whom the opposite of such exalted, proud states finds expression. He despises them. One notices right away that in this first kind of morality the antithesis "good" and "bad" means about the same as "eminent" and "despicable" (the antithesis "good" and "evil" is of a different origin). The cowardly, the timid, the petty, those whose thinking is confined to utility, are despised; similarly, the suspicious with their side-long glances, the self-abasing, the dog-like kind of human being who let themselves be maltreated, the miserly flatterers and, above all, the liars—it is a fundamental tenet of all aristocrats that the common people are untruthful. "We, the truthful." Thus the nobility of ancient Greece referred to themselves. It is obvious that moral designations were everywhere applied first to *human beings* and were only derivatively and later applied to *actions*. For which reason it is a gross error when moral historians start out from questions like, "why is sympathetic behavior commended?" The noble type of human being feels *himself* to be a determiner of values; he does not need to be approved of; he judges "what is harmful to me is harmful in itself"; he knows himself to be that which first confers honor upon things; he is a *creator of values*. He honors whatever he recognizes in himself. A morality of this kind is self-glorifying. In the foreground, we find the feeling of fullness, of overflowing power, the happiness of high tension, the consciousness of a wealth that would like to give and bestow—the noble man also helps the unfortunate, but not, or hardly at all, out of sympathy, but more from an impulse engendered by the superabundance of power. The noble man honors himself as one who is powerful and also as one who has power over himself, as one who knows how to speak and to be silent, as one who delights in subjecting himself to severity and hardness, and as one who has respect for all that is severe and hard. "Wotan put a hard heart into my breast," says an old Scandinavian Saga. This is the kind of poetic expression which proceeds quite fittingly from the soul of a proud Viking. Such a type of man is actually proud of the fact that he is not made for pity; for which reason the hero of the Saga adds the warning: "whoever does not already have a hard heart when young will never have one." Those noble and courageous individuals who think in this way are furthest from that morality which precisely sees in sympathy or in acting on behalf of others or in *désintéressement*, the distinguishing characteristic of the moral. Belief in oneself, pride in oneself, a fundamental hostility and irony against "selflessness" belong just as definitely to noble morality as does a light-hearted disdain and caution towards sympathy and the "warm heart." It is the powerful who know how to honor; it is their art, their discovery. Profound reverence for age and tradition—all law rests on this double reverence—belief and prejudice in favor of ancestors and unfavorable to the new-comers is typical in the morality of the powerful; and if, conversely, "men of ideas" believe almost instinctively in "progress" and "the future" and are ever more lacking in respect toward the old, this already suffices to betray the ignoble origin

of these "ideas." A morality of the ruling class is however most particularly alien and aggravating to present-day taste in the severity of its basic principle, that one can only have duties toward one's equals; that, against beings of lower rank, against all that is alien, one may behave as one thinks fit or "as the heart desires" and, in any case, "beyond good and evil": it is here that pity and the like belong. The capacity for and obligation to prolonged gratitude and prolonged revenge—both only amongst one's equals—fineness in retaliation, the idea of refinement in friendship, a certain necessity to have enemies (as outlets, so to speak, for the emotions of envy, aggressiveness, arrogance,—at bottom in order to be capable of being a good friend): all these are typical characteristics of the noble morality which, as indicated, is not the morality of "modern ideas" and is therefore at present difficult to sympathize with as also to unearth and uncover.

It is otherwise with the second type of morality, the *slave morality*. Suppose that the violated, the oppressed, the suffering, the enslaved, those who are weary and uncertain of themselves were to moralize: what would be the common characteristic of their moral evaluations? In all probability, a pessimistic suspicion directed against the entire condition of mankind will come to expression, perhaps a condemnation of man, together with his condition. The slave looks unfavorably upon the virtues of the powerful. He is skeptical and distrustful. He is subtly distrustful of all the good that is honored there—he would like to convince himself that even happiness is not genuine there. Conversely, those qualities which serve to alleviate the suffering of existence are brought to prominence and flooded with light. Here we find pity, the kind and helpful hand, the warm heart, patience, diligence, humility and friendliness are honored,—for here these are the most useful qualities and virtually the only means of enduring the burden of existence. Slave morality is essentially a morality of utility. This is the locus for the origination of that famous antithesis of "good" and "evil." Power and dangerousness are located in the sphere of evil, as also a certain fearfulness and a fineness and strength which do not let contempt get started. According to slave morality therefore evil arouses fear; according to master morality, it is precisely the good which arouses and which seeks to arouse fear, while the "bad" man is taken to be contemptible. The antithesis reaches its highest point when finally, as a result of slave morality, a taint of depreciation now also gets attached to the good of the morality—however slight and well-intentioned it may be—because, in the slavish way of thinking, the good man must at all costs be the innocuous man. He is good natured, easily taken in, a little stupid perhaps, *un bonhomme*. Wherever slave-morality gets the upper hand, language displays a tendency to bring the words "good" and "stupid" closer together.

One last, fundamental distinction: the longing for *freedom*, the instinct for happiness, and the refinement of the feeling of freedom belong just as necessarily to slave morals and morality as artistry and enthusiasm in reverence and dedication are the regular symptoms of an aristocratic way of thinking and evaluating. From this it becomes immediately intelligible why love as *passion*—it is our European speciality—must undoubtedly be of noble origin. As is well known, its discovery is due to the Provencal knightly poets, those splendid, ingenious men of the "gai saber," to which Europe owes so much and almost itself.

[228] May I be forgiven the discovery that all Moral Philosophy hitherto has been tedious and should be classified as a soporific—and that, in my eyes, "virtue" has been impaired by nothing more than by the tediousness of its advocates; although I should not be thought to have overlooked their general usefulness. Much hangs on the fact that as few human beings as possible think about morality;—consequently, a *very great deal* hangs on the fact that morality should not one day become interesting! But not to worry! Things are no different today than they always were. I see no one in Europe who has (or promotes) any idea that thinking about morality might be carried out in a dangerous, captivating or seductive way—that a *fatality* might lurk therein! Consider, for example, the indefatigable, unavoidable English Utilitarians, how ponderously and respectably they walk in Bentham's footsteps, walking along (a Homeric metaphor says it better) even as he himself had walked in the footsteps of the respectable Helvetius (no, this was not a dangerous man, this Helvetius. . . .). No new thought. Nothing in the way of a subtler turn or expression of an old thought, not even a real history of what had been thought before; on the whole an impossible literature unless one knows how to salt it with

some malice. For that old English vice which is called *cant* and consists in *moral tartuffery* has slipped into these moralists too (whom one certainly has to read with circumspection, if one has to read them at all)—only this time hidden under the new form of the scientific spirit. Moreover, a secret struggle against the pangs of conscience is not lacking, a struggle from which it is only natural that a race of former Puritans will suffer in all their scientific dealings with morality. (Is not a moralist the opposite of a Puritan? Namely as a thinker who takes morality to be questionable, worthy of interrogation, in short, as a problem? Should moralizing not be—immoral?) In the last analysis they all want *English* morality to be proved right insofar precisely as humanity or the "general utility" or "the happiness of the greatest number"—no! England's happiness—is best served thereby. They would like at all costs to convince themselves that the striving after *English* happiness, I mean after comfort and fashion, (and, above all, after a seat in Parliament) is, at the same time, the true path of virtue; indeed, that whatever virtue there has been in the world thus far has consisted in just such a striving. Not one of these ponderous, conscience stricken herd animals (who have undertaken to advocate the cause of egoism as the cause of the general welfare) wants to know or even suspect that the "general welfare" is not an ideal, is not a goal, not even a concept that can be specified in some way, but is simply an emetic—that what is right for one simply can not be right for the Other, that the requirement of one morality for all is precisely detrimental to the higher man, in short, that there is an *order of rank* between man and man and consequently also between one morality and another. They are a modest and thoroughly mediocre type of man, these utilitarian Englishmen, and, as was noted above, in so far as they are tedious, one can not think highly enough of their utility. They should even be *encouraged* as has, in part, been attempted in the following rhymes.

Hail to you brave fashion setter
For ever, longer will be better
Always stiff in hand and knee
Uninspiring, ne'er a joker
Everlastingly mediocre
Sans genie et sans esprit

Peter Kropotkin
(1842–1921)

Mutual Aid: A Factor of Evolution [7]

Introduction

[T]o reduce animal sociability to *love* and *sympathy* means to reduce its generality and its importance, just as human ethics based upon love and personal sympathy only have contributed to narrow the comprehension of the moral feeling as a whole. It is not love to my neighbour—whom I often do not know at all—which induces me to seize a pail of water and to rush towards his house when I see it on fire; it is a far wider, even though more vague feeling or instinct of human solidarity and sociability which moves me. So it is also with animals. It is not love, and not even sympathy (understood in its proper sense) which induces a herd of ruminants or of horses to form a ring in order to resist an attack of wolves; not love which induces wolves to form a pack for hunting; not love which induces kittens or lambs to play, or a dozen of species of young birds to spend their days together in the autumn; and it is neither love nor personal sympathy which induces many thousand fallow-deer scattered over a territory as large as France to form into a score of separate herds, all marching towards a given spot, in order to cross there a river. It is a feeling infinitely wider than love or personal sympathy—an instinct that has been slowly developed among animals and men in the course of an extremely long evolution, and which has taught animals and men alike the force they can borrow from the practice of mutual aid and support, and the joys they can find in social life.

The importance of this distinction will be easily appreciated by the student of animal psychology, and the more so by the student of human ethics. Love, sympathy and self-sacrifice certainly play an immense part in the progressive development of our moral feelings. But it is not love and not even sympathy upon which Society is based in mankind. It is the conscience—be it only at the stage of an instinct—of human solidarity. It is the unconscious

recognition of the force that is borrowed by each man from the practice of mutual aid; of the close dependency of every one's happiness upon the happiness of all; and of the sense of justice, or equity, which brings the individual to consider the rights of every other individual as equal to his own. Upon this broad and necessary foundation the still higher moral feelings are developed. . . .

. . . [T]here are a number of evolutionists who may not refuse to admit the importance of mutual aid among animals, but who, like Herbert Spencer, will refuse to admit it for Man. For primitive Man—they maintain—war of each against all was *the* law of life. In how far this assertion, which has been too willingly repeated, without sufficient criticism, since the times of Hobbes, is supported by what we know about the early phases of human development, is discussed in the chapters given to the Savages and the Barbarians.

The number and importance of mutual-aid institutions which were developed by the creative genius of the savage and half-savage masses, during the earliest clan-period of mankind and still more during the next village-community period, and the immense influence which these early institutions have exercised upon the subsequent development of mankind, down to the present times, induced me to extend my researches to the later, historical periods as well; especially, to study that most interesting period—the free mediaeval city-republics, of which the universality and influence upon our modern civilization have not yet been duly appreciated. And finally, I have tried to indicate in brief the immense importance which the mutual-support instincts, inherited by mankind from its extremely long evolution, play even now in our modern society, which is supposed to rest upon the principle: "every one for himself and the State for all," but which it never has succeeded, nor will succeed in realizing. [pp. xii–xv]

Self-assertion has played a significant role in the evolution of mankind, but it is "something quite different from, and far larger and deeper than, the petty, unintelligent narrow-mindedness, which, with a large class of writers, goes for 'individualism' and 'self-assertion'." Beyond the self-assertion that is profit seeking there is another self-assertion that is

[7] Rev. ed. (London: William Heinemann, 1904; first published 1902).

constructive in building institutions. "Nor have history-making individuals been limited to those whom the historians have represented as heroes" (pp. xvi–xvii).

Ch I: Mutual Aid Among Animals

The conception of struggle for existence as a factor of evolution, introduced into science by Darwin and Wallace, has permitted us to embrace an immensely wide range of phenomena in one single generalization, which soon became the very basis of our philosophical, biological, and sociological speculations. An immense variety of facts:—adaptations of function and structure of organic beings to their surroundings; physiological and anatomical evolution; intellectual progress, and moral development itself, which we formerly used to explain by so many different causes, were embodied by Darwin in one general conception. We understood them as continued endeavours—as a struggle against adverse circumstances—for such a development of individuals, races, species and societies, as would result in the greatest possible fulness, variety, and intensity of life. It may be that at the outset Darwin himself was not fully aware of the generality of the factor which he first invoked for explaining one series only of facts relative to the accumulation of individual variations in incipient species. But he foresaw that the term which he was introducing into science would lose its philosophical and its only true meaning if it were to be used in its narrow sense only— that of a struggle between separate individuals for the sheer means of existence. And at the very beginning of his memorable work he insisted upon the term being taken in its "large and metaphorical sense including dependence of one being on another, and including (which is more important) not only the life of the individual, but success in leaving progeny." [*Origin of Species*, Chap. iii.]

While he himself was chiefly using the term in its narrow sense for his own special purpose, he warned his followers against committing the error (which he seems once to have committed himself) of overrating its narrow meaning. In *The Descent of Man* he gave some powerful pages to illustrate its proper, wide sense. He pointed out how, in numberless animal societies, the struggle between separate individuals for the means of existence disappears, how *struggle* is replaced by *co-operation*, and

how that substitution results in the development of intellectual and moral faculties which secure to the species the best conditions for survival. He intimated that in such cases the fittest are not the physically strongest, nor the cunningest, but those who learn to combine so as mutually to support each other, strong and weak alike, for the welfare of the community. "Those communities," he wrote, "which included the greatest number of the most sympathetic members would flourish best, and rear the greatest number of offspring" (2nd edit., p. 163). The term, which originated from the narrow Malthusian conception of competition between each and all, thus lost its narrowness in the mind of one who knew Nature.

Unhappily, these remarks, which might have become the basis of most fruitful researches, were overshadowed by the masses of facts gathered for the purpose of illustrating the consequences of a real competition for life. . . . Nay, on the very pages just mentioned, amidst data disproving the narrow Malthusian conception of struggle, the old Malthusian leaven reappeared—namely, in Darwin's remarks as to the alleged inconveniences of maintaining the "weak in mind and body" in our civilized societies (ch. v). As if thousands of weak-bodied and infirm poets, scientists, inventors, and reformers, together with other thousands of so-called "fools" and "weak-minded enthusiasts," were not the most precious weapons used by humanity in its struggle for existence by intellectual and moral arms, which Darwin himself emphasized in those same chapters of *Descent of Man*.

It happened with Darwin's theory as it always happens with theories having any bearing upon human relations. Instead of widening it according to his own hints, his followers narrowed it still more. And while Herbert Spencer, starting on independent but closely-allied lines, attempted to widen the inquiry into that great question, "Who are the fittest?" . . . the numberless followers of Darwin reduced the notion of struggle for existence to its narrowest limits. They came to conceive the animal world as a world of perpetual struggle among half-starved individuals, thirsting for one another's blood. They made modern literature resound with the war-cry of *woe to the vanquished*, as if it were the last word of modern biology. They raised the "pitiless" struggle for personal advantages to the height of a biological principle which man must submit to as well, under the menace of otherwise succumbing in a world based upon mutual extermination. Leaving aside the economists who know of natural science but a few words borrowed from second-hand vulgarizers, we must recognize that even the most authorized exponents of Darwin's views did their best to maintain those false ideas. . . .

. . . Huxley's view of nature had as little claim to be taken as a scientific deduction as the opposite view of Rousseau, who saw in nature but love, peace, and harmony destroyed by the accession of man. In fact, the first walk in the forest, the first observation upon any animal society, or even the perusal of any serious work dealing with animal life . . . cannot but set the naturalist thinking about the part taken by social life in the life of animals, and prevent him from seeing in Nature nothing but a field of slaughter, just as this would prevent him from seeing in Nature nothing but harmony and peace. Rousseau had committed the error of excluding the beak-and-claw fight from his thoughts; and Huxley committed the opposite error; but neither Rousseau's optimism nor Huxley's pessimism can be accepted as an impartial interpretation of nature.

As soon as we study animals—not in laboratories and museums only, but in the forest and the prairie, in the steppe and the mountains—we at once perceive that though there is an immense amount of warfare and extermination going on amidst various species, and especially amidst various classes of animals, there is, at the same time, as much, or perhaps even more, of mutual support, mutual aid, and mutual defence amidst animals belonging to the same species or, at least, to the same society. Sociability is as much a law of nature as mutual struggle. Of course it would be extremely difficult to estimate, however roughly, the relative numerical importance of both these series of facts. But if we resort to an indirect test, and ask Nature: "Who are the fittest: those who are continually at war with each other, or those who support one another?" we at once see that those animals which acquire habits of mutual aid are undoubtedly the fittest. They have more chances to survive, and they attain, in their respective classes, the highest development of intelligence and bodily organization. If the numberless facts which can be brought forward to support this view are taken into account, we may safely say that mu-

tual aid is as much a law of animal life as mutual struggle, but that, as a factor of evolution, it most probably has a far greater importance, inasmuch as it favours the development of such habits and characters as insure the maintenance and further development of the species, together with the greatest amount of welfare and enjoyment of life for the individual, with the least waste of energy. [pp. 1–6]

The very faculties which help in survival—language, imitation, accumulation of experience—are social products. A review of mutual aid in human history shows that while warriors fought and exterminated each other, the masses continued to live their daily lives and to carry on their daily toil. Study is needed of that daily life and how the masses maintained their own social organization, their mutual aid and support, even under theocracy or autocracy. Even when the state crushed liberties, the current of mutual aid flowed on. The masses, by creating new economic and social institutions, ethical systems and religions, gradually extended mutual aid to larger and larger aggregates. This has been hindered by the state's claim to be the sole representative of union between its subjects and initiator of further development. By absorbing social functions the state favored an unbridled, narrow-minded individualism and relieved citizens of their obligations to one another. Biology read this individualism into the animal world, and history and political economy proclaimed its importance.

Ch VII: Mutual Aid Amongst Ourselves

It seems, therefore, hopeless to look for mutual-aid institutions and practices in modern society. What could remain of them? And yet, as soon as we try to ascertain how the millions of human beings live, and begin to study their everyday relations, we are struck with the immense part which the mutual-aid and mutual-support principles play even now-a-days in human life. Although the destruction of mutual-aid institutions has been going on in practice and theory, for full three or four hundred years, hundreds of millions of men continue to live under such institutions; they piously maintain them and endeavour to reconstitute them where they have ceased to exist. In our mutual relations every one of us has his moments of revolt against the fashionable individualistic creed of the day, and actions in which men are guided by their mutual-aid inclinations constitute so great a part of our daily intercourse that if a stop to such actions could be put all further ethical progress would be stopped at once. Human society itself could not be maintained for even so much as the lifetime of one single generation. [pp. 228–229]

The usual history, concentrating on military power, autocracy, and rule by the richer classes, has given a one-sided picture. The undoubted origin of our ethical conceptions lies in the practice of mutual aid.

18

Ethics of Self-Realization: Green, Bradley, Bosanquet

In the last part of the nineteenth century and the beginning of the twentieth, the growing strength of evolutionism and the continued vigor of utilitarianism provoked a reaction. Against the naturalization of man and ethics implicit in evolutionism, it was argued that consciousness and self-consciousness—that which allows humans to stand apart from the world and to frame ideas of what the world should be and of loyalties and ideals—cannot be explained by natural laws. Utilitarianism provides no bridge between the individual and the community when the community is taken as the aggregate of individuals, each seeking his own happiness; hence there is no rational ground for any concern for the common good. The intransigent character of this problem can be seen best in the way Henry Sidgwick (1838–1900) analyzed ethical egoism in his classic *The Methods of Ethics* (1874). In the posthumous sixth edition (1901) the editor includes in the introduction a manuscript in which Sidgwick describes his quest in ethical theory. The Utilitarianism of Mill gave him "relief from the ap-

parently external and arbitrary pressure of moral rules which I had been educated to obey, and which presented themselves to me as to some extent doubtful and confused; and sometimes, even when clear, as merely dogmatic, unreasoned, incoherent." [1] He was attracted by Mill's double view—that each man seeks his own happiness and that he ought to seek the general happiness—but eventually found that it did not cohere. Thus he set off on the quest for the relation of duty and interest. The path led from Mill to Kant, from Kant to Butler, from Butler back to Aristotle. Butler persuaded him that man is under the dual guidance of self-interest and conscience; Aristotle seemed to be presenting largely the common sense morality of the cultivated Greek. What Sidgwick had first seen as the confused intuitions of his moral education he now came to see as a system of rules tending to the promotion of general happiness. To this his attitude was

[1] *The Methods of Ethics*, 6th ed. (London: Macmillan, 1901), p. xv.

474

"Adhere generally, deviate and attempt reform only in exceptional cases in which,—notwithstanding the roughness of hedonistic methods,—the argument against Common Sense is decisive." [2]

But the relation of individual and general interest still lacked a basis. Many practical paths between them could be traced, such as the frequent coincidence of individual and general happiness, the existence of sympathy and the personal experience of it, the hopes of future alignment of general and individual well-being. But in decision in the present, Sidgwick says in the concluding chapter of the sixth edition (dealing with the mutual relations of the different approaches), the egoist can claim that a person is concerned with the quality of his own existence in a way in which he is not concerned with that of others. Hence he can regard it as irrational to sacrifice his own happiness to that of another. Such egoism sets itself forth as rational and right, and there appears to be no ultimate proof that it is irrational and wrong. The only resort is to a basic intuition—as clearly axiomatic as any axiom in arithmetic or geometry—that "it is 'right' and 'reasonable' for me to treat others as I should think that I myself ought to be treated under similar conditions, and to do what I believe to be ultimately conducive to universal Good or Happiness." [3] Lacking a theological guarantee of rewards and punishments, practical reason cannot resolve a serious conflict between self-interest and duty.

A different approach to the conflict of self-interest and duty is taken by self-realization ethics. This is the path followed by some philosophical idealists in the latter part of the nineteenth century. Hoping to halt the naturalization of man in evolutionary theory and the almost predatory individualism in ethics, they renewed the struggle in ethical theory on what

it is to be an individual, with greater vigor and more refinement. Its effort was to find a spiritual principle *within* the human being, in knowledge as well as morals, and a social character *within* what it means to be a self.

The central figures in Britain were T. H. Green, F. H. Bradley, and Bernard Bosanquet. In Green there is a strong mixture of the Hegelian and the Kantian. Bradley and Bosanquet are more explicitly neo-Hegelian, but their general world view shifts to a less temporal systemic wholeness of things. The readings select from Green his criticism of utilitarianism and evolutionary ethics; from Bradley, his social grounding of ethics, and from Bosanquet his conception of the state as an ethical whole.

T. H. Green
(1836–1882)

Green's assessment of evolutionary ethics is that the existence of knowledge in human thought and the sense of the moral in human consciousness cannot be explained by anything less than a unifying spiritual principle within. Just as knowledge cannot be reduced to collections of sensations (as in the empiricist tradition of Hume), so morality cannot be reduced to the conflict of desires. Similarly, he is critical of the utilitarian conceptions of the individual (simply a collection of discrete experiences and desires) and of the community (simply a collection of individuals). A truer understanding of the self and its unified development restores its relation to the community. Green carried his outlook into practice by supporting movements for social reform in England, for a greater role by government in ensuring protection of children against child labor, for factory legislation, and other social services. This was consonant with his view that the community had the positive

[2] Ibid., p. xx.
[3] Ibid., p. 505.

responsibility for the development of the individual in his self-relization.

He first examines the consequences of an evolutionary reduction of man to a part of the natural world.

Prolegomena to Ethics [4]

If it is the chief business of the moralist to distinguish the nature and origin of the pleasures and pains which are supposed to be the sole objects of human desire and aversion, to trace the effect upon conduct of the impulses so constituted, and to ascertain the several degrees in which different courses of action, determined by anticipation of pleasure and pain, are actually productive of the desired result; then the sooner the methods of scientific experiment and observation are substituted for vague guessing and an arbitrary interpretation by each man of his own consciousness, the better it will be. Ethics, so understood, becomes to all intents and purposes a science of health, and the true moralist will be the physiologist who, making the human physique his specialty, takes a sufficiently wide view of his subject. [p. 4]

There is an alternative: a moral sense that is a determining agent in the inner life and of which no natural history can be given. Now grant that the evolutionists have a theory that

professes to explain, on the method of a natural history conducted according to the principle of evolution, the process by which the human animal has come, according to the terminology in vogue, to exhibit the phenomena of a moral life—to have a conscience, to feel remorse, to pursue ideals, to be capable of education through appeals to the sense of honour and of shame, to be conscious of antagonism between the common and private good, and even sometimes to prefer the former. [p. 9]

This will still not be enough. The moralist should explain not only how men act, but how they *ought* to act. It is obvious that "to a being who is simply a result of natural forces an in-

junction to conform to their laws is unmeaning." Hence an evolutionary moralist must abolish the practical or prescriptive part of morals:

He will not mock the misery of him who fails, nor flatter the self-complacency of him who prospers, by speaking of a happiness that is to be obtained by conformity to the laws of nature, when he knows that, according to his own principles, it is a struggle for existence determined by those laws which has brought the one to his wretchedness and the other to his contentment. He will rather set himself to show how the phraseology of 'ought' and 'ought not,' the belief in a good attainable by all, the consciousness of something that should be though it is not, may according to his philosophy be accounted for. Nor, if he has persuaded himself that the human consciousness, as it is, can be physically accounted for, will he find any further difficulty in thus explaining that language of moral injunction which forms so large an element in its expression. He will probably trace this language to the joint action of two factors—to the habit of submission to the commands of a physical or political superior, surviving the commands themselves and the memory of them, combined with that constant though ineffectual wish for a condition of life other than his own, which is natural to a being who looks before and after over perpetual alternations of pleasure and pain.

The elimination of ethics, then, as a system of precepts, involves no intrinsic difficulties other than those involved in the admission of a natural science that can account for the moralisation of man. The discovery, however, that our assertions of moral obligation are merely the expression of an ineffectual wish to be better off than we are, or are due to the survival of habits originally enforced by physical fear, but of which the origin is forgotten, is of a kind to give us pause. It logically carries with it the conclusion, however the conclusion may be disguised, that, in inciting ourselves or others to do anything because it ought to be done, we are at best making use of a serviceable illusion. And when this consequence is found to follow logically from the conception of man as in his moral attributes a subject of natural science, it may lead to a reconsideration of a doctrine which would otherwise have

[4] Oxford: Clarendon Press, 1883.

been taken for granted as the most important outcome of modern enlightenment. As the first charm of accounting for what has previously seemed the mystery of our moral nature passes away, and the spirit of criticism returns, we cannot but enquire whether a being that was merely a result of natural forces could form a theory of those forces as explaining himself. We have to return once more to that analysis of the conditions of knowledge, which forms the basis of all Critical Philosophy whether called by the name of Kant or no, and to ask whether the experience of connected matters of fact, which in its methodical expression we call science, does not presuppose a principle which is not itself any one or number of such matters of fact, or their result.

Can the knowledge of nature be itself a part or product of nature, in that sense of nature in which it is said to be an object of knowledge? This is our first question. If it is answered in the negative, we shall at least have satisfied ourselves that man, in respect of the function called knowledge, is not merely a child of nature. We shall have ascertained the presence in him of a principle not natural, and a specific function of this principle in rendering knowledge possible. The way will then be so far cleared for the further question which leads us, in the language of Kant, from the Critique of Speculative to that of Practical Reason: the question whether the same principle has not another expression than that which appears in the determination of experience and through it in our knowledge of a world—an expression which consists in the consciousness of a moral ideal and the determination of human action thereby. [pp. 10–11]

The emphasis throughout is on the distinction between mere wants and consciously designed objects that would embody the wants.

It is this consciousness which yields, in the most elementary form, the conception of something that *should be* as distinct from that which *is*, of a world of practice as distinct from that world of experience of which the conception arises from the determination by the Ego of the receptive senses. [pp. 91–92]

Appetites or wants become motives in human beings only with the presentation of the want by self-conscious subjects to themselves, along with the idea of self-satisfaction in the filling of the want. A desire implies a distinction of the self from its desire and the real world, a consciousness of the real world as not at that point in harmony with it, and an effort to adjust the world to procure satisfaction of the desire (p. 137). The *ought* is not, however, primary in the Kantian sense. Underlying it is the idea of an absolute or common good, "a good common to the person conceiving it with others, and good for him and them, whether at any moment it answers their likings or no" (p. 213).

F. H. Bradley
(1846–1924)

The dominant direction of idealist ethics became the search for system in life and consciousness, and the interpretation of the systematizing tendency as self-expression or self-realization. In this sense the Hegelian influence predominated over the Kantian. It is most militantly expressed in F. H. Bradley's *Ethical Studies*, which has remained the standard text for self-realizationist ethics.

Ethical Studies [5]

The preface to the first edition states the conviction that in the end ethical theories rest on metaphysical and psychological preconceptions. The key to understanding moral ideas of responsibility and moral ideals lies in taking seriously the common man's moral beliefs rather than theoretical distortions issuing from an erroneous psychology. For example, determinists would have us not responsible for our actions because in principle they are predictable. The plain man, however, would not ob-

[5] London: Henry S. King, 1876.

ject to predictions of what he does if they are deduced from his *character* and not from a wholly external set of facts. From this it is a short philosophical step to the kind of self-determination as freedom that had been sketched in outline by Kant and given social content by Hegel, including the justice of punishment, not as medicine for reforming the individual nor as external sanction but as an imputation of guilt. The necessitarian (determinist) ignores the rational self as will and the act of volition that alone gives meaning to imputing the act and guilt to a person.

The fundamental ideas of the hedonistic calculus are criticized: pleasure is so fleeting that the very idea of summing its flux makes no sense. Similarly, Kant's duty for duty's sake is too abstract in emphasizing only the form of the will and not its empirical content. Bradley's own view is presented in a chapter entitled, "My Station and Its Duties." The good will, for morality, is the will of living finite beings. It is both above us and within us.

It is an organism and a moral organism; and it is conscious self-realization, because only by the will of its self-conscious members can the moral organism give itself reality. It is the self-realization of the whole body, because it is one and the same will which lives and acts in the life and action of each. It is the self-realization of each member, because each member can not find the function, which makes him himself, apart from the whole to which he belongs; to be himself he must go beyond himself, to live his life he must live a life which is not *merely* his own, but which, none the less, but on the contrary all the more, is intensely and emphatically his own individuality. . . . It is real, and real for me. It is in its affirmation that I affirm myself, for I am but as a 'heart-beat in its system.' And I am real in it; for, when I give myself to it, it gives me the fruition of my own personal activity, the accomplished ideal of my life which is happiness. In the realized idea which, superior to me, and yet here and now in and by me, affirms itself in a continuous process, we have found the end, we have found self-realization, duty, and happiness in one;—yes, we have found ourselves, when we have found our station and its duties, our function as an organ in the social organism. [pp. 147–148]

The point of the notion of a person's station in life, taken for granted in a nineteenth-century class society, is that the self is social to the core; if stripped of the language of culture, ambition, occupational division, roles, and models of ordinary life, it will be found empty; and it never has existed first by itself without these elements of its "station."

He grows up in an atmosphere of example and general custom, his life widens out from one little world to other and higher worlds, and he apprehends through successive stations the whole in which he lives, and in which he has lived. Is he now to try and develope his 'individuality,' his self which is not the same as other selves? Where is it? What is it? Where can he find it? The soul within him is saturated, is filled, is qualified by, it has assimilated, has got its substance, has built itself up from, it *is* one and the same life with the universal life, and if he turns against this he turns against himself; if he thrusts it from him, he tears his own vitals; if he attacks it, he sets his weapon against his own heart. He has found his life in the life of the whole, he lives that in himself, 'he is a pulse-beat of the whole system, and himself the whole system.' [p. 156]

Systems and institutions, from the family to the nation, are the body of the moral life, while its spirit is the will of the members, as organs of the whole. Hence a purely personal morality is an unreality, just as moral institutions without personal morality are carcasses.

To be moral, I must will my station and its duties; that is, I will to particularize the moral system truly in a given case; and the other side to this act is, that the moral system wills to particularize itself in a given station and functions, *i.e.* in my actions and by my will. . . . The objective organism, the systematized moral world, is the reality of the moral will; my duties on the inside answer to due functions on the outside. [p. 163]

The antithesis of individualism and despotism is thus broken down by understanding the community as the real moral organism. Morality is evident then because it exists all around us, and the member's realization of the whole within itself is necessary for achieving his individuality.

Bradley's general philosophy as developed in later works on logic and metaphysics has the same holistic character: in every judgment the real subject is the whole of reality, so that to say, for example, "Socrates is mortal," is more accurately to say, "The world accepts the connection Socrates-mortal." All judgments are partially true and partially false, and the whole truth is to be found only in the whole of reality.

In the case of morality, since the nature of man is being worked out in history—an evolution that humanizes man and realizes him as an infinite whole—the station and its duties at any time are relative, but still real.

Morality is "relative," but is none the less real. At every stage there is the solid fact of a world so far moralized. There is an objective morality in the accomplished will of the past and present, a higher self worked out by the infinite pain, the sweat and blood of generations, and now given to me by free grace and in love and faith as a sacred trust. It comes to me as the truth of my own nature, and the power and the law, which is stronger and higher than any caprice or opinion of my own. [p. 172]

In this Hegelian (not Darwinian) sense, Bradley accepts "evolution." But it requires a qualification of his notion of my station and its duties, for some few may detach themselves from the present state in the light of a greater perfection. Not realized in their own community, they begin to think of a goodness that transcends any particular community. Accordingly Bradley goes on to consider ideal morality. It is not a morality that can take the place of social morality but arises from the effort to resolve the conflicts and contradictions inevitable to any social morality.

From a twentieth-century view, it is clear that part of the force in the outlook of Bradley

and Green comes from the critique of individualistic psychology and the social theory of utilitarianism. In their understanding of both the integration of a self and the pervasive role of social influence in human development they are much closer to the lessons of contemporary psychology and social science. Self-realizationist ethics also has metaphysical themes, often with theological overtones, carrying the values of a spirituality beyond the pursuit of self-interest. Interestingly, their ethic had room for different social commitments: Green worked out a social liberalism with an emphasis on public welfare, whereas Bradley remained highly conservative in his social judgments. Bosanquet's writings on the state as the all-inclusive community were to have an even more turbulent social career.

Bernard Bosanquet
(1848–1923)

Bosanquet wrote widely on metaphysics, logic, value theory, and social philosophy. In the theory of knowledge he opposes both rationalist intellectual intuitions and empiricist sensory atoms. Interpretation enters everywhere, and the test of truth is coherence. This is, however, a matter of degree. Principles furnished by the intellect are acceptable to the extent that they serve a unifying function in the body of knowledge, and items of sense are likewise intelligible by virtue of their function of furthering the coherence of that body. Reality or Truth is the systematic totality or "Absolute"; it is an organic whole, neither (epistemologically) a deductive system nor (metaphysically) a separate superreality. To traditional religion this verged on pantheism.

In discussing values Bosanquet shifts the emphasis from the temporal achievement of ends or purposes through means to their systematic character. In ordinary life we think of the relation of means and ends as temporal: the means has value because of the end it will produce. But this is the finite or partial perspective: it considers only a possibly valuable end in isolation and the resources available to realize it. To determine whether it is a really valuable end, we would have to place it in the system in which it plays a part. The same holds for a means. Value thus pertains ultimately not to partial individuality but to the supreme value of the whole.

Bosanquet applies these abstract reflections to the relation of the individual and the state.

The Philosophical Theory of the State [6]

Ch IV: The Problem of Political Obligation More Radically Treated

1. The reader will no doubt have observed that the theory dealt with in the last chapter [Mill on liberty and Spencer] belongs to the general type of what is currently known as Individualism. For several reasons I have preferred not to make use of this hackneyed word. In the first place, it is very hackneyed; and the employment of such terms takes all life and expressiveness out of philosophy. And, in the next place, Individualism may mean many things, and in its fullest, which is surely, for the student of philosophy, its truest meaning, it is far too good for the theories under discussion. An "Individual" may be "individual" or indivisible because he has so little in him, that you cannot imagine it possible to break him up into lesser parts; or because, however full and great his nature, it is so thoroughly one, so vital and so true to itself, that, like a work of art, the whole of his being cannot be separated into parts without ceasing to be what it essentially is. In the former case the "individual" is an "atom"; in the latter he is "a great individuality." The sense in which we shall make use of the notion of the individual, so far as we use it at all, will be the latter and not the former. And, therefore, we shall as far as possible discard the hackneyed

[6] London: Macmillan, 1899.

term "Individualism," which embodies the former meaning only.

If then we are to coin an expression which will indicate the common features of the theories outlined in the previous chapter, we may venture upon some such phrase as *"prima facie* theories," or "theories of the first look." By this I do not mean that they stand in the same rank with the views of the Greek thinkers, who, undisturbed by previous speculation, saw the great facts of social experience with a freshness and wholeness of vision with which they can never be seen again. The "first look" of our own day is of a different kind. It is the first look of the man in the street or of the traveller, struggling at a railway station, to whom the compact self-containedness and self-direction of the swarming human beings before him seems an obvious fact, while the social logic and spiritual history which lie behind the scene fail to impress themselves on his perceptive imagination.

We see then that these theories of the first appearance are mainly guided by this impression of the natural separateness of the human unit. For this reason, as we noted, the experience of self-government is to them an enigma, with which they have to compromise in various ways. And because their explanations of it are not true explanations but only compromises, they rest on no principle, and dictate no consistent attitude. For Bentham all solid right is actually in the State, though conceived by himself as a means to individual ends; for Mill, it is divided between the State and the individual, by a boundary which cannot be traced and therefore cannot be respected; for Herbert Spencer all right is in the individual, and the State has become little more than a record office of his contracts and consents.

The assumption common to the theories in question is dictated by their very nature. It is not precisely, as is often supposed to be the case, that the individual is the end to which Society is a means. Such a definition fails to assign a character which is distinctive for any social theories whatever. For Society, being, at the lowest rate, a plurality of individuals, whatever we say of the individual may be construed as true of Society and *vice versa*, so long as all individuals are understood in the same sense as one. Thus the "means" and the "ends" are liable to change places, as, for practical purposes, we saw that they did in Bentham. The ethical term "altruism" illustrates this principle. It shows that by taking "the individual" as the "end," nothing is determined as to the relation between each individual and all, and it remains a matter of chance how far it is required of "each" individual, in the name of the welfare of "the individual," to sacrifice himself to "all."

The fact is that the decisive issue is not whether we call the "individual" or "society" the "end"; but what we take to be the nature at once of individuals and of society. This is the question of principle; and views which are at one in this have nothing which can in principle keep them apart, although they may diverge to the seemingly opposite poles of the liberty of each and the welfare of all. We have observed this sliding from one narrowness to its opposite, as between Bentham, Mill, and Herbert Spencer.

The root idea then, of the views which we have been discussing, is simply that the individual or society—it makes no difference which we take—is what it *prima facie* appears to be. . . .

[According to such theories the social whole is] composed of units A, B, C, etc., who, *as they stand, and just as they seem to us when we rub against them in daily intercourse,* are taken to be the organs and centres of human life. From this assumption all the rest follows. Each of us, A, B, C, and all the others, seems to be, and to a great extent in the routine of life actually is, self-complete, self-satisfied, and self-willed. To each of us, A, B, or C, all the rest are "others." They are "like" him; they are "repetitions" of him, but they are not himself. He knows that they are something to himself; but this "something" is still "something else," and even in ethical reflection he is apt to call his recognition of it "altruism"—an indefinite claim and feeling, touching his being at its margin of contact with neighbouring circles, the centres of which are isolated.

To the individual and society thus conceived—A, B, C, and the rest—it is plain that government can be nothing but self-protection. It is, in fact, a form of the impact of "others," scientifically minimised, and accepted because it is minimised. For this reason it is, as we saw throughout, alien to the self, and incapable of being recognised as springing from a common root with the spontaneous life which we pretend to be aware of only within our private magic circle. Then the forcible impact of B and C upon the circle of A is a necessary evil, a diminution, *pro tanto*, of A. And the more altruistic

A is, the more he will recognise this, as affecting not himself only, but B and C also.

It is for this reason that, on the views in question, all law and government necessarily remain formal and negative as compared with the substantive and positive ends of the self. The maintenance of "liberty," of the circular or hexagonal fences round A, B, C, and the rest, is conceived as involving no determinate type of life, no relation to the ends which the units pursue within their hexagons. If in any way the self went beyond itself, and A recognised a positive end and nature which peremptorily bound him to B and the others, it would be impossible to keep this nature and end from reflecting themselves in the determinate content of the conditions of association between them. The assumption would be destroyed which keeps "government" alien to "self," and it would be possible to consider in what sense and for what reason the nature of a spiritual animal turns against itself with the dualism which the paradox of self-government embodies, and that in pursuit of its true unity. [pp. 79–84]

An alternative conception of the relation of the individual and society can be based on Rousseau's idea of the *general will.* There is a moral and collective body that is a common self, and a "real will" as opposed "to our trivial and rebellious moods," an organic unity as contrasted with a mere aggregate, a distinction between real and apparent interest (even in the case of private interests).

In order to obtain a full statement of what we will, what we want at any moment must at least be corrected and amended by what we want at all other moments; and this cannot be done without also correcting and amending it so as to harmonise it with what others want, which involves an application of the same process to them. . . . Such a process of harmonising and readjusting a mass of data to bring them into a rational shape is what is meant by criticism. And criticism, when applied to our actual will, shows that it is not our real will; or, in the plainest language, that what we really want is something more and other than at any given moment we are aware that we will, although the wants which we are aware of lead up to it at every point. [p. 119]

In the light of such ideas the concepts of liberty and the state are refashioned.

Ch VI: The Conception of Liberty, as Illustrated by the Foregoing Suggestions

1. . . . [W]e can speak, without a contradiction, of being forced to be free. It is possible for us to acquiesce, as rational beings, in a law and order which on the whole makes for the possibility of asserting our true or universal selves, at the very moment when this law and order is constraining our particular private wills in a way which we resent, or even condemn. Such a law and order, maintained by force, which we recognise as on the whole the instrument of our greatest self-affirmation, is a system of rights; and our liberty, or to use a good old expression, our liberties, may be identified with such a system considered as the condition and guarantee of our becoming the best that we have it in us to be, that is, of becoming ourselves. [p. 127]

4. . . . Any system of institutions which represents to us, on the whole, the conditions essential to affirming such a will, in objects of action such as to constitute a tolerably complete life, has an imperative claim upon our loyalty and obedience as the embodiment of our liberty. The only question that can arise is whether the system is that which it pretends to be. But even if rebellion is a duty, it can only be so because the imperative obligation, as we recognise it, is irreconcilable with the particular system which claims our obedience in its name. The imperative claim of the will that wills itself is our own inmost nature, and we cannot throw it off. This is the ultimate root of political obligation. [p. 149]

5. . . . The State . . . is not merely the political fabric. The term State accents indeed the political aspect of the whole, and is opposed to the notion of an anarchical society. But it includes the entire hierarchy of institutions by which life is determined, from the family to the trade, and from the trade to the Church and the University. It includes all of them, not as the mere collection of the growths of the country, but as the structure which gives life and meaning to the political whole, while receiving from it mutual adjustment, and therefore expansion and a more liberal air. The State, it might be said, is thus conceived as the operative criticism of all institutions—the modification and adjustment by which they are capable of playing a rational part in the object of human will. And criticism, in this sense, is the life of institutions. . . . It follows that the State, in this sense, is, above all things, not a number of persons, but a working conception of life. . . . But a complete reflective conception of the end of the State, comprehensive and free from contradiction, would mean a complete idea of the realisation of all human capacity, without waste or failure. Such a conception is impossible owing to the gradual character of the process by which the end of life, the nature of the good, is determined for man. The Real Will, as represented by the State, is only a partial embodiment of it.

. . . The State is the fly-wheel of our life. Its system is constantly reminding us of duties, from sanitation to the incidents of trusteeship, which we have not the least desire to neglect, but which we are either too ignorant or too indolent to carry out apart from instruction and authoritative suggestion. We profit at every turn by institutions, rules, traditions, researches, made by minds at their best, which, through State action, are now in a form to operate as extensions of our own minds. . . . All individuals are continually reinforced and carried on, beyond their average immediate consciousness, by the knowledge, resources, and energy which surround them in the social order, with its inheritance, of which the order itself is the greatest part. . . . [pp. 150–153]

Views of the state such as Bosanquet's were influential and controversial in the early twentieth century when a growing nationalism found congenial ideas of duty to the state. (Comparable and even more extreme theories calling for individual readiness to sacrifice were prevalent in a Germany that had only recently achieved nationhood in Bismarck's wars against Austria and France.) Philosophical irrationalism combined a rejection of reason with an adulation of violence as expressive of vital will. Thus a spirit quite unlike Bosanquet's found its way into cultural circles. The most virulent form of this irrationalism was Mussolini's view of the individual as a molecule in the state.

The prominence assigned the state in these

theories was resisted in many quarters, but particularly by the dominant liberalism and the utilitarian tradition. Bertrand Russell, who briefly had been entranced by Hegel, thought it right to disobey the state and went to prison for his opposition to British participation in World War I. Marxian theory, of course, condemned the state as the executive arm of the dominant class rather than the ethical unification of the whole society. Strong movements in liberalism and socialism ventured pluralist ideas of social organization, regarding the state as simply one institution among many. For example, guild socialism proposed that society be organized by occupational representation, with a central coordinating body of limited tasks. The United States, with its entrenched individualism, did not feel this whole struggle, for its political structure was then closer to Spencer's purely "policeman theory of the state," in which individuals pursue their own plans and interests while the state acts largely to prevent violent conflict. Interestingly, Josiah Royce (1855–1916), the outstanding proponent of philosophical idealism in the United States (although not tied to self-realizationists), much as he valued the sense of community, tied moral consciousness not to the state but to the phenomenon of loyalty, in which the individual chooses his own cause or commitment to an ideal, and through this to the development of a generalized loyalty to loyalty.[7]

The longer-range contributions of the self-realizationist ethics were thus to reveal the complexity of the individual, to insist on interpretations of individuality as a focus in ethical theory, and to preserve some element of loyalty or communal commitment beyond individual desire or preference. These became part of the agenda for the twentieth century.

[7] *The Philosophy of Loyalty* (New York: Macmillan, 1908).

The Twentieth Century

Ethics in the twentieth century has been rich and varied. Accordingly it is here presented in the diversity of its schools. Starting with a vast inheritance, not only of theories but of problems, it debated whether right or good, or perhaps virtue, is primary; increasingly sharp distinctions of fact and value, theory and practice, social and individual; whether to gear ethics to universal rules or particular decisions; duels between absolutism and relativism; even the radical possibility that ethics is noncognitive rather than cognitive; whether ethics is autonomous and independent, or dependent on accumulated knowledge. While some moral philosophers refined and sharpened these problems, others sought to reinterpret and even dissolve them, particularly by resort to the psychological and social sciences. At the same time a general rising sense of the pervasiveness of moral problems and of questions of moral decision in one area after another has brought a larger awareness of the need for guiding practical moral action and so of the opportuneness of theoretical redirection in ethics.

Making peace between the right and the good has always been a difficult task. The conceptual struggle for primacy between these two notions continued into our century. The ancient tradition and the utilitarian in modern times refers everything ultimately to the good, whereas Kant gives primacy to duty. A utilitarianism in terms of welfare dominated the earlier part of the twentieth century, to be challenged in the second half of the century by a renewed rights approach, most evident in the appeal to human rights and justice (Chapter 23). Some attempts were made to fit right and good together. W. D. Ross's *The Right and the Good* (1930) treated them as coordinate notions contingently related, while C. I. Lewis (Chapter 21) assigned them different functions. In the 1920s and 1930s John Dewey proposed a comprehensive theory of their relationship (Chapter 21). In the 1970s Ronald Dworkin suggested a derivation of both sides from the idea of equality; others have attempted to undercut the sharp opposition of the two (Chapter 23).

Today there is a renewed interest in the third option—virtue. The moral aim here, reminiscent of the ancient Stoics, is to develop the kind of character with which a person can face changing obligations or altered goals and goods. Whether this is not simply a pendulum swing in ethical theory may depend on whether it becomes informed by the psychology of personality and character and the historical understanding of their social determinants, as well as on the basic aspirations embedded in the virtues.

The twentieth-century dichotomy of *fact* and *value* generalizes the more traditional dichotomy of *is* and *ought*. Hume expressed surprise that reasonings about what *is* the case so often ended up with judgments about what *ought* to be the case, and Kant made the sharpest distinction between the *ought* of morality and the *is* of scientific propositions. Later the value side of the dichotomy came to include not merely the *ought* but also the *good* or the *worthwhile* or the *valuable*. This problem appeared in Mill's attempt to go from what is desired to what is desirable. In the twentieth century it became a commonplace—permeating not only moral philosophy but the social sciences and education—that facts and values were utterly distinct, that science was concerned with facts and not with values, that it had accordingly no responsibilities as science to anything but truth. It carried the implication that moral judgments, since not factual, are incapable of scientific verification.

Related to the fact-value question is whether there is moral *knowledge*. One path takes Hume's formulation, "morals are more properly felt than judged of," perhaps more literally than he intended. Both emotivist and ordinary language ethics construe moral utterances as psychological expressions functioning practically instead of as assertive propositions (Chapter 21). Others, however, turn to the idea of reason or rationality, to see what moral propositions or mandates can be derived from it; many find methods and imperatives common to science and ethics, allowing of no break with the cognitive (Chapter 21).

The relation of theory and practice crosses with the cognitive-noncognitive and fact-value issues through an increasing emphasis on the role of moral utterances as practical rather than theoretical. Practices and institutions were taken to have a constitutive role rather than being simply a field of application for preestablished moral ideas (Rawls, Chapter 23). In the 1970s problems of practice—medical ethics, environmental ethics, legal ethics, ethics of technology—came to occupy a major place in the work of moral philosophers. Their feedback to theoretical problems remains still to be estimated. Since mid-century, decision and policy sciences have become more closely linked with ethical theory. With growing emphasis on practice and its problems, the tendency has grown (in line with pragmatist analysis—Chapter 21) to see theory linked to test and use.

Since at least the seventeenth century ethics has been constructed on an individualist basis with social conclusions drawn from it, rather than on a social basis with individual morality finding its place within it. Thus social contract theory, though aiming at social conclusions, generally begins with the individual. Kant and the Utilitarians do the same. The basic individualism continued into the twentieth century, except where Hegelian influence was strong, as in Marxian ethics, or where it combined with Darwinian influence, as in Dewey. In spite of its subtleties, the individualist approach has difficulties in meeting large-scale social problems. Increasingly, the question is raised whether the individualist formulation does not disguise its social character (e.g., Foot, Chapter 20). Indeed, the analytic approach in the second half of the century, in spite of its individualism, came to see the practical as involving *social* practices, and the rules guiding these practices as essentially traditional or social. Others attempt to refashion the problem (Dewey, Chapter 21; Buber, Chapter 22).

Whether morality primarily involves moral laws and universals and moral essences, or whether it is directed to particular decisions, continued to be a perennial problem. In the early part of the century, phenomenological ethics stressed the intuitive grasp of moral essences as prior to questions of application (Chapter 22). W. D. Ross, and H. A. Prichard in *Moral Obligation* (1949), although both believed that we grasp moral truths by intuition, put forward contrasting views of what our intuition grasps: Ross thought we grasped universal rules, but since they were only *prima facie* and in practice would conflict, we had certainty only in the rules, not in their application; for Prichard we grasp with certainty what is right or wrong in the particular situation, and our rules reflect only rough generalizations. Later in the century, here-and-now decision emerged as a central moral phenomenon for theories as wide apart as the existentialist, with its focus on absolute responsibility (Sartre, Chapter 22), and mathematical decision theory in policy science.

Traditional attempts to affirm a single morality for all mankind were for the most part absolutistic, whether on the basis of religion, reason, or a fixed human nature. Religious wars and conflicts about reason and human nature had not shaken the conviction that there is a definite right and wrong. On the other hand, relativism was stimulated by the discovery of variation in moral judgment (particularly among different peoples) and the suspicion that no ultimate resolution of differences was possible. Some philosophers simply abandoned the whole attempt to find what was natural for human beings, as had the Skeptics in ancient times. Others took a position of qualified relativism, as did Hume, for whom virtue is relative to the utilities of different societies.

Ethical relativism took the offensive on a broader scale in the twentieth century, largely because it seemed a lesson from anthropology. Edward Westermarck's *Ethical Relativity* (1932), resulting from a quarter-century's comparative study of the moral beliefs of different societies, concluded:

> that the moral consciousness is ultimately based on emotions, that the moral judgment lacks objective validity, that the moral values are not absolute but relative to the emotions they express.[1]

[1] Edward Westermarck, *Ethical Relativity* (Patterson, N.J.: Littlefield, Adams & Co., 1960; originally published 1932), p. 289.

Then Ruth Benedict's *Patterns of Culture* (1934) gave new shape to the controversy. Whereas Westermarck had dealt with discrete moral items and separate institutions (such as the history of marriage), for Benedict relativity meant different total configurations of cultures. Human living takes different ultimate forms in different societies, and—the moral implication seemed to be—the differences should be respected and the various patterns regarded as "equally valid." Benedict was responding to the mounting racism of the period and in part making a plea for tolerance. Critics quickly differentiated the descriptive variation of moral patterns from the ethical position of liberal tolerance, which would be sorely tested by the brutalities of the Nazi pattern.

What lesson is to be drawn from the variety in the moral patterns?[2] The problem need not be cross-cultural. It is raised also by variations among individuals in the same culture. Emotivism accepted the fact of ultimate difference (Chapter 20), while phenomenologists attempted direct refutation by insisting on the objectivity of values (Chapter 22).

Finally, a question that became particularly acute in our century is that of the independence or autonomy of ethics.[3] At one extreme it was argued, on grounds of either subject matter or method, that biology, psychology, history, metaphysics, and religion are irrelevant to moral judgment. At the other extreme it was argued that ethics cannot be isolated but is related to and has to draw on the full range of human knowledge. The controversy raged through the whole century. The extreme opposing views are represented by Moore (Chapter 19) and Dewey (Chapter 21). In between, positivist and analytic ethics argued that *metaethics*—a purely logical-linguistic analysis of ethical ideas—is the proper business of moral philosophy. Scientifically minded philosophers, (e.g., R. B. Perry, Stephen Pepper, Abraham Edel) defended the dependence of ethical theory on biological, psychological, social, and historical materials.[4] Of course, no one denied that the best knowledge available should be used for *means* to good ends; the issue was rather the meaning of ethical ideas and what they presuppose. At stake were different ideas of the enterprise of ethics.

Closely related was the question of how to construe the relation of ethical theory and practical moral problems. While some saw "applied ethics" as a

---

[2] Benedict went on in later work to look for cross-cultural bases of assessment. Philosophers also went into the field to study the moral patterns, and attempted to analyze and estimate the impact of the variety. See Richard B. Brandt, *Hopi Ethics* (1954), and John Ladd, *The Structure of a Moral Code* (1957), dealing with the Navaho. For analyses of ethical relativity, see Abraham Edel, *Ethical Judgment: The Use of Science in Ethics* (1955); Richard B. Brandt, *Ethical Theory, The Problems of Normative and Critical Ethics* (1959), Chapter 11; and May Edel and Abraham Edel, *Anthropology and Ethics* (1959, 1970).

[3] This is to be distinguished from the claims for the autonomy of the individual, the individualist ideal of a maximum field of free judgment and decision for the person.

[4] Perry's *General Theory of Value* (1926) built ethical theory on a biopsychological concept of interest. Pepper's *The Sources of Value* (1958) used the concept of purpose, from the psychologist E. C. Tolman, as a theoretical foundation stone. Edel's *Ethical Judgment* (1955) examined each of the human sciences in turn to see what contribution they made to ethical theory.

straightforward task of applying moral principles to particular situations and professions, others were working out complex models of interrelation. This problem and the growing consciousness of the role that the whole range of knowledge has to play in ethics are major issues on the contemporary agenda for ethics (Chapter 24).

19

The Autonomy of Ethics

Twentieth-century ethical discussion, at least in the English-speaking world, is often counted as beginning with G. E. Moore's *Principia Ethica* (1903) and its thesis—that good, the basic concept of ethics, is unanalyzable and to be grasped only by a special kind of intuition. Although the thesis was controversial, antagonists and protagonists alike accepted his statement of the problem: "What is the nature of the evidence, by which alone any ethical proposition can be proved or disproved, confirmed or rendered doubtful?" And all accepted that much more analysis of ethical ideas was needed than the tradition had provided.

According to Moore, writers on ethics had confused two questions: What things have intrinsic value and ought to exist for their own sake (that is, are intrinsically *good*), and what actions ought we to perform? On the first, his fundamental question, Moore not only distinguished instrumental good from intrinsic good but also what *things* are good from what is the meaning of the term "good." His thesis was that "good" cannot be defined because

it designates a simple quality that cannot be broken up into parts. In this respect it is like "yellow": while we can say many things about yellow, such as that it is a primary color and has a certain wave length, when we ask what yellow is we can only say that it is what it is and nothing else. So too we know the property good immediately; it cannot be reduced to simple terms; it is unique and unanalyzable. The only kinds of statements that can be made about it are synthetic ones about whether and to what degree an object (whether complex or simple) has this simple property or about causal relations between other things and those that have this property.

In addition Moore called *good* a "nonnatural" quality, a much disputed concept he later abandoned. Originally this meant just that *good* was not part of the description one would give of a thing, but rather an attribute that could be (properly) considered only after the description (e.g., friendship, pleasure, consciousness of pleasure) was complete. *Natural* properties were descriptive of objects in the world, whether ordinary objects, scientific ones, or metaphysical and theological. To identify good with pleasure or the will of God was for Moore a basic fallacy—he called it the "naturalistic fallacy." His arguments in the first chapter of *Principia* are worth careful examination, especially what came to be known as the "open-question argument"—that you could always ask of any proposed definition of good whether the object appearing in the defining role, say *pleasure*, was itself good. That such a question is meaningful shows that the idea of good has a surplus meaning beyond pleasure. The effect is to make good or intrinsic value indefinable and entirely cut off from all forms of fact. Thus Moore is committed in his theory of *good* to the sharpest of separations between values and facts; no facts, whether about happiness, or psychology, history, biology, or theology, can settle the question of what is good. Good can only be intuited by the individual who holds up in his or her mind the object that is under consideration. Chapters II to IV of *Principia* are especially interesting for the way in which they examine utilitarian, evolutionist, and metaphysical theory to find the naturalistic fallacy being committed or, as we would say in more recent terminology, the values being smuggled in through concepts of needs, adaptation and development, survival of the fittest, nature of reality, and so on.

On the question of what actions we ought to perform, that is, the question of right and duty, Moore's answer is different. The question concerns ways in which we can produce the greatest good in the world (thus "right" is defined in terms of "good") and involves empirical issues of causation. No moral *rule* can sell itself as self-evident or authoritative without an examination of its empirical claims. But when Moore looks at this process he finds it so complicated that the only reasonable thing he thinks we can do is to conform to customary or generally accepted rules, whatever they may be. So what started out as a tough attitude toward morality turns into a soft acceptance. Nevertheless, the total effect of Moore's theory was felt as liberating, since on the fundamental question of the good (on which judgments of right depend) decision lies with the vision (intuition) of the individual; it is not a theory of empirical learning or verification. It fed into the stream of twentieth-century demand for individual *autonomy*.

A new generation in moral philosophy turning its back on the nineteenth century took from Moore the notion that here was a new logical way of doing ethics that broke with old mistaken ways. That is how he was greeted and how he continued to be regarded when twentieth-century philosophy began to look back to its revolutionary changes. Nevertheless there was controversy from the beginning. Bernard Bosanquet wrote in a review of Moore's book,

He has hampered himself with ideas not less dogmatic than those of the most hide-bound orthodoxy; and he is not yet therefore a critic in the true sense, a critic who can take the standpoint of that which he criticizes.[1]

For the most part, in twentieth-century analytic ethics Moore was treated with intellectual piety even when not followed. He was always said to have an important point, but not exactly what he had taken it to be. Each writer offered his own interpretation of what Moore should have said to make his point.

The selections from Moore show the structure of his thesis. The selection from John Maynard Keynes shows the direct impact of Moore's theory on a generation of students at Cambridge at the beginning of the century.

[1] *Mind*, n.s., 13 (April 1904): 261.

G. E. Moore
(1873–1958)

Principia Ethica [2]

The preface complains that moral philosophers try to answer questions without first analyzing them. Two questions should be distinguished:

These two questions may be expressed, the first in the form: What kind of things ought to exist for their own sakes? the second in the form: What kind of actions ought we to perform? I have tried to shew exactly what it is that we ask about a thing, when we ask whether it ought to exist for its own sake, is good in itself or has intrinsic value; and exactly what it is that we ask about an action, when we ask whether we ought to do it, whether it is a right action or a duty.

But from a clear insight into the nature of these two questions, there appears to me to follow a second most important result: namely, what is the nature of the evidence, by which alone any ethical proposition can be proved or disproved, confirmed or rendered doubtful. Once we recognise the exact meaning of the two questions, I think it also becomes plain exactly what kind of reasons are relevant as arguments for or against any particular answer to them. It becomes plain that, for answers to the *first* question, no relevant evidence whatever can be adduced: from no other truth, except themselves alone, can it be inferred that they are either true or false. We can guard against error only by taking care, that, when we try to answer a question of this kind, we have before our minds that question only, and not some other or others; but that there is great danger of such errors of confusion I have tried to shew, and also what are the chief precautions by the use of which we may guard against them. As for the *second* question, it becomes equally plain, that any answer to it *is* capable of proof or disproof—that, indeed, so many different considerations are relevant to its truth or falsehood, as to make the attainment of probability very difficult, and the attainment of certainty impossible. Never-

theless the *kind* of evidence, which is both necessary and alone relevant to such proof and disproof, is capable of exact definition. Such evidence must contain propositions of two kinds and of two kinds only: it must consist, in the first place, of truths with regard to the results of the action in question—of *causal* truths—but it must *also* contain ethical truths of our first or self-evident class. Many truths of both kinds are necessary to the proof that any action ought to be done; and any other kind of evidence is wholly irrelevant. . . .

. . . I have endeavoured to discover what are the fundamental principles of ethical reasoning; and the establishment of these principles, rather than of any conclusions which may be attained by their use, may be regarded as my main object. I have, however, also attempted, in Chapter VI, to present some conclusions, with regard to the proper answer of the question 'What is good in itself?' which are very different from any which have commonly been advocated by philosophers. I have tried to define the classes within which all great goods and evils fall; and I have maintained that very many different things are good and evil in themselves, and that neither class of things possesses any other property which is both common to all its members and peculiar to them.

In order to express the fact that ethical propositions of my *first* class are incapable of proof or disproof, I have sometimes followed Sidgwick's usage in calling them 'Intuitions.' But I beg it may be noticed that I am not an 'Intuitionist,' in the ordinary sense of the term. Sidgwick himself seems never to have been clearly aware of the immense importance of the difference which distinguishes his Intuitionism from the common doctrine, which has been generally been called by that name. The Intuitionist proper is distinguished by maintaining that propositions of my *second* class—propositions which assert that a certain action is *right* or a *duty*—are incapable of proof or disproof by any enquiry into the results of such actions. I, on the contrary, am no less anxious to maintain that propositions of *this* kind are *not* 'Intuitions,' than to maintain that propositions of my *first* class *are* Intuitions.

Again, I would wish it observed that, when I call such propositions 'Intuitions,' I mean *merely* to assert that they are incapable of proof; I imply nothing whatever as to the manner or origin of our cognition of them. Still less do I imply (as most

[2] Cambridge: Cambridge University Press, 1965; originally published 1903.

Intuitionists have done) that any proposition what-ever is true, *because* we cognise it in a particular way or by the exercise of any particular faculty: I hold, on the contrary, that in every way in which it is possible to cognise a true proposition, it is also possible to cognise a false one. [pp. viii–x]

Since there are too many things to be dealt with to judge particular goods, "it is not the business of the ethical philosopher to give per-sonal advice or exhortation" (p. 3). It is the business of the philosopher, however, to de-cide what general things are good or bad (Chapter VI). The philosopher's job is thus not identified purely with analysis, as later move-ments that utilized his ideas maintained in sharply distinguishing metaethics from norma-tive ethics—the former analyzing ethical dis-course, the latter making moral judgments.

Moore regards his analysis as dealing not with language but with qualities we experience and realities we discern. Thus, although the intellectual grandfather of much of the techni-cal moral philosophy of the mid-century, he is not himself a partisan of linguistic analysis as it came to be known. Nevertheless, Moore shares with this later analysis the aim of giving the *correct analysis* of the ideas with which he deals—good and right and other ethical no-tions—not, as a pragmatist might take the aim, of designing a conceptual program to be judged by what it could accomplish.

The selections are organized to show as sys-tematically as possible in brief compass how Moore carries out the program stated in his preface.

(A) Treatment of good or intrinsic value as a simple object of thought and the sole ethical term with reference to which all others must be explicated.

(B) Demonstration that good cannot be iden-tified with any natural or metaphysical property. The "naturalistic fallacy" is the name for such attempts.

(C) Critique of other moral philosophies, to show that they do commit the naturalistic fallacy.

(D) How statements about intrinsic values are established or accepted.

(E) How, and with what certainty, state-ments of right, duty, or obligation are established.

(F) What things are found to have intrinsic value and the method of determination.

(A) Good as a Simple Object of Thought

[T]his question, how 'good' is to be defined, is the most fundamental question in all Ethics. That which is meant by 'good' is, in fact, except its con-verse 'bad,' the *only* simple object of thought which is peculiar to Ethics. [p. 5]

Whenever we judge that a thing is 'good as a means,' we are making a judgment with regard to its causal relations: we judge *both* that it will have a particular kind of effect, *and* that that effect will be good in itself. [p. 22]

Such judgments are not usually universally true, and may be generally true at one period but not at another. Even more:

[W]e require to know not only that one good effect will be produced, but that, among all subsequent events affected by the action in question, the balance of good will be greater than if any other possible action had been performed. [pp. 22–23]

Of "right":

In short, to assert that a certain line of conduct is, at a given time, absolutely right or obligatory, is obviously to assert that more good or less evil will exist in the world, if it be adopted than if anything else be done instead. [p. 25]

"Right" and "duty" are not significantly dif-ferent from "expedient" or "useful." The belief that there is such a distinction comes from the fact that some classes of action excite specifi-cally moral sentiments and that we tend to speak of "duties" generally in cases where many individuals are commonly tempted not to do the actions (pp. 167–169).

Of "good as a part":

To have value merely as a part is equivalent to having no value at all, but merely being a part of that which has it. [p. 35] The part of a valuable whole retains exactly the same value when it is, as when it is not, a part of that whole. If it had value under other circumstances, its value is not any greater, when it is part of a far more valuable whole; and if it had no value by itself, it has none still, however great be that of the whole of which it now forms a part. We are not then justified in asserting that one and the same thing is under some circumstances intrinsically good, and under others not so. [p. 30]

Wholes are organic:

The value of a whole must not be assumed to be the same as the sum of the values of its parts [p. 28], [or in more general terms, for organic unities] *the value of such a whole bears no regular proportion to the sum of the values of its parts.* [p. 27]

Of "virtue":

Accordingly a virtue may be defined as an habitual disposition to perform certain actions, which generally produce the best possible results. [p. 172]

Of "interest":

When we ask the question, 'Is this really to my interest?' we appear to be asking exclusively whether its *effects upon me* are the best possible; and it may well happen that what will affect me in the manner, which is really the best possible, will not produce the best possible results on the whole. . . . By 'interested' actions are *mainly* meant those which, whether a means to the best possible or not, are such as have their most obvious effects on the agent; which he generally has no temptation to omit; and with regard to which we feel no moral sentiment. That is to say, the distinction is not primarily ethical. [pp. 170–171]

Of "my good": The interpretation of this term disposes peremptorily of Sidgwick's claim that egoism is rational.

What, then, is meant by 'my own good'? In what sense can a thing be good *for me*? It is obvious, if we reflect, that the only thing which can belong to me, which can be *mine*, is something which is good, and not the fact that it is good. When therefore, I talk of anything I get as 'my own good,' I must mean either that the thing I get is good, or that my possessing it is good. In both cases it is only the thing or the possession of it which is *mine*, and not *the goodness* of that thing or that possession. There is no longer any meaning in attaching the 'my' to our predicate, and saying: The possession of this *by me* is *my* good. Even if we interpret this by 'My possession of this is what *I* think good,' the same still holds: for *what* I think is that my possession of it is good *simply*; and, if I think rightly, then the truth is that my possession of it *is* good simply—not, in any sense, *my* good; and, if I think wrongly, it is not good at all. In short, when I talk of a thing as 'my own good' all that I can mean is that something which will be exclusively mine, as my own pleasure is mine (whatever be the various senses of this relation denoted by 'possession'), is also *good absolutely*; or rather that my possession of it is *good absolutely*. The *good* of it can in no possible sense be 'private' or belong to me; any more than a thing can *exist* privately or *for* one person only. The only reason I can have for aiming at 'my own good,' is that it is *good absolutely* that what I so call should belong to me—*good absolutely* that I should *have* something, which, if I have it, others cannot have. But if it is *good absolutely* that I should have it, then everyone else has as much reason for aiming at *my* having it, as I have myself. If, therefore, it is true of *any* single man's 'interest' or 'happiness' that it ought to be his sole ultimate end, this can only mean that *that* man's 'interest' or 'happiness' is *the sole good, the* Universal Good, and the only thing that anybody ought to aim at. What Egoism holds, therefore, is that *each* man's happiness is the sole good—that a number of different things are *each* of them the only good thing there is—an absolute contradiction! No more complete and thorough refutation of any theory could be desired.

60. Yet Prof. Sidgwick holds that Egoism is rational; and it will be useful briefly to consider the reasons which he gives for this absurd conclusion. 'The Egoist,' he says (last Chap. sec. 1), 'may avoid the proof of Utilitarianism by declining to affirm,' either 'implicitly or explicitly, that his own greatest

happiness is not merely the ultimate rational end for himself, but a part of Universal Good.' And in the passage to which he here refers us, as having there 'seen' this, he says: 'It cannot be proved that the difference between his own happiness and another's happiness is not *for him* all-important' (iv. ii, sec. 1). What does Prof. Sidgwick mean by these phrases 'the ultimate rational end for himself,' and *'for him* all-important'? He does not attempt to define them; and it is largely the use of such undefined phrases which causes absurdities to be committed in philosophy. [pp. 98–99]

(B) The Naturalistic Fallacy

6. What, then, is good? How is good to be defined? Now, it may be thought that this is a verbal question. A definition does indeed often mean the expressing of one word's meaning in other words. But this is not the sort of definition I am asking for. Such a definition can never be of ultimate importance in any study except lexicography. . . . My business is solely with that object or idea, which I hold, rightly or wrongly, that the word is generally used to stand for. What I want to discover is the nature of that object or idea, and about this I am extremely anxious to arrive at an agreement.

But, if we understand the question in this sense, my answer to it may seem a very disappointing one. If I am asked 'What is good?' my answer is that good is good, and that is the end of the matter. Or if I am asked 'How is good to be defined?' my answer is that it cannot be defined, and that is all I have to say about it. But disappointing as these answers may appear, they are of the very last importance. To readers who are familiar with philosophic terminology, I can express their importance by saying that they amount to this: That propositions about the good are all of them synthetic and never analytic; and that is plainly no trivial matter. And the same thing may be expressed more popularly, by saying that, if I am right, then nobody can foist upon us such an axiom as that 'Pleasure is the only good' or that 'The good is the desired' on the pretence that this is 'the very meaning of the word.'

7. Let us, then, consider this position. My point is that 'good' is a simple notion, just as 'yellow' is a simple notion; that, just as you cannot, by any manner of means, explain to any one who does not already know it, what yellow is, so you cannot

explain what good is. Definitions of the kind that I was asking for, definitions which describe the real nature of the object or notion denoted by a word, and which do not merely tell us what the word is used to mean, are only possible when the object or notion in question is something complex. You can give a definition of a horse, because a horse has many different properties and qualities, all of which you can enumerate. But when you have enumerated them all, when you have reduced a horse to his simplest terms, then you can no longer define those terms. They are simply something which you think of or perceive, and to any one who cannot think of or perceive them, you can never, by any definition, make their nature known. [pp. 6–7]

10. . . . Consider yellow, for example. We may try to define it, by describing its physical equivalent; we may state what kind of light-vibrations must stimulate the normal eye, in order that we may perceive it. But a moment's reflection is sufficient to shew that those light-vibrations are not themselves what we mean by yellow. *They* are not what we perceive. Indeed we should never have been able to discover their existence, unless we had first been struck by the patent difference of quality between the different colours. The most we can be entitled to say of those vibrations is that they are what corresponds in space to the yellow which we actually perceive.

Yet a mistake of this simple kind has commonly been made about 'good.' It may be true that all things which are good are *also* something else, just as it is true that all things which are yellow produce a certain kind of vibration in the light. And it is a fact, that Ethics aims at discovering what are those other properties belonging to all things which are good. But far too many philosophers have thought that when they named those other properties they were actually defining good; that these properties, in fact, were simply not 'other,' but absolutely and entirely the same with goodness. This view I propose to call the 'naturalistic fallacy' and of it I shall now endeavour to dispose.

11. Let us consider what it is such philosophers say. And first it is to be noticed that they do not agree among themselves. They not only say that they are right as to what good is, but they endeavour to prove that other people who say that it is something else, are wrong. One, for instance, will affirm that good is pleasure, another, perhaps, that

good is that which is desired; and each of these will argue eagerly to prove that the other is wrong. But how is that possible? One of them says that good is nothing but the object of desire, and at the same time tries to prove that it is not pleasure. But from his first assertion, that good just means the object of desire, one of two things must follow as regards his proof:

(1) He may be trying to prove that the object of desire is not pleasure. But, if this be all, where is his Ethics? The position he is maintaining is merely a psychological one. Desire is something which occurs in our minds, and pleasure is something else which so occurs; and our would-be ethical philosopher is merely holding that the latter is not the object of the former. But what has that to do with the question in dispute? His opponent held the ethical proposition that pleasure was the good, and although he should prove a million times over the psychological proposition that pleasure is not the object of desire, he is no nearer proving his opponent to be wrong. . . . Well, that is one alternative which any naturalistic Ethics has to face; if good is *defined* as something else, it is then impossible either to prove that any other definition is wrong or even to deny such definition.

(2) The other alternative will scarcely be more welcome. It is that the discussion is after all a verbal one. When A says 'Good means pleasant' and B says 'Good means desired,' they may merely wish to assert that most people have used the word for what is pleasant and for what is desired respectively. And this is quite an interesting subject for discussion: only it is not a whit more an ethical discussion than the last was. Nor do I think that any exponent of naturalistic Ethics would be willing to allow that this was all he meant. They are all so anxious to persuade us that what they call the good is what we really ought to do. . . .

12. . . . If I were to imagine that when I said 'I am pleased,' I meant that I was exactly the same thing as 'pleased,' I should not indeed call that a naturalistic fallacy, although it would be the same fallacy as I have called naturalistic with reference to Ethics. The reason of this is obvious enough. When a man confuses two natural objects with one another, defining the one by the other, if for instance, he confuses himself, who is one natural object, with 'pleased' or with 'pleasure' which are others, then there is no reason to call the fallacy

naturalistic. But if he confuses 'good,' which is not in the same sense a natural object, with any natural object whatever, then there is a reason for calling that a naturalistic fallacy; its being made with regard to 'good' marks it as something quite specific, and this specific mistake deserves a name because it is so common. As for the reasons why good is not to be considered a natural object, they may be reserved for discussion in another place. But, for the present, it is sufficient to notice this: Even if it were a natural object, that would not alter the nature of the fallacy nor diminish its importance one whit. All that I have said about it would remain quite equally true: only the name which I have called it would not be so appropriate as I think it is. And I do not care about the name: what I do care about is the fallacy. It does not matter what we call it, provided we recognise it when we meet with it. It is to be met with in almost every book on Ethics; and yet it is not recognised: and that is why it is necessary to multiply illustrations of it, and convenient to give it a name. . . . [pp. 10–14]

13. . . . (1) The hypothesis that disagreement about the meaning of good is disagreement with regard to the correct analysis of a given whole, may be most plainly seen to be incorrect by consideration of the fact that, whatever definition be offered, it may be always asked, with significance, of the complex so defined, whether it is itself good. To take, for instance, one of the more plausible, because one of the more complicated, of such proposed definitions, it may easily be thought, at first sight, that to be good may mean to be that which we desire to desire. Thus if we apply this definition to a particular instance and say 'When we think that A is good, we are thinking that A is one of the things which we desire to desire,' our proposition may seem quite plausible. But, if we carry the investigation further, and ask ourselves 'Is it good to desire to desire A?' it is apparent, on a little reflection, that this question is itself as intelligible, as the original question 'Is A good?'—that we are, in fact, now asking for exactly the same information about the desire to desire A, for which we formerly asked with regard to A itself. But it is also apparent that the meaning of this second question cannot be correctly analysed into 'Is the desire to desire A one of things which we desire to desire?': we have not before our minds anything so complicated as the question 'Do we desire to desire to desire to desire

A?' Moreover any one can easily convince himself by inspection that the predicate of this proposition—'good'—is positively different from the notion of 'desiring to desire' which enters into its subject: 'That we should desire to desire A is good' is *not* merely equivalent to 'That A should be good is good.' It may indeed be true that what we desire to desire is always also good; perhaps, even the converse may be true: but it is very doubtful whether this is the case, and the mere fact that we understand very well what is meant by doubting it, shews clearly that we have two different notions before our minds.[3]

(2) . . . [W]hoever will attentively consider with himself what is actually before his mind when he asks the question 'Is pleasure (or whatever it may be) after all good?' can easily satisfy himself that he is not merely wondering whether pleasure is pleasant. And if he will try this experiment with each suggested definition in succession, he may become expert enough to recognise that in every case he has before his mind a unique object, with regard to the connection of which with any other object, a distinct question may be asked. Every one does in fact understand the question 'Is this good?' When he thinks of it, his state of mind is different from what it would be, were he asked 'Is this pleasant, or desired, or approved?' It has a distinct meaning for him, even though he may not recognise in what respect it is distinct. Whenever he thinks of 'intrinsic value,' or 'intrinsic worth,' or says that a thing 'ought to exist,' he has before his mind the unique object—the unique property of things—which I mean by 'good.' Everybody is constantly aware of this notion, although he may never become aware at all that it is different from other notions of which he is also aware. But, for correct ethical reasoning, it is extremely important that he should become aware of this fact; and, as soon as the nature of the problem is clearly understood, there should be little difficulty in advancing so far in analysis. [pp. 15–17]

The conclusion, that good or intrinsic value is "a simple, indefinable, unanalysable object of thought" (p. 21) makes complete the isolation of intrinsic value from any kind of fact.

[3] This is the open-question argument.

The confusion of questions of intrinsic value and those of obligation, which involve causality, leads to serious errors: "Either it is assumed that nothing has intrinsic value which is not possible, or else it is assumed that what is necessary must have intrinsic value" (p. 26). Both assumptions are false: something that does not and cannot exist presumably may be intrinsically valuable; and the fact that something happens necessarily does not endow it with such value. Any claim that judgments of intrinsic value have a metaphysical base rests upon the failure to perceive that any truth which asserts " 'This is good in itself' is quite unique in kind—that it cannot be reduced to any assertion about reality, and therefore must remain unaffected by any conclusions we may reach about the nature of reality" (p. 114).[4]

(C) Critique of Other Theories

Chapters 2, 3, and 4 are critical of naturalistic ethics, hedonism, and metaphysical ethics. In claims about the good, factual assertions are disentangled from statements of intrinsic value. The view that nature fixes what is health, so that the normal state of the organism is good, is met with the question whether excellence may not lie in the abnormal or the extraordinary (pp. 42–43). To equate health with the good is to commit the naturalistic fallacy; no matter how obvious the goodness of health may be, the question is still logically open. "That health, *when* the word is used to denote something good, is good, goes no way at all to shew that health, when the word is used to denote something normal, is also good" (p. 43). Spencer is charged with committing the fallacy by equating "good" and "more

[4] A clear statement of this sweeping isolation of value from the nature of the world is found in Moore's review of Brentano's *The Origin of the Knowledge of Right and Wrong*: "No ethical proposition of this form is such that, if a certain thing exists, it is true, whereas, if that thing does not exist, it is false. All such ethical truths are true, *whatever the nature of the world may be.*" (*International Journal of Ethics* 14 [October 1903]: 116)

evolved"; the latter is a factual question according to its own criteria. The hedonistic thesis, "Pleasure is the only thing which is good in itself," also commits the naturalistic fallacy. In general, both naturalistic and hedonistic ethics identify good with a natural property of one or another kind. A natural property is one that we can think of as existing in time (p. 41), that is, as part of the description of a natural object. Good, though a property of natural objects, is not a natural property, for we cannot think of good existing in time by itself as we can think of yellow; rather, good is a nonnatural property.

If indeed good were a feeling, as some would have us believe, then it would exist in time. But that is why to call it so is to commit the naturalistic fallacy. It will always remain pertinent to ask, whether the feeling itself is good; and if so, then good cannot itself be identical with any feeling. [p. 41]

The arguments against different forms of metaphysical ethics follow largely the same lines. For example, to identify what ought to be with what is commanded by some real supersensible authority is open to the same kind of objections (p. 128). Similar difficulties face the view that something is good means that it is willed in a certain way.

(D) How Statements about Intrinsic Value Are Established

It has been pointed out that one difference between a judgment which asserts that a thing is good in itself, and a judgment which asserts that it is a means to good, consists in the fact that the first, if true of one instance of the thing in question, is necessarily true of all; whereas a thing which has good effects under some circumstances may have bad ones under others. Now it is certainly true that all judgments of intrinsic value are in this sense universal. [p. 27]

The method which I employed in order to shew that pleasure itself was not the sole good, was that of considering what value we should attach to it, if it existed in absolute isolation, stripped of all its usual accompaniments. And this is, in fact, the only method that can be safely used, when we wish to discover what degree of value a thing has in itself. [p. 91]

Pleasure cannot be the sole good because a world consisting of pleasure is of much less value than a world of pleasure together with the consciousness of it.

The method which must be employed in order to decide the question 'What things have intrinsic value, and in what degrees?' has already been explained. . . . In order to arrive at a correct decision on the first part of this question, it is necessary to consider what things are such that, if they existed *by themselves*, in absolute isolation, we should yet judge their existence to be good; and, in order to decide upon the relative *degrees* of value of different things, we must similarly consider what comparative value seems to attach to the isolated existence of each. [p. 187]

The seeing or insight in the judging of such situations is self-evident, but "self-evident"

means properly that the proposition so called is evident or true, *by itself* alone; that it is not an inference from some proposition other than *itself*. The expression does *not* mean that the proposition is true, because it is evident to you or me or all mankind, because in other words it appears to us to be true. That a proposition appears to be true can never be a valid argument that true it really is. [p. 143]

Self-evidence is not proof:

Following the method established by our first discussion, I claimed that the untruth of this proposition [pleasure alone is good] was self-evident. I could do nothing to *prove* that it was untrue; I could only point out as clearly as possible what it means, and how it contradicts other propositions which appear to be equally true. My only object in all this was, necessarily, to convince. But even if I did convince, that does not prove that we are right. [pp. 144–145]

Yet, having asked the question, we are more likely to be right than Bentham, Mill, and Sidgwick, who confused the question they purported to answer with another.

(E) Statements of Right, Duty, and Obligation

Questions about right, duty, and ought involve causal judgments about what will produce the greatest value.

89. . . . All moral laws, I wish to shew, are merely statements that certain kinds of actions will have good effects. The very opposite of this view has been generally prevalent in Ethics. 'The right' and 'the useful' have been supposed to be at least *capable* of conflicting with one another, and, at all events, to be essentially distinct. It has been characteristic of a certain school of moralists, as of moral common sense, to declare that the end will never justify the means. What I wish first to point out is that 'right' does and can mean nothing but 'cause of a good result,' and is thus identical with 'useful'; whence it follows that the end always will justify the means, and that no action which is not justified by its results can be right. . . .

That the assertion 'I am morally bound to perform this action' is identical with the assertion 'This action will produce the greatest possible amount of good in the Universe' has already been briefly shewn . . .; but it is important to insist that this fundamental point is demonstrably certain. This may, perhaps, be best made evident in the following way. It is plain that when we assert that a certain action is our absolute duty, we are asserting that the performance of that action at that time is unique in respect of value. But no dutiful action can possibly have unique value in the sense that it is the sole thing of value in the world; since, in that case, *every* such action would be the *sole* good thing, which is a manifest contradiction. And for the same reason its value cannot be unique in the sense that it has more intrinsic value than anything else in the world; since *every* act of duty would then be the *best* thing in the world, which is also a contradiction. It can, therefore, be unique only in the sense that the whole world will be better, if it be performed, than if any possible alternative were taken. And the question whether this is so cannot possibly depend solely on the question of its own intrinsic value. For any action will also have effects different from those of any other action; and if any of these

have intrinsic value, their value is exactly as relevant to the total goodness of the Universe as that of their cause. It is, in fact, evident that, however valuable an action may be in itself, yet, owing to its existence, the sum of good in the Universe may conceivably be made less than if some other action, less valuable in itself, had been performed. But to say that this is the case is to say that it would have been better that the action should not have been done; and this again is obviously equivalent to the statement that it ought not to have been done—that it was not what duty required. 'Fiat iustitia, ruat caelum' can only be justified on the ground that by the doing of justice the Universe gains more than it loses by the falling of the heavens. It is, of course, possible that this is the case: but, at all events, to assert that justice *is* a duty, in spite of such consequences, is to assert that it is the case.

Our 'duty,' therefore, can only be defined as that action, which will cause more good to exist in the Universe than any possible alternative. And what is 'right' or 'morally permissible' only differs from this, as what will *not* cause *less* good than any possible alternative. When, therefore, Ethics presumes to assert that certain ways of acting are 'duties' it presumes to assert that to act in those ways will always produce the greatest possible sum of good. If we are told that to 'do no murder' is a duty, we are told that the action, whatever it may be, which is called murder, will under no circumstances cause so much good to exist in the Universe as its avoidance.

90. But, if this be recognised, several most important consequences follow, with regard to the relation of Ethics to conduct.

(1) It is plain that no moral law is self-evident, as has commonly been held by the Intuitional school of moralists. . . . It is, indeed, possible that some of our immediate intuitions are true; but since *what* we intuit, *what* conscience tells us, is that certain actions will always produce the greatest sum of good possible under the circumstances, it is plain that reasons can be given, which will shew the deliverances of conscience to be true or false.

91. (2) In order to shew that any action is a duty, it is necessary to know both what are the other conditions, which will, conjointly with it, determine its effects; to know exactly what will be the effects of these conditions; and to know all the events which will be in any way affected by our action

throughout an infinite future. We must have all this causal knowledge, and further we must know accurately the degree of value both of the action itself and of all these effects; and must be able to determine how, in conjunction with the other things in the Universe, they will affect its value as an organic whole. And not only this: we must also possess all this knowledge with regard to the effects of every possible alternative; and must then be able to see by comparison that the total value due to the existence of the action in question will be greater than that which would be produced by any of these alternatives. But it is obvious that our causal knowledge alone is far too incomplete for us ever to assure ourselves of this result. Accordingly it follows that we never have any reason to suppose that an action is our duty: we can never be sure that any action will produce the greatest value possible.

Ethics, therefore, is quite unable to give us a list of duties: but there still remains a humbler task which may be possible for Practical Ethics. Although we cannot hope to discover which, in a given situation, is the best of all possible alternative actions, there may be some possibility of shewing which among the alternatives, *likely to occur to any one,* will produce the greatest sum of good. This second task is certainly all that Ethics can ever have accomplished: and it is certainly all that it has ever collected materials for proving; since no one has ever attempted to exhaust the possible alternative actions in any particular case. Ethical philosophers have in fact confined their attention to a very limited class of actions, which have been selected because they are those which most commonly occur to mankind as possible alternatives. [pp. 146–150]

A complicating factor is the fact that judging right conduct requires reference to effects in an infinite future. It is doubtful that ethics can establish the utility of rules other than those generally practiced. Even in established rules, "though we may be sure that there are cases where the rule should be broken, we can never know which those cases are, and ought, therefore, never to break it" (pp. 162–163). Strong probability favors adhering to existing custom even if it is a bad one, although the individual's example in breaking the rule may be for the good.

(F) What Does Have Intrinsic Value?

113. If, now, we use this method of absolute isolation, and guard against these errors, it appears that the question we have to answer is far less difficult than the controversies of Ethics might have led us to expect. Indeed, once the meaning of the question is clearly understood, the answer to it, in its main outlines, appears to be so obvious, that it runs the risk of seeming to be a platitude. By far the most valuable things, which we know or can imagine, are certain states of consciousness, which may be roughly described as the pleasures of human intercourse and the enjoyment of beautiful objects. No one, probably, who has asked himself the question, has ever doubted that personal affection and the appreciation of what is beautiful in Art or Nature, are good in themselves; nor, if we consider strictly what things are worth having *purely for their own sakes,* does it appear probable that any one will think that anything else has *nearly* so great a value as the things which are included under these two heads. I have myself urged in Chap. III (sec. 50) that the mere existence of what is beautiful does appear to have *some* intrinsic value; but I regard it as indubitable that Prof. Sidgwick was so far right, in the view there discussed, that such mere existence of what is beautiful has value, so small as to be negligible, in comparison with that which attaches to the *consciousness* of beauty. This simple truth may, indeed, be said to be universally recognised. What has *not* been recognised is that it is the ultimate and fundamental truth of Moral Philosophy. That it is only for the sake of these things— in order that as much of them as possible may at some time exist—that any one can be justified in performing any public or private duty; that they are the *raison d'être* of virtue; that it is they—these complex wholes *themselves,* and not any constituent or characteristic of them—that form the rational ultimate end of human action and the sole criterion of social progress: these appear to be truths which have been generally overlooked.

That they are truths—that personal affections and aesthetic enjoyments include *all* the greatest, and *by far* the greatest, goods we can imagine, will, I hope, appear more plainly in the course of that analysis of them, to which I shall now proceed. All the things, which I have meant to include under the above descriptions, are highly complex *organic unities;* and in discussing the consequences, which follow from this fact, and the elements of which they are composed, I may hope at the same time both to confirm and to define my position. [pp. 188–189]

Some among Moore's specific findings depart from ordinary judgment, most strikingly: "[I]t appears that knowledge, though having little or no value by itself, is an absolutely essential constituent in the highest goods, and contributes immensely to their value" (p. 199). Beauty loses its independent character: "beautiful" is used to denote "that of which the admiring contemplation is good in itself" (p. 208). Pains, as may be expected, are found to be great positive evils (p. 212); on the other hand, adding pain to a villain decreases the evil (pp. 213–214).

That things intrinsically good or bad are many and various; that most of them are 'organic unities,' in the peculiar and definite sense to which I have confined the term; and that our only means of deciding upon their intrinsic value and its degree, is by carefully distinguishing exactly what the thing is, about which we ask the question, and then looking to see whether it has or has not the unique predicate 'good' in any of its various degrees: these are the conclusions, upon the truth of which I desire to insist. [p. 223]

John Maynard Keynes
(1883–1946)

My Early Beliefs [5]

[F]or us, those who were active in 1903 . . . Moore completely ousted McTaggart, Dickinson, Russell. The influence was not only overwhelming; . . . it was exciting, exhilarating, the beginning of a renaissance, the opening of a new heaven on a

new earth, we were the forerunners of a new dispensation, we were not afraid of anything. . . .

Now what we got from Moore was by no means entirely what he offered us. He had one foot on the threshold of the new heaven, but the other foot in Sidgwick and the Benthamite calculus and the general rules of correct behaviour. There was one chapter in the *Principia* of which we took not the slightest notice.[6] We accepted Moore's religion, so to speak, and discarded his morals. Indeed, in our opinion, one of the greatest advantages of his religion, was that it made morals unnecessary—meaning by 'religion' one's attitude towards oneself and the ultimate and by 'morals' one's attitude towards the outside world and the intermediate. To the consequences of having a religion and no morals I return later.

. . . Nothing mattered except states of mind, our own and other people's of course, but chiefly our own. These states of mind were not associated with action or achievement or with consequences. They consisted in timeless, passionate states of contemplation and communion, largely unattached to 'before' and 'after.' Their value depended, in accordance with the principle of organic unity, on the state of affairs as a whole which could not be usefully analysed into parts. For example, the value of the state of mind of being in love did not depend merely on the nature of one's own emotions, but also on the worth of their object and on the reciprocity and nature of the object's emotions; but it did not depend, if I remember rightly, or did not depend much, on what happened, or how one felt about it, a year later, though I myself was always an advocate of a principle of organic unity through time, which still seems to me only sensible. The appropriate objects of passionate contemplation and communion were a beloved person, beauty and truth, and one's prime objects in life were love, the creation and enjoyment of aesthetic experience and the pursuit of knowledge. Of these love came a long way first. But in the early days under Moore's influence the public treatment of this and its associated acts was, on the whole, austere and platonic.

---

[5] From *Two Memoirs* (New York: Augustus M. Kelly, 1949), pp. 82–89.

[6] The chapter on right and duty. Keynes later says, "The large part played by considerations of probability in his theory of right conduct was, indeed, an important contributory cause to my spending all the leisure of many years on the study of that subject" (p. 95).

Some of us might argue that physical enjoyment could spoil and detract from the state of mind as a whole. . . .

Our religion closely followed the English puritan tradition of being chiefly concerned with the salvation of our own souls. The divine resided within a closed circle. There was not a very intimate connection between 'being good' and 'doing good'; and we had a feeling that there was some risk that in practice the latter might interfere with the former. But religions proper, as distinct from modern 'social service' pseudo-religions, have always been of that character; and perhaps it was a sufficient offset that our religion was altogether unworldly—with wealth, power, popularity or success it had no concern whatever, they were thoroughly despised.

How did we know what states of mind were good? This was a matter of direct inspection, of direct unanalysable intuition about which it was useless and impossible to argue. In that case who was right when there was a difference of opinion? There were two possible explanations. It might be that the two parties were not really talking about the same thing, that they were not bringing their intuitions to bear on precisely the same object, and, by virtue of the principle of organic unity, a very small difference in the object might make a very big difference in the result. Or it might be that some people had an acuter sense of judgment, just as some people can judge a vintage port and others cannot. On the whole, so far as I remember, this explanation prevailed. In practice, victory was with those who could speak with the greatest appearance of clear, undoubting conviction and could best use the accents of infallibility. Moore at this time was a master of this method—greeting one's remarks with a gasp of incredulity—*Do* you *really* think *that*, an expression of face as if to hear such a thing said reduced him to a state of wonder verging on imbecility, with his mouth wide open and wagging his head in the negative so violently that his hair shook. *Oh!* he would say, goggling at you as if either you or he must be mad; and no reply was possible. Strachey's methods were different; grim silence as if such a dreadful observation was beyond comment and the less said about it the better, but almost as effective for disposing of what he called death-packets. Woolf was fairly good at indicating a negative, but he was better at producing the effect that it was useless to argue with *him* than at crushing *you*.

Dickinson knew how to shrug his shoulders and retreat unconvinced, but it was retreat all the same. As for Sheppard and me we could only turn like worms, but worms who could be eventually goaded into voluble claims that worms have at least the *right* to turn. Yet after all the differences were about details. Broadly speaking we all knew for certain what were good states of mind and that they consisted in communion with objects of love, beauty and truth.

I have called this faith a religion, and some sort of relation of neo-platonism it surely was. But we should have been very angry at the time with such a suggestion. We regarded all this as entirely rational and scientific in character. Like any other branch of science, it was nothing more than the application of logic and rational analysis to the material presented as sense-data. Our apprehension of good was exactly the same as our apprehension of green, and we purported to handle it with the same logical and analytical technique which was appropriate to the latter. Indeed we combined a dogmatic treatment as to the nature of experience with a method of handling it which was extravagantly scholastic. Russell's *Principles of Mathematics* came out in the same year as *Principia Ethica;* and the former, in spirit, furnished a method for handling the material provided by the latter. Let me give you a few examples of the sort of things we used to discuss.

If A was in love with B and believed that B reciprocated his feelings, whereas in fact B did not, but was in love with C, the state of affairs was certainly not so good as it would have been if A had been right, but was it worse or better than it would become if A discovered his mistake? If A was in love with B under a misapprehension as to B's qualities, was this better or worse than A's not being in love at all? If A was in love with B because A's spectacles were not strong enough to see B's complexion, did this altogether, or partly, destroy the value of A's state of mind? Suppose we were to live our lives backwards, having our experiences in the reverse order, would this affect the value of our successive states of mind? If the states of mind enjoyed by each of us were pooled and then redistributed, would this affect their value? How did one compare the value of a good state of mind which had bad consequences with a bad state of mind which had good consequences? In valuing the consequences did one assess them at their actual value as it turned out eventually to be, or their probable value at the time? If at their probable value, how much evidence as to possible consequences was it one's duty to collect before applying the calculus? Was there a separate objective standard of beauty? Was a beautiful thing, that is to say, by definition that which it was good to contemplate? Or was there an actual objective quality 'beauty,' just like 'green' and 'good'? And knowledge, too, presented a problem. Were all truths equally good to pursue and contemplate?—as for example the number of grains in a given tract of sea-sand. We were disposed to repudiate very strongly the idea that useful knowledge could be preferable to useless knowledge. But we flirted with the idea that there might be some intrinsic quality—though not, perhaps, quite on a par with 'green' and 'good' and 'beautiful'—which one could call 'interesting,' and we were prepared to think it just possible that 'interesting' knowledge might be better to pursue than 'uninteresting' knowledge. Another competing adjective was 'important,' provided it was quite clear that 'important' did not mean 'useful.' Or to return again to our favourite subject, was a violent love affair which lasted a short time better than a more tepid one which endured longer? We were inclined to think it was. But I have said enough by now to make it clear that the problems of mensuration, in which we had involved ourselves, were somewhat formidable.

It was all under the influence of Moore's method, according to which you could hope to make essentially vague notions clear by using precise language about them and asking exact questions. It was a method of discovery by the instrument of impeccable grammar and an unambiguous dictionary. 'What *exactly* do you mean?' was the phrase most frequently on our lips. If it appeared under cross-examination that you did not mean *exactly* anything, you lay under a strong suspicion of meaning nothing whatever. It was a stringent education in dialectic; but in practice it was a kind of combat in which strength of character was really much more valuable than subtlety of mind. In the preface to his great work, bespattered with the numerous italics through which the reader who knew him could actually hear, as with Queen Victoria, the vehemence of his utterance, Moore begins by saying that error is chiefly 'the attempt to answer questions, without first discovering precisely *what* question it is which you desire to answer. . . . Once we recognise the exact meaning of the two questions, I think it also becomes plain exactly what kind of reasons are relevant as arguments for or against any particular answer to them.' So we spent our time trying to discover *precisely what* questions we were asking, confident in the faith that, if only we could ask precise questions, everyone would know the answer. Indeed Moore expressly claimed as much.

20

Emotivism and Ordinary Language Analysis

Two related movements contributed an important linguistic dimension to twentieth-century ethical theory. The earlier, Logical Positivism, began in the 1920s in meetings of the Vienna Circle, a group that sought to bring a scientific outlook to philosophy. They were reacting largely against the reigning European metaphysics and epistemology, which they regarded as obscurantist, as raising meaningless and therefore insoluble questions. They emphasized "logical" to distinguish themselves from British empiricism as well as from the Comtean positivism of the nineteenth century. The movement quickly spread to other centers in Germany and Poland. Its influence was growing when, under the Nazi threat, the groups were dispersed to England and North America. In the United States, Logical Positivism mellowed somewhat in exchange with an already well developed philosophy of science and became known as Logical Empiricism. In both countries it was early popularized by A. J. Ayer's *Language, Truth and Logic* (1936).

The second movement, developed especially at Oxford, was Ordinary Language Analysis. Its influence spread in the late 1940s and remained strong well into the 1970s in England and America. Both movements agreed that the task of philosophy had been generally misconstrued: it is not a set of substantive truths, but an activity directed toward clarifying and precising language. But where positivists were interested above all in the language of science, especially the languages of formal logic and mathematics, ordinary language analysts turned rather to the clarification of terms and concepts of natural language, the common or ordinary ways of speaking. The positivists were inspired by the formalism in the new logic of Alfred North Whitehead and Bertrand Russell (*Principia Mathematica* [1910]) and by the way in which concepts were handled in the new physics of Einstein. They thus looked to the construction of technical languages by which they hoped to replace the confusions of ordinary language. Oxford analysis, on the other hand, found wisdom embedded in ordinary language and sought to clarify or to dissolve philosophical problems by strict attention to its subtleties. It explored in detail the multiple uses of language beyond its familiar function as description and carried this exploration into the language of psychology, education, politics, law, and above all, morals. On principle it offered little in the way of a general theory of analysis, but it agreed with positivism that ethics is isolated from science, description from evaluation, and that the language of morals is distinctive in use or meaning.

Logical Empiricism and the Emotive Theory

If philosophy is to be rid of its preoccupation with meaningless questions, early on the agenda must be what is a meaningful question or statement. Here logical empiricists used a dichotomy at least as old as Hume, between analytic statements and empirical statements. To qualify as meaningful—that is, as true or false—a declarative sentence had to be one or the other.

Analytic statements are true or false by virtue of the meanings of their components. There is no need of verifying experience for "All oranges are fruit" or "The cephalic index is the maximum width divided by the maximum length of the skull multiplied by 100." The meaning of the words that compose them is a matter of convention. Considering Kant's *synthetic a priori* the citadel of rationalism and mathematics its strongest case, logical positivists challenged Kant's account of mathematics: they treated pure mathematics as analytic, and in the case of geometry distinguished it as a mathematical (formal) discipline and as a physical (interpreted) discipline. They regarded the latter as empirical, since it was a matter of experimental physics whether our space is Euclidean or, as Einstein had shown, non-Euclidean. (The sharpness with which they set off the analytic from the empirical or from wider contexts of assumptions and presuppo-

sitions set in motion a raging controversy in succeeding decades.)[1]

Statements that are not analytic are meaningful if they are capable of verification or falsification, or are confirmable or disconfirmable, by appeal to observation and experience. These are synthetic or factual statements. But much of our discourse is neither empirical nor logical and mathematical—for example, metaphysical assertions about what is real, or theological propositions about God's nature. Positivists took these to be noncognitive; any attempt to see them as cognitive is either nonsense or bad grammar. Similarly with aesthetic and moral judgments, or value judgments generally: they fail to be cognitive and meaningful, being neither true by definition nor verifiable in a public and objective way. Similarly, strictly speaking, imperatives, optatives, and exclamations are also noncognitive. This was not, of course, intended to imply that noncognitive utterances are unimportant.

Among themselves, positivists differed in their accounts of noncognitive assertions. Russell, although not a positivist, at one point translated "This is good" into an optative "Would that everybody desired this." Carnap took "Stealing is wrong" as a disguised imperative, equivalent to "Don't steal" or "Thou shalt not steal." Ayer interpreted it as expressive, giving vent to a feeling of horror, such as saying "Stealing!!!" He distinguished such moral uses of language from descriptions of moral experience—these are psychological or sociological statements. The proper and sole business of ethics is the linguistic analysis of ethical terms; hence ethics is a purely logical-linguistic business and makes no moral judgments. The correct analysis of such assertions discovers their emotive status. Ayer did not confine that status wholly to what was

[1] The distinction was challenged notably by W. V. Quine ("Two Dogmas of Empiricism," *Philosophical Review*, 1951), who argued that it is at most a matter of degree, marking how tenaciously a proposition will be held in the face of recalcitrant experience.

happening to the person in the expressive act; he also noted that the act might be directed to encouraging attitudes in others.

This interpersonal role of moral or normative assertion was given a primary place in the work of Charles L. Stevenson, who developed the emotive theory systematically. Beginning with the phenomenon of moral disagreement his *Ethics and Language* (1944) offers an emotive interpretation of disagreement and of ethical utterances and argument generally. Stevenson shared Ayer's view of ethics as limited to the analysis of moral terms; he described it as a neutral discipline, one that uses only logical-linguistic or methodological tools in the interest of clarity, and labeled it *metaethics*. No matter how much else in the emotive theory was revised, the sharp distinction between metaethics and normative or substantive moral judgment governed much of moral philosophy into the 1970s.

Stevenson combined positivism with two other strands. One came from literary criticism under the influence of such works as C. K. Ogden and I. A. Richards's *The Meaning of Meaning* (1923); their subtitle, *A Study of the Influence of Language upon Thought and of the Science of Symbolism*, shows the direction of the growing linguistic studies. Indeed, Stevenson carried his analysis beyond ethics and tried to develop a general category of emotive meaning. The other strand is Moore's ethics, which influenced Stevenson during his studies in Cambridge. But where Moore had identified intrinsic value as a nonnatural quality, Stevenson took the allegedly nonnatural part to be a surplus beyond the descriptive and reinterpreted it as persuasive, not merely expressive (as Ayer had done). Moral utterance combines, then, a description of one's inner state and an effort to urge it upon others.

Emotivism provoked strong emotions. It was often charged with promoting irrationality by its depiction of the moral judge using rhetorical and emotional devices to change and influence attitudes. Also challenged was Ste-

venson's claim that the logical-linguistic analysis of the use of ethical terms is neutral and presupposes only the value of clarity and similar purely methodological values. Behind the stance of neutrality, critics argued, was an advocacy of individualism.[2] Not all positivists subscribed to the emotive theory. Moritz Schlick's *Problems of Ethics* (1939) takes an almost utilitarian approach to ethics. Others carried out the logical positivist program in ethics by constructing technical logics: deontic logics to formalize the logic of "ought" and axiological logics for preference or "better."[3]

Ordinary Language Analysis

The work of ordinary language analysis can be seen as in part rejection, in part extension, of the emotivist approach. It kept the sharp methodological distinction between metaethics and normative ethics, and therefore assumed that analysis was a self-enclosed activity. Its data consist of people's moral discourse. Also like emotivism, it took moral utterance to have practical or prescriptive functions, not cognitive or descriptive ones. But ordinary language analysis is critical of emotivism as much too wholesale, much too crude. David Falk, for example, criticized Stevenson for putting all the fine shades into the one category of persuasive meaning.[4] Thus a narrative can be as effective as a prescription to teach a moral lesson; or again, impersonal pleading can be a guiding influence without coercion. "I want you to

[2] For example, Margaret MacDonald thought Stevenson's view an "exaggerated moral protestantism" for its "romantic preoccupation with a personal gospel and a private missionary society" ("Ethics and the Ceremonial Use of Language," in Max Black, ed., *Philosophical Analysis* [Englewood Cliffs, N.J.: Prentice-Hall, 1963], p. 206).
[3] G. H. Von Wright, *Norm and Action* (1963) and *The Logic of Preference* (1963), and Sören Halldén, *On the Logic of Better* (1957).
[4] "Guiding and Goading," *Mind* 42 (April 1953): 145–171.

. . ." creates a reason, but good reasons have to be distinguished from valid reasons and sufficient reasons, as well as from preponderant reasons (despite counterreasons). Moral speaking is not reporting, nor is it telling; but one can report what is "demanded" by the nature of the act and its circumstances, and one can teach a person to appreciate something.

In extended studies in the 1950s others developed the complex character of moral discourse. Stephen Toulmin's *Reason in Ethics* (1953) distinguished different levels of justification in which are found different kinds of "good reasons." Richard M. Hare's *The Language of Morals* (1952) pressed the prescriptive character of moral utterances. While "right" and "ought" are prescriptive, "good" is commendatory and not to be given a descriptive meaning. In *Freedom and Reason* (1963) Hare added the requirement of universalization: in using moral terms one implies that the prescription is addressed to or will hold for all. (His theory was accordingly labeled "universal prescriptivism.") P. H. Nowell-Smith's *Ethics* (1954), a full-scale examination of the problems of ethical theory, with many detailed analyses of the impact of linguistic analysis, listed as uses for value words:

to express tastes and preferences, to express decisions and choices, to criticize, grade, and evaluate, to advise, admonish, warn, persuade and dissuade, to praise, encourage and reprove, to promulgate and draw attention to rules; and doubtless for other purposes also.[5]

The shift away from emotivism was not just a matter of multiplying functions. It was a major shift in attitude to language from the positivist attitude that ordinary language is encrusted ignorance to be reconstructed by technical formal language systems. In the *informalists*, as the ordinary language analysts were

[5] P. H. Nowell-Smith, *Ethics* (Baltimore: Penguin, 1954), p. 98.

sometimes called, a number of influences were converging: the conceptual analysis of W. D. Ross and H. A. Prichard; the later work of Ludwig Wittgenstein, eventually to be published as *Philosophical Investigations* (1955), and of course the pervasive influence of G. E. Moore, with his open-question argument and his emphasis on good as bearing more than descriptive meaning.

Further influences were Gilbert Ryle's exploration of the riches of ordinary language in *Concept of Mind* (1949) and *Dilemmas* (1954). Ryle argued that every term in ordinary language had its own logic, its own implicit rules for use; thus there was quite an extensive "informal logic" of notions such as pleasure. He even regarded formal logic as simply the artificial drilling of a few selected words such as "and," "or," "if" according to strict rules, but—except for its artificiality—no different in kind from the logic of ordinary words. In John L. Austin's intensive concern with the practical uses of language—in *Philosophical Papers* (1961) and *How to Do Things with Words* (1962)—there was a kind of veneration for ordinary language as a storehouse of wisdom accumulated in the long march of tradition, reminiscent of the way in which lawyers and jurists look upon the common law. Austin paid special attention to the *performative* uses of language, that is, how practical effects are not merely signaled but actually instituted by set expressions—for example, the "I do" of the marriage ceremony marks the moment when the marriage legally begins to exist, the "You're out" of the baseball umpire establishes the authoritative fact. In many cases to state a fact or to describe is at the same time to prescribe. Austin pointed out that very few of the statements we make are just true or false; they may also be fair or unfair, felicitous or infelicitous, exaggerated, rough, adequate or inadequate. Accordingly he called for a study of all the possible forces of utterances and regarded his discovery of performatives as just a start. The cognitive use of language is simply one of the multiplicity of uses; there is no linguistic justification for setting it off as a separate realm of "fact."

Although ordinary language analysts substituted for talk of the "meaning" of terms that of the "uses" of terms, the contexts in which they examined uses were linguistic, not psychological, social, or even historical. At most they reached out to so-called "nonformal" conditions of discourse: for example, if I say "you" it presupposes your presence, whereas presence is not a necessary condition if I say "he."

Still, from the outset a social dimension was latent. Thus it was an easy step from the exploration of use to the analysis of practices, that is, ways of doing things or arrangements governed by rules. For example, John Rawls's early article "Two Concepts of Rules," [6] in exploring promise keeping as a practice, circumvented the traditional options for justifying the obligation to keep a promise—either the utilitarian appeal to the greatest well-being or the intuitionist claim of its self-evidence. If to say "I promise" is to take on an obligation by invoking a practice (a performatory act in Austin's sense), then it is like any other institutional act with its constituent rules. The promiser abdicates title to act in accordance with utilitarian or prudential considerations. The justification of having such a practice as promise keeping, on the other hand, may itself be utilitarian, just as, say, the justification of check cashing in banks is utilitarian. The appeal to such a notion as a practice, while clearly social, rarely went further into the historical with its view of growth, development, and change.[7]

The selections for the emotive theory, from A. J. Ayer and from Stevenson's chief earlier article, show the theory as it was being expounded in a fresh and challenging way. From the materials in ordinary language analysis we offer samples to exhibit some of its several major lessons for ethics. Nowell-Smith shows how linguistic analysis is used to break down the search for a single meaning for an ethical term, and how the contextual use analysis of "ought" affects even our understanding of the phenomenon of conscience. The selection from J. L. Austin comes closest to an exposition of method; he not only stakes out a domain of excuses and justifications but suggests how its exploration can replace the traditional philosophical approach to the general problems of freedom and responsibility. H. L. A. Hart's classic paper illustrates the practical uses of language, in law as well as ethics.[8] Philippa Foot's "Approval and Disapproval," arguing that erroneous assumptions about the psychology of feeling mislead us into regarding morality as a purely individual phenomenon, shows clearly the latent concern of linguistic analysis with the social dimension.

A. J. Ayer
(1910–)

Language, Truth and Logic [9]

Chapter VI: Critique of Ethics and Theology

The ordinary system of ethics, as elaborated in the works of ethical philosophers, is very far from being a homogeneous whole. Not only is it apt to contain pieces of metaphysics, and analyses of non-ethical concepts: its actual ethical contents are themselves of very different kinds. We may divide them, indeed, into four main classes. There are, first of all, propositions which express definitions of ethical terms, or judgements about the legitimacy or possi-

---

[6] *Philosophical Review* 64 (1955): 3–32. For his own view, see Chapter 23.

[7] Nietzsche long ago had pointed out that for promising to make sense as a practice, there has to be some predict-□ility of actions, and this, he said, presupposes that man □ready been sufficiently *domesticated*!

[8] Hart changed his mind on some of the issues involved.

[9] A. J. Ayer, *Language, Truth and Logic* (London, 1936; 2d ed, 1946). The selection is from *Language, Truth and Logic* (New York: Dover, nd), pp. 103–108.

bility of certain definitions. Secondly, there are propositions describing the phenomena of moral experience, and their causes. Thirdly, there are exhortations to moral virtue. And, lastly, there are actual ethical judgements. It is unfortunately the case that the distinction between these four classes, plain as it is, is commonly ignored by ethical philosophers; with the result that it is often very difficult to tell from their works what it is that they are seeking to discover or prove.

In fact, it is easy to see that only the first of our four classes, namely that which comprises the propositions relating to the definitions of ethical terms, can be said to constitute ethical philosophy. The propositions which describe the phenomena of moral experience, and their causes, must be assigned to the science of psychology, or sociology. The exhortations to moral virtue are not propositions at all, but ejaculations or commands which are designed to provoke the reader to action of a certain sort. Accordingly, they do not belong to any branch of philosophy or science. As for the expressions of ethical judgements, we have not yet determined how they should be classified. But inasmuch as they are certainly neither definitions nor comments upon definitions, nor quotations, we may say decisively that they do not belong to ethical philosophy. A strictly philosophical treatise on ethics should therefore make no ethical pronouncements. But it should, by giving an analysis of ethical terms, show what is the category to which all such pronouncements belong. And this is what we are now about to do.

A question which is often discussed by ethical philosophers is whether it is possible to find definitions which would reduce all ethical terms to one or two fundamental terms. But this question, though it undeniably belongs to ethical philosophy, is not relevant to our present enquiry. We are not now concerned to discover which term, within the sphere of ethical terms, is to be taken as fundamental; whether, for example, "good" can be defined in terms of "right" or "right" in terms of "good," or both in terms of "value." What we are interested in is the possibility of reducing the whole sphere of ethical terms to non-ethical terms. We are enquiring whether statements of ethical value can be translated into statements of empirical fact.

That they can be so translated is the contention of those ethical philosophers who are commonly called subjectivists, and of those who are known as utilitarians. For the utilitarian defines the rightness of actions, and the goodness of ends, in terms of the pleasure, or happiness, or satisfaction, to which they give rise; the subjectivist, in terms of the feelings of approval which a certain person, or group of people, has towards them. Each of these types of definition makes moral judgements into a sub-class of psychological or sociological judgements; and for this reason they are very attractive to us. For, if either was correct, it would follow that ethical assertions were not generically different from the factual assertions which are ordinarily contrasted with them; and the account which we have already given of empirical hypotheses would apply to them also.

Nevertheless we shall not adopt either a subjectivist or a utilitarian analysis of ethical terms. We reject the subjectivist view that to call an action right, or a thing good, is to say that it is generally approved of, because it is not self-contradictory to assert that some actions which are generally approved of are not right, or that some things which are generally approved of are not good. And we reject the alternative subjectivist view that a man who asserts that a certain action is right, or that a certain thing is good, is saying that he himself approves of it, on the ground that a man who confessed that he sometimes approved of what was bad or wrong would not be contradicting himself. And a similar argument is fatal to utilitarianism. We cannot agree that to call an action right is to say that of all the actions possible in the circumstances it would cause, or be likely to cause, the greatest happiness, or the greatest balance of pleasure over pain, or the greatest balance of satisfied over unsatisfied desire, because we find that it is not self-contradictory to say that it is sometimes wrong to perform the action which would actually or probably cause the greatest happiness, or the greatest balance of pleasure over pain, or of satisfied over unsatisfied desire. And since it is not self-contradictory to say that some pleasant things are not good, or that some bad things are desired, it cannot be the case that the sentence "x is good" is equivalent to "x is pleasant," or to "x is desired." And to every other variant of utilitarianism with which I am acquainted the same objection can be made. And therefore we should, I think, conclude that the validity of ethical judgements is not determined by the felicific tendencies of actions, any more than by the nature of people's feelings; but that it must be regarded as "absolute" or "intrinsic," and not empirically calculable.

If we say this, we are not, of course, denying that it is possible to invent a language in which all ethical symbols are definable in non-ethical terms, or even that it is desirable to invent such a language and adopt it in place of our own; what we are denying is that the suggested reduction of ethical to non-ethical statements is consistent with the conventions of our actual language. That is, we reject utilitarianism and subjectivism, not as proposals to replace our existing ethical notions by new ones, but as analyses of our existing ethical notions. Our contention is simply that, in our language, sentences which contain normative ethical symbols are not equivalent to sentences which express psychological propositions, or indeed empirical propositions of any kind.

It is advisable here to make it plain that it is only normative ethical symbols, and not descriptive ethical symbols, that are held by us to be indefinable in factual terms. There is a danger of confusing these two types of symbols, because they are commonly constituted by signs of the same sensible form. Thus a complex sign of the form "x is wrong" may constitute a sentence which expresses a moral judgement concerning a certain type of conduct, or it may constitute a sentence which states that a certain type of conduct is repugnant to the moral sense of a particular society. In the latter case, the symbol "wrong" is a descriptive ethical symbol, and the sentence in which it occurs expresses an ordinary sociological proposition; in the former case, the symbol "wrong" is a normative ethical symbol, and the sentence in which it occurs does not, we maintain, express an empirical proposition at all. It is only with normative ethics that we are at present concerned; so that whenever ethical symbols are used in the course of this argument without qualification, they are always to be interpreted as symbols of the normative type.

In admitting that normative ethical concepts are irreducible to empirical concepts, we seem to be leaving the way clear for the "absolutist" view of ethics—that is, the view that statements of value are not controlled by observation, as ordinary empirical propositions are, but only by a mysterious "intellectual intuition." A feature of this theory, which is seldom recognized by its advocates, is that

it makes statements of value unverifiable. For it is notorious that what seems intuitively certain to one person may seem doubtful, or even false, to another. So that unless it is possible to provide some criterion by which one may decide between conflicting intuitions, a mere appeal to intuition is worthless as a test of a proposition's validity. But in the case of moral judgements, no such criterion can be given. Some moralists claim to settle the matter by saying that they "know" that their own moral judgements are correct. But such an assertion is of purely psychological interest, and has not the slightest tendency to prove the validity of any moral judgement. For dissentient moralists may equally well "know" that their ethical views are correct. And, as far as subjective certainty goes, there will be nothing to choose between them. When such differences of opinion arise in connection with an ordinary empirical proposition, one may attempt to resolve them by referring to, or actually carrying out, some relevant empirical test. But with regard to ethical statements, there is, on the "absolutist" or "intuitionist" theory, no relevant empirical test. We are therefore justified in saying that on this theory ethical statements are held to be unverifiable. They are, of course, also held to be genuine synthetic propositions.

Considering the use which we have made of the principle that a synthetic proposition is significant only if it is empirically verifiable, it is clear that the acceptance of an "absolutist" theory of ethics would undermine the whole of our main argument. And as we have already rejected the "naturalistic" theories which are commonly supposed to provide the only alternative to "absolutism" in ethics, we seem to have reached a difficult position. We shall meet the difficulty by showing that the correct treatment of ethical statements is afforded by a third theory, which is wholly compatible with our radical empiricism.

We begin by admitting that the fundamental ethical concepts are unanalysable, inasmuch as there is no criterion by which one can test the validity of the judgements in which they occur. So far we are in agreement with the absolutists. But, unlike the absolutists, we are able to give an explanation of this fact about ethical concepts. We say that the reason why they are unanalysable is that they are mere pseudo-concepts. The presence of an ethical symbol in a proposition adds nothing to its factual content. Thus if I say to someone, "You acted wrongly in stealing that money," I am not stating anything more than if I had simply said, "You stole that money." In adding that this action is wrong I am not making any further statement about it. I am simply evincing my moral disapproval of it. It is as if I had said, "You stole that money," in a peculiar tone of horror, or written it with the addition of some special exclamation marks. The tone, or the exclamation marks, adds nothing to the literal meaning of the sentence. It merely serves to show that the expression of it is attended by certain feelings in the speaker.

If now I generalise my previous statement and say, "Stealing money is wrong," I produce a sentence which has no factual meaning—that is, expresses no proposition which can be either true or false. It is as if I had written "Stealing money!!"—where the shape and thickness of the exclamation marks show, by a suitable convention, that a special sort of moral disapproval is the feeling which is being expressed. It is clear that there is nothing said here which can be true or false. Another man may disagree with me about the wrongness of stealing, in the sense that he may not have the same feelings about stealing as I have, and he may quarrel with me on account of my moral sentiments. But he cannot, strictly speaking, contradict me. For in saying that a certain type of action is right or wrong, I am not making any factual statement, not even a statement about my own state of mind. I am merely expressing certain moral sentiments. And the man who is ostensibly contradicting me is merely expressing his moral sentiments. So that there is plainly no sense in asking which of us is in the right. For neither of us is asserting a genuine proposition.

What we have just been saying about the symbol "wrong" applies to all normative ethical symbols. Sometimes they occur in sentences which record ordinary empirical facts besides expressing ethical feeling about those facts: sometimes they occur in sentences which simply express ethical feeling about a certain type of action, or situation, without making any statement of fact. But in every case in which one would commonly be said to be making an ethical judgement, the function of the relevant ethical word is purely "emotive." It is used to express feeling about certain objects, but not to make any assertion about them.

It is worth mentioning that ethical terms do not serve only to express feeling. They are calculated also to arouse feeling, and so to stimulate action. Indeed some of them are used in such a way as to give the sentences in which they occur the effect of commands. Thus the sentence "It is your duty to tell the truth" may be regarded both as the expression of a certain sort of ethical feeling about truthfulness and as the expression of the command "Tell the truth." The sentence "You ought to tell the truth" also involves the command "Tell the truth," but here the tone of the command is less emphatic. In the sentence "It is good to tell the truth" the command has become little more than a suggestion. And thus the "meaning" of the word "good," in its ethical usage, is differentiated from that of the word "duty" or the word "ought." In fact we may define the meaning of the various ethical words in terms both of the different feelings they are ordinarily taken to express, and also the different responses which they are calculated to provoke.

Charles Leslie Stevenson
(1908–1979)

The Emotive Meaning of Ethical Terms [10]

I

Ethical questions first arise in the form "Is so and so good?", or "Is this alternative better than that?" These questions are difficult partly because we don't quite know what we are seeking. We are asking, "Is there a needle in that haystack?" without even knowing just what a needle is. So the first thing to do is to examine the questions themselves. . . .

The present paper is concerned wholly with this preliminary step of making ethical questions clear. In order to help answer the question "Is X good?" we must *substitute* for it a question which is free from ambiguity and confusion. . . .

[10] Charles Leslie Stevenson, "The Emotive Meaning of Ethical Terms," *Mind* 46 (January 1937): 14–31. The selection is from pp. 14–20.

Let us now turn to our particular task—that of giving a relevant definition of "good." Let us first examine some of the ways in which others have attempted to do this.

The word "good" has often been defined in terms of *approval,* or similar psychological attitudes. We may take as typical examples: "good" means *desired by me* (Hobbes); and "good" means *approved by most people* (Hume, in effect). It will be convenient to refer to definitions of this sort as "interest theories.". . .

Now many have maintained that interest theories . . . neglect the very sense of "good" which is most vital. And certainly, their arguments are not without plausibility.

Only . . . what *is* this "vital" sense of "good"? The answers have been so vague, and so beset with difficulties, that one can scarcely determine.

There are certain requirements, however, with which this "vital" sense has been expected to comply—requirements which appeal strongly to our common sense. It will be helpful to summarize these, showing how they exclude the interest theories:

In the first place, we must be able sensibly to *disagree* about whether something is "good." This condition rules out Hobbes's definition. For consider the following argument: "This is good." "That isn't so; it's not good." As translated by Hobbes, this becomes: "I desire this." "That isn't so, for *I* don't." The speakers are not contradicting one another, and think they are, only because of an elementary confusion in the use of pronouns. The definition, "good" means *desired by my community,* is also excluded, for how could people from different communities disagree? [a]

In the second place, "goodness" must have, so to speak, a magnetism. A person who recognizes X to be "good" must *ipso facto* acquire a stronger tendency to act in its favour than he otherwise would have had. This rules out the Humian type of definition. For according to Hume, to recognize that something is "good" is simply to recognize that the majority approve of it. Clearly, a man may see that the majority approve of X without having, himself, a stronger tendency to favour it. This requirement excludes any attempt to define "good"

in terms of the interest of people *other* than the speaker.[b]

In the third place, the "goodness" of anything must not be verifiable solely by use of the scientific method. "Ethics must not be psychology." This restriction rules out all of the traditional interest theories, without exception. It is so sweeping a restriction that we must examine its plausibility. What are the methodological implications of interest theories which are here rejected?

According to Hobbes's definition, a person can prove his ethical judgments, with finality, by showing that he is not making an introspective error about his desires. According to Hume's definition, one may prove ethical judgments (roughly speaking) by taking a vote. *This* use of the empirical method, at any rate, seems highly remote from what we usually accept as proof, and reflects on the complete relevance of the definitions which imply it.

But aren't there more complicated interest theories which are immune from such methodological implications? No, for the same factors appear; they are only put off for a while. Consider, for example, the definition: "X is good" means *most people would approve of X if they knew its nature and consequences.* How, according to this definition, could we prove that a certain X was good? We should first have to find out, empirically, just what X was like, and what its consequences would be. To this extent the empirical method, as required by the definition, seems beyond intelligent objection. But what remains? We should next have to discover whether most people would approve of the sort of thing we had discovered X to be. This couldn't be determined by popular vote—but only because it would be too difficult to explain to the voters, beforehand, what the nature and consequences of X really were. Apart from this, voting would be a pertinent method. We are again reduced to counting noses, as a *perfectly final* appeal.

Now we need not scorn voting entirely. A man who rejected interest theories as irrelevant might readily make the following statement: "If I believed that X would be approved by the majority, when they knew all about it, I should be strongly *led* to say that X was good." But he would continue: *"Need* I say that X was good, under the circumstances?

---

[a] See G. E. Moore's *Philosophical Studies,* pp. 332–334.

[b] See G. C. Field's *Moral Theory,* pp. 52, 56–57.

Wouldn't my acceptance of the alleged 'final proof' result simply from my being democratic? What about the more aristocratic people? They would simply say that the approval of most people, even when they knew all about the object of their approval, simply had nothing to do with the goodness of anything, and they would probably add a few remarks about the low state of people's interests." It would indeed seem, from these considerations, that the definition we have been considering has presupposed democratic ideals from the start: it has dressed up democratic propaganda in the guise of a definition.

The omnipotence of the empirical method, as implied by interest theories and others, may be shown unacceptable in a somewhat different way. Mr. G. E. Moore's familiar objection about the open question is chiefly pertinent in this regard. No matter what set of scientifically knowable properties a thing may have (says Moore, in effect), you will find, on careful introspection, that it is an open question to ask whether anything having these properties is *good*. It is difficult to believe that this recurrent question is a totally confused one, or that it seems open only because of the ambiguity of "good." Rather, we must be using some sense of "good" which is not definable, relevantly, in terms of anything scientifically knowable. That is, the scientific method is not sufficient for ethics.[c]

These, then, are the requirements with which the "vital" sense of "good" is expected to comply: (1) goodness must be a topic for intelligent disagreement; (2) it must be "magnetic"; and (3) it must not be discoverable solely through the scientific method.

II

Let us now turn to my own analysis of ethical judgments. First let me present my position dogmatically, showing to what extent I vary from tradition.

I believe that the three requirements, given above, are perfectly sensible; that there is some *one* sense

of "good" which satisfies all three requirements; and that no traditional interest theory satisfies them all. But this does not imply that "good" must be explained in terms of a Platonic Idea, or of a Categorical Imperative, or of an unique, unanalyzable property. On the contrary, the three requirements can be met by a *kind* of interest theory. *But we must give up a presupposition which all the traditional interest theories have made.*

Traditional interest theories hold that ethical statements are *descriptive* of the existing state of interests—that they simply *give information* about interests. (More accurately, ethical judgments are said to describe what the state of interests is, was, or will be, or to indicate what the state of interests *would* be under specified circumstances.) It is this emphasis on description, on information, which leads to their incomplete relevance. Doubtless there is always *some* element of description in ethical judgments, but this is by no means all. Their major use is not to indicate facts, but to *create an influence*. Instead of merely describing people's interests, they *change* or *intensify* them. They *recommend* an interest in an object, rather than state that the interest already exists.

For instance: When you tell a man that he oughtn't to steal, your object isn't merely to let him know that people disapprove of stealing. You are attempting, rather, to get *him* to disapprove of it. Your ethical judgment has a quasi-imperative force which, operating through suggestion, and intensified by your tone of voice, readily permits you to begin to *influence*, to *modify*, his interests. If in the end you do not succeed in getting *him* to disapprove of stealing, you will feel that you've failed to convince him that stealing is wrong. You will continue to feel this, even though he fully acknowledges that you disapprove of it, and that almost everyone else does. When you point out to him the consequences of his actions—consequences which you suspect he already disapproves of—these *reasons* which support your ethical judgment are simply a means of facilitating your influence. If you think you can change his interests by making vivid to him how others will disapprove of him, you will do so; otherwise not. So the consideration about other people's interest is just an additional means you may employ, in order to move him, and is not a part of the ethical judgment itself. Your ethical judgment

[c] See G. E. Moore's *Principia Ethica*, chap. i. I am simply trying to preserve the spirit of Moore's objection, and not the exact form of it.

doesn't merely describe interests to him, it directs his very interests. The difference between the traditional interest theories and my view is like the difference between describing a desert and irrigating it.

Another example: A munition maker declares that war is a good thing. If he merely meant that he approved of it, he would not have to insist so strongly, nor grow so excited in his argument. People would be quite easily convinced that he approved of it. If he merely meant that most people approved of war, or that most people would approve of it if they knew the consequences, he would have to yield his point if it were proved that this wasn't so. But he wouldn't do this, nor does consistency require it. He is not *describing* the state of people's approval; he is trying to *change* it by his influence. If he found that few people approved of war, he might insist all the more strongly that it was good, for there would be more changing to be done.

This example illustrates how "good" may be used for what most of us would call bad purposes. Such cases are as pertinent as any others. I am not indicating the *good* way of using "good." I am not influencing people, but am describing the way this influence sometimes goes on. If the reader wishes to say that the munition maker's influence is bad—that is, if the reader wishes to awaken people's disapproval of the man, and to make him disapprove of his own actions—I should at another time be willing to join in this undertaking. But this is not the present concern. I am not using ethical terms, but am indicating how they *are* used. The munition maker, in his use of "good," illustrates the persuasive character of the word just as well as does the unselfish man who, eager to encourage in each of us a desire for the happiness of all, contends that the supreme good is peace.

Thus ethical terms are *instruments* used in the complicated interplay and readjustment of human interests. This can be seen plainly from more general observations. People from widely separated communities have different moral attitudes. Why? To a great extent because they have been subject to different social influences. Now clearly this influence doesn't operate through sticks and stones alone; words play a great part. People praise one another, to encourage certain inclinations, and blame one another, to discourage others. Those of forceful personalities issue commands which weaker people, for complicated instinctive reasons, find it difficult to disobey, quite apart from fears of consequences. Further influence is brought to bear by writers and orators. Thus social influence is exerted, to an enormous extent, by means that have nothing to do with physical force or material reward. The ethical terms facilitate such influence. Being suited for use in *suggestion*, they are a means by which men's attitudes may be led this way or that. The reason, then, that we find a greater similarity in the moral attitudes of one community than in those of different communities is largely this: ethical judgments propagate themselves. One man says "This is good"; this may influence the approval of another person, who then makes the same ethical judgment, which in turn influences another person, and so on. In the end, by a process of mutual influence, people take up more or less the same attitudes. Between people of widely separated communities, of course, the influence is less strong; hence different communities have different attitudes.

In *Ethics and Language* (1944) Stevenson further developed the theory. Once again, the focus is ethical disagreement. Disagreement in belief is distinguished from disagreement in attitude, the latter being "an opposition of purposes, aspirations, wants, preferences, desires, and so on." [11] Instead of definitions of ethical terms, working models for them are proposed. For example,

(1) "This is wrong" means *I disapprove of this; do so as well.*
(2) "He ought to do this" means *I disapprove of his leaving this undone; do so as well.*
(3) "This is good" means *I approve of this; do so as well.* [12]

The crucial consequence of these models comes in Chapter VII, "Validity," which asks what kind of relation can obtain between a set of reasons and an ethical conclusion. The

[11] *Ethics and Language* (New Haven: Yale University Press, 1944), p. 3.
[12] Ibid., p. 21.

relation cannot be deductive or inductive. And to accept any ethical method to determine validity is itself a moral act, involving an attitude. It follows that the relation of belief and attitude is causal, not logical; beliefs may, but do not always, determine the acceptance of an attitude. Chapter X argues that definitions of moral terms are *persuasive*—for example, to define "right" as that which produces the greatest happiness for the greatest number is to advocate democracy; or to define "good" in terms of a reasoned preference is to advocate rationality.

The initial picture of disagreement was between at least two parties, and Stevenson's models were fashioned for such a situation. Eventually, he had to face the question whether—as decision became central in ethical analysis—his models could apply to the decision of a single individual. In *Facts and Values* (1963) he supplemented disagreement in attitude with uncertainty in attitude.[13] The situation is thus seen as one part of a personality attempting to control another part, as in Freud's account of conflicts of supergo and id. It would thus appear that internal decision is no more rational than interpersonal argument.

Interestingly, despite what might seem to be a relativistic denial of absolute moral judgment, Stevenson is highly critical of ethical relativism. He epitomizes relativism as forcing "good" to have the meaning of "considered good" and "justified" the meaning of "is considered justified"; by a special metatheory for the utterance, it abstains from making ethical judgments. Stevenson says it substitutes the indirect discourse for the direct discourse, thus replacing ethical participation with social science fact.[14]

---

[13] Charles L. Stevenson, *Facts and Values: Studies in Ethical Analysis* (New Haven: Yale University Press, 1963), "Retrospective Comments," pp. 191–203.
[14] Ibid., "Relativism and Nonrelativism in the Theory of Value," pp. 91–92.

P. H. Nowell-Smith
(1914–   )

Ethics [15]

Ch 18: Conscience

At the end of chapter 16 I suggested that the actual power of conscience was more obvious than its authority and that a man might be a slave to his own conscience; and in chapter 12 I said that it was logically odd to say 'This is the morally better course; but I shall do that.' These paradoxes must now be explained.

It might seem to be tautologous to say that a man ought to do what his conscience tells him to do; for is not the Voice of Conscience precisely the voice that tells him what he ought to do? But this argument is plainly specious; for a decision to do something never follows logically from a command to do it. 'I ought' never follows from 'You ought,' and if Conscience is described—as it is both in philosophical literature and common speech—as a voice that tells you what you ought to do, its function is that of advising, exhorting, or commanding, not of deciding or choosing. 'Everyone ought to obey his conscience' is a general moral commandment issued to everyone, including the speaker; it is not a logical truism.

Nor can this conclusion be evaded by saying that the voice of conscience is infallible, that 'you ought' entails 'I ought' in the special case in which it is conscience that issues the command. For if this were so we should have to say that men can mistake some other voice, perhaps that of the Freudian Father-Substitute, for that of conscience; and we should have no way of distinguishing the true conscience from the false except by saying that the 'you ought' is a genuine command of conscience only in cases in which it does entail 'I ought.' Nothing is more certain than the fact that the consciences of different men conflict; and, even if it were true that Jones necessarily thinks Smith a better man if he follows his conscience (which I have given reasons for doubting), it is certainly untrue that Jones always thinks that Smith's conscience has given the right commands.

---

[15] The selection is from Nowell-Smith, *Ethics*, pp. 260–265.

The philosophical tradition that treats conscience as an internal judge is partly responsible for the theory that conscience has "manifest authority"; for judges are notoriously people who have authority. If conscience is the court from which there is no appeal, it is tautological to say that it is right for a man to obey his conscience, since conscience is, by definition, the authority competent to judge what is right and what is wrong. But we must not confuse the office of the judge with that of the advocate. The role of the former is to pronounce a verdict, that of the latter to plead a cause.

The confusion is reached in the following way. 'I ought' is used to express a verdict or decision. It differs from 'I shall' in that, while 'I shall' can be used to express any decision, 'I ought' is only used to express decisions of a certain kind, namely those based on rules. It is for this reason that it is logically odd to say "I know I ought to do X, but shall I do it?" Unless 'shall I?' is being used in a predictive sense to be considered later, a man who says it has not yet reached a decision and cannot, in consequence, say 'I ought' in the judicial, verdict-giving sense.

But 'I ought' is also used, not to express a decision, but in the course of making up one's mind before a decision has been reached. A man may hesitate between two moral principles and say to himself at one time 'I ought to do X' and at another 'But on the other hand I ought to do Y' or he may contrast 'I ought' with 'I should like to.' In the first of these cases he is hesitating between two moral principles, in the second between acting on a moral principle and acting on some other motive. But in neither case has he arrived at a verdict. In the first case it is quite natural to represent the two 'oughts' as being spoken by internal moral authorities advising or telling him what to do; and in the second to represent the conflict as one between the Voice of Conscience and Desire. But these are the voices of advocates, not of judges; and what they say is, not 'I ought,' but 'you ought.'

The difference between 'you ought' and 'I ought' is obscured by two facts, one empirical and one logical. In the first place moral struggles are comparatively rare; we have often only to recognize the 'you ought' of conscience to pass immediately to the 'I ought' of decision. (Whether we carry out the decision is another matter; we may lack self-control.) And secondly our talk *about* moral judgments, as opposed to the expressions we use in *making* moral judgements or decisions, is always put in indirect speech. And here both the verdict-giving 'I ought' and the self-hortatory 'you ought' become 'he ought.' In a description of a man making up his mind about a course of action "He thinks that he ought to do X" might mean "He is saying to himself 'You ought to do X,'" i.e. he is telling himself what to do. But it might also mean "He is saying to himself 'I ought to do X,'" i.e. he has arrived at a decision about what to do.

Duty and Inclination. This way of representing deliberation as a conflict between voices or forces is not wholly unnatural. But if either the metaphor of the council chamber or that of the conflict of mechanical forces is taken too seriously it leads to highly paradoxical results. According to some psychologists the Voice of Conscience in an adult is the ghost or memory of the father who told him what to do when he was a child and punished him for not doing it. Now so long as psychologists confine themselves to describing and explaining empirical phenomena and do not draw moral conclusions, there is no reason why a philosopher should quarrel with them; and if he does, he ought to produce evidence that rebuts the psychologists' explanation. But philosophers often object to this account of the genesis of conscience on the grounds that it ignores the peculiar moral authority of conscience. They claim rightly that we are under no necessary obligation to do what the voice of conscience tells us if this voice is really what the psychologists say it is. But in their account of decision and obligation they tend to reproduce the very feature that makes the psychologist's account irrelevant to the question whether I ought to obey my conscience. Conscience, they say, is a special non-natural voice that speaks with authority; but they still represent it as a voice which issues orders. And if this is what it is it will always make sense for me to ask whether I ought to do what my conscience tells me to do. For a moral decision is a decision to act on a principle that one freely accepts, not a decision to act on a principle on which one is told to act. The 'voice' or 'force' to which conscience is likened in the council chamber and mechanical metaphors is one of the participants in the contest and cannot be identified with the person who decides between the participants. To make a moral decision is neither to be ordered (though it may be a decision to obey an order) nor to be the prize of a victorious inner force (though it may be a decision to follow a certain inclination); it is to *decide*; and this is something that *I* do, not something that is done by voices or forces inside me.

Some philosophers will object to this account of the difference between the self-hortatory 'you ought' and the verdict-giving 'I ought' on the grounds that, in the special case of conscience, the two are identical. My conscience, they will say, *is* myself. While they are prepared to talk of desires or inclinations as internal forces which operate on 'me,' the 'self' or 'self-acting-in-accordance-with-conscience' is, as it were, the billiard-ball on which these forces act. The only difference between the case of the billiard ball and that of the self is that, whereas the behaviour of the billiard ball is completely determined by the forces acting on it, the self is capable of spontaneous action. I choose freely only when I am not obliged by my desires or inclinations but do what my 'self' decides to do.

But this theory seriously distorts our account both of choosing and of responsibility. I shall consider its application to responsibility in the next chapter and confine myself here to the suggested analysis of choice. Moral conflict is now represented as a battle between 'me' (or my 'self' or 'my conscience') and 'my desires'; and if this is so it is nonsense to ask whether or not I can choose to overcome a particular desire. For 'I' am now represented as one of the participants in the conflict. Either I win or I lose. If I win, I act freely because my action is that of the self-propelled conscience or conscience-propelled self; if I lose, I do not act freely, because the action is that of a desire which is not me at all. But in neither case can I choose between what I ought to do and what I want to do.

I have already suggested that it is paradoxical to represent all motives other than the sense of duty as 'forces' which oblige me to act as I do, since this entails that I do not act freely when I do what I want to do; and I suggested that a worse paradox was to follow. It is this. There can be no such thing as intentional or even voluntary wrong-doing, and therefore no such thing as just blame or punishment. In the mouth of a Socrates or a Spinoza there would be nothing strange about this conclusion; for Socrates thought no wrong-doing could be voluntary and was puzzled to know how any man

could deserve blame, and Spinoza was prepared to push the theory to its inevitable conclusion and say that blame is never justified. A wise man tries to understand why men behave as they do; only a fool blames them.

But the theory of the self-propelling conscience is often found in conjunction with the view that conscientiousness is the only virtue and acting against one's conscience the only vice. And it is this combination that is paradoxical, since on this theory a conscientious action is the only type of free action, all actions prompted by desire being unfree. If conscience wins the day I act freely and am good; if desire wins the day, I am bad but *I* do not choose to do what I do. Now all this may be true; but, if so, ordinary men have for centuries been labouring under a profound delusion. For nothing is more certain than that they believe that a man can choose to do what is wrong and that he chooses in exactly the same sense of 'choose' as he does when he chooses to do what is right or when he chooses to do something in a case in which morality is not involved. No doubt there are many differences between choosing the path of duty and choosing a place for a holiday; but it is paradoxical to suggest that we have to do with different senses of the word 'choose.'

The linguistic analysis of "ought" outlined here is carried out in greater detail by Paul W. Taylor in *Normative Discourse* (Englewood Cliffs, N.J.: Prentice-Hall, 1961), Chapter 7. Taylor distinguishes "I ought," "you ought," and "he ought." The first is decisional, the second is advisory, and the third is evaluative. The distinctions are based not only on the function but on nonformal conditions: for example, "you ought" requires the presence of the person; "he ought" does not. There are also temporal distinctions: for example, after-the-event oughts are said to be evaluative, never prescriptive; pre-event oughts may be prescriptive or evaluative depending on circumstances and personal pronoun, and whether they express value judgments of the act or the agent, whether they tell or advise, etc. Thus if we ask "What is the meaning of 'ought'?" we cannot expect a *general* answer.

J. L. Austin
(1911–1960)

A Plea for Excuses [16]

The subject of this paper, *Excuses*, is one not to be treated, but only to be introduced, within such limits. It is, or might be, the name of a whole branch, even a ramiculated branch, of philosophy, or at least of one fashion of philosophy. I shall try, therefore, first to state *what* the subject is, *why* it is worth studying, and *how* it may be studied, all this at a regrettably lofty level: and then I shall illustrate, in more congenial but desultory detail, some of the methods to be used, together with their limitations, and some of the unexpected results to be expected and lessons to be learned. Much, of course, of the amusement, and of the instruction, comes in drawing the coverts of the microglot, in hounding down the minutiae, and to this I can do no more here than incite you. But I owe it to the subject to say, that it has long afforded me what philosophy is so often thought, and made, barren of—the fun of discovery, the pleasures of co-operation, and the satisfaction of reaching agreement.

What, then, is the subject? I am here using the word "excuses" *for a title,* but it would be unwise to freeze too fast to this one noun and its partner verb: indeed for some time I used to use "extenuation" instead. Still, on the whole "excuses" is probably the most central and embracing term in the field, although this includes others of importance— "plea," "defence," "justification," and so on. When, then, do we "excuse" conduct, our own or somebody else's? When are "excuses" proffered?

In general, the situation is one where someone is *accused* of having done something, or (if that will keep it any cleaner) where someone is *said* to have done something which is bad, wrong, inept, unwelcome, or in some other of the numerous possible ways untoward. Thereupon he, or someone on his behalf, will try to defend his conduct or to get him out of it.

One way of going about this is to admit flatly

that he, X, did do that very thing, A, but to argue that it was a good thing, or the right or sensible thing, or a permissible thing to do, either in general or at least in the special circumstances of the occasion. To take this line is to *justify* the action, to give reasons for doing it: not to say, to brazen it out, to glory in it, or the like.

A different way of going about it is to admit that it wasn't a good thing to have done, but to argue that it is not quite fair or correct to say *baldly* "X did A." We may say it isn't fair just to say X did it; perhaps he was under somebody's influence, or was nudged. Or, it isn't fair to say baldly he *did* A; it may have been partly accidental, or an unintentional slip. Or, it isn't fair to say he did simply A—he was really doing something quite different and A was only incidental, or he was looking at the whole thing quite differently. Naturally these arguments can be combined or overlap or run into each other.

In the one defence, briefly, we accept responsibility but deny that it was bad: in the other, we admit that it was bad but don't accept full, or even any, responsibility.

By and large, justifications can be kept distinct from excuses, and I shall not be so anxious to talk about them because they have enjoyed more than their fair share of philosophical attention. But the two certainly can be confused, and can *seem* to go very near to each other, even if they do not perhaps actually do so. You dropped the tea-tray: Certainly, but an emotional storm was about to break out: or, Yes, but there was a wasp. In each case the defence, very soundly, insists on a fuller description of the event in its context; but the first is a justification, the second an excuse. Again, if the objection is to the use of such a dyslogistic verb as "murdered," this may be on the ground that the killing was done in battle (justification) or on the ground that it was only accidental if reckless (excuse). It is arguable that we do not use the terms justification and excuse as carefully as we might; a miscellany of even less clear terms, such as "extenuation," "palliation," "mitigation," hovers uneasily between partial justification and partial excuse; and when we plead, say, provocation, there is genuine uncertainty or ambiguity as to what we mean—is *he* partly responsible, because he roused a violent impulse or passion in me, so that it wasn't truly or merely

[16] J. L. Austin, "A Plea for Excuses," *Proceedings of the Aristotelian Society* 57 (1956–1957): 1–30. The selection is from pp. 1–8.

me acting "of my own accord" (excuse)? Or is it rather that, he having done me such injury, I was entitled to retaliate (justification)? Such doubts merely make it the more urgent to clear up the usage of these various terms. But that the defences I have for convenience labeled "justification" and "excuse" are in principle distinct can scarcely be doubted.

This then is the sort of situation we have to consider under "excuses." I will only further point out how very wide a field it covers. We have of course to bring in the opposite numbers of excuses—the expressions that *aggravate,* such as "deliberately," "on purpose" and so on, if only for the reason that an excuse often takes the form of a rebuttal of one of these. But we have also to bring in a large number of expressions which at first blush look not so much like excuses as like accusations—"clumsiness," "tactlessness," "thoughtlessness" and the like. Because it has always to be remembered that few excuses get us out of it *completely:* the average excuse, in a poor situation, gets us only out of the fire into the frying pan—but still, of course, any frying pan in a fire. If I have broken your dish or your romance, maybe the best defence I can find will be clumsiness.

Why, if this is what "excuses" are, should we trouble to investigate them? It might be thought reason enough that their production has always bulked so large among human activities. But to moral philosophy in particular a study of them will contribute in special ways, both positively towards the development of a cautious, latter-day version of conduct, and negatively towards the correction of older and hastier theories.

In ethics we study, I suppose, the good and the bad, the right and the wrong, and this must be for the most part in some connexion with conduct or the doing of actions. Yet before we consider what actions are good or bad, right or wrong, it is proper to consider first what is meant by, and what not, and what is included under, and what not, the expression "doing an action" or "doing something." These are expressions still too little examined on their own account and merits, just as the general notion of "saying something" is still too lightly passed over in logic. There is indeed a vague and comforting idea in the background that, after all, in the last analysis, doing an action must come

down to the making of physical movements with parts of the body; but this is about as true as that saying something must, in the last analysis, come down to making movements of the tongue.

The beginning of sense, not to say wisdom, is to realise that "doing an action," as used in philosophy,[a] is a highly abstract expression—it is a stand-in used in the place of any (or almost any?) verb with a personal subject, in the same sort of way that "thing" is a stand-in for any (or when we remember, almost any) noun substantive, and "quality" a stand-in for the adjective. Nobody, to be sure, relies on such dummies quite implicitly quite indefinitely. Yet notoriously it is possible to arrive at, or to derive the idea for, an over-simplified metaphysics from the obsession with "things" and their "qualities." In a similar way, less commonly recognised even in these semi-sophisticated times, we fall for the myth of the verb. We treat the expression "doing an action" no longer as a stand-in for a verb with a personal subject, as which it has no doubt some uses, and might have more if the range of verbs were not left unspecified, but as a self-explanatory, ground-level description, one which brings adequately into the open the essential features of everything that comes, by simple inspection, under it. We scarcely notice even the most patent exceptions or difficulties (is to think something, or to say something, or to try to do something, to do an action?), any more than we fret, in the *ivresse des grandes profondeurs,* as to whether flames are things or events. So we come easily to think of our behaviour over any time, and of a life as a whole, as consisting in doing now action A, next action B, then action C, and so on, just as elsewhere we come to think of the world as consisting of this, that and the other substance or material thing, each with its properties. All "actions" are, as actions (meaning what?), equal, composing a quarrel with striking a match, winning a war with sneezing: worse still, we assimilate them one and all to the supposedly most obvious and easy cases, such as posting letters or moving fingers, just as we assimilate all "things" to horses or beds.

If we are to continue to use this expression in sober philosophy, we need to ask such questions

---

[a] This use has little to do with the more down-to-earth occurrences of "action" in ordinary speech.

as: Is to sneeze to do an action? Or is to breathe, or to see, or to checkmate, or each one of countless others? In short, for what range of verbs, as used on what occasions, is "doing an action" a stand-in? What have they in common, and what do those excluded severally lack? Again we need to ask how we decide what is the correct name for "the" action that somebody did—and what, indeed, are the rules for the use of "the" action, "an" action, "one" action, a "part" or "phase" of an action and the like. Further, we need to realise that even the "simplest" named actions are not so simple—certainly are not the mere makings of physical movements, and to ask what more, then, comes in (intentions? conventions?) and what does not (motives?), and what is the detail of the complicated internal machinery we use in "acting"—the receipt of intelligence, the appreciation of the situation, the invocation of principles, the planning, the control of execution and the rest.

In two main ways the study of excuses can throw light on these fundamental matters. First, to examine excuses is to examine cases where there has been some abnormality or failure: and as so often, the abnormal will throw light on the normal, will help us to penetrate the blinding veil of ease and obviousness that hides the mechanisms of the natural successful act. It rapidly becomes plain that the breakdowns signalised by the various excuses are of radically different kinds, affecting different parts or stages of the machinery, which the excuses consequently pick out and sort out for us. Further, it emerges that not *every* slip-up occurs in connexion with *every*thing that could be called an "action," that not every excuse is apt with every verb—far indeed from it: and this provides us with one means of introducing some classification into the vast miscellany of "actions." If we classify them according to the particular selection of breakdowns to which each is liable, this should assign them their places in some family group or groups of actions, or in some model of the machinery of acting.

In this sort of way, the philosophical study of conduct can get off to a positive fresh start. But by the way, and more negatively, a number of traditional cruces or mistakes in this field can be resolved or removed. First among these comes the problem of Freedom. While it has been the tradition to present this as the "positive" term requiring elucida-

tion, there is little doubt that to say we acted "freely" (in the philosopher's use, which is only faintly related to the everyday use) is to say only that we acted *not* un-freely, in one or another of the many heterogeneous ways of so acting (under duress, or what not). Like "real," "free" is only used to rule out the suggestion of some or all of its recognised antitheses. As "truth" is not a name for a characteristic of assertions, so "freedom" is not a name for a characteristic of actions, but the name of a dimension in which actions are assessed. In examining all the ways in which each action may not be "free," *i.e.*, the cases in which it will not do to say simply "X did A," we may hope to dispose of the problem of Freedom. Aristotle has often been chidden for talking about excuses or pleas and overlooking "the real problem": in my own case, it was when I began to see the injustice of this charge that I first became interested in excuses.

There is much to be said for the view that, philosophical tradition apart, Responsibility would be a better candidate for the role here assigned to Freedom. If ordinary language is to be our guide, it is to evade responsibility, or full responsibility, that we most often make excuses, and I have used the word myself in this way above. But in fact "responsibility" too seems not really apt in all cases: I do not exactly evade responsibility when I plead clumsiness or tactlessness, nor, often, when I plead that I only did it unwillingly or reluctantly, and still less if I plead that I had in the circumstances no choice: here I was constrained and have an excuse (or justification), yet may accept responsibility. It may be, then, that at least two key terms, Freedom and Responsibility, are needed: the relation between them is not clear, and it may be hoped that the investigation of excuses will contribute towards its clarification.[b]

---

[b] Another well-flogged horse in these same stakes is Blame. At least two things seem confused together under this term. Sometimes when I blame X for doing A, say for breaking the vase, it is a question simply or mainly of my disapproval of A, breaking the vase, which unquestionably X did: but sometimes it is, rather, a question simply or mainly of how far I think X responsible for A, which unquestionably was bad. Hence if somebody says he blames me for something, I may answer by giving a *justification*, so that he will cease to disapprove of what I did,

So much, then, for ways in which the study of excuses may throw light on ethics. But there are also reasons why it is an attractive subject methodologically, at least if we are to proceed from "ordinary language," that is, by examining *what we should say when*, and so why and what we should mean by it. Perhaps this method, at least as *one* philosophical method, scarcely requires justification at present—too evidently, there is gold in them thar hills: more opportune would be a warning about the care and thoroughness needed if it is not to fall into disrepute. I will, however, justify it very briefly.

First, words are our tools, and, as a minimum, we should use clean tools: we should know what we mean and what we do not, and we must forearm ourselves against the traps that language sets us. Secondly, words are not (except in their own little corner) facts or things: we need therefore to prise them off the world, to hold them apart from and against it, so that we can realise their inadequacies and arbitrarinesses, and can re-look at the world without blinkers. Thirdly, and more hopefully, our common stock of words embodies all the distinctions men have found worth drawing, and the connexions they have found worth marking, in the lifetimes of many generations: these surely are likely to be more numerous, more sound, since they have stood up to the long test of the survival of the fittest, and more subtle, at least in all ordinary and reasonably practical matters, than any that you or I are likely to think up in our armchairs of an afternoon—the most favoured alternative method.

In view of the prevalence of the slogan "ordinary language," and of such names as "linguistic" or "analytic" philosophy or "the analysis of language," one thing needs specially emphasising to counter misunderstandings. When we examine what we should say when, what words we should use in what situations, we are looking again not *merely* at words (or "meanings," whatever they may be) but also at the realities we use the words to talk about: we are using a sharpened awareness of words to sharpen our perception of, though not as the final arbiter of, the phenomena. For this reason I think it might be better to use, for this way

of doing philosophy, some less misleading name than those given above—for instance, "linguistic phenomenology," only that is rather a mouthful.

H. L. A. Hart
(1907–   )

The Ascription of Responsibility and Rights [17]

There are in our ordinary language sentences whose primary function is not to describe things, events, or persons or anything else, nor to express or kindle feelings or emotions, but to do such things as claim rights ("This is mine"), recognise rights when claimed by others ("Very well this is yours"), ascribe rights whether claimed or not ("This is his"), transfer rights ("This is now yours"), and also to admit or ascribe or make accusations of responsibility ("I did it," "He did it," "You did it"). My main purpose in this article is to suggest that the philosophical analysis of the concept of a human action has been inadequate and confusing, at least in part because sentences of the form "He did it" have been traditionally regarded as primarily descriptive whereas their principal function is what I venture to call *ascriptive*, being quite literally to ascribe responsibility for actions much as the principal function of sentences of the form "This is his" is to ascribe rights in property. Now ascriptive sentences and the other kinds of sentences quoted above, though they may form only a small part of our ordinary language, resemble in some important respects the formal statements of claim, the indictments, the admissions, the judgments, and the verdicts which constitute so large and so important a part of the language of lawyers; and the logical peculiarities which distinguish these kinds of sentences from descriptive sentences, or rather from the theoretical model of descriptive sentences with which philosophers often work, can best be grasped by consider-

---

or else by giving an *excuse*, so that he will cease to hold me, at least entirely and in every way, responsible for doing it.

[17] H. L. A. Hart, "The Ascription of Responsibilities and Rights," *Proceedings of the Aristotelian Society* 49 (1948–1949): 171–194.

ing certain characteristics of legal concepts, as these appear in the practice and procedure of the law rather than in the theoretical discussions of legal concepts by jurists who are apt to be influenced by philosophical theories. Accordingly, in the first part of this paper I attempt to bring out some of these characteristics of legal concepts; in the second, I attempt to show how sentences ascribing rights function in our ordinary language and also why their distinctive function is overlooked; and in the third part I attempt to make good my claim that sentences of the form "He did it" are fundamentally ascriptive and that some at any rate of the philosophical puzzles concerning "action" have resulted from inattention to this fact.

I

As everyone knows, the decisive stage in the proceedings of an English law court is normally a *judgment* given by the court to the effect that certain facts (Smith put arsenic in his wife's coffee and as a result she died) are true and that certain legal consequences (Smith is guilty of murder) are attached to those facts. Such a judgment is therefore a compound or blend of facts and law. . . . Now there are several characteristics of the legal element in these compounds or blends which conspire to make the way in which facts support or fail to support legal conclusions, or refute or fail to refute them, unlike certain standard models of how one kind of statement supports or refutes another upon which philosophers are apt to concentrate attention. . . .

[One is that legal concepts have] a vagueness of character very loosely controlled by judicial traditions of interpretation and it has the consequence that usually the request for a definition of a legal concept—"What is a trespass?" "What is a contract?"—cannot be answered by the provision of a verbal rule for the translation of a legal expression into other terms or one specifying a set of necessary and sufficient conditions. . . .

But there is another characteristic of legal concepts of more importance for my present purpose which . . . can be seen by examining the distinctive ways in which legal utterances can be challenged. For the accusations or claims upon which law courts adjudicate can usually be challenged or opposed

in two ways. First, by a denial of the facts upon which they are based . . . and secondly by something quite different, namely, a plea that although all the circumstances are present on which a claim could succeed, yet in the particular case, the claim or accusation should not succeed because other circumstances are present which brings the case under some recognised head of exception, the effect of which is either to defeat the claim or accusation altogether or to "reduce" it so that only a weaker claim can be sustained. Thus a plea of "provocation" in murder cases, if successful, "reduces" what would otherwise be murder to manslaughter; and so in a case of contract a defence that the defendant has been deceived by a material fraudulent misrepresentation made by the plaintiff entitles the defendant in certain cases to say that the contract is not valid as claimed nor "void" but "voidable" at his option. In consequence, it is usually not possible to define a legal concept such as "trespass" or "contract" by specifying the necessary and sufficient conditions for its application. For any set of conditions may be adequate in some cases but not in others and such concepts can only be explained with the aid of a list of exceptions or negative examples showing where the concept may not be applied or may only be applied in a weakened form.

This can be illustrated in detail from the law of contract. When the student has learnt that in English law there are positive conditions required for the existence of a valid contract, *i.e.,* at least two *parties*, an *offer* by one, *acceptance* by the other, a *memorandum* in writing in some cases and *consideration*, his understanding of the legal concept of a contract is still incomplete and remains so even if he has learnt the lawyers' technique for the interpretation of the technical but still vague terms, "offer," "acceptance," "memorandum," "consideration." For these conditions, although necessary, are not always sufficient and he has still to learn what can *defeat* a claim that there is a valid contract, even though all these conditions are satisfied. That is the student has still to learn what can follow on the word "unless" which should accompany the statement of these conditions. This characteristic of legal concepts is one for which no word exists in ordinary English. The words "conditional" and "negative" have the wrong implications, but the law has a word which with some hesitation I borrow and extend: this is the word "*defeasible*" used of a legal interest in property which is subject to termination or "*defeat*" in a number of different contingencies but remains intact if no such contingencies mature. In this sense then, contract is a defeasible concept. [pp. 170–175]

Some have taken those defenses that refer to the defendant's knowledge and will and interpreted them as the general formula that "true, full and free" consent of the parties is a necessary condition of a valid contract. This is profoundly misleading, because

it suggests that there are certain psychological elements required by the law as necessary conditions of contract and that the defences are merely admitted as negative *evidence* of these. But the defence, *e.g.*, that B entered into a contract with A as a result of the undue influence exerted upon him by A, is not evidence of the absence of a factor called "true consent," but one of the multiple criteria for the use of the phrase "no true consent." To say that the law requires true consent is therefore, in fact, to say that defences such as undue influence or coercion, and any others which should be grouped with them, are admitted. And the practice of law . . . makes this clear; for no party attempting to enforce a contract is required to give evidence that there was "true, full and free consent," though in special cases where some person in a fiduciary position seeks to enforce a bargain with the person in relation to whom he occupies that position, the onus lies upon him to prove that no influence was, in fact, exerted. But, of course, even here the proof consists simply in the exclusion of those facts which ordinarily constitute the defence of undue influence, though the onus in such cases is by exception cast on the plaintiff. . . .

The principal field where jurists have I think created difficulties for themselves (in part under the influence of the traditional philosophical analysis of action) by ignoring the essentially defeasible character of the concepts they seek to clarify is the Criminal Law. There is a well-known maxim, "*actus non est reus nisi mens sit rea*," which has tempted jurists (and less often judges) to offer a general theory of

"the mental element" in crime (*mens rea*) of a type which is logically inappropriate just because the concepts involved are defeasible and are distorted by this form of definition. . . . [W]hat is meant by the mental element in criminal liability (*mens rea*) is only to be understood by considering certain defences or exceptions, such as Mistake of Fact, Accident, Coercion, Duress, Provocation, Insanity, Infancy, most of which have come to be admitted in most crimes and in some cases exclude liability altogether, and in others merely "reduce" it. The fact that these are admitted as defences or exceptions constitutes the cash value of the maxim "*actus non est reus nisi mens sit rea*." But in pursuit of the will o' the wisp of a general formula, legal theorists have sought to impose a spurious unity (as judges occasionally protest) upon these heterogeneous defences and exceptions, suggesting that they are admitted as merely evidence of the absence of some single element ("intention") or in more recent theory, two elements ("foresight" and "voluntariness") universally required as necessary conditions of criminal responsibility. And this is misleading because what the theorist misrepresents as evidence negativing the presence of necessary mental elements are, in fact, multiple criteria or grounds defeating the allegation of responsibility. But it is easy to succumb to the illusion that an accurate and satisfying "definition" can be formulated with the aid of notions like "voluntariness" because the logical character of words like "voluntary" is anomalous and ill-understood. They are treated in such definitions as words having positive force, yet, as can be seen from Aristotle's discussion in Book III of the Nicomachean Ethics, the word "voluntary" in fact serves to exclude a heterogeneous range of cases such as physical compulsion, coercion by threats, accidents, mistakes, etc., and not to designate a mental element or state; nor does "involuntary" signify the absence of this mental element or state. . . .

Consideration of the defeasible character of legal concepts helps to explain how statements of fact support or refute legal conclusions. . . . [S]ince the judge is literally deciding that on the facts before him a contract does or does not exist, and to do this is neither to describe the facts nor to make inductive or deductive inferences from the statement of facts, what he does may be either a *right* or a *wrong* decision or a *good* or *bad* judgment and can be either *affirmed* or *reversed* and (where he has no jurisdiction to decide the question) may be *quashed* or *discharged*. What cannot be said of it is that it is either *true* or *false*, logically necessary or absurd. [pp. 177–182]

II

If we step outside the law courts we shall find that there are many utterances in ordinary language which are similar in important respects in spite of important differences, to the judicial blend of law and fact. [p. 183]

. . . [C]onsider now sentences where the words used derive their meaning from legal or social institutions, for example, from the institution of property, but are simple non-technical words. Such are the simple indicative sentences in which the possessive terms "mine," "yours," "his" appear as grammatical predicates. "This is mine," "This is yours," "This is his" are primarily sentences for which lawyers have coined the expression "operative words" and Mr. J. L. Austin the word "performatory." By the utterance of such sentences, especially in the present tense, we often do not describe but actually perform or effect a transaction; with them we *claim* proprietary rights, *confer* or *transfer* such rights when they are claimed, *recognise* such rights or *ascribe* such rights whether claimed or not, and when these words are so used they are related to the facts that support them much in the same way as the judge's decision. But apart from this, these sentences, especially in past and future tenses, have a variety of other uses not altogether easy to disentangle from what I have called their primary use, and this may be shown by a sliding scale of increasing approximation to a pure descriptive use as follows:

(*a*) First, the operative or performatory use. "This is yours" said by a father handing over his gold watch to his son normally effects the transfer of the father's rights in the watch to the son; that is, makes a gift of it. But said by the elder son at the end of a dispute with his brother over the family possessions, the utterance of such a sentence constitutes a recognition of the rights of the younger son and abandons the claims of the elder. Of course, difficulties can arise in various ways over such cases analogous to the problems that confront the Judge: we can ask whether the use of the words is a valid

method of making gifts. If English law is the criterion, the answer is "yes" in the example given; but it would be "no" if what the father had pointed to was not his watch but his house, though in this case it may be that we would consider the son morally entitled to the house and the father morally bound to make it over to him. This shows that the rules which are in the background of such utterances are not necessarily legal rules. But the case to which I wish to draw attention is that where we use such sentences not to transfer or confer rights, but to ascribe or recognise them. For here, like a Judge, the individual decides, *on* certain facts, that somebody else has certain rights and his recognition is like a judgment, a blend of fact and rule if not of law. [pp. 184–186]

III

. . . I now wish to defend the similar but perhaps more controversial thesis that the concept of a human action is an ascriptive and a defeasible one, and that many philosophical difficulties come from ignoring this and searching for its necessary and sufficient conditions. The sentences "I did it," "you did it," "he did it" are, I suggest, primarily utterances with which we *confess* or *admit* liability, make accusations, or *ascribe* responsibility; and the sense in which our actions are ours is very much like that in which property is ours. . . . Of course, like the utterances already examined, connected with the non-descriptive concept of property, the verb "to do" and generally speaking the verbs of action, have an important descriptive use, especially in the present and future senses, their ascriptive use being mainly in the past tense. . . .

I can best bring out my point by contrasting it with what I think is the mistaken, but traditional philosophical analysis of the concept of an action. "What distinguishes the physical movement of a human body from a human action?" is a famous question in philosophy. The old-fashioned answer was that the distinction lies in the occurrence before or simultaneously with the physical movement of a mental event related (it was hoped) to the physical movement as its psychological cause, which event we call "having the intention" or "setting ourselves" or "willing" or "desiring" to do the act in question. The modern answer is that to say that X performed an action is to assert a categorical proposition about the movement of his body, *and* a general hypothetical proposition or propositions to the effect that X would have responded in various ways to various stimuli, or that his body would not have moved as it did or some physical consequence would have been avoided, had he chosen differently, etc. Both these answers seem to me to be wrong or at least inadequate in many different ways, but both make the common error of supposing that an adequate analysis can be given of the concept of a human action in any combination of the descriptive sentences, categorical or hypothetical, or any sentences concerned wholly with a single individual. To see this, compare with the traditional question about action the question "What is the difference between a piece of earth and a piece of property?" Property is not a descriptive concept, and the difference between "this is a piece of earth" or "Smith is holding a piece of earth" on the one hand, and "this is someone's property" and "Smith owns a piece of property" on the other cannot be explained without reference to the non-descriptive utterances by means of which laws are promulgated and decisions made or at the very least without reference to those by which rights are recognised. Nor, I suggest, can the difference between "His body moved in violent contact with another's" and "He did it" (*e.g.*, "He hit her") be explained without reference to the non-descriptive use of sentences by which liabilities or responsibility are ascribed. What is fundamentally wrong in both the old and the new version of the traditional analysis of action as a combination of physical and psychological events or a combination of categorical and hypothetical descriptive sentences, is its mistake in identifying the meaning of a non-descriptive utterance ascribing responsibility in stronger or weaker form, with the factual circumstances which support or are good reasons for the ascription. In other words, though of course not all the rules in accordance with which, in our society, we ascribe responsibility are reflected in our legal code nor vice versa, yet our concept of an action, like our concept of property, is a social concept and logically dependent on accepted rules of conduct. It is fundamentally not descriptive, but ascriptive in character; and it is a defeasible concept to be defined through exceptions and not by a set of necessary and sufficient conditions whether physical or psychological. [pp. 187–189]

Philippa R. Foot
(1920–   )

Approval and Disapproval [18]

When anthropologists or sociologists look at contemporary moral philosophy they must be struck by a fact about it which is indeed remarkable: that morality is not treated as essentially a social phenomenon. Where they themselves would think of morals first of all in connection with moral teaching, and with the regulation of behaviour in and by society, philosophers commonly take a different starting-point. What the philosopher does is to ask himself what it is to make a moral judgment, or take up a moral attitude, and he tries to give the analysis in terms of elements such as feeling, action, and thought, which are found in a single individual. Controversy persists between emotivists, prescriptivists, and those who have been labelled 'neo-naturalists' as to just which elements are needed and how they must be combined; all are agreed, however, in looking to the individual for their location. We are first to find out how it must be with him if he is to think something right or wrong, or to have an attitude such as that of moral approval; then we may go on, if we choose, to talk of shared moral beliefs and of the mechanism by which morality is taught. The essentials are found in the individual; social practices come in at a later stage in the story.

In a way it is strange that so few people question the methodological assumption just described, since we are well aware that many concepts cannot be analysed without the mention of social facts. For example it is a commonplace that writing a cheque, or going bankrupt, is impossible without the existence of particular social institutions such as banks and debts; no one would think that he could say what it is to write a cheque without giving an account of the social practices which give these marks on these bits of paper their significance. Examples may easily be multiplied. One recognizes at once, for instance, that voting is something that a man can do only in the right social setting. Other people come in to the matter not just as being voted for,

---

[18] Philippa Foot, "Approval and Disapproval," in *Law, Morality, and Society: Essays in Honour of H. L. A. Hart*, ed. P. M. S. Hacker and J. Raz (Oxford: Clarendon Press, 1977), pp. 229–246. The selection is from pp. 229–234.

but also as the creators or perpetuators of the arrangements which make voting possible. Voting requires conventions about what counts as voting, and voting on a certain side; and a special piece of social stage-setting is needed for each election in so far as lists of candidates must be drawn up, or the possible choices established in some other way.

We are, therefore, well aware that the analysis of certain concepts cannot proceed without the description of social institutions and conventions. Why is it thought that we can ignore such things in analysing the fundamental concepts of ethics? One answer is that it is the attitude, not the act, of approval that we speak about in our moral philosophy, and that it is easier to believe that acts may require an appropriate social setting than that attitudes may do so. Another answer is that we have in mind the analysis of emotions such as fear, and that for these concepts the individualistic assumption seems to be justified. Whatever precisely is to be said about fear, however such elements as feelings, desires, actions, and thoughts are involved in *being afraid*, it does not seem necessary to look beyond the individual in order to understand the concept. Other people come in as the possible objects of fear, and conventions are needed for its verbal expression; but there seems to be no reason why a single individual should not feel fear whatever the social setting in which he finds himself. In this instance it is, therefore, right to start with the individual, going on, if one chooses, to shared fears and fears that can be attributed to social groups. No fact about society is implied by the attribution of fear to an individual as facts about society are implied by saying that he voted or signed a cheque. There are, therefore, mental concepts for which the individualist assumption is correct. The question is whether it is also right for the case of approval and disapproval. Are approving and disapproving more like voting in this respect, or more like feeling afraid?

The thesis to be put forward in this paper is that it is no more possible for a single individual, without a special social setting, to approve or disapprove than it is for him to vote. This will be argued for non-moral approval and disapproval; moral attitudes will be considered briefly later on.

It is evident that there is one case of approval which is more like voting than feeling fear so far as the relation to a specific social setting is concerned; this is the case of approval by an inspector passing e.g. plans for buildings in a city. The distinguishing mark of this kind of approval (apart from the fact that it is opposed to rejection rather than disapproval) is that the approving is something done, whether by a performative use of 'I approve' or by some other recognized device; if told that the inspector has approved the plans we can ask 'When did he do so?' asking not for the period during which he had the attitude (which perhaps he never did) but rather for the time at which the act of approval was performed. For such an act of approval a special social setting is obviously required. In the first place anyone who approves plans must be appointed to do so; the appointment may be formal or informal, but it must exist. Someone not designated as competent in the matter cannot be said to approve the plans; if he imagines himself to be doing so he must also imagine himself to occupy the relevant position. Moreover to each inspecting position belong not only conditions of appointment but also the standards which are to be used by the inspector. He is required to see if certain standards are met, and this is one of the things that makes his act one of approving rather than merely giving permission. In some cases he will be given the tests that he must apply; in others he will rather judge, in his own way, how far particular ends are served, as a school inspector may license a school on the basis of his judgment, however arrived at, that the pupils are well educated and cared for.

It is clear that we cannot describe this kind of approving without mentioning the social practices which create and maintain the position of inspector. There is, it seems, no need to prove the thesis of this paper so far as the acts of approval are concerned; the debatable proposition concerns the attitudes not the acts. It does not, however, seem right to argue from the features of one to the features of the other. No doubt it is not an accident that we use the same word 'approval' in both cases; but who can say just where the similarities lie?

We must, then, start afresh and ask whether the attitudes of approval and disapproval can exist only in a determinate social setting? Why is it commonly supposed that nothing of the kind is required? The main reason is, I think, that approving and disapproving are thought to be rather like wanting and not wanting. The chief element in their composition is supposed to be a readiness to work towards or away from some result, or perhaps from some *kind* of result. When one approves of the thing one is thought to favour it, which means working towards it, and the ill-defined term of art 'pro-attitude' is used to slide between wanting and approving.

I shall first try to show that such things as promoting and wanting are quite different from approving, and that wanting and promoting may exist without the possibility of approving; the same going for the opposites. For this I shall use a number of examples, all of approval and disapproval on non-moral grounds. Let us consider, for instance, parents who approve or disapprove of the marriage of one of their children; it is common for parents to do so, and we understand very well what this means. We notice, however, that a stranger cannot approve or disapprove of the marriage as the parents can, and we must ask why this is so. Why is it that I can approve of my own daughter's marriage, or disapprove of it, but not of the marriage of some girl who is not a relative, or even a friend? (Perhaps I have read of her in the local paper, or heard of her from a gossiping neighbour.) No doubt it will be objected that approval and disapproval of a marriage is not in fact confined to parents or even relatives and friends. For surely many white men in South Africa disapprove of the marriage of any white man's daughter to any black man, and surely there are grounds on which even reasonable people might disapprove of the marriage of some girl with whom they had no special connection, for instance because it was a case of child marriage, or a marriage that was forced upon the girl. This is true, but it should be noticed that these examples all come within the sphere of public manners and morals. The fact that anyone can approve or disapprove on such grounds is something we shall discuss later on.[19] It is enough for the present argument, which confines itself to other areas, that there are grounds on which a parent can disapprove and a stranger cannot. Parents may disapprove of their daughter's

marriage because the man is too old for her, or not rich enough, or not well enough connected; they may disapprove because they think that the marriage will not work out well, or because the family's honour or pride is at stake. Now the very same opinions may be held by someone unconnected with the family. Why is it that this other person cannot disapprove? One might think that it is because the stranger will not care about the girl's fortunes, or the fortunes of the family. But this may not be true. One may very well care about what happens to a stranger, either through a kindly disposition, or because there is some other factor at work. Then one will hope that the marriage will not take place and be sorry if it does; but it will still be wrong to say that one approves or disapproves. Nor is it a matter of having or not having actual power. Perhaps the parents are not able to influence what happens, and perhaps the stranger has this power; he decides to prevent the marriage, and by some means or other, perhaps by an anonymous letter to one of the parties, he is able to do so.

Nor does this appear to be an isolated case, which might be thought to depend on some ancient ritual aspect of parental approval. One can find other examples with the greatest ease. Suppose, for instance, that an elderly couple are thinking of retiring to some seaside resort, and the evidence is against the success of the venture. A relative or close friend who knows how things are likely to turn out may therefore disapprove of the idea. But what about a stranger? Or what about one who though a neighbour is not a friend? He too is of the opinion that if they go they will regret it, and being of a kindly disposition he cares, and may actually care more than the friends and relations, about whether they are unhappy or not. Moreover, he may, by chance, be in a better position than the others to make a difference to what the old people do. Perhaps there is only one bungalow in the seaside town, and he can buy it himself; or perhaps he can send an anonymous letter that will frighten them off. Even with the caring, and the power, we still cannot say of him that he disapproves of their idea unless, surreptitiously, we introduce some new role for him, such as that of the family doctor or the social worker in charge of elderly persons' welfare. If, not having such a position, he went and offered them *advice* he would merely be impertinent or officious; if,

---

[19] Moral approval is open to everyone because of the universal character of morality. Foot later says:

In matters of morality we do not need experts, and such things as relationships are irrelevant to moral approval and disapproval. If anyone can approve or disapprove on moral grounds, then everyone can do so, or any sane person over a certain age. What is understood is that anyone is to listen to anyone when considerations are brought forward which are moral considerations. [p. 241]

however, he said that he disapproved he would be saying something that could not, in the circumstances, be true. . . .

It seems, therefore, that there is this first difference between approval and disapproval and, e.g., wanting and liking. What anyone can want or like is not restricted, logically speaking, by facts about his relationship to other people, as for instance that he is the parent or friend of one, and engaged in a joint enterprise with another. Such facts can, however, create possibilities of approving and disapproving that would otherwise not exist.

21

Pragmatism

Pragmatism introduces new dimensions into ethical theory: it looks at moral problems as just that, problems to be solved in an open-ended world of change and novelty. Its emphasis on the experiential base of knowledge focuses on corrigibility. It thus opens possibilities of control and direction that stem from inventive capacities to see and diagnose difficulties, to frame goals, and to plan.

Pragmatism began in informal meetings of a group associated with Harvard, including Chauncey Wright (1830–1875), a skilled mathematician also concerned with the evolution of self-consciousness; Charles Sanders Peirce (1839–1914), who made significant contributions to logic, scientific method, and semantics; William James (1842–1910), a psychologist as well as a philosopher when those disciplines were closely allied; and Oliver Wendell Holmes (1841–1935), later on the Supreme Court. From the outset their discussions were deeply influenced by Kant's view of the activity of the knower in constructing the categories by which knowledge and perception are organized. But they also sought to come to terms with the newer developments in mathematics and the experimental sciences, and with the implications of the Darwinian revolution concerning, above all, the biological basis of consciousness and its utility. Thinking is an evolutionary instrument enabling men to survive and perhaps to flourish, to construct theories by which to understand and come to grips with the world, even to fashion a fulfilling social environment. Thus in contrast to the "fixed" categories of Kant, conceptual structures are tentative, open to revision in the light of an accumulating experience that embeds the successes and failures of tests and practical consequences. Ideas are thus dynamic, and serve as plans of action; knowledge and science function in the broad context of human enterprise.

Central to the understanding of pragmatism is Peirce's definition of concepts or meanings, although it was utilized in vastly different ways not only by pragmatists but by scientists.[1] All organisms develop habits and patterned ways

---

[1] See, for example, Percy Bridgman's discussion of operationalism in his *The Logic of Modern Physics* (1927).

of response. In humans, inquiry is continuous with such adaptive behavior and is directed toward discovery. Habits include settled beliefs and ideas of how to satisfy needs. When these habits are blocked, in conflict, or inadequate, they result in uneasiness, doubt, hesitation, which then stimulates inquiry that restores the smooth functioning. The meaning of an idea is the set of test results experienced under given conditions—that is, the consequences that follow in the behavior of the objects under consideration. Meaning is therefore expressible as a set of conditional (if-then) statements relating tests and anticipated experiential results. Since the function of thought is to produce habits of action, to discover the meaning of an idea is to look at the habits of behavior it involves. At its best, the mode of such inquiry is scientific method producing well-supported beliefs.

Others carried the pragmatic approach beyond Cambridge, giving it a wider perspective—both as to geography and as to problems. John Dewey (1859–1952) added a social dimension, enriched by exchange and cooperation with psychologists, philosophers, sociologists (G. H. Mead, J. H. Tufts, and Albion Small), economists (Thorstein Veblen), and historians (Charles Beard). Mead in particular focused pragmatism on interpersonal relations. The impact of this group was felt in different ways in educational thought and experiment, and importantly found its way into the American legal tradition—Cardozo, Brandeis, Pound, and the legal realists—inspiring a distinctive cast to American jurisprudence that attends to the consequences and functional character of law as integral to its nature. Back at Harvard, C. I. Lewis (1883–1964) developed his own brand of strongly Kantian conceptualistic pragmatism. Pragmatism was thus a well-established outlook when positivism became influential in America; indeed it helped create a cordial reception for the European movement, for both shared the need to hold philosophy to scientific standards. But pragmatists of

whatever flavor disagreed critically with the positivist separation of value and fact, and with the isolation of thinking from doing. Thus the later pragmatism has a place in the naturalistic rejoinder to ethical emotivism and to the noncognitive value theory.

Pragmatism is more an outlook than a school; it shares broad commitments rather than specific doctrines. Today it touches the way problems are framed, even by those who do not regard themselves as pragmatists. Hence it will be found to have a place in a larger naturalism and in connection with logical positivism, but also to share much with phenomenology, to respect the self-realizationist view of character and virtue, and now and then to echo something of the existentialist's tragic sense of life.

In this chapter we present the ethics of pragmatism from Dewey and Lewis. The introduction includes James inasmuch as he provides a psychological background for both.

Classical Pragmatists

WILLIAM JAMES (1842–1910)

James faced directly a crisis posed by evolution: how to preserve that part of our nature shared with animals without discounting what makes for our humanness: rich capacities for feeling (aesthetic, moral, social), sense of self and self-consciousness, prepared response in the face of foreseen consequences. His account of consciousness in *The Principles of Psychology* (1890) challenged both faculty psychology and the impoverished reigning associationist view of ideas as discrete repeatable elements that combine and recombine episodically: such a view isolates ideas from action and cannot account for inventiveness, planning, and our distinctive ways of learning. By enlarging the range of confirmatory experience beyond

Peirce's, James gave meaning a broader and more humanistic scope. Such meanings, insofar as they are expectations, not only can be tested but help prepare modes of response. Accordingly consciousness functions in guiding the whole organism.

Experience comes as a flow of initially undifferentiated feelings, not only those that derive from sensation, but also desires, willings, fugitive fears, satisfactions, resentments, discomforts. This instates as genuine experience peripheral feelings and relations; a sense of relevance and problematic, of likeness and difference, of the reasonable, of mind and self.

From this flow of consciousness we carve out concepts (repeatable ideas), building on perceived likenesses and similarities, discounting the fullness and uniqueness of each moment to transform the manifold of sense into a world of stable objects and meanings. We go on to construct abstract patterns even further removed from the initially experienced—linear orderings (say of colors, shapes, or preferences), spaces, narratives, histories. All this is unstable, changing, as accumulating experience notes discrepancies, as expectations are unfulfilled, and as unprecedented situations arise. Insight often brings novel ways of perceiving, not unrelated to past experience but reassessing it.

Even personal identity is built from primitive feelings of continuity and appropriation (*my* thought) and from the sense of activity obscurely felt viscerally, as in breathing. From these we construct a concept of self, or rather selves, for each of us is many selves. Most broadly we are all that we call mine—our bodies, clothes, friends, property, style. We are also social selves, the self we show our colleagues, friends, teammates. Indeed, not only the way we perceive but the way we perceive that we are perceived expands and contracts the fortunes of the self, its reputation, honor, disgrace. Finally, what we most often feel to be our true self is the self as spirit—our intellectual capacities, aspirations, sensibilities.

Seldom are these selves all integrated, all together at peace. They often move in conflicting directions—the material self toward self-preserving acts, the social self toward recognition from others, and the self as spirit toward self-improvement and self-criticism. Withal we carry around general tones of self-esteem and self-abasement that are as primitive as rage and pain. Even the *ego*, taken as unifying *I* or agent, is rooted in transitive feelings like appropriation discoverable in experience. For some purposes I am the "same" person as yesterday, whereas for other purposes and contexts I am quite another person.

As there are many selves, so there are many worlds "fixed" by an implicit claim to objective reference and consolidated in language. Science, answering our curiosity and need for prediction and coherence, constructs a world of facts and physical laws. We also construct a world of goods and betters, with ideals (i.e., serviceable guides to be tested and corrected in experience) of what could be for ourselves and our community. Were this world to contain only physical laws, without a God or even an interested spectator, there would be no sense in declaring one state better than another, and no status for good and evil, right and obligation, or even the pleasant and painful. A world of sentient beings is the only habitat for moral relations and moral law. The moral center is constituted by concrete acts of valuing, of fixing the better and worse in what can and cannot satisfy needs, wants, and interests of particular individuals. Similarly, obligation can exist only in a world which harbors demands that win respect and acknowledgment as legitimate claims.

Since the satisfaction of every need and demand is a prima facie good, in the best imaginable moral world all would be satisfied without mutual harm. Imagine shooting and hunting without harming beast or fish. But our world is vastly more recalcitrant and penurious in its satisfactions. The tragic situation is that a right scale of priorities is an altogether practical need and that some part of the ideal must be butchered. What is more, we come already biased, born into a society whose ideals are already ordered.

The guiding principle must be to satisfy as many demands as possible. Those ideals are highest which prevail at least cost, and sacrifice the least number of ideals. Still, vanquished ideals must not be lost. "The course of history is nothing but the story of men's struggles from generation to generation to find a more and more inclusive order." Society has settled into one sort of equilibrium after another by social discoveries analogous to those of science. Polyandry, polygamy, slavery, private warfare and liberty to kill, judicial torture, and arbitrary royal power have slowly succumbed to actually aroused complaints; and though the ideals of some are worse off for each improvement, yet the total number finding shelter in our civilized society is vastly greater than in a savage one. Thus while the evolving system is better than any individual could make, no given equilibrium is final; our present laws and customs will in turn be overthrown by a newly discovered order that will hush up complaints without provoking still louder ones.

While we take great risks in breaking away from customary morality to grasp at a larger ideal than it permits, still we must experiment; for pent up under every system of rules are innumerable persons upon whom it weighs and whose good it suppresses. Private property, for all its utilities, covers abuses when it is shamelessly asserted that one of the prime functions of national government is to help the adroiter citizen grow rich. The tyranny of the marriage institution (generally so beneficent) brings unnamed and unnamable sorrows. And so on for the rest.

Our moral world is thus unfinished and in the making. No previously fashioned ethical rules will suffice. There are few absolute evils and no nonmoral goods, and the highest ethical life consists in challenging rules grown too narrow for the present case. Every real dilemma betokens a unique situation and calls for novelty and increased knowledge. In an actual moral decision, the exact mix of ideals to be realized and disappointed is without precedent or preexisting rule.

James is probably better known today for his less scientific works—for example, "Moral Equivalent of War," which while preserving the martial ideals of courage, discipline, and energy, redirects them away from brutality. He is not embarrassed to ask "Is Life Worth Living?" and "What Makes Life Worth Living?" Perhaps most familiar are *The Will to Believe* and *The Varieties of Religious Experience*. A popular style often obscures the grounding of his position in experience, even in physiology, and his concern to make explicit the assumptions we rely on but seldom expose. Thus the "will to believe" is not a license for wishful believing; it is rightfully applied only where evidence is equally balanced for alternative hypotheses or plans of action, where further facts are unavailable, where the matter is momentous and choice is forced (not to choose is equivalent to one of the choices). Only then is it legitimate to risk belief and action along the optimally promising line, which sometimes renders judgments self-fulfilling. And in religion, James's concern is not orthodoxy or creed but authenticity of feeling, the feeling that our strivings are serious and significant. The seriousness involves an open world—we are not passive observers but participants in a real struggle whose outcome is in balance and may be tipped by our choices and decisions. Opportunities and novelties are genuine and call on an energy deep within ourselves that strengthens resolve, sometimes in small ways, sometimes in dramatic ones, to remake ourselves and our society.

JOHN DEWEY (1859–1952)

Where Peirce and James wrote little systematically on ethical theory, so that the outlines need to be filled in, Dewey wrote so extensively, touched so many of the concrete issues, broadening morals to their institutional settings, that a brief summary is daunting. Three features are constant. First, he persistently attacks entrenched *dualisms* of philosophy—theory and practice, individual and social, means and ends, morals and science (a "scandal"). Second, he opens the philosophical portals to *change*. Change is inevitable: in language, customs, institutions, and morals. It is all around us: cities grow, industrialization develops, populations alter, physical resources are discovered and depleted; catastrophes alter history. The human problem is how to learn to understand and direct change. Dewey had early acquired an approach to problems in terms of a total field and developing structure; he never lost this total view of life experience as growth coming from the effort to steer a way in a field of transaction within a physical and social environment. Life is this transaction or working-with, even as we change our environment and ourselves. Finally, there is his pervasive notion of the *social*. While all thought and action are individual, in that the individual makes decisions, their content is social throughout, in the materials drawn on, in the habits or culture acquired, in the formulation of problems, in the resources available. Thus in *Human Nature and Conduct* (1922) the self is a social development of habit (culture) that organizes impulse. Intelligence is understood in a special sense, less as an individual endowment than as the social habits of inquiry, a social resource on which individuals may draw; science, especially as carried on today, is clearly a social enterprise. Even individualism should be understood as a social category (*Individualism Old and New*, 1929). Different ideals of individualism—such as the "rugged individual" of the frontier, or the self-centered, aggressive competitor of a laissez-faire economy—take shape under specific social and cultural conditions. In modern conditions, the way is open for an individuality as a type of character that gives freer rein to human growth and cooperation.

Dewey taught at Minnesota, at Michigan, and then at Chicago, where he was intensely aware of social and political conflicts, of social experiment (as in Hull House, where ideals of welfare and social work developed), and he himself organized experiments in education in the lower grades. From Chicago he went to Columbia, and during his career he traveled (after World War I), in Mexico, Russia, and Turkey, and for an extended period lectured in Japan and China. He was constantly involved in matters of public interest, including international affairs. He gave a course at Columbia together with Franz Boas, the founder of modern scientific anthropology; he wrote jointly with sociologists like Albion Small and with political scientists like A. F. Bentley (a father of pressure group theory), and his *Ethics* is coauthored with James H. Tufts, a fellow philosopher. He joined in cooperative courses with judges and lawyers at Columbia Law School and his influence on Cardozo, Brandeis, and the legal realists was important. And, of course, his part in educational life and theory in America is legend.

The special turn Dewey gave to moral and social thought came from his concern with a theory of method—one that stays close to our problem-solving behavior. Its psychological basis is to be found in an article that was to mark the beginning of functionalism as a movement in psychology.[2] Dewey is criticizing the way that continuous behavior was partitioned into two entities: the stimulus or sensory input as one event, and as a succeeding and separate event, the motor response. He argues that it is a mistake to separate the sensory from the motor; seeing, for example, is as much muscular, involving the holding of the head, the control of the eyes, and so forth, while directed movement involves a continual

[2] "The Reflex Arc Concept in Psychology," *Psychological Review* 3 (1896): 357–370.

direction by kinesthetic and visual cues. More important, stimulus and response are simply functional, not existential, differences that reflect our interest in analyzing a situation. Indeed what might be regarded as response in one description may serve as stimulus to a further response. Neither can stand alone, for involved is an integrated process, a kind of continuous feedback, when the behavior is well established and habitual. The smooth flow may be interrupted. For example, where stimulus is ambiguous or (equivalently) appropriate response is uncertain or in conflict with other possible responses, hesitation and doubt result. This gives time to diagnose the situation. A kind of rudimentary inquiry is instituted to explore what gave rise to the interruption, to uncover further clues in the situation (a stimulus description), and to determine a course of action (a response description).

This pattern, much modified, serves as a model for Dewey's setting of inquiry in a problematic situation. It appears as intelligence in *Human Nature and Conduct,* and as the search for reasonable decision in *Theory of Valuation.* Ongoing experience is blocked (sensed as a problem), allowing for deliberation about what is amiss, a look at the conditions, alternate hypotheses for resolution to be considered and imaginatively projected. The challenge to the partitioning of stimulus/response is later met in the challenge of means/end and value/fact in what is a continuity of experience.

Dewey's revisions imparted to experience a feedback continuity, an integrated character with conceptual distinctions indicative of aspects rather than separate entities, and a constantly purposive selectivity. This is the origin of his emphatic view that there is no sharp separation of fact and value, that values are involved in and embodied in factual knowledge and factual knowledge involved in valuation and evaluation; that in both cases there is a *contextual setting* that is rich in complexity both for understanding and for efforts at control.

Dewey directed his theory of inquiry against philosophies of science that, stressing only the deductive and inductive aspects of knowledge, thrust aside the questions of discovery and inventiveness. Deductive and axiomatized science of course gives great power; but that is when the principles are already given. The important role of the search for principles can be seen readily not only in the history of science but in the common operations of the legal system, where the question of what principles (laws) to bring to bear on particular cases are of the essence. Induction is based on the line-up of particulars; but a sophisticated induction has to ask how those particulars are themselves secured and how they are interpreted. It is such questions that bring into focus the fact that science is replete with values: not only the general ones of consistency and system and the ideal of truth, but the particular ones of what constraints are involved in warranting one rather than another conclusion in experiment and action, what features are to be selected, or in short, how the problem of problematic structure back of all inquiry is intended—not as a feature of application merely, but as an integral part of method, just as the deductive and inductive procedures are. Hence he speaks of *intelligence,* as embracing discovery and novelty and inventiveness, rather than simply of *reason.*

Aligning ethical theory and science as inquiry leads Dewey to a different view of ethical theory. It must remain in touch with the moral situation, with actual conflicts and quandaries. A moral situation is not one where we are tempted to deviate from what we know to be right, but one where we do not know and have to decide what we ought to do. As in science, moral theory seeks to solve a problem and to resolve an indeterminate situation. There can be no final catalogue of rules of obligation or of goods or objectives, and the hope of a finished set of moral rules covering every decision is misleading.

Ends-in-view are set up as hypotheses for

solving the problem, and these ends can be corrected, amplified, altered in the process. We cannot put everything on the line at once. It is just as in science: there are always more constant assumptions within which experiment and evaluation take place, even though in the longer run these may themselves be brought to a test, again within a framework of other assumptions. Hence the fallibilism of science is also the fallibilism of morals.

Dewey's analysis of morals is generalized in the *Theory of Valuation* (1939). Evaluation goes on in all fields, wherever people seek criteria for decision and its justification: assessing real estate, quality control in industry, grading examinations, as well as adjudicating the conflict of goods and obligations. It cannot be understood in purely emotive terms, for even emotions become indicative of needs and directions of effort required; nor merely in terms of felt satisfactions or pleasures, for these are always set in a complex of conditions, required means, and consequences. Nor again by a sharp separation of fact and value, for what is held as factual and what as valuational varies with the demands of different contexts, and each always contains some of the other. Evaluation is thus the broadest feature of inquiry into the problems of men, in the effort to fashion instruments for the guidance of life.

The history of moral philosophy adds another dimension to the nature of moral inquiry. It is usually represented as a struggle between different theories—Platonic, Aristotelian, Utilitarian, Kantian, Self-realizationist, and so on. From his restudy of the history of ethics Dewey came to the view that the theories represented specializations focusing on differing aspects of the tasks of morality. The *good* was essentially devoted to finding criteria to face the complexities of conflicting needs and desires. The *right* and the *ought* recognized the group character of human life and the consequent claims and responsibilities among people. Conceptions of virtue and vice embodied the importance of character and the sensitive responses of people

to one another; he might have added what was obvious in his own attention to education, the need of each generation to cultivate character of some sort in the oncoming generation. Dewey concluded that the conflicts between ethical theories thus in part reflect different social needs at different times—a large Roman empire needs a conception of law, an Athenian democratic assembly legislates directly in terms of a conceived good—and in part constitute a genuine moral problem rather than just a theoretical choice, as when goods and obligations are in conflict. But in all cases, the task of ethics is not to rest with the problem but to seek resources and fresh ideas for resolving it, refining principles and rules, refining and concretizing ideals, and developing more sensitive character. And all this goes on as a social enterprise in the midst of change.

Dewey's theory of inquiry and associated values permeates his practical and social thought. He is of course widely known for his educational theory, which centers on the need to cultivate human beings whose freedom lies in their ability and readiness for reflection, cooperative deliberation, and initiative. This "progressive education," far different from the stereotype of complete permissiveness, is socially needed, particularly when the development of industrialism requires broad initiative to face the problems of continual change. Sharing with Mill the conviction that social institutions are to be judged by the extent to which they bring greater education and participation to people at large, he carried this democratic commitment into both economics and the theory of history. In economics, free market enterprise is already on the wane before growing corporate enterprise; a more socialized economy is needed, not one that involves regimentation and repression but one that encourages worker participation in planning. In historical interpretation, social revolutions are periods in which the failure to achieve institutional changes to meet altered conditions reaches a breaking point; the success of a revolution lies in a psychological change in the whole population, an awakening to broad participation in reconstruction. A broader liberalism could minimize the need for revolutions; the office of liberalism is to mediate social transitions and to minimize the violence and repression that so often succeed them. Economic determinism would be correct if people do not plan and intervene; people, taking thought together, are able to influence the course of events and exert a measure of control on human life and welfare.

The same basic emphasis on social construction is found in Dewey's writings on religion and art. The core of religion is not its traditional supernaturalism but its lifting people from their narrow concerns to a communal sharing of life and aims. In art what should be stressed is the character of aesthetic experience in all of life, not the institutionalization of art works in elitist centers for the few.

C. I. Lewis
(1883–1964)

Lewis contributes to ethical theory by showing the continuity of valuations and judgments of the good with empirical knowledge generally and by giving an account of moral imperatives according to which, far from signaling the noncognitive, they are of the same order as the prescriptive and regulative features essential to all serious undertakings, including science. Involved here is a deep respect for human talents—especially the human ways of learning by testing and trial, by funding the successes and failures, and by searching for effective rules of that experience. Philosophers often forget that we do not come empty-handed to their problems. Philosophy does not create rationality; we start with all kinds of presystematic commitments about what is real, true, just, good, and satisfying, as well as what

is valid in argument and cogent in reasoning. Philosophy's job is not to start from scratch but to build on these commitments and to make explicit, clarify, and systematize what is implicit in them, eliciting those higher-ordered principles of thinking and doing that reflect criteria immanent in most critical judgments. Philosophy is neither a science nor a substitute for one; its job is to forge normative critiques, such as rules of valid inference that we call logic, the canons of empirical evidence that can be called a critique of cogency, and ethics, the critique of ourselves in action.

Lewis's point of departure is mathematical logic, particularly *Principia Mathematica*, and the philosophy of science. He was troubled by the *Principia's* definition of "material implication," from which it follows technically that a false proposition implies any proposition, and a true proposition is implied by any. This scarcely captures what we ordinarily mean— that is, intend—when we say that one thing "follows from" another. Lewis explored alternative definitions of "implies" that would better represent the ordinary sense of "follows from" and provide a more useful scientific sense of "implies." The systems built on these alternate definitions, though different from that of the *Principia*, turn out to be internally consistent. Thus a choice between logics does not depend on logic alone but on extralogical or pragmatic considerations of simplicity or effectiveness for a problem or task.

Broad lessons are involved: one is the recognition that just as logic provides rules for guiding consistent concludings and inferrings, so critiques generally provide binding rules for their domain. Further, just as choice and definitions (meanings or intentions) have a role in logic, so they have a role in what the mind brings to knowledge in the way of structuring the felt or sensibly given. Empirical knowledge or belief lies in the interplay of sensibility with the meanings or categories contributed by the knower. Here Lewis combines a Kantian insight into the constructive role of the knower with James's insight into the knower's options.

Analysis of Knowledge and Evaluation (1946) traces the long route from sensible experience to claims of objective belief—from experience reported as "This looks red" to "This is objectively red"—and the even longer path to laws and full theory. Along this route are met the complexities of theory construction, concept formation, the role of purpose and planning, as well as systematic correction in the face of new experience. Knowledge—beliefs making objective knowledge claims—involves a whole set of envisaged consequences, themselves the product of past experience, that if fulfilled would strengthen the probability of the belief. Knowledge claims are predictions (reminiscent of Peirce), and we weave patterns of concepts that depend, at least in part, on tests and actions that we may perform. Successes and failures of such expectations become a new justifying base for revised predictions. As we become self-conscious and develop canons of empirical knowledge and method implicit in all these procedures, we have the *critique of cogency*, a critique developing rules that warrant empirical conclusions.

Knowledge is not only active but also for the sake of action: as guide to what to pursue and what to avoid, what in our future we can control and what is unavoidable. To know, then, is to apprehend the future as qualified by values that decision and action may realize. It is only because we are creatures of desires and preferences that knowledge has any function; and it is only as we act, predict, conclude, test, that we gain knowledge. This is the setting for the account of value.

The same route from observation and objective claims to theory lies between what is felt good or satisfying and objective judgments of good or value, and finally a full theory of value. Valuations—objective judgments of what is good, worthwhile, or valuable—are a kind of empirical knowledge. They are grounded in concrete experience of felt goodness and satisfaction; they are predictions no different from empirical knowledge generally in what determines their truth or falsity, their justification and validation. Of course such judgments are more complex; for example, they involve a kind of double prediction, not only of what consequences will ensue but of what their value quality will be. Further, there are many dimensions of good—intrinsic, instrumental, contributory, individual, and social. The contributory well illustrates the complexities, for it involves judging what is good on the whole—a good concert, a good marriage, even a life good on the whole.

There is no simple step from objective value judgments to a right decision of consequences that are right to bring about. Conflict is likely between our goods and others' goods, or for that matter between our own long- and short-term goods. And the factors of risk and remoteness make matters even more difficult.

Here Lewis begins to come to grips with traditionally vexing problems: the relation and priorities of the good and the right (e.g., the relation of utilitarianism and Kantianism), the cognitive status of imperatives, and the grounds by which the interest of others is to be consolidated in our own decisions.

Now while value and good are properties of consequences, rightness is a property of decision, carrying a sense of urgency, constraint, and imperativeness. Value judgments are necessary and antecedent, but not sufficient. What is needed is a principle or justifying rule of rightness that legislates the choice, that authorizes, for example, the claim of the interest of others on our conduct, or prescribes a prudential preference for long-term over immediate goods.

The question of how moral imperatives can themselves be justified and whether they are cognitive has already been provided for. The sense of the imperative—of prescription, responsibility, and obligation—does not arise uniquely with moral judgments; nor the normative distinctively with justice. The search for a right decision is pervasive; it is sought wherever deliberation is in point, whether it is in cooking, business deals, chess, or dieting. And when a right decision is arrived at and taken to be justified, we feel ourselves constrained or bound to follow its advice, not only on a particular occasion but as a rule constraining all like cases. If we did not feel ourselves bound by a justified rule, then deliberation would indeed be pointless.

Of course such rules are hypothetical, contingent on engaging in the enterprise. We are not obligated by the rules of chess if we choose not to play; even the pursuit of wealth and health are in some sense optional. If, however, there are activities that we cannot avoid, then their rules, since always in force, have the character of a categorical imperative. We really have no choice, if we are to reason at all, but to be bound by the critique of consistency; and if we seek to guide our action by reliable prediction, we are bound by the critique of cogency. These epitomize what we mean by being rational—the necessity to decide and to decide from reasons, to learn distinctively from experience by teasing out of it lessons and principles and rules that are implicit in our best reflective judgments, to formulate such rules for addressing the future and to feel ourselves constrained by these lessons. No reason can be given other than that to be rational is to be concerned about the future and to wish not to regret those decisions that are in our control.

It is a rational imperative to be concerned with both the quality of our own lives and our own conduct as it affects others. To search for guidance here has given rise classically to the moral critiques of prudence and justice—rules concerning our own conduct in pursuit of self-determined objectives, and rules or imperatives concerning the claims made by the interest of others on our own action. As with critiques generally, neither prescribes a single course; they allow leeway for the integration of various interests and the consideration of special conditions. And they are complexly in-

terrelated with other critiques: neither prudential nor just decision could be warranted that flies in the face of cogent and objective fact. Further, the critique of justice presumes and builds on that of prudence, for it is only through our own experience that we can come to appreciate that others have the possibilities to enjoy and suffer, to plan the quality of their lives—all on a par with ours—and that they too are restrained by foresight. Thus for Lewis, the critique of justice is the socially significant counterpart of prudence. To its imperative need be added only the impartiality that is guaranteed by the generality of any rule. Our history is replete with formulations of such an imperative—from the Golden Rule to Bentham's insistence on counting every person as one to Kant's categorical imperative.

For Lewis there is a further dimension to the claim that we are imperatively social: not merely that individual and social goals and projects are interwoven, but that the distinctive ways of accumulating experience and the distinctive modes of intelligent and reasonable response are themselves the products of a social evolution that is at least in part self-conscious. Perhaps this is clearest in the history of science and its record of learning from failure, of capitalizing on successes, and of developing the critiques of consistency and cogency. Here truth itself is a common social objective enduring over time and resting on institutionalizing the exchange and communication of information, the freedom of inquiry and of education. Similar considerations apply, even more obviously, to the development of technology, which has exponentially increased not only opportunities for individual enjoyment but the ability to control and make certain the realization of our plans. This too is a common objective, for clearly the evolution of science and technology depends on social agencies of transmission and supportive social structures. And science and its values then have a setting in a larger pattern of morals that depends on social relationships which are themselves evolving. These spread over the more complex structural relationships of individual and group, and group with group, expansion of responsibilities and of roles, greater leisure and participation, and greater freedom for initiative at the same time that there is growing dependence on the group. For Lewis, morality as a social critique is larger than justice narrowly construed as impartiality. Given that we have a common interest in maintaining social institutions of transmission and regulation, the moral critique is the critique of institutions and practices that are not merely instrumental to the good life but constitutive within it. This requires institutionalizing even the canons of social criticism. The critique seeks not merely to defend the status quo and to avoid the errors of the past, but to invent fresh forms and norms that further encourage the development of personality and affiliative relations.

The interplay between imperatives, empirical judgments, and moral decision constitutes a large circle of principles, growing knowledge, alternatives, trial, and correction. There is no easy way out. Imperatives do not prescribe a particular course of action but leave to empirical science, knowledge of ourselves, and institutions and our historical development the task of working out what is possible. For example, among moral achievements we reckon today the greater degree of liberty and autonomy and the right to participate in a common life and its formulation of policy. But the increasing complexities of social structure generate their own larger need for the agencies of control and restraint. What is to be the exact mixture of the opposites under particular social conditions is a matter of experiment and social learning.

As compared to Dewey, an interesting contrast of emphasis is discernible. Lewis is concerned with the building up of reliable knowledge for use in action, and much of his technical epistemological theory elaborates the fine points of the structure of knowledge.

Dewey focuses rather on the situation of action and the need for imagination and initiative, which in a new unique situation will require an alteration in the developed structure. The two emphases are thus complementary. Both recognize the basic social character of morality and the way an experimental attitude and the possibilities of correction are always inherent in moral processes.

John Dewey
(1859–1952)

Ethics, Part II: *Theory of the Moral Life* [3]

X: The Nature of Moral Theory

1. Reflective Morality and Ethical Theory . . . Moral theory begins, in germ, when any one asks "Why should I act thus and not otherwise? Why is this right and that wrong? What right has any one to frown upon this way of acting and impose that other way?" Children make at least a start upon the road of theory when they assert that the injunctions of elders are arbitrary, being simply a matter of superior position. Any adult enters the road when, in the presence of moral perplexity, of doubt as to what it is right or best to do, he attempts to find his way out through reflection which will lead him to some principle he regards as dependable.

Moral theory cannot emerge when there is positive belief as to what is right and what is wrong, for then there is no occasion for reflection. It emerges when men are confronted with situations in which different desires promise opposed goods and in which incompatible courses of action seem to be morally justified. Only such a conflict of good ends and of standards and rules of right and wrong calls forth personal inquiry into the bases of morals. A critical juncture may occur when a person, for

---

[3] The selection is from John Dewey and James H. Tufts, *Ethics*, rev. ed. (New York: Henry Holt, 1932; originally published 1908). The chapters on moral theory were written by Dewey.

example, goes from a protected home life into the stress of competitive business, and finds that moral standards which apply in one do not hold in the other. Unless he merely drifts, accommodating himself to whatever social pressure is uppermost, he will feel the conflict. If he tries to face it in thought, he will search for a reasonable principle by which to decide where the right really lies. In so doing he enters into the domain of moral theory, even if he does so unwittingly.

For what is called moral theory is but a more conscious and systematic raising of the question which occupies the mind of any one who in the face of moral conflict and doubt seeks a way out through reflection. In short, moral theory is but an extension of what is involved in all reflective morality. There are two kinds of moral struggle. One kind, and that the most emphasized in moral writings and lectures, is the conflict which takes place when an individual is tempted to do something which he is convinced is wrong. Such instances are important practically in the life of an individual, but they are not the occasion of moral theory. The employee of a bank who is tempted to embezzle funds may indeed try to argue himself into finding reasons why it would not be wrong for him to do it. But in such a case, he is not really thinking, but merely permitting his desire to govern his beliefs. There is no sincere doubt in his mind as to what he should do when he seeks to find some justification for what he has made up his mind to do.

Take, on the other hand, the case of a citizen of a nation which has just declared war on another country. He is deeply attached to his own State. He has formed habits of loyalty and of abiding by its laws, and now one of its decrees is that he shall support war. He feels in addition gratitude and affection for the country which has sheltered and nurtured him. But he believes that this war is unjust, or perhaps he has a conviction that all war is a form of murder and hence wrong. One side of his nature, one set of convictions and habits, leads him to acquiesce in war; another deep part of his being protests. He is torn between two duties: he experiences a conflict between the incompatible values presented to him by his habits of citizenship and by his religious beliefs respectively. Up to this time, he has never experienced a struggle between the two; they have coincided and reinforced one an-

other. Now he has to make a choice between competing moral loyalties and convictions. The struggle is not between a good which is clear to him and something else which attracts him but which he knows to be wrong. It is between values each of which is an undoubted good in its place but which now get in each other's way. He is forced to reflect in order to come to a decision. Moral theory is a generalized extension of the kind of thinking in which he now engages.

There are periods in history when a whole community or a group in a community finds itself in the presence of new issues which its old customs do not adequately meet. The habits and beliefs which were formed in the past do not fit into the opportunities and requirements of contemporary life. The age in Greece following the time of Pericles was of this sort; that of the Jews after their captivity; that following the Middle Ages when secular interests on a large scale were introduced into previous religious and ecclesiastic interests; the present is preëminently a period of this sort with the vast social changes which have followed the industrial expansion of the machine age.

Realization that the need for reflective morality and for moral theories grows out of conflict between ends, responsibilities, rights, and duties defines the service which moral theory may render, and also protects the student from false conceptions of its nature. The difference between customary and reflective morality is precisely that definite precepts, rules, definitive injunctions and prohibitions issue from the former, while they cannot proceed from the latter. Confusion ensues when appeal to rational principles is treated as if it were merely a substitute for custom, transferring the authority of moral commands from one source to another. Moral theory can (i) generalize the types of moral conflicts which arise, thus enabling a perplexed and doubtful individual to clarify his own particular problem by placing it in a larger context; it can (ii) state the leading ways in which such problems have been intellectually dealt with by those who have thought upon such matters; it can (iii) render personal reflection more systematic and enlightened, suggesting alternatives that might otherwise be overlooked, and stimulating greater consistency in judgment. But it does not offer a table of commandments in a catechism in which answers are as definite as are the questions which are asked. It can render personal choice more intelligent, but it cannot take the place of personal decision, which must be made in every case of moral perplexity. [pp. 173–176]

Aristotle's formulation of the conditions for a moral act is accepted: that the doer know what he is doing and choose the act, and that the act be voluntary (in the sense that it expresses a formed and stable character). Every act has a potential moral significance through its consequences, though not all turn out to be consciously moral. Acts may be habitual, but habit reaches down into the very structure of the self, in that it solidifies or weakens desires. "[C]onduct and character are strictly correlative. Continuity, consistency, throughout a series of acts is the expression of the enduring unity of attitudes and habits. Deeds hang together because they proceed from a single and stable self" (p. 183). Similarly, both the Kantian emphasis on motive and the Benthamite emphasis on consequences are one-sided. Motive is not to be identified with a personal feeling, but with attitudes and predispositions toward ends embodied in action. Both foresight of consequences and the part played by personal disposition, character, and attitude are important.

5. *Present Need of Theory* We have already noted in passing that the present time is one which is in peculiar need of reflective morals and of a working theory of morals. The scientific outlook on the world and on life has undergone and is still undergoing radical change. Methods of industry, of the production, and distribution of goods have been completely transformed. The basic conditions on which men meet and associate, in work and amusement, have been altered. There has been a vast dislocation of older habits and traditions. Travel and migration are as common as they were once unusual. The masses are educated enough to read and a prolific press exists which supplies cheap reading matter. Schooling has ceased to be the privilege of the few and has become the right and even the enforced duty of the many. The stratification of society into classes each fairly homogeneous in itself has been broken into. The area of contacts with persons and populations alien to our bringing up and traditions has enormously extended. A ward of a large city in the United States may have persons of from a score to fifty racial origins. The walls and barriers that once separated nations have become less important because of the railway, steamship, telegraph, telephone, and radio.

Only a few of the more obvious changes in social conditions and interests have been mentioned. Each one of them has created new problems and issues that contain moral values which are uncertain and disputed. Nationalism and internationalism, capital and labor, war and peace, science and religious tradition, competition and coöperation, *laissez faire* and State planning in industry, democracy and dictatorship in government, rural and city life, personal work and control *versus* investment and vicarious riches through stocks and bonds, native born and alien, contact of Jew and Gentile, of white and colored, of Catholic and Protestant, and those of new religions: a multitude of such relationships have brought to the fore new moral problems with which neither old customs nor beliefs are competent to cope. In addition, the rapidity with which social changes occur brings moral unsettlement and tends to destroy many ties which were the chief safeguards of the morals of custom. There was never a time in the history of the world when human relationships and their accompanying rights and duties, opportunities and demands, needed the unremitting and systematic attention of intelligent thought as they do at present.

There are those who tend to minimize the importance of reflection in moral issues. They hold that men already know more morally than they practice and that there is general agreement among men on all moral fundamentals. Usually such persons will be found to adhere to some especial tradition in whose dogmas they find final and complete authority. But in fact the agreement exists to a large extent only with reference to concepts that are taken vaguely and apart from practical application. Justice: to be sure; give to each that which is his due. But is individualistic competitive capitalism a just system? or socialism? or communism? Is inheritance of large fortunes, without rendering of personal service to society, just? What system of taxation is just? What are the moral claims of free-trade and protection? What would constitute a just system of the distribution of national income? Few would question the desirability of chastity, but there are a multitude of interpretations of its meaning. Does it mean that celibacy is more pleasing to God than marriage? This idea is not generally held today, but its former vogue still affects the beliefs and practices of men and women. What is the relation of chastity as a moral idea to divorce, birth control, state censorship of literature? Human life is sacred. But what about many of the health-destroying practices and accident-inducing practices of modern industry? What about war, preparation for which absorbs the chief part of the revenue of modern States?

And so we could go down the list of all the time-honored virtues and duties, and show that changes in conditions have made what they signify for human action a matter of uncertainty and controversy. The ultimate difference, for example, between the employing and the employed in industry is one of moral criteria and outlook. They envisage different values as having a superior claim. The same is evidently even more true of the convinced nationalist and internationalist, pacifist and militarist, secularist and devotee of authoritatively revealed religion. Now it is not held for a moment that moral theory can give direct and final answers to these questions. But it is held that they cannot be dealt with by adherence to mere tradition nor by trusting to casual impulse and momentary inspiration. Even if all men agreed sincerely to act upon the principle of the Golden Rule as the supreme law of conduct, we should still need inquiry and thought to arrive at even a passable conception of what the Rule means in terms of concrete practice under mixed and changing social conditions. Universal agreement upon the abstract principle even if it existed would be of value only as a preliminary to coöperative undertaking of investigation and thoughtful planning; as a preparation, in other words, for systematic and consistent reflection.

6. *Sources of Moral Theory* No theory can operate in a vacuum. Moral as well as physical theory requires a body of dependable data, and a set of intelligible working hypotheses. Where shall moral theory find the material with which to satisfy these needs?

1. While all that has been said about the extent of change in all conditions of life is true, nevertheless there has been no complete breach of continuity. From the beginning of human life, men have arrived at some conclusions regarding what is proper and fair in human relationships, and have

engaged in working out codes of conduct. The dogmatist, whether made so by tradition or through some special insight which he claims as his own, will pick out from the many conflicting codes that one which agrees the most closely with his own education and taste. A genuinely reflective morals will look upon all the codes as possible *data;* it will consider the conditions under which they arose; the methods which consciously or unconsciously determined their formation and acceptance; it will inquire into their applicability in present conditions. It will neither insist dogmatically upon some of them, nor idly throw them all away as of no significance. It will treat them as a storehouse of information and possible indications of what is now right and good.

2. Closely connected with this body of material in codes and convictions, is the more consciously elaborated material of legal history, judicial decisions, and legislative activity. Here we have a long experimentation in working out principles for direction of human beings in their conduct. Something of the same kind is true of the workings of all great human institutions. The history of the family, of industry, of property systems, of government and the state, of education and art, is full of instructions about modes of human conduct and the consequences of adopting this or that mode of conduct. Informal material of the same sort abounds in biographies, especially of those who have been selected as the great moral teachers of the race.

3. A resource which mankind was late in utilizing and which it has hardly as yet begun to draw upon adequately is found in the various sciences, especially those closest to man, such as biology, physiology, hygiene and medicine, psychology and psychiatry, as well as statistics, sociology, economics, and politics. The latter upon the whole present problems rather than solutions. But it is well to get problems more clearly in mind, and the very fact that these social disciplines usually approach their material independently of consideration of moral values has a certain intellectual advantage for the moralist. For although he still has to translate economic and political statement over into moral terms, there is some guarantee of intellectual objectivity and impartiality in the fact that these sciences approach their subject-matter in greater detachment from preformed and set moral convictions, since the latter may be only the prejudices of tradition or temperament. From the biological and psychological sciences, there are

derivable highly valuable techniques for study of human and social problems and the opening of new vistas. For example, the discovery of the conditions and the consequences of health of body, personal and public, which these sciences have already effected, opens the way to a relatively new body of moral interests and responsibilities. It is impossible any longer to regard health and the conditions which affect it as a merely technical or physical matter. Its ramifications with moral order and disorder have been clearly demonstrated.

4. Then there is the body of definitely theoretical methods and conclusions which characterize European history for the last two thousand years, to say nothing of the doctrines of Asiatic thinkers for a still longer period. Keen intellects have been engaged in analysis and in the development of directive principles on a rational basis. Alternative positions and their implications have been explored and systematically developed. At first sight, the variety of logically incompatible positions which have been taken by theorists may seem to the student to indicate simply a scene of confusion and conflict. But when studied more closely they reveal the complexity of moral situations, a complexity so great that while every theory may be found to ignore factors and relations which ought to be taken into account, each one will also be found to bring to light some phase of the moral life demanding reflective attention, and which, save for it, might have remained hidden. The proper inference to be drawn is not that we should make a mechanical compromise or an eclectic combination of the different theories, but that each great system of moral thought brings to light some point of view from which the facts of our own situations are to be looked at and studied. Theories afford us at least a set of questions with which we may approach and challenge present conditions. [pp. 188–193]

Three Independent Factors in Morals [4]

In the time I have at my disposal I will not attempt to prove that this idea of the nature of conflict is an abstract and arbitrary simplification, so much so that it runs counter to every empirical observa-

[4] From John Dewey, "Three Independent Factors in Morals," trans. Jo Ann Boydston, *Educational Theory*, 16 (July 1966): 197–209.

tion of fact. I can only express, briefly and in passing, the idea that moral progress and the sharpening of character depend on the ability to make delicate distinctions, to perceive aspects of good and of evil not previously noticed, to take into account the fact that doubt and the need for choice impinge at every turn. Moral decline is on a par with the loss of that ability to make delicate distinctions, with the blunting and hardening of the capacity of discrimination. Posing this point without undertaking to prove it, I shall content myself with presenting the hypothesis that there are at least three independent variables in moral action. Each of these variables has a sound basis, but because each has a different origin and mode of operation, they can be at cross purposes and exercise divergent forces in the formation of judgment. From this point of view, uncertainty and conflict are inherent in morals; it is characteristic of any situation properly called moral that one is ignorant of the end and of good consequences, of the right and just approach, of the direction of virtuous conduct, and that one must search for them. The essence of the moral situation is an internal and intrinsic conflict; the necessity for judgment and for choice comes from the fact that one has to manage forces with no common denominator.

By way of introduction, let us see what is involved. We know that there are two opposing systems of moral theory: the morality of ends and the morality of laws. The dominating, the only, and monistic principle of the first, is that of ends which, in the final analysis, can be reduced to one single end, supreme and universal good. The nature of this end, this good, has been discussed frequently. Some say that it is happiness (*eudaemonia*), others pleasure, still others, self-realization. But, in every respect, the idea of Good, in the sense of satisfaction and of achievement, is central. The concept of right, to the extent it is distinguished from good, is derivative and dependent; it is the means or the manner of attaining the good. To say that an act is consonant with right, legitimate or obligatory, is to say that its accomplishment leads to the possession of the good; otherwise, it is senseless. In the morality of laws, this concept is reversed. At the heart of this morality is the idea of law which prescribes what is legitimate or obligatory. Natural goods are the satisfaction of desires and the accomplishment of purposes; but natural goods have nothing in common except in name, with moral Good. Moral good becomes that which is in agreement with juridical imperative, while the opposite is not true.

Now I would like to suggest that good and right have different origins, they flow from independent springs, so that neither of the two can derive from the other, so that desire and duty have equally legitimate bases and the force they exercise in different directions is what makes moral decision a real problem, what gives ethical judgment and moral tact their vitality. I want to stress that there is no uniform, previous moral presumption either in one direction or in the other, no constant principle making the balance turn on the side of good or of law; but that morality consists rather in the capacity to judge the respective claims of desire and of duty from the moment they affirm themselves in concrete experience, with an eye to discovering a practical middle footing between one and the other—a middle footing which leans as much to one side as to the other without following any rule which may be posed in advance.

So much for preliminary considerations; the essential problem I propose to discuss is the source and the origin in concrete experience of what I have called independent variables. What reasons are there for accepting the existence of these three factors?

First, no one can deny that impulses, appetites, and desires are constant traits in human action and have a large part in determining the direction conduct will take. When impulse or appetite operate without foresight, one does not compare or judge values. The strongest inclination carries one along and effort follows its direction. But when one foresees the consequences which may result from the fulfillment of desire, the situation changes. Impulses which one cannot measure as impulses become measurable when their results are considered; one can visualize their external consequences and thus compare them as one might two objects. These acts of judgment, of comparison, of reckoning, repeat themselves and develop in proportion to the increase in capacity for foresight and reflection. Judgments applied to such a situation can be thoroughly examined, corrected, made more exact by judgments carried over from other situations; the results of previous estimates and actions are available as working materials.

In the course of time two moral concepts have been formed. One of these is that of Reason as a function which moderates and directs impulses by considering the consequences they entail. The "Reason" thus conceived is nothing but the ordinary faculty of foresight and of comparison; but that faculty has been elevated to a higher order of dignity and named eulogistically by virtue of what it accomplishes, or the order and system it introduces into the succession of acts which constitute conduct.

The other concept we see emerging from moral experience is that of *ends* forming a united and coherent system and merging into one generalized and comprehensive end. As soon as foresight is used to summon objective consequences, the idea of an end is self-apparent; consequences are the natural limit, the object, the end of the action envisaged. But it is significant that from the moment particular acts of judgment become organized into the general moral function called reason, a classification of ends is established; estimates found correct about one are applied in thought to others. Our first ancestors were preoccupied quite early with goals such as health, wealth, courage in battle, success with the other sex. A second level was reached when men more reflective than their fellows ventured to treat those different generalized ends as elements of an organized plan of life, ranking them in a hierarchy of values, going from the least comprehensive to the most comprehensive, and thus conceived the idea of a single end, or in other words, of a good to which all reasonable acts led.

When that process was accomplished, one form of moral theory had been established. To take a broad view of the history of thought, it might be said that it was Greek thinkers who gave articulate expression to that distinctive phase of experience, who left as a lasting contribution to moral theory the concept of ends in terms of perfection, of achievement, and, therefore, of a final end or Good—a concept which is a hierarchical organization of ends. They stressed the intimate relationship between that organization and Reason. Let us further note that Greek philosophy as a whole considered the universe a cosmos in which all natural processes tended to achieve themselves in rational and ideal forms, so that their view of human conduct was simply an extension of the idea that they applied to the universe. Law was conceived as the expression of reason, not as will or command, but in effect a succession of changes leading to the realization of an end.

Although the moral heritage of the Greeks constitutes an important phase of human moral experience, it cannot be said that their concept applies to morals in its fullest extension. It seems to me that it was a natural consequence of the peculiar nature of the Greek city for Greek philosophers to consider social obligations and claims among the ends subject to reason. Because there was an intimate and vital relation between the problems of state and the interests of the citizens in Athens, which has served as a model for philosophers, legislation was discussed and considered to the point that (theoretically at least) it was the manifestation of reflective intelligence. Greek cities were small enough so that it was possible to consider formal political decisions as an expression of the reasoned thought of the group, that is to say, directed toward purposeful goals, whereas laws based on the *fiat* of the will were considered arbitrary and tyrannical and those born of passion, confused and perverse.

However, in all probability, it was impossible in that social environment to identify law with moral obligation by a rational adjustment of means to ends. Moreover, the Greeks' lack of success in politics, their incorrigible instability, their factious spirit, brought discredit to the idea of the intuition of ends: the calculation of means constituted the sound and solid base of social relations. In any event, the practice of the Romans shows us that the sense of order, the desire for a stable government and administration led to quite a different conception of reason and of law. Reason became a type of cosmic force constituting the structure of things, forcing them to adapt to each other and to exert themselves in the same direction: law was simply the manifestation of that great ordering force. Functions, duties, relations—not of means to ends but of mutual adaptation—of correspondence and reciprocal harmony, became the center of moral theory.

That concept also corresponds to a fact of everyday experience. Communal life has its own particular requirements and forms. By the simple fact of living and acting, each member of the group tries, however unconsciously, to bend others to his purposes, to make others co-operate in his plan of life. There is no normal person who does not struggle to influence the conduct of others in some way. Parents and all those who govern are particularly well placed to insist on actions conforming to their requests, to obtain obedience and submission; but even infants, to the extent of their resources, make claims, give orders, and express desires they hope to establish as norms of conduct in others. For a

person trying to impose his will, such conduct is natural behavior because it is a part of carrying out his own plan; for the one who accedes to requirements imposed, there will be a feeling of arbitrariness unless they happen to coincide with his personal interest. But he also makes requirements of other people, so that he finally develops a pattern or system, more or less reciprocal according to social conditions, of *desiderata* generally accepted or at least admitted without overt rebellion. From the viewpoint of those who set forth these *desiderata*, they are rights; from the viewpoint of those who submit to them, they are duties. The whole of the established system, to the extent it is accepted without violent protest, constitutes the principle of authority—*Jus, Recht, Droit*—which becomes current, that is, socially accepted, as an exchange of requirements and responses.

It seems to me quite evident that in their origins and in their natural mode of manifestation, these demands on the conduct of others are an independent variable with regard to the principle of teleological, rational ends and good. It is a fact that this or that individual exerts claims on other people for the satisfaction of this or that desire. But this fact does not make his desire a right; it does not confer moral authority on it; of itself and in itself it is more a manifestation of power than of right. To become a right, the claim should be recognized and have behind it not only the power of the claimant but the emotional and intellectual assent of the group. Naturally, one can object that even here good is still the dominant principle, the right being but a means of realizing it; however, we are no longer dealing with the individual end of an isolated person, but the welfare of the group. Such an objection conceals the fact that the "good" and the "end" have now taken on a new and intrinsically different meaning. These terms no longer designate what will satisfy the purpose of an individual, but what the individual recognizes as important and valid from the viewpoint of the social group. The right, in the eyes of the other person, becomes a demand, a requirement, to which he is obliged to submit. To the extent he recognizes that the requirement is clothed with authority and does not solely express an external force to which he would be prudent to submit, it is "good," in the sense that it is right— that is self-evident; but it is no longer a particular good as are objects to which desire is naturally directed. In truth, the requirement appears to be a frustrating element, opposed to natural desire, otherwise it would not be perceived as an obligation which must be acknowledged. With time and through the action of habit, the requirement in question can become an object of desire; when that happens, it loses the character of right and of authority and becomes simply a good.

The point that I want to emphasize is this: there is a difference in nature, both in origin and in mode of operation, between an object which seems capable of satisfying desire and which is thereby a good, and an object which sets up a demand on our conduct which we must acknowledge. One cannot be reduced to the other.

Empirically, there is a third independent variable in morals. We praise or blame the conduct of other people; we approve or disapprove, encourage or condemn, reward or punish. These actions occur after another person has acted or in anticipation of a certain mode of conduct on his part. Westermarck maintained that sympathetic response is the first source of morals at any time and in any place. Although I doubt, for reasons indicated earlier, that it is the only source, it is undeniable that a sympathetic response, accompanied by approval, is an empirical phenomenon which is spontaneous and powerful in morals. Generally approved actions and dispositions constitute virtues from the beginning; those which are generally disapproved constitute vices. Praise and blame are natural responses of human nature to the acts of other people. They are especially marked when the act implies danger for the one who accomplishes it and becomes heroic, or when he goes against customs of the group and becomes disreputable. But praise and blame are so spontaneous, so natural, and as we said, so instinctive, that they have nothing to do with considerations on which the satisfaction of desire depends, nor with the questions of requirements towards others. They lack the element of rationalization, of reflection, characteristic of ends, and the element of social constraint which characterizes right. Along with rewards and punishments, they act as reflexes of virtue or of vice to sanction right; to the extent individuals seek the esteem of others, they serve in particular cases as auxiliaries of deliberation about ends. But as a category and principle, the virtuous differs from good and from right. Good, I have said, is ascribable to deliberation about desires and intentions; right, obligation, is dependent upon requirements which have social authority and force; virtues are dependent upon approbation.

If one observes the whole development of morals in England, one cannot help but note that that country was influenced by the idea of approval and disapproval as much as Greece was by the existence of generalized norms, and as Rome by the exercise of social authority. Many characteristics of English morals can only be explained by remembering that this problem is paramount even when writers seem preoccupied with other questions. Consider, for example, the role played by the idea of sympathy, the tendency to regard benevolence as the source of every good and of every obligation because it is essentially the object of approbation (as sympathy is the agent of approbation). Consider the illogical combination in English utilitarianism of pleasure as end or good and the inclination to seek happiness for all as worthy of approval. The important place which such concepts have in English morals doubtless shows an inclination in English society to consider first of all the reaction of individuals to the conduct of their neighbors, as opposed to the tendency to rationalize morals according to norms or a tendency to attach highest importance to a public system of obligations constituting the law.

In calling these elements independent variables, I do not attempt to deny that they are intertwined in moral situations found in common experience. An example of this is occurring today. Moral problems exist because we have to reconcile certain elements which come from each of the different sources. If each principle were separate and supreme, I do not see how it could cause difficulties and moral uncertainties. Good would simply be opposed to bad, justice to injustice, virtue to vice. In other words, we would clearly distinguish what satisfies desire from what frustrates it. We would commit errors of judgment in certain cases but these would not affect the distinction of the categories. Similarly, we would without difficulty make a distinction between what is recognized and licit and what is forbidden and illicit; between what is approved and encouraged and what is disapproved and punished.

However, in reality, the different lines of distinction cut across each other. What is good from the viewpoint of desire is bad from the viewpoint of social requirements; what is bad from a personal point of view may be warmly recommended by public opinion. Each conflict is real and sharp and we must find the means of reconciling opposing facts. It sometimes happens that what is officially and legally forbidden is the object of tolerance or of encouragement by society. Witness the prohibition of alcoholic drinks in the United States; or enlarging our field of observation, the difficulties children find themselves in because of the divergence between something which is publicly blamed but permitted by private customs or even, in practice, praised and considered a triumph of crafty cleverness or of desirable ambition. The system of rational goods or of officially and publicly recognized duties in the Anglo-Saxon countries is in marked contrast with the schema of virtues which assure economic success, a fact which explains in some measure our reputation for hypocrisy. In the face of the role played by the real conflict of forces in moral situations and the manifest uncertainty about which side to take, I am inclined to think that one of the causes of the inefficiency of moral theories resides in their attachment to the unitary concept, which has led them to simplify moral life excessively. The result is an abyss between the involved realities of practice and the abstract forms of the system. A moral philosophy which frankly recognizes the impossibility of reducing all the elements of moral situations to one single principle, one which would admit that every human being can only do his best to shift for himself among the disparate forces, would throw light on our real difficulties and would help us make a more accurate estimate of competing factors. It would be necessary to sacrifice the idea that there exists, theoretically and beforehand, a unique and ideally correct solution for every difficulty into which a person will be thrown. Personally, I believe that this sacrifice, far from being a loss, would be a gain. By turning our attention from rules and rigid standards, it would lead us to take fuller consideration of the specific elements which necessarily enter into every situation where we must act. [pp. 199–204]

Ethics, Part II: *Theory of the Moral Life*

Dewey attempts to show not only that different human processes enter into morality but that the history of ethics shows successive one-sided emphases on each aspect. A fuller theory of ethics must therefore be more comprehensive and appreciate the interlocking and the conflicts in the three aspects.[5]

Chapter XIV, "Moral Judgment and Knowledge," reckons with the place of immediate sensitivity and reflection, conscience and principles, in moral judgment. Of special interest is the contrast of rules and principles:

A genuine principle differs from a rule in two ways: (a) A principle evolves in connection with the course of experience, being a generalized statement of what sort of consequences and values tend to be realized in certain kinds of situations; a rule is taken as something ready-made and fixed. (b) A principle is primarily intellectual, a method and scheme for judging, and is practical secondarily because of what it discloses; a rule is primarily practical. [pp. 304–305]

A moral principle is thus not a command, but a tool for analyzing special situations.

Chapter XV exemplifies Dewey's distinctive analysis of ethical issues, especially in the treatment of egoism and altruism, and moral responsibility. The former focuses on the kind of self that is being developed and the institutions that cultivate it, rather than attempting a general moral disproof of egoism. The latter regards responsibility, not in the traditional way as retrospective, but as prospective. This is not a shift from free will to "manipulation" of what people become; it is rather the identification of freedom in persons with the power to learn and the concept of responsibility as an instrument in guiding learning.

XV: The Moral Self

3. *Egoism and Altruism* . . . The real moral question is what *kind of* a self is being furthered and formed. And this question arises with respect to both one's own self and the selves of others. An intense emotional regard for the welfare of others, unbalanced by careful thought, may actually result in harm to

[5] For a fuller discussion, see the chapters entitled "Ends, the Good and Wisdom," "Right, Duty, and Loyalty," and "Approbation, the Standard and Virtue."

others. Children are spoiled by having things done for them because of an uncontrolled "kindness"; adults are sometimes petted into chronic invalidism; persons are encouraged to make unreasonable demands upon others, and are grieved and hurt when these demands are not met; charity may render its recipients parasites upon society, etc. The goodness or badness of *consequences* is the main thing to consider, and these consequences are of the same nature whether they concern *my*self or *your*self. The kind of objects the self wants and chooses is the important thing; the *locus* of residence of these ends, whether in you or in me, cannot of itself make a difference in their moral quality.

The idea is sometimes advanced that action is selfish just because it manifests an interest, since every interest in turn involves the self. Examination of this position confirms the statement that everything depends upon the *kind* of self which is involved. It is a truism that all action springs from and affects a self, for *interest* defines the self. Whatever one is interested in is in so far a constituent of the self, whether it be collecting postage stamps, or pictures, making money, or friends, attending first nights at the theater, studying electrical phenomena, or whatever. Whether one obtains satisfaction by assisting friends or by beating competitors at whatever cost, the interest of the self is involved. The notion that therefore all acts are equally "selfish" is absurd. For "self" does not have the same significance in the different cases; there is always a self involved but the different selves have different values. A self changes its structure and its value according to the kind of object which it desires and seeks; according, that is, to the different kinds of objects in which active interest is taken.

The identity of self and act, the central point in moral theory, operates in two directions. It applies to the interpretation of the quality and value of the act and to that of the self. It is absurd to suppose that the difference between the good person and the bad person is that the former has no interest or deep and intimate concern (leading to personal intimate satisfaction) in what he does, while the bad person is one who does have a personal stake in his actions. What makes the difference between the two is the *quality* of the interest that characterizes them. For the quality of the interest is dependent upon the nature of the object which arouses it and to which it is attached, being trivial, momentous;

narrow, wide; transient, enduring; exclusive, inclusive in exact accord with the object. When it is assumed that because a person acts from an interest, in and because its fulfillment brings satisfaction and happiness, he therefore always acts selfishly, the fallacy lies in supposing that there is a separation between the self and the end pursued. If there were, the so-called end would in fact be *only* a means to bringing some profit or advantage to the self. Now this sort of thing does happen. A man may use his friends, for example, simply as aids to his own personal advancement in his profession. But in this case, he is *not* interested in them as friends or even as human beings on their own account. He is interested in what he can get out of them; calling them "friends" is a fraudulent pretense. In short, the essence of the whole distinction between selfishness and unselfishness lies in what sort of object the self is interested. [pp. 327–328]

5. Responsibility and Freedom . . . Now the commonest mistake in connection with the idea of responsibility consists in supposing that approval and reprobation have a retrospective instead of prospective bearing. The possibility of a desirable *modification* of character and the selection of the course of action which will make that possibility a reality is the central fact in responsibility. The child, for example, is at first held liable for what he has done, not because he deliberately and knowingly intended such action, but in order that *in the future* he may take into account bearings and consequences which he has failed to consider in what he *has* done. Here is where the human agent differs from a stone and inanimate thing, and indeed from animals lower in the scale.

It would be absurd to hold a stone responsible when it falls from a cliff and injures a person, or to blame the falling tree which crushes a passerby. The reason for the absurdity is that such treatment would have and could have no conceivable influence on the future behavior of stone or tree. They do not interact with conditions about them so as to learn, so as to modify their attitudes and dispositions. A human being is held accountable in order that he may learn; in order that he may learn not theoretically and academically but in such a way as to modify and—to some extent—remake his prior self. The question of whether he might when he acted have acted differently from the way in which he did act is irrelevant. The question is whether he is capable of acting differently *next* time; the practical importance of effecting changes in human character is what makes responsibility important. Babes, imbeciles, the insane are not held accountable, because there is incapacity to learn and to change. With every increase of capacity to learn, there develops a larger degree of accountability. The fact that one did not deliberate before the performance of an act which brought injury to others, that he did not mean or intend the act, is of no significance, save as it may throw light upon the kind of response by others which will render him likely to deliberate next time he acts under similar circumstances. The fact that each act tends to *form*, through habit, a self which will perform a certain kind of acts, is the foundation, theoretically and practically of responsibility. We cannot undo the past; we can affect the future.

Hence responsibility in relation to control of our reactions to the conduct of others is twofold. The persons who employ praise and blame, reward and punishment, are responsible for the selection of those methods which will, with the greatest probability, modify in a desirable way the future attitude and conduct of others. There is no inherent principle of retributive justice that commands and justifies the use of reward and punishment independently of their consequences in each specific case. To appeal to such a principle when punishment breeds callousness, rebellion, ingenuity in evasion, etc., is but a method of refusing to acknowledge responsibility. Now the consequence which is most important is that which occurs in personal attitude: confirmation of a good habit, change in a bad tendency.

The point at which theories about responsibility go wrong is the attempt to base it upon a state of things which *precedes* holding a person liable, instead of upon what ensues in consequence of it. One is held responsible in order that he may *become* responsible, that is, responsive to the needs and claims of others, to the obligations implicit in his position. Those who hold others accountable for their conduct are themselves accountable for doing it in such a manner that this responsiveness develops. Otherwise they are themselves irresponsible in their own conduct. The ideal goal or limit would be that each person should be completely responsive in all his actions. But as long as one meets new conditions this goal cannot be reached; for

where conditions are decidedly unlike those which one has previously experienced, one cannot be sure of the rightness of knowledge and attitude. Being held accountable by others is, in every such instance, an important safeguard and directive force in growth.

The idea of freedom has been seriously affected in theoretical discussions by misconceptions of the nature of responsibility. Those who have sought for an antecedent basis of and warrant for responsibility have usually located it in "freedom of the will," and have construed this freedom to signify an unmotivated power of choice, that is an arbitrary power to choose for no reason whatever except that the will does choose in this fashion. It is argued that there is no justice in holding a person liable for his act unless he might equally have done otherwise—completely overlooking the function of being held to account in improving his future conduct. A man might have "acted otherwise than he did act" *if* he had been a different kind of person, and the point in holding him liable for what he did do (and for being the kind of person he was in doing it) is that he may *become* a different kind of self and henceforth choose different sorts of ends.

In other words, freedom in its practical and moral sense (whatever is to be said about it in some metaphysical sense) is connected with possibility of growth, learning and modification of character, just as is responsibility. [pp. 337–339]

C. I. Lewis
(1883–1964)

Turning Points in Ethical Theory [6]

There are, I think, three outstanding concepts in ethics: the good, the right, and the just. A particular ethical theory is largely, if not wholly, determined by its analysis of these concepts, and its manner of conceiving their relations to one another.

Justice is, plainly, a derivative concept here. What

[6] The selection is from "Turning Points in Ethical Theory," in *Collected Papers of Clarence Irving Lewis,* ed. John D. Goheen and John L. Mothershead, Jr. (Stanford, Calif.: Stanford University Press, 1970), pp. 215–227.

is just is what is right toward others—what is right in view of our social relationships. Good and right have, each of them, a much wider application than just. Right is what is correct, justified, valid, imperative. The distinction of right and wrong extends over the whole field of man's decisions and his deliberate doing. It applies to all our thinking and inferring, as the distinction between valid and invalid conclusions, and between beliefs which are justified as against those which are mistaken or delusive. It applies to doing as directed to any purpose or kind of purpose, to artistic doing, to any manner of technical doing, and to doing and decisions to do which, like getting one's own breakfast or choosing a comfortable pair of shoes, are as free as possible from any responsibility to other persons. There is, correspondingly, the logically right or wrong, the cognitively valid or invalid, the prudentially justified or unjustified, as well as the artistically right, the politically right, the right answer in arithmetic, the right investment to choose, and the right way to make friends and impress people. In brief, 'right' connotes critique.

Good and bad likewise have wide application, beyond what concerns our relations to others, and are thus just or unjust. Good applies to whatever gratifies or satisfies, or conduces to satisfaction, and hence is desirable and rationally to be wished. The concept of justice occupies so prominent a place in ethics, in spite of being obviously derivative, for two reasons: first, because it seems to require some peculiar principle, not called for in the case of other kinds of right doing, to cover right doing toward others; and second, because so many thinkers in the field of ethics speak and write as if moral rightness and wrongness were exclusively a matter of our obligations to other persons.

Let us grant that this question of justice is the most exigent of moral problems, and what any ethical theory has to say about it is the most important feature of that ethics. But is it in fact the only question of morals? For example, are merely prudential problems questions of ethics, and is it the business of ethics to elicit rules of prudence? If you say "Yes," you outrage any who would follow Kant; and if you say "No," you flout Bentham and the utilitarians. Extraordinary as it may seem at this date, there never has been any clear and common understanding as to what the boundaries of ethics are and what the subject of ethical study is.

I do not think it important how we divide up our problems—though I do think it ought to be recognized as indicating an extraordinary lack if there is to be no attempt at systematic study of right and wrong doing in general and beyond the bound of justice and injustice merely. And I do suggest that the whole business of the conduct of life, and of rightness and wrongness in such conduct at large, is a vitally needed study with which no one can in fact fail to concern himself, and that all questions falling within this broader field are affected with a sense of the moral, because all decisions of the conduct of life must be affected with a sense of right or wrong. If ethics is to be restricted to what concerns justice only, then this broader field of right and wrong doing in general might be called 'practical philosophy,' and ethics will be merely one branch of it.

I would further draw attention to the trouble which ethics has encountered in finding any clear, intelligible, and generally accepted answer to the principal question of justice: the question, namely, "Is it my duty to act with equal regard for the interests of others as for my own; and if so, why?" Could it be that the reason for this difficulty lies in overlooking the fact that right and wrong toward others is only one species of right and wrong; and that we are unlikely to find the root of the imperative of justice if that imperative be thought of as *sui generis* and without parallel? If justice and injustice are one species of right or wrong doing in general, then it might be that the imperative of justice is simply one mode or one application of an imperative which is more general. In that case, it would not be surprising that if we wait to raise the question of the validity of imperatives of action until the specific question of right action toward others comes in view, what we can then find to say about it may prove to be too little and too late.

I wish to suggest that this approach to the question of justice is the auspicious one, from the point of view of theoretical understanding, and that it is best to begin by investigating the broader topic of right and wrong in general, and the imperative in general, and of principles of validity and critique over the whole scope of them. That takes in the normative in general. But it will be obvious that I could not even outline so large a project here. I can only touch upon it here and there, hoping to indicate points which have special importance and are such as can be suggested briefly.

'Right' and its inverse 'wrong' concern some

property or character of acts—of whatever is done by decision, and is subject to criticism and such that the doer may be called upon, or call upon himself, to justify it. These terms 'right' and 'wrong' are extended, by that metonymy which characterizes the use of language in general, to whatever connects itself with rightness in action or wrongness in action. But the first and literal meaning, from which the further senses of them derive, is one in which their application is confined to acts, and to acts which are deliberate or corrigible.

I shall wish to use the words 'act' and 'action' here in the above meaning, confining their application to what is done by decision and excluding incorrigible behavior and even unconsidered behavior, except so far as the failure to *consider* it would itself be a matter calling for correction. This is a narrower sense than the common sense usage, but frequent in ethics since it confines act to the sense of 'conduct.' On another point, however, I would use 'act' and 'activity' more widely than is usual by extending these terms to include decisions themselves. Deciding not only is of the essence of any deliberate doing, but deciding is itself an activity, subject to critique and calling for justification. In fact, though a physical doing is not the same fact as the decision to do it, any physical doing is right or is wrong just in case it is something done by decision and that decision is right or is wrong. Rightness and wrongness of decision are, thus, the root of rightness and wrongness in general. All decisions are right or wrong, and nothing else is right or wrong except as it flows from a decision which is right or wrong, or is something the decision to do or to bring about would be right or wrong. And all decisions are right or wrong, justified or unjustified, because all decisions are subject to some imperative. That is right which accords with the imperative and that is wrong which contravenes it.

There will be some, I am sure, who will fail to recognize this fact because, by habit of thought, they associate this word 'imperative' exclusively with felt obligation to others. I can do no more than suggest here very briefly that there are other imperatives than the imperative of justice, and that they are familiar.

There is, for example, the imperative to rightness in inference—the imperative to be consistent in our thinking, by reason of which we are constrained to cry "Touché" when we are found inconsistent or if we refuse a conclusion whose premises we have accepted. At the present moment in history, it is customary to think of principles of logic as formulating a certain kind of fact, and not as normative rules, the adherence to which is an acknowledged dictate for the conduct of our thought. But that there is this normative function of them, determinative of what is justified and is unjustified in conclusions reached, will hardly be denied. At a later point, I shall wish to revert to the kind of facts which logic is supposed to formulate.

Also, believing in general, and disbelieving, have their imperative. And in passing, let us remind ourselves that the greater part of what is called knowing is merely giving credence according to the evidence. The constraint so to conduct our decisions of belief is familiar. There are things we should like to believe but are obliged to consider doubtful. Also we sometimes say regretfully, "That I have to accept as fact." If there are any who could overlook this manner of imperative, it might be persons who conform to it habitually because for them obedience to it represents a bent of mind and professional self-discipline, and any recognized wishful thinking they almost automatically repudiate.

Prudent behavior is also a matter having its imperative. Whether prudential principles are taken to be included in or excluded from ethics, at least it is clear that they concern a problem different from that of social justice. And if prudence lies nearer to inclination, at least we observe in children that prudent decision and action are neither automatic nor dictated by felt inclination; and any of us who has ever postponed a task too long for our own best interests will be able to take the point that prudential dictates operate as imperatives. In fact, the prudential offers a particularly favorable example for distinguishing between inclination and any sense of the imperative, while still observing that the imperative in general cannot be identified with the socially obligatory. [pp. 215–218]

I have suggested that without values there would be no imperative, but if we seek to derive the imperative straight from value, we are bound to miss its distinctive character. The imperative is imperative whether we like it or not. And it is most clearly discerned where it stands opposed to what we wish. But I have also suggested that we shall not easily see the nature of it by looking to that particular imperative which obliges us to respect the good of others.

Rather our sense of the imperative is simply our

sense of fact—but of fact as not immediate. I have used the example of our serious judgment when our own good life is critically in question. It is that same imperative which, as even Hume acknowledged, obliges us practically to act as if our cognitive apprehensions are significant of a real objective world in which we can make valid predictions of the future, in the light of past experience, whether we consider the premises of that practical attitude theoretically sufficient or not. If one makes this investment or takes this job, or studies for this profession or marries at this age, the facts of what will happen and whether they will make for a good life are difficult matters. The consequences of our decision once effected are then out of our hands, and even if we can foretell the future, or estimate it accurately so far as its other features go, we can still blunder devastatingly by mistaking what value-quality will be found in that which we predict and to which we so commit ourselves. To rush in from present inclination and uncriticized emotion is precisely what we would avoid. This is prudential judgment, if you will, though if you say that 'prudence' is a poor word for the responsible attitude, sure, I shall agree and applaud. Our aim is to respect the future fact as that fact will be when it comes: to appreciate it or realize it in that nature it will have experienced, and not as envisaged now in our attempted imaginative presentation of it—colored, it may be, by wishful thinking or romantic daydream. We have two kinds of facts here to respect: the cause-effect facts of natural consequences of our present choice of action, and the value-facts of these consequences as satisfying or dissatisfying ingredients in a life to be lived. From both points of view, our only clues now when we must decide are some manner of immediate presentments. But we would govern our decision not by the immediate quality of this presentment but by the character of what it represents. To heed this imperative will be to decide and to act here and now in view of the objective realities our immediate presentments mediate instead of deciding and doing as present feeling inclines us. [pp. 221–222]

. . . Animals act toward the future and adaptively to future fact. But we suppose that their doing so requires an instinct whose emotive power as now felt exceeds that of any presently opposing inclination. Men are not moved and deterred by the strength of now felt apprehensive feeling but by

the sense of an imperative to objectivity in decision. It is so that I would describe the imperative as a felt ingredient in human experience. And the principle of it is simply the principle of objectivity: respect realities apprehended for what they objectively are, and not by reference to your subjective feeling, not according to the quality and intensity of the immediate feeling which mediates them for your apprehension. In other words, be rational, not emotional. Be governed by your intellectual integrity, not by your uncriticized feelings. Taking this as the basic principle of right decision in general, and of moral conduct in the widest sense of 'moral,' is—I hope you note—the exact antithesis of an emotive theory of morals.

And correlatively, this view connects itself with a conception of cognition which, instead of contrasting indicative statements of fact with hortations, persuasions and advice, would point to the essential connection of every statement of fact with corresponding imperatives of action. But these imperatives, unlike commands from one of us to another, or persuasions intended to cozen those addressed into doing what we wish, are such as appeal to the integrity of the one addressed and advise him in the light of it, but do not trespass upon that integrity or upon his freedom of decision and of action. [pp. 222–223]

. . . The small child who, seeing the glowing stove, feels the urge to touch it and does so, injures only himself. And so likewise in the case of the careless adult, or the occasional pathological mind with the urge to self-inflicted pain. But let us observe that what this trivial example illustrates is the imperative to the good life. The tendency to sacrifice future goods to present urges, especially if the contemplated future be remote, is more frequent, and lapses from the dictate of the principle of objectivity are there more common. The dictate to respect the objective fact of your future satisfactions and griefs for the realities they are, and not to prejudice them by doing as momentarily pleases you—not to sacrifice your birthright for some mess of pottage—is not quite so trivial as our example seems, but the principle is the same. And here too, let us observe, if the validity of this imperative to have regard for a good life on the whole should be challenged by some fool who says, "If I do this I prejudice my interests of ten years from now—so what?" there is nothing to reply. And if his present urges affect our own interests also, there is nothing left but to protect ourselves, as best we may.

It is a common failing of our human nature not to see or feel remote and future interests full size—e.g., to postpone study to the week before exams—and it is by reason of that kind of fact that the principle of objectivity as the dictate of prudence and the good life has the status of an imperative. But it is a dictate which must be self-imposed, and whose validity must be self-acknowledged, or it has none. [pp. 223–224]

Working from a minimal formal idea of prudence, Lewis insists that an imperative principle of such a sort is necessary. What the content of prudence is involves an empirical study of life. Even a Cyrenaic formula, a principle of acting on impulse on each occasion, could count as a prudential principle if it were a thought-out conclusion about how life is to be carried out, not, however, if it were unreflective egoism. Prudence can be a rich notion—expressing a right ordering of life or segments of it in a community where there are mutual undertakings, cooperative behavior with diverse roles, a measure of competition, and freedom for self-determination of goals and their pursuit. The demand for a principle of justice, directed to relations among persons, has this kind of setting.

But what of the distinctively ethical imperative: the imperative of justice? I suggest that we do not have to look in any theoretical dark corner for it; the main consideration is right there in plain sight. The other fellow's joys and sorrows are exactly as real and as poignant as your own. Respect them for the objective realities they are, instead of according to any weakly felt and vicarious immediate feeling of sympathy with which they may afflict you. There is more than that, of course, to the question of egoism versus altruism. But time is too short to go into it. If it is the imperative of justice that is wanted, then it is in the principle of objectivity, in application to the question of decisions and actions affecting others. And if one have no sense of this as a valid imperative, then perhaps there is nothing for the rest of us to do but banish him as one we cannot admit to our company and treat as a fellow. [p. 225]

Lewis attempts the formulation of an imperative of justice in two of his other works, *The Ground and Nature of the Right* (1955) and *Our Social Inheritance* (1957). The object is to come to grips with the predicament of Sidgwick, who had concluded that no rule obliges you to take account of others' interests so long as you do not expect them to sacrifice for you. Lewis, recognizing the more complex sociability of human social inheritance—as opposed to Sidgwick's individual contractual relations—experiments with a variety of formulations, some minimal like the Kantian, others stronger—for example, that nothing should be acceptable to you in making a decision with consequences for others that would not be acceptable to you if you were in their place. A clear statement of the dialectic of individual and community that underlies the search for a principle is found in another essay: [7]

When we come to the ethical questions of justice, and the seeming divergence to the dictate of prudence, on occasion, from the dictate of justice, then let us not forget two things: first, that if one should ask, "What is it that is most indispensable to the individual good of any human?" the readiest and most plausible answer must be, "The privilege of living in a good human society, profiting from its spiritual inheritance of ideas, and sharing in its cooperative institutions, preserved and furthered by its mores" but second, if any community ask itself, "What is it that is most indispensable to our ongoing life, to the distinctive character of the life we share, the source of all we cherish, and the hope of all further social achievement?" there the discerning answer is, "The fact that our social order is composed of autonomous individuals, capable of thinking and learning otherwise than by being told, and subject to their own self-criticism and the ultimate authority of their own self-government in action."

[7] "The Individual and the Social Order," in *Collected Papers of Clarence Irving Lewis*, p. 214.

If we suppress that self-governing initiative, we destroy that only root from which all that we possess has come to be and from which alone can spring any social advance to be hoped for in the future.

The formulation of rational imperatives requires hard work. To understand the impera-tive of consistency required the full twentieth-century development of logical theory; and the imperative of cogency presupposes an understanding of how science operates, which has taken centuries to unfold. Comparable reflective labors on the self and social history are required to understand prudence and justice.

22

Phenomenological Description and Existential Decision

Phenomenology and Existentialism are closely related movements that originated in Germany and France in the early part of the century and spread in the English-speaking world around mid-century. Phenomenology looked to consciousness as knowing, while Existentialism addressed man's situation in the world and his ethical responsibilities.

Phenomenological Description

Edmund Husserl (1859–1938) founded modern phenomenology in the first decade of the century. Its distinctive initial feature was its method, which Husserl saw as carrying through the methodic doubt of Descartes in a truly radical way: to study conscious experience and to describe it without making any presuppositions. Descartes had been on the right track, but he then enshrined dualism as a categorial divide of mind and body, inner

and outer, subjective and objective. Since natural science was concerned with the physical and biological world, inner experience—consciousness—was regarded as unscientific, unless it could be "reduced" to the physical. Yet if we stow all that is characteristically human in the subjective, we are then forced to look for values in some inner realm divorced from science, to debate only whether they are beliefs or feelings. This whole mess is of our own making. The remedy lies in careful phenomenological inspection of direct experience.

In 1913 the first issue of the journal of the phenomenological movement, edited by Husserl, announced a platform:

It is not a system that the editors share. What unites them is the common conviction that it is only by a return to the primary sources of direct intuition and to insights into the essential structures derived from them that we shall be able to put to use the great traditions of philosophy with their concepts and problems; only thus shall we be in a position to clarify such concepts intuitively, to restate the

555

problems on an intuitive basis, and thus, eventually, to solve them, at least in principle.[1]

Two notes are sounded here. One is the call for a direct encounter with experience without presupposition, sometimes sloganized as "To the Things Themselves" (*Zu den Sachen*). The second is the conviction that the output of this encounter would be knowledge of *essences*. Joining these two claims, phenomenologists span rationalism and empiricism: by the first claim they aim to be radical empiricists; through the second, they are aligned with rationalism. Husserl himself thought that by the phenomenological method he could transform philosophy into a discipline as rigorous as science, though different and foundational to it. Few followed him in this. He insisted that a critical step in the method was to "bracket" existence, that is, to postpone any assumption as to the existence of what was being studied, particularly the physical presupposition that out there there are objects to be experienced and the psychological presupposition that there is a subject doing the experiencing. Few practiced the method with the rigor he expected. His designated successor, Martin Heidegger, moved away even from the analysis of consciousness, bracketing even it, and took Being as more fundamental. Others regarded phenomenology as a method only, and refused to follow Husserl's apparent move into idealism. It is therefore impossible to give a precise account of the nature of phenomenology that will include everyone who wrote under its banner. Still, there is no doubt that Husserl's example seemed to indicate a new direction in values and ethics.

Broadly speaking, in ethics phenomenology opposes reductionism and relativism. The antireductionism is rooted in the conviction that a full description of pure consciousness would show experience to be much richer than philosophers hitherto had recognized. Husserl did most of his work in epistemology, relying on William James in attacking the copy theory of perception. Others, extending the method into the domain of values, argue that a faithful description of experience shows the inadequacy of "reducing" concepts such as justice, friendship, punishment, sympathy, and so on, to complexes, however sophisticated, of utilities or pleasures. Phenomenological analyses of emotions and feelings have attempted to rescue them from "reduction" to inner feelings or even outward acts. Thus Max Scheler (1874–1928) rescues love and hatred in *The Nature of Sympathy* and rancor (*ressentiment*) elsewhere. It is similarly a mistake to reduce values to facts, or facts to values, or for that matter, to reduce the distinction to the inner and outer, or subjective and objective. Experience is simply richer than these categories permit. Frithjof Bergmann, writing in the 1970s, conveys this sense, discussing the qualities to be found in experience:

What we notice is the stark and unqualified 'givenness' of these qualities. They present themselves and they confront us. If we set aside all explanatory frameworks and assumptions, even those that are only hazy shadows and habits, and make the effort to see clearly nothing but the actual brute experience of them (and that is at least a large part of what Husserl meant by his 'return to the facts') then we are struck by the simple 'thereness' of them. We look and we *see* that this gesture is clumsy while that one is graceful. We listen and we *hear* the sadness of a little tune.[2]

It might appear that to confine oneself to experience is severely limiting. Phenomenologists argue that a fundamental feature of consciousness is that it is *intentional*: every act of consciousness is consciousness *of* something (its "object"). Thus a complete description of

[1] *Jahrbuch für Philosophie und phänomenologische Forschung.* Quoted in Herbert Spiegelberg, *The Phenomenological Movement: A Historical Introduction* (The Hague: Nijhoff, 1965), p. 5.

[2] "The Experience of Values," *Inquiry* 16, no. 3 (Autumn 1973): 251.

an experience must include its object. By "object" is not meant an actually physical object, but that which the consciousness is directed to, what it is "of." Phenomenologists study human capacities by examining the distinctive features of the field of consciousness, which cannot be characterized as either inner or outer. Thus seeing and hearing are studied, not just by looking at the acts, but by including the seen and the heard; thinking, by examining the structure of knowledge as well as the processes of speaking and symbolizing; laughing, by looking at the comic and its nature as well as to strains and releases in the economy of the self. The acts of consciousness themselves are to be thought of, not as separate, but as a joint fulfillment of the capacities and the structures in a unified activity. Such a philosophical perspective would speak in the same tones of a spreading feeling of shame and a blush advancing over the cheek as it would of a reddish sunrise spreading over the sky.

The phenomenological approach possesses a rich bundle of features and accordingly permits different emphases and different directions. The selections sample these: Bergmann emphasizes the immediacy and in-the-world character of the experience of values, qualities there already and not constructed by us, and examines their role in rule formation. Buber turns to interpersonal experience and the differences within it, exploring, for example, how a unifying intimacy differs from a scrutinizing distancing.

A second feature of phenomenological ethics is its opposition to relativism. Although the method begins with a particular experience—whether seeing a red particular or beholding a compassionate action—what it grasps or intuits is an *essence* of, for example, the color red or the feeling compassion. This essence is not the old Platonic universal, nor the Aristotelian cognition. As Scheler says:

An essence, or whatness, is in this sense *as such* neither universal nor particular. The essence red,

for example, is given in the universal concept as well as in each perceivable nuance of this color. The differences between universal and particular meanings come about only in relation to the objects in which an essence comes to the fore. Thus, an essence becomes *universal* if it comes to the fore in a plurality of otherwise different objects as an identical essence: in all and everything that "has" or "bears" this essence. The essence can, on the other hand, also constitute the nature of an *individual thing* without ceasing to be such an *essence*.[3]

What we learn in intuiting such an essence, Scheler insists, is *a priori*—given or prior to all experience (of this kind). He denies that such intuitions can be assimilated to ordinary perception and thought working in tandem, or to willing; the former provides only access to the intuition, whereas the latter is subsequent to the value-intuition. Value-essences as direct object of intuition claim objectivity, against a background of changing contexts and historical transformations. Values have also to be distinguished from the *bearers* of these values, the things or actions which are thought to express them. Relativity applies not to the values themselves, but to their bearers.

Hartmann's *Ethics* (1926) develops a similar, though variant, approach. Here too the phenomenological weapon wielded is the feeling-intuition of essences; no matter what actions are the carriers, it is the essence of nobility, fidelity, justice, courage, and the rest, that we intuit in observing the action. For Hartmann, direct valuational insight is directed to ideal self-existent values, which he calls the realm of ideal ought-to-be. This pure realm is sharply distinguished from two subordinate realms: that of positive ought-to-be, those values appropriate to a given state of existence; and, most concretely, the domain of the ought-to-do, the duties and obligations incumbent on

[3] *Formalism in Ethics and Non-Formal Ethics of Value*, trans. Manfred S. Frings and Roger L. Funk (Evanston: Northwestern University Press, 1973; original German edition 1913–1916), pp. 48–49.

particular people in virtue of the situation in which they find themselves. Hartmann's heaven of values, unlike Plato's forms, is pluralistic and does not converge on a single unitary Good. Its rich constellations are not even necessarily consistent with one another: they may point in different directions, as do, for example, strict justice and brotherly love. In dealing with moral disagreement, then, Hartmann offers three possibilities. First, he invokes a theory of moral blindness to explain the simple inability to see a value. Second, in some cases where we seem to ignore a value, it is simply that we are so intent on other values that we are prevented from seeing the value in question; he quaintly speaks of this as passing on the other side of the street. Finally, even for one whose sight is sound and who has not overlooked the values involved there is often still the need to select some values at the cost of others. Accordingly, guilt in human conduct is unavoidable; but to bear it is part of a responsible self. Hence the religious view of divine forgiveness, in removing this guilt, goes morally astray.

Phenomenological intuition is not simple inspection, immune to revision in the light of further experience. A phenomenologist is not committed to the first intuited result; it is possible that a wider range of experience will lead to deeper intuitive apprehensions. But it is our apprehension that is revised, not the essence apprehended. For example, suppose we ask what the essence of compassion is. We might begin with specific cases of compassion, real or imaginary, and inspect them closely for qualities of experience, for example certain kinds of feelings, certain kinds of relations between subject and object, intentions, results, and so on. Gradually the essence will crystallize in consciousness: that is what compassion is. From inspection of various putative acts of compassion it becomes clear that purposes such as impressing one's friends, or justifying an income tax deduction are excluded by the essence. One might go on to ask whether compassion is a quality only of persons, and not

of social practices. Consider the case of a community whose practice it is to pass a closed box containing money to a family thought to be in need—for example, due to death or illness. It is expected that the recipients will either open and take money from it (if they are in need) or contribute to it and then hand it back to be passed to the next family. No one knows whether the family has taken or given. If it gave, is it a pure case of compassion? Is compassion a quality of the whole practice? One might want to inquire into the relationship between essences, for example, that between the essences of compassion and of pity: how might they be distinguished in, say, a helpful response to a handicapped person? Again, one inspects cases. The differences between them is a matter finally of *seeing*. If we are asked *how* we see this, we can only point to the items in the action that carry the essence: that an act was of pity rather than of compassion might be indicated by the giver's embarrassment or oversolicitousness, or his too loudly lamenting the plight of the handicapped. Thus inspection of varieties of cases leads to a more refined intuition.[4] In any case, the phenomenologist claims that we can and do see the essence of compassion. Furthermore, the same intuition tells us not only what compassion is—its "whatness"—but that it is a positive value.

The scientifically minded epistemologist might object that compassion is not a given, but an intellectual conception we bring to bear on experience. Like all concepts compassion is open to refinement, splitting up, and reassortment in further experience. The epistemologist might point to the fact that the concept has a history of change and refinement, such as its earlier association with the feeling aspect of beneficence and benevolence, Hobbes's theoretical analysis of compassion in terms of a person's feeling how he or she would suffer

---

[4] For a full account of the method, extended to seven steps, see Spiegelberg, *The Phenomenological Movement*, pp. 655–698.

in the same situation, and Butler's and Smith's arguments for an original relation of sympathy. The differentiation of pity and compassion to the scientifically minded is less a matter of given qualitative experience and more a product of a more sophisticated psychology of personality. The alleged direct intuition is rather the habitual application of an intellectual concept carrying along with it a penumbra of typical instances and indices.

Despite its internal differences, controversies and obscurities, phenomenology had liberating effects. It gave all disciplines permission to explore direct experience, defying the accumulated warnings of traditional scientific methodology not to trespass on the subjective, the qualitative, or the introspective. This proved especially important for psychology. Gestalt psychologists, vehemently antibehavioristic, took the perceptual field as the object of direct study. They denied their methods were introspective, for they were not looking *within* but describing the experiential field: for example, how two measurably identical lines look different in length when arrow heads at their ends point inward or outward; how hearing a tune differs from hearing the notes; how far ahead the rails appear to be parallel and where they converge; how, when the train we are riding in is moving past telephone poles and we see the poles flying past the window. Gestalt psychology opened up whole areas of phenomena for systematic study, illustrated here by the selection from Duncker.

Social psychology too was allowed to raise questions of how the world and human relations *looked* to participants: what different kinds of natural and social situations *meant* to those who were placed within them; what the different ways are in which one experiences being with other people; how people look on nature: as something to be conquered or exploited, as something they either stand outside of or feel part of, as within or beyond manipulation and control. Sociologists studying ethnic and racial problems could examine not merely how one group treated another, but how they

looked upon one another. The impact of this approach became evident when women's groups engaged in "consciousness raising": there was little need to explain that it meant looking at what it means to be a woman from the viewpoint of a woman. Anthropology could explore not only the different customs of different peoples, but how they oriented themselves to the world around them—in space, in time (whether they lived in the present or worked chiefly for the future or looked back to the past), in interpersonal relations (whether they saw other people as collaborators or as rivals).

This essentially descriptive phenomenological analysis contributed also to practical and normative disciplines. Psychiatrists, who had dealt with their patients' depression in terms of guilt feelings or had invoked theoretical causal hypotheses of how guilt arises (e.g., from early parental threats), now tried first to understand how the world looked to their patients. Educators asked themselves what precisely being a child meant in terms of how the child saw the world and adults. (As Maria Montessori had a room constructed so proportioned that adults could simulate a child's experience of normal sized furniture, for example, having to jump to reach the soap dish on the bathroom sink.) Questions of responsibility, punishment, treatment, desirable practices and institutions, were all affected by the insights of such extended analysis.

Existentialist Decision

Two lines of thought converge in existentialism. One is phenomenology, from which it took the method, although it turned away from Husserl's concern with the foundations of knowledge toward a concern with human action. The other is that associated with Soren Kierkegaard (1813–1855), a Dane who passionately defended the inner, the personal, the particular, against Hegelian system building and absolutes.

At the center is the German philosopher Martin Heidegger (1884–1976). Although his major work, *Being and Time*, appeared in the phenomenological yearbook it decisively broke with Husserl in declaring that the problem for philosophy is not knowledge but Being. He rejected Husserl's bracketing of existence, but still employed a reinterpreted and extended phenomenological method to analyze the fundamental structures of Being. It is impossible briefly to convey the power and energy of Heidegger's writing, and impossible even at length to secure agreement on what for him the problem of Being was. What is clear, though, is that he seemed to many of his contemporaries to be challenging at the most fundamental level philosophical traditions as ancient as Plato, and forging a new and striking vocabulary through which to do it. Thus a central concept is *Dasein* (sometimes translated as "Humanbeing," that is, the kind of Being humans exhibit). Dasein is said to have the character of being "thrown" into the world, it is discussed in such terms as authenticity/inauthenticity, its relation to the world is said to be "Concern," and our understanding of Being is said to come through Anxiety. To many of his contemporaries, this seemed a form of obscure mysticism; but to others it was profound. Although it now seems that the personal and the authentic, Kierkegaard's themes, were not at all what Heidegger had in mind—he persistently disclaimed the label "existentialist"—the effect of his language was to direct attention toward what are now commonly thought "existential" themes: anguish, solitude, the authentic, freedom, responsibility, and so on.

In France, Jean-Paul Sartre (1905–1979) became the existentialist *par excellence*. He too began from phenomenology, but he merged it more directly with Kierkegaard. Sartre was prominent not merely because of his many novels and plays as well as his similarly passionate philosophical writing, but because of his militant participation in French political life:

in the resistance movement during the 1940s, against French colonial activities in Algeria in the 1950s, and in the student protest movement of the 1960s. Through it all ran a central moral theme, that of "engagement" in practice.

After World War II existentialism became popular in the Anglo-American world. For a time it was in vogue to search out existentialist strains in virtually all philosophers, from Socrates on. Religions and philosophies developed their own existentialist wings. The common concern was the human predicament: individuals abandoned without guidance in a condition of risk and uncertainty, left to make their own free decisions on their own full responsibility—how to face crisis, how to live, and how to die. Eventually existentialism left center stage as later (particularly French) philosophies came to the forefront in rapid succession—structuralism, hermeneutics, deconstructionism. But a number of philosophers still remained for whom the human predicament was critical and to whom the label "existentialist" still clung.

An early example is the Spanish philosopher Miguel de Unamuno (1864–1936), whose *Tragic Sense of Life* (1912) stressed the in-the-world character of philosophy, as against the autonomy of abstract thought or philosophical system:

> Philosophy is a product of the humanity of each philosopher, and each philosopher is a man of flesh and bone who addresses himself to other men of flesh and bone like himself. And, let him do what he will, he philosophizes not with reason only, but with the will, with the feelings, with the flesh and with the bones, with the whole soul and the whole body. It is the man that philosophizes.[5]

Unamuno regards Spinoza's *Ethics* as a philosophy of despair in spite of Spinoza's remark

---

[5] Miguel de Unamuno, *The Tragic Sense of Life*, trans. J. E. Crawford Flitch (New York: Dover, 1954), p. 28. This edition contains an excellent introduction to Unamuno's thought by Salvador de Madariaga.

that no topic is of less concern to the free man than death. In Unamuno's view, one thinks of death only in the vain endeavor to be free of it, for at bottom in human beings there is a hunger for immortality. Indeed the will to live is assimilated to this hunger for immortality, which in turn is assimilated to love.[6] Gradually Unamuno's view of the human predicament emerges: the philosopher seeks rational grounds for what he wills, particularly in ideas of God, but reason at best yields skepticism.

And in this abyss the scepticism of the reason encounters the despair of the heart, and this encounter leads to the discovery of a basis—a terrible basis!—for consolation to build on.[7]

Here is the existentialist touch: one does not run away from the predicament; it becomes the basic building-block for life's attitudes. The man who says in his heart that there is no God is wicked, for saying it in his heart; a righteous man well could say it in his head![8] Faith is simply the will not to die, and in a certain sense creates its object.[9] And so in the end it is clear that "it is the conflict itself, it is this self-same passionate uncertainty, that unifies my actions and makes me live and work."[10] His final injunction is:

[A]ct in such a way as to make our annihilation an injustice, in such a way as to make our brothers, our sons, and our brothers' sons, and their sons' sons, feel that we ought not to have died.[11]

Philosophy is the science of the tragedy of life.[12]

Existentialism is far from the traditional moral philosophy that sought a fixed basis in the moral law enjoined by God or in a well-designed human nature or in the habits of custom and tradition. It is not necessarily tied to a religious belief, as can be seen from Sartre's secular existentialism. His specific account of the basic predicament is of course different from Unamuno's; Sartre's stresses the loneness of the individual and the ultimacy of his decision and responsibility. Each decision is unique, not because the situation is complex but because to decide is to exercise complete freedom. Any attempt to bind present decision to preexistent standards is characterized as an inauthentic flight from responsibility. Even appealing to one's own principles will not do, since the selection of the principle to apply on the present occasion is still a matter of personal choice. (It is as if to take out a magazine subscription for a full year, rather than to renew with each issue, is to abandon responsibility.) Sartrean ethics thus postulates complete freedom and calls for complete responsibility, against determinisms that shape people's expectations and engender moral compromises.

The tone of Sartre's view of ethics is clear in a little essay he wrote on the occasion of the liberation of France.[13] It begins with the startling dictum: "We were never more free than during the German occupation." Even under those conditions—the loss of rights, the silencing, the insults, deportation, and death—"every accurate thought was a conquest . . . every one of our gestures had the weight of a solemn commitment." The implication is that the peace of ordinary life, with its pursuits and lesser problems, obscures the character of the moral. "And the choice that each of us made of his life and of his being was an authentic choice because it was made face to face with death, because it could always have been expressed in these terms: 'Rather death than. . . .' "

As a translation of moral utterance, this rings truer than, say, Stevenson's "I approve of this:

---

[6] Ibid., p. 39.
[7] Ibid., p. 105.
[8] Ibid., p. 184.
[9] Ibid., p. 192.
[10] Ibid., p. 270.
[11] Ibid., p. 269.
[12] Ibid., p. 320.

[13] "The Republic of Silence," trans. Ramon Guthrie, in *The Republic of Silence*, ed. A. J. Liebling (New York: Harcourt, Brace, 1947), pp. 498–500.

do so as well" (see Chapter 20), especially in the context of life in which Sartre offers it. It is sobering, however, to observe how naturally such a formula as Sartre's rises to the lips of a terrorist making nonnegotiable demands. It raises the question of whether it is by the kind of death or the kind of life that ultimately morality is to be understood.

Nicolai Hartmann
(1882–1950)

Ethics [14]

Hartmann compares the insight of self-existent values with mathematical insight. His adherence to absolute values compels him to deal with cases of people who ignore them or even deny them; here he invokes the theory of moral blindness.

Ch XVI: The Ideal Self-Existence of Values

(a) The Self-Existence of Values for Knowledge. Values have self-existence. . . . Values subsist independently of the consciousness of them. Consciousness can grasp or miss them, but cannot make them or spontaneously decree them. This does not hold true of the material. By his co-operation a subject can very well—within certain limits—produce the material (for example, he can set up a relation of confidence): but he cannot thereby prevent such a material from being of value—or the contrary. Such a material simply "is" so, without any co-operation, and even if it is believed not to be so. Hence, concerning the characteristics which values have, the proposition holds good that they have self-existence. [p. 218]

(d) The Elhico-Ideal Self-Existence of Values. . . . The moral judgment of values, which declares that a

breach of trust is revolting or that malicious joy in another's misfortune is reprehensible, does not refer to the sensation as revolting or reprehensible. The judgment is rather itself this sensation, or its expression. What it means is something else, an objective revoltingness and reprehensibleness, which is independent of the sensation. It means something objective, something existing in itself. But, of course, a self-existence that is of an ideal nature.

In harmony with this is the conviction, which accompanies every genuine judgment of values, that everyone else must judge in the same way and have the same impression. And here also the universality and necessity, which betray themselves in such a conviction, are not a psychological factum. For, actually, other persons occasionally feel and judge otherwise. And the one judging knows, or may very well know, of the deviation of the judgment of others from his own.

But it is here just as it is with mathematical insight. Not everyone is capable of it; not everyone has the eye, the ethical maturity, the spiritual elevation, for seeing the situation as it is. Nevertheless, the universality, necessity and objectivity of the valuational judgment hold good in idea. For this universality does not at all mean that everyone is capable of the insight in question. It only means that whoever is capable of it—that is, whoever has attained the adequate mentality—must necessarily feel and judge thus and not otherwise. This is a quite commonplace truth. Not everyone, for instance, has sense and understanding for the moral value of a noble-minded act matured in quiet meditation, or of consideration for others practised in a fine way; but everyone who has the understanding for them must judge them as something of value and must respect the personality of the doer.

In this sense—the only one under consideration—moral judgment and the primal moral feeling which underlies it are universal, necessary and objective. In this sense also the value expressing itself in the judgment is independent of the subject who judges. It has as genuine an ideal self-existence as any mathematical law.

The principle that values have an ideal self-existence has a striking significance for ethics. It affirms more than the mere apriority of valuational discernment and the absoluteness of discerned values. It affirms that there is a realm of values subsisting for itself, a genuine *kosmos noetos* which

[14] Nicolai Hartmann, *Ethics*, 3 vols., trans. Stanton Coit (London: George Allen & Unwin; New York: The Macmillan Company, 1932; original German edition 1926). The selection is from vol. 1.

exists beyond reality just as much as beyond consciousness—an ethical ideal sphere, not manufactured, invented or dreamed, but actually existing
and capable of being grasped in the phenomenon
of the feeling for values—a sphere which perdures
side by side with the ethical real and the ethical
actual sphere, just as the logical ideal realm exists
side by side with the ontological real and the
gnoseological positive realm.

(e) Valuational Delusion and Blindness. The doctrine
of apriority and that of self-existence are not identical. To see the truth of the former is relatively easy;
it was sufficient to understand that standards of
value are the presupposition of moral phenomena.
But prejudices, arbitrary assumptions, presenta-
tions, emotional attitudes can also be a priori. Now
values announce themselves primarily as enlist-
ments of emotion. They are therefore exposed to
doubt as to their objectivity so much the more, because feelings are less objective than discernments.

The concept of self-existence first raises them
above all such doubts. But it itself is rooted in the
fact that it is as little possible to summon up arbitrarily a sense of value as it is to construct a mathematical truth arbitrarily. In both cases there is an
objectively beheld existent, which presents itself
and which the feeling, the intuition, the thought
only follows but cannot dominate. We can experience as valuable only what in itself is so. We may
of course also be incapable of such an experiencing:
but if we are in general capable of it, we can experience the value only as it is in itself, but not as it is
not. The sense of value is not less objective than
mathematical insight. Its object is only more veiled
through the emotional character of the act; it must
be especially raised above the act, if we want to
become aware of it. But even this later making of
it known to ourselves can change nothing in the
structure of the object (the value).

The opposite question here forces itself to the
front, whether the evidence of the primary discernment of value is not also subject to delusion. And
it is natural to believe that, if there is valuational
delusion, the self-existence of values becomes again
doubtful and gives way to a certain relativity.

That is a great mistake. On the contrary, where
there are delusion and error, these consist of non-
agreement with the fact. The fact, as something
fixed and independent of the truth or error of the

knowledge—that is, the fact as something existing
in itself—is precisely the presupposition of delusion;
otherwise delusion would not be delusion. But the
"fact" is in this case the value itself. Accordingly,
if anything is proof for the self-existence of values,
it is exactly the phenomenon of delusion.

If values were only things posited by the subject,
if they consisted of nothing except the act of valuing—that is, of the evaluating sense as such—then
every chance enlistment of feeling would be as justifiable as every other. Valuational delusion would
then be altogether impossible.

But there are many authenticated delusions as
to values, even falsifications which rest upon perversions of the sense of values, as in the manifestations of resentment. These manifestations, as well
as their exposure through normal moral feelings,
would be an impossibility—that is, they would not
be falsifications, if the genuine values which were
lacking did not have a self-existence independent
of them. It is possible to be mistaken and to be set
right only where the object is a fixed one and has
its own definite character which is not changed by
being understood or misunderstood.

The ordinary kind of delusion as to values is of
course purely negative, the incapacity to discrimi-
nate, valuational blindness. But this is not delusion
proper, but only a defect of the sense of value concerning a definite point. It stands on all fours with
the theoretical incapacity of the mathematically untrained and untalented person. There are such
things as education and lack of education of the
sense of values, talent and lack of talent for the
discernment of them. There is such a thing as individual maturity of the power of discrimination in
the individual man, and there is a historical maturity
in mankind. Whether the latter always means progress must remain undecided; possibly it brings with
it a narrowness of the consciousness of values, so
that there is always lost on the one side what is
gained on the other. Perhaps there is also an enlargement of the field of valuational vision. But the
fact is that we always survey only a limited section
of the realm of values, while we remain blind to
the other sections. That is the reason why the historical shifting of our gaze, with its circle of light, on
the plane of self-existent values—which is reflected
in the multiplicity and transiency of moral systems—is so very instructive for philosophical investigation. And at the same time the reason lies here

why this shifting and this variability do not constitute a "transvaluation of values," but a revaluation and reorientation of human life. Values do not change, but our insight into them changes. The insight however changes, because the values themselves and their ideal order do not change with the movements of the mental eye, and because they are objective and self-existent. [pp. 225–229]

Frithjof H. Bergmann
(1930–   )

The Experience of Values [15]

Bergmann, professor of philosophy at the University of Michigan, regards as a common tacit presupposition of contemporary value theory, that the world is value-neutral. This drains all the content out of a rich vocabulary of values and puts it on the factual or descriptive side, leaving for the domain of values only bare approval and disapproval. Different moral philosophers go astray to argue about degrees of evaluative force, supporting reasons, whether reasons are merely persuasive or strictly logical; or again (among cognitivists) whether value properties are natural or nonnatural, whether values are reducible to desires or something else. In short, they do everything but look at the rich panoply of values.

I. The World Is Not 'Neutral'

. . . Telling me that I should think in terms of a simple positive or negative value, or in terms of 'goodness' and 'badness' is a little like asking me to go through a museum and telling me that I can only either shake my head or otherwise nod it. I could do that, of course, and I could shake or nod with more or less vigor, but it would be ludicrously confining, and I certainly could not communicate what I felt. Moreover—and this is the point—the

situation would not change much if I had permission to use as many purely descriptive, valuationally neutral words as I liked and could shake or nod my head in addition. A painting might seem impressive, majestic, coy, timid, self-conscious, or sentimental; or it might be grotesque, clownish, boorish, or severe or ascetic. Each of these words would be normally regarded as having some evaluative ingredient; but if I were told to make the descriptive content explicit, to articulate that part and only that part of its meaning in words, I would not know how to do it. What is the strictly descriptive content of 'grotesque' for example? I can think of words that are more or less close to it in meaning, like 'ghoulish,' 'clumsy,' 'untoward,' 'fantastic,' or 'ugly,' but these are, if anything, more evaluative and certainly not purely descriptive. [pp. 249–250]

This is not just to increase the parameters on the value side, beyond "negative" and "positive." It challenges any attempt to divide the descriptive and the evaluative as if they were simply compounded.

The purpose behind the hard look at these qualities is of course not to reject the fact/value distinction in general. Naturally there are contexts in which this categorization is useful. But that is not the issue. What I am saying is that this separation does not *work* for the qualities under discussion. Nor is this argument on its way to the conclusion that values and facts are so exquisitely blended that it is impossible to sort them apart. At stake is something completely different. It is this: The basic orientation, the kind of 'stance' that one adopts toward the whole issue of values, and derivatively from that, toward the question of how one should live, is powerfully influenced by the subterranean conceptions that we have tried to bring to the surface. These ideas exist not only in philosophy but are pervasive. (Every time you are challenged to 'stick to the facts' and not make value judgments you are in their presence.) Thus far, I have only made them explicit and set them into confrontation with a class of qualities that do not seem to fit into this framework. The eventual aim of this is not any one specific conclusion. The idea is rather to dissolve a conceptual pattern that has ordered the general approach to the theory of values, that has marked out the points

[15] Frithjof Bergmann, "The Experience of Values," *Inquiry* 16, 3 (Autumn 1973): 247–279.

that are regarded as problems and has defined what may count as their solution. In short: the aim is to achieve a new perception and a different orientation. [pp. 251–252]

It is wrong to think of ourselves as mere outsiders to the world, observing it from the outside. So to conceptualize our relation to the world fails to recognize that the world *acts* on us: when we are tempted by a cigarette or a drink of whiskey we think of these as neutral objects and of the drama of acceptance or rejection as taking place entirely inside us.

Take a situation that is very threatening. Imagine a tree falling down in your direction. Does it really make sense to believe that we do not perceive the danger directly but that the 'neutral' tree causes a sensation in us and that the whole response of our body is produced by it? But if not, then why should the experience of being charmed or tempted be metaphysically so different from that of terror? For that matter, what of other organisms? Are we to suppose that they too respond largely to their own sensations? If so, would this assumption not conflict with everything we know about awareness in the lower forms of life? Moreover, is this not in any case an inherently strange view of organisms? Is it not a needlessly complex theory of how organisms interact with their environment? Still further, what of Gestalt Psychology, or of Piaget's contention that infants perceive (in his terminology) 'affective qualities' *before* they have either a concept of self, or of their own body? There are other, similar questions, but in the end some very simple points are stronger.

It is a matter of immediate experience. If we simply look and see (not in any special 'bracketed' or Husserlian manner, but just with open eyes) we notice that this is plainly not what happens. In these situations there often is no sensation inside us. It may sound strange, but if one wanted to describe these experiences correctly one would have to say that it is the cigarette itself, or the drink itself that has the quality of 'being-tempting.' And the same is true for the falling, threatening tree, for a leaf that is luxurious, for a vulnerable face, or a voice that is revolting. The main pattern in all these situations is that of a presentation. One *confronts*. Just as earlier we noted that no seam separates fact from

value, so we now contend that there is no duality of indifferent, neutral stimulus and value-quality-endowed sensation. In direct experience these qualities are not by-products. On the contrary, they 'come first,' their assertion is immediate, and it is they who in turn evoke effects. They are of one piece with the 'given' and are encountered as integral with it. . . .

To say all this is not simply to propose an 'alternative conceptual framework.' It involves a different experience of oneself and of the world. There should be a powerful sense of displacement, of an outward shift; the discovery that much to which we had so far given only a doubtful, internal, flimsy existence is in fact real, and out there, and substantial. [pp. 253–254]

Qualities cannot be classified as subjective or objective. For example, the sadness of music or its majestic character or the oppressive silence of a room entered is a matter of direct experience. True, the perception of these qualities is dependent on our sense organs; but so is our perception of color. We do distinguish the music being sad from our having a feeling of sadness and the feeling of silence from the silence in the room.

II. Sketch of a Theory

We perform the virtuosities of our surgical thinking in the dim light that falls through heavy and cracked metaphors. Above all we needed to *see* the new and different pattern that a less obstructed light reveals. If we now have this otherwise arranged perception, we can begin to trace the alterations engendered by it in the evolving structure of a theory.

As long as the world is seen as a gray collage of facts one problem stands unavoidably in the center: the question of how values are 'justified.' If the given is thought to be bare fact, and values are conceptualized as fundamentally different, the issue of their entrance, of their arrival in this strange domain, has to arise. From the outset, the discussion takes the form of a search: where in this great wall of facts is the chink through which values come in? And what gives them a creditable base? This is now radically changed. There is of course still a problem of 'justification' but it no longer has the same meaning, or the same size. To say it first bluntly: there no longer is any question about how values 'come in,' or about the nature of their 'derivation' from facts, for the plain reason that they are there from the beginning, and that they are not 'secondary' to facts.

The psychologies of the two positions stand at opposite poles: the former is reminiscent of a Beckett landscape. An expanse of broken slate, dejected feet shuffling through stones, moving them, playing with hope to make hopeless time pass. The view to which we have come has its analogue in a sense of pressure. Now there is no question of looking for one thing that perhaps merits attachment, instead there is too much. Values clamor, crowd in, and exhaust us. One looks for a bench to find a rest from them.

But let us look at this contrast closely, and examine the workings of some details in the two schemes. On the traditional and customary view, we encounter this problem whenever a particular specific judgment is questioned, and we want to 'justify' it in the face of this doubt. If we have condemned a given action as wrong, and someone intercedes with the question 'Why do you think so?' we have to support our judgment. The question therefore centers on how we do this and in what the nature and quality of the mustered support consists.

The most prestigious and usual answer has been that we perform a deduction. In practical terms this means that we look for a generalization from which the particular judgment can be derived; i.e. we justify our judgment by referring the particular case to a more general rule, and by showing that it is an instance falling under the principle we have invoked.

Take an example: If a conversation started with my saying that it was rotten of you to lie, and you turned and asked 'Why?' then the justification of my condemnation would move one level up to a more general rule—to something like 'dishonesty is in general bad'—and from that my individual judgment on the lie could then be deduced. But if you were serious you very likely would not be ultimately satisfied with this answer. You would be apt to feel that this only shifts the place of the problem. So you might press further and ask what entitles me to such confidence in this rule, and how I propose to justify it. This would set off a repetition

of the same procedure. To satisfy the renewed demand I would move up yet another level of generality, and invoke a still higher rule. But there is no reason why this process should come to a halt there. [pp. 261–263]

Eventually and inevitably we are driven to a most general ultimate principle (the first cardinal rule of our moral position). It is different when this is challenged, for there is no more general principle from which to derive it. The resulting impasse has led many philosophers to the conviction that values are ultimately without justification, that they cannot be defended rationally but only clung to blindly.

This overall schematization of what in fact occurs and of where the main problems lie, changes completely as soon as we replace the first premise of the 'nothing-but factual world' with the axiom that things are sad and alluring, horrible, magnificent, and disgusting in their own right. If a specific, initial judgment is questioned, then the obvious way to support and justify it *in this new framework* is not by deduction. One does not turn upward to a general rule, but on the contrary to the object, as it were 'downward.' The slow systematic ascent hence does not even begin, and it therefore does not end in a blind shaft.

But we had better take one step at a time. The whole foregoing discussion was intended to lay the foundations on which we can now proceed to build. The upshot of it is in essence that the qualities whose status we examined at length constitute the base, the solid fundament, on which the theory and praxis of valuing rests. The judgments that ascribe these qualities to an object or an action are basic. They exist on the ground-level, and are the elementary particles from which the rest is built up. (There is an analogy here to the 'report-sentences' of some Phenomenalists.) Their 'justification,' i.e. the kind of support that validates or establishes them, is quite simply that they are true, that they correspond, that the quality which they predicate is in fact there.

Involved in the actual making of these judgments is nothing more complicated than whatever is required for assertions like 'this is red,' or 'this is green.' If these statements presuppose the application of certain criteria and rules, then the same is true for our ability to say that something is sad or frightening or vulgar. But the crucial point is that it is *no more* than this, that only criteria of *that* sort, and *that* kind of use of them, are in play. Specifically, it is not a precondition that there be some more abstract or ultimate 'standard,' or a general measure or criterion of 'goodness' or 'value.' In short, we need only the ability to recognize qualities and to use words.

There are of course instances of disagreement. But we have already seen that these are not nearly as common as one is apt to imagine, and that the metaphysical status of these qualities is in any case not radically affected by their occurrence. We can now add to this that we are not reduced to a dumb pointing when our judgment conflicts with that of others. How very far we are from this helpless silence comes into sharper focus if we distinguish the question of what gives legitimacy to a judgment—which in this case is the sheer 'there-ness' of the quality—from the quite different question of how we conduct ourselves when there are disputes. Nothing could be more mistaken than the fear that we could only 'agree to disagree' and then part. This specter haunts the discussion of values in the framework that we have discarded. For us it is the other way around. There is no end to what we could do, and the limits are set only by our patience. A complete psychoanalysis, for example, may help someone see that his mother is really 'aggressive.' And entire college curricula are meant to cultivate the ability to recognize some of these qualities in poems or plays. Just as painters spend a life-time learning how to see colors. So it is not at all as if there is 'no more to be said' if I call it magnificent and you think it grotesque. We could talk about nothing else for the next ten years, if that is how we wanted to spend our lives. And this has theoretical importance: it means that we do not substitute innumerable little impasses on the ground for the single big impasse at the top.

The next logical question is, how do we ever come to formulate general rules from these beginnings, and what is it that finally makes something 'bad' or 'good'? Here we should not overlook the possibility that someone might decline to go on. There is nothing insane, or nihilistic in the position that only these particularistic judgments are to be made, and it would be utterly wrong to think that such a person

'had no values.' What he would not have are *principles,* but that is not the same thing.

Still, how could we move beyond these pointillistic judgments if that is what we wanted to do, and how is their justification to be conceived?

Into the framework of an otherwise neutral world the idea of goodness breaks with a sharp abruptness. There it appears as a *novum,* as *the* contrast, in short as 'value' against a uniform backdrop of facts. This changes drastically once the full qualities have been restored to the outside that we confront. In the new framework, good or bad are not at all the value-terms *par excellence.* They do not have the central place assigned to them in most recent philosophical writings. The judgments close to the base that we have been discussing are all in all the more precise, the more discriminating, and the more informative evaluations. The strain is on, and our perceptivities are exerted, when we say of a dance, that it is 'fluffy,' or of a piece of music, that it 'clowns.' (And that is still only the surface. When we want to come closer, single words do not cut a sharp enough pattern. Then only images and metaphors draw a thin enough line.) Compared to that, 'good' and 'bad' only sort sheep from goats. In most circumstances these are precisely *not* the words that can be used for a genuine assessment. When that is asked for, we use another much more richly qualified language.

This is the vocabulary that critics use. The discovery and articulation of these qualities *is* the critic's performance. One might say, that he uses the language of the myriad qualities when he is serious, when he is writing his book on Blake, or on Kafka or Yeats. And that is why a real appraisal often needs an entire book. It is only because there are other contexts, and because other purposes have to be served, that cruder and blunter judgments are also felled. Books must be reviewed—one doesn't want to waste one's investment—and for that a more abstract and loose-shanked set of terms will still do. Yet even there (in his newspaper column) the critic will still avoid 'good' and 'bad,' or 'ugly' and 'beautiful.' They are too slap-dash (and intellectually snubnosed) even for a morning-after review. They operate too much like the man in Hesse's parable who divided all things only into those he could eat and those he could not eat. This kind of yes/no judgment a critic might only make in exasperation, when his children have worn through the last thread of his patience: 'No you can't go—because it is bad.'

And is the critic's hierarchy of language so different from our own? What words do we use when in talking to a friend late at night the improbable is granted, and we say what we think? Do we ever judge a man, an action, or anything to be simply 'bad' or 'good' if we take the time to be precise?

Still, we need a rigorously formulated account of how a concept like good does function. (Even if it were only to understand *why* it is so blunt.) That there are many uses goes without saying. One, however, seems to be central. In that use the word 'good' works in important ways like a generic term. It groups or orders the concrete, low-level qualities, and makes assertions in an abbreviated, short-hand fashion about whole sets or classes of them. If the subject were, for example, plays, then the lower, or intermediate level judgments might deal with qualities like the 'clarity of structure,' the 'economy of style,' the 'deftness of characterization,' the 'intellectual substance,' and so forth, while judgments concerning the 'goodness' of a play would be quick summations that presuppose and *tally* these evaluations. The manner of this reduction to a single denominator is of course flexible and subject to change. A play, to be good, must not possess one set of qualities that all good plays have in common. If it lacks structure but is very witty it can still be good. So one might say that the idea of goodness is like a minimum that the sum-total of these qualities must reach on balance. And this is one of the principal reasons for the *essential* vagueness and uninformativeness of the word. It only conveys the *result* of a very general weighing. Everything else—which qualities were weighed and how they have been reduced—is omitted.

The fact that we can arrive at this kind of tallied judgment does *not* mean that there is after all a positive or a negative 'value component' in each of these qualities. But the connection is important: the fact that this is *not* the case shows further how very gross the word 'good' really is. It means that judgments which pronounce something 'good' are not the outcome of a genuine adding or subtracting (give 'six' for sensitivity, take away 'three' for rashness), or of a fine-spun calculation. They *cannot* be, since the basic qualities are not sufficiently commensurate for that.

And here lies perhaps the crassest error of the theory of value. It is one thing for a theory to be exact. It is quite another thing if a theory makes the phenomena with which it deals more 'geometric' than they actually are. Then the theory is wrong. The best theory of value is not the theory that reduces the activity of evaluating most nearly to a calculus, but the theory that comes closest to the truth.

Which qualities must be present in a given case, and to what degree, is to some extent fixed by convention. There is a rough consensus on what makes a fuse, a hammer, a painting, or a person 'good.' (This is no different from the understanding attached to other classifying terms.) It works rather like a check-list, and we perform a task similar to those which some workers execute on assembly lines. We simply know which properties are expected, very like a man who is testing radio tubes.

Of course this is not all. Often, though not always, another aspect comes into play, and that side is best understood on the analogy of a 'special place' in a room, or garden, or to 'the place of honor' at table. The fact that there is such a place is also, as it were, a social given. The aura with which it is invested, the distinction it confers, are relatively stable. They constitute a kind of instrument furnished by society and language—it is the use to which we put it that is more up to us.

Prose, for example, needed to have a measured and gracious elegance to be 'good' in the early nineteenth century, but in a very gradual process the quality of elegance has been demoted. For the structural design of the theory of value it is important to understand that this sort of alteration results from a host of small-scaled reconsiderations, and even from shifts in perception: that the general thrust is *up* from the specific and concrete, and not *down*—via deduction—from general criteria and standards. The same is true on the more private plane. As we compare countless passages of prose, and become by slow degrees more aware of what elegance sometimes hides, and of the sacrifices it exacts—as we begin to see strength and economy where before we noticed only roughness—we gradually approach the point where we are ready to bring the cruder and more general level into line. We reach a decision and cross elegance from the list.

The genesis and justification of principles and rules follow essentially the same scheme. A rule, such as that prose should be lucid or transparent, has the same relationship to the more interesting, more perceptual judgments that the notion of 'good' prose has to them. Again one has to tally the many qualities of many instances of prose and reduce them to one denomination. If many of the cases that were on balance 'good,' were also at the same time lucid or transparent, then one can tentatively postulate this general rule. But its force would be no greater than the examples on which it rests. In this case one could cite the prose of Tolstoy, of Heine, and of Lichtenberg to support this rule, while the works of Joyce or Faulkner could be adduced against it. This being so, one would not set great store by it. Instead one would introduce qualifications until some principle might be discovered, that conformed more closely to one's more concrete judgments.

The rules with which we judge our own and others' actions have the same foundation. The general proscription against lies has its actual final base only in the qualities of individual deceptions. It is a giant structure, but in the last analysis it rests on the loss of pride, or the isolation, in short on all the qualities produced in the great complexity of circumstances, by all manner of dishonesties. That measures the force to which this rule—or any other principle of conduct—is entitled. The rest, its authority beyond that, is insupportable excess.

This means that all valuational principles stand theoretically only until further notice. They all live by the grace of the more particular, concrete judgments that they entail. If there is conflict, then there may of course be reason for delay (considerations of consistency and so forth), but in the long run the concrete and perceptual judgments must prevail. The generalizations have to yield and are rejected or revised to suit the level of experience.

This Primacy of the Concrete is not at all put forward as a radical reversal. On the contrary, this is one place where our framework means only to produce a theory that is in line—and as intelligent—as parts of our practice already are. In the whole domain of art we have come to act on it, and there it is nearly banal. The testimonial that painters and composers violate old catechisms, and that their work succeeds precisely *because* of this, has been so faithfully repeated, that the mere crudity and fallibility of rules sounds by now like a middle-aged and mellow proposition that would be noddingly acknowledged. So, of course, would the idea that

the rules of art are mere abstractions from the best art of the past, and that it is therefore the rules that must adjust themselves to art, and not the other way around.

But when it comes to conduct and to morality, then the situation is weirdly ambiguous and inconsistent. On the one hand we have begun to give priority to the concrete in actual practice. Especially when there is openly acknowledged conflict, in the debates over Capital Punishment or Birth Control, for instance, less and less weight is given to the high-flying arguments from the necessity of retribution, and gradually more and more is said about the concrete consequences. Single cases of prisoners in death-row, or of 16 year-old mothers are looked at closely, and we have moved some distance toward the idea that the laws and rules have to be changed until they conform to our individual judgments. This 'turn to the concrete' may actually be the larger revolution. The other changes in our values and morality, compared to it, are small effects. Still, on the other hand, there remains the feeling that first principles must be adhered to, that they are somehow sacrosanct and sacred, and that morality could not survive without them.

It is this inconsistency that our framework allows us to eliminate, or that it compels us to abandon. There is no reason why what we already do in the sphere of art, and with conduct when it is controversial, should not be extended to the whole domain of values. The general status of the rules of conduct is not different from that of the precepts of art. Both derive from the same foundation and should be treated in accord with it.

This means of course that they are all subject to revision. But the loss of the presumption to infallibility (or *a priori*-ty, or even permanence) seems small compared to the gain of a solid base. Yet there are other changes. Really one's whole relationship to the rules of conduct becomes different. It is no longer necessary to struggle for some deep and main foundation stone. The existence of values is quite secure; no leap of faith or any other act on our part is needed to prevent their metaphysical disintegration. Just as with art: rules are clumsy and make-shift things. Of course we need them: we could not possibly evaluate each situation fully; the effort of perception would exhaust us; a great deal must be filtered out and simplified to keep us sane. Still, that is all 'principles' are: tools for crude, perfunctory estimations, which cannot serve us once we need to be precise. When we are not just flipping cards across a table but face a real decision, then all the rules are nothing but coy preparations. We have not begun until we face our situation in the same solitude in which we encounter books.

The categorical principles are no longer the main beams from which all other values hang. They are more like a grid that covers up and blocks out. Those who always follow them don't use their eyes.

All the same, we eventually do build a whole hierarchical structure of rules; and in this construction all levels are constantly in interaction with all other parts. Individual perceptions from the ground are pitted against high and ancient virtues; the most general rules are applied to everything that is subsumed beneath them and are yet at the same time revised and tested. All the intermediate levels are continuously matched against each other, and anything can be standard at one moment, and be on trial at the next. The whole system is thus in an unceasing flux. One never questions the whole body of rules and judgments at one and the same time. If one rule becomes problematic, other rules are still employed in the evaluation. Only gradually are all the rules held at one time replaced by others. It is possible to end up with a completely new system, but it happens as in a card game where one may get a totally new hand by exchanging two cards several times. The whole process moves slowly toward some coherence, but never reaches it; for long before all the rules conform to the concrete perceptions and particular judgments, these, influenced by the new rules, have themselves changed. [pp. 264–271]

Karl Duncker
(1903–1940)

Ethical Relativity? (*An Enquiry into the Psychology of Ethics*) [16]

Duncker examines the problem of ethical relativity from the base of Gestalt psychology.

[16] Karl Duncker, "Ethical Relativity? (An Enquiry into the Psychology of Ethics)," *Mind* 48 (January 1939): 39–57. The selection is from pp. 39–44.

He argues that the "same" action may have different "situational meanings."

1. The Problem

What is meant by "ethical relativity"? That morals vary no one will deny. They are undoubtedly different at different times and in different places.

There is a widespread view that the sole invariant of morals is their *sociological* function to secure the preservation and welfare of a social group. This function, however, is external to the *psychological* situation. There may, of course, be cases in which conduciveness to social welfare figures as a motive and thus becomes part of the psychological situation, but these are exceptional rather than typical.

There is according to this thesis of ethical relativity nothing invariable within the psychological content of morality. Any conceivable behaviour may, in appropriate historical or ethnological circumstances, take its turn in fulfilling the function of social expediency. . . .

2. Three Examples of Ethical Variability

Here are some instances of moral variability. In ancient times, and especially throughout the Middle Ages, it was considered immoral or even sinful to practice "usury," *i.e.* to take interest on money lent. With the rise of capitalism the same practice gradually lost its moral stigma and forced its way into respectability. Now economists are not slow in pointing out that circumstances, the enormous increase of commerce and industrial investments, no longer permitted of those old moral fetters. Morals had to yield to altered circumstances. (They always show a considerable inertia, but in the end they are bound to give way.) The case of usury thus presents a fair example of the same act's having at different times a different moral value.

To take another example: decency in dress is admittedly of the utmost variability. There is no degree of concealment between nudity and the swathings of a Moslem woman which is not, somewhere or other, found to represent the fine border-line between the decent and the indecent. Even in our own community standards vary. A bathing dress is taboo in the street. A woman may show herself undressed in the presence of her male physician, but not in that of her male acquaintances. Prof.

Sumner would appear to be quite justified in saying that "the *mores* can make everything right." [a] Customs are, of course, in their turn shaped by all sorts of circumstances and necessities.

One more example from the classical store of comparative anthropology: there have been many peoples, all the world over, who indulged in the practice of killing new-born infants or superannuated parents. To our civilised minds this appears to be a rude custom. Here again the particular act has undergone a radical change in moral valuation. We can no doubt link up the difference in custom with different circumstances, such as the hardships of a nomadic life, the domination of the group, the various superstitious beliefs, etc. But our understanding of the causes does not seem to obviate the ethical difference.

For the moment these three examples may suffice to make it clear that the theory of ethical relativism could not possibly be wrong if the only factors to be considered were the act, the sociological function and the circumstances.

3. *Psychological Analysis of the Examples*

Let us, however, subject our examples to a psychological analysis. In the case of "usury" the act in question was "the taking of interest on money lent," which we found to have been repudiated at one time and recommended at another. But do we in both cases deal with the *same* act? Is money always identical with money, or interest with interest? From a genetical point of view the usage of the identical word is well justified. But in early stages of civilisation loans were employed predominantly for consumption, whereas in capitalism loans are employed mainly as capital for profitable production. That makes all the difference. Where the borrower borrows in order to gain, it is only fair to make the lender a partner in the undertaking by paying him some "share in the profit." Interest no longer means an exploitation of necessities or passions. It has changed its typical "*meaning*." [b] Of course, this is due to changed economical circum-

stances, to the increase of productive investments, etc. However, these circumstances do not remain external to the act, but enter into the psychological essence of the objects dealt with in the act. They provide what I shall call the "*pattern of situational meanings.*" It is on this pattern of situational meanings that the moral essence of an act, its ethical quality and value, depends. [c] *In our example we have not two different ethical valuations of usury, but two different meanings of money-lending each of which receives its specific valuation.*

Before proceeding any further on theoretical lines I will give some additional empirical data, this time concerning infanticide and the killing of the old.

. . . Peter Kolben, in his *Present State of the Cape of Good Hope*,[d] gives us the following account, "a little meliorated," of Hottentot feelings with regard to exposing superannuated parents to starvation in a solitary hut:

> If you represent to the Hottentots, as I have done very often, the inhumanity of this custom, they are astonished at the representation, as proceeding, in their opinion, from an inhumanity of our own. The custom, in their way of thinking, is supported by very pious and very filial considerations. "Is it not a cruelty," they ask you, "to suffer either man or woman to languish any considerable time under a heavy, motionless old age? Can you see a parent or relative shaking and freezing under a cold, dreary, heavy, useless old age, and not think, in pity of them, of putting an end to their misery by putting, which is the only means, an end to their old days?"

. . . .

I think everybody would agree that the mere fact of "killing" is too abstract a topic to allow of any serious ethical consideration. Many people, however, seem to believe that "killing superannuated parents" is sufficiently concrete. But is it really? "Killing an aged parent" may, according to circumstances, mean sparing him the miseries of a lingering death or an existence which, as a born warrior, he must feel to be exceedingly dull and unworthy; or it may mean protecting him against injuries from

---

[a] Sumner, *Folkways*, ch. 15.

[b] Even in earlier times interest was sometimes defended as meaning a "compensation for the risk" (*cf.* the *foenus nauticum*).

[c] Note how the sociological understanding is necessary for, but not identical with, the ethical understanding.

[d] p. 319 (London 1731).

enemies or beasts, or causing him to enter the happy land which is not open save to those who die by violence. Such "meanings" clearly give to the act a quality of benevolence rather than of cruelty. But even where it is not performed out of benevolence it may still be in full accordance with the victim's feelings. For he has done the same sort of thing to his elders, he has known his own fate all his life long, and he knows that neither will the next generation be exempted. That is to say, the being killed "means" to him about as natural a thing as death itself means to us. On the other hand, what is done to him may be done for the benefit of the group. He is of no further use, and life may be hard and food scarce to the point of starvation. Surely, then, it is more reasonable to cast off that part of the ballast than to kill young and healthy members. Or, again, the old man may be sacrificed (as a "substitute") in order to appease the gods and avert from the tribe their anger as embodied in some epidemic, famine, flood, etc.

To say that this is a credit to the group spirit at the cost of filial piety is to leave two important features out of account. In the first place the aged parent is not only a victim but a subject apt to appreciate the call of the hour himself. It may be his point of honour to die for the group. Assuredly the victim's own view of the matter is a most essential constituent of what I have called the "pattern of situational meanings." In the second place it is a mistake tacitly to substitute one's own individualistic outlook for that of a primitive group. Where the individual is felt to be a mere "limb of the group body" we should be the less surprised at the body's decision to sacrifice one of its limbs.

This meaning of a man as a "limb" rather than a "person of his own" is extremely important for a genuine *ethical* understanding of many other phenomena. For instance, blood-revenge is not genuinely understood unless one takes into consideration that the victim is felt to be just an organ, the available "vulnerable spot" of the other clan, which, as a collective whole, is felt to be the real offender. Neither is it justifiable to treat of infanticide without enquiring into the meaning of the infant in question: whether it is conceived of as an inanimate thing, a limb of the group, a piece of property belonging to the pater familias, a person of its own, or finally as an immortal soul (which would be doomed to everlasting perdition if it died unbaptised).

4. Confrontation of Formulae

Locke [in whom the thesis of ethical relativism has found its classical formulation] wondered why the principle (note what he calls a principle) "parents, preserve and cherish young children" had not received any general consent throughout history. Well, if one leaves out "meanings," *i.e.* if one fails to define the situation in psychological terms, how can one expect to meet with general consent? *For ethical valuation is not concerned with acts as abstract events in space-time. The ethical essence of an act depends upon its concrete pattern of situational meanings.* The term "situational meanings" is meant to convey the notion of "relevant features of the actual psychological situation with reference to which the subject behaves." It should be emphasised that personal reactions are not made direct to the "stimuli" (the positivistic-behaviourist fallacy!), but to the psychological situation which is a joint product of stimuli, beliefs, sentiments, etc.—We have seen that the "same" things and acts, in short the same materials, may have different meanings (Wertheimer). And the reverse is no less true: different materials may have the same meaning. Now, if our moral valuation depends upon meanings it is not fair to connect it with meaningless, with abstract acts. But this, precisely, is what ethical relativism does.

In place of the relativistic formula: morals depend on circumstances according to the function of social expediency—I put forward the following three statements: An act which receives a positive valuation must needs satisfy certain functions of promoting, or at least agreeing with, the social good in the given circumstances. But whether a given act can be positively valued from an *ethical* point of view, depends upon the meanings involved, according to certain basic invariable relationships. And, in their turn, these meanings depend upon the circumstances. (Meanings are, as it were, a reflection of the circumstances within the inner, psychological make-up of the ethical situation. Meanings are not identical with circumstances. The meaning of interest is that it is a share in the profit. The corresponding circumstances are capitalism as a whole. Again, the Christian meaning of a human being is that it is an immortal soul. The responsible circumstances are for the most part still a problem for the sociologist.)

The new formula indicates, besides a sociological

invariant, certain invariable relationships between valuations and meanings. They amount to this: given the same situational meanings an act is likely to receive the same ethical valuation. If an act is found to receive different valuations at different times or places, this is generally found to be due to different meanings.

Martin Buber
(1878–1965)

Buber is the best known of those who, searching for authenticity, shifted attention from the individual to interpersonal relations. He shares the practical motivation of existentialists. His is also a religious philosophy in taking divinity as the background to genuine human relations. But what stands out in the way he philosophizes is his use of a phenomenological approach. He looks directly and primarily at the quality of immediate experience, meaning by it the whole vital attitude, not just conscious experience. The basic distinction is between *relation* and *self-distancing*. The former, which is the direct relation of the I to another addressed as Thou, is characterized by intimacy and absorption. In self-distancing, seen at its clearest in science, the world and everything in it—person and thing alike—becomes *object*. Since knowledge is necessary for human life, the impersonal attitude, an easy way out, becomes pervasive. We begin to see other people as objects. Therefore a genuine effort is required to restore relation.

The idea of relation has wide moral and social implications. It fits neatly into the common recognition of modern alienation and carries important lessons for education, psychiatry, and social philosophy. Reliance on impersonal institutions and the flight to a subjective hedonistic ethic are correlative consequences of the breakdown of genuine interpersonal relations. Hence small face-to-face communities (such as the Israeli kibbutz) are preferable to large sociopolitical organizations.

The idea of interpersonal relations has been variously interpreted, embodied in different philosophies of man and expressing different values of human orientation. The counters with which they all deal are persons, their interrelation, community, and (in religious philosophies) God. They all locate reality in one or another place in the complex of these counters. Buber speaks as if life lights up primarily in the direct dialogue of I and Thou, with God in the background tapped as a source of energy. Although equally opposed as Buber is to the intense individualism of modern life, others present the relation of persons as more indirect. Jacques Maritain (*The Person and the Common Good* [1947]) has the relation go from the person to God and through God to the other person—the brotherhood of man rests on the fatherhood of God. Karol Wojtyla (Pope John Paul II) insists on the real priority of the individual person:

This relation or complex of relations which constitutes the definite plurality of personal subjects as a social unity may be considered not so much as an objective reality which qualifies all and every one in this plurality, but rather on the basis of the consciousness and experience of all its members and to some degree of each of them. It is only in this latter mode that we treat the reality of community and touch upon its proper meaning.[17]

Wojtyla suggests a similar secondary status for the I-and-Thou in their relation:

It is sometimes maintained that "I" is, so to speak, constituted by "you." . . . The fundamental fact is that the "you" is always, like "me," someone or some other "I." Owing to this fact about the starting point of the relation "I-you," there is a cer-

---

[17] "The Person: Subject and Community," *Review of Metaphysics* 33 (December 1979), p. 290.

tain plurality of personal subjects, namely, the minimal plurality of one plus one.[18]

The entry into the relation with another would not then be a kind of merging but the meeting of independent beings.

In these various patterns of relation of persons, found by a sensitive phenomenology, it is possible that the controversy is less over what the real character of the relation is and more a matter of different possible fashionings of human experience. If so, then the disagreements are essentially normative, namely, what kind of relation is humanly more valuable.

I and Thou [19]

If I face a human being as my *Thou*, and say the primary word *I-Thou* to him, he is not a thing among things, and does not consist of things.

This human being is not *He* or *She*, bounded from every other *He* and *She*, a specific point in space and time within the net of the world; nor is he a nature able to be experienced and described, a loose bundle of named qualities. But with no neighbour, and whole in himself, he is *Thou* and fills the heavens. This does not mean that nothing exists except himself. But all else lives in *his* light.

Just as the melody is not made up of notes nor the verse of words nor the statue of lines, but they must be tugged and dragged till their unity has been scattered into these many pieces, so with the man to whom I say *Thou*. I can take out from him the colour of his hair, or of his speech, or of his goodness. I must continually do this. But each time I do it he ceases to be *Thou*.

And just as prayer is not in time but time in prayer, sacrifice not in space but space in sacrifice, and to reverse the relation is to abolish the reality, so with the man to whom I say *Thou*. I do not meet with him at some time and place or other. I can set him in a particular time and place; I must continually do it: but I set only a *He* or a *She*, that is an *It*, no longer my *Thou*.

So long as the heaven of *Thou* is spread out over me the winds of causality cower at my heels, and the whirlpool of fate stays its course.

I do not experience the man to whom I say *Thou*. But I take my stand in relation to him, in the sanctity of the primary word. Only when I step out of it do I experience him once more. In the act of experience *Thou* is far away.

Even if the man to whom I say *Thou* is not aware of it in the midst of his experience, yet relation may exist. For *Thou* is more than *It* realises. No deception penetrates here; here is the cradle of the Real Life. [pp. 8–9]

The world of *It* is set in the context of space and time.

The world of *Thou* is not set in the context of either of these.

The particular *Thou*, after the relational event has run its course, *is bound* to become an *It*.

The particular *It*, by entering the relational event, *may* become a *Thou*.

These are the two basic privileges of the world of *It*. They move man to look on the world of *It* as the world in which he has to live, and in which it is comfortable to live, as the world, indeed, which offers him all manner of incitements and excitements, activity and knowledge. In this chronicle of solid benefits the moments of the *Thou* appear as strange lyric and dramatic episodes, seductive and magical, but tearing us away to dangerous extremes, loosening the well-tried context, leaving more questions than satisfaction behind them, shattering security—in short, uncanny moments we can well dispense with. For since we are bound to leave them and go back into the "world," why not remain in it? Why not call to order what is over against us, and send it packing into the realm of objects? Why, if we find ourselves on occasion with no choice but to say *Thou* to father, wife, or comrade, not say *Thou* and mean *It*? To utter the sound *Thou* with the vocal organs is by no means the same as saying the uncanny primary word; more, it is harmless to whisper with the soul an amorous *Thou*, so long as nothing else in a serious way is meant but *experience* and *make use of*.

It is not possible to live in the bare present. Life would be quite consumed if precautions were not taken to subdue the present speedily and thoroughly. But it is possible to live in the bare past, indeed only in it may a life be organised. We only

---

[18] Ibid., p. 292.
[19] The selection is from Martin Buber, *I and Thou*, trans. Ronald Gregor Smith (Edinburgh: T. & T. Clark, 1937).

need to fill each moment with experiencing and using, and it ceases to burn.

And in all the seriousness of truth, hear this: without *It* man cannot live. But he who lives with *It* alone is not a man. [pp. 33–34]

Spirit in its human manifestation is a response of man to his *Thou*. Man speaks with many tongues, tongues of language, of art, of action; but the spirit is one, the response to the *Thou* which appears and addresses him out of the mystery. Spirit is the word. And just as talk in a language may well first take the form of words in the brain of the man, and then sound in his throat, and yet both are merely refractions of the true event, for in actuality speech does not abide in man, but man takes his stand in speech and talks from there; so with every word and every spirit. Spirit is not in the *I*, but between *I* and *Thou*. It is not like the blood that circulates in you, but like the air in which you breathe. Man lives in the spirit, if he is able to respond to his *Thou*. He is able to, if he enters into relation with his whole being. Only in virtue of his power to enter into relation is he able to live in the spirit.

But the destiny of the relational event is here set forth in the most powerful way. The stronger the response the more strongly does it bind up the *Thou* and banish it to be an object. Only silence before the *Thou*—silence of *all* tongues, silent patience in the undivided word that precedes the formed and vocal response—leaves the *Thou* free, and permits man to take his stand with it in the reserve where the spirit is not manifest, but *is*. Every response binds up the *Thou* in the world of *It*. That is the melancholy of man, and his greatness. For that is how knowledge comes about, a work is achieved, and image and symbol made, in the midst of living beings.

But that which has been so changed into *It*, hardened into a thing among things, has had the nature and disposition put into it to change back again and again. This was the meaning in that hour of the spirit when spirit was joined to man and bred the response in him—again and again that which has the status of object must blaze up into presentness and enter the elemental state from which it came, to be looked on and lived in the present by men.

The fulfilment of this nature and disposition is thwarted by the man who has come to terms with the world of *It* that it is to be experienced and used.

For now instead of freeing that which is bound up in that world he suppresses it, instead of looking at it he observes it, instead of accepting it as it is, he turns it to his own account.

Take knowledge: being is disclosed to the man who is engaged in knowing, as he looks at what is over against him. He will, indeed, have to grasp as an object that which he has seen with the force of presence, he will have to compare it with objects, establish it in its order among classes of objects, describe and analyse it objectively. Only as *It* can it enter into the structure of knowledge. But when he saw it, it was no thing among things, no event among events, but exclusively present. Being did not share itself with him in terms of the law that was afterwards elicited from the appearance, but in terms of its very self. When a man thinks a general thought in this connexion he is merely unravelling the tangled incident; for it was seen in particular form, in what was over against him. Now the incident is included in the *It* of knowledge which is composed of ideas. He who frees it from that, and looks on it again in the present moment, fulfils the nature of the act of knowledge to be real and effective *between* men. But knowledge can also be managed in such a way that it is affirmed that "this, then, is how the matter stands, the thing is called this, made in this way, its place is over there"; that which has become *It* is left as *It*, experienced and used as *It*, appropriated for the undertaking to "find one's bearings" in the world, and then to "conquer" it.

So too in art: form is disclosed to the artist as he looks at what is over against him. He banishes it to be a "structure." This "structure" is not in a world of gods, but in this great world of men. It is certainly "there," even if no human eye seeks it out; but it is asleep. . . .

It is not as though scientific and aesthetic understanding were not necessary; but they are necessary to man that he may do his work with precision and plunge it in the truth of relation, which is above the understanding and gathers it up in itself.

And, thirdly, there is pure effective action without arbitrary self-will. This is higher than the spirit of knowledge and the spirit of art, for here the mortal bodily man does not need to mix himself with the more lasting stuff, but himself outlasts it as structure; encircled by the sounding music of his living speech he reaches the starry heaven of the spirit. Here the *Thou* appeared to the man out of deeper mystery, addressed him even out of the darkness, and he responded with his life. Here the word has from time to time become life, and this life is *teaching*. This life may have fulfilled the law or broken it; both are continually necessary, that spirit may not die on earth. This life is presented, then, to those who come later, to teach them not what is and must be, but how life is lived in the spirit, face to face with the *Thou*. That is, it is itself ready on every occasion to become *Thou* for them, and open up the world of *Thou*—no; it is not ready: it continually approaches and touches them. But they, having become disinclined and unfitted for the living dealings that would open the world to them, are fully equipped with information. They have pinned the person down in history, and secured his words in the library. They have codified, in exactly the same way, the fulfilment or the breaking of the law. Nor are they niggards with admiration and even idolatry, amply mixed with psychology, as befits modern man. O lonely Face like a star in the night, o living Finger laid on an unheeding brow, o fainter echoing footstep!

The development of the function of experiencing and using comes about mostly through decrease of man's power to enter into relation.

How does this same man, who made spirit into a means of enjoyment for himself, behave towards the beings that live round about him?

Taking his stand in the shelter of the primary word of separation, which holds off the *I* and the *It* from one another, he has divided his life with his fellow-men into two tidily circled-off provinces, one of institutions and the other of feelings—the province of *It* and the province of *I*.

Institutions are "outside," where all sorts of aims are pursued, where a man works, negotiates, bears influence, undertakes, concurs, organises, conducts business, officiates, preaches. They are the tolerably well-ordered and to some extent harmonious structure, in which, with the manifold help of men's brains and hands, the process of affairs is fulfilled.

Feelings are "within," where life is lived and man recovers from institutions. Here the spectrum of the emotions dances before the interested glance. Here a man's liking and hate and pleasure are indulged, and his pain if it is not too severe. Here he is at home, and stretches himself out in his rocking-chair.

Institutions are a complicated market-place, feelings a boudoir rich in ever-changing interests.

The boundary line, to be sure, is constantly in danger since the wanton feelings break in at times on the most objective institutions; but with united goodwill it may be restored.

Most difficult of all is the reliable drawing of the boundary line in the realms of so-called personal life. In marriage, for instance, the line is occasionally not to be fully drawn in any simple way; but in the end it is possible. In the realms of so-called public life it can be perfectly drawn. Let it be considered, for instance, how faultlessly, in the year of the parties and the groups with their "movements" which aimed at being above parties, the heaven-storming sessions on the one hand, and on the other hand business, creeping along the ground (smoothly like a machine or slovenly and organically), are separated from one another.

But the separated *It* of institutions is an animated clod without soul, and the separated *I* of feelings an uneasily fluttering soul-bird. Neither of them knows man: institutions know only the specimen, feelings only the "object"; neither knows the person, or mutual life. Neither of them knows the present: even the most up-to-date institutions know only the lifeless past that is over and done with, and even the most lasting feelings know only the flitting moment that has not yet come properly into being. Neither of them has access to real life. Institutions yield no public life, and feelings no personal life.

That institutions yield no public life is realised by increasing numbers, realised with increasing distress: this is the starting-point of the seeking need of the age. That feelings yield no personal life is understood only by a few. For the most personal life of all seems to reside in feelings, and if, like the modern man, you have learned to concern yourself wholly with your own feelings, despair at their unreality will not easily instruct you in a better way—for despair is also an interesting feeling.

The men who suffer distress in the realisation that institutions yield no public life have hit upon an expedient: institutions must be loosened, or dissolved, or burst asunder, by the feelings themselves; they must be given new life from the feelings, by the introduction into them of the "freedom of feeling." If the mechanical State, say, links together citizens alien to one another in their very being, without establishing, or promoting, a being together, let the State, these men say, be replaced by the community of love; and this community will arise when people, out of free, abundant feeling, approach and wish to live with one another. But it is not so. The true community does not arise through peoples having feelings for one another (though indeed not without it), but through, first, their taking their stand in living mutual relation with a living Centre, and, second, their being in living mutual relation with one another. The second has its source in the first, but is not given when the first alone is given. Living mutual relation includes feelings, but does not originate with them. The community is built up out of living mutual relation, but the builder is the living effective Centre.

Further, institutions of the so-called personal life cannot be given new life by free feeling (though indeed not without it). Marriage, for instance, will never be given new life except by that out of which true marriage always arises, the revealing by two people of the *Thou* to one another. Out of this a marriage is built up by the *Thou* that is neither of the *I*'s. This is the metaphysical and metapsychical factor of love to which feelings of love are mere accompaniments. He who wishes to give new life to marriage from another source is not essentially different from him who wishes to abolish it. Both clearly show that they no longer know the vital factor. And indeed, if in all the much discussed erotic philosophy of the age we were to leave out of account everything that involves experience in relation to the *I*, that is, every situation in which the one is not present to the other, given present status by it, but merely enjoys itself in the other— what then would be left?

True public and true personal life are two forms of connexion. In that they come into being and endure, feelings (the changing content) and institutions (the constant form) are necessary; but put together they do not create human life: this is done by the third, the central presence of the *Thou*, or rather, more truly stated, by the central *Thou* that has been received in the present.

The primary word *I-It* is not of evil—as matter is not of evil. It is of evil—as matter is, which presumes to have the quality of present being. If a man lets it have the mastery, the continually growing world of *It* overruns him and robs him of the reality of his own *I*, till the incubus over him and the ghost within him whisper to one another the confession of their non-salvation. [pp. 39–46]

Jean-Paul Sartre
(1905–1979)

Existentialism [20]

When we conceive God as the Creator, He is generally thought of as a superior sort of artisan. Whatever doctrine we may be considering, whether one like that of Descartes or that of Leibnitz, we always grant that will more or less follows understanding or, at the very least, accompanies it, and that when God creates He knows exactly what He is creating. Thus, the concept of man in the mind of God is comparable to the concept of paper-cutter in the mind of the manufacturer, and, following certain techniques and a conception, God produces man, just as the artisan, following a definition and a technique, makes a paper-cutter. Thus, the individual man is the realisation of a certain concept in the divine intelligence.

In the eighteenth century, the atheism of the *philosophes* discarded the idea of God, but not so much for the notion that essence precedes existence. To a certain extent, this idea is found everywhere; we find it in Diderot, in Voltaire, and even in Kant. Man has a human nature; this human nature, which is the concept of the human, is found in all men, which means that each man is a particular example of a universal concept, man. . . .

Atheistic existentialism, which I represent, is more coherent. It states that if God does not exist, there is at least one being in whom existence precedes essence, a being who exists before he can be defined by any concept, and that this being is man, or, as Heidegger says, human reality. What is meant here by saying that existence precedes essence? It means that, first of all, man exists, turns up, appears on the scene, and, only afterwards, defines himself. If man, as the existentialist conceives him, is indefinable, it is because at first he

[20] The selection is from Jean-Paul Sartre, *Existentialism*, trans. Bernard Frechtman (New York: Philosophical Library, 1947). (This lecture is sometimes given as "Existentialism and Humanism.")

is nothing. Only afterward will he be something, and he himself will have made what he will be. Thus, there is no human nature, since there is no God to conceive it. Not only is man what he conceives himself to be, but he is also only what he wills himself to be after this thrust toward existence.

Man is nothing else but what he makes of himself. Such is the first principle of existentialism. It is also what is called subjectivity, the name we are labeled with when charges are brought against us. But what do we mean by this, if not that man has a greater dignity than a stone or table? For we mean that man first exists, that is, that man first of all is the being who hurls himself toward a future and who is conscious of imagining himself as being in the future. Man is at the start a plan which is aware of itself, rather than a patch of moss, a piece of garbage, or a cauliflower; nothing exists prior to this plan; there is nothing in heaven; man will be what he will have planned to be. Not what he will want to be. Because by the word "will" we generally mean a conscious decision, which is subsequent to what we have already made of ourselves. I may want to belong to a political party, write a book, get married; but all that is only a manifestation of an earlier, more spontaneous choice that is called "will." But if existence really does precede essence, man is responsible for what he is. Thus, existentialism's first move is to make every man aware of what he is and to make the full responsibility of his existence rest on him. And when we say that a man is responsible for himself, we do not only mean that he is responsible for his own individuality, but that he is responsible for all men.

The word subjectivism has two meanings, and our opponents play on the two. Subjectivism means, on the one hand, that an individual chooses and makes himself; and, on the other, that it is impossible for man to transcend human subjectivity. The second of these is the essential meaning of existentialism. When we say that man chooses his own self, we mean that every one of us does likewise; but we also mean by that that in making this choice he also chooses all men. In fact, in creating the man that we want to be, there is not a single one of our acts which does not at the same time create an image of man as we think he ought to be. To choose to be this or that is to affirm at the same time the value of what we choose, because we can never choose evil. We always choose the good, and nothing can be good for us without being good for all.

If, on the other hand, existence precedes essence, and if we grant that we exist and fashion our image at one and the same time, the image is valid for everybody and for our whole age. Thus, our responsibility is much greater than we might have supposed, because it involves all mankind. If I am a workingman and choose to join a Christian trade-union rather than be a communist, and if by being a member I want to show that the best thing for man is resignation, that the kingdom of man is not of this world, I am not only involving my own case—I want to be resigned for everyone. As a result, my action has involved all humanity. To take a more individual matter, if I want to marry, to have children; even if this marriage depends solely on my own circumstances or passion or wish, I am involving all humanity in monogamy and not merely myself. Therefore, I am responsible for myself and for everyone else. I am creating a certain image of man of my own choosing. In choosing myself, I choose man.

This helps us understand what the actual content is of such rather grandiloquent words as anguish, forlornness, despair. As you will see, it's all quite simple.

First, what is meant by anguish? The existentialists say at once that man is anguish. What that means is this: the man who involves himself and who realizes that he is not only the person he chooses to be, but also a law-maker who is, at the same time, choosing all mankind as well as himself, can not help escape the feeling of his total and deep responsibility. Of course, there are many people who are not anxious; but we claim that they are hiding their anxiety, that they are fleeing from it. Certainly, many people believe that when they do something, they themselves are the only ones involved, and when someone says to them, "What if everyone acted that way?" they shrug their shoulders and answer, "Everyone doesn't act that way." But really, one should always ask himself, "What would happen if everybody looked at things that way?" There is no escaping this disturbing thought except by a kind of double-dealing. A man who lies and makes excuses for himself by saying "not everybody does that," is someone with an uneasy conscience, because the act of lying implies that a universal value is conferred upon the lie.

Anguish is evident even when it conceals itself. This is the anguish that Kierkegaard called the anguish of Abraham. You know the story: an angel has ordered Abraham to sacrifice his son; if it really were an angel who has come and said, "You are Abraham, you shall sacrifice your son," everything would be all right. But everyone might first wonder, "Is it really an angel, and am I really Abraham? What proof do I have?"

There was a madwoman who had hallucinations; someone used to speak to her on the telephone and give her orders. Her doctor asked her, "Who is it who talks to you?" She answered, "He says it's God." What proof did she really have that it was God? If an angel comes to me, what proof is there that it's an angel? . . . If a voice addresses me, it is always for me to decide that this is the angel's voice; if I consider that such an act is a good one, it is I who will choose to say that it is good rather than bad. [pp. 16–24]

When we speak of forlornness, a term Heidegger was fond of, we mean only that God does not exist and that we have to face all the consequences of this. The existentialist is strongly opposed to a certain kind of secular ethics which would like to abolish God with the least possible expense. About 1880, some French teachers tried to set up a secular ethics which went something like this: God is a useless and costly hypothesis; we are discarding it; but, meanwhile, in order for there to be an ethics, a society, a civilization, it is essential that certain values be taken seriously and that they be considered as having an *a priori* existence. It must be obligatory, *a priori*, to be honest, not to lie, not to beat your wife, to have children, etc., etc. So we're going to try a little device which will make it possible to show that values exist all the same, inscribed in a heaven of ideas, though otherwise God does not exist. In other words—and this, I believe, is the tendency of everything called reformism in France— nothing will be changed if God does not exist. We shall find ourselves with the same norms of honesty, progress, and humanism, and we shall have made of God an outdated hypothesis which will peacefully die off by itself.

The existentialist, on the contrary, thinks it very distressing that God does not exist, because all possibility of finding values in a heaven of ideas disappears along with Him; there can no longer be an *a priori* Good, since there is no infinite and perfect consciousness to think it. Nowhere is it written that the Good exists, that we must be honest, that we must not lie; because the fact is we are on a plane where there are only men. Dostoievsky said, "If God didn't exist, everything would be possible." That is the very starting point of existentialism. Indeed, everything is permissible if God does not exist, and as a result man is forlorn, because neither within him nor without does he find anything to cling to. He can't start making excuses for himself.

If existence really does precede essence, there is no explaining things away by reference to a fixed and given human nature. In other words, there is no determinism, man is free, man is freedom. On the other hand, if God does not exist, we find no values or commands to turn to which legitimize our conduct. So, in the bright realm of values, we have no excuse behind us, nor justification before us. We are alone, with no excuses.

That is the idea I shall try to convey when I say that man is condemned to be free. Condemned, because he did not create himself, yet, in other respects is free; because, once thrown into the world, he is responsible for everything he does. The existentialist does not believe in the power of passion. He will never agree that a sweeping passion is a ravaging torrent which fatally leads a man to certain acts and is therefore an excuse. He thinks that man is responsible for his passion. [pp. 25–28]

To give you an example which will enable you to understand forlornness better, I shall cite the case of one of my students who came to see me under the following circumstances: his father was on bad terms with his mother, and, moreover, was inclined to be a collaborationist; his older brother had been killed in the German offensive of 1940, and the young man, with somewhat immature but generous feelings, wanted to avenge him. His mother lived alone with him, very much upset by the half-treason of her husband and the death of her older son; the boy was her only consolation.

The boy was faced with the choice of leaving for England and joining the Free French Forces—that is, leaving his mother behind—or remaining with his mother and helping her to carry on. He was fully aware that the woman lived only for him and that his going-off—and perhaps his death—would plunge her into despair. He was also aware that every act that he did for his mother's sake was a sure thing, in the sense that it was helping her to carry on, whereas every effort he made toward going off and fighting was an uncertain move which might run aground and prove completely useless; for example, on his way to England he might, while passing through Spain, be detained indefinitely in a Spanish camp; he might reach England or Algiers and be stuck in an office at a desk job. As a result, he was faced with two very different kinds of action: one, concrete, immediate, but concerning only one individual; the other concerned an incomparably vaster group, a national collectivity, but for that very reason was dubious, and might be interrupted en route. And, at the same time, he was wavering between two kinds of ethics. On the one hand, an ethics of sympathy, of personal devotion; on the other, a broader ethics, but one whose efficacy was more dubious. He had to choose between the two.

Who could help him choose? Christian doctrine? No. Christian doctrine says, "Be charitable, love your neighbor, take the more rugged path, etc., etc." But which is the more rugged path? Whom should he love as a brother? The fighting man or his mother? Which does the greater good, the vague act of fighting in a group, or the concrete one of helping a particular human being to go on living? Who can decide *a priori?* Nobody. No book of ethics can tell him. The Kantian ethics says, "Never treat any person as a means, but as an end." Very well, if I stay with my mother, I'll treat her as an end and not as a means; but by virtue of this very fact, I'm running the risk of treating the people around me who are fighting, as means; and, conversely, if I go to join those who are fighting, I'll be treating them as an end, and, by doing that, I run the risk of treating my mother as a means.

If values are vague, and if they are always too broad for the concrete and specific case that we are considering, the only thing left for us is to trust our instincts. That's what this young man tried to do; and when I saw him, he said, "In the end, feeling is what counts. I ought to choose whichever pushes me in one direction. If I feel that I love my mother enough to sacrifice everything else for her—my desire for vengeance, for action, for adventure—then I'll stay with her. If, on the contrary, I feel that my love for my mother isn't enough, I'll leave."

But how is the value of a feeling determined? What gives his feeling for his mother value? Precisely the fact that he remained with her. I may say that I like so-and-so well enough to sacrifice a certain amount of money for him, but I may say

so only if I've done it. I may say "I love my mother well enough to remain with her" if I have remained with her. The only way to determine the value of this affection is, precisely, to perform an act which confirms and defines it. But, since I require this affection to justify my act, I find myself caught in a vicious circle.

On the other hand, Gide has well said that a mock feeling and a true feeling are almost indistinguishable; to decide that I love my mother and will remain with her, or to remain with her by putting on an act, amount somewhat to the same thing. In other words, the feeling is formed by the acts one performs; so, I can not refer to it in order to act upon it. Which means that I can neither seek within myself the true condition which will impel me to act, nor apply to a system of ethics for concepts which will permit me to act. You will say, "At least, he did go to a teacher for advice." But if you seek advice from a priest, for example, you have chosen this priest; you already knew, more or less, just about what advice he was going to give you. In other words, choosing your adviser is involving yourself. The proof of this is that if you are a Christian, you will say, "Consult a priest." But some priests are collaborating, some are just marking time, some are resisting. Which to choose? If the young man chooses a priest who is resisting or collaborating, he has already decided on the kind of advice he's going to get. Therefore, in coming to see me he knew the answer I was going to give him, and I had only one answer to give: "You're free, choose, that is, invent." No general ethics can show you what is to be done; there are no omens in the world. The Catholics will reply, "But there are." Granted—but, in any case, I myself choose the meaning they have. [pp. 28–33]

The Emotions: Outline of a Theory [21]

Involved with Sartre's analysis is a definite theory of the emotions, which breaks with fairly dominant conceptions of the time.

In many of [Janet's] descriptions he lets it be understood that the sick person throws himself into

[21] The selection is from Jean-Paul Sartre, *The Emotions: Outline of a Theory*, trans. Bernard Frechtman (New York: Philosophical Library, 1948), pp. 31–32.

the inferior behavior *in order not* to maintain the superior behavior. Here it is the sick person himself who proclaims himself checked even before having undertaken the struggle, and the emotive behavior comes to *mask* the impossibility of maintaining the adapted behavior. Let us again take the example which we cited earlier: a sick girl comes to Janet; she wants to confide the secret of her turmoil, to describe her obsession minutely. But she is unable to; such social behavior is too hard for her. *Then* she sobs. But does she sob *because* she cannot say anything? Are her sobs vain attempts to act, a diffuse upheaval which represents the decomposition of too difficult behavior? Or does she sob precisely *in order not to say anything*? At first sight, the difference between these two interpretations seems slight; in both hypotheses there is behavior which is impossible to maintain; in both there is substitution for behavior by diffuse manifestations. Janet also passes easily from one to the other; that is what makes his theory ambiguous. But in reality, these two theories are separated by an abyss. The first, in effect, is purely mechanistic and—as we have seen—rather close to the essence of that of James. The second, on the contrary, really brings us something new; it alone really deserves the title of a psychological theory of the emotions; it alone sees emotion as behavior. That is because, if we reintroduce finality here, we can understand that emotional behavior is not a disorder at all. It is an organized system of means aiming at an end. And this system is *called* upon to mask, substitute for, and reject behavior that one cannot or does not want to maintain. By the same token, the explanation of the diversity of emotions becomes easy; they represent a particular subterfuge, a special trick, each one of them being a different means of eluding a difficulty.

Being and Nothingness [22]

Part One, Ch Two: Bad Faith

II. Patterns of Bad Faith. Take the example of a woman who has consented to go out with a particular man for the first time. She knows very well the

[22] The selection is from Jean-Paul Sartre, *Being and Nothingness*, trans. Hazel E. Barnes (New York: Philosophical Library, 1956).

intentions which the man who is speaking to her cherishes regarding her. She knows also that it will be necessary sooner or later for her to make a decision. But she does not want to realize the urgency; she concerns herself only with what is respectful and discreet in the attitude of her companion. She does not apprehend this conduct as an attempt to achieve what we call "the first approach"; that is, she does not want to see possibilities of temporal development which his conduct presents. She restricts this behavior to what is in the present; she does not wish to read in the phrases which he addresses to her anything other than their explicit meaning. If he says to her, "I find you so attractive!" she disarms this phrase of its sexual background; she attaches to the conversation and to the behavior of the speaker, the immediate meanings, which she imagines as objective qualities. The man who is speaking to her appears to her sincere and respectful as the table is round or square, as the wall coloring is blue or gray. The qualities thus attached to the person she is listening to are in this way fixed in a permanence like that of things, which is no other than the projection of the strict present of the qualities into the temporal flux. This is because she does not quite know what she wants. She is profoundly aware of the desire which she inspires, but the desire cruel and naked could humiliate and horrify her. Yet she would find no charm in a respect which would be only respect. In order to satisfy her, there must be a feeling which is addressed wholly to her *personality*—i.e., to her full freedom— and which would be a recognition of her freedom. But at the same time this feeling must be wholly desire; that is, it must address itself to her body as object. This time then she refuses to apprehend the desire for what it is; she does not even give it a name; she recognizes it only to the extent that it transcends itself toward admiration, esteem, respect and that it is wholly absorbed in the more refined forms which it produces, to the extent of no longer figuring anymore as a sort of warmth and density. But then suppose he takes her hand. This act of her companion risks changing the situation by calling for an immediate decision. To leave the hand there is to consent in herself to flirt, to engage herself. To withdraw it is to break the troubled and unstable harmony which gives the hour its charm. The aim is to postpone the moment of decision as long as possible. We know what happens next; the young woman leaves her hand there, but she *does not notice* that she is leaving it. She does not notice because it happens by chance that she is at this moment all intellect. She draws her companion up to the most lofty regions of sentimental speculation; she speaks of Life, of her life, she shows herself in her essential aspect—a personality, a consciousness. And during this time the divorce of the body from the soul is accomplished; the hand rests inert between the warm hands of her companion—neither consenting nor resisting—a thing.

We shall say that this woman is in bad faith. But we see immediately that she uses various procedures in order to maintain herself in this bad faith. She has disarmed the actions of her companion by reducing them to being only what they are; that is, to existing in the mode of the in-itself.[23] But she permits herself to enjoy his desire, to the extent that she will apprehend it as not being what it is, will recognize its transcendence. Finally while sensing profoundly the presence of her own body—to the degree of being disturbed perhaps—she realizes herself as *not being* her own body, and she contemplates it as though from above as a passive object to which events can *happen* but which can neither provoke them nor avoid them because all its possibilities are outside of it. What unity do we find in these various aspects of bad faith? It is a certain art of forming contradictory concepts which unite in themselves both an idea and the negation of that idea. The basic concept which is thus engendered, utilizes the double property of the human being, who is at once a *facticity* and a *transcendence*. These two aspects of human reality are and ought to be capable of a valid coordination. But bad faith does not wish either to coordinate them or to surmount them in a synthesis. Bad faith seeks to affirm their identity while preserving their differences. It must affirm facticity as *being* transcendence and transcendence as *being* facticity, in such a way that at the instant when a person apprehends the one, he can find himself abruptly faced with the other. [pp. 55–56]

If man is what he is, bad faith is forever impossible and candor ceases to be his ideal and becomes

instead his being. But is man what he is? And more generally, how can he *be* what he is when he exists as consciousness of being? If candor or sincerity is a universal value, it is evident that the maxim "one must be what one is" does not serve solely as a regulating principle for judgments and concepts by which I express what I am. It posits not merely an ideal of knowing but an ideal of *being;* it proposes for us an absolute equivalence of being with itself as a prototype of being. In this sense it is necessary that we *make ourselves* what we are. But what *are we* then if we have the constant obligation to make ourselves what we are, if our mode of being is having the obligation to be what we are?

Let us consider this waiter in the café. His movement is quick and forward, a little too precise, a little too rapid. He comes toward the patrons with a step a little too quick. He bends forward a little too eagerly; his voice, his eyes express an interest a little too solicitous for the order of the customer. Finally there he returns, trying to imitate in his walk the inflexible stiffness of some kind of automaton while carrying his tray with the recklessness of a tight-rope-walker by putting it in a perpetually unstable, perpetually broken equilibrium which he perpetually reestablishes by a light movement of the arm and hand. All his behavior seems to us a game. He applies himself to chaining his movements as if they were mechanisms, the one regulating the other; his gestures and even his voice seem to be mechanisms; he gives himself the quickness and pitiless rapidity of things. He is playing, he is amusing himself. But what is he playing? We need not watch long before we can explain it: he is playing *at being* a waiter in a café. There is nothing there to surprise us. The game is a kind of marking out and investigation. The child plays with his body in order to explore it, to take inventory of it; the waiter in the café plays with his condition in order to *realize* it. This obligation is not different from that which is imposed on all tradesmen. Their condition is wholly one of ceremony. The public demands of them that they realize it as a ceremony; there is the dance of the grocer, of the tailor, of the auctioneer, by which they endeavour to persuade their clientele that they are nothing but a grocer, an auctioneer, a tailor. A grocer who dreams is offensive to the buyer, because such a grocer is not wholly a grocer. Society demands that he limit himself to his function as a grocer, just as the soldier at

---

[23] For Sartre the world is divided into two species of being: *in-itself* (the being of things) and *for-itself* (the being of human beings). The important contrast is that things are complete in their being, while humans are incomplete in that their future remains open.

attention makes himself into a soldier-thing with a direct regard which does not see at all, which is no longer meant to see, since it is the rule and not the interest of the moment which determines the point he must fix his eyes on (the sight "fixed at ten paces"). There are indeed many precautions to imprison a man in what he is, as if we lived in perpetual fear that he might escape from it, that he might break away and suddenly elude his condition.

In a parallel situation, from within, the waiter in the café can not be immediately a café waiter in the sense that this inkwell *is* an inkwell, or the glass is a glass. It is by no means that he can not form reflective judgments or concepts concerning his condition. He knows well what it "means": the obligation of getting up at five o'clock, of sweeping the floor of the shop before the restaurant opens, of starting the coffee pot going, *etc.* He knows the rights which it allows: the right to the tips, the right to belong to a union, etc. But all these concepts, all these judgments refer to the transcendent. It is a matter of abstract possibilities, of rights and duties conferred on a "person possessing rights." And it is precisely this person *who I have to be* (if I am the waiter in question) and who I am not. It is not that I do not wish to be this person or that I want this person to be different. But rather there is no common measure between his being and mine. It is a "representation" for others and for myself, which means that I can be he only in *representation*. But if I represent myself as him, I am not he; I am separated from him as the object from the subject, separated *by nothing*, but this nothing isolates me from him. I can not be he, I can only play *at being* him; that is, imagine to myself that I am he. And thereby I affect him with nothingness. In vain do I fulfill the functions of a café waiter. I can be he only in the neutralized mode, as the actor is Hamlet, by mechanically making the *typical gestures* of my state and by aiming at myself as an imaginary café waiter through those gestures taken as an "analogue." What I attempt to realize is a being-in-itself of the café waiter, as if it were not just in my power to confer their value and their urgency upon my duties and the rights of my position, as if it were not my free choice to get up each morning at five o'clock or to remain in bed, even though it meant getting fired. As if from the very fact that I sustain this role in existence I did not transcend it on every

side, as if I did not constitute myself as one *beyond* my condition. Yet there is no doubt that I *am* in a sense a café waiter—otherwise could I not just as well call myself a diplomat or a reporter? But if I am one, this can not be in the mode of being in-itself. I am a waiter in the mode of *being what I am not.* [pp. 58–60]

Even sincerity as a goal is undercut.

In the final analysis the goal of sincerity and the goal of bad faith are not so different. To be sure, there is a sincerity which bears on the past and which does not concern us here; I am sincere if I confess *having had* this pleasure or that intention. We shall see that if this sincerity is possible, it is because in his fall into the past, the being of man is constituted as a being-in-itself. But here our concern is only with the sincerity which aims at itself in present immanence. What is its goal? To bring me to confess to myself what I am in order that I may finally coincide with my being; in a word, to cause myself to be, in the mode of the in-itself, what I am in the mode of "not being what I am." Its assumption is that fundamentally I am already, in the mode of the in-itself, what I have to be. Thus we find at the base of sincerity a continual game of mirror and reflection, a perpetual passage from the being which is what it is, to the being which is not what it is and inversely from the being which is not what it is to the being which is what it is. And what is the goal of bad faith? To cause me to be what I am, in the mode of "not being what one is," or not to be what I am in the mode of "being what one is." We find here the same game of mirrors. [pp. 65–66]

Through shame the presence of other people is felt. (Note the power of phenomenological description here.)

Part Three, Ch One: The Existence of Others

I. The Problem. Consider for example shame. . . . [I]ts structure is intentional; it is a shameful apprehension *of* something and this something is *me.* I am ashamed of what I *am.* Shame therefore realizes an intimate relation of myself to myself. Through shame I have discovered an aspect of *my* being. Yet although certain complex forms derived from shame can appear on the reflective plane, shame is not originally a phenomenon of reflection. In fact no matter what results one can obtain in solitude by the religious *practice* of shame, it is in its primary structure shame *before somebody*. I have just made an awkward or vulgar gesture. This gesture clings to me; I neither judge it nor blame it. I simply live it. I realize it in the mode of for-itself. But now suddenly I raise my head. Somebody was there and has seen me. Suddenly I realize the vulgarity of my gesture, and I am ashamed. It is certain that my shame is not reflective, for the presence of another in my consciousness, even as a catalyst, is incompatible with the reflective attitude; in the field of my reflection I can never meet with anything but the consciousness which is mine. But the Other is the indispensable mediator between myself and me. I am ashamed of myself *as I appear* to the Other.

By the mere appearance of the Other, I am put in the position of passing judgment on myself as on an object, for it is as an object that I appear to the Other. Yet this object which has appeared to the Other is not an empty image in the mind of another. Such an image in fact, would be imputable wholly to the Other and so could not "touch" me. I could feel irritation, or anger before it as before a bad portrait of myself which gives to my expression an ugliness or baseness which I do not have, but I could not be touched to the quick. Shame is by nature *recognition*. I recognize that I *am* as the Other sees me. There is however no question of a comparison between what I am for myself and what I am for the Other as if I found in myself, in the mode of being of the For-itself, an equivalent of what I am for the Other. In the first place this comparison is not encountered in us as the result of a concrete psychic operation. Shame is an immediate shudder which runs through me from head to foot without any discursive preparation. In addition the comparison is impossible; I am unable to bring about any relation between what I am in the intimacy of the For-itself, without distance, without recoil, without perspective, and this unjustifiable being-in-itself which I am for the Other. There is no standard here, no table of correlation. Moreover the very notion of *vulgarity* implies an inter-monad relation. Nobody can be vulgar all alone! [pp. 221–222]

Part Four, Ch One: Being and Doing: Freedom

III. Freedom and Responsibility. The essential consequence of our earlier remarks is that man being condemned to be free carries the weight of the whole world on his shoulders; he is responsible for the world and for himself as a way of being. We are taking the word "responsibility" in its ordinary sense as "consciousness (of) being the incontestable author of an event or of an object." In this sense the responsibility of the for-itself is overwhelming since he is the one by whom it happens that *there is* a world; since he is also the one who makes himself be, then whatever may be the situation in which he finds himself, the for-itself must wholly assume this situation with its peculiar coefficient of adversity, even though it be insupportable. He must assume the situation with the proud consciousness of being the author of it, for the very worst disadvantages or the worst threats which can endanger my person have meaning only in and through my project; and it is on the ground of the engagement which I am that they appear. It is therefore senseless to think of complaining since nothing foreign has decided what we feel, what we live, or what we are.

Furthermore this absolute responsibility is not resignation; it is simply the logical requirement of the consequences of our freedom . . . for what happens to a man through other men and through himself can be only human. The most terrible situations of war, the worst tortures do not create a non-human state of things; there is no non-human situation. It is only through fear, flight, and recourse to magical types of conduct that I shall decide on the non-human, but this decision is human, and I shall carry the entire responsibility for it. But in addition the situation is *mine* because it is the image of my free choice of myself, and everything which it presents to me is *mine* in that it represents me and symbolizes me. Is it not I who decide the coefficient of adversity in things and even their unpredictability by deciding myself?

Thus there are no *accidents* in a life; a community event which suddenly bursts forth and involves me in it does not come from the outside. If I am mobilized in a war, this war is *my* war; it is in my image and I deserve it. I deserve it first because I could always get out of it by suicide or by desertion; these ultimate possibles are those which must always be present for us when there is a question of envisaging a situation. For lack of getting out of it, I have *chosen* it. This can be due to inertia, to cowardice in the face of public opinion, or because I prefer certain other values to the value of the refusal to join in the war (the good opinion of my relatives, the honor of my family, *etc.*). Any way you look at it, it is a matter of a choice. This choice will be repeated later on again and again without a break until the end of the war. . . .

. . . There can be no question of considering it as "four years of vacation" or as a "reprieve," as a "recess," the essential part of my responsibilities being elsewhere in my married, family, or professional life. In this war which I have chosen I choose myself from day to day, and I make it mine by making myself. If it is going to be four empty years, then it is I who bear the responsibility for this.

Finally, as we pointed out earlier, each person is an absolute choice of self from the standpoint of a world of knowledges and of techniques which this choice both assumes and illumines; each person is an absolute upsurge at an absolute date and is perfectly unthinkable at another date. It is therefore a waste of time to ask what I should have been if this war had not broken out, for I have chosen myself as one of the possible meanings of the epoch which imperceptibly led to war. I am not distinct from this same epoch; I could not be transported to another epoch without contradiction. Thus I *am* this war which restricts and limits and makes comprehensible the period which preceded it. In this sense we may define more precisely the responsibility of the for-itself if to the earlier quoted statement, "There are no innocent victims," we add the words, "We have the war we deserve." Thus, totally free, undistinguishable from the period for which I have chosen to be the meaning, as profoundly responsible for the war as if I had myself declared it, unable to live without integrating it in *my* situation, engag-

ing myself in it wholly and stamping it with my seal, I must be without remorse or regrets as I am without excuse; for from the instant of my upsurge into being, I carry the weight of the world by myself alone without anything or any person being able to lighten it.

Yet this responsibility is of a very particular type. Someone will say, "I did not ask to be born." This is a naive way of throwing greater emphasis on our facticity. I am responsible for everything, in fact, except for my very responsibility, for I am not the foundation of my being. Therefore everything takes place as if I were compelled to be responsible. I am *abandoned* in the world, not in the sense that I might remain abandoned and passive in a hostile universe like a board floating on the water, but rather in the sense that I find myself suddenly alone and without help, engaged in a world for which I bear the whole responsibility without being able, whatever I do, to tear myself away from this responsibility for an instant. For I am responsible for my very desire of fleeing responsibilities. To make myself passive in the world, to refuse to act upon things and upon Others is still to choose myself, and suicide is one mode among others of being-in-the-world. . . .

. . . The one who realizes in anguish his condition of *being* thrown into a responsibility which extends to his very abandonment has no longer either remorse or regret or excuse; he is no longer anything but a freedom which perfectly reveals itself and whose being resides in this very revelation. But as we pointed out at the beginning of this work, most of the time we flee anguish in bad faith. [pp. 553–556]

23

Human Rights, Justice, and Welfare

In the twentieth century three conspicuous claimants to provide foundations for ethics have been proposed: *human rights, justice,* and commonweal or *welfare.* Each has, of course, historical antecedents: human rights, in the natural rights theories of the seventeenth and eighteenth centuries; justice, in the long tradition that includes Plato's rendering of the key virtues in a way of life and Kant's basic moral principle of respect for the person, and of course, in the legal tradition that takes justice as its central ideal; welfare, in the utilitarian tradition with its social ideal of the greatest happiness of the greatest number.

Each claimant has developed more refined modern versions as it meets newer problems and attempts to remedy old defects with new models and new conceptual tools, frequently those developed in other disciplines. Thus the freshness of Rawls's (1971) framework, built on the idea of justice as fairness, lies in how he uses contemporary ideas of decision theory and economics in analyzing the process and reckonings of contract formation. Rights the-

ory forced its way on to the agenda of public discussion after World War II by the United Nations Declaration of Human Rights. It provoked different theoretical analyses of rights. On the one hand some, such as Robert Nozick (*Anarchy, State, and Utopia,* 1974), would resist an expansive tendency. On the other hand Alan Gewirth goes so far as to assert, "Every person has a basic right not to have cancer inflicted on him by the action of other persons." [1] Nozick's explicit basis is Lockean, while Gewirth's analysis rests on connecting rights with the concept of reason in a refined version of Kantian ideas, as worked out in his *Reason and Morality* (1978). Richard B. Brandt's *A Theory of the Good and the Right* (1979) follows the utilitarian path; but it discards the oversimplifications of that school's history, refines its concepts, and replaces its psychological and economic presuppositions with more vigorous contemporary materials. The concept of wel-

---

[1] *Human Rights: Essays in Justification and Applications* (Chicago: University of Chicago Press, 1982), p. 181.

586

fare has also begun to depart from the narrow individualism of the utilitarian tradition and to look to a more communitarian conception of the commonweal.

The claimants draw their strength from different but occasionally overlapping segments of human problems. Welfare has its base in the ordinary working of a society. It is obvious that questions of social policy—national defense, maintenance of high employment, protection of the environment and public health, and the rest—are constantly being decided on grounds of common welfare. The rights concept has its base in the protection of traditional liberties, so widely outraged in the history of our century, and in the effort to weave them into a pattern for social policy. The justice framework has a hold both on the common ideas of fairness and on the obvious need for some system of social peace and order on which to build the pursuit of human goods.

The three concepts need not confront one another with theoretical hostility. Every concept of welfare has room within its scheme for rights and justice, every concept of rights bids for human well-being and justice, and every notion of justice embraces rights and points to welfare. Similar moral principles and liberties may be supported by all three schemes, as freedom of thought and discussion appeared as a natural right in the work of Jefferson and Paine while it was equally supported on utilitarian grounds by Mill. On the other hand, when each framework claims to be *the* foundation of ethics, conflict is inevitable. Each claims the authority to constrain, delimit, and in effect define the others—for example, when a rights theory attacks a welfare conception as sacrificing the individual to social ends, or when a welfare conception criticizes a "rugged individualism," or when a justice theory criticizes as unfair the stringent assertion of individual rights.

We may accordingly look first into each of these conceptions and postpone the question whether reconciliation is possible till after the selections have been examined.

Human Rights

Basic or human rights have an absoluteness: it is wrong to violate a human right merely to achieve a greater good. As a human right, it falls to the lot of *each* and *every* human being. Thus human rights has two faces: it is individualistic when the focus is on protecting an individual's rights against all others, whatever their opinion or interest; it is universalistic when the focus is on securing a right for everybody. We may expect therefore that a human rights doctrine will have a reversible career, now demanding absolutely for all, now defending the individual absolutely against all.

The concern for human rights grew after World War II, in the United Nations Declaration of Human Rights (1948), in the succession of liberation movements, and thereafter in the struggles of world politics. The advances made under the appeal to rights might have been achieved on utilitarian principles too, but utilitarianism seemed to lack the stringency required. Where power belonged to entrenched minorities buttressed by traditional rights, human rights spoke for the majority's need to counter the minority's traditional rights with the absolutism of other, newer rights. In other cases, where advanced industrialism had brought benefits to majorities, the appeal for disadvantaged minorities had to say that majorities were not enough.

The UN Declaration went beyond the traditional items of basic personal security and freedom rights of the eighteenth century to include social and economic rights; it also went beyond general or abstract statement to specify detailed rights—for example, holidays with pay and a secret ballot. Again, particularly on matters of economic rights, it had to face issues between capitalism and socialism. For example, on property, in a UNESCO symposium that reports some of the preliminary debates and proposals, we find, "Every man has the right to private property in so far as it is necessary for his personal use and the use of his family; no other form of property is in itself a fundamental right." [2] This would remove from the protection of a human right property possessed by corporations. But the actual UN Declaration says (Article 17): "Every one has a right to own property alone as well as in association with others." Most startlingly, the Declaration has no hesitation in giving expression to new rights, abstract or concrete. Thus Article 23 states the right to form trade unions. Harold Laski, in the UNESCO symposium, pointed out that freedom of association by trade unions had been granted in England as recently as 1871, in France in 1884, and in Germany in Bismarck's time, and had been sanctioned only partially in the United States in 1935.[3] Article 27 gives everyone the right to share in scientific advancement and benefits. Under the inspiration of such an active exploration of new rights (whether conceived as constructed or discovered) it is not surprising that the various liberation movements concentrated on categories of persons discriminated against, yielding a focus on rights of previously colonial countries, of women, of the handicapped, and so on.

The chief theoretical problem a rights theory faces is how to establish the list of rights (see Felix Cohen, question 6) and how to handle a conflict of rights. A work such as Robert Nozick's *Anarchy, State, and Utopia* is in effect a defense of property and contract rights against the newer, upstart rights. The problem of the conflict of rights concerns less their legitimacy than which should yield under what circumstances to others. The most effective use of the framework will of course be seen in dealing with fundamental issues such as protecting the person against torture. The more numerous the rights, the greater the need for some principles of ordering that carry one outside the framework itself, unless the comparative strength of rights is itself regarded as a matter of intuition—and here intuitions will differ. Thus where the costs of satisfying the right to social services grow high we witness revolts against taxation as an inroad on rights of property, though other rights (such as national defense) may not be asked to share the cost. Is this to be regarded as the superiority of property rights over welfare rights, or rather as the selfish failure of people to support human rights? The rights framework, in rejecting the balancing and weighing so notable in utilitarianism, has its own problems of balancing. Yet this does not mean that its rejection of cost-benefit attitudes is without content. A familiar example today is the issue whether cost-benefit analysis should be admitted as a consideration in environmental protection, cutting the extent of pollution control in industrial production. If stated wholly within a rights framework, it is a conflict of the right to life and health versus the right to property and free enterprise. The complexity of these issues, both as problems of theoretical framework and as problems of application, is therefore very great.

The writings on the theory of rights show a marked shift of emphasis over several decades. Felix Cohen states the problems; subsequent papers in both moral and legal philosophy defend the concept and try to set off its distinctive features (as in Dworkin's account) or send out peace feelers to other accounts (also as in Dworkin); still later works attempt fuller study of varieties of rights theories, of different possible relations to other ethical approaches, and in general (see Becker) attempt to give rights a systematic place in a broader ethical theory.

---

[2] Proposed by the UNESCO Committee on the theoretical bases of human rights. See *Human Rights, Comments and Interpretations,* a symposium edited by UNESCO (New York: Columbia University Press, 1949), Appendix II.
[3] Ibid., p. 78.

Recently a feminist critique of the rights conception has emerged, not to supplant the content of remedial justice but to pinpoint its structure as distinctively masculine. Carol Gilligan, in examining differences in the responses of men and women to moral problems and their modes of reasoning, finds a contrast between an isolating individualist mode of decision involving commitment to ultimate intellectual-moral principles and decision in terms of human relatedness and mutual responsibility.[4] The former expresses a masculine ideal of autonomy, the latter a feminine ideal of care. Such differences appear to be supported by the male-female differences that Helen Block Lewis has found in a reappraisal of the emotions: here shame, an emotion that involves relation to others, appears to be more characteristic of female development in our society; whereas guilt, inner and isolating, is more characteristic of male development.[5]

Justice

The same social and historical factors that led to the reemergence of rights theory provided as fertile a soil for the resurgence of justice as primary, rather than derivative, in ethics. John Rawls's *A Theory of Justice* (1971) overrode the current division of metaethics and normative ethics and went directly to normative problems. His theory has at least three important features that stem both from the history of ethics and from the moral tradition of classic liberalism.

One feature is equalitarianism: everyone is entitled to an equal share unless the structure replacing the equality works out better for all and improves the expectations of the least advantaged. This has moved beyond Kant's respect for every person and the meritocratic conception in which greater abilities merit greater rewards.

Another feature is reliance on social contract—in his case, the unanimous agreement of individuals about the principles of justice that are to be the social foundations. The unanimity is aided by the minimal terms on which he constructs justice. In this respect, a comparison with Hobbes is suggestive. Hobbes derives his morality in large measure from the need for peace and order, but more as a means, or at least a necessary condition, to a variety of human goals than as an end in itself. So too Rawls argues that individuals will in fact agree on minimal formulations of justice if they act under a "veil of ignorance"—that is, if they do not know where their own position will fall: whether they will be male or female, master or servant, rich or poor, healthy or sick. In this way they will be compelled to be impartial and hence their agreements will be fair. Rawls's theory aims at a formulation of basic principles for all time. Of course when it comes to the application of the principles—but only then—knowledge of economics, social arrangements, and so on become relevant. This approach is in marked contrast with that of a Dewey or a Marx, who in different ways bring to the determination of principles the maximum of knowledge in its growth and who want morality to be affected by changes in human production and control.

A third feature is the importance of liberty. Not only does it enter as a principle in the theory of justice, but it seems to be what makes possible a broader conception of the good; for

[4] Gilligan's study analyzes responses to the tests devised by Lawrence Kohlberg. He takes moral development of the individual to go through fixed stages: punishment-obedience, instrumentality (means-end), "good-boy–nice-girl," law and order, social contract (with a utilitarian character), and universal ethical principle. Few individuals reach the top level.

[5] *Shame and Guilt in Neurosis* (1971) and *Psychic War in Men and Women* (1976). Lewis's previous work, with H. A. Witkin, on perceptual style also found a difference between preponderantly male field-independence and preponderantly female field-dependence—that is, between making perceptual judgments on inner, bodily cues or on outer, environmental cues.

once the social order has been established, there is less need to constrain individuals' freely pursuing their own conceptions of the good.

The impact of *A Theory of Justice* was immediate and dramatic, and reached beyond philosophy. It was widely reviewed in the popular press, where it was often regarded as an important restatement of postwar liberalism with strong political implications. Around it has grown virtually an academic mini-industry, involving not just philosophers, many of whom found it liberating, but economists, political scientists, and lawyers—some to explore its implications, some to challenge the technical models he took from their fields. Rawls was attacked for being both too little and too much equalitarian. But perhaps the feature that drew most controversy was his revised contractualism, in particular over what principles would be a rational choice in the original position: some argued that the utilitarian principle would be a rational choice; others that principles different from Rawls's would arise from a greater willingness to risk. A still deeper critique challenged the posture of neutrality in the choice of principles:

[S]ome things may be primary goods only relative to the social institutions in which persons who have these preferences find themselves. . . . Wealth and power, for instance, may be essential for the attainment of a person's ends in some kinds of societies but not in others. Indeed, there are possible life plans in which possession of wealth and power are genuine nuisances. I think this social relativization holds for a broad range of things and seriously restricts the class of primary goods.[6]

This is a modern version of the difficulty that from the seventeenth century has so burdened social contract theory—how far the foundation of the theory requires the social and the historical.

[6] Michael Teitelman, "The Limits of Individualism," *Journal of Philosophy* 69 (October 1972): 550–551.

Welfare

Utilitarianism has continued its effort to establish and justify moral rules and generalizations on the basis of a more refined calculation of utilities and a more sophisticated identification of goods in terms of some notion of pleasure or happiness or some substitute for it, and to state some general well-being derived from the spread of individual well-being.

On the use of moral rules, a basic distinction is between *act* and *rule* utilitarianism. In the former, the task of moral decision is to calculate full utilities for each particular situation. The rule utilitarian points to the need for acting according to rules in the particular situation because of the utilities of the practice that the rule embodies. Rules are also embodied in character and virtue and in how the self is developed. The act utilitarian regards appeal to rules as only a secondhand procedure, made necessary by practical shortcomings, to be replaced where possible by particular-oriented calculations. The distinction itself has had its critics, who object that any description of a particular situation is already of a given sort or a given kind, therefore already brought under a rule: a right decision in any one situation is implicitly for all situations of that kind. The issue is not whether to have a rule, but what degree of generality is to be employed—whether a high-order rule such as "Don't harm a human being" or a lower-order rule such as "Don't harm this human being just because you are angry and think you can get away with it." There is no single answer about what level of generality is required for what kind of situation; hence no choice can be made between rule and act utilitarianism.

On the identification of goods in terms of pleasures produced, experimentation has been continuous. The basic question is whether selecting some unit other than pleasure-pain would provide a more fruitful and determinate mode of reckoning value. Moore substituted the intrinsic value of well-demarcated states of affairs, each intuitively assessed. Others, moved by critiques of pleasure as subjective, volatile, and evanescent, sought instead some underlying unit in terms of whose functioning pleasure and pain might themselves be understood. Ralph Barton Perry (1876–1957) proposed *interests* (*General Theory of Value*, 1926), which could be extended to animal life generally. Stephen Pepper (1891–1972) fastened on the more complex phenomenon of *purposive behavior* and attempted from an examination of its structure to give an account of the variety of values (*The Sources of Value*, 1958). Still others, hopeful that in the Freudian theory of the underlying "mechanism" of pleasure a more solid base for it would be found, held on to pleasure.

The choice of appropriate unit thus became a disputed matter. Economists, who had once hoped to use a Benthamite model, eventually gave up on a scientific use of pleasure-pain. They adopted the more general idea of individual *preferences* (or, better, *preferential dispositions*), for the most part identified with choice. These preferences could cover not merely the content of choice but even procedural principles—for example, whether in a situation of risk an individual prefers minimal danger or maximum gain. The shift from pleasure to preferences involves serious issues, in part epistemological—whether the individual knows best what pleases him—and in part moral—whether individuals should have the last word about their values.

From the work of economists came the greatest technical refinement in deriving general well-being from profiles of individual preference. They devised ways of depicting "utility functions" for the individual and for the group; discussed the possibility of interpersonal comparison of preferences, which would enable us to judge that one person's preferences were better than another's (and to a great extent decided against it); separated the different strands in the decision process; gave a clearer picture of what is entailed in "maximization," and so on. Unfortunately, the net results for deriving the general well-being have been thin. They are generally associated with the ideas of Vilfredo Pareto (1848–1923): a situation is "Pareto optimal" when no one can become better off ("better" being judged in terms of the individual's own preferences) without someone else becoming worse off. Welfare is thus increased by a policy that gives someone more without giving anyone else less. Situations can be constructed, however, where general welfare is greatly improved if a few are made somewhat worse off (see the Braybrooke selection), raising the question whether a preference account of social welfare is too restrictive. Further, "Arrow's theorem" suggests that no democratic decision procedure is possible whereby a social policy is derivable from individual preferences unless some values are assumed or dictated.[7]

Interpersonal utility comparison is the crux; without it the individual seems to have an ultimate veto over what is to be regarded as the social good. But to deny interpersonal comparison runs counter to well established intuitions and usage. John C. Harsanyi writes in "Morality and the Theory of Rational Behavior,"

In everyday life we make, or at least attempt to make, interpersonal utility comparisons all the time. When we have only one nut left at the end of a trip, we may have to decide which particular member of our family is in greatest need of a little extra food. Again, we may give a book or a concert ticket or a free invitation to a wine-tasting fair to one friend rather than to another in the belief that the former would enjoy it more than the latter would. I do not think it is the task of a philosopher or a social scientist to deny the obvious fact that people often feel quite capable of making such comparisons. Rather, his task is to explain how we ever managed

[7] Kenneth Arrow, *Social Choice and Individual Values* (New Haven and New York: Yale University Press and Wiley, 1951; 2d ed., 1963).

to make such comparisons—as well or as badly as we do make them.[8]

Harsanyi thinks we do this by an imaginative empathy that, since we project ourselves into the position of others and judge by how we should feel or judge from there, presupposes a basic similarity of people. This is a necessary a priori postulate; without it, we will not be able to make the interpersonal utility comparisons by which we can go beyond giving to every individual a veto. ("I cannot let *all* the members of my family go hungry because I have philosophical scruples about interpersonal comparisons and cannot make up my mind.") At the same time, he distinguishes between rational and irrational preferences:

All we have to do is to distinguish between a person's manifest preferences and his true preferences. His manifest preferences are his actual preferences as manifested by his observed behaviour, including preferences possibly based on erroneous factual beliefs, or on careless logical analysis, or on strong emotions that at the moment greatly hinder rational choice. In contrast, a person's true preferences are the preferences he *would* have if he had all the relevant factual information, always reasoned with the greatest possible care, and were in a state of mind most conducive to rational choice.[9]

Social utility, in his view, must take account of only true preferences. And he also disqualifies rational but antisocial preferences, such as "sadism, envy, resentment, and malice."

If Harsanyi's ultimate base turns out to be a moral necessity, Kenneth Arrow's rejection of interpersonal comparison is frankly a moral individualism:

[A] difficulty is that reducing an individual to a specified list of qualities is denying his individuality

in a deep sense. In a way that I cannot articulate well and am none too sure about defending, the autonomy of individuals, an element of mutual incommensurability among people seems denied by the possibility of interpersonal comparisons. No doubt it is some such feeling as this that has made me so reluctant to shift from pure ordinalism, despite my desire to seek a basis for a theory of justice.[10]

If what is at stake is the search for a common good or community interest, conceived in Benthamite fashion as a sum of pleasures of individuals or as the more sophisticated maximization of preferences, then so far it has proved unpersuasive. Other writers, seeking ways to mitigate the sheer individualism of the utilitarian tradition, look to a fresh interpretation of welfare to provide a genuinely social good. They reject the equation of welfare or happiness with satisfaction of preferences, although they may recognize a limited role for preference to ensure some degree of individual autonomy. There are, for example, *pluralistic* conceptions that depart from a single or monistic treatment of happiness or the good. (See Braybrooke's treatment of happiness as one of the goods of diverse sort that go along together in an integrated way in a given time and place.)

Quality of life is another notion offered to replace general happiness. It can, of course, apply to the individual, just as happiness does. And indeed, some studies in the economics of income—apart from the general notion of "standard of living"—attempt to calculate what constitutes "disposable income," that which individuals may spend in accordance with their preferences, over and above income required for the necessities of life. But such individualistic reduction by-passes the novel social force of the concept. This comes from the recognition of communal problems. In environmental studies, pollution of the

---

[8] "Morality and the Theory of Rational Behavior," in *Utilitarianism and Beyond*, ed. Amartya Sen and Bernard Williams (Cambridge: Cambridge University Press, 1982), pp. 49–50.

[9] Ibid., p. 55.

[10] Kenneth J. Arrow, "Extended Sympathy and the Possibility of Social Choice," *American Economic Review* 62 (1977): 225.

atmosphere or toxicity of the surroundings (including water supply) can readily be seen as features of the community's life without reference to individual discomforts.[11] The same holds for crowding consequent on overpopulation or conditions of widespread insecurity of one sort or another. Again, once the concept has been fashioned it begins to throw fresh light on existent conditions. For example, studies of the problems of the handicapped, or the plight of the aged, or the feminization of poverty, or attitudes to death and dying become increasingly cast as problems of quality of life. The obvious present requirement is to develop adequate indexes for quality of life (such as rates of infant mortality, crime, literacy, life expectancy). Indexes need not have the same status: some may be necessary conditions for survival, others may be cultural, established as lessons of historical experience—such as freedom of thought and expression, participation in social decision making, extent of opportunities for the development of talent, or a creative enjoyment of one's work.

Understood thus, the notion of quality of life differs from utopian ideals. It is not presented as something that will be achieved in the long run, whether by effort or by the wheels of history or both. It is not the Hegelian ideal of a rational state, the Marxian conception of an eventual communism, or the Spencerian notion of a mode of life of an ideal individual in an ideal society that is the end product of evolution fusing egoism and altruism. Quality of life refers instead to problems of the present, or the foreseeable future, to be tackled by present generations. Study of the problems may carry us into their conditions and historical development.

Even so, quality of life may not be a sufficiently rich concept. To those for whom the temporal, developmental, and historical factors are of great importance in understanding social welfare, quality of life may prove too limited. They look at welfare in the context of the history of humankind—the growth of knowledge and techniques, the major transformations in modes of life, the opportunities grasped or missed, the alternative paths that are now open and the traps to avoid. This conception of welfare, which departs from the individualistic model, is pluralistic; it does not operate with utopias but insists that a historical perspective is necessary to understand where the human goods are to be found, both those specific to a particular period as well as those that are perennial. The view of history taken by such a conception is not deterministic but makes room for human effort and human knowledge as vital forces. When the concept of welfare is given such a broad scope, the notion of human *goods* becomes again congenial, and it ties in readily with traditional ideals of social progress.[12]

---

[11] See papers in Ronald O. Clarke and Peter List, eds., *Environmental Spectrum* (New York: Van Nostrand, 1974).

[12] Such conceptions are less common in recent philosophical literature than among philosophically minded social scientists who try to map the outlines of a possible future, using the lessons of the past. A good example is Kenneth Boulding's *The Meaning of the 20th Century: The Great Transition* (1964). In his account of the contours of a second great transition (the first had been from "precivilized" to "civilized" society) to "postcivilized society" (the technological or developed society), Boulding sketches conditions and changes and alternatives, and possible goods and traps and tasks. There are reflections on history, sociological conditions, and the impact of technological change. The historical panorama includes accounts of the productive growth that made the abolition of slavery possible; moral changes in the family; the impact of population changes on attitudes to children and sex; growing bases for a common culture and the multiplicity of social types; the quality of human life and dignity; the possibilities of eliminating war, poverty and disease; conditions that assist in self-mastery; speculation on new forms of ethical development and new ethical standards; and sources of creativity. In more traditional writings all this would have been sorted differently: on the one hand, the moral patterns and ethical theory; on the other, hypotheses about significant social and technological conditions and the historical development that are taken to have had different types of impact on the moral and the ethical. Doubtless

United Nations Universal Declaration of Human Rights (1948)

The Universal Declaration of Human Rights furnishes the essential materials for the twentieth-century discussion of rights.

Whereas recognition of the inherent dignity and of the equal and inalienable rights of all members of the human family is the foundation of freedom, justice and peace in the world,

Whereas disregard and contempt for human rights have resulted in barbarous acts which have outraged the conscience of mankind, and the advent of a world in which human beings shall enjoy freedom of speech and belief and freedom from fear and want has been proclaimed as the highest aspiration of the common people,

Whereas it is essential, if man is not to be compelled to have recourse, as a last resort, to rebellion against tyranny and oppression, that human rights should be protected by the rule of law,

Whereas it is essential to promote the development of friendly relations between nations,

Whereas the peoples of the United Nations have in the Charter reaffirmed their faith in fundamental human rights, in the dignity and worth of the human person and in the equal rights of men and women and have determined to promote social progress and better standards of life in larger freedom,

Whereas Member States have pledged themselves to achieve, in cooperation with the United Nations, the promotion of universal respect for and observance of human rights and fundamental freedoms,

Whereas a common understanding of these rights and freedoms is of the greatest importance for the full realization of this pledge,

Now, therefore,

The General Assembly,

Proclaims this Universal Declaration of Human Rights as a common standard of achievement for all peoples and all nations, to the end that every individual and every organ of society, keeping this Declaration constantly in mind, shall strive by teaching and education to promote respect for these rights and freedoms and by progressive measures, national and international, to secure their universal and effective recognition and observance, both among the peoples of Member States themselves and among the peoples of territories under their jurisdiction.

Article 1. All human beings are born free and equal in dignity and rights. They are endowed with reason and conscience and should act towards one another in a spirit of brotherhood.

Article 2. Everyone is entitled to all the rights and freedoms set forth in this Declaration, without distinction of any kind, such as race, colour, sex, language, religion, political or other opinion, national or social origin, property, birth or other status.

Furthermore, no distinction shall be made on the basis of the political, jurisdictional or international status of the country or territory to which a person belongs, whether it be independent, trust, non-self-governing or under any other limitation of sovereignty.

Article 3. Everyone has the right to life, liberty and the security of person.

Article 4. No one shall be held in slavery or servitude; slavery and the slave trade shall be prohibited in all their forms.

Article 5. No one shall be subjected to torture or to cruel, inhuman or degrading treatment or punishment.

Article 6. Everyone has the right to recognition everywhere as a person before the law.

Article 7. All are equal before the law and are entitled without any discrimination to equal protection of the law. All are entitled to equal protection against any discrimination in violation of this Declaration and against any incitement to such discrimination.

Article 8. Everyone has the right to an effective remedy by the competent national tribunals for acts violating the fundamental rights granted him by the constitution or by law.

Article 9. No one shall be subjected to arbitrary arrest, detention or exile.

Article 10. Everyone is entitled in full equality to a fair and public hearing by an independent and impartial tribunal, in the determination of his rights

---

this would make clearer the specific lines of theoretical interrelationship. But in his tracing of a large-scale historical transformation, Boulding has fashioned a contemporary conception of social welfare; its lesson is how deeply the moral is rooted in the historical and cultural milieu.

and obligations and of any criminal charge against him.

Article 11.——1. Everyone charged with a penal offence has the right to be presumed innocent until proved guilty according to law in a public trial at which he has had all the guarantees necessary for his defence.

2. No one shall be held guilty of any penal offence on account of any act or omission which did not constitute a penal offence, under national or international law, at the time when it was committed. Nor shall a heavier penalty be imposed than the one that was applicable at the time the penal offence was committed.

Article 12. No one shall be subjected to arbitrary interference with his privacy, family, home or correspondence, nor to attacks upon his honour and reputation. Everyone has the right to the protection of the law against such interference or attacks.

Article 13.——1. Everyone has the right to freedom of movement and residence within the borders of each state.

2. Everyone has the right to leave any country, including his own, and to return to his country.

Article 14.——1. Everyone has the right to seek and to enjoy in other countries asylum from persecution.

2. This right may not be invoked in the case of prosecutions genuinely arising from non-political crimes or from acts contrary to the purposes and principles of the United Nations.

Article 15.——1. Everyone has the right to a nationality.

2. No one shall be arbitrarily deprived of his nationality nor denied the right to change his nationality.

Article 16.——1. Men and women of full age, without any limitation due to race, nationality or religion, have the right to marry and to found a family. They are entitled to equal rights as to marriage, during marriage and at its dissolution.

2. Marriage shall be entered into only with the free and full consent of the intending spouses.

3. The family is the natural and fundamental group unit of society and is entitled to protection by society and the State.

Article 17.——1. Everyone has the right to own property alone as well as in association with others.

2. No one shall be arbitrarily deprived of his property.

Article 18. Everyone has the right to freedom of thought, conscience and religion; this right includes freedom to change his religion or belief, and freedom, either alone or in community with others and in public or private, to manifest his religion or belief in teaching, practice, worship and observance.

Article 19. Everyone has the right to freedom of opinion and expression; this right includes freedom to hold opinions without interference and to seek, receive and impart information and ideas through any media and regardless of frontiers.

Article 20.——1. Everyone has the right to freedom of peaceful assembly and association.

2. No one may be compelled to belong to an association.

Article 21.——1. Everyone has the right to take part in the Government of his country, directly or through freely chosen representatives.

2. Everyone has the right of equal access to public service in his country.

3. The will of the people shall be the basis of the authority of government; this will shall be expressed in periodic and genuine elections which shall be by universal and equal suffrage and shall be held by secret vote or by equivalent free voting procedures.

Article 22. Everyone, as a member of society, has the right to social security and is entitled to realization, through national effort and international cooperation and in accordance with the organization and resources of each State, of the economic, social and cultural rights indispensable for his dignity and the free development of his personality.

Article 23.——1. Everyone has the right to work, to free choice of employment, to just and favourable conditions of work and to protection against unemployment.

2. Everyone, without any discrimination, has the right to equal pay for equal work.

3. Everyone who works has the right to just and favourable remuneration insuring for himself and his family an existence worthy of human dignity, and supplemented, if necessary, by other means of social protection.

4. Everyone has the right to form and to join trade unions for the protection of his interests.

Article 24. Everyone has the right to rest and leisure, including reasonable limitation of working hours and periodic holidays with pay.

Article 25.——1. Everyone has the right to a

standard of living adequate for the health and well-being of himself and of his family, including food, clothing, housing and medical care and necessary social services, and the right to security in the event of unemployment, sickness, disability, widowhood, old age or other lack of livelihood in circumstances beyond his control.

2. Motherhood and childhood are entitled to special care and assistance. All children, whether born in or out of wedlock shall enjoy the same social protection.

Article 26.——1. Everyone has the right to education. Education shall be free, at least in the elementary and fundamental stages. Elementary education shall be compulsory. Technical and professional education shall be made generally available and higher education shall be equally accessible to all on the basis of merit.

2. Education shall be directed to the full development of the human personality and to the strengthening of respect for human rights and fundamental freedoms. It shall promote understanding, tolerance and friendship among all nations, racial or religious groups, and shall further the activities of the United Nations for the maintenance of peace.

3. Parents have a prior right to choose the kind of education that shall be given to their children.

Article 27.——1. Everyone has the right freely to participate in the cultural life of the community, to enjoy the arts and to share in scientific advancement and its benefits.

2. Everyone has the right to the protection of the moral and material interests resulting from any scientific, literary or artistic production of which he is the author.

Article 28. Everyone is entitled to a social and international order in which the rights and freedoms set forth in this Declaration can be fully realized.

Article 29.——1. Everyone has duties to the community in which alone the free and full development of his personality is possible.

2. In the exercise of his rights and freedoms, everyone shall be subject only to such limitations as are determined by law solely for the purpose of securing due recognition and respect for the rights and freedoms of others and of meeting the just requirements of morality, public order and the general welfare in a democratic society.

3. These rights and freedoms may in no case be exercised contrary to the purposes and principles of the United Nations.

Article 30. Nothing in this Declaration may be interpreted as implying for any State, group or person any right to engage in any activity or to perform any act aimed at the destruction of any of the rights and freedoms set forth herein.

Felix S. Cohen
(1907–1953)

Human Rights: An Appeal to Philosophers [13]

After three decades it is refreshing again to consider the seven questions about human rights posed by Felix S. Cohen to the 1952 annual meeting of the American Philosophical Association and to wonder how many have been answered. The occasion was dramatic: a refugee ship was being turned away from the ports of one country after another and lay off American shores. Apparently Cohen does not expect the seventh question (what in doubtless preinflationary terms he calls "the $64 question") to be tackled until the first six are reckoned with.

Perhaps the greatest of all the riddles that the Sphinx of History has put before our generation is the problem of how, if at all, men of different races, conflicting religions, and opposing economic and political faiths, can live together on a shrinking earth. This is the kind of problem on which human beings have habitually turned to philosophers for guidance. We all know the penalty that the Sphinx imposes for failure to answer such riddles. And so today the peoples of the world ask for philosophical vision in meeting the practical question: What rights, if any, can a man claim of me not because he is my brother or my neighbor or my colleague or co-religionist or fellow-citizen, but just because he's human?

This is a practical lawyer's appeal for help on behalf of clients to whom the question of human

[13] Felix S. Cohen, "Human Rights: An Appeal to Philosophers," *Review of Metaphysics* 6 (June 1953): 617–622.

rights is particularly pressing. It so happens that some of these clients are aliens, not citizens, so they can't very well talk or worry about rights of citizenship. Many of them are without property, and so not deeply interested in rights of property. Many of them have no jobs, and so are not particularly interested in the rights of labor. But all of them are human, and if that gives them any rights, they would like to know, and I, as their lawyer, would like to know, what those rights are. And so I come to a forum of the wise men of America searching for light on that problem. If I can return to my clients with even one lighted candle, that would be better than sitting and cursing the darkness. But I should like to return with a whole candelabra of seven candles illuminating seven questions that seem to me to be at the heart of the world's great darkness today.

Question 1

The first of these questions is a very modest one, which might be answered not only by utilitarians and anti-utilitarians, Thomists and anti-Thomists, Marxists and anti-Marxists, but even by those philosophers who think that ethical statements are neither true nor false but only animal noises, like the barking of dogs or the song of the mocking-bird, which are intended to influence the behavior of other animals and frequently do. Our first question, then, is: *When people discourse on human rights, what light does such discussion throw upon the character and motivations of the discussants?*

This, I submit, is a significant question even if there are no human rights. Even outside the field of ethics we often find in a statement more information about the speaker than about the object of his discourse. One may disbelieve in witches and yet find significance in the fact that the State of Delaware and, until 1935 or so, the Federal Government have declared witchcraft to be a punishable offense. That may not tell us much about witches but it does tell us something about the State of Delaware and the Federal Government. Consider, for example, a completely Machiavellian cynic who views the discussion of human rights as a process of noisemaking by which rival diplomats seek to put their adversaries in corners and bid against each other for the support of the wretched of the earth. May not such an amoralist teach us something about the motivations and significant conditions of assertions about

human rights, and thus help us to understand what goes on in the heart and nerve centers of the world?

Question 2

Our second question, again, might be answered by any philosopher, even by one who thinks that ethical discussion does not consist of true or false statements, any more than chess. But if ethical discussion is a game, with influences upon human behavior constituting the stakes, it is at least an important and exciting game. And we can certainly ask: *How do people in fact reach agreements on basic objectives?* Is the shift in language from "I want" to "You and I each have a right" a part of the process of overcoming our egocentric predicaments, and perhaps also our ethnocentric and politicocentric predicaments? Does not civilized society rest in large part upon the distinction that most of us learn in childhood between wanting something and recognizing the right of another to grant or withhold that which is desired? What is there about the process of rational discussion that can lead us not only to change the desires of others but even to curb our own desires, and thus reach agreements where hostility once existed? Surely this is a question on which any philosophy of human nature should have light to shed.

Question 3

My third question is again addressed to cynics and skeptics as well as to believers in the existence of moral knowledge. Suppose we begin with the cynical observation that language is an invention for concealing human thought. We note then that some words carry remarkable powers in this direction. For example, in the "Universal Declaration of Human Rights" on December 19, 1948, some 48 nations agreed that nobody should "arbitrarily" be deprived of his property (Article 17) or his nationality (Article 15) or be subjected to "arbitrary arrest" (Article 9) or "arbitrary interference with his privacy" (Article 12). Does such an agreement mean more than a statement that we are against sin? Doesn't the use of the word "arbitrary" in such clauses constitute the clearest evidence of the wide diversity that exists in the world today as to what can properly justify invasions of privacy, arrest, expatriation, or the expropriation of private property? And from this perspective we may ask: *How do people use language to conceal disagreements on basic objectives?*

Are there some terms like "arbitrary" or "reasonable" which can serve us as semantic guideposts to the areas of significant disagreement on the content of human rights? Certainly, a sophisticated philosophy of language should be able to cast great light on the actual extent of human agreement and disagreement.

Question 4

There is a fourth question on which a practising lawyer may appeal to philosophers for help without limiting his appeal to those who take ethics seriously as a field of true or false opinions. That is the question which is integral to any philosophy of history, and basic to any philosophy of legal history, the question, namely: *How do the social arrangements that we call rules of law come into being?* The idea of a universal human right, I take it, comes to mankind only after a long history of family rights, tribal rights, and other rights limited to particular groups. One finds perhaps the first adumbration of the idea of human rights in the words of a great law teacher:

> The stranger that sojourneth with you shall be unto you as the home-born among you, and thou shalt love him as thyself; for ye were strangers in the land of Egypt. (Lev. XIX, 34)

Somewhat the same idea is implicit in the Aristotelian doctrine of natural rights, especially in its stoic interpretation. But only with the union of the Hebraic and Hellenic traditions in scholastic philosophy do we find the idea of human rights put forward in all its boldness, most eloquently, I think, in the discourse of Francisco Vitoria, *De Indis,* in 1532, with its insistence that American Indians, Moslems, and other unbelievers, living in sin, have certain rights just because they are human. Kant, in 1784, in his *Idea of Universal History from a Cosmopolitical Point of View,* with uncanny gifts of prophecy, described the events of our day, the fumbling and halting efforts at agreement among peoples in conflict. These efforts he saw as a final projection, upon the international sphere, of that dialectic process by which man's "unsocial sociability" hammers agreement out of natural antagonisms and thus begins "to arrange for a great future political body, such as the world has never yet seen." Have 168

years of second thoughts added to Kant's vision of the events of our day or to Vitoria's expression of basic human aspirations?

Question 5

The questions put so far are not specifically ethical, although they may illumine our understanding of the events on which some of us seek to form ethical judgments. There remain some questions which are specifically ethical and which will therefore be dismissed as nonsense by those who deny the possibility of knowledge of the good. Now, whether or not goodness is relative, certainly nonsense is relative. Perhaps a recognition of the relativity of nonsense may save us from the wasted effort of seeking wisdom concerning ethical truth or modern art from those who consider ethical truth or modern art special forms of nonsense. Let me then limit my remaining questions to those who can conceive the possibility of true or false ethical judgments, and I include in this category relativists as well as absolutists, since even a relativist's value judgments are true or false when his moral perspective or field is fully defined. The first of these specifically ethical or meta-ethical questions is simply: *What ethical implications follow logically from the assertion or denial of any given human right?* Is there, for example, a difference between the goodness of life and the right to life? Surely, if the logical analysis of ethical systems is a proper part of philosophy, philosophers ought to be able to show how a system qualifies or defines the propositions it contains, and if philosophers can do this they can surely help a practical lawyer to avoid the waste of effort that is inherent in the pursuit of a plurality of mutually incompatible ideals.

Question 6

The next basic question on which I and many others look for light from ethical philosophers is the question: *What sort of evidence can establish a human right?* Even if we agree that no formulation yet achieved of human rights is entirely accurate, can we say, at least, that some statements are more inaccurate than others? And if so, which? If we agree that Jones has no right to live, does this throw any evidenciary light on the proposition that all men have a right to live? Or can we blithely accept both propositions as true? And can we then charge any logician who rejects this happy tolerance with usurpation of judicial functions or with contempt of court? Or, to put the matter more generally, by what scientific, unscientific, or pre-scientific, procedure can we achieve greater accuracy in our further formulation of ethical judgments in the field of human rights?

Question 7

We come finally to the $64 question, to which all our other questions are somehow preliminary: *Are there any human rights, and if so, what are they?*

Now it may be supposed that only some extraordinary coincidence would lead philosophers who disagree as to the meaning of the word "right," and disagree as to the criteria for testing ethical truth, to any consensus as to the content of human rights. But this would be an over-hasty assumption. If we take, for example, the proposition in Article I of the "Universal Declaration of Human Rights" that "all human beings . . . should act towards one another in a spirit of brotherhood," I think we are likely to find this proposition generally defended by utilitarians on the ground that in the long run more human misery is avoided by brotherly regard for other humans than by any contrary principle. We are likely to find Thomists, I think, generally supporting the brotherhood principle on the further ground that we are all under a divine duty to recognize each other as children of a single heavenly Father. The Hegelian proponent of self-development as the highest human good may join in the consensus on the ground that unfraternal hatreds impede the human development of both the hater and the hated. Perhaps the Yogi, if not the Commissar, may join the consensus on the ground that the sense of egocentric individuality is an illusion, and that the sense of union, dimly perceived in the notion of brotherhood, is a necessary approach to understanding and to the peace that passeth understanding. But whatever the different paths that lead us together, and whatever may be the further paths by which we shall separate when we come to pass judgment on pressing political controversies, the fact that today so many different philosophies can find even a small area of common intersection and moral consensus, seems to me to be one of the great significant facts of our

age. To explore that significance seems a task worthy of all our efforts.

Ronald Dworkin
(1931–   )

Philosophy and Politics [14]

In an interview with Bryan Magee, taped for the BBC in 1975–1977, Dworkin reviews the current state of political philosophy, particularly the contrasting positions of John Rawls and Robert Nozick. The selection is from his answer to Magee's request that he summarize his own view, as contained in *Taking Rights Seriously* (1977). His fundamental aim is

to contest the assumption that any of the conventional base liberties we call rights are in conflict with equality at any fundamental level. Individual rights, in my view, make most sense if we conceive them as necessary to any defensible theory of what equality requires. I want to change the terms of the orthodox debate by asking, about any claim of an individual right to liberty, not 'How much equality must we give up to respect this right adequately?' but rather 'Is this right necessary to protect equality?' I want to defend liberalism from the charge that it protects individuals at the cost of the welfare of those at the bottom of society. . . . I have tried to argue that economic equality and the familiar individual rights stem from the same fundamental conception of equality as independence, so that equality is the motor of liberalism, and every defence of liberalism is also a defence of equality.

[Magee asks:] But isn't the idea of individual rights opposed to another political ideal, namely the idea that political decisions should aim to serve not the special interests of particular individuals demanding their 'rights,' but the general good?

[Dworkin:] Yes, that is so, at least on the surface. Indeed, I think that the only clear and useful definition of what a right is uses this opposition between

[14] Ronald Dworkin and Bryan Magee, "Philosophy and Politics," in *Men of Ideas*, ed. Bryan Magee (New York: Viking, 1978), pp. 255–259.

rights and the general welfare. Someone has a right, in this strong and useful sense, when he is entitled to insist on doing something or having something even though the general welfare is harmed thereby. So someone has a genuine right to free speech only if he is entitled to speak his mind on political matters even when, for some reason, the average person in the community is made worse off when he does so. Rights, on this account, are trumps held by individuals over the general or average good. (This notion of what rights are may not be exactly in accordance with the ordinary usage of the word 'right,' which is inexact and lumps many different sorts of situations together under that one title. But the definition does show that, although Rawls does not use the word 'right' very much in his book, his basic liberties are in fact rights in the sense I am using, because the basic liberties have priority over improvements in the condition of the worst-off group, and *a fortiori* in the average welfare.) One virtue of this account of rights is that it shows that rights cannot be taken for granted, or simply taken as axiomatic, as Nozick takes his right to personal liberty and property to be. After all, if someone is entitled to insist on something even though others suffer more in welfare than he gains, then he is making a very strong claim that begs for a justification. If it really would threaten economic stability to permit an individual to criticize the Government whenever and wherever he wishes, and many people would then suffer, then it is not intuitively obvious that he is entitled to criticize it in that event. If we believe that he does have a right to speak freely even in that circumstance (which I do) then we must show why.

You might think that there are various strategies available. We might try to find some value that is different from and more important than the value of the general good, perhaps the value of individual self-development, or something of the kind. We might then say that since self-development is more important than the general welfare, and since freedom of speech even in situations in which the general welfare suffers is essential to self-development, individuals must have a right to free speech. That general strategy has in fact often been tried by people anxious to defend individual rights, but I do not think it can succeed. Self-development may be important, but if so then it is a value that *enters into* the calculation of the general welfare. If the general welfare would be advanced by forbidding

someone to speak in certain circumstances, then this must be because the damage to the welfare of other individuals, collectively, outweighs the loss in self-development of the person forbidden to speak. Perhaps the self-development of others is threatened if they lose jobs because of economic instability.

I argue for a very different strategy in defence of rights. I want to show, not that rights are necessary because of a fundamental value that is in opposition to the general welfare, but rather that the idea of rights and the idea of the general welfare are *both* rooted in the same more fundamental value. After all, just as it seems arbitrary to insist on rights as fundamental and axiomatic, it seems equally arbitrary to insist on the general welfare as of fundamental or axiomatic importance. It is frequently thought that the general welfare is of fundamental importance because pleasure (or happiness, or the satisfaction of desires or preferences) is a good in itself. Suppose a particular economic decision (like an incomes policy) will disadvantage some people but work to the long-term benefit of more people. Then, on this theory, it will produce more pleasure (or happiness) overall, after subtracting the pain caused to the few from the pleasure given to the many, than the opposite decision would produce. If pleasure is a good in itself, then it is better to have more rather than less of it overall, and that is why the general welfare, rather than benefit to particular individuals, is of decisive importance.

But this defence of the idea of the general welfare, though familiar, seems very weak. Isn't it absurd to suppose that pleasure (or happiness, or the satisfaction of desires) is a good in itself? Some of Rawls's best arguments are directed to showing that this idea is in fact as absurd as it seems. So if we really do think that the general welfare is an important consideration in political affairs, we must find a better explanation of why. I think we can find a better explanation in the idea of equality. If one decision would benefit a great many people to a certain degree and harm a few others to the same degree, and the governors of society choose the opposite decision, then they are showing favouritism to the few. The only way to treat all citizens as equals is to show the same concern for the fate of each; it follows that, all else being equal, a gain to many must be preferred over a gain to a few. Bentham (whose utilitarian philosophy provides the most dramatic defence of the idea of the general welfare) made this point himself. He said that the strategy of pursuing the general welfare counts each man as one and no one as more than one.

So the idea of the general welfare is in fact rooted in the more fundamental idea of equality. But (as I said earlier) that fundamental idea also supports the idea of individual rights as, under certain circumstances, trumps over the general welfare. The apparent opposition between rights and the general good, on which the definition I proposed relies, is just an opposition on the surface. The package of the two ideas—allowing the general welfare to be a good justification of political decisions in the normal case but providing individual rights as trumps over that justification in exceptional cases—serves equality better than simply allowing the general welfare to be the ultimate justification in all cases.

I cannot, in the space we have available, defend this claim in detail, but let me give some idea of how the defence would proceed. Take economic rights, for example, like the right to a decent standard of living in a society with enough total resources to provide that standard for everyone. Overall economic policy should aim at improving the average welfare. That means that if one economic policy would improve the condition of the community considered as a whole it should be chosen over another policy that would improve the condition of some smaller group more. So much is required by a general egalitarian attitude, because otherwise the claims of each member of the smaller class would have been preferred over the claims of each member of the larger, more inclusive community. But if some people, because of their special circumstances—because they are crippled, or lack talents prized in the market, or for some such reason—end up below the minimum standard of living required to lead a decent, self-fulfilling life *at all*, then the general egalitarian justification of the original choice has gone haywire in their case, and must be corrected by recognizing that they have a right to a minimum standard even if the general welfare is not as high as it would be by ignoring them. That is what it comes to, on this account, to claim an economic right for them.

The familiar political rights that form Rawls's basic liberties are also capable of an egalitarian justification. Parliamentary democracy is an egalitarian way of deciding what the criminal laws of a community, for example, shall be. The criminal laws are designed to protect the general welfare, and equality demands that each citizen have the same voice in determining what the shape of the general welfare is for this purpose. But suppose one citizen or one group is despised by the rest, for his race or his political convictions or his personal morality. In that case there is a danger that the rest will gang up on him and make criminal laws specifically aimed against him, not because the general welfare will really be improved in this way, but out of contempt and prejudice. Equality therefore demands that he have a right—perhaps embedded in a constitution, as such rights are in the United States—against the workings of the legislature. Even if the legislature *thinks* that it would improve the general welfare to prohibit someone from advocating a particular form of government, or from criticizing the economic policies of the present government, he has a right that it does not actually do so. Once again, that is an egalitarian constraint on the workings of a fundamentally egalitarian institution. This description is, as I said, not an argument, but only a general summary of the arguments I provide in the book you mentioned.

Lawrence C. Becker
(1939–   )

Individual Rights [15]

In a paper that ranges widely over the contemporary literature, Becker considers four issues that are crucial for a rights theory: the *place* of rights (that is, "their importance relative to other sorts of considerations"), the *definition* of various types of rights, the *justification* of rights, and the *scope* of rights. (The selection omits his treatment of scope.)

The Place of Rights

Moral arguments produce a bewildering array of claims and counter-claims. Amnesty International says that everyone has a right not to be tortured. The torturers say that the benefits they want

[15] "Individual Rights," in *And Justice for All*, ed. Tom Regan and Donald Van DeVeer (Totowa, N.J.: Rowman and Littlefield, 1982), pp. 197–216.

outweigh the costs to the victims, and that they (the torturers) have an obligation to carry out the orders of their superiors. But what kind of human being could do the things that Amnesty International describes? Could anyone you admire systematically, maliciously, and in cold blood administer crippling beatings day after day, electric shocks to the genitals, starvation diets, and the like? Not likely—because we have standards of character and conduct that we expect people to live up to no matter how serious the consequences. . . . And so it goes. Duties are pitted against desires, rights against consequences, ideals against practicality, social welfare against individual welfare, cost-benefit analysis against obligations.

Rights are just one of the many sorts of considerations that go into moral arguments. But rights have a special prominence in popular rhetoric, in political debate, in legal argument, and in moral philosophy. The most poignant claims of oppressed people are put in terms of rights to freedom and equality. Counterclaims from people in power are put in terms of rights to liberty and property. Pro- anti-abortion battles are waged over the right to life and a woman's right to control her body. All sorts of political action groups form around rights: civil rights, women's rights, prisoners' rights, children's rights, gay rights, the rights of the handicapped. The list is long and familiar.

What is not so familiar is the difficulty of getting a satisfactory account of the *place* of rights in moral arguments. Consider property rights. If I own some land, I have a bundle of rights with respect to it. But what rights? And how are they related to other important considerations? Suppose, due to a drought, my land now contains the only source of water for hundreds of miles. Do I have the right to withhold that water from my neighbors, or from travellers? Do I have the right to sell it at an exorbitant price? Do I have the right to sell it at all? Perhaps life-threatening emergencies override my rights. (Or perhaps those in need have rights to life that override my property rights.) And what about zoning? Suppose I want to develop my land, but my neighbors think a development would lessen the value of their own property, disturb their peace and quiet, and generally degrade the quality of their environment. Should I have the right, because I own the land, to do what I choose? Or should the interests, desires and welfare of my neighbors prevent me?

These questions illustrate the problem of establishing the proper place of rights in moral argument. Are rights the most important kind of moral considerations? Or just one of many? Do rights automatically take priority over everything else? Or must they always be balanced against other factors?

Here is an instructive conceit—instructive, that is, if you can study it with a straight face. The basic metaphor comes from the contemporary legal theorist Ronald Dworkin,[a] but he had the good taste not to elaborate it.

Think of a card game called Moral Argument. The cards—sometimes called "considerations" are divided into four suits: Rights, Consequences, Ideals, and Desires. (In real moral arguments, of course, the considerations are more numerous and divided somewhat differently. There is normally a place for Needs, for example, as well as for Duties, Social Goals, Social Welfare, and so on. But this is a simplified game.)

In this game, Rights is the most powerful suit, analogous to Spades in an ordinary deck of playing cards. Consequences, Ideals, and Desires follow in descending order.

Each suit is double, however. Each positive consideration—Ace, King, Queen, and so on—is matched by a negative one in the same suit. So there is a +10 of Desires, but also a −10. Each suit thus has 26 cards, and there are 104 in the full deck.

Moral Argument is a four-handed game. There is no bidding. The players merely "make arguments" (tricks) by laying down considerations (cards) in turn. The Dealer leads, and positive and negative considerations are played in turn. (If the Dealer plays a negative, West must play a positive, North must respond with a negative, and East ends the argument with a positive consideration.)

The object of the game is to take arguments (take tricks) by either nullifying or besting the considerations already on the table. You nullify a 3 with the other 3 of the same suit, for example. You best a 3 with a 4 or better of the same suit—or with a 3 or better of a more powerful suit. (Remember that the weakest suit is Desires, followed up the scale by Ideals, Consequences, and Rights.)

Here is a sample of play. Dealer leads with a small negative Desire—say a −4. West nullifies it with a +4 of the same suit. North bests both of those considerations with a −10 Ideal, and East takes the argument with a +10 Consequence. Simple game.

Now imagine that there are two radically different ways of playing Moral Argument. The standard "weak" game is the one I just described. It is played by most competitors. But certain hard-nosed tournament players favor a "strong" game in which one or more of the suits can be trump. And there are disputes about this, too. Hedonists make Desires trump. Utilitarians favor Consequences. And Intuitionists play a rather messy game in which any one of the suits—or none at all—may be trump depending on the circumstances in which the game is being played.

The toughest game of all is played by a few hardy Rights Theorists. (Detractors call this version Social Suicide.) In this game Rights are always trump. They take any argument constructed from considerations of Consequences, Ideals, and Desires. In such a game the following scenario is common: Dealer leads with a positive ideal—not a particularly high one, perhaps. Something like "Write good letters to your lover." West counters with a big negative desire: "I hate writing letters." North bests both of those with a big consequence: "What would the world be like if everyone were so selfish?" And then East takes the argument with the lowest right in the deck: "I don't have to if I don't want to." Not a game for the faint of heart.

The metaphor points to the problem of deciding how important rights are going to be in moral argument. And the different versions of the game correspond roughly to the various logical possibilities.

It is unlikely that anyone actually favors the strict "Rights are trump" rule, even though some writers occasionally speak as though they do. Dworkin says:

> Individual rights are political trumps . . . Individuals have rights, when, for some reason, a collective goal is not a sufficient justification for denying them what they wish.[b]

Harvard philosopher Robert Nozick opens his book this way:

Individuals have rights, and there are things no person or group may do to them (without violating their rights.) So strong and far-reaching are these rights that they raise the question of what, if anything, the state and its officials may do. How much room do individual rights leave for the state?[c]

Alan Gewirth, a philosopher at the University of Chicago, says:

> Whatever else may be demanded of moral rules and principles, they cannot be held to fulfill even their minimal point if they do not require that persons be protected in their rights . . .[d]

And Harvard law professor Charles Fried, says that "the violation of a right is always wrong."[e]

But in fact all of these writers would reject the view that just any right must be honored regardless of the consequences. If I have a right to the last bit of sugar in the vicinity (because I just bought it, though the shopkeeper has not yet handed it over), and it is suddenly needed to save the life of a diabetic who has collapsed on the floor next to me, does my right to the sugar trump her desperate need for it? No serious rights theorist would say so. Most acknowledge that rights can be overridden in emergencies—at least those rights that are not essential for one's health or survival. Furthermore, even basic rights may conflict to produce difficult cases. Nozick raises the case of the "innocent shield"—an innocent person used as a shield by an attacker. May you kill the shield to save your life?[f] It is unclear.

The fact is, however, that most rights are thought of as having built-in exceptions. John Locke, for example, in Chapter V of his *Second Treatise of Government*, argued that people were entitled to property rights in whatever they acquired through their labor—but only if they left as much and as good for others. Current discussions of Locke's "labor theory" of property rights agree that this

---

[b] *Ibid.*

[c] Robert Nozick, *Anarchy, State and Utopia* (New York, Basic Books, 1974), p. ix.
[d] Alan Gewirth, *Reason and Morality* (Chicago, University of Chicago Press, 1978).
[e] Charles Fried, *Right and Wrong* (Cambridge, Harvard U. Press, 1978), p. 108.
[f] Nozick, pp. 34–35.

qualification is necessary.[g] And yet another qualification is introduced by those who divide rights into strong or basic ones (such as rights to life and well-being) and weak or non-basic ones, and then hold that only the basic ones are trumps. Some of what Dworkin says can be understood this way.[h]

In any case, most rights theorists take a position roughly equivalent to the standard game—the game in which rights are merely the most powerful considerations in moral argument rather than trumps. The Ace of Rights beats any other Ace, but the 2 of Rights doesn't.

Alternatives. Even this position gets strong opposition, however. Some people want to think of rights simply as rules of thumb which place the burden of proof on anyone who wants to go against them.[i] Such a conception of rights amounts to this: If I want to do something and you don't want me to do it, so far we have a standoff. But if I have a right to do it, there is no standoff. Unless you come forward with a good argument against my plan, I may disregard your wishes and go ahead. On this view, rights amount to something more than ordinary moral considerations, but not very much more.

We leave rights theory altogether if we hold that rights are actually subordinate to other considerations. This corresponds to playing the Moral Argument game with Consequences, or Ideals, or even Desires on top. And if we play the "messy" version—letting intuitions decide when to treat Rights as trump and when to treat some other suit (or none) as trump, we have also abandoned rights theory.

The choice we make about the place of rights in moral argument is a crucial one. Our political system differs from Great Britain's on this issue. They do not have a bill of rights which is immune from repeal through the ordinary legislative process. We do. And the Western liberal democracies generally differ from revolutionary socialist regimes on the importance of individual rights. The philosophical basis for this important choice ultimately depends on the definitions of various types of rights, and on the sorts of justification we can give for them. [pp. 197–200]

Types of Rights

Getting a General Definition. . . . [R]ights have a few common elements which are important. One is that rights are more than just norms, or expectations, or standards of conduct. They are rules which define the boundaries of what is "owed" to a specified group of people (the right holders) by another group (the right respecters). . . .

This feature of rights accounts for two other general characteristics. One has to do with gratitude and indebtedness. When you respect my rights, you haven't done me a favor. I don't "owe" you anything for it—not even gratitude. (Though civility is not out of place.) . . . The other characteristic is that rights are supposed to be enforceable in a way that mere ideals or desires are not. If I simply want you to do something for me and you do not, that is too bad for me. Depending on the circumstance, it might not be good of you to refuse, but if all I have on my side is the fact that I want your help, I do not have any business twisting your arm for it. If I have a right to your help, however, and you refuse it, some sort of arm-twisting is presumably in order. I say some sort because of course the extent of it depends on the sort of right involved. If the right is a moral but not a legal one, verbal demands are frequently as far as one can go. But the general principle is important: If I have a right to it I can justifiably take steps to extract it from you if you fail to hand it over.

If rights are to be enforceable, however, they must be specific. They must indicate *who* has the right against whom, what the *content* of the right is, and what *kind of enforcement* is appropriate. Some claims of rights are criticized on just this ground. What could "Everyone has a right to an education" mean? If it means that everyone has a right to go to school, then we can readily understand how it could be enforced. If it means more than that (say, for example, that the state has a duty to see to it that everyone actually learns calculus), could it be enforced at all? If it cannot be enforced, is it really a "right"? . . .

So to summarize: Rights are rules that define what is owed to some (the right holders) by others. Rights

---

[g] See Nozick, pp. 178–182, and Lawrence C. Becker, *Property Rights: Philosophic Foundations* (Boston, Routledge, 1977) Chapter Four.

[h] Dworkin, p. 191.

[i] See R. G. Frey, *Rights and Interest* (Oxford, Oxford University Press, 1980).

may be demanded and enforced. They are therefore part of our system of permissions and requirements.

Beyond that, because rights are so various, there is not much else one can usefully say about their general nature. [p. 203]

The Justification of Rights

Even so, the common elements I have described are enough by themselves to pose special problems for justification. Rights are very stringent moral considerations—regardless of whether they are trumps. And if they are treated as trumps, the justification problem is even more difficult. There is no generally agreed upon general justification at present—not even a generally agreed upon strategy. What we have instead are some commonsense convictions buttressed with a variety of more or less unsatisfactory arguments.

The commonsense convictions are these: . . . Each one of us has an importance, a worth, a "dignity" that makes it wrong for others to abuse us or use us, against our will, without a very strong moral justification. We are justified in demanding such respect; it is owed to us. And if we don't get it, we are justified in using coercion to get it. In this sense at least we have rights—and they are "natural" rights because they are justified independently of any special agreement or contract we have made, or any special form of government we live under, or any special role or status we have in society. These "natural" rights include at least all the standard negative ones found in the criminal law of every country: e.g., rights to be free from murder, battery, assault, and so forth. Whether they also include other negative rights—such as the right not to give self-incriminating testimony—is a disputed point. Whether they include some positive rights as well—rights, say, to a decent standard of living— is also disputed.

What is not disputed—at the level of commonsense—is the conviction that we also have a welter of "conventional" rights—rights that come from government guarantees, contracts we have made, and special roles we occupy. The problem of justification is a double one: to examine the arguments for both natural and conventional rights.

The general strategies for a reasoned justification are fairly limited in number. I shall not consider, here, the various religious positions, and the relativ-

istic view that whatever is believed in a given society is "moral" for members of that society. I am only concerned here with the problem of whether we can construct a secular, reasoned justification for rights. The leading candidates are utilitarian, contractarian, rationalist, and intuitionist lines of argument. But I shall also discuss the possibility of deriving natural rights from the prior existence of conventional ones, and the possibility that being a "person" is by itself a sufficient condition for having rights.

The Utility of Rights. The most obvious approach to justification is to point out the usefulness, or "utility," of rights. . . . Crudely put, the principle would be: Figure out, in each case, what would produce the greatest good for the greatest number (i.e., what would maximize aggregate welfare), and then do it. This is called *act-utilitarianism*.

The problem is that in the real world we cannot operate that way. We not only don't have the time for such case-by-case analysis (sometimes decisions have to be made instantly), but we usually lack the information necessary for figuring out what all the consequences will be. On the other hand, we do know, from human history as a whole, that certain *kinds* of acts usually turn out to have more bad consequences than good ones. Murder, torture, rape, theft, and so on are examples. The obvious solution is to identify the sorts of acts that are usually bad on balance. Next, for each type of act, identify the unusual circumstances in which it is likely to be good (the murder of a Hitler, perhaps). Then write a rule about every type of act. Example: Thou shalt not murder (except for Hitler). The thought is that if we live by these rules, we will maximize welfare in the long run because we will make fewer errors than we would if we were to try to calculate the consequences in each case. If that is so, then everyone should live by the rules—even when the rules are onerous, inconvenient, costly, and seem to lead to bad rather than good consequences in a particular case. This is *rule-utilitarianism*.

The way rights get into this picture is that some of these utilitarian rules will impose duties on us— duties that correlate with claim-rights. Other rules will define liberties, and powers, and immunities. Some of these rules will apply only to special circumstances (in marriage, for example). They will define conventional rights. Others—the ones about murder, perhaps—will apply across the board and define "natural" rights. The strength of the rules—whether rights are trumps or not—will also depend on utility. Does it usually turn out for the best when a given right is treated as a trump? What about compensation? What about enforcement? The rule-utilitarian will calculate the consequences of all these factors for each right and work out a full definition of the right.

As a strategy for justifying rights, however, rule-utilitarianism has one glaring difficulty. (This is quite apart from the well-known general difficulties of utilitarianism: e.g., What reason do I have for maximizing aggregate welfare rather than merely my own? What is aggregate welfare? A total of some sort? An average? What is individual welfare and how is it measured? And so on.)

The problem is this: Every rule (defining a right) has exceptions. And exceptions are added to or subtracted from the rules on the basis of our experience with the consequences. So the rules are in flux. . . . All rules have the form "Do x—unless it would be better if you didn't"! Not much of a rule. And "the right not to be tortured unless it would be better (for social welfare) if you were," is not much of a right, either! This is just another way of playing Moral Argument with Consequences as trump. [pp. 203–205]

Rights as Part of the Social Contract. Social contract theory seems a promising alternative. Its controlling idea is agreement, and it uses agreement to solve the problems of political authority and justice. What gives government its authority? The consent of the governed, say social contract theorists. . . . [I]f people agree to a decision in advance, that decision is a fair one—a "just" one. . . .

So perhaps when it comes to deciding what the basic structure of society should be, we should use social agreement or consent as the test—rather than social utility. (After all, the parties to the social contract will probably do their best to calculate the consequences anyway, as the basis for deciding what to consent to.)

Problems arise immediately. An actual, explicit contract is out of the question as the basis for any large, ongoing society. Even if one could start from scratch and get all the adults to agree, what would be the justification for holding children, immigrants, and succeeding generations to the agreement? What

if they were to demand a renegotiation on the grounds that they were not part of the original process? If actual, explicit agreement is the test, won't every social contract have to be renegotiated for every new member? Further, actual consent is a slippery notion. There are the problems of tacit consent. (If I live quietly in a society, accepting the benefits of its laws, have I consented to them? Am I obligated to obey them?) And there are the problems of symbolic consent. (Do I have to take an oath, or can I just throw my hat in the air and shout for joy?)

Most serious of all, there are the problems of nonvoluntary and uninformed agreement. Consent can be manipulated. People who are ignorant of the consequences for themselves, or who are impulsive, or careless, or under pressure, often make bad bargains. And sometimes the options are so limited that the "agreement" is a farce. [p. 206]

Rationalistic Arguments. A strikingly different strategy is employed by people who attempt to derive rights from the nature of moral agency itself. A *moral agent* is someone who is capable of the sort of actions that we are willing to praise or blame, morally. An amoeba moves, but we don't blame it for what it does. Some humans also escape moral and legal responsibility for their actions—through diminished capacity or insanity. Why is this? What makes someone a moral agent?

A full answer to that question is a large task, but here we only have to pay attention to one important feature of moral agents: they are "rational"—at least in the very weak sense that they have a conception of what is good for them and strive to get it. Another way of saying this is to say that moral agents are purposive: their acts (at least some of them) are goal-directed. Never mind for the moment that agents have radically different goals, and that some agents are very active in pursuit of their goals while others are rather passive. Never mind that some agents are selfish while others are not. We are for the moment only concerned with this one "formal" or "contextual" feature of agency: purposiveness. What does it mean for rights?

Alan Gewirth has recently argued[j] that *every* moral agent is forced to claim, on pain of self-

[j] Gewirth, *Reason and Morality.*

contradiction, that *all* moral agents have equal rights to freedom and well-being. This conclusion does not say directly that moral agents "have" rights; it only says that they must claim that they do. But Gewirth says that much is enough.

In outline, his argument goes this way. First he notes that, by definition, agents regard their own purposes as good. Not necessarily as "morally good," but good enough to strive for. A consequence of this, Gewirth says, is that agents must regard the things necessary to purposive action *per se* as "necessary goods"—that is, as goods that they "must" have to carry out their purposes. These necessary goods are certain minimal levels of freedom and well-being.

The next step is to make the transition from necessary goods to rights. Every agent must make the following claim, as we have already seen: "My freedom and well-being are necessary goods." This claim is, Gewirth says, equivalent to "I must have freedom and well-being." And that claim is tantamount to claiming rights to freedom and well-being for oneself.

The final step is to show that because agents lay claim to rights for themselves on this basis, they are logically committed to holding that all other agents have the same rights. The reason is simple. Being a purposive agent is a sufficient condition for claiming rights in one's own case. It therefore follows that it must be a sufficient condition in every other similar case—that is, for every other purposive agent. Thus all moral agents—merely by virtue of their nature as rational, purposive creatures—must hold that all such agents have rights to freedom and well-being.

There are at least two problems with this approach, however. One is the proposition that the goods necessary for my purposive activity are "normatively necessary goods." The other is the contention that "my freedom and well-being are necessary goods" entails the assertion "I have rights to freedom and well-being." Gewirth has arguments for these moves, of course, and is aware of the objections to them, but some critics remain unconvinced. [pp. 207–208]

Rights and Persons. Less overtly rationalistic arguments about the relation between "personhood" and rights have also been offered. Their thought is that there must be something about simply being a person—some property of personhood—which generates rights. . . .[k]

These arguments begin with descriptions (sometimes value-loaded ones). Persons are sharply distinguished from "things." Persons think, feel, hope, care, plan, and strive. Persons do not just live; they have *lives*. Persons (even the worst of them) have a worth, a dignity, an intrinsic value which must be respected. Persons, simply by their nature, "have a claim" on our feelings and our conduct. To "use" persons as "things" is to *de*-personalize them—to deny the *fact* of their personhood. Besides: People—our handiest examples of personhood—actively demand our respect. In a very real sense, to fail to demand at least minimal respect is to fail to be a "fully human" individual. (Think of the kind of passivity, servility, and loss of self-esteem that we call "dehumanizing.") So isn't the recognition of human rights just a logical consequence of the recognition of someone as a person? (Note the similarity to Gewirth's general strategy.)

The problem, however, is again the connection between the "facts" about persons and the very special sort of moral consideration that rights are. No characteristic of persons—or combination of characteristics—seems sufficient to generate rights by itself. People make claims, but so what? They surely don't have rights to everything they claim. So which claims are valid ones? We need a separate argument—from utility, perhaps, or from contract, or from necessity a la Gewirth—to answer that question. Similarly for other properties of person. People have interests, projects, desires, feelings, fears, expectations, needs, and hopes. They have worth and dignity. But none of these things is sufficient to generate rights. My "worth" may entail that you should admire me, respect me, and value me. But how does it entail that I have a "right" of some sort against you? [p. 209]

Intuitionist Arguments. Yet rights remain a prominent feature of the moral landscape. People just do draw lines beyond which they will not go. They request, want, hope, strive, and negotiate, but they also demand, insist, and refuse. Whether these rebellion points and demand points are explicitly

[k] See Charles Fried, *Right and Wrong*, and (perhaps) A. I. Melden, *Rights and Persons* (Berkeley, U. of California Press, 1977).

expressed in the language of rights or not, they are equivalent to claims of right. . . .

Some theorists have decided to turn this situation to their advantage by treating rights as basic, or axiomatic features of morality. . . .[16] [p. 210]

. . . Arguments certainly must stop somewhere. But can rights possibly be such stopping places? Aren't there radical disagreements among moral agents about what rights people have? And don't those disagreements weaken the intuitionist position? . . .

People's intuitions on rights turn out to differ so much—on the details of negative rights and the very existence of positive ones—that intuitionism fares no better than the other justifications. This fact, combined with the difficulty of distinguishing intuitions on these matters from arbitrary cultural conditioning, makes intuitionistic arguments *for rights* very weak. [p. 211]

Carol Gilligan
(1936–   )

In a Different Voice [17]

Gilligan's critique aims not to remove the appeal to rights but to understand its isolating tendency and to seek an integrated pattern of self that involves both individualism and responsibility.

[W]omen not only define themselves in a context of human relationship but also judge themselves in terms of their ability to care. Women's place in man's life cycle has been that of nurturer, caretaker, and helpmate, the weaver of those networks of relationships on which she in turn relies. But while women have thus taken care of men, men have, in their theories of psychological development, as in their economic arrangements, tended to assume or devalue that care. When the focus on individua-

tion and individual achievement extends into adulthood and maturity is equated with personal autonomy, concern with relationships appears as a weakness of women rather than as a human strength.

. . . The repeated finding of . . . studies is that the qualities deemed necessary for adulthood—the capacity for autonomous thinking, clear decision-making, and responsible action—are those associated with masculinity and considered undesirable as attributes of the feminine self. The stereotypes suggest a splitting of love and work that relegates expressive capacities to women while placing instrumental abilities in the masculine domain. Yet looked at from a different perspective, these stereotypes reflect a conception of adulthood that is itself out of balance, favoring the separateness of the individual self over connection to others, and leaning more toward an autonomous life of work than toward the interdependence of love and care.

The discovery now being celebrated by men in mid-life of the importance of intimacy, relationships, and care is something that women have known from the beginning. . . . [P]sychologists have neglected to describe its development. In my research, I have found that women's moral development centers on the elaboration of that knowledge and thus delineates a critical line of psychological development in the lives of both of the sexes. The subject of moral development not only provides the final illustration of the reiterative pattern in the observation and assessment of sex differences in the literature of human development, but also indicates more particularly why the nature and significance of women's development has been for so long obscured and shrouded in mystery.

The criticism that Freud makes of women's sense of justice, seeing it as compromised in its refusal of blind impartiality, reappears not only in the work of Piaget but also in that of Kohlberg. . . .

Yet herein lies a paradox, for the very traits that traditionally have defined the "goodness" of women, their care for and sensitivity to the needs of others, are those that mark them as deficient in moral development. In this version of moral development, however, the conception of maturity is derived from the study of men's lives and reflects the importance of individuation in their development. . . .

When one begins with the study of women and

[16] For the arguments on axiomatic treatment of rights see Chapter 9.
[17] Carol Gilligan, *In a Different Voice: Psychological Theory and Women's Development* (Cambridge, Mass.: Harvard University Press, 1982).

derives developmental constructs from their lives, the outline of a moral conception different from that described by Freud, Piaget, or Kohlberg begins to emerge and informs a different description of development. In this conception, the moral problem arises from conflicting responsibilities rather than from competing rights and requires for its resolution a mode of thinking that is contextual and narrative rather than formal and abstract. This conception of morality as concerned with the activity of care centers moral development around the understanding of responsibility and relationships, just as the conception of morality as fairness ties moral development to the understanding of rights and rules. [pp. 17–19]

. . . [A] morality of rights and noninterference may appear frightening to women in its potential justification of indifference and unconcern. At the same time, it becomes clear why, from a male perspective, a morality of responsibility appears inconclusive and diffuse, given its insistent contextual relativism. Women's moral judgments thus elucidate the pattern observed in the description of the developmental differences between the sexes, but they also provide an alternative conception of maturity by which these differences can be assessed and their implications traced. The psychology of women that has consistently been described as distinctive in its greater orientation toward relationships and interdependence implies a more contextual mode of judgment and a different moral understanding. Given the differences in women's conceptions of self and morality, women bring to the life cycle a different point of view and order human experience in terms of different priorities. [p. 22]

. . . When assertion no longer seems dangerous, the concept of relationships changes from a bond of continuing dependence to a dynamic of interdependence. Then the notion of care expands from the paralyzing injunction not to hurt others to an injunction to act responsively toward self and others and thus to sustain connection. A consciousness of the dynamics of human relationships then becomes central to moral understanding, joining the heart and the eye in an ethic that ties the activity of thought to the activity of care.

Thus changes in women's rights change women's moral judgments, seasoning mercy with justice by enabling women to consider it moral to care not only for others but for themselves. The issue of inclusion first raised by the feminists in the public domain reverberates through the psychology of women as they begin to notice their own exclusion of themselves. When the concern with care extends from an injunction not to hurt others to an ideal of responsibility in social relationships, women begin to see their understanding of relationships as a source of moral strength. But the concept of rights also changes women's moral judgments by adding a second perspective to the consideration of moral problems, with the result that judgment becomes more tolerant and less absolute.

As selfishness and self-sacrifice become matters of interpretation and responsibilities live in tension with rights, moral truth is complicated by psychological truth, and the matter of judgment becomes more complex. [p. 149]

John Rawls
(1921–   )

A Theory of Justice [18]

The selection presents Rawls's initial sketch of the theory.

§ 3. *The Main Idea of the Theory of Justice*

My aim is to present a conception of justice which generalizes and carries to a higher level of abstraction the familiar theory of the social contract as found, say, in Locke, Rousseau, and Kant. In order to do this we are not to think of the original contract as one to enter a particular society or to set up a particular form of government. Rather, the guiding idea is that the principles of justice for the basic structure of society are the object of the original agreement. They are the principles that free and rational persons concerned to further their own interests would accept in an initial position of equality as defining the fundamental terms of their association. These principles are to regulate all further agreements; they specify the kinds of social cooperation that can be entered into and the forms of government that can be established. This way of

[18] From John Rawls, *A Theory of Justice* (Cambridge, Mass.: Harvard University Press, Belknap Press, 1971).

regarding the principles of justice I shall call justice as fairness.

Thus we are to imagine that those who engage in social cooperation choose together, in one joint act, the principles which are to assign basic rights and duties and to determine the division of social benefits. Men are to decide in advance how they are to regulate their claims against one another and what is to be the foundation charter of their society. Just as each person must decide by rational reflection what constitutes his good, that is, the system of ends which it is rational for him to pursue, so a group of persons must decide once and for all what is to count among them as just and unjust. The choice which rational men would make in this hypothetical situation of equal liberty, assuming for the present that this choice problem has a solution, determines the principles of justice.

In justice as fairness the original position of equality corresponds to the state of nature in the traditional theory of the social contract. This original position is not, of course, thought of as an actual historical state of affairs, much less as a primitive condition of culture. It is understood as a purely hypothetical situation characterized so as to lead to a certain conception of justice. Among the essential features of this situation is that no one knows his place in society, his class position or social status, nor does any one know his fortune in the distribution of natural assets and abilities, his intelligence, strength, and the like. I shall even assume that the parties do not know their conceptions of the good or their special psychological propensities. The principles of justice are chosen behind a veil of ignorance. This ensures that no one is advantaged or disadvantaged in the choice of principles by the outcome of natural chance or the contingency of social circumstances. Since all are similarly situated and no one is able to design principles to favor his particular condition, the principles of justice are the result of a fair agreement or bargain. For given the circumstances of the original position, the symmetry of everyone's relations to each other, this initial situation is fair between individuals as moral persons, that is, as rational beings with their own ends and capable, I shall assume, of a sense of justice. The original position is, one might say, the appropriate initial status quo, and thus the fundamental agreements reached in it are fair. This explains the propriety of the name "justice as fairness": it conveys the idea that the principles of justice are agreed to in an initial situation that is fair. The name does not mean that the concepts of justice and fairness are the same, any more than the phrase "poetry as metaphor" means that the concepts of poetry and metaphor are the same.

Justice as fairness begins, as I have said, with one of the most general of all choices which persons might make together, namely, with the choice of the first principles of a conception of justice which is to regulate all subsequent criticism and reform of institutions. Then, having chosen a conception of justice, we can suppose that they are to choose a constitution and a legislature to enact laws, and so on, all in accordance with the principles of justice initially agreed upon. Our social situation is just if it is such that by this sequence of hypothetical agreements we would have contracted into the general system of rules which defines it. Moreover, assuming that the original position does determine a set of principles (that is, that a particular conception of justice would be chosen), it will then be true that whenever social institutions satisfy these principles those engaged in them can say to one another that they are cooperating on terms to which they would agree if they were free and equal persons whose relations with respect to one another were fair. They could all view their arrangements as meeting the stipulations which they would acknowledge in an initial situation that embodies widely accepted and reasonable constraints on the choice of principles. The general recognition of this fact would provide the basis for a public acceptance of the corresponding principles of justice. No society can, of course, be a scheme of cooperation which men enter voluntarily in a literal sense; each person finds himself placed at birth in some particular position in some particular society, and the nature of this position materially affects his life prospects. Yet a society satisfying the principles of justice as fairness comes as close as a society can to being a voluntary scheme, for it meets the principles which free and equal persons would assent to under circumstances that are fair. In this sense its members are autonomous and the obligations they recognize self-imposed.

One feature of justice as fairness is to think of the parties in the initial situation as rational and mutually disinterested. This does not mean that the parties are egoists, that is, individuals with only certain kinds of interests, say in wealth, prestige, and domination. But they are conceived as not taking an interest in one another's interests. They are to presume that even their spiritual aims may be opposed, in the way that the aims of those of different religions may be opposed. Moreover, the concept of rationality must be interpreted as far as possible in the narrow sense, standard in economic theory, of taking the most effective means to given ends. I shall modify this concept to some extent, as explained later (§ 25),[1] but one must try to avoid introducing into it any controversial ethical elements. The initial situation must be characterized by stipulations that are widely accepted.

In working out the conception of justice as fairness one main task clearly is to determine which principles of justice would be chosen in the original position. To do this we must describe this situation in some detail and formulate with care the problem of choice which it presents. These matters I shall take up in the immediately succeeding chapters. It may be observed, however, that once the principles of justice are thought of as arising from an original agreement in a situation of equality, it is an open question whether the principle of utility would be acknowledged. Offhand it hardly seems likely that persons who view themselves as equals, entitled to press their claims upon one another, would agree to a principle which may require lesser life prospects for some simply for the sake of a greater sum of advantages enjoyed by others. Since each desires to protect his interests, his capacity to advance his conception of the good, no one has a reason to acquiesce in an enduring loss for himself in order to bring about a greater net balance of satisfaction. In the absence of strong and lasting benevolent impulses, a rational man would not accept a basic

structure merely because it maximized the algebraic sum of advantages irrespective of its permanent effects on his own basic rights and interests. Thus it seems that the principle of utility is incompatible with the conception of social cooperation among equals for mutual advantage. It appears to be inconsistent with the idea of reciprocity implicit in the notion of a well-ordered society. Or, at any rate, so I shall argue.

I shall maintain instead that the persons in the initial situation would choose two rather different principles: the first requires equality in the assignment of basic rights and duties, while the second holds that social and economic inequalities, for example inequalities of wealth and authority, are just only if they result in compensating benefits for everyone, and in particular for the least advantaged members of society. These principles rule out justifying institutions on the grounds that the hardships of some are offset by a greater good in the aggregate. It may be expedient but it is not just that some should have less in order that others may prosper. But there is no injustice in the greater benefits earned by a few provided that the situation of persons not so fortunate is thereby improved. The intuitive idea is that since everyone's well-being depends upon a scheme of cooperation without which no one could have a satisfactory life, the division of advantages should be such as to draw forth the willing cooperation of everyone taking part in it, including those less well situated. Yet this can be expected only if reasonable terms are proposed. The two principles mentioned seem to be a fair agreement on the basis of which those better endowed, or more fortunate in their social position, neither of which we can be said to deserve, could expect the willing cooperation of others when some workable scheme is a necessary condition of the welfare of all. Once we decide to look for a conception of justice that nullifies the accidents of natural endowment and the contingencies of social circumstance as counters in quest for social and political advantage, we are led to these principles. They express the result of leaving aside those aspects of the social world that seem arbitrary from a moral point of view.

The problem of the choice of principles, however, is extremely difficult. I do not expect the answer I shall suggest to be convincing to everyone. It is, therefore, worth noting from the outset that justice as fairness, like other contract views, consists of

---

[1] § 25. The concept of rationality invoked here, with the exception of one essential feature, is the standard one familiar in social theory. Thus in the usual way, a rational person is thought to have a coherent set of preferences between the options open to him. He ranks these options according to how well they further his purposes; he follows the plan which will satisfy more of his desires rather than less, and which has the greater chance of being successfully executed. The special assumption I make is that a rational individual does not suffer from envy. He is not ready to accept a loss for himself if only others have less as well. He is not downcast by the knowledge or perception that others have a larger index of primary social goods. Or at least this is true as long as the differences between himself and others do not exceed certain limits, and he does not believe that the existing inequalities are founded on injustice or are the result of letting chance work itself out for no compensating social purpose. [p. 143]

two parts: (1) an interpretation of the initial situation and of the problem of choice posed there, and (2) a set of principles which, it is argued, would be agreed to. One may accept the first part of the theory (or some variant thereof), but not the other, and conversely. The concept of the initial contractual situation may seem reasonable although the particular principles proposed are rejected. To be sure, I want to maintain that the most appropriate conception of this situation does lead to principles of justice contrary to utilitarianism and perfectionism, and therefore that the contract doctrine provides an alternative to these views. Still, one may dispute this contention even though one grants that the contractarian method is a useful way of studying ethical theories and of setting forth their underlying assumptions.

Justice as fairness is an example of what I have called a contract theory. Now there may be an objection to the term "contract" and related expressions, but I think it will serve reasonably well. Many words have misleading connotations which at first are likely to confuse. The terms "utility" and "utilitarianism" are surely no exception. They too have unfortunate suggestions which hostile critics have been willing to exploit; yet they are clear enough for those prepared to study utilitarian doctrine. The same should be true of the term "contract" applied to moral theories. As I have mentioned, to understand it one has to keep in mind that it implies a certain level of abstraction. In particular, the content of the relevant agreement is not to enter a given society or to adopt a given form of government, but to accept certain moral principles. Moreover, the undertakings referred to are purely hypothetical: a contract view holds that certain principles would be accepted in a well-defined initial situation.

The merit of the contract terminology is that it conveys the idea that principles of justice may be conceived as principles that would be chosen by rational persons, and that in this way conceptions of justice may be explained and justified. The theory of justice is a part, perhaps the most significant part, of the theory of rational choice. Furthermore, principles of justice deal with conflicting claims upon the advantages won by social cooperation; they apply to the relations among several persons or groups. The word "contract" suggests this plurality as well as the condition that the appropriate division of advantages must be in accordance with principles acceptable to all parties. The condition

of publicity for principles of justice is also connoted by the contract phraseology. Thus, if these principles are the outcome of an agreement, citizens have a knowledge of the principles that others follow. It is characteristic of contract theories to stress the public nature of political principles. Finally there is the long tradition of the contract doctrine. Expressing the tie with this line of thought helps to define ideas and accords with natural piety. There are then several advantages in the use of the term "contract." With due precautions taken, it should not be misleading.

A final remark. Justice as fairness is not a complete contract theory. For it is clear that the contractarian idea can be extended to the choice of more or less an entire ethical system, that is, to a system including principles for all the virtues and not only for justice. Now for the most part I shall consider only principles of justice and others closely related to them; I make no attempt to discuss the virtues in a systematic way. Obviously if justice as fairness succeeds reasonably well, a next step would be to study the more general view suggested by the name "rightness as fairness." But even this wider theory fails to embrace all moral relationships, since it would seem to include only our relations with other persons and to leave out of account how we are to conduct ourselves toward animals and the rest of nature. I do not contend that the contract notion offers a way to approach these questions which are certainly of the first importance; and I shall have to put them aside. We must recognize the limited scope of justice as fairness and of the general type of view that it exemplifies. How far its conclusions must be revised once these other matters are understood cannot be decided in advance. [pp. 11–17]

§ 11. Two Principles of Justice

I shall now state in a provisional form the two principles of justice that I believe would be chosen in the original position. In this section I wish to make only the most general comments, and therefore the first formulation of these principles is tentative. As we go on I shall run through several formulations and approximate step by step the final statement to be given much later. I believe that doing this allows the exposition to proceed in a natural way.

The first statement of the two principles reads as follows:

First: each person is to have an equal right to the most extensive basic liberty compatible with a similar liberty for others.

Second: social and economic inequalities are to be arranged so that they are both (a) reasonably expected to be to everyone's advantage, and (b) attached to positions and offices open to all.

There are two ambiguous phrases in the second principle, namely "everyone's advantage" and "open to all." Determining their sense more exactly will lead to a second formulation of the principle in § 13. The final version of the two principles is given in § 46. . . .[2]

[2] § 46. *First Principle*

Each person is to have an equal right to the most extensive total system of equal basic liberties compatible with a similar system of liberty for all.

Second Principle

Social and economic inequalities are to be arranged so that they are both:

(a)   to the greatest benefit of the least advantaged, consistent with the just savings principle, and
(b)   attached to offices and positions open to all under conditions of fair equality of opportunity.

First Priority Rule (The Priority of Liberty)

The principles of justice are to be ranked in lexical order and therefore liberty can be restricted only for the sake of liberty.

There are two cases:

(a)   a less extensive liberty must strengthen the total system of liberty shared by all;
(b)   a less than equal liberty must be acceptable to those with the lesser liberty.

Second Priority Rule (The Priority of Justice over Efficiency and Welfare)

The second principle of justice is lexically prior to the principle of efficiency and to that of maximizing the sum of advantages; and fair opportunity is prior to the difference principle. There are two cases:

(a)   an inequality of opportunity must enhance the opportunities of those with the lesser opportunities.
(b)   an excessive rate of saving must on balance mitigate the burden of those bearing this hardship.

General Conception

All social primary goods—liberty and opportunity, income and wealth, and the bases of self-respect—are to be distributed equally unless an unequal distribution of any or all of these goods is to the advantage of the least favored. [pp. 302–303]

By way of general comment, these principles primarily apply, as I have said, to the basic structure of society. They are to govern the assignment of rights and duties and to regulate the distribution of social and economic advantages. As their formulation suggests, these principles presuppose that the social structure can be divided into two more or less distinct parts, the first principle applying to the one, the second to the other. They distinguish between those aspects of the social system that define and secure the equal liberties of citizenship and those that specify and establish social and economic inequalities. The basic liberties of citizens are, roughly speaking, political liberty (the right to vote and to be eligible for public office) together with freedom of speech and assembly; liberty of conscience and freedom of thought; freedom of the person along with the right to hold (personal) property; and freedom from arbitrary arrest and seizure as defined by the concept of the rule of law. These liberties are all required to be equal by the first principle, since citizens of a just society are to have the same basic rights.

The second principle applies, in the first approximation, to the distribution of income and wealth and to the design of organizations that make use of differences in authority and responsibility, or chains of command. While the distribution of wealth and income need not be equal, it must be to everyone's advantage, and at the same time, positions of authority and offices of command must be accessible to all. One applies the second principle by holding positions open, and then, subject to this constraint, arranges social and economic inequalities so that everyone benefits.

These principles are to be arranged in a serial order with the first principle prior to the second. This ordering means that a departure from the institutions of equal liberty required by the first principle cannot be justified by, or compensated for, by greater social and economic advantages. The distribution of wealth and income, and the hierarchies of authority, must be consistent with both the liberties of equal citizenship and equality of opportunity.

It is clear that these principles are rather specific in their content, and their acceptance rests on certain assumptions that I must eventually try to explain and justify. A theory of justice depends upon a theory of society in ways that will become evident as we proceed. For the present, it should be observed that the two principles (and this holds for all formulations) are a special case of a more general conception of justice that can be expressed as follows.

> All social values—liberty and opportunity, income and wealth, and the bases of self-respect—are to be distributed equally unless an unequal distribution of any, or all, of these values is to everyone's advantage.

Injustice, then, is simply inequalities that are not to the benefit of all. Of course, this conception is extremely vague and requires interpretation.

As a first step, suppose that the basic structure of society distributes certain primary goods, that is, things that every rational man is presumed to want. These goods normally have a use whatever a person's rational plan of life. For simplicity, assume that the chief primary goods at the disposition of society are rights and liberties, powers and opportunities, income and wealth. (Later on in Part Three the primary good of self-respect has a central place.) These are the social primary goods. Other primary goods such as health and vigor, intelligence and imagination, are natural goods; although their possession is influenced by the basic structure, they are not so directly under its control. Imagine, then, a hypothetical initial arrangement in which all the social primary goods are equally distributed: everyone has similar rights and duties, and income and wealth are evenly shared. This state of affairs provides a benchmark for judging improvements. If certain inequalities of wealth and organizational powers would make everyone better off than in this hypothetical starting situation, then they accord with the general conception.

Now it is possible, at least theoretically, that by giving up some of their fundamental liberties men are sufficiently compensated by the resulting social and economic gains. The general conception of justice imposes no restrictions on what sort of inequalities are permissible; it only requires that everyone's position be improved. We need not suppose anything so drastic as consenting to a condition of slavery. Imagine instead that men forego certain political rights when the economic returns are significant and their capacity to influence the course of policy by the exercise of these rights would be marginal in any case. It is this kind of exchange which the two principles as stated rule out; being arranged in serial order they do not permit exchanges between basic liberties and economic and social gains. The serial ordering of principles expresses an underlying preference among primary social goods. When this preference is rational so likewise is the choice of these principles in this order. [pp. 60–63]

Now the second principle insists that each person benefit from permissible inequalities in the basic structure. This means that it must be reasonable for each relevant representative man defined by this structure, when he views it as a going concern, to prefer his prospects with the inequality to his prospects without it. One is not allowed to justify differences in income or organizational powers on the ground that the disadvantages of those in one position are outweighed by the greater advantages of those in another. Much less can infringements of liberty be counterbalanced in this way. Applied to the basic structure, the principle of utility would have us maximize the sum of expectations of representative men (weighted by the number of persons they represent, on the classical view); and this would permit us to compensate for the losses of some by the gains of others. Instead, the two principles require that everyone benefit from economic and social inequalities. It is obvious, however, that there are indefinitely many ways in which all may be advantaged when the initial arrangement of equality is taken as a benchmark. How then are we to choose among these possibilities? The principles must be specified so that they yield a determinate conclusion. I now turn to this problem. [pp. 64–65]

David Braybrooke
(1924–   )

Three Tests for Democracy [19]

Braybrooke argues that a society is democratic to the extent that it respects personal rights, promotes human welfare, and reflects in its policies and government the collective preferences of its people. Part Two, "Human

[19] David Braybrooke, *Three Tests for Democracy: Personal Rights, Human Welfare, Collective Preference* (New York: Random House, 1968).

Welfare," considers the second test and analyzes the concept of welfare by contrasting it first with the notion of rights and then with the notion of preferences.

1: Welfare Distinguished from Rights

1.1 Logically Distinct Considerations. The considerations raised by the concepts of rights and of welfare are distinct logically. Moreover, in practice—the practice of evaluating policies and governments—they demand separate attention, because they are not constantly associated even as empirical matters. Yet the two subjects are connected in so many ways, both in fact and in supposition, that the difference between them needs to be insisted upon.

Welfare is a very broad concept. It may be held to include moral welfare as well as material welfare (though material welfare is basic); and moral welfare has something to do with rights. A person could not be said to be looking out for the moral welfare of a child if he did not observe the child's rights; inform the child of them as need be; teach the child to respect the rights of others.

These rights, again—both the child's and other people's—might be considered devices for protecting welfare; they may even have been deliberately designed to function as such devices. But if this is true—if rights are devices for protecting people's welfare—then a government's respect for rights will be a test of its effective concern for welfare. Rights might in fact be the only devices steadily operating on behalf of welfare. They might cover between them, furthermore, all the provisions for welfare yet thought of. Property, livelihood, education, the use of public facilities, health, even companionship might all be subjects wholly regulated by particular rights. To a considerable extent they already are. In what sense, then, are rights and welfare distinct considerations?

A beginning toward seeing them as distinct considerations may be made by recalling that non-democrats (like King John's unruly barons) may be champions of rights; yet be interested, more or less frankly, only in their own welfare, as provided for by these rights and otherwise. The rights of some people—the barons—may not at all entail, or even aim at, the welfare of other people—the people who do not happen to be barons.

Just as clearly, the welfare of one and the same set of people is a consideration distinct from their rights. For those rights—a particular assortment of particular social devices—may not suffice at all to protect their welfare. The rights of the villeins against the barons, one imagines, did not suffice (though those rights existed). The barons' own rights may not have sufficed even for barons. They may, for example, have frustrated economic innovations from which the barons would have benefited; and without these innovations the barons may have done rather poorly.

Welfare and rights are logically such different subjects that the one may be invoked while the other (without inconsistency) is disregarded. Marxist writers concern themselves with human welfare, but avoid endorsing rights for fear of compromising themselves with bourgeois ideology. One can imagine a society maintaining comprehensive provisions for human welfare without anyone ever invoking or discussing personal rights. If the provisions fail in any particular, the questions raised would be questions about efficiency; or about the adequacy of the provisions, considered as comprehensive plans.

On the other hand, people may champion rights without being interested in welfare at all, even (it may appear) their own. If they have any reasons purporting to justify the rights they champion, these reasons may be theological ones. They may say, for example, that God has imposed a system of rights and duties on men, and done so for His own good reasons, which men may speculate about, but must respect however obscure they may be. [pp. 87–89]

1.2. Welfare as an Argument for Rights. . . . Some utilitarians believe that welfare reduces to happiness and happiness to pleasure; and some of these, at least in the past, have believed that the happiness of groups of people can be measured by a felicific, that is to say, hedonistic calculus. Other utilitarians do not believe either of these things; they accept the ingredients of welfare as maybe irreducibly diverse. For them (and, I think, in ordinary language generally) welfare functions as a convoy concept, within which a number of particular considerations float on their own bottoms and can be separately observed to keep up with the rest or lag behind. Among these considerations, the ingredients of welfare, figure food; safety; clothing; shelter; medical care; education; congenial employment; companionship. One can treat happiness as another particular ingredient of welfare, to be added to the convoy; or recognize that all the other ingredients mentioned contribute to making happiness possible, though happiness itself (unlike the other considerations) is rarely a direct object of social policy. [p. 92]

2: Evidence for Welfare Shaped by Census-Notion

2.2. Conflicts Between Census Topics. People who frankly accept the concept of welfare as a convoy concept . . . must face the . . . complication that these considerations sometimes conflict. Policies better as regards the supply of food may be worse, for example, as regards education or congenial employment. These different ingredients of welfare may then require to be weighed against one another. [p. 111]

There is a temptation in this subject to try for general solutions in advance of particular conflicts. Certainly it must be granted that it would be much tidier and more convenient to have the means for a general solution. Bentham was trying for such a means when he projected the felicific calculus. A calculus might serve if the different aspects of welfare could be systematically reduced in advance to a unique basis (like pleasure). The difficulty is that the concept of welfare, as we now understand it, does not have such a basis. Though there is no need to exaggerate the amount of possible conflict that the concept in its present condition is liable to generate, it is a fact that the particular aspects of welfare are not exhaustively enumerable. There is no standard list, but rather a great number of partly overlapping terms, which are subject to increase. Furthermore, the aspects are not so well coordinated that an exhaustive system of priorities, which would rule out any conflicts, can be discovered by analysis. To provide such a system of priorities by stipulation would beg particular policy questions, which the concept as it stands leaves open.

The present concept of welfare is in fact set up so as to leave particular conflicts to be settled in particular circumstances. It is in this respect (in contrast to the concept of rights) designedly *ad hoc* and advantageously so. To understand the concept, one must resist the natural desire for a tidy general solution. One must also resist what in this case leads to the same thing, the characteristic ambition of

philosophical analysis to give complete analyses, which indicate in advance the truth-conditions for every application of the concepts analyzed. The concept of welfare turns out to be a sort of concept that does not admit of complete analysis in this sense. For the analysis to be complete, one would have to state in advance how all the particular considerations bearing upon the truth-conditions for the use of "welfare" are related, to the point of saying what follows for the affirmation or denial of general statements claiming improvements in welfare. Now, the various ingredients of welfare certainly form considerations bearing upon the truth-conditions for the use of the concept. But the coordination of these ingredients (e.g., of safety and morale) is left to particular circumstances (where, e.g., a relatively big improvement in morale may warrant some reduction in safety—or vice versa).

2.3. A New Assessment of Utilitarianism. These remarks have some significance for the assessment of utilitarianism—the misnamed ethics of human welfare. Controversies about utilitarianism have frequently revolved about the question whether happiness or pleasure (as reckoned by the felicific calculus, or by some other means) could be the sole ultimate criterion for good or evil. Many counterutilitarian arguments have taken the line that whether or not the calculus could be carried out, happiness could not be the sole criterion, because there were a number of other valuable things contributing to human well-being that might conflict with happiness or at least be desired in addition to it.

These arguments have succeeded far enough to make it a sensible precaution for utilitarianism to acknowledge the weight of the other considerations, even while their relation to happiness remains uncertain. But on neither side of the controversy have philosophers given much attention to the problem of how any of these considerations, happiness or the others in the convoy, apply in the absence of a calculus. It can hardly be maintained that these considerations do not get attention in practice; evidence about them provides familiar occasions for debate and investigation. In philosophy, too, their application has often been called for; yet a mystery has been left standing as to how their application is to be carried out.

The counterutilitarian arguments mentioned have the further defect of being slightly beside the point. Bentham's commitment to the project of the felicific calculus and the terms in which he concentrated attention on happiness as a matter to be reduced to algebraic sums of pleasures and pains warrant attack. But deeper attention to the topics being agitated would show that even for his own purposes it was a mistake for Bentham to concentrate upon happiness—just as it was a mistake for him to rely on the idea of the calculus. Bentham's practical purposes in policy-making—and the chief part of his purposes in ethical theory, where he was above all concerned to knock out judgments opposed to human welfare and happiness—could have been accomplished without using a supposedly comprehensive and completely analyzed standard, entirely fixed in advance. A convoy concept, under which happiness sailed together with a number of other considerations, would have served him better. [pp. 112–115]

3: Welfare Distinguished from Preferences

3.1. Conflation of Welfare with Preferences. A number of impressive lines of reasoning converge in support of conflating the subject of welfare with the subject of preferences. Some of them arise outside economic theory to reinforce those that arise within.

Among the considerations arising outside economic theory are these: It is certainly true that the happiness or welfare of any sane, normal adult will be diminished if he is not allowed to follow his own preferences in many matters. There are, in other words, some ingredients of welfare (taking welfare as a convoy concept) which depend upon the expression and satisfaction of preferences.

This scope for preferences—for freedom of choice—has compelling moral attractions of yet another order: for we think that the dignity of human persons requires respect for such freedom, and requires its exercise, too. (Otherwise a species of satisfaction that was obtained through drugs or through the electrical stimulation of the brain might suffice morally as a substitute for happiness.) Again, there is a famous thesis in philosophy—the thesis of Socrates that virtue is knowledge—which correctly reminds us of difficulties in conceiving of a person failing to choose what he firmly knows to be best for him and—perhaps not so correctly—encourages us to believe that given suitable information people can be counted on to make the right choices.

We might wonder, will right for them be right for all; but the present presupposition would be

that in the market we are dealing not with controversies about what is morally right, but with the pursuit of happiness, given that a necessary minimum set of moral rules have been accepted and satisfied. We might wonder also whether the participants in the market do in fact have sufficient information to choose what is best for them; and this doubt cannot be easily laid to rest. The strongest answer that can be maintained at this point seems to be the hypothesis that imperfect as their information may be, individual participants do have some advantages in information over people other than themselves; and that these advantages can neither be compensated for nor realized through institutions other than the market. [pp. 122–123]

At bottom, welfare includes many matters, evidence as to which may run contrary to evidence as to the accommodation of preferences: food; safety; clothing; shelter; medical care; education; congenial employment; companionship. When evidence on these matters does conflict with evidence about preferences, evidence about preferences will be superseded, for it has at most a presumptive claim to being evidence about welfare. An economy in which a single rich maharajah held sway over millions of half-starved untouchables might have arrived at a Pareto optimum, so long as the maharajah did not care to change. But assuming that a redistribution of income could be carried out without the economy collapsing, it would have to be said that the economy was very far from doing as much as it could for the welfare of the people involved. Now, not only the peculiarly irrelevant stand of the Pareto welfare criterion would be overborne by the evidence in such a case (as would the felicific calculus as commonly understood). Even if the millions of half-starved untouchables sincerely expressed themselves as preferring a state of affairs that contributed so much to the comfort of the maharajah and so little to their own necessities, it would have to be said, again in the ordinary sense of "welfare," that their preferences notwithstanding, their welfare was not being served.

Economists working with the Pareto criterion do not mean to deny that welfare in the ordinary sense may not be served when the criterion is satisfied. They would point out that in adopting the Pareto criterion they were deliberately abstracting from the distribution of property and income. (They are not quite so clear or frank about departing from the ordinary sense of "welfare," perhaps because they have forgotten that even if everyone's preferences were attended to, the observed results might not promote welfare.)

Deliberately it may have been; but deliberately does not excuse them. For any contention about welfare that they put forward using the Pareto criterion demands qualification—in big capital letters—to the effect that the distribution of property and income has not been questioned. To be sure of preventing misunderstanding, the qualification should really extend to explaining how crucial an omission this is. If accommodating preferences is to be taken as tantamount to promoting welfare, then at the very least one might expect it to be stipulated that everyone's preferences are to be counted fairly—which means, either equally as between persons, or unequally only in ways consistent with variations in deservingness. Evidence about welfare must be consistent with elementary considerations of social justice; otherwise it cannot be accepted, as in the ordinary sense of "welfare" it is bound to be accepted, as favoring an action, policy, or government. [pp. 129–130]

3.3 Influence of Preferences on the Concept of Welfare. The subject of preferences must be distinguished emphatically from the subject of human welfare. Yet it cannot be denied that the very meaning of the concept of welfare, as well as its application to the evaluation of policies and government, depends in various ways on preferences. What is congenial employment if it is not somehow consistent with a man's preferences? Yet people may seek employment or companionship on terms that reflect their preferences but do not in fact offer any objective prospect of satisfying their aims. They may not know what employment they will in the end find congenial, or what sort of company they will find companionable. On the other hand, they may in fact be satisfied with employment or with a species of companionship that fall far short of what could be provided for them. The fact that a man, lacking in experience or imagination, is satisfied with extraordinarily long hours and primitive conditions of work, or with having a few people to speak to daily who remember his name, does not imply that his welfare is being looked after. Preferences do not imply satisfaction; satisfaction does not imply welfare.

Logically, therefore, occasions may appear on which governments can promote welfare only if

they override preferences; and in fact some social policies generally approved of by advocates of democracy aim at providing for people's welfare in spite of people's preferences to the contrary. Sometimes the people whose welfare will be provided for are the same people as those whose preferences will be overridden. At the very least, a democrat might want proof in such cases that the preferences of the people affected will change in favor of the policies after the consequences of these have been felt. But overriding people's preferences on the pretext of providing for their welfare can excuse all sorts of tyrannies, gross and petty. It is so dangerous to liberty and so objectionable to anyone who cherishes liberty that even a proof of the kind mentioned will seldom suffice. Generally speaking, once the difference between welfare and preferences has been made clear, advocates of democracy might well be inclined to respect preferences even when the preferences run counter to the evidence of welfare—as regards the same people. The scruples associated with the Pareto criterion are in this connection democratic scruples. However, even democrats ordinarily very scrupulous about attending to people's preferences do not always insist upon this condition. They do not insist upon it, for example, in the case of children, or in provisions for the insane. They will not tolerate a child's growing up entirely without benefit of schooling; they will have madmen restrained from cutting themselves up with knives.

Moreover, it is quite a different matter (though still so repugnant as to be avoided when it is morally possible to avoid doing so) to proceed against people's preferences when these run counter to other people's welfare. Social policies are frequently undertaken by modern governments, and approved by advocates of democracy evaluating those governments, which aim at providing for some people's welfare regardless of other people's preferences. The people opposed now, because the policies will reduce their comforts or undermine their status, may be expected to continue opposed. They may even become embittered opponents, with stronger preferences to the contrary, after the policies have been carried out. Their preferences will nonetheless not be given as much weight under most modern governments as considerations of welfare, at any rate when these are urgent. If a progressive income tax turns out to be a necessary means to financing a program for reducing infant mortality among the poor, then (other things being equal) the concept of welfare, as it is actually used to evaluate governments and policies, motivates the adoption of a progressive income tax. [pp. 133–136]

3.4. The Definition of Human Welfare. How much has the preceding discussion accomplished toward the definition of "human welfare"? The discussion did not begin with a definition, and it would have been unnecessarily restrictive to require one at the beginning. Very often, a philosophical discussion must search for a definition that no one knows how to produce straight off. . . .

Welfare, according to the results achieved in this discussion, is something different from rights; and also something different from preferences. Like either of these concepts, the concept of welfare may be used in a perfectionist way, with a stringent individualism ready to condemn a government or policy as soon as one case of deficiency is discovered. But it is most often used on the assumption that the issue in hand requires a comparative judgment of different governments or different policies, both of which may be imperfect. When it is applied, under the auspices of such an assumption, the conclusive form of evidence sought is the form of a comparative census. Comparative censuses may also be made respecting rights and preferences. The difference from welfare at this point lies in the more extensive variety of particular considerations that press for attention under the heading of welfare.

The variety of considerations has been illustrated by mentioning food; safety; clothing; shelter; medical care; education; congenial employment; companionship. This list, however, is not especially privileged as to the categories mentioned; nor is it complete. "Welfare" is a convoy concept under which an indefinite number of particular considerations, even now increasing in variety, may be marshaled. Now, these particular considerations may conflict with each other on occasion; but it is a mistake to try to settle such conflicts in advance by taking them into account in the definition of welfare. All one can say is that the conflicts will be settled *ad hoc*, according to marginal differences in accommodating various considerations in particular circumstances. But it is important and illuminating to say this; it gives further light as to just what sort of concept the concept of welfare happens to be. [pp. 142–143]

Conflict or Detente?

There remains the question whether theories of rights, justice, and welfare are reconcilable. One way is to find a common concept from which the different approaches may be derived and to incorporate them within a larger framework. Thus Ronald Dworkin suggests (*Taking Rights Seriously*, 1977) that both a rights approach and a welfare approach can be derived from the democratic idea of equality. Hence the difference between the approaches might be referred rather to different domains or problems in which each would be relevant and serviceable. This avenue of reconciliation becomes more profitable as we see how frequently the battle of schools is reduced to slogans—the utilitarian recast as "cost-benefit analysis," the Kantian as "respect for persons," and rights theory as the weapon of the underprivileged. Such sloganizing can veil the full riches of each theory and how it deals with the values central to the others.

Another proposal is to undercut the separateness of the conceptions by analyzing more precisely their respective key ideas. Thus Andrew Oldenquist ("Rules and Consequences")[20] challenges the whole distinction between teleological and deontological ethics (utilitarian and Kantian). He analyzes elements in the idea of action and shows how each of the allegedly opposing theoretical types simply organizes differently the same basic materials so as to yield surface differences without ethically relevant differences. Bentham thinks of an act in narrow behavioral terms so that all the significant features are regarded as consequences (e.g., the act is moving the finger, so that firing the gun and killing someone are consequences); Kant puts all the significant features into a broadly formulated maxim (e.g., killing a person when he hinders one's important projects), and so he can regard ethical decision as internal and not dependent on

[20] *Mind* 75 (1966): 180–186.

consequences. There may be value differences between Kant and Bentham, but the fundamental difference by which their theories are often cast—one evaluating by motives and internal factors, the other by external consequences—falls by the way.

A third route to reconciliation is to deny the primacy of these concepts, or indeed of any one concept, and to regard the appeals to rights, justice, or welfare as specialized conceptions within the same family. Thus a pragmatist approach would focus on how problems arise from the conflicts in particular situations and would take these three concepts as components in our total resources for dealing with these problems. None of the three concepts is everywhere privileged; sometimes a problem seems better addressed as a matter of rights, sometimes as justice, sometimes as welfare, sometimes as an amalgam of these concepts, and sometimes we find we need to discover fresh ways of resolution.

Such different ways of going about the use of theories in ethics raises an important further problem—the need for a careful reassessment of the role and tasks of an ethical theory. This is considered in the next chapter.

24

✤

Agenda: Looking Toward the Next Century

Many philosophers in our century championed on principle the self-sufficiency of ethical theory. On the one hand, some insulated theory from practice because they took the task of philosophy to be that of clarifying ethical language or concepts (Ayer, Stevenson; see Chapter 20); others, while accepting the role of theory as a guide to action, held that theory has nothing to learn from application because ethical principles are rationally provided (Gewirth, *Reason and Morality*, 1978) or because moral values are directly perceived (Hartmann, Bergmann; see Chapter 22). On the other hand, some, subscribing to a separation of fact from value, insulated ethical theory from other fields. Recently, however, these isolating bulwarks have begun to weaken. The urgency of moral problems in a changing world and criticisms of the sharp theory-practice distinction have compelled ethical theory to explore its interplay with practice. Further, as the role of selective value components in science have come to be recognized and the critical role in ethics of presuppositions of what human beings and their worlds are like is ac-

knowledged, the hard separation of fact and value has been wearing thin. In any case, these two matters—how practice is related to theory, and how the accelerating range of knowledge and experience is to be integrated in ethical theory—are clearly on the present agenda of ethical theory. They call for a reassessment of the nature and functions of ethical theories themselves.

Ethics and Practice

Beginning in the 1970s, a concern with practical moral problems began to invade college teaching, textbook publishing, and even research. Generally associated with universities, institutes and centers have appeared dealing with philosophy and public policy, applied philosophy, ethics and the life sciences, business ethics, and so on. Much of the work is cooperative: philosophers participating on ethics committees, doing rounds with physicians, learning in detail about the way cases are analyzed.

Novel problems of a new technology—organ transplantation, artificial prolongation of life, artificial insemination, genetic control, and embryo transplantation—soon generated a cohesive body of dilemmas. Joined with more traditional issues of abortion, euthanasia, and the like, they mark out a vigorous field of bioethics. Doctor-patient relations were re-examined. Informed consent and new sensitivity about human subjects in medical (as well as psychological) research led to the formulation or revision of professional codes. Attitudes toward death and ways of relating to the dying, as well as a growing sociomedical field of gerontology, intensified issues of professional responsibility. Undoubtedly other factors contributed: law suits and the increasingly high cost of malpractice insurance make even the hardened professional eager to have determinate rules of responsibility.

Urgent social-moral problems include pollution and waste disposal; responsibility for workers' health, well-being, and retirement; questions of acceptable margins of risk and distribution of costs; responsibility for the character of products and fears about the cultural mechanization of life. Dilemmas for individuals are accentuated by the institutions and practices in which technology is enmeshed—thus the whistle blower who puts the general well-being above loyalty to the employer is regarded both as an informer and as a hero. And overwhelming is the problem of nuclear energy in war and in peace.

Technology, so often in the past regarded as a neutral instrument, with moral issues relegated to the ends for which it is employed, presents a multitude of problems, social as well as individual. Those who view it positively point to the potential for increased power; they argue that if it is used for destructive purposes, or if its rapid advance upsets social arrangements and generates unemployment, such

problems reflect not on technology as such but on the unreadiness of people. Others argue that technology has a momentum beyond our control, that its demands enslave human beings, impersonalize human situations, and degrade the environment and quality of life, making us an extension of the machine rather than the machine our servant.[1] Yet others, taking a middle ground, attribute such consequences to special types of technology, such as large-scale technology,[2] or to a lack of wisdom or leadership in facing the social consequences of technological advance—arguing, for example, that robotics could bring great savings in labor without increasing unemployment if the working day were cut and the values of leisure cultivated.[3] In short, the more central technology becomes to our mode of life, the more central moral outlooks become.

This same multiplication of moral problems is found in areas that in the past got along with a few code rules.[4] Today moral philosophers are dealing with problems of ethics in the legal profession, in police work and criminal justice, in psychiatry, in familial and parental relations, in nursing, in teacher-student relations, and in countless other areas. And of course there are the current forms of the traditional ethics of political and economic life—democratic participation, distributive justice, national and international relations, and discrimination.

The expanding scope of the moral today is reminiscent of the medievals, who saw moral

---

[1] Jacques Ellul, *The Technological Society* (1952).

[2] E. F. Schumacher, *Small Is Beautiful: Economics as if People Mattered* (1973).

[3] Wassily W. Leontief, "The Distribution of Work and Income," *Scientific American* 247 (September 1982): 188–204.

[4] It is amusing to read collections of codes of ethics a bare half-century ago. For example, the iceman is expected to give correct weight, be friendly and courteous, and obey the Ten Commandments (Edgar L. Heermance, *Codes of Ethics: A Handbook* [1924], pp. 239 ff.) Perhaps the auto mechanic and the TV repairer today raise comparable problems, but with more vulnerable customers.

questions wherever they turned. It is no longer possible to slice off a special department of moral questions, allowing matters of business and politics to be settled solely on their own grounds. Moral principles are appealed to and moral questions are raised appropriately in any area of human life.

Those working especially from an older juridical model think of their work as "applied ethics," parallel to that of an engineer, who gives answers by applying an already formulated general theory to a situation. This *administrative* approach assumes that an ethical theory can be established independently and before the practical problem is faced; the practical then becomes a matter of its *application.* Thus textbooks on "applied ethics" or one of its fields first present the various theories—Kantian, utilitarian, contractarian—and then, going to the field of problems, show how applying the different theories may lead to different results. On the whole, however, the demand is not so much to give authoritative answers to moral problems as to design and explore options and alternatives, to examine contexts and specify the terms by which decision may be reached. This approach to the relation of ethical theory to practice looks to theory for suggestions on how a practical situation might be analyzed; but the practice itself is not just an entity to which the theory is applied; it is rather an active *decision* in which the theory itself is being put to the test. This *heuristic* approach (the theory functioning as a lead for finding out or trying out) starts from the moral problem and feels no pressure to adopt antecedently one of the theories. It expects to find one theory more helpful in certain kinds of problems and another theory more helpful in others. Whereas the administrative approach regards the theory as authoritative for practice, the heuristic regards theories as furnishing intellectual instruments for practice and assigns the moral philosopher a role quite different from older conceptions of moral mon-

arch or secular priest. The critical difference is that the administrative does not look to practice for help in deciding the worth of a theory, whereas the heuristic expects practice to help decide not merely the scope but also the worth of a theory. Of course practice is not the sole arbiter: the relation is like that of theory and experiment in science—experience helps to refine and establish the theory and the theory helps predict further experience. So too, ethical theory guides practice in multiple ways, while practice helps to refine and assess theory.

The administrative approach regards the relation of theory to practice as fairly straightforward. The heuristic sees it as extremely complex—selecting formulations of the problem and principles to be employed. Environmental ethics is a good example of an area in which the opposing approaches have been particularly marked. In the administrative mood, utilitarian ethics prompts cost-benefit analyses in which the preservation of resources becomes subordinate to the accumulation of satisfying consumer goods, while a rights framework presses its often bizarre search for the rights of animals and trees and mother nature. By contrast a heuristic approach—such as Mark Sagoff's "On Teaching Environmental Ethics" [5] —shows where each mode of analysis leads when pressed as encompassing, and how the inquirer is led to a deeper vision of complexities and of the obligations of individuals in the midst of unresolved issues of policy. The suggestion is that moral philosophy may have to absorb and digest the complexities of contemporary practical life if it is to carry out its traditional function of moral guidance. It is not peculiar to ethics that even at this late date we cannot tell whether there will remain a plurality of theories or whether, as each is refined and altered, they will converge. Physics itself falls short of an integrating, unified theory. At present the complexity of moral

[5] *Metaphilosophy* 2 (July–October 1980): 307–325.

problems, reinforced by the impact of the revived concern for practice, weighs heavily on the side of the heuristic approach as the more mature account of how ethical theories operate.

Mobilizing Knowledge for Morality

Ethical theory has much to gain from a better understanding of the kinship of morality with other institutions and from insights provided by science and the humanities where they touch its central notions. Ethical theory builds in assumptions about criteria of cogent argument, human nature and its intellectual and emotional capabilities, the character of social development, and views of the world as recalcitrant or responsive to controlled change. If ethics is to fine-tune its theory to advancing human knowledge, it cannot coast on older or common sense ideas but must consciously and continuously cultivate its relations to other disciplines. A great deal of work now going on in many disciplines has relevance to the study of morality and the development of ethical theory. The contributions from these disciplines are diverse. Some offer useful models or at least suggestive analogies; some help to clarify ideas already involved in moral discourse; some set moral ideas in historical context and relate them to human development; some call attention to constraints on human nature; some challenge traditional assumptions. Sometimes too when ethics forces questions to be debated in another field—as it frequently does in jurisprudence and in history—both fields gain as a result. It is worth illustrating the variety of mutual relations in our century.

As law is close kin to morality, so jurisprudence is kin to ethical theory. Central to both ethics and jurisprudence are decision and decision making. Both involve the selection of relevant rules and facts, both are constrained by precedent and tradition while taxed by novelty and change, and both work with the adversarial, or at least with alternatives. But the formal structure of legal institutions magnifies, and hence allows us to see more clearly in its explicit processes and in its division of labor (lawgiver, judge, advocates, and enforcement officer), what in moral decision may be wrapped in a single, inner, debating consciousness.

Like ethics, jurisprudence has been divided on the question of autonomy. There is one tendency to regard law as an independent and self-sufficient system (whether as common law or, in John Austin's positivistic tradition, as expressive of sovereign power). Another view holds that law—as one instrument for promoting social purposes—responds to changing conditions and emerging needs. Such dependence was traced in the early period of American jurisprudence in this century by judges (Oliver Wendell Holmes, Benjamin Cardozo, Louis Brandeis), by professors of law (Roscoe Pound, Karl Llewellyn), and by an occasional philosopher (Morris Raphael Cohen). The contrast on the issue of autonomy is sharp in the critical debate between H. L. A. Hart and Lon Fuller over whether a Nazi law when invoked in a post-Nazi German court was to be regarded as law though unethical (Hart) or as not law because not ethical (Fuller).

Specific ethical concepts—justice, equity, and natural law—do of course have a role in law. Some features of the legal system may also be seen as deliberately providing a place for moral or quasi-moral judgments to break through the more formal structure. For instance, Sanford Kadish and Mortimer Kadish (*Discretion to Disobey* [1973]) examine the exercise of discretion by juries and prosecuting officials as an informal mechanism by which decision can conform to morality in cases where the formal operations of the law threaten to produce injustice.

The history of jurisprudence is thus an admirable intellectual laboratory for studying the interaction of rules, principles, policies, and ideals.

Specific legal fields and their central concepts also furnish guides and suggestions for specific ethical ideas. Legal analyses of contract and its conditions illuminate different aspects of promising, agreement, commitment, and expression of will, as well as relations of expectation and reliance, and the extent to which they form dependable patterns. Legal analyses of property and power, property and personality, and types of corporeal and incorporeal property contribute to greater sharpness in ethical treatments of property concepts as well as to moral evaluation of different property systems. And of course theories of responsibility in ethics are enriched by the comparative analyses of liability and responsibility in the legal theory of torts and crimes.

Emanating from biology, evolutionary theory has served philosophy as a powerful scientific model of a nonmechanistic and nonpredictive theory. The ecological model, in exposing broader vulnerabilities, calls for correspondingly broad responsibilities. The rapid development of genetics—the discovery of DNA and its structure and the consequent "genetic revolution"—has jeopardized the distinction between the natural and the artificial or "unnatural," and threatens to unravel the historical association of the "natural," the "unalterable," and the genetic (as opposed to the environmental). When in the late 1970s the U.S. Supreme Court considered whether a newly "manufactured" life form could be patented (it could), a fresh examination of the nature of life and the nature of property (reminiscent of the eighteenth-century debate on slavery) ensued. Biologists also entered the ethical arena, most recently in the acrimonious debate over sociobiology. Sociobiologists claim that patterns of altruism, that is, sacrifice, can be explained by genetic mechanisms of evolutionary survival, and hence that moral philosophy and other humanistic disciplines are superfluous.

At the beginning of the century, when philosophy and psychology were joined, the relevance of psychology to ethics was a given, but when a strict behaviorism took over academic psychology it found little place for the treatment of morals. In the 1940s, however, Gordon Allport reopened discussion of the self and its values. Self-development, personality, and the development of attitudes and norms became flourishing topics in personality psychology and social psychology (Muzafer Sherif, Hadley Cantril, and Kurt Lewin). Research on democracy and authoritarianism attempted largely to explain the distortion of values in Nazi Germany.[6] Although some psychologists carried on their research on values in the familiar neutral spirit of simply describing and seeking to explain phenomena, it proved difficult to avoid evaluation, particularly when dealing with the development of the self and personality. Even in examining the perception of value, the largely antirelativistic Gestalt social psychology (Wolfgang Köhler, Solomon Asch, Tamara Dembo, and Karl Duncker) saw the perception as an actual grasping of values. Developmental studies sometimes moved from an analysis of human needs and the process of actualizing the whole man to a full-fledged ethics reminiscent of nineteenth-century moral philosophy (Abraham Maslow). Similarly, when developmental psychology, building on the work of Jean Piaget, turned to explicitly moral themes (e.g., Lawrence Kohlberg), notions of "higher stages" carried obviously evaluative dimensions. Experimental social psychology also turned to moral subjects, such as honesty and conformity. Stanley Milgram experimented in the 1970s on how far people will go for the sake of obeying authority. Equity theorists (e.g., Elaine Walzer) tried to formulate predictive measures for

[6] Else Frenkel-Brunswik and others on the antidemocratic personality; Lewin and others on democratic and nondemocratic children's play groups.

analyzing the conditions under which people will judge themselves as unjustly benefiting or losing. More indirectly related to ethics, cognitive psychology along with artificial intelligence brings out the role of rules and intellectual patterning. Today moral phenomena are a recognized field of inquiry (e.g., Robert Coles on the child's experience of morality, Christopher Lasch on narcissism and alienation in our culture, Robert Bellah and others on individualism and commitment).

Freudian thought, of course, pervaded the century. Initially, psychoanalysis was taken to have reduced giving reasons (in an evidential sense) to rationalization; in fact it had provided ways to distinguish these. The specific material uncovered in psychoanalysis can help persons to become more rational by strengthening the ego in controlling the id (initial drives) and in pushing back the superego (the purely authoritarian mandates transmitted through parental influence in a nonrational way). Thus we can become conscious of our "mechanisms of defense" (Anna Freud) and so work for more rational ways of dealing with the world. Ego psychologists studied the child's developing ability to cope with reality (Heinz Hartmann, Ernst Kris, David Rapaport). Others emphasized the role of culture in development and studied cultural patterns to see which encourage and which inhibit psychic health (Karen Horney, Harry Stack Sullivan, Erik Erikson). Thus Erich Fromm dealt explicitly with moral character: *Escape from Freedom* (1941) is a study of the psychological sources of Nazism; *Man for Himself* (1947)—inspired by a study of the history of ethics—combined Freudian psychology with cultural orientations to classify and distinguish types of character, including the forms of conscience involved. Fromm hoped that by altering interpersonal relations and familial and economic institutions an authoritarian conscience could be replaced by a humanistic one. Psychologists influenced by psychoanalysis also began to study human emotions more intensively—for exam-

ple, shame and guilt (Gerhart Piers and Milton Singer, Helen Block Lewis).

The social sciences have furnished a variety of leads. Anthropology continued to fuel the debates over ethical relativism and provided empirical descriptions of cultural diversity under different social conditions. In the 1930s some social anthropologists moved from the ethnographic presentation of different practices and institutions of primitive societies to eliciting different value attitudes—for example, Malinowski on sex and repression, Margaret Mead on different attitudes toward sex and aggression, cooperation and competition; or in a more unified way, Ruth Benedict on patterns of culture that she formulated in almost value terms. The direct turn to values as a major topic in the 1950s involved for many the assumption that values themselves were an independent variable in the large-scale explanation of the behavior of a people, that to understand the direction of the countries of the new and expanded post–World War II world we had to grasp their different value orientations in an integrated way. The methodology of value study became a significant theme, particularly to show how values could be studied empirically rather than by introspection alone. For example, the Harvard Value Studies (Clyde Kluckhohn and others) examined five cultures of Southwestern America—Zuni, Navaho, Mormon, Texan-American, and Spanish-American—and attempted to map comparative values in areas as far apart as household operations, law, religion, music, orientations in time, and property. Others went more directly to the value configurations of total cultural traditions (e.g., the Comparative Studies of Cultures and Civilizations, edited by Robert Redfield and Milton Singer). In any case, anthropological studies of cultures carried out in the second half of the century—whether of Asian, African, or Pacific cultures, or of particular areas of self-study in the home culture (as in urban anthropology)—give prominent place to pinpointing values, if not cast largely in value terms (see Clifford Geertz, *The Inter-pretation of Cultures* [1973]).

Anthropologists at times have been seriously concerned with the practical value aspects of their discipline. In the latter days of the British Empire, British anthropologists worried about whether the knowledge they were furnishing provided instruments for colonial repression. American anthropologists have turned down research in projects that would assist covert political control in Latin America (e.g., Project Camelot). During World War II, however, anthropologists were enlisted to study value patterns at a distance for its utility in dealing with other countries—from what foods to prepare for liberated countries to the role of conceptions of duty in the process of surrender.[7]

Similarly sociology had its concern with values and value patterns—for example, Robert Lynd and Helen Lynd's studies of "Middletown," small-group studies (e.g., gangs and street-corner groups), the culture of poverty—promoted often by institutional problems and urgent social issues, for example, race relations, cross-generational relations, the various movements of liberation, attempts to understand and predict political trends, and contrasts between rural and urban society.

On the whole, two distinct attitudes toward values were found. One, perhaps the more traditional, insists with Max Weber that science should be descriptive and value-free, and the scientist neutral in his work. The other finds sociology taking an active evaluative role, whether consciously or not, and inclined to a participatory role in value conflicts (the Lynds, C. Wright Mills, Alvin Gouldner, Irving Horowitz). Thus Horowitz's *Taking Lives; Genocide and State Power* (1980) traces the relations between genocide and incipient trends in current institutions. Similarly, Michel Foucault has been influential in raising moral questions

about the long-term effects of institutions, such as hospitals and asylums.

The influence of economics on developing ideas of utility has already been noted (Chapter 23, on welfare). By broadening utility theory into a general theory of value it led to the exploration of values in all fields—aesthetic, religious, economic, and physical, as well as moral. It also promoted an idea of rationality identified with the maximizing strategies of economic competition.

The growth of the natural sciences as a great collective enterprise has given science almost a moral character, as historians of science have noted recently.[8] Two features stand out as suggestive for ethics. The fact that science has relinquished claims to certainty in favor of constant revision and self-correction suggests to ethics that it might better think in terms of the growth and adventure of moral experience instead of striving for absolute moral laws. Second, as the sciences constantly seek to refine the operations that enter into the meaning of their concepts (and thus enable theory to be tested), so ethics might explore more profoundly the repertoire of human feelings and responses and the various conditions under which they occur.

As the ideas of chance and contingency were tamed by the mathematics of probability, all fields came to appreciate the probable and to recognize that partial control admits of rationality. This suggests that ethical rules need not lose their weight for being open-ended or subject to exceptions. Just as physics survived indeterminacy, so ethics need not be threatened by the possibility that there is not a definitive answer to every moral problem.

The contributions of ideas of probability to the analysis of moral and value problems have not been only of this general sort. The close association between ethics and *decision theory*

---

[7] Ruth Benedict, *The Chrysanthemum and the Sword* (1946), on Japanese ethics.

[8] Thomas Kuhn's work on revolutions in science, and controversies about the role of social and value outlooks in the development of scientific theory.

goes beyond a general concern with the practical. On the mathematical side, decision theory had long recognized that optimal decision requires a probability scale on which the events on which interest centered could be assigned a numerical value, a value scale by which desirabilities or utilities were ordered, and a strategy (for example, to maximize possible gains or minimize possible losses). As long as these three were separate avenues, the concern of ethics (or more broadly, value theory) lay with the value scale alone. Recently attempts have been made to factor both the values and the probabilities in choices. Increasing demands from industry for theoretical tools to be used in quality control and in guiding the ordering of production prompted the forging of new and refined mathematical tools to analyze strategies (as in the theory of games). The parallel in ethics is a reorientation toward the problem of decision in situations of indeterminate knowledge or under risk (as for example in Dewey's reorientation of the moral situation). Approaches in these terms have generated a whole area of inquiry, of which Bentham's cost-benefit analysis was perhaps the ancestor.[9]

The relevance of linguistics and logic to ethics needs no further comment. Throughout the century they combined to deepen traditional inquiries into the structure of moral judgments, the way they are shaped and what is involved in their form, as well as how far they can be organized in logical systems. One school even defined ethics as the analysis of moral discourse (Chapter 20).

The intimate connection of religion and ethics is part of the whole historical story of this book. The newer movements in religion in the twentieth century—including the meeting of Eastern and Western religions, the emergence of strongly moralistic social activism (liberation theologies, resurgence of fundamentalisms)—pose serious problems for ethics, at least in the relation of moral belief and social change, the meaning of community, and doubtless numerous questions about the place of faith. Ethics has always gone to literature for plotting moral situations and delineating moral emotions (often more richly than the psychological sciences of the day) but has only rarely mined the resources of literature for theory—such as patterns of virtue (Jane Austen) or the nature of the human situation (Dostoyevsky) or the possibilities of resolving ultimate conflict (Sophocles versus Aeschylus) or for hypothetical experiments (e.g., utopias). The general theory of the arts, on the other hand, has continually focused on the character of immediate and intrinsic value, although for the most part as an isolated experience.

History, perhaps the most influential humanistic discipline for ethics, chronicles the past with its welter of forces—economic, political, social, religious, intellectual. History attempts to discover laws, trace lines of development or even progress, and derive lessons in the belief (George Santayana) that those who will not learn from their past mistakes are bound to repeat them. Works of history that impinge on morality and ethical theory include not only narrative but social, political, and intellectual history, as well as histories of morality and ethics, and philosophies of history.

Historical materials have constantly raised moral issues and offered moral lessons. It once was commonplace for historians to pass moral judgment on the acts of kings and statesmen. Even now the question is often raised whether the responsibility of guiding states and nations does not call for actions that trespass on individual morality. In history different programs of human life seek their moral justification. When we ask whether nationalism has been a good or an evil, we look to the wars nationalism has generated as well as to the loyalties and cohesions it has made possible. History offers great scope for surmise and reflection:

[9] See, for example, C. West Churchman, *Prediction and Optimal Decision: Philosophical Issues of a Science of Values* (Englewood Cliffs, N.J.: Prentice-Hall, 1961).

Is revolution invariably followed by counter-revolution? Are the freedoms of the revolution paid for in subsequent forms of enslavement? Do the gods, as the ancients believed, make mad those whom they are about to destroy—for example, entrenched classes maintaining privilege in the face of their inevitable destruction? What changes in institutional structure bring about what benefits? For example, if India and China move from arranged marriages to marriage by individual romantic selection, will this bring greater happiness without diminishing family stability?

History also provides evidence for the way morality changes and for the kinds of causes or influences that incline, if not determine, directions of change. An excellent example, though much debated, concerns the rise of the Protestant ethic and to what degree it supported or was supported by rising capitalism (Max Weber, R. H. Tawney).

For the most part ethical theory has ignored its own sociohistorical context. Much of the history of philosophy is written as if philosophy were self-contained, Plato setting the problem for Aristotle, and Kant for Hegel, and Bentham for Mill. Occasionally philosophers admit cultural and social factors—for example, they may see Aristotle's theory of the mean as a reflection of the general Greek avoidance of extremes ("Nothing in excess"); or see seventeenth-century contractualism as the break with feudal concepts of natural places and loyalties for different classes. The growth of philosophy of history in the nineteenth century prompted a more systematic view of the relation of ethical ideas to social conditions. Mill correlates the growth of individual liberty with stages of social development and the growth of opportunities. Hegelians see history as unfolding rationally, with the shape of ethics suited to each successive spirit of the age. Marxians connect ideas and ethical theories to the stages of development of the forces and relations of production.

This emphasis on social and technological factors is congenial to twentieth-century social thought, which tends to be more pluralistic and less given to fixed schemes. Ethical ideas are not just reactions but may be genuine efforts to meet the challenges and problems generated by these social conditions. From this perspective the conflicts of ethical theories also have a social dimension. Take, for example, the central controversy in ethics during the 1930s over whether ultimate disagreement on values could be settled rationally or only by war and social strife (Chapter 20). In the literature of the period some stressed the ultimacy of moral disagreement (the emotive theory), others the possibilities of rational intelligence; still others began to define morality itself as the search for compromise, while yet others rested morality on ultimate commitments that had only to be *willed*. The problem was rendered more acute by the setting of the broader fact-value dichotomy, which so isolated ethics from factual and rational (e.g., scientific) considerations that no appeal to such evidence could be decisive. The controversies over cultural and ethical relativity in the social sciences belong to the same period. It is a ready hypothesis that the historical background of this prevalent problem—the bitter clash of social systems of the era, particularly the utter disparity between the values of Nazism and those of Western liberalism—made the problem a central one. Once World War II began, the need to feel the rightness of one's struggle became a serious moral factor. Ralph Barton Perry wrote a book entitled *Our Side Is Right* (1942) and Julian Huxley said in his Romanes Lecture of 1943:

We live under the grim material necessity of defeating the Nazi system, ethics and all, but no less under the spiritual and intellectual necessity not merely of feeling and believing but *knowing* that Nazi ethics are not just different from ours, but wrong and false; or at least less right and less true.[10]

[10] "Evolutionary Ethics," in T. H. Huxley and Julian Huxley, *Touchstone for Ethics* (New York: Harper, 1947), p. 114.

Much of the continuing discussion of the relation of fact and value was carried by this impetus. At the same time the seriousness of practical decision both in individual and in social contexts shifted the focus to decision itself as a vital act. In Sartre's concept of freedom (Chapter 22) the existentialist view of ultimate responsibility seemed to be modeled directly on the predicament of the individual in the French Resistance.

After World War II an activist tone entered moral philosophy. It matched the need for rebuilding and fitted admirably the growing sense that we needed to remake our world and could do it with a greater hope of control. The breakdown of colonialism and the succession of liberation movements raised fresh problems of liberty, equality, justice, and human rights (Chapter 23). If the problem of equality was old, the scope of racial and sexual equality gave it a character that permeated the whole pattern of life. Similar changes had come in the concept of democracy, with the growing demands for participation in the determination of social policies. In addition, rapid technological changes effected profound changes in social life, such as the shift to dominantly urban life, with its attendant problems of individualism and alienation.

Thus the development of new problems thrust ethics into a critical position in all fields. That moral philosophy turned to matters of application and practice surprised no one but moral philosophers themselves.

The complex movements considered here concerning the relation of ethical theory to moral practice and to advancing knowledge have converged to clarify the nature and function of ethical theories themselves as guiding morality. In Chapter 1 we distinguished the morality of a community and the ethical theory that is a reflective effort to explain, systematize, justify, and guide that morality. We have seen theory and morality interrelating in different ways. Sometimes the ethical theory helped

to readjust the morality, especially when the latter had grown out of tune with the changed conditions of social life; thus natural rights theory challenged long accepted vested interests. At other times changed moral demands called for a fresh ethical theory that would do them greater justice. Thus when equalitarian sentiment surged into morality and generated a movement for the abolition of slavery, it found expression also in the ethical theories of Bentham and Kant—in the first as a rule that every person count as one, in the second as respect for the person and universal legislation for all mankind. Some of these moral gains have been stabilized and extended in our time through these ideas: witness the reduction of many forms of discrimination and an acknowledged social responsibility for the impoverished.

Serious moral disagreements remain: on sex, abortion, pornography, euthanasia, capital punishment, specific responsibilities of various professions, economic distribution, responsibilities to Third World countries. Further, while many conflicts appear initially as an issue of means or as purely technical matters—such as economic sanctions and toxic waste disposal—their analysis quickly stumbles on appropriate moral balance and fairness.

The extent of such conflicts gives us a measure of the greater need for ethical theory. Moral debate is full of appeals to the individual's right to judge for himself or herself, the authority of traditional values, the ideals of liberty and equality, the need for community. To understand their meaning, their different weights, costs, and gains, is the work of ethical theory with its striving for the systematic organization of ideas. Take, for example, the strides of individualism and its ideals of autonomy. Their liberating role has been paid for by the threat of alienation and moral isolation. This accounts for the widespread yearning for community, for the concentration in theory on the issue of egoism versus altruism, for the frequently expressed fears of "moral relativism" or lapsing into individual "hedonism" and "consumerism." More positively, this pressure is manifest in the frequent revival in ethics of questions of the nature of friendship or the relation of love and sex, or the investigations into the moral dimensions of the affective side of life.

Moral philosophy is now in a period in which the expansion and refinement of ethical theory has become a pressing need. Even the current concern with practical problems depends for its success on the degree to which it deploys adequate theory. This does not of course mean that an ethical theory can of itself furnish a moral catalogue for practice. The distance between theory and decision in morality is often as great as the distance between theory and observation in science, but it has to be traversed if we are to have reliable decision. A reader once complained to John Dewey that his book on ethics had not provided answers to moral problems. Dewey agreed in his reply but pointed out that the complaint asked the author to do what, on the very theory of the book, was the job of the reader.

The various ethical theories examined in this book are not then to be seen as a gallery of position portraits, some of which are to be simply rejected and others simply accepted. They appear as an increasingly rich array of different perspectives that add to insight into morality and practice and furnish improved instruments for deciding issues and resolving conflicts. No theory at any stage can expect to have finality or to stand alone, and none henceforth can dispense with critique as a continuing central component.

If our judgment is correct, that ethical theory is on the verge of expansion, growth, and refinement, and if it is to be of human service, then its development is a moral demand. Since a large portion of the readers of this book will doubtless be the younger generation, we wish you well in the task.

INDEX

Abelard, Peter, 91, 104, 106, 110–116
Abraham the patriarch, 91, 107, 114, 579
Accountability (*see* Responsibility)
Acquired sit (*see* Virtue, intellectual)
Acquisition
  commonwealth by (*see* Commonwealth)
  of property (*see* Trade)
Action, 54, 60, 121, 124, 125, 126–127, 437
  consequences of (*see* Consequences)
  decision as, 551
  good or evil, 123–124, 126, 145, 146–147, 312–
    313
  kinds of, 40–41, 309
  propriety of, 266–267
  responsibility for, 524–525
  worth of, 336
Active citizens (*see* Citizens)
Act utilitarianism (*see* Utilitarianism)
Adultery, 48, 87, 88, 92, 124, 150, 259
Affection, personal (*see* Love
Affections (*see* Passions)
Agents, moral, 606–607
Agreement and disagreement, 512, 514, 515,
    567, 606
Agreement of the People, 200, 210, 212–213
Aid, mutual, 470–473
Alcheic, 258, 259
America, 288, 383
American Revolution, 202
Analytic statements, 327n, 505
Ancient ethics, 5–102
Anger (*see also* Righteous indignation), 49, 76–
    77, 92, 111
Anguish, 578
Animal motion (*see* Passions)
Animals
  benevolence in, 208–209
  capable of expression, 59
  incapable of
    covenant, 189
    voluntariness, 52
  not morally weak, 56
  production by, 405–406

social, 194, 456–457, 458, 470, 471–472
  treatment of, 313n, 356
Anthropology, 627
Antipater, 74–75
Antithesis (*see* Dialectic)
A posteriori statements, 327n
Appetite (*see also* Passions), 477
  aversion and, 180–181
  distinguished from
    choice, wish, and opinion, 52
    self-love, 229–230
  opposed to reason, 56
  voluntariness and, 52
Applied ethics, 486, 488–489, 500, 621–624
Approval (*see* Blame and praise)
A priori statements, 327n, 341
Aquinas, Thomas, 104, 108, 117–141
Arbitration, 192
Aristocracy, 66, 466–467
Aristotle, 36n, 38–68, 70, 71, 90–91, 117
  cited by
    Aquinas, 121, 122, 123, 124, 125, 129, 140
    Hart, 523
    Ockham, 147, 151
  compared to
    Hegel, 372–373
    Posidonius, 71
  medieval church and, 104
Arrow, Kenneth, 591, 592
Art, 35–36, 263–264, 321, 382–383, 415, 569, 575
Ascription of responsibility (*see* Responsibility)
Assembly, right of, 434
Assistance, mutual, 470–473
Association of ideas (*see* Ideas)
Associations, political (*see* Commonwealth;
    Polis; State, The)
Astronomy, 166–168
Ataraxia (*see also* Peace of mind), 72, 86
Atheism, 577
Atoms, 70, 72, 83, 87
Augustine, 70, 90, 92, 96–102, 106, 164n
  cited by
    Abelard, 114, 115, 124

Aquinas, 133, 136, 139
Ockham, 150
Austin, J. L., 507–508, 518–521
Autonomy
  of ethics, 488, 490–503
  of persons, 329, 330, 345–356
Aversion (*see* Appetite)
Axioms, moral, 204–205
Ayer, A. J., 505–506, 508–511

Bacon, Francis, 171–172
Bad faith, 581–583
Badness (*see* Evil)
Banneker, Benjamin, 282–283
Bare use (*see* Use, right of)
Barter (*see* Trade)
Beauty, 500, 501
Becker, Lawrence C., 601–608
Being, 89–90
Belief (*see* Opinion)
Benevolence
  in Aquinas, 135–136
  in Bentham, 312, 314
  in Butler, 228–230
  in Cumberland, 208–209
  fund of, 318
  in Hume, 241, 246, 251–252
  in Kant, 352–353
Bentham, Jeremy, 296–324, 328, 414
Bermann, Frithjof H., 556, 557, 564–570
Berkeley, Bp. George, 225–226
Bias (*see* Prejudice)
Biology (*see also* Sociobiology), 625
Birthright, 210, 213, 215, 289
Blame and praise (*see also* Contumely; Excuses), 77, 127, 266–267, 269, 459, 520n, 546
Blindness, moral (*see* Self-deception)
Blossius, 71
Boniform faculty, 207
Bosanquet, Bernard, 479–482
Boulding, Kenneth, 593n–594n
Bourgeoisie (*see* Middle class)
Bracketing (*see also* Suspension of judgment), 556, 565
Bradley, F. H., 477–479
Braybrooke, David, 592, 614–629
Breach
  of friendship (*see* Friendship)
  of promise (*see* Promise)
Britain, 321, 323, 369, 546
Buber, Martin, 557, 573–577
Burke, Edmund, 287–292, 317
Butler, Joseph, 227–232

Calculus, felicific (*see* Felicific calculus)
Cambridge Platonists, 199, 201–209
Capitalism (*see* Communism)
Capital punishment (*see* Punishment)
Care (nurture), 608–609
Casuistics, 353–354, 355, 357, 423
Categorical imperative, 328–329, 330, 340–341, 343, 346, 419
Causality, 235–237, 327
Cave, image of the, 30–31
Celibacy, 28n, 106
Cesena, Michael, 152
Changuis, 258
Charity (*see* Benevolence)
Chastity (*see* Sex)
Children (*see also* Family; Marriage), 433, 572, 618
  incapable of voluntariness, 52, 314, 549
  in *polis*, 24–25
  sin in, 100–101, 150
Choice, 52
Christianity (*see* Hebraic-Christianity)
Chrysippus, 71, 73, 74
Church property, 154
Cicero, 71, 73, 74–75, 107, 286n
Circumstances, 122, 124–125, 151, 242–243, 308, 309, 423
Citizens (*see also* Subjects of commonwealth), 281–282, 284, 361, 444
  rights of, 292–293, 361, 613
City-state (*see* Polis)
Civil constitutions (*see* Constitutions)
Civil disobedience (*see* Civil obedience)
Civil law, 178, 318–321
  self-executing, 316–317
Civil obedience, 104–105, 117, 134–135, 196, 197, 238–239
Civil rights, 292–293, 361, 613
Clarke, Samuel, 205–207
Classes, social (*see* Social classes)
Cleanthes (Fourlian), 252
Cleanthes (Stoic), 71
Cleitophon, 16–17
Cleomenes, 71
Clothing, decent, 570
Cognition (*see* Knowledge)
Cognitive relativism (*see* Relativism)
Cohen, Felix S., 588, 596–599
Coke, Sir Edward, 174
Commandments, Ten, 2, 91, 92–93, 132–133
Commerce (*see* Trade)
Common law, 174
Common tribunal, 323–324
Commonweal (*see* Welfare)

Commonwealth (*see also* Community; Government; *Polis*; State, The), 193–197, 222, 261, 291

Communism, 28n, 64, 391–394, 406–407, 416, 447–449, 450

Community (*see also* Commonwealth; Mutual aid; *Polis*; State, The), 101, 222, 304, 371, 373–374, 475

Commutative justice, 136, 191

Compassion (*see also* Sympathy), 558–559

Compromise, 291

Compulsion, 50–51, 428–429

Conflict (*see also* War), 185
  of duties, 353, 423, 579–580
  moral, 540–541, 546–547, 601–604, 619–620
  of rights, 588, 600–601

Conscience, 134, 230–231, 232, 355–356, 424, 458, 515–517
  right of (*see also* Religious freedom), 293, 434
  vs. civil law, 178
  vs. self-interest, 269–271

Consciousness, 474, 477, 500, 556–557

Consent (*see* Agreement and disagreement; Intention)

Consequences, 312–313, 386, 537, 548

Constitutions (*see also* specific kinds, e.g., Republic), 10, 32–34, 46, 53, 65–68, 299

Constraint, 50–51, 428–429

Contemplation, 120

Contentment, 420

Contract, 166, 293
  in Becker, 606
  in Burke, 291–292
  in Cudworth, 203–204
  in Engels, 410
  in English law, 522–523
  in Hegel, 385
  in Hobbes, 177–178, 188–191
  in Hume, 238
  in Kant, 330, 331, 359
  in Locke, 216–217, 219, 222
  in Putney Debates, 211
  in Rawls, 589, 609–614
  in Rousseau, 279–281

Contumely, 191, 357, 436

Convenience (*see* Expedience)

Convention (*see* Promise)

Conventionality (*see also* Habit), 53, 87, 290, 437, 491
  in Hume, 237, 238, 248

Copernicus, Nicolaus, 166, 326

Corrective justice, 52

Court, common, 323–324

Covenant (*see* Contract)

Crime (*see* Punishment)

Criminal law, 523

Criterion, 86

Criticism, 481, 482, 567–568

Cromwell, Oliver, 200, 210, 211, 214

Cruelty, 190, 191, 594, 601–602

Cudworth, Ralph, 202–204

Cumberland, Richard, 207–209

Currency, 62–63

Custom (*see* Conventionality)

Cynics, 71

Cyrenaics, 83, 553

Darwin, Charles, 38, 452–460

Death, 72, 81, 84, 150, 151, 196, 561

Decalogue, 2, 91, 92–93, 132–133

Decent dress, 570

Decision (*see* Responsibility)

Declaration of Independence, 278, 281, 283, 292

Declaration of the Rights of Man and of Citizens, 278, 279, 281–282, 286–287

Defenses (*see* Excuses)

De Gouges, Olympe, 283–284

Deliberation, 52, 181–182, 538, 540

Delusion (*see* Self-deception)

Demerit (*see* Worth)

Democracy, 33–34, 65–66, 67, 278, 370, 614

Democritus, 72

Deontology, 302

Descartes, René, 169–170

Desire (*see* Appetite)

Despair, 576

Despotism (*see* Tyranny)

De Unamuno, Miguel, 560–561

Devil, 93, 101, 102

Dewey, John, 532–536, 539–549

Dialectic, 8, 11, 32, 373–374, 375–376, 384, 503

Dignity (*see* Worth)

Diogenes Laertius, 72, 73, 81n

Diogenes of Babylonia, 74–75

Diogenes the Cynic, 71, 88

Disagreement (*see* Agreement and disagreement)

Disappointment (*see* Expectation)

Disapproval (*see* Blame and praise)

Discrimination (*see* Prejudice)

Dislike (*see* Resentment)

Disobedience, civil (*see* Civil obedience)

Disposition, mental, 311–312

Distribution of wealth (*see* Wealth)

Distributive justice, 52, 136, 191

Divine law (*see also* Eternal law), 107, 135

Divine right of kings, 199, 216, 217

Divine will, 302, 332, 346

Division of labor, 23–24, 389

Dominion (*see also* Ownership; Property; Use, right of), 153–154
Dress, decent, 570
Drunkenness, 55, 56, 150, 192, 314, 316
Duncker, Karl, 570–573
Duns Scotus, 142, 148
Duty (*see also* Deontology; Obligation)
   in Bentham, 313–314
   conflict of, 353, 423, 579–580
   distinguished from
     ends, 351–352
     law, 351
   in Kant, 335–336, 341–342, 350, 356–358, 429, 455
   in Moore, 499–500
   as pure respect for law, 336–338, 350
   as purpose of moral speculation, 240
   of sovereign, 273
   vs. self-interest, 475
Dworkin, Ronald, 588, 599–601, 602, 603, 604, 619

Ecclesiastical property, 154
Economics, 165, 288, 299, 416, 450–451, 627
   marginalist, 301–302, 319
   Marxist, 392–393, 402–403
Education, 24–25, 31, 78–79, 247, 421, 596, 604
   progressive, 535
   state and, 442, 461–462
Egalitarianism (*see* Equality)
Egoism, 494–495
Elections (*see* Voting)
Emotions (*see* Feelings)
Emotive theory, 506, 508–515, 552
Empiricism (*see also* Sensation), 171–173, 223–224, 234
   Logical, 504–506
End in itself, 419, 425, 480–481
   action as, 54
   beauty as, 500
   good will as, 335
   happiness as, 43, 352
   man as, 92, 330, 344, 574
   personal affection as, 500
   pleasure as, 82 310, 419, 498
   rationality as, 343, 344
   virtue as, 74, 256
End (purpose) (*see* Intention)
Ends, Kingdom of, 344–345
Enemies, 14–16, 92, 253, 336, 458n
Engels, Frederick, 368, 390, 400–404, 409–412
England (*see* Great Britain)
Enlightenment, 227, 276, 325
Enmity (*see* Resentment)

Envy, 50
Epictetus, 72, 77–79
Epicureanism, 70, 72, 81–86, 101
Epistemology (*see* Knowledge)
Equality, 192, 210, 217, 221–222, 401–403
   in Bentham, 303, 319
   in Dworkin, 600–601
   in Mill, 428
   of property, 244, 384–385
   in Rawls, 589, 611
   of representation, 213–215, 261, 282, 446, 595
   of rights, 280–281, 358, 361
   state of (*see* State of nature)
   in United Nations, 594
Equity, 53–54, 192
Essence (*see also* Forms, Platonic), 557
Eternal law (*see also* Divine law), 107, 126–127, 130
Ethical relativism (*see* Relativism)
Ethical theory (*see* Ethics)
Ethics (*see also* Metaethics), 1–4
   autonomy of, 488, 490–503
   defined by
     Bentham, 313–314
     Hobbes, 193
     Kant, 351
   history of, 629–630
   normative, 492
   practical, 486, 488–489, 500, 621–624
   relation to other disciplines, 4, 624–630
European politics (*see* Politics)
Evidence, 425, 492–493, 551, 598–599
Evil (*see also* Action, good or evil; Sin; Vice), 96, 142n, 231–232
Evolution, 367, 452–473
   of man, 72, 464
   of society, 462–466, 476–477
Exchange of property (*see* Property; Trade)
Excuses (*see also* Justification), 518–521, 523, 579
Existentialism, 559–562, 577–585
Exodus, 92–93
Expectation, 319–320
Expedience, 431–432
Experience, 416
   necessary to
     morality, 41, 330, 332–333
     practical wisdom, 54, 334, 340
   in phenomenology, 556
   in pragmatism, 529, 531, 542–543
Exploitation, 397, 411–412, 467
Expression, right of, 286–287, 434, 435–436, 595
External form, 105, 193
External sanctions (*see* Sanctions)

Factual knowledge (*see* Knowledge)

Factual use (*see* Use, right of)

Fact/value distinction, 564–566

Fairness (*see* Justice)

Faith, bad, 581–583

Fallacy, naturalistic, 491, 493, 495–496, 497–498

Fame, love of (*see also* Pride), 253, 459

Family (*see also* Children; Marriage), 58–59, 63, 295–296, 400

Fancy value, 345

Fate, 74

Fear, 189, 190

Feelings (*see also* Passions; Sensation), 239–240, 254–256, 556, 576, 580–581

Felicific calculus, 300, 301, 306–307, 615, 616–617

Felicity (*see* Happiness)

Feminism (*see also* Women), 589, 609

Feudalism, 104, 105, 393, 396, 402–403

Foot, Philippa R., 508, 525–528

Force, 50–51, 428–429

Forlornness, 579

Forms, Platonic (*see also* Essence), 10–11

Fornication (*see* Sex)

Fourli, 258–259

France, 321, 323, 368

Franchise (*see* Voting)

Franciscans (*see* Friars Minor)

Freedom (*see* Liberty; Religious freedom)

Free will (*see* Will)

French Revolution, 275–276, 289–292

Friars Minor, 143–144, 152, 154, 155, 158

Friendship, 14–16, 42, 49, 56–57, 66, 431

Functionalism, 533–534

Galilei, Galileo, 167

General will (*see* Will)

Geocentric astronomy, 166

Geographical morality, 287

Geometry, 69

Germany, 368, 372

Gestalt psychology (*see* Psychology)

Gewirth, Alan, 586, 603, 606–607

Gilligan, Carol, 589, 608–609

Glaucon, 9, 20–24, 31, 36

Glorious Revolution (*see* Revolution in England)

God (*see also* One, The; Religion)
  covenant with, 189
  as creator, 40n, 452–453, 577
  existence of, 327, 332, 579
  freedom of, 145–146
  Hebraic-Christian, 91–102
  impersonality of, 41
  love for, 151
  as source of law (*see* Divine law)
  will of, 302, 332, 346

Golden Rule, 329, 422, 463, 542

Goodness (*see also* Value [Ideal])
  of action (*see* Action)
  in Aquinas, 131
  in Aristotle, 42–43
  in Bentham, 310
  in Bergmann, 567–569
  in Darwin, 459
  distinguished from welfare, 329
  in Hobbes, 180–181
  intuited, 490
  in Kant, 334, 335, 338
  in Moore, 490–491, 493–494
  in Plato, 21
  in Stevenson, 512

Good, The, 11–12, 40, 73, 418, 543

Good will (faculty) (*see* Will)

Good will (kindliness) (*see* Benevolence)

Gospels (*see also* Matthew, Gospel of), 107n, 157, 187

Gouges, Olympe de, 283–284

Gouze, Marie, 283–284

Government (*see also* Constitutions)
  employees, 317n
  genesis of, 293
  interference of, 442, 450–451
  limits of, 292, 303
  provides for human wants, 290
  representative, 442–446
  rewards and punishes, 308–309, 316–317
  as self-protection, 481

Graeco-Roman philosophy, 69–102

Gratian, 104, 105, 106, 110

Gratitude and ingratitude, 254–255, 267–269, 604

Great Britain, 321, 323, 369, 546

Greatest Happiness Principle (*see* Utility)

Great men, 379–380, 439, 454, 468

Greece, 7–8, 69

Greek philosophy (*see* Hellenistic philosophical schools)

Green, T. H., 475–477

Grotius, Hugo, 108, 173

Guardians (*see* Rulers)

Gulki, 258

Habit (*see also* Conventionality), 130, 238, 456, 457
  virtue formed by, 45–46, 127, 147, 148–149

Happiness (*see also* Quality of life), 43, 285–286, 334–335, 340, 352, 420
  in Aquinas, 120, 129

in Aristotle, 43–44
in Bentham, 301
calculus of (*see* Felicific calculus)
contentment and, 420
as duty, 336, 352
in Kant, 334, 335, 336, 340, 346
law and, 129
in Mill, 421, 426–427
in More, 207
of others, 250, 314, 342, 352, 425
wealth and, 319
welfare and, 616
Harsanyi, John C., 591–592
Hart, H. L. A., 508, 521–525
Hartmann, Nicolai, 557–558, 562–564
Hatred (*see* Resentment)
Heaven, right of, 158
Hebraic-Christianity, 69, 70, 90–102, 104, 454, 580
Hedonism (*see also* Pleasure), 72, 179–180, 298, 498
Hedonistic calculus, 300, 301, 306–307, 615, 616–617
Hegel, G. W. F., 371–389, 390–391, 403
Heidegger, Martin, 560
Heliocentrism, 69, 166
Hellenistic philosophical schools, 70–90
Heretics, 135, 179, 191, 435–436
Heroes, 379–380, 439, 454, 468
Historical men (*see* Heroes)
History, 102, 363–365, 373, 374, 376–384, 628–629
Hobbes, Thomas, 108, 175–197
Homosexuality, 88, 315–316n
Honesty, 314, 316
Household (*see* Family)
Human rights, 587–589, 594–609
Hume, David, 232–264
Husserl, Edmund, 555–556
Hutcheson, Francis, 232–233
Huxley, Julian, 465–466, 629
Huxley, T. H., 454, 462–466

Idea
of the Good (*see* Good, The)
in Hegel, 378, 380
Ideas, 234, 235
Platonic (*see* Forms, Platonic)
Ignorance, 8, 51, 121–122, 126, 610
Imagination, 180
Immortality, 36, 561
Imperative (*see also* Law), 339–341, 551–554
categorical, 328–329, 330, 340–341, 343, 346, 419

Imperfect duty (*see* Duty in Kant)
Impressions (*see* Sensation)
Incestuous marriage, 88, 113, 260, 321
Indignation, righteous, 50
Individualism, 301–302, 373, 440–441, 480, 486–487, 533
Induction, 236, 237
Industrial revolution, 276, 299
Informalism (*see* Ordinary Language Analysis)
In foro externo, 105, 193
In foro interno (*see* Internal forum)
Inquiry, scientific, 38, 39–40, 172
Insanity (*see* Madness)
Institution, commonwealth by (*see* Commonwealth)
Institutions, social, 482, 576–577
Instrumental power (*see* Power)
Intellect (*see* Virtue; Will)
Intellectualism, 107
Intellectual rights, 292
Intelligence, personification of, 88, 89, 90
Intemperance (*see* Drunkenness)
Intention (*see also* Motivation), 110–111, 112–115, 119–120, 309, 351–352
Interest (finance) (*see* Usury)
Interesting perceptions (*see* Perceptions)
Interest, self- (*see* Self-love)
Internal forum (*see also* Conscience), 105–106, 193
Internal sanctions (*see* Conscience; Sanctions)
International law (*see* War)
Interpersonal relations, 573–577, 608
Intoxication (*see* Drunkenness)
Intrinsice value (*see* End in itself)
Intuitionism (*see also* Moral sense intuitionists), 492–493, 499, 510, 607–608
Invective (*see* Contumely)
Ireton, Henry, 210, 211–212, 213, 214–215
Irrationality (*see also* Appetite; Feelings; Madness; Passions), 45
Isidore of Seville, 103
"Is-ought" problem, 238, 257 477, 486
Ius, 71, 75, 108–109, 144, 152, 156

James, William, 529, 530–532
Job, 91, 92–95
John XXII, Pope, 152–159
John Paul II, Pope, 573–574
Judaism (*see* Hebraic-Christianity)
Judgment, suspension of (*see* Suspension of judgment)
Jurisprudence (*see also* Law), 624–625
Jus (see Ius)

Justice (*see also* Natural right; Positive right), 101, 190–191, 242–243, 358, 427–432
  in Aquinas, 136
  in Aristotle, 52, 60
  commutative, 136, 191
  corrective, 52
  distributive, 52, 136, 191
  in Hume, 242–243
  in Kant, 358–363
  in Lewis, 549–551
  in Mill, 427–432
  in Plato, 13–27
  in Rawls, 610–614
  in twentieth century, 589–590
Justification
  of rights, 605
  of values, 565–567
Just war, 136

Kant, Immanuel, 92, 276, 325–366, 374, 386–387, 418–419
Kepler, Johann, 167
Keynes, John Maynard, 501–503
Killing (*see also* Murder; Punishment; Self-defense; Suicide), 93, 106, 137–138, 219, 571–572
Kingdom of ends, 344–345
Kings (*see* Rulers)
Knowledge, 8, 9, 223–224, 479, 486, 537, 575
  constituent of highest goods, 501
  derives from Forms, 10–11
  exercise of, 55
  factual, 235
  scientific, 55, 148, 418, 534
Kropotkin, Peter, 455, 470–473

Labor
  of appropriation, 221, 244, 385
  division of, 23–24, 389
  unions, 588, 595
Laborers (*see* Working class)
Language (*see also* Ordinary Language Analysis), 300–301, 456, 521–524
Law (*see also* specific categories of law, e.g., Natural law; *see also* Imperative; Jurisprudence), 129, 173–174, 336–337, 338, 349–351, 522–523
  defined, 75, 87, 129–130, 133–134
Lawful rights (*see* Legal rights)
Lawyers, 139, 174, 320
Legal language, 521–524
Legal rights, 158, 427
Legal theory, 173–174

Legislation, civil (*see* Civil law)
Legislator, universal (*see* Will)
Levellers, 200, 209–216)
Lewis, C. I., 530, 536–539, 549–554
Liberalism, 368–369, 599
Liberty (*see also* God, freedom of; Religious freedom), 67, 195–197, 303, 318, 378, 469
  defined, 143n, 186, 404
  in Dewey, 548–549
  in existentialism, 561
  in Mill, 432–442
  in nineteenth century, 369–370
  of the press (*see* Expression, right of)
  in Rawls, 589–590
  in Sartre, 579, 584–585
  state of (*see* State of nature)
  of the will (*see* Will, freedom of)
License, 155–156, 158
  Life, quality of, 592–593
Lilburne, John, 210
Locke, John, 201, 216–224, 603
Logical Empiricism, 504–506
Lombard, Peter, 106, 110
Love (*see also* Benevolence; Self-love; Sympathy), 151, 356–357, 500
Lucretius, 72, 83–86
Luxury (*see also* Money; Wealth), 263–264, 319, 388, 408
Lying (*see also* "Noble Lie"), 332, 354–355, 569

Madness, 55, 150, 183, 314, 549, 579, 618
Manicheanism, 92, 96
Marcus Aurelius, 72, 79–81
Marginalist economics, 301–302, 319
Market value, 345
Marriage (*see also* Children; Family), 385, 406–407, 409–411, 442, 527–528
  as I/Thou relation, 577
  incestuous, 88, 113, 260, 321
  right of, 595
Marx, Karl, 368, 390–400, 404–409, 411–412
Marxism (*see* Communism; Economics, Marxist)
Master morality, 467–468
Mathematics (*see also* Felicific calculus; Geometry), 54, 55, 505, 562, 563, 627–628
  adumbrates Forms, 11, 32
  as model for ethics, 204–206
Matthew, Gospel of, 95–96
Maxim, universal, 337–338, 341, 342
Mean, The (*see also* Compromise), 41, 42, 47–50
Measurement of happiness (*see* Felicific calculus)

Median, The (*see* Mean, The)

Medieval ethics, 103–159

Menoeceus, 81

Mental disposition, 311–312

Mental state, 501, 502

Mercantilism, 262–263

Merit (*see* Worth)

Metaethics, 492, 506

Metaphysics, 327, 418

Middle class, 66–67, 299, 393–394, 396–397, 402–403, 417

Mill, James, 413, 417

Mill, John Stuart, 369, 413–451, 456n

Mind

  peace of (*see* Peace of mind)

  rights of the, 292

  state of, 501, 502

Modern ethics, 163–174

Monasticism (*see* Religious orders)

Money (*see also* Luxury; Wealth), 49, 52, 221, 262–263, 341–342, 408–409

  currency, 62–63

  diminishing marginal utility of, 319

Moore, G. E., 490–501

Moral agents, 606–607

Moral Argument (card game), 602–603, 604, 606

Moral axioms, 204–205

Moral blindness (*see* Self-deception)

Moral conflict (*see* Conflict)

Moral philosophy (*see* Ethics)

Moral relativism (*see* Relativism)

Moral sense intuitionists (*see also* Intuitionism), 227

Moral theory (*see* Ethics)

Moral virtue (*see* Virtue)

Moral weakness, 55–56

More, Henry, 204–205, 207

Motivation (*see also* Intention), 309–311, 314, 328, 422, 597

Murder, 257, 271–272, 362–363

Mutual aid, 470–473

Naturalistic fallacy, 491, 493, 495–496, 497–498

Natural law, 71, 106–107, 130–133, 173, 186–187, 190–193

Natural power (*see* Power)

Natural right, 136, 153, 154–155, 158

Natural rights, 108, 278–297

Natural science (*see* Science)

Natural wit (*see* Virtue, intellectual)

Nature, state of (*see* State of nature)

Neoplatonism (*see also* Cambridge Platonists), 70, 73, 88–90, 502

Newton, Issac, 168

Nicholas III, Pope, 154

Nietzsche, Friedrich, 454–455, 466–469

Nineteenth-century ethics, 367–483

"Noble Lie," 24, 32

Noemata, 204–205

Nonpositive moral science (*see* Ethics)

Normative ethics, 492

Nowell-Smith, P. H., 507, 515–517

Nozick, Robert, 586, 588, 599, 600, 603

Oaths, 78, 190

Obedience, civil (*see* Civil obedience)

Obligation (*see also* Duty), 203, 206, 332, 339, 350

Ockham, William, 108, 141–159

Oligarchy, 32–33, 65–66

One, The (*see also* God), 73, 88–90

Opinion (*see also* Expression, right of), 11, 52, 56, 77, 435–436

Orders, religious (*see* Religious orders)

Ordinary Language Analysis, 504–505, 506–508

Organic unities, 500, 501, 502

Original rights (*see* Natural rights)

"Othello," 282–283

"Ought" problem, 238, 257, 477, 486

Overton, Richard, 210

Ownership (*see also* Dominion; Property; Use, right of), 359–360, 384, 524

Pact (*see* Contract)

Pain (*see* Pleasure)

Paine, Thomas, 292–294

Palamedes, 258–259

Panaetius, 71

Pantheism, 70, 479

Paraphrasis, 300–301

Pareto, Vilfredo, 591, 617–618

Parliament, 199–201, 212

Partiality (*see* Prejudice)

Passions (*see also* Appetite; Feelings), 52, 180, 229–230, 232

  in Hegel, 378–382

  in Hobbes, 182, 183, 186

Passive citizens (*see* Citizens)

Patriotism, 540, 579–580

Paul the Apostle, 90, 92, 101, 105

Paulus, 107

Peace, 35, 101–102, 186, 192, 323, 363, 365–366

  of mind (*see also* Ataraxia), 80, 182

Perceptions, 234, 257, 307–308

Perfect duty (*see* Duty in Kant)

Persons, 285, 330, 344, 384, 574, 607
    relations between, 573–577, 608
    respect for, 350, 605
    respect of (*see* Prejudice)
Petty, Maximilian, 210, 214
Phenomenology, 487, 555–559, 562–577
    Philo Judaeus, 90
Philosophers, 28, 78
"Philosopher, The" (*see* Aristotle)
Plato (*see also* Neoplatonism), 7–37, 65, 89, 418
Platonic forms (*see* Forms, Platonic)
Platonists, Cambridge, 199, 201–209
Pleasure (*see also* Hedonism; Preferences),
        34–35, 56–57, 64, 100, 113, 181
    in Aristotle, 57–58
    in Bentham, 301–302, 310
    as end in itself, 82, 310, 419, 498
    and pain, 47, 49, 72, 303, 349
        measurement of (*see* Felicific calculus)
Plotinus, 73, 88–90
Polemarchus, 9, 13, 16–17
Polis (*see also* Commonwealth; Community;
        Government; State, The), 23–30, 39, 58–
        59, 545
Political associations (*see* Commonwealth;
        Polis; State, The)
Political revolution (*see* Revolution)
Politics, 43, 165–166
Poor-laws (*see* Poverty)
Posidonius, 71
Positive moral science (*see* Ethics)
Positive right, 136, 154–155
Positivism, 530
Possession (*see* Dominion; Ownership)
Poverty, 321, 363, 388, 460–461, 627
Power, 184, 218
Practical ethics (*see* Ethics)
Practical wisdom, 54–55, 334
Pragmatism, 529–554
Praise (*see* Blame and praise)
Predestination, 101
Preferences (*see also* Pleasure), 591, 617–619
Prejudice (*see also* Toleration and intolerance),
        136, 192, 287–288, 428
Press, liberty of (*see* Expression, right of)
Price, 105–106
Price, Richard, 284–287, 289
Pride (*see also* Fame, love of), 101
Private deontology, 302
Private ethics (*see* Ethics)
Private property (*see* Property)
Privilege, 291, 302, 303
Probity, 314, 316
Production, 60, 392, 395, 405–406
Progressive education, 535

Proletariat (*see* Working class)
Promise (*see also* Contract), 188, 246, 330, 337–
        338, 340, 341–342
    in Mill, 428, 431
    in Rawls, 508
Proof (*see* Evidence)
Property (*see also* Dominion; Ownership; Use,
        right of), 60, 138, 244–245, 246, 285, 320,
        330
    abolition of, 398–399
    ecclesiastical, 154
    equality of, 244, 289, 384–385
    exchange of, 61–63
    family relations and, 295–296
    labor of appropriation and, 221, 405
    in Marxian economics, 404, 406, 407
    in Middle Ages, 105–106
    in Mill, 446–449
    offenses against, 316
    in *polis*, 28n
    qualifications, 67–68, 210–211, 214–215
    rights, 152–159, 404, 524, 602
    slaves as, 60–61
    systems compared, 64–65
    in United Nations, 588, 595
Proprietorship (*see* Dominion; Ownership)
Propriety (*see* Action)
Protestant Reformation, 164
Prudence, 128–129, 147–150, 313, 315, 339–340,
        538, 551–553
Psychology, 72, 559, 625–626
Ptolemaic astronomy, 166
Publication, right of (*see* Expression, right of)
Public justice (*see* Justice)
Public utility (*see* Utility)
Public worth (*see* Worth)
Punishment (*see also* Killing; Sanctions), 47, 139
    in Abelard, 115–116
    in Bentham, 313–316
    in Hegel, 385
    in Hobbes, 191
    in Kant, 358, 362–363
    in Locke, 218
    in Mill, 429, 430
    in Smith (Adam), 267–269
Purpose (*see* Intention)
Putney Debates, 200, 210, 211–216
Pyrrhonism, 86–88
Pythagoreans, 48

Quality of life, 592–593

Rainborough, Col. Thomas, 210, 214, 215
Rank, social (*see* Social classes)

Rationalism, 169–171, 201–209, 234–235
Rationality, 41, 44, 237, 610–611
  as end in itself, 343, 344
  in history, 376–377
  vs. sentiment, 239–240, 254–256
  vs. taste, 256
Rawls, John, 586, 589–590, 609–614
Reason (faculty) (*see* Rationality)
Reciprocity, 52
Reductionism, 556–557
Reflection (*see* Deliberation)
Reformation, Protestant (*see* Protestant Reformation)
Reform movements, 288, 299–300, 317n
Regret, 51, 424, 458–459
Relativism, 8, 73, 88, 479, 487–488, 515
  in Duncker, 570–573
  opposed by phenomenology, 557
Religion (*see also* God), 178–179, 190, 332, 382, 501, 628
  in England, 199–200, 201, 212, 502
  in Hellenistic period, 70
Religious freedom, 286
Religious orders (*see also* Friars Minor), 28n, 106
Remorse (*see* Regret)
Representation (*see* Equality)
Representative government, 442–446
Republic, 331, 366
Research, scientific, 38, 39–40, 172
Resentment, 267–269, 440, 458n
Respect, 356, 357
  for law, 336–337, 338, 349–350
  for persons, 350, 605
  of persons (*see* Prejudice)
Responsibility, 521–525, 561, 578, 584–585
Retail trade (*see* Trade)
Retaliation (*see* Punishment)
Revolution
  Age of, 275–366
  in America, 202
  in England, 199–201, 286
  in France, 275–276, 289–292
  industrial, 276, 299
  in *polis*, 32
  scientific, 166–168
  unlawful, 361–362
Reward (*see* Punishment)
Rich, Col. Nathaniel, 215
Riches (*see* Wealth)
Right
  natural (*see* Natural right)
  positive, 136, 154–155
Righteous indignation, 50
Rightful use (*see* Use, right of)

Rights (*see also* classes of rights, e.g., Natural rights; and specific rights, e.g., Use, right of)
  of citizenship (*see* Civil rights)
  conflict of, 588, 600–601
  declarations of, 281–282, 284, 594–596
  distinguished from welfare, 615
  equality of, 280–281, 358, 361
  justification of, 605
  transference of, 187–188, 280, 290
  utility of, 605–606
  of women, 284, 294–296, 410
Robbery (*see* Theft)
Roman law, 104, 105, 173
Roman philosophy (*see* Graeco-Roman philosophy)
Rousseau, Jean Jacques, 278, 279–281
Rulers, 13, 24, 28–29, 59, 273, 322, 344–345
  divine right of, 199, 216, 217
Rule utilitarianism (*see* Utilitarianism)

Sacrifice, 352, 421–422, 457–458
Sanctions (*see also* Punishment), 306, 423–425
Sarcasm (*see* Contumely)
Sartre, Jean-Paul, 560, 561–562, 577–585
Satan, 93, 101, 102
Science, 54, 415, 627
  of morals (*see* Ethics)
  social, 559, 626–627
Scientific inquiry (*see* Scientific research)
Scientific knowledge, 55, 148, 418, 534
Scientific research, 38, 39–40, 172
Scientific revolution, 166–168
Scottish Enlightenment (*see* Enlightenment)
Scotus, Duns (*see* Duns Scotus)
Secrecy, 324
Security, 72, 303, 318, 319–320, 430
  social, 595
Sedition (*see* Revolution)
Self-conceit, 349–350
Self-consciousness (*see* Consciousness)
Self-deception, 355, 423, 563–564
Self-defense, 138, 178, 187, 433
Self-evident principles, 131, 148, 222, 278, 284, 498, 499
Self-executing law (*see* Civil law)
Self-existence of values, 562–563
Self-government (*see* Ethics)
Self-incrimination, 139, 178, 605
Self-interest (*see* Self-love)
Self-love (*see also* Egoism), 229–230, 248–249, 251, 318, 338, 495
  vs. conscience, 269–271
  vs. duty, 475

Self-love (*continued*)
  object of interest and, 548
  as universal law, 341, 349
Self-realization, 474–489
Self-sacrifice (*see* Sacrifice)
Self-sufficiency, 43–44, 101
Seneca, 71–72, 76–77, 107, 134
Sensation (*see also* Empiricism), 11, 38, 70, 72
Sensibility, 308
Sentiment (*see* Feelings)
Serfdom (*see* Slavery)
Sermon on the Mount, 92
Sex (*see also* Adultery; Homosexuality; Marriage), 2, 78, 247, 315, 316, 410–411
Sextus Empiricus, 72–73, 86–88
Shame, 583–584, 589
Ship, simile of the, 29
Sidgwick, Henry, 474–475
Simonides, 13–15
Sin, 92, 94, 100–101, 106, 110–116, 186, 401–402
Sincerity, 583
Situational meaning, 571, 572–573
Skepticism, 70, 72–73, 86–88
Skill, imperative of, 339, 340
Slave morality, 467, 468–469
Slavery, 220, 387–388, 394, 466–467, 594
  in America, 282–283
  in Athens, 7
  in British Empire, 321n
  property and, 60–61
Sleep, 45, 55, 56
Smith, Adam, 23n, 264–273
Smith, P. H. Nowell (*see* Nowell-Smith, P. H.)
Social animals (*see* Animals)
Social classes (*see also* Middle class; Social station; Working class), 9–10, 393, 400–401
Social contract (*see* Contract)
Social Darwinism, 454–455, 462–466
Social institutions, 482, 576–577
Socialism (*see* Communism)
Social psychology (*see* Psychology)
Social science, 559, 626–627
Social security, 595
Social station (*see also* Social classes), 478
Social utility (*see* Utility)
Sociobiology, 455
Sociology, 627
Socrates, 8–9, 13–37
  mentioned, 55, 56, 71, 72, 418, 516, 617
Sophists, 8, 418
Soul, 9–10, 26–27, 44–45
  immortality of, 36, 561
Sovereigns (*see* Rulers)
Sovereignty, 143, 165–166, 195, 280, 282, 440–441, 443

Speech, right of (*see* Expression, right of)
Spencer, Herbert, 453–454, 460–462
Spirit, World-, 378, 379, 381
State education, 442, 461–462
State of mind, 501, 502
State of nature, 85–86, 217–219, 280, 358–359
  fictional, 243–244, 359
  as slavery, 388
  war as, 285
State of war (*see* War)
State, The (*see also* Commonwealth; Community; Government; *Polis*), 381–382, 482–483
Station, social (*see* Social station)
Stealing (*see* Theft)
Stevenson, Charles Leslie, 506, 511–515
Stoicism, 70, 71–72, 73–81
Struggle for existence (*see* Social Darwinism)
Suarez, Francisco, 108
Subjective volition (*see* Passions)
Subjectivism, 578
Subjects of commonwealth (*see also* Citizens), 195–197
Suffrage (*see* Voting)
Suicide, 137, 341, 354, 584, 585
Supermen, 379–380, 439, 454, 468
Survival of the fittest (*see* Social Darwinism)
Suspension of judgment (*see also* Bracketing), 87, 255
Syllogistic reasoning, 38, 55
Sympathy (*see also* Compassion; Mutual aid), 237–238, 250–251, 265, 266, 267, 456, 457
Synthesis (*see* Dialectic)
Synthetic statements, 327n, 495, 505, 510

Taste (esthetics), 256, 302, 318, 434
Teleology, 39–40, 331, 372–373
Temptation, 100
Ten Commandments, 2, 91, 92–93, 132–133
Theft, 93, 112, 124, 359, 401, 511
  by Augustine, 99–100
Thesis (*see* Dialectic)
Thrasymachus, 9, 16–20
Timocracy, 33
Toleration and intoleration (*see also* Prejudice), 293
Torture (*see* Cruelty)
Trade, 61–63, 105, 139–141, 213, 262, 442
  unions, 588, 595
Tragedy, 36n, 38, 41
Tranquillity (*see* Peace of mind)
Transference of rights (*see* Rights)
Tribunal, common, 323–324
Truthfulness, 49

Twentieth-century ethics, 485–631
Tyranny, 19, 34, 135, 260, 433–434

Ulpian, 106–107
Unamuno, Miguel de, 560–561
*United Nations Universal Declaration of Human
    Rights*, 587–588, 594–596, 597, 599
Unities, organic (*see* Organic unities)
Universal legislator (*see* Will)
Universal maxim, 337–338, 341, 342
Universals, Platonic (*see* Forms, Platonic)
Usefulness (*see* Utility)
Use, right of (*see also* Dominion; Ownership;
    Property), 152–153, 154–156
Usufruct, 152
Usurpation (*see* Theft)
Usury, 105, 141, 570, 571
Utilitarianism, 298, 414–415, 417–432, 469, 590,
    605–606, 616–617
Utility, 56–57, 245, 411–412, 427–432, 605–606
    in Becker, 605–606
    in Bentham, 303–307
    in Hume, 245, 247–249, 254, 260
    in Hutcheson, 233
    in Marx and Engels, 411–412
    in Rawls, 611
    in Smith (Adam), 272

Value/fact distinction, 564–566
Value (ideal) (*see also* Goodness), 558, 562–
    563, 565–567
Value (worth) (*see* Worth)
Vengeance (*see* Punishment)
Vice (*see also* specific vices, e.g., Adultery), 48,
    254, 257, 318
Virtue (*see also* specific virtues, e.g., Truthful-
    ness), 8, 57, 150–151, 353, 485–486, 617
    defined, 47, 255, 353, 494
    as end in itself, 74, 256
    happiness and, 426
    intellectual, 45, 54–55, 127–128, 182–183
    moral, 45, 128–129, 148–150
    in *polis*, 25–26
    prudence and, 149–150
Vituperation (*see* Contumely)
Volition (*see* Will)
Volitional law, 173
Voluntariness and involuntariness, 50–52,
    121, 523

Voluntarism, 107–108, 144–145
Voluntary motions (*see* Passions)
Voting (*see also* Property qualifications), 210–
    211, 445–446, 512, 525–526, 595

Waiter, illustration of the, 582–583
War, 185, 197, 219–220, 243, 285, 584–585
    international law and, 322–323
    just, 136
    patriotism and, 540, 579–580
    in *polis*, 23–24
Weakness, moral, 55–56
Wealth (*see also* Luxury; Money), 13, 62–63,
    319, 329, 408, 446–447
Welfare, 590–593, 599–601, 615–619
Whole, The, 494
Wickedness (*see* Evil)
Wildman, John, 210, 212
Will, 97–98, 101, 182, 338–339, 342, 344
    freedom of, 327, 329, 346–349, 403–404
    general, 279, 280–281, 360–361, 481
    of God, 302, 332, 346
    good, 334–335, 346–347
    intellect and
        in Aquinas, 120, 122–123
        in Middle Ages, 107
        in Ockham, 144
Wisdom, practical, 54–55, 334
Wish, 52
Wit (*see* Virtue, intellectual)
Wojtyla, Karol, 573–574
Wollstonecraft, Mary, 294–296
Women (*see also* Feminism), 7, 27–28, 400, 406–
    407, 608–609
    rights of, 284, 294–296, 410
Work, 595
Working class (*see also* Government employ-
    ees), 228, 397–398, 404–406, 444–445, 449
World-historical persons (*see* Heroes)
World-Spirit, 378, 379, 381
Worship (*see* Religion)
Worth (*see also* Fancy value; Market value),
    184, 240, 241, 267–269, 330, 345
    of action, 336
    intrinsic (*see* End in itself)
Wrong (*see* Evil)

Zeno, 71, 72, 73–74

About The Authors

ABRAHAM EDEL is research professor of philosophy at the University of Pennsylvania. Previously he had been professor of philosophy at the City College of New York and distinguished professor at CUNY's Graduate Center. His publications include eleven books, most recently *Aristotle and His Philosophy* and the three-volume *Science, Ideology, and Value*, and over a hundred papers. He was recently the first Romanell lecturer of the APA. He has been president of Amintaphil, and of the American Society for Value Inquiry, and vice-president of the Eastern Division, APA. In 1986 he was the subject of *Ethics, Science, and Democracy*, a volume of essays in his honor.

ELIZABETH FLOWER, long-time professor of philosophy at the University of Pennsylvania, is known for her work in American philosophy and in the history and interdisciplinary relations of ethics. Her writings include the two-volume *A History of Philosophy in America* (with Murray Murphey), now a standard work in the field; numerous journal articles; and papers in collaborative volumes on ethical theory and problems of value and method in relation to law, education, and social theory. She has lectured widely in Latin America and written on its philosophical developments. She has been visiting professor at Barnard, and Truax professor at Hamilton; spent research years as fellow of the National Humanities Center and the Dewey Foundation; and served as secretary-treasurer of the Eastern Division of the American Philosophical Association.

FINBARR O'CONNOR is associate professor of philosophy at Beaver College. His writings include *Deviance and Decency: The Ethics of Research with Human Subjects* (with Carl Klockars), *Writing in the Arts and Sciences* and *Readings in the Arts and Sciences* (with Elaine Maimon, Gerald Belcher, Gail Hearn, and Barbara Nodine), and the forthcoming *Thinking, Reasoning, and Writing* (with Elaine Maimon and Barbara Nodine). He has published articles in ethics, political philosophy, and in the relation of logic to problem solving.